TREATMENT OF CHILDHOOD DISORDERS

Treatment of Childhood Disorders

Second Edition

Edited by

ERIC J. MASH
University of Calgary

RUSSELL A. BARKLEY
University of Massachusetts Medical Center

THE GUILFORD PRESS
New York   London

© 1998 The Guilford Press
A Division of Guilford Publications, Inc.
72 Spring Street, New York, NY 10012
http://www.guilford.com

Printed in the United States of America

This book is printed on acid-free paper.

Last digit is print number: 9   8   7   6   5   4   3   2   1

Library of Congress cataloging-in-publication data
is available from the Publisher.

ISBN 1-57230-276-3

*To the memory of Dennis P. Cantwell, MD (1939–1997),
the Joseph Campbell Professor
of Child Psychiatry at the Neuropsychiatric Institute
of the University of California at Los Angeles.
Dr. Cantwell was an exceptional scientist/practitioner
who made numerous contributions
to the understanding, classification, and treatment
of childhood mental disorders over the more than 30 years
of his professional career in child psychiatry.
Children with developmental, learning,
and psychiatric disorders could not have had a better friend,
advocate, and scientist in the mental health profession.*

Contributors

Sandra T. Azar, PhD, Department of Psychology, Clark University, Worcester, MA

Russell A. Barkley, PhD, Departments of Psychiatry and Neurology, University of Massachusetts Medical Center, Worcester, MA

Billy A. Barrios, PhD, Department of Psychology, University of Mississippi, University, MS

Sandra A. Brown, PhD, Departments of Psychiatry and Psychology, University of California at San Diego, La Jolla, CA; Psychology Service, Veterans Healthcare System, San Diego, CA

Laurie E. Cutting, PhD, Department of Neurology, Kennedy Krieger Institute, Johns Hopkins University School of Medicine, Baltimore, MD

Kenneth A. Dodge, PhD, Department of Psychology and Human Development, Vanderbilt University, Nashville, TN

John P. Foreyt, PhD, Department of Medicine, Baylor College of Medicine, Houston, TX

Sharon L. Foster, PhD, California School of Professional Psychology—San Diego, San Diego, CA

Benjamin L. Handen, PhD, Child Development Unit, Children's Hospital of Pittsburgh, Pittsburgh, PA

Alan E. Kazdin, PhD, Department of Psychology, Yale University, New Haven, CT

G. Reid Lyon, PhD, Human Learning and Behavior Branch, Center for Research for Mothers and Children, National Institute of Child Health and Human Development, National Institutes of Health, Bethesda, MD

Paul L. Marciano, PhD, Department of Psychology, Davidson College, Davidson, NC

Eric J. Mash, PhD, Department of Psychology, University of Calgary, Calgary, Alberta, Canada

Steven A. McFadyen-Ketchum, PhD, Department of Psychology and Human Development, Vanderbilt University, Nashville, TN

Jill K. McGavin, PhD, Psychology Service, Department of Veterans Affairs Medical Center, Houston, TX

Robert J. McMahon, PhD, Department of Psychology, University of Washington, Seattle, WA

Mark G. Myers, PhD, Department of Psychiatry, University of California at San Diego, La Jolla, CA; Psychology Service, Veterans Healthcare System, San Diego, CA

Crighton Newsom, PhD, Southwest Ohio Developmental Center, Batavia, OH

Stan L. O'Dell, PhD, Department of Psychology, University of Mississippi, University, MS

Walker S. Carlos Poston II, PhD, Baylor College of Medicine, Houston, TX

Arthur L. Robin, PhD, Department of Pediatrics, Wayne State University, School of Medicine, Detroit, MI

Peter W. Vik, PhD, Department of Psychology, Idaho State University, Pocatello, ID

Karen C. Wells, PhD, Family Studies Program and Clinic, Department of Psychiatry and Behavioral Sciences, Duke University Medical Center, Durham, NC

Allen A. Winebarger, PhD, Department of Psychology, Grand Valley State University, Allendale, MI

David A. Wolfe, PhD, Department of Psychology, University of Western Ontario, London, Ontario Canada

Vicky Veitch Wolfe, PhD, Division of Child and Adolescent Psychology, London Health Sciences Center, London, Ontario, Canada

Preface

The intention of this book remains the same as that of its predecessor—to create a resource that would be at once scholarly and applied, and would continue to address the relative dearth of information on empirically based treatments for childhood psychopathological disorders. Its sister volume, Mash and Terdal's *Assessment of Childhood Disorders* (New York: Guilford Press, 1997), was just recently updated and republished in a third edition—making it imperative that this companion volume likewise be brought up to date, given the years that have elapsed since its initial publication. Once more we have tried to select well-regarded experts, highly knowledgeable and experienced in their respective domains of treatment, to convey a sense to the reader of the state-of-the-art of treatments for childhood disorders. We are most grateful that many of the authors from the first edition agreed to update their chapters, despite their hectic schedules and other pressing commitments, so that readers might have the benefit of the additional decade's worth of wisdom they have gleaned. Once more we charged them with the mission of providing as timely an overview and critique as possible of the various scientifically based treatment methods most often applied to the disorders in which they specialized, raising along the way critical issues they discerned within these fields of study. Fads, fancies, New Age remedies, dogmatic therapies, and the treatments *du jour* of the latest therapeutic gurus were to be eschewed in favor of a focus on treatments for which there were sound scientific rationales as well as evidence of efficacy and effectiveness. We were delighted with the resulting chapters and the clear evidence that this mission was fulfilled.

As we noted in the first edition, an effort to capture the dynamic nature of the empirically supported child treatment literature is akin to taking still snapshots of brief moments in the life of a family. The slice of life so rendered suggests what came before and hints at the shadows of things yet to come, but remains merely a cross-sectional representation of an otherwise continuously changing entity. Our current effort to describe the state of this family of treatments is another representation. In comparison to our last snapshots of the available treatments for children, it is immediately clear from the present ones that much has changed. Treatments that were once young and promising have now matured. Some have not withstood the tooth of time and trial particularly well. Indeed, a few have passed away in their infancy or found their initial promise unfulfilled. Others, however, have blossomed with their maturation to fully grown and well-established treatment approaches, even giving us offspring to continue the family line. New members of the treatment family have joined up with this literature as well, some wholly unanticipated in the first volume. Marriages between some treatments have occurred, to the benefit of those children having a particular disorder; other unions have failed to survive the trials of empirical tests. Regardless of the state of flux of this family tree of treatments, we believe the authors have done a superb job in capturing the status of their respective members of this treatment genealogy, offering up suggestions for their improvement, and indicating the future directions in which treatments for their respective disorders are likely to proceed.

We owe gratitude to many who have helped us over the course of this project. First among these are the authors of these chapters, who once again graciously tolerated our editorial feedback while richly educating us about their fields of treatment specialization in the process. We are deeply indebted to them for doing so. During the preparation of this book, Eric J. Mash was supported, in part, by a grant from the Killam Foundation and the Office of the Vice President of Research at the University of Calgary. This support is gratefully acknowledged. Russell A. Barkley was financially supported, in part, by grants from the National Institute of Mental Health (Nos. MH45714 and MH41583) and the National Institute for Child Health and Human Development (No. HD28171). The contents of this book, however, are solely our responsibility and do not necessarily represent the official views of these institutes. Russell A. Barkley was also financially supported during this time by funds from the Department of Psychiatry, University of Massachusetts Medical Center, to the chairman of which, Paul Appelbaum, MD, he is most grateful. We also sincerely appreciate the exceptional assistance of the editorial production department of The Guilford Press with the publishing of this text. Likewise, we wish to thank our friends Seymour Weingarten and Robert Matloff, Editor in Chief and President, respectively, of The Guilford Press for their continued support and encouragement of this new and expanded edition of this volume. And, last but not least, we remain continually appreciative of the support of our respective family members—Heather Mash and Pat, Steve, and Ken Barkley—for their relinquishing of family time so that we might bring this second edition to fruition and on to market. Once more, we are most thankful for their bountiful support of our editorial and writing efforts.

ERIC J. MASH, PHD
University of Calgary

RUSSELL A. BARKLEY, PHD
University of Massachusetts Medical Center

Contents

PART V   CHILDREN AT RISK

PART VI   PROBLEMS OF ADOLESCENCE

PART I
INTRODUCTION

CHAPTER 1

Treatment of Child and Family Disturbance: A Behavioral–Systems Perspective

Eric J. Mash
University of Calgary

Each year nearly 3 million children and adolescents in North America receive some type of mental health services, at an estimated cost of $1.5 billion or more (Weisz & Weiss, 1993). The behavioral, psychological, social, physical, and learning problems for which children are referred to professionals for help are numerous and varied (Achenbach, 1982; Cicchetti & Cohen, 1995a, 1995b; Hersen & Ammerman, 1995; Mash & Barkley, 1996; Mash & Terdal, 1997a; Quay & Werry, 1986). Adaptation difficulties that lead to referral for services frequently reflect developmentally and/or situationally inappropriate or exaggerated expressions of behavior that may at times also occur in children who are not referred (Achenbach, Howell, Quay, & Conners, 1991; Mash & Dozois, 1996). As a result, decisions concerning the evaluation and treatment of any child are embedded within the child's social and cultural milieu, and are always the result of ongoing judgments that are either made or not made by significant individuals in the child's environ-

ment, usually parents and teachers (Mash & Terdal, 1997b). The professionals who evaluate and treat disturbed children and their families come from a variety of disciplines and backgrounds. They include psychologists, educators, pediatricians, child psychiatrists, nurses, social workers, speech and language pathologists, physical and occupational therapists, day care specialists, and others. It is not surprising, therefore, that a tremendous number and diversity of treatments for children and families exist (Johnson, Rasbury, & Siegel, 1997; Kratochwill & Morris, 1993; Mash & Barkley, 1989; Walker & Roberts, 1992), with some conservative estimates listing well over 200 different varieties of psychosocial intervention alone (Kazdin, 1988b).

In light of the heterogeneity of circumstances leading up to and surrounding the identification, referral, evaluation, and treatment of children with problems, it is believed that these activities are best depicted as ongoing decision-making/problem-solving processes (e.g., Evans & Meyer, 1985; Herbert, 1987; Kanfer & Schefft, 1988; Mash, 1989; Schroeder & Gordon, 1991). These processes are directed at providing answers to such questions as these:

- Should this child's difficulties be treated?
- What are the projected outcomes in the absence of treatment?
- What types of treatment are likely to be most effective?
- What types of treatment are likely to be the most efficient and cost-effective?
- Who is (are) the best person(s) to provide treatment?
- What are the most appropriate settings (e.g., clinic, home, classroom, community) in which to carry out treatment?
- Which types of intervention are likely to be the most acceptable to the child, parents, and other family and community members?
- When should treatment be initiated and when should it be terminated?
- What changes or adjustments in treatment are needed as intervention progresses?
- Is the intervention having the desired impact and are these effects maintained over time?
- Has the treatment resulted in clinically meaningful changes for the child and family?

The ultimate goal of this iterative decision-making process should be to achieve effective solutions to the problems being faced by children and their families and to promote and enhance long-term adjustments.

It is my view, and that of the authors represented in this book, that decisions concerning these and other related questions are best made when they are based on a consistently applied theoretical framework, well-established research findings relevant to both normal and deviant child and family functioning, empirically supported treatment procedures, and operational rules that are sensitive to the realities and changing demands of clinical practice and to the broader societal context in which treatments are carried out. Kazdin (1997) has provided a useful framework that is consistent with the general behavioral–systems orientation of this volume, in which the steps needed to advance the development of effective treatments for children and families are specified (see Table 1.1). This model emphasizes the importance of theory and

TABLE 1.1. A Model for Developing Effective Treatments: Steps toward Progress

1. Conceptualization of the dysfunction: Propose key areas, processes, and mechanisms that relate to the development, onset, and escalation of dysfunction.
2. Research on processes related to dysfunction: Test proposed processes in relation to the dysfunction.
3. Conceptualization of treatment: Propose key areas, processes, and mechanisms through which treatment may achieve its effects and how the procedures relate to these processes.
4. Specification of treatment: Operationalize the procedures, preferably in manual form, that identify how one changes the key processes. Provide material to codify the procedures, to evaluate treatment integrity, and to replicate in research and practice.
5. Tests of treatment outcome: Test the impact of treatment drawing on diverse designs (e.g., open [uncontrolled] studies, single-case designs, and full-fledged clinical trials) and types of studies (e.g., dismantling, parametric studies, and comparative outcome studies) are relevant.
6. Tests of treatment processes: Identify whether the intervention techniques, methods, and procedures within treatment actually affect those processes that are critical to the model.
7. Tests of the boundary conditions and moderators: Examine the child, parent, family, and contextual factors with which treatment interacts. The boundary conditions or limits of application are identified through interactions of treatment and diverse attributes within empirical tests.

Note. From Kazdin (1997 p. 117). Reprinted by permission.

data about specific childhood disorders, and the need for carefully specified and empirically supported treatment strategies with known boundary conditions. Although such an amalgamation of theory, research, and practice is more an ideal than a fact at the present time, current behavioral–systems perspectives seem to approximate this integration most closely, and it is these approaches upon which this volume is based.

Although most practicing child and family therapists continue to identify their approach as "eclectic," the use of behavioral and cognitive-behavioral strategies is especially predominant with children and families, with 50% or more of all clinical child and pediatric psychologists identifying with these orientations (O'Leary, 1984a). Nevertheless, we believe that the complexity of childhood disorders, the diversity of circumstances under which they occur and are treated, the evolving nature of cognitive-behavioral treatments, current efforts to integrate different therapy orientations (e.g., Fauber & Kendall, 1992; Goldfried, 1995; Kendall, 1982; Norcross & Goldfried, 1992), the widespread use of combined and multimodal treatments (e.g., Kazdin, 1996a), and uncertainties regarding the clinical significance and long-term effectiveness of current treatments for children (Weisz, in press; Weisz, Han, & Valeri, 1997), would contraindicate a rigid adherence to *any* narrowly defined therapeutic perspective.

It is the purpose of this initial chapter to provide an overview of recent developments, conceptual issues, and practical concerns associated with the treatment of child and family disturbances from a behavioral–systems perspective, and also to describe some of the common features of this approach. The general themes that are raised in this introductory chapter are elaborated in the chapter discussions of specific child and family disorders that follow.

HISTORICAL ANTECEDENTS AND EARLY DEVELOPMENTS

There have been several descriptions of the early development of behavioral and cognitive-behavioral approaches to the treatment of children and families (e.g., Kazdin, 1978; O'Leary & Wilson, 1987; Ollendick, 1986; Ollendick & Cerny, 1981; Ross, 1981). This development is briefly highlighted here. Although it is possible to find examples of the application of behavioral principles with children throughout the history of humankind (Lasure & Mikulas, 1996), systematic behavioral applications are usually identified as beginning with the rise of behaviorism in the early 1900s, as reflected in the classic studies on the conditioning and elimination of children's fears (Jones, 1924; Watson & Rayner, 1920), and Pavlov's experimental research that established the foundations for classical conditioning. The period from 1930 to 1950 represented child behavior therapy's latency period, with a few reports in the 1930s describing the treatment of isolated problems such as bedwetting (Mowrer & Mowrer, 1938), stuttering (Dunlap, 1932), and fears (Holmes, 1936; Weber, 1936).

It was not until the 1950s and early 1960s that behavior therapy began to emerge as a systematic approach to the treatment of child and family disorders. The classic works of Wolpe (1958), Salter (1949), Lazarus (1958; Lazarus & Abramovitz, 1962), Skinner (1953), Eysenck (1960), and Bijou (Bijou & Baer, 1961) all contributed to behavior therapy's early development. The behavioral approaches that emerged during the 1950s and early 1960s were counterreactions to the then-dominant psychodynamic perspective. Most behavioral work with children was carried out with mentally retarded or severely disturbed youngsters, for whom psychoanalytic practices were perceived as not being very effective or appropriate. Much of this work took place in institutions or classrooms—settings that were thought to provide the kind of environmental control needed to "modify" behavior effectively. Early case studies were designed primarily to demonstrate the applicability of one learning principle or another, and showed relatively little concern for the clinical significance of treatment or its long-term impact on the child and family. As Wachtel (1977) pointed out, many of the most prominent figures in the early behavior therapy movement were psychologists who were almost exclusively experimental researchers, with little or no clinical experience. In retrospect, early case reports underestimated the complexity of clinical phenomena and failed to communicate the subtleties needed to understand and mediate the gap between laboratory-based principles of behavior change and clinical practice (Kazdin, 1988a).

The case study phase of behavior modification is perhaps most clearly illustrated in the 1965 volume edited by Ullmann and Krasner, entitled *Case Studies in Behavior Modification.* The childhood behaviors treated in these case reports included phobias, thumb sucking, eliminative disturbances, tantrums, isolate behavior, crying, crawling, vomiting, hyperactivity, and noncompliance. Most of these studies devoted little attention to the larger social or cultural networks in which these specific behavior problems occurred, or to issues such as generalization, follow-up, the possible negative effects of treatment, or the clinical significance of change. With few exceptions, they also ignored or minimized diagnostic considerations, comorbid conditions, developmental factors, cognitive processes, possible biological determinants, the use of medications, and therapeutic processes such as resistance or the therapist–client relationship.

Early behavioral work with children and families was derived primarily from an operant/reinforcement tradition. A major development in the field was the establishment of the *Journal of Applied Behavior Analysis* in 1968, which provided an outlet for treatment studies with children, and also served to define, shape, and reshape the field of applied behavior analysis (Baer, Wolf, & Risley, 1968, 1987). The establishment of journals such as *Behaviour Research and Therapy* and *Behavior Therapy,* and later *Child and Family Behavior Therapy, Behavior Modification, Journal of Behavior Therapy and Experimental Psychiatry*, *Behavioral Assessment, Cognitive Therapy and Research,* and *Cognitive and Behavioral Practice*, further legitimized and promoted behavioral and cognitive-behavioral applications in clinical child psychology.

Work during the late 1960s foreshadowed developments of the 1970s, as reflected in several noteworthy clinical research programs and publications. Tharp and Wetzel's (1969) *Behavior Modification in the Natural Environment* provided a model that redirected intervention into the community and provided a beginning systems framework for treatment. Mischel's (1968) *Personality and Assessment* focused attention on the importance of examining behavior in relation to context and established the conceptual foundations upon which behavioral assessment was built. Bandura's (1969) *Principles of Behavior Modification* and Kanfer and Phillips's (1970) *Learning Foundations of Behavior Therapy* placed behavioral approaches more squarely within a clinical context, broadened the range of principles upon which behavioral procedures were based, and laid the groundwork for the many cognitive approaches that were to develop in the 1970s and beyond. Kanfer and Saslow's (1965, 1969) model for "behavioral diagnosis" established the complex network of factors that needed to be considered in treatment, and by doing so provided a beginning decision-making approach to treatment. Patterson's (Patterson, Ray, & Shaw, 1968) work with antisocial children extended the locus of behavioral intervention from the child to the family, and from the clinic to the home and classroom. The work of operant psychologists such as Lindsley, Bijou, Baer, Wolf, Risley, Hopkins, and many others refined many of the behavioral procedures and extended them across a range of settings, especially the classroom. Finally, Lovaas's early work with children with autism established the range of procedures to be used in working with children with developmental disabilities, and also provided the needed impetus for addressing such important issues as generalization, the appropriateness of using aversive procedures in a clinical context, and ethical issues in behavior therapy more generally (Lovaas, Freitag, Gold, & Kasorla, 1965). Although there were undoubtedly other important developments during the late

1960s, the aforementioned seem especially noteworthy in retrospect.

It is difficult to place the events of the 1970s and later into a neat temporal perspective, partly as a function of the tremendous change and growth in cognitive-behavioral concepts and applications that have taken place. However, the continuing work of several investigators served to firmly establish the new conceptual and technological base for child and family cognitive-behavioral therapy. Patterson's (Patterson, Reid, Jones, & Conger, 1975) and Wahler's (1975) programs for antisocial children; Forehand and McMahon's (1981) systematic program of child management training for parents of oppositional children; Lovaas's continuing work with young children with autism (Lovaas, Koegel, Simmons, & Long, 1973); O'Leary's classroom interventions (O'Leary, Becker, Evans, & Saudargas, 1969); Barkley's (1987) program for teaching child management skills to parents of children with what is now known as Attention-Deficit/Hyperactivity Disorder (ADHD); Meichenbaum's (1977) promotion of cognitive-behavior modification; Kendall's (1991; Kendall & Braswell, 1985) cognitive-behavioral strategies for impulsive children and for children with anxiety disorders; and the systematic interventions and ecological applications by operant psychologists in classroom, day care, group home, and work environments all served to shape the field. As described in the sections that follow, further expansion and extensions of this work in the 1980s and 1990s have moved behavioral applications into cognitive and affective processes, family intervention, health psychology, behavioral pediatrics, community intervention, environmental engineering, clinical process, and early intervention and prevention. The cumulative impact of Alan Kazdin's writings and research over the past 25 years has been monumental: His work has helped to bring cognitive-behavioral approaches into mainstream clinical child psychology; has done much to bridge the gaps between work in clinical child psychology, child psychiatry, and developmental psychopathology; and has provided the impetus for the current emphasis on the need for empirically supported child and family interventions. All of the aforementioned developments have resulted in most practicing behavior therapists identifying with a cognitive-behavioral orientation (Elliott, Miltenberger, Kaster-Bundgaard, & Lumley, 1996), and an integration of cognitive-behavioral approaches within the more general field of clinical child psychology.

RECENT DEVELOPMENTS

A number of recent conceptual, methodological, and societal developments have shaped, and continue to shape, current cognitive-behavioral approaches to the treatment of child and family disorders. These include the following:

1. A growing recognition of the need for a systems perspective to guide cognitive-behavioral assessment and treatment (e.g., Emery, Fincham, & Cummings, 1992; Foster & Robin, Chapter 12, this volume; Henggeler, Schoenwald, & Pickrel, 1995; Kanfer & Schefft, 1988).
2. An increased developmental emphasis in the design and implementation of cognitive-behavioral treatments (e.g., Harris & Ferrari, 1983; Kendall, Lerner, & Craighead, 1984; Meyers & Cohen, 1990; Peterson, 1996).
3. An increased sensitivity to the role of individual differences, including personality, gender, ethnic, cultural, and biological factors, in moderating the effectiveness of treatment (e.g., Haynes & Uchigakiuchi, 1993b; Iwamasa, 1996; Neal-Barnett & Smith, 1996; Russo & Budd, 1987; Strayhorn, 1987).
4. A heightened interest in the potential utility of clinical diagnosis and empirical classification as decision aids in formulating effective treatments (e.g., Achenbach, 1993; Achenbach & McConaughy, 1997; Harris & Powers, 1984; Mash & Terdal, 1997b).
5. A growing view of cognitive-behavioral intervention as a collaborative clinical decision-making process (e.g., Evans & Meyer, 1985; Herbert, 1987; Kanfer & Busemeyer, 1982; Nezu & Nezu, 1989, 1993; Webster-Stratton & Herbert, 1994).
6. An increased emphasis on prevention, and the development of early intervention programs for high-risk children, youths, and families (e.g., Clarke et al., 1995; Conduct Problems Prevention Research Group, 1992; Dunst, Trivette, & Deal, 1988; McEachin, Smith, & Lovaas, 1993; Peterson & Mori, 1985; Peters & McMahon, 1996; Peterson, Zink, & Downing, 1993; Roberts & Peterson, 1984).
7. A focus on the interrelated influences of child cognitions and affects on behavior, as assessed and treated within the context of ongoing social interactions (e.g., Gottman & Katz, 1996; Lochman, 1987; Finch, Nelson, & Ott, 1993; Kendall, 1991; Schwebel & Fine, 1992).
8. An increased emphasis on the treatment of childhood disorders in the context of the family (Henggeler et al., 1997; Henggeler & Borduin, 1990; Mash & Johnston, 1996; Schwebel & Fine, 1994), including efforts to integrate individual and family therapy approaches (Fauber & Long, 1991), and the extensive involvement of family members in treatment programs for a wide range of childhood disorders.
9. The proliferation of cognitive-behavioral practices in health care settings and their application to a growing number of health-related problems (e.g., Gross & Drabman, 1990; Karoly, 1988; Koetting, Peterson, & Saldana, 1997; Roberts, 1995).
10. A growing acceptance of the notion that individualized treatments should also be population-specific, focusing on parameters that are relevant to particular types of childhood disorders (Kazdin, 1997; Lee & Mash, 1990; Mash & Barkley, 1989; Mash & Terdal, 1997b).
11. An increased emphasis on the use of multimodal and combined (e.g., behavior therapy and medication) intervention strategies (Kazdin, 1996a).
12. A growing recognition of the general importance of accountability in treatment, with a concomitant emphasis on the need for empirically supported treatments (Hibbs & Jensen, 1996; Hoagwood, Hibbs, Brent, & Jensen, 1995; Weisz, in press) and for cost-effective interventions such as group treatments (Hoag & Burlingame, 1997; Stoiber & Kratochwill, in press) and behavioral consultations (Sheridan, Kratochwill, & Bergan, 1996).
13. An increasing emphasis on the detailed specification of treatment strategies and procedures, as reflected in a growing number of treatment manuals for such child and adolescent disorders as conduct problems (Barkley, 1997b; Forehand & McMahon, 1981; Henggeler, 1991), anxiety disorders (Albano, Marten, & Holt, 1991; Kendall, Kane, Howard, & Siqueland, 1992; Knox, Al-

bano, & Barlow, 1993), depression (Clarke & Lewinsohn, 1995; Stark & Kendall, 1996), and relationship violence (Wolfe et al., 1996).

14. Increased attention to models of child and family intervention that are sensitive to changing societal demographics and needs (American Psychological Association, 1996), the realities and constraints of present-day health care delivery systems (Mash & Hunsley, 1993; Norcross, Karg, & Prochaska, 1997; Roberts & Hurley, 1997; Strosahl, 1994, 1996), and the everyday demands of clinical practice (Adelman, 1995; Clement, 1996; Kazdin, 1997).

Behavioral–Systems Perspective

Perhaps the most striking development in child and family cognitive-behavioral therapy has been the increasing tendency to design and implement treatments based on a systems perspective of child and family functioning (Mash, 1989; Miller & Prinz, 1990). This approach is consistent with a more general trend toward the use of systems models in related fields, such as developmental psychology (e.g., Bronfenbrenner, 1986; Cowan, 1997; Fogel & Thelan, 1987), developmental psychopathology (Sameroff, 1995), and family therapy (Gurman & Kniskern, 1991). Many of the other developments that have occurred in child and family cognitive-behavioral therapy appear to be either directly or indirectly related to the adoption of a systems perspective. Although a thorough presentation of contemporary systems models for child and family treatment is beyond the scope of this chapter (see Steinglass, 1987, for an overview), concepts that are especially relevant for cognitive-behavioral clinical practice include (1) a view of child and family disorders as constellations of interrelated response systems and subsystems; (2) the need to consider the child and family's entire situation when assessing the impact of any single variable; (3) the idea that similar behaviors may be the result of different sets of initiating factors; (4) a recognition that intervention is likely to lead to multiple outcomes, including readjustments of relationships within the family system (e.g., Brunk, Henggeler, & Whelan, 1987); and (5) the notion that family systems and subsystems possess dynamic properties and are constantly changing over time (Hollandsworth, 1986). As will be illustrated throughout this volume, all of these

concepts have important implications for the manner in which treatments are selected, implemented, and evaluated.

Isolated elements of a systems formulation have characterized behavioral and cognitive-behavioral approaches to child and family treatment throughout their inception and development. For example, concepts such as situationism (Mischel, 1968), social learning (Bandura, 1969, 1986), reciprocity (Patterson, 1976, 1982), behavioral ecology (Willems, 1974), intervention in the natural environment (Tharp & Wetzel, 1969), response classes (Voeltz & Evans, 1982), triple-response-system assessment (Eifert & Wilson, 1991), keystone behaviors (Wahler, 1975), setting events (Wahler & Fox, 1981; Wahler & Graves, 1983), stimulus generalization (Stokes & Baer, 1977), and response generalization (Kazdin, 1982b) all suggest the complex interplay of variables associated with a systems orientation. However, it is only recently that explicit systems formulations have been brought to bear in child and family behavior therapy, both as a general therapeutic orientation (e.g., Alexander & Parsons, 1982; Robin & Foster, 1989) and in specific areas such as conduct problems (Henggeler & Borduin, 1990), autism (Harris, 1984), school and learning problems (Evans & Meyer, 1985), and child abuse (Azar & Wolfe, Chapter 10, this volume).

Progression toward a systems perspective has resulted in a number of related developments in the cognitive-behavioral treatment of child and family disorders, including (1) continued extension of cognitive-behavioral practices into new areas; (2) an emphasis on the use of combined and multimodal treatments; (3) increasing specialization; (4) a broadening of treatment goals; (5) a growing recognition of the need for multidisciplinary approaches to treatment; and (6) an expanded concept of treatment to include a range of treatment delivery models.

Extension into New Areas

The range of individual response systems (e.g., behavioral, cognitive, emotional, physical), family subsystems (e.g., mother–child, father–child, marital, sibling), and settings (e.g., home, classroom, day care, outpatient clinic, hospital, summer camp, workplace) encompassed by a systems perspective has promoted the extension of cognitive-behavioral practices into new problem areas, with different populations, and in new settings. Perhaps the most visible extension has been in the area of pediatric and health psychology (e.g., Gross & Drabman, 1990; Roberts,

1995). The range of problems treated also continues to grow, as interventions have become increasingly sensitive to the interrelationships among the behavioral, emotional, cognitive, and physical manifestations of child and family disorders (e.g., Crick & Dodge, 1994; Kendall, 1987). Applications in the areas of social competence (e.g., Lochman, 1988; Lochman & Wells, 1996; McFadyen-Ketchum & Dodge, Chapter 6, this volume), sexual abuse (e.g., Wolfe & Birt, 1997), childhood and adolescent depression (e.g., Kazdin & Marciano, Chapter 4, this volume; Stark, Rouse, & Livingston, 1991), teenage drinking and other substance misuse (e.g., Myers, Brown, & Vik, Chapter 15, this volume), accident prevention (e.g., Peterson & Mori, 1985), and childhood anxiety disorders (e.g., Barrios & O'Dell, Chapter 5, this volume) illustrate this growth.

Use of Combined and Multimodal Treatments

The multidimensional nature of the causes and contexts of child and family disorders; the limited therapeutic effects of single-modality treatments; and the desire for more powerful treatments to produce clinically significant, generalizable, and long-lasting effects have led to an increased use of combined and multimodal treatments (Kazdin, 1996a). The term "combined treatments" generally refers to the use of two or more interventions, each of which can stand on its own as a treatment strategy. In some instances, combinations of stand-alone interventions may cross conceptual approaches—for example, when cognitive-behavioral and pharmacological treatments are used for children with ADHD (Arnold, Abikoff, & Wells, 1997; Barkley, 1990) or children with Obsessive–Compulsive Disorder (Piacentini & Graae, 1997), or when cognitive-behavioral treatment and family therapy are combined (Fauber & Kendall, 1992). In other instances, combined treatments may be derived from the same overall conceptual approach—for example, the use of social skills training and cognitive restructuring in a group treatment program for adolescents with Social Phobia (Marten, Albano, & Holt, 1991) or individual behavior management and family behavior therapy in the treatment of children with oppositional disorders (Fauber & Long, 1991).

There are numerous theoretical, practical, and evaluation issues associated with the use of combined treatments. Paramount among these are the need for models to guide decision mak-

ing with respect to when, how, and under what circumstances combined treatments are to be used, and the need for a variety of research strategies to determine the incremental gains, synergistic effects, and conditions associated with the effective use of combined treatments. Clearly, more treatment is not synonymous with more *effective* treatment, and in the absence of decision rules and research to guide when combined treatments are to be used there is the potential danger of using cost-inefficient, time consuming, and potentially detrimental treatments in an effort to introduce the most "powerful" intervention possible using an "everything but the kitchen sink" model of service delivery. Kazdin (1996a) has presented a detailed and thought provoking discussion of these and many other issues related to the use of combined treatments.

Increasing Specialization

Extension of cognitive-behavioral practice into new areas has also been accompanied by increasing differentiation and specialization. Such specialization indicates a recognition of the unique developmental demands, setting events, controlling variables, and intervention requirements associated with particular age groups, problems, and settings. In referring to developments in child behavior therapy, Hersen and Van Hasselt (1987) noted that "the field has become more differentiated, with many of our colleagues specializing in the treatment of certain age groups and particular disorders. As time goes on we see fewer generalists in behavior therapy with children and adolescents" (p. xi). The chapters in this volume bear witness to the fact that the conceptual formulations, clinical procedures, and operational rules associated with different kinds of childhood disorders are quite different, and that effective intervention requires a thorough understanding of the specific parameters and empirical findings associated with particular clusters of problems, situations, and risk factors.

Broadening of Treatment Goals

The systems perspective in child and family cognitive-behavioral therapy also has implications for the manner in which treatment goals are defined and the range of treatment outcomes evaluated. Although early behavioral interventions were criticized for their overemphasis on management, compliance, and the short-term reduction of symptomatic distress (e.g., Winett & Winkler, 1972), recent applications have shown an increasing sensitivity to the need to develop skills and competencies in both the child and his or her social environment, and to minimize adverse outcomes through the use of maintenance and prevention strategies. As Blechman (1985) has stated, "Children with behavior problems deserve more in the way of treatment than training to conform quietly to the demands of poorly functioning homes and schools. Contemporary behavior therapy aspires to reshape the social environment, so that family and classroom foster children's social, emotional, and intellectual competence" (p. ix). The focus of treatment needs to be on changes that make a meaningful difference in the child's life, and producing changes that are statistically significant may not be sufficient in achieving this objective.

Current cognitive-behavioral treatments are directed at the family and/or peer group, and not just the child (e.g., Howard & Kendall, 1996). An increasing number of studies support the notion that more effective treatment outcomes are achieved when treatment focuses on the child *and* on relevant family subsystems. For example, in treating conduct-disordered children, Dadds, Schwartz, and Sanders (1987) compared child management training alone with a combined child management training plus partner support training package, which focused on reducing marital conflict and improving communication and problem solving. Although there were no group differences immediately following treatment, the partner support condition was associated with better child and family outcomes at a 6-month follow-up for families in which there was marital discord. Other studies have found that the addition of a family component to treatment that focused on interactions, managing emotion, communication, and problem solving significantly enhanced short-term outcome and long-term maintenance in children with anxiety disorders (Barrett, Dadds, & Rapee, 1996).

These findings, and those from many other investigations to be discussed throughout this volume, all reinforce the notion that treatment goals should focus on building skills in the child and his or her social environment that will facilitate long-term adjustment, and not just on the elimination of problem behaviors and/or the short-term reduction of subjective distress. Although symptom reduction is one important goal of therapy, other treatment goals and outcomes are also of crucial importance to the child, family, and society at large. These include

(1) outcomes related to child functioning, such as changes in symptoms, degree of impairment in functioning, prosocial competence, and academic performance; (2) outcomes related to family functioning, such as level of family dysfunction, marital and sibling relationships, stress, quality of life, burden of care, and family support; (3) outcomes of societal importance, such as the child's participation in school-related activities (increased attendance, reduced truancy, reduction in school dropout), decreased involvement in the juvenile justice system, reduced need for special services, reduction in accidental injuries or substance misuse, and enhancement of physical and mental health (Kazdin, 1997).

Cognitive-behavioral therapies have typically emphasized the goal of helping children and families to achieve control over their thoughts and feelings as a vehicle for behavior change. A recent trend in work with adults is toward helping some clients accept rather than control their thoughts and feelings as a key element for behavior change (e.g., Jacobson & Christensen, 1996). Although experiential acceptance and its relationship to behavior change in interventions with children and families have not received systematic attention to date, there has been an implicit emphasis on this goal in several applications of work with children and families. For example, treatments for children with ADHD and developmental disabilities are often directed at helping parents accept their reactions to their child's condition while providing them with alternative strategies for coping with their own reactions and their child's behavior (Barkley, 1997b). Some treatments for adolescents with Social Phobia help children understand and accept the adaptive nature of anxiety as a normal reaction to perceived threat as one element of treatment (Marten et al., 1991). The goal of acceptance in the context of the rapid developmental change and malleability that characterizes childhood is likely to be controversial and in some ways antagonistic with the current emphasis on prevention. On the other hand, an accumulating body of evidence suggesting the importance of early dispositions and styles of information processing and emotion regulation for a number of childhood disorders, such as ADHD, early-onset Conduct Disorder, anxiety disorders, autism, and learning disabilities, suggests that a recognition and acceptance of these "basic" tendencies by the child and family may be an important element for teaching coping strategies and achieving effective behavior change. This hypothesis is worthy of further exploration.

Multidisciplinary Perspective

The adoption of a systems viewpoint has also reinforced the need for a multidisciplinary perspective in the cognitive-behavioral treatment of child and family disorders. As stated by Kanfer and Schefft (1988), "The systems approach implies the relevance of different knowledge bases, particularly the social and biological sciences. It is multidisciplinary, and effective treatment often requires familiarity with information that cuts across disciplines" (p. 19). The interlocking network of physical, behavioral, social, and learning difficulties that characterizes most childhood disorders necessitates a multidisciplinary approach to both treatment and prevention (e.g., Jason, Felner, Hess, & Moritsugo, 1987). The coordinated use of medication and psychosocial interventions for children with ADHD (e.g., Barkley, Chapter 2, this volume; Pelham & Murphy, 1986), autism (e.g., Schroeder, Gualtieri, & Van Bourgondien, 1986), anxiety disorders (Piacentini & Graae, 1997), and childhood depression (e.g., Kazdin & Marciano, Chapter 4, this volume) illustrates this point, as does the integration of cognitive-behavioral procedures with effective teaching strategies for learning-disabled children (e.g., Lyon & Cutting, Chapter 9, this volume), or with required medical procedures in the case of children with a chronic illness (e.g., Johnson & Rodrigue, 1997).

Expanded Concept of Treatment and Range of Treatment Delivery Models

The complexity of a systems framework underscores the notion that different child and family problems and circumstances require different solutions. Conventional models of cognitive-behavioral treatment have consisted of brief time-limited interventions focusing on already-identified problems. Treatment is carried out for several weeks or months, until the problem is eliminated, at which time the treatment is withdrawn. Even within this model it has been recognized that concerted efforts must be made both during, and to a lesser extent after, treatment is terminated if gains are to be maintained (Mash & Terdal, 1980). Although conventional models of treatment may be appropriate for many acute or focal problems of mild severity, it is clear that other treatment delivery models

may be needed for more complex, severe, or chronic difficulties.

As possible alternatives to the conventional care model of treatment, Kazdin (1997) has highlighted two types of continuing care models. The first is a "chronic care model," in which treatment is maintained and adjusted in the same way that it would be for children with a chronic illness such as diabetes mellitus or asthma. Ongoing treatment is needed to insure that the benefits of treatment are maintained. ADHD and early-onset Conduct Disorder are two long-term and persistent problems in which a chronic care model of treatment may be needed. The second approach to continuing care is a "dental-care model," in which ongoing follow-ups are carried out on a regular basis following initial treatment, in much the same way that regular dental checkups are recommended at 6-month intervals. Follow-ups may be conducted on a periodic basis at prescribed intervals or on an "as-needed" basis related to emergent issues in development and adjustment.

Conventional models of treatment, in which a child is seen individually by a therapist for a limited number of treatment sessions in the clinic, fail to recognize the many other options for helping children with problems that are available and that are currently being used. These options include many different treatment agents (e.g., parents, teachers, siblings, peers, foster parents) and settings (e.g., home, school, community, residential, day care, summer camps, foster homes). Current behavioral–systems approaches to child and family treatment recognize the need for a continuum of intervention activities and treatment delivery models ranging from primary prevention programs to targeted preschool and early-school interventions, to focused intensive treatments for severe and chronic problems. An illustration of one such intervention continuum, and the wide range of intervention and prevention activities encompassed under the concept of "treatment" with children and families, is shown in Figure 1.1 (Adelman & Taylor, 1993).

Developmental Emphasis

Early behavioral applications were decidedly insensitive to the need for incorporating developmental information into their assessments and treatments. This was due in part to their almost exclusive reliance on principles of learning such as positive reinforcement, negative reinforcement, extinction, and punishment, which were presumed to apply universally across all age groups and populations without regard for developmental status. Recent cognitive-behavioral work has become increasingly sensitive to the developmental issues surrounding diagnosis (e.g., Peterson, Burbach, & Chaney, 1989), assessment (e.g., Mash & Terdal, 1990, 1997b; Yule, 1993), and treatment (e.g., Harris & Ferrari, 1983; Kendall et al., 1984; McMahon & Peters, 1985; Meyers & Cohen, 1990). Also, behavioral conceptualizations of child and family disturbance have increasingly attempted to conceptualize, describe, predict, and suggest ways to alter the developmental progression of child and family disorders—for example, in the cases of antisocial children (Dishion, French, & Patterson, 1995), children with autism (e.g., Lovaas, 1987), children with ADHD (Barkley et al., 1997), or children who have been abused or neglected (e.g., Azar & Wolfe, Chapter 10, this volume). Although this increased developmental emphasis continues to be an exciting and needed direction in the field, the incorporation of developmental findings and principles into cognitive-behavioral practice is a complex affair, and, to date, the degree to which it has been accomplished remains rudimentary at best.

Part of the difficulty in achieving a clinical–developmental integration is in specifying precisely what such an integration would require. At its simplest level, and the one that has characterized behavioral approaches to date, a developmental emphasis involves some recognition (1) that the child's age, developmental level, and gender play a significant role in determining the methods of treatment that are likely to be most effective; and (2) that normative information about development may facilitate clinical decision making by suggesting such things as the boundaries for normal development, when intervention is or is not required, and what constitute appropriate treatment goals. Normative information may also provide a basis for evaluating the clinical significance of change. For example, Kazdin, Esveldt-Dawson, French, and Unis (1987) found that even though a problem-solving skills training program was more effective than a relationship-oriented approach in treating conduct-disordered children, the adjustment of these children was still outside the norms for a nonclinical population at a 1-year follow-up. Similarly, Barkley, Guevremont, Anastopoulos, and Fletcher (1992) found that although adolescents with ADHD improved following treatment, most did not show clinically significant

improvements when their functioning was compared with the functioning of control children.

At a more complex level, a developmental emphasis would require the incorporation of developmental principles and findings into our conceptualizations of child and family psychopathology—such that treatments are sensitive not only to a child's age and sex, but also to ongoing developmental *processes* as they unfold and interact with and within one or more dynamic and changing social systems. At this level, our treatments not only would be sensitive to developmental parameters, but would be *derived from* our knowledge of relevant developmental processes, including neurodevelopmental processes (Courchesne, Townsend, & Chase, 1995; cognition (Noam, Chandler, & LaLonde, 1995), attachment (Rutter, 1997), self-control (Barkley, 1997a), and emotion regulation (Cicchetti, Ackerman, & Izard, 1995). However, the principles and processes that are deemed to be most important vary across developmental theories; the empirical base describing these processes is just beginning to emerge from recent longitudinal investigations; and the decision rules by which developmental knowledge can be translated into clinical practice are not well developed at this time. In light of this, there is likely to be continued exploration of the boundaries for developmental applications of cognitive-behavioral treatments with children and families. Recent research in the emergent field of developmental psychopathology has provided a growing empirical base to guide these new interventions (Cicchetti & Cohen, 1995a, 1995b).

Within the field of developmental psychopathology, organizational–developmental positions that consider development as involving progressive reorganizations in response to changing environmental demands (e.g., Cicchetti & Cohen, 1995c), and models that conceptualize early development in terms of child and family coping responses (e.g., Emery & Kitzmann, 1995; Tronick & Gianino, 1986), seem especially consistent with a cognitive-behavioral perspective. Within these views, the origins of child and family disorders are seen as involving breakdowns in adaptational processes. For a variety of reasons, both the child and family fail to cope adequately with either normative or nonnormative events. These models consider adaptational outcomes in relation to the complex interaction between and among external events, perceptual and cognitive appraisals of such events, internal conditions

Intervention Continuum	Types of Activities (directed at system changes and individual needs)

Primary prevention ("public health")

1. Programs designed to promote and maintain

   - safety (at home and at school)
   - physical and mental health (including healthy start initiatives, immunizations, substance abuse prevention, violence prevention, health/mental health education, sex education and family planning, and so forth)

2. Preschool programs (encompassing a focus on health and psychosocial development)

   - parent education and support
   - day care
   - early education
   - identification and amelioration of physical and mental health and psychosocial problems

Early-age targeted intervention

3. Early school adjustment program

   - welcoming and transition support into school life for students and their families (especially immigrants)
   - personalized instruction in the primary grades
   - additional support in class for identified students
   - parent involvement in problem solving
   - comprehensive and accessible psychosocial and physical and mental health programs (primary grades)

Early-after-onset correction

4. Improvement and augmentation of ongoing regular support

   - preparation and support for school and life transitions
   - teaching "basics" of remediation to regular teachers (including use of available resource personnel, peer and volunteer support)
   - parent involvement in problem solving
   - providing support for parents in need
   - comprehensive and accessible psychosocial and physical and mental health programs (including interventions for students and families targeted as high risks—all grades)
   - emergency and crisis prevention and response mechanisms

5. Interventions prior to referral for intensive treatments

   - staff development (including consultation)
   - short-term specialized interventions (including resource teacher instruction and family mobilization; programs for pregnant minors, substance abusers, gang members, and other potential dropouts)

6. Intensive treatments—referral to and coordination with

   - special education
   - dropout recovery and follow-up support
   - services for severe/chronic psychosocial/mental/physical health problems

Treatment for severe/chronic problems

FIGURE 1.1. From prevention to treatment: A continuum of programs for amelioration of learning, behavior, and socioemotional problems. From Adelman and Taylor (1993, p. 279). Copyright 1993 by Wadsworth, Inc. Reprinted by permission of Brooks/Cole Publishing Company.

(e.g., values, physical status, personality traits), external resources for coping (e.g., social support), decision-making processes, and preferred coping strategies.

Age

A common assumption in the treatment of children has been that interventions directed at younger children are likely to be more effective. In part, this is because younger children are presumed to be more malleable than older children, and because maladaptive patterns of behavior have had less time to become well established. Some indirect support for this assumption comes from a meta-analysis ("meta-analyis" is a technique for pooling research findings across studies) carried out by Weisz, Weiss, Alicke, and Klotz (1987), who found a mean effect size of 0.92 for treatment studies with children aged 4–12, compared with a mean effect size of 0.58 for children aged 13–18. However, findings between age and outcome are inconsistent, with one recent meta-analysis reporting the largest effect size for adolescents (Weisz, Weiss, Han, Granger, & Morton, 1995).

Age effects in treatment are also likely to interact with the type of treatment under consideration. For example, in one meta-analysis of studies using just cognitive-behavioral therapy it was predicted that effect sizes would be larger for adolescents than younger children, because adolescents function at a higher cognitive level and thus are more likely to learn the cognitive skills needed in treatment. This prediction was supported, with an effect size of 0.92 for 11- to 13-year-old adolescents, compared with effect sizes of 0.55 in children aged 7–11 years and 0.57 in children aged 5–7 years (Durlak, Fuhrman, & Lampman, 1991). Although both common sense and clinical sensitivity would indicate that different approaches are required for children of different ages, few empirical studies have demonstrated specific cognitive-behavioral strategies to be more or less effective with children of different ages.

More importantly, the issue is not so much one of differential effectiveness of the same treatment procedure at different ages, but rather the extent to which we can identify specific age-related developmental processes and capacities and incorporate them into treatment in order to produce more effective outcomes. At best, age is a summary measure of many diverse developmental influences—biological, social, cognitive, and contextual, each of which is deserving of attention in its own right (Weisz, in press). For ex-

ample, at what ages can mental imagery be used in reducing fears, or can cognitive self-instruction be employed in regulating impulsive behavior? How might the application of a time-out procedure be different for 3- to 5-year-olds versus school-age children? How might explanations of procedures be adjusted to take into account a child's cognitive capabilities? In one study, Wurtele, Marrs, and Miller-Perrin (1987) found that participant modeling procedures were more effective than symbolic modeling procedures in teaching personal safety skills to kindergarten children, although this difference was not significant at a 6-week follow-up. These authors emphasized the importance of including active rehearsal in programs for young children, and noted that some prevention studies have found that young children may have difficulty understanding the abstract concepts involved in a cognitive approach.

Gender

Few studies have examined the general effectiveness of treatment as a function of children's gender and findings in this area are variable. In one meta-analysis of treatment outcome studies, Casey and Berman (1985) found that the percentage of boys in the sample was negatively correlated with treatment outcome. Weisz, Weiss, Alicker, and Klotz (1987) found no difference in mean effect size for treatment studies with males versus females. And Weisz, Weiss, et al. (1995) found mean effect sizes for adolescent girls that were approximately twice as large as those for adolescent boys and for younger children of both genders. As with age, a critical question related to gender differences is how information regarding these differences might suggest different treatment strategies. To date, few cognitive-behavioral treatment studies have directly addressed this question. However, numerous studies have reported sex differences in the expression of childhood disorders (Zahn-Waxler, 1993; Zoccolillo, 1993), and these may suggest different intervention protocols for boys versus girls. To illustrate, a few of these studies are described below.

Moran and Eckenrode (1988) examined the relationship between social stress and depression in adolescent males and females. It was found that female early adolescents were significantly more affected by social stress than male agemates, but that older males and females were similarly affected. Other studies (e.g., Nolen-Hoeksema, Girgus, & Seligman, 1988) have shown peer popularity or rejection to be more highly correlated with depression in girls than in boys. Such findings suggest that interventions directed at enhancing peer relationships may be especially critical for young adolescent females.

Block and Gjerde (1990) found that the predictors at age 14 of depressive symptomatology at age 18 were quite different for boys versus girls. Fourteen-year-old girls subsequently expressing depressive tendencies were described as vulnerable, anxious, somaticizing, and showing generally low esteem. In contrast, 14-year-old boys who later showed high depressive symptomatology tended to show an early lack of concern for satisfying interpersonal relationships, and subsequent antisocial and hostile characteristics. Introspective concern with self-adequacy seemed to be a less salient issue for boys. For boys, early intellective *in*competence predicted later depressive symptoms, whereas for girls early intellective competence predicted depressive symptomatology.

Block, Block, and Keyes (1988) found that the personality concomitants and antecedents of drug use differed somewhat as a function of gender and the drug used. At age 14, the use of marijuana was related to ego undercontrol, while the use of harder drugs reflected an absence of ego resiliency, with undercontrol also being a contributing factor. For girls, adolescent drug use was related to both undercontrol and lower ego resiliency at 3 to 4 years of age; for boys, preschool undercontrol was a strong predictor of adolescent drug use, but there was no impact of ego resiliency. Early family environments that were characterized by an unstructured and laissez-faire atmosphere, with little pressure to achieve, were related to adolescent drug use in girls but not in boys. For boys only, drug use was related to an IQ decline from age 11 to 18.

Recent studies of the psychophysiology of disruptive behavior in boys versus girls suggest that girls' disruptive behavior may be more closely connected than boys' disruptive behavior to experiences of anxiety (Zahn-Waxler, Cole, Welsh, & Fox, 1995), and that although rates of disruptive behavior are lower in girls than in boys, girls show a higher incidence of comorbid disorders (Zahn-Waxler, 1993). Such findings would suggest that different interventions may be needed for girls and boys with disruptive behavior disorders. For example, combined interventions that focus both on conduct problems and on anxiety and mood disorders may be especially important in treating the comorbid conditions observed in females with disruptive behavior disorders.

Recent research has also found that girls are more likely than boys to be emotionally upset by aggressive social exchanges (Crick, 1995). Moreover, when angry, girls are more likely than boys to use indirect and relational forms of aggression, such as verbal insults, gossip, tattling, ostracism, threatening to withdraw one's friendship, getting even, or third-party retaliation (Crick, Bigbee, & Howes, 1996). As girls move into adolescence, the function of their aggressive behavior increasingly centers around group acceptance and affiliation, whereas for boys aggression remains confrontational in nature. These findings suggest different avenues for the treatment of aggression in girls versus boys.

There also may be gender differences in children's preferences for treatment agents. For example, Winter, Hicks, McVey, and Fox (1988) found that children's choices regarding the people (i.e., peers, parents, experts) they would consult for different types of problems varied as a function of the children's age and sex. Furthermore, in choosing consultants, females valued familiarity, whereas males valued expertise. Although a number of the studies just described do not address treatment concerns directly, their findings do suggest that the focus of both treatment and prevention efforts needs to be different for boys and girls of different ages (Kavanagh & Hops, 1994).

Norms

The uses of normative information in cognitive-behavioral assessment have received extensive discussion (e.g., Edelbrock, 1984; Hartmann, Roper, & Bradford, 1979; Mash & Terdal, 1997b), and many of these uses parallel those for treatment. Briefly, such normative information is important in identifying problems, evaluating parental and teacher expectations, identifying difficulties that are likely to be chronic versus those that are common and transient, deciding when treatment is indicated, establishing treatment goals, suggesting different forms of treatment, and evaluating the clinical significance of change.

Normative information may also suggest possible goals for prevention studies. For example, Kline, Canter, and Robin (1987) reported that 15%–40% of junior and senior high school students may experience problems related to alcohol use, and found that measures of family functioning such as disengagement, poor communication, and family approval of alcohol were highly predictive of teenage drinking. Rubenstein, Heeren, Houssman, Rubin, and Stechler

(1988) reported that 20% of the adolescents in their high school sample were suicidal, and virtually indistinguishable on all measures from their hospitalized suicidal sample. Of the high school sample of adolescents, 75% had received no therapeutic intervention in the year of their suicide attempt. Carlson, Asarnow, and Orbach (1987) reported that although rates of completed suicide were low prior to the age of 14 years, suicidal ideation and nonfatal suicide attempts were not uncommon in preadolescent children. Such ideation and nonfatal attempts have been noted prior to fatal suicides, and they sometimes occur in the context of depression. The normative information derived from the Rubenstein et al. and Carlson et al. studies suggests that there are significant numbers of unidentified and/or untreated suicidal adolescents in the public schools, and that there is a need for early intervention and prevention programs in this area.

Recognition of Individual Differences

Cognitive-behavioral approaches have shown a growing concern for individual differences in inborn and/or acquired characteristics of both children and parents in mediating treatment outcomes. Characteristics such as child temperament, personality disorders, parental anxiety and depression, and the generalized expectations and attributions of parents have all been identified as possible mediators. In addition to basic biological differences (e.g., temperament, social inhibition, arousability, threshold to novel events, emotion regulation, sensitivity to aversive stimuli), background characteristics (e.g., intelligence, social status, family configuration) may also influence the child's and family's style of social problem solving, their attributional processes, and their reactions to specific types of treatment. For example, in the case of parents, generalized expectancies concerning what the future holds, referred to as "dispositional optimism or pessimism" (Scheier & Carver, 1985), could determine the success of behavioral parent training programs, to the extent that they influence the parental coping mechanisms that are invoked. Optimists focus on active problem solving in coping with stress, whereas pessimists focus on their feelings of distress, disengage from goal-directed activities, and give up their goals when obstacles intervene (Carver & Scheier, 1986).

Maternal depression and anxiety, parental psychopathy, parental substance misuse, marital conflict, parent attributional styles, and parenting self-esteem are examples of other parent characteristics that have been shown to be related to treatment outcomes. It has also been found that family members of children with problems have an elevated risk of psychopathology across a wide range of childhood disorders (e.g., ADHD, anxiety, depression), often for the same or similar disorders as their children. This possibility needs to be carefully considered in treatment, since many cognitive-behavioral interventions with children rely extensively on the involvement of family members in treatment, and the presence of a disorder in a parent may interfere with treatment efficacy if not also addressed. For example, it was found that a mother with ADHD did better in parent training when her own ADHD was treated with medication (Evans, Vallano, & Pelham, 1994).

One child characteristic that seems especially important for both treatment and prevention is intelligence, which appears to be an attenuating factor for many different kinds of problems (e.g., Lynam, Moffitt, & Stouthamer-Loeber, 1993). For example, Kandel et al. (1988) reported that in a group at high risk for criminality, seriously criminal cohort members evidenced lower IQ scores than cohort members with no criminal registration. Their interpretation was that within the high-risk group higher IQ led to school success and greater rewards, which in turn led to greater attachment to school and bonding to the conventional social order. Also, Schonfeld, Shaffer, O'Conner, and Portnoy (1988) have reported a direct link between deficiencies in cognitive functioning and Conduct Disorder in boys, and argue that the nature of this deficiency is one of acculturational learning broadly defined, rather than a narrowly focused social-cognitive deficit.

Recent research has found that cognitive-behavioral interventions with community-based samples of parents and children may not be as effective as interventions with parents and children who are referred to clinics for treatment, and that community-identified samples may be less likely to participate fully in treatment and more likely to terminate treatment prematurely (Barkley, Chapter 2, this volume). Understanding the individual differences that may contribute to such differential participation rates and treatment outcomes in community samples seems especially important in the context of current prevention efforts directed at children and families whose problems have not yet resulted in referral. In this regard, one characteristic that may be especially important is the parent's (and child's) "readiness for change." We need to understand the structural stages and processes of change that support or impede such readiness.

Clinical Diagnosis and Empirical Classification

Early cognitive-behavioral treatments minimized the need for formal clinical diagnosis and/or assignment to groups based on empirical classification procedures, and emphasized the importance of individualized behavioral assessments. However, current research and practice has increasingly acknowledged the potential benefits to be derived from the use of standardized diagnostic systems such as the fourth edition of the *Diagnostic and Statistical Manual of Mental Disorders* (DSM-IV; American Psychiatric Association, 1994) or the 10th revision of *International Classification of Diseases* (ICD-10; World Health Organization, 1992); multivariate classification strategies (e.g., Achenbach, 1993, 1995; Reynolds & Kamphaus, 1992); and classification models based upon a developmental perspective (e.g., Garber, 1984; Zero to Three/National Center for Clinical Infant Programs, 1994). Such approaches are intended to supplement rather than replace the individualized and contextually grounded assessments characteristic of an individualized and ongoing behavioral/functional analysis (Carr, 1994; Hayes & Follette, 1992; Haynes & Uchigakiuchi, 1993a; Mash & Terdal, 1997b).

Many treatment programs have been instituted with poorly or globally defined groups of children and with little regard for comorbidity or family or cultural context. Classification efforts focusing on the refinement and development of subtypes of child and family disorders have potential for determining the kinds of treatments that are likely to be most effective for individuals and families showing particular constellations of characteristics (e.g., client–treatment matching). Categorization efforts to date have attempted to subtype disturbed children on the basis of dimensions such as social withdrawal (Rubin & Stewart, 1996), styles of social information processing (Milich & Dodge, 1984), and peer social status (Lochman & Lampron, 1986), comorbid disorders (Caron & Rutter, 1991), and types of violence (Tolan & Guerra, 1994) and aggression (Crick & Dodge, 1996), to name a few. To illustrate in the case of aggression, "re-

active aggression" occurs in response to actions by others, whereas "proactive aggression" involves taking the offensive without provocation through domination, bullying, or threats. Reactive aggression is associated with deficits and distortions in children's taking in and interpreting information in social situations, including a limited use of social information in reaching interpersonal decisions and a tendency to think that others have bad intentions. In contrast, proactive aggression is associated with a restricted and mostly aggressive behavioral repertoire (Crick & Dodge, 1996). Subgrouping children based on the dimension of proactive versus reactive aggression may lead to a relative difference in treatment emphasis: greater use of cognitive strategies in the case of children who display reactive aggression, and greater use of skill-based or problem-solving strategies in the case of the latter.

The importance of differential diagnosis is also evident in the work on conduct-disordered children with and without comorbid disorders such as ADHD or anxiety disorders (Hinshaw & Anderson, 1996; Lynam, 1996, 1997). Children with diagnoses of Conduct Disorder *and* ADHD show a more diverse and serious pattern of antisocial behavior than children with a diagnosis of Conduct Disorder alone. When ADHD is present, the onset of Conduct Disorder is earlier, the developmental progression from less serious to more serious antisocial behavior may be more rapid, and the risk for psychopathy may be greater than for case of Conduct Disorder alone. In other instances, when Conduct Disorder is accompanied by anxiety, the conduct problem symptoms may be less severe. These differences in behavior and outcomes related to comorbid conditions and developmental history in the case of children with Conduct Disorder suggest the need for different treatment recommendations based on these factors.

Therapy as a Collaborative Decision-Making Process

A number of writers have emphasized the need for a collaborative clinical decision-making approach to cognitive-behavioral interventions with disturbed children and families (Herbert, 1987; Kanfer & Busemeyer, 1982; Nezu & Nezu, 1989, 1993; Webster-Stratton & Herbert, 1994). In many ways, this approach extends and formalizes the everyday decision-making/problem-solving processes used by parents (e.g.,

Holden, 1985), teachers (Evans & Meyer, 1985), children (Urbain & Kendall, 1980), and adolescents (Tisdelle & St. Lawrence, 1988). The models presented by Kanfer (Kanfer & Busemeyer, 1982; Kanfer & Schefft, 1988), Evans and Meyer (1985), Herbert (1981, 1987), Webster-Stratton and Herbert (1994), and Henggeler et al. (1994) provide excellent descriptions of a collaborative decision-making perspective. In contrast to earlier cognitive-behavioral approaches, which were concerned with the use of specific techniques derived from principles of learning, decision-making approaches emphasize the collaborative and flexible application and reapplication of a variety of treatment strategies over time as needed. Decisions concerning the utilization of specific procedures are made within a broader clinical context that takes into account the phase of treatment (Kanfer & Schefft, 1988), the cognitive activities and potential decision-making biases of the clinician (e.g., Kanfer, 1985; Tabachnik & Alloy, 1988); and the social context and values surrounding treatment. Although collaborative decision-making approaches are still under development, some of their more common features include an emphasis on the use of flexible and ongoing decisional strategies (Kanfer & Busemeyer, 1982); a systems orientation (Evans, 1985); the development of generic strategies intended to optimize the effectiveness of more specific target-oriented tactics (Kanfer & Schefft, 1988); creation of a favorable therapeutic environment; identification and elaboration of decision points in treatment (e.g., seeking help, terminating treatment); client participation in decision making; and a sensitivity to the varying needs of different treatment phases.

An emphasis on the flexible use of strategies as a medium in which specific cognitive-behavioral techniques are applied is perhaps the major distinguishing feature of these approaches. As reflected in the following quotations, the concern is with process and not just with techniques. In describing their model of educational decision making, Evans and Meyer (1985) state:

Our approach involves an extension and elaboration of standard behavior modification methods. It is a "second generation" of behavior modification in which the focus is no longer simply on the derivation of techniques from learning principles, but on how these principles may be most effectively adapted to the instructional situation and extended to deal with the total educational needs of the child. This volume

is about educational programming, not just the design of isolated behavioral interventions; about clinical strategies and the values that influence clinical decisions, not just techniques that produce behavior change. (p. 2)

And Herbert (1987), in a practical manual for treating children's problems, states: "There is no one way of carrying out assessments and behavioural programmes. There is nothing preordained about the ordering of the steps suggested" (p. v).

Although the flexibility inherent in the approach being described here has some appeal, there is a need for specific guidelines concerning how clinical *strategies* are to be implemented from a cognitive-behavioral perspective with children and families. As Kanfer and Schefft (1988) note, there are many descriptions of therapy methods (e.g., biofeedback, modeling, parent training, cognitive change methods, relationship enhancement methods), but "there are only a few books that offer clinicians a conceptually consistent framework for structuring each step of the change process, regardless of the specific treatment used" (p. xvi). Implicit in a probabilistic decision-making approach is the notion that there are many different ways to achieve the same treatment objective and that it is possible to identify alternative treatment goals and choices for the same client, depending on the circumstances. There is no proposed solution that can be rigidly adhered to, since each step in treatment is presumed to generate new information that requires ongoing adjustments in the program. In light of the many possible choices that are involved, further elaboration and empirical validation of the decision rules to be used in treatment are clearly needed, in much the same way that specific techniques have been described and validated. Although the desirability of such validation has been acknowledged, it remains to be seen whether systematic quantification of the complex judgmental process involved in treatment is even possible (Kanfer & Schefft, 1988).

Any decision rules in treatment are likely to be contextually specific, and there is a need to identify the parameters under which specific rules may or may not apply. I believe that the accumulated knowledge concerning *specific* childhood disorders represents a critical dimension for clinical decision making, and this view is reflected in the organization of the current volume. A host of other factors also contribute to the selection and sequencing of treatments for children and families, including characteristics of the family subsystems that are involved (e.g., child, parent–child, marital, sibling) and their cultural context; the overt versus covert nature of the problem; characteristics of the primary agent of treatment (e.g., therapist, parent, teacher, child); the treatment setting (e.g., home, classroom); applicable psychological principles and techniques; empirical support for the efficacy and effectiveness of specific treatments for particular problems; and the therapist's orientation (Wolfe & Goldfried, 1988). Collaborative therapeutic decision making is an interactive process that incorporates information from each of these areas and more in formulating an overall intervention strategy.

Decision-making frameworks also emphasize the importance of adapting decision-making rules to the various phases of treatment (e.g., therapist's response to a missed first vs. a missed tenth treatment session), and several writers have delineated such phases. For example, Kanfer and Schefft (1988) describe seven phases of treatment: (1) role structuring and the creation of a therapeutic alliance; (2) developing a commitment for change; (3) the behavioral analysis; (4) negotiating treatment objectives and methods; (5) implementing treatment and maintaining motivation; (6) monitoring and evaluating progress; and (7) maintenance, generalization, and termination of treatment.

Herbert (1987) has presented three general phases. The first, initial screening, involves explaining the therapist's role, identifying problems, identifying the child's and family's assets, specifying the desired outcomes, constructing a problem profile, teaching clients to think in antecedent–behavior–consequence (A-B-C) terms, and establishing problem priorities. The second phase, moving from data collection to problem formulation, includes specifying relevant situations, assessing the extent and severity of the problem, providing the clients with appropriate materials, and determining the frequency and intensity of the problem. The third phase, intervention, involves planning treatment, formulating objectives, selecting procedures and methods, developing a treatment plan, working out practicalities of implementation, evaluating the plan, initiating the program, phasing out intervention, and conducting follow-up.

Conceptual models and decision guides to therapeutic choices within each of these phases for specific problems are just beginning to emerge in cognitive-behavioral child and family interventions, and it is not possible to do justice

to the many complexities involved in this brief introductory discussion. The interested reader may wish to consult Evans and Meyer (1985), Herbert (1987), and Kanfer and Schefft (1988) for particularly detailed accounts of how collaborative decisional models can be implemented in different types of therapeutic contexts.

Emphasis on Prevention

Cognitive-behavioral approaches have shown a growing concern for both primary and secondary prevention programs for children and families (e.g., Conduct Problems Prevention Research Group, 1997; Rickel & Allen, 1987; Roberts & Peterson, 1984). These programs have included interventions with high-risk populations directed at minimizing the likelihood of several known adverse outcomes (e.g., the sequelae associated with abusive family situations); interventions directed at reducing the future risk of specific problems, such as the misuse of alcohol or drugs; interventions designed to facilitate transitions and to minimize their negative impact (e.g., new school, foster placement); interventions intended to increase the child's and family's general adaptive competencies (e.g., early social skills training); and interventions designed to increase the child's and family's overall health, safety, and physical well-being (Jason, 1980).

Some examples of areas in which prevention efforts have been carried out include accident prevention (e.g., Christopherson, 1986; Mori & Peterson, 1986; Wright, Flagler, & Friedman, 1988), child abduction (e.g., Flanagan, 1986), sexual abuse (e.g., Harvey, Forehand, Brown, & Holmes, 1988; Wurtele, Kast, & Kondrick, 1988; Wurtele et al., 1987), practicing safer sex (e.g., Gordon & Craver, 1988), seat belt use (Malenfant, Wells, Van Houten, & Williams, 1996), teaching emergency fire safety skills to blind children and adolescents (e.g., Jones, Sisson, & Van Hasselt, 1984), and reducing relationship violence in teens (Wolfe et al., 1996).

In one prevention study, Markman, Floyd, Stanley, and Storaasli (1988) provided premarital intervention utilizing a cognitive-behavioral approach that included communication and problem-solving skills training, clarifying and sharing expectations, and sensual/sexual enhancement. Although there were no differences in self-reported relational quality at posttreatment, there were differences $1\frac{1}{2}$ years later that were maintained at 3 years. Markman et al.

(1988) suggest that their premarital intervention served to reduce the declines in marital quality that occur in most relationships over time. Similar longitudinal studies involving premarital or prenatal interventions that focus on parent–child relationships and the prevention of possible child and family disorders are needed.

Although investigations of child and parent behaviors have typically employed causal models in which single factors are hypothesized to uniquely determine outcomes, a number of studies across a wide variety of domains, such as IQ (e.g., Sameroff, Seifer, Barocas, Zax, & Greenspan, 1987), behavior disorders (e.g., Rutter, Tizard, Yule, Graham, & Whitmore, 1976), and child abuse (e.g., Egeland, Jacobvitz, & Sroufe, 1988), have shown that combinations of risk factors provide the best predictions of outcome (Mash & Dozois, 1996). In light of this, it follows that early prevention strategies should encompass multiple areas of child and family functioning. However, in considering a number of factors that have been shown to relate to child competence (e.g., maternal mental health, maternal anxiety, parental perspectives, maternal interactive behavior, maternal education, occupation of head of household, minority group status, family social support, family size, and stressful life events), Sameroff et al. (1987) noted that there is a large difference between the number of variables affecting a child's competence and the number that can be changed by our interventions. Only stress is likely to change by itself (for better or for worse), and psychological interventions for the individual often come down to altering maternal interactive behavior and maternal anxiety.

The fact that early circumstances and early personality characteristics seem to foreshadow so many later childhood disorders reinforces the need for early intervention. For example, in a study by Block et al. (1988), personality dimensions such as undercontrol and ego resiliency at 3 and 4 years were predictive of adolescent drug use 10 or 11 years later. Lerner, Hertzog, Hooker, Hassibi, and Thomas (1988) analyzed data from the New York Longitudinal Study and found two separate dimensions of negative emotional behavior—aggression (aggression, undercompliance, disobedience) and affect (anxiety, dissatisfaction, depression)—both at ages 1–6 and at ages 7–12. There was a substantial amount of developmental stability in individual differences on these dimensions, with autoregressive coefficients of .97 and .91 for aggression and affect, respectively. Aggression at age

7–12 was the best predictor of adolescent adjustment problems. Affect did not predict social maladjustment independent of aggression. These and many other findings suggest that it is especially critical that interventions alter the course of early aggressive behavior, if later child maladjustment is to be prevented.

Cognition and Affect

Current cognitive-behavioral interventions with children and families have given increased attention to cognitive and affective processes in treatment. The growth of cognitive-behavioral therapy with children has continued unabated since the early 1970s. The 1980s and the 1980s have also witnessed a greater concern for the affective components of child and family disorders, including child and maternal anxiety and depression, and the interactions between children and parents, peers, and spouses during emotionally charged social situations.

Cognitive-Behavioral Therapy

There are now many descriptions of behavioral interventions that take both child (Kendall, 1991; Harris, Wong, & Keogh, 1985) and family (Foster & Robin, Chapter 12, this volume) cognitions into account. Although the long-term effectiveness of cognitive-behavioral interventions with children has yet to be determined (Lochman, 1988), and the concordance between cognitive-behavioral theory and therapy is not always clear (see Beidel & Turner, 1986, for a critique), a number of shared assumptions characterize current approaches:

1. Psychological disturbances are, in part, the result of faulty thought patterns that include deficiencies in cognitive mediators and distortions in both cognitive content (e.g., erroneous beliefs) and cognitive process (e.g., irrational thinking and faulty problem solving). A range of cognitive distortions and attributional biases have been identified in studies of depressed (e.g., Asarnow, Carlson, & Guthrie, 1987), aggressive (McFadyen-Ketchum & Dodge, Chapter 6, this volume), and anxious (e.g., Bell-Dolan, 1995; Bell-Dolan & Wessler, 1994) children. For example, Lochman (1987) found that during social interaction, aggressive boys tended to minimize perceptions of their own aggressiveness and to perceive their partners as more aggressive than they were. There is also some evidence of the specificity of cognitive distortions across different child psychiatric

populations (e.g., Siqueland, Kendall, Stoff, & Pollack, 1987). The presence of cognitive distortions in disturbed populations is suggestive, but there is a need for longitudinal studies that would establish causal relationships between early cognitive distortions and later childhood psychopathology.

2. A goal of treatment is to identify maladaptive cognitions and to replace them with more adaptive ones.

3. The manner in which children and parents think about their environment determines their reactions to it (Meichenbaum, 1977).

4. Cognitive appraisals need to be evaluated in the context of ongoing social interaction (Gottman & Levenson, 1986). For example, Lochman (1987) found that nonaggressive boys in the early stages of conflict tended to assume greater responsibility for aggression, and suggested that this attribution of greater self-blame might motivate their efforts to modulate the expression of hostility. In contrast, if aggressive boys blamed others, they might begin to justify their subsequent peer aggression and engage in conflict escalation.

5. Interventions need to take into account both the developmental continuities and changes in children's cognitive appraisals over time (e.g., Lochman, 1988; Mahoney & Nezworski, 1985).

If cognitive approaches to treatment are to be systematically evaluated, it will also be important to improve our methodologies for assessing those cognitions that are being targeted for change—for example, attributional styles, cognitive errors, and irrational beliefs (e.g., Robins & Hinkley, 1989)—and also to establish the relationship between cognitive changes and long-term behavioral outcomes.

Emotional Factors in Relationships

The progression in emphasis of behavioral treatments has been from behaviors, to cognitions, to emotions, to strategies that attempt to integrate information from all three areas. The more recent interest in affect has included the following:

1. The development and refinement of interventions for disturbances that are predominantly affective in nature, such as childhood and adolescent depression (e.g., Kazdin & Marciano, Chapter 4, this volume) and anxiety disorders (e.g., Barrios & O'Dell, Chapter 5, this volume).

2. A concern for the ways in which emotional processes (e.g., arousal) moderate the expression of other types of behavior, such as social aggression (e.g., Lochman, 1988).

3. A concern for the ways in which the child's emotional status affects social-cognitive processes, such as attributions of causality (e.g., McFadyen-Ketchum & Dodge, Chapter 6, this volume).

4. A concern for the manner in which the emotional environment of the child's larger social system—for example, maternal depression (e.g., Patterson, 1982), maternal anxiety (e.g., Turner, Beidel, & Costello, 1987), maternal arousability (e.g., Wolfe & Bourdeau, 1987), marital conflict (e.g., Gottman & Levenson, 1986), and/or family communication (Gottman, Katz, & Hooven, 1997)—affects the child's functioning.

The interest in affective processes has led to the development of such interventions as anger management and stress management training for both children and parents. It should be recognized that training (in child management, for example) that occurs under safe, sterile conditions may not simulate the real-life context in which these skills must be exercised. Parenting in relatively unhurried and unstressful circumstances, versus parenting in situations where the child or parent is stressed, irritable, or rushed, may require very different skills. Interventions are required that will generalize to the emotionally charged situations that often set the stage for family conflict (Foster & Robin, Chapter 12, this volume).

Population Specificity

Although cognitive-behavioral interventions have maintained their idiographic focus on individuals, individual behaviors, and treatment individualization as the "categorical imperative" in therapy (Wolpe, 1986), there is an increasing sensitivity to the unique characteristics and treatment needs associated with particular populations of children and families (Mash & Terdal, 1997b). For example, Ollendick and Cerny (1981) stated that "although basic concepts of behavior therapy may not change across populations, the manner in which those concepts are applied to particular populations may vary considerably" (p. 3). While the latter part of this statement is undoubtedly true, it may well be that the basic concepts of cognitive-behavioral therapy (e.g., relevant principles, conceptual framework for treatment, model of childhood disorder) also vary from population to population. As will be illustrated throughout this volume, intervention models need to be directed at the specific child and family characteristics that have been shown to be important for different disorders. Training protocols for parents of children with mental retardation (e.g., Baker, 1980), parents of defiant children (e.g., Barkley, 1997b), or abusive parents (e.g., Azar & Wolfe, Chapter 10, this volume) are likely to be quite different, as are the social skills training programs employed with conduct-disordered (e.g., McMahon & Wells, Chapter 3, this volume) versus autistic (e.g., Newsom, Chapter 8, this volume) children. An emphasis on populations rather than techniques in behavior therapy seems especially relevant for clinical practice, because, as noted by Kazdin (1988b, p. 3), "clinically, the major concern is not what the effects are of a particular treatment across a host of problem areas, but rather what the options are and what 'works' for a specific clinical problem."

CHILDHOOD DISORDERS

Consistent with a population-specific treatment focus, current cognitive-behavioral approaches acknowledge the importance of considering specific clinical problems as representing constellations of child–environment symptoms that commonly occur together (Mash & Terdal, 1997b). Such an approach capitalizes on established bodies of knowledge concerning the expression, prevalence, etiology, associated characteristics, prognosis, and prescribed treatments for specific problems, and attempts to use this information in order to design individualized programs of intervention.

The types of childhood problems that have most often been identified in clinical and empirical classification efforts are reflected in the major headings and subheadings of DSM-IV (American Psychiatric Association, 1994). Although there are many unresolved conceptual and empirical issues surrounding all of the currently available classification systems for childhood disorders (Achenbach, 1985; Mash & Terdal, 1997b), the DSM-IV categories are useful in orienting the reader to the types of childhood disorders that will be discussed throughout this text. The disorders presented in these Tables are not intended to be exhaustive of all DSM diag-

TABLE 1.2. DSM-IV Categories for Developmental and Learning Disorders, Usually First Diagnosed in Infancy, Childhood, or Adolescence

Mental Retardation

  Mild, Moderate, Severe, Profound,
    Severity Unspecified

Learning Disorders

  Reading Disorder
  Mathematics Disorder
  Disorder of Written Expression
  Learning Disorder Not Otherwise Specified

Motor Skills Disorder

  Developmental Coordination Disorder

Communication Disorders

  Expressive Language Disorder
  Mixed Receptive–Expressive Language Disorder
  Language Disorder
  Phonological Disorder
  Stuttering
  Communication Disorder Not Otherwise Specified

Pervasive Developmental Disorders

  Autistic Disorder
  Rett's Disorder
  Childhood Disintegrative Disorder
  Asperger's Disorder
  Pervasive Developmental Disorder Not Otherwise Specified

noses that apply to children. Rather, they are intended to provide an overview of the range and variety of disorders that typically occur during childhood and for which children are most commonly referred for treatment. Further details concerning the characteristics of children with these problems are included in each of the chapters that follow and in Mash and Barkley (1996).

Table 1.2 lists DSM-IV developmental and learning disorders which are usually first diagnosed in infancy, childhood, or adolescence. These include Mental Retardation; pervasive developmental disorders such as Autistic Disorder; specific problems related to reading and mathematics; and language and communication difficulties. A number of these disorders constitute chronic conditions that often reflect deficits in capacity rather than performance difficulties per se.

Table 1.3 lists the DSM-IV categories for additional disorders that are usually first diagnosed in infancy, childhood, or adolescence. These disorders have traditionally been thought of as first occurring in childhood, or as exclu-

TABLE 1.3. DSM-IV Categories for Additional Disorders Usually First Diagnosed in Infancy, Childhood, or Adolescence

Attention-Deficit and
Disruptive Behavior Disorders

  Attention-Deficit/Hyperactivity Disorder
    Predominantly Inattentive Type
    Predominantly Hyperactive–Impulsive Type
    Combined Type
    Attention-Deficit/Hyperactivity Disorder
      Not Otherwise Specified
  Conduct Disorder
  Oppositional Defiant Disorder
  Disruptive Behavior Disorder
    Not Otherwise Specified

Feeding and Eating Disorders
of Infancy or Early Childhood

  Pica
  Rumination Disorder
  Feeding Disorder of Infancy or Early Childhood

Tic Disorders

  Tourette's Disorder
  Chronic Motor or Vocal Tic Disorder
  Transient Tic Disorder
  Tic Disorder Not Otherwise Specified

Elimination Disorders

  Encopresis
  Enuresis

Other Disorders of Infancy,
Childhood, or Adolescence

  Separation Anxiety Disorder
  Selective Mutism
  Reactive Attachment Disorder of Infancy or
    Early Childhood
  Stereotypic Movement Disorder
  Disorder of Infancy, Childhood, or Adolescence
    Not Otherwise Specified

sive to childhood, and as requiring operational criteria different from those used to define disorders in adults.

Table 1.4 lists disorders that can be diagnosed in children (e.g., mood disorders, anxiety disorders, Schizophrenia) but that are not listed in DSM-IV as distinct disorders that first occur during childhood, or that require operational criteria that are different from those used for adults. In many ways the DSM-IV distinction between child and adult categories is arbitrary, and more a reflection of our current lack of knowledge concerning the continuities between child and adult disorders than of the existence of qualitatively distinct conditions. Recent efforts to diagnose ADHD in adults illustrate this prob-

lem. Although the criteria for ADHD were derived from work with children, and the disorder is included in the DSM-IV section for disorders that are usually first diagnosed in infancy, childhood, or adolescence, these criteria are also used to diagnose adults even though they do not fit the expression of the disorder in adults very well (Barkley, 1996). The more general issue here is whether there is a need for separate diagnostic criteria for children versus adults, or whether we can use the same criteria for both groups by adjusting them to take into account differences in developmental status—for example, by requiring fewer symptoms, different symptoms, or a shorter duration of impaired functioning.

Finally, Table 1.5, lists DSM-IV categories for other conditions that are not defined as mental disorders but that may be a focus of clinical attention during childhood. The categories included are the ones that seem especially relevant to children, in that they emphasize relational problems, maltreatment, and academic and adjustment difficulties.

Since the criteria for judging abnormality in children are to a large extent social in nature, what constitutes a problem, and the likelihood of referral for treatment, will depend greatly upon the norms and expectations of key individuals in the child's environment. Children may not be accurate reporters of their own distress, especially when describing externalizing difficulties such as social aggression. The discrepancy in what constitutes "normal" for different individuals is illustrated in the following extreme example reported by Donnellan (1988):

> For two years the mother of a young man with autism would correct her son by saying, "Don't do that. It doesn't look normal." The son would stop the inappropriate behavior. Then she would add, "You want to look normal, don't you?" The son would say, "Yes." Then one day, it occurred to the mother to ask her son, "Do you know what normal means?" "Yes," he said, and the mother was impressed. She pushed for his definition. He said, "It's the second button from the left on the washing machine."

NEED FOR EFFECTIVE INTERVENTIONS

In spite of frequently acknowledged inconsistencies in the manner in which childhood disorders are conceptualized, defined, diagnosed, and assessed (Mash & Terdal, 1997a), epidemiological

TABLE 1.4.   Selected Categories for Disorders of Childhood or Adolescence Not Listed Separately in DSM-IV as Ones Usually First Diagnosed in Infancy, Childhood, or Adolescence

Mood Disorders

  Depressive Disorders
    Major Depressive Disorder
    Dysthymic Disorder
  Bipolar Disorders

Anxiety Disorders

  Specific Phobia, Social Phobia, Obsessive–Compulsive Disorder, Posttraumatic Stress Disorder, Panic Disorder, Generalized Anxiety Disorder, Acute Stress Disorder, Anxiety Disorder Due to . . . . (Indicate the General Medical Condition)

Somatoform Disorders

Factitious Disorders

Dissociative Disorders

Sexual and Gender Identity Disorders

Eating Disorders

Sleep Disorders

Schizophrenia and Other Psychotic Disorders

Substance-Related Disorders

Impulse-Control Disorders Not Elsewhere Classified

Adjustment Disorders

Personality Disorders

TABLE 1.5.   Selected DSM-IV Categories for Other Conditions That May Be a Focus of Clinical Attention during Childhood but Are Not Defined as Mental Disorders

Relational Problems

  Relational Problem Related to a General Mental Disorder or General Medical Condition
  Parent–Child Relational Problem
  Sibling Relational Problem
  Relational Problem Not Otherwise Specified

Problems Related to Abuse or Neglect

  Physical Abuse of Child
  Sexual Abuse of Child
  Neglect of Child

Additional Conditions That May Be a Focus of Clinical Attention

  Bereavement
  Borderline Intellectual Functioning
  Academic Problem
  Child or Adolescent Antisocial Behavior
  Identity Problem

---

studies have been surprisingly consistent in their overall findings, reporting that between 5% and 15% of children and adolescents exhibit some type of emotional disturbance (Mash & Dozois, 1996). Although such incidence figures vary as a function of the child's age, type of disorder, gender, socioeconomic status (SES), ethnicity, and geographical region, they do indicate a rather substantial need for effective child mental health services (Kazdin, 1988b). If preventive psychological and health-related services for high-risk populations, such as children who have been physically or sexually abused (e.g., Wekerle & Wolfe, 1996), infants with interactional disturbances (e.g., Lyons-Ruth, Zeanah, & Benoit, 1996), learning-disabled youths (e.g., Lyon, 1996), chronically ill children (e.g., Johnson & Rodrigue, 1997), children and adolescents with HIV/AIDS (Kalichman, 1997; Thomason, Bachanas, & Campos, 1996), or potential accident victims (e.g., Peterson & Brown, 1994), were also taken into account, this need

would be considerably greater (e.g., Rickel & Allen, 1987).

It would also appear that most children who are in need of psychological services do not receive them (Kazdin, 1988b). Estimates indicate that only 20%–33% of children with clinically significant disturbances actually receive treatment (Knitzer, 1982), and that children with more severe dysfunctions may be slightly less likely to receive help (Sowder, 1975). On the other hand, the transient nature of many types of psychological disturbances during childhood would suggest that not all children exhibiting disorders are best served through the provision of specialized psychological services. For many children, community, school, and other health care services may adequately address the personal and social adjustment difficulties they are experiencing.

EFFECTIVENESS OF COGNITIVE-BEHAVIORAL TREATMENTS FOR CHILDREN

The effectiveness of cognitive-behavioral treatments for children needs to be considered in relation to empirical evidence regarding the efficacy of psychotherapy with children more generally, since it is not clear that cognitive-behavioral procedures are more effective than alternative approaches (Ollendick, 1986). The current emphasis on empirically supported treatments has focused attention on psychotherapy outcome studies with adults and this has resulted in spillover effects to studies of interventions for children (Seligman, 1995).

It was only about a decade ago that several researchers called attention to the scarcity of well-controlled outcome research on any form of therapy for children (e.g., Kendall & Koehler, 1985). For example, Kazdin (1988b) stated that "progress in the area of child treatment has been slow. There are many different treatments. . . . The great majority of these have not been shown to be effective. Even more regrettably, most of these techniques have never been carefully evaluated" (p. 9). This state of affairs has been steadily changing, and the number of controlled outcome investigations for a wide range of childhood disorders has increased dramatically over the past decade. Nevertheless, the proportion of controlled outcome studies with children and families still pales in comparison to studies of psychotherapy with adults (Hibbs & Jensen, 1996). Even more scarce in the child therapy literature are controlled studies of treatment processes such as the therapeutic relationship or treatment noncompliance (DiGiuseppe, Linscott, & Jilton, 1996; Shelton, Levy, & Contributors, 1981).

Several broad-based meta-analytic reviews of treatment outcome studies with children have been conducted (Casey & Berman, 1985; Kazdin, Bass, Ayers, & Rodgers, 1990; Weisz, Weiss, Alicke, & Klotz, 1987; Weisz, Weiss, et al., 1995), as have more focused meta-analytic reviews of cognitive-behavioral therapy (Durlak, et al., 1991). The central findings from these reviews have been presented by Weisz (in press) and by Weisz and Weiss (1993), and have been summarized as follows (Kazdin, 1996b, p. 11):

1. The changes achieved by children receiving psychotherapy are greater than those for children not receiving therapy. This result has been consistent across reviews.

2. The size of the mean treatment effects for treatment versus no treatment are in the order of 0.7 to 0.8 across a broad range of treatment techniques, problems, and ages. These effect sizes are comparable to those reported for adults and fall in the range typically considered to be "large."

3. The effects of treatment have not been shown to be reliably different for internalizing (e.g., depression, anxiety, social withdrawal) versus externalizing (e.g., ADHD, Conduct Disorder) disorders.

4. Treatment effects tend to be durable, with effects measured at follow-up being similar to those found immediately following treatment. In general, follow-up intervals average about 6 months.

5. Treatment effect sizes are about twice as large for problems that are specifically targeted in treatment as they are for changes in nonspecific areas of functioning. This suggests that treatments are producing focused (e.g., anxiety reduction) rather than nonspecific or global effects (e.g., feeling good).

Types of treatments—for example behavioral versus nonbehavioral, or individual techniques within a given class of treatments—do not vary consistently in their relative effectiveness. Where differences have been found, they have favored cognitive and behavioral treatments over nonbehavioral treatments such as client-centered counseling or insight-oriented therapy (Weisz, Weiss, et al., 1995), although these findings have been challenged on both conceptual and methodological grounds. For example, Weisz, Weiss, Alicke, and Klotz (1987) employed meta-analysis to investigate the effectiveness of psychotherapy with children and adolescents. They examined 108 well-designed outcome studies with participants aged 4–18. Findings showed that the average treated youngster was better adjusted than 79% of those not treated. These authors also found that behavioral treatments proved to be more effective than nonbehavioral treatments, regardless of the client's age, therapist's experience, or type of problem treated. The mean effect size for behavioral treatments was 0.88, compared with a mean effect size of 0.42 with nonbehavioral approaches. However, when comparisons were excluded in which the outcome measure was similar to the treatment procedure, this difference was nonsignificant. Weisz, Weiss, Alicke, and Klotz (1987) then reintroduced into their analysis those studies where inclusion of such outcome measures was deemed to be a fair test, and again found the behavioral procedures to be superior. These authors concluded that, overall, their findings make a case for the superiority of behavioral over nonbehavioral approaches in the treatment of children.

In considering the findings of the meta-analyses that have compared behavioral and nonbehavioral approaches, it is important to note that these meta-analyses have included mostly studies involving group comparisons. This selection criterion probably underestimates the documented successes of cognitive-behavioral procedures with children in studies employing single-subject research designs (e.g., Barlow & Hersen, 1984; Kazdin, 1982a). Although suggestions have been presented for using meta-analysis with within-subject designs (White, Rusch, Kazdin, & Hartmann, 1989), such analyses have received minimal attention. One exception is a recent meta-analysis of school interventions for ADHD children that included between-subject, within-subject, and single-case studies (DuPaul & Eckert, 1997). The overall mean effect size for contingency management procedures was 0.6 for between-subject designs, nearly 1.0 for within-subject designs, and approximately 1.4 for single-case experimental designs. To date, other forms of therapy have not received the rigorous empirical evaluations characteristic of the behavioral strategies used in many single-case studies, so direct comparisons across approaches cannot be made.

Although the meta-analytic findings present a generally positive picture of psychotherapy with children, and of behavioral and cognitive-behavioral approaches in particular, there are a number of important caveats. Weisz and colleagues (see Weisz & Weiss, 1993) have noted the important distinction between "research therapy" (i.e., therapy as carried out in laboratory outcome studies) and "clinic therapy" (i.e., child therapy as carried out in clinics). Relative to research therapy, clinic therapy is typically conducted with more severe cases (some of whom are coerced into treatment), is directed at a heterogeneous set of problems and children, focuses on multiple problems and goals, and is carried out in clinic or hospital settings by professional career therapists with large caseloads. In general, clinic therapy is generally less structured and more flexible, and it uses proportionately more nonbehavioral methods such as psychodynamic and eclectic approaches. In stark contrast to the meta-analytic findings for research therapy, as described above, similar analyses for nine studies of clinic therapy produced minimal effect sizes ranging from -0.40 to $+0.29$, with a mean effect size across studies of 0.01 (Weisz, Donenberg, Han, & Weiss, 1995).

Similarly, other community-based mental health delivery systems for children have not found incremental improvement in outcomes related to the availability of comprehensive services. For example, in one large-scale study, the Fort Bragg Project, an integrated continuum of services was successfully implemented that provided good access, greater continuity of care, more client satisfaction, and treatment of children in less restrictive environments. However, costs were higher, and clinical outcomes were no better than those at a comparison site that provided services in a conventional manner (Bickman, 1996, 1997). These and other findings suggest that conventional services for children may be of limited effectiveness, and that integrating these interventions into more coordinated systems of care also results in minimal support for the beneficial effects of treatment (Weisz, in press). However, it is generally recognized that studies of child therapy outcomes in settings where it is typically conducted are few in number, and that it would be premature to draw any conclusions from the findings from clinic and community studies until more empirical data about therapy in practice are available (Shadish et al., 1997).

There is a clear need for additional information on the effectiveness of conventional forms of treatment for children. However, as Kazdin (1997) and Weisz (in press) note, it is not just that more research is needed, but also that a different kind of research is needed—research that focuses on the conditions under which therapy for children is normally provided and on the therapies used most often in clinic settings. If systematic investigations of conventional treatments continue to provide weak results, further attention to the *reasons* for the large discrepancy between research therapy and clinic therapy will be needed. Since research therapy generally includes more behavioral and cognitive-behavioral treatments, and since these approaches are often not the first choices of treatment for most practitioners, one possible conclusion is that clinic therapy with children might be enhanced if cognitive-behavioral therapies were used more often. However, conclusions about the exportability of these therapies may be premature when we consider that the conditions under which cognitive-behavioral therapies have been evaluated are quite different from those in which therapy is typically conducted in clinics. Empirically supported treatments need to be taken out of the laboratory and evaluated in clinic practice before their generalizability can be assessed (Weisz, in press).

The evaluation of cognitive-behavioral treatments for children is compounded by the fact that comprehensive multifaceted cognitive-behavioral programs are usually used, and it is difficult to evaluate the specific elements within such multimodal packages. Also, different aspects of a child's environment (e.g., with different family members, in different settings) are involved in treatment, and changes may occur not only in the child, but also in other systems in which the child functions (i.e., spillover effects). For example, as children come to view themselves as more competent and less avoidant, parents' perceptions about what their children can and can't do may change as well. As a result, parents may begin to respond differently to their children, and their own feelings and functioning are improved (Kendall & Flannery-Schroeder, in press). These more general spillover effects of treatment have not received sufficient attention in research to date. Moreover, in light of the rapid changes that take place during childhood, treatments that produce short-term effects are probably less meaningful in the evaluation of childhood disorders than they might be in that of adult disorders (Kazdin, 1988b). Consequently, more studies of long-term adjustment following treatment are needed, although such studies are difficult to conduct (e.g., Mash & Terdal, 1980).

Finally, and perhaps most importantly, blanket claims concerning the general effectiveness of cognitive-behavioral therapies for children and families make little sense. As Bornstein, Kazdin, and McIntyre (1985) have noted, "Behavior therapy is not a monolithic, monomethodological approach. The area incorporates widely diverse methods and techniques with differential efficacy. To draw reasonable conclusions, we must examine the individual literatures for each technique as it is applied to specific problems" (p. 837).

GENERAL FEATURES OF A COGNITIVE-BEHAVIORAL PERSPECTIVE

A cognitive-behavioral perspective to the treatment of child and family disorders involves a problem-solving approach to treatment—one that is guided by a conceptual viewpoint and certain assumptions about child and family functioning, adheres to certain methodologies, and utilizes techniques that have empirical support and are evaluative, in the sense that they are self-correcting and constantly changing. More than a decade ago, a review of input from several major figures in the field of child behavior therapy and elsewhere, Ollendick (1986) concluded that the major points emphasized in defi-

nitions of a behavioral perspective to child treatment are these: "(1) principles of behavioral psychology, most notably principles of learning; (2) use of strategies or procedures that are methodologically sound and empirically validated; and (3) application of such principles and procedures to adjustment problems of children and adolescents." (p. 527).

In the years following this review, it has become apparent that the principles upon which cognitive-behavioral applications with children and families are based are increasingly heterogeneous; they encompass elements derived from the areas of learning, cognitive psychology, developmental psychology, developmental psychopathology, social psychology, and the neurosciences. The appropriateness of such a conceptual expansion has not gone uncontested (e.g., Levis, 1988), but the current state of affairs seems to be the result of a gradual, 30+-year evolution in behavior therapy away from an ideological emphasis on principles of learning to a pragmatic search for effective treatments, regardless of their theoretical origins (e.g., London, 1972). Although the development of a consistent conceptual framework is important for organizing cognitive-behavioral research and practice with children and families, a framework that is based exclusively on the extrapolation of laboratory principles of learning to the clinical context seems far too narrow, and the current commitment in cognitive-behavioral therapy is as much to empirical as to conceptual ties (e.g., Mash, 1989; Kazdin, 1988a). As noted by Ross (1981), "The touchstone of a behavioral technique is whether it has objective, observable referents that permit one to put its validity to empirical test—not whether it fits neatly into the procrustean bed of one theory or another" (p. 2).

Given that cognitive-behavioral approaches are so thoroughly committed to a foundation of empiricism, the persistent contradictions between the vagaries and complexities of clinical practice and the rigor of laboratory–clinical research have been a continuing struggle. It is often the case that clinical realities require research-based treatment protocols to be altered or set aside in the interests of responsible practice. Some have suggested that the resolution of this paradox involves constructing a knowledge base for the therapeutic enterprise from *both* sources, although experience over the past half century tells us that this is more easily said than done (Goldfried & Wolfe, 1996).

Interestingly, the epistemological alliance between clinic and laboratory, as reflected in a scientific orientation to clinical practice, has been a double-edged sword for cognitive-behavioral approaches to child and family behavior therapy. This alliance has embraced two premises, both of which have been challenged as providing a suitable model for practice.

Laboratory Research and Clinical Practice

The first premise is that cognitive-behavioral clinical practice is based upon methods derived from empirically supported psychological principles including, but not restricted to, those derived from studies of learning and cognition. The validity of this premise has been challenged from within and from outside the field. For example, in his text on child behavior therapy, Ross (1981) stated, "It would be folly to assert that everything a behavior therapist does in the course of a treatment program, let alone in an individual treatment session, is explicitly and directly derived from empirically supported psychological principles" (p. 2). Similarly, Wachtel (1977), a psychoanalyst, noted:

> The more sophisticated among behavior therapists recognize that there is often only a loose, analogic connection between the methods they use and the learning experiments on which the methods are purportedly based. The various models of learning derived from experimental research serve only as stimulating guiding metaphors for much of the clinical work in the behavioral tradition. . . . but they can be mischievous when the connection between clinic and laboratory is exaggerated or misconstrued for purposes of polemic or myth. (p. 8)

Wachtel went on:

> Behavior therapists are often effective precisely because they are not behavioristic in any narrowly construed way. In their clinical work they find it necessary to make inferences and to concern themselves with what their patients want and feel as well as what they do. Most of the practicing behavior therapists with whom I have discussed this issue have acknowledged privately that what they actually do looks quite different from what one would expect from reading the literature. (p. 8)

In support of this general view, findings from a survey by Morrow-Bradley and Elliot (1986) that was carried out over a decade ago indicated that only a very small proportion of practicing clinicians reported using research findings as a basis for their practice. However, more recent reports suggest that this situation is changing, with substantial numbers of clinicians indicating that research findings are useful in guiding their clinical practice (Beutler, Williams, Wakefield, & Entwistle, 1995). Apparently the road from clinical practice to the laboratory is less well traveled, however, with researchers being less likely to attempt to understand the problems that face clinical practitioners.

Empiricism and Clinical Practice

The second premise is that cognitive-behavioral clinical practice is closely wedded to empiricism, involving the collection of objective data prior to, during, and following treatment. However, guidelines for the uses of data collection in clinical practice are not readily available, and the extent to which such data collection facilitates meaningful outcomes in therapy has not been empirically documented. For example, Herbert (1987), in discussing his treatment manual for working with children and families, has stated:

> It [the manual] fails if it leads to some facile "cookbook" application of techniques, or a mechanical insistence on numbers and measurement. The virtues of operationism can turn into quantiphrenia, which acts to the detriment of warm empathic interactions with parents and children. The emphasis on rigorous thinking and scientific assessment in this book is not meant to be at the expense of clinical art and sensitivity. "Scientism," a Pharasaical adherence to the letter rather than the spirit of the scientific method is to be avoided at all costs. (pp. 6–7)

The current emphasis on treatment accountability in mental health services for children and families has led to a renewed interest in data collection in clinical practice and to the development of meaningful and workable assessment and evaluation protocols for assessing treatment outcomes in the clinical context (Ogles, Lambert, & Masters, 1996). The long-standing recognition by cognitive-behavioral therapists of the importance of empirically guided clinical practice makes them especially sensitive to and equipped for meeting current health care system requirements for greater accountability in practice.

PROTOTYPE FOR A BEHAVIORAL–SYSTEMS APPROACH

The basic model for the treatment of childhood disorders from a behavioral–systems perspective involves a blend of epistemological assumptions; psychological principles; research findings; specific techniques (literally hundreds); operational rules for the selection and implementation of these techniques in relation to specific problems, concerns, and settings; and the continuous evaluation of short- and long-term outcomes. Given the complexity of conditions and processes encompassed by this perspective, any single model that attempts to capture the processes of therapeutic intervention will of necessity be an oversimplification. Although there are no necessary or defining characteristics of a behavioral–systems approach to intervention with children and families, the following conceptual, strategic, and procedural points, taken together, provide a general prototype for some of its more commonly occurring features.

Commitment to a Consistent Theoretical Framework

Cognitive-behavioral perspectives adhere to the general belief that good theory generates good practice, and that a consistent but flexible theoretical framework regarding behavior change principles and the nature and development of childhood disorders is needed to guide our intervention efforts (Bornstein & van den Pol, 1985; Herbert, 1987; Ollendick & Cerny, 1981). For the reasons mentioned earlier, the epistemological framework for cognitive-behavioral interventions has been changing and evolving. Although a general commitment to a variety of cognitive-behavioral theories and models continues (e.g., instrumental, operant, respondent, drive reduction, mediational, observational/social learning, cognitive-behavior modification, applied behavior analysis), current approaches are perhaps best represented by a systems point of view. As noted by Kanfer and Schefft (1988), systems models provide the clinician with a perspective that will help to "guide decisions concerning what observations to make, what empirical data to select from various sciences, and at what systems level effective interventions should be conducted" (p. 19).

Within a general systems framework, the theoretical models being used to guide our treat-

ments for disturbed children and families are becoming increasingly population-specific. For example, Patterson's (1986) performance model for social aggression suggests the importance of several molar and microlevel variables that are important to address in interventions with families of antisocial children. These include the extent to which a child is rejected or perceived as antisocial by others; the likelihood of the child's unprovoked negative behavior toward parents and siblings, and its duration; the extent to which parents monitor their children and spend time with them; and the parents' inept discipline, as reflected in their use of explosive forms of punishment, negative actions and reactions, and inconsistent/erratic behavior.

As will be illustrated throughout this volume, the theoretical models underlying various child and family problems suggest very different sets of variables that are important in treatment (Mash & Barkley, 1996). The conceptual frameworks that guide our interventions with ADHD, anxious, depressed, abused, mentally retarded, or learning-disabled children are likely to be quite different from one population to another. Models of service delivery for children with developmental disabilities are typically based on teaching long-term management and coping strategies, whereas intervention models for many other childhood disorders are based on a curative or corrective view that we can go in, fix the problem, and then terminate treatment. However, as I have noted, it is becoming more apparent that many childhood disorders that were previously treated from a curative perspective (e.g., Conduct Disorder, ADHD) may be more appropriately considered from a chronic illness model of coping and long-term management (Barkley, Chapter 2, this volume; Kazdin, 1988b).

Conceptualization of Childhood Disorders

Although the number of child and family dysfunctions is large, a broad conceptualization of how such dysfunctions develop is needed in order to gather and organize information for assessment and treatment (Mash & Dozois, 1996). What is observed and emphasized during assessment and treatment will depend on the therapist's assumptions concerning child and family development, including the importance ascribed to social context, sociocultural norms, and biological factors. In light of the multiple etiologies underlying any child or family problem, all of these determinants will be involved, although their relative emphasis may vary depending on the particular condition. Childhood disorders have been viewed as learned maladaptive habits, as physical defects and deficits, as failures in the adaptational process, and as system breakdowns. All of these views have some validity.

Most childhood disorders are best conceptualized as representing failures in adaptation on the part of the child and his or her social environment, and therapy is directed at corrective actions that will permit successful adaptation (or, in a preventive model, that will prevent or decrease the likelihood of future breakdowns). From a behavioral–systems perspective, childhood disorders are viewed as representing exaggerations, insufficiencies, handicapping combinations, situationally inappropriate behaviors, or developmentally atypical expressions of behavior that are common to all children at certain ages. Although some childhood disorders such as autism may represent qualitatively distinct conditions (Kazdin & Kagan, 1994), for the most part dysfunction is a matter of quantitative rather than qualitative variation in the expression of behavior, and the principles underlying the development and modification of normal and abnormal behaviors are presumed to be similar. As I have noted, there is also an increasing acceptance of the view of childhood problems as constellations of behaviors, cognitions, and emotions, and not simply as isolated responses (Mash & Dozois, 1996).

Importance of Reciprocal Influences

A behavioral–systems perspective recognizes the importance of the reciprocal influences that occur both within and between individuals (Bandura, 1986). Numerous studies have demonstrated reciprocity in parent–child and marital interactions across a wide range of disorders (e.g., Houts, Shutty, & Emery, 1985; Patterson, 1982; Patterson, Reid, & Dishion, 1992). At a more molar level, adult reactions are affected by the age, gender, physical attractiveness, and temperament of a child (Mash, 1984). Child characteristics will also influence parental disciplinary practices. For example, mothers may exhibit more helping and rewarding behavior toward anxious children, and more controlling and restrictive behavior toward conduct problem or hyperactive children. Unidirectional models of in-

tervention, which fail to recognize the ongoing reciprocal social influences that characterize most child and family disorders, are not likely to be very effective.

Empirically Based Treatment and Clinical Sensitivity

In a relative sense, treatment from a cognitive-behavioral perspective is based on empirical data and well-documented theories, rather than on an accumulation of clinical folklore and experience. As much as possible, the description and treatment of child and family disorders from this perspective employ objectively defined terms and measurable operations, and are based on a quantitative analysis of actual performance (e.g., behavioral, cognitive, physiological), including a description of proximal and distal antecedent and consequent events. Many writers have adopted the view that the analytic approach and empirical methodologies that characterize cognitive-behavioral interventions are far more important dimensions than the model of behavior change ascribed to.

In spite of the acknowledged importance of an empirical perspective, there is a growing appreciation of some of the difficulties inherent in such an approach. For example, in describing their systems-oriented approach, Kanfer and Schefft (1988) state:

> While parameters and details may vary across clients and treatment settings, the approach presented here has wide applicability. It presumes that an empirical knowledge base is indispensable. But there is simply not sufficient scientific knowledge available at present (or may never be) to guide a therapist's action in all detail. Therefore, the empirical knowledge base has to be supplemented by extrapolations from personal experience, subjective judgments, and the realities of the present situation. But whenever strategies and tactics derived from scientific principles *are* available, intuition and subjectivity should never be substituted for them. (pp. xvii–xviii)

Thus, empirically grounded, behavioral intervention with children and families also constitutes a craft—one that involves "a subtle amalgam of art and applied science," and that requires careful study and supervised practice (Herbert, 1987, p. 6).

Combined Emphasis on Contemporaneous and Distal Controlling Events

From a behavioral–systems perspective, controlling variables that are contemporaneous and present in the immediate situation have been given special emphasis in assessment and treatment. This is in contrast to orientations that focus on historical or temporally remote events. This emphasis on contemporaneous influences reflects the view that such events are likely to be more accessible and therefore more easily incorporated into our change efforts. This is especially so when a primary emphasis is placed on external environmental events, as was the case with many of the early behavioral approaches. However, with the integration of the role of cognitive mediators into behavior therapy, symbolic processes give historical events contemporaneous representation, and any designation of what is considered contemporaneous and what is not becomes arbitrary and often difficult to make.

In addition, numerous studies have established the important influence of extrasituational and temporally remote events on family functioning. External stressors such as marital discord (e.g., O'Leary, 1984b), negative interactions with neighbors or friends (e.g., Wahler, 1980), or neighborhood social disorganization (e.g., Caspi & Moffitt, 1995) may have direct effects on a mother's immediate reactions to her child's behavior. Behavioral intervention programs that do not take these and other such events within the child's larger social system into account have not proved to be very effective (Patterson, 1982, 1996). The combined emphasis on proximal and distal, microlevel and molar controlling events is evident in the multimodal intervention strategies presented throughout this volume.

Important Role of Assessment

Cognitive-behavioral assessment and intervention are viewed as complementary and interactive. Initial intervention follows from a systematic behavioral or functional analysis that considers the different system parameters and levels that are likely to be important for a particular child or family (Cone, 1997). Behavioral analyses have typically involved a single-level and linear consideration of antecedents, behav-

iors, and consequences (the A-B-C model). Although this approach continues to have enormous heuristic value in organizing information for intervention, it is limited in describing complex system relationships and the possible organizing role of cognitions and plans. Grawe and his coworkers (as described in Kanfer & Schefft, 1988, pp. 181–182) have presented an adaptation of the A-B-C model, referred to as "vertical" or "hierarchical" behavioral analysis. In this model, behavior is seen as being organized at hierarchical levels; the top of the hierarchy consists of themes, or beliefs and motives, that are related to specific responses in a situation. Hierarchical behavioral analysis appears to be a promising approach to organizing assessment information within a behavioral–systems perspective.

Terdal and I (Mash & Terdal, 1997a) have described child and family behavior assessment as involving a range of deliberate problem-solving strategies for understanding both disturbed and nondisturbed children and their social systems, including their families and peer groups. These strategies employ a flexible and ongoing process of hypothesis testing regarding the nature of the problem, its causes, likely outcomes in the absence of intervention, and the anticipated effects of various treatments. Such hypothesis testing should be based upon an understanding of the general theories, principles, and techniques of psychological assessment (e.g., Anastasi & Urbina, 1997; Cronbach, 1990; Sattler, 1992, 1998); information concerning normal child and family development (e.g., Mussen, 1983); and knowledge of populations of children and families showing similar types of problems, including information about incidence, prevalence, developmental characteristics, biological factors, and system parameters (e.g., Lewis & Miller, 1990; Mash & Barkley, 1996; Quay & Werry, 1986).

We (Mash & Terdal, 1997b) have described a number of commonly occurring conceptual, strategic, and procedural features of behavioral–systems assessments that, for the most part, parallel those associated with cognitive-behavioral treatment. These include the following:

1. An emphasis on conceptualizations of personality and abnormal behavior that give greater relative emphasis to the child's thoughts, feelings, and behaviors as they occur in specific situations than

to global underlying traits or dispositions.

2. An approach that is predominantly idiographic and individualized. Greater relative emphasis is given to understanding the individual child and family than to nomothetic comparisons that describe individuals primarily in relation to group norms.

3. An emphasis on the role of situational influences on behavior and the need to assess them in formulating effective treatments.

4. A recognition of the changes over time and reorganizations that often characterize child and family behavior, cognitions, and emotions.

5. A systems-oriented approach directed at describing and understanding the characteristics of children and families; the contexts in which these characteristics are expressed; and the structural organizations and functional relationships that exist between situations and behaviors, thoughts, and emotions.

6. An emphasis on contemporary controlling variables, in addition to the role of historical and more distal setting events.

7. A view of behaviors, cognitions, and affects as direct samples of the domains of interest, rather than as signs of some underlying or remote causes.

8. A focus on assessment information that is directly relevant to treatment, including such activities as pinpointing goals; selecting targets for intervention; choosing, designing, or implementing interventions; and evaluating therapy outcomes.

9. A reliance on a multimethod approach involving the flexible use of different informants and a variety of procedures, including observations, interviews, and questionnaires.

10. The use of a relatively low level of inference in interpreting assessment findings.

11. An ongoing and self-evaluating approach to assessment, with the need for further assessment being dictated in part by the efficacy of methods in facilitating desired treatment outcomes.

12. Assessment strategies—in particular, decisions regarding which variables to assess—that are guided by (a) knowledge concerning the characteristics of the child and family being assessed, and (b) the research literature on specific disorders (Mash & Barkley, 1996). Where assessments are theoretically driven, theories should be closely tied to the data.

The interested reader may wish to consult a number of comprehensive books and book chapters that review the underlying conceptual models and methods characteristic of behavioral assessment in general (e.g., Ciminero, Calhoun, & Adams, 1986; Mash & Hunsley, 1990; Nelson & Hayes, 1986), and child and family behavioral assessment in particular (e.g., Bornstein & van den Pol, 1985; Mash & Terdal, 1997a, 1997b; Ollendick & Hersen, 1984).

Ongoing Evaluation of Outcomes

Although it is recognized that clinical practice dictates a priority on the discovery of solutions rather than the demonstration of a functional relation between treatment and performance, accountability has been and continues to be a central characteristic of cognitive-behavioral interventions with children and families. Single-subject designs, which are presumed to be more applicable in the clinical context than comparison group designs, have been developed to document the relation between treatment and outcome (e.g., Barlow & Hersen, 1984; Kazdin, 1998).

Idiographic Emphasis

A behavioral–systems perspective recognizes that within groups of children showing common symptom clusters, variation among individuals is the norm. Children and families with the same disorder may have different etiologies that are represented both in past events and in current controlling conditions. For example, with Conduct Disorder, the etiology may involve early ADHD, family interaction, or cultural influences. One major implication for intervention is that different treatments may be required for the same phenotypic expression of a disorder. Idiographic analyses permit this type of individualization of treatments for children within particular diagnostic categories.

Importance of Contextual Events

Cognitive-behavioral approaches are especially sensitive to the impact of situational context on behavior and the need to incorporate contextual information into treatment. Many studies have shown how context moderates the expression of behaviors, cognitions, and affects. For example, Asarnow et al. (1987) found that the negative biases of children aged 8–13 was not generalized across all situational contexts. Similarly, with aggressive boys, Lochman (1987) found that attributional processes were distorted only when a child was interacting with another boy who had a different behavioral status (e.g., nonaggressive with aggressive vs. aggressive with nonaggressive or nonaggressive with nonaggressive), and who was typically much more aggressive or nonaggressive than himself. Interventions need to be sensitive to these types of situational variations. Within a behavioral–systems framework for intervention, it is also important to identify the complex interrelationships among settings. For example, Pettit, Dodge, and Brown (1988) found that several dimensions of family experience were predictive of classroom social competence and problem solving. However, although early family experience with peers had a direct impact on peer outcomes, the impact of exposure to maternal values and expectations on social competence with peers was mediated by the child's social problem-solving skills. Such findings suggest the need to consider family relationship factors when designing preventive interventions in the area of classroom social competence.

Context also moderates the effectiveness of treatment, as, for example, when intervention takes place in the home versus the classroom. Expectations and responses of family members, teachers, and the child's peers all interact in determining the expression of childhood disorders as well as the impact of various treatment strategies.

Family Involvement in Treatment

The behavioral–systems view often means that the child, family members, and other significant individuals will be actively involved in all phases of treatment. Koocher and Pedulla (1977) found that 94% of therapists reported seeing both parent and child, and 23% reported teacher involvement as well. Early behavioral views promoted the idea that the most effective change agents would be individuals in the child's natural environment, such as parents and teachers (Tharp & Wetzel, 1969). Although the "child as target" focus of this viewpoint is somewhat antagonistic to current systems formulations, it was seen as both conceptually relevant and eco-

nomical, and it spawned a rich and continuing tradition in child cognitive-behavioral therapy of involving parents (e.g., Dangel & Polster, 1984), teachers (e.g., Alberto & Troutman, 1982), peers (e.g., Strain, 1981), and siblings as change agents for children with a wide range of disorders.

The assumption that individuals in the child's natural environment are likely to be the most effective change agents has not been systematically tested. However, the meta-analysis by Weisz, Weiss, Alicke, and Klotz (1987) suggested an interaction between the agent of intervention and the nature of the child's problem. It was found that paraprofessionals and graduate students were equally effective as therapists in the treatment of undercontrolled types of problems, such as aggression and impulsivity, but that professionals were more effective in treating disorders of overcontrol, such as phobias and shyness. Also, graduate students and paraprofessionals were more effective with younger than with older children, whereas this was not the case for professionals. These findings suggest that the applicability of cognitive-behavioral models of parent training may depend on the nature of the disorder and the age of the child, although many other factors would also need to be considered in determining the primary agent of change.

A number of additional concerns must be addressed when involving parents as therapists for their own children. For example, the relationships between family resources, well-being, and adherence to prescribed regimens would suggest that before parents are asked to carry out child-level interventions, efforts to meet more basic family needs must be made in order for parents to have the time, energy, and personal investment to work with their own children in a therapeutic or educational capacity (Dunst et al., 1988).

Importance of Cognitive Processes

Current practices emphasize that understanding the cognitive processes of both the child and significant others is essential to understanding and treating childhood disorders (Finch et al., 1993; Kendall, 1991; Schwebel & Fine, 1994). Behavioral–systems interventions are based on developing new behaviors, response strategies, and coping skills, and these types of learning are mediated by the beliefs, perceptions, expectations, and attributions of children and their families (Herbert, 1987).

There has been an increasing emphasis on the role of social cognition in both the developmental and clinical literatures (e.g., Miller, 1988). For example, in examining the link between family experience, social problem-solving skills, and children's social competence, Pettit et al. (1988) found that the strongest predictors of social competence were mothers' biased expectations (attributions of hostile intent). These authors suggest a developmental path running from maternal attitudes, values, and expectations to child social cognition to child social competence with peers. There seems to be a covert but pervasive influence of maternal attitudes, values, and expectations, and through verbal means mothers may exert a more subtle influence on their children than through other direct forms of control, such as harsh discipline. Pettit et al. (1988) hypothesize that through exposure to deviant maternal values, a child may learn to process social information in a deviant way when interacting with peers, and then may come to be perceived by teachers and peers as socially incompetent. Putallaz (1987) reported that mothers' social values, as expressed in their advised solutions to a hypothetical situation involving their children being teased, were predictive of children's social status in the classroom. However, solutions involving other social situations, such as entry into a new group, were not predictive. Such findings reinforce the need for a contextually specific approach to cognitive as well as behavioral interventions.

Development of Operational Rules for Implementing Treatment

The availability of operational rules for interpreting principles, in formulating assessment and treatment strategies, is limited. However, the form that such rules might take has been suggested by several investigators (Kazdin, 1997). For example, in the context of early intervention, Dunst et al. (1988, pp. 48–49) presented four general operating rules, each specifying a pragmatic relationship between an outcome and the action that has the greatest probability of achieving a desired goal:

1. To promote positive child, parent, and family functioning, base intervention efforts on family-identified needs, aspirations, and personal projects.
2. To enhance successful efforts toward meeting needs, use existing family functioning style (strengths and capabilities) as a basis

for promoting the family's ability to mobilize resources.
3. To insure the availability and adequacy of resources for meeting needs, place major emphasis on strengthening the family's personal social network as well as promoting utilization of untapped but potential sources of informal aid and assistance.
4. To enhance a family's ability to become more self-sustaining with respect to meeting its needs, employ helping behaviors that promote the family's acquisition and use of competencies and skills necessary to mobilize and secure resources.

In the context of educational interventions for handicapped learners, Evans, Meyer, Derer, and Hanashiro (1985) suggest that because of the limited availability of educational programming time in proportion to the learning needs of handicapped children, and because most excess behaviors can be effectively decreased by meeting educational needs rather than by behavior reduction procedures, "direct programming to modify a behavior should be considered a priority *only when unavoidable*" (p. 45; emphasis in original).

The Important Role of Neurobiological Processes

The role of neurobiological processes, including basic maturational changes, has received increasing attention in cognitive-behavioral approaches to the treatment of childhood disorders. Studies of the effects of endocrine products, metabolites, neurotransmitters, and genetic structures on behavioral predispositions (e.g., Cicchetti & Cohen, 1995a, 1995b) have necessitated a reappraisal of several learning-based theories and treatment approaches (Kanfer & Schefft, 1988; O'Leary & Wilson, 1987). Genetically influenced constitutional factors provide the medium in which psychological principles operate to produce both adaptive and maladaptive behavior. Biological determinants, biochemical disorders, or physical diseases frequently set limits on the skills a given child or family can learn; in turn, these limits influence decisions concerning the type of treatment that is likely to be most effective (Mash & Dozois, 1996; Ross, 1981).

The possible involvement of organic illness in many forms of childhood disorder necessitates an active collaboration with medical specialists. Strayhorn (1987) has presented several general guidelines in assessing the possibility of organic illness (e.g., toxic, traumatic, infectious, idiopathic, neoplastic, nutritional, collagen vascular/autoimmune, congenital/hereditary, endocrine, vascular, metabolic, and degenerative). An organic contribution is seen as more likely when functioning is grossly impaired, when there is a loss of previous ability in intellectual functioning, when explanations based on other grounds are not readily available, and when there are physical complaints and symptoms in addition to psychological ones.

Current cognitive-behavioral practices are based upon a wide net of research findings, including those emanating from the biological sciences. This has led to the identification of important organismic variables and to information concerning the manner in which such variables interact with environmental factors in determining behavioral outcomes. For example, the relationship between child temperament and the quality of early parent–child relationships may be mediated by social class, suggesting that early intervention with difficult infants may be more critical for low-SES families. Some longitudinal studies (e.g., Cohen, Velez, Brook, & Smith, 1989), have found that pre- and perinatal problems, as well as illnesses, accidents, and hospitalizations in early childhood, pose a biological risk for future psychopathology in children. Interestingly, these studies have tended to find that biological risk factors such as perinatal and early somatic problems are nonspecific, placing a child at increased risk for all kinds of problems (including both externalizing and internalizing disorders, as well as substance misuse). Implicit in such findings is the notion that experiential factors in a family may mediate the expression of a disorder and should therefore be a high priority for intervention.

Concern for Treatment Generalization

Within a behavioral–systems framework, choices concerning the target of intervention, the agent of intervention, the setting in which intervention occurs, and the nature of the intervention should be based upon one's predictions concerning the generalizability of effects that can be achieved by intervening in one aspect of the family system versus another. The intent is to make choices that will maximize the impact of treatment throughout the relevant systems in which the child functions. Treatment generalization has been conceptualized as occurring across

settings (e.g., clinic to home), across responses and response systems (i.e., from targeted to untargeted behaviors), over time (i.e., durable effects), and to other family members (e.g., from target child to sibling). Findings from numerous investigations indicate that unless systematic steps are taken in treatment to promote generalization, it will not occur, and several writers have offered suggestions as to how generalization might be enhanced (e.g., Stokes & Baer, 1977). These suggestions have included the use of cognitive-behavioral therapy procedures, the enlistment of mediators in the child's natural environment, the use of multicomponent treatment strategies that focus on several family subsystems (e.g., parent–child and marital), the employment of self-management programs, and the use of specific operant procedures such as fading. The emphasis on cognitive processes and self-control in treatment has been viewed as one way of increasing generalization, by providing the child with internal self-regulators that will continue to operate across settings and time in the absence of external controls. This hypothesis has not, however, been systematically tested, and studies are needed to determine whether the use of cognitive therapies do in fact produce more generalized or more durable treatment effects with children and families, relative to other forms of treatment that do not include cognitive components.

Although follow-up studies have become increasingly common in the cognitive-behavioral literature, there is still a great need for studies that evaluate the long-term impact of child and family interventions. Complex issues surrounding the choice of follow-up intervals remain (e.g., Mash & Terdal, 1980), and the rapid developmental changes that characterize child and adolescent development make the assessment of long-term outcomes that much more difficult. A few investigators have suggested the possibility of "sleeper effects" in treatment; that is, performance at follow-up may actually be better than that immediately following treatment. This improvement has been hypothesized to be a function of the cumulative benefits derived from the continuing use of skills that were learned during treatment and the positive impact that such skills might have on a child's social system. Further investigation of possible "sleeper effects" is needed, and in doing so, it will be important to consider such posttreatment improvements against a baseline of growing maturity.

Several studies have found that treatments focusing on multiple family and school subsystems tend to produce more durable outcomes. For example, Dadds et al. (1987) found that child management training alone resulted in 6-month relapses in child problems, parent reports of difficulties, and marital dissatisfaction in families with marital discord. However, such relapses were less prevalent in families where child management training had been supplemented with partner support training in conflict resolution, communication, and problem solving. Epstein, Wing, Koeske, and Valoski (1987) found that at a 5-year follow-up of their diet management program, the children who had received combined parent and child training showed significantly greater weight reduction when compared to children who had been trained without their parents, or to controls. One-third of the children in the parent and child training group were within 20% of normal weight, in comparison with only 5% of the controls.

Interest in Treatment Processes

A growing recognition of the importance of the general therapeutic milieu in moderating the effectiveness of cognitive-behavioral techniques has resulted in a greater interest in understanding treatment processes (e.g., resistance, treatment termination, treatment dropout). Although most forms of cognitive-behavioral intervention require a cooperative therapeutic relationship with children, parents, and teachers, it is not always the case that these individuals are motivated for change (e.g., Chamberlain, Patterson, Reid, Kavanagh, & Forgatch, 1984). Consequently, there may be a need for special strategies designed to increase client involvement in order to reduce the likelihood that premature intervention will lead to resistance and premature treatment termination (e.g., Ellis, 1985).

Kanfer and Schefft (1988) have described resistance and treatment noncompliance as representing a discrepancy between the client's behavior and the therapist's expectations. They also note that there are many sources of noncompliance that need to be examined, including such things as client anxieties and self-doubts (e.g., fear of the future, giving up a known life pattern for a new and possible worse state); client skill deficits; insufficient therapeutic structure or guidance; no motivation for change, due to secondary gain from symptoms; a countertherapeutic support network; and the client's

lack of confidence in his or her ability to carry out therapeutic assignments. Understanding the different sources of therapeutic noncompliance will lead to different strategies for dealing with it in treatment.

Premature treatment termination has also been a concern in cognitive-behavioral work with children and families. The fact that as many as 40% to 60% of cases receiving outpatient care drop out of treatment make this a significant concern (Kazdin, 1996c). In the review of child treatment outcome studies conducted by Weisz, Weiss, Alicke, and Klotz (1987), the mean number of therapy sessions was 9.5. However, this review also supported the idea that more intensive forms of treatment may produce more beneficial effects. In light of this, understanding the factors surrounding treatment dropout and developing methods to minimize them are priorities in cognitive-behavioral intervention. In a study by Weisz, Weiss, and Langmeyer (1987), dropouts and continuers in child psychotherapy were compared on a variety of child and family characteristics that included child demographic variables, therapist variables, child problems, and parent perception variables. Surprisingly, the two groups were virtually indistinguishable on the basis of these characteristics. Weisz, Weiss, and Langmeyer (1987) suggested that source of referral and caretaker symptomatology—factors that were not included in their study—may be more important factors in determining whether or not families drop out of treatment.

In a recent study that focused on children with conduct problems, Kazdin (1996c) identified a number of factors that were associated with a greater risk of dropping out of treatment. Among these were lower income, dangerous neighborhood, younger mothers, one-parent families, greater perceived stress, maternal history of antisocial behavior, greater severity and duration of child conduct problem symptoms, greater number of parent-reported symptoms, below-normal intelligence, poor school functioning, harsh parenting practices, and contacts with deviant peers. Kazdin (1996c, pp. 146–147) summarized his findings as follows:

1.　Several factors increase the risk of families dropping out of treatment. Although many of these are related, they make separate contributions to predicting early termination from treatment.

2. The factors that predict early termination are much the same as those that predict poor long term prognosis in children with conduct problems.

3. It is possible to reliably predict early treatment termination based on the identified risk factors.

4. Current parent psychopathology does not seem to predict early treatment termination.

5. Those high-risk families who continue in treatment do not profit very much from seeing treatment to the end of its course.

These findings suggest the need for decision models that view dropping out of treatment in the larger context of service delivery and utilization and that focus on a wide variety of barriers to service utilization and their interaction (Kazdin, 1996c). Such decision models will need to be developed in the context of different childhood disorders, since, although there is likely to be some overlap, the barriers for children with conduct problems (e.g., socioeconomic disadvantage) are likely to differ from those for children with anxiety disorders (e.g., reluctance of parents to seek treatment) or children with autism (e.g., high burden of care).

Emphasis on Self-Regulation, Self-Management, and Self-Control

A number of cognitive-behavioral models for intervention have emphasized the importance of examining self-regulatory systems as the basis for treatment (e.g., Kanfer & Schefft, 1988; Karoly, 1981). Self-initiated, self-maintained, and self-corrective internal processes, including self-observation, self-monitoring, self-reinforcement, imaging, planning, and decision making, have the potential for maintaining behavior over protracted periods of time, and by doing so can decrease the individual's dependence on environmental and biological factors. A self-management approach seems especially relevant for children and families, in that many of the disorders to be discussed in this volume represent a failure to develop (or a breakdown in) self-regulatory skills. Recent early-intervention models that have emphasized family needs assessment and concepts such as empowerment are consistent with the self-regulatory approach.

Self-management and self-regulation therapies are directed at teaching such processes as setting goals, evaluating norms and standards,

monitoring and evaluating problem situations, planning, solving problems, examining choices, anticipating outcomes, employing self-reward and self-punishment, and understanding the relationships between cognitions and behavior. Appropriate use of these strategies assists the child and family in developing control over their behavior; over certain physiological reactions, such as anxiety, anger, and the experience of pain; and over cognitive or imaginally mediated reactions, such as intrusive thoughts, negative self-appraisals, or undesirable urges (Kanfer & Schefft, 1988). Achieving such control is intended to make the child and family more proactive in their behavior, so that they are able to anticipate potentially conflictual situations, and have available a variety of mechanisms permitting them to cope effectively.

Concern for Ethical Standards

Criticism of some of the early behavior therapy practices, especially the use of aversive controls, has led to a special concern for the development of ethical standards for behavioral intervention. Minimum ethical standards for practice have been presented and include such things as selecting treatment goals and procedures that are in the best interests of the client; making sure that client participation is active and voluntary; keeping records that document the effectiveness of treatments in achieving its objectives; protecting the confidentiality of the therapeutic relationship; and insuring the qualifications and competencies of the therapist (e.g., MacDonald, 1986). Guidelines for the responsible use of aversive procedures in behavioral intervention have also been developed (Favell et al., 1982), although the use of such procedures with children continues to decline.

Use of Specific Techniques and Technology

The specific techniques that have been used in behavioral interventions for children and families are numerous; they are described in great detail throughout the chapters of this volume in relation to specific disorders. Some of the more commonly utilized general techniques are parent management training; modeling and role playing; relaxation procedures; desensitization and its many variants; exposure and response prevention; self-control and self-management methods; basic operant techniques, such as differential reinforcement, shaping, fading, punishment, and time out; cognitive change procedures, such as cognitive restructuring, stress inoculation, and cognitive coping strategies; social skills training; token systems; behavioral contracting; and environmental engineering.

Although, as noted earlier, flexibility is required in the clinical context, efforts to describe behavioral programs in as precise and replicable a fashion as possible have resulted in the availability of many useful assessment and intervention technologies. These include many detailed therapists' manuals for the assessment and treatment of a variety of child and family disorders (e.g., Albano et al., 1991; Barkley, 1997b; Blechman, 1985; Clarke & Lewinsohn, 1995; Evans & Meyer, 1985; Fleischman, Horne, & Arthur, 1983; Forehand & McMahon, 1981; Henggeler, 1991; Herbert, 1987; Kendall & Braswell, 1985; Kendall et al., 1992; Knox et al., 1993; Stark & Kendall, 1996); training materials and handouts for parents (e.g., Bernal & North, 1978); videotaped sequences of parent–child interaction (e.g., Wolfe & LaRose, 1986); computer simulations for training (e.g., Lambert, 1987); programs for data collection and treatment implementation utilizing microprocessors (e.g., Romanczyk, 1986); and filmed presentations of treatment programs (e.g., Houts, Whelan, & Peterson, 1987). Such technology is not intended to be a substitute for sound clinical decision making, but it does permit the training, transmission, and further evaluation of empirically well-documented techniques and procedures. The availability of these technologies is viewed as an important distinguishing characteristic of a behavioral–systems approach to intervention.

Use of Multiple Indicators to Assess Treatment Outcomes

A behavioral–systems perspective recognizes the need to use multiple indicators to assess the impact of treatment. Such indicators include reduction in symptoms; improvements in adjustment at home, at school, or in the community; increases in self-reported happiness and well-being; evaluations of relatives and friends that things are better; and prevention of possible further deterioration in the child's and family's adjustment. A concern for the clinical significance of therapeutic change has increased. Not only is it important to demonstrate behavioral changes, but it is essential that the magnitude and quality of these changes place the child and family within the boundaries of developmental, sociocultural, and personal norms for adjustment.

Concern for Consumer Satisfaction and the Acceptability of Treatments

A number of studies have examined the acceptability to consumers of a variety of cognitive-behavioral interventions, and the possible factors mediating such acceptance (e.g., Elliott, 1988; Kazdin, 1981, 1984; LeBow, 1982; McMahon & Forehand, 1983; Witt & Elliott, 1986). For example, Tarnowski, Kelly, and Mendlowitz (1987) examined pediatric nurses' acceptability ratings of six behavioral interventions. Interventions directed at increasing desired behaviors were rated as more acceptable than reductive treatments, and treatment acceptability varied as a function of behavior problem severity. The medical severity of the child's condition did not significantly influence ratings. Furey and Basili (1988) attempted to predict consumer satisfaction in parent training for noncompliant children, and noted the importance of predicting what "consumer satisfaction" is going to be in advance, rather than determining what it is after the fact. Although clients' rights to self-determination, ethical and legal considerations, and common sense would certainly dictate the use of client-preferred treatment procedures, it has also been assumed that procedures that are perceived as objectionable or offensive by children and families will not be very effective, and that procedures that are preferred over others are likely to be more effective. However, the relationships between acceptability and outcome are just beginning to be empirically investigated.

The assessment of the social validity of interventions includes expanding the definition of "consumers" to acknowledge the range of community members and health care delivery personnel who are likely to influence the survival and effectiveness of an intervention program; assessing underrepresented populations, particularly lower-SES families and minority group members; and increasing the involvement of consumers in the planning and evaluation of cognitive-behavioral programs, so as to educate consumers to make better informed decisions about intervention (Schwartz & Baer, 1991).

Need to Consider Ethnic and Cultural Factors in Assessment and Treatment

In light of the family's central importance as a social unit and transmitter of sociocultural values, it is especially critical that interventions concerned with child behavior, child rearing, and other family issues establish some degree of congruence between the cognitive–behavior therapy program and the sociocultural milieu in which it is carried out (Tharp, 1991). Often the rules that govern behavior and expectations for children are more explicit than those describing social intercourse among adults. The need to give greater attention to the cultural context of children and families participating in cognitive-behavioral interventions has received increased attention. This is evidenced in a recent call to consider parenting values and behaviors of specific ethnic minority groups (African, Asian, Latino, and Native Americans) in parent management training (Forehand & Kotchick, 1996) and in a special journal series devoted to ethnic and cultural diversity in cognitive and behavioral practice (Iwamasa, 1996). A consideration of treatment in relation to specific values, norms, expectations, and prescribed behaviors for different social classes within cultures; across families that vary in their religious belief systems; for new immigrants; and across cultures is essential. Although cognitive-behavioral procedures have certainly been applied across many different ethnic groups and cultures, cross-cultural assessment and treatment have received only minimal attention to date.

SUMMARY AND CONCLUSIONS

In this chapter, I have presented some of the major characteristics of a behavioral–systems perspective on the treatment of child and family disorders. The behavioral–systems perspective is depicted as a decision-making approach to treatment and prevention; it is based on a consistently applied theoretical framework, well-established research findings relevant to both normal and deviant child and family functioning, empirically supported treatment procedures, and operational rules that conform to the realities and changing demands of clinical practice. Recent developments in the field have included a growing systems emphasis; greater sensitivity to developmental factors; and an increased recog-

nition of the importance of individual differences, biological determinants, and emotional, cognitive, and cultural factors in treatment. A need for the further development of cognitive-behavioral treatment strategies that are sensitive to specific clinical problems is emphasized. The population-specific chapter presentations that follow provide detailed discussions of many of the issues that have been highlighted in this introductory presentation.

ACKNOWLEDGMENTS

During the preparation of this chapter, I was supported by a grant from the Killam Foundation and the Office of the Vice-President of Research at the University of Calgary. This support is gratefully acknowledged.

REFERENCES

Achenbach, T. M. (1982). *Developmental psychopathology* (2nd ed.). New York: Wiley.

Achenbach, T. M. (1985). *Assessment and taxonomy of child and adolescent psychopathology.* Beverly Hills, CA: Sage.

Achenbach, T. M. (1993). *Empirically based taxonomy: How to use syndromes and profile types derived from the CBCL/4–18, TRF, and YSF.* Burlington: University of Vermont, Department of Psychiatry.

Achenbach, T. M. (1995). Diagnosis, assessment, and comorbidity in psychosocial treatment research. *Journal of Abnormal Child Psychology, 23*, 45–65.

Achenbach, T. M., Howell, C. T., Quay, H. C., & Conners, C. K. (1991). National survey of problems and competencies among four- to sixteen-year-olds. *Monographs of the Society for Research in Child Development, 56*(3, Serial No. 225).

Achenbach, T. M., & McConaughy, S. H. (1997). *Empirically based assessment of child and adolescent psychopathology: Practical applications* (2nd ed.). Thousand Oaks, CA: Sage.

Adelman, H. S. (1995). Clinical psychology: Beyond psychopathology and clinical interventions. *Clinical Psychology: Science and Practice, 2*, 28–44.

Anselm, H. S., & Taylor, L. (1993). *Learning problems and learning disabilities: Moving forward.* Pacific Grove, CA: Brooks/Cole.

Albano, M., Marten, P. A., & Holt, C. B. (1991). *Cognitive-behavioral group treatment of adolescent social phobia.* Unpublished manual, Anxiety Disorders Clinic, University of Louisville.

Alberto, P. A., & Troutman, A. C. (1982). *Applied behavior analysis for teachers: Influencing student performance.* Columbus, OH: Charles E. Merrill.

Alexander, J. G., & Parsons, B. V. (1982). *Functional family therapy.* Monterey, CA: Brooks/Cole.

American Psychological Association. (1996). *Violence and the family: Report of the American Psychological Association Presidential Task Force on Violence and the Family.* Washington, DC: Author.

American Psychiatric Association. (1994). *Diagnostic and statistical manual of mental disorders (4th ed.).* Washington, DC: Author.

Anastasi, A., & Urbina, S. (1997). *Psychological testing* (7th ed.). Upper Saddle River, NJ: Prentice Hall.

Arnold, L. E., Abikoff, H. B., & Wells, K. C. (1997). National Institute of Mental Health Collaborative Multimodal Treatment Study of Children with ADHD (the MTA): Design challenges and choices. *Archives of General Psychiatry, 54,* 865–868.

Asarnow, J., Carlson, G. A., & Guthrie, D. (1987). Coping strategies, self-perceptions, hopelessness, and perceived family environments in depressed and suicidal children. *Journal of Consulting and Clinical Psychology, 55,* 361–366.

Baer, D. M., Wolf, M. M., & Risley, T. R. (1968). Some current dimensions of applied behavior analysis. *Journal of Applied Behavior Analysis, 1,* 91–97.

Baer, D. M., Wolf, M. M., & Risley, T. R. (1987). Some still-current dimensions of applied behavior analysis. *Journal of Applied Behavior Analysis, 20,* 313–327.

Baker, B. L. (1980). Training parents as teachers of their developmentally disabled children. In S. Saizinger, J. Antrobus, & J. Glick (Eds.), *The ecosystem of the sick child* (pp. 201–216). New York: Academic Press.

Bandura, A. (1969). *Principles of behavior modification.* New York: Holt, Rinehart & Winston.

Bandura, A. (1986). *Social foundations of thought and action: A social cognitive theory.* Englewood Cliffs, NJ: Prentice-Hall.

Barkley, R. A. (1987). *Defiant children: A clinician's manual for parent training.* New York: Guilford Press.

Barkley, R. A. (1990). *Attention-Deficit Hyperactivity Disorder: A handbook for diagnosis and treatment.* New York: Guilford Press.

Barkley, R. A. (1996). Attention-Deficit/Hyperactivity Disorder. In E. J. Mash & R. A. Barkley (Eds.), *Child psychopathology* (pp. 63–112). New York: Guilford Press.

Barkley, R. A. (1997a). *ADHD and the nature of self-control.* New York: Guilford Press.

Barkley, R. A. (1997b). *Defiant children: A clinician's manual for parent training* (2nd ed.). New York: Guilford Press.

Barkley, R. A., Guevremont, D. C., Anastopoulos, A. D., & Fletcher, K. E. (1992). A comparison of three family therapy programs for treating family conflicts in adolescents with Attention-Deficit Hyperactivity Disorder. *Journal of Consulting and Clinical Psychology, 60,* 450–462.

Barkley, R. A., Shelton, T. L., Crosswait, C., Moorehouse, M., Fletcher, K., Barrett, S., Jenkins, L., & Metevia, L. (1997). Preliminary findings of an early intervention program with aggressive hyperactive children. In C. F. Ferris & T. Grisso (Eds.), *Understanding aggressive behavior in children* (pp. 277–289). New York: New York Academy of Sciences.

Barlow, D. H., & Hersen, M. (1984). *Single case experimental designs: Strategies for studying behavior change* (2nd ed.). New York: Pergamon Press.

Barrett, P. M., Dadds, M. R., & Rapee, R. M. (1996). Family treatment of childhood anxiety: A controlled trial. *Journal of Consulting and Clinical Psychology, 64,* 333–342.

Beidel, D. C., & Turner, S. M. (1986). A critique of the theoretical bases of cognitive-behavior theories and therapy. *Clinical Psychology Review, 6,* 177–197.

Bell-Dolan, D. (1995). Social cue interpretation of anxious children. *Journal of Clinical Child Psychology, 24,* 1–10.

Bell-Dolan, D. J., & Wessler, A. E. (1994). Attributional style of anxious children: Extensions from cognitive theory and research on adult anxiety. *Journal of Anxiety Disorders, 8,* 79–96.

Bernal, M. E., & North, J. (1978). A survey of parent training manuals. *Journal of Applied Behavior Analysis, 11,* 533–544.

Beutler, L. E., Williams, R. E., Wakefield, P. J., & Entwistle, S. R. (1995). Bridging scientist and practitioner perspectives in clinical psychology. *American Psychologist, 50,* 984–994.

Bickman, L. (1996). A continuum of care: More is not always better. *American Psychologist, 51,* 689–701.

Bickman, L. (1997). Resolving issues raised by the Fort Bragg evaluation: New directions for mental health services research. *American Psychologist, 52,* 562–565.

Bijou, S. W., & Baer, D. M. (1961). *Child development: Systematic and empirical theory.* New York: Appleton-Century-Crofts.

Blechman, E. A. (1985). *Solving child behavior problems at home and school.* Champaign, IL: Research Press.

Block, J., & Gjerde, P. F. (1990). Depressive symptoms in late adolescence: A longitudinal perspective on personality antecedents. In J. E. Rolf, A. Masten, D. Cicchetti, K. Neuchterlein, & S. Weintraub (Eds.), *Risk and protective factors in the development of psychopathology* (pp. 334–360). New York: Cambridge University Press.

Block, J., Block, J. H., & Keyes, S. (1988). Longitudinally foretelling drug usage in adolescence: Early childhood personality and environmental precursors. *Child Development, 59,* 336–355.

Bornstein, P. H., Kazdin, A. E., & McIntyre, T. J. (1985). Characteristics, trends, and future directions in child behavior therapy. In P. H. Bornstein &

A. E. Kazdin (Eds.), *Handbook of clinical behavior therapy with children* (pp. 833–850). Homewood, IL: Dorsey Press.

Bornstein, P. H., & van den Pol, R. A. (1985). Models of assessment and treatment in child behavior therapy. In P. H. Bornstein & A. E. Kazdin (Eds.), *Handbook of clinical behavior therapy with children* (pp. 44–74). Homewood, IL: Dorsey Press.

Bronfenbrenner, U. (1986). Ecology of the family as a context for human development: Research perspectives. *Developmental Psychology, 22,* 723–742.

Brunk, M., Henggeler, S. W., & Whelan, J. P. (1987). Comparison of multisystemic therapy and parent training in the brief treatment of child abuse and neglect. *Journal of Consulting and Clinical Psychology, 55,* 171–178.

Carlson, G., Asarnow, J. R., & Orbach, I. (1987). Developmental aspects of suicidal behavior in children. *Journal of the American Academy of Child and Adolescent Psychiatry, 26,* 186–192.

Caron, C., & Rutter, M. (1991). Comorbidity in child psychopathology: Concepts, issues, and research strategies. *Journal of Child Psychology and Psychiatry, 32,* 1063–1080.

Carr, E. G. (1994). Emerging themes in the functional analysis of problem behavior. *Journal of Applied Behavior Analysis, 27, 393–399.*

Carver, C. S., & Scheier, M. F. (1986, August). *Dispositional optimism: A theoretical analysis and implications for the self-regulation of behavior.* Paper presented at the annual meeting of the American Psychological Association, Washington, DC.

Casey, R. J., & Berman, J. S. (1985). The outcome of psychotherapy with children. *Psychological Bulletin, 98,* 388–400.

Caspi, A., & Moffitt, T. E. (1995). The continuity of maladaptive behavior: From description to understanding in the study of antisocial behavior. In D. Cicchetti & D. J. Cohen (Eds.), *Developmental psychopathology: Vol. 2. Risk, disorder, and adaptation* (pp. 472–511). New York: Wiley.

Chamberlain, P., Patterson, G. R., Reid, J. B., Kavanagh, K., & Forgatch, M. (1984). Observation of client resistance. *Behavior Therapy, 15,* 144–155.

Christopherson, E. R. (1986). Accident prevention in primary care. *Pediatric Clinics of North America, 33,* 925–933.

Cicchetti, D., Ackerman, B. P., & Izard, C. E. (1995). Emotions and emotion regulation in developmental psychopathology. *Development and Psychopathology, 7,* 1–10.

Cicchetti, D., & Cohen, D. J. (Eds.). (1995a). *Developmental psychopathology: Vol. 1. Theory and methods.* New York: Wiley.

Cicchetti, D., & Cohen, D. J. (Eds.). (1995b). *Developmental psychopathology: Vol. 2. Risk, disorder, and adaptation.* New York: Wiley.

Cicchetti, D., & Cohen, D. J. (1995c). Perspectives on developmental psychopathology. In D. Cicchetti & D. J. Cohen (Eds.), *Developmental psychopathology: Vol. 1. Theory and methods* (pp. 3–20). New York: Wiley.

Ciminero, A. R., Calhoun, K. S., & Adams, H. E. (Eds.). (1986). *Handbook of behavioral assessment* (2nd ed.). New York: Wiley-Interscience.

Clarke, G. N., Hawkins, W., Murphy, M., Sheeber, L. B., Lewinsohn, P. M., & Seeley, M. S. (1995). Targeted prevention of unipolar depressive disorder in an at-risk sample of high school adolescents: A randomized trial of a group cognitive intervention. *Journal of the American Academy of Child and Adolescent Psychiatry, 34,* 312–321.

Clarke, G., & Lewinsohn, P. M. (1995). *The Adolescent Coping with Stress Class: Leader manual.* Unpublished manual. Oregon Health Sciences University.

Clement, P. W. (1996). Evaluation in private practice. *Clinical Psychology: Science and Practice, 3,* 146–159.

Cohen, P., Velez, C. N., Brook, J. S., & Smith, J. (1989). Mechanisms of the relation between perinatal problems, early childhood illness, and psychopathology in late childhood and adolescence. *Child Development, 60,* 701–709.

Conduct Problems Prevention Research Group. (1992). A developmental and clinical model for the prevention of Conduct Disorder: The FAST Track Program. *Development and Psychopathology, 4,* 509–527.

Conduct Problems Prevention Research Group. (1997, April). *Prevention of antisocial behavior: Initial findings from the Fast Track project.* Symposium presented at the biennial meeting of the Society for Research in Child Development, Washington, DC.

Cone, J. D. (1997). Issues in functional analysis in behavioural assessment. *Behaviour Research and Therapy, 35,* 259–275.

Courchesne, E., Townsend, J., & Chase, C. (1995). Neurodevelopmental principles guide research on developmental psychopathologies. In D. Cicchetti & D. J. Cohen (Eds.), *Developmental psychopathology: Vol. 1. Theory and methods* (pp. 195–226). New York: Wiley.

Cowan, P. A. (1997). Beyond meta-analysis: A plea for a family systems view of attachment. *Child Development, 68,* 601–603.

Crick, N. R. (1995). Relational aggression: The role of intent attributions, feelings of distress, and provocation type. *Development and Psychopathology, 7,* 313–322.

Crick, N. R., Bigbee, M. A., & Howes, C. (1996). Gender differences in children's normative beliefs about aggression: How do I hurt thee? Let me count the ways. *Child Development, 67,* 1003–1014.

Crick, N. R., & Dodge, K. A. (1994). A review and reformulation of social information processing mechanisms in children's social adjustment. *Psychological Bulletin, 115,* 74–101.

Crick, N. R., & Dodge, K. A. (1996). Social information-processing mechanisms in reactive and proactive aggression. *Child Development, 67,* 993–1002.

Cronbach, L. J. (1990). *Essentials of psychological testing* (5th ed.). New York: Harper & Row.

Dadds, M. R., Schwartz, S., & Sanders, M. R. (1987). Marital discord and treatment outcome in behavioral treatment of child conduct disorders. *Journal of Consulting and Clinical Psychology, 55,* 396–403.

Dangel, R. F., & Polster, R. A. (Eds.). (1984). *Parent training: Foundations of research and practice.* New York: Guilford Press.

DiGiuseppe, R., Linscott, J., & Jilton, R. (1996). Developing the therapeutic alliance in child–adolescent psychotherapy. *Applied & Preventive Psychology, 5,* 85–100.

Dishion, T. J., French, D. C., & Patterson, G. R. (1995). The development and ecology of antisocial behavior. In D. Cicchetti & D. J. Cohen (Eds.), *Developmental psychopathology: Vol. 2. Risk, disorder, and adaptation* (pp. 421–472). New York: Wiley.

Donnellan, A. M. (1988, February). Our old ways just aren't working. *Dialect* (Newsletter of the Saskatchewan Association for the Mentally Retarded).

Dunlap, K. (1932). *Habits: Their making and unmaking.* New York: Liveright.

Dunst, C., Trivette, C. & Deal, A. (1988). *Enabling and empowering families: Principles and guidelines for practice.* Cambridge, MA: Brookline Books.

DuPaul, G. J., & Eckert, T. L. (1997). The effects of school-based interventions for Attention Deficit Hyperactivity Disorder: A meta-analysis. *School Psychology Digest, 26,* 5–27.

Durlak, J. A., Fuhrman, T., & Lampman, C. (1991). Effectiveness of cognitive-behavior therapy for maladapting children: A meta-analysis. *Psychological Bulletin, 110,* 204–214.

Edelbrock, C. (1984). Developmental considerations. In T. H. Ollendick & M. Hersen (Eds.), *Child behavioral assessment: Principles and procedures* (pp. 20–37). New York: Pergamon Press.

Egeland, B., Jacobvitz, D., & Sroufe, L. A. (1988). Breaking the cycle of abuse. *Child Development, 59,* 1080–1088.

Eifert, G. H., & Wilson, P. H. (1991). The triple response approach to assessment: A conceptual and methodological reappraisal. *Behaviour Research and Therapy, 29,* 283–292.

Elliott, A. J., Miltenberger, R. G., Kaster-Bundgaard, J., & Lumley, V. (1996). A national survey of assessment and therapy techniques used by behavior therapists. *Cognitive and Behavioral Practice, 3,* 107–125.

Elliott, S. N. (1988). Acceptability of behavioral treatments: Review of variables that influence treatment selection. *Professional Psychology: Research and Practice, 19,* 68–80.

Ellis, A. (1985). *Overcoming resistance: Rational–emotive therapy with difficult clients.* New York: Springer.

Emery, R. E., Fincham, F. D., & Cummings, E. M. (1992). Parenting in context: Systemic thinking about parental conflict and its influence on children. *Journal of Consulting and Clinical Psychology, 60,* 909–912.

Emery, R. E., & Kitzmann, K. M. (1995). The child in the family: Disruptions in family functioning. In D. Cicchetti & D. J. Cohen (Eds.), *Developmental psychopathology: Vol. 2. Risk, disorder, and adaptation.* (pp. 3–33). New York: Wiley.

Epstein, L. H., Wing, R. R., Koeske, R., & Valoski, A. (1987). Long-term effects of family based treatment of childhood obesity. *Journal of Consulting and Clinical Psychology, 55,* 91–95.

Evans, I. M. (1985). Building systems models as a strategy for target behavior selection in clinical assessment. *Behavioral Assessment, 7,* 21–32.

Evans, I. M., & Meyer, L. H. (1985). *An educative approach to behavior problems: A practical decision model for interventions with severely handicapped learners.* Baltimore: Paul H. Brookes.

Evans, I. M., Meyer, L. H., Derer, K. R., & Hanashiro, R. Y. (1985). An overview of the decision model. In I. M. Evans & L. H. Meyer, *An educative approach to behavior problems: A practical decision model for interventions with severely handicapped learners* (pp. 43–61). Baltimore: Paul H. Brookes.

Evans, S. W., Vallano, G., & Pelham, W. (1994). Treatment of parenting behavior with a psychostimulant: A case study of an adult with Attention-Deficit Hyperactivity Disorder. *Journal of Child and Adolescent Psychopharmacology, 4,* 63–69.

Eysenck, H. J. (Ed.). (1960). *Behavior therapy and the neuroses.* New York: Pergamon Press.

Fauber, R. L., & Kendall, P. C. (1992). Children and families: Integrating the focus of interventions. *Journal of Psychotherapy Integration, 2,* 107–123.

Fauber, R. L., & Long, N. (1991). Children in context: The role of the family in child psychotherapy. *Journal of Consulting and Clinical Psychology, 59,* 813–820.

Favell, J. E., Azrin, N. H., Baumeister, A. A., Carr, E. G., Dorsey, M. F., Forehand, R., Foxx, R. M., Lovaas, O. I., Rincover, A., Risley, T. R., Romancyzk, R. O., Russo, D. C., Schroeder, S. R., & Solnick, J. V. (1982). The treatment of self-injurious behavior (AABT Task Force Report, Winter 1982). *Behavior Therapy, 13,* 529–554.

Finch, A. J., Jr., Nelson, W. M., III, & Ott, E. S. (Eds.). (1993). *Cognitive-behavioral procedures with children and adolescents: A practical guide.* Needham Heights, MA: Allyn & Bacon.

Flanagan, R. (1986). Teaching young children responses to inappropriate approaches by strangers in public places. *Child and Family Behavior Therapy, 8,* 27–43.

Fleischman, M. J., Horne, A. M., & Arthur, J. L. (1983). *Troubled families: A treatment program.* Champaign, IL: Research Press.

Fogel, A., & Thelan, E. (1987). Development of early expressive and communicative action: Reinterpreting the evidence from a dynamic systems perspective. *Developmental Psychology, 23,* 747–761.

Forehand, R. L., & Kotchick, B. A. (1996). Cultural diversity: A wake-up call for parent training. *Behavior Therapy, 27,* 187–206.

Forehand, R. L., & McMahon, R. J. (1981). *Helping the noncompliant child: A clinician's guide to parent training.* New York: Guilford Press.

Furey, W. M., & Basili, L. (1988). Predicting consumer satisfaction in parent training for noncompliant children. *Behavior Therapy, 19,* 555–564.

Garber, J. (1984). Classification of child psychopathology: A developmental perspective. *Child Development, 55,* 30–48.

Goldfried, M. R. (1995). *From cognitive-behavior therapy to psychotherapy integration: An evolving view.* New York: Springer.

Goldfried, M. R., & Wolfe, B. E. (1996). Psychotherapy practice and research: Repairing a strained relationship. *American Psychologist, 51,* 1007–1016.

Gordon, J. R., & Craver, J. N. (1988, January). *Safer sex: A self help manual.* Unpublished manual, University of Washington School of Social Work.

Gottman, J. M., & Katz, L. F. (1996). Parental meta-emotion philosophy and the emotional life of families: Theoretical models and preliminary data. *Journal of Family Psychology, 10,* 243–268.

Gottman, J. M., Katz, L. F., & Hooven, C. (1997). *Meta-emotion: How families communicate emotionally.* Mahwah, NJ: Lawrence Erlbaum.

Gottman, J. M., & Levenson, R. W. (1986). Assessing the role of emotion in marriage. *Behavioral Assessment, 8,* 31-48.

Gross, A. M., & Drabman, R. S. (Eds.). (1990). *Handbook of clinical behavioral pediatrics.* New York: Plenum Press.

Gurman, A. S., & Kniskern, D. P. (Eds.). (1991). *Handbook of family therapy* (Vol. 2). New York: Brunner/Mazel.

Harris, K. R., Wong, B. L., & Keogh, B. K. (Eds.). (1985). Cognitive-behavior modification with children: A critical review of the state of the art [Special issue]. *Journal of Abnormal Child Psychology, 3,* 329–476.

Harris, S. L. (1984). The family of the autistic child: A behavioral systems view. *Clinical Psychology Review, 4,* 227–239.

Harris, S. L., & Ferrari, M. (1983). Developmental factors in child behavior therapy. *Behavior Therapy, 14,* 54–72.

Harris, S. L., & Powers, M. D. (1984). Diagnostic issues. In T. H. Ollendick & M. Hersen (Eds.), *Child behavioral assessment: Principles and procedures* (pp. 38–57). New York: Pergamon Press.

Hartmann, D. P., Roper, B. L., & Bradford, D. C. (1979). Some relationships between behavioral and traditional assessment. *Journal of Behavioral Assessment, 1,* 3–21.

Harvey, P., Forehand, R., Brown, C., & Holmes, T. (1988). The prevention of sexual abuse: Examination of the effectiveness of a program with kindergarten-age children. *Behavior Therapy, 19,* 429–435.

Hayes, S. C., & Follette, W. C. (1992). Can functional analysis provide a substitute for syndromal classification? *Behavioral Assessment, 14,* 345–365.

Haynes, S. N., & Uchigakiuchi, P. (1993a). Functional analytic causal models and the design of treatment programs: Concepts and clinical applications with childhood behavior problems. *European Journal of Psychological Assessment, 9,* 189–205.

Haynes, S. N., & Uchigakiuchi, P. (1993b). Incorporating personality trait measures in behavioral assessment: Nuts in a fruitcake or raisins in a Mai Tai? *Behavior Modification, 17,* 72–92.

Henggeler, S. W. (1991, April). *Treating conduct problems in children and adolescents: An overview of the multisystemic approach with guidelines for intervention design and implementation.* Charleston Division of Children, Adolescents and Their Families, South Carolina Department of Mental Health.

Henggeler, S. W., & Borduin, C. M. (1990). *Family therapy and beyond: A multisystemic approach to treating the behavior problems of children and adolescents.* Pacific Grove, CA: Brooks/Cole.

Henggeler, S. W., Rowland, M. D., Pickrel, S. G., Miller, S. L., Cunningham, P. B., Santos, A. B., Schoenwald, S. K., Randall, J., & Edwards, J. E. (1997). Investigating family-based alternatives to institution-based mental health services for youth: Lessons learned from the pilot study of a randomized field trial. *Journal of Clinical Child Psychology, 26,* 226–233.

Henggeler, S. W., Schoenwald, S. K., & Pickrel, S. G. (1995). Multisystemic therapy: Bridging the gap between university- and community-based treatment. *Journal of Consulting and Clinical Psychology, 63,* 709–717.

Henggeler, S. W., Schoenwald, S. K., Pickrel, S. G., Brondino, S. J., Borduin, C. M., & Hall, J. A. (1994). *Treatment manual for family preservation using multisystemic therapy.* Charleston: South Carolina Health and Human Services Finance Commission.

Herbert, M. (1981). *Behavioural treatment of problem children: A practice manual.* London: Academic Press.

Herbert, M. (1987). *Behavioural treatment of children with problems: A practice manual* (2nd ed.). London: Academic Press.

Hersen, M., & Ammerman, R. T. (Eds.). (1995). *Advanced abnormal child psychology.* Hillsdale, NJ: Erlbaum.

Hersen, M., & Van Hasselt, V. B. (Eds.). (1987). *Behavior therapy with children and adolescents: A clinical approach.* New York: Wiley.

Hibbs, E. D., & Jensen, P. S. (Eds.). (1996). *Psychosocial treatments for child and adolescent disorders: Empirically based strategies for clinical practice.* Washington, DC: American Psychological Association.

Hinshaw, S. P., & Anderson, C. A. (1996). Conduct and oppositional disorders. In E. J. Mash & R. A.

Barkley (Eds.), *Child psychopathology* (pp. 113–149). New York: Guilford Press.

Hoag, M. J., & Burlingame, G. M. (1997). Evaluating the effectiveness of child and adolescent group treatment: A meta-analytic review. *Journal of Clinical Child Psychology, 26,* 234–246.

Hoagwood, K., Hibbs, E., Brent, D., & Jensen, P. (1995). Introduction to the special section: Efficacy and effectiveness in studies of child and adolescent psychotherapy. *Journal of Consulting and Clinical Psychology, 63,* 683–687.

Holden, G. W. (1985). Analyzing parental reasoning with microcomputer-presented problems. *Simulation and Games, 16,* 203–210.

Hollandsworth, J. G., Jr. (1986). *Physiology and behavior therapy.* New York: Plenum Press.

Holmes, F. B. (1936). An experimental investigation of a method of overcoming children's fears. *Child Development, 7,* 6–30.

Houts, A. C., Shutty, M. S., & Emery, R. E. (1985). The impact of children on adults. In B. B. Lahey & A. E. Kazdin (Eds.) *Advances in clinical child psychology* (Vol. 8, pp. 267–307). New York: Plenum Press.

Houts, A. C., Whelan, J. P., & Peterson, K. (1987). Filmed versus live delivery of full-spectrum home training for primary enuresis: Presenting the information is not enough. *Journal of Consulting and Clinical Psychology,* 55, 902–906.

Howard, B., & Kendall, P. C. (1996). *Cognitive-behavioral family therapy for anxious children: Therapist manual.* Ardmore, PA: Workbook.

Iwamasa, G. Y. (1996). Introduction to the special series: Ethnic and cultural diversity in cognitive and behavioral practice. *Cognitive and Behavioral Practice, 3,* 209–213.

Jacobson, N. S., & Christensen, A. (1996). *Integrative couple therapy: Promoting acceptance and change.* New York: Norton.

Jason, L. A. (1980). Prevention in the schools. In R. H. Price, R. F. Ketterer, B. C Bader, & J. Morahan (Eds.), *Prevention in mental health: Research, policies, and practices.* Beverly Hills, CA: Sage.

Jason, L. A., Felner, R. D., Hess, R., & Moritsugo, J. N. (1987). *Prevention: Toward a multidisciplinary approach.* New York: Haworth Press.

Johnson, J. H., Rasbury, W. C., & Siegel, L. J. (1997). *Approaches to child treatment: Introduction to theory, research, and practice* (2nd ed.). Needham Heights, MA: Allyn & Bacon.

Johnson, S. B., & Rodrigue, J. R. (1997). Health-related disorders. In E. J. Mash & L. G. Terdal (Eds.), *Assessment of childhood disorders* (3rd ed., pp. 481–519). New York: Guilford Press.

Jones, M. C. (1924). A laboratory study of fear: The case of Peter. *Journal of Genetic Psychology, 31,* 308–315.

Jones, R. T., Sisson, L. A., & Van Hasselt, V. B. (1984). Emergency fire-safety skills for blind children and adolescents: Group training and generalization. *Behavior Modification, 8,* 267–286.

Kalichman, S. C. (1997). HIV prevention for youth. *Child, Youth, and Family Services Quarterly, 20*(1), 1–3.

Kandel, E., Mednick, S. A., Kirkegaard-Sorensen, L., Hutchings, B., Knop, J., Rosenberg, R., & Schulsinger, F. (1988). IQ as a protective factor for subjects at high risk for antisocial behavior. *Journal of Consulting and Clinical Psychology, 56,* 224–226.

Kanfer, F. H. (1985). Target selection for clinical change programs. *Behavioral Assessment, 7,* 7–20.

Kanfer, F. H., & Busemeyer, J. R. (1982). The use of problem-solving and decision-making in behavior therapy. *Clinical Psychology Review, 2, 239–266.*

Kanfer, F. H., & Phillips, J. S. (1970). *Learning foundations of behavior therapy.* New York: Wiley.

Kanfer, F. H., & Saslow, G. (1965). Behavioral analysis: An alternative to diagnostic classification. *Archives of General Psychiatry, 12,* 529–538.

Kanfer, F. H., & Saslow, G. (1969). Behavioral diagnosis. In C. M. Franks (Ed.), *Behavior therapy: Appraisal and status* (pp. 417–444). New York; McGraw-Hill.

Kanfer, F. H., & Schefft, B. K. (1988). *Guiding the process of therapeutic change.* Champaign, IL: Research Press.

Karoly, P. (1981). Self-management problems in children. In E. J. Mash & L. G. Terdal (Eds.), *Behavioral assessment of childhood disorders* (pp. 79–126). New York: Guilford Press.

Karoly, P. (Ed.). (1988). *Handbook of child health assessment: Biopsychosocial perspectives.* New York: Wiley-Interscience.

Kavanagh, K., & Hops, H. (1994). Good girls? Bad boys?: Gender and development as contexts for diagnosis and treatment. In T. H. Ollendick & R. J. Prinz (Eds.), *Advances in clinical child psychology* (Vol. 16, pp. 45–79). New York: Plenum Press.

Kazdin, A. E. (1978). *History of behavior modification.* Baltimore: University Park Press.

Kazdin, A. E. (1981). Acceptability of child treatment techniques: The influence of treatment efficacy and adverse side effects. *Behavior Therapy, 12,* 493–506.

Kazdin, A. E. (1982a). *Single-case research designs: Methods for clinical and applied settings.* New York: Oxford University Press.

Kazdin, A. E. (1982b). Symptom substitution, generalization, and response covariation: Implications for psychotherapy outcome. *Psychological Bulletin, 91,* 349–365.

Kazdin, A. E. (1984). Acceptability of aversive procedures and medication as treatment alternatives for deviant child behavior. *Journal of Abnormal Child Psychology, 12,* 289–302.

Kazdin, A. E. (1988a). Behavior therapy and the treatment of clinical dysfunction. *Contemporary Psychology, 33,* 686–687.

Kazdin, A. E. (l988b). *Child psychotherapy: Developing and identifying effective treatments.* New York: Pergamon Press.

Kazdin, A. E. (1996a). Combined and multimodal treatments in child and adolescent psychotherapy: Issues, challenges, and research directions. *Clinical Psychology: Science and Practice, 3,* 69–100.

Kazdin, A. E. (1996b). Developing effective treatments for children and adolescents. In E. D. Hibbs & P. S. Jensen (Eds.), *Psychosocial treatments for child and adolescent disorders: Empirically based strategies for clinical practice* (pp. 9–18). Washington, DC: American Psychological Association.

Kazdin, A. E. (1996c). Dropping out of child psychotherapy: Issues for research and practice. *Clinical Child Psychology and Psychiatry, 1,* 133–156.

Kazdin, A. E. (1997). A model for developing effective treatments: Progression and interplay of theory, research, and practice. *Journal of Clinical Child Psychology, 26,* 114–129.

Kazdin, A. E. (1998). *Research design in clinical psychology* (3rd ed.). Needham Heights, MA: Allyn & Bacon.

Kazdin, A. E., Bass, D., Ayers, W. A., & Rodgers, A. (1990). Empirical and clinical focus of child and adolescent psychotherapy research. *Journal of Consulting and Clinical Psychology, 62,* 100–110.

Kazdin, A. E., Esveldt-Dawson, K., French, N. H., & Unis, A. S. (1987). Problem-solving skills training and relationship therapy in the treatment of antisocial child behavior. *Journal of Consulting and Clinical Psychology, 55,* 76–85.

Kazdin, A. E., & Kagan, J. (1994). Models of dysfunction in developmental psychopathology. *Clinical Psychology: Science and Practice, 1,* 35–52.

Kendall, P. C. (1982). Integration: Behavior therapy and other schools of thought. *Behavior Therapy, 13,* 550–571.

Kendall, P. C. (1987). Ahead to basics: Assessments with children and families. *Behavioral Assessment, 9,* 321–332.

Kendall, P. C. (Ed.). (1991). *Child and adolescent therapy: Cognitive-behavioral procedures.* New York: Guilford Press.

Kendall, P. C., & Braswell, L. (1985). *Cognitive-behavioral therapy for impulsive children.* New York: Guilford Press.

Kendall, P. C., & Flannery-Schroeder, E. (in press). Methodological issues in treatment research for anxiety disorders in youth. *Journal of Abnormal Psychology.*

Kendall, P. C., Kane, M., Howard, B., & Siqueland, L. (1992). *Cognitive-behavioral therapy for anxious children.* Ardmore, PA: Workbook.

Kendall, P. C., & Koehler, C. (1985). Outcome evaluation in child behavior therapy: Methodological and conceptual issues. In P. H. Bornstein & A. E. Kazdin (Eds.), *Handbook of clinical behavior therapy with children* (pp. 75–122). Homewood, IL: Dorsey Press.

Kendall, P. C., Lerner, R. M., & Craighead, W. E. (1984). Human development and intervention in child psychopathology. *Child Development, 55,* 71–82.

Kline, R. B., Canter, W. A., & Robin, A. (1987). Parameters of teenage alcohol use: A path analytic conceptual model. *Journal of Consulting and Clinical Psychology, 55,* 521–528.

Knox, L. S., Albano, A. M., & Barlow, D. H. (1993). *Treatment of OCD in children: Exposure and response prevention.* Unpublished manuscript, Anxiety Disorders Clinic, University of Louisville.

Knitzer, J. (1982). *Unclaimed children: The failure of public responsibility to children and adolescents in need of mental health services.* Washington, DC: Children's Defense Fund.

Koetting, K., Peterson, L., & Saldana, L. (1997). Survey of pediatric hospitals' preparation programs: Evidence of the impact of health psychology research. *Health Psychology, 16,* 147–154.

Koocher, G. P., & Pedulla, B. M. (1977). Current practices in child psychotherapy. *Professional Psychology: Research and Practice, 8,* 275–287.

Kratochwill, T. R., & Morris, R. J. (Eds.). (1993). *Handbook of psychotherapy with children and adolescents.* Needham Heights, MA: Allyn & Bacon.

Lambert, M. E. (1987). A computer simulation for behavior therapy training. *Journal of Behavior Therapy and Experimental Psychiatry, 18,* 245–248.

Lasure, L. C., & Mikulas, W. L. (1996). Biblical behaviour modification. *Behaviour Research and Therapy, 34,* 563–566.

Lazarus, A. A. (1958). New methods in psychotherapy: A case study. *South African Medical Journal, 32,* 660–664.

Lazarus, A. A., & Abramovitz, A. (1962). The use of "emotive imagery" in the treatment of children's phobias. *Journal of Mental Science, 108,* 191–195.

LeBow, J. (1982). Consumer satisfaction with mental health treatment. *Psychological Bulletin, 91,* 244–259.

Lee, C. M., & Mash, E. J. (1990). Behaviour therapy. In B. Tonge, G. D. Burrows, & J. Werry (Eds.), *Handbook of studies on child psychiatry* (pp. 415–430). Amsterdam: Elsevier.

Lerner, J. V., Hertzog, C., Hooker, K. A., Hassibi, M., & Thomas, A. (1988). A longitudinal study of negative emotional states and adjustment from early childhood through adolescence. *Child Development, 59,* 356–366.

Levis, D. J. (1988). Integration of behavioral theory and practice. *The Behavior Therapist, 11,* 75.

Lewis, M., & Miller, S. M. (Eds.). (1990). *Handbook of developmental psychopathology: Perspectives in developmental psychology* (pp. 475–485). New York: Plenum Press.

Lochman, J. E. (1987). Self- and peer perceptions and attributional biases of aggressive and nonaggressive boys in dyadic interactions. *Journal of Consulting and Clinical Psychology, 55,* 404–410.

Lochman, J. E. (1988). *Effectiveness of a cognitive-behavioral intervention with aggressive boys.* Unpublished manuscript, Duke University Medical Center.

Lochman, J. E., & Lampron, L. B. (1986). Situational social problem-solving skills and self esteem of aggressive and nonaggressive boys. *Journal of Abnormal Child Psychology, 14,* 605–617.

Lochman, J. E., & Wells, K. C. (1996). A social-cognitive intervention with aggressive children: Prevention effects and contextual implementation issues. In R. DeV. Peters & R. J. McMahon (Eds.), *Preventing childhood disorders, substance abuse, and delinquency* (pp. 111–143). Thousand Oaks, CA: Sage.

London, P. (1972). The end of ideology in behavior modification. *American Psychologist, 27,* 913–920.

Lovaas, O. I. (1987). Behavioral treatment and normal educational and intellectual functioning in young autistic children. *Journal of Consulting and Clinical Psychology, 55,* 3–9.

Lovaas, O. I., Freitag, G., Gold, V. J., & Kasorla, I. C. (1965). Experimental studies in childhood schizophrenia: Analysis of self-destructive behavior. *Journal of Experimental Child Psychology, 2,* 67–84.

Lovaas, O. I., Koegel, R., Simmons, J. Q., & Long, J. S. (1973). Some generalization and follow-up measures on autistic children in behavior therapy. *Journal of Applied Behavior Analysis, 6,* 131–166.

Lynam, D. R. (1996). Early identification of chronic offenders: Who is the fledgling psychopath? *Psychological Bulletin, 120,* 209–234.

Lynam, D. R. (1997). Pursuing the psychopath: Capturing the fledgling psychopath in a nomological net. *Journal of Abnormal Psychology, 106,* 425–438.

Lynam, D. R., Moffitt, T. E., & Stouthamer-Loeber, M. (1993). Explaining the relation between IQ and delinquency: Race, class, test motivation, school failure, or self-control. *Journal of Abnormal Psychology, 102,* 187–196.

Lyon, R. (1996). Learning disabilities. In E. J. Mash & R. A. Barkley (Eds.), *Child psychopathology* (pp. 390–435). New York: Guilford Press.

Lyons-Ruth, K., Zeanah, C. H., & Benoit, D. (1996). Disorder and risk for disorder during infancy and toddlerhood. In E. J. Mash & R. A. Barkley (Eds.), *Child psychopathology* (pp. 457–491). New York: Guilford Press.

MacDonald, L. (1986). Ethical standards for therapeutic programs in human services: An evaluation model. *The Behavior Therapist, 9,* 213–215.

Mahoney, M. J., & Nezworski, M. T. (1985). Cognitive-behavioral approaches to children's problems. *Journal of Abnormal Child Psychology, 13,* 467–476.

Malenfant, L., Wells, J. K., Van Houten, R., & Williams, A. F. (1996). The use of feedback signs to increase observed daytime seat belt use in two cities in North Carolina. *Accident Analysis and Prevention, 28,* 771–777.

Markman, H. J., Floyd, F. J., Stanley, S. M., & Storaasli, R. D. (1988). Prevention of marital distress: A longitudinal investigation. *Journal of Consulting and Clinical Psychology, 56,* 210–217.

Marten, P. A., Albano, A. M., & Holt, C. S. (1991, January). *Cognitive-behavioral group treatment of adolescent social phobia with parent participation.* Unpublished manual, Department of Psychology, University of Louisville.

Mash, E. J. (1984). Families with problem children. In A. Doyle, D. Gold, & D. Moskowitz (Eds.), *Children in families under stress* (pp. 65–84). San Francisco: Jossey-Bass.

Mash, E. J. (1989). Treatment of child and family disturbance: A behavioral-systems perspective. In E. J. Mash & R. A. Barkley (Eds.), *Treatment of childhood disorders* (pp. 3–36). New York: Guilford Press.

Mash, E. J., & Barkley, R. A. (Eds.). (1989). *Treatment of childhood disorders.* New York: Guilford Press.

Mash, E. J., & Barkley, R. A. (Eds.). (1996). *Child psychopathology.* New York: Guilford Press.

Mash, E. J., & Dozois, D. J. A. (1996). Child psychopathology: A developmental–systems perspective. In E. J. Mash & R. A. Barkley (Eds.), *Child psychopathology* (pp. 3–60). New York: Guilford Press.

Mash, E. J., & Hunsley, J. (1990). Behavioral assessment: A contemporary approach. In A. S. Bellack, M. Hersen, & A. E. Kazdin (Eds.), *International handbook of behavior modification and therapy* (2nd ed., pp. 87–106). New York: Plenum Press.

Mash, E. J., & Hunsley, J. (1993). Behavior therapy and managed mental health care: Integrating effectiveness and economics in managed mental health care. *Behavior Therapy, 24,* 67–90.

Mash, E. J., & Johnston, C. (1996). Family relationship problems: Their place in the study of psychopathology. *Journal of Emotional and Behavioral Disorders, 4,* 240–254.

Mash, E. J., & Terdal, L. G. (1980). Follow-up assessments in behavior therapy. In P. Karoly & J. J. Steffan (Eds.), *The long-range effects of psychotherapy: Models of durable outcome* (pp. 99–147). New York: Gardner Press.

Mash, E. J., & Terdal, L. G. (1990). Assessment strategies in clinical behavioral pediatrics. In A. M. Gross & R. S. Drabman (Eds.), *Handbook of clinical behavioral pediatrics* (pp. 49–79). New York: Plenum Press.

Mash, E. J., & Terdal, L. G. (Eds.). (1997a). *Assessment of childhood disorders* (3rd ed.). New York: Guilford Press.

Mash, E. J., & Terdal, L. G. (1997b). Assessment of child and family disturbance: A behavioral–systems approach. In E. J. Mash & L. G. Terdal (Eds.), *Assessment of childhood disorders* (3rd ed., pp. 3–68). New York: Guilford Press.

McEachin, J. J., Smith, T., & Lovaas, O. I. (1993). Long-term outcome for children with autism who received early intensive behavioral treatment. *American Journal on Mental Retardation, 97,* 359–372.

McMahon, R. J., & Forehand, R. (1983). Consumer satisfaction in behavioral treatment of children: Types, issues, and recommendations. *Behavior Therapy, 14,* 209–225.

McMahon, R. J., & Peters, R. D. (Eds.). (1985). *Childhood disorders: Behavioral–developmental approaches.* New York: Brunner/Mazel.

Meichenbaum, D. (1977). *Cognitive behavior modification.* New York: Plenum Press.

Meyers, A. W., & Cohen, R. (1990). Cognitive-behavioral approaches to child psychopathology: Present status and future directions. In M. Lewis & S. M. Miller (Eds.), *Handbook of developmental psychopathology: Perspectives in developmental psychology* (pp. 475–485). New York: Plenum Press.

Milich, R., & Dodge, K. A. (1984). Social information processing in child psychiatric populations. *Journal of Abnormal Child Psychology, 13,* 471–490.

Miller, G. E., & Prinz, R. J. (1990). Enhancement of social learning family interventions for childhood Conduct Disorder. *Psychological Bulletin, 108,* 291–307.

Miller, S. A. (1988). Parents' beliefs about children's cognitive development. *Child Development, 59,* 259–285.

Mischel, W. (1968). *Personality and assessment.* New York: Wiley.

Moran, P., & Eckenrode, J. (1988). *Social stress and depression during adolescence: Gender and age differences.* Unpublished manuscript, Department of Human Development and Family Studies, Cornell University.

Mori, L., & Peterson, L. (1986). Training preschoolers in home safety skills to prevent inadvertent injury. *Journal of Clinical Child Psychology, 15,* 106–114.

Morrow-Bradley, C., & Elliot, R. (1986). Utilization of psychotherapy research by practicing psychotherapists. *American Psychologist, 41,* 188–197.

Mowrer, O. H., & Mowrer, W. M. (1938). Enuresis: A method for its study and treatment. *American Journal of Orthopsychiatry, 8,* 436–459.

Mussen, P. H. (General Ed.). (1983). *Handbook of child psychology* (4th ed., 4 vols.). New York: Wiley.

Neal-Barnett, A. M., & Smith, Sr., J. M. (1996). African American children and behavior therapy: Considering the Afrocentric approach. *Cognitive and Behavioral Practice, 3,* 351–369.

Nelson, R. O., & Hayes, S. C. (Eds.). (1986). *Conceptual foundations of behavioral assessment.* New York: Guilford Press.

Nezu, A. M., & Nezu, C. M. (1989). *Clinical decision making in behavior therapy: A problem-solving perspective.* Champaign, IL: Research Press.

Nezu, A. M., & Nezu, C. M. (1993). Identifying and selecting target problems for clinical interventions: A problem-solving model. *Psychological Assessment, 5,* 254–263.

Noam, G. G., Chandler, M., & LaLonde, C. (1995). Clinical–developmental psychology: Constructivism and social cognition in the study of psychological dysfunctions. In D. Cicchetti & D. J. Cohen (Eds.), *Developmental psychopathology: Vol 1. Theory and methods* (pp. 424–464). New York: Wiley.

Nolen-Hoeksema, S., Girgus, J. S., & Seligman, M. E. P. (1988, March). *A longitudinal study of depression in pre-adolescents: Sex differences in depression and related factors.* Paper presented at the meeting of the Society for Research on Adolescence, Alexandria, VA.

Norcross, J. C., & Goldfried, M. R. (Eds.). (1992). *Handbook of psychotherapy integration.* New York: Basic Books.

Norcross, J. C., Karg, R. S., & Prochaska, J. O. (1997). Clinical psychologists in the 1990s: II. *The Clinical Psychologist, 50*(3), 4–11.

Ogles, B. M., Lambert, M. J., & Masters, K. S. (1996). *Assessing outcome in clinical practice.* Needham Heights, MA: Allyn & Bacon.

O'Leary, K. D. (1984a). The image of behavior therapy: It's time to take a stand. *Behavior Therapy, 15,* 219–233.

O'Leary, K. D. (1984b). Marital discord and children: Problems, strategies, methodologies and results. In A. Doyle, D. Gold, & D. S. Moskowitz (Eds.). *Children in families under stress* (pp. 35–36). San Francisco: Jossey-Bass.

O'Leary, K. D., Becker, W. C., Evans, M. B., & Saudargas, R. A. (1969). A token reinforcement program in a public school: A replication and systematic analysis. *Journal of Applied Behavior Analysis, 2,* 3–13.

O'Leary, K. D., & Wilson, G. T. (1987). *Behavior therapy: Application and outcome* (2nd ed.). Englewood Cliffs, NJ: Prentice-Hall.

Ollendick, T. H. (1986). Behavior therapy with children and adolescents. In S. L. Garfield & A. E. Bergin (Eds.), *Handbook of psychotherapy and behavior change* (3rd ed., pp. 565–624). New York: Wiley.

Ollendick, T. H., & Cerny, J. A. (1981). *Clinical behavior therapy with children.* New York: Plenum Press.

Ollendick, T. H., & Hersen, M. (Eds.). (1984). *Child behavioral assessment: Principles and procedures.* New York: Pergamon Press.

Patterson, G. R. (1976). The aggressive child: Victim and architect of a coercive system. In E. J. Mash, L. A. Hamerlynck, & L. C. Handy (Eds.), *Behavior modification and families* (pp. 267–316). New York: Brunner/Mazel.

Patterson, G. R. (1982). *Coercive family process.* Eugene, OR: Castalia.

Patterson, G. R. (1986). Performance models for antisocial boys. *American Psychologist, 41,* 432–444.

Patterson, G. R. (1996). Some characteristics of a developmental theory for early-onset delinquency. In M. F. Lenzenweger & J. J. Haugaard (Eds.), *Fron-*

tiers of developmental psychopathology (pp. 81–124). New York: Oxford University Press.

Patterson, G. R., Ray, R. S., & Shaw, D. A. (1968). Direct intervention in families of deviant children [Special issue]. *Oregon Research Institute Research Bulletin, 8.*

Patterson, G. R., Reid, J. B., & Dishion, T. J. (1992). *Antisocial boys.* Eugene, OR: Castalia.

Patterson, G. R., Reid, J. B., Jones, R. R., & Conger, R. E. (1975). *A social learning approach to family intervention: Families with aggressive children* (Vol. 1). Eugene, OR: Castalia.

Pelham, W. E., & Murphy, H. A. (1986). Attention deficit and conduct disorders. In M. Hersen (Ed.), *Pharmacological and behavioral treatment: An integrative approach* (pp. 108–148). New York: Wiley.

Peters, R. DeV., & McMahon, R. J. (Eds.). (1996). *Preventing childhood disorders, substance abuse, and delinquency.* Thousand Oaks, CA: Sage.

Peterson, L. (1996). Establishing the study of development as a dynamic force in health psychology. *Health Psychology, 15,* 155–157.

Peterson, L., & Brown, D. (1994). Integrating child injury and abuse–neglect research: Common histories, etiologies, and solutions. *Psychological Bulletin, 116,* 293–315.

Peterson, L., Burbach, D. J., & Chaney, J. (1989). Developmental issues. In C. G. Last & M. Hersen (Eds.), *Handbook of child psychiatric diagnosis* (pp. 463–482). New York: Wiley.

Peterson, L., & Mori, L. (1985). Prevention of child injury: An overview of targets, methods, and tactics for psychologists. *Journal of Consulting and Clinical Psychology, 53,* 58–595.

Peterson, L., Zink, M., & Downing, J. (1993). Childhood injury prevention. In D. S. Glenwick & L. A. Jason (Eds.), *Promoting health and mental health in children, youth, and families* (pp. 51–73). New York: Springer.

Pettit, G. S., Dodge, K. A., & Brown, M. M. (1988). Early family experience, social problem solving patterns, and children's social competence. *Child Development, 59,* 107–120.

Piacentini, J., & Graae, F. (1997). Childhood OCD. In E. Hollander & D. Stein (Eds.), *Obsessive–compulsive disorders: Diagnosis, etiology, treatment* (pp. 23–46). New York: Marcel Dekker.

Prochaska, J. O. (1994). Strong and weak principles for progressing from precontemplation to action on the basis of twelve problem behaviors. *Health Psychology, 13,* 47–51.

Putallaz, M. (1987). Maternal behavior and children's sociometric status. *Child Development, 58,* 324–340.

Quay, H. C., & Werry, J. S. (Eds.). (1986). *Psychopathological disorders of childhood* (3rd ed.). New York: Wiley.

Reynolds, C. R., & Kamphaus, R. W. (1992). *Behavior Assessment System for Children (BASC).* Circle Pines, MN: American Guidance Service.

Rickel, A. U., & Allen, L. (1987). *Preventing maladjustment from infancy through adolescence.* Newbury Park, CA: Sage.

Roberts, M. C. (Ed.). (1995). *Handbook of pediatric psychology* (2nd ed.). New York: Guilford Press.

Roberts, M. C., & Hurley, L. K. (1997). *Managing managed care.* New York: Plenum Press.

Roberts, M. C., & Peterson, L. (Eds.). (1984). *Prevention of problems in childhood: Psychological research and applications.* New York: Wiley.

Robin, A. L., & Foster, S. L. (1989). *Negotiating parent–adolescent conflict: A behavioral–family systems approach.* New York: Guilford Press.

Robins, C. J., & Hinkley, K. (1989). Social-cognitive processing and depressive symptoms in children: A comparison of measures. *Journal of Abnormal Child Psychology, 17,* 29–36.

Romancyzk, R. G. (1986). *Clinical utilization of microcomputer technology.* New York: Pergamon Press.

Ross, A. (1981). *Child behavior therapy: Principles, procedures and empirical basis.* New York: Wiley.

Rubenstein, J. L., Heeren, T., Houssman, D., Rubin, C., & Stechler, G. (1988, March). *Suicidal behavior in "normal" adolescents: Risk and protective factors.* Paper presented at the biennial meeting of the Society for Research on Adolescence, Alexandria, VA.

Rubin, K. H., & Stewart, S. L. (1996). Social withdrawal. In E. J. Mash & R. A. Barkley (Eds.), *Child psychopathology* (pp. 277–307). New York: Guilford Press.

Russo, D. C., & Budd, K. S. (1987). Limitations of operant practice in the study of disease. *Behavior Modification, 11,* 264–285.

Rutter, M. (1997). Clinical implications of attachment concepts: Retrospect and prospect. In L. A. Atkinson & K. J. Zucker (Eds.), *Attachment and psychopathology* (pp. 17–46). New York: Guilford Press

Rutter, M., Tizard, J., Yule, W., Graham, P., & Whitmore, K. (1976). Research report: Isle of Wight studies, 1964–1974. *Psychological Medicine, 6,* 313–332.

Salter, A. (1949). *Conditioned reflex therapy.* New York: Capricorn.

Sameroff, A. J. (1995). General systems theories and developmental psychopathology. In D. Cicchetti & D. J. Cohen (Eds.), *Developmental psychopathology: Vol 1. Theory and methods* (pp. 659–695). New York: Wiley.

Sameroff, A. J., Seifer, R., Barocas, R., Zax, M., & Greenspan, S. (1987). Intelligence quotient scores of 4-year-old children: Social–environmental risk factors. *Pediatrics, 79,* 343–350.

Sattler, J. M. (1992). *Assessment of children: Revised and updated third edition.* San Diego, CA: Jerome M. Sattler, Publisher.

Sattler, J. M. (1998). *Clinical and forensic interviewing of children and families: Guidelines for the mental health, education, pediatric, and child mal-*

treatment fields. San Diego, CA: Jerome M. Sattler, Publisher.

Scheier, M. F., & Carver, C. S. (1985). Optimism, coping and health: Assessment and implications of generalized outcome expectancies. *Health Psychology, 4,* 219–247.

Schonfeld, I. S., Shaffer, D., O'Conner, P., & Portnoy, S. (1988). Conduct Disorder and cognitive functioning: Testing three causal hypotheses. *Child Development, 59,* 993-1007.

Schroeder, C. S., & Gordon, B. N. (1991). *Assessment and treatment of childhood problems: A clinician's guide.* New York: Guilford Press.

Schroeder, S. R., Gualtieri, C. T., & Van Bourgondien, M. E. (1986). Autism. In M. Hersen (Ed.), *Pharmacological and behavioral treatment: An integrative approach* (pp. 89–107). New York: Wiley.

Schwartz, I. S., & Baer, D. M. (1991). Social validity assessments: Is current practice state of the art? *Journal of Applied Behavior Analysis, 24,* 189–204.

Schwebel, A. I., & Fine, M. A. (1992). Cognitive–behavioral family therapy. *Journal of Family Psychotherapy, 3,* 73–91.

Schwebel, A. I., & Fine, M. A. (1994). *Understanding and helping families: A cognitive–behavioral approach.* Hillsdale, NJ: Erlbaum.

Seligman, M. E. P. (1995). The effectiveness of psychotherapy: The *Consumer Reports* study. *American Psychologist, 50,* 965–974.

Shadish, W. R., Matt, G. E., Navarro, A. M., Siegle, G., Crits-Christoph, P., Hazelrigg, M. D., Jorm, A. F., Lyons, L. C., Nietzel, M. T., Prout, H. T., Robinson, L., Smith, M. L., Svartberg, M., & Weiss, B. (1997). Evidence that therapy works in clinically representative conditions. *Journal of Consulting and Clinical Psychology, 65,* 355–365.

Shelton, J. L., Levy, R. L., & contributors. (1981). *Behavioral assignments and treatment compliance: A handbook of clinical strategies.* Champaign, IL: Research Press.

Sheridan, S. M., Kratochwill, T. R., & Bergan, J. R. (1996). *Conjoint behavioral consultation: A procedural manual.* New York: Plenum Press.

Siqueland, L., Kendall, P. C., Stoff, D., & Pollack. L. (1987). *Cognitive distortions and deficiencies in child psychiatric populations.* Unpublished manuscript, Department of Psychology, Temple University.

Skinner, B. F. (1953). *Science and human behavior.* New York: Macmillan.

Sowder, B. J. (1975). *Assessment of child mental health needs* (Vols. 1–8). McLean, VA: General Research Corporation.

Stark, K. D., & Kendall, P. C. (1996). *Treating depressed children: Therapist manual for "taking action."* Ardmore, PA: Workbook.

Stark, K. D., Rouse, L. W., & Livingston, R. (1991). Treatment of depression during childhood and adolescence: Cognitive-behavioral procedures for the individual and family. In P. C. Kendall (Ed.), *Child and adolescent therapy: Cognitive-behavioral procedures* (pp. 165–206). New York: Guilford Press.

Steinglass, P. (1987). A systems view of family interaction and psychopathology. In T. Jacob (Ed.), *Family interaction and psychopathology: Theories, methods, and findings* (pp. 25–65). New York: Plenum Press.

Stoiber, K. C., & Kratochwill, T. R. (Eds.). (in press). *Handbook of group intervention for children and families.* Boston: Allyn & Bacon.

Stokes, T. F., & Baer, D. M. (1977). An implicit technology of generalization. *Journal of Applied Behavior Analysis, 10,* 349–367.

Strain, P. S. (Ed.). (1981). *The utilization of peers as behavior change agents.* New York: Plenum Press.

Strayhorn, J. M., Jr. (1987). Medical assessment of children with behavioral problems. In M. Hersen & V. B. Van Hasselt (Eds.), *Behavior therapy with children and adolescents: A clinical approach* (pp. 50–74). New York: Wiley.

Strosahl, K. D. (1994). Entering the new frontier of managed mental health care: Gold mines and land mines. *Cognitive and Behavioral Practice, 1,* 5–23.

Strosahl, K. D. (1996). Confessions of a behavior therapist in primary care: The odyssey and the ecstasy. *Cognitive and Behavioral Practice, 3,* 1–28.

Tabachnik, N., & Alloy, L. B. (1988). Clinician and patient as aberrant actuaries: Expectation-based distortions in assessment of covariation. In L. Y. Abramson (Ed.), *Social cognition and clinical psychology* (pp. 295–365). New York: Guilford Press.

Tarnowski, K. J., Kelly, P. A., & Mendlowitz, D. R. (1987). Acceptability of behavioral pediatric interventions. *Journal of Consulting and Clinical Psychology, 55,* 435–436.

Tharp, R. G. (1991). Cultural diversity and treatment of children. *Journal of Consulting and Clinical Psychology, 59,* 799–812.

Tharp, R. G., & Wetzel, R. J. (1969). *Behavior modification in the natural environment.* New York: Academic Press.

Thomason, B. T., Bachanas, P. J., & Campos, P. E. (1996). Cognitive behavioral interventions with persons affected by HIV/AIDS. *Cognitive and Behavioral Practice, 3,* 417–442.

Tisdelle, D. A., & St. Lawrence, J. S. (1988). Adolescent interpersonal problem-solving skills training: Social validation and generalization. *Behavior Therapy, 19,* 171–182.

Tolan, P. H., & Guerra, N. (1994, July). *What works in reducing adolescent violence: An empirical review of the field.* Boulder, CO: Center for the Study and Prevention of Violence.

Tronick, E., & Gianino, A. (1986). Interactive mismatch and repair: Challenges to the coping infant. *Zero to Three, 6,* 1–6.

Turner, S. M., Beidel, D. C., & Costello, A. (1987). Psychopathology in the offspring of anxiety disorders patients. *Journal of Consulting and Clinical Psychology, 55,* 229–235.

Ullmann, L. P., & Krasner, L. (Eds.). (1965). *Case studies in behavior modification.* New York: Holt, Rinehart & Winston.

Urbain, E. S., & Kendall, P. C. (1980). Review of social-cognitive problem-solving interventions with children. *Psychological Bulletin, 88,* 109–143.

Voeltz, L. M., & Evans, I. M. (1982). The assessment of behavioral interrelationships in child behavior therapy. *Behavioral Assessment, 4,* 131–165.

Wachtel, P. L. (1977). *Psychoanalysis and behavior therapy.* New York: Basic Books.

Wahler, R. G. (1975). Some structural aspects of deviant child behavior. *Journal of Applied Behavior Analysis, 8,* 27–42.

Wahler, R. G. (1980). The insular mother: Her problems in parent–child treatment. *Journal of Applied Behavior Analysis, 13,* 207–219.

Wahler, R. G., & Fox, J. J. (1981). Setting events in applied behavior analysis: Toward a conceptual and methodological expansion. *Journal of Applied Behavior Analysis, 14,* 327–338.

Wahler, R. G., & Graves, M. G. (1983). Setting events in social networks: Ally or enemy in child behavior therapy? *Behavior Therapy, 14,* 19–36.

Walker, C. E., & Roberts, M. C. (Eds.). (1992). *Handbook of clinical child psychology* (2nd ed.). New York: Wiley.

Watson, J. B., & Rayner, R. (1920). Conditioned emotional reactions. *Journal of Experimental Psychology, 3,* 1–14.

Weber, J. (1936). An approach to the problem of fear in children. *Journal of Mental Science, 82,* 136–147.

Webster-Stratton, C., & Herbert, M. (1994). *Troubled families—problem children: Working with parents: A collaborative process.* Chichester, England: Wiley.

Weisz, J. R. (in press). Empirically supported treatments for children and adolescents: Efficacy, problems, and prospects. In K. S. Dobson & K. D. Craig (Eds.), *Best practice: Developing and promoting empirically validated interventions.* Thousand Oaks, CA: Sage.

Weisz, J. R., Donenberg, G. R., Han, S. S., & Weiss, B. (1995). Bridging the gap between laboratory and clinic in child and adolescent psychotherapy. *Journal of Consulting and Clinical Psychology, 63,* 688–701.

Weisz, J. R., Han, S. S., & Valeri, S. M. (1997). More of what?: Issues raised by the Fort Bragg study. *American Psychologist, 52,* 541–545.

Weisz, J. R., & Weiss, B. (1993). *Effects of psychotherapy with children and adolescents.* Newbury Park, CA: Sage.

Weisz, J. R., Weiss, B., Alicke, M. D., & Klotz, M. L. (1987). Effectiveness of psychotherapy with children and adolescents: A meta-analysis for clinicians. *Journal of Consulting and Clinical Psychology, 55,* 542–549.

Weisz, J. R., Weiss, B., Han, S. S., Granger, D. A., & Morton, T. (1995). Effects of psychotherapy with children and adolescents revisited: A meta-analysis of treatment outcome studies. *Psychological Bulletin, 117,* 450–468.

Weisz, J. R., Weiss, B., & Langmeyer, D. B. (1987). Giving up on child psychotherapy: Who drops out? *Journal of Consulting and Clinical Psychology, 55,* 916–918.

Wekerle, C., & Wolfe, D. A. (1996). Child maltreatment. In E. J. Mash & R. A. Barkley (Eds.), *Child psychopathology* (pp. 492–537). New York: Guilford Press.

White, D. M., Rusch, F. R., Kazdin, A. E., & Hartmann, D. P. (1989). Applications of meta analysis in individual-subject research. *Behavioral Assessment, 11,* 281–296.

Willems, E. P. (1974). Behavioral technology and behavioral ecology. *Journal of Applied Behavior Analysis, 7,* 151–165.

Winett, R. A., & Winkler, R. C. (1972). Current behavior modification in the classroom: Be still, be quiet, be docile. *Journal of Applied Behavior Analysis, 5,* 499–504.

Winter, M. G., Hicks, R., McVey, G., & Fox, J. (1988). Age and sex differences in choice of consultant for various types of problems. *Child Development, 59,* 1046–1055.

Witt, J. C., & Elliott, S. N. (1986). Acceptability of classroom management procedures. In T. R. Kratochwill (Ed.), *Advances in school psychology* (pp. 251–288). Hillsdale, NJ: Erlbaum.

Wolfe, B. E., & Goldfried, M. R. (1988). Research on psychotherapy integration: Recommendations and conclusions from an NIMH workshop. *Journal of Consulting and Clinical Psychology, 56,* 448–451.

Wolfe, D. A., & Bourdeau, P. A. (1987). Current issues in the assessment of abusive and neglectful parent–child relationships. *Behavioral Assessment, 9,* 271–290.

Wolfe, D. A., & LaRose, L. (1986). *Child videotape series* [Videotape]. London, Ontario: University of Western Ontario.

Wolfe, D. A., Wekerle, C., Gough, R., Reitzel-Jaffe, D., Grasley, C., Pittman, A., Lefebve, L., & Stumpf, J. (1996). *The youth relationships manual: A group approach with adolescents for the prevention of woman abuse and the promotion of healthy relationships.* Thousand Oaks, CA: Sage.

Wolfe, V. V., & Birt, J. (1997). Child sexual abuse. In E. J. Mash & L. G. Terdal (Eds.), *Assessment of childhood disorders* (3rd ed., pp. 569–623). New York: Guilford Press.

Wolpe, J. (1958). *Psychotherapy by reciprocal inhibition.* Stanford, CA: Stanford University Press.

Wolpe, J. (1986). Individualization: The categorical imperative of behavior therapy practice. *Journal of Behavior Therapy and Experimental Psychiatry, 17,* 145–153.

World Health Organization. (1992). *The ICD-10 classification of mental and behavioural disorders:*

Clinical descriptions and diagnostic guidelines. Geneva: Author.

Wright, L., Flagler, S., & Friedman, A. G. (1988). Assessment for accident prevention. In P. Karoly (Ed.), Handbook of child health assessment: *Biopsychosocial perspectives* (pp. 491–518). New York: Wiley-Interscience.

Wurtele, S. K., Kast, L. C., & Kondrick, P. A. (1988). *Measuring young children's responses to sexual abuse prevention programs: The What-If Situations Test.* Unpublished manuscript, Department of Psychology, Washington State University.

Wurtele, S. K., Marrs, S. R., & Miller-Perrin, C. L. (1987). Practice makes perfect?: The role of participant modeling in sexual abuse prevention programs. *Journal of Consulting and Clinical Psychology, 55,* 599–602.

Yule, W. (1993). Developmental considerations in child assessment. In T. H. Ollendick & M. Hersen (Eds.), *Handbook of child and adolescent assessment* (pp. 15–25). Needham Heights, MA: Allyn & Bacon.

Zahn-Waxler, C. (1993). Warriors and worriers: Gender and psychopathology. *Development and Psychopathology, 5,* 79–89.

Zahn-Waxler, C., Cole, C. M., Welsh, J. D., & Fox, N. A. (1995). Psychophysiological correlates of empathy and prosocial behaviors in preschool children with behavior problems. *Development and Psychopathology, 7,* 27–48.

Zero to Three/National Center for Clinical Infant Programs. (1994). *Diagnostic classification of mental health and developmental disorders of infancy and early childhood (Diagnostic Classification: 0–3).* Washington, DC: Author.

Zoccolillo, M. (1993). Gender and the development of conduct disorder. *Development and Psychopathology, 5,* 65–78.

PART II

BEHAVIOR DISORDERS

CHAPTER 2

Attention-Deficit/ Hyperactivity Disorder

Russell A. Barkley

University of Massachusetts Medical Center

Over the past century, numerous diagnostic labels have been given to clinically referred children having significant deficiencies in behavioral inhibition, sustained attention, resistance to distraction, and the regulation of activity level. "Attention-Deficit/Hyperactivity Disorder" (ADHD) is the term most recently used to capture this developmental disorder (American Psychiatric Association, 1994). Previously employed terms have included "brain-injured child syndrome," "hyperkinesis," "hyperactive child syndrome," "minimal brain dysfunction," and "Attention Deficit Disorder (with or without Hyperactivity)." Such relabeling every decade or so reflects a shifting emphasis on the primacy of certain symptoms, based, in part, on the substantial research conducted each year on ADHD.

This chapter provides a critical overview of the treatments that have some efficacy for the management of ADHD as shown through scientific research. That literature is voluminous, however, and so space here permits only a brief discussion and critique of each of the major treatments. More detailed discussions of these treatments can be found in various texts (Barkley, 1990, 1997a, in press-b; Goldstein & Goldstein, 1990; DuPaul & Stoner, 1994; Shaywitz & Shaywitz 1992; and Weiss, 1992). I begin with a brief overview of the history of

ADHD. More thorough treatments of that topic can be found in my other writings (Barkley, 1990, in press-a), and those by Kessler (1980), Schachar (1986), and Werry (1992). This historical overview is followed by brief summaries of the disorder's nature, prevalence, developmental course, and etiologies. Subsequently, the main purpose of this chapter is addressed through a critical overview of various treatments for the disorder. No information on the assessment of ADHD is provided here, due to both space limitations and the availability of more detailed information on this topic elsewhere (Barkley, 1997a, 1997b, in press-b).

OVERVIEW OF ATTENTION-DEFICIT/HYPERACTIVITY DISORDER

History

George Still (1902) presented the first clinical description of children having the symptoms of ADHD, and the first attempt to conceptualize the disorder in a series of three lectures to the Royal College of Physicians in England. Still described children in his clinical practice who were quite aggressive, defiant, resistant to discipline, highly emotional, poorly inhibited, and otherwise lacking in self-control. Most were also excessively active, distractible, and poor at sustaining their attention to tasks. Such children would probably now be viewed as having not only ADHD, but also Oppositional Defiant Disorder (ODD) or even Conduct Disorder (CD) (American Psychiatric Association, 1994).

Still argued that these children had serious defects in the moral control of behavior, which arose from a deficiency in volitional inhibition. He argued that variation in moral control and volitional inhibition existed within the normal population as a result of both environmental and innate factors. However, he seemed to believe that when such defects were seen to the severe degree observed in clinic cases, the deficiencies were most often the result of biological factors rather than lack of adequate childrearing or training. He posited a possible hereditary transmission of these characteristics in some children, whereas in others it might be acquired as a result of pre-, peri-, or postnatal central nervous system damage. In some cases it could even be transient, corresponding with the acute phases of certain brain diseases or infections. Consistent with later research, Still found that more males than females displayed such problems.

During the next 35 years, few papers appeared on this subject in children, largely as a consequence of two world wars. Those papers that were published in relation to the disorder or its symptoms focused either on the encephalitis epidemic of the early part of this century as causal of such symptoms or on the motor restlessness that characterized these children (Childers, 1935; Levin, 1938), rather than on their disturbances in self-regulation and social conduct. More widespread interest in these children did not emerge until after World War II. At that time, the highly influential writings of Strauss, Lehtinen, and their colleagues (Strauss & Lehtinen, 1947) appeared, advocating that restless and inattentive behavior was *de facto* evidence of brain damage in children. These authors reasoned that if hyperactivity, inattention, and impulsivity could arise from brain damage, then the manifestation of such behaviors must be indicative of brain injury in such children, even in cases where a history supporting the brain injury was not evident. The term "minimal brain damage" was coined to refer to these children, and strict guidelines were advocated for their education.

Increasing emphasis on excessive motor activity as the central symptom of the disorder arose from the 1950s through the 1970s. Some

authors (Laufer, Denhoff, & Solomons, 1957) posited a possible defect in the filtering of stimuli in the central nervous system as the cause, allowing excessive stimulation to reach the cortex. Others later viewed the disorder as simply one of a daily rate of motor activity level significantly deviant from that of normal children (Chess, 1960; Werry & Sprague, 1970), without reference to its origins. Conclusions concerning brain damage as a cause of hyperactivity became less frequent over time, though the belief remained that problems in brain functioning seemed related to the disorder. This resulted in a softening of the terminology for the disorder from "minimal brain damage" to "minimal brain dysfunction" (Wender, 1971). Eventually, the link with neurological damage was dropped from the diagnostic terminology, and the disorder was simply referred to as "hyperactive child syndrome" (Chess, 1960) or "Hyperkinetic Reaction of Childhood" (American Psychiatric Association, 1968). Its association with abnormal brain functioning remained strong until the 1970s, when a series of publications refuted the syndromal nature of the disorder and its relationship to brain damage (Rie & Rie, 1980; Rutter, 1977).

By the mid-1970s, a growing body of evidence suggested that hyperactive children also had major deficits with sustained attention and impulse control (Douglas, 1972). Douglas (1972, 1980, 1983; Douglas & Peters, 1979) argued that the disorder consisted of impairments in (1) investment, organization, and maintenance of attention; (2) the inhibition of impulsive responding; (3) the modulation of arousal levels to meet situational demands; and (4) a strong tendency to seek immediate reinforcement. Excessive motor activity was viewed as being problematic, but not as central to the disorder as the attentional and inhibitory problems. The American Psychiatric Association (1980) eventually relabeled the disorder as "Attention Deficit Disorder (with or without Hyperactivity)" in the third edition of the *Diagnostic and Statistical Manual of Mental Disorders* (DSM-III), in part as a result of Douglas's influential reviews on the field. The change in nomenclature and diagnostic criteria heralded by the DSM-III essentially demoted the symptom of hyperactivity to that of an unnecessary or simply related characteristic of these children, yet one that could be used to create subtypes of the disorder based on its presence or absence.

Later in the 1980s, the disorder was relabeled yet again as "Attention-Deficit/Hyperactivity

Disorder" in the DSM-III-R (American Psychiatric Association, 1987), suggesting a reemergence of the importance of hyperactivity as one of the central features of the disorder, equal in import to the other two (inattention, impulsiveness). The subtyping scheme of "without Hyperactivity" was demoted in this revision, not because children who are primarily inattentive do not exist, but because it was unclear at the time whether they represented a true subtype of this disorder or a separate diagnostic entity altogether (Barkley, 1990; Carlson, 1986). Clinicians could label such children as having "Undifferentiated Attention Deficit Disorder," but no criteria for diagnosis were provided, nor was the relationship of this disorder to ADHD clarified. More research was recommended before the answers to these issues could guide such a taxonomic enterprise. Across the 1980s, many scientists came to posit that the central deficiency in ADD/ADHD children was one of poor executive functioning or self-regulation of behavior (Barkley, 1981, 1989a; Douglas, 1983, 1989; Kendall & Braswell, 1985; Routh, 1978). This trend continues to the present (Barkley, 1994, 1997a, 1997b; see below), resembling in some respects a return to the earlier notions of Still (1902) that deficits in volitional inhibition and moral regulation of behavior explain the disorder.

In 1994, when the DSM was once again revised (DSM-IV; American Psychiatric Association, 1994), several important changes were added to the diagnostic criteria. These are discussed below, but suffice it to say here that the option of diagnosing children with a subtype of the disorder characterized by primary attention problems without hyperactivity or impulsiveness has been restored to this taxonomy. This is despite continuing scientific uncertainty over whether children who are primarily inattentive actually represent a subtype of ADHD or an entirely separate disorder (Barkley, 1990; Barkley, Grodzinsky, & DuPaul, 1992; Goodyear & Hynd, 1992; Lahey & Carlson, 1992).

Primary Symptoms

Children having ADHD, by definition, display difficulties with attention relative to normal children of the same age and sex. However, attention is a multidimensional construct that can refer to alertness, arousal, selective or focused attention, sustained attention, distractibility, or span of apprehension, among others (Barkley, 1988; Hale & Lewis, 1979; Mirsky, 1996). Research to date suggests that, among these elements, ADHD children most likely have their greatest difficulties with sustaining attention to tasks, persistence of effort, or vigilance (Douglas, 1983). These difficulties are sometimes apparent in free-play settings (Barkley & Ullman, 1975; Routh & Schroeder, 1976), but they are more evident in situations requiring sustained attention to dull, boring, repetitive tasks (Luk, 1985; Milich, Loney, & Landau, 1982; Ullman, Barkley, & Brown, 1978).

Often accompanying this difficulty with sustained attention is a deficiency in inhibiting behavior, or impulsiveness. Like attention, impulsiveness is also multidimensional in nature (Milich & Kramer, 1985). Rather than a deficit in cognitive reflectiveness, the deficit of ADHD children here is mainly in the capacity to inhibit or delay prepotent responses, particularly in settings in which those responses compete with rules (Barkley, 1997c, 1997d). A "prepotent response" is that which would gain the immediate reinforcement (reward or escape) available in a given context, or which has a strong history of such reinforcement in the past. Those with ADHD have difficulties with sustained inhibition of such dominant responses over time (Gordon, 1979), poor delay of gratification (Rapport, Tucker, DuPaul, Merlo, & Stoner, 1986), or impaired adherence to commands to inhibit behavior in social contexts (Kendall & Wilcox, 1979). This inhibitory deficit may also include a difficulty with interrupting an ongoing response pattern (Schachar, Tannock, & Logan, 1993), particularly when given feedback about performance and errors. In the latter case, a perseveration of responding may be evident despite negative feedback concerning performance, which may reflect an insensitivity to errors (Sergeant & van der Meere, 1988).

Numerous studies exist showing ADHD children to be more active, restless, and fidgety than normal children (Barkley & Cunningham, 1979; Porrino et al., 1983; Teicher, Ito, Glod, & Barber, 1996). As with the other symptoms, there are significant situational fluctuations in this symptom (Jacob, O'Leary, & Rosenblad, 1978; Luk, 1985; Porrino et al., 1983). It has not always been convincingly shown that hyperactivity distinguishes ADHD from other clinic-referred groups of children (Firestone & Martin, 1979; Sandberg, Rutter, & Taylor, 1978; Shaffer, McNamara, & Pincus, 1974; Werry, Elkind, & Reeves, 1987; Werry, Reeves, & Elkind, 1987). Some studies suggest that it may be the pervasiveness of the hyperactivity across settings that separates ADHD from other diagnostic categories of children (Taylor, 1986). The hyperactivity has been shown to decline significantly across the elementary school years, while problems with attention persist at relatively stable levels during this same period of development in ADHD children (Hart, Lahey, Loeber, Applegate, & Frick, 1995). One explanation that may account for such a state of affairs is that the hyperactivity reflects an early developmental manifestation of a more central deficit in behavioral inhibition. Studies that have factor-analyzed behavior ratings certainly show that hyperactivity and poor impulse control form a single dimension of behavior, as indicated in the DSM-IV (Achenbach & Edelbrock, 1983; DuPaul, 1991; Goyette, Conners, & Ulrich, 1978; Hinshaw, 1987). This deficit in inhibition is increasingly reflected in poor self-regulation over development, even though the difficulties with excessive activity level may wane with maturation (Barkley, 1997d).

Difficulties with adherence to rules and instructions are also evident in ADHD children (American Psychiatric Association, 1994; Barkley, 1981, 1989a). Care is taken here to exclude poor rule-governed behavior that may stem from sensory handicaps (e.g., deafness), impaired language development, or defiance or oppositional behavior. ADHD children show significant problems in complying with parental and teacher commands (Barkley, 1985; Danforth, Barkley, & Stokes, 1991; Whalen, Henker, & Dotemoto, 1980), with experimental instructions in the absence of the experimenter (Draeger, Prior, & Sanson, 1986), and with directives to defer gratification or resist temptations (Campbell, Szumowski, Ewing, Gluck, & Breaux, 1982; Hart et al., 1995; Rapport, Tucker, et al., 1986). Like the other symptoms, rule-governed behavior is a multidimensional construct (Hayes, 1987; Zettle & Hayes, 1982). It remains to be shown which of these are specifically impaired in ADHD.

Diagnostic Criteria

Between 1980 and the present, efforts have been made to develop more specific guidelines for the classification of children as having ADHD. These efforts have been increasingly based on an empirical approach to developing a taxonomy of child psychopathology. Although preliminary guidelines appeared in the DSM-II (American Psychiatric Association, 1968), these consisted of a single sentence along with the admonition not to grant the diagnosis if demonstrable brain injury were present. A more concerted effort at developing criteria appeared in the DSM-III (American Psychiatric Association, 1980), though it was still unempirical. These criteria were not examined in any field trial, but were developed primarily from expert opinion. In the DSM-III-R (American Psychiatric Association, 1987), an attempt was made to draw upon the results of factor-analytic studies of child behavior rating scales in selecting symptoms that might be included for ADHD (Spitzer, Davies, & Barkley, 1990). A small-scale field trial employing 500 children from multiple clinical sites was conducted to narrow down the potential list of symptoms, and a cutoff score on this list was chosen that best differentiated ADHD children from other diagnostic groups.

In DSM-IV (American Psychiatric Association, 1994), the criteria are based on a better field trial and more thorough analysis of its results (Lahey et al., 1994). These criteria appear in Table 2.1. Despite their empirical foundation, there remain a few problems with the DSM-IV criteria. Questions remain about developmental sensitivity to the disorder and gender discrimination in diagnosis; there is a wholly unempirically justified age of onset of 7 years; and there is a vexing requirement for cross-setting impairment, which is confounded with the problem of parent–teacher agreement (Barkley, 1996). Also problematic for the generality of these criteria is the fact that the field trial used primarily male European American children, ages 4–16 years. To the extent that clinicians wish to apply the DSM criteria to females or to groups of different ages or ethnic characteristics, adjustments may be required. Moreover, clinicians should consider children whose symptoms began sometime during the childhood years (prior to age 13) as having valid cases of ADHD, rather than adhering strictly to the DSM criterion of 7 years as the age of onset for a valid case (Barkley & Biederman, 1997).

Prevalence and Sex Ratio

The DSM-IV cites a prevalence of 3%–5% of school-age children as probably having ADHD. In his review, Szatmari (1992) found that the prevalence varied from a low of 2% to a high of 6.3%. Most fell within the range of 4.2% to 6.3%. Other studies not included in Szatmari's review have found similar prevalence rates in elementary school-age children, ranging from a low of 2.5% to a high of 6.4% (DuPaul, 1991;

Lambert, Sandoval, & Sassone, 1978; Pelham, Gnagy, Greenslade, & Milich, 1992); a very high rate of 14.3% was found in one study (Trites, Dugas, Lynch, & Ferguson, 1979). In large part, differences in prevalence rates across studies are due to different methods of selecting samples, to differences in the nature of the populations themselves (urban vs. rural, etc.), to differing definitions for the disorder, and certainly to the variation in ages of the samples. Males are approximately three times more likely than females to have ADHD. The disorder decreases in both sexes across development.

Onset, Course, and Outcome

Studies of the developmental course and outcome of ADHD children have been numerous (see Weiss & Hechtman, 1993, for a review) and can only be briefly summarized here. Although some ADHD children are reported to have been difficult in their temperament since birth or early infancy (Barkley, DuPaul, & McMurray, 1990; Ross & Ross, 1976), the majority appear to be identifiable by their caregivers as deviant from normal between 3 and 4 years of age (Barkley, Fischer, Newby, & Breen, 1987; Loeber, Green, Lahey, Christ, & Frick, 1992; Ross & Ross, 1982). However, it may be several years later before such children are brought to the attention of professionals (Safer & Allen, 1976). During their preschool years, ADHD children are often excessively active, mischievous, noncompliant with parental requests, and difficult to toilet-train (Campbell, 1990; Campbell, Schleifer, & Weiss, 1978; Hartsough & Lambert, 1985; Mash & Johnston, 1982). Parental distress over child care and management is likely to reach its zenith when the children are between 3 and 6 years of age, declining thereafter as the children's deficits in attention and rule following improve (Barkley, Karlsson, & Pollard, 1985; Mash & Johnston, 1983). Yet, into the elementary school years, the stress parents report in raising ADHD children remains considerably higher than that for parents of children in control groups (Anastopoulos, Guevremont, Shelton, & DuPaul, 1992; Fischer, 1990; Mash & Johnston, 1983). Parents of ADHD teenagers likewise report high levels of stress and family conflict with these youths, particularly if the youths carry a comorbid diagnosis of ODD (Barkley, Anastopoulos, Guevremont, & Fletcher, 1992; Barkley, Fischer, Edelbrock, & Smallish, 1991).

By entry into formal schooling (6 years of age), most ADHD children have become recognizably deviant from normal peers in their poor sustained attention, impulsivity, and restlessness. Difficulties with aggression, defiance, or oppositional behavior may now have emerged, if they did not earlier in development (Ross & Ross, 1982). ADHD children developing conduct problems or antisocial behaviors are likely to veer into a more severe path of maladjustment in later years than are those ADHD children who do not develop such behaviors or do so only to a limited degree. During these elementary school years, the majority of ADHD children have varying degrees of poor school performance—usually related to failure to finish assigned tasks in school or as homework, disruptive behavior during class activities, and poor peer relations with schoolmates. Learning disabilities in the areas of reading, spelling, math, handwriting, and language may also be manifested by a significant minority of ADHD children, requiring additional special educational assistance beyond that typically needed to manage the ADHD symptoms.

As teenagers, a small percentage of ADHD children will have "outgrown" their symptoms, in that they now fall within the broadly defined normal range in their symptom deviance. However, perhaps as many as 43%–80% (Barkley, Fischer, Edelbrock, & Smallish, 1990; Biederman, Faraone, Milberger, Guite, et al., 1996; Mannuzza et al. 1991; Weiss & Hechtman, 1993) continue to have the disorder into adolescence. At home, family conflicts may continue or even increase (Barkley, Anastopoulos et al., 1992; Fletcher, Fischer, Barkley, & Smallish, 1996) and may now center around the failure of the ADHD teens to accept responsibility for performing routine tasks, difficulties with their being trusted to obey rules when away from home, and trouble with the problem-solving approaches that parents and ADHD adolescents attempt to use in resolving conflicts (e.g., authoritarianism, high emotion, excessive use of ultimatums, etc.) (Edwards, 1995; Robin, 1990). Among the subset of youths who have had significant earlier problems with aggressive and oppositional behavior, delinquency and CD are more likely to emerge (if they have not done so already) as these adolescents spend greater amounts of unsupervised time in the community (Barkley, Fischer, et al., 1990; Mannuzza et al., 1991; Satterfield, Hoppe, & Schell, 1982; Satterfield, Swanson, Schell, & Lee, 1994; Weiss & Hechtman, 1993). Greater-than-normal sub-

TABLE 2.1.   DSM-IV Criteria for ADHD

A. Either (1) or (2):
  (1) six (or more) of the following symptoms of **inattention** have persisted for at least 6 months to a degree that is maladaptive and inconsistent with developmental level:
  Inattention
  (a) often fails to give close attention to details or makes careless mistakes in schoolwork, work, or other activities
  (b) often has difficulty sustaining attention in tasks or play activities
  (c) often does not seem to listen when spoken to directly
  (d) often does not follow through on instructions and fails to finish schoolwork, chores, or duties in the workplace (not due to oppositional behavior or failure to understand instructions)
  (e) often has difficulty organizing tasks and activities
  (f) often avoids, dislikes, or is reluctant to engage in tasks that require sustained mental effort (such as schoolwork or homework)
  (g) often loses things necessary for tasks or activities (e.g., toys, school assignments, pencils, books, or tools)
  (h) is often easily distracted by extraneous stimuli
  (i) is often forgetful in daily activities
  (2) six (or more) of the following symptoms of **hyperactivity–impulsivity** have persisted for at least 6 months to a degree that is maladaptive and inconsistent with developmental level:
  Hyperactivity
  (a) often fidgets with hands or feet or squirms in seat
  (b) often leaves seat in classroom or in other situations in which remaining seated is expected
  (c) often runs about or climbs excessively in situations in which it is inappropriate (in adolescents or adults, may be limited to subjective feelings of restlessness)
  (d) often has difficulty playing or engaging in leisure activities quietly
  (e) is often "on the go" or often acts as if "driven by a motor"
  (f) often talks excessively
  Impulsivity
  (g) often blurts out answers before the questions have been completed
  (h) often has difficulty awaiting turn
  (i) often interrupts or intrudes on others (e.g., butts into conversations or games)
B. Some hyperactive–impulsive or inattentive symptoms that caused impairment were present before age 7 years.

C. Some impairment from the symptoms is present in two or more settings (e.g., at school [or work] and at home).

D. There must be clear evidence of clinically significant impairment in social, academic, or occupational functioning.

E. The symptoms do not occur exclusively during the course of a Pervasive Developmental Disorder, Schizophrenia, or other Psychotic Disorder, and are not better accounted for by another mental disorder (e.g., Mood Disorder, Anxiety Disorder, Dissociative Disorder, or a Personality Disorder).
  Code based on type:
  314.01 Attention-Deficit/Hyperactivity Disorder, Combined Type: if both Criteria A1 and A2 are met for the past 6 months.
  314.00 Attention-Deficit/Hyperactivity Disorder, Predominantly Inattentive Type: if Criterion A1 is met but Criterion A2 is not met for the past 6 months.
  314.01 Attention-Deficit/Hyperactivity Disorder, Predominantly Hyperactive-Impulsive Type: if Criterion A2 is met but Criterion A1 is not met for the past 6 months.
  Coding note: For individuals (especially adolescents and adults) who currently have symptoms that no longer meet full criteria, "In Partial Remission" should be specified.

Note. From American Psychiatric Association (1994, pp. 83–85). Copyright 1994 by the American Psychiatric Association. Reprinted by permission.

stance experimentation and misuse are likely to occur within the adolescent years, mainly among ADHD youths with comorbid CD (Barkley, Fischer, et al., 1990; Gittelman, Man- nuzza, Shenker, & Bonagura, 1985; Thompson, Riggs, Mikulich, & Crowley, 1996; Weiss & Hechtman, 1993) or bipolar disorders (Biederman et al., 1997). And an increasing number of studies have replicated and extended the original report of Weiss and Hechtman (1986) suggesting that ADHD teenagers have a greater number of automobile accidents and speeding citations than normal teens (Barkley, Guevremont, Anastopoulos, DuPaul, & Shelton, 1993; Barkley, Murphy, & Kwasnik, 1996; Nada-Raja, et al., 1997). Research also suggests that up to 30% may fail to complete high school, and that most fail to pursue college programs after high school (Weiss & Hechtman, 1993). Certainly, the outcome of childhood ADHD in the adolescent years is far more negative than previous clinical lore had postulated.

Less research exists on the adult outcome of ADHD children. What does exist suggests that from 8% to 65% may continue to have the disorder, or at least symptoms of ADHD that significantly affect their lives (Fischer, Barkley, Fletcher, & Smallish, 1997; Mannuzza, Gittelman-Klein, Bessler, Malloy, & LaPadula, 1993; Weiss & Hechtman, 1993). The more recent studies using more modern diagnostic criteria for ADHD appear to demonstrate higher rates of persistence of the disorder than do earlier follow-up studies. Interpersonal problems continue to plague as many as 75% and demoralization and low self-esteem are commonplace (Weiss & Hechtman, 1993). Juvenile convictions and symptoms of adult antisocial personality may occur in 23% to 45% (Farrington, Loeber, & van Kammen; 1987; Mannuzza et al., 1993), while 27% or more may be alcoholic (Loney, Whaley-Klahn, Kosier, & Conboy, 1981). Hence, adult disorders appear to exist that either are identical to the childhood disorder or may be the outcomes of earlier ADHD symptoms in childhood. Such outcomes may range from residual ADHD symptoms that impair home or work adjustment (Wender, Reimherr, & Wood, 1981) to Major Depression, Substance Dependence or Abuse, and Antisocial Personality Disorder.

Related Characteristics

Children with ADHD have a higher likelihood than non-ADHD peers of having other medical, developmental, adaptive, behavioral, emotional, and academic difficulties. Delays in intelligence, academic achievement, and motor coordination are more prevalent in ADHD children than in matched samples of normal children or even in siblings (August, Realmuto, MacDonald, Nuget, & Crosby, 1996; Cantwell & Satterfield, 1978; Carte, Nigg, & Hinshaw, 1996; Denckla & Rudel, 1978; Hinshaw, 1992a), as are delays in adaptive functioning more generally (Greene et al., 1996; Roizen, Blondis, Irwin, & Stein, 1994; Stein, Szumowski, Blondis, & Roizen, 1995). As noted earlier, ADHD children are more likely to have coexisting ODD and CD symptoms than normal children (Barkley, DuPaul, & McMurray, 1990; Biederman, Faraone, & Lapey, 1992; Eiraldi, Power, & Nezu, 1997). Depression, anxiety disorders, and juvenile-onset bipolar disorders also appear to be more common in children with ADHD than would be expected in a normal population (Biederman, Faraone, Mick, Moore, & Lelon, 1996; Biederman, Faraone, Mick, Wozniak, et al., 1996; Jensen, Shervette, Xenakis, & Richters, 1993; Perrin & Last, 1996; Tannock, in press). The severity of the ADHD symptoms may in part predict the severity of these comorbid conditions (Gabel, Schmidtz, & Fulker, 1996). Certainly, problems with peer acceptance and in peer interactions are commonly documented in children with ADHD (Cunningham & Siegel, 1987; Erhardt & Hinshaw, 1994; Pelham & Bender, 1982; Hubbard & Newcomb, 1991; Johnston, Pelham, & Murphy, 1985). ADHD children appear to have more minor physical anomalies than normal children (Quinn & Rapoport, 1974; Trites, Tryphonas, & Ferguson, 1980) and may be physically smaller than normal children, at least during childhood (Spencer et al., 1996). They may also have more sleep difficulties than normal children (Ball & Koloian, 1995; Hartsough & Lambert, 1985; Kaplan, McNichol, Conte, & Moghadam, 1987). However, prior beliefs that ADHD may have a higher-than-normal association with either allergies or asthma have not been corroborated by later research (Biederman, Milberger, Faraone, Guite, & Warburton, 1994; McGee, Stanton, & Sears, 1993).

Research on the family interactions of ADHD children suggests that their symptoms produce significant alterations in family functioning, particularly in those children who are also manifesting problems with oppositional and defiant behavior. ADHD children have been shown to be less compliant, more negative, and less able to sustain compliance than normal children during task completion with their mothers (Barkley, Karlsson, & Pollard, 1985; Campbell, 1975; Cunningham & Barkley, 1979; Danforth et al., 1991; Mash & Johnston, 1982). Their mothers are more directive and negative, and less rewarding and responsive to their children's behavior, than mothers of normal children. There appears to be less conflict in the task-related interactions of older ADHD children than in those of younger age groups (Barkley, Karlsson, & Pollard, 1985; Mash & Johnston, 1982). However, older ADHD children remain deviant from same-age children in their noncompliance and parent–child conflicts, even into adolescence (Barkley et al., 1992; Fletcher et al., 1996). Not surprisingly, these interaction problems are significantly greater in those ADHD teens having ODD than in those without this comorbid disorder. It is also not surprising, then, that parents of ADHD children report significantly greater stress in their parental roles than do parents of normal children (Baldwin, Brown, & Milan, 1995; Anastopoulos et al., 1992; Fischer, 1990; Mash & Johnston, 1990). Studies evaluating the impact of stimulant medication on these interactions suggest that the greater directiveness and negative behavior of the mothers of ADHD children may be reactions to their children's noncompliance and poor self-control rather than a cause of these problems (Barkley & Cunningham, 1978; Barkley, Karlsson, Pollard, & Murphy, 1985; Barkley, Karlsson, Strzelecki, & Murphy, 1985; Danforth et al., 1991). Moreover, these conflicts in social interactions appear to exist in the relations of ADHD children with their fathers (Tallmadge & Barkley, 1983), as well as those with peers (Cunningham & Siegel, 1987) and teachers (Whalen et al., 1980).

Etiologies

The proposed etiologies for ADHD are too numerous to review here in any detail. I concentrate on only those for which there is substantial empirical support.

Neurological Factors

Although brain damage was initially proposed as a chief cause of ADHD symptoms (Still, 1902; Strauss & Lehtinen, 1947), later reviews of the evidence suggest that fewer than 5% of ADHD children have neurological findings consistent with such an etiology (Rutter, 1977). Nevertheless, brain damage to the prefrontal cortex, and particularly to the orbital–prefrontal region, has frequently been associated with the symptoms typifying ADHD (Fuster, 1989). And abnormally low birth weight (Breslau et al., 1996; Schothurst & van Engeland, 1996; Szatmari, Saigal, Rosenbaum, & Campbell, 1993) has also been consistently shown to be associated with risk for ADHD, probably through its relationship to abnormal or immature brain development. Possible neurotransmitter dysfunctions or imbalances have been proposed, chiefly on the basis of ADHD children's responses to differing drugs, but little direct evidence is available and many of the early studies were inconsistent in their results (Shaywitz, Shaywitz, Cohen, & Young, 1983; Zametkin & Rapoport, 1986). An interaction among several neurotransmitters, such as dopamine and norepinephrine, may account better for the results of these studies than does positing a single transmitter deficit (Pliszka, McCracken, & Maas, 1996).

Difficulties with neuropsychological tests presumed to assess frontal lobe executive functioning have been repeatedly found in children and adults with ADHD (for reviews, see Barkley, 1997c, 1997d; Barkley, Grodzinsky, & DuPaul, 1992; Goodyear & Hynd, 1992). Physiological functioning in certain brain regions has also been shown to be reduced significantly below normal levels, as measured by decreased cerebral blood flow, particularly to the prefrontal and striatal regions (Lou, Henriksen, & Bruhn, 1984; Lou, Henriksen, Bruhn, Borner, & Nielsen, 1989; Sieg, Gaffney, Preston, & Hellings, 1995) and by decreased brain electrical activity, particularly in prefrontal regions (Hastings & Barkley, 1978; Klorman, 1992; Kuperman, Johnson, Arndt, Lindgren, & Wolraich, 1996). Reduced brain metabolic activity has also been found in ADHD adults and adolescent females with ADHD (Ernst et al., 1994; Zametkin et al., 1990, 1993).

Several recent studies have employed modern magnetic resonance imaging technology to evaluate the structural volumes in various regions of the brain in children with ADHD. These studies have consistently demonstrated significantly reduced regions in the right prefrontal cortex, the striatum, the corpus callosum, and the right cerebellum in children having ADHD (Baumgardner et al., 1996; Castellanos et al., 1994, 1996; Filipek et al., 1997; Hynd et al., 1993; Semrud-Clikeman et al., 1994). Such reduced volume in the right prefrontal and striatal regions is associated with significantly greater difficulties with behavioral inhibition (Casey et al., 1997).

Food Additives and Toxins

Although various environmental toxins, such as food additives, refined sugars, and allergens (Feingold, 1975; Taylor, 1980), have been proposed as causal of ADHD, more rigorous investigations have failed to yield much supportive evidence (Conners, 1980; Gross, 1984; Mattes

& Gittelman, 1981; Wolraich, Milich, Stumbo, & Schultz, 1985; Wolraich, Wilson, & White, 1995). Some evidence of a correlational nature exists to show that elevated blood lead levels in children may be related to excessive activity and inattention (David, 1974; de la Burde & Choate, 1972, 1974; Gittelman & Eskinazi, 1983; Needleman et al. 1979; Needleman & Bellinger, 1984), but the relationships found between lead levels and symptoms of ADHD remain modest in magnitude and controversial in their interpretations (Fergusson, Fergusson, Horwood, & Kinzett, 1988). Maternal alcohol consumption and cigarette smoking during pregnancy (Denson, Nanson, & McWatters, 1975; Milberger, Biederman, Faraone, Chen, & Jones, 1996; Shaywitz, Cohen, & Shaywitz, 1980; Streissguth et al., 1984; Streissguth, Bookstein, Sampson, & Barr, 1995) have both shown associations with the degree of ADHD symptoms in the offspring of these mothers.

Genetics

One of the most exciting areas of current research into the etiologies of ADHD involves the role of heredity generally and molecular genetics specifically. Twin studies of the heritability of ADHD may tell us as much about potential environmental contributions to this disorder as genetic ones. For years, researchers have noted the higher prevalence of psychopathology in the parents and other relatives of children with ADHD (Cantwell, 1975). In particular, higher rates of ADHD, conduct problems, substance misuse, and depression have been repeatedly observed in these studies (Barkley, DuPaul, & McMurray, 1990a; Biederman et al., 1992; Pauls, 1991). When ADHD children have been separated into those with and without CD, it has been shown that the conduct problems, substance misuse, and depression in the parents are more closely related to the presence of CD than to that of ADHD (Barkley, Fischer, et al., 1991; Lahey et al., 1988). Yet rates of hyperactivity or ADHD remain high even in relatives of the group of ADHD children without CD. Research shows that between 10% and 35% of the immediate family members of children with ADHD are also likely to have the disorder, with the risk to siblings of the ADHD children being approximately 32% (Biederman et al., 1992; Biederman, Faraone, Keenan, Knee, & Tsuang, 1990; Pauls, 1991; Welner, Stewart, Palkes, & Wish, 1977). Even more striking, recent research shows that if a parent has ADHD, the risk to the offspring is 57% (Biederman, Faraone, et al.,

1995). Thus, ADHD clusters among biological relatives of children or adults with the disorder, strongly implying a hereditary basis for this condition.

Another line of evidence for genetic involvement in ADHD has emerged from studies of adopted children. Cantwell (1975) and Morrison and Stewart (1973) both reported higher rates of hyperactivity in the biological parents of hyperactive children than in the adoptive parents of such children. A later study (van den Oord, Boomsma, & Verhulst, 1994), using biologically related and unrelated pairs of international adoptees, identified a strong genetic component (47% of the variance) for the Attention Problems dimension of the Child Behavior Checklist. This particular scale has a strong association with a diagnosis of ADHD (Biederman et al., 1994) and is often used in research in selecting subjects with the disorder.

Studies of twins provide the strongest evidence for a hereditary contribution to ADHD. Early studies demonstrated a greater agreement (concordance) for symptoms of hyperactivity and inattention between monozygotic (MZ) than between dizygotic (DZ) twins (O'Connor, Foch, Sherry, & Plomin, 1980; Willerman, 1973). Studies of very small samples of twins (Heffron, Martin, & Welsh, 1984; Lopez, 1965) found complete (100%) concordance for MZ twins for hyperactivity, but far less agreement for DZ twins. Other twin studies using much larger samples have found a substantial hereditary contribution to the symptoms comprising ADHD, accounting for 50% to 98% of the variance among individuals in these symptoms (Edelbrock, Rende, Plomin, & Thompson, 1995; Goodman & Stevenson, 1989; Levy & Hay, 1992). For instance, Gilger, Pennington, and DeFries (1992) found that if one twin was diagnosed as ADHD, the concordance for the disorder was 81% in MZ twins and 29% in DZ twins. More recent twin studies have been remarkably consistent with this conclusion, demonstrating that the majority of variance (70%–80%) in the trait of inattention–hyperactivity–impulsivity is due to genetic factors (averaging approximately 80%). The more extreme the scores along this trait happen to be, the more the genetic contribution may increase, although this point is debatable (Faraone, 1996; Gjone, Stevenson, & Sundet, 1996; Gjone, Stevenson, Sundet, & Eilertsen, 1996; Rhee, Waldman, Hay, & Levy, 1995; Silberg et al., 1996; Thapar, Hervas, & McGuffin, 1995; van den Oord, Verhulst, & Boomsma, 1996).

But twin studies can also tell us about environmental contributions to the expression of a trait (Faraone, 1996; Pike & Plomin, 1996; Plomin, 1995). Across the twin studies conducted to date, the results have been quite consistent in demonstrating that the shared environment contributes little, if any, explanation to individual differences in the trait underlying ADHD (hyperactivity–impulsivity–inattention), accounting for only up to 6% of the variance among individuals (Sherman, McGue, & Iacono, 1997; Silberg et al., 1996). A recent study suggests, however, that shared environmental factors may play a small role in the continuity of these behavior problems over development (van den Oord & Rowe, 1997).

These twin studies can also indicate the extent to which individual differences in ADHD symptoms are the result of nonshared environmental factors. To date, studies have suggested that approximately 15%–30% percent of the variance in hyperactive–impulsive–inattentive behavior or ADHD symptoms can be attributed to nonshared environmental (nongenetic) factors (Sherman et al., 1997; Silberg et al., 1996). Thus, if researchers are interested in identifying environmental contributors to ADHD, these twin studies suggest that such research should focus on those biological, interactional, and social experiences that are specific and unique to the individual and are not part of the common environment to which other siblings have been exposed.

Several teams of investigators are now pursuing molecular genetic studies of ADHD children and their family members. Quantitative genetic analyses of the large sample of families studied in Boston by Biederman and his colleagues suggest that a single gene may account for the expression of the disorder (Faraone et al., 1992), though other investigators believe it may be a polygenetic trait (Cook, Stein, & Leventhal, 1997). The focus of research was initially on the dopamine type 2 gene, given findings of its increased association with alcoholism, Tourette's Disorder, and ADHD (Blum, Cull, Braverman, & Comings, 1996; Comings et al., 1991), but others have failed to replicate these findings (Gelernter et al., 1991; Kelsoe et al., 1989). More recently, the dopamine transporter gene has been implicated in ADHD (Cook et al., 1997, in press). Another gene related to dopamine, the D4RD (repeater gene), was recently found to be overrepresented in the seven-repetition form of the gene in children with ADHD (Lahoste et al., 1996). This gene has previously been shown to be related to novelty-seeking behavior in studies of personality. Both of these more recent findings are being replicated in an ongoing study by Swanson and colleagues (J.M. Swanson, personal communication, November 1996). Clearly, research into the genes involved in ADHD promises to be an exciting and fruitful area of research endeavor over the next decade as the human genome is better mapped and better understood.

Social Causes

A few environmental theories of ADHD have been proposed—for example, that ADHD is due to increased cultural tempo (Block, 1977) or to poor parental management of the child (Jacobvitz & Sroufe, 1987; Silverman & Ragusa, 1992; Willis & Lovaas, 1977). But these theories have not been clear in articulating just how deficits in behavioral inhibition and attention could arise from such social factors. Nor have these theories received much support in the available literature (see Danforth et al., 1991, concerning child management issues). In view of the twin studies discussed above, which show minimal or nonsignificant contributions of the common or shared environment to the expression of symptoms of ADHD, theories based entirely on social explanations of the origins of ADHD are difficult to take seriously any longer. Still, despite the large role heredity seems to play in ADHD symptoms, they remain malleable to unique environmental influences and nonshared social learning. The actual severity of the symptoms, the continuity of those symptoms over development, the types of secondary symptoms, and the outcome of the disorder are related in varying degrees to environmental factors (Biederman, Faraone, Milberger, Curtis, et al., 1996; van den Oord & Rowe, 1997; Weiss & Hechtman, 1993).

CONCEPTUALIZATION OF THE DISORDER

Until recently, ADHD has lacked a reasonably credible scientific theory to explain its basic nature and associated symptoms and to link it with normal developmental processes. Consequently, the vast majority of research into the treatment of ADHD has remained exploratory in nature, rather than being based upon any theory of the disorder. Treatments were tried principally because they had shown some efficacy for other

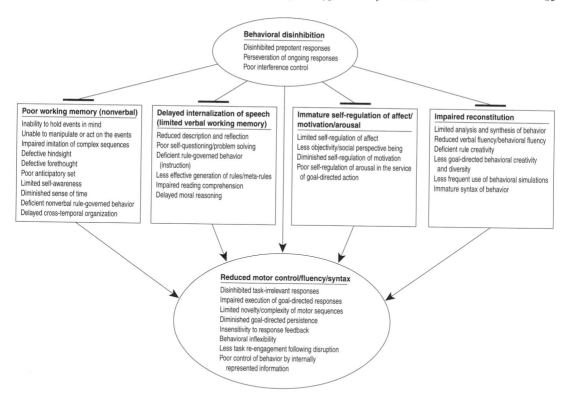

FIGURE 2.1. Diagram of the theoretical model linking behavioral disinhibition to disrupted executive functions and reduced motor control in ADHD. From Barkley (1997). Copyright 1997 by The Guilford Press. Reprinted by permission.

disorders (e.g., behavior modification with the mentally retarded) or were discovered to have beneficial effects primarily by accident (e.g., stimulant medications). Thus, treatment decisions have not been guided as much by a scientific theory as by pragmatics; whatever seems to work is retained, and whatever doesn't is discarded, with little guidance from any sound theoretical rationale.

At present, however, the neuropsychological, neuroimaging, and genetic studies described above are beginning to set clear limits not only on theories about the origins of ADHD, but on theories of its nature as well. Any credible theory on the nature of ADHD must now posit psychological constructs that are related to the normal development of inhibition, self-regulation, and executive functioning, and must explain how these may go awry in ADHD. And such a theory will need to argue that these constructs arise from the functions of the prefrontal–striatal network and its interconnections with other brain regions that appear to subserve the executive functions and self-control. Individual differences in these cognitive functions will probably be shown to have a substantial hereditary contribution, given the results of twin studies to date. I have been working on just such a theoretical conceptualization of ADHD over the past 5 years (see Barkley, 1997c, 1997d). This is briefly discussed below, followed by a discussion of its implications for the management of ADHD. The model is founded on the premise that ADHD consists mainly of a developmental delay in behavioral inhibition—an assertion for which there is substantial research support (for reviews, see Barkley, 1997c, 1997d; Pennington & Ozonoff, 1996).

Behavioral Inhibition, Executive Functions, and Time

This theory, in essence, is a model linking behavioral inhibition to the executive functions and self-regulation. It is shown in Figure 2.1, where it is rephrased in terms of the deficiencies that are hypothesized to exist in ADHD. As can be seen here, behavioral inhibition occupies a central point in relationship to four other executive functions, which are dependent upon it for their own effective execution. These four executive functions subserve human self-regulation, bringing behavior (motor control) progressively more under the control of internally represented information, time, and the probable future, and wresting it from control by the immediate context and the temporal now. This functions to maximize future consequences for the individual over merely immediate ones.

The model does not apply to those having what used to be called Attention Deficit Disorder without Hyperactivity, or what is now called ADHD, Predominantly Inattentive Type. This theory has been derived from earlier theories on the evolution of human language (Bronowski, 1977) and the functions of the prefrontal cortex (Goldman-Rakic, 1995; Fuster, 1989). The evidence for the model as applied to ADHD and for the assertions made below is reviewed elsewhere (Barkley, 1997c, 1997d).

Behavioral Inhibition

Behavioral inhibition involves (1) the capacity to inhibit prepotent responses, creating a delay in the response to an event (response inhibition). There may be two other inhibitory processes related to it, which, at least for the moment, I have combined into a single construct concerning inhibition. These two other processes are (2) the capacity to interrupt ongoing responses, given feedback about performance (particularly those response patterns that are proving ineffective) and (3) the protection of this delay in responding, the self-directed actions occurring within it, and the goal-directed behaviors they create from interference by competing events and their prepotent responses ("interference control"). "Prepotent responses" are defined as those for which immediate reinforcement, both positive and negative, is available for their performance, or for which there is a strong history of reinforcement in this context. Through the postponement of the prepotent response and the creation of this protected period of delay, the occasion is set for the four executive functions (covert, self-directed actions) to act effectively in modifying the individual's eventual response(s) to the event. The chain of goal-directed, temporally governed, and future-oriented behaviors set in motion by these acts of self-regulation is then protected from interference during its performance by this same process of inhibition (interfer-

ence control). And even if disrupted, the individual retains the capacity or intention (via working memory) to return to the goal-directed actions until the outcome is successfully achieved or judged to be no longer necessary.

Nonverbal Working Memory (Covert Self-Directed Sensing)

"Nonverbal working memory" is the ability to maintain mental information on-line that will be used subsequently to control a motor response. These prolonged mental representations of events, achieved by covertly sensing to the self, can also be stored in long-term memory for later retrieval back into working memory when their information may be pertinent to considering a response to a current event. This recall of past events for the sake of preparing a current response represents "hindsight" or the "retrospective function" of working memory (Bronowski, 1977; Fuster, 1989). To carry out such a process, events must be tagged in some way concerning their sequence or temporal order. And this retention of events in a temporal sequence has been shown to contribute to the subjective estimation of psychological time (Michon, 1985). Analysis of temporal sequences of events for recurring patterns can then be used to conjecture hypothetical future events—the individual's best guess as to what may happen next or later in time, based upon the detection of recurring patterns in past event sequences. This extension of hindsight forward into time also creates "forethought" or the "prospective function" of working memory, forming a temporally symmetrical counterpart to the retrospective function of hindsight (Bronowski, 1977; Fuster, 1989). And from this sense of future probably emerges the progressively greater valuation of future consequences over immediate ones that takes place not only throughout child development, but into young adult life as well (Green, Fry, & Meyerson, 1994). All of this permits the individual to create a preparation or intention to act, sometimes called an "anticipatory set" (Fuster, 1989). In so doing, the individual is now capable of the cross-temporal organization of behavior—that is, the linking of events, responses, and their eventual consequences via their representation in working memory, despite what may be considerable gaps among them in real time. Thus, self-regulation relative to time arises as a consequence of working memory and the internally represented information it provides for the control and guidance of behavior over time.

Internalization of Speech

One of the more fascinating developmental processes witnessed in children is the progressive internalization or privatization of their originally public, other-directed speech. During the early preschool years, speech, once developed, is initially employed for communication with others. As behavioral inhibition progresses, the delays in responding it permits allows language to be turned on the self. Language is now not just a means of influencing the behavior of others, but provides a means of reflection (self-directed description) as well as a means for controlling one's own behavior (Berk, 1992, 1994; Bronowski, 1977; Diaz & Berk, 1992). Self-directed speech progresses from being public, to being subvocal, to finally being private, all over the course of perhaps 6–10 years. With this progressive privatization of speech comes the increasing amount of control it permits over behavior (Berk, 1992; Berk & Potts, 1992; Kopp, 1982). Language in general, and rules (behavior-specifying stimuli) in particular, gain an increasing degree of control over motor behavior; this results in a tremendously increased capacity for self-control, planfulness, and goal-directed behavior. This developmental progression of public speech to private, covert self-directed speech gives rise to verbal thought and thus, I believe, to verbal working memory (Barkley, 1997d).

Self-Regulation of Affect/Motivation/Arousal

Figure 2.1 also shows that behavioral inhibition sets the occasion for the self-regulation of affect, motivation, and arousal. The inhibition of the initial prepotent response includes the inhibition of the initial emotional and motivational valence that it may have elicited. The delay in responding this creates allows the child time to engage in self-directed actions that will modify both the eventual response to the event and the emotional reaction that may accompany it. This is believed to permit greater objectivity on the part of the child in determining an eventual response to an event (Bronowski, 1977). But it is not just affect that is being managed by the development of self-regulation, but drive and motivation as well (Fuster, 1989), given that they are inherently linked (Ekman & Davidson, 1994; Lang, 1995). This capacity to privately manipulate and modulate emotional and motivational states eventually permits the child to induce drive or motivational states that may be required for the initiation and maintenance of goal-directed behavior (Barkley, 1997d).

Reconstitution

It has been argued (Bronowski, 1977) that the use of language to represent the objects, actions, and properties that exist in the world provides a means by which the world, through internalized speech, can be taken apart and recombined, just as is done with the parts of speech that represent that world. The delay in responding that behavioral inhibition permits allows time for events and the responses associated with them to be mentally represented and then disassembled, so as to extract more information about the event before preparing a response to it. Internal speech permits analysis and out of this process comes its complement—synthesis. Just as the parts of speech can be recombined to form new sentences, the parts of the world represented in speech are likewise recombined to create entirely new ideas about the world (Bronowski, 1977) and entirely new responses to that world. It becomes obvious when speech is task- or goal-directed, as it requires the rapid, efficient, and often novel combination of the parts of speech into entire messages that represent the ideas of the individual. This reconstitutive function does not apply simply to the domain of language, but to all human behavior, thereby providing a means to synthesize novel behavioral sequences in the service of problem solving and goal-directed action (Barkley, 1997d; Fuster, 1989). The capability of synthesizing new behaviors out of the individual's existing repertoire also requires that a set of rules be used to construct such response sequences, and these rules form the syntax of behavioral sequences (Fuster, 1989).

Motor Control/Fluency/Syntax

Over development, inhibition and the executive functions it supports permit the construction and execution of increasingly lengthy, complex, hierarchically organized, and novel chains of goal-directed behavior, protecting them from disruption by interference until they have been completed. This end is achieved by generating internally represented information that serves to take over the control of behavior from the moment and immediate setting, and to direct behavior toward time and the probable or anticipated future. Such internal control over behavior not only gives behavior a greater flexibility and fluency, but also grants it a more determined, persistent, reasoned, intentional, and purposive quality—an appearance of volition and will that even William James (1890) and Charles Darwin

(1871/1992) recognized as arising from internally guided behavior.

Application of the Model to ADHD

The impairment in behavioral inhibition occurring in ADHD is hypothesized to disrupt the efficient execution of these executive functions, thereby delimiting the capacity for self-regulation. The result is an impairment in the cross-temporal organization of behavior and in the guidance and control of behavior by internally represented information. This inevitably leads to a reduction in the maximization of long-term consequences for the individual.

Undoubtedly, this theory requires a great deal of research to clarify the nature of each component in the model; to evaluate the strength of the relationship of behavioral inhibition to each executive function and of the executive functions to one another; to elucidate the developmental progression of each component and their ordering; and to critically test some of the previously unexpected predictions of the model as applied to ADHD (e.g., the diminished sense of time in ADHD, the impact of ADHD on analysis–synthesis and creativity, etc.). These issues are discussed in greater detail elsewhere (Barkley, 1997d). What research is available, however, seems to be reasonably consistent with the components set forth in the model (Barkley, 1997c, 1997d).

How is the problem with inattention in ADHD accounted for in this model? It will be necessary to distinguish between two forms of sustained attention that are traditionally confused in the research literature on ADHD. The first I have called "contingency-shaped attention" (Barkley, 1997c), which refers to persistent responding in a situation as a function of the motivational or reinforcement properties of that context and specifically the contingencies of reinforcement provided by the task or activity. Such responding is directly dependent on the immediate environmental contingencies, and so is described as contingency-shaped. This form of attention is not affected by ADHD.

As children mature, a second form of sustained attention emerges that is better termed "goal-directed persistence." It arises as a direct consequence of the development of self-regulation by internally generated information. It derives from the development of a progressively greater capacity by the child to hold events, goals, and plans in mind (working memory), to adhere to rules governing behavior and to formulate and follow such rules as need be, and to self-induce motivational or drive states supportive of the plans and goals formulated by the individual so as to maintain goal-directed behavior. The interaction of the components of the model in the performance of self-regulation permits substantially longer, complex, flexible, and novel chains of behavior to be constructed and sustained, despite interruptions, until the goal is attained. Such behavior is less dependent upon the current context and its immediate contingencies for its performance. It may even be associated with a state of self-imposed deprivation from reinforcement (or, less often, with infliction of immediate aversive or punitive states) if, in so doing, later consequences are maximized over immediate ones. It is this type of goal-directed persistence arising out of self-regulation that is impaired by ADHD.

TREATMENT APPROACHES

It is fair to say that advances made in the treatment of ADHD since the first edition of this chapter (Barkley, 1989b) have been relatively circumscribed and have mainly occurred in the area of psychopharmacology rather than that of psychosocial treatments. This is not to say that more information on the prevailing treatments has not been gained over this decade; that is hardly the case. It is to say that no significant breakthroughs in the treatment of the disorder have been forthcoming. Most of the research has served to clarify the efficacy (or lack of it) of already extant treatment approaches, or their combinations. Indeed, some recent findings concerning multimodality treatments have been especially sobering. Before the efficacy of specific treatments for ADHD is discussed, it will be helpful to reexamine some traditional assumptions about the treatment of this disorder. They are being called into question not only by the theoretical model presented above, but by the results of research on the etiologies of the disorder and on the efficacy of particular treatments.

Reexamining Treatment Assumptions

Advances in research on the etiologies of ADHD and in theoretical models about the disorder seem to suggest why few treatment breakthroughs, especially in the psychosocial arena, have occurred. The information yielded from these sources increasingly points to ADHD as being a developmental disorder of probable neurogenetic origins in which some unique environmental factors play a role in expression of the disorder, though a far smaller role than genetic ones do. And so new treatments are unlikely to be discovered at this time that would result in an amelioration of the disorder, since they are unlikely to correct the underlying neurological substrates or genetic mechanisms that are contributing so strongly to it. As with the learning disabilities and mental retardation, which appear to have relatively analogous etiologies, treatment is actually management. It is management of a chronic developmental condition and involves finding means to cope with, compensate for, and accommodate to the developmental deficiencies. These means also include the provision of symptomatic relief, such as that obtained by various medications. And, given the relatively greater contribution of genotype than of environment in explaining individual differences in the symptoms of the disorder, it is highly likely that treatments for ADHD, while providing improvements in the symptoms, do little to change the rank ordering of such individuals relative to each other in their posttreatment levels of ADHD (for general discussions of this issue in developmental psychology and clinical interventions, see Scarr, 1992; Scarr & McCartney, 1983; Rutter, 1997). It is also likely that such treatments, particularly in the psychosocial realm, will prove to be specific to the treatment setting, showing minimal generalization unless active arrangements for its occurrence are made.

The theoretical model of ADHD discussed above suggests other reasons why treatment efects may be so limited. According to this model, ADHD does not result from a lack of skill, knowledge, or information. It is therefore not going to respond well to interventions emphasizing the transfer of knowledge or of skills, as might occur in psychotherapy, social skills training, cognitive therapies, or academic tutoring. Instead, ADHD is viewed as a disorder of performance—of doing what one knows, rather than knowing what to do. It is more a disorder of "when" behavior should be performed than of "how" to perform it. Like patients with injuries to the frontal lobes, those with ADHD find that the disorder has partially cleaved or dissociated intellect from action, or knowledge from performance. Thus, the individuals with ADHD may know how to act, but may not act that way when placed in social settings where such ac-

tions would be beneficial to them. The timing and timeliness of behavior are also being disrupted more in ADHD than is the basic knowledge or skill about behavior.

From this vantage point, treatments for ADHD will be most helpful when they assist with the performance of particular behaviors at the *points of performance* in the natural environments where and when such behaviors should be performed. A corollary of this is that the further away in space and time a treatment is from these points of performance, the less effective it is likely to be in assisting with the management of ADHD (Goldstein & Ingersoll, 1993). Not only is assistance at the "points of performance" going to prove critical to treatment efficacy, but so is assistance with the time, timing, and timeliness of behaviors in those with ADHD, not just in the training of the behaviors themselves (Barkley, 1997d).

Nor will there necessarily be any lasting value or maintenance of treatment effects from such assistance, if it is summarily removed within a short period of time once the individual is performing the desired behaviors. For, as the model discussed above implies, the value of such treatments lies not only in providing assistance with eliciting behaviors that are already likely to be in the individual's repertoire at the points of performance where their display is critical, but in maintaining the performance of those behaviors over time in that natural setting. Disorders of performance like ADHD create great consternation among those in the mental health and educational arenas of service, because at the core of such problems is the vexing issue of just how to get people to behave in ways that they know are good for them, yet that they seem unlikely, unable, or unwilling to perform. Conveying more knowledge does not prove as helpful as altering the motivational parameters associated with the performance of those behaviors at their appropriate points of performance. Coupled with this is the realization that such behavior changes are maintained only so long as those environmental adjustments or accommodations are maintained as well. To expect otherwise would seem to approach the treatment of ADHD with outdated or misguided assumptions about its essential nature.

The conceptual model of ADHD introduced above brings with it other implications for the management of ADHD, which are too numerous to discuss in detail here (see Barkley, 1997d). However, some of them are briefly mentioned below:

1. If the process of regulating behavior by internally represented forms of information (the internalization of behavior) is delayed in those with ADHD, then they will be best assisted by "externalizing" those forms of information; the provision of physical representations of that information will be needed in the natural settings at the points of performance. Since covert or private information is weak as a source of stimulus control, making that information overt and public may assist with strengthening control of behavior by that information.

2. The organization of the individual's behavior both within and across time is one of the ultimate disabilities rendered by the disorder. ADHD is to time what nearsightedness is to spatial vision: It has created a temporal myopia in which behavior is governed even more than in normal individuals by events close to or within the temporal now and immediate context, rather than by internal information that pertains to longer-term, future events. Those with ADHD can be expected to be assisted, then, by making time itself more externally represented; by reducing or eliminating gaps in time among the components of a behavioral contingency (event, response, outcome); and by serving to bridge such temporal gaps related to future events with the assistance of caregivers and others.

3. Given that the model hypothesizes a deficit in internally generated and represented forms of motivation that are needed to subserve goal-directed behavior, those with ADHD will require the provision of externalized sources of motivation. For instance, the provision of artificial rewards, such as tokens, may be needed throughout the performance of a task or goal-directed behavior when there are otherwise few or no such immediate consequences associated with that performance. Such artificial reward programs become for ADHD children like prosthetic devices or mechanical limbs to the physically disabled, allowing them to perform more effectively in some tasks and settings where they otherwise would have considerable difficulty. The motivational disability created by ADHD makes such motivational prostheses nearly essential for most children with ADHD.

Ineffective or Unproven Therapies

A great many treatments have been attempted with ADHD children over the past century—far too numerous to review here (for reviews, see Ingersoll & Goldstein, 1993; Ross & Ross, 1976, 1982). Vestibular stimulation (Arnold,

Clark, Sachs, Jakim, & Smithies, 1985), running (Hales & Hales, 1985), biofeedback and relaxation training (Richter, 1984), and electroencephalographic biofeedback or neurofeedback (Lubar & Lubar, 1984; Linden, Habib, & Radojevic, 1996), among others, have been described as potentially effective in either uncontrolled case reports, small series of case studies, or in some treatment versus no-treatment comparisons; yet well-controlled experimental replications of their efficacy are lacking. Many dietary treatments, such as the removal of additives, colorings, or sugar from the diet or the addition of high doses of vitamins, minerals, or other "health food" supplements to the diet, have proven very popular despite minimal or no scientific support (Conners, 1980; Haslam, Dalby, & Rademaker, 1984; Ingersoll & Goldstein, 1993; Milich, Wolraich, & Lindgren, 1986; Wolraich et al., 1995). Certainly traditional psychotherapy and play therapy have not proven especially effective for ADHD (see Ross & Ross, 1976).

The provision of cognitive-behavioral treatment, or cognitive therapy, was previously felt to hold some promise for children with ADHD (Douglas, 1980; Kendall & Braswell, 1985; Meichenbaum & Goodman, 1971). Indeed, a few small-scale studies suggested some benefits to this form of treatment when used with ADHD children (Fehlings, Roberts, Humphries, & Dawe, 1991). But this form of treatment has been recently challenged as being seriously flawed from the conceptual (Vygotskian) point of view on which the treatment was initially founded (Diaz & Berk, 1995). And its efficacy for impulsive children or those with ADHD has been repeatedly called into question by the rather poor or limited results of empirical research (Abikoff, 1985, 1987; Abikoff & Gittelman, 1985). In one of the most ambitious cognitive-behavioral programs ever undertaken, involving the training of parents, teachers, and children, researchers found significant treatment effects on only one of a large variety of dependent measures: class observations of off-task/disruptive behavior (Bloomquist, August, & Ostrander, 1991). And even this treatment effect was not maintained at a 6-week follow-up. Reviews of this literature using meta-analyses have typically found the effect sizes to be only about a third of a standard deviation, and in many studies even less than this (Baer & Nietzel, 1991; Dush, Hirt, & Schroeder, 1989). Although such treatment effects may at times rise to the level of statistical significance, they are nonetheless of only modest clinical importance, and usually are to be found mainly on relatively circumscribed lab measures (Brown, Wynne, et al., 1986) rather than more clinically important measures of functioning in natural settings.

The theoretical model of ADHD discussed above may offer some explanation for such limited treatment effects. For one thing, the model implies that the acquisition of skills is not likely to prove particularly useful in the treatment of ADHD, given that the children's primary problem lies more in the realm of performance than of knowledge. Cognitive-behavioral treatment is predominantly a skills training program and does little to address the performance problems of those with the disorder. But the theoretical model also suggests that there is a developmental delay in self-speech and its internalization, which makes teaching verbal self-instruction procedures questionable as a means of treatment. Such self-speech may have less stimulus control over motor behavior in these children than in normal children. Moreover, the problem with self-speech lies downstream from the problem with response inhibition, and thus self-instruction training is focusing on a secondary consequence of ADHD rather than on its primary deficit. Such a theoretical position would tend to call into serious question the utility of cognitive-behavioral therapies for children with ADHD, at least as the major modality of intervention. For all of these reasons, then, this form of treatment will not receive any further attention here.

Similarly, social skills training will receive little coverage here. Again, this is largely due to the fact that reviews of this treatment as applied specifically to children with ADHD have been quite discouraging (Hinshaw, 1992b; Hinshaw & Erhardt, 1991; Whalen & Henker, 1991). ADHD children certainly have serious difficulties in their social interactions with peers (Cunningham, Siegel, & Offord, 1985; Erhardt & Hinshaw, 1994; Hubbard & Newcomb, 1991; Pelham & Bender, 1982; Whalen & Henker, 1992). This seems to be especially true for that subgroup having significant levels of comorbid aggression (Hinshaw, 1992b; Erhardt & Hinshaw, 1994), in which more than 50% of the variance in peer ratings of children whom they disliked was predicted by this behavior alone. As Hinshaw (1992b) has summarized, the social interaction problems of children with ADHD are quite heterogeneous; they are not likely to respond to a treatment package that focuses only on social approach strategies and that treats all

ADHD children as if they shared common problems in their peer relationship difficulties. Nor are either the actual sources of these peer difficulties or the mechanisms by which they operate especially clear at this time (with the exception of aggressive behavior, as noted above). For instance, do ADHD children actually lack the knowledge of proper social skills, or is it that they know how to act with others but do not do so at the points of performance in social interactions where such skills would be useful? The theoretical model presented earlier would suggest that the latter is likely to be more of a problem than the former, at least for children having ADHD without significant aggression. Teaching them additional skills is not so much the issue as is assisting them with the performance of the skills they have *when* it would be useful to do so *at the points of performance* where such skills are most likely to enhance the children's long-term social acceptance. Those ADHD children with comorbid aggression may well have additional problems with their peer perceptions—particularly with the motives they attribute to others for their behavior, as well as with information processing about social interactions (Dodge, 1989; Milich & Dodge, 1984). This combination of perceptual/information–processing deficits with problems in the performance of social skills during social interactions with others may make ADHD children with aggression particularly resistant to social skills training (Hinshaw, 1992b). And so, until more evidence for the efficacy of social skills training for ADHD children is forthcoming, this form of treatment will receive no further coverage here.

Those treatments with some proven efficacy, which will be the subjects of the remainder of this chapter are as follows: (1) psychopharmacological therapy (Barkley, in press-b); (2) parent training in contingency management methods (Anastopoulos, Shelton, DuPaul, & Guevremont, 1993); (3) classroom applications of contingency management techniques (DuPaul & Eckert, 1997); and (4) assorted combinations of these approaches. Besides these interventions, therapists should also be cognizant of the availability of special educational programs for ADHD children, which are now mandated under the Individuals with Disabilities in Education Act and Section 504 of the Civil Rights Act (DuPaul & Stoner, 1994; Latham & Latham, 1992). The determination of eligibility for such programs is often a major referral concern of parents or teachers; clinicians must therefore be familiar with federal, state, and local regulations regarding placement in such programs.

None of the presently recommended treatments are at all curative of ADHD symptoms. Their value lies in the temporary reduction of symptom levels or in the reduction of related behavioral and emotional difficulties, such as defiance and conduct problems, depression and low self-esteem, or academic underachievement. When such treatments are removed, the level of ADHD symptoms appears to return to pretreatment ranges of deviance. Their effectiveness in improving prognosis, then, rests on their being maintained over long periods of time (often years). Even this practice, however, has only sparse research support (Satterfield, Satterfield, & Cantwell, 1981), owing in large part to the difficulties inherent in conducting long-term treatment research. Several efforts to study the efficacy of long-term treatment more rigorously will receive some mention below.

Psychopharmacological Therapy

Research suggests that at least three classes of psychotropic drugs have proven useful in the management of ADHD symptoms: the stimulants, the antidepressants, and the antihypertensives. Use of each of these types of medications, however, has been founded on virtual chance discoveries of their effectiveness, and not as yet on any theoretical rationale (Bradley, 1937; Winsberg, Bialer, Kupietz, & Tobias, 1972). However, such a rationale may be emerging in view of recent theoretical models (such as the one discussed above) that emphasize poor behavioral inhibition as probably being central to the nature of the disorder. Moreover, findings from neurological research indicate that brain regions subserving such inhibition appear to be involved in the etiology of ADHD, and that stimulants seem to produce their greatest effects within these same brain regions (Volkow et al., 1995, 1997). Until recently, it was not clear precisely how these medications affected brain function, and particularly what their sites and neurochemical modes of action might be. It now appears as if the major therapeutic effects of the drugs are achieved through alterations in frontal–striatal activity (Volkow et al., 1997), via their impact on at least three or more neurotransmitters important to the functioning of this region and related to response inhibition: dopamine, norepinephrine, epinephrine, and perhaps also serotonin (Pliszka et al., 1996). The direct rationale, then, for employing the stimu-

lant medications with ADHD children may be that they directly, if only temporarily, improve the deficiencies in these neural systems related to behavioral inhibition and self-regulation.

Stimulant Medication

Since Bradley (1937) first (accidentally) discovered their successful use with behavior problem children, the stimulants have received an enormous amount of research—far more than any known treatment for any childhood psychiatric disorder. The results overwhelmingly indicate that these medications are quite effective for the management of ADHD symptoms in most children older than 5 years (Barkley, 1977b; Barkley et al., in press-b; Greenhill & Osmon, 1991; Swanson, McBurnett, Christian, & Wigal, 1995). For children between 4 and 5 years of age, the response rate is probably much less, and for those under 3 years of age, the drugs are not recommended for use. The effectiveness of these medications has led to their widespread use with ADHD children, with approximately 2.8% of the school-age population being treated with stimulants for possible ADHD symptoms (Safer, Zito, & Fine, 1996). With the recognition that these medications may be just as useful for ADHD adolescents and adults (Coons, Klorman, & Borgstedt, 1987a, 1987b; Mattes, Boswell, & Oliver, 1984; Spencer et al., 1995; Wender, Reimherr, Wood, & Ward, 1985), their frequency of prescription is only likely to increase, particularly within these older age groups.

The most commonly prescribed stimulants are methylphenidate (Ritalin), d-amphetamine (Dexedrine), and pemoline (Cylert). Adderall is a recently approved stimulant compound for use in the management of ADHD. It is a combination of different forms of amphetamine that is reported by the manufacturer to be significantly effective in the treatment of symptoms of ADHD. Little published research on the medication is available at this time, but given the similarity of the medication to the previously studied compounds of d-amphetamine and l-amphetamine, there is little reason to believe that this new combination of amphetamines would not be just as efficacious.

Methylphenidate and d-amphetamine are the most commonly prescribed medications for ADHD. They are rapidly acting stimulants, producing effects on behavior within 30 to 45 minutes after oral ingestion of their standard preparations, and peaking in their behavioral effects within 2 to 4 hours (Barkley et al., in press).

Their utility in managing behavior quickly dissipates within 3 to 7 hours, although minuscule amounts of the medication may remain in the blood for up to 24 hours (Cantwell & Carlson, 1978; Dulcan, 1990; Greenhill & Osmon, 1991). Because of their short half-life, they are often prescribed in twice- or thrice-daily doses. Although they were once used predominantly for school days, there is an increasing clinical trend toward usage throughout the week as well as during school vacations, particularly for children with more severe ADHD and/or conduct problems. This is the result of more recent discoveries that the growth of ADHD children on stimulants is not as seriously affected as was once believed (Spencer et al., 1996), and so the rationale for universal drug holidays is no longer justifiable. Both methylphenidate and d-amphetamine come in slow-release preparations that may reduce the number of daily doses children require for management of their ADHD (see Barkley et al., in press; Dulcan, 1990). Pemoline is also a slow-release form of stimulant medication that has been modestly popular in the management of ADHD children. But the risks that it poses for problems with liver functioning in children, and a recent report of a series of deaths due to such dysfunctioning, have led the manufacturer to issue a warning to physicians that this drug no longer be considered a first-line agent in the management of ADHD (personal communication with Abbott Laboratories, December 1996).

The behavioral improvements produced by methylphenidate and d-amphetamine are in sustained attention, impulse control, and reduction of task-irrelevant activity, especially in settings demanding restraint of behavior (Barkley, 1977b; Barkley et al., in press; Rapport & Kelly, 1993; Swanson, McBurnett, et al., 1995; Taylor, 1986). Generally noisy and disruptive behavior also diminishes with medication. ADHD children may become more compliant with parental and teacher commands, are better able to sustain such compliance, and often increase their cooperative behavior toward others with whom they may have to accomplish a task as a consequence of stimulant treatment (Barkley et al., 1984; Cunningham, Siegel, & Offord, 1985; Whalen et al., 1980; see also Danforth et al., 1991, for a review). Recent research suggests that ADHD children are also able to perceive the medication as beneficial to the reduction of ADHD symptoms and even describe improvements in their self-esteem (DuPaul, Anastopoulos, Kwasnik, Barkley, & McMurray, 1996), though they may

report somewhat more side effects than do their parents and teachers.

Improvements in other domains of behavior in children with ADHD have also been demonstrated. The effects of stimulants on aggressive behavior were once thought to be less clear-cut (Taylor, 1986), but most recent studies tend to find reductions in this behavior in ADHD children demonstrating abnormally high levels of pretreatment aggressiveness (Barkley, McMurray, Edelbrock, & Robbins, 1989; Murphy, Pelham, & Lang, 1992). The quality of children's handwriting may also improve with medication (Lerer, Lerer, & Artner, 1977). Academic productivity (i.e., the number of problems completed) and accuracy of work completion also increase, in some cases dramatically, as a function of medication (Pelham, Bender, Caddell, Booth, & Moorer, 1985; Rapport, DuPaul, Stoner, & Jones, 1986; Rapport & Kelly, 1993). However, the effects of medication are idiosyncratic (see Rapport, DuPaul, et al., 1986), with some children showing maximal improvement at lower doses, while others are most improved at higher doses of medication. Much controversy remains over whether these immediate improvements in academic performance translate into greater gains in academic achievement (the level of difficulty of academic material mastered by a child) over longer-term use of the medications (Barkley & Cunningham, 1978; Schachar & Tannock, 1993). Nevertheless, the stimulants appear to remain useful in the management of ADHD over extended periods of time (Schachar & Tannock, 1993; Zeiner, 1995). It seems best to conclude that the stimulants produce significant improvement in academic accuracy and productivity, but not in the long-term achievement of ADHD children.

The most frequently occurring side effects of the stimulants are mild insomnia and appetite reduction, particular at the noon meal (Barkley, 1977b; Barkley, McMurray, Edelbrock, & Robbins, 1990). Temporary growth suppression may accompany stimulant treatment, but is not generally severe or especially common (Spencer et al., 1996); it can be managed by insuring that adequate caloric and nutritional intake is maintained through shifting the distribution of food intake to other times of the day, when the child is more amenable to eating (Taylor, 1986). Some children become irritable and prone to crying late in the afternoon, when their medication may be wearing off. This may be accompanied by an increase in hyperactivity. A small percentage of ADHD children may complain of stomachaches and headaches when treated with stimulants, but these tend to dissipate within a few weeks of beginning medication or can be managed by reducing the dose. In approximately 1% to 2% of ADHD children treated with stimulants, motor or vocal tics may occur (Barkley et al., in press). In children who already exhibit tics, these can be mildly exacerbated by stimulant treatment in some cases, but may even be improved in others (Gadow, Sverd, Sprafkin, Nolan, & Ezor, 1995). It now appears to be relatively safe to use stimulant medications with children with ADHD and comorbid tic disorders, but to be prepared to reduce the dose or discontinue medication should the children experience a drug-related exacerbation of their tic symptoms.

It has been difficult to establish any reliable predictors of response to stimulant medication in ADHD children. Those characteristics having the most consistent relationship to response have been pretreatment levels of poor sustained attention and hyperactivity (Barkley, 1976; Buitelaar, van der Gaag, Swaab-Barneveld, & Kuiper, 1995; Taylor, 1983). The more deviant children are before treatment on such factors, the better their response to medication is likely to be. Predictors of adverse responding have not been as well studied. What research exists suggests that higher pretreatment levels of anxiety are associated with poorer responding to stimulants (Buitelaar et al., 1995; DuPaul, Barkley, & McMurray, 1994; Taylor, 1983).

There is little doubt now that the stimulant medications are the best-studied and most effective treatment for the symptomatic management of ADHD and its secondary consequences. As a result, for many children with moderate to severe levels of ADHD, stimulants may be the first treatments employed in their clinical management. Other treatments may often be required as adjuncts, given that medication typically does not address all of the presenting problems shown by these children. And current formulations of stimulant medications do not provide continuous treatment across the entire day, leaving periods of time when only psychosocial management methods can be used. The following issues should be considered in the decision to employ medication for the management of ADHD: (1) the age of the child; (2) duration and severity of symptoms; (3) the risk of injury to the child (through either accident or abuse) posed by the present severity of symptoms; (4) the success of prior treatments; (5) relatively normal levels of anxiety; (6) the absence of stimulant abuse by the child/adolescent or caregivers; and (7) the likelihood that the parents will employ the medication responsibly, in compliance with physician recommendations.

Several suggested paradigms for evaluating stimulant drug response in individual cases have been reported (Barkley et al., 1988; Pelham, 1987; Rapport, DuPaul, et al., 1986). Table 2.2 illustrates the sequence of events involved in a medication trial at the University of Massachusetts Medical Center; it is acknowledged that this constitutes more of an ideal approach to medication management than that likely to be occurring in most pediatric practices. The approach assumes that the child has received a satisfactory diagnostic workup, which has resulted in the child's being diagnosed with ADHD of a sufficient severity to warrant participation in such a medical trial. The trial includes the traditional initial medical checkup to insure that the child has no preexisting conditions that might contraindicate or complicate the medication trial (such as cardiac problems, unusually high levels of anxiety, or a prior history of stimulant misuse, among others). This is followed by the child's receiving a baseline evaluation on the measures to be collected across the weeks of the trial. The child's participation is then scheduled for a 4-week drug–placebo trial, during which the child is tested on three different doses of medication (typically methylphenidate at 5, 10, and 15 mg, given morning and noon) and a placebo (lactose powder placed in gelatin capsules). Each drug condition lasts for 7–10 days before the child progresses to the next drug condition. The order of the drug conditions is random, except that the 10- and 15-mg conditions are paired such that the 10-mg condition always precedes the 15-mg condition. This is done to reduce the possibility of unnecessary side effects being provoked by beginning the trial at an initially excessive dose. Arrangements are made to have the noon dose of medication given at school on school days. The parents, teachers, child, and clinical assistant conducting the weekly assessment of the child are all kept blind to the order of medication doses and placebo until the end of the trial.

At the end of each week, the child is given a continuous-performance test (CPT) of attention and impulse control at the clinic and parents and teachers complete rating scales about the child's behavior during that week. One rating scale assesses the symptoms of ADHD as well as ODD (see Barkley, 1997a), while another is used to obtain information about side effects the child may have experienced that week (see Barkley, 1990, in press-b). A third rating scale completed only by the teacher assesses work productivity and accuracy (the Academic Performance Rating Scale; see Barkley, 1990). Teacher comments are also collected by telephone each week, as are parent comments during the weekly clinic visit. Also during each weekly clinic visit, the child is given a set of math problems of appropriate grade level to perform while seated alone in a clinic playroom. Observations are taken of the child from behind a one-way mirror, and the observations are coded on the Restricted Academic Situation coding sheet (see Barkley, 1990) for behaviors related to ADHD (e.g., off task, fidgets, plays with objects, out of seat, etc.). In addition, the amount of work attempted and the accuracy of that work are scored.

At the end of the 4-week trial, the results are tabulated, and a recommendation is made concerning possible continuation of the medication (and, if so, which dose seems most effective). Children not found to be responsive to this stimulant may be tried on another, recommended for a trial of an antidepressant, or referred back to the treating physician with recommendations to pursue appropriate psychosocial and educational management strategies.

Antidepressant Medication

Clinicians have increasingly turned to the use of the tricyclic antidepressants, such as imipramine and desipramine, for the management of ADHD symptoms. In part this has been due to the occasional negative (and often underserving) publicity that the stimulants, especially methylphenidate, have received in the popular media. But the rise in antidepressant use may also have resulted from cases where stimulants have been contraindicated or have not been especially effective, or where significant comorbid mood disturbance may exist (Ryan, 1990). Less is known about the pharmacokinetics and behavioral effects of the antidepressants in children with ADHD than is known about the stimulants. However, research on these compounds, particularly desipramine, has increased in the last decade and generally supports their efficacy in the management of ADHD (Wilens, Biederman, Baldessarini, et al., 1996). Often given twice daily (morning and evening), these medications are longer-acting than the stimulants: as a result, it takes longer to evaluate the therapeutic value of any given dose (Viesselman, Yaylayan, Weller, & Weller, 1993). Some research suggests that low doses of the tricyclics may mimic stimulants in producing increased vigilance and sustained attention and decreased impulsivity. As a result, disruptive

and aggressive behavior may also be reduced. Elevation in mood may also occur, particularly in those children in whom significant pretreatment levels of depression and anxiety exist (Pliszka, 1987). Rapoport and Mikkelsen (1978) and Ryan (1990) reported that treatment effects may diminish over time, however; thus the tricyclics, unlike the stimulants, cannot be used as long-term therapy for ADHD.

The most common side effects of the tricyclics are drowsiness during the first few days of treatment, dry mouth, constipation, and flushing. Less likely yet more important are the cardiotoxic effects, such as possible tachycardia or arrhythmia, and even coma or death in cases of overdose (Viesselman et al., 1993). Some children may develop sluggish reactions in focusing of the optic lens, which may mimic nearsightedness. These reactions are not permanent, dissipating when treatment is withdrawn. Skin rash is occasionally reported and usually warrants ceasing drug treatment.

In general, it seems that the tricyclic antidepressants may be useful in the short-term treatment of ADHD children when the stimulants cannot be used, or when significant mood disturbances accompany the ADHD symptoms (Pliszka, 1987; Ryan, 1990). However, the cardiac functioning of children must be properly evaluated before treatment and then must be periodically monitored throughout the course of treatment, given the apparent risks of the tricyclic antidepressants for impairing cardiac functioning (see Wilens, Biederman, Baldessarini, et al., 1996, for a review and guidelines for monitoring children on tricyclic antidepressants).

Antihypertensive Medication

In the late 1980s, a small number of research papers appeared suggesting that the antihypertensive drug clonidine (Catapres) may be beneficial in the management of ADHD symptoms, particularly in the reduction of hyperactivity and overarousal (Hunt, Caper, & O'Connell, 1990). The drug is believed to act as an alpha-2-adrenergic agonist that ultimately inhibits the release of norepinephrine, increases dopamine turnover, and reduces blood serotonin levels (Werry & Aman, 1993). Changes in behavior may be the result of the general sedation produced by the medication. A large-scale study in The Netherlands also reported significant improvements in behavior in hyperkinetic children placed on this medication (Gunning, 1992). The limited research to date suggests that clonidine is much less effective than the stimulants at improving inattention and school productivity, but may be equally efficacious in the reduction of hyperactivity and moodiness. The drug may also be useful in managing the sleep disturbances that some ADHD children may experience (Prince, Wilens, Biederman, Spencer, & Wozniak, 1996).

The recent trend in clinical practice of combining clonidine with methylphenidate was abruptly questioned on July 13, 1995, when several cases of sudden death in children using this combination were reported on National Public Radio. Although investigation of these cases did not provide convincing evidence that this drug combination resulted in these fatalities (Fenichel, 1995; Popper, 1995), several prominent investigators have raised serious questions about this drug combination, given what is known about the pharmacology of both and the utter lack of any research on the efficacy and safety of the combination (Swanson, Flockhart, et al., 1995). Additional cases involving clinically significant side effects apparently resulting from this combination were recently reported (Cantwell, Swanson, & Connor, 1997). Werry and Aman (1993) have recommended that clonidine be employed in the treatment of ADHD only when stimulants have proven ineffective or are contraindicated; this seems to be sound advice, in view of the limited scope of research to date on this medication for management of ADHD. Its combination with the stimulants should be undertaken only in rare cases and with the utmost care and monitoring until more research on this drug combination becomes available.

Behavior Management

The initial rationale for the use of behavior modification techniques with ADHD children was often founded on their success in the management of behavior problems among mentally retarded children, and on the purported limitations and potential side effects of stimulant drug therapy (Mash & Dalby, 1978; Pelham & Sams, 1992), rather than on behavior modification's own merits for the management of ADHD. By themselves, such arguments provide a rather nonspecific rationale for undertaking such treatment. Moreover, at least one of these reasons can now be seen to have been based on outdated information concerning the side effects of stimulants, which are clearly more benign than were previously thought to be the case (Barkley et al., 1989). The behavioral improvements resulting from the use of simulant medications are typically as great as or greater than those resulting from behavior modification; moreover, stimulant use frequently results in greater improvements in academic productivity (Carlson, Pelham, Milich, & Dixon, 1992; Horn et al., 1991; Pelham et al., 1988). Given this state of affairs, such medications may be viewed by some as the preferred first-line treatment for ADHD in place of behavior modification, or at least seen as necessary in combination with behavior modification methods to achieve maximal treatment effects (Carlson et al., 1992; Horn et al., 1991; Pelham et al., 1988). A more convincing justification for using behavior modification techniques in treating ADHD is the argument that since referral of children for ADHD is based in part on the social distress they have created for their caregivers, an intervention that attempts to change the interaction between children and their caregivers should be quite useful (Werry & Sprague, 1970).

A variation on this theme once provided an even more direct rationale for using behavioral interventions with ADHD children. Willis and Lovaas (1977) proposed that ADHD reflects poor stimulus control of behavior by parental commands, resulting from the inconsistent or inadequate use of child management methods by the parents: thus, training parents in more consistent and effective child management should reduce or even eliminate the ADHD symptoms. However, such a theory of ADHD can now be dismissed on the grounds that the inconsistent, negative, or punitive management techniques of some parents of ADHD children have been shown to be more often associated with the ODD frequently seen in conjunction with ADHD than with the ADHD itself (Barkley, Anastopoulos, et al., 1992; Fletcher et al., 1996; Johnston, 1996). Moreover, research suggests that the negative and controlling behavior of parents toward their ADHD children is more a reaction to than a cause of their children's inappropriate behavior (Barkley, 1985; Danforth et al., 1991). Also, some parents of ADHD children do not show such poor management skills. Finally, parent training does not normalize the ADHD symptoms of children, nor do its effects generalize to no-treatment settings such as school, where ADHD symptoms may be equally problematic (see below). Thus, the evidence seems to be against the concept of "bad parenting" as a primary etiology of ADHD (see "Etiologies," above), and so this rationale cannot be considered a reasonable justification for undertaking parent training with ADHD children.

TABLE 2.2.   **Procedures Employed in a Stimulant Medication Trial for ADHD Children**

1. Initial diagnostic evaluation documenting presence and severity of ADHD, and justifying initiation of stimulant medication trial is conducted.
2. Brief medical evaluation and physical exam are performed to rule out conditions that may contra-indicate the use of stimulant medication or dictate closer monitoring during trial (e.g., tic disorders, high levels of anxiety, cardiac abnormalities, etc.). Parent signs informed consent for the drug trial at this time. Prescriptions are prepared by pharmacy for three different dose levels of stimulant medication (typically methylphenidate given at doses of 5, 10, and 15 mg, morning and noon) and a placebo (lactose powder in gelatin capsules); 7- to 10-day supply of each prepared. Each drug condition lasts 1 week, and order of drug conditions is quasi-random (highest dose is always preceded by moderate dose).
3. Baseline evaluation is conducted in the clinic, using the measures to be repeated weekly across the trial:
   a. Parent and teacher rating scales of ADHD and ODD symptoms (teacher scales are collected by mail). (See Barkley, 1997a.)
   b. Parent and teacher rating scales of stimulant medication side effects. (See Barkley, 1990.)
   c. Teacher rating scale of academic performance. (See Barkley, 1990.)
   d. Continuous-performance test (CPT—Conners Continuous Performance Test, Gordon Diagnostic System, or Test of Variables of Attention).
   e. Observation of behavior during clinic performance of academic work. (See Barkley, 1990.)
4. Drug trial is initiated, with evaluation in #3 above repeated at the end of each week.
5. At end of trial, results are tabulated and reviewed by psychologist and physician. Greater emphasis is placed on parent and teacher reports than on measures collected in the clinic (CPT and observations).
6. Parents are contacted by telephone by physician for review of results and final disposition.
7. Report is prepared for referring physician and parents concerning results of trial.

But with the recent trend toward viewing ADHD as a potential problem in response inhibition and self-regulation in children, and the secondary consequences this may create for their poor self-motivation to persist at assigned tasks (Barkley, 1997d), a persuasive, theoretically based rationale for employing behavioral interventions with ADHD may now exist. If ADHD is in fact a developmental delay in the self-regulation of behavior through internal means of representing information and motivating goal-directed behavior, then interventions that directly alter the nature of the stimuli controlling behavior, as well as the pattern, timing, or salience of such consequences, by socially arranged means should be useful—at least for symptomatic reduction in some settings and tasks. Such procedures for the manipulation of antecedent and consequent events are precisely those provided by the behavior therapies. A logical extension of this argument holds, however, that such socially arranged means of addressing this neurologically based dysregulation will not alter the underlying neurophysiological basis for it. These techniques must be employed across situations over extended time intervals (months to years), much as prosthetic devices (e.g., hearing aids, mechanical limbs, etc.) are employed to compensate for physically handicapping conditions. Premature removal of the socially arranged motivational programs can be predicted to result in an eventual return to pretreatment

levels of the behavioral symptoms. Also, use of the behavioral techniques in only one environment is unlikely to affect rates of ADHD symptoms in other, untreated settings unless generalization has been intentionally programmed to occur across such settings. The research reviewed below for the various behavioral techniques seems to support this interpretation.

Direct Application of Behavior Therapy Methods in the Laboratory

A number of early studies evaluated the effects of reinforcement and punishment, usually response cost, on the behavior and cognitive performance of ADHD children. These studies usually indicated that the performance of ADHD children on tasks measuring vigilance or impulse control can be immediately and significantly improved by the use of contingent consequences (Firestone & Douglas, 1975, 1977; Patterson, 1965; Worland, 1976; Worland, North-Jones, & Stern, 1973). In some cases, the behavior of ADHD children approximated that of normal control children. However, none of these studies examined the degree to which such changes generalized to the natural environments of the children, calling into question the clinical efficacy of such an approach. Given the findings of highly limited generalization of treatment effects for the classroom interventions described below, it is unlikely that behavioral techniques implemented only in the clinic or laboratory will carry over into the home or school settings of these children with formal programming for such generalization.

Another problem with past laboratory research has been its relatively exclusive focus on response consequences as a means of altering ADHD symptoms, as opposed to altering the stimuli that may control or set the occasion for ADHD symptoms. To their credit, some investigators have examined stimulus control procedures. Zentall (1985), in her thorough review of the literature up to that time on situational factors related to ADHD symptoms, concluded that the degree of structure (e.g., task vs. free play), extent of shared attention (e.g., one-to-one interaction vs. group settings), and presence or absence of an adult were not reliably associated with significant differences in the levels of ADHD symptoms. Instead, she argued that the difficulty of the task assigned to ADHD children, and especially the degree of environmental stimulation, greatly determined the level of hyperactivity and inattention displayed by these children. In a series of studies, Zentall and her colleagues (see Zentall, 1985) showed that increasing relevant intratask stimulation and novelty, as well as reducing task complexity, resulted in declines in ADHD symptoms. In contrast, providing extratask stimulation, especially during difficult or complex tasks, increased ADHD symptoms and proved more disruptive to the performance of these children on academic tasks. Perhaps related to this is the observation of Douglas (1983) that repeating task instructions frequently throughout a task enhanced the performance of ADHD children to within normal limits in laboratory studies. Hence, a possible behavioral treatment of ADHD children besides altering response consequences may be to alter the stimulus properties of settings and especially tasks assigned to ADHD children. Making tasks more novel and stimulating through the use of added color, motor participation by the child, frequent shifts in the nature of the task, increased rate of presentation of the material, frequent repetition of the task instructions, and greater enthusiasm and theatrics by the instructor during teaching of the task may make ADHD children more attentive, less active, and more productive in such tasks. Moreover, reducing the length of the task by creating smaller task units and providing frequent breaks from the task could also achieve improved task performance.

Another means of altering stimulus control parameters to enhance the task performance of ADHD children may be to increase the use of externally and concretely represented time limits and rules with particular tasks. Such time limits and rules may be internally or cognitively represented in normal children and help serve stimulus control functions in maintaining on-task behaviors. Yet such internal cues may be weak or inconsistently effective in mediating the behavior of ADHD children, as discussed in the theoretical model presented earlier. For instance, when normal children are assigned school tasks to complete and are orally given a time limit in which to do so, their perceptions of elapsed time and cognitive iteration of rules for on-task behavior (e.g., "Stay on task, don't space out, don't bug others, etc.") may function to maintain task performance for adequate periods of time. The behavior of ADHD children seems to be less controlled by such internal perceptions of time and self-statements or at least inconsistently controlled by them (see Barkley, 1997d). These children could be assisted by the use of portable timers placed on children's desks and set to reflect the elapsed time available for task performance, as well as by small "reminder" cards placed on their desks during individual desk work. Such "reminder" cards might list in bold print four or more rules for on-task behavior, similar to the internal self-statements described above. I have employed a similar tactic of enhancing stimulus control by allowing ADHD children to clip small portable tape players to their belts with earphones attached, to permit them to listen to "nag" tapes while they are performing individual desk assignments in class. These tapes are recorded by the parents and consist of periodic reminders to "stay on task, finish your work, and don't daydream," as well as reminders of how pleased the parents will be if the children complete that assignment on time. Clinical experience with these techniques, however, suggests that they must eventually be paired with a program of response consequences in order for adequate stimulus control to be maintained. Despite clinical anecdotes supporting the value of these methods, much research needs to be done to test the efficacy of these stimulus control programs more rigorously.

Paniagua (1987) has also evaluated the contribution of stimulus control to the management of ADHD children. Using a method known as "correspondence training," he has attempted to establish greater control over ADHD symptoms through commands and rules previously stated publicly by the children. "Correspondence" refers to the degree of concordance between public statements by children as to what they will do and the actual behavior they subsequently display in that setting—in essence, the degree of agreement between "saying" and "doing." In this paradigm, ADHD children are requested to state publicly how they will behave in an immediately subsequent situation. Their behavior in that situation is then observed, after which they are reinforced or punished for the degree of correspondence. Results have suggested that under such conditions, ADHD children significantly reduce their levels of inattention and overactivity during task performance, as well as their levels of aggressive behavior during peer interactions. These preliminary findings with a small sample (*n* = 3) of 7- to 10-year-old ADHD children were quite promising, suggesting that self-instruction followed by reinforcement for the degree of rule–behavior correspondence may be yet another way of improving the performance of ADHD children through stimulus manipulations. However, work by Hayes et al. (1985) has suggested that such self-statements must be publicly made in order to be effective, because they serve as a form of public goal setting for which social consequences can be made contingent. Future research needs to show that the children's own statements are serving as the controlling stimuli in such paradigms, rather than the presence of the examiner during the task.

Training Parents in Child Behavior Management Methods

Despite the plethora of research on parent training in child behavior modification (Dangel & Polster, 1984), only a small amount have examined the efficacy of this approach with children specifically selected for hyperactive or ADHD symptoms. What limited research exists can be interpreted with cautious optimism as supporting the use of behavioral parent training with ADHD children (Anastopoulos et al., 1992; Bidder, Gray, & Newcombe, 1978; Dubey, O'Leary, & Kaufman, 1983; Firestone, Kelly, Goodman, & Davey, 1981; Horn, Iolongo, Popovich, & Peradotto, 1987; O'Leary, Pelham, Rosenbaum, & Price, 1976; Pollard, Ward, & Barkley, 1984; Strayhorn & Weidman, 1989, 1991). One of the few studies to conduct a follow-up reevaluation 1 year after treatment, however, found that the families receiving parent training were no longer different from the control group, although the children's school behavior was rated by teachers as significantly better

than that of children in the control group (Strayhorn & Weidman, 1991).

The treatment techniques used to date have primarily consisted of training parents in general contingency management tactics, such as contingent application of reinforcement or punishment following appropriate or inappropriate behaviors. Reinforcement procedures have typically relied on praise or tokens, while punishment methods have usually been loss of tokens or time out from reinforcement. Why these particular methods were chosen, or what specific target behaviors they were used with, have often gone unreported. At least one study (Bidder et al., 1978) employed a shaping procedure to modify hyperactivity directly. ADHD children were required to sit for progressively longer periods of time while working on assigned tasks with their mothers, for which they were presumably reinforced.

I (Barkley, 1997a) have developed a parent training program for ADHD children, the methods of which have been borrowed from research indicating their efficacy in managing defiant and oppositional children. The rationale for the program is twofold. First, it is hypothesized that ADHD children may have a specific deficit in rule-governed behavior, or the stimulus control of behavior by commands, rules, and self-directed speech (Barkley, 1989a, 1990, 1997d). Unlike a similar theory by Willis and Lovaas (1977), this one does not stipulate that the problem has arisen from poor child management by parents, but instead proposes a neurophysiological deficiency underlying the problem with rules. Consequently, parents are going to need to use more explicit, systematic, externalized, and compelling methods of presenting rules and instructions to ADHD children, and of providing consequences for their compliance with them, than are likely to be needed with normal children. Second, there exists a considerable overlap of ODD with ADHD in clinic-referred ADHD children, and such children are recognized to have poorer adolescent and young adult outcomes (Hinshaw, 1987; Paternite & Loney, 1980; Weiss & Hechtman, 1993). Hence, treatment must be provided for the oppositional defiant behaviors associated with ADHD in such cases. The most useful vehicle for doing so seems to be parent training in behavioral techniques applied contingently for compliance or noncompliance (Barkley, 1997a).

The program consists of 10 sessions plus a review/booster session, with 1- to 2-hour weekly training sessions provided either to individual families or in groups. Each step is described in detail elsewhere (Barkley, 1997a), but is briefly presented below:

1. *Review of information on ADHD.* In the first session, the therapist provides a succinct overview of the nature, developmental course, prognosis, and etiologies of ADHD. Providing the parents with additional reading materials, such as a book for parents (Barkley, 1995), can be a useful addition to this session. Professional videotapes that present such an overview are also available (Barkley, 1992a, 1992b), and these can be loaned to parents for review at home and sharing with relatives or teachers, as needed. Such a session is essential in parent training to dispel a number of misconceptions parents often have about ADHD in children. A recent study suggests that just this provision of information can result not only in improved parental knowledge about ADHD, but also in improved parental perceptions of the degree of deviance of their children's behavioral difficulties (Andrews, Swank, Foorman, & Fletcher, 1995).

2. *The causes of oppositional defiant behavior.* Next, parents are provided with an in-depth discussion of those factors identified in past research as contributing to the development of defiant behavior in children (for reviews, see Barkley, 1997a; Loeber, 1991; Patterson, 1982; Patterson, Dishion, & Reid, 1992). Essentially, four major contributors are discussed: (a) child characteristics, such as health, developmental disabilities, and temperament; (b) parent characteristics similar to those described for the child; (c) situational consequences for oppositional and coercive behavior; and (d) stressful family events. Parents are taught that where problems exist in (a), (b), and (d), they increase the probability of children's displaying bouts of coercive, defiant behavior. However, the consequences for such defiance, (c), seem to determine whether that behavior will be maintained or even increased in subsequent situations where commands and rules are given. Such behavior appears to function primarily as escape/avoidance learning, in which oppositional behavior results in a child's escaping from aversive parent interactions and task demands, thus negatively reinforcing the child's coercion. As in the first session, this content is covered so as to correct parents' potential misconceptions about defiance (e.g., it is primarily attention-getting in nature). This session can be augmented by the use of two professional videotapes on the nature of

oppositional defiant behavior and its management (Barkley, 1997e, 1997f).

3. *Developing and enhancing parental attention.* Patterson (1965, 1982) has suggested that the value of verbal praise and social reinforcement for oppositional or hyperactive children is greatly reduced, making it weak as a reinforcer for compliance. In this session, parents are trained in more effective ways of attending to child behavior so as to enhance the value of their attention to their children. The technique consists of verbal narration and occasional positive statements to a child, with attention being strategically deployed only when appropriate behaviors are displayed by the child. Parents are taught to ignore inappropriate behaviors, but to greatly increase their attention to ongoing prosocial and compliant child behaviors.

4. *Attending to child compliance and independent play.* This session extends the techniques developed in Session 3 to instances when parents issue direct commands to children. Parents are trained in methods of giving effective commands, such as reducing question-like commands (e.g., "Why don't you pick up your toys now?"), increasing imperatives, eliminating setting activities that compete with task performance (e.g., television), reducing task complexity, and so on. They are then encouraged to begin using a more effective commanding style and to pay immediate positive attention when their children initiate compliance. As part of this assignment, parents are asked to increase the frequency with which they give brief commands to their children this week and to reinforce each command obeyed. Research suggests that these brief commands are more likely to be obeyed, thereby providing excellent training opportunities for attending to compliance. In this session, parents are also trained to provide more positive attention frequently and systematically when their children are engaged in nondisruptive activities while the parents must be occupied with some other work or activity. Essentially, the method taught here amounts to a shaping procedure, in which parents provide frequent praise and attention for progressively longer periods of child nondisruptive activities.

5. *Establishing a home token economy.* As noted above in discussing the theoretical model of ADHD, children with this disorder may require more frequent, immediate, and salient consequences for appropriate behavior and compliance in order to maintain it. If this is correct, then instituting a home token economy is critical

to addressing these difficulties with intrinsically generated and represented motivation by bringing more salient external consequences, more immediately, and more frequently to bear on child compliance than is typically the case. The parent handout for this step of the program is shown in Table 2.3, so as to illustrate the sort of advice that must be conveyed to parents in creating such a home motivational program.

In establishing this program, the parents list most of the children's home responsibilities and privileges and then assign values of points or chips to each. The parents are encouraged to have at least 12 to 15 reinforcers on the menu so as to maintain the motivating properties of the program. Generally, plastic chips are used with children aged 8 or younger, as they seem to value the tangible features of the tokens. For those 9 years old or older, points recorded in a notebook seem sufficient.

During the first week of this program, parents are not to fine children or remove points for misconduct. The program is for rewarding good behavior only. Parents are also asked to be liberal in awarding chips to children for even minor instances of appropriate conduct. However, chips are given only for obeying first requests. If a command must be repeated, it must still be obeyed, but the opportunity to earn chips has been forfeited. Parents are also encouraged to give bonus chips for good attitude or emotional regulation in their children. For instance, if a command is obeyed quickly, without complaint, and with a positive attitude, parents may give a child additional chips beyond those typically given for that job. When this is done, parents are to expressly note that the awarding of the additional chips is for a positive attitude. Families are encouraged to establish and maintain such programs for at least 6 to 8 weeks, to allow for the newly developed interaction patterns spawned by such programs to become habit patterns in dealing with child compliance.

6. *Implementing time out for noncompliance.* Parents are now trained to use response cost (removal of points or chips) contingent on noncompliance. In addition, they are trained in an effective technique for time out from reinforcement, to be used with two serious forms of defiance that may continue to be problematic despite the use of the home token economy. These two misbehaviors are selected in consultation with the parents and typically involve a type of command or household rule that the child continues to defy despite parental use of previous treatment strategies. Time out is limited to these two forms of misconduct so as to keep it from being used excessively during the next week.

The time-out procedure taught to parents often differs from that commonly used by them. First, the time out is to be implemented shortly after noncompliance by a child begins. Parents often wait until they are very upset with a child before instituting punishment, often repeating their commands frequently to the child in the interim. In this program, parents issue a command, wait 5 seconds, issue a warning, wait another 5 seconds, and then take the child to time out immediately should compliance not have begun to these commands or warnings. Second, children are not given control over the time-out interval, as they often are in many households. For instance, parents often place children in time out and then say that the children can leave time out when they are quiet, when they are ready to do as the parents asked, or when a timer signals the end of the interval. In each of these cases, determination as to when the time-out interval ends is no longer under the parents' control. This program teaches parents simply to tell a child not to leave the time-out chair until given permission to do so. Three conditions must be met by the child before time out ends, and these are in a hierarchy: (a) The child must serve a minimum sentence in time out, usually 1 to 2 minutes for each year of his or her age; (b) the child must then become quiet for a brief period of time, so as not to have disruption associated with the parents' approaching the time-out chair and talking to the child; and (c) the child must then agree to obey the command. Failure of the child to remain in time out until all three conditions are met is dealt with by additional punishment. The consequence is tailored to meet parental wishes, but may consist of a fine within the home token system, extension of the time-out interval by an additional 5 or 10 minutes, or placement of the child in his or her bedroom. In the latter case, toys or other entertaining activities are previously removed from the bedroom, and the door to the room may be closed and locked to preclude further escape from the punishment.

7. *Extending time out to additional noncompliant behaviors.* In this session, no new material is taught to parents. Instead, any problems with previously implementing time out are reviewed and corrected. Parents may then extend their use of time out to one or two additional noncom-

pliant behaviors with which a child may still have trouble.

8. *Managing noncompliance in public places.* Parents are now taught to extrapolate their home management methods to troublesome public places, such as stores, church, and restaurants. Using a "think aloud–think ahead" paradigm, parents are taught to stop just before entering a public place, review two or three rules with the child that the child may previously have defied, explain to the child what reinforcers are available for obedience in the place, then explain what punishment may occur for disobedience, and finally assign the child an activity to perform during the outing. Parents then enter the public place and immediately begin attending to and reinforcing ongoing child compliance with the previously stated rules. Time out or response cost is used immediately for disobedience.

Time out in a public place may require slight modification from its use at home. For instance, parents may be taught to stand a child against the farthest wall from the central aisle of a store to serve as the time-out location. If this is inconvenient, then taking the child to a restroom or having him or her face the side of a display cabinet may be adequate substitutes. If these are unavailable, then taking the child outside the building to face the front wall or returning to the car can be used for time out. When none of these locations seem appropriate, parents can be trained to use a delayed-punishment contingency. In this case, the parent carries a small spiral notebook to the public place and, before entering the building, indicates that rule violations will be recorded in the book and the child will serve time out for them upon return home from this trip. I encourage parents to keep a picture of the child sitting in time out at home with this notebook and to show it to the child before entering the public building. This serves as a reminder to the child of what may be in store should a rule be violated. Whenever time out is used in a public place, it need not be for as long an interval as at home. I have found that half of the usual time out interval may be sufficient for public misbehavior, given the richly reinforcing activities in public places from which the child has just been removed.

9. *Improving child school behavior from home: The daily school behavior report card.* This session is a recent addition (Barkley, 1997a) to the original parent training program and is designed to help parents assist their children's teachers with the management of classroom behavior problems. The session focuses on

training parents in the use of a home-based reward program, in which children are evaluated on a daily school behavior report card by their teachers, and this card serves as the means by which consequences later in the day will be dispensed at home for classroom conduct. The card can be designed to address class behavior, recess or free-time behavior, or more specific behavioral targets for any given child. The consequences provided at home typically consist of the rewarding or removal of tokens or points within the home token system as a function of the ratings given by teachers on this daily behavioral report card.

10. *Managing future misconduct.* By now, parents should have acquired an effective repertoire of child management techniques. The goal of this session is to get parents to think about how these may be implemented in the future if some other forms of noncompliance develop. The therapist challenges the parents with misbehaviors they have not seen yet and asks them to explain how they might use their recently acquired skills to manage these problems.

11. *One-month review/booster session.* In what is typically the final session, the concepts taught in earlier sessions are briefly reviewed, problems that have arisen in the last month are discussed, and plans are made for their correction. Other sessions may be needed to deal with additional issues that persist, but for most families, the previous 10 sessions appear adequate for improving rates of compliant behavior in ADHD children.

The program is intended for children aged 2 to 11 years for whom oppositional defiant behavior is an issue. Studies examining the efficacy of this particular parent training program with ADHD children have consistently reported significant improvements in child behavior as a function of the parents' acquisition of these child management skills (Anastopoulos et al., 1993; Johnston, 1992; Pisterman et al., 1989). Results suggest that up to 64% of families experience clinically significant change or recovery (normalization) of their child's disruptive behavior as a consequence of this program (Anastopoulos et al., 1993). However, improvements in behavior may be more concentrated in the realm of aggressive and defiant child behavior than in that of inattentive–hyperactive symptoms (Johnston, 1992). All of these studies have relied on clinic-referred families, in most of which the parents sought the assistance of mental health professionals for their children. In contrast to the results of research with such motivated families, my colleagues and I recently found that when such a clinic-based parent training program was offered to parents of preschool children identified at kindergarten enrollment as having significant levels of aggressive–hyperactive–impulsive behavior, most either did not attend training or attended unreliably (Barkley, Shelton, et al., 1996). Moreover, no significant improvements in child behavior were found even among those who did attend at least some of the training sessions. Cunningham, Bremmer, and Boyle (1995) have recently shown that such parent training programs may be more cost-effective, reach more severely disruptive children and more minority families, and possibly be more effective for them if they are provided as group training classes offered through neighborhood public schools in the evenings with paraprofessionals as trainers.

For teenagers with ADHD and oppositional behavior, I have often recommended a family training program that includes problem-solving and communication training (PSCT), developed by Robin and Foster (1989; see Foster & Robin, Chapter 12, this volume; see also Forgatch & Patterson, 1987). My colleagues and I have now had the opportunity to examine the efficacy of the Robin and Foster program with ADHD teenagers having significant family conflicts (Barkley, Guevremont, Anastopoulos, & Fletcher, 1992). This program was compared against the parent training program described above (Barkley, 1997a), which was modified somewhat for use with adolescents. It was also compared against the family therapy program developed by Minuchin and Fishman (1981). Families in each group received 8–10 sessions of therapy, and multiple outcome measures of family conflict were collected, including videotaped parent–teen interactions. Results indicated that all three treatments produced statistically significant improvements in the various self-report ratings of family conflict, but no significant improvements in the direct observations of parent–teen interactions. When statistics evaluating individual change and recovery were applied to these data, they revealed that only 5%–30% of the families in these programs improved reliably as a result of treatment and that only 5%–20% had recovered (reached normalization) in their level of conflicts, with no significant differences among the groups in these reliable change and recovery percentages. Such results are quite disappointing and suggest that the power of treatment needs to be enhanced in

various ways if it is to be of much value to most families of ADHD adolescents experiencing significant family conflict. My colleagues and I are now conducting a study to examine this issue. Treatment has been enhanced by increasing the number of sessions to 18, encouraging greater involvement by fathers in therapy, and combining the behavioral parent training and PSCT programs, among other changes.

Training Teachers in Classroom Management

Somewhat more research has examined the application of behavior management methods with ADHD children in the classroom than in parent training. Moreover, there is a voluminous literature on the application of classroom management methods to disruptive child behaviors, many of which include the typical symptoms of ADHD. This research clearly indicates the effectiveness of behavioral techniques in the short-term treatment of academic performance problems in ADHD children.

A recent meta-analysis of the research literature on classroom behavioral interventions for ADHD covered 70 separate experiments of various within- and between-subject designs, as well as single-case designs (DuPaul & Eckert, 1997). This review found an overall mean effect size for contingency management procedures of 0.60 for between-subject designs, nearly 1.00 for within-subject designs, and approximately 1.40 for single-case experimental designs. Interventions aimed at improving academic performance through the manipulation of the curriculum, antecedent conditions, or peer tutoring produced approximately equal or greater effect sizes. In contrast, cognitive-behavioral treatments used in the school setting were significantly less effective than these other two forms of interventions. Thus, despite some initial findings of rather limited impact of classroom behavior management on children with ADHD (Abikoff & Gittelman, 1984), more recent studies such as those by Pelham and colleagues (Pelham et al., 1988; Carlson et al., 1992), and the totality of the extant literature reviewed by DuPaul and Eckert (1997), suggest that behavioral and academic interventions in the classroom can be effective in improving behavioral problems and academic performance in children with ADHD. The behavior of these children, however, may not be fully normalized by these interventions.

As noted above in regard to laboratory applications of behavior therapy techniques, research suggests some promise in the use of stimulus

TABLE 2.3.   Parent Handout on Establishing a Home Token System

The Home Poker Chip/Point System

When trying to manage a child with behavioral problems, it is common to find that praise is not enough to motivate the child to do chores, follow rules, or to obey commands. As a result, it is necessary to set up a more powerful program to motivate the child. One such program that has been very successful with children is the Home Poker Chip Program (for children 4 to 7 years old) or the Home Point System (for 8-year-olds and older children). Your therapist will explain in detail how to set up such a program, but here are the steps to follow:

The Home Poker Chip Program

1. Find or buy a set of plastic poker chips. If the child is 4 or 5 years old, then each chip, regardless of color, represents 1 chip. For 6- to 8-year-olds, the colors can represent different amounts: white = 1 chip, blue = 5 chips, and red = 10 chips. If you use the colors this way, take one of each color, tape it to a small piece of cardboard, and write on each chip how many chips it is worth. Post this card somewhere so your child can easily refer to it.
2. Sit down and explain to your child that you feel he or she has not been rewarded enough for doing nice things at home and you want to change all that. You want to set up a new reward program so your child can earn nice privileges and things for behaving properly. This sets a very positive tone to the program.
3. You and your child should make a nice bank in which he or she will keep the chips the child will earn. A shoe box, coffee can (with a dull edge on the rim), a plastic jar, etc., can serve as a bank. Have some fun decorating it with your child.
4. Now, you and your child should make up a list of the privileges you want your child to earn with the poker chips. These should include not just occasional special privileges (going to movies, roller skating, buying a toy) but also the everyday privileges your child takes for granted (television, video games, special toys already in the home, riding a bike, going over to a friend's home, etc.). Your therapist will explain what types of privileges you might include on this list. Be sure to have at least 10, and preferably 15, rewards on this list.
5. Now make up a second list that will contain the jobs and chores you often ask this child to perform. These can be typical household chores such as setting the table for a meal, clearing the table after a meal, cleaning a bedroom, making a bed, emptying wastebaskets, etc. Also put on the list things like getting dressed for school, getting ready for bed, washing and bathing, brushing teeth, or any other self-help tasks you give a child that normally pose a problem for you. Your therapist can help you decide what types of jobs to put on this list for your child's age group and special problems.
6. Next, take each job or chore and decide how much you feel it is worth in chips. For 4- and 5-year-olds, assign from 1 to 3 chips for most tasks, and perhaps 5 for really big jobs. For 6- to 8-year-olds, use a range of 1 to 10 chips and perhaps give a larger amount for big jobs. Remember, the harder the job, the more chips you will pay.
7. Take a moment and add up approximately how many chips you think your child will earn in a typical day if he or she does most of these jobs. Then, remembering this number, decide how many chips your child should have to pay for each of the rewards you listed. We generally suggest that two-thirds of the child's daily chips should be spent on his or her typical daily privileges. This allows the child to save about one-third of his or her chips every day toward the purchase of some of the very special rewards on the list. Don't worry about the exact numbers to use here. Just use your judgment as to how much each reward should cost, be fair, and charge more chips for the special rewards and less for the daily ones.
8. Be sure to tell your child that he or she will have a chance to earn "bonus" chips when he or she performs a chore in a nice, prompt, and pleasant manner. You will not give these bonus chips all the time, but should give them when your child has done a job in an especially pleasant and prompt manner.
9. Be sure to tell the child that chips will only be given for jobs that are done on the first request. If you have to repeat a command to the child, he or she will not receive any chips for doing it.
10. Finally, be sure to go out of your way this week to give chips away for any small appropriate behavior. Remember, you can reward a child even for good behaviors that are not on the list of jobs. Be alert for opportunities to reward the child.

NOTE: DO NOT TAKE CHIPS AWAY THIS WEEK FOR MISBEHAVIOR!!! You can do that when your therapist tells you to, but otherwise chips are to be used ONLY as rewards this week, not taken away as punishment.

The Home Point System

1. Get a notebook, and set it up like a checkbook with five columns, one each for the date, the item, deposits, withdrawals, and the running balance. When your child is rewarded with points, write the job in under "item" and enter the amount as a "deposit." Add it to the child's balance. When your child buys a privilege

(continued)

TABLE 2.3. (*continued*)

with his or her points, note the privilege under "item," place this amount in the "withdrawal column," and deduct this amount from the "balance." The program works just like the chip system except that points are recorded in the book instead of using poker chips.

2. Make up the lists of rewards/privileges and jobs as in the chip program above. Be sure to give the same explanation to the child as to why the point system is being set up. Again, your therapist can help you with these lists.

3. When you get ready to determine how much each job should be paid in points, use larger numbers than in the chip program. We generally use a range of 5 to 25 points for most daily jobs and up to 200 points for very big jobs. Typically, you might consider paying 15 points for every 15 minutes of extended work a child has to do.

4. Then add up how many points you feel your child will earn on an average day for doing his routine jobs. Use this number to decide how much to charge for each privilege. Be sure the child has about one-third of his or her daily points free to save up for special privileges. Your therapist can help you in deciding how much to charge for each reward.

5. Follow the same guidelines in using the point system as were given above for the chip program this week. Do not fine the child any points for misbehavior and pay points to the child only if he or she listens to the first command or request. Only parents are to write in the point notebook.

Other Reminders

Review the list of rewards and jobs every month or so and add new ones to each list as you deem necessary. Check with your child for new rewards he or she may want on the list.

You can reward your child with chips or points for almost any form of good behavior. They can even be used in conjunction with Step #3 to reward your child for not bothering or interrupting your work.

Do not give the chips or points away before the child has done what he or she was told to do. Only afterwards. But be as quick as possible in rewarding the child for compliance. Don't wait to reward!

Both parents should use the chip or point system to make it as effective as possible.

When you give points or chips for good behavior, smile, and tell the child what you like that he or she has done.

Note. From Barkley (1997a). Copyright 1997 by The Guilford Press. Reprinted by permission.

control procedures with ADHD children, many of which can be readily adapted to the classroom. Reducing task length, "chunking" tasks into smaller units to fit more within a child's attention span, and setting quotas for the child to achieve within shorter time intervals may increase the success of the ADHD child with academic work (see Allyon & Rosenbaum, 1977; DuPaul & Stoner, 1994; Pfiffner & Barkley, 1990). As Zentall (1985) has already documented, the use of increased stimulation within the task (e.g., color, shape, texture, rate of stimulus presentation) may enhance attention to academic tasks in ADHD children. In addition, teaching styles may play an important role in how well ADHD children attend to lectures by a teacher. More vibrant, enthusiastic teachers who move about more, engage children frequently while teaching, and allow greater participation of the children in the teaching activity may increase sustained attention to the task at hand. Zentall has also shown that permitting ADHD children to move or participate motorically while learning a task may improve attention and performance. The use of written, displayed rules

and timers for setting task time limits, as already described, may further benefit ADHD children in the classroom.

A number of studies have also shown that the contingent application of reinforcers for reduced activity level or increased sustained attention can rapidly alter ADHD children's levels of hyperactivity and inattention (see Allyon & Rosenbaum, 1977; DuPaul & Eckert, 1997; Schulman, Stevens, Suran, Kupst, & Naughton, 1978). Usually these programs incorporate token rewards, since some research suggests that praise may not be sufficient to increase or maintain normal levels of on-task behavior in hyperactive children (Pfiffner & Barkley, 1990; Pfiffner, Rosen, & O'Leary, 1985). Several studies have shown that group-administered rewards (i.e., rewards for all children in class contingent on the performance of one child) are as effective as individually administered rewards (Rosenbaum, O'Leary, & Jacob, 1975). One of the problems arising in such research, however, was the demonstration that simply reinforcing greater on-task behavior and decreased activity level did not necessarily translate into increased work productivity or accuracy (Marholin & Steinman, 1977). Since the latter are the ultimate goals of behavioral intervention in the classroom, these results were somewhat dismaying. Research now suggests that reinforcing the products of classroom behavior (i.e., number and accuracy of problems completed) results not only in increased productivity and accuracy, but also indirectly in declines in off-task and hyperactive behavior (Allyon, Layman, & Kandel, 1975; Allyon & Rosenbaum, 1977; Marholin & Steinman, 1977; Pfiffner, Rosen, & O'Leary, 1985).

A serious limitation of these promising results has been the lack of follow-up on the maintenance of these treatment gains over time. In addition, none of these studies examined whether generalization of behavioral control occurred in other school settings, where no treatment procedures were in effect. Other studies employing a mixture of cognitive-behavioral and contingency management techniques have failed to find such generalization with ADHD children (Barkley, Copeland, & Sivage, 1980), suggesting that improvements derived from classroom management methods are quite situation-specific and may not generalize or be maintained once treatment has been terminated.

The role of punishment in the management of classroom behavior in ADHD children has been less well studied. Pfiffner, O'Leary, Rosen, and Sanderson (1985) evaluated the effects of continuous and intermittent verbal reprimands and response cost on off-task classroom behaviors. They found that although each of these treatments significantly reduced disruptive and off-task behavior, the continuous use of response cost (loss of recess time) was most effective. Allyon and Rosenbaum (1977) also reported on the initial success of adding response cost contingencies to an ongoing classroom token economy. However, after less than 1 week, disruptive behavior returned to baseline levels despite the punishment contingency.

In a later paper, Pfiffner and O'Leary (1987) determined that the use of positive reinforcement for controlling ADHD behaviors in the classroom was not sufficient to maintain improved behavior in these children unless punishment in the form of response cost was added to the program. The addition of response cost further increased rates of on-task behavior and academic accuracy. These gains in behavior could then be maintained by an all-positive program once the response cost procedure was gradually withdrawn. However, abrupt withdrawal of the punishment contingency resulted in declines in

on-task behavior and accuracy, suggesting that the manner in which response cost techniques are implemented and then faded out of classroom management programs is important in the maintenance of initial treatment gains. In general, the efficacy of response cost procedures with ADHD children has been well documented (Firestone & Douglas, 1975, 1977; DuPaul, Guevremont, & Barkley, 1992; Gordon, Thomason, & Cooper, 1990; Rapport, Murphy, & Bailey, 1980, 1982).

What conclusions can be drawn from this literature indicate that contingency management methods can produce immediate, significant, short-term improvement in the behavior, productivity, and accuracy of ADHD children in the classroom. Secondary or tangible reinforcers are more effective in reducing disruptive behavior and increasing performance than are attention or other social reinforcers. The use of positive reinforcement programs alone does not seem to result in as much improvement, nor does it maintain that improvement over time as well, as does the combination of token reinforcement systems with a punishment such as response cost (i.e., removal of tokens or privileges). Such findings would be expected from the theoretical model of ADHD discussed earlier, which suggests a decreased power to self-regulate motivation and a delay in the development of internalized speech and the rule-governed behavior it affords in children with this disorder. What little evidence there is, however, suggests that treatment gains are unlikely to be maintained in these children once treatment has been withdrawn, and that improvements in behavior probably do not generalize to settings where no treatment is in effect.

Two additional classroom management techniques may prove of value in treating ADHD children, but their effectiveness remains to be more rigorously studied. One involves the use of a transmitter and receiver/counter for implementing an in-class token system. The device, known as the Attention Training System,[1] consists of a small transmitter clipped to the belt of a teacher and a second counting device/receiver placed on a child's desk. The counter is turned on when the child is given an assignment to do at his or her desk. Every minute, the counter adds a point on the face of the device, and the cumulative points can be exchanged later for other rewards. Whenever the teacher witnesses the child off task or disrupting the class, he or she presses a button on the transmitter, which activates a red light on top of the receiver and deducts a point from the face of the counter.

This method of utilizing a combined token reinforcement/response cost procedure eliminates one of the major difficulties in implementing class token systems—the need for proximity of the teacher to the child to administer the contingencies. After initially demonstrating its efficacy with ADHD children (Rapport et al., 1980), Rapport et al. (1982) compared this procedure to stimulant medication for improving attention and academic productivity of two ADHD children in a classroom setting. The response cost procedure was superior to methylphenidate alone in increasing both attention and productivity during academic tasks. Others have reported successful results for this approach with ADHD children in a series of single-case designs (DuPaul et al., 1992; Gordon et al., 1990), suggesting that it may be worthwhile to explore its efficacy in larger-scale group treatment studies.

Another promising method deserving of further evaluation is the use of home-based contingencies for in-class behavior and performance. Atkinson and Forehand (1979) reviewed the literature up to the late 1970s and found that the method offered some usefulness for managing disruptive classroom behavior, but that much more rigorous research was required to evaluate its promise. As discussed above in connection with my parent training program (see also Barkley, 1997a), the method involves having a teacher rate a child's daily school performance one or more times throughout a school day. These ratings are then sent home with the child for review by the parents. The parents then dispense rewards and punishments (usually response cost) at home, contingent upon the content of these daily ratings. O'Leary et al. (1976) employed this procedure for 10 weeks with nine hyperkinetic children and documented significant improvements on teacher ratings of classroom conduct and hyperkinesis as compared to a no treatment control group. Others have similarly found such home–school behavioral report cards to be useful, either alone or in combination with parent and teacher training in behavior management, in the treatment of ADHD children (Allyon, Garber, & Pisor, 1975; O'Leary & Pelham, 1978; Pelham et al., 1988).

The range of accommodations that can be suggested for assisting individuals with ADHD in the classroom is rather substantial. To illustrate the point, consider the list provided in Table 2.4 of various treatment recommendations that might be conveyed to school staff members dealing with children or adolescents having ADHD. Such recommendations range from altering the productivity requirements, classroom seating arrangements, and even teaching style, to instituting classroom token systems and daily school report cards linked to home-based token reward programs, to suggestions concerning classroom punishment methods. Some of the recommendations are based mainly on common sense and clinical wisdom, while others are derived from the scientific literature on treatments used in classrooms with ADHD children. Not all will prove appropriate or effective for all ADHD children, as any school intervention plan must be tailored to the issues involved in any particular case of ADHD.

Although little research has been done on the subject, it is likely that certain aspects of the teacher's personality, the presence of psychological difficulties in the teacher, the compatibility of teacher and student characteristics, and the teacher's philosophy of child behavior management contribute to the success or failure of any contingency management methods to be used in the classroom and the success of the ADHD child in that classroom more generally (Greene, 1996). In my experience, I have found that the two greatest hindrances to implementing these methods are the time available to the teacher for doing so and his or her attitude toward behavioral techniques in general. Many regular education classes have 22 to 26 children, making it difficult for a teacher to implement these procedures rigorously in what little time he or she may have for any individual child. This problem can be partly remedied by keeping the methods relatively simple or by having an aide assigned to the class temporarily to assist with the initial implementation of the program. Should this prove infeasible or ineffective, and should the child's ADHD symptoms be severe enough, placement of the child in a smaller, special educational classroom for part or all of the school day may help. Special education teachers often have much more training and experience in contingency management methods and typically have the time as well as the teacher assistants to implement them.

Overcoming an antagonistic philosophy held by a teacher is more difficult. Some teachers have had negative experiences with poorly designed behavioral techniques, or they may simply feel that they are dehumanizing and mechanistic to children or fail to address a child's "true, inner" emotional disturbance. In such cases, I have often sought a change of classrooms for an ADHD child. In extreme circumstances, I recommend that the parents place the child in another school, where teachers may be more amenable to providing the additional time and special techniques ADHD children require for improved classroom adjustment (see Pfiffner & Barkley, 1990).

Combined Interventions

As should have been gathered from the discussion above, psychopharmacological and behavioral treatments are not, by themselves, typically adequate to address all of the difficulties likely to be presented by clinic-referred ADHD children. Optimal treatment is likely to consist of a combination of many of these approaches for maximal effectiveness (Carlson et al., 1992; Pelham et al., 1988; Horn et al., 1991). Some research studies have examined the utility of such treatment packages, with interesting results. It appears that in many studies, the combination of contingency management training of parents or teachers with stimulant drug therapies is generally little better than either treatment alone for the management of ADHD symptoms (Firestone et al., 1981; Gadow, 1985; Pollard et al., 1983; Wolraich, Drummond, Saloman, O'Brien, & Sivage, 1978). One study (Abikoff & Gittelman, 1984) found that classroom behavioral interventions mildly improved the deviant behavior of ADHD children but did not bring such levels of behavior within the normal range. Medication, in contrast, rendered most children normal in classroom behavior. Others have found more impressive results for classroom behavior management methods (Carlson et al., 1992; DuPaul & Eckert, 1997; Pelham et al., 1988), but also found that the addition of medication provided improvements beyond those achieved by behavior management alone. Moreover, such a combination may result in the need for less intense behavioral interventions or lower doses of medication than might be the case if either intervention were used alone. Where there is an advantage to behavioral interventions, it appears to be in reliably increasing rates of academic productivity and accuracy (Allyon & Rosenbaum, 1977; Gadow, 1985; Wolraich et al., 1978). Yet here too, stimulant medication has shown positive effects (Pelham et al., 1988). Despite some failures to obtain additive effects for these two treatments, their combination may still be advantageous, given that the stimulants are not usually used in the late afternoons or evenings— times when parents may need effective behavior management tactics to deal with the ADHD symptoms. Moreover, between 8% and 25% of ADHD children do not respond positively to the stimulant medications (Barkley, 1977a; Barkley et al., 1989), making behavioral interventions one of the few scientifically proven alternatives for these cases.

Several studies have examined the effects of combining stimulant medication with cognitive-behavioral interventions. Horn, Chatoor, and Conners (1983) examined the separate and combined effects of d-amphetamine and self-instructional training with a 9-year-old inpatient ADHD child. The combined program was more effective in increasing on-task behavior during classwork and decreasing teacher ratings of ADHD symptoms. However, academic productivity was improved only by the use of direct reinforcement for correct responses. In contrast, using group comparison designs, Brown, Borden, Wynne, Schleser, and Clingerman (1986) and Brown, Wynne, and Medenis (1985) found no benefits of combined drug and cognitive-behavioral interventions over either alone on similar domains of functioning of ADHD children. A later study by Horn et al. (1991) likewise did not find the combination of treatments to be superior to medication alone. Similarly negative results were found by Cohen, Sullivan, Minde, Novak, and Helwig (1981) for kindergarten-age ADHD children at a 1-year follow-up evaluation.

Some successes for combined medication and self-evaluation procedures have been reported (Hinshaw, Henker, & Whalen, 1984a) when social skills such as cooperation have been targets of intervention. Yet, when these same investigators attempted to teach anger control strategies to ADHD children to enhance self-control during peer interactions, no benefits of a combined intervention were found beyond those achieved by self-control training alone (Hinshaw, Henker, & Whalen, 1984b). The self-control techniques were the most successful in teaching these children specific coping strategies to employ in provocative interactions with peers, which usually led to angry reactions from the ADHD children. Medication, in contrast, served only to lower the overall level of anger responses, but did not enhance the application of specific anger control strategies. These studies suggest that each form of treatment may have highly specific and unique effects on some aspects of social behavior but not on others.

Some investigators have evaluated the effects of behavioral parent training in contingency management, both alone and combined with self-control therapy (Horn et al., 1987), on home and school behavioral problems. The results failed to find any significant advantage for the combined treatments. Both self-control training and behavioral parent training alone improved home behavior problems, but neither resulted in any generalization of treatment effects to the school, where no treatment had occurred. Since a no-treatment group was not employed in this study, however, it is not possible to conclude that these effects were due to treatment rather than to nonspecific effects (e.g., maturation, therapist attention, regression effects, etc.). A later study by Horn and colleagues (Horn, Ialongo, Greenberg, Packard, & Smith-Winberry, 1990) did find such a treatment combination to be superior to either treatment used alone in producing a significantly larger number of treatment responders. Once again, however, no generalization of the results to the school setting occurred.

Satterfield, Satterfield, and Cantwell (1980) have attempted to evaluate the effects of individualized multimodality intervention provided over extensive time periods (up to several years) on the outcome of ADHD boys. Interventions included medication, behavioral parent training, individual counseling, special education, family therapy, and other programs as needed by each individual. Results suggest that such an individualized program of combined treatments continued over longer time intervals can produce improvements in social adjustment at home and school, rates of antisocial behavior, substance misuse, and academic achievement. These results seem to be sustained across at least a 3-year follow-up period (Satterfield, Cantwell, & Satterfield, 1979; Satterfield et al., 1981; Satterfield, Satterfield, & Schell, 1987). Although these findings suggest great promise for the possible efficacy of multimodality treatment extended over years for children with ADHD, the lack of random assignment and more adequate control procedures in this series of studies limits the ability to attribute the improvements obtained in this study directly to the treatments employed. And these limitations certainly preclude establishing which of the treatment components was most effective. Still, studies such as these and others (Carlson et al., 1992; Pelham et al., 1988) have raised hopes that multimodality treatment can be effective for ADHD if extended over long intervals of time. They have led to a historic venture by the National Institute of Mental Health to evaluate the effects of such treatment for ADHD more systematically in a multisite collaborative study (Richters et al., 1995). The results of this study, however, are not yet available.

Intensive, Multimodal Treatment Programs

Two of the most well-known and well-regarded multimodality intervention programs are (1) the summer treatment program developed by William Pelham and colleagues and conducted at Western Psychiatric Institute in Pittsburgh (Pelham & Hinshaw, 1992), and (2) the University of California at Irvine/Orange County Department of Education (UCI/OCDE) intervention developed by James Swanson, Linda Pfiffner, Keith McBurnett, and Dennis Cantwell (see Pfiffner & Barkley, 1990). The latter program incorporates a number of features of the program developed by Pelham's group, as well as some components of the multimodal program conducted by Stephen Hinshaw, Barbara Henker, and Carol Whalen at the University of California at Los Angeles. All three of these programs rely on four major components of treatment: (1) parent training in child behavior management; (2) classroom implementation of behavior modification techniques; (3) social skills training; and (4) stimulant medication, in some cases. Whereas the Pelham et al. program is conducted during the summer months in a residential, camp-style setting, the UCI/OCDE program is a year-round day-school-style program. After describing these two programs, I describe a multimethod early intervention project for kindergarten children carried out by our group at the University of Massachusetts Medical Center in conjunction with the Worcester Public Schools (the UMass/WPS project).

The Summer Day Treatment Program

The program developed by Pelham and colleagues is conducted in a day treatment environment with a summer school/camp-like format. Daily activities include several hours of classroom instruction, which also incorporates behavior modification methods such as token economies, response cost, and time out from reinforcement. In addition, sports and recreational activities are arranged each day, during which behavioral management programs are operative as well. The program also includes parent training, peer relationship training, and a follow-up protocol to enhance the likelihood that treatment gains will be maintained after leaving the program. During their stay at the camp, some children may be tested on stimulant medication; a double-blind, placebo-controlled procedure is used, in which a child is tested on several different doses of medication while teacher ratings and behavioral observations are collected across the different camp activities.

Pelham and colleagues have used this setting and the larger programmatic context to conduct more focused research investigations into the effectiveness of classroom behavior management procedures alone, stimulant medication alone, and their combination in managing ADHD symptoms and improving academic performance and social behavior. Some of the components of this day treatment program have been evaluated previously, such as classroom contingency management, and have been found to produce significant short-term improvements in children with ADHD. And they clearly seem to do so in this context as well (Carlson et al., 1992; Pelham et al., 1988). But other components of the program have not been so well evaluated previously for their efficacy with children having ADHD, such as social skills training. And although parents' ratings before and after their children's participation indicate that 86% believe their ADHD children have improved through their participation in the program, no data have been published as yet on whether the gains made during the treatment program are maintained in the normal school and home settings after the children terminate their participation in this program.

The UCI/OCDE Program

The UCI/OCDE program provides weekday treatment for ADHD children in kindergarten through fifth grade in a school-like atmosphere, using classes of 12–15 children. The clinical interventions rely chiefly on a token economy program for the management of behavior in the classrooms and a parent training program conducted through both group and individual treatment sessions. Some training of self-monitoring, evaluation, and reinforcement also occurs as part of the class program. In addition, children receive daily group instruction in social skills as part of the classroom curriculum, and some of these behaviors may be targeted for modification outside of the group instruction time by using consequences within the classroom token economy. Before returning to their regular public schools, some children may participate in a transition school program that focuses on more advanced social skills as well as behavior modification programs, to facilitate the transfer of learning to their regular school setting. Some children within this program may also be receiving stimulant medication as needed for management of their ADHD symptoms.

Although this program has served as an exemplar for many others, published research on its efficacy has not been available. Granted, the parent training program and classroom behavior modification methods are highly similar to those used in published studies that have found them to be effective, at least in the short term, so long as they are in use (Barkley, 1990, 1997a; DuPaul & Eckert, 1997; Pelham & Sams, 1992). But the actual extent to which this particular program achieves its stated goals—specifically, the generalization of treatment gains to nontreatment settings, as well as the maintenance of those gains after children return to their public schools—has not been systematically evaluated in studies.

The UMass/WPS Early Intervention Project

More recently, my colleagues and I have completed a multimethod early intervention project for kindergarten children (ages 4–6 years) having significant problems with hyperactivity and aggression, at least 70% of whom qualified for a clinical diagnosis of ADHD (see Barkley, Shelton, et al., 1996, for a preliminary report). This program did not utilize clinic-referred children, whose parents and even teachers may be highly motivated to cooperate with treatment. Instead, children were identified at kindergarten registration as being at high risk for hyperactive–aggressive behavior, and were randomly assigned to one of four intervention groups for their entire kindergarten year. One group received a 10-week group parent training program followed by monthly booster session group meetings. Otherwise, the children participated in the standard public school kindergarten program offered by the WPS system. The second group was assigned to a special enrichment kindergarten classroom in which the children received accelerated instruction in academic skills, social skills training, classroom contingency management procedures (token systems and other reinforcements, response cost, time out, etc.), and cognitive therapy (self-instruction training) as part of their full-day kindergarten program. These special classes contained 12–16 hyperactive–aggressive children in each and were held in two neighborhood elementary schools in the WPS system, to which the children were provided with busing. Children in this special classroom also received several months of follow-up consultation to their teachers when they returned to their regular public schools for their first grade

TABLE 2.4.   A Typical Range of Treatment Suggestions for Classroom Behavior Management of Children and Adolescents with ADHD

Decrease Work Load to Fit Child's Attentional Capacity
- Smaller quotas for productivity
- More frequent but shorter work periods
- Lower accuracy quotas that increase over time with child's success
- Don't send unfinished classwork home
- Eliminate high-appeal distractors

Alter Teaching Style and Curriculum
- Allow some restlessness at work area
- Be animated, theatrical, and responsive
- Use participatory teaching with activities
- Computer-based drills and instructions
- Stay flexible, open to unusual teaching approaches to lessons
- Don't reinforce speed of responding
- Reward thoughtful "think aloud" approach
- Sit child close to teacher's work area
- Intersperse low- with high-interest tasks
- Use occasional brief exercise breaks
- Schedule more difficult subjects in A.M.
- Use direct instruction type curriculum materials

Make Rules External
- Signs that signal rule periods
- Posters listing rules for work periods
- Cards on desks with rules for desk work
- Child verbally restates rules before entering the next activity
- Child uses self-instruction during work
- Child recites rules to others before work
- Use tape-recorded cues to facilitate on-task behavior, which child listens to privately on a portable tapeplayer while working
- Have child prestate goals for work periods in advance

Frequency of Rewards and Fines
- Token economies
- Use Attention Training System (Gordon Systems, DeWitt, NY)
- Use tape-recorded tones for self-reward (see Barkley, Copeland, & Sivage, 1980)
- Have access to rewards several times/day

Increase Immediacy of Consequences—Act, Don't Yack!
- Stop repeating your commands
- Avoid lengthy reasoning over misbehavior

Increase Magnitude/Power of Rewards
- Token systems are great for this
- Have parents send in preferred toys or games
- Get a video-game donated to classroom
- Use home-based reward program (daily school behavior report card) (see Barkley, 1997a)
- Try group rewards if child meets quotas

Set Time Limits for Work Completion
- Use timers if possible for external time references
- Use tape-recorded time prompts with decreasing time counts

Develop Hierarchy of Classroom Punishments
- Head down at desk
- Response cost (fines in token system)
- Time out in corner
- Time out at school office
- Suspension to office (in school)

If all fail, schedule meeting with parents and consider special educational referral

Coordinate Home and School Consequences
- Daily school report card/rating form
- Daily home–school journal
- Gradually move to weekly monitoring

Manage Your Own Stress/Frustration Levels
- Stay calm when ADHD child is emotional
- Keep wits when reacting to misconduct
- Think ahead, have a management plan
- Periodically remember child is disabled
- Ask for backup help as needed
- Seek out advice from older teachers of behavior disorder children

Tips to Improve Teen School Performance
- Daily school assignment notebook with verification and cross-checking
- In-class cueing system for off-task behavior and disruption
- Assign a daily "case manager" or organizational "coach"
- Daily/weekly school conduct card with home–school point system
- Extra set of books maintained at home
- Additional school/home tutoring as needed

Note. From R. A. Barkley (1997g). Copyright 1997 by R. A. Barkley. Reprinted by permission.

year. A third group received both the parent training and enrichment classroom treatments, while a fourth group received no special services except for the initial evaluation and periodic reevaluations.

All children have been followed for 2 years after their participation in these treatment programs. Results to date have indicated no beneficial effect of the parent training program, in large part because more than 60% of the parents did not attend the training classes regularly, if at all. The enrichment classroom produced a significant improvement in the children's classroom behavior and social skills during the kindergarten year, but did not result in any change in behavior in the home as rated by parents. Nor did it produce greater gains in academic achievement skills than those experienced by the control groups not receiving this classroom program. Moreover, the results of the classroom appear to have attenuated during the follow-up period. Such results are rather sobering in view of the large investment of money, time, and staff training. Parent training programs for children at high risk for school and home behavior problems may not be especially effective in families identified through such community screening programs, largely because of poor parental motivation and investment in the training program. And even where classroom interventions are successful in the short-term, "active" treatment phase, their effects may diminish or disappear with time after children leave the treatment environment. This study suggests that the rather positive treatment outcome results for families who seek treatment and, by inference, are motivated to change themselves and their ADHD children may not be readily extrapolated to families of similarly deviant children who have not sought treatment but are identified through community screening programs.

Developmental Considerations

Not all of the treatments reviewed above are appropriate for all ADHD individuals of all ages. A clinician attempting to select an appropriate therapy or therapies for ADHD needs to consider the developmental characteristics of the child, not to mention the psychological adjustment of the parents, their willingness to carry out or cooperate with the treatments recommended, the degree of family intactness, the extent to which their insurance or managed health care plan may cover (or not cover) the recommended services, and even the availability of particular resources for such treatments within a geographic region. Given the strong hereditary nature of the disorder, a clinician is likely to find that at least one parent is similarly affected. Although no research is available to suggest how ADHD in a parent may affect the daily management of and psychological risks for an ADHD child, it is unlikely to be an effect that is particularly beneficial. Hence, treatment may be

needed for any parental psychological or psychiatric difficulties, along with those proposed for the ADHD child.

Regardless of the child's age, the most important first step in treatment apart from diagnosis is the education of the parents and family about the nature of ADHD and related issues. Not only does clinical wisdom dictate this, but there is some small-scale research to suggest that such reeducation of parents does alter their perceptions of their children's deviance and their own stress in the care of such children (Andrews et al., 1995). A similar reeducation process may be needed for some teachers and preschool staff as well prior to undertaking formal behavior management or medication treatment programs, so that the educators will have a better understanding of the likely etiologies of the child's difficulties, as well as the most effective ways to approach their management (Greene, 1996).

When one considers the issue of age alone, it is clear that stimulant medication is not typically recommended or especially useful for children below 4 years of age and may be of only modest benefit to those 4–5 years of age (Barkley et al., in press). And so at the preschool age, treatment may consist entirely of providing training to the parents in child behavior management methods. As part of this consultation, advising parents on the importance of childproofing their home against the possibility of accidental injuries or poisonings is critical, given the greater proneness of ADHD children to such accidents. Some consultation with the preschool teaching staff may also be needed for those ADHD children who are participating in preschool programs and whose behavior is problematic in such settings. These consultations should also focus mainly upon contingency management methods that may prove useful for managing the particular problems in the preschool setting.

For the elementary-age child, the increased importance of school in the child's life brings with it an increased likelihood of behavioral and performance problems in this setting, beyond those settings that may have proven problematic during the preschool years. The broader or more numerous social settings in which the ADHD child may now be participating bring with them additional responsibilities for the child—to behave well, follow established rules, interact cooperatively with peers, and generally display greater powers of self-regulation than was the case in earlier years. Associated with this expanded opportunity for difficulties outside of the home comes the increased likelihood of difficulties with peer relationships, both at school and in the larger community in which the ADHD child may now be more frequently interacting with others (i.e., Scouts, sports, clubs, church functions, etc.). Interventions must now focus on addressing not only the parent–child conflicts that may have arisen earlier in the preschool years, but the teacher–child and peer–child conflicts that may arise in the child's participation in school and community activities. The classroom contingency management procedures discussed earlier are well suited to this age group of children, as are some of the social skills training programs, though the latter still need to have their efficacy reasonably well established for children with ADHD. The disorders that tend to co-occur with ADHD, such as the learning disabilities, may make their presence more obvious during this developmental period and may necessitate additional interventions beyond those specifically targeted to the child's ADHD-related problems. The increased probability of positive responding to stimulant medication at this age now makes this treatment approach a more viable option for the elementary-age ADHD child. Again, however, the presence of comorbid conditions, such as anxiety or tic disorders, may alter this treatment regimen by making it necessary to consider other medications in addition to or in lieu of the stimulants.

Adolescence brings with it additional considerations in the selection of possible treatments for the teenager's ADHD and associated problems. The increased desires for autonomy from parents, for involvement in decision making that pertains to oneself, and for the approval of one's peer group introduce new issues into treatment planning. The cooperation of the teen with any treatments recommended for ADHD may now become the most salient or even the sole issue in treatment efficacy, forcing greater attention from professionals to the feelings, desires, and involvement of the teen in treatment planning and greater care in the negotiation with the teen for his or her cooperation with those plans (see Robin, 1990). Simply training the parents in the same behavior management methods as would have sufficed in earlier years will not be sufficient, since this approach has shown steep declines in its efficacy with the adolescent age group, as discussed earlier. Family therapy with the teen actively involved now becomes necessary, so as to negotiate the treatment plan with

the teen and seek his or her cooperation with it. Programs such as that described in this text by Robin and Foster (Chapter 12), which emphasize problem-solving training, communication training, and the altering of unreasonable interpersonal beliefs on the parts of parents and teens, become of equal or greater importance to the success of treatment than simply working with parents exclusively on the management of behavioral consequences in the home. Certainly the wider geographic range in the community over which the ADHD adolescent is now likely to be roaming (often without parental supervision), the larger number of activities in which the teen may participate, the increased number of peers and adults with whom the teen may now interact, and the increased privileges and responsibilities that may be given to the teen by virtue of his or her age all conspire to broaden the possible opportunities for problems with which the teen and parents must now deal. For instance, the teen's conduct at shopping malls, libraries, convenience stores, recreational parks, and even school facilities after hours may now become a potential problem and source of conflict with parents, not to mention local authorities. The combination of the ADHD teen's bursting sexuality at this age with his or her immature self-regulatory powers makes this domain of adolescent adaptive functioning an increasingly important one for parents, if not for the teen, given the demonstrably greater risks of ADHD teens for adolescent pregnancies and sexually transmitted diseases (which have been recently documented in my own longitudinal study). Although advice about birth control may seem to be a simple solution to this issue, the teen's cooperation with such advice once more becomes the key ingredient to success or failure in the efforts to assist the teen with more effective and adaptive conduct at critical points of performance in his or her daily life. And the opportunities for the adolescent to obtain driving privileges after 16 years of age in most states brings with it a whole host of new potential problems for the adolescent and parents. As noted earlier, adolescents and young adults with ADHD have significantly and substantially increased risks for negative driving outcomes (e.g., speeding and vehicular crashes) over those normally associated with teenage drivers, who are already the highest-risk driving age group.

Along with this broadening of treatment participants to include the teenager's active involvement comes a broadening of the number of participants in any school-based interventions as well. By adolescence, if not earlier, teens will have a far larger number of teachers, coaches, and other school staff members with whom to contend, none of whom exercises sole responsibility for the success of a teen's school day. Enlisting the assistance of seven or more teachers, several coaches, guidance counselors, school office staffers, and others in the contemporary middle school or high school environment of the ADHD teen is a daunting and usually unsuccessful task. Finding anyone in the school environment willing to monitor and assist with the teen's activities, organization, and responsibilities across an entire school day often becomes the first order of business in a school intervention plan for a teenager with ADHD. Such a person—the teen's "case manager" or organizational "coach"—can serve as the conduit through which recommendations from the professional are passed on to the other teachers and school staffers working with the teen. Conversely, this pivotal person serves as the means by which information about the teen's conduct and performance, and about the success of any earlier treatment ventures, is communicated to those mental health or medical professionals advising school personnel on the teen's treatment plan. And this "coach" can further serve the important role of periodically meeting with the teen briefly across the school day to monitor the teen's behavior, to see that the teen has obtained necessary information on school assignments, to provide a public accounting of the teen's performance of his or her prior agreements about school performance, and to provide motivational support to the teen for persisting with the plan and meeting obligations at school. The use of stimulant medications with this age group is likely to be as efficacious as it is with younger children having ADHD. Yet the more salient issue now is enlisting an adolescent's cooperation with the medication regimen, especially in view of the adolescent's desire not to be different from the chosen peer group in any way that might invite criticism.

Culminating this stage of adolescent development will be the myriad conflicts that may arise in the normal course of launching the ADHD older teen or young adult into gainful employment and eventually completely independent living, or at least into college and the semi-independent living arrangements often associated with it. Although medication treatment, family therapy, and comparable school-based interventions may be needed for the adolescent making

the transition to postsecondary education, the lion's share of the responsibility for getting help now rests squarely with the older teen or young adult, whose investment in and cooperation with treatment programs become the most important treatment issues. For the teen not going on for such education, the need to find appropriate employment and to see that such employment succeeds becomes an issue for both teen and parents. Vocational assessments and counseling may now be required as part of the intervention plan for the older adolescent. So may some assistance from parents or others with the young adult's bids for semi-independent or totally independent living arrangements; with the responsible management of the young person's increased income and opportunities to obtain easy credit; and with the moderation of his or her use of now-legal substances, such as tobacco and alcohol. All of these appear to be more problematic areas of adaptive functioning for ADHD teens and young adults than for their normal peers.

CONCLUSION

This chapter has discussed ADHD as a developmental disability in the domains of sustained attention, impulse control, and the regulation of activity level to situational demands. It arises during early childhood, is often relatively pervasive or cross-situational, and is typically chronic in nature. Current research suggests that among these deficits, the deficiency in behavioral inhibition may be most central to the disorder. My recently formulated neuropsychological theory of ADHD posits that this developmental delay in response inhibition disrupts the performance of four executive functions that are dependent upon such inhibition for their own effectiveness. These executive functions constitute private or covert forms of self-directed action that generate internally represented information; they are the means by which human self-regulation arises and succeeds. This internally held information serves to wrest behavior from control by the immediate context and temporal now, and to direct behavior toward time and the conjectured future, giving human behavior its purposive, intentional, reasoned, and future-oriented qualities. Thus it is easy to see how a deficit in inhibition such as that occurring in ADHD disrupts these executive functions and the self-regulation they afford, returning behavior to its more primitive stage of control by the moment.

Present knowledge strongly points to a biological predisposition to the disorder, with multiple etiologies being implicated. Chief among them, however, are genetic and neurological factors. ADHD has been shown over the past decade to be a strongly heritable condition. Recent neuroimaging research points to problems in the embryological development of the prefrontal lobes and the frontal–striatal network as probably involved in the genesis of ADHD. Environmental influences appear to play some role, albeit a more modest one than once believed, in determining the severity of ADHD symptoms, the continuity of the disorder over development, and the development of some comorbid disorders (such as ODD and CD). Unique environmental events appear to be more important in the expression of the symptoms, whereas shared or common environmental factors may contribute more to the continuity of disorder across development.

The treatment of ADHD requires expertise in many different treatment modalities, no single one of which can address all of the difficulties likely to be experienced by such individuals. Among the available treatments, education of parents, family members, and teachers about the disorder; psychopharmacology (chiefly stimulant medications); parent training in effective child behavior management methods, classroom behavior modification methods; and academic interventions, and special educational placement appear to have the greatest efficacy or promise of efficacy for children with ADHD. To these must often be added family therapy that emphasizes problem-solving and communication skills; the coordination of multiple teachers and school staff members across the high school day; assisting the ADHD teen with expanded responsibilities, opportunities, and privileges; and the preparation of the teen for eventual independent living and self-support. To be effective in altering eventual prognosis, treatments must be maintained over extended time periods (months to years), with periodic reintervention as needed across the life course of the individual. Moreover, as the individual matures, enlisting his or her cooperation with and investment in the long-term intervention program becomes increasingly important.

NOTE

1. Available from Gordon Systems, Inc., P.O. Box 746, DeWitt, NY 13214.

REFERENCES

Abikoff, H. (1985). Efficacy of cognitive training interventions in hyperactive children: A critical review. *Clinical Psychology Review, 5,* 479–512.

Abikoff, E. (1987). An evaluation of cognitive behavior therapy for hyperactive children. In B. Lahey & A. Kazdin (Eds.), *Advances in clinical child psychology* (Vol. 10, pp. 171–216). New York: Plenum Press.

Abikoff, H., & Gittelman, R. (1984). Does behavior therapy normalize the classroom behavior of hyperactive children? *Archives of General Psychiatry, 41,* 449–454.

Abikoff, H., & Gittelman, R. (1985). Hyperactive children treated with stimulants: Is cognitive training a useful adjunct? *Archives of General Psychiatry, 42,* 953–961.

Achenbach, T. M., & Edelbrock, C. (1983). *Manual for the Child Behavior Checklist and Revised Child Behavior Profile.* Burlington: University of Vermont, Department of Psychiatry.

Allyon, T., Garber, S., & Pisor, K. (1975). The elimination of discipline problems through a combined school–home motivational system. *Behavior Therapy, 6,* 616–626.

Allyon, T., Layman, D., & Kandel, H. (1975). A behavioral–educational alternative to drug control of hyperactive children. *Journal of Applied Behavior Analysis, 8,* 137–146.

Allyon, T., & Rosenbaum, M. (1977). The behavioral treatment of disruption and hyperactivity in school settings. In B. Lahey & A. Kazdin (Eds.), *Advances in clinical child psychology* (Vol. 1, pp. 83–118). New York: Plenum Press.

American Psychiatric Association. (1968). *Diagnostic and statistical manual of mental disorders* (2nd ed.). Washington, DC: Author.

American Psychiatric Association. (1980). *Diagnostic and statistical manual of mental disorders* (3rd ed.). Washington, DC: Author.

American Psychiatric Association (1987). *Diagnostic and statistical manual of mental disorders* (3rd ed., rev.). Washington, DC: Author.

American Psychiatric Association (1994). *Diagnostic and statistical manual of mental disorders* (4th ed.). Washington, DC: Author.

Anastopoulos, A. D., Guevremont, D. C., Shelton, T. L., & DuPaul, G. J. (1992). Parenting stress among families of children with Attention Deficit Hyperactivity Disorder. *Journal of Abnormal Child Psychology, 20,* 503–520.

Anastopoulos, A. D., Shelton, T. L., DuPaul, G. J., & Guevremont, D. C. (1993). Parent training for Attention-Deficit Hyperactivity Disorder: Its impact on parent functioning. *Journal of Abnormal Child Psychology, 21,* 581–596.

Andrews, J. N., Swank, P. R., Foorman, B., & Fletcher, J. M. (1995). Effects of educating parents about ADHD. *The ADHD Report, 3*(4), 12–13.

Arnold, L. E., Clark, D. L., Sachs, L. A., Jakim, S., & Smithies, C. (1985). Vestibular and visual rotational stimulation as treatment for attention deficit and hyperactivity. *American Journal of Occupational Therapy, 39,* 84–91.

Atkinson, B. M., & Forehand, R. (1979). Home-based reinforcement programs designed to modify classroom behavior: A review and methodological evaluation. *Psychological Bulletin, 86,* 1298–1308.

August, G. J., Realmuto, G. M., MacDonald, A. W., Nugent, S. M., & Crosby, R. (1996). Prevalence of ADHD and comorbid disorders among elementary school children screened for disruptive behavior. *Journal of Abnormal Child Psychology, 24,* 571–596.

Baer, R. A., & Nietzel, M. T. (1991). Cognitive and behavioral treatment of impulsivity in children: A meta-analytic review of the outcome literature. *Journal of Clinical Child Psychology, 20,* 400–412.

Baldwin, K., Brown, R. T., & Milan, M. A. (1995). Predictors of stress in caregivers of attention deficit hyperactivity disordered children. *American Journal of Family Therapy, 23,* 149–160.

Ball, J. D., & Koloian, B. (1995). Sleep patterns among ADHD children. *Clinical Psychology Review, 15,* 681–691.

Barkley, R. A. (1976). Predicting the response of hyperkinetic children to stimulant drugs: A review. *Journal of Abnormal Child Psychology, 4,* 327–348.

Barkley, R. A. (1977a). The effects of methylphenidate on various measures of activity level and attention in hyperkinetic children. *Journal of Abnormal Child Psychology, 5,* 351–369.

Barkley, R. A. (1977b). A review of stimulant drug research with hyperactive children. *Journal of Child Psychology and Psychiatry, 18,* 137–165.

Barkley, R. A. (1981). *Hyperactive children: A handbook for diagnosis and treatment.* New York: Guilford Press.

Barkley, R. A. (1985). The social interactions of hyperactive children: Developmental changes, drug effects, and situational variation. In R. McMahon & R. Peters (Eds.), *Childhood disorders: Behavioral–developmental approaches* (pp. 218–243). New York: Brunner/Mazel.

Barkley, R. A. (1988). Attention. In M. Tramontana & S. Hooper (Eds.), *Assessment issues in child neuropsychology* (pp. 145–176). New York: Plenum Press.

Barkley, R. A. (1989a). The problem of stimulus control and rule-governed behavior in children with Attention Deficit Disorder with Hyperactivity. In L. Bloomingdale & J. Swanson (Eds.), *Attention Deficit Disorders: Current concepts and emerging trends in attentional and behavioral disorders of childhood* (pp. 203–228). New York: Pergamon Press.

Barkley, R. A. (1989b). Attention Deficit–Hyperactivity Disorder. In E. J. Mash & R. A. Barkley (Eds.), *Treatment of childhood disorders* (pp. 39–72). New York: Guilford Press.

Barkley, R. A. (1990). *Attention-Deficit Hyperactivity Disorder: A handbook for diagnosis and treatment.* New York: Guilford Press.

Barkley, R. A. (1992a). *ADHD: What do we know?* [Videotape]. New York: Guilford Press.

Barkley, R. A. (1992b). *ADHD: What can we do?* [Videotape]. New York: Guilford Press.

Barkley, R. A. (1994). Impaired delayed responding: A unified theory of Attention Deficit Hyperactivity Disorder. In D. K. Routh (Ed.), *Disruptive behavior disorders: Essays in honor of Herbert Quay* (pp. 11–57). New York: Plenum Press.

Barkley, R. A. (1995). *Taking charge of ADHD: The complete, authoritative guide for parents.* New York: Guilford Press.

Barkley, R. A. (1996). Attention-Deficit/Hyperactivity Disorder. In E. J. Mash & R. A. Barkley (Eds.), *Child psychopathology* (pp. 63–112). New York: Guilford Press.

Barkley, R. A. (1997a). *Defiant children: A clinician's manual for assessment and parent training* (2nd ed.). New York: Guilford Press.

Barkley, R. A. (1997b). Attention-deficit/hyperactivity disorder. In E. J. Mash & L. G. Terdal (Eds.), *Assessment of childhood disorders* (3rd ed., pp. 71–129). New York: Guilford Press.

Barkley, R. A. (1997c). Behavioral inhibition, sustained attention, and executive functions: Constructing a unifying theory of ADHD. *Psychological Bulletin, 121,* 65–94.

Barkley, R. A. (1997d). *ADHD and the nature of self-control.* New York: Guilford Press.

Barkley, R. A. (1997e). *Understanding the defiant child* [Videotape]. New York: Guilford Press.

Barkley, R. A. (1997f). *Managing the defiant child* [Videotape]. New York: Guilford Press.

Barkley, R. A. (1997g). *Manual to accompany the workshop on Attention-Deficit/Hyperactivity Disorder.* Worcester, MA: Author.

Barkley, R. A. (in press-a). Theories of Attention Deficit Hyperactivity Disorder. In H. C. Quay & A. E. Hogan (Eds.), *Handbook of disruptive behavior disorders.* New York: Plenum Press.

Barkley, R. A. (in press-b). *Attention-Deficit/Hyperactivity Disorder: A handbook for diagnosis and treatment* (2nd ed.). New York: Guilford Press.

Barkley, R. A., Anastopoulos, A. D., Guevremont, D. G., & Fletcher, K. F. (1992). Adolescents with Attention Deficit Hyperactivity Disorder: Mother–adolescent interactions, family beliefs and conflicts, and maternal psychopathology. *Journal of Abnormal Child Psychology, 20,* 263–288.

Barkley, R. A., & Biederman, J. (1997). Towards a broader definition of the age of onset criterion for Attention Deficit Hyperactivity Disorder. *Journal of the American Academy of Child and Adolescent Psychiatry, 36,* 1204–1210.

Barkley, R. A., Copeland, A. P., & Sivage, C. (1980). A self-control classroom for hyperactive children. *Journal of Autism and Developmental Disorders, 10,* 75–89.

Barkley, R. A., & Cunningham, C. E. (1978). Do stimulant drugs improve the academic performance of hyperkinetic children?: A review of outcome research. *Journal of Clinical Pediatrics, 17,* 85–92.

Barkley, R. A., DuPaul, G. J., & Connor, D. (in press). Stimulants. In J. Werry & M. Aman (Eds.), *A practitioner's guide to psychoactive drugs for children and adolescents.* New York: Plenum Press.

Barkley, R. A., DuPaul, G. J., & McMurray, M. B. (1990). A comprehensive evaluation of Attention Deficit Disorder with and without Hyperactivity. *Journal of Consulting and Clinical Psychology, 58,* 775–789.

Barkley, R. A., Fischer, M., Edelbrock, C. S., & Smallish, L. (1990). The adolescent outcome of hyperactive children diagnosed by research criteria: I. An 8 year prospective follow-up study. *Journal of the American Academy of Child and Adolescent Psychiatry, 29,* 546–557.

Barkley, R. A., Fischer, M., Edelbrock, C. S., & Smallish, L. (1991). The adolescent outcome of hyperactive children diagnosed by research criteria: III. Mother–child interactions, family conflicts, and maternal psychopathology. *Journal of Child Psychology and Psychiatry, 32,* 233–256.

Barkley, R. A., Fischer, M., Newby, R., & Breen, M. (1988). Development of a multi-method clinical protocol for assessing stimulant drug responses in ADHD children. *Journal of Clinical Child Psychology, 17,* 14–24.

Barkley, R. A., Grodzinsky, G., & DuPaul, G. (1992). Frontal lobe functions in Attention Deficit Disorder with and without Hyperactivity: A review and research report. *Journal of Abnormal Child Psychology, 20,* 163–188.

Barkley, R. A., Guevremont, D. C., Anastopoulos, A. D., & Fletcher, K. E. (1992). A comparison of three family therapy programs for treating family conflicts in adolescents with Attention-Deficit Hyperactivity Disorder. *Journal of Consulting and Clinical Psychology, 60,* 450–462.

Barkley, R. A., Guevremont, D. G., Anastopoulos, A. D., DuPaul, G. J., & Shelton, T. L. (1993). Driving-related risks and outcomes of Attention Deficit Hyperactivity Disorder in adolescents and young adults: A 3–5 year follow-up survey. *Pediatrics, 92,* 212–218.

Barkley, R. A., Karlsson, J., & Pollard, S. (1985). Effects of age on the mother–child interactions of hyperactive children. *Journal of Abnormal Child Psychology, 13,* 631–638.

Barkley, R. A., Karlsson, J., Pollard, S., & Murphy, J. (1985). Developmental changes in the mother–child interactions of hyperactive boys: effects of two doses of Ritalin. *Journal of Child Psychology and Psychiatry, 26,* 705–715.

Barkley, R. A., Karlsson, J., Strzelecki, E., & Murphy, J. (1984). Effects of age and Ritalin dosage on the mother–child interactions of hyperactive children. *Journal of Consulting and Clinical Psychology, 52,* 750–758.

Barkley, R. A., McMurray, M. B., Edelbrock, C. S., & Robbins, K. (1989). The response of aggressive and nonaggressive ADHD children to two doses of methylphenidate. *Journal of the American Academy of Child and Adolescent Psychiatry, 28,* 873–881.

Barkley, R. A., McMurray, M. B., Edelbrock, C. S., & Robbins, K. (1990). Side effects of methyphenidate in children with attention deficit hyperactivity disorder: A systematic, placebo–controlled evaluation. *Pediatrics, 86,* 184–192.

Barkley, R. A., Murphy, K. R., & Kwasnik, D. (1996). Motor vehicle driving competencies and risks in teens and young adults with ADHD. *Pediatrics, 98,* 1089–1095.

Barkley, R. A., Shelton, T. L., Crosswait, C., Moorehouse, M., Fletcher, K., Barrett, S., Jenkins, L., & Metevia, L. (1996). Preliminary findings of an early intervention program for aggressive hyperactive children. *Annals of the New York Academy of Sciences, 794,* 277–289.

Barkley, R. A., & Ullman, D. G. (1975). A comparison of objective measures of activity and distractibility in hyperactive and nonhyperactive children. *Journal of Abnormal Child Psychology, 3,* 231–244.

Baumgardner, T. L., Singer, H. S., Denckla, M. B., Rubin, M. A., Abrams, M. T., Colli, M. J., & Reiss, A. L. (1996). Corpus callosum morphology in children with Tourette syndrome and Attention Deficit Hyperactivity Disorder. *Neurology, 47,* 477–482.

Berk, L. E. (1992). Children's private speech: An overview of theory and the status of research. In R. M. Diaz & L. E. Berk (Eds.), *Private speech: From social interaction to self-regulation* (pp. 17–54). Hillsdale, NJ: Erlbaum.

Berk, L. E. (1994, November). Why children talk to themselves. *Scientific American,* pp. 78–83.

Berk, L. E., & Potts, M. K. (1991). Development and functional significance of private speech among Attention-Deficit Hyperactivity Disorder and normal boys. *Journal of Abnormal Child Psychology, 19,* 357–377.

Bidder, R. T., Gray, O. P., & Newcombe, R. (1978). Behavioural treatment of hyperactive children. *Archives of Disease in Childhood, 53,* 574–579.

Biederman, J., Faraone, S. V., Keenan, K., Knee, D., & Tsuang, M. T. (1990). Family–genetic and psychosocial risk factors in DSM-III Attention Deficit Disorder. *Journal of the American Academy of Child and Adolescent Psychiatry, 29,* 526–533.

Biederman, J., Faraone, S. V., & Lapey, K. (1992). Comorbidity of diagnosis in Attention-Deficit Hyperactivity Disorder. *Child and Adolescent Psychiatric Clinics of North America, 1*(2), 335–360.

Biederman, J., Faraone, S. V., Mick, E., Moore, P., & Lelon, E. (1996). Child Behavior Checklist findings further support comorbidity between ADHD and Major Depression in a referred sample. *Journal of the American Academy of Child and Adolescent Psychiatry, 35,* 734–742.

Biederman, J., Faraone, S. V., Mick, E., Spencer, T., Wilens, T., Kiely, K., Guite, J., Ablon, J. S., Reed,

E., & Warburton, R. (1995). High risk for Attention Deficit Hyperactivity Disorder among children of parents with childhood onset of the disorder: A pilot study. *American Journal of Psychiatry, 152,* 431–435.

Biederman, J., Faraone, S. V., Mick, E., Wozniak, J., Chen, L., Ouellette, C., Marrs, A., Moore, P., Garcia, J., Mennin, D., & Lelon, E. (1996). Attention-Deficit Hyperactivity Disorder and juvenile mania: An overlooked comorbidity. *Journal of the American Academy of Child and Adolescent Psychiatry, 35,* 997–1008.

Biederman, J., Faraone, S., Milberger, S., Curtis, S., Chen, L., Marrs, A., Ouellette, C., Moore, P., & Spencer, T. (1996). Predictors of persistence and remission of ADHD into adolescence: Results from a four-year prospective follow-up study. *Journal of the American Academy of Child and Adolescent Psychiatry, 35,* 343–351.

Biederman, J., Faraone, S. V., Milberger, S., Guite, J., Mick, E., Chen, L., Mennin, D., Marrs, A., Ouellette, C., Moore, P., Spencer, T., Norman, D., Wilens, T., Kraus, I., & Perrin, J. (1996). A prospective 4-year follow-up study of Attention-Deficit Hyperactivity and related disorders. *Archives of General Psychiatry, 53,* 437–446.

Biederman, J., Milberger, S., Faraone, S. V., Guite, J., & Warburton, R. (1994). Associations between childhood asthma and ADHD: Issues of psychiatric comorbidity and familiarity. *Journal of the American Academy of Child and Adolescent Psychiatry, 33,* 842–848.

Biederman, J., Milberger, S., Faraone, S. V., Kiely, K., Guite, J., Mick, E., Ablon, J. S., Warburton, R., Reed, E., & Davis, S. G. (1995). Impact of adversity on functioning and comorbidity in children with Attention-Deficit Hyperactivity Disorder. *Journal of the American Academy of Child and Adolescent Psychiatry, 34,* 1495–1503.

Biederman, J., Wilens, T., Mick, E., Faraone, S. V., Weber, W., Curtis, S., Thornell, A., Pfister, K., Jetton, J. G., & Soriano, J. (1997). Is ADHD a risk factor for psychoactive substance use disorders?: Findings from a four-year prospective follow-up study. *Journal of the American Academy of Child and Adolescent Psychiatry, 36,* 21–29.

Biederman, J., Wozniak, J., Kiely, K., Ablon, S., Faraone, S., Mick, E., Mundy, E., & Kraus, I. (1995). CBCL clinical scales discriminate prepubertal children with structured-interview-derived diagnosis of mania from those with ADHD. *Journal of the American Academy of Child and Adolescent Psychiatry, 34,* 464–471.

Block, G. H. (1977). Hyperactivity: A cultural perspective. *Journal of Learning Disabilities, 110,* 236–240.

Bloomquist, M. L., August, G. J., & Ostrander, R. (1991). Effects of a school-based cognitive-behavioral intervention for ADHD children. *Journal of Abnormal Child Psychology, 19,* 591–605.

Blum, K., Cull, J. G., Braverman, E. R., & Comings, D. E. (1996). Reward deficiency syndrome. *American Scientist, 84,* 132–145.

Bradley, W. (1937). The behavior of children receiving benzedrine. *American Journal of Psychiatry, 94,* 577–585.

Breslau, N., Brown, G. G., DelDotto, J. E., Kumar, S., Exhuthachan, S., Andreski, P., & Hufnagle, K. G. (1996). Psychiatric sequelae of low birth weight at 6 years of age. *Journal of Abnormal Child Psychology, 24,* 385–400.

Bronowski, J. (1977). *A sense of the future.* Cambridge, MA: MIT Press.

Brown, R. T., Borden, K. A., Wynne, M. E., Schleser, R., & Clingerman, S. T. (1986). Methylphenidate and cognitive therapy with ADD children: A methodological reconsideration. *Journal of Abnormal Child Psychology, 14,* 481–497.

Brown, R. T., Wynne, M. E., Borden, K. A., Clingerman, S. R., Geniesse, R., & Spunt, A. L. (1986). Methylphenidate and cognitive therapy in children with Attention Deficit Disorder: A double-blind trial. *Journal of Developmental and Behavioral Pediatrics, 7,* 163–170.

Brown, R. T., Wynne, M. E., & Medenis, R. (1985). Methylphenidate and cognitive therapy: A comparison of treatment approaches with hyperactive boys. *Journal of Abnormal Child Psychology, 13,* 69–88.

Buitelaar, J. K., van der Gaag, R. J., Swaab-Barneveld, H., & Kuiper, M. (1995). Prediction of clinical response to methylphenidate in children with Attention-Deficit Hyperactivity Disorder. *Journal of the American Academy of Child and Adolescent Psychiatry, 34,* 1025–1032.

Cadoret, R. J., & Stewart, M. A. (1991). An adoption study of attention deficit/hyperactivity/aggression and their relationship to adult antisocial personality. *Comprehensive Psychiatry, 32,* 73–82.

Campbell, S. B. (1975). Mother–child interactions: A comparison of hyperactive, learning disabled, and normal boys. *American Journal of Orthopsychiatry, 45,* 51–57.

Campbell, S. B. (1990). *Behavior problems in preschool children.* New York: Guilford Press.

Campbell, S. B., Schleifer, M., & Weiss, G. (1978). Continuities in maternal reports and child behaviors over time in hyperactive and comparison groups. *Journal of Abnormal Child Psychology, 6,* 33–45.

Campbell, S. B., Szumowski, E. K., Ewing, L. J., Gluck, D. S., & Breaux, A. M. (1982). A multidimensional assessment of parent-identified behavior problem toddlers. *Journal of Abnormal Child Psychology, 10,* 569–592.

Cantwell, D. P. (1975). *The hyperactive child.* New York: Spectrum.

Cantwell, D. P., & Carlson, G. (1978). Stimulants. In J. Werry (Ed.), *Pediatric psychopharmacology* (pp. 171–207). New York: Brunner/Mazel.

Cantwell, D. P., & Satterfield, J. H. (1978). The prevalence of academic underachievement in hyperactive children. *Journal of Pediatric Psychology, 3,* 168–171.

Cantwell, D. P., Swanson, J., & Connor, D. F. (1997). Case study: Adverse response to clonidine. *Journal of the American Academy of Child and Adolescent Psychiatry, 36,* 539–544.

Carlson, C. L. (1986). Attention Deficit Disorder Without Hyperactivity: A review of preliminary experimental evidence. In B. Lahey & A. Kazdin (Eds.), *Advances in clinical child psychology* (Vol. 9, pp. 153–176). New York: Plenum Press.

Carlson, C. L., Pelham, W. E., Jr., Milich, R., & Dixon, J. (1992). Single and combined effects of methylphenidate and behavior therapy on the classroom performance of children with Attention-Deficit Hyperactivity Disorder. *Journal of Abnormal Child Psychology, 20,* 213–232.

Carte, E. T., Nigg, J. T., & Hinshaw, S. P. (1996). Neuropsychological functioning, motor speed, and language processing in boys with and without ADHD. *Journal of Abnormal Child Psychology, 24,* 481–498.

Casey, B. J., Castellanos, F. X., Giedd, J. N., Marsh, W. L., Hamburger, S. D., Schubert, A. B., Vauss, Y. C., Vaituzis, A. C., Dickstein, D. P., Sarfatti, S. E., & Rapoport, J. L. (1997). Implication of right frontostriatal circuitry in response inhibition and Attention-Deficit/Hyperactivity Disorder. *Journal of the American Academy of Child and Adolescent Psychiatry, 36,* 374–383.

Castellanos, F. X., Giedd, J. N., Eckburg, P., Marsh, W. L., Vaituzis, C., Kaysen, D., Hamburger, S. D., & Rapoport, J. L. (1994). Quantitative morphology of the caudate nucleus in Attention Deficit Hyperactivity Disorder. *American Journal of Psychiatry, 151,* 1791–1796.

Castellanos, F. X., Giedd, J. N., Marsh, W. L., Hamburger, S. D., Vaituzis, A. C., Dickstein, D. P., Sarfatti, S. E., Vauss, Y. C., Snell, J. W., Lange, N., Kaysen, D., Krain, A. L., Ritchhie, G. F., Rajapakse, J. C., & Rapoport, J. L. (1996). Quantitative brain magnetic resonance imaging in Attention-Deficit Hyperactivity Disorder. *Archives of General Psychiatry, 53,* 607–616.

Chess, S. (1960). Diagnosis and treatment of the hyperactive child. *New York State Journal of Medicine, 60,* 2379–2385.

Childers, A. T. (1935). Hyper-activity in children having behavior disorders. *American Journal of Orthopsychiatry, 5 ,* 227–243.

Cohen, N. J., Sullivan, J., Minde, K., Novak, C., & Helwig, C. (1981). Evaluation of the relative effectiveness of methylphenidate and cognitive behavior modification in the treatment of kindergarten-aged hyperactive children. *Journal of Abnormal Child Psychology, 9,* 43–54.

Comings, D. E., Comings, B. G., Muhleman, D., Dietz, G., Shahbahrami, B., Tast, D., Knell, E., Kocsis, P., Baumgarten, R., Kovacs, B. W., Levy, D. L., Smith, M., Kane, J. M., Lieberman, J. A., Klein, D. N., MacMurray, J., Tosk, J., Sverd, J., Gysin, R., & Flanagan, S. (1991). The dopamine D2 receptor locus as a modifying gene in neuropsychiatric disorders. *Journal of the American Medical Association, 266,* 1793–1800.

Conners, C. K. (1980). *Food additives and hyperactive children.* New York: Plenum Press.

Cook, E. H., Stein, M. A., Krasowski, M. D., Cox, N. J., Olkon, D. M., Kieffer, J. E., & Leventhal, B. L. (1993). Association of Attention Deficit Disorder and the dopamine transporter gene. *American Journal of Human Genetics, 56,* 993–995.

Cook, E. H., Stein, M. A., & Leventhal, D. L. (1997). Family-based association of Attention-Deficit/Hyperactivity Disorder and the dopamine transporter. In K. Blum (Ed.), *Handbook of psychiatric genetics* (pp. 297–310). New York: CRC Press.

Coons, H. W., Klorman, R., & Borgstedt, A. D. (1987a). Effects of methylphenidate on adolescents with a childhood history of Attention Deficit Disorder: I. Clinical findings. *Journal of the American Academy of Child and Adolescent Psychiatry, 26,* 363–367.

Coons, H. W., Klorman, R., & Borgstedt, A. D. (1987b). Effects of methylphenidate on adolescents with a childhood history of Attention Deficit Disorder: II. Information processing. *Journal of the American Academy of Child and Adolescent Psychiatry, 26,* 368–374.

Cunningham, C. E., & Barkley, R. A. (1979). The interactions of hyperactive and normal children with their mothers during free play and structured task. *Child Development, 50,* 217–224.

Cunningham, C. E., Bremmer, R., & Boyle, M. (1995). Large group community-based parenting programs for families of preschoolers at risk for disruptive behaviour disorders: Utilization, cost effectiveness, and outcome. *Journal of Child Psychology and Psychiatry, 36,* 1141–1159.

Cunningham, C. E., & Siegel, L. S. (1987). Peer interactions of normal and attention-deficit disordered boys during freeplay, cooperative task, and simulated classroom situations. *Journal of Abnormal Child Psychology, 15,* 247–268.

Cunningham, C. E., Siegel, L. S., & Offord, D. R. (1985). A developmental dose response analysis of the effects of methylphenidate on the peer interactions of attention deficit disordered boys. *Journal of Child Psychology and Psychiatry, 26,* 955–971.

Danforth, J. S., Barkley, R. A., & Stokes, T. F. (1991). Observations of parent–child interactions with hyperactive children: Research and clinical implications. *Clinical Psychology Review, 11,* 703–727.

Dangel, R. F., & Polster, R. A. (Eds.). (1984). *Parent training: Foundations of research and practice.* New York: Guilford Press.

Darwin, C. (1992). *The descent of man and selection in relation to sex.* Chicago: Encyclopedia Britannica. (Original work published 1871)

David, O. J. (1974). Association between lower level lead concentrations and hyperactivity. *Environmental Health Perspective*, 17–25.

de la Burde, B., & Choate, M. (1972). Does asymptomatic lead exposure in children have latent sequelae? *Journal of Pediatrics, 81*, 1088–1091.

de la Burde, B., & Choate, M. (1974). Early asymptomatic lead exposure and development at school age. *Journal of Pediatrics, 87*, 638–642.

Denckla, M. B., & Rudel, R. G. (1978). Anomalies of motor development in hyperactive boys. *Annals of Neurology, 3*, 231–233.

Denson, R., Nanson, J. L., & McWatters, M. A. (1975). Hyperkinesis and maternal smoking. *Canadian Psychiatric Association Journal, 20*, 183–187.

Diaz, R. M., & Berk, L. E. (Eds.). (1992). *Private speech: From social interaction to self-regulation.* Hillsdale, NJ: Erlbaum.

Diaz, R. M., & Berk, L. E. (1995). A Vygotskian critique of self-instructional training. *Development and Psychopathology, 7*, 369–392.

Dodge, K. A. (1989). Problems in social relationships. In E. J. Mash & R. A. Barkley (Eds.), *Treatment of childhood disorders* (pp. 222–246). New York: Guilford Press.

Douglas, V. I. (1972). Stop, look, and listen: The problem of sustained attention and impulse control in hyperactive and normal children. *Canadian Journal of Behavioural Science, 4*, 259–282.

Douglas, V. I. (1980). Higher mental processes in hyperactive children: Implications for training. In R. Knights & D. Bakker (Eds.), *Treatment of hyperactive and learning disordered children* (pp. 65–92). Baltimore: University Park Press.

Douglas, V. I. (1983). Attention and cognitive problems. In M. Rutter (Ed.), *Developmental neuropsychiatry* (pp. 280–329). New York: Guilford Press.

Douglas, V. I. (1989). Can Skinnerian theory explain attention deficit disorder? A reply to Barkley. In L. M. Bloomingdale & J. Swanson (Eds.), *Attention deficit disorder: Current concepts and emerging trends in attentional and behavioral disorders of childhood* (pp. 235–254). New York: Pergamon.

Douglas, V. I., & Peters, K. G. (1979). Toward a clearer definition of the attentional deficit of hyperactive children. In G. A. Hale & M. Lewis (Eds.), *Attention and cognitive development* (pp. 173–248). New York: Plenum Press.

Draeger, S., Prior, M., & Sanson, A. (1986). Visual and auditory attention performance in hyperactive children: Competence or compliance. *Journal of Abnormal Child Psychology, 14*, 411–424.

Dubey, D. R., O'Leary, S. G., & Kaufman, K. F. (1983). Training parents of hyperactive children in child management: A comparative outcome study. *Journal of Abnormal Child Psychology, 11*, 229–246.

Dulcan, M. K. (1990). Using psychostimulants to treat behavioral disorders in children and adolescents. *Journal of Child and Adolescent Psychopharmacology, 1*, 7–20.

DuPaul, G. R. (1991). Parent and teacher ratings of ADHD symptoms: Psychometric properties in a community-based sample. *Journal of Clinical Child Psychology, 20*, 2425–253.

DuPaul, G. J., Anastopoulos, A. D., Kwasnik, D., Barkley, R. A., & McMurray, M. B. (1996). Methylphenidate effects on children with Attention Deficit Hyperactivity Disorder: Self-report of symptoms, side-effects, and self-esteem. *Journal of Attention Disorders, 1*, 3–15.

DuPaul, G. J., Barkley, R. A., & McMurray, M. B. (1994). Response of children with ADHD to methylphenidate: Interaction with internalizing symptoms. *Journal of the American Academy of Child and Adolescent Psychiatry, 93*, 894–903.

DuPaul, G. J., & Eckert, T. L. (1997). The effects of school-based interventions for Attention Deficit Hyperactivity Disorder: A meta-analysis. *School Psychology Digest, 26*, 5–27.

DuPaul, G. J., Guevremont, D. C., & Barkley, R. A. (1992). Behavioral treatment of Attention-Deficit Hyperactivity Disorder in the classroom: The use of the Attention Training System. *Behavior Modification, 16*, 204–225.

DuPaul, G. J., & Stoner, G. (1994). *ADHD in the schools: Assessment and intervention strategies.* New York: Guilford Press.

Dush, D. M., Hirt, M. L., & Schroeder, H. E. (1989). Self-statement modification in the treatment of child behavior disorders: A meta-analysis. *Psychological Bulletin, 106*, 97–106.

Edelbrock, C. S., Rende, R., Plomin, R., & Thompson, L. (1995). A twin study of competence and problem behavior in childhood and early adolescence. *Journal of Child Psychology and Psychiatry, 36*, 775–786.

Edwards, G. (1995). Patterns of paternal and maternal conflict with adolescents with ADHD. *The ADHD Report, 3*(5), 10–11.

Eiraldi, R. B., Power, T. J., & Nezu, C. M. (1997). Patterns of comorbidity associated with subtypes of Attention-Deficit/Hyperactivity Disorder among 6- to 12-year-old children. *Journal of the American Academy of Child and Adolescent Psychiatry, 36*, 503–514.

Ekman, P., & Davidson, R. J. (1994). *The nature of emotion: Fundamental questions.* New York: Oxford University Press.

Erhardt, D., & Hinshaw, S. P. (1994). Initial sociometric impressions of Attention-Deficit Hyperactivity Disorder and comparison boys: Predictions from social behaviors and from nonbehavioral variables. *Journal of Consulting and Clinical Psychology, 62*, 833–842.

Ernst, M., Liebenauer, L. L., King, A. C., Fitzgerald, G. A., Cohen, R. M., & Zametkin, A. J. (1994). Reduced brain metabolism in hyperactive girls. *Journal of the American Academy of Child and Adolescent Psychiatry, 33*, 858–868.

Faraone, S. V. (1996). Discussion of "Genetic influence on parent-reported attention-related problems in a Norwegian general population twin sample." *Journal of the American Academy of Child and Adolescent Psychiatry, 35,* 596–598.

Faraone, S. V., Biederman, J., Chen, W. J., Krifcher, B., Keenan, K., Moore, C., Sprich, S., & Tsuang, M. T. (1992). Segregation analysis of Attention Deficit Hyperactivity Disorder. *Psychiatric Genetics, 2,* 257–275.

Farrington, D. P., Loeber, R., & van Kammen, W. B. (1987, October). *Long-term criminal outcomes of hyperactivity–impulsivity–attention deficit and conduct problems in childhood.* Paper presented at the meeting of the Society for Life History Research, St. Louis, MO.

Fehlings, D. L., Roberts, W., Humphries, T., & Dawe, G. (1991). Attention Deficit Hyperactivity Disorder: Does cognitive behavioral therapy improve home behavior? *Journal of Developmental and Behavioral Pediatrics, 12,* 223–228.

Feingold, B. (1975). *Why your child is hyperactive.* New York: Random House.

Fenichel, R. R. (1995). Combining methylphenidate and clonidine: The role of post-marketing surveillance. *Journal of Child and Adolescent Psychopharmacology, 5,* 155–156.

Fergusson, D. M., Fergusson, I. E., Horwood, L. J., & Kinzett, N. G. (1988). A longitudinal study of dentine lead levels, intelligence, school performance, and behaviour. *Journal of Child Psychology and Psychiatry, 29,* 811–824.

Filipek, P. A., Semrud-Clikeman, M., Steingard, R. J., Renshaw, P. F., Kennedy, D. N., & Biederman, J. (1997). Volumetric MRI analysis comparing subjects having Attention-Deficit Hyperactivity Disorder with normal controls. *Neurology, 48,* 589–601.

Firestone, P., & Douglas, V. (1975). The effects of reward and punishment on reaction times and autonomic activity in hyperactive and normal children. *Journal of Abnormal Child Psychology, 3,* 201–216.

Firestone, P., & Douglas, V. I. (1977). The effects of verbal and material reward and punishers on the performance of impulsive and reflective children. *Child Study Journal, 7,* 71–78.

Firestone, P., Kelly, M. J., Goodman, J. T., & Davey, J. (1981). Differential effects of parent training and stimulant medication with hyperactives. *Journal of the American Academy of Child Psychiatry, 20,* 135–147.

Firestone, P., & Martin, J. E. (1979). An analysis of the hyperactive syndrome: A comparison of hyperactive, behavior problem, asthmatic, and normal children. *Journal of Abnormal Child Psychology, 7,* 261–273.

Fischer, M. (1990). Parenting stress and the child with attention deficit hyperactivity disorder. *Journal of Clinical Child Psychology, 19,* 337–346.

Fischer, M., Barkley, R. A., Fletcher, K., & Smallish, L. (1997, June). *The persistence of ADHD into young adulthood: It depends on the informant.* Paper presented at the meeting of the International Society for Research in Child and Adolescent Psychopathology, Paris.

Fletcher, K., Fischer, M., Barkley, R. A., & Smallish, L. (1996). A sequential analysis of the mother–adolescent interactions of ADHD, ADHD/ODD, and normal teenagers: Neutral and conflict discussions. *Journal of Abnormal Child Psychology, 24,* 271–298.

Forgatch, M., & Patterson, G. R. (1987). *Parents and adolescents living together* (2 vols.). Eugene, OR: Castalia.

Fuster, J. M. (1989). *The prefrontal cortex.* New York: Raven Press.

Gabel, S., Schmitz, S., & Fulker, D. W. (1996). Comorbidity in hyperactive children: Issues related to selection bias, gender, severity, and internalizing symptoms. *Child Psychiatry and Human Development, 27,* 15–28.

Gadow, K. D. (1985). Relative efficacy of pharmacological, behavioral, and combination treatments for enhancing academic performance. *Clinical Psychology Review, 5,* 513–533.

Gadow, K. D., Sverd, J., Sprafkin, J., Nolan, E. E., & Ezor, S. N. (1995). Efficacy of methylphenidate for Attention-Deficit Hyperactivity Disorder in children with tic disorder. *Archives of General Psychiatry, 52,* 444–455.

Gelernter, J. O., O'Malley, S., Risch, N., Kranzler, H. R., Krystal, J., Merikangas, K., & Kennedy, J. L. (1991). No association between an allele at the D2 dopamine receptor gene (DRD2) and alcoholism. *Journal of the American Medical Association, 266,* 1801–1807.

Gilger, J. W., Pennington, B. F., & DeFries, J. C. (1992). A twin study of the etiology of comorbidity: Attention-Deficit Hyperactivity Disorder and dyslexia. *Journal of the American Academy of Child and Adolescent Psychiatry, 31,* 343–348.

Gittelman, R., & Eskinazi, B. (1983). Lead and hyperactivity revisited. *Archives of General Psychiatry, 40,* 827–833.

Gittelman, R., Mannuzza, S., Shenker, R., & Bonagura, N. (1985). Hyperactive boys almost grown up: I. Psychiatric status. *Archives of General Psychiatry, 42,* 937–947.

Gjone, H., Stevenson, J., & Sundet, J. M. (1996). Genetic influence on parent-reported attention-related problems in a Norwegian general population twin sample. *Journal of the American Academy of Child and Adolescent Psychiatry, 35,* 588–596.

Gjone, H., Stevenson, J., Sundet, J. M., & Eilertsen, D. E. (1996). Changes in heritability across increasing levels of behavior problems in young twins. *Behavior Genetics, 26,* 419–426.

Goldstein, S., & Goldstein, M. (1990). *Managing attention disorders in children.* New York: Wiley.

Goldstein, S., & Ingersoll, B. (1993). Controversial treatments for ADHD: Essential information for clinicians. *The ADHD Report, 1* (3), 4–5.

Goldman-Rakic, P. S. (1995). Architecture of the prefrontal cortex and the central executive. *Annals of the New York Academy of Sciences, 769,* 71–83.

Gomez, R., & Sanson, A. V. (1994). Mother–child interactions and noncompliance in hyperactive boys with and without conduct problems. *Journal of Child Psychology and Psychiatry, 35,* 477–490.

Goodman, J. R., & Stevenson, J. (1989). A twin study of hyperactivity: II. The aetiological role of genes, family relationships, and perinatal adversity. *Journal of Child Psychology and Psychiatry, 30,* 691–709.

Goodyear, P., & Hynd, G. (1992). Attention Deficit Disorder with (ADD/H) and without (ADD/WO) Hyperactivity: Behavioral and neuropsychological differentiation. *Journal of Clinical Child Psychology, 21,* 273–304.

Gordon, M. (1979). The assessment of impulsivity and mediating behaviors in hyperactive and non-hyperactive children. *Journal of Abnormal Child Psychology, 7,* 317–326.

Gordon, M., Thomason, D., & Cooper, S. (1990, August). *Non-medical treatment of ADHD/hyperactivity: The Attention Training System.* Paper presented at the 98th Annual Convention of the American Psychological Association, Boston.

Goyette, C. H., Conners, C. K., & Ulrich, R. F. (1978). Normative data for Revised Conners Parent and Teacher Rating Scales. *Journal of Abnormal Child Psychology, 6,* 221–236.

Green, L., Fry, A. F., & Meyerson, J. (1994). Discounting of delayed rewards: A life-span comparison. *Psychological Science, 5,* 33–36.

Greene, R. W. (1996). Students with Attention-Deficit Hyperactivity Disorder and their teachers: Implications of a goodness-of-fit perspective. In T. Ollendick & R. J. Prinz (Eds.), *Advances in clinical child psychology* (Vol. 18, pp. 205–230). New York: Plenum Press.

Greene, R. W., Biederman, J., Faraone, S. V., Ouellette, C. A., Penn, C., & Griffin, S. M. (1996). Toward a psychometric definition of social disability in children with Attention-Deficit Hyperactivity Disorder. *Journal of the American Academy of Child and Adolescent Psychiatry, 35,* 571–578.

Greenhill, L. L., & Osmon, B. B. (1991). *Ritalin: Theory and patient management.* New York: Mary Ann Liebert.

Gross, M. D. (1984). Effects of sucrose on hyperkinetic children. *Pediatrics, 74,* 876–878.

Gunning, B. (1992). *A controlled trial of clonidine in hyperkinetic children.* Unpublished doctoral dissertation, University of Amsterdam: The Netherlands.

Haenlein, M., & Caul, W. F. (1987). Attention Deficit Disorder with Hyperactivity: A specific hypothesis of reward dysfunction. *Journal of the American Academy of Child and Adolescent Psychiatry, 26,* 356–362.

Hale, G. A., & Lewis, M. (1979). *Attention and cognitive development.* New York: Plenum Press.

Hales, D., & Hales, R. (1985). Using the body to mend the mind. *American Health,* pp. 27–31.

Hart, E. L., Lahey, B. B., Loeber, R., Applegate, B., & Frick, P. J. (1995). Developmental changes in Attention-Deficit Hyperactivity Disorder in boys: A four-year longitudinal study. *Journal of Abnormal Child Psychology, 23,* 729–750.

Hartsough, C. S., & Lambert, N. M. (1985). Medical factors in hyperactive and normal children: Prenatal, developmental, and health history findings. *American Journal of Orthopsychiatry, 55,* 190–201.

Haslam, R. H. A., Dalby, J. T., & Rademaker, A. W. (1984). Effects of megavitamin therapy on children with Attention Deficit Disorders. *Pediatrics, 74,* 103–111.

Hastings, J. E., & Barkley, R. A. (1978). A review of psychophysiological research with hyperactive children. *Journal of Abnormal Child Psychology, 7,* 413–447.

Hayes, S. (1989). *Rule-governed behavior.* New York: Plenum Press.

Hayes, S. C., Rosenfarb, I., Wulfert, E., Munt, E. D., Korn, Z., & Zettle, R. D. (1985). Self-reinforcement effects: An artifact of social standard setting? *Journal of Applied Behavior Analysis, 18,* 201–214.

Heffron, W. A., Martin, C. A., & Welsh, R. J. (1984). Attention Deficit Disorder in three pairs of monozygotic twins: A case report. *Journal of the American Academy of Child Psychiatry, 23,* 299–301.

Hinshaw, S. P. (1987). On the distinction between attentional deficits/hyperactivity and conduct problems/aggression in child psychopathology. *Psychological Bulletin, 101,* 443–447.

Hinshaw, S. P. (1992a). Externalizing behavior problems and academic underachievement in childhood and adolescence: Causal relationships and underlying mechanisms. *Psychological Bulletin, 111,* 127–155.

Hinshaw, S. P., & Erhardt, D. (1992b). Interventions for social competence and social skill. *Child and Adolescent Psychiatric Clinics of North America, 1*(2), 539–552.

Hinshaw, S. P., & Erhardt, D. (1991). Attention-Deficit Hyperactivity Disorder. In P. C. Kendall (Ed.), *Child and adolescent therapy: Cognitive-behavioral procedures* (pp. 98–128). New York: Guilford Press.

Hinshaw, S. P., Henker, B., & Whalen, C. K. (1984a). Cognitive-behavioral and pharmacologic interventions for hyperactive boys: Comparative and combined effects. *Journal of Consulting and Clinical Psychology, 52,* 739–749.

Hinshaw, S. P., Henker, B., & Whalen, C. K. (1984b). Self-control in hyperactive boys in anger-inducing situations: Effects of cognitive-behavioral training and of methylphenidate. *Journal of Abnormal Child Psychology, 12,* 55–77.

Horn, W. F., Chatoor, I., & Conners, C. K. (1983). Additive effects of dexedrine and self-control training: A multiple assessment. *Behavior Modification, 7,* 383–402.

Horn, W. F., Iolongo, N., Greenberg, G., Packard, T., & Smith-Winberry, C. (1990). Additive effects of behavioral parent training and self-control therapy with attention deficit hyperactivity disordered children. *Journal of Clinical Child Psychology, 19,* 98–110.

Horn, W. F., Ialongo, N., Pascoe, J. M., Greenberg, G., Packard, T., Lopez, M., Wagner, A., & Puttler, L. (1991). Additive effects of psychostimulants, parent training, and self-control therapy with ADHD children. *Journal of the American Academy of Child and Adolescent Psychiatry, 30,* 233–240.

Horn, W. F., Ialongo, N., Popovich, S., & Peradotto, D. (1987). Behavioral parent training and cognitive-behavioral self-control therapy with ADD-H children: Comparative and combined effects. *Journal of Clinical Child Psychology, 16,* 57–68.

Hubbard, J. A., & Newcomb, A. F. (1991). Initial dyadic peer interaction of Attention Deficit-Hyperactivity Disorder and normal boys. *Journal of Abnormal Child Psychology, 19,* 179–195.

Hunt, R. D., Caper, L., & O'Connell, P. (1990). Clonidine in child and adolescent psychiatry. *Journal of Child and Adolescent Psychopharmacology, 1,* 87–102.

Hynd, G. W., Hern, K. L., Novey, E. S., Eliopulos, D., Marshall, R., Gonzalez, J. J., & Voeller, K. K. (1993). Attention-Deficit Hyperactivity Disorder and asymmetry of the caudate nucleus. *Journal of Child Neurology, 8,* 339–347.

Ingersoll, B. D., & Goldstein, S. (1993). *Attention Deficit Disorder and learning disabilities: Realities, myths, and controversial treatments.* New York: Doubleday.

Jacob, R. G., O'Leary, K. D., & Rosenblad, C. (1978). Formal and informal classroom settings: Effects on hyperactivity. *Journal of Abnormal Child Psychology, 6,* 47–59.

Jacobvitz, D., & Sroufe, L. A. (1987). The early caregiver–child relationship and Attention-Deficit Disorder with Hyperactivity in kindergarten: A prospective study. *Child Development, 58,* 1488–1495.

James, W. (1890). *The principles of psychology* (2 vols.). New York: Henry Holt.

Jensen, P. S., Shervette, R. E., III, Xenakis, S. N., & Richters, J. (1993). Anxiety and depressive disorders in Attention Deficit Disorder with Hyperactivity: New findings. *American Journal of Psychiatry, 150,* 1203–1209.

Johnston, C. (1992, February). *The influence of behavioral parent training on inattentive–overactive and aggressive–defiant behaviors in ADHD children.* Poster presented at the annual meeting of the International Society for Research in Child and Adolescent Psychopathology, Sarasota, FL.

Johnston, C. (1996). Parent characteristics and parent–child interactions in families of nonproblem children and ADHD children with higher and lower levels of oppositional–defiant behavior. *Journal of Abnormal Child Psychology, 24,* 85–104.

Johnston, C., Pelham, W. E., &. Murphy, H. A. (1985). Peer relationships in ADDH and normal children: A developmental analysis of peer and teacher ratings. *Journal of Abnormal Child Psychology, 13,* 89–100.

Kagan, J. (1966). Reflection–impulsivity: The generality and dynamics of conceptual tempo. *Journal of Abnormal Psychology, 71,* 17–24.

Kaplan, B. J., McNichol, J., Conte, R. A., & Moghadam, H. K. (1987). Sleep disturbance in preschool-aged hyperactive and nonhyperactive children. *Pediatrics, 80,* 839–844.

Kelsoe, J. R., Ginns, E. I., Egeland, J. A., Gerhard, D. S., Goldstein, A. M., Bale, S. J., & Pauls, D. L. (1989). Re-evaluation of the linkage relationship between chromosome 11p loci and the gene for bipolar affective disorder in the Old Order Amish. *Nature, 342,* 238–243.

Kendall, P. C., & Braswell, L. (1985). *Cognitive-behavioral therapy for impulsive children.* New York: Guilford Press.

Kendall, P. C., & Wilcox, L. E. (1979). Self-control in children: Development of a rating scale. *Journal of Consulting and Clinical Psychology, 47,* 1020–1029.

Kessler, J. W. (1980). History of minimal brain dysfunction. In H. E. Rie & E. D. Rie (Eds.), *Handbook of minimal brain dysfunction: A critical view* (pp. 18–52). New York: Wiley.

Klorman, R. (1992). Cognitive event-related potentials in Attention Deficit Disorder. In S. E. Shaywitz & B. A. Shaywitz (Eds.). *Attention Deficit Disorder comes of age: Toward the twenty-first century* (pp. 221–244). Austin, TX: Pro-Ed.

Kopp, C. B. (1982). Antecedents of self-regulation: A developmental perspective. *Developmental Psychology, 18,* 199–214.

Kuperman, S., Johnson, B., Arndt, S., Lindgren, S., & Wolraich, M. (1996). Quantitative EEG differences in a nonclinical sample of children with ADHD and undifferentiated ADD. *Journal of the American Academy of Child and Adolescent Psychiatry, 35,* 1009–1017.

Lahey, B. B., Applegate, B., McBurnett, K., Biederman, J., Greenhill, L., Hynd, G., Barkley, R. A., Newcorn, J., Jensen, P., Richters, J., Garfinkel, B., Kerdyk, L., Frick, P. J., Ollendick, T., Perez, D., Hart, E. L., Walkman, I., & Shaffer, D. (1994). DSM-IV field trials for Attention Deficit/Hyperactivity Disorder in children and adolescents. *American Journal of Psychiatry, 151,* 1673–1685.

Lahey, B. B., & Carlson, C. L. (1992). Validity of the diagnostic category of Attention Deficit Disorder without Hyperactivity: A review of the literature. In S. E. Shaywitz & B. A. Shaywitz (Eds.). *Attention deficit disorder comes of age: Toward the twenty-first century* (pp. 119–144). Austin, TX: Pro-Ed.

Lahey, B. B., Pelham, W. E., Schaughency, E. A., Atkins, M. S., Murphy, H. A., Hynd, G. W., Russo, M., Hartdagen, S., & Lorys-Vernon, A. (1988). Dimensions and types of Attention Deficit Disorder with Hyperactivity in children: A factor and cluster-analytic approach. *Journal of the American Academy of Child and Adolescent Psychiatry, 27,* 330–335.

Lahoste, G. J., Swanson, J. M., Wigal, S. B., Glabe, C., Wigal, T., King, N., & Kennedy, J. L. (1996). Dopamine D4 receptor gene polymorphism is associated with Attention Deficit Hyperactivity Disorder. *Molecular Psychiatry, 1,* 121–124.

Lambert, N. M., Sandoval, J., & Sassone, D. (1978). Prevalence of hyperactivity in elementary school children as a function of social system definers. *American Journal of Orthopsychiatry, 48,* 446–463.

Lang, P. J. (1995). The emotion probe: Studies of motivation and attention. *American Psychologist, 50,* 372–385.

Latham, P., & Latham, R. (1992). *ADD and the law.* Washington, DC: JKL Communications.

Laufer, M., Denhoff, E., & Solomons, G. (1957). Hyperkinetic impulse disorder in children's behavior problems. *Psychosomatic Medicine, 19,* 38–49.

Lerer, R. J., Lerer, P., & Artner, J. (1977). The effects of methylphenidate on the handwriting of children with minimal brain dysfunction. *Journal of Pediatrics, 91,* 127–132.

Levin, P. M. (1938). Restlessness in children. *Archives of Neurology and Psychiatry, 39,* 764–770.

Levy, F., & Hay, D. (1992, February). *ADHD in twins and their siblings.* Paper presented at the annual meeting of the International Society for Research in Child and Adolescent Psychopathology, Sarasota, Florida, February.

Linden, M., Habib, T., & Radojevic, V. (1996). A controlled study of the effects of EEG biofeedback on cognition and behavior of children with Attention Deficit Disorder and learning disabilities. *Biofeedback and Self-Regulation, 21,* 35–50.

Loeber, R. (1991). Development and risk factors of juvenile antisocial behavior and delinquency. *Clinical Psychology Review, 10,* 1–42.

Loeber, R., Green, S. M., Lahey, B. B., Christ, M. A. G., & Frick, P. J. (1992). Developmental sequences in the age of onset of disruptive child behaviors. *Journal of Child and Family Studies, 1,* 21–41.

Loney, J., Whaley-Klahn, M. A., Kosier, T., & Conboy, J. (1981, November). *Hyperactive boys and their brothers at 21: Predictors of aggressive and antisocial outcomes.* Paper presented at the meeting of the Society of Life History Research, Monterey, CA.

Lopez, R. (1965). Hyperactivity in twins. *Canadian Psychiatric Association Journal, 10,* 421–426.

Lou, H. C., Henriksen, L., & Bruhn, P. (1984). Focal cerebral hypoperfusion in children with dysphasia and/or Attention Deficit Disorder. *Archives of Neurology, 11,* 825–829.

Lou, H. C., Henriksen, L., Bruhn, P., Borner, H., & Nielsen, J. B. (1989). Striatal dysfunction in attention deficit and hyperkinetic disorder. *Archives of Neurology, 46,* 48–52.

Lubar, J., & Lubar, J. (1984). Electroencephalographic biofeedback of SMR and beta for treatment of Attention Deficit Disorders in a clinical setting. *Biofeedback and Self-Regulation, 9,* 1–23.

Luk, S. (1985). Direct observations studies of hyperactive behaviors. *Journal of the American Academy of Child Psychiatry, 24,* 338–344.

Mannuzza, S., Klein, R. G., Bonagura, N., Malloy, P., Giampino, T. L., & Addalli, K. A. (1991). Hyperactive boys almost grown up: V. Replication of psychiatric status. *Archives of General Psychiatry, 48,* 77–83.

Mannuzza, S., Gittelman-Klein, R., Bessler, A., Malloy, P., & LaPadula, M. (1993). Adult outcome of hyperactive boys: Educational achievement, occupational rank, and psychiatric status. *Archives of General Psychiatry, 50,* 565–576.

Marholin, D., & Steinman, W. M. (1977). Stimulus control in the classroom as a function of the behavior reinforced. *Journal of Applied Behavior Analysis, 10,* 465–478.

Mash, E. J., & Dalby, T. (1978). Behavioral interventions for hyperactivity. In R. L. Trites (Ed.), *Hyperactivity in children: Etiology, measurement, and treatment implications* (pp. 161–216). Baltimore: University Park Press.

Mash, E. J., & Johnston, C. (1982). A comparison of the mother–child interactions of younger and older hyperactive and normal children. *Child Development, 53,* 1371–1381.

Mash, E. J., & Johnston, C. (1983). Parental perceptions of child behavior problems, parenting self-esteem, and mothers' reported stress in younger and older hyperactive and normal children. *Journal of Consulting and Clinical Psychology, 51,* 68–99.

Mash, E. J., & Johnston, C. (1990). Determinants of parenting stress: Illustrations from families of hyperactive children and families of physically abused children. *Journal of Clinical Child Psychology, 19,* 313–328.

Mattes, J. A., Boswell, L., & Oliver, H. (1984). Methylphenidate effects on symptoms of Attention Deficit Disorder in adults. *Archives of General Psychiatry, 41,* 1059–1063.

Mattes, J. A., & Gittelman, R. (1981). Effects of artificial food colorings in children with hyperactive symptoms. *Archives of General Psychiatry, 38,* 714–718.

McGee, R., Stanton, W. R., & Sears, M. R. (1993). Allergic disorders and Attention Deficit Disorder in children. *Journal of Abnormal Child Psychology, 21,* 79–88.

Meichenbaum, D., & Goodman, J. (1971). Training impulsive children to talk to themselves: A means of developing self-control. *Journal of Abnormal Psychology, 77*, 115–126.

Michon, J. (1985). Introduction. In J. Michon & T. Jackson (Eds.), *Time, mind, and behavior*. Berlin: Springer-Verlag.

Milberger, S., Biederman, J., Faraone, S. V., Chen, L., & Jones, J. (1996). Is maternal smoking during pregnancy a risk factor for Attention Deficit Hyperactivity Disorder in children? *American Journal of Psychiatry, 153*, 1138–1142.

Milich, R., & Dodge, K. A. (1984). Social information processing in child psychiatry populations. *Journal of Abnormal Child Psychology, 12*, 471–490.

Milich, R., & Kramer, J. (1985). Reflections on impulsivity: An empirical investigation of impulsivity as a construct. In K. Gadow & I. Bialer (Eds.), *Advances in learning and behavioral disabilities* (Vol. 3, pp. 117–150). Greenwich, CT: JAI Press.

Milich, R., Loney, J., & Landau, S. (1982). The independent dimensions of hyperactivity and aggression: A validation with playroom observation data. *Journal of Abnormal Psychology, 91*, 183–198.

Milich, R., Wolraich, M., & Lindgren, S. (1986). Sugar and hyperactivity: A critical review of empirical findings. *Clinical Psychology Review, 6*, 493–513.

Minuchin, S., & Fishman, H. C. (1981). *Family therapy techniques*. Cambridge, MA: Harvard University Press.

Mirsky, A. F. (1996). Disorders of attention: A neuropsychological perspective. In R. G. Lyon & N. A. Krasnegor (Eds.), *Attention, memory, and executive function* (pp. 71–96). Baltimore: Paul H. Brookes.

Morrison, J., & Stewart, M. (1973). The psychiatric status of the legal families of adopted hyperactive children. *Archives of General Psychiatry, 28*, 888–891.

Murphy, D. A., Pelham, W. E., & Lang, A. R. (1992). Aggression in boys with Attention Deficit-Hyperactivity Disorder: Methylphenidate effects on naturalistically observed aggression, response to provocation, and social information processing. *Journal of Abnormal Child Psychology, 20*, 451–465.

Nada-Raja, S., Langley, J. D., McGee, R., Williams, S. M., Begg, D. J., & Reeder, A. I. (1997). Inattentive and hyperactive behaviors and driving offenses in adolescence. *Journal of the American Academy of Child and Adolescent Psychiatry, 36*, 515–522.

Needleman, H. L., & Bellinger, D. (1984). The developmental consequences of childhood exposure to lead: Recent studies and methodological issues. In B. B. Lahey & A. E. Kazdin (Eds.), *Advances in clinical child psychology* (Vol. 7, pp. 195–220). New York: Plenum Press.

Needleman, H. L., Gunnoe, C., Leviton, A., Reed, R., Peresie, H., Maher, C., & Barrett, P. (1979). Deficits in psychologic and classroom performance of children with elevated dentine lead levels. *New England Journal of Medicine, 300*, 689–695.

O'Connor, M., Foch, T., Sherry, T., & Plomin, R. (1980). A twin study of specific behavioral problems of socialization as viewed by parents. *Journal of Abnormal Child Psychology, 8*, 189–199.

O'Leary, S. G., & Pelham, W. E. (1978). Behavior therapy and withdrawal of stimulant medication in hyperactive children. *Pediatrics, 61*, 211–216.

O'Leary, R. D., Pelham, W. E., Rosenbaum, A., & Price, G. H. (1976). Behavioral treatment of hyperkinetic children: An experimental evaluation of its usefulness. *Clinical Pediatrics, 15*, 510–515.

Paniagua, F. A. (1987). Management of hyperactive children through correspondence training procedures: A preliminary study. *Behavioral Residential Treatment, 2*, 1–23.

Paternite, C., & Loney, J. (1980). Childhood hyperkinesis: Relationships between symptomatology and home environment. In C. K. Whalen & B. Henker (Eds.), *Hyperactive children: The social ecology of identification and treatment* (pp. 105–141). New York: Academic Press.

Patterson, G. R. (1965). Responsiveness to social stimuli. In L. Krasner & L. P. Ullman (Eds.), *Research in behavior modification: New developments and implications* (pp. 157–178). New York: Holt, Rinehart & Winston.

Patterson, G. R. (1982). *Coercive family process*. Eugene, OR: Castalia.

Patterson, G. R., Dishion, T., & Reid, J. (1992). *Antisocial boys*. Eugene, OR: Castalia.

Pauls, D. L. (1991). Geenetic factors in the expression of Attention-Deficit Hyperactivity Disorder. *Journal of Child and Adolescent Psychopharmacology, 1*, 353–360.

Pelham, W. E. (1987). What do we know about the use and effects of CNS stimulants in the treatment of ADD? In J. Loney (Ed.), *The hyperactive child: Answers to questions about diagnosis, prognosis, and treatment* (pp. 99–110). New York: Haworth Press.

Pelham, W. E., & Bender, M. E. (1982). Peer relationships in hyperactive children: Description and treatment. In K. D. Gadow & I. Bialer (Eds.), *Advances in learning and behavioral disabilities* (Vol. 1, pp. 365–436). Greenwich, CT: JAI Press.

Pelham, W. E., Bender, M. E., Caddell, J., Booth, S., & Moorer, S. R. (1985). Methylphenidate and children with Attention Deficit Disorder. *Archives of General Psychiatry, 42*, 948–952.

Pelham, W. E., Gnagy, E. M., Greenslade, K. E., & Milich, R. (1992). Teacher ratings of DSM-III-R symptoms for the disruptive behavior disorders. *Journal of the American Academy of Child and Adolescent Psychiatry, 31*, 210–218.

Pelham, W. E., & Hinshaw, S. P. (1992). Behavioral intervention for attention deficit hyperactivity disorder. In S. M. Turner, K. S. Calhoun, & H. E. Adams (Eds.), *Handbook of clinical behavior therapy* (2nd ed., pp. 259–283). New York: Wiley.

Pelham, W. E., & Sams, S. E. (1992). Behavior modification. *Child and Adolescent Psychiatric Clinics of North America, 1*(2).

Pelham, W. E., Schnedler, R. W., Bender, M. E., Nilsson, D. E., Miller, J., Budrow, M. S., Ronnel, M., Paluchowski, C., & Marks, D. A. (1988). The combination of behavior therapy and methylphenidate in the treatment of Attention Deficit Disorders: A therapy outcome study. In L. Bloomingdale (Ed.), *Attention Deficit Disorders* (Vol. 3, pp. 29–48). New York: Pergamon Press.

Pennington, B. F., & Ozonoff, S. (1996). Executive functions and developmental psychopathology. *Journal of Child Psychology and Psychiatry, 37*, 51–87.

Perrin, S., & Last, C. G. (1996). Relationship between ADHD and anxiety in boys: Results from a family study. *Journal of the American Academy of Child and Adolescent Psychiatry, 35*, 988–996.

Pfiffner, L. J., & Barkley, R. A. (1990). Educational management. In R. A. Barkley, *Attention-Deficit Hyperactivity Disorder: A handbook for diagnosis and treatment* (pp. 498–539). New York: Guilford Press.

Pfiffner, L. J., & O'Leary, S. G. (1987). The efficacy of all-positive management as a function of the prior use of negative consequences. *Journal of Applied Behavior Analysis, 20*, 265–271.

Pfiffner, L. J., O'Leary, S. G., Rosen, L. A., & Sanderson, W. C., Jr. (1985). A comparison of the effects of continuous and. intermittent response cost and reprimands in the classroom. *Journal of Clinical Child Psychology, 14*, 348–352.

Pfiffner, L. J., Rosen, L. A., & O'Leary, S. G. (1985). The efficacy of an all-positive approach to classroom management. *Journal of Applied Behavior Analysis, 18*, 257–261.

Pike, A., & Plomin, R. (1996). Importance of nonshared environmental factors for childhood and adolescent psychopathology. *Journal of the American Academy of Child and Adolescent Psychiatry, 35*, 560–570.

Pisterman, S., McGrath, P., Firestone, P., Goodman, J. T., Webster, I., & Mallory, R. (1989). Outcome of parent-mediated treatment of preschoolers with Attention Deficit Disorder with Hyperactivity. *Journal of Consulting and Clinical Psychology, 57*, 628–635.

Pliszka, S. R. (1987). Tricyclic antidepressants in the treatment of children with Attention Deficit Disorder. *Journal of the American Academy of Child and Adolescent Psychiatry, 26*, 127–132.

Pliszka, S. R., McCracken, J. T., & Maas, J. W. (1996). Catecholamines in Attention-Deficit Hyperactivity Disorder: Current perspectives. *Journal of the American Academy of Child and Adolescent Psychiatry, 35*, 264–272.

Plomin, R. (1995). Genetics and children's experiences in the family. *Journal of Child Psychology and Psychiatry, 36*, 33–68.

Pollard, S., Ward, E. M., & Barkley, R.. A. (1983). The effects of parent training and Ritalin on the parent–child interactions of hyperactive boys. *Child and Family Behavior Therapy, 5*, 51–69.

Popper, C. W. (1995). Combining methylphenidate and clonidine: Pharmacologic questions and new reports of sudden death. *Journal of Child and Adolescent Psychopharmacology, 5*, 157–166.

Porrino, L. J., Rapoport, J. L., Behar, D., Sceery, W., Ismond, D. R., & Bunney, W. E. (1983). A naturalistic assessment of the motor activity of hyperactive boys. *Archives of General Psychiatry, 40*, 681–687.

Prince, J. B., Wilens, T. E., Biederman, J., Spencer, T. J., & Wozniak, J. (1996). Clonidine for sleep disturbances associated with Attention-Deficit Hyperactivity Disorder: A systematic chart review. *Journal of the American Academy of Child and Adolescent Psychiatry, 35*, 599–605.

Prior, M., Wallace, M., & Milton, L. (1984). Schedule-induced behavior in hyperactive children. *Journal of Abnormal Child Psychology, 12*, 227–244.

Quinn, P. O., & Rapoport, J. L. (1974). Minor physical anomalies and neurologic status in hyperactive boys. *Pediatrics, 53*, 742–747.

Rapoport, J., & Mikkelsen, E. (1978). Antidepressants. In J. Werry (Ed.), *Pediatric psychopharmacology* (pp. 208–233). New York: Brunner/Mazel.

Rapport, M. D., DuPaul, G. J., Stoner, G., & Jones, J. T. (1986). Comparing classroom and clinic measures of Attention Deficit Disorder: Differential, idiosyncratic, and dose–response effects of methylphenidate. *Journal of Consulting and Clinical Psychology, 54*, 334–341.

Rapport, M. D., & Kelly, K. L. (1993). Psychostimulant effects on learning and cognitive function. In J. L. Matson (Ed.), *Handbook of hyperactivity in children* (pp. 97–135). Needham Heights, MA: Allyn & Bacon.

Rappoport, M. D., Murphy, A., & Bailey, J. S. (1980). The effects of a response cost treatment tactic on hyperactive children. *Journal of School Psychology, 18,* 98–111.

Rapport, M. D., Murphy, A., & Bailey, J. S. (1982). Ritalin versus response cost in the control of hyperactive children: A within-subject comparison. *Journal of Applied Behavior Analysis, 15*, 205–216.

Rapport, M. D., Tucker, S. B., DuPaul, G. J., Merlo, M., & Stoner, G. (1986). Hyperactivity and frustration: The influence of control over and size of rewards in delaying gratification. *Journal of Abnormal Child Psychology, 14*, 191–204.

Rhee, S. H., Waldman, I. D., Hay, D. A., & Levy, F. (1995). Sex differences in genetic and environmental influences on DSM-III-R Attention-Deficit Hyperactivity Disorder (ADHD). *Behavior Genetics, 25*, 285.

Richter, N. C. (1984). The efficacy of relaxation training with children. *Journal of Abnormal Child Psychology, 12*, 319–344.

Richters, J. E., Arnold, E., Jensen, P. S., Abikoff, H., Conners, C. K., Greenhill, L. L., Hechtman, L., Hinshaw, S. P., Pelham, W. E., & Swanson, J. M. (1995). NIMH Collaborative Multisite Multimodal Treatment Study of Children with ADHD: I. Background and rationale. *Journal of the American Academy of Child and Adolescent Psychiatry, 34,* 987–1000.

Rie, H. E., & Rie, E. D. (Eds.). (1980). *Handbook of minimal brain dysfunction: A critical view.* New York: Wiley.

Robin, A. R. (1990). Training families with ADHD adolescents. In R. A. Barkley, *Attention-Deficit Hyperactivity Disorder: A handbook for diagnosis and treatment* (pp. 462–497). New York: Guilford Press.

Robin, A. R., & Foster, S. (1989). *Negotiating parent–adolescent conflict: A behavioral–family systems approach.* New York: Guilford Press.

Roizen, N. J., Blondis, T. A., Irwin, M., & Stein, M. (1994). Adaptive functioning in children with Attention-Deficit Hyperactivity Disorder. *Archives of Pediatric and Adolescent Medicine, 148,* 1137–1142.

Rosenbaum, A., O'Leary, K. D., & Jacob, R. G. (1975). Behavioral intervention with hyperactive children: Group consequences as a supplement to individual contingencies. *Behavior Therapy, 6,* 315–323.

Ross, D. M., & Ross, S. A. (1976). *Hyperactivity: Research theory and action.* New York: Wiley.

Ross, D. M., & Ross, S. A. (1982). *Hyperactivity: Current issues, research, and theory* (2nd ed.). New York: Wiley.

Routh, D. K. (1978). Hyperactivity. In P. Magrab (Ed.), *Psychological management of pediatric problems* (pp. 3–48). Baltimore: University Park Press.

Routh, D. K., & Schroeder, C. S. (1976). Standardized playroom measures as indices of hyperactivity. *Journal of Abnormal Child Psychology, 4,* 199–207.

Rutter, M. (1977). Brain damage syndromes in childhood: Concepts and findings. *Journal of Child Psychology and Psychiatry, 18,* 1–21.

Rutter, M. (1997). Nature–nurture integration: The example of antisocial behavior. *American Psychologist, 52,* 390–398.

Ryan, N. D. (1990). Heterocyclic antidepressants in children and adolescents. *Journal of Child and Adolescent Psychopharmacology, 1,* 21–32.

Safer, D. J., & Allen, R. (1976). *Hyperactive children.* Baltimore: University Park Press.

Safer, D. J., Zito, J. M., & Fine, E. M. (1996). Increased methylphenidate usage for Attention Deficit Disorder in the 1990s. *Pediatrics, 98,* 1084–1088.

Sandberg, S. T., Rutter, M., & Taylor, E. (1978). Hyperkinetic disorder in psychiatric clinic attendees. *Developmental Medicine and Child Neurology, 20,* 279–299.

Satterfield, J. H., Cantwell, D. P., & Satterfield, B. T. (1979). Multimodality treatment: A one-year follow-up of 84 hyperactive boys. *Archives of General Psychiatry, 36,* 965–974.

Satterfield, J. H., Hoppe, C. M., & Schell, A. M. (1982). A prospective study of delinquency in 110 adolescent boys with Attention Deficit Disorder and 88 normal adolescent boys. *American Journal of Psychiatry, 139,* 795–798.

Satterfield, J. H., Satterfield, B. T., & Cantwell, D. P. (1980). Multimodality treatment: A two-year evaluation of 61 hyperactive boys. *Archives of General Psychiatry, 37,* 915–919.

Satterfield, J. H., Satterfield, B. T., & Cantwell, D. P. (1981). Three-year multimodality treatment study of 100 hyperactive boys. *Journal of Pediatrics, 98,* 650–655.

Satterfield, J. H., Satterfield, B. T., & Schell, A. M. (1987). Therapeutic interventions to prevent delinquency in hyperactive boys. *Journal of the American Academy of Child and Adolescent Psychiatry, 26,* 56–64.

Satterfield, J. H., Swanson, J., Schell, A., & Lee, F. (1994). Prediction of antisocial behavior in Attention-Deficit Hyperactivity Disorder boys from aggression/defiance scores. *Journal of the American Academy of Child and Adolescent Psychiatry, 33,* 185–190.

Scarr, S. (1992). Developmental theories for the 1990s: Development and individual differences. *Child Development, 63,* 1–19.

Scarr, S., & McCartney, K. (1983). How people make their own environments: A theory of genotype → environment effects. *Child Development, 54,* 424–435.

Schachar, R. J. (1986). Hyperkinetic syndrome: Historical development of the concept. In E. Taylor (Ed.), *The overactive child* (pp. 19–40). Philadelphia: J. B. Lippincott.

Schachar, R. J., & Tannock, R. (1993). Childhood hyperactivity and psychostimulants: A review of extended treatment studies. *Journal of Child and Adolescent Psychopharmacology, 3,* 81–98.

Schachar, R. J., Tannock, R., & Logan, G. (1993). Inhibitory control, impulsiveness, and Attention Deficit Hyperactivity Disorder. *Clinical Psychology Review, 13,* 721–740.

Schothorst, P. F., & van Engeland, H. (1996). Long-term behavioral sequelae of prematurity. *Journal of the American Academy of Child and Adolescent Psychiatry, 35,* 175–183.

Schulman, J. L., Stevens, T. M., Suran, B. G., Kupst, M. J., & Naughton, M. J. (1978). Modification of activity level through biofeedback and operant conditioning. *Journal of Applied Behavior Analysis, 11,* 145–152.

Semrud-Clikeman, M., Filipek, P. A., Biederman, J., Steingard, R., Kennedy, D., Renshaw, P., & Bekken, K. (1994). Attention-Deficit Hyperactivity Disorder: Magnetic resonance imaging morphometric analysis of the corpus callosum. *Journal of the American Academy of Child and Adolescent Psychiatry, 33*, 875–881.

Sergeant, J. A., & van der Meere, J. (1988). What happens when the hyperactive child commits an error? *Psychiatry Research, 24*, 157–164.

Shaffer, D., McNamara, N., & Pincus, J. H. (1974). Controlled observations on patterns of activity, attention, and impulsivity in brain-damaged and psychiatrically disturbed boys. *Psychological Medicine, 4*, 4–18.

Shaywitz, S. E., Cohen, D. J., & Shaywitz, B. E. (1980). Behavior and learning difficulties in children of normal intelligence born to alcoholic mothers. *Journal of Pediatrics, 96*, 978–982.

Shaywitz, S. E., & Shaywitz, B. A. (1992). *Attention deficit disorder comes of age.* Austin, TX: Pro-Ed.

Shaywitz, S. E., Shaywitz, B. A., Cohen, D. J., & Young, J. G. (1983). Monoaminergic mechanisms in hyperactivity. In M. Rutter (Ed.), *Developmental neuropsychiatry* (pp. 330–347). New York: Guilford Press.

Sherman, D. K., McGue, M. K., & Iacono, W. G. (1997). Twin concordance for Attention Deficit Hyperactivity Disorder: A comparison of teachers' and mothers' reports. *American Journal of Psychiatry, 154*, 532–535.

Sieg, K. G., Gaffney, G. R., Preston, D. F., & Hellings, J. A. (1995). SPECT brain imaging abnormalities in Attention Deficit Hyperactivity Disorder. *Clinical Nuclear Medicine, 20*, 55–60.

Silberg, J., Rutter, M., Meyer, J., Maes, H., Hewitt, J., Simonoff, E., Pickles, A., Loeber, R., & Eaves, L. (1996). Genetic and environmental influences on the covariation between hyperactivity and conduct disturbance in juvenile twins. *Journal of Child Psychology and Psychiatry, 37*, 803–816.

Silverman, I. W., & Ragusa, D. M. (1992). Child and maternal correlates of impulse control in 24-month old children. *Genetic, Social, and General Psychology Monographs, 116*, 435–473.

Spencer, T. J., Biederman, J., Harding, M., O'Donnell, D., Faraone, S. V., & Wilens, T. E. (1996). Growth deficits in ADHD children revisited: Evidence of disorder-associated growth delays? *Journal of the American Academy of Child and Adolescent Psychiatry, 35*, 1460–1469.

Spencer, T. J., Wilens, T., Biederman, J., Faraone, S. V., Ablon, J. S., & Lapey, K. (1995). A double-blind, crossover comparison of methylphenidate and placebo in adults with childhood-onset Attention-Deficit Hyperactivity Disorder. *Archives of General Psychiatry, 52*, 434–443.

Spitzer, R. L., Davies, M., & Barkley, R. A. (1990). The DSM-III-R field trial for the disruptive behavior disorders. *Journal of the American Academy of Child and Adolescent Psychiatry, 29*, 690–697.

Stein, M. A., Szumowski, E., Blondis, T. A., & Roizen, N. J. (1995). Adaptive skills dysfunction in ADD and ADHD children. *Journal of Child Psychology and Psychiatry, 36*, 663–670.

Still, G. F. (1902). Some abnormal psychical conditions in children. *Lancet, i,* 1008–1012, 1077–1082, 1163–1169.

Strauss, A. A., & Lehtinen, J. E. (1947). *Psychopathology and education of the brain-injured child.* New York: Grune & Stratton.

Strayhorn, J. M., & Weidman, C. S. (1989). Reduction of attention deficit and internalizing symptoms in preschoolers through parent–child interaction training. *Journal of the American Academy of Child and Adolescent Psychiatry, 28*, 888–896.

Strayhorn, J. M., & Weidman, C. S. (1991). Follow-up one year after parent–child interaction training: Effects on behavior of preschool children. *Journal of the American Academy of Child and Adolescent Psychiatry, 30*, 138–143.

Streissguth, A. P., Bookstein, F. L., Sampson, P. D., & Barr, H. M. (1995). Attention: Prenatal alcohol and continuities of vigilance and attentional problems from 4 through 14 years. *Development and Psychopathology, 7*, 419–446.

Streissguth, A. P., Martin, D. C., Barr, H. M., Sandman, B. M., Kirchner, G. L., & Darby, B. L. (1984). Intrauterine alcohol and nicotine exposure: Attention and reaction time in 4 year-old children. *Developmental Psychology, 20*, 533–541.

Swanson, J. M., Flockhart, D., Udrea, D., Cantwell, D., Connor, D., & Williams, L. (1995). Clonidine in the treatment of ADHD: Questions about safety and efficacy. *Journal of Child and Adolescent Psychopharmacology, 5*, 301–304.

Swanson, J. M., McBurnett, K., Christian, D. L., & Wigal, T. (1995). Stimulant medications and the treatment of children with ADHD. In T. H. Ollendick & R. J. Prinz (Eds.), *Advances in clinical child psychology* (Vol. 17, pp. 265–322). New York: Plenum Press.

Szatmari, P. (1992). The epidemiology of Attention-Deficit Hyperactivity Disorders. *Child and Adolescent Psychiatric Clinics of North America, 1*(2), 361- 372.

Szatmari, P., Saigal, S., Rosenbaum, P., & Campbell, D. (1993). Psychopathology and adaptive functioning among extremely low birthweight children at eight years of age. *Development and Psychopathology, 5*, 345–357.

Tallmadge, J., & Barkley, R. A. (1983). The interactions of hyperactive and normal boys with their mothers and fathers. *Journal of Abnormal Child Psychology, 11*, 565–579.

Tannock, R. (in press). Attention Deficit Disorders with anxiety disorders. In T. E. Brown (Ed.), *Subtypes of Attention Deficit Disorders in children, adolescents, and adults.* Washington, DC: American Psychiatric Press.

Taylor, E. A. (1983). Drug response and diagnostic validation. In M. Rutter (Ed.), *Developmental neuropsychiatry* (pp. 348–368). New York: Guilford Press.

Taylor, E. A. (1986). Childhood hyperactivity. *British Journal of Psychiatry, 149*, 562–573.

Taylor, J. F. (1980). *The hyperactive child and the family*. New York: Random House.

Teicher, M. H., Ito, Y., Glod, C. A., & Barber, N. I. (1996). Objective measurement of hyperactivity and attentional problems in ADHD. *Journal of the American Academy of Child and Adolescent Psychiatry, 35*, 334–342.

Thapar, A., Hervas, A., & McGuffin, P. (1995). Childhood hyperactivity scores are highly heritable and show sibling competition effects: Twin study evidence. *Behavior Genetics, 25*, 537–544.

Thompson, L. L., Riggs, P. D., Mikulich, S. K., & Crowley, T. J. (1996). Contribution of ADHD symptoms to substance problems and delinquency in conduct-disordered adolescents. *Journal of Abnormal Child Psychology, 24*, 325–347.

Trites, R. L., Dugas, F., Lynch, G., & Ferguson, B. (1979). Incidence of hyperactivity. *Journal of Pediatric Psychology, 4*, 179–188.

Trites, R. L., Tryphonas, H., & Ferguson, H. B. (1980). Diet treatment for hyperactive children with food allergies. In R. Knight & D. Bakker (Eds.), *Treatment of hyperactive and learning disordered children* (pp. 151–166). Baltimore: University Park Press.

Ullman, D. G., Barkley, R. A., & Brown, H. W. (1978). The behavioral symptoms of hyperkinetic children who successfully responded to stimulant drug treatment. *American Journal of Orthopsychiatry, 48*, 425–437.

van den Oord, E. J. C. G., Boomsma, D. I., & Verhulst, F. C. (1994). A study of problem behaviors in 10- to 15-year-old biologically related and unrelated international adoptees. *Behavior Genetics, 24*, 193–205.

van den Oord, E. J. C. G., & Rowe, D. C. (1997). Continuity and change in children's social maladjustment: A developmental behavior genetic study. *Developmental Psychology, 33*, 319–332.

van den Oord, E. J. C. G., Verhulst, F. C., & Boomsma, D. I. (1996). A genetic study of maternal and paternal ratings of problem behaviors in 3 year-old twins. *Journal of Abnormal Psychology, 105*, 349–357.

Viesselman, J. O., Yaylayan, S., Weller, E. B., & Weller, R. A. (1993). Antidysthymic drugs (antidepressants and antimanics). In J. S. Werry & M. G. Aman (Eds.), *A practitioner's guide to psychoactive drugs for children and adolescents* (pp. 239–268). New York: Plenum Press.

Volkow, N. D., Ding, Y., Fowler, J. S., Wang, G., Logan, J., Gatley, J. S., Dewey, S., Ashby, C., Lieberman, J., Hitzemann, R., & Wolf, A. P. (1995). Is methylphenidate like cocaine?: Studies on their pharmacokinetics and distribution in the human brain. *Archives of General Psychiatry, 52*, 456–463.

Volkow, N. D., Wang, G., Fowler, J. S., Logan, J., Angrist, B., Hitzemann, R., Lieberman, J., & Pappas, N. (1997). Effects of methylphenidate on regional brain glucose metabolism in humans: Relationship to dopamine D$_2$ receptors. *American Journal of Psychiatry, 154*, 50–55.

Weiss, G. (Ed.). (1992). *Attention Deficit Hyperactivity Disorder* [Special issue]. *Child and Adolescent Psychiatric Clinics of North America, 1*(2).

Weiss, G., & Hechtman, L. (1986). *Hyperactive children grown up*. New York: Guilford Press.

Weiss, G., & Hechtman, L. (1993). *Hyperactive children grown up* (2nd ed.). New York: Guilford Press.

Welner, Z., Welner, A., Stewart, M., Palkes, H., & Wish, E. (1977). A controlled study of siblings of hyperactive children. *Journal of Nervous and Mental Disease, 165*, 110–117.

Wender, P. H. (1971). *Minimal brain dysfunction in children*. New York: Wiley.

Wender, P. H., Reimherr, F. W., & Wood, D. R. (1981). Attention Deficit Disorder ("minimal brain dysfunction") in adults. *Archives of General Psychiatry, 38*, 449–456.

Wender, P. H., Reimherr, F. W., Wood, D., & Ward, M. (1985). A controlled study of methylphenidate in the treatment of Attention Deficit Disorder, Residual Type, in adults. *American Journal of Psychiatry, 142*, 547–552.

Werry, J. S. (1992). History, terminology, and manifestations at different ages. *Child and Adolescent Psychiatric Clinics of North America, 1*(2), 297–310.

Werry, J. S., & Aman, M. G. (1993). Anxiolytics, sedatives, and miscellaneous drugs. In J. S. Werry & M. G. Aman (Eds.), *A practitioner's guide to psychoactive drugs for children and adolescents* (pp. 391–416). New York: Plenum Press.

Werry, J. S., Elkind, G. S., & Reeves, J. S. (1987). Attention deficit, conduct, oppositional, and anxiety disorders in children: III. Laboratory differences. *Journal of Abnormal Child Psychology, 15*, 409–428.

Werry, J. S., Reeves, J. C., & Elkind, G. S. (1987). Attention deficit, conduct, oppositional, and anxiety disorders in children: I. A review of research on differentiating characteristics. *Journal of the American Academy of Child and Adolescent Psychiatry, 26*, 133–143.

Werry, J. S., & Sprague, R. L. (1970). Hyperactivity. In C. G. Costello (Ed.), *Symptoms of psychopathology* (pp. 397–417). New York: Wiley.

Whalen, C. K., & Henker, B. (1991). Therapies for hyperactive children: Comparisons, combinations, and compromises. *Journal of Consulting and Clinical Psychology, 59*, 126–137.

Whalen, C. K., & Henker, B. (1992). The social profile of Attention-Deficit Hyperactivity Disorder: Five fundamental facets. *Child and Adolescent Psychiatric Clinics of North America, 1*(2), 395–410.

Whalen, C. K., Henker, B., & Dotemoto, S. (1980). Methylphenidate and hyperactivity: Effects on teacher behaviors. *Science, 208*, 1280–1282.

Wilens, T. E., Biederman, J., Baldessarini, R. J., Geller, B., Schleifer, D., Spencer, T. J., Birmaher, B., & Goldblatt, A. (1996). Cardiovascular effects of therapeutic doses of tricyclic antidepressants in children and adolescents. *Journal of the American Academy of Child and Adolescent Psychiatry, 35*, 1491–1501.

Willerman, L. (1973). Activity level and hyperactivity in twins. *Child Development, 44*, 288–293.

Willis, T. J., & Lovaas, I. (1977). A behavioral approach to treating hyperactive children: The parent's role. In J. B. Millichap (Ed.), *Learning disabilities and related disorders* (pp. 119–140). Chicago: Year Book Medical.

Winsberg, B. G., Bialer, I., Kupietz, S., & Tobias, J. (1972). Effects of imipramine and dextroamphetamine on behavior of neuropsychiatrically impaired children. *American Journal of Psychiatry, 128*, 1425–1431.

Wolraich, M., Drummond, T., Saloman, M. K., O'Brien, M. L., & Sivage, C. (1978). Effects of methylphenidate alone and in combination with behavior modification procedures on the behavior and academic performance of hyperactive children. *Journal of Abnormal Child Psychology, 6*, 149–161.

Wolraich, M., Milich, R., Stumbo, P., & Schultz, F. (1985). The effects of sucrose ingestion on the behavior of hyperactive boys. *Pediatrics, 106*, 675–682.

Wolraich, M. L., Wilson, D. B., & White, J. W. (1995). The effect of sugar on behavior or cognition in children: A meta-analysis. *Journal of the American Medical Association, 274*, 1617–1621.

Worland, J. (1976). Effects of positive and negative feedback on behavior control in hyperactive and normal boys. *Journal of Abnormal Child Psychology, 4*, 315–325.

Worland, J., North-Jones, M., & Stern, J. A. (1973). Performance and activity of hyperactive and normal boys as a function of distraction and reward. *Journal of Abnormal Child Psychology, 1*, 363–377.

Zametkin, A. J., Liebenauer, L. L., Fitzgerald, G. A., King, A. C., Minkunas, D. V., Herscovitch, P., Yamada, E. M., & Cohen, R. M. (1993). Brain metabolism in teenagers with Attention-Deficit Hyperactivity Disorder. *Archives of General Psychiatry, 50*, 333–340.

Zametkin, A. J., Nordahl, T. E., Gross, M., King, A. C., Semple, W., Rumsey, J., Hamburger, S., & Cohen, R. M. (1990). Cerebral glucose metabolism in adults with hyperactivity of childhood onset. *New England Journal of Medicine, 323*, 1361–1366.

Zametkin, A. J., & Rapoport, J. L. (1986). The pathophysiology of Attention Deficit Disorder with Hyperactivity: A review. In B. Lahey & A. Kazdin (Eds.), *Advances in clinical child psychology* (Vol. 9, pp. 177–216). New York: Plenum Press.

Zeiner, P. (1995). Body growth and cardiovascular function after extended treatment (1.75 years) with methylphenidate in boys with Attention-Deficit Hyperactivity Disorder. *Journal of Child and Adolescent Psychopharmacology, 5*, 129–138.

Zentall, S. S. (1984). Context effects in the behavioral ratings of hyperactivity. *Journal of Abnormal Child Psychology, 12*, 345–352.

Zentall, S. S. (1985). A context for hyperactivity. In K. Gadow (Ed.), *Advances in learning and behavioral disabilities* (Vol. 4, pp. 273–343). Greenwich, CT: JAI Press.

Zettle, R. D., & Hayes, S. C. (1982). Rule-governed behavior: A potential theoretical framework for cognitive-behavioral therapy. In P. C. Kendall (Ed.), *Advances in cognitive-behavioral research* (Vol. 1, pp. 73–118). New York: Academic Press.

CHAPTER 3

Conduct Problems

Robert J. McMahon
University of Washington

Karen C. Wells
Duke University Medical Center

Conduct problems in children constitute a broad range of "acting-out" behaviors, ranging from annoying but relatively minor behaviors such as yelling, whining, and temper tantrums to aggression, physical destructiveness, and stealing. Typically, these behaviors do not occur in isolation but as a complex or syndrome, and there is strong evidence to suggest that oppositional behaviors (e.g., noncompliance, argumentativeness) are developmental precursors to more serious forms of antisocial behavior. When displayed as a cluster, these behaviors have been referred to as "oppositional," "antisocial," and "conduct-disordered" (see Hinshaw & Anderson, 1996, for a thorough discussion of terminology). In this chapter, we use the term "conduct problems" (CP) to refer to this constellation of behaviors. Terminology from the *Diagnostic and Statistical Manual of Mental Disorders* (DSM; American Psychiatric Association, 1980, 1987, 1994) is used only in those instances in which a formal DSM diagnosis is being discussed or referred to (e.g., Conduct Disorder [CD], Oppositional Defiant Disorder [ODD]).

The primary purpose of this chapter is to present and critically evaluate the interventions currently employed with children with CP. We first present an overview of CP in children and ado-

lescents, followed by a description of the assessment of CP. The former section includes brief descriptions of CP, associated characteristics, and developmental pathways. We also discuss various associated child characteristics, familial and peer influences, and broader contextual influences. In the section on assessment, we present an overview of methods and processes that are currently employed with children with CP in different contexts.

CONDUCT PROBLEMS IN CHILDREN AND ADOLESCENTS[1]

Epidemiology

CP is among the most frequently occurring child behavior disorders, with prevalence rates ranging from 2% to 9% for CD and 6% to 10% for ODD in various nonclinic samples (as summarized in Costello, 1990). Children with CP also make up the largest single source of referrals to outpatient and inpatient child mental health settings, accounting for one-third to one-half of referrals (Kazdin, 1995b; Sholevar & Sholevar, 1995). Prevalence rates have been shown to vary as a function of age and sex of the child, as well as the type of CP behavior. For example, younger children are more likely to engage in oppositional behaviors, whereas older children and adolescents are more likely to engage in more covert CP behavior (e.g., stealing). In general, boys are more likely to begin engaging in overt CP behaviors earlier and at higher rates than girls throughout the developmental period.2 During adolescence, gender differences in prevalence decrease dramatically; this seems to be largely accounted for by an increase in the number of girls engaging in covert CP behaviors.

There is a high degree of continuity in CP behaviors from early childhood to later childhood (e.g., Campbell, 1995), from childhood to adolescence (e.g., Lahey et al., 1995; Offord et al., 1992), and from adolescence to adulthood (e.g., Farrington, 1995; Rutter, Harrington, Quinton, & Pickles, 1994). There is evidence for cross-generational consistency as well (Huesmann, Eron, Lefkowitz, & Walder, 1984). Stability also appears comparable for boys and girls (Coie & Dodge, 1998; Stanger, Achenbach, & Verhulst, 1997). Both boys and girls with CP are at increased risk as adults for engaging in criminal activity (e.g., Kratzer & Hodgins, 1997); girls also seem to be more at risk for a broad array of other adverse outcomes, including various internalizing disorders (Bardone, Moffitt, Caspi, Dickson, & Silva, 1996).

Classification

There are a number of current approaches to the description and classification of CP behavior. In the DSM-IV (American Psychiatric Association, 1994), the two diagnostic categories that are most relevant to CP are ODD and CD. The essential feature of ODD is a repetitive pattern in which the child is defiant, disobedient, negative and hostile toward authority figures. The pattern of behavior must have a duration of at least 6 months, and at least four of the following eight behaviors must be present: losing temper, arguing with grownups, defying or not complying with grownups' rules or requests, deliberately doing things that annoy other people, blaming others for own mistakes, being touchy or easily becoming annoyed by others, exhibiting anger and resentment, and showing spite or vindictiveness. The behaviors must have a higher frequency than is generally seen in other children of similar developmental level and age. Furthermore, the behaviors must lead to meaningful impairment in academic and social functioning.

The essential feature of CD is a recurrent, persistent pattern of behavior in which the child violates the basic rights of others or major age-appropriate societal norms or rules (American Psychiatric Association, 1994). At least 3 of the 15 behaviors listed below must have been present in the past 12 months, with at least one of the behaviors present in the past 6 months. The behaviors are categorized into four groups: aggressiveness to people and animals (bullying, fighting, using a weapon, physical cruelty to people, physical cruelty to animals, stealing with confrontation of victim, forced sexual activity); property destruction (fire setting, other destruction of property); deceptiveness or theft (breaking and entering, lying for personal gain, stealing without confronting victim); and serious rule violations (staying out at night [before age 13], running away from home, being truant [before age 13]).

Two subtypes of CD are described in the DSM-IV; these are differentiated on the basis of the child's age at the appearance of the first symptom of CD. The Childhood-Onset Type is defined by the onset of at least 1 of the 15 behaviors prior to 10 years of age, whereas CD behavior does not appear until age 10 or older in the Adolescent-Onset Type. Although ODD includes behaviors (e.g., noncompliance) that are also included in CD, it does not involve the more serious behaviors that represent violations of either the basic rights of others or age-appropriate societal norms or rules. Thus, if a child meets the diagnostic criteria for both disorders, only the diagnosis of CD is made.

Field trials for assessing the psychometric properties of the DSM-IV diagnoses of ODD and CD have demonstrated that the internal consistency and test–retest reliabilities of the DSM-IV versions are higher than those of their DSM-III-R counterparts (Lahey et al., 1994). The validity of the Childhood-Onset and Adolescent-Onset Types of CD has also been supported, in that children with the Childhood-Onset Type were more likely to display more aggressive symptoms, to be boys, and to receive additional diagnoses of ODD and Attention-Deficit/Hyperactivity Disorder (ADHD) (Waldman & Lahey, 1994).

Multivariate statistical approaches to classification have identified other dimensions on which CP behaviors can be subtyped, in addition to age of onset. Loeber and Schmaling (1985a) have proposed a bipolar unidimensional typology of "overt" and "covert" CP behaviors. Overt CP

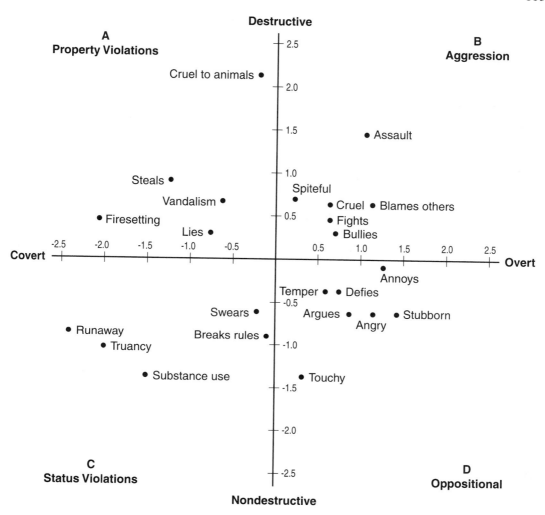

FIGURE 3.1. Meta-analysis of parent and teacher ratings of child CP using multidimensional scaling. Reprinted from Frick et al. (1993). Copyright 1993 by Elsevier Science Ltd. Reprinted by permission.

behaviors include those that involve direct confrontation with or disruption of the environment (e.g., aggression, temper tantrums, argumentativeness), whereas covert CP behaviors include those that usually occur without the awareness of adult caretakers (e.g., lying, stealing, fire setting). In a recent extension of this investigation, Frick et al. (1993) conducted a meta-analysis of 60 factor analyses with more than 28,000 children. They identified a similar "overt–covert" dimension, but also extracted a second bipolar dimension of "destructive–nondestructive." When individual CP behaviors were plotted, four subtypes were obtained: "property violations," "aggression," "status violations," and

"oppositional" (see Figure 3.1). Symptoms of CD fall into the first three quadrants, whereas symptoms of ODD fall into the fourth quadrant. Cluster analyses of an independent sample of clinic-referred boys aged 7–12 indicated one group of boys who displayed high elevations on the oppositional quadrant score and moderate elevations on the aggression quadrant score, and another group of boys who showed high elevations on the property violations, oppositional, and aggression quadrant scores. These clusters approximated those groups of boys who received diagnoses of ODD and CD, respectively.

Noncompliance (i.e., excessive disobedience to adults) appears to be a keystone behavior in the development of both overt and covert CP. Loeber and Schmaling (1985a) found that noncompliance is positioned near the zero point of their unidimensional overt–covert scale of CP behaviors. Patterson and colleagues (e.g., Chamberlain & Patterson, 1995; Patterson, Reid, & Dishion, 1992) have developed a comprehensive theoretical model for the development and maintenance of CP; in their model, early child noncompliance not only is the precursor of severe manifestations of CP behaviors later in childhood and adolescence, but plays a role in these children's subsequent academic and peer relationship problems as well. Walker and Walker (1991) have stressed the role of compliance and noncompliance in the classroom. There is also empirical support for the premise that noncompliance appears early in the progression of CP, and continues to be manifested in subsequent developmental periods (e.g., Edelbrock, 1985; Loeber et al., 1993; Patterson et al., 1992). Low levels of compliance are also associated with referral for services in children with CP (Dumas, 1996). Furthermore, intervention research has shown that when child noncompliance is targeted, there is often concomitant improvement in other CP behaviors as well (Russo, Cataldo, & Cushing, 1981; Wells, Forehand, & Griest, 1980).

Focusing specifically on aggressive behavior, Vitiello and Stoff (1997) recently reviewed the evidence for qualitatively distinct subtypes as they relate to childhood psychopathology. Research using a variety of theoretical models and methods has identified evidence for dichotomous subtypes. For example, Dodge (1991; Dodge & Coie, 1987) has distinguished between "reactive" and "proactive" forms of aggression. The former is a response to perceived provocation, whereas the latter occurs as a means of obtaining some self-serving outcome. Differential responses from teachers and peers have been noted as a function of these subtypes (e.g., Day, Bream, & Pal, 1992), although many aggressive children display both types of aggression (Dodge & Coie, 1987). Others have made a distinction between "affective" and "predatory" aggression (Vitiello, Behar, Hunt, Stoff, & Ricciuti, 1990). Affective aggression tends to be defensive, explosive, and uncontrolled; is generally accompanied by anger or fear and by high levels of arousal; and is more likely to be associated with neurotransmitter abnormalities (Stoff & Cairns, 1996). Predatory aggression is less likely to be associated with affective instability,

is goal-oriented, is associated with low arousal, and is offensive (aimed at securing a positive outcome for the aggressor).

Bullying, a form of CP behavior occurring primarily in school settings, has received increasing attention. Several recent authoritative reviews have appeared on this topic (Farrington, 1993; Olweus, 1992). The general definition of "bullying" has included physical, verbal, or psychological attack or intimidation that is intended to cause fear, distress, or harm to the victim. Direct bullying, which is more characteristic of boys, involves physical and direct verbal attacks. Indirect bullying, which is more characteristic of girls, involves efforts by the bully to isolate and exclude the victim from the social group and includes behaviors such as slandering, spreading rumors, and manipulating friendships (similar to the construct of "relational aggression" identified by Crick & Grotpeter, 1995).

The prevalence of bullying is alarmingly high. Cross-national studies indicate that between 10% and 23% of children are involved in bullying interactions as either bullies or victims (Pepler, Craig, Ziegler, & Charach, 1993). Playgrounds and hallways are the locations where bullying is most likely to occur, with a lesser amount of playground supervision being associated with a greater amount of bullying. Researchers in this area emphasize that adults (teachers and parents) are relatively unaware of the extent of and harm created by the problem and that teachers intervene to help victims very infrequently; peers intervene approximately three times more often than teachers to stop bullying (Craig & Pepler, 1995), but even they are more likely to observe or even to collaborate than to help the victim.

Relatively less research has been conducted on covert types of CP. Research has focused on children who steal, and, more recently, on children who set fires. Lying continues to be significantly underresearched compared to other covert CP.

There is a paucity of longitudinal research on children who steal, although retrospective reports suggest developmental sequences for stealing, such that minor forms of theft (e.g., shoplifting) seem to occur prior to more serious forms of theft (e.g., car theft) (Le Blanc & Frechette, 1989; Loeber, 1988). Much of the work on stealing has been conducted by Patterson and his colleagues. Children who steal exhibit levels of aversive behavior that are comparable to those of nonreferred children, although children who engage in both stealing and social aggression are even more aversive than children who are socially aggressive but who do not steal (Loeber & Schmaling, 1985b; Patterson, 1982). It also appears that children who steal are older at time of referral than children referred for overt types of CP (Moore, Chamberlain, & Mukai, 1979; Reid & Hendricks, 1973) and are at greater risk for committing delinquent offenses as adolescents (Loeber & Schmaling, 1985b; Moore et al., 1979).

Patterson (1982) has reported that the parents of children who steal are more distant and less involved in interactions with their children than are either parents of nonreferred children or parents of children who are socially aggressive. The mothers and siblings of children who are socially aggressive are more coercive than their counterparts in nonreferred families or families in which the children steal. Loeber and Schmaling (1985b) found that families with children who are socially aggressive and those with children who both fought and stole were more likely to demonstrate poorer monitoring skills and to have rejecting mothers. Fathers of children who steal also appear to be less involved in the discipline process than fathers of socially aggressive or normal children (Loeber, Weissman, & Reid, 1983).

Lying, defined as a "verbal statement intended to deceive" (Stouthamer-Loeber, 1986, p. 268), may be one of the first covert CP behaviors to appear (Edelbrock, 1985) and is highly correlated with stealing (especially in adolescents). For example, the correlations between lying and stealing in 4th-, 7th-, and 10th-grade boys were .39, .59, and .74, respectively (Stouthamer-Loeber & Loeber, 1986). Based on the findings of the meta-analytic study conducted by Loeber and Schmaling (1985a), Stouthamer-Loeber (1986) concluded that although lying loads most heavily on the covert dimension of CP, it is also related (albeit less strongly) to overt CP. Lying did correlate significantly with fighting in a community sample of 4th-, 7th-, and 10th-grade boys (r's = .50–.65) (Stouthamer-Loeber & Loeber, 1986), particularly when it occurred in conjunction with stealing. Furthermore, early lying has been shown to be predictive of later recidivism (Loeber & Dishion, 1983).

Childhood fire setting is quite common and potentially very serious in its effects. Prevalence estimates have ranged from 3% to 35% across epidemiological, outpatient, and inpatient samples (Achenbach & Edelbrock, 1981; Heath, Hardesty, Goldfine, & Walker, 1983; Kolko & Kazdin, 1988). Fire setting tends to be associated with other CP behaviors. Although only a relatively small proportion of children with CP engage in fire-setting behavior (e.g., 5% in Jacobson's [1985] outpatient sample in London), most, but not all, fire setters demonstrate other CP behaviors (i.e., can be considered to display the "syndrome" of CP). For example, 74% of the children who set fires in both outpatient (Jacobson, 1985) and inpatient (Kazdin & Kolko, 1986) samples received a diagnosis of CD. In addition, youth with CP who also set fires seem to have more severe levels of CP behavior and to have a history of previous fire setting (Forehand, Wierson, Frame, Kemptom, & Armistead, 1991; Hanson, Mackay-Soroka, Staley, & Poulton, 1994).

In terms of other behavioral and family characteristics, fire setters have been identified as displaying lower social competence and poorer academic performance than controls (Kolko & Kazdin, 1991a; Kolko, Kazdin, & Meyer, 1985). Their parents show significantly greater dysfunction, in terms of psychiatric symptoms; higher levels of depression; and lower levels of affection, consensus, and overall adjustment in their dyadic relationship. The latter findings were demonstrated for parents of fire setters largely independently of the contribution of CD, suggesting that there is even more parent and family dysfunction in families of fire setters than in non-fire setting populations with CD (Kazdin & Kolko, 1986).

In the clinical literature, a number of typologies of juvenile fire setting exist. For example, Humphreys, Kopet, and Lajoy (1993) have described typologies that include "curiosity" fire setters (who are typically younger children), "crisis" fire setters (for whom fire setting is associated with stress or high negative affect), "delinquent" fire setters (for whom fire setting is a deliberate violation of others' rights), and "severely disturbed" fire setters (who exhibit major affective instability or disturbed thinking). Although these typologies of fire setting have a certain appeal in terms of face validity, there has been very little empirical validation. An exception is the study by Kolko and Kazdin (1991b), who divided fire setters into high versus low subgroups on both curiosity and anger motivation. Heightened curiosity as a motive was associated with greater psychopathology (both CP and internalizing problems), fire-setting risk, and fire involvement, whereas heightened anger was associated only with fire-setting risk and fire-setting involvement.

Associated/Comorbid Conditions

Children with CP are at increased risk for manifesting a variety of other behavior disorders and adjustment problems as well. These include ADHD; various internalizing disorders, such as anxiety and depressive disorders and Somatization Disorder (e.g., Loeber & Keenan, 1994); substance use disorders; psychopathy (Frick, O'Brien, Wootton, & McBurnett, 1994); and academic underachievement (Hinshaw, 1992). In their review of the relationship of CP to various comorbid conditions, Loeber and Keenan (1994) have stressed the importance of considering the temporal ordering of comorbid conditions, as well as the different patterns and influences of these comorbid disorders for boys versus girls. Although girls are less likely to display CP than are boys, when girls do display CP, they may be more likely than boys to develop one or more of these comorbid disorders.

ADHD is the comorbid condition most commonly associated with CP, and is thought to precede the development of CP in the majority of cases. In fact, some investigators consider ADHD (or, more specifically, the impulsivity or hyperactivity components of ADHD) to be the "motor" that drives the development of early-onset CP, especially for boys (e.g., Coie & Dodge, 1998; Loeber & Keenan, 1994; White et al., 1994). Coexisting ADHD also predicts a more negative life outcome than does CP alone (see Abikoff & Klein, 1992, and Hinshaw, Lahey, & Hart, 1993, for reviews).

Internalizing disorders, such as the depressive and anxiety disorders and Somatization Disorder, also co-occur with CP at rates higher than expected by chance (see Zoccolillo, 1992). In most cases, CP precedes the onset of depressive symptoms (Loeber & Keenan, 1994), although in some cases depression may precipitate CP behavior (e.g., Kovacs, Paulauskas, Gatsonis, & Richards, 1988). Risk for suicidality has also been shown to increase as a function of preexisting CP (e.g., Capaldi, 1991, 1992), and this risk appears to be higher for girls than for boys (Loeber & Keenan, 1994).

The picture for anxiety disorders and Somatization Disorder is somewhat less clear. Loeber and Keenan (1994) indicate that anxiety disorders do co-occur with CP at a greater than chance level, especially for girls. In some studies, boys with CP and comorbid anxiety disorders are less seriously impaired than are children with CP alone (e.g., J. L. Walker et al., 1991); in other studies, the presence of a comorbid anxiety disorder has not been shown to have a differential effect (e.g., Campbell & Ewing, 1990). A separate but related body of research on shy/withdrawn children who also display CP behaviors suggests that they may be at increased risk for negative life outcomes than children who display only CP (e.g., McCord, 1988; Serbin, Peters, McAffer, & Schwartzman, 1991). Somatization Disorder has been shown to co-occur in some adolescents with CP (Lilienfeld, 1992). Although the base rate of this disorder alone is much higher in girls than in boys, its comorbid occurrence with CP may actually be higher in boys (Offord, Alder, & Boyle, 1986).

Although not all youths who use substances have a history of CP, both longitudinal and cross-sectional studies have documented that preexisting CP constitutes a significant risk factor for substance use (e.g., Hawkins, Catalano, & Miller, 1992; Loeber, 1988). This may be particularly true for girls (Loeber & Keenan, 1994). In addition, concurrent substance use may increase the risk of more serious delinquent behavior.

Psychopathy, which is characterized by superficial charm, lack of concern for others, lack of guilt, and absence of anxiety, has recently been investigated in samples of school-age children by Frick and his colleagues (Christian, Frick, Hill, Tyler, & Frazer, 1997; Frick et al., 1994). CP and psychopathy were moderately correlated, but they displayed differential associations on a number of variables. Psychopathy was positively associated with sensation seeking and negatively correlated with anxiety, whereas CP was not associated with sensation seeking and was positively correlated with anxiety. Children with ODD or CD who also displayed psychopathic characteristics were more likely to have more diverse and serious CP, an increased likelihood of parental Antisocial Personality Disorder (APD), and an increased likelihood of police contacts.

An association between CP and academic underachievement has long been noted. In a comprehensive review, Hinshaw (1992) concluded that during preadolescence, this relationship is actually a function of comorbid ADHD, rather than of CP per se. In adolescence, the relationship is more complex, with preexisting ADHD (and perhaps other neuropsychological deficits), a history of academic difficulty and failure, and long-standing socialization difficulties with family and peers all playing interacting roles.

Developmental Progressions

The preceding description of CP and various co-morbid conditions fails to convey three different but related considerations that must guide assessment and intervention procedures for children with CP: the developmental, contextual, and transactional aspects of CP (Mash & Dozois, 1996; McMahon & Estes, 1997). With respect to developmental considerations, it is clear that the behavioral manifestations of CP (as well as the base rates of various comorbid disorders) change over time. With respect to context, the development and maintenance of CP are influenced by genetic/constitutional characteristics of the child (e.g., temperament), family (parent–child interaction, parenting practices and social cognition, parental personal and marital adjustment), peers (the "deviant peer group"), and broader ecologies (the school, neighborhood, and community). Ethnicity and cultural considerations may also apply to these contexts (e.g., Prinz & Miller, 1991). By "transactional," we mean that these developmental and contextual processes unfold over time and continuously influence one another.

Space considerations preclude an extensive description of the roles these various developmental, contextual, and transactional influences play in the development and maintenance of CP. Instead, we present summary descriptions of two developmental progressions of CP as a means of illustrating many of these influences.[3] The reader is referred to several recent excellent reviews on CP for more extensive treatment of these issues (Coie & Dodge, 1998; Dishion, French, & Patterson, 1995; Hinshaw & Anderson, 1996; Kazdin, 1995b; Moffitt, 1993).

Early-Starter Pathway

The more thoroughly delineated pathway, and the one that seems to have the more negative long-term prognosis, has been variously referred to as the "early-starter" (Patterson, Capaldi, & Bank, 1991), "childhood-onset" (Hinshaw et al., 1993), "life-course-persistent" (Moffitt, 1993), or "aggressive–versatile" (Loeber, 1988) pathway. The Childhood-Onset Type of CD in DSM-IV (American Psychiatric Association, 1994) would seem to be a likely diagnostic outcome of this pathway.

The early-starter pathway is characterized by the onset of CP in the preschool and early school-age years, and by a high degree of continuity throughout childhood and into adolescence and adulthood. It is thought that these children progress from relatively less serious (e.g., noncompliance, temper tantrums) to more serious (e.g., aggression, stealing, substance misuse) CP behaviors over time; that overt behaviors (e.g., defiance, fighting) appear earlier than covert behaviors (e.g., lying, stealing); and that later CP behaviors expand the children's behavioral repertoire rather than replacing earlier behaviors (Edelbrock, 1985; Frick et al., 1993; Lahey & Loeber, 1994). Furthermore, there is an expansion of the settings in which the CP behaviors occur over time, from the home to other settings such as the school and the broader community.

There is a growing body of evidence concerning the many individual, familial, and broader contextual factors that may increase the likelihood of a child's entering and progressing along the early-starter pathway. As noted above, a number of researchers have proposed that early hyperactivity is a significant (and perhaps necessary) risk factor for the early-starter pathway (e.g., Loeber & Keenan, 1994; Moffitt, 1993). Certainly, there is ample evidence that children who display both CP and hyperactivity display more serious and higher levels of CP, and that they have a poorer prognosis than do children with CP or hyperactivity only (see reviews by Abikoff & Klein, 1992, and Hinshaw et al., 1993). Moffitt (1993) has suggested that subtle neuropsychological variations in the infant's central nervous system increase the likelihood that the infant will be "temperamentally difficult," displaying such characteristics as irritability, hyperactivity, impulsivity, and the like. Such a child is thought to be predisposed to the development of subsequent behavior problems, because of the increased likelihood of maladaptive parent–child interactions.

Temperament has often been found to have a low to moderate relation to subsequent CP in early and middle childhood (e.g., Bates, Bayles, Bennett, Ridge, & Brown, 1991; Webster-Stratton & Eyberg, 1982) and in late childhood and adolescence (Caspi, Henry, McGee, Moffitt, & Silva, 1995; Olweus, 1980). Other investigators have shown that the combination of difficult temperament in infancy with other concurrently measured risk factors, such as maternal perception of difficulty, male gender, prematurity, and low socioeconomic status (SES) (Sanson, Oberklaid, Pedlow, & Prior, 1991) or inappropriate parenting (Bates et al., 1991), is what best predicts subsequent CP.

The development of the child's social-cognitive skills may also be affected by the neuropsychological deficits noted above. Dodge and colleagues (Coie & Dodge, 1998; Crick & Dodge, 1994) have demonstrated that children with CP display a variety of deficits in the processing of social information. For example, children with CP have been shown to have deficits in encoding (e.g., lack of attention to relevant social cues, hypervigilant biases), to make more hostile attributional biases and errors in the interpretation of social cues, to have deficient quantity and quality of generated solutions to social situations, to evaluate aggressive solutions more positively, and to be more likely to decide to engage in aggressive behavior. These deficiencies and biases in social-cognitive skills have been shown to predict the subsequent development of CP in kindergarten, and are associated with parental report of earlier harsh disciplinary practices (Weiss, Dodge, Bates, & Pettit, 1992).

These child characteristics (i.e., difficult temperamental style and deficits in social information processing) may then predispose the child to both the development of an insecure attachment to the parent (Greenberg, Speltz, & DeKlyen, 1993) and a coercive style of parent–child interaction (Patterson et al., 1992). Both of these interaction patterns have been implicated in the development of CP. However, the relationship between insecure (avoidant or ambivalent) patterns of attachment in infancy and later CP has been inconsistent, with high-risk families (e.g., low-SES families, single parents) more likely to exhibit such an association than low-risk families (Greenberg et al., 1993). More recently, Lyons-Ruth (1996) has noted the stronger association between "disorganized" (Main & Solomon, 1990) patterns of infant attachment and subsequent CP. In addition, cross-sectional studies with clinic-referred oppositional children (primarily boys) demonstrated that they were much more likely than nonreferred children to display the preschool analogue of disorganized attachment ("controlling–disorganized" attachment) (Greenberg, Speltz, DeKlyen, & Endriga, 1991; Speltz, Greenberg, & DeKlyen, 1990). Furthermore, ratings of attachment security and separation were powerful discriminators of clinic–nonclinic status (Speltz, DeKlyen, Greenberg, & Dryden, 1995). Attachment researchers (e.g., Greenberg et al., 1993; Lyons-Ruth, 1996) have noted the necessity of adopting a transactional perspective, in that attachment security is probably mediated by other risk or protective factors (e.g., parenting

practices, maternal depression, family adversity) over time.

The critical role of parenting practices in the development and maintenance of CP has been well established (Kendziora & O'Leary, 1992; Loeber & Stouthamer-Loeber, 1986; Patterson et al., 1992). The most comprehensive family-based formulation for the early-starter pathway has been the coercion model developed by Patterson and his colleagues (Patterson, 1982; Patterson et al., 1992; Snyder, 1995). The model describes a process of "basic training" in CP behaviors, which occurs in the context of an escalating cycle of coercive parent–child interactions in the home that begins prior to school entry. The proximal cause for entry into the coercive cycle is thought to be ineffective parental management strategies, particularly in regard to child compliance with parental directives during the preschool period. As this process continues over long periods, significant increases in the rate and intensity of these coercive behaviors occur as family members are reinforced by engaging in aggressive behaviors. Furthermore, the child also observes his or her parents engaging in coercive responses, and this provides the opportunity for modeling of aggression to occur (Patterson, 1982).

The findings from several longitudinal studies are consistent with the coercion model (e.g., Bates et al., 1991; Campbell, 1991, 1995). For example, several studies conducted by Campbell (1991) and her colleagues have shown that high levels of externalizing behavior problems during the preschool period, in conjunction with high levels of negative maternal control in observed parent–child interactions and maternal personal and/or familial distress, predict subsequent externalizing problems several years later.

Various other risk factors that may have an impact on the family and serve to precipitate or maintain child CP have been identified. These include familial factors, such as parental social cognitions (e.g., perceptions of the child), parental personal and marital adjustment, and other familial stressors, as well as certain extrafamilial factors. Less clear are the mechanisms by which these factors exert their effects on CP and on one another, the extent to which child CP may reciprocally influence them, and the role of timing and duration (Kazdin, 1995b). For example, these risk factors may have a direct effect on child CP, or they may exert their effects by disrupting parenting practices (Patterson et al., 1992). In some cases, the "risk" factor may be a *result* of CP, rather than a potential cause. With these caveats in mind, we note some of the relationships of these factors to CP.

Parents of children with CP display more maladaptive social cognitions, and they experience more personal (e.g., depression, antisocial behavior), interparental (marital problems), and extrafamilial (e.g., isolation) distress, than do parents of nonreferred children. It has been suggested that these stressors may interact to impede parental tracking of child behavior and lead to perceptual biases (Wahler & Dumas, 1989). With respect to social cognitions, Johnston (1996) has proposed a model that places parental cognitions (expectancies, perceptions, and attributions concerning child behavior and sense of parenting efficacy) in a mediational role vis-à-vis parenting behavior. Parents of clinic-referred children with CP are more likely to misperceive child behaviors (Holleran, Littman, Freund, & Schmaling, 1982; Middlebrook & Forehand, 1985; Wahler & Sansbury, 1990), to have fewer positive and more negative family-referent cognitions (Sanders & Dadds, 1992), and to perceive CP behaviors as intentional and to attribute them to stable and global causes (Baden & Howe, 1992). Sense of parenting efficacy has been shown to relate negatively to child CP in both clinic-referred and nonreferred samples (e.g., Johnston & Mash, 1989; Roberts, Joe, & Rowe-Hallbert, 1992).

Maternal depression is related to a broad spectrum of child behavior disorders, including CP (e.g., Cummings & Davies, 1994b; Forehand, Furey, & McMahon, 1984). Some evidence suggests not only that maternal depression may adversely affect the mothers' parenting behavior, but also that it may negatively bias maternal perceptions of children with CP (e.g., Dumas & Serketich, 1994; Fergusson, Lynskey, & Horwood, 1993; Forehand, Lautenschlager, Faust, & Graziano, 1986). However, others have presented evidence suggesting that depressed mothers do not possess a negative perceptual bias in their reports of their children's CP behaviors and that they may be accurate reporters (Richters, 1992). Recent investigators have suggested that chronicity of maternal depression may be particularly related to child CP (Alpern & Lyons-Ruth, 1993; Fergusson & Lynskey, 1993).

Parental antisocial behavior has received increasing attention as both a direct and an indirect influence on the development and maintenance of CP. Links between parental criminality, aggressive behavior, and a diagnosis of APD and childhood delinquency, aggression, and CD/

ODD diagnoses have been reported by a number of investigators (see Frick & Jackson, 1993, for a review). This association appears specific to CP, occurs more frequently in parents whose children are diagnosed with CD rather than ODD (but see Frick et al., 1993), and is not associated with increased occurrence of ADHD or other child disorders (Frick et al., 1992). There is some evidence to suggest that parental antisocial behavior may play a more central role than other risk factors in its effect on parenting practices and child CP (e.g., Frick et al., 1992; Patterson & Capaldi, 1991; Patterson et al., 1992). For example, parenting and marital status were not associated with child CP independently of parental APD (Frick et al., 1992).

Similarly, parental substance misuse has been associated with child CP and substance use, at least partly because of its association with disrupted parenting practices (Dishion, Reid, & Patterson, 1988; Patterson et al., 1992; Wills, Schreibman, Benson, & Vaccaro, 1994). Observations of parent–child interactions in families with parental alcohol problems suggest that the parents are less able to engage their children and are less congenial (Jacob, Krahn, & Leonard, 1991; Whipple, Fitzgerald, & Zucker, 1995). In a review of laboratory studies examining the effects of alcohol consumption on parent–child interaction, Pelham and Lang (1993) concluded not only that alcohol consumption had a deleterious effect on parenting practices, but that the children's inappropriate behavior increased parental alcohol consumption (for parents with a positive family history of alcohol problems) and distress (for all parents).

Marital distress and conflict have been shown to be associated with child CP, negative parenting behavior, and parental perceptions of child maladjustment (Amato & Keith, 1991; Cummings & Davies, 1994a). The most commonly offered hypothesis for the relationship has been that marital distress or conflict interferes with the parents' ability to engage in appropriate parenting practices, which then leads to child CP; however, other explanations are possible (see Rutter, 1994). These include direct modeling of aggressive and coercive behavior, and the cumulative stressful effects of such conflict, including maternal depression. It has been suggested that both child CP and parental marital distress/conflict may be the result of parental antisocial behavior (Frick, 1994). Child characteristics such as age and gender appear to moderate the relationship between specific aspects of marital adjustment and CP (Dadds & Powell, 1991; Katz

& Gottman, 1993). Some investigators (e.g., Abidin & Brunner, 1995; Jouriles et al., 1991; Porter & O'Leary, 1980) have focused more narrowly on specific aspects of marital conflict that relate directly to parenting, such as disagreement over child-rearing practices, marital conflict in a child's presence, or the strength of the parenting alliance. There is some indication that these more narrowly focused constructs may demonstrate stronger relationships to CP than may broader constructs such as marital distress.

Parents of children with CP also appear to experience higher frequencies of stressful events—both minor ones (e.g., daily hassles) and events of a more significant nature (e.g., unemployment, major transitions) (Patterson, 1983; Webster-Stratton, 1990b). The effects of stress on child CP may be mediated through such parenting practices as disrupted parental discipline (e.g., Forgatch, Patterson, & Skinner, 1988; Snyder, 1991) and maladaptive parental social cognitions (Johnston, 1996; Middlebrook & Forehand, 1985; Wahler & Dumas, 1989).

CP has been associated with a number of extrafamilial factors (Coie & Jacobs, 1993), such as low SES (Dodge, Pettit, & Bates, 1994), neighborhood risk (Attar, Guerra, & Tolan, 1994; Duncan, Brooks-Gunn, & Klebanov, 1994), and parental insularity/low social support (Jennings, Stagg, & Connors, 1991; Wahler, Leske, & Rogers, 1979). Some parents of children with CP may be quite isolated from friends, neighbors, and the community. Wahler and his colleagues have developed a construct called "insularity," which is defined as a "specific pattern of social contacts within the community that is characterized by a high level of negatively perceived coercive interchanges with relatives and/or helping agency representatives and by a low level of positively perceived supportive interchanges with friends" (Wahler & Dumas, 1984, p. 387). Insularity is positively related to negative parent behavior directed toward children and oppositional child behavior directed toward parents (Dumas & Wahler, 1985; Wahler, 1980). It has also been associated with poor maintenance of treatment effects (e.g., Dumas & Wahler, 1983). Thus, when a mother has a large proportion of aversive interactions outside the home, the interactions between the mother and her child in the home are likely to be negative as well.

Upon school entry, this child's coercive style of interaction is likely to extend to interactions with teachers and peers, resulting in frequent disciplinary confrontations with school personnel, rejection by peers, and continued coercive interchanges with parents (some of which now center around school-related problems) (e.g., Patterson et al., 1992). Difficulties in the acquisition of basic academic skills are most likely consequences of the preexisting neuropsychological deficits noted above (which now may be manifested as verbal deficits, self-control difficulties, social-cognitive deficits and biases, and/or ADHD), as well as the child's coercive interactional style. The CP behaviors may become more serious, more frequent, and more covert (e.g., stealing) during the elementary school years.

By age 10 or 11, this recurrent constellation of negative events places the child at increased risk for association with a deviant peer group in middle school and high school (with a likely escalation in the CP behaviors) and/or for depression. The role of the peer group in the maintenance and escalation of CP behaviors during middle and late childhood and early adolescence has been documented in several longitudinal investigations, in terms of both peer rejection (e.g., Coie, Lochman, Terry, & Hyman, 1992) and subsequent involvement with antisocial peers (e.g., Dishion, Patterson, Stoolmiller, & Skinner, 1991). Children with CP (particularly boys) are also at increased risk for depression by the time they reach adolescence (see Ollendick & King, 1994).

It is not surprising that adolescents who have progressed along the early-starter pathway are at significant risk for continuing to engage in more serious CP behaviors throughout adolescence and into adulthood (e.g., Farrington, 1995; Moffitt, 1993; Rutter et al., 1994). As adults, not only are such individuals at high risk for subsequent diagnosis of APD; they are also at increased risk for other psychiatric diagnoses and a variety of negative life outcomes (e.g., lower occupational adjustment and educational attainment, poorer physical health).

Late-Starter Pathway

A second major pathway for the development of CP has been proposed, but there has been less consistency in how it has been described. In general, this second pathway begins in adolescence rather than early childhood; it is also thought to result in less serious forms of CP (e.g., property offenses rather than violent offenses) and to have a higher rate of desistance. However, more children are involved in this pathway than in the early-starter pathway (e.g.,

24% vs. 7%, respectively, in the Dunedin Multidisciplinary Health Study; Moffitt, Caspi, Dickson, Silva, & Stanton, 1996). It has been referred to as the "late-starter" (Patterson et al., 1991), "adolescent-onset" (Hinshaw et al., 1993), "adolescence-limited" (Moffitt, 1993), or "nonaggressive–antisocial" (Loeber, 1988) pathway. The Adolescent-Onset Type of CD in DSM-IV would seem to be a likely diagnostic outcome of this pathway.

Empirical support for the late-starter pathway has been recently provided in both epidemiological (e.g., McGee, Feehan, Williams, & Anderson, 1992; Moffitt, 1990; Moffitt et al., 1996) and high-risk (Loeber et al., 1993) samples. In the Dunedin sample, a large increase in nonaggressive (but not aggressive) CP behaviors has been noted between ages 11 and 15 for both boys and girls (McGee et al., 1992). Moffitt (1990) found that the late starters made up 73% of her delinquent sample of boys at age 13, and had levels of CP behaviors at age 13 comparable to those displayed by the early-starter boys. However, in contrast to the early-starter boys, the late-starter boys had engaged in very low levels of CP in childhood, and there was no evidence of Verbal IQ deficits, reading difficulties, preexisting family adversity, temperamental difficulty (Moffitt et al., 1996), or perinatal or motor skills difficulties. Furthermore, they were less likely to have been convicted of violent criminal offenses than were the early-starter boys (Moffitt et al., 1996). Similarly, Capaldi and Patterson (1994) presented data on a high-risk sample indicating that late-starter boys were less likely than early-starter boys to live in families characterized by inappropriate parental discipline practices, unemployment, divorce, parental antisocial behavior, and low SES.

Patterson et al. (1991) have hypothesized that the process leading to the late-starter pathway begins in families that have marginally effective family management skills as a result either of significant stressors (e.g., divorce, unemployment) or of the typical strains placed on families as children become adolescents. Inadequate parental supervision and the relative lack of supervision in middle and high school increase the likelihood of significant involvement in a deviant peer group. However, because these adolescents have a higher level of social skills and a longer learning history of employing such skills successfully than do early starters, they are far less likely to continue to engage in CP behaviors than are early starters. Moffitt (1993) has conjectured that participation in CP behaviors by late starters is a form of social mimicry of early starters that is one way of asserting independence from the family. The basis for desistance among the late starters is thought to be the gradual increase in opportunities to engage in more legitimate adult roles and activities as these adolescents grow older. Whether these suppositions about desistance will prove to be valid has yet to be determined; Hämäläinen and Pulkkinen (1996) found that late starters constituted nearly one-third of their group of young adult (age 27) criminal offenders. However, it is the case that there is a dramatic decline in CP behaviors by early adulthood (e.g., Farrington, 1986).

Although the pathways described above are certainly not fully developed at this time, they do provide a conceptual framework for the assessment and treatment of children with CP. We now turn to a discussion of the assessment process itself.

ASSESSMENT

In this section of the chapter, we provide an overview of the methods and processes currently employed in the assessment of children with CP. As knowledge of the characteristics, causes, and correlates of CP has grown, the scope of assessment has broadened as well. Primary areas to be assessed include child behavior per se and in an interactional context; associated child characteristics and disorders, such as temperament and ADHD; and familial and extrafamilial factors, such as parenting practices, parents' and teachers' social cognitions, personal and marital adjustment of the parents, parental stress, maternal insularity, and parental satisfaction with treatment. In each of these areas, the particular methods (e.g., interviews, questionnaires, observations) that have proven to have the greatest utility with children with CP are presented here. For a more extensive description and evaluation of these assessment methods, see McMahon and Estes (1997).

Child Behavior Per Se and in an Interactional Context

In order to obtain an accurate representation of the referred child's CP behavior, particularly with regard to its interactional aspects, the therapist[4] must rely on multiple assessment methods, including interviews with the parents, child, and other relevant parties (e.g., teachers); behavioral rating scales; and behavioral observations in the clinic, home, and/or school settings.

Interviews

Interviews conducted with children with CP and their families, and other important adults, can be divided into two general categories: clinical interviews and structured diagnostic interviews.

Because parent–child interactions are an important etiological factor in CP, the clinical interview with the parent is of major importance. The primary purpose of the interview is to determine the nature of the typical parent–child interactions that are problematic, the antecedent stimulus conditions under which CP behaviors occur, and the consequences that accompany such behaviors. A number of interview formats are available to aid the clinician in structuring the information obtained from the parents. Some of the formats, such as those presented by Forehand and McMahon (1981) and Wahler and Cormier (1970), are structured around problematic situations (e.g., bedtime, sibling interactions), whereas others are structured according to different child behaviors (e.g., Patterson, Reid, Jones, & Conger, 1975).

An individual interview with the child may or may not provide useful content-oriented information, depending upon the age and/or developmental level of the child and the nature of the specific child behaviors. Children below the age of 10 are not usually reliable reporters of their own behavioral symptoms (Edelbrock, Costello, Dulcan, Kalas, & Conover, 1985). Loeber and Schmaling (1985b) have suggested that when one is assessing overt types of CP behaviors such as fighting, maternal and teacher reports may be preferable to child reports, since these children often underestimate their own aggressive behavior. Alternatively, because of the nature of covert types of CP behaviors such as stealing, more valid reports of these behaviors are more likely to be obtained from a child.[5] However, informal interviews can be extremely useful, even with a younger child, in that they can provide the therapist with an opportunity to assess the child's perception of why he or she has been brought to the clinic and can provide a subjective evaluation of the child's cognitive, affective, and behavioral characteristics (Bierman, 1983).

When the presenting problems include classroom behavior or academic underachievement,

an interview with the child's teacher(s) is appropriate. Breen and Altepeter (1990) have provided an outline for a brief interview with a teacher, which can be conducted at the school or by telephone. Situationally formatted interview guides based on Barkley's (1981) School Situations Questionnaire or Wahler and Cormier's (1970) preinterview checklists can be employed in conjunction with specific questions related to the child's problem behaviors. Contextual factors, such as classroom rules of conduct, teacher expectations, and the behavior of other children in the classroom, are important as well.

Structured interviews have been used in efforts to improve the reliability and validity of diagnostic interviewing (using DSM criteria), particularly for research purposes; however, these interviews are also used in clinical settings, usually in conjunction with other assessment techniques (Kamphaus & Frick, 1996). They can be employed with multiple informants such as parents, children, and sometimes teachers. The structured diagnostic interviews most commonly employed with children with CP are the Diagnostic Interview Schedule for Children (DISC; Shaffer, Fisher, Piacentini, Schwab-Stone, & Wicks, 1991; Shaffer et al., 1993) and the Diagnostic Interview for Children and Adolescents (DICA; Boyle et al., 1993; Herjanic & Reich, 1982; Reich & Welner, 1988). For reviews of these and other structured diagnostic interviews, refer to Bird and Gould (1995), Edelbrock and Costello (1988), and Hodges and Zeman (1993).

An alternative approach to interviewing children has been developed by McConaughy and Achenbach (1994). The Semistructured Clinical Interview for Children and Adolescents (SCICA) is a broad interview administered to children (ages 6–18) that employs a protocol of open-ended questions to assess a variety of areas of child functioning. Dimensional scores similar to those obtained from various versions of the Child Behavior Checklist (CBCL) family of instruments (Achenbach, 1993; see below) can also be derived from these items, but only for children aged 6–12. Kolko and Kazdin have developed several semistructured interviews for parents and children that have been used to assess various aspects of fire setting and match play in inpatient, outpatient, and community samples of children. Examples include the Firesetting History Screen (Kolko & Kazdin, 1988), the Firesetting Risk Interview (Kolko & Kazdin, 1989a), and the Children's Firesetting Interview

(Kolko & Kazdin, 1989b). Evidence for the reliability and validity of these interviews is encouraging.

The interview as an assessment tool does not end with the first contact, but continues throughout intervention formulation and implementation. The interview is used to obtain information necessary for the development of interventions, to assess the effectiveness of the intervention and its implementation, and to alter the intervention if necessary (Breen & Altepeter, 1990).

Behavioral Rating Scales

Behavioral rating scales are assessment instruments that are completed by adults or the child in reference to the child's behavior or characteristics. They are very useful as screening devices, both for covering a broad range of CP behaviors and for assessing the presence of other child behavior disorders. Some of the rating scales can provide data relevant to diagnostic decisions. Behavioral rating scales are currently regarded as excellent measures of parental and teacher perceptions of the child, and as such have been extensively employed as treatment outcome and social validation measures in treatment studies with children with CP and their families.

Although there are many behavioral rating scales (see Kamphaus & Frick, 1996, for a review), several have been recommended as most appropriate for clinical and research use with children with CP (McMahon & Estes, 1997). The CBCL family of instruments (Achenbach, 1993) is designed for use with children between the ages of 2 and 18. There are parallel forms of the CBCL for parents (CBCL/2–3, CBCL/4–18), teachers (Teacher's Report Form, or TRF), youths (Youth Self-Report, or YSR), and observers (Direct Observation Form, or DOF). The interview (SCICA) and observation (DOF) versions are described elsewhere.

The CBCL, TRF, and YSR are highly similar in terms of structure, items, scoring, and interpretation. They are designed to be self-administered, and each can usually be completed in 15–20 minutes. The CBCL currently consists of two different rating scales: one completed by parents of children aged 4–18 (CBCL/4–18; Achenbach, 1991a) and another rating scale completed by parents of children aged 2–3 (CBCL/2–3; Achenbach, 1992). The TRF is completed by teachers of children between the ages of 5 and 18, and the YSR is completed by children from 11 to 18 years of age. The instruments include sections concerning Competence and Problem items (the CBCL/2–3 includes only Problem items). The Problem items are scored and presented as a profile that indicates the child's standing on two broad-band (Internalizing, Externalizing) and eight narrow-band syndromes (there are six narrow-band syndromes on the CBCL/2–3). A Total Problem score can be obtained as well. The 1991 Profiles have separate norms for boys and girls at two age levels (4–11 [5–11 on the TRF], and 12–18). The Externalizing dimension on the CBCL/4–18, TRF, and YSR includes CP behaviors on two of the narrow-band scales (Aggressive Behavior, Delinquent Behavior). On the CBCL/2–3, the Aggressive and Destructive narrow-band scales include CP behaviors. The Competence scales on the 1991 Profiles include items related to various activities, social relationships, and success in school.

The psychometric properties of the various forms of the CBCL, the TRF, and the YSR are described thoroughly in their respective manuals (Achenbach, 1991a, 1991b, 1991c; 1992). The CBCL/4–18 and the TRF are sensitive to treatment changes resulting from parent training and child cognitive-behavioral therapy (e.g., Eisenstadt, Eyberg, McNeil, Newcomb, & Funderburk, 1993; Kazdin, Bass, Siegel, & Thomas, 1989; Kendall, Reber, McLeer, Epps, & Ronan, 1990; Webster-Stratton & Hammond, 1997) interventions for the treatment of CP.

The various CBCL measures offer a number of compelling advantages. First, they are among the few behavioral rating scales to assess prosocial behaviors. Second, their psychometric qualities are adequate, and extensive normative data are provided for children of different ages and sexes. Third, the development of equivalent forms for different informants should maximize the amount of information that can be gathered about a child and should permit comparisons across informants and situations. Fourth, the provision of both broad-band and narrow-band syndromes (including broad coverage of CP behaviors) means that the CBCL instruments can be used for both general and more specific purposes, including classification, screening, diagnosis, and treatment evaluation. With children with CP, the comprehensive coverage can be useful in screening for some of the disorders that are often comorbid with CP, such as ADHD and depression. However, it is important to note some of the limitations of the CBCL family of instruments as well. These include a limited assessment of social competence; use of a normative sample that excluded children who had recently received mental health services; and limited sensitivity to behaviors occurring in the subclinical range. In addition, it is essential to note that the interpretations of both broad- and narrow-band scale scores from the 1991 revision of the CBCL family of instruments are not necessarily comparable to those obtained from previous versions (see Drotar, Stein, & Perrin, 1995, and Kamphaus & Frick, 1996, for more details).

Various other behavioral rating scales, completed by parents, teachers, or children, focus on specific aspects of CP. Two examples of parent or teacher report measures are the Eyberg Child Behavior Inventory and the Sutter–Eyberg Student Behavior Inventory (ECBI and SESBI; Eyberg, 1992). The ECBI is completed by parents and is intended for use with children aged 2–16. The 36 items describe specific CP behaviors (primarily overt) and are scored on both a frequency-of-occurrence scale and a yes–no problem identification scale. Both scales have been shown to discriminate children with CP from other clinic-referred children and from nonreferred children (Burns & Patterson, 1990; Burns, Patterson, Nussbaum, & Parker, 1991; Eyberg, 1992; Eyberg & Colvin, 1994) and to be sensitive to treatment effects from parent training interventions with young children (e.g., Eisenstadt et al., 1993; McNeil, Eyberg, Eisenstadt, Newcomb, & Funderburk, 1991; Webster-Stratton & Hammond, 1997).

The SESBI is identical in format to the ECBI. Standardization studies have been done on the SESBI with preschoolers (Burns, Sosna, & Ladish, 1992; Funderburk & Eyberg, 1989) and with children in kindergarten through 6th grade (Burns & Owen, 1990; Burns, Walsh, & Owen, 1995). The SESBI has been shown to be sensitive to the effects of a parent training intervention (McNeil et al., 1991).

Children whose scores exceed the cutoff points on the ECBI or the SESBI are probably a heterogeneous group who may present with ADHD as well as ODD or CD. Given the increasing attention paid to the comorbidity of ADHD and CP, this represents a potentially serious limitation of the ECBI. Despite this potential limitation, the ECBI and SESBI show promise as useful rating scales in clinical settings, where they can be employed as screening instruments and as treatment outcome measures for disruptive behavior (broadly defined) as rated by parents and teachers. However, their unidimensional assessment of disruptive behaviors limits their utility as broad-band screening instruments. In situations in which a broader screening is desired or when information pertinent to differential diagnosis is sought, then use of the CBCL and TRF is recommended.

An example of a child self-report measure that focuses specifically on CP is the Self-Report Delinquency Scale (SRD; Elliott, Huizinga, & Ageton, 1985). The SRD is probably the most widely used youth self-report measure of CP behavior. It consists of 47 items that are derived from offenses listed in the Uniform Crime Reports and covers index offenses (e.g., stole motor vehicle, aggravated assault), other delinquent behaviors (e.g., hit parent, panhandled), and drug use. The SRD is intended for use by 11- to 19-year-olds, who report on the frequency of engagement in each behavior over the past year. It has been employed primarily in epidemiological and community samples to assess prevalence of CP (e.g., Elliott et al., 1985; Loeber, Stouthamer-Lober, Van Kammen, & Farrington, 1989), but it has also been employed as a measure of intervention outcome in clinic-referred samples (e.g., Henggeler, Melton, Brondino, Scherer, & Hanley, 1997; Kazdin, Mazurick, & Siegel, 1994; Kazdin, Siegel, & Bass, 1992). Pretreatment levels of CP behavior as assessed by the SRD were predictive of teacher ratings of child behavior problems following a cognitive-behavioral therapy intervention (Kazdin, 1995a).

Behavioral Observation

Direct behavioral observation has long been a critical component of the assessment of children with CP and their families and teachers, both for delineating specific patterns of maladaptive parent–child or teacher–child interaction and for assessing change in those interactions as a function of treatment. More recently, observational data have been compared with data gathered via other methods to assist the clinician in determining whether the focus of treatment should be on the adult–child interaction or on adult perceptual and/or personal adjustment issues.

Space limitations preclude an extensive review of the many behavioral observation systems currently in use for assessing interactions of children with CP in the clinic, home, and school settings. We describe three widely used, structured, microanalytic observation procedures available for assessing parent–child interactions in the clinic: the Behavioral Coding System developed by Forehand and his colleagues (BCS; Forehand & McMahon, 1981), the Dyadic Parent–Child Interaction Coding System II (DPICS II; Eyberg, Bessmer, Newcomb, Edwards, & Robinson, 1994), and the Interpersonal Process Code (IPC; Rusby, Estes, & Dishion, 1991). The BCS and the DPICS II are modifications of the assessment procedure developed by Hanf (1970) for the observation of parent–child interactions in the clinic. The IPC is a descendant of the Family Interaction Coding System, developed by Patterson and his colleagues (Patterson, Ray, Shaw, & Cobb, 1969; Reid, 1978), and the Family Process Code (Dishion et al., 1984). All three of these systems have also been employed in home observations.

Both the BCS and DPICS II place the parent–child dyad in standard situations that vary in the degree to which parental control is required, ranging from a free-play situation to one in which the parent directs the child's activity. In each system, various parent and child behaviors are scored, many of which emphasize parental antecedents (e.g., commands) and consequences (e.g., praise, time out) for child compliance or noncompliance. Both systems have adequate psychometric properties and have been extensively employed as intervention outcome measures.

The IPC has been used in a number of different interactional contexts, such as teaching and free-play situations in the clinic with young school-age children and their families; problem solving in the clinic with preadolescents and their families; live playground observations; and family therapy process. Different settings require flexibility regarding the placement of the observer, instructions to the participants, and the length of the observation. The IPC consists of three behavioral dimensions: activity (e.g., on-task, off-task), content (i.e., verbal, nonverbal, physical), and affect (e.g., happy, aversive, sad). Psychometric properties are adequate, and preliminary data from a prevention program for children with CP and their families show that the IPC is sensitive to treatment effects (Reid, Eddy, Bank, & Fetrow, 1994).

The use of the preceding observation systems in the home setting for practicing clinicians is desirable, but rare for obvious reasons. The coding systems are relatively complex and require lengthy periods to train observers and to maintain adequate levels of reliability. The observations themselves are usually lengthy as well. As a consequence, the use of structured clinical observations to assess parent–child interactions is

recommended (McMahon & Estes, 1997). In addition, simplified versions of both the DPICS II and the BCS have been developed recently (Eyberg et al., 1994; McMahon & Estes, 1993). These adaptations are designed to reduce training demands, and may ultimately prove to be more useful to clinicians.

Behavioral observation systems designed specifically for assessing CP behaviors in the school setting have received relatively less attention. Both the BCS and IPC have been adapted for use in the school (e.g., Breiner & Forehand, 1981; Rusby et al., 1991). Adoption of one of these coding systems does have the advantage of facilitating cross-situational comparisons during the assessment process. The DOF of the CBCL (Achenbach, 1991a) may be used as part of a multimodal assessment with the other versions of the CBCL described above. Yielding Internalizing, Externalizing, and Total Problem scores as well as scores for six narrow-band problem scales and a measure of on-task behavior, the DOF is relatively simple to use; it has been shown to discriminate between referred and nonreferred children in the classroom, as well as between children with externalizing behavior problems and children with other behavior problems. Pepler and Craig (1995) have developed an innovative observational methodology for assessing elementary-school-age children's peer interactions on school playgrounds using wireless microphones and remote video cameras.

"Academic engaged time" (AET) is the amount of time a child appropriately engaged in on-task behavior during classtime (Walker, Colvin, & Ramsey, 1995). Walker et al. have developed a simple stopwatch recording method for assessing AET, in which children are observed during two 15-minute periods. AET has been shown to correlate positively with academic performance (Walker, 1995) and to discriminate boys at risk for CP from boys not at risk (e.g., Walker, Shinn, O'Neill, & Ramsey, 1987).

An alternative to observations by independent observers in the natural setting is to train significant adults in the child's environment to observe and record certain types of child behavior. An added advantage is the opportunity to assess low-rate behaviors such as stealing or fire setting. The most widely used procedure of this type is the Parent Daily Report (PDR; Chamberlain & Reid, 1987), a parent observation measure that is typically administered during brief telephone interviews. Current versions consist of 22–34 negative overt and covert behaviors common to children (Chamberlain & Reid, 1987; Patterson & Bank, 1986; Webster-Stratton & Spitzer, 1991). Parents are asked whether any of the targeted behaviors have occurred in the past 24 hours. Some versions also record the setting in which the problem behavior is occurring (home, school, community, other) or parental disciplinary practices. There is also a parallel form for children (see Patterson & Bank, 1986). The Daily Telephone Discipline Interview (Webster-Stratton & Spitzer, 1991) was developed as an addendum to the PDR to provide more detailed information about parental interventions subsequent to child misbehavior reported on the PDR. The PDR has been employed on a pretreatment basis to assess the magnitude of behavior problems, to monitor the progress of the family during therapy, and to assess treatment outcome.

Walker (1995) presents guidelines and examples of simple observation procedures appropriate for use by teachers in the classroom. He suggests that the stopwatch method of assessing AET, described above, may be employed by teachers to assess the amount of prosocial behavior directed by a child with CP to his or her peers on the playground.

Few assessment instruments have focused primarily on covert, as opposed to overt, forms of CP behavior (Miller & Klungness, 1989). A brief daily interview similar to the PDR for collecting parent report data on stealing has been developed by Jones (1974). The Telephone Interview Report on Stealing and Social Aggression (TIROSSA) has adequate test–retest reliability and is sensitive to the effects of treatment procedures designed to reduce stealing (Reid, Hinojosa Rivera, & Lorber, 1980).

Hinshaw, Heller, and McHale (1992) developed a clinic-based protocol to assess the covert CP behaviors of stealing, property destruction, and cheating in samples of boys (aged 6–12) with ADHD (most of whom also had ODD or CD) and a comparison group. Each child was asked to complete an academic worksheet alone in a room that contained a completed answer sheet, money, and toys. Stealing was measured by conducting a count of objects in the room immediately following the work session, whereas property destruction and cheating were assessed by ratings derived from observing the child's behavior during the session. Each of these observational measures of covert CP was correlated with parental ratings on the Delinquency scale of the CBCL.

Associated Child Characteristics

A brief developmental and medical history of the child should be obtained, usually as part of the initial interview with the parents. The purpose of this line of questioning is to determine whether any medical factors may be associated with the development or maintenance of the child's CP behaviors (e.g., neurological injury or disease, hearing difficulties), and whether the child's early temperament may have been a contributing factor in the development of a coercive style of parent–child interaction. If desired, child temperament may be assessed in a more formal manner by standardized parent interviews or parent-completed questionnaires; however many of these present difficulties in terms of lengthy administration and scoring procedures, and/or problems with respect to the adequacy of their psychometric properties (see Slabach, Morrow, & Wachs, 1991, for a review).

As noted above, children with CP may also present with a variety of other behavior disorders, including ADHD, internalizing disorders (especially depression, and to a lesser extent anxiety disorders and Somatization Disorder), and substance use disorders. Behavioral rating scales that provide information about a wide range of narrow-band behavior disorders, such as the CBCL family of instruments (Achenbach, 1993), can serve as useful screening devices, as can brief questions in the initial interview about these problems. A behavioral rating scale to assess psychopathy (the Psychopathy Screening Device; Frick & Hare, in press) has recently been developed, and is completed by parents and teachers. It seems especially promising in terms of its potential for identifying children with CP who also exhibit manifestations of the psychopathy construct (Christian et al., 1997; Frick et al., 1994).

As noted above children with CP frequently have problems with peer interactions. If information from interviews, behavioral rating scales (e.g., the Social Competence scales of the CBCL; Achenbach, 1991a), and observations indicate that this is a problem area for a particular child, additional assessment of the child's social skills is necessary. (See Bierman & Welsh, 1997, for a review.)

If the presenting problem concerns classroom behavior, a functional analysis of the problem behaviors should also include an assessment of the child's academic behavior. Although interviews, observations, and rating scales can provide information concerning the child's academic behavior, additional evaluation in the form of intelligence and achievement tests is necessary to determine whether the child may have learning difficulties in addition to CP. Walker (1995) discusses the use of a standardized method for retrieving and using school records (School Archival Records System; H. M. Walker, Block-Pedego, Todis, & Severson, 1991) with children with CP. Lyon (1994) provides a complete review of assessment strategies with which to evaluate learning problems.

Familial and Extrafamilial Factors

McMahon and Estes (1997) have delineated six areas that are relevant to the assessment of children with CP: parenting practices; parents' (and teachers') social cognitions; parents' perceptions of their own personal and marital adjustment; parental stress; parental functioning in extrafamilial social contexts; and parental satisfaction with treatment.

As noted above, parenting practices have typically been assessed via direct observation of parent–child interaction. Several questionnaires also have been specifically designed to assess parenting practices. These questionnaires may be potentially quite useful as adjuncts to behavioral observations and/or to assess parental behaviors that either occur infrequently or are otherwise difficult to observe (e.g., physical discipline, parental monitoring practices), as screening instruments, and to measure the effects of parent training interventions. Examples include the Parenting Scale (Arnold, O'Leary, Wolff, & Acker, 1993), the Parent Practices Scale (Strayhorn & Weidman, 1988), and the Alabama Parenting Questionnaire (Frick, 1991). These measures are employed with children aged 2 to 13; development of a similar instrument that is appropriate for parents of adolescents is needed. None of the measures has yet been employed to assess treatment outcome for parents of children with CP, although the Parent Practices Scale was used in this way with a sample of children with mixed behavior problems (Strayhorn & Weidman, 1989).

Parental and teacher perceptions of the child, rather than child behaviors per se, may be the best predictors of referral for CP types of behavior. The behavioral rating scales described above are the most readily available sources of such data, although written, audiotaped, or videotaped vignettes describing various child behaviors or parent–child interactions have also been employed. When examined in the context of be-

havioral observation data and the clinician's own impressions, these perception measures can be important indicators as to whether the informants (parents, teachers) appear to have a perceptual bias in their assessment of the referred child's behavior.

Several measures that assess aspects of parental self-esteem (e.g., satisfaction, self-efficacy, and locus of control with the parenting role) are the Parenting Sense of Competence Scale (as adapted by Johnston & Mash, 1989), the Cleminshaw–Guidubaldi Parent Satisfaction Scale (Guidubaldi & Cleminshaw, 1985), and the Parental Locus of Control Scale (Campis, Lyman, & Prentice-Dunn, 1986).

To assess the extent to which parents' personal and marital adjustment problems may be playing a role in the child's presenting behavior problems, a set of screening procedures that includes brief questions in the initial interviews with the parents and child and certain parental self-report measures can be utilized. Maternal depression has been the most widely investigated personal adjustment problem in parents of children with CP, and the Beck Depression Inventory (Beck, Rush, Shaw, & Emery, 1979) has been the most frequently employed measure. Parental antisocial behavior has been assessed with structured diagnostic interviews and the Minnesota Multiphasic Personality Inventory, although Zucker and Fitzgerald (1992) have developed a more specific self-report instrument, the Antisocial Behavior Checklist, that shows promise. With respect to substance use, some of the more frequently employed screening instruments that may prove useful in working with parents of children with CP include the short version of the Michigan Alcoholism Screening Test (Selzer, Vinokur, & van Rooijen, 1975), the Drug Abuse Screening Test (Skinner, 1982), and the Alcohol Use Disorders Identification Test (Saunders, Aasland, Babor, de la Fuente, & Grant, 1993).

With respect to marital discord, the Marital Adjustment Test (Locke & Wallace, 1959) and the Dyadic Adjustment Scale (Spanier, 1976) have been the most widely used instruments with parents of children with CP. There is some evidence to suggest that marital conflict, rather than general marital adjustment, has a stronger relationship with child CP behavior. Two questionnaires are often used to assess general marital conflict: the O'Leary–Porter Scale (Porter & O'Leary, 1980), and the Conflict Tactics Scale–Partner (Straus, 1979, 1990). Instruments designed to measure parenting-related conflict have also been developed, such as the Parenting

Alliance Inventory (Abidin, 1988), Child Rearing Disagreements (Jouriles et al., 1991), and the Parent Problem Checklist (Dadds & Powell, 1991).

Two types of measures that assess stress have been employed with parents of children with CP: general measures of stress, such as life event scales, and specific measures of parenting-related stress. Examples of the former include the Life Experiences Survey (Sarason, Johnson, & Siegel, 1978) and the Family Events List (Patterson, 1982). Measures specific to parenting-related stress include Parenting Daily Hassles (Crnic & Greenberg, 1990) and the Parenting Stress Index (Abidin, 1995). The Parenting Stress Index has been extensively employed with parents of children with CP, both in terms of predicting CP and with respect to treatment outcome and dropout (e.g., Abidin, Jenkins, & McGaughey, 1992; Kazdin, 1990; Webster-Stratton, 1994).

With respect to extrafamilial functioning, the Community Interaction Checklist (CIC; Wahler et al., 1979) has been extensively employed in research with children with CP and their families. The CIC is a brief interview designed to assess maternal insularity and is usually administered on multiple occasions. As noted above, classification as insular on the CIC is a strong predictor of poor maintenance of the effects of parent training interventions for children with CP (e.g., Dumas & Wahler, 1983; Wahler, 1980).

Finally, it is important to assess the social validity of treatment with children with CP and their families. Parental satisfaction with treatment, which is one form of social validity, may be assessed in terms of satisfaction with the outcome of treatment, therapists, treatment procedures, and teaching format (McMahon & Forehand, 1983). At present, no single consumer satisfaction measure is appropriate for use with all types of interventions for children with CP and their families. The Parent's Consumer Satisfaction Questionnaire (Forehand & McMahon, 1981; McMahon, Tiedemann, Forehand, & Griest, 1984) is an example of one such measure designed to evaluate parental satisfaction with a particular parent training program designed to modify child noncompliance and other CP behaviors.

An Assessment Model

The delineation of different developmental pathways of CP has a number of important implications for the assessment of children with CP (McMahon & Estes, 1997). First, the assessment must be developmentally sensitive, not only with respect to the child's age and sex, but also in terms of the child's status and progression on a particular developmental pathway of CP. The possibility of comorbid conditions, such as ADHD and internalizing disorders, should also be investigated. The assessment must also be contextually sensitive, and must provide for the assessment not only of child CP behaviors and other behavior problems, but also of other child characteristics and of familial and peer influences. Furthermore, this assessment must examine the broader ecologies of home, school, neighborhood, and community, to the extent that each is warranted. Cultural sensitivity in the development, administration, and interpretation of assessment instruments also requires increased attention (Prinz & Miller, 1991). Finally, the clinician needs to recognize the transactional nature of these developmental and contextual processes, and to conduct the assessment accordingly.

It is readily apparent that a proper assessment of the child with CP must make use of multiple methods (e.g., behavioral rating scales, direct observation, interviews) completed by multiple informants (parents, teachers, the child himself or herself) concerning the child's behavior in multiple settings (e.g., home, school), and that the familial and extrafamilial context in which the child functions must also be assessed (McMahon & Estes, 1997). However, in cost-effectiveness terms, to conduct such a broad-based assessment with every child who is referred would be prohibitively expensive, and the incremental utility of each additional assessment measure or content area with respect to improving our treatment selecting capabilities would be suspect as well (Mash & Terdal, 1997).

A "multiple-gating" approach to screening is an example of one strategy for employing multiple assessment measures that may prove to be cost-effective (e.g., Reid, Baldwin, Patterson, & Dishion, 1988; Walker et al., 1995). In this approach, less costly assessment procedures, such as brief interviews and behavioral rating scales, can be employed as screening instruments with all children who are clinic-referred for the treatment of CP. More expensive methods, such as observations in the home or school, can be used to assess only that subgroup of children for whom the less expensive methods have indicated the desirability of further assessment. An analogous strategy could be followed in the assessment of other child characteristics and familial and extrafamilial factors, in that low-cost methods such as interview questions (e.g., questions concerning the child's temperament) and/or brief self-report measures (e.g., the Beck Depression Inventory) would be employed as screening measures. Should additional assessment in these areas be warranted, then a more thorough (and expensive) assessment could be conducted.

The ultimate goal of the assessment process is, of course, to facilitate selection of the most appropriate treatment strategy or strategies. Algorithms for matching clinic-referred families with specific interventions exist (e.g., Blechman, 1981; Embry, 1984), but they have been quite limited in scope, have not been closely tied to underlying assessment strategies, and have not yet been empirically tested. A comprehensive, empirically based treatment selection model for children with CP is sorely needed. The more clinically oriented strategies for integrating and interpreting information from comprehensive assessments, such as those presented by Sanders and Lawton (1993) and Kamphaus and Frick (1996), are a step in the right direction.

TREATMENT

As demonstrated in the preceding material, CP is multifaceted in the diversity of specific behaviors manifested, the ages of the children who engage in these behaviors, and the settings in which the behaviors occur. Not surprisingly, a plethora of interventions have been developed to deal with the various manifestations of CP (e.g., Kazdin, 1995b). In an attempt to impose some structure in our discussion of this array of interventions, we adopt the following organizational scheme. Psychosocial interventions designed to deal with overt and covert CP behaviors are discussed separately. Although noncompliance is characteristic of both overt and covert forms of CP, it has been typically dealt with in treatment programs designed to deal with overt CP behaviors (e.g., Forehand & McMahon, 1981; Patterson et al., 1975), and so is discussed in that section of the chapter. For each of the major subtypes of CP, we describe family-based interventions (e.g., parent training), community-based programs (e.g., Achievement Place, Treatment Foster Care), school-based interventions (e.g., classroom contingency management programs), and skills training approaches (e.g., so-

cial skills training, anger control training). For each type of program, interventions that are available for, and appropriate to, the preadolescent (3–12 years of age) and the adolescent (13 and older) are described. For each intervention, we provide a description and briefly review the empirical evidence concerning its effectiveness. Following the review of psychosocial interventions for overt and covert CP, we discuss psychopharmacological and preventive interventions. In the final section of the chapter, we discuss a number of issues related to the development, selection, and evaluation of these interventions, such as generalization and social validity, the prediction of outcome, and comparative efficacy.

Psychosocial Interventions for Overt CP

The majority of psychosocial interventions directed to children with CP have been designed for the treatment of overt as opposed to covert CP, probably because of the disruptive effects of those behaviors on parents, siblings, teachers, peers, and others. Because current theoretical (e.g., Patterson et al., 1992) and empirical (e.g., Loeber & Stouthamer-Loeber, 1986) writings indicate the primary role of the family in the development and maintenance of CP, we focus first on interventions directed at the child with CP in the context of the family.

Family-Based Interventions with Preadolescents

Approaches to treating children with CP in the family have typically been based on a social-learning-based "parent training" model of intervention (Kazdin, 1995b; Miller & Prinz, 1990). The underlying assumption of this model is that some sort of parenting skills deficit has been at least partly responsible for the development and/or maintenance of the CP behaviors. The core elements of the parent training approach have been delineated by a number of authors (e.g., Dumas, 1989; Kazdin, 1995b; Miller & Prinz, 1990). They include the following:

1. Intervention is conducted primarily with the parents, with relatively less therapist–child contact.

2. There is a refocusing from a preoccupation with CP behaviors to an emphasis on prosocial goals.

3. The content of these programs typically includes instruction in the social learning princi-

ples underlying the parenting techniques; training in defining, monitoring, and tracking child behavior; training in positive reinforcement procedures, including praise and other forms of positive parent attention, and token or point systems; training in extinction and mild punishment procedures such as ignoring, response cost, and time out in lieu of physical punishment; training in giving clear instructions or commands; and problem solving.

4. There is extensive use of didactic instruction, modeling, role playing, behavioral rehearsal, and structured homework exercises.

Parent training interventions have been successfully utilized in the clinic and home settings, have been implemented with individual families or with groups of families, and have involved some or all of the instructional techniques listed above. O'Dell (1985) has provided an extensive review of the myriad parametric considerations involved in parent training.

Although the short-term efficacy of behavioral parent training in producing changes in both parent and child behaviors has been demonstrated repeatedly (e.g., O'Dell, 1974; Serketich & Dumas, 1996), the generalization of those effects has been less consistently documented. Forehand and Atkeson (1977) discussed four major types of generalization relevant to parent training interventions with children. "Setting generalization" refers to the transfer of treatment effects to settings in which treatment did not take place (e.g., from the clinic to the home), whereas "temporal generalization" pertains to the maintenance of treatment effects following termination. "Sibling generalization" concerns the transfer of the newly acquired parenting skills to untreated siblings in the family, and the siblings' responding in the desired manner. "Behavioral generalization" refers to whether targeted changes in specific CP behaviors are accompanied by improvements in other nontargeted behaviors.

Pertinent to the generalization of effects is the "social validity" of the intervention, which refers to whether therapeutic changes are "clinically or socially important" for the client (Kazdin, 1977a, p. 429). Parent training interventions for the treatment of children with CP have demonstrated their generalizability and social validity to varying degrees—some quite impressively, others not at all. As a consequence of this emphasis on the generalization and social validity of treatment effects, and the increased awareness of the multiple causal and maintain-

ing factors for CP, the parent training model has been broadened to what is referred to as "behavioral family therapy" (Griest & Wells, 1983; Wells, 1985). This model is an attempt to acknowledge and incorporate into treatment the variety of child and parent variables that have been implicated in the development and maintenance of CP, such as parental personal adjustment and perceptions of the child, and child characteristics such as temperament and attributional style. Johnston (1996) has recently presented a model for conceptualizing various types of parental cognitions and their role in family-based interventions with children with CP. Miller and Prinz (1990) provide a thorough discussion and review of various enhancements to the basic parent training model as a means of enhancing generalization and social validity.

We present several parent training/behavioral family therapy programs as examples of state-of-the-art family-based interventions for preadolescent children with CP. Descriptions of the clinical procedures utilized in these programs are widely available, and each of the programs has been extensively evaluated.

The first parent training program is specifically designed to treat noncompliance in younger children (3–8 years of age). As noted above, noncompliance is regarded as a keystone behavior in the development and maintenance of CP. The program was originally developed by Hanf (1969, 1970; Hanf & Kling, 1973), but has been modified and subsequently evaluated by several independent groups of clinical researchers, including Forehand and his colleagues (Forehand & McMahon, 1981), Webster-Stratton (1996a), and Eyberg (e.g., Eyberg, Boggs, & Algina, 1995). As presented by Forehand and McMahon (1981), the Helping the Noncompliant Child parent training program employs a controlled learning environment in which a parent is taught to change maladaptive patterns of interaction with a child. Sessions are typically conducted in a clinic setting with individual families rather than in groups. Ideally, treatment occurs in playrooms equipped with one-way mirrors for observation, sound systems, and "bug-in-the-ear" devices (Farrall Instruments) by which the therapist can communicate unobtrusively with the parent, although these are not necessary for successful implementation of the program. A number of discrete parenting skills are taught to the parent by way of didactic instruction, modeling, and role playing. The parent also practices the skills in the clinic with the child while receiving prompting and feedback from the therapist by means of the bug-in-the-ear device. Finally, the parent employs these newly acquired skills in the home setting.

The treatment program consists of two phases. During the differential-attention phase of treatment (Phase I), the parent learns to break out of the coercive cycle of interaction with the child by increasing the frequency and range of social attention and by reducing the frequency of competing verbal behavior. The primary goal is to establish a positive, mutually reinforcing relationship between the parent and child. The parent is first taught to attend to and describe the child's appropriate behavior while eliminating commands, questions, and criticisms. The second segment of Phase I consists of teaching the parent to use verbal and physical attention contingent upon compliance and other appropriate behaviors, and to ignore minor inappropriate behaviors. Homework is assigned in the form of daily 10-minute practice sessions with the child, using the skills taught in the clinic. The parent is also required to develop programs for use outside the clinic, designed to increase at least two child behaviors by means of the new skills.

Phase II of the treatment program consists of teaching the parent to use appropriate commands and a time-out procedure to decrease noncompliant behavior exhibited by the child. The parent is taught to give direct, concise commands one at a time, and to allow the child sufficient time to comply.[6] If compliance is initiated, the parent is taught to praise or attend to the child. If compliance is not initiated, the parent learns to implement a 3-minute time-out procedure. Following time out, the command that originally elicited noncompliance is repeated. Compliance is followed by contingent attention from the parent. When the parent is able to administer the command–warning–time-out sequence successfully in the clinic, he or she is instructed to begin using the procedure for noncompliance at home. Finally, parents are taught to use permanent "standing rules" as an occasional supplement to this sequence.

Progression to each new skill in the treatment program is determined by the use of behavioral and temporal (number of sessions) criteria. These criteria insure that the parent has attained an acceptable degree of competence in a particular skill before being taught additional parenting techniques, and allow for the individualization of the treatment program by allocating training time more efficiently. For complete details of this parent training program, see Forehand and McMahon (1981).

The Helping the Noncompliant Child parent training program has been extensively evaluated in terms of its short-term effectiveness, generalization, and social validity (see McMahon & Forehand, 1984). Short-term effectiveness and setting generalization from the clinic to the home have been demonstrated for both parent and child behaviors, as well as parents' perceptions of their children (e.g., Peed, Roberts, & Forehand, 1977). Furthermore, these improvements occur regardless of families' SES (Rogers, Forehand, Griest, Wells, & McMahon, 1981) or age of the children (within the 3- to 8-year-old age range) (McMahon, Forehand, & Tiedemann, 1985). Two studies have failed to find evidence for setting generality to the classroom, but there was also no evidence of a behavioral contrast effect, since there were no systematic increases or decreases in child deviant behavior in the classroom (Breiner & Forehand, 1981; Forehand et al., 1979).

The temporal generalization of this parent training program has been documented in several studies (Baum & Forehand, 1981; Forehand & Long, 1988; Forehand, Rogers, McMahon, Wells, & Griest, 1981; Forehand, Steffe, Furey, & Walley, 1983; Forehand et al., 1979; Long, Forehand, Wierson, & Morgan, 1994), with follow-up assessments ranging from 6 months to 14 years after treatment termination. Forehand and Long (1988) demonstrated that, relative to a nonreferred "normal" sample, a sample of children who had participated in the parent training program 4.5 to 10.5 years earlier (and who were now between the ages of 11 and 15) were functioning well. Long et al. (1994) reported similar findings at an 11- to 14- year follow-up. Sibling generalization has been demonstrated by Humphreys, Forehand, McMahon, and Roberts (1978), who showed that mothers employed the skills they had learned in the parent training program with untreated siblings, who responded by being more compliant to maternal directives. Finally, improvement in child compliance has been shown to be accompanied by decreases in other overt CP behaviors, such as aggression, tantrums, destructiveness, and inappropriate verbal behavior, thereby supporting the behavioral generalization of the program (Wells, Forehand, & Griest, 1980).

With respect to the social validity of the Forehand and McMahon (1981) program, children's compliance and inappropriate behavior have improved to within the normal range by the end of treatment, although mothers' perceptions of the children's adjustment appear to lag slightly behind the children's behavioral improvements (Forehand, Wells, & Griest, 1980). However, by 2 months after the conclusion of treatment, mothers' perceptions are consistent with the children's improved behavior and are comparable to those of mothers of "normal" children. High parental ratings of the acceptability of (Cross Calvert & McMahon, 1987), and satisfaction with (Baum & Forehand, 1981; Forehand et al., 1980; McMahon et al., 1984), the parent training program in general and its components have also been documented.

Several procedures have been evaluated as adjuncts to the basic parent training program. These include maternal (Wells, Griest, & Forehand, 1980) and child (Baum, Reyna McGlone, & Ollendick, 1986) self-control procedures; training of parents in the social learning principles underlying the parent training program (McMahon, Forehand, & Griest, 1981); expanded exemplars of common parent–child situations ("simulation training"; Powers & Roberts, 1995); and a multimodal treatment package ("parent enhancement therapy") designed to enhance general family functioning, which includes components related to parental perceptions of the child's behavior, marital adjustment, parental personal adjustment, and the parents' extrafamilial relationships (Griest et al., 1982). In general, these studies have supported the efficacy of these adjunctive procedures in enhancing the generalization and/or maintenance of treatment effects, over and above those gains obtained in the basic parent training program.

Two studies have compared the effects of this parent training program with other treatments for children with CP. Wells and Egan (1988) found that the parent training program was more effective than family systems therapy on observational measures of parent and child behaviors. The two treatment groups did not differ on parental self-report measures of personal (depression, anxiety) or marital adjustment. Baum et al. (1986) reported that a group version of the parent training program (with or without the child self-control adjunct noted above) was more effective at posttreatment and at a 6- to 8-month follow-up than a parent discussion group based on the Systematic Training for Effective Parenting (STEP) program (Dinkmeyer & McKay, 1976).

A second parent training program for young (3- to 8-year-old) children with CP, which includes some components of the Hanf (1969) and Forehand and McMahon (1981) programs, is the videotape modeling/group discussion (BA-SIC) program developed by Webster-Stratton (1996a). What is unique about this particular intervention is its use of a standard package of 10 videotape programs of modeled parenting skills shown by a therapist to groups of parents. The 250 vignettes (each of which lasts approximately 2 minutes) include examples of parents interacting with their children in both appropriate and inappropriate ways. After each vignette, the therapist leads a discussion of the relevant interactions and solicits parental responses to the vignettes. In this particular program, the children do not attend the therapy sessions, although parents are given homework exercises to practice various parenting skills with their children. The videotapes and associated therapist manuals are commercially available.

Several outcome studies have evaluated the immediate and longer-term effects of this parent training approach. The first study (Webster-Stratton, 1981, 1982a, 1982b), which employed a sample of nonreferred mothers, reported positive changes in mothers' and children's behaviors and in maternal perceptions of the children's adjustment at posttreatment, compared to those of a waiting-list control group. Mothers also reported high levels of satisfaction with the treatment program. At a 1-year follow-up, most of the parental perceptions and mother and child behaviors were maintained or continued to improve; however, there was a significant decrease in mothers' confidence in their parenting skills and perceived ability to manage their children's behavior problems.

In the second study, Webster-Stratton (1984) employed a sample of 35 mothers of clinic-referred children with CP. Mothers were randomly assigned to either the BASIC program, an individual parent training program, or a waiting-list control. The individual parent training program, the content of which was comparable to that of the BASIC program, employed one-to-one sessions with a therapist, a mother, and her child. Positive changes in both treatment conditions at posttreatment, compared to the waiting-list control condition, were obtained on a variety of treatment outcome measures. At a 1-year follow-up, most of these changes were maintained; in fact, the children's noncompliance and deviant behavior had continued to decrease. Parental satisfaction with treatment was also maintained at the 1-year follow-up. What is also of interest is that there were virtually no differences between the two treatment groups at posttreatment and at the follow-up. Given that therapist time per client was five times greater for the individual parent training condition than for the BASIC condition, the latter program appears to represent a cost-effective alternative to the traditional parent training format of individual consultation with a single family, at least for families of young children with CP.

A component analysis of the BASIC program was conducted with a sample of mothers and fathers of 114 children with CP (Webster-Stratton, 1989, 1990a; Webster-Stratton, Hollinsworth, & Kolpacoff, 1989; Webster-Stratton, Kolpacoff, & Hollinsworth, 1988). Parents were randomly assigned to either the BASIC program, self-administered videotape modeling (with no therapist feedback or group discussion), group discussion alone, or a waiting-list control condition. Each of the three treatment conditions was superior to the waiting-list control condition on most of the various outcome measures (Webster-Stratton et al., 1988), and these improvements were maintained at a 1-year follow-up (Webster-Stratton et al., 1989). However, the BASIC program appeared to be somewhat more effective than the other two treatment conditions, and both mothers and fathers reported somewhat greater satisfaction with the BASIC program than with the other conditions (Webster-Stratton, 1989). At a 3-year follow-up, only the parents in the BASIC condition reported stable improvements in their children's behavior problems (Webster-Stratton, 1990a). These findings again support the short-term effectiveness and temporal generalization of the BASIC program, and suggest the power of the videotape modeling component.

Webster-Stratton (1996a) has described the development of several adjuncts to the BASIC program. The ADVANCE program, which consists of 14 sessions and 60 videotaped vignettes, focuses on the enhancement of parental interpersonal skills. Parents who received the ADVANCE component following participation in the BASIC parent training program reported greater improvements in communication, problem-solving skills, and consumer satisfaction than did parents who received only the BASIC program (Webster-Stratton, 1994). The KIDVID program, which is conducted with children and consists of 22 sessions and more than 100 videotape vignettes, focuses on child social skills training and classroom behavior. The KIDVID adjunct, whether alone or in conjunction with BASIC and ADVANCE, resulted in child improvements in problem solving and conflict management skills with peers (Webster-Stratton & Hammond, 1997). However, the combined

parent and child intervention had the most robust improvements in child behavior at a 1-year follow-up. Most recently, Webster-Stratton (1996c) demonstrated that the combination of the BASIC program with an adjunct to promote teachers' classroom management skills and their promotion of parental involvement in school (PARTNERS) resulted in greater positive parent and child behavior changes in a sample of Head Start families than did the regular Head Start program.

As noted above, the work of Gerald Patterson and his associates at the Oregon Social Learning Center (OSLC) with children with CP and their families has been seminal in the development of the theoretical and empirical knowledge base concerning CP. Patterson's efforts over the past 30 years have also been extremely influential with respect to the development and evaluation of family-based intervention strategies for children with CP. Here, we briefly review Patterson's parent training program for preadolescent children (3–12 years of age) who engage in overt CP. OSLC intervention programs for children who steal and for adolescents with CP are described later in the chapter.

The parent training program for preadolescent aggressive children is delineated in the treatment manual by Patterson et al. (1975) and has been summarized by Forgatch (1991). Prior to beginning treatment, parents are given a copy of either *Living with Children* (Patterson, 1976) or *Families* (Patterson, 1975a), to provide a conceptual background for the specific skills training in the treatment sessions and to facilitate generalization and maintenance. For some families, simply reading the book may lead to a significant reduction in observed child deviant behaviors (Patterson, 1975b). After completion of the reading assignment, the next step is to teach the parents to pinpoint the problem behaviors of concern. The parents then learn to track the child's behavior. Parents choose two or three behaviors (one of which is usually noncompliance) to observe for a 1-hour period each day for a week. Once the parents are pinpointing and tracking these child behaviors appropriately, they are assisted in establishing a positive reinforcement system, using points, backup reinforcers such as privileges or treats, and social reinforcement (i.e., praise). Over time, the tangible reinforcers are faded. After the point system is well established, the parents are taught to use a 5-minute time-out procedure for noncompliance or aggressive behavior. Response cost (e.g., loss of privileges) and work chores are also sometimes used with older children. As treatment progresses, parents become increasingly responsible for designing and implementing behavior management programs for various child behaviors. Parents are also taught to monitor or supervise their children, even when they are away from home. Problem-solving and negotiation strategies are taught to the parents at this point in treatment. Patterson and Chamberlain (1988) estimate that approximately 30% of treatment time is devoted to dealing with such problems as marital difficulties, parental personal adjustment problems, and family crises.

The parent training program for preadolescent children with CP has been extensively evaluated at OSLC and in community settings. Patterson, Cobb, and Ray (1973) treated 13 consecutive referrals of boys with CP and their families. Behavioral observation data indicated that 9 of the 13 families demonstrated improvements equal to or greater than 30% reduction from baseline levels of observed deviant behavior. In subsequent replication studies, similar effects were obtained (Patterson, 1974; Patterson & Reid, 1973). Improvements in maternal perceptions of the children's adjustment have also been reported, and there is evidence for generalization across settings, time (up to 2 years posttreatment), behavior, and siblings (e.g., Arnold, Levine, & Patterson, 1975; Horne & Van Dyke, 1983; Patterson, 1974; Patterson & Fleischman, 1979; Patterson & Forgatch, 1995). The program has been shown to have comparable effects for families with older (6.5 to 12.5 years old) and younger (2.5 to 6.5 years old) children, although families with older children were more likely to drop out of treatment (Dishion & Patterson, 1992).

Early attempts by other investigators to replicate Patterson's procedures and methodology met with mixed results (Eyberg & Johnson, 1974; Ferber, Keeley, & Shemberg, 1974). The results of later studies have been more promising. Comparable findings to those reported by Patterson (1974) have been obtained in a mixed sample of children who stole or who were socially aggressive (Fleischman, 1981), and for a subset of children who were socially aggressive (Weinrott, Bauske, & Patterson, 1979). These families were treated by clinicians who, although affiliated with Patterson, had not participated in the 1974 investigation and were not supervised by the OSLC staff during the course of the studies. Not only were positive treatment effects maintained at a 1-year follow-up, but standardization of treatment procedures and use of a group format in the replication studies reduced treatment time per family from 31 hours to 13–16 hours. Fleischman and Szykula (1981) conducted another replication study in a community setting with 50 families, and reported comparable improvements at posttreatment and at a 1-year follow-up.

The OSLC group has also conducted a number of comparison studies. Early investigations comparing the parent training program with attention placebo (Walter & Gilmore, 1973) and waiting-list control (Wiltz & Patterson, 1974) conditions reported significant reductions in targeted deviant child behaviors, whereas there were no significant changes for the comparison groups. However, small sample sizes, short treatment intervals, and other methodological difficulties limited the significance of the findings. A later study (Patterson, Chamberlain, & Reid, 1982) randomly assigned 19 families to parent training or waiting-list control conditions. The control condition actually became a comparison treatment condition by default, since eight of nine families obtained treatment from various clinicians in the community. Treatment ranged from "eclectic" to behavioral in orientation. Observational data in the home indicated significant reductions in child deviant behavior for the parent training program only. However, both groups demonstrated significant improvements on the PDR with respect to frequency of parent-reported problem behaviors.

Preliminary findings from a large-scale comparative study at OSLC were reported by Patterson and Chamberlain (1988) and Reid (1987). Seventy families with children with CP (aged 6 to 12 years) were randomly assigned to parent training ($n = 50$) or to a community agency employing eclectic family therapy ($n = 20$). Preliminary findings based on the first 34 families in the study indicate significant reductions in child CP behaviors for families in the parent training condition, but no significant reduction for children in the family therapy condition (Reid, 1987). Only mothers in the parent training condition also demonstrated significant reductions in self-reported levels of depression.

Family-Based Interventions with Adolescents

Patterson and his colleagues have modified their parent training intervention for use with adolescents with CP (Bank, Marlowe, Reid, Patterson, & Weinrott, 1991; Forgatch & Patterson, 1989; Patterson & Forgatch, 1987). Modifications for delinquent adolescents include the following: (1) In addition to targeting prosocial and CP behaviors, parents also target any other behaviors that they believe put the adolescent at risk for further delinquency (e.g., class attendance, sassing the teacher, homework, spending time with "bad" companions, curfew violations, drug use); (2) there is a strong emphasis on parental monitoring/supervision of the adolescent, especially with respect to the adolescent's school attendance, behavior, and academic performance; (3) in lieu of the time-out procedure, punishment procedures include work details, point loss, restriction of free time, and restitution of stolen/damaged property; (4) the parents are asked to report legal offenses to juvenile authorities and then to act as advocates for the adolescent in court (as a way of decreasing the likelihood of the child's being removed from the home); and (5) there is greater involvement of the adolescent in treatment sessions, especially with regard to the formulation and monitoring of behavioral contracts with the parents (Bank et al., 1991).

The relative efficacy of this approach to dealing with adolescents has been examined by Bank et al. (1991). Fifty-five chronically delinquent boys (mean age of 14 years, with an average of eight previous offenses) were randomly assigned to parent training or existing services provided by the court and community agencies. These services included behavioral-family systems therapy and, for many of the adolescents, group counseling concerning drug use. The primary outcome measure was rate of official offenses as documented by the court, although home observation and PDR data were collected on families in the parent training condition (the court refused to permit the collection of treatment outcome data for the comparison condition). Families in the parent training condition received an average of 45 hours of treatment, half of which took place over the phone. Nearly half of those families received additional booster sessions during follow-up as well.

During the treatment year, adolescents in the parent training condition evidenced a greater reduction in total and nonstatus (but not status) offense rates than the adolescents in the comparison condition. By the first year after treatment, however, offense rates for the two conditions were comparable, and remained so throughout the 3-year follow-up. Adolescents in the parent training condition also spent less time in institutions than their counterparts during the treatment year and the first and second years of follow-up, at an estimated savings of over $100,000 over the 3-year period. There was no improvement in family interactions (as noted in the home observation data) as a function of treatment for the parent training condition, although parents did report significant decreases in targeted inappropriate behaviors (especially stealing) on the PDR. Despite these somewhat positive findings, Bank et al. (1991) are pessimistic as to the feasibility of this approach on a larger scale, given the extreme distress of the families and the high likelihood of therapist burnout. Instead, they argue for intervention with these families at an earlier stage, before the problems have increased to such severity and duration.

Another family-based intervention for adolescents engaging in CP behaviors has been developed and evaluated by James Alexander and his colleagues at the University of Utah. "Functional Family Therapy" (FFT; Alexander & Parsons, 1982; Barton & Alexander, 1981) represents a unique integration and extension of family systems and behavioral perspectives. The model has also incorporated cognitive and affective perspectives (Alexander, Jameson, Newell, & Gunderson, 1996). In the early stages of the development of FFT, Alexander employed a "matching-to-sample" approach in which behavior patterns that distinguished deviant families from their nondeviant counterparts were first identified, and then etiologically significant subsets of those patterns were chosen as targets of intervention (Morris, Alexander, & Waldron, 1988). Although early investigations of the efficacy of FFT were positive (see below), the model has been expanded to deal more successfully with those families more resistant to change.

In its current form, FFT consists of five components (Alexander, Waldron, Newberry, & Liddle, 1988). The introduction/impression phase is concerned with family members' expectations prior to therapy and in the initial sessions. Preliminary analogue investigations suggest the importance of identifying and modifying family members' blaming attributions in initial therapy sessions with families of delinquent adolescents (Alexander, Waldron, Barton, & Mas, 1989). In the assessment phase, the clinician identifies the behavioral, cognitive, and emotional expectations of each family member, as well as the family processes in need of change (e.g., interpersonal functions such as closeness and distance). The goal of the induction/therapy phase is to modify the inappropriate attributions and expectations of family members. Various cognitive therapy techniques, especially relabeling, are employed. Relabeling is defined as the "verbal portrayal of any 'negative' family (or individual) behavior in a benign or benevolent light by describing the 'positive' antonym properties of the behavior, and by portraying family members as victims rather than perpetrators" (Morris et al., 1988, p. 112). This reattribution process among family members is seen as necessary, but not sufficient, for successful treatment. Actual behavior change must follow. In the behavior change/education phase, various behavioral techniques are employed, including communication skills training, behavioral contracting, and contingency management. In the generalization/termination phase, the therapist's job is to facilitate maintenance of therapeutic gains while also fostering the family's independence from the therapy context through gradual disengagement. It is also during this phase that relevant extrafamilial factors (e.g., school, the legal system) are dealt with as necessary.

Most of the empirical research on the efficacy of FFT was conducted in the 1970s, prior to the inclusion of the cognitive and affective components described above. A series of three studies was conducted, using a single sample of 86 status delinquents and their families (Alexander & Parsons, 1973; Klein, Alexander, & Parsons, 1977; Parsons & Alexander, 1973). Families were randomly assigned to FFT or to one of several comparison conditions (no treatment, client-centered counseling, or psychodynamic counseling). At the conclusion of treatment, families in the FFT condition performed better than families in the comparison conditions on a number of communication variables assessed in a 20-minute family discussion (e.g., greater equality in talk time, less silence, and increased interruptions). An examination of juvenile court records 6–18 months after treatment indicated that adolescents in the FFT condition had a significantly lower recidivism rate (26%), compared to adolescents in the no-treatment (50%), client-centered counseling (47%), and psychodynamic counseling (73%) conditions (Alexander & Parsons, 1973). Within the FFT condition, a poorer outcome on the behavioral family interaction measures was associated with an increased likelihood of recidivism, thus lending direct support to the relationship between the two measures. Finally, Klein et al. (1977) reported a decreased probability of sibling involvement in the juvenile courts over a period of 2.5 to 3.5 years following the families' participation in FFT. Whereas only 20% of the siblings in the FFT condition had subsequent court contact, the percentages were 40%, 59%, and 63% for the no-treatment, client-centered counseling, and psychodynamic counseling conditions, respectively.

These earlier investigations focused on the families of adolescent delinquents with relatively minor status offenses. The current version of FFT, in conjunction with supportive adjuncts such as remedial education and job training, has been shown to be effective with multiply offending, previously incarcerated delinquents (Barton, Alexander, Waldron, Turner, & Warburton, 1985). In this investigation, adolescents who participated in FFT were less likely to be charged with committing an offense in the 15-month follow-up period than were adolescents placed in group homes (60% vs. 93%). FFT participants who did commit additional offenses committed significantly fewer offenses than adolescents in the group home condition.

Gordon, Arbuthnot, and their colleagues (Gordon, Arbuthnot, Gustafson, & McGreen, 1988; Gordon, Graves, & Arbuthnot, 1995) have successfully employed a slightly modified version of FFT (longer treatment, treatment in the home as opposed to clinic, and longer training and supervision of therapists) with a sample of 27 disadvantaged rural families of delinquent adolescents, many of whom were multiple offenders. Recidivism rates for the FFT and comparison (probation-only) groups at a 2.5-year follow-up were 11% and 67%, respectively. Reduced recidivism rates were noted for both males and females (Gordon et al., 1988). In a subsequent follow-up when the subjects were 20 to 22 years old, Gordon et al. (1995) reported recidivism rates of 9% and 41% for the FFT and comparison groups, respectively. Recidivism occurred entirely among the males; none of the females in either group recidivated during this second follow-up period.

The "Multisystemic Therapy" (MST) approach to treating adolescents with CP emphasizes both the interactional nature of adolescent psychopathology and the role of multiple systems in which the adolescent is embedded, such as the family, school, and peer group (Henggeler & Borduin, 1990; Henggeler, Schoenwald, Borduin, Rowland, & Cunningham, in press). The family is viewed as a core focus of the intervention. Assessment and treatment are concerned with the adolescent as an individual, his or her role in the various systems, and the interrelationships among those systems. Therapists intervene at one or more levels as required, and employ a variety of therapy approaches, such as family therapy, school consultation, peer intervention strategies, marital therapy, or individual therapy. Treatment techniques are similarly wide-ranging, and may include traditional family therapy procedures (e.g., paradoxical intent) as well as behavioral and cognitive-behavioral techniques (e.g., reinforcement, contingency contracting, self-instructions) (Schoenwald, Henggeler, Pickrel, & Cunningham, 1996). Clinicians are guided by a set of nine treatment principles (e.g., "Focus on systemic strengths," "Promote responsible behavior and decrease irresponsible behavior among family members," "Interventions should be developmentally appropriate.") (Henggeler et al., in press).

Most of the evaluations of MST have been conducted with samples of juvenile offenders (many of whom were chronic and/or violent offenders), although the effectiveness of MST with adolescent sexual offenders has also been investigated. Henggeler et al. (1986) conducted an evaluation of the efficacy of MST with inner-city adolescent delinquents, most of whom were repeat offenders, and their families ($n = 57$). At the conclusion of treatment, parents in the MST condition reported fewer behavior problems, whereas parents of adolescents in an alternative mental health services condition ($n = 23$) and in the normal control condition ($n = 44$) reported no change. Families in the MST condition had also improved at posttreatment on several observational measures of family interaction (based on a family discussion exercise), whereas the families in the alternative treatment condition either did not change or deteriorated on those measures from pretreatment to posttreatment.

Henggeler, Melton, and Smith (1992) assessed the effects of MST with a sample of 84 violent, chronic juvenile offenders (mean age = 15.2 years). The offenders, who averaged 3.5 previous offenses, were randomly assigned to receive either MST or "usual services" through the Department of Youth Services. One year following referral, youths whose families had participated in MST reported fewer CP behaviors and were less likely to have been arrested or incarcerated than youth in the comparison group. Families that received MST also reported greater cohesion and less peer aggression than families in the comparison group. MST was not differentially effective as a function of either demographic characteristics (e.g., sex, ethnicity, SES, previous arrests) or psychosocial variables (e.g., family relations, parental symptomatology). However, emotional bonding with peers was a significant predictor of lower frequencies

of rearrests. In a follow-up study conducted 2.4 years postreferral, survival analyses indicated the temporal generalization of the superiority of MST (Henggeler, Melton, Smith, Schoenwald, & Hanley, 1993). Thirty-nine percent of the MST group had not been rearrested, compared to 20% of the comparison group.

MST has also been compared to individual therapy in a sample of 176 adolescent chronic offenders (Borduin et al., 1995). At posttreatment, MST families reported more positive family relations, lower levels of parental symptomatology, and decreased child behavior problems, compared to the individual therapy group. Observed family interactions were also more positive in the MST group. At a 4-year follow-up assessment of arrest records, 26% of the MST group had been rearrested, compared to 71% of the individual therapy group. In addition, youths in the MST group were arrested for less serious (i.e., nonviolent) crimes than youths in the individual therapy group.

MST is less effective and dropout appears higher (see Henggeler, Pickrel, Brondino, & Crouch, 1996) when less intensive training procedures (similar to those found in community mental health settings) are employed (Henggeler et al., 1997). More specifically, there was no weekly consultation with an "expert" in MST (a standard component of implementation procedures for MST) during a community-based trial in which MST was compared to usual services. Although adolescent symptomatology and incarceration were reduced significantly at posttreatment and at a 1.7-year follow-up, respectively, the overall effects of MST were not as strong as reported in previous trials. Henggeler et al. (1997) demonstrated that higher treatment adherence ratings were associated with more positive outcomes.

MST has also been shown to be effective with other CP-related behaviors. Henggeler et al. (1991) reported lower rates of self-reported "soft" drug use (alcohol, marijuana) in the Henggeler et al. (1992) sample and lower rates of substance-related arrests (4% vs. 16%) in the Borduin et al. (1995) sample for those youths who received MST than for youths in the comparison groups. MST may also have positive effects with adolescent sexual offenders (Borduin, Henggeler, Blaske, & Stein, 1990). At a 3-year follow-up, youths in the MST group were less likely to have been rearrested for sexual offenses than were youths who had received individual therapy (13% vs. 75%). However, the sample size in this study was quite small ($n = $

16) and the dropout rate was high (6 of the 16 subjects were rearrested during the course of intervention), so these findings must be considered preliminary.

Community-Based Programs

The systematic development and evaluation of community-based residential programs for aggressive and delinquent adolescents began over 30 years ago. The impetus came from judicial writings that highlighted ineffective and abusive institutional programs for delinquent youths, and at a national level, from the Presidential Commission on Law Enforcement and the Administration of Justice (1967), which severely criticized traditional institutional programs for being inhumane, expensive, and ineffective. In response to these forces, there has been increasing recognition that community-based programs must be developed in an attempt to address the complications presented by juvenile offenders (i.e., adjudicated aggressive and assaultive youths) who also display other emotional or behavioral conditions. Fagan (1991) has emphasized that it is frequently unclear whether the juvenile justice system or the mental health system has primary responsibility for these youths, with the result that neither does an effective job with them; each system frequently seeks to transfer these problem youths back to the other one. In addition, there has been a recent trend back toward punishment and retribution and away from rehabilitation as policy goals in the juvenile justice system (Fagan, 1991).

State-government-based programs have attempted to redress some of these problems by providing mental health services to youths who are also involved in the juvenile justice system because of their violent or aggressive behaviors. Examples of these efforts are the New York State Mobile Mental Health Teams program and North Carolina's Willie M program.

The New York program is an interagency approach (Fagan, 1991). Teams consist of Department of Mental Health staff members (psychologists, psychiatric social workers, nurses) who travel in mobile units, 4 days a week, to juvenile correctional facilities (training schools, residential centers) to assist program staffs by providing mental health evaluations, treatment plan development, follow-up on treatment plans, crisis intervention, and ongoing staff training. The program reaches all levels of security and attempts to provide mental health interventions to all youth with CP within the juvenile corrections department. Unfortunately, though it is ambitious in its goals and scope, the New York program has not received systematic evaluation.

North Carolina's Willie M program is another comprehensive state system; arising out of a class action lawsuit (Willie M. v. Hunt et al., 1979), it attempts to provide violent or assaultive youths with accompanying "emotional, mental, or neurological handicaps" with appropriate services. The heart of the program is a case management therapeutic approach, in which managers oversee the development and execution of individualized treatment plans for program participants. Youths are referred to appropriate, existing community services in the least restrictive environment. Unfortunately, despite a multimillion-dollar price tag, program evaluations have not indicated measurable, relative gains for Willie M program participants (Weisz, Walter, Weiss, Fernandez, & Mikow, 1990).

Achievement Place/Teaching Family Model.
Broad-based community treatment programs such as the two mentioned above, despite having considerable face validity and being based on well-intentioned efforts to treat youths with serious CP in the least restrictive setting possible, have suffered from a lack of empirical evaluation or from results that call their effectiveness into question. Recent reviews have questioned the effectiveness of case management-based approaches that attempt to direct youths into traditional treatments in the community (Weisz et al., 1990). For these reasons, more focused and specific models of community-based treatment have been evaluated. The Achievement Place model, an exemplar of a theoretically driven, empirically evaluated, focused intervention, was originally developed in 1967 and has become the prototypical community-based residential program for aggressive and delinquent adolescents.

The Achievement Place program is currently known as the Teaching-Family Model (TFM). There are now more than 250 group homes employing the TFM, serving over 1,500 children at a time (Fixsen & Blase, 1993; Wolf, Kirigin, Fixsen, Blase, & Braukmann, 1995). Each TFM group home is run by a young married couple, referred to as "teaching parents." The teaching parents undergo a rigorous 1-year training program and are certified by the Teaching-Family Association. Currently, there are no free-standing TFM group homes. All bona fide TFM group homes are affiliated with a training site or center that was certified by the Teaching-Family

Association as capable of providing the full complement of training, consultation, and evaluation services (Kirigin, 1996). There are typically five to eight adolescents ranging from 12 to 16 years of age in each group home; most are adjudicated delinquents, although more recently the program has expanded to include children and adolescents with a variety of presenting problems (Kirigin, 1996). While living in the group home, the adolescents attend local schools and are involved in community activities. The primary treatment components of TFM include a multilevel point system, self-government procedures (daily family conferences, a peer manager), social skills training, academic tutoring, and a home-based reinforcement system for monitoring school behavior. The average stay for a participant in the program is about 1 year (Kirigin, 1996).

Over the years, there has been increasing emphasis on the development of a positive relationship between each youth and the teaching parents, and upon the creation of a humane environment, in addition to the more traditional behavioral skills training and motivational procedures described in the earlier publications. Also, the program has expanded dramatically to include multiple layers of teaching parents, trainers, consultants, and evaluators, who create an integrated system of training, services, and reciprocal feedback systems that facilitate quality control. Community consumers (e.g., judges, community boards, teachers in local schools) are included in the evaluation system to insure that youths are receiving optimal care and that the program is responsive to youths' and communities' needs (Wolf et al., 1995).

The TFM's approach to treating adolescents with CP has been extensively evaluated, both in terms of formative evaluations of program components and with regard to treatment outcome. Formative evaluations have validated teaching procedures for social, academic, and self-care behaviors; vocational training procedures; the token reinforcement and self-government systems; and the home-based report card systems. These in-house evaluations have made extensive use of the assessment of social validity as a means of refining the program. Targets of those assessments have included the adolescents themselves; the teaching parents; and personnel in schools, juvenile courts, and social welfare agencies (Willner, Braukmann, Kirigin, & Wolf, 1978; Wolf et al., 1995).

The effectiveness of TFM has been assessed by its developers (e.g., Kirigin, Braukmann, At-

water, & Wolf, 1982), and by an independent evaluation team (Weinrott, Jones, & Howard, 1982). Although the investigations differed in scope, the findings were similar. Kirigin et al. (1982) compared 13 TFM group homes with 9 "traditional" community-based residential programs. Court/police records were collected for the year preceding treatment, the period during treatment, and the year after treatment. During treatment, there was a lower percentage of TFM participants (both boys and girls) engaging in offenses, as well as fewer recorded offenses, than for participants in the other group homes. There was no difference between the two treatment conditions on these measures during the year following treatment. Consumer satisfaction ratings by the adolescent participants and by school personnel, as well as a composite measure of consumer satisfaction, favored the TFM group homes.

In an independent evaluation of the cost-effectiveness of TFM, Weinrott et al. (1982) examined 26 TFM group homes housing 354 adolescents and 25 community-based comparison programs (nearly all of which were group homes) that housed 363 adolescents. Data collection occurred at intake, during the treatment period, and for each of 3 years following treatment. The TFM programs were 22% less expensive than the comparison programs on a cost-per-youth basis and 7% cheaper on a per diem basis. To assess the relative effectiveness of the interventions, the programs were compared on four composite indices: deviant behavior (court records and self-reports of delinquent behavior), education, occupation, and social/personality. The two groups differed only on the education index, with the TFM approach being slightly more successful in slowing a decline in grade point average and in raising the percentage of courses passed. In a separate analysis, Howard, Jones, and Weinrott (1981, cited in Weinrott et al., 1982) found that TFM was perceived to be more effective than the comparison programs by various community groups (i.e., teachers, court workers, and social services personnel).

A third study expanded the comparison group design and included multiple measures of effectiveness obtained from youths, staff members, school records, and official police and court files. The results of this study (Kirigin & Wolf, 1994; Wolf, Braukmann, & Kirigin Ramp, 1987) replicated earlier findings of immediate treatment effectiveness on officially recorded delinquency, social skills, school grades, and youth satisfaction. However, as in the earlier study, treatment effects dissipated once the youths left the program.

In summary, the TFM's approach to treating adolescent delinquents appears to be more effective than comparison programs while the adolescents are active participants. However, once the adolescents complete treatment and leave the group home setting, those differences disappear (Kirigin, 1996). The issue of whether TFM is better than either no intervention at all or institutional treatment has not been addressed. With respect to cost-effectiveness, TFM is cheaper than alternative group homes. However, both approaches are very expensive; only 45% of the adolescents complete treatment; and by 2–3 years later, there are few meaningful differences between treatment completers and dropouts (Weinrott et al., 1982). Suggestions to decrease the costs associated with TFM have included better selection and training of the teaching parents (so that they stay with TFM longer than the current average of 18 months) and operating the group homes at capacity (Weinrott et al., 1982). With respect to enhancing efficacy, TFM proponents have stressed the necessity of a greater emphasis on the transition from the group home back to the family of origin, as well as on the use of treatment strategies to facilitate maintenance (Kirigin, 1996; Willner et al., 1978; Wolf et al., 1995).

In summary, community-based residential programs for adolescents with severe CP have progressed from the inhumane "warehouses" of many years ago to programs that, though more humane and placing greater emphasis on the need for intervention, have little evidence for efficacy. Even programs such as the TFM, with its rigorous standards for staff training, quality control, and multilevel evaluation, have been disappointing in demonstrating long-term treatment effects, even though significant effects have been noted during the active treatment phase. Such results have prompted calls for an emphasis on a continuum of intervention services for youths with severe CP (Fagan, 1991; Wolf et al., 1995). After more restrictive treatment, stepping down to a short- or long-term supportive foster family model may be indicated for some youths. In this approach, specially trained foster parents would provide care and treatment for a single adolescent, possibly into early adulthood. Interestingly, just such a "treatment foster care" approach has been advocated by a variety of authors (Chamberlain, 1994; Hawkins, Meadowcroft, Trout, & Luster, 1985; Hudson, Nutter, & Galaway, 1994).

Treatment Foster Care. In addition to the data on limited treatment generalization once adolescents leave a group home or residential setting, there are a number of compelling reasons for training foster parents to care for a single adolescent with CP. First, over the past 10 years there has been a dramatic increase in the number of adolescents with severe behavioral problems who are placed outside of their family homes into institutional or residential care. In some cases, restrictive settings may be needed to protect the community; however, in other cases less restrictive (and expensive) out-of-home care may be sufficient. In addition, foster care may provide a step-down from restrictive care, as indicated above. Second, given that association with deviant peers in adolescence is a strong predictor of involvement in and escalation of CP behaviors (e.g., Dishion et al., 1991), the logic of placing youngsters displaying CP behaviors together in groups has been questioned (e.g., Dishion & Andrews, 1995). Such groups can potentially facilitate further bonding and development of common social identities among deviant group members.

Treatment foster care models are seeing a proliferation in use and evaluation. In a recent meta-analytic review, Reddy and Pfeiffer (1997) analyzed 40 published studies (encompassing 12,282 subjects) that employed some kind of treatment foster care model for a variety of child and adolescent populations. There were large positive effects on increasing the placement stability of difficult-to-place and difficult-to-maintain youths and on increasing their social skills, and medium positive effects on reducing behavior problems, improving psychological adjustment, and reducing restrictiveness of postdischarge placement.

Over the past 10 years, Chamberlain and her colleagues at OSLC have developed and systematically evaluated a multicomponent intervention for youths with CP that is called Treatment Foster Care (TFC; e.g., Chamberlain, 1994; Chamberlain & Moore, in press; Chamberlain & Reid, 1994). This program is based on previous intervention work from OSLC and was also influenced by the work of Hawkins (1989) and his colleagues (Hawkins et al., 1985), who were the first to use treatment foster care in community-based settings. The key components of the TFC intervention include: (1) recruitment and up to 20 hours of preservice training for foster parents in a social-learning-based parent training model; (2) ongoing case management consisting of individualized consultation to foster parents, weekly group foster parent meetings, and 24-hour on-call services for crisis management and support to foster parents; (3) daily structure and telephone contact support; (4) school consultation, consisting of teaching foster parents school advocacy skills and setting up a home–school daily report card for the adolescent; (5) family therapy with biological parents (or relatives), to coordinate gradual transfer of care from the TFC parents to the home, if possible; and (6) individual therapy for skills training in problem solving, anger management, educational issues, and other individual issues. This may be especially important for delinquent and aggressive females, who have a very high rate of previous sexual abuse, as well as more numerous and severe family disruptions (Chamberlain & Reid, 1994).

The TFC program has been evaluated in several outcome studies. The first study (Chamberlain, 1990) used a posthoc, nonrandomized design; it compared 16 aggressive adolescents (aged 12 to 18) who had been committed to a juvenile corrections institution but then diverted to TFC, with 16 matched control adolescents in group residential treatment. The experimental TFC subjects fared better than the control subjects on gross measures of outcome, with a significantly greater rate of program completion, significantly fewer days spent in incarceration 1 and 2 years after treatment, and consequently a significant cost savings to the community.

Because of these encouraging preliminary findings, three subsequent experimental trials have been conducted. Chamberlain and Reid (1991) randomly assigned 19 adolescents with CP discharged from the state hospital to postdischarge TFC treatment or to control treatment consisting of traditional community placements (e.g., group homes, training school). There were significantly greater reductions in PDR ratings of behavior problems at 3 months for TFC subjects than for control subjects, and a trend for differences at 7 months. There was also a significantly shorter time from referral to placement for TFC subjects, with associated cost savings. However, social competence and problem-solving skills did not improve for either group.

Another study was conducted with a sample of regular foster parents and the children placed in their care (Chamberlain, Moreland, & Reid, 1992). This study compared one group of foster parents, who received the TFC model of training and support plus a small increase in their monthly stipend, to a control group of foster parents who received only the increased stipend. The enhanced TFC group had increased foster parent retention rates, increased ability to manage child behavior problems, decreased reports of child behavior problems, and decreased number of disrupted placements over the 2-year study period.

Chamberlain and Moore (in press) randomly assigned 80 boys referred for out-of-home care due to chronic delinquency to either TFC or one of 11 existing group care placements. Preliminary data on 68 boys who completed a 6-month follow-up showed significant differences in frequency of arrest, timing of arrests, incarceration and runaway rates, and boys' self-reports of problem behavior frequency, all in favor of TFC. Interestingly, TFC boys spent significantly more time with adults than the group care boys did, and the group care boys spent significantly more time with delinquent peers than the TFC boys did. Consistent with previous research on risk factors, time spent associating with delinquent peers and consistency of discipline administered by adults *during placement* predicted the total number and seriousness of arrests at a 1-year follow-up; more deviant peer contact and less discipline were associated with greater and more serious arrests. This finding validates the importance of intervening on these two variables in intervention programs, and suggests that it is easier to supervise and discipline a boy who has severe problems with delinquency when he is not part of a group of peers with the same type of problems.

Chamberlain and Reid (1994) examined the effects of TFC on adolescent boys and girls. At the beginning of the intervention, boys had higher rates of CP (as measured by the PDR) than did girls. However, for boys CP behaviors decreased over the 6-month intervention period, while for girls they actually increased! Program completion rates were comparable between boys and girls, and both groups demonstrated comparable levels of arrest rates by 1 year after treatment (boys did show greater improvement than girls with respect to property crimes, but not for status offenses or person-to-person crimes). Chamberlain and Reid postulate that the treatment pattern found for the girls may be a reflection of their greater history of sexual abuse (49% vs. 11%); additional analyses suggested that history of sexual abuse, regardless of gender, was associated with greater pretreatment risk and more total arrests and arrests for status offenses over the 1-year follow-up.

These studies, taken together, lend strong support to the multicomponent TFC program as an effective and cost-efficient intervention for seriously delinquent and aggressive youths requiring out-of-home placement. The program is multicomponent and staff- and time-intensive; however, it still results in greater cost savings than traditional group home and residential placement do. A hallmark of the program is the provision of some adjunctive services that are individualized to meet the needs of youths and their families, similar to MST (Henggeler & Borduin, 1990).

Day Treatment Programs.   Another type of community-based intervention that falls at a more intermediate level of care is the day treatment program. Although these programs represent a wide array of services, we present the following description of a multicomponent approach to day treatment with preadolescent children with CP presented by Kolko (in press). The program is oriented toward maintaining each child in the community; meeting for several hours per week; providing exposure to peer and staff role models and multimodal services (e.g., cognitive-behavioral skills training, contingency management, parent training, school consultation); addressing multiple clinical targets (e.g., children, parents, and teachers); and conducting routine weekly monitoring and follow-up. The program is conducted after school, on Saturday mornings, and during the summer. A group of children participating in the day treatment program improved with respect to in-program assessments of aggression and property destruction; however, noncompliance was not affected. There was some evidence for setting generalization to the home and to the school, based on parent and teacher reports. The children and parents both reported high levels of consumer satisfaction with the program.

Grizenko, Papineau, and Sayegh (1993) reported that preadolescent children with CP who participated in their day treatment program showed greater gains on parental ratings of child measures of behavior (including CP) and on the children's self-perceptions of adjustment than did children in a waiting-list control group. Peer, family, and academic functioning was not differentially affected by the intervention at the posttreatment assessment. By a 6-month follow-up, children who had participated in the day treatment program had improved significantly on all of the measures except academics.

School-Based Treatment

A major problem in providing treatment for children with CP in the school setting is the current definition of "serious emotional disturbance" in Public Law 94–142 and its amendments (P. L. 99–457), which specifically exclude children who are "socially maladjusted unless it is determined that they are seriously emotionally disturbed" (U.S. Department of Health, Education, and Welfare, 1977, p. 42478) (Executive Committee of the Council for Children with Behavioral Disorders, 1987; Walker & Fabre, 1987). In spite of challenges at multiple levels to the assumptions behind this exclusion (e.g., Nelson, Rutherford, Center, & Walker, 1991), by federal mandate most children with CP are technically ineligible for special education assistance.

In addition to this formalized exclusion of many children with CP from special education services, most of the treatment research conducted in the school setting has failed to include a comprehensive assessment of children referred for school problems to ascertain whether they meet objective and/or clinical criteria for the diagnosis of CD or ODD; behavior is often defined as "inappropriate" and worthy of intervention if teachers and/or parents define it as such. Nevertheless, there is adequate reason to believe that this literature can provide useful guidelines for the treatment of children with CP in school settings. Although these children are often globally described as "disruptive," as "socially maladjusted," and as displaying "high rates of inappropriate behavior," an examination of the behaviors targeted for treatment in these studies reveals such overt CP behaviors as noncompliance to teacher requests or classroom rules, disturbing others, aggression, tantrums, and excessive verbal outbursts. The few investigations that have dealt with covert CP behaviors in the school are described later in the chapter.

Even if CP behaviors are not occurring initially in the school setting, research on behavioral covariation and setting generality in behavioral treatment programs indicates that (1) when CP behaviors are treated in the clinic or home environment, similar behaviors in school may remain unchanged (e.g., Breiner & Forehand, 1981; Forehand et al., 1979); (2) a behavioral contrast effect may occur, in which deviant school behavior increases as home disruption decreases (e.g., Johnson, Bolstad, & Lobitz, 1976; Walker, Hops, & Johnson, 1975); or (3) setting generalization may occur (e.g., Fellbaum, Daly, Forrest, & Holland, 1985; McNeil et al., 1991). Because some children do not show generalization of positive treatment effects to the school setting when CP behaviors are treated in the clinic or at home, it is necessary to monitor the school behavior of these children throughout and following treatment to ascertain whether interventions specific to the school setting are needed. It is also necessary to have an armamentarium of treatment strategies available for school intervention once the need for treatment is identified.

In this section of the chapter, we highlight some of the major types of psychosocial interventions that have been applied to overt CP behaviors in the school. A comprehensive review of the myriad intervention procedures that have been employed for these and related problems (such as academic achievement per se and peer relationship difficulties) is beyond the scope of this chapter. The reader is referred to McFadyen-Ketchum and Dodge, Chapter 6, and Lyon and Cutting, Chapter 9, this volume; Brewer, Hawkins, Catalano, and Neckerman (1995); Goldstein (1995); and Pfiffner and Barkley (in press).

Classroom and Playground Behavior Management Strategies. In their classic book on classroom behavior management strategies, O'Leary and O'Leary (1977) discuss the importance of teachers' behavior in modifying children's disruptive classroom behavior. Many of the earliest studies in classroom behavior therapy focused on contingency arrangements in the interactions of teachers and students. For example, a number of studies have shown that teacher praise for appropriate behavior, especially when coupled with ignoring of inappropriate behaviors, can effectively reduce classroom disruption (Becker, Madsen, Arnold, & Thomas, 1967; Brown & Elliot, 1965). In these strategies, teachers are taught to notice instances of appropriate behavior that are the prosocial opposites of the children's target CP behaviors, and to praise and otherwise reward the children when prosocial behaviors occur. Although teachers often protest that "I routinely praise my students," naturalistic observation studies show that rates of positive teacher attention to prosocial behavior are surprisingly low, and may be insufficient for increasing and maintaining the prosocial classroom behavior of children with mild levels of CP (Martens & Hiralall, 1997; Strain, Lambert, Kerr, Stagg, & Lenkner, 1983; White, 1975). It is also important to note that studies with children engaging in more severe negative/aggressive behaviors have shown that praise alone can have a neutral or even negative effect (Walker et al., 1995).

Other elements of effective classroom management include the establishment of clear rules and directions; use of programmed instructional materials that pace a student's academic progress at his or her own rate; provision of positive and corrective feedback; use of classroom token economies; and, for disruptive behaviors that cannot be ignored, the use of reprimands, time out, and response cost contingent upon the occurrence of CP behaviors. Although some studies demonstrate that each of these procedures alone can exert control over CP behaviors (e.g., Proctor & Morgan, 1991), clinically significant changes are most likely to occur when treatment strategies are combined (Greenwood, Hops, Delquadri, & Guild, 1974; O'Leary, Becker, Evans, & Saudargas, 1969). In fact, results of an accumulating body of research indicate that combining positive and negative approaches to contingency management produces effects superior to and more powerful than those of either positive-alone or negative-alone approaches (e.g., Pfiffner & O'Leary, 1987; Pfiffner, Rosen, & O'Leary, 1985; Shores, Gunter, & Jack, 1993; Walker & Hops, 1993; Walker et al., 1995).

Although instituting changes in teachers' social behavior can be an effective approach for modifying some children's CP behaviors, there are a number of disadvantages to such an approach. First, some teachers resent the implication that somehow their behavior is responsible for some children's misconduct, and they are resistant to consultation regarding how to change their own social behavior. In addition, some investigators have shown that teachers who have higher baseline levels of teaching self-efficacy are less accepting of behavioral consultation (Dunson, Hughes, & Jackson, 1994) and perceive less positive outcomes from consultation (Hughes, Grossman, & Barker, 1990). Other investigators have discussed the fact that changes in teacher social behavior alone may be effective with mildly disruptive children, but for children displaying more severely deviant classroom behavior, more powerful procedures are necessary (O'Leary et al., 1969; Walker, Hops, & Fiegenbaum, 1976). As noted earlier, several studies have demonstrated that changing teacher's social behavior alone is not sufficient to change extremely disruptive children's behavior and that combined strategies are necessary for these students.

For these reasons, investigators have turned their attention to the use of token reinforcement systems in the classroom. Token reinforcement programs typically involve three basic ingredients: (1) a set of instructions to the class about the behaviors that will be reinforced; (2) a means of making a potentially reinforcing stimulus (usually called a "token") contingent upon behavior; and (3) a set of rules governing the exchange of tokens for backup reinforcers (O'Leary & Drabman, 1971). Typical examples of classroom target behaviors have been paying attention, remaining seated, raising hands before speaking, facing the front of the room, not running, not talking out, and accurately completing class assignments. Many of these behaviors are incompatible with the aggressive and oppositional behaviors of children with CP.

A variety of systems can be developed for the delivery of tokens to children; specific details should always be worked out with each individual classroom teacher, so that the system fits as smoothly as possible into ongoing classroom routine. For example, in special education classrooms with a small teacher-to-pupil ratio, the teacher(s) may be able to monitor and rate children's behavior every 10–15 minutes. In large classrooms, teachers may do well to rate behavior and dispense tokens at the end of each class.

Token reinforcement programs have been evaluated singly and in combination with other classroom management strategies by a number of investigators, and substantial behavioral improvement with use of token systems has been shown (for reviews, see Abramowitz & O'Leary, 1991, and Kazdin, 1977b). There may be differences in the effectiveness of token programs when individual versus group contingencies are used. Pigott and Heggie (1986) reviewed 20 studies that directly compared these two strategies. In individual contingencies, individual children are reinforced solely on the basis of their own performance. In group contingencies, three or more children are reinforced on the basis of the overall performance of the group or a significant proportion thereof. Group contingencies were superior to individual ones when academic performance was the target behavior, whereas there was no consistent differential effect when social responses were the target behaviors. Group contingencies have been associated with an increase in verbal threats among classmates, however, and this potential effect should

be strongly considered in deciding between the use of group or individual contingencies.

An example of a program employing interdependent group contingencies bears special mention. The Good Behavior Game (Barrish, Saunders, & Wolf, 1969; Deitz, 1985; Medland & Stachnik, 1972) is an approach that capitalizes on team competitiveness and group social conformity. The classroom is divided into two or more teams. Each team receives marks against itself based on violations of posted rules by individual team members. Reinforcement is provided to both teams if a maximum threshold of total marks is not exceeded by both teams. Otherwise, the team with the fewest marks wins and receives reinforcement. A variant of this procedure, the Good Behavior Game Plus Merit (Darveaux, 1984), also allows students to earn merit points for their team for accurate academic assignment completion.

The effectiveness (Barrish et al., 1969) and acceptability to teachers (Tingstrom, 1994) of the Good Behavior Game have been demonstrated. Interestingly, teachers evaluated the Good Behavior Game Plus Merit as less acceptable than the basic version. Tingstrom speculates that because the Plus Merit variant is more complex and requires more time to implement, teachers are less accepting of the procedure, even though it targets positive behaviors in addition to negative behaviors. The Good Behavior Game has also been implemented in a large-scale, preventive intervention program (see the "Prevention" section of this chapter).

A number of investigators have examined the extent to which the effects of multicomponent treatment programs involving teacher training and token economies generalize across time and settings. In some of the earliest studies to examine these questions, little evidence for generalization was found (Kuypers, Becker, & O'Leary, 1968; O'Leary et al., 1969; Walker & Hops, 1976). On the other hand, there is some evidence that positive treatment effects will be maintained across time, although the duration of follow-up has ranged only from 3 to 12 weeks (Greenwood et al., 1974; Greenwood, Hops, & Walker, 1977; Walker & Hops, 1976). Treatment-acquired gains do not appear to generalize well from one academic year to the next when no attempts at facilitating generalization are implemented (Walker et al., 1975).

For all these reasons, Walker, Hops, and their colleagues have conducted a number of studies evaluating strategies to enhance generalization and maintenance of treatment effects acquired in multicomponent classroom programs. Walker and Buckley (1972) treated children for 2 months in a token economy classroom and then randomly assigned them to one of three maintenance strategies or a control group before returning them to their regular classrooms. In a "peer reprogramming" strategy, the target children's regular classroom peers were trained to support positive behavior and to ignore minor disruption. In addition, target children earned points for appropriate behavior that were exchangeable for rewards for the entire class. In an "equating stimulus conditions" strategy, essential elements of the experimental classroom procedures were transferred directly to the children's regular classroom. In a "teacher training" condition, teachers learned general principles of behavior modification and were encouraged to implement programs in their own classrooms. Peer reprogramming and equating stimulus conditions were significantly more effective than teacher training or no generalization programming in facilitating transfer of positive treatment effects to the regular classroom.

Walker et al. (1975) implemented a regular classroom maintenance program after 4 months of intensive treatment in a special classroom. In this study, classroom maintenance involved not only teacher training, but weekly meetings with the teachers in which feedback was provided regarding the level of the children's training. In addition, teachers earned credit hours as well as course grades contingent upon continued improvement in the children's behavior. The effects of the combined treatment (intensive treatment plus maintenance program) generalized to a significantly greater degree in the subsequent academic year than did treatment effects for subjects who did not receive maintenance strategies.

One of the most comprehensive systems for school-based behavior management is the four-component system developed by the Center at Oregon for Research in the Behavioral Education of the Handicapped (CORBEH) during the 1970s for children in mainstream kindergarten through fourth-grade classrooms (Hops & Walker, 1988; Walker, Hops, & Greenwood, 1984). Two of the four components are specifically designed to deal with CP behaviors, such as acting-out disruptive behavior and social aggression. The other two components address low academic survival skills and social withdrawal. Each component uses a teacher consultant (e.g., counselor, school psychologist) as the primary delivery agent, with control ultimately transferred to the classroom teacher and/or playground supervisor.

The Contingencies for Learning Academic and Social Skills (CLASS) program is designed to decrease disruptive behaviors in various school settings (i.e., classroom, cafeteria, hallways, playground). Behavioral techniques include a token economy with a response cost component, contingency contracting, teacher praise, school and home rewards, and 1-day suspensions for certain serious acting-out behaviors (Walker & Hops, 1979). During the first week, the consultant implements the procedures; then the program is shifted to the classroom teacher, who assumes primary control of the daily procedures with the support and assistance of the consultant. Over the next 5 weeks, the program is extended over the entire day, and there is a gradual fading from tangible rewards to social reinforcement in the natural environment. Because each child's progress through the program is performance-based, the actual length of the program varies from 6 to 10 weeks (Walker & Hops, 1979).

The Reprogramming Environmental Contingencies for Effective Social Skills (RECESS) program focuses on the remediation of social aggression with peers on the playground and in the classroom (Walker, Hops, & Greenwood, 1993) and is designed for children in kindergarten through third grade. RECESS consists of four program components: (1) systematic training in cooperative, positive, social behavior via prepared scripts, discussion, and role playing for the child with CP and the entire class; (2) a response cost system in which points are lost for aggressive social behavior and rule infractions; (3) praise by the RECESS consultant, teacher, and playground supervisor for positive, cooperative, interactive behavior; and (4) concurrent group and individual reward contingencies, with group activity rewards available at school and individual rewards available at home (Walker et al., 1995). The program is administered in four phases: recess only, extension to the classroom, fading, and then maintenance.

Walker, Hops, and Greenwood (1981) and Walker et al. (1995) present data indicating that RECESS has a very powerful effect on reducing negative/aggressive behavior on the playground and in the classroom. The program requires 40–45 hours of consultant time over a 2- to 3-month period, however, and may therefore be used only for the most aggressive, antisocial students or when the school has made a firm, programmatic commitment to the institution of a powerful intervention program for its aggressive students in special education. Like the other CORBEH packages, RECESS includes built-in fading and maintenance procedures.

All of the CORBEH packages were developed and evaluated through a systematic three-phase process: component evaluation and package development in an experimental classroom, adaptation and standardization of package components, and field testing under normal conditions of use (Walker, Hops, & Greenwood, 1984). The CLASS program has been implemented and evaluated with 119 children in this process in both urban and rural settings (Walker et al., 1984). Field trial evaluations indicate not only that the CLASS program was effective in increasing the level of appropriate behaviors among children in the classroom, compared to acting-out children who did not participate in the program, but that these effects were maintained at a 1-year follow-up (Hops et al., 1978). Furthermore, examination of student files 1.5 to 3 years after the program indicated that students who had participated in the CLASS program were less likely to have been placed in special education settings. The CLASS program has also been successfully implemented in Costa Rica, although the magnitude of treatment effects was somewhat reduced (Walker, Fonseca Retana, & Gersten, 1988). Most recently, the CLASS program has been included in a multicomponent prevention program for high-risk children in kindergarten (Walker et al., 1995).

The RECESS program has also been extensively validated in experimental and field settings (Walker et al., 1981). This program is quite effective in reducing the rate of negative/aggressive social responses of the target children, compared to untreated controls. However, empirical data with respect to its generalization once the program has ended are lacking.

At an even broader level of systems conceptualization and intervention, Sugai, Kameenui, and Colvin (1990, 1993) have developed a school-wide intervention model called Project PREPARE, to enable special and general educators to meet classroom and school-wide disciplinary needs. As such, it is a universal intervention designed to change the entire environment around children with CP. It is also a staff development model designed to enable educators to handle as many problems as possible at the school level rather than on a case-by-case basis. Such a program requires a school-wide commitment, but also reflects a growing opinion that schools must become increasingly invested in playing a key role in coordinating and implementing comprehensive intervention models for prevention and remediation of child CP (Brewer et al., 1995; Walker & Sylwester, 1991).

Project PREPARE interventions involve three major components: (1) school-wide strategies to teach expected behaviors, (2) clear delineation of behaviors requiring office referrals versus those managed by the staff, and (3) staff training in managing problem behavior as a team. Preliminary data from an experimental versus a control school show significant and substantial reductions in disruption, harassment, fighting, and defiance by children, and in the percentage of detentions, suspensions, and office referrals, in the experimental versus the control school (reported in Walker et al., 1995). Although such interventions require considerable commitment at a systems level, behavioral consultants may find districts and schools increasingly willing to make such a commitment, as the prevalence of CP displayed in schools has risen and schools find themselves confronted with management of increasing numbers of youths with CP.

In summary, it is clear that teacher training and consultant-assisted implementation of behavior therapy programs (such as token economies) in the classroom and on the playground can significantly improve children's socially aggressive and disruptive behavior in the school environment, and in some cases can improve these children's academic achievement as well. In addition, maintenance and generalization strategies can be built into treatment to enhance the probability that treatment-acquired gains will transfer to other class periods and even into the next academic year. The problem with these programs is that they can be quite expensive in terms of the amount of consultant time necessary to train teachers to implement programs appropriately. In addition, the studies by Walker and his colleagues showed that weekly posttraining meetings with teachers may be necessary to maintain treatment-acquired gains. Teachers may not have the time to devote to the program and may be especially reluctant if only one or two children in the entire classroom require intervention. Therefore, these approaches may be most productive in special education classes in which the entire class needs and participates in treatment.

Home-Based Reinforcement Programs.   One procedure that has proven useful in regular classrooms is the use of home-based reinforcement programs (see Kelley, 1990). With home-based reinforcement programs, a concerted effort is made to relieve the teacher of many of the aspects of managing a behavioral system, and to place some of the responsibility for implementation of the program on the parents and even on the child himself or herself.

The first step in initiating a home-based reinforcement program is deciding on the behaviors that will be targeted for monitoring and consequences. In work with children with CP, these may include not only CP behaviors to be decreased, but also social, academic, or study behaviors to be increased. Usually, consultation with the teacher occurs to determine the relevant target behaviors for a particular child. In addition, a monitoring interval is selected, ranging from as frequently as every 4–8 minutes to once per day. Some studies have had teachers observe and rate children's behavior at frequent intervals. Although no empirical studies exist of the most effective and efficient monitoring intervals, children with severe, pervasive, and high-frequency CP behaviors may need more frequent monitoring intervals.

Once the decisions described above are made, an index card or other reporting sheet listing the target behaviors is prepared, and the teacher monitors and rates the child's behavior at the prescribed interval on a card or sheet. Although in some research studies the experimenter has provided the teacher with the daily report form, the more common clinical situation is for parents to prepare the form listing the target behaviors, and to give it to the child each morning to take to school. Often the card is taped to the child's desk. It is the child's responsibility to keep track of the card and then to take the card home at the end of the day. Backup consequences are provided by the parent at home, contingent upon the child's meeting certain pre-arranged criteria. Failure to produce a card at the end of the day results in loss of all rewards available in the system for that evening. The result is that children quickly learn not to "lose" their cards (Ayllon, Garber, & Pisor, 1975).

Studies have varied in the extent to which the clinician or experimenter has consulted with the parents regarding the home backup reinforcers. Ayllon et al. (1975) had a single 2-hour meeting with parents, and in some cases only telephone contact. Parents were informed about the home-based reward system for their children, and they were told to use their own judgment in selecting rewards and sanctions that had worked for them

in the past. At the other end of the spectrum, Schumaker, Hovell, and Sherman (1977) sent a clinician to students' homes to draw up lists of privileges and to negotiate systems for exchanging points earned at school for privileges at home. Weekly home visits occurred throughout the study, and twice-weekly telephone contact was made with each family. Although the procedure followed by Schumaker et al. may not be clinically feasible, the one followed by Ayllon et al. may not be sufficient or appropriate for some families. For example, in families in which rewards are scarce and punishment is impulsive, irrational, or abusive, clinicians need to take greater responsibility for working out the details of the backup system of consequences with the parents in therapy sessions.

A number of studies have evaluated the efficacy of home-based reinforcement programs for school behavior problems (for reviews, see Abramowitz & O'Leary, 1991; Atkeson & Forehand, 1979; Kelley, 1990). Target populations have ranged from kindergartners (Budd, Liebowitz, Riner, Mindell, & Goldfarb, 1981; Lahey et al., 1977) to middle school students (Schumaker et al., 1977) to predelinquent youths in group home placement (Bailey, Wolf, & Phillips, 1970). Backup reinforcers have ranged from praise delivered by teachers and/or parents to concrete, detailed home-based reinforcement systems. Thus, positive effects of the daily report card systems have been demonstrated across a variety of subject and treatment parameters.

Subsequent studies have generally confirmed the positive effects of home-based reinforcement systems implemented by the child's own parents. Ayllon et al. (1975) implemented a home-based reinforcement system with disruptive third-graders in public school after a teacher-administered token system failed to effect sustained improvements in classroom behavior. The system involved one global daily report and minimal parent consultation regarding home consequences. Nevertheless, the system was highly effective in reducing classroom disruption.

Schumaker et al. (1977) also demonstrated the efficacy of a home-based reinforcement program involving daily report, praise, and home privileges in a multiple-baseline-across-subjects design, using "problem" junior high school students. In addition, these investigators showed that although praise alone may result in transient improvements in school behavior, the greatest, most sustained improvements are achieved when contingent privileges are provided at home. Similarly, Budd et al. (1981) found that praise in the absence of home-based privileges was not sufficient to reduce the disruptive behavior of kindergarten children with serious behavior disorders. By contrast, Lahey et al. (1977) showed that praise alone delivered by parents contingent upon receipt of daily report cards was sufficient to improve the behavior of mildly disruptive kindergarten students. The discrepancy in the results of these three studies is probably related to the different ages of the subject populations (parental praise is more likely to function as a powerful reinforcer for younger than for older students) and to behavior problem severity (more severe behavior problems may require more concrete backup reinforcers). More recently, Rosen, Gabardi, Miller, and Miller (1990) showed that the combination of reinforcement plus response cost may be more effective than reinforcement alone in home-based reinforcement programs, mimicking the effects obtained with classroom-based contingencies.

The social validity of home-based reinforcement systems has been examined with respect to acceptability. Teachers rated home-based reinforcement as more acceptable than token economies, time out, and ignoring, and less acceptable than praise or response cost (Witt, Martens, & Elliott, 1984). Students (fifth- to ninth-graders) preferred home-based praise over home-based reprimands, teacher praise, and teacher reprimands (Turco & Elliott, 1986).

Interventions for Homework Problems.   Another arena of academically targeted behavioral intervention in which teachers and parents are linked is children's homework problems. Research indicates that, aside from ability, time spent on homework is the best predictor of student grades and achievement (Keith, 1982), and that homework has a positive impact on school outcome (Miller & Kelley, 1991). Parental involvement in homework has a favorable impact on a child's schoolwork (Anesko & O'Leary, 1982; Bien & Bry, 1980).

Miller and Kelley (1991) have reviewed interventions for improving homework performance. Parent training (Anesko & O'Leary, 1982) and goal setting (Kahle & Kelley, 1994) are two strategies that have demonstrated efficacy in decreasing behavior problems and improving homework accuracy among children with homework problems. In both strategies, parent–child dyads are first taught to establish homework routines, including setting up a time and place

for doing homework. In parent training, parents are also taught to target behaviors that interfere with homework and to provide contingent positive attention and other consequences for behavioral alternatives. In goal setting, parents are taught to help the child divide homework into small, specific goals, and to establish a time limit for completion and criteria for accuracy. Daily and weekly rewards are then negotiated and administered for reaching goals.

In a recent comparison of these two strategies with families of children in grades 2–4, Kahle and Kelley (1994) found that goal setting was more effective than parent training or a homework monitoring control condition in improving homework accuracy and correct answers per minute. In addition, goal setting was associated with greater child consumer satisfaction than was parent training (parent consumer satisfaction was equally high for both conditions). However, the two interventions and the monitoring control were comparable in reducing homework-related behavior problems, suggesting the important role of parental monitoring in this aspect of homework. Forgatch and Ramsey (1994) have shown that establishing homework routines and setting up parental monitoring and reinforcement contracts can be taught to parents and junior high school students via videotaped instruction, resulting in similar effects.

It should be noted that these strategies (parent training, goal setting, and monitoring) include parent involvement in the homework process, validating the finding from large-scale research that parental involvement has a favorable effect on children's overall academic performance. The only difference in the strategies lies in the particular techniques that parents implement with their children, with slightly more favorable outcomes achieved when parents assist their children specifically with goal setting.

Interventions for Child Compliance/Noncompliance.   As noted above, noncompliance is considered to be a keystone behavior in the development of CP. Walker and Walker (1991) report that child compliance and noncompliance are rated by teachers as among the most and least acceptable classroom behaviors, respectively. They provide a number of guidelines and procedures for increasing compliance and decreasing noncompliance in the classroom. These include structuring the classroom in terms of classroom rules that communicate teacher expectations concerning academic performance and behavior; posting a daily schedule of classroom activities; making class-wide and/or individual activity rewards available for following classroom rules; and planning the physical arrangement of the classroom to accommodate different activities. In addition, concrete suggestions for improving teacher relationships with students and managing difficult teacher–student interactions that involve noncompliance are provided.

Interventions for School Bullying. As noted in a previous section, bullying is a form of CP behavior that has received increased attention. Large-scale efforts to introduce and evaluate school-wide antibullying programs have occurred in Scandinavia (Olweus, 1993), in England (Smith & Sharp, 1994a), and in Canada (Pepler, Craig, Ziegler, & Charach, 1993, 1994). These programs are both systems- and person-oriented (Olweus, 1992); that is, they are directed at both the school as a system and at the level of individual bullies, victims, and their parents. Although component analyses have not been conducted, Olweus believes that both major components are necessary, and that the typical clinical approach of intervening at the individual level will not be sufficient to achieve a meaningful outcome.

Key elements of the whole-school approach are the school's taking responsibility for bullying and giving it a high priority; increasing awareness of bullying by teachers, peers, and parents; publicizing explicit school policies and classroom rules that devalue and communicate low tolerance and negative consequences for bullying; discussing bullying in the curriculum; encouraging peer disapproval of bullying; encouraging bystanders to help victims and report bullying to teachers; and instituting better adult supervision at recess (Farrington, 1993; Olweus, 1992). Examples of interventions at the individual level include serious talks with bullies; letters home to parents and parent meetings; implementation of negative consequences for bullying (time outs, privilege removal); social skills training for victims; encouraging victims to report bullying incidents to adults; and assigning older children to "shadow" victims to observe the bullying and report it to teachers (Farrington, 1993; Pepler et al., 1993).

The most important evaluation of the whole-school approach to bullying was conducted by Olweus (1990, 1991, 1996) in Norway. Olweus's intervention was a nationwide campaign to intervene in grades 4–7 with an antibullying, whole-school approach to intervention following the suicides of several victims of bullies. Evaluation of the effects of the intervention was based on data from approximately 2,500 students in Bergen schools, using a quasi-experimental design. Outcome data were derived from a student self-report questionnaire. Results after 8 months and 20 months of intervention showed marked reductions in the level of bully–victim problems for both boys and girls. Similar effects were found on an aggregated peer-rating variable. There was also a reduction in covert CP behaviors, such as vandalism, theft, and truancy. This is an interesting, unintended effect that may have arisen from the general increase in adult monitoring and supervision. Finally, there was an increase in student satisfaction with school life, especially at recess.

A similar program, based closely on the model implemented in Norway, was introduced in 23 schools in the United Kingdom by Smith and his colleagues (Smith & Sharp, 1994a, 1994b). In addition to the basic Olweus program elements, this variation also included bully courts and the "Heartstone Odyssey" (a story that introduces experiences of racial harassment). The U.K. program has produced results similar to those presented by Olweus (Smith & Sharp, 1994a).

Pepler, Craig, and their colleagues (Pepler et al., 1993, 1994) have conducted an evaluation of the Toronto Anti-Bullying Intervention, a whole-school approach modeled after Olweus's program and developed and implemented with the cooperation of the Toronto Board of Education. Like the Olweus program, the Toronto program involved intervention components at the school, parent, classroom/peer, and individual levels, similar to those described above. Results of this study confirmed that bullying is a stable and pervasive problem in schools. Over an 18-month whole-school intervention program implemented in four Toronto schools, there were some improvements in students' reports of bullying as assessed at individual, peer, and school levels, as well as increases in teachers' interventions to stop bullying. However, there were no differences in students' discussions of bully–victim problems with their parents and, unfortunately, victim reports of racial bullying increased.

Skills Training Approaches

Since the first edition of this chapter was published, several systematic programs of research have evaluated skills training programs for children with CP. Although the particular foci of these programs may vary, they share an emphasis on remediating or changing the skill deficiencies and dysfunctions displayed by a child with CP. The historical evolution of this research has followed a path from early emphasis on the behavioral aspects of social skills, to a later emphasis on the cognitive aspects of social/interpersonal behavior, to a still more recent emphasis on comprehensive, multicomponent programs. As the interventions have become more complex, so too have the theoretical models underpinning these interventions. The following is a brief overview of some of the current major skills training models of intervention for children with CP.

One of the first skills-based models of intervention for children with CP was social skills training. As noted above, children with CP often evidence poor peer relations, experience peer rejection, and display social skills deficits. Furthermore, they may display immaturity of moral reasoning and judgment (Chandler & Moran, 1990; Gregg, Gibbs, & Basinger, 1994; Nelson, Smith, & Dodd, 1990). Theoretical models underpinning social skills training have emphasized that children who display such deficits in prosocial interpersonal reasoning and skills will resort to CP behaviors in order to secure rewards from the social environment. Therefore, direct training in moral reasoning and/or social skills has been hypothesized to be a potentially viable treatment method for these youths. Social skills training typically involves modeling, role playing, coaching and practice, feedback, and positive reinforcement.

One of the first evaluations of a social skills training approach was the well-designed investigation reported by Spence and Marzillier (1981), in which 76 adolescent male delinquents (aged 10–16) were randomly assigned to a social skills training group, an attention placebo group, or a no-treatment group. The social skills training program included twelve 1-hour sessions with youths in groups of four. Training procedures included instructions, discussion, live and videotaped modeling, role plays, videotaped feedback, social reinforcement, and homework tasks. Skills taught were individually tailored to each adolescent, based on a needs assessment. Results of both multiple-baseline-across-behaviors and group-comparison designs indicated specific improvements in many individual social skills on the analogue assessment tests for the social skills training group, but not for the attention placebo or no-treatment control groups. Furthermore, these improvements were maintained at a 3-month follow-up assessment. However, there was no evidence of generalized differential changes in staff ratings of social skills; self-report of social problems; observer ratings of friendliness, social anxiety, social skills, and employability; social workers' ratings of improvements in family work, school, and social relationships; self-report of delinquent offenses; or police convictions.

Subsequent studies with CP youths have also produced positive effects using social skills training. Michelson et al. (1983) studied a clinical population of 61 boys (aged 8 to 12 years) with CP, comparing social skills training, interpersonal problem solving, and a nondirective control condition. Using a comprehensive assessment strategy, the study indicated that the social skills and interpersonal problem-solving treatments resulted in significant changes on parent, teacher, and self-report ratings, and on peer sociometric ratings at posttreatment. At the 1-year follow-up, the social skills treatment group maintained gains and continued to show modest improvement, whereas the other two groups manifested significant declines. Bierman and her colleagues (Bierman, 1989; Bierman, Miller, & Staub, 1987) engaged aggressive–rejected boys in grades 1 to 3 and competent peers in enjoyable activities together and provided individual and group reinforcement, coaching, and shaping of social skills. These investigators reported reduced CP behaviors and improved peer acceptance at 1-year follow-up following a 10-session program.

With respect to moral reasoning, it has been demonstrated that higher levels can be facilitated by relatively brief discussion groups (8–20 sessions) composed of behavior-disordered (Arbuthnot & Gordon, 1986) or incarcerated delinquent (Gibbs, Arnold, Ahlborn, & Cheesman, 1984) adolescents. However, only the Arbuthnot and Gordon study included measures of behavioral functioning to assess whether changes in moral reasoning are associated with behavior change. Following participation in a "moral dilemma discussion group" that met for 45 minutes per week over 16–20 weeks in the school, adolescents with CP had fewer referrals to the principal for disciplinary reasons, were less tardy, had higher grades in the humanities and social sciences, and had fewer police or court contacts than adolescents in a no-treatment control condition. At a 1-year follow-up, these between-group differences were still evident, although both groups had virtually eliminated any police or court contacts. It should also be noted that there were no differences between the groups on teacher ratings of the adolescents' behavior, either at posttreatment or at the 1-year follow-up.

Other studies using this approach show that though intervention may stimulate more mature moral judgment, the reduction of CP behaviors does not necessarily follow (Gibbs et al., 1984; Power, Higgins, & Kohlberg, 1989). Interestingly, the Arbuthnot and Gordon (1986) study, which did find positive changes on indices of CP behaviors, also included techniques to develop social skills. Insofar as the Arbuthnot and Gordon intervention included such techniques, it may be that the singular results in terms of changes in indices of CP may be mainly attributable to the social skills training rather than to the moral reasoning component.

Because single-component programs may produce limited results, some investigators have combined different approaches to skills training into multicomponent treatment packages. Goldstein and his colleagues developed a 10-week curriculum called Aggression Replacement Training (ART; Goldstein, Glick, Reiner, Zimmerman, & Coultry, 1986), which combines interventions designed to enhance social skills (Structured Learning Training; Goldstein & Pentz, 1984), anger control (Anger Control Training; Feindler, Marriott, & Iwata, 1984), and moral reasoning (Moral Education). More recently, the program has been expanded to a 50-skill curriculum (Goldstein & Glick, 1994). Preliminary evaluations in two juvenile correctional facilities suggested differential improvements on analogue measures of social skills (and sometimes on a measure of the moral development) for adolescent males who participated in ART as opposed to those in either a brief-instruction or a no-treatment control group (Glick & Goldstein, 1987). Subsequent evaluations in community settings employing ART with adolescents with CP showed evidence of significantly improved skills across a variety of domains targeted in treatment. Evidence for generalization to the community after release was limited to global ratings completed by probation officers in initial studies. More recently, 3-month rearrest data have been collected, showing significantly fewer arrests for youths receiving ART (Goldstein & Glick, 1994). At a 1-year follow-up, social workers rated youths who had received ART more highly on a variety of indices of adjustment. Taken together, these studies suggest that ART does have the potential for facilitating improvement across a broad array of skills deficits (especially if it were to be com-

bined with one of the family-based interventions described earlier in this chapter), and for reducing recidivism rates in offending adolescents with CP.

A more recent multicomponent skills training intervention has been described by Gibbs, Potter, Barriga, and Liau (1996). This treatment program, called EQUIP, combines social skills training, moral reasoning, and problem solving in group meetings that emphasize positive peer culture. Behavioral methods, such as self-monitoring in daily homework assignments, are also included. The effectiveness of EQUIP has been evaluated in a controlled outcome study with 15- to 18-year old incarcerated juvenile male offenders (Leeman, Gibbs, & Fuller, 1993). The experimental condition was compared to both no treatment and attention placebo (a brief motivational induction) control conditions. Outcome measures assessed both institutional and postrelease conduct, as well as mediating processes of social skills and moral judgment. Institutional conduct gains were highly significant for the EQUIP group relative to the control groups in terms of self-reported misconduct, staff-filed incident reports, and unexcused absences from schools. Twelve months after subjects' release from the institution, the recidivism rate for EQUIP participants remained low and stable (15%), whereas the likelihood of recidivism for untreated subjects (41%) climbed. Social skills also improved significantly for EQUIP participants and were significantly correlated with self-reported institutional conduct gains. These studies suggest that multicomponent skills training programs are more effective than single-component programs and may result in more significant long-term effects as well.

Several of the programs in skills-based intervention research have been based upon a cognitive model of psychopathology in youths that began to gain prominence after the earlier models, which focused more exclusively on behavior. The cognitive model has been articulated most forcefully by Kendall (Kendall, 1985, 1991; Kendall & MacDonald, 1993) and by Dodge and his associates in the latter's social information-processing model of social competence in children (Coie & Dodge, 1998; Crick & Dodge, 1994; see also McFadyen-Ketchum & Dodge, Chapter 6, this volume). A fundamental assumption of this model is that when children with CP encounter an anger- or frustration-arousing event (often an interpersonal interaction), their emotional, physiological, and behavioral reactions are determined by their cognitive perceptions and appraisals of that event, rather than by the event itself. Intervening at the level of these cognitive processes then becomes the most important focus of treatment. Children with CP appear to display both deficiencies (a lack or insufficient amount of cognitive activity in situations in which this would be useful) and distortions (active but maladaptive cognitive contents and processes) in their cognitive functioning (Crick & Dodge, 1994; Kendall, 1991; Kendall & MacDonald, 1993).

The program of cognitive-behavioral treatment research most directly connected to the social information-processing model is that developed by Lochman and his colleagues. Based originally on Novaco's (1978) model of anger arousal, and subsequently heavily influenced by Dodge's (1986) social information-processing model, this treatment program has evolved from a 12-session school-based program called Anger Coping (Lochman, Lampron, Gemmer, & Harris, 1987) to a 33-session program called Coping Power (the latter also supplemented by a parent training intervention) (Lochman & Wells, 1996). Elementary-school-age children with CP meet once a week in pull-out groups of six during the school day and participate in sessions that have specific goals, objectives, and exercises. Although designed for use in school, the program can be implemented in a clinic setting as well.

The exercises in the Anger Coping and Coping Power interventions are designed to provide children with practice in cognitive and behavioral skills associated with each stage of the social information-processing model. Children practice reviewing examples of social encounters and discussing social cues and possible motives of people in the situations. As weeks go by, they receive *in vivo* practice in problem-solving elements: identifying problems, generating many possible solutions to problems, and evaluating solutions using prosocial judgment criteria. They role-play enactments of behavioral responses to social situations, and then receive reinforcement and feedback. Children also receive training in strategies for increasing awareness of feelings and physiological states.

After skills for managing anger arousal in problem situations are practiced, exercises designed to induce affective arousal in the groups are introduced. Children are supported in the use of anger control strategies and anger-reducing self-talk. In the Coping Power intervention, sessions have been expanded in number and complexity to focus on an expanded range of skills and social contexts that children must negotiate

(e.g., family interactions, sibling interactions, organization skills for homework completion).

Lochman and colleagues have conducted a series of studies aimed at evaluating the effects of the Anger Coping program with boys with CP (Lochman, 1985; Lochman, Burch, Curry, & Lampron, 1984; Lochman & Curry, 1986; Lochman, Nelson, & Sims, 1981). In their first uncontrolled study (Lochman et al., 1981), 12 children who participated in the cognitive-behavioral intervention showed significant decreases from pre- to posttreatment on teacher ratings of aggressiveness in the classroom and increases in on-task behavior. The children tended to have fewer acting-out behaviors on a teacher report behavioral rating scale. A subsequent controlled evaluation (Lochman et al., 1984) confirmed that the cognitive-behavioral program was more effective than either goal setting alone or no treatment in reducing disruptive, aggressive, off-task behavior in the classroom. Also, the addition of a goal-setting strategy (in which children set daily behavioral goals that were monitored and reinforced by their teachers) to the cognitive intervention resulted in greater reductions in aggressive behavior than did the cognitive intervention alone. In a subsequent study looking at the parameters of treatment, Lochman (1985) found that longer-duration treatment (18 sessions) produced more significant changes in classroom behavior than did a 12-session intervention.

Maintenance effects of the Anger Coping intervention have also been examined. Lochman and Lampron (1988) examined a subsample of boys in the original Lochman et al. (1984) study. Maintenance effects were examined on independently observed classroom behavior at a 7-month follow-up. Boys with CP who had received the Anger Coping intervention had significantly higher levels of on-task behavior and lower levels of passive off-task behavior than untreated controls did. However, significant posttreatment reductions in disruptive off-task behavior were not maintained at a 7-month follow-up.

Subsequently, Lochman (1992) examined the 3-year follow-up effects of the Anger Coping intervention. Follow-up effects were most evident on substance use outcomes. Treated boys with CP had significantly lower levels of drug and alcohol use than untreated boys with CP; furthermore, the treated boys' level of substance use was similar to the level displayed by nonproblem boys. Three-year maintenance effects were not observed for independently observed classroom behavior, except for boys who had received booster sessions in the second year (who did show lower levels of off-task behavior). These booster sessions' effects have served as part of the rationale for extending the Anger Coping program to its current iteration (Coping Power), which covers 33 sessions over 2 school years.

Guerra and Slaby (1990) developed and evaluated a 12-session program based on the same social information-processing model as that underpinning Lochman's work, but targeted toward male and female adolescents incarcerated for aggressive offenses. In this program, adolescents learned social problem-solving skills, addressed and modified beliefs supporting a broad and extensive use of aggression as a legitimate activity, and learned cognitive self-control skills to control impulsive responding. Relative to an attention placebo control group, the aggressive adolescents who received treatment showed greater social problem-solving skills, greater reductions in some beliefs associated with aggression, and greater reductions on staff ratings of aggressive, impulsive, and inflexible behavior. In addition, posttest aggression was related to change in cognitive factors. Unfortunately, no differences were noted between groups on recidivism rates 24 months after release from the institution, although there seemed to be a trend toward lower recidivism for those who received the active treatment.

Another line of programmatic skills-based research heavily influenced by the cognitive behavioral model is that of Kazdin and his colleagues. Called "Problem Solving Skills Training" (PSST; Kazdin, 1996b), this model emphasizes primarily the latter stages of the information-processing model (skills for problem identification, solution generation and evaluation, solution selection, and enactment). Preadolescent children with CP receive training and *in vivo* practice in these problem-solving skills, and then learn to apply the skills to interpersonal, impersonal, and academic tasks. PSST is administered individually over 20 sessions, each of which lasts approximately 45 minutes.

In the first evaluation of this model (Kazdin, Esveldt-Dawson, French, & Unis, 1987b), 56 children (aged 7–13) who were inpatients on a psychiatric unit were randomly assigned to PSST, a nondirective relationship therapy condition, or an attention placebo control condition. Parent and teacher ratings on both behavior problem and social adjustment scales were collected at pre- and posttreatment and at a 1-year follow-up. PSST demonstrated a clear superiority over the relationship therapy and attention placebo control conditions on both parent and teacher ratings at posttreatment and the 1-year follow-up. Children in the PSST condition were also more likely to move to within or near the normal range on these measures, although it is important to note that most of the children in this group were still outside this range on measures of behavior problems in the home and school.

Kazdin et al. (1989) reported no difference in 1-year follow-up effects obtained from PSST with or without *in vivo* practice in a mixed sample of inpatient and outpatient children. Children who received client-centered relationship therapy did not improve. Thus, PSST seems to produce improvements in children with serious, aggressive CP as well as in children with mild to moderate CP treated on an outpatient basis.

In another investigation with an inpatient sample, Kazdin, Esveldt-Dawson, French, and Unis (1987a) obtained similar results when PSST combined with a parent training intervention (the latter based on Patterson et al., 1975) was compared to an attention placebo control condition. In a more recent study, the unique and combined effects of PSST and parent training were evaluated (Kazdin et al., 1992). Results at a 1-year follow-up indicated that combining these two forms of treatment was more effective than either one alone. Children in the combined group fell within the normative range of CP behaviors according to parent report; all treatment groups were rated in the normative range by teacher report.

Kendall et al. (1990) evaluated a 20-session cognitive-behavioral treatment program anchored in the cognitive model of youth psychopathology described earlier and based on the Kendall and Braswell (1985, 1993) treatment manual. The program was implemented with 6- to 13-year-old youths psychiatrically hospitalized and formally diagnosed with CD. Cognitive-behavioral treatment was compared to supportive and insight-oriented therapy, commonly used in psychiatric hospitals, in a crossover design. Results indicated the superiority of cognitive-behavioral treatment on measured teacher ratings of self-control and prosocial behavior and on self-reports of perceived social competence. However, not all measures evidenced gains. Nevertheless, the difference between the percentage of children who moved from deviant to within the nondeviant range of behavior was significantly higher for the cognitive-behavioral program, supporting the greater clinical significance of this treatment. In a similar study with psychiatrically hospitalized inpatient children, Kolko, Loar, and Sturnick (1990) showed improvements in dimensions of children's assertiveness, staff sociometric ratings, role-play performances, and *in vivo* behavioral observations of individual social skills for children who received social-cognitive skills training relative to children receiving an activity group.

Feindler has developed and refined an anger control training program for adolescents called "Chill Out" (Feindler, 1990, 1991, 1995; Feindler & Guttman, 1994). As the name implies, Chill Out is anchored in a model that assumes that anger motivates much of the aggressive behavior of adolescents with CP and that interventions focused on reducing anger will impact aggressive behavior. Furthermore, based on Novaco's (1978) model, anger is assumed to consist of physiological, cognitive, and behavioral components. More recently, Feindler's conceptualization of the cognitive components of anger has incorporated the findings from research on the social information-processing model (Crick & Dodge, 1994). Following from this tripartite model of anger, the Chill Out program focuses on three major intervention target categories: Arousal Management Training (relaxation training procedures), Cognitive Restructuring (addressing hostile and dysfunctional attributions), and Behavioral Skills Training (assertion, communication, and problem-solving skills).

Although there have been increasing theoretical and technical refinements to the Chill Out program over recent years, the empirical foundation of the program rests on two studies conducted in the 1980s. In the first study (Feindler et al., 1984), 36 junior high school students with a history of high rates of classroom and/or community disruption were randomly assigned to the treatment program or a no-treatment control condition. Students completed self-report measures of locus of control, means–ends problem solving, and impulsivity. Teachers completed ratings of self-control and kept daily records of fines incurred for aggressive behavior in an already ongoing contingency management system. The Chill Out program met for ten 50-minute sessions over 7 weeks. The data collected at a 5-week follow-up provided minimal support for the efficacy of the treatment program. Students who received the program did perform better than the students in the no-treatment control condition on some self-report measures, and

teachers rated the former more highly on the self-control measure. However, there were no between-group differences on the behavioral fines (the most direct measure of actual behavior in this study) or on the other self-report measures.

This program was also adapted for use with male adolescent psychiatric inpatients, most of whom had been diagnosed with CD (Feindler, Ecton, Kingsley, & Dubey, 1986). Although there were significant posttreatment differences between the Chill Out and no-treatment control groups on the Matching Familiar Figures Test and child care staff ratings of self-control, the groups differed on only 3 of 11 behavioral measures in role-play tests at posttreatment. Daily records of discipline interactions on the ward indicated a significant decrease in general rule violations for the Chill Out group and an increase in those violations for the control group. There were no group differences at posttreatment with respect to violations for physical aggression. Thus, this study produced mixed results on behavioral outcomes; the broad-based efficacy of this anger control training program for adolescents has yet to be clearly demonstrated.

Another line of theoretically driven programmatic intervention research has recently been reported by Blechman, Prinz, and Dumas (Blechman, Dumas, & Prinz, 1994; Prinz, Blechman, & Dumas, 1994). The theoretical model underpinning this intervention approach has been presented in elegant detail by Blechman, Prinz, and Dumas (1995) and Blechman (1996). Briefly, this is a developmental model of coping and competence that attempts to incorporate the now voluminous literature on risk factors for CP into an integrated theory of prediction and intervention. The coping–competence model organizes the empirically identified correlates of a high-risk developmental trajectory into first-order and second-order constructs, and specifies interdependent pathways of influence among surface characteristics of individuals, risk–protection variables, competence, and life outcomes (Blechman et al., 1995).

An intervention program anchored in the coping–competence model has been developed (Blechman et al., 1994) and recently evaluated (Prinz et al., 1994). The program is a school-based intervention designed to support prosocial coping (rather than to remediate skills deficits) with emotional, social, and achievement challenges faced by high-risk *and* competent youths. The program includes competent, low-risk youths in groups with highly aggressive youths in order to provide role models in prosocial coping. Without any public labeling, youths identified as competent and aggressive are invited to participate in self-management "clubs." The primary goal of self-management club meetings is to encourage prosocial coping through "information exchange," in which children are encouraged to share information about controllable and uncontrollable challenges in their lives. Information exchange centers around describing situations, sharing thoughts and feelings, and cooperating in discussing possible coping mechanisms (Blechman et al., 1994). Ideally, families are engaged in a process that begins with home visits and proceeds to parent training with parents of both high-risk and competent youths.

Prinz et al. (1994) evaluated the Peer Coping Skills (PCS) training program based upon the model (with the exception that no family intervention was provided in this study) described above, with 100 first- to third-grade children with and without CP. The children were compared to 96 similarly identified children who received minimal classroom intervention. In each PCS intervention group, half of the children engaged in CP and half did not. After 22 sessions of intervention (posttreatment) and at a 6-month follow-up, children in the PCS group (both those with and without CP) significantly improved prosocial coping via information exchange, and their social skills improved compared to control subjects who showed no improvement. For children with CP, PCS training produced a significant reduction in teacher-rated aggression in comparison to controls, although the mean level of aggression at posttreatment was still in the clinical range. Peer ratings of social acceptance did not show significant change. No iatrogenic effects were noted on the children without CP by virtue of their being in groups with children with CP. In fact, as noted earlier, the children with CP also showed significant improvements in prosocial coping, compared to their counterparts who did not participate in the PCS intervention (Prinz et al., 1994).

Psychosocial Interventions for Covert CP

Whereas psychosocial interventions for overt CP behaviors have been evaluated extensively in home, school, and community settings, there are relatively less data concerning interventions of any type for covert types of CP behaviors. However, the attention being given to some of these covert behaviors (especially fire setting) and their treatment is increasing, due to the rising recognition that when both overt and covert behaviors are present, the child's CP is more serious and may have a poorer long-term outcome. In addition, covert CP often represents serious violations of the rights of others, provoking concern from the community. In this section of the chapter, we describe interventions that have been designed to treat stealing, lying, and fire setting. (Interventions for substance use, which is often considered to be a manifestation of covert CP, are described in the chapter by Myers, Brown, & Vik, Chapter 14, this volume.)

Stealing

There is a consensus that the identification/labeling of stealing is the key to developing a successful intervention for this behavior (Barth, 1987; Miller & Klungness, 1989; Patterson et al., 1975). Because of the low base rate and covert nature of stealing, firsthand, immediate detection of all stealing events by parents, teachers, or others is not a feasible goal. Therefore, "stealing" is operationally defined as "the child's taking, or being in possession of, anything that does not clearly belong to him [or her]" (Barth, 1987, p. 151). Table 3.1 contains an elaboration of this definition, as well as instructions for caregivers on how to respond to stealing behavior. Although adoption of this definition of stealing may result in instances in which the child is incorrectly labeled as having stolen, the alternative of not being able to treat the stealing behavior effectively is regarded as the greater of the two evils.

In the first edition of this chapter, we indicated that the most systematic work on the treatment of covert CP had been conducted by Patterson, Reid, and their colleagues at OSLC with respect to family-based interventions for treating stealing. That remains true today. The OSLC group developed a specialized approach to social-learning-based family therapy with children who display stealing and other covert CP behaviors (Patterson et al., 1975; Reid et al., 1980)—one that takes into account the definitional and detection problems inherent in treating covert CP behaviors, and also attempts to make a direct impact on the parenting variables strongly associated with delinquency (i.e., parental involvement, monitoring, and parental discipline practices). The failure of parents of children who steal to monitor their children's whereabouts or

TABLE 3.1.   Instructions to Caregivers for Defining and Providing Consequences for Stealing

1. The most important part of working to decrease stealing is *defining stealing as stealing. Stealing is defined as the child's taking, or being in possession of, anything that does not clearly belong to him [or her]*. Parents, teachers, or other adults are the only judges. They may label an act as stealing by observing it, by having it reported to them, or by noticing that something is missing. There is no arguing about guilt or innocence. It is the child's job to be sure that he [or she] is not accused. The value of the object is irrelevant. Trading and borrowing are not permissible. Any "purchases" that the child brings home must be accompanied by a receipt. Otherwise they are to be returned and consequences instituted.
2. Once the behavior of stealing has been labeled, then the consequences are to be applied. Avoid discussions, shaming, or counseling.
3. Every stealing event must be so labeled and consequences given.
4. Avoid using excessive detective tactics (such as searches); just keep your eyes open, and investigate the origins of new property.
5. Consequences for stealing should be work restrictions and loss of privileges for the day of the stealing, and basic privileges only on the following weekend. There should be no other consequences such as humiliations or beatings. Special privileges can be earned again on the following day.
6. Remember: Stealing goes hand in hand with wandering and with your not knowing the whereabouts of your child. Check-in times are recommended if stealing is a problem.
7. Do not tempt your child. Keep items like those that your child has stolen in the past away from him or her. For example, avoid leaving your wallet or cigarette packs in view or unwatched.
8. Stealing may occur no matter how many possessions your child has, so giving him or her everything is not a successful approach to ending stealing. Your child should, however, have some way of earning his or her own money so that he or she may have a choice of things to buy.

Note. From Barth (1987). Copyright 1987 by Plenum Publishing Corporation. Reprinted by permission.

to be involved with the children to any great extent compounds the difficulty of designing effective family-based interventions.

In the OSLC approach to the treatment of stealing, the standard parent training program for treating overt CP behaviors is implemented first, because these behaviors covary with the lower-rate covert CP behaviors in many children. In addition, the standard OSLC program addresses two of the three important parenting structures

noted earlier (i.e., poor discipline practices and parental involvement with the child). Next, parents are taught to identify stealing using an operational definition similar to the one presented above, and to monitor its occurrence on a daily basis. Much discussion and role playing of these procedures occur in therapy sessions.

Once the operational definition of stealing is accepted by the parents (a process that can involve a great deal of therapy time), parents are taught to administer a mild consequence immediately contingent upon each and every suspected stealing event. The consequence (e.g., 1–2 hours of hard work around the home) is kept at a mild level because the child will be inaccurately accused from time to time. The implementation of this approach involves much support, telephone contact, and discussion. Check-in systems are instituted for families in which infrequent monitoring occurs. In addition, it would seem important to incorporate therapeutic strategies for involving fathers in the therapy process, given the relationship between uninvolved fathers and stealing (Frick, 1994; Loeber et al., 1983).

In a study that remains the most systematic evaluation of treatment focused specifically on stealing behavior, Reid et al. (1980) evaluated the effectiveness of this modified approach to behavioral family therapy for 5- to 14-year-old children with CP who were referred for stealing. In this study, 28 families of children with CP who stole received treatment. The mean amount of therapist contact was 32 hours. Outcome measures consisted of parent reports of stealing on the TIROSSA, parent reports of other referral problems on the PDR, and a deviant behavior summary score in home observations conducted by trained independent observers. Results indicated significant decreases in parent-reported stealing events and other referral problems from pre- to posttreatment and at a 6-month follow-up. The observed deviant behavior scores decreased nonsignificantly. However, as might be expected, aversive social behaviors in the families were not high to begin with in this sample of children who stole. A waiting-list control group, in which parent report data on stealing were collected at baseline, at the end of the parent training program for dealing with overt CP, and following the treatment package for stealing, indicated that significant reductions in parent-reported stealing did not occur until after the treatment for stealing was implemented. However, large differences in baseline levels of stealing limit the utility of this comparison.

In another study by the OSLC group with chronic delinquents, described earlier in this chapter, Bank et al. (1991) found some empirical support for the efficacy of this family-based approach with the subset of adolescents who engaged in both overt and covert CP behaviors. Parent-reported stealing (as noted on the PDR) was reduced to zero at treatment termination.

Stealing has also been approached from a more traditional family therapy model. Seymour and Epston (1989) treated 45 consecutive cases of childhood stealing with an approach that "regraded" the child from "stealer" to "honest person." Therapists focused questions in such a way as to "externalize the symptom," a framework promulgated by White (1986), and assisted the child and the parents to engage together in working against the stealing. Thereafter, techniques were very similar to those employed by Reid et al. (1980). Emphasis was placed on suspicion of stealing; on responding to stealing with work chore consequences; and on "honesty tests," in which items of interest were left around the house, and the child was reinforced by parents for not stealing. Although no control group was employed, Seymour and Epston (1989) reported significant changes from pre- to posttreatment in stealing. Fifty-four percent of the cases reported no stealing at a 2-month follow-up, and an additional 40% reported only one to three instances. At a 1-year follow-up, levels of stealing remained low. Sixty-two percent of parents reported no instances of stealing and 19% of parents reported that stealing was "substantially reduced."

Although the results of family-based intervention studies are suggestive, the effects of treatment on stealing were assessed from parent report measures. Given the problems these parents have with respect to effective monitoring of their children's behavior, future investigators should attempt to include some treatment component directed specifically to parental monitoring (see Dishion & McMahon, in press). Not only is this a worthwhile target of intervention in its own right, but effective monitoring of the child's behavior and whereabouts would seem to be a prerequisite for accurate recording on such measures as the TIROSSA and PDR. Another critical issue that must be addressed pertains to the generalizability of family-based interventions for stealing in other settings, such as the school or the community at large. Although there are effective treatment procedures for dealing with stealing in the school setting (see below), identifying and stopping stealing in public places such as stores is very difficult.

Henderson (1981, 1983) developed an Individualized Combined Treatment (ICT) program for children and adolescents who report that they want to stop stealing. This approach has three broad components: (1) self-control of the internal environment; (2) adult or responsible-other control of the external environment; and (3) personalization of the program by the therapist. In the first component, Henderson teaches relaxation skills in an effort to countercondition internal arousal stimuli, which he maintains are often associated with stealing. In therapy sessions, the child is asked to imagine himself or herself in theft situations and then to relax and imagine walking away. In this way, relaxation and imagery are also conceptualized as self-control techniques, which are later extended to the external environment. Heart rate biofeedback is used to facilitate relaxation. Parents are asked to provide stealing opportunities or "traps" for the child in the home so that the child has an opportunity to practice self-control strategies. Bonuses in a reward system are provided for not stealing. The "traps" are gradually made less obvious, and items are made easier to take without being caught.

To provide external controls for not stealing, some system for monitoring "not stealing" must be implemented. Henderson (1981) advocates the use of a "not-stealing diary." Two types of entries are made in the diary: (1) any length of time that the stealer has been observed by a responsible adult not to have stolen; and (2) times of departure and arrival noted by responsible adults at both ends of a journey (e.g., from home to school). If the times logged in conform to appropriate travel time, then an assumption is made that no stealing has occurred. Daily time "not stealing" is computed, and such time is rewarded with backup privileges and activities. These reinforcers are selected so that they are related in some way to the child's motive for stealing (see Barth, 1987). For example, if the child seems to steal for "kicks," then an appropriate backup reinforcer might be a roller-coaster ride at an amusement park.

Henderson (1981, 1983) presented descriptive data on 10 children (8–15 years of age) who were treated with the ICT program. Compared to 17 other children who were treated for stealing at the same clinic with a variety of other treatment procedures, only 20% of the children who received the ICT program were reported to have stolen in the 2-year period following treatment, whereas 60%–75% of the other children were reported to have stolen. Although the descriptive data on this approach to treatment are certainly encouraging, systematic evaluation of the program with appropriate controls needs to be undertaken.

Several case studies with an individual child or adolescent have reported the successful use of self-control training plus family contingency contracting (Stumphauzer, 1976), covert sensitization (Cautela, 1967), and response cost (loss of access to social contact with a preferred adult) (Wetzel, 1966).

A few studies have focused on the reduction of stealing in elementary school classrooms. Because of its relatively controlled and geographically confined nature, the classroom may be amenable to more systematic monitoring of stealing behavior and to the implementation of differential reinforcement procedures for not stealing than is the case when treatment is implemented in the home setting (see Reid, 1984). For example, with respect to the detection and monitoring of stealing, one teacher marked all of the target student's personal and school items with a green circle. "Stealing" was then defined as "having items not marked with green circles on your person, desk, or supply box" (Rosen & Rosen, 1983, p. 58), and the teacher checked those areas every 15 minutes. In another study designed to reduce classroom-wide stealing, 10 standard items (e.g., nickels, Magic Markers, erasers) were placed around the classroom each day, and their presence or absence was noted at 15-minute intervals (Switzer, Deal, & Bailey, 1977).

The three studies that have examined procedures to reduce classroom stealing have all utilized some form of response cost for stealing and positive reinforcement for periods of non-stealing (Brooks & Snow, 1972; Rosen & Rosen, 1983; Switzer et al., 1977). In all cases, the frequency of stealing was significantly reduced when either group or individual contingencies were applied. Group contingencies that are applied to an entire classroom may be considered as adjuncts to individualized sets of contingencies when one is designing an intervention for stealing by an individual child.

Although none of these studies formally assessed the generalization of treatment effects across settings or behaviors, anecdotal data indicated that there was a decrease in stealing of nontargeted items (Switzer et al., 1977) and of disruptive acting-out behaviors (Rosen & Rosen, 1983). In the latter case, informal reports

from the teacher and parents suggested decreases in stealing behavior in other areas of the school (e.g., cafeteria) and at home. Behavioral generalization of school-based intervention effects to stealing has been demonstrated in at least one instance. As noted above, reductions in stealing at school (as well as other covert behaviors such as vandalism and truancy) were found as a result of implementing the antibullying program designed by Olweus (1990, 1991, 1996).

In their review of the treatment of nonconfrontative stealing in elementary-school-age children, Miller and Klungness (1986) raise some important issues that must be considered in the detection, monitoring, and treatment of stealing in the classroom. The use of unannounced theft probes (Switzer et al., 1977) or systematic searches (Rosen & Rosen, 1983) raises important legal and ethical issues. The use of group contingencies has the potential for several undesirable side effects, such as increased negative peer pressure and/or rejection (Pigott & Heggie, 1986) and the possibility that children may eventually choose not to report stealing because they do not want to lose access to the reward. In the Switzer et al. (1977) investigation, peer sociometric ratings prior to and after the implementation of the group contingency, as well as unobtrusive audiotaping of the children's conversations when the teacher left the classroom after each stealing incident, did not indicate the presence of any of these negative effects. However, more systematic and practical methods of monitoring such potential negative side effects are essential.

Miller and Klungness (1989) make several recommendations about interventions to reduce the occurrence of stealing. First, they recommend that therapists emphasize the accurate labeling and consistent detection of stealing. Second, therapists should place an emphasis on promoting effective child management skills with parents. Third, with motivated children, Miller and Klungness recommend the use of child self-control procedures in addition to external controls employed by parents. Fourth, the intervention should designate alternative behaviors to reinforce, in order to counteract the withdrawal of reinforcement that has been attendant to stealing. Fifth, it is important to implement system-level changes, such as increased supervision of children at recess and in school hallways. Although the recommendations of Miller and Klungness have not been evaluated, they are consistent with the treatment package designed and evaluated by Reid and his colleagues.

To our knowledge, the effects of medication on stealing have been examined in only one study (Hinshaw et al., 1992). The effects of methylphenidate on covert CP in boys with ADHD were investigated in a laboratory paradigm designed to provide an occasion for stealing, cheating, and property destruction. In a drug–placebo crossover design, drug treatment resulted in significant decreases in stealing and property destruction, observed surreptitiously in the laboratory. However, cheating *increased* when the children were taking methylphenidate.

Lying

To our knowledge, there have been no reports of formalized interventions to deal with lying. Stouthamer-Loeber (1986) has suggested that younger children, whose lies are more transparent and easily detectable, should be easier to treat. She advocates an educational approach in which a parent instructs a child in the difference between what is true and not true, and provides training in empathy and/or perspective taking. For older children, she suggests an approach similar to that described above by Reid et al. (1980) for stealing. If a parent suspects that a child is lying, the child must prove that he or she is being truthful to avoid a negative consequence. Stouthamer-Loeber also stresses the necessity of focusing on increasing parental monitoring of the child in interventions designed to decrease lying.

Fire Setting

Although fire setting is often (but not always) associated with a diagnosis of CD and is a more advanced, extreme, or complex type of CP (Forehand et al., 1991; Hanson et al., 1994; Kazdin & Kolko, 1986), it has been recognized as requiring a specific treatment focus in addition to standard psychosocial treatments for CP.

There are a number of case studies in the treatment literature involving both behavioral and nonbehavioral treatments (Kolko, 1985). Treatments have included contingency management procedures, negative practice in fire setting as a satiation and extinction procedure, prosocial skills training in the expression of anger and other emotional arousal, and family therapy (Kolko, 1996). Kolko (1983) and McGrath, Marshall, and Prior (1979) employed multicomponent treatment packages including fire safety instruction along with behavioral components. One study involved behavioral intervention focused on fire setting, but targeted comorbid CP and depression as well (Cox-

Jones, Lubetsky, Fultz, & Kolko, 1990). These case studies served as a prelude to more recent group experimental designs involving intervention for fire setters.

In the first of these more recent studies, Kolko, Watson, and Faust (1991) evaluated the effects of a brief cognitive-behavioral skills training curriculum on reducing laboratory analogue measures of fire-related behaviors, as well as increasing fire safety knowledge. The subjects were 24 psychiatrically hospitalized children randomly assigned to a cognitive-behavioral treatment group or to a fire assessment and awareness control group. The cognitive-behavioral group emphasized fire safety concepts and preventive skills training. The second group met with a nurse to discuss fire-setting behavior. In this study, the cognitive-behavioral condition was associated with significantly greater reductions in contact with fire-related toys and matches in an analogue task and an increase in fire safety knowledge. At a 6-month follow-up, parents reported less involvement with fire for children in the cognitive-behavioral condition.

In addition to the psychological treatments just reviewed, another approach to intervention has occurred outside the realm of mental health. This approach is implemented by trained firefighters in the community. Two national organizations sponsor community-based intervention programs for juvenile fire setters. One was developed by the U. S. Federal Emergency Management Agency (FEMA) and one by the National Firehawk Foundation. Both emphasize detection and assessment of the fire setter and rely heavily on fire safety education, although Firehawk programs also match fire setters with firefighters who serve as mentors and role models (Kolko, 1988). Systematic, controlled evaluations of these programs are scarce. A recent evaluation of educational materials (a brief brochure) alone or in conjunction with an adaptation of the FEMA program or referral to a mental health specialist showed statistically and clinically significant reductions in frequency and seriousness of fire setting at a 1-year follow-up assessment, regardless of intervention condition (Adler, Nunn, Northam, Lebnan, & Ross, 1994). Thus, the multicomponent FEMA intervention was no more effective than the provision of educational materials.

Because fire safety education alone provides for significant reductions in fire setting, Kolko and his colleagues have designed an experiment to test the comparative effects of fire safety education as implemented in community settings (such as the FEMA program) and psychosocial treatment as implemented in mental health settings (Kolko, 1996). In this study, psychosocial treatment consisted of cognitive-behavioral procedures designed to modify the characteristics and correlates of fire setting. Specifically, children learn graphing techniques to relate fire-setting motives to specific events or affective states, problem-solving skills, and assertion skills. Parents receive parent management training with special emphasis on child monitoring. Boys aged 5 to 12 who set fires were randomly assigned to the two treatments. Although this study is ongoing, initial analyses have revealed significantly greater reductions in child reports of fire involvement in psychosocial treatment versus fire safety skills treatment and reductions in parent-reported fire involvement for both groups. Definitive results await study completion.

Psychopharmacological Treatment

The history of psychopharmacological treatment of children with CP dates back to a landmark paper by Bradley (1937) on the use of amphetamines in children with behavior disorders. As the field of childhood psychopharmacology has grown and methods for diagnostic specification and symptom measurement have improved, studies evaluating drug treatment for children with the DSM-IV attention-deficit and disruptive behavior disorders (i.e., ADHD, CD, and ODD) have become increasingly numerous and sophisticated. By far the greatest research attention in this field has been directed to evaluations of drug treatment of children with what we now call ADHD; there are literally thousands of studies documenting the efficacy of stimulant medication treatment for symptoms associated with ADHD (Swanson, 1993). In the last 15 years, psychopharmacological treatment of children with primary CP has received increasing attention by both clinicians and researchers. Although no specific antiaggressive drug is currently available, a number of drugs are used by clinicians, and some have been evaluated in controlled research for their secondary antiaggressive properties (Vitiello & Stoff, 1997). What follows is a selective review of the research evaluations of various classes of drug treatments for children with CP, highlighting emerging theoretical and empirical issues related to selection of a drug treatment strategy. The reader is also referred to several excellent recent reviews of this area (Campbell & Cueva, 1995; Campbell, Gonzalez, & Silva, 1992; Connor & Steingard, 1996; Kruesi & Lelio, 1996; Werry, 1994).

Psychostimulants

Although ADHD is the only well-established indication for psychostimulants (the primary exemplars used in treatment studies are methylphenidate, dextroamphetamine, and pemoline), an early study using informal staff observations (Bradley, 1937) and later studies using quantified formal parent and teacher reports (Conners, 1969, 1972) indicated that stimulant drug treatment reduced ratings of aggression in children with disruptive behavior. Because ADHD has a very high rate of comorbidity with CP, more recent studies have begun specifically to investigate the effect of stimulant medication on the co-occurring CP behaviors of children selected on the basis of a primary diagnosis of ADHD, using more objective, direct observational methods.

In spite of the fact that low base rates of CP behavior in some naturalistic settings present problems in measurement and interpretation, there is a growing body of evidence that stimulant drugs do exert an effect, reducing the CP behaviors of ADHD children. Hinshaw, Buhrmester, and Heller (1989) showed that weight-adjusted doses of 0.6 mg/kg methylphenidate produced reductions in retaliatory aggression during verbal taunting from peers in a laboratory-type setting. In another study, in which several additional categories of physical and verbal aggression were assessed in order to increase the density of behavior observed during direct observations, Hinshaw, Henker, Whalen, Erhardt, and Dunnington (1989) reported that both 0.3 and 0.6 mg/kg of methylphenidate significantly reduced noncompliance and aggression in the classroom and on the playground of a summer school research program.

In the first observational study of stimulant medication effects on aggressive behavior in a truly naturalistic, nonresearch setting (a public school), Gadow, Nolan, Sverd, Sprafkin, and Paolicelli (1990) reported a highly significant effect of methylphenidate on physical aggression and a marginally significant effect on verbal aggression during a recess situation, although no effects were found during lunchtime.

As noted above, medication effects on covert CP have also been reported in boys with ADHD (Hinshaw et al., 1992). Methyphenidate resulted in significant decreases in stealing and property destruction, as observed in an analogue laboratory paradigm. Interestingly, cheating *increased* with drug treatment—an effect that Hinshaw et al. attributed to increased on-task involvement associated with primary stimulant medication.

We know of only two (unpublished) studies that have evaluated stimulant medication effects in children referred for and selected on the basis of a primary, formal diagnosis of CD according to DSM criteria. In the first study (Abikoff, Klein, Klass, & Ganeles, 1987), marked stimulant medication effects were observed on a broad spectrum of CP behaviors. However, even though heroic efforts were made in this study to recruit children with a sole diagnosis of CD, 90% of the sample had co-occurring ADHD. In the second study, which compared methylphenidate, lithium, and placebo, methylphenidate produced improvement over placebo in measures of CP in 80 children and adolescents diagnosed with CD, whereas lithium did not (Klein, Abikoff, Klass, Shah, & Seese, 1994).

The results of these and other studies provide increasing support for the conclusion that stimulant medications produce reductions in CP in children selected on the basis of primary diagnoses of ADHD or CD (see also Hinshaw, 1991). Because comorbidity of ADHD and CP is probably the rule rather than the exception in clinical samples (Abikoff & Klein, 1992), these findings bear significantly on treatment considerations for children with CP.

Although at this stage of research it appears prudent to suggest that stimulant medication treatment should be considered when CP co-occurs with ADHD, it seems likely that future research will demonstrate that pure CP may also be significantly affected by stimulants. Finally, almost all extant studies have evaluated stimulant medication effects on CP against a background of a more or less intensive, structured psychosocial treatment program. For this and other reasons, most prominent childhood psychopharmacologists recommend that stimulant medications be tried after, or along with, a trial of intensive psychosocial treatment (e.g., Kruesi & Lelio, 1996; Werry, 1994).

Lithium

Lithium carbonate has revolutionized the treatment of bipolar affective disorder in adults and has been used in children and adolescents for control of severe aggression with an affective component. Recommendations for its use come primarily from the work of Campbell and her colleagues. This group has conducted two sepa-

rate, large-scale, double-blind, placebo-controlled studies in children who were formally diagnosed with CD characterized by aggressive and explosive behaviors, and who were hospitalized following outpatient treatment failure.

In the first study (Campbell et al., 1984), 61 children aged 5 to 12 were randomly assigned to receive lithium, haloperidol, or placebo in a 4-week treatment trial. Lithium and haloperidol were both statistically and clinically superior to placebo on Aggression, Hostility, and Hyperactivity factors of the Children's Psychiatric Rating Scale (CPRS) and on Clinical Global Impressions (CGI) ("Special Feature," 1985). Twice as many children improved on lithium as on haloperidol, and lithium was associated with significantly fewer adverse side effects. Therefore, in a replication study with a larger sample of aggressive, explosive, hospitalized children with CD, lithium was compared only with placebo (Campbell et al., 1995). Effects on the Aggression factor of the CPRS and the CGI were found but more modest effects on other measures were obtained. Neither study found significant effects on the Aggression factor of the Conners Rating Scales; however, the authors argue for the greater ecological validity of the CPRS in the hospital setting.

The two other well-controlled studies of lithium in treatment of diagnosed CD in children produced negative results. However, several design and sample differences may account for the discrepancy in findings and point to possible predictors of successful treatment with lithium. In the first negative study, Rifkin et al. (1989) studied inpatients with a diagnosis of CD. The lithium treatment trial lasted only 2 weeks (as opposed to up to 6 weeks in the Campbell et al. [1984, 1995] studies) and the majority of the Rifkin et al. subjects were female (as opposed to the Campbell et al. studies, where the vast majority were male). Because 2 weeks probably represents an inadequate treatment trial, and because CD in females and males may represent different underlying subclasses of the disorder, the results of the Rifkin et al. and Campbell et al. studies may not be comparable.

In the second negative study (Klein et al., 1994), 80 outpatient children and adolescents with diagnoses of CD were randomly assigned to lithium, methylphenidate, or placebo. Lithium did not produce improvement compared to placebo. However, in this study children were outpatients and "only a few" displayed "explosively dangerous outbursts" (Klein, 1991, p. 120), as opposed to the inpatient population in the Campbell et al. (1984, 1995) studies, for whom "explosiveness" was one of the selection criteria.

These differences in the positive and negative studies have led to the speculation that lithium is most likely to be effective with severe, aggressive manifestations of CP. Furthermore, they add to the growing literature suggesting that subtyping CP may be important in clinical considerations and in future pharmacological treatment trials. Specifically, lithium may be more likely to lead to improvement in children with CP with an explosive (affective) component. Finally, because lithium was found in a direct comparison to be equally effective to a commonly used neuroleptic medication, haloperidol, but had fewer and milder adverse side effects, it should be considered a more conservative pharmacological approach than neuroleptics (see below) for treatment-resistant children with explosive CP. However, lithium is itself associated with possible side effects, such as weight gain, urinary frequency or polyuria, nausea, tremors, ataxia, and slurred speech, especially in younger children (Hagino et al., 1995). Consideration of demonstrated efficacy in controlled research only with treatment-resistant, hospitalized children, coupled with concern about toxicity, side effects, and the necessity for regular monitoring of blood levels, has led psychopharmacologists to recommend lithium treatment for CP only in exceptional circumstances (e.g., a very cooperative family), and with explosively aggressive children for whom other treatments have failed (e.g., Werry, 1994).

Clonidine

Clonidine is an alpha-adrenergic agonist originally used in adults as an antihypertensive agent. It has been used in adult psychiatry to lower activation in a variety of disorders of arousal, such as Posttraumatic Stress Disorder, other anxiety disorders, and mania. Although the Food and Drug Administration (FDA) has not approved any uses of clonidine in the treatment of children and adolescents, and despite the virtual absence of controlled treatment trials in children, we mention it here because there is evidence that it is increasingly being prescribed by clinicians for children with CP (Stoewe, Kruesi, & Lelio, 1995).

An open, uncontrolled study of clonidine in 17 children aged 5 to 15 with severe, treatment-resistant CP, who manifested cruel behavior and property destruction, showed a significant decrease in aggression in 15 of the 17 children (Kemph, DeVane, Levin, Jarecke, & Miller, 1993). Gamma-aminobutyric acid plasma levels increased during clonidine treatment and correlated with the reduction in aggression. In the only controlled trial to date, Hunt, Minderaa, and Cohen (1986) used clonidine for 10 boys with ADHD. Although the treatment targets were primary ADHD symptoms, teachers reported that children were "less aggressive and explosive."

These studies, along with the predicted effect of clonidine on adrenergic centers related to the arousal system, may be responsible for the increased usage by clinicians of clonidine with CP children and adolescents, especially those prone to irritability and explosive outbursts. However, these studies are merely suggestive. Evidence for efficacy from controlled research is lacking, and the increase in prescribing practices is therefore not well-justified empirically. Further research on the efficacy of clonidine with CP is greatly needed.

Other Psychopharmacological Agents

Antipsychotics (Neuroleptics). Antipsychotic medications (e.g., chlorpromazine, thioridazine, haloperidol) have been used historically to treat CP in children, especially those who are hospitalized chronically or who display mental retardation. They have proven aggression suppression effects in animal and human research (Stoewe et al., 1995), although it is not clear whether this is a true antiaggressive property or the result of nonspecific, sedative effects (Miczek & Barry, 1976). Several controlled trials have demonstrated the efficacy of antipsychotics in reducing aggression, fighting, explosiveness, and hostility, mostly with hospitalized, inpatient child populations (e.g., Campbell et al., 1984; Greenhill, Solomon, Pleak, & Ambrosini, 1985). Nevertheless, interest in and use of neuroleptics to control aggression have declined substantially, due to the increased variety of other available drug treatments and the potentially severe adverse effects of neuroleptics. Short-term side effects include acute dystonic reactions. Tardive and withdrawal dyskinesias (which may be severely disabling and irreversible) have been documented in 8%–51% of child patients treated with neuroleptics, and neuroleptic malignant syndrome (a potentially life-threatening condition) has been reported in a small number of cases. For these reasons, in spite of their potential efficacy in controlling aggression, most clinicians are wary of prescribing neuroleptics to children, and their use should be considered only in the most severe and treatment-refractory cases.

Anticonvulsants. The use of anticonvulsants for control of CP emanates from observations of the sudden onset and episodic nature of rage outbursts in some aggressive individuals, and the speculation that these are secondary to abnormal electrical activity in the limbic system, especially the temporal lobe. These drugs reduce the excitability of neurons, especially when they are overactive.

Carbamazepine has been the most studied anticonvulsant in children with CP. Several open (noncontrolled) trials have suggested positive effects of carbamazepine on symptoms of aggression, hyperactivity, and delinquency, and on severity ratings of assaultiveness (Kafantaris et al., 1992; Mattes, 1990; Vincent, Unis, & Hardy, 1990). However, a recent double-blind placebo-controlled trial of carbamazepine with children who received well-established diagnoses of CD and exhibited symptoms of severe aggressiveness and explosiveness found that carbamazepine was not superior to placebo, even at optimal daily doses (Cueva et al., 1996). In addition, the drug was associated with adverse side effects. The sample was rather small ($n = 22$), probably restricting power to detect a difference in this study. In addition, placebo responders were identified initially and eliminated from subsequent study, providing a very stringent test of the drug. The negative results of this study challenge the results of the open trials and suggest that further research is needed to support the use of anticonvulsants for children with CP.

Antidepressants. Clinical use of antidepressants for treatment of CP in children has been stimulated by the higher-than-chance comorbidity rates for depression and CP (estimates range from 23% to 37%); by an early clinical report of 13 comorbid boys who experienced improvement in depression and in CP symptoms with imipramine treatment (Puig-Antich, 1982); by evidence for altered serotonergic function in children with CP and in aggression (Reis, 1975); and by evidence for effectiveness of antidepressants in children with ADHD (Biederman, Baldessarini, Wright, Keenan, & Faraone, 1993).

Nevertheless, tricyclic antidepressants have not proven to be significantly more effective than placebo in children with depression (Jensen, Ryan, & Prien, 1992), weakening the rationale for their use for children who are comor-

bid for CP and depression. In addition, there are no controlled trials of antidepressants in treatment of children with primary diagnoses related to CP. One open trial of 75 mg of trazadone with three children presenting with serious problems of aggression showed significant decreases in aggression (Ghaziuddin & Alessi, 1992). In another open trial of trazadone with hospitalized children displaying a variety of disruptive behavior disorders, CP improved significantly (Zubieta & Alessi, 1992). However, as we have concluded for other drug classes, further controlled research with children with primary CP is needed before strong conclusions of efficacy can be drawn. In addition, because of the potential for cardiac arrhythmias, and because of rare but disturbing reports of deaths in children treated with antidepressants (Riddle et al., 1991), adverse effects must be strongly considered in the benefit–risk ratio assessment.

Aggression Subtypes and Psychopharmacological Treatment

Throughout this section, we have repeated the observations of several childhood psychopharmacologists that aggression with an explosive, affective component and/or rage seems to be more responsive to pharmacotherapy than does instrumental, controlled aggression without an affective component. Campbell et al. (1992) go so far as to say that "pharmacotherapy is appropriate only for aggressive and destructive behaviors accompanied by explosiveness" (p. 70). Although this recommendation seems extreme, especially in light of studies demonstrating stimulant medication effects in mild to moderate overt CP (i.e., aggression) and on covert CP behaviors, there is a growing opinion among childhood psychopharmacologists that aggression subtypes exist and that these have implications for use of a drug treatment strategy.

Vitiello and Stoff (1997) argue that children with the affective subtype of CP should be more responsive to pharmacological and psychosocial interventions aimed at decreasing arousal, hostility, and impulsivity. In contrast, the predatory subtype, which is more goal-oriented, is less likely to respond to drug treatment and more likely to respond to manipulation of environmental reinforcers via traditional contingency management strategies. These ideas are very intriguing, and we echo the call by other researchers for studies examining the interaction of aggression subtype with outcome of pharmacological as well as psychosocial treatments.

In closing this section, we reiterate that good controlled trials of pharmacotherapy for CP alone are relatively lacking. Studies of comorbid CP in children with a diagnosis of ADHD are accumulating, and indicate beneficial treatment effects on both the overt and covert CP behavior symptoms of children with ADHD. Therefore, for children comorbid for ADHD and CP, most childhood psychopharmacologists now recommend a trial of stimulant medication as the first choice when drug treatment is being considered. Likewise, for children comorbid with CP and depression, antidepressants are often considered, despite the dearth of evidence for efficacy of antidepressants for pure depression in children and adolescents.

For children and adolescents with severe or treatment-refractory aggression accompanied by an explosive or affective component, other drug classes with effects on arousal systems and affect modulation have been used. The greatest evidence for efficacy with this subtype exists for lithium and the antipsychotics, with lithium by far being the safer of these two drug classes; other drugs reviewed here must be considered experimental at this time. Nevertheless, they are increasingly being used by clinicians in spite of the lack of solid evidence for their effectiveness.

Any consideration of use of drugs with children must include careful review of their putative benefits against their side effects. A review of the side effects associated with different drugs is well beyond the scope of this chapter. Physicians considering drug treatment are referred to other authoritative reviews of drug side effects (Kruesi & Lelio, 1996; Werry & Aman, 1993). Likewise, all clinicians prescribing drugs to children must familiarize themselves with FDA regulations and *Physicians' Desk Reference* guidelines. Psychoactive drugs should be prescribed judiciously and only with careful clinical and laboratory monitoring. All prominent child psychopharmacologists recommend that drug treatment be used in conjunction with active psychosocial treatment or after the demonstrated failure of psychosocial treatment. We strongly concur with these recommendations.

PREVENTION

The prevention of CP has received increasing interest and attention over the past 10 years. This has been partly due to advances made in the delineation of developmental pathways of CP (especially the early-starter pathway) and the risk and protective factors associated with progression on this pathway (McMahon, 1994). Increased interest in prevention has also evolved from the successes and limitations of the treatment-focused interventions described in earlier sections of this chapter. With a few exceptions (such as parent training with young children with CP), the effects of single-component treatments have demonstrated limited generalizability, especially over time (see below). Nonetheless, it has been argued that well-designed treatment research with single-intervention components lays the foundation for the selection of components in multicomponent preventive interventions (Dodge, 1993).

To a certain extent, the distinction between treatment and prevention of CP is often difficult to make, since preventive interventions have usually (although not always) targeted younger children who are already engaging in some type of CP behavior (Coie & Dodge, 1998). One distinction is that treatment involves referral for assistance, whereas participation in prevention is usually determined by screening. This is a tenuous distinction at best. For example, a number of family-based interventions that were developed as treatments for CP have recently been identified as model family interventions for delinquency prevention (Office of Juvenile Justice and Delinquency Prevention, 1996). Such treatment approaches include the parent training programs developed by Forehand and McMahon (1981) and Webster-Stratton (1996a), FFT (Alexander & Parsons, 1982), MST (Henggeler & Borduin, 1990; Henggeler et al., in press), and TFC (Chamberlain, 1994).

Two broad classes of interventions are applicable to the prevention of CP: early intervention programs that are not focused on CP per se, and interventions that specifically target the prevention of CP. Space considerations preclude a detailed description of the many programs that have been developed or that are in progress for the prevention of CP. Reviews of such efforts may be found in Brewer et al. (1995), Kazdin (1995b), McCord and Tremblay (1992), Peters and McMahon (1996), and Yoshikawa (1994).

Early Intervention

There is evidence that early intervention programs (i.e., those that are implemented during the infancy and/or preschool periods) may have long-term effects on reducing the occurrence of CP behavior (for reviews, see Hawkins, Catalano, & Brewer, 1995; Yoshikawa, 1994;

Zigler, Taussig, & Black, 1992). These long-term effects have been noted in later childhood and adolescence, and in at least one case into adulthood (Schweinhart, Barnes, & Weikart, 1993). This is of particular interest, because prevention of CP has not typically been an explicit goal of these interventions. Four programs that have demonstrated such long-term effects are the Perry Preschool Program (Berrueta-Clement, Schweinhart, Barnett, Epstein, & Weikart, 1984), the Houston Parent–Child Development Center's program (Johnson & Walker, 1987), the Syracuse University Family Development Research Program (Lally, Mangione, Honig, & Wittner, 1988), and the Yale Child Welfare Project (Seitz, Rosenbaum, & Apfel, 1985). Yoshikawa (1994) notes four common elements of these interventions: (1) Each intervention included both family support and child education components; (2) the intervention was implemented during the child's first 5 years; (3) the intervention lasted for at least 2 years (range = 2 to 5 years); and (4) the intervention had short- to medium-term effects on risk factors shown to be associated with CP.

Preventive Interventions Focused on CP

At least two generations of preventive interventions have been designed specifically to prevent CP. The first generation of interventions, which began in the 1980s, are now reporting their findings. We briefly describe three of these earlier prevention trials.

The Seattle Social Development Project (Hawkins, Catalano, Morrison, et al., 1992; Hawkins, Von Cleve, & Catalano, 1991; O'Donnell, Hawkins, Catalano, Abbott, & Day, 1995) began in first grade, with elements of intervention implemented at various points between first and sixth grades. The classroom intervention consisted of proactive classroom management, interactive teaching, and cooperative learning strategies. Children also received a social problem-solving curriculum in first grade and training in refusal skills in sixth grade. The parent training component involved a series of voluntary workshops focusing on child behavior management, parental academic support, and prevention of child substance use. Unfortunately, parental involvement in the workshops was very low, so this aspect of the intervention does not appear to have received an adequate test. O'Donnell et al. (1995) have reported findings through sixth grade. Girls had lower rates of substance use initiation, and boys demonstrated less involvement with antisocial peers and a tendency for less initiation of delinquency.

A universal preventive intervention trial carried out by Kellam and his colleagues in Baltimore conducted intervention in first and second grades using the Good Behavior Game (Barrish et al., 1969; Deitz, 1985; Medland & Stachnik, 1972) described earlier (Kellam & Rebok, 1992). (A second intervention, Mastery Learning, focused on enrichment of the reading curriculum. However, because it was not intended to affect CP behaviors, it is not described here.) At the end of first grade, boys who participated in the Good Behavior Game were rated as having lower levels of aggression on both teacher ratings and peer sociometrics; girls were rated lower on aggression on the teacher ratings, but not on the sociometrics (Dolan et al., 1993). By the end of sixth grade, effects of the Good Behavior Game on teacher-rated aggression were limited only to boys who had exhibited initially high levels of aggression; there were no effects of the intervention for girls or for boys with lower levels of aggression (Kellam, Rebok, Ialongo, & Mayer 1994).

The prevention trial conducted by Tremblay and his colleagues (Tremblay, Masse, Pagani, & Vitaro, 1996; Tremblay et al., 1992) in Montreal employed a sample of boys who were identified as aggressive and disruptive in kindergarten. The boys were randomly assigned to intervention, a no-intervention control, or attention placebo conditions. Intervention occurred in second and third grade, and combined a parent training component with child social skills training. The parent training component was based on the work of Patterson et al. (1975), and the social skills training focused on prosocial skills and self-control. To date, annual assessments have been conducted from ages 10 through 15. During elementary school (ages 10 through 12), boys in the intervention condition were less likely to be described as having serious difficulties by teachers and peers, were more likely to have a more positive peer group (Vitaro & Tremblay, 1994), and were less likely to have engaged in delinquent behavior than boys in the control conditions (Tremblay et al., 1992). During early adolescence (to age 15), boys who received the intervention were less likely to be involved with gangs; were less involved in delinquent behavior; and were less likely to be arrested, to have their friends arrested, and to engage in substance use (Tremblay et al., 1996; Tremblay, Pagani-Kurtz, Masse, Vitaro, & Pihl,

1995). Intervention did not affect early sexual intercourse, and the earlier positive effects in elementary school on school adjustment were not maintained. However, the Montreal study has presented some of the most encouraging findings to date about the long-term maintenance of interventions that focus specifically on the prevention of CP.

A second generation of prevention trials specifically focused on CP is currently underway. These trials tend to provide more comprehensive intervention components and to implement the interventions for a longer period of time than the earlier prevention trials. An example, which represents a next step in the iteration of such large-scale, intervention-focused, longitudinal experimental studies, is the Fast Track Project (Conduct Problems Prevention Research Group, 1992). This multisite collaborative study is following a high-risk sample of almost 900 children who have been identified by both teachers and parents as displaying high rates of CP behaviors during kindergarten, as well as approximately 385 children who constitute a representative sample from the same schools as the high-risk children. The neighborhoods in which these children live are in urban, suburban, and rural communities. There is adequate representation of girls (approximately 30%) and minorities (approximately 50%, most of whom are African American), so that it will be possible to examine both the developmental course and the effects of intervention with various subgroups of children.

The children are being followed on an annual basis from kindergarten through high school. Assessments include interviews with the children, parents, and teachers; observations of parent–child interaction and child interactions in the classroom and on the playground; peer sociometric interviews; and archival school, police, and court records.

Half of the children in the high-risk sample are participating in an intensive and long-term intervention that is designed to address the developmental issues involved in the early starter pathway of CP. The intervention begins in grade 1 and continues through grade 10. However, there are two periods of intensive intervention: school entry (grades 1–2) and the transition into middle school (grades 5–6). The intervention at school entry targets proximal changes in six domains: (1) disruptive behaviors in the home; (2) disruptive and off-task behaviors in the school; (3) social-cognitive skills pertaining to affect regulation, and social problem-solving

skills; (4) peer relations; (5) academic skills; and (6) the family–school relationship. Integrated intervention components include parent training, home visiting, social skills training, academic tutoring, and a teacher-based classroom intervention. (See Bierman, Greenberg, & the Conduct Problems Prevention Research Group, 1996, and McMahon, Slough, & the Conduct Problems Prevention Research Group, 1996, for detailed descriptions of the first phase of the intervention.) The intervention at entry into middle school includes developmentally appropriate interventions in the domains described above, with increasing emphasis placed upon parental monitoring of the child, identity development and goal setting, affiliation with an age-appropriate peer group, and development of a mentoring relationship with a same-sex adult.

Initial evaluations of the effects of the intervention have been encouraging, with hypothesized changes in the domains described above being obtained at the end of first grade, and with other analyses suggesting that changes in parent and teacher reports of child CP behaviors are accounted for by changes in the hypothesized parent and child mediating variables (Conduct Problems Prevention Research Group, 1997a, 1997b).

ISSUES IN INTERVENTION EFFECTIVENESS

In this section of the chapter, we address some of the major issues pertaining to interventions with children with CP. These issues include generalization and social validity; predictors of outcome; and comparisons of the relative effectiveness of interventions with that of control conditions (no treatment, attention placebo, etc.) and of other forms of intervention.

Generalization and Social Validity

In an earlier section of the chapter, we have employed Forehand and Atkeson's (1977) classification of various types of generalization (setting, temporal, sibling, and behavioral) as an introduction to our evaluation of various family-based interventions with children with CP. With respect to such interventions with preadolescent children and their families (e.g., Forehand & McMahon, 1981; Patterson et al., 1975; Webster-Stratton, 1996a), there have been a number of investigations assessing the various types of generalization; these have, for the most part, supported the effectiveness of behavioral parent training programs.

Each of the three programs described earlier in the chapter has documented setting generalization from the clinic to the home for parent and child behavior and for parents' perception of the child's adjustment (e.g., Fleischman, 1981; Peed et al., 1977; Taplin & Reid, 1977; Webster-Stratton, 1984). Temporal generalization of treatment effects has also been demonstrated over follow-up periods of 1 to 3 years (e.g., Baum & Forehand, 1981; Patterson & Fleischman, 1979; Patterson & Forgatch, 1995; Webster-Stratton, 1990a; Webster-Stratton et al., 1989). Maintenance of effects for the Forehand and McMahon (1981) parent training program has been demonstrated for up to 4.5 years after treatment (Baum & Forehand, 1981), and less rigorous studies done 4.5 to 14 years after treatment suggest that the children were functioning well compared to their peer groups in terms of parent-, teacher-, and self-reported adjustment (Forehand & Long, 1988; Long et al., 1994). Other parent training programs with young children with CP have also demonstrated long-term temporal generalization effects of 3 years or more (e.g., Daly, Holland, Forrest, & Fellbaum, 1985; Strain, Steele, Ellis, & Timm, 1982).

Several investigators have now assessed setting generalization from the clinic or home setting to the school. In their meta-analytic study, Serketich and Dumas (1996) reported an effect size of 0.73 for parent training when the outcome was based on teacher report. Whereas several investigators have reported evidence of generalization in the form of teacher ratings of child CP behavior (e.g., Fellbaum et al., 1985; Sayger, Horne, & Glaser, 1993; Webster-Stratton et al., 1988), McNeil et al. (1991) demonstrated generalization to the classroom using both observational data and teacher ratings of CP behaviors (but not of teacher-rated social competence or observed on-task behavior). McNeil et al. also demonstrated that change in home behavior was positively correlated with changes in school behavior (based on parent and teacher ratings, respectively). Evidence of behavioral contrast effects (e.g., Johnson et al., 1976; Wahler, 1975) has occasionally been found. Other investigators have failed to find evidence of generalization to the school or of maintenance of this generalization (e.g., Breiner & Forehand, 1981; Forehand et al., 1979; Patterson & Forgatch, 1995; Webster-Stratton et al., 1989). Based on this research, we suggest that when a child presents with problems in both the home and school set-

tings, improvement in school functioning should not necessarily be expected to occur as a function of family-based intervention in the home; rather, intervening directly in the school may be required. Furthermore, the therapist should monitor the child's behavior in the school, regardless of whether this was an initial referral problem, because of the possibility of a behavioral contrast effect.

Both the Forehand and McMahon (1981) and Patterson et al. (1975) parent training programs have demonstrated sibling generalization at the end of treatment (Arnold et al., 1975; Horne & Van Dyke, 1983; Humphreys et al., 1978), and this generalization has been maintained at 6-month (Arnold et al., 1975) and 1-year (Horne & Van Dyke, 1983) follow-ups for Patterson's program. However, it should be noted that many of the siblings in the Arnold et al. investigation had been directly involved in the actual treatment program. Evidence for sibling generalization, based on parental ratings of siblings' behavior on the ECBI, has been reported by Brestan, Eyberg, Boggs, and Algina (1997).

Behavioral generalization from the treatment of child noncompliance to other deviant behaviors (e.g., aggression, temper tantrums) has been demonstrated for both the Forehand and McMahon (Wells, Forehand, & Griest, 1980) and Webster-Stratton (1984) parent training programs for younger children with CP, as well as by other parent trainers (e.g., Russo et al., 1981). Significant reductions in a composite measure of observed coercive child behaviors and in PDR scores over the course of treatment suggest that Patterson's parent training program for preadolescent children with CP also manifests behavioral generality (e.g., Fleischman, 1981; Fleischman & Szykula, 1981; Patterson, 1974), although it should be noted that Patterson and Reid (1973) did not find generalization of treatment effects from targeted to nontargeted observed deviant behaviors.

The social validity of family-based interventions with children with CP has been assessed by a number of methods, including measures of consumer satisfaction completed by the parents (see McMahon & Forehand, 1983), measures of treatment acceptability (e.g., Cross Calvert & McMahon, 1987), and by determining the clinical significance of posttreatment improvements. All three parent training programs for preadolescents have provided strong evidence of consumer satisfaction at posttreatment and/or follow-up periods of a year or more (e.g., Baum & Forehand, 1981; McMahon et al., 1984;

Patterson et al., 1982; Webster-Stratton, 1984, 1989). They have also provided normative comparisons indicating that by the end of treatment, child and/or parent behavior more closely resembles that in nonreferred families (e.g., Forehand et al., 1980; Patterson, 1974; Webster-Stratton, 1990a; Webster-Stratton et al., 1989). In their meta-analytic review of parent training, Serketich and Dumas (1996) reported that 17 of 19 intervention groups dropped below the clinical range after treatment on at least one measure, and that 14 groups did so on all measures.

It is apparent that evidence for the generalization and social validity of family-based interventions with preadolescent children with CP is extensive and, for the most part, positive. A number of studies (many of them conducted by Forehand, Sanders, and Dadds and their colleagues) have examined the role of adjunctive treatments in facilitating generalization and/or social validity, over and above that obtained by standard parent training programs. Adjunctive treatments have included components designed to facilitate maternal self-control/self-management (Sanders, 1982; Sanders & Glynn, 1981; Wells, Griest, & Forehand, 1980); child self-control (Baum et al., 1986); parental knowledge of social learning principles (McMahon, Forehand, & Griest, 1981); generalization to specific settings in the home and community (Powers & Roberts, 1995; Sanders & Christensen, 1985; Sanders & Dadds, 1982); marital support, communication, and problem solving (Dadds, Sanders, Behrens, & James, 1987; Dadds, Sanders, & James, 1987; Dadds, Schwartz, & Sanders, 1987; Webster-Stratton, 1994); discrimination training for mothers ("synthesis teaching"; Wahler, Cartor, Fleischman, & Lambert, 1993); and parental social support (Dadds & McHugh, 1992). One of the more comprehensive adjuncts to date is "Parent Enhancement Therapy" (Griest et al., 1982), which includes components related to parental perceptions of the child's behavior, marital adjustment, parental personal adjustment, and the parents' extrafamilial relationships. Similarly, Prinz and Miller (1994) developed an "enhanced" version of parent training that incorporated supportive discussions with the parent about other issues of concern. The utility of these adjunctive treatments when they are employed in conjunction with the basic parent training programs lends support to the current movement toward a broader behavioral family therapy model of intervention (Griest & Wells, 1983). (However, it is important to note that not all of these adjunctive procedures have resulted in enhanced generalization or social validity; see, e.g., Dadds & McHugh, 1992.)

With respect to family-based treatments with adolescents, there have been encouraging developments with respect to the generalization and social validity of this approach. However, investigators either have failed to assess adolescent and parent behavior in the home (e.g., Alexander & Parsons, 1973; Henggeler et al., 1986) or have failed to find changes in that setting (Bank et al., 1991). Bank et al. did find significant decreases in targeted delinquent and predelinquent behaviors as reported by parents on the PDR.

Setting and temporal generalization have usually been assessed via some measure of recidivism, the use of which is fraught with methodological problems (see Gordon & Arbuthnot, 1987). Although the results of the Bank et al. (1991) investigation were not supportive of temporal generalization (offense rates for the two conditions were comparable at each of the three follow-up years), Alexander and Parsons (1973) reported reduced recidivism rates at a 6- to 18-month follow-up for adolescents who had participated in FFT, compared to other forms of family therapy. Reduced recidivism for participants in Gordon's adaptation of FFT over a 5-year posttreatment interval has been documented with serious juvenile offenders (Gordon et al., 1988, 1995). Evidence for the temporal generalization of MST for periods of up to 4 years after treatment has also been provided (Borduin et al., 1995; Henggeler et al., 1992, 1993).

FFT also appears to reduce the likelihood of subsequent court involvement by siblings of the identified client, thus providing some evidence of sibling generalization for this intervention (Gordon & Arbuthnot, 1987; Klein et al., 1977). Henggeler et al. (1991) reported that MST also resulted in lower rates of self-reported "soft" drug use and lower rates of substance-related arrests, providing support for behavioral generalization. The social validity of these interventions has not been formally assessed.

With respect to other forms of intervention with children and adolescents with CP, somewhat less attention has been paid to generalization and social validity. However, many of these other interventions are now providing evidence for some aspects of generalization and social validity. As noted above, treatment effects from community-based programs for adolescents, such as TFM (Achievement Place), have not been found to show setting generalization to the home environment or temporal generalization when measures of recidivism are employed (e.g., Kirigin et al., 1982; Kirigin & Wolf, 1994; Weinrott et al., 1982). These investigations do indicate that TFM possesses a high degree of social validity in how it is perceived by program participants and members of the community. Weinrott et al. demonstrated that although the TFM group homes may not have been more effective than alternative group homes, they were less costly. The data concerning the temporal generalization of TFC are more encouraging. For example, Chamberlain (1990) reported significantly fewer days incarcerated at both 1- and 2-year follow-ups for adolescents who had participated in TFC as opposed to traditional group homes. Some evidence for setting generalization to home and school and for temporal generalization has been presented for day treatment programs for children with CP (Grizenko et al., 1993; Kolko, in press).

To our knowledge, the setting generalization to the home of school-based interventions for children with CP has not been assessed. This is potentially of considerable import, given the previously noted findings of occasional generalization or behavioral contrast effects in the school as a function of family-based treatments. Even more restricted forms of setting generalization (e.g., generalization of effects from one class period to another) have usually not been assessed. The available evidence suggests that various school-based interventions often exert their effects only in those classes in which the procedures are implemented (e.g., O'Leary et al., 1969; Walker & Hops, 1976), although use of experimenter-selected material reinforcers (as opposed to child-selected activity reinforcers) did facilitate setting generalization for a token system (Stumpf & Holman, 1985).

Temporal generalization has been largely ignored, except for the investigations by the CORBEH group. The CORBEH studies have shown that multicomponent treatment packages do not generalize well from one academic year to the next when no generalization training is attempted (Walker et al., 1975). The CLASS program has demonstrated maintenance of treatment effects over a 1-year period, but weekly booster sessions may need to be held with the teachers during this period (Hops et al., 1978). The temporal generalization of the RECESS program has not been assessed, but Walker et al. (1981) note some anecdotal reports of decay of treatment effects when the program is eventually turned over to the school's playground supervisors. Shorter follow-up intervals (3 to 12 weeks)

have been employed in investigations examining token economy and teacher contingency management interventions (Greenwood et al., 1974, 1977; Walker & Hops, 1976).

The issue of behavioral generalization of these school-based interventions for overt CP is a critical one. It is essential that investigators who elect to target overt CP behaviors in the classroom examine the effects of their interventions not just on these behaviors, but also in terms of whether the intervention ultimately leads to adaptive changes in children's academic achievement, social adjustment, and so on (see Klein, 1979; Winett & Winkler, 1972). This issue has been largely ignored. (There is at least one study in which changes in academic behavior, as a function of academic tutoring, have led to decreases in CP behaviors at school; see Coie & Krehbiel, 1984.)

Similarly, the social validity of these school-based interventions has not received systematic attention. The CLASS program appears to reduce demand for special educational services for its participants over at least a 3-year follow-up (Hops et al., 1978), and program consultants perceive their training and the program very positively (e.g., Walker et al., 1988). Teachers perceive the basic Good Behavior Game to be more acceptable than a more complex version (Tingstrom, 1994). The acceptability of home-based reinforcement systems to teachers and students has also been documented (Turco & Elliott, 1986; Witt et al., 1984). Parents reported equally high levels of satisfaction with goal-setting and parent training interventions to improve children's homework problems, but children were more satisfied with the goal-setting intervention (Kahle & Kelley, 1994).

With respect to the various school-based intervention programs for dealing with bullying, there is some evidence for setting, temporal, and behavioral generalization, as well as for social validity. In Olweus's (1990, 1991, 1996) intervention, reductions in bullying were noted not only at school, but on the way to and from school as well. Reductions in bullying were maintained up to 20 months after the program was implemented. (However, it should be noted that the intervention was in effect throughout this period, so, technically speaking, it is not a true maintenance effect.) Reductions were also noted in other CP behaviors, including fighting, stealing, truancy, and vandalism. Finally, increases in student satisfaction with the school were noted, providing evidence for the social validity of the intervention.

In the Pepler et al. (1993, 1994) adaptation of this intervention, the investigators noted an increase in racial bullying, even as other forms of bullying decreased. It is not clear whether this is a behavioral contrast effect, or simply an increase that would have occurred regardless of the intervention.

With respect to skills training treatments for children and adolescents with CP, conclusions regarding the generalization of treatment effects of some interventions have been limited somewhat because of many investigators' reliance on analogue measures and settings to assess treatment effectiveness. In the studies that assessed treatment outcome in naturalistic settings, generalization often either was not assessed or failed to occur (e.g., Guerra & Slaby, 1990; Spence & Marzillier, 1981). Generalization of at least some treatment effects to other settings up to a 1-year follow-up period has been demonstrated for some social skills (e.g., Michelson et al., 1983) and moral reasoning skills (e.g., Arbuthnot & Gordon, 1986) interventions. Evidence of setting generalization to the classroom (e.g., Lochman et al., 1984), to psychiatric inpatient units (e.g., Feindler et al., 1986), and to community functioning (Goldstein & Glick, 1994) for some of the anger control training interventions has been demonstrated. Maintenance of these effects has been assessed for up to 3 years (Lochman, 1992). Lochman reported that effects were found in the classroom at 3 years after treatment, but only if the boys had received booster sessions during the second year following intervention. Lower levels of self-reported substance use were found, providing some support for behavioral generalization as well. Multicomponent skills training programs such as ART (Goldstein et al., 1986) and EQUIP (Leeman et al., 1993) may ultimately result in enhanced generalization, although this has yet to be documented.

The strongest demonstration of generalization for the skills training approaches has been presented by Kazdin (1996b). Not only were children who participated in PSST while they were inpatients in a psychiatric unit rated more highly on both parent and teacher report measures (observational measures were not employed) after treatment than were children in either relationship therapy or attention placebo control conditions, but this superiority was maintained at a 1-year follow-up (Kazdin et al., 1987b, 1989). Similar findings were obtained when PSST was combined with a parent training intervention and compared to an attention placebo control

condition (Kazdin et al., 1987a, 1992). Thus, these data provide evidence not only for temporal generalization, but for setting generalization to the home and to school, since intervention occurred primarily with inpatient samples of children.

There is also evidence for the social validity of some skills training approaches. Some social skills researchers (e.g., Willner et al., 1978) have utilized social-validational techniques in a sophisticated manner in their development of teaching procedures for the skills training interventions, and others (e.g., Prinz et al., 1994) have employed assessments of consumer satisfaction from the perspectives of children, parents, and teachers. Kazdin and his colleagues (1987a, 1987b, 1989, 1992) found that children in the PSST condition (alone or in combination with parent training) were more likely to move within or near the normal range on some of the parent and teacher report measures than were children in the other conditions. These data provide evidence for the social validity of PSST, although Kazdin has been careful to note that many of these children still function outside the normal range.

A discussion of the generalization of treatment effects in dealing with covert CP is limited almost entirely to investigations that have dealt with stealing. A study by the OSLC group provides some limited evidence for setting, temporal, and behavioral generalization. Reid et al. (1980) noted parent-reported decreases in stealing and other referral problems at posttreatment and at a 6-month follow-up. However, decreases were not observed on an observational measure of child aversive behavior. Furthermore, Moore et al. (1979) have presented data suggesting that children referred to OSLC for stealing (only some of whom completed treatment) were at great risk for being labeled as delinquent 2 to 9 years later. Seymour and Epston (1989) reported decreased frequency of stealing at 2- and 12-month follow-ups, based on parent report. To our knowledge, no one has attempted to assess generalization or behavioral contrast effects of family-based treatments for stealing to other settings, such as the school or community.

In school-based interventions for stealing, Rosen and Rosen (1983) reported maintenance of effects at 1 month for their single subject, and anecdotal reports of decreased stealing of nontargeted items (Switzer et al., 1977) and of disruptive acting-out behaviors (Rosen & Rosen, 1983) provide minimal support for behavioral generalization. In the latter study, informal teacher and parent reports also suggested a decrease in stealing in other areas of the school and at home. With respect to social validity, methylphenidate reduced levels of stealing (and property damage) to levels comparable to those displayed by a normal comparison sample of boys; however, cheating actually increased as a function of the medication (Hinshaw et al., 1992).

There is minimal evidence concerning the generalization of interventions for fire setting. At a 6-month follow-up, parents reported less overall involvement with fire for children who had participated in a cognitive-behavioral intervention focused on fire safety and prevention skills training than for children who had participated in a discussion control condition (Kolko et al., 1991). Adler et al. (1994) reported comparable intervention effects at a 1-year follow-up for an educational brochure, whether alone or in conjunction with a FEMA program or referral to a mental health specialist.

The assessment of the generalization of effects of psychopharmacological treatments has been extremely limited, and has tended to be confined to studies of methylphenidate. Because the primary clinical use of stimulant medications such as methylphenidate has been to improve attention and decrease impulsivity in children diagnosed with ADHD, the effectiveness of this medication in decreasing both overt (e.g., aggression) and covert (e.g., stealing; Hinshaw et al., 1992) types of CP might be considered evidence of behavioral generalization. Reductions in aggression have been noted in multiple settings as well, including the laboratory, classroom, and playground (e.g., Gadow et al., 1990; Hinshaw, Buhrmester, & Heller, 1989; Hinshaw, Henker, et al., 1989).

Some preventive interventions have presented impressive evidence for long-term temporal generalization. For example, several early intervention programs implemented during infancy and preschool have documented preventive effects on CP behaviors in later childhood and adolescence (e.g., Berrueta-Clement et al., 1984; Johnson & Walker, 1987; Lally et al., 1988; Seitz et al., 1985). The effects of the Perry Preschool Program on CP have been demonstrated at age 27 (Schweinhart et al., 1993). Among the preventive interventions that have focused specifically on CP, the Montreal prevention trial (Tremblay et al., 1995, 1996) has demonstrated the strongest evidence for temporal generalization, with preventive effects noted at age 15. However, earlier effects on school adjustment were not maintained into adolescence. Kellam et al. (1994) have demonstrated preventive effects on aggressive behavior 4 years following intervention (i.e., in grade 6), but only for boys with initially high levels of aggression.

Predictors of Outcome

We have described a broad spectrum of interventions for the treatment and prevention of CP in children and adolescents. These interventions have varied tremendously in their demonstrated effectiveness, both in terms of immediate outcome and in terms of the generalization of these effects. In this section of the chapter, we discuss various predictors of outcome, not only with respect to positive treatment effects, but also with respect to decreasing dropouts (i.e., increasing parent and child engagement). As in other areas, most of the extant research has assessed predictors of outcome for interventions designed to treat overt CP. Most of that research has been carried out with family-based interventions for preadolescents (i.e., parent training) and, to a lesser extent, with cognitive-behavioral skills training. We have divided our review into child and family characteristics and characteristics of intervention (e.g., client engagement–resistance, therapist characteristics).

Child Characteristics

A myriad of characteristics of the child with CP could conceivably affect outcome in a differential manner. These include the nature of the CP behaviors (e.g., subtype, severity, duration); comorbid disorders (e.g., ADHD); the child's age, gender, and race; and variables such as temperament, problem-solving abilities, attributional biases, and so on. With the few exceptions described here, there has been a dearth of research in this area. Particularly serious omissions are the lack of data related to the nature of the CP behaviors and to the presence of comorbid disorders, especially ADHD. In terms of subtypes of CP, there is some evidence to suggest that children with CP who exhibit "explosive" aggression may be more responsive to lithium (Campbell et al., 1984, 1995).

More severe or frequent levels of CP at pretreatment have been associated with dropout and negative outcome at posttreatment and at follow-up for parent training interventions (e.g., Dumas, 1984b; Holden, Lavigne, & Cameron, 1990; Patterson & Forgatch, 1995; Ruma, Burke, & Thompson, 1996; Webster-Stratton, 1996b). Similar findings have been noted by

Kazdin (1990, 1995a; Kazdin, Mazurick, & Bass, 1993; Kazdin, Mazurick, & Siegel, 1994) for skills training, parent training, or their combination, and for interventions to decrease fire setting (Adler et al., 1994; Kolko et al., 1991). Other investigators have not found initial severity of child CP behaviors to be associated with treatment outcome or dropout (e.g., Fleischman, 1981; Henggeler et al., 1992). In contrast, Lochman, Lampron, Burch, and Curry (1985) found that greater reductions in disruptive/aggressive off-task behavior in the classroom following their anger control intervention were predicted by higher initial rates of this behavior. Similarly, in their school-based preventive intervention, Kellam et al. (1994) reported that higher levels of severity of CP behaviors in grade 1 were associated with intervention effects (for boys only) at grade 6.

Several investigators have found that relatively younger children are more likely to succeed in treatment (Strain et al., 1982; Strain, Young, & Horowitz, 1981) and that their families are less likely to drop out of parent training interventions (Dishion & Patterson, 1992; Fleischman, 1981; Scott & Stradling, 1987) than are older children and their families. McMahon et al. (1985) reported no differential treatment effects for their parent training program, either at posttreatment or at a 2-month follow-up, as a function of the children's age (which ranged from 3 to 8 years). However, a meta-analytic study of parent training (Serketich & Dumas, 1996) found larger effect sizes for parent training conducted with elementary-school-age children than with preschool-age children. Within an elementary-school-age sample, Kolko (in press) found that younger children were more responsive to a day treatment intervention than were older children. Kazdin (1995a) reported that age was not related to outcome in his intervention (PSST, parent training, or the combination). Age was also not a significant predictor of response to intervention for fire setting in two different studies (Adler et al., 1994; Kolko et al., 1991).

The question of whether interventions for CP are equally effective for boys and girls has, for the most part, been ignored. Most investigators have typically employed samples composed entirely of boys or have failed to analyze their outcome data separately by gender of the children. Several investigators have reported no differential effects on outcome as a function of child gender for parent training (e.g., Strain et al., 1981, 1982; Webster-Stratton, 1996b), family-

based interventions with adolescents (e.g., Henggeler et al., 1992), or skills training (alone or in combination with parent training) (e.g., Gibbs et al., 1984; Kazdin, 1995a; Kazdin et al., 1993). The most comprehensive assessment of the effects of child gender on outcome has been presented by Webster-Stratton (1996b). She reported that boys and girls responded in a similarly favorable fashion to her parent training intervention, and that these effects were maintained at 1- and 2-year follow-ups. Predictors of outcome in the school were similar, but in the home, pretreatment level of CP behaviors was the best predictor of outcome for boys at follow-up, whereas for girls, maternal negativity and depression and paternal negativity and life stress were the best predictors. Gordon et al. (1988, 1995) reported reduced recidivism rates for both male and female adolescent delinquents following completion of a modified version of FFT; recidivism was virtually eliminated for the girls. Chamberlain and Reid (1994) found that whereas reports of boys' behavior on the PDR improved during their participation in TFC, girls' behavior during the intervention actually got worse. However, completion rates of the program and follow-up arrest data were similar. A history of sexual abuse, regardless of gender, was associated with poorer outcome. Similar findings have been reported with response to a day treatment program (Kolko, in press). Two of the school-based prevention programs have reported differential effects of intervention favoring boys over girls (e.g., Hawkins et al., 1991; Kellam et al., 1994). In both cases, these effects were further qualified, in that effects were found only for boys who exhibited high initial levels of CP behaviors (Kellam et al., 1994) or who were white (Hawkins et al., 1991).

A similar lack of knowledge exists concerning the relative effectiveness of interventions for CP with children of different ethnicities (Forehand & Kotchick, 1996; Hammond & Yung, 1993; Prinz & Miller, 1991). In many cases, samples consisted of children from different ethnic backgrounds; however, no assessment was made of whether ethnicity served as a predictor or moderator of intervention outcome or of dropout. Strain et al. (1981, 1982) did not find ethnicity to predict outcome at posttreatment outcome and follow-up after a parent training intervention; Henggeler et al. (1992) reported a similar finding for MST. However, minority status was associated with dropout from another parent training program (Holden et al., 1990) and from Kazdin's (1996b) intervention (PSST, parent training, or the combination) (Kazdin et al., 1993). Some investigators have reported positive intervention findings with African-American samples for skills training interventions (e.g., Kendall et al., 1990; Lochman et al., 1981). On the other hand, Hawkins et al. (1991) reported that the effects of their school-based prevention program at the end of second grade were limited to European American boys; the intervention was not shown to be effective with African American children or with European American girls.

Other individual-difference variables have been examined even less frequently. With respect to cognitive interventions, Dodge (1985) has stressed the importance of the accurate identification and assessment of the particular processing deficits that are operating for an individual child. Attributional biases that arise from faulty formal information analysis should respond best to self-instructional interventions, whereas more affectively driven attributions indicate alternative interventions, such as extinguishing the negative affective response. Lochman et al. (1985) found that lower initial levels of interpersonal problem-solving abilities and higher parental ratings of a child's somatization predicted a positive response on parental ratings of the child's aggression following participation in anger control training. Children with lower perceived levels of hostility and a more internalized attributional style at pretreatment had a more positive outcome following a cognitive-behavioral social problem-solving intervention (Kendall, Ronan, & Epps, 1991).

Family Characteristics

Family characteristics that have been investigated include parental behavior, perceptions of the child's adjustment, and personal and marital adjustment; extrafamilial characteristics such as insularity; and structural variables such as family composition (single-parent vs. two-parent households) and SES.

With respect to parental behaviors, Dumas (1984b) reported that mothers classified as treatment "failures" (dropouts or cases showing inadequate improvement in child and maternal behaviors) were more aversive and indiscriminate at baseline than mothers who ultimately succeeded in the parent training program. Dropouts from this type of intervention have also been noted to emit higher rates of maternal commands (McMahon, Forehand, Griest, & Wells, 1981). Both maternal and paternal "negativity" predicted girls' but not boys' CP behaviors at

home 1 to 2 years posttreatment (Webster-Stratton, 1996b). Patterson and Forgatch (1995) reported that both pre- and posttreatment levels of parental monitoring and posttreatment levels of problem solving predicted child arrest and out-of-home placement 2 years later. In an evaluation of the TFC intervention, foster parents' frequent use of appropriate discipline (along with the adolescent spending less time with delinquent peers) predicted the number and seriousness of subsequent arrests (Chamberlain & Moore, in press). Parental perceptions of children's adjustment prior to treatment have not been associated with treatment outcome (Dumas, 1984a; Dumas & Albin, 1986) or with dropout (McMahon, Forehand, Griest, & Wells, 1981), although maternal shifts to fewer blaming attributions and indiscriminate reactions and to more specific and less global summary descriptions of the children have been shown to be associated with maintenance of treatment effects (Wahler & Afton, 1980; Wahler et al., 1993).

The role of parental personal and marital adjustment in predicting treatment outcome is somewhat unclear. Parenting locus of control did not influence dropout from the Forehand and McMahon parent training program, although parents who completed the program displayed a more internalized parenting locus of control at posttreatment (Roberts et al., 1992). Maternal adult attachment status has been recently demonstrated to moderate the relationship between pretreatment and follow-up (1 to 3.5 years) levels of child CP (Routh, Hill, Steele, Elliott, & Dewey, 1995), in that this relationship held only when mothers were insecurely attached. Maternal depression (as measured by the Beck Depression Inventory) has been shown to predict dropout (McMahon, Forehand, Griest, & Wells, 1981) and failure to participate in an 8-month follow-up assessment (Griest, Forehand, & Wells, 1981) for the Forehand and McMahon (1981) parent training program. Both maternal and paternal depression and negative life events have been significant predictors of outcome either at posttreatment or at follow-up for parent training (e.g., Webster-Stratton, 1985b, 1996b; Webster-Stratton & Hammond, 1990) and skills training (alone or with parent training) (Kazdin, 1990, 1995a; Kazdin et al., 1993) interventions. Kazdin et al. (1993) reported that a maternal history of childhood antisocial behavior was also associated with dropout from his intervention (PSST, parent training, or the combination). Dumas and Albin (1986) found maternal report of psychopathological symptoms to account for

17% of the variance in predicting treatment outcome in their sample of 82 families; however, Henggeler et al. (1992) did not find parental symptomatology to be associated with the outcome of MST.

For the most part, level of marital satisfaction has not been found to differentially affect treatment outcome and generalization at posttreatment or brief follow-up assessments (Brody & Forehand, 1985; Dadds, Schwartz, & Sanders, 1987; Forehand, Griest, Wells, & McMahon, 1982). For example, Forehand et al. (1982) reported comparable improvements in parents' and children's behavior and in parental perceptions of the children's behavior at posttreatment and at a 2-month follow-up, regardless of level of marital satisfaction prior to treatment. However, Dadds, Schwartz, and Sanders (1987) failed to find maintenance of the effects of parent training at a 6-month follow-up for maritally distressed families; this suggests that over longer periods of time, marital distress may ultimately impede temporal generalization. In addition, paternal marital satisfaction was found to be a predictor of posttreatment (but not 1-year follow-up) success for both observed paternal and child behavior (Webster-Stratton & Hammond, 1990).

Although there is evidence that fathers' behaviors and/or perceptions regarding their children with CP change as a function of participation in parent training interventions (e.g., Eyberg & Robinson, 1982; Taplin & Reid, 1977; Webster-Stratton, 1985a, 1994; Webster-Stratton et al., 1988), whether or not such participation enhances outcome and generalization is unclear. The relatively few studies to address this issue have generally not indicated the necessity of including the father in parent training; however, those studies suffer from a number of methodological weaknesses (e.g., small sample size, nonrandom assignment to groups, lack of follow-up data, reliance on self-report data) (Budd & O'Brien, 1982; Coplin & Houts, 1991). Webster-Stratton and Hammond (1990) found that predictors of successful outcome at posttreatment and at a 1-year follow-up were similar for mothers and fathers when parental ratings of child behavior served as the measure of outcome.

Similarly, single-parent status has failed to emerge as a consistent predictor of treatment outcome when examined as an entity. Although a number of investigators have reported single-parent status to be associated with increased risk of dropping out of parent training or with a lack of treatment success (e.g., Dumas & Albin, 1986; Strain et al., 1981, 1982; Webster-Stratton, 1985a, 1985b; Webster-Stratton & Hammond, 1990), other investigators have failed to obtain similar results (e.g., Dumas & Wahler, 1983; Fleischman, 1981; Holden et al., 1990). In one investigation, single mothers were *less* likely to drop out than were married mothers (Scott & Stradling, 1987). Serketich and Dumas (1996) did not find either single-parent status or SES to be associated with effect size in their meta-analytic study of parent training outcome. Similar findings have been reported with respect to Kazdin's (1996b) intervention (PSST, parent training, or the combination) (Kazdin, 1995a) and to interventions for fire setting (Kolko et al., 1991), although Kazdin et al. (1993) did find that single-parent status was associated with dropout.

Lower SES has been associated with subsequent dropout in at least one parent training program (McMahon, Forehand, Griest, & Wells, 1981), although for mothers who complete that program, SES did not affect treatment outcome (Rogers et al., 1981). Similar findings have been reported with respect to dropout from Kazdin's (1996b) intervention (PSST, parent training, or the combination) (Kazdin, 1990; Kazdin et al., 1993), and to outcome for other parent training interventions (e.g., Holden et al., 1990; Thompson, Grow, Ruma, Daly, & Burke, 1993) and for MST (Henggeler et al., 1992). As noted above, maternal insularity has been associated with failure to maintain improvements in parent and child behavior (Wahler, 1980; Wahler & Afton, 1980). In those earlier studies, insularity was confounded with socioeconomic disadvantage, in that all of the insular mothers were also highly disadvantaged. Dumas and Wahler (1983) conducted two studies in which they examined the relative predictive power of maternal insularity and socioeconomic disadvantage at a 1-year follow-up. The latter measure was a composite index made up of six sociodemographic variables: family income, maternal education, family composition (one-parent vs. two-parent families), family size, source of referral, and area of residence. The index of socioeconomic disadvantage and maternal insularity each contributed unique variance to predicting outcome, and together they accounted for 49% of the variance in both studies. Noninsular but disadvantaged families (or vice versa) had approximately a 50% chance of having a favorable outcome, whereas those mothers who were insular and disadvantaged were virtually assured of failure at the 1-year follow-up. Other investigators have reported similar findings with similar indices of socioeconomic disadvantage (Dumas, 1986; Routh et al., 1995; Webster-Stratton, 1985b), and with cumulative counts of total risk factors (e.g., Kazdin et al., 1993; Prinz & Miller, 1994). It is interesting to note that use of a composite index may enhance predictability of outcome (at least with respect to parent training), over and above the use of single indices.

Characteristics of Intervention

There has been significant progress over the past few years in the attention paid to the role of engagement in interventions for children with CP. Of prime importance has been the development of conceptual frameworks for examining the engagement process in general (e.g., Kazdin, Holland, & Crowley, 1997; Prinz & Miller, 1996; Webster-Stratton & Herbert, 1993, 1994) and therapist behavior in particular (e.g., Patterson & Chamberlain, 1994). Prinz and Miller present four domains that they posit affect parental engagement in family-based interventions for CP: (1) parents' personal expectations, attributions, and beliefs (e.g., expectations about the nature of the intervention, attributions about the source of the child's problem and/or about their own self-efficacy) (see also Johnston, 1996); (2) situational demands and constraints (e.g., financial and social stressors, marital and personal adjustment, daily hassles, and competing demands of other activities); (3) intervention characteristics (e.g., group vs. individual parent training, home vs. clinic delivery, type of intervention, homework); and (4) relationships with the therapist. In an earlier study, Prinz and Miller (1994) demonstrated that participation variables (e.g., in-session quality of participation, homework completion) were stronger predictors of dropout than were various child and family characteristics. Kazdin et al. (1997) present a similar "barriers-to-treatment" model. Their model focuses on (1) stressors and obstacles that compete with intervention; (2) intervention demands and issues; (3) perceived relevance of the intervention; and (4) relationship with the therapist. Kazdin et al. demonstrated that these aspects of engagement added additional explanatory variance to predicting dropout from intervention (PSST, parent training, or a combination), over and above that provided by the child, parent, and family factors described above. Furthermore, there was a clear dose–response relationship between the number of barriers experienced by the family and the likelihood of subsequent dropout.

The work of Webster-Stratton and her colleagues (e.g., Webster-Stratton & Herbert, 1994; Webster-Stratton & Spitzer, 1996) has been especially innovative, as it has involved the use of qualitative research methods to describe the process of intervention from the perspective of the parents. Participants in the BASIC version of her parent training program went through five phases during the course of intervention (Spitzer, Webster-Stratton, & Hollinsworth, 1991): acknowledging the problem, alternating despair and hope, "tempering the dream" (settling for less than total recovery), tailoring the program to their own family situations, and coping effectively. Parents' experiences during a 3-year period following the intervention have also been analyzed (Webster-Stratton & Herbert, 1994; Webster-Stratton & Spitzer, 1996).

The importance of the therapist's establishing a collaborative relationship with the parent during parent training has been emphasized, and therapist activities in such a relationship have been delineated (Sanders & Dadds, 1993; Webster-Stratton & Herbert, 1993, 1994). For example, Webster-Stratton and Herbert have delineated a number of roles for the therapist in the context of the BASIC parent training program (Webster-Stratton, 1996a): building a supportive relationship, empowering parents, active teaching, interpreting, "leading" (e.g., dealing with resistance), and "prophesying" (e.g., anticipating problems and setbacks, resistance to change, and positive change/success). These roles are probably applicable to other family-based interventions for children with CP as well.

Other investigators have examined the role of therapist characteristics in predicting the outcome of interventions with children or adolescents with CP. Alexander, Barton, Schiavo, and Parsons (1976) examined the role of therapist characteristics in predicting outcome (as defined by completion of treatment and recidivism rate) for families that participated in FFT. Prior to the start of treatment, graduate student therapists were rated on a variety of characteristics that clustered into two dimensions. Relationship characteristics included affect-behavior integration, warmth, and humor, whereas Structuring characteristics included directiveness and self-confidence. The Relationship dimension accounted for 45% of the variance in predicting treatment outcome; the Structuring dimension accounted for an additional 15% of the variance. Additional research from this group suggests that therapist gender is associated both with different verbal styles for parents and adolescents and with different therapist responses in the first sessions of FFT (Mas, Alexander, & Barton, 1985; Newberry, Alexander, & Turner, 1991), and that reframing statements are associated with more positive within-session attitudes with adolescents than with mothers (Robbins, Alexander, Newell, & Turner, 1996).

Researchers involved with TFM (Achievement Place) have also provided data concerning the relationship of the therapist's (in this case, the teaching parent's) behavior to intervention outcome (see Braukmann, Ramp, Tigner, & Wolf, 1984, for a review). As noted earlier, teaching parents undergo an intensive year-long training process. Use of the particular teaching behaviors (description, demonstration, use of rationales, providing opportunities for practicing behaviors, providing positive consequences) is positively correlated with higher levels of youth satisfaction and negatively correlated with self-reports of delinquency. Teaching parents' use of such relationship-building behaviors as joking, showing concern, and enthusiasm has also been shown to increase youths' satisfaction with the interactions (Willner et al., 1977).

Patterson and his colleagues have an ongoing program of research that has focused on the role of parental resistance in the OSLC parent training intervention. Patterson and Chamberlain (1994) have presented a conceptualization of parental resistance that includes both within-session resistance (refusal, stated inability to perform) and out-of-session resistance (failure to do homework). Initial resistance is thought to be a function of the parent's history of parent–child interaction, preexisting parental psychopathology, and social disadvantage, as well as therapist behavior (Patterson & Chamberlain, 1988). Patterson and Chamberlain (1994) have demonstrated that these contextual variables are associated with parental resistance throughout parent training. According to their "struggle hypothesis," parental resistance is expected to increase initially, but then eventually to decrease as the parent begins to meet with success.

High levels of resistance in the first two therapy sessions are associated with subsequent dropout (Chamberlain, Patterson, Reid, Kavanagh, & Forgatch, 1984). In one study, the directive therapist behaviors of "teach" and "confront" increased the likelihood of parental noncooperative behavior within the session, whereas supportive and facilitative therapist behaviors had the opposite effect (Patterson & Forgatch, 1985). This poses an intriguing paradox for therapists: The directive therapist behaviors

that seem to be intrinsic to parent training also seem to be those that predict parent noncompliance during treatment. Patterson and Forgatch conclude that two sets of therapist skills are required: "standard" parent training skills, and "relationship characteristics" (to use Alexander et al.'s [1976] term) to deal with parental noncompliance. Growth curve analyses of parental resistance over the course of parent training have shown a pattern of increasing resistance that peaks at about the midpoint, followed by a gradual decrease in resistance (Stoolmiller, Duncan, Bank, & Patterson, 1993). In addition, Stoolmiller et al. reported that chronic maternal resistance (i.e., failure to work through resistance issues) was associated with child arrest over a 2-year follow-up period. In general, these findings are supportive of the struggle hypothesis proposed by Patterson and Chamberlain (1994).

Comparison Studies

We divide our discussion of comparison studies into those comparing interventions with (1) no-treatment, waiting-list, attention placebo, or normal control conditions; and (2) other forms of intervention.

Control Conditions

Each of the three parent training programs described earlier in the chapter (Forehand & McMahon, 1981; Patterson et al., 1975; Webster-Stratton, 1996a) has been positively evaluated in comparison with no-treatment and waiting-list control conditions (e.g., Peed et al., 1977; Webster-Stratton, 1984; Wiltz & Patterson, 1974) or an attention placebo condition (Walter & Gilmore, 1973). Furthermore, comparisons with groups of nonreferred "normal" children and their parents have indicated greater similarity in parent and child behaviors and/or parental perceptions of children after treatment (e.g., Forehand et al., 1980; Patterson, 1974). Other investigators have also reported the superiority of parent training over waiting-list control conditions (e.g., Bernal, Klinnert, & Schultz, 1980; Sayger, Horne, Walker, & Passmore, 1988; Scott & Stradling, 1987), although Bernal et al. did not find any differences at posttreatment for parent and child behaviors observed in the home. However, nonrandom assignment to the waiting-list condition and other methodological difficulties limit the robustness of their findings.

Family-based interventions with adolescents have also demonstrated superiority over no-treatment control conditions. FFT (Alexander & Parsons, 1982) has been shown to lead to greater changes in family communication immediately after treatment and to lower recidivism at 6–18 months after treatment (Alexander & Parsons, 1973; Parsons & Alexander, 1973), as well as to a greater decrease in sibling involvement with the juvenile courts over a 2.5- to 3.5-year follow-up period (Klein et al., 1977). Parental perceptions of their adolescents' adjustment improved significantly as a function of MST (Henggeler et al., 1986), whereas there was no change in a normal comparison group.

Grizenko et al. (1993) compared children in a multicomponent day treatment program to children in a waiting-list control condition. Children in the intervention condition displayed greater improvements in parents' ratings of child behavior problems and in the children's self-report of personal adjustment.

Several evaluations of school-based interventions with children with CP have employed control groups. For example, the comprehensive CLASS and RECESS programs developed by the CORBEH group have been shown to be effective, compared to no-treatment control conditions (e.g., Hops et al., 1978; Walker et al., 1981, 1988). The preliminary investigation of the school-wide intervention model developed by Sugai et al. (1990, 1993) employed a comparison with a nonintervention control school. A no-contact condition was employed by Kahle and Kelley (1994) in their evaluation of different strategies for improving homework performance. In evaluating the national implementation of his bullying intervention program, Olweus (1996) utilized an age cohort quasi-experimental design that permitted time-lagged comparisons between intervention children and children of the same age who had not yet received the intervention.

Investigators evaluating skills training treatments for children with CP have, for the most part, done an exemplary job of including no-treatment and/or attention placebo comparison conditions in those evaluations. Both behavioral (e.g., Spence & Marzillier, 1981) and cognitive-behavioral (e.g., Kazdin et al., 1987b; Lochman et al., 1984; Prinz et al., 1994) interventions have consistently demonstrated superiority over the comparison conditions on a variety of measures. Similarly, multicomponent skills training interventions have also demonstrated their superiority over no-treatment and/or attention placebo comparison conditions (e.g., Glick & Goldstein, 1987; Kazdin et al., 1987a; Leeman

et al., 1993). Unfortunately, as noted above, generalization of these effects to naturalistic settings and over time has not always occurred.

The only study to employ a control condition in evaluating the effects of a psychosocial intervention for covert CP was Reid et al.'s (1980) investigation concerning stealing. Inclusion of a nonrandomly assigned subgroup of families that served as a waiting-list control group suggested that parental reports of decreased stealing were a function of the treatment program and not simply due to the passage of time. Using a drug–placebo crossover design, Hinshaw et al. (1992) found that boys with ADHD who were treated with methylphenidate engaged in less stealing and property destruction than when they were receiving a drug placebo; furthermore, these levels were comparable to those exhibited by a normal control sample.

Several other studies have investigated the relative effectiveness of methylphenidate and a drug placebo in affecting overt CP (e.g., Hinshaw, Buhrmester, & Heller, 1989; Hinshaw, Henker, et al., 1989; Klein et al., 1994). Double-blind placebo trials have also been conducted with lithium (e.g., Campbell et al., 1984, 1995; Klein et al., 1994), clonidine (Hunt et al., 1986), and carbamazepine (Cueva et al., 1996).

The large-scale preventive interventions described above have consistently compared their preventive interventions to no-intervention control groups. This is true for both early intervention programs (e.g., Berrueta-Clement et al., 1984) and those that have focused specifically on CP (e.g., Tremblay et al., 1996). The Montreal study (Tremblay et al., 1996) also employed an attention placebo condition. Some of the school-based preventive interventions have employed both separate control schools and control classrooms within intervention schools (e.g., Kellam & Rebok, 1992).

Other Interventions as Comparisons

As evidence for the efficacy of various interventions with children with CP has accumulated, increased attention has been focused on the relative efficacy of these interventions compared to other forms of treatment. Family-based interventions with preadolescents have been compared with family systems therapies (e.g., Patterson & Chamberlain, 1988; Wells & Egan, 1988), the STEP program (Baum et al., 1986), client-centered therapy (Bernal et al., 1980), and available community mental health services (Patterson et al., 1982). With the exception of the Bernal et al. investigation, which indicated superiority of behavioral parent training over client-centered therapy on parent report measures at posttreatment but not at 6- and 12-month follow-ups, the other comparative investigations have supported the relative efficacy of behavioral parent training.

Family-based interventions with adolescents have also been compared with a variety of alternative treatments. Both the OSLC program (Bank et al., 1991) and MST (Borduin et al., 1995; Henggeler et al., 1986, 1992, 1997) have been favorably compared with "existing services" conditions, which provide the standard array of mental health or probation services available to delinquent adolescents in those communities. For example, in the Bank et al. investigation, these services included family therapy of an unspecified nature and, for many of the youths, group sessions concerning drug use. In a series of investigations examining the efficacy of FFT (Alexander & Parsons, 1973; Klein et al., 1977; Parsons & Alexander, 1973), both client-centered and psychodynamic counseling conditions were included. These alternative treatments proved to be no more effective (and sometimes less effective) than the no-treatment control condition with this sample of adolescent status offenders and their families. Barton et al. (1985) demonstrated that multiply offending adolescents receiving FFT had a lower recidivism rate over a 15-month follow-up period than did comparable adolescents in an alternative treatment condition (primarily group homes). Similarly, Gordon's adaptation of FFT has been shown to be significantly more effective than probation only (Gordon et al., 1988, 1995).

Community-based residential programs such as TFM (Achievement Place; Kirigin, 1996) have not fared as well in comparison with their counterparts, and have not, to our knowledge, been compared with no-treatment or attention placebo control conditions. As noted above, several evaluations have indicated that the superiority of TFM over other types of group homes is limited, for the most part, to the period when the youths are active participants in the program (e.g., Kirigin & Wolf, 1994; Kirigin et al., 1982; Weinrott et al., 1982; Wolf et al., 1987).

Therapeutic foster care, as exemplified by TFC (Chamberlain, 1994), has been compared to a variety of existing community services, such as group homes and/or training schools (Chamberlain, 1990; Chamberlain & Moore, in press; Chamberlain & Reid, 1991). TFC has also been compared to a condition in which foster

parents were untrained (Chamberlain et al., 1992). As noted above, TFC has been demonstrated to be more effective in outcome and in cost than these alternative services.

Several studies have compared various forms of treatment in the school. For example, studies have shown that combined interventions that include both positive and negative contingencies are more effective than either alone (see Rosen et al., 1990; Walker et al., 1995); other studies have assessed the relative effectiveness of individual versus group contingencies in token programs (see Pigott & Heggie, 1986). Kahle and Kelley (1994) compared parent training, goal setting, and parental monitoring alone as interventions for improving homework performance.

Various types of skills training interventions have been compared with each other or with other forms of intervention. Kazdin et al. (1987b, 1989) reported the superiority of PSST with inpatient and outpatient children over a nondirective relationship therapy condition, both at treatment termination and at a 1-year follow-up. Similar cognitive-behavioral skills interventions have been shown to be more effective than supportive/insight-oriented therapy (Kendall et al., 1990) and an inpatient activity group (Kolko et al., 1990). Michelson et al. (1983) reported that behavioral social skills training was superior to cognitive-behavioral skills training in maintenance of effects. Finally, Kazdin et al. (1992) reported that the combination of parent training and PSST was superior to either intervention alone.

With respect to interventions for covert CP behaviors, several investigators have compared multiple interventions. Henderson (1983) presented descriptive data suggesting that children who received his behavioral ICT program engaged in stealing less frequently over a 2-year period than children who had received a variety of other interventions, singly or in combination (e.g., counseling, placement in a residential setting or special education class). Kolko et al. (1991) reported that a cognitive-behavioral group treatment that focused on fire safety skills training was superior to a discussion group. In an ongoing study of the relative effectiveness of fire safety skills training administered in community versus mental health settings, Kolko (1996) reported comparable reductions in fire involvement based on parent report, but greater reductions in fire involvement for the psychosocial treatment based on child report. Adler et al. (1994) found no advantage of adding an adaptation of the community-based FEMA intervention program to the provision of basic educational materials, whether referral to a mental health specialist was involved or not.

In a few studies, the relative effectiveness of two medications for dealing with CP behaviors has been assessed. Klein et al. (1994) reported methylphenidate to be more effective than lithium, which was comparable to the placebo in an outpatient sample of children diagnosed with CD. However, in an inpatient sample of children with CD, lithium and haloperidol were both more effective than a placebo (Campbell et al., 1984). More children responded positively to lithium than to haloperidol, and there were many fewer side effects.

Preventive interventions focused on CP have usually not been systematically compared with other preventive interventions. Kellam and Rebok (1992) compared the Good Behavior Game with a Mastery Learning intervention designed to improve reading achievement. Because the Mastery Learning intervention was not expected to have a direct effect on CP behaviors, it has been labeled as an "active control" by Kellam et al. (1994, p. 261).

CONCLUSIONS

In this chapter, we have provided an overview of the characteristics of children with CP and their families, outlined suggested assessment strategies, and described and critically evaluated a variety of interventions. In this section of the chapter, we briefly summarize the most salient points of our review concerning intervention, with particular emphasis on changes since the first edition of this chapter appeared in 1989. We conclude by providing some suggestions for future research.

It is still the case that studies of family-based interventions with preadolescent children with CP (i.e., parent training, behavioral family therapy) continue to constitute the largest and most sophisticated body of intervention research in this area, and to present the most promising results. Not only has immediate treatment outcome been quantified by changes in parents' and children's behavior and in parental perceptions of the children's adjustment in a large number of investigations, but generalization of such effects to the home, over reasonable follow-up periods (3 years posttreatment and longer), to untreated siblings, and to untreated behaviors has been demonstrated for many of these families as well. The social validity of these effects has also been documented by a number of the parent training programs. Several of the most extensively validated parent training programs (Forehand & McMahon, 1981; Patterson et al., 1975; Webster-Stratton, 1996a) provide commercially available therapist manuals and/or materials, which should aid in the dissemination of these programs and facilitate replication by investigators not associated with their original development and evaluation.

Investigators associated with these family-based interventions have broadened the basic parent training model to enhance outcome and generalization. This has resulted in the assessment of a wide variety of variables in predicting the outcome of this type of intervention (the ongoing development and elaboration of which is now referred to as the "behavioral family therapy" model; Griest & Wells, 1983), as well as in the development of adjunctive treatment modules to deal with marital conflict, parental distress, and the like.

One of the most significant advances over the past 10 years has been the application and evaluation of family-based approaches with adolescents who are engaging in serious and chronic delinquent offending. Although the overall body of research is not as extensive as that supporting family-based interventions with preadolescents, there have been some very encouraging findings from different investigators. For example, results of evaluations of Gordon et al.'s (1988, 1995) adaptation of FFT suggest that FFT is effective not only with the status offenders treated in the earlier outcome studies, but with more serious offenders as well. Most significant, however, has been the series of large-scale studies by Henggeler and his colleagues (e.g., Borduin et al., 1995; Henggeler et al., 1992) that have demonstrated the effectiveness and generalization of MST with chronic and severe offenders. The emphases on focusing on multiple risk factors in multiple social contexts, and on using carefully selected, developmentally appropriate interventions, represent a state-of-the-art approach for dealing with severe CP. It is also consistent with more prevention-oriented approaches to CP. Also noteworthy are the attempts by these investigators to delineate the key principles of the intervention (Henggeler et al., in press) and to disseminate the intervention in "real-life" settings (e.g., Henggeler et al., 1997).

Community-based residential programs, such as TFM (Achievement Place; Willner et al., 1978), have yet to demonstrate their superiority to nonbehavioral interventions of this type in terms of reducing recidivism once adolescents have left the treatment setting. Systematic programming of aftercare services is widely recognized as necessary if residential programs are to have a meaningful long-term impact on the behavior of adolescents with CP. Other systems of care, such as the TFC program developed and evaluated by Chamberlain and her colleagues (e.g., Chamberlain, 1994; Chamberlain & Moore, in press), appear promising. TFC seems to represent an important component in a continuum of services for children and adolescents with CP; in some cases, it may represent an alternative to residential placements. Day treatment programs, such as those described by Kolko (in press) and Grizenko et al. (1993), may also prove to be useful avenues of intervention, although they require more extensive evaluation.

Evaluation of school-based interventions with children with CP continues to be hindered by a number of definitional and assessment problems. Although there have been dozens of studies documenting strategies for producing changes in "disruptive" or "acting-out" behavior in the classroom, it is unclear what proportion of the children in those studies were engaging in significant levels of CP behaviors. There have not been many new developments in classroom management procedures for dealing with children with CP. The focus seems to have shifted toward school-based approaches, either as stand-alone packages of interventions such as CLASS and RECESS (Hops & Walker, 1988; Walker et al., 1984) and Project PREPARE (Sugai et al., 1990, 1993), or as part of a multicomponent intervention such as Fast Track (Conduct Problems Prevention Research Group, 1992).

Skills training approaches have continued to be widely employed with children with CP and have focused on social skills, anger control, interpersonal problem solving, moral reasoning, and the like. These interventions are being derived from increasingly sophisticated and developmentally sensitive theoretical models. Although some of these interventions have not demonstrated evidence of generalization to settings outside the treatment context, the situation has improved significantly since we last reviewed this area. Lochman's anger control program (e.g., Lochman et al., 1984) and Kazdin's (1996b) PSST are notable for the rigor and extent of the evaluations of their respective interventions. (However, as noted above, the latter has relied exclusively on parent and teacher report to assess outcome at home and at school.) Kazdin's evaluations have also suggested the enhanced effectiveness of combining PSST with a parent training intervention (Kazdin et al., 1992).

There continues to be a relative dearth of knowledge about the development, assessment, and treatment of covert CP, such as stealing, lying, and fire setting. The OSLC intervention to treat stealing (Reid et al., 1980) has not been well evaluated, and seems limited to stealing that comes to the attention of the parents. There is even less empirical support for other interventions that address stealing. Although there has been a significant increase in knowledge concerning the phenomenology of childhood fire setting, with a corresponding development of clinically useful assessment methods, these advances have not yet been translated into clearly effective interventions for fire setting. There is little empirically evaluated information to guide the clinician in the selection of treatment methods for these problems, although empirical validation of typologies of fire setting (e.g., Kolko & Kazdin, 1991b) may lead to enhanced intervention.

The application of psychopharmacological interventions to CP in children and adolescents is a relatively new phenomenon. Evidence that stimulant medications such as methylphenidate may decrease both overt (aggression) and some covert (stealing) CP behaviors in children who are comorbid for both ADHD and CP is encouraging (e.g., Abikoff et al., 1987; Hinshaw et al., 1992). However, these findings should be considered suggestive. Some studies indicate that lithium may be effective in treating children who exhibit "explosive" forms of aggressive behavior (e.g., Campbell et al., 1984). However, there are conflicting findings, and additional research is needed to clarify the situation. Of particular importance is the need to disentangle medication effects from those of ongoing psychosocial interventions in applied evaluations, and to determine whether there are synergistic effects. At present, there is little evidence for the clinical utility of other medications for treating CP.

Interest in interventions for the *prevention* of CP has burgeoned over the past 10 years. There is now evidence from a variety of early intervention programs that they may have long-term preventive effects with respect to CP (Yoshikawa,

1994). Other preventive interventions have focused specifically on the prevention of CP. These programs have taken many forms, ranging from universal school-based interventions such as that reported by Kellam and Rebok (1992) to ones that intervene in multiple social contexts such as the school and home with high-risk populations (e.g., Conduct Problems Prevention Research Group, 1992). The preventive intervention described by Tremblay et al. (1996) has presented some of the strongest data indicating the long-term effectiveness of such a preventive approach.

Advances

We would like to note what we see as some significant advances in the field that have direct implications for intervention with children and adolescents with CP. First and foremost, we view the tremendous growth in knowledge concerning the early-starter pathway of CP as the most significant advance. By delineating the developmental trajectory that these children follow (development), by elaborating on the various risk and protective factors that affect this trajectory (context), and by identifying potential windows of opportunity in which intervention may be most salient because of the interplay of these developmental and contextual processes over time (transaction), therapists and clinical researchers have been presented with a conceptual model that can help to guide assessment and the design and selection of interventions (McMahon & Estes, 1997). Forehand and Wierson (1993) have provided a number of examples of how developmental theory can be utilized in designing interventions for children with CP. The Fast Track preventive intervention (Conduct Problems Prevention Research Group, 1992) is one example of how the early-starter model has guided the timing, content, and focus of the intervention.

A second advance that is closely tied to the first has been the development and evaluation of multicomponent interventions to address the multiple social systems affecting the child with CP. These combined interventions have included adjunctive procedures to a single intervention (e.g., training in social learning principles; McMahon, Forehand, & Greist, 1981), multiple interventions of the same type (e.g., CLASS; Walker & Hops, 1979), and multiple interventions of different types (e.g., MST; Henggeler & Borduin, 1990; Henggeler et al., in press). Multicomponent interventions have been applied in prevention contexts (e.g., Tremblay et al., 1996) as well.

However, we concur with the cautions provided by Kazdin (1996a) in his thoughtful discussion of the conceptual and methodological issues involved in the use of multicomponent interventions. Simply providing more types of interventions is unlikely to be effective in the treatment and prevention of CP. We have been impressed with the conceptual and empirical bases for the nature and timing of these combined interventions. Use of a developmental model of CP (e.g., Forehand & Wierson, 1993) and a careful assessment (McMahon & Estes, 1997) are essential first steps in the selection and integration of components for intervening with CP. It is also the case that much more work needs to be done in regard to this treatment selection process (Kazdin, 1996a; see also below).

A third advance is the increased attention being paid to evaluating interventions with the most difficult-to-treat segment of the spectrum of children with CP—that is, multiply offending chronic adolescent delinquents. The evaluations of MST (Henggeler & Borduin, 1990; Henggeler et al., in press), Gordon et al.'s (1988, 1995) adaptation of FFT, and TFC (Chamberlain, 1994) are especially encouraging in this regard.

A fourth advance has been the increased attention given to the prevention of CP. Development of the prevention perspective has been stimulated in part by increased knowledge about the early-starter pathway of CP. That early intervention programs can have long-term preventive effects on CP (Yoshikawa, 1994) is especially intriguing. It also provides some support for suggestions that family-based interventions such as parent training may have significant preventive effects if they are applied during the preschool period (Reid, 1993; Sanders, 1996). More intensive and broadly focused interventions that target those populations at highest risk for CP (e.g., Conduct Problems Prevention Research Group, 1992; Tremblay et al., 1996) also appear promising, but we must await the long-term outcomes of such programs.

A fifth advance concerns the clinical and empirical interest in describing important elements of family engagement and resistance in parent training interventions for CP (e.g., Kazdin et al., 1997; Patterson & Chamberlain, 1994; Prinz & Miller, 1996; Webster-Stratton & Herbert, 1994; Webster-Stratton & Spitzer, 1991). Particularly important has been the development of conceptual models (e.g., Kazdin et al., 1997; Prinz &

Miller, 1996) to guide research in this area. Similar attention needs to be directed to process issues pertaining to the engagement of children with CP in child-focused interventions.

Areas of Needed Research

We would like to highlight five areas that we feel require additional attention. The first has to do with the development of reliable and valid treatment selection guidelines. As we and others (e.g., Kazdin, 1996a) have noted, a comprehensive, empirically based treatment selection model for children with CP is greatly needed. We believe that the early-starter pathway is a useful starting point for such an endeavor, in that it provides guidance concerning the extent of CP behavior and the contexts in which it is most likely to occur.

A second area of concern has to do with the serious lack of attention paid to issues of comorbidity in the development and evaluation of interventions for children with CP. For example, although it is widely known that there is an extremely high rate of comorbidity between CP and ADHD, most interventions have been developed to deal with either CP or ADHD, not both. A recent investigation by Barkley et al. (1996) is one of the few intervention studies to specifically target children who are comorbid for ADHD and CP. Similar concerns could be raised with respect to various other comorbid disorders, such as depression and anxiety. The important work by Frick and his colleagues (e.g., Christian et al., 1997) concerning psychopathy in children suggests that different interventions may be needed when children present with both CP and psychopathic features.

A third area of concern is the failure of researchers and clinicians alike to attend to the possibility of gender differences in the development of CP, their sequelae, and their prevention and treatment. Although there is now a significant amount of research being directed to the possibility of different developmental trajectories and sequelae of CP for girls and boys, this has not carried over into intervention research. In fact, as noted above, most investigators have not even assessed whether their interventions are differentially effective with boys and girls. Although there is some evidence to suggest that girls may respond to current interventions comparably to boys, this does not preclude the possibility that gender-specific interventions might result in greater effectiveness and/or generalization.

Even less attention has been applied to the question of whether the effectiveness of current interventions is moderated by the ethnicity of children with CP. Prinz and Miller (1991) suggest three levels at which interventions for children with CP can be made more culturally sensitive. First, the interface between the intervention and the cultural group can be enhanced (e.g., by matching the ethnicity of the intervention staff to that of the target population). Second, the content of the intervention can be adapted for a particular ethnic group (e.g., by tailoring materials or examples to enhance the relevance of the intervention). Third, an intervention that is specifically developed for a particular ethnic group can be developed. An example of this approach is presented by Hammond and Yung (1993), who describe a violence prevention program for African American adolescent males.

Finally, it is important to raise the issue of possible iatrogenic effects as a function of intervention. Two examples of how such effects may occur are provided. As early as 1985, Elliott et al. cautioned that group-based approaches to treating delinquents may actually contribute to the maintenance and furtherance of delinquent activities. Interesting data from Dishion and Andrews (1995), in which high-risk adolescents who received group-based treatment alone actually showed increases in CP behaviors from pre- to posttreatment, support such a notion; they contribute to a rationale for development of treatments that minimize the influence of adolescent peers and immerse the youngsters in nondelinquent settings. It is important to note that this iatrogenic effect may be age-specific to adolescents. Investigations that have employed peer groups of younger children with CP have not found these negative effects. However, it may also be the case that the inclusion of low-risk children or adolescents ("norms") in these groups may decrease the likelihood of negative effects (e.g., Bierman et al., 1987; Prinz et al., 1994; Tremblay et al., 1995). Further research is clearly indicated to delineate the parameters of this phenomenon.

A second example of potential iatrogenic effects pertains to the use of psychopharmacological treatments for CP. Negative physical side effects are a potential risk with any medication; they should be considered in selecting the medication, and should be monitored throughout the intervention. For example, Campbell et al. (1984) reported that lithium and haloperidol were comparable in the extent to which they decreased explosive aggressive behaviors in a sample of inpatient children. However, lithium had significantly fewer adverse side effects than haloperidol, indicating that it would be a better choice. The possibility of psychosocial iatrogenic effects from these medications should also be considered (Gadow, 1991). These might include children's developing external attributions of control, learning to use medication as a way of coping with stress, or possibly becoming more likely to develop later substance use problems. Hinshaw et al. (1992) reported that although methylphenidate reduced stealing and property destruction in a sample of boys with ADHD, cheating was increased!

In conclusion, we are encouraged by the significant advances that have been made in knowledge concerning the development, assessment, and intervention with children with CP over the past 10 years. We are also sobered and challenged by the limitations of what is still unknown about how best to prevent and treat CP. Our hope is that the issues raised in this chapter will serve as an impetus for clinicians and researchers alike to address these limitations.

ACKNOWLEDGMENTS

Preparation of this chapter was partially supported by National Institute of Mental Health Grant No. R18 MH50951 to Robert J. McMahon, and by Center for Substance Abuse Prevention Grant No. 1UR6SPO7956–01 and National Institute on Drug Abuse Grant No. DA08453–04 to Karen C. Wells. We would like to acknowledge with appreciation the clerical, administrative, and editorial assistance of Jill Smith, Delphine Mozlowski, and Matt Vrablik.

NOTES

1. This material is based on McMahon and Estes (1997).

2. Gender is the most consistently documented risk factor for CP (Robins, 1991). However, much of the research on CP has focused exclusively on boys, or, when girls have been included, has failed to consider possible gender effects. Space considerations preclude discussion of possible factors and processes that may be responsible for these sex differences. Instead, the reader is referred to Eme and Kavanaugh (1995), Zahn-Waxler (1993), and Zoccolillo (1993).

3. Portions of this section are based on McMahon (1994).

4. We use the term "therapist" in the broadest sense in this chapter, to include anyone engaged in the delivery of treatment or prevention activities.

5. However, given the strong positive correlations between stealing and lying noted above, children who steal may not be veridical in their self-reports.

6. These commands are referred to as "alpha commands." "Beta commands" are those to which the child has no opportunity to demonstrate compliance because of vagueness or parental interruption (e.g., "Act your age").

REFERENCES

Abidin, R. R. (1988). *Parenting Alliance Inventory.* Unpublished scale, University of Virginia.

Abidin, R. R. (1995). *Parenting Stress Index—professional manual* (3rd ed.). Odessa, FL: Psychological Assessment Resources.

Abidin, R. R., & Brunner, J. F. (1995). Development of a Parenting Alliance Inventory. *Journal of Clinical Child Psychology, 24,* 31–40.

Abidin, R. R., Jenkins, C. L., & McGaughey, M. C. (1992). The relationship of early family variables to children's subsequent behavioral adjustment. *Journal of Clinical Child Psychology, 21,* 60–69.

Abikoff, H., & Klein, R. G. (1992). Attention-Deficit Hyperactivity and Conduct Disorder: Comorbidity and implications for treatment. *Journal of Consulting and Clinical Psychology, 60,* 881–892.

Abikoff, H., Klein, R., Klass, E., & Ganeles, D. (1987, October). Methylphenidate in the treatment of conduct disordered children. In H. Abikoff (Chair), *Diagnosis and treatment issues in children with disruptive behavior disorders.* Symposium conducted at the annual meeting of the American Academy of Child and Adolescent Psychiatry, Washington, DC.

Abramowitz, A. J., & O'Leary, S. G. (1991). Behavioral interventions for the classroom: Implications for students with ADHD. *School Psychology Review, 20,* 220–234.

Achenbach, T. M. (1991a). *Manual for the Child Behavior Checklist/4–18 and 1991 Profile.* Burlington: University of Vermont, Department of Psychiatry.

Achenbach, T. M. (1991b). *Manual for the Teacher's Report Form and 1991 Profile.* Burlington: University of Vermont, Department of Psychiatry.

Achenbach, T. M. (1991c). *Manual for the Youth Self-Report and 1991 Profile.* Burlington: University of Vermont, Department of Psychiatry.

Achenbach, T. M. (1992). *Manual for the Child Behavior Checklist/2–3 and 1992 Profile.* Burlington: University of Vermont, Department of Psychiatry.

Achenbach, T. M. (1993). Implications of multiaxial empirically based assessment for behavior therapy with children. *Behavior Therapy, 24,* 91–116.

Achenbach, T. M., & Edelbrock, C. S. (1981). Behavioral problems and competencies reported by parents of normal and disturbed children aged four through sixteen. *Monographs of the Society for Research in Child Development, 46* (Serial No. 188).

Adler, R., Nunn, R., Northam, E., Lebnan, V., & Ross, R. (1994). Secondary prevention of childhood firesetting. *Journal of the American Academy of Child and Adolescent Psychiatry, 33,* 1194–1202.

Alexander, J. F., Barton, C., Schiavo, R. S., & Parsons, B. V. (1976). Systems–behavioral intervention with families of delinquents: Therapist characteristics, family behavior, and outcome. *Journal of Consulting and Clinical Psychology, 44,* 656–664.

Alexander, J. F., Jameson, P. B., Newell, R. M., & Gunderson, D. (1996). Changing cognitive schemas: A necessary antecedent to changing behaviors in dysfunctional families? In K. S. Dobson & K. D. Craig (Eds.), *Advances in cognitive-behavioral therapy* (pp. 174–191). Thousand Oaks, CA: Sage.

Alexander, J. F., & Parsons, B. V. (1973). Short-term behavioral intervention with delinquent families: Impact on family process and recidivism. *Journal of Abnormal Psychology, 81,* 219–225.

Alexander, J. F., & Parsons, B. (1982). *Functional Family Therapy.* Monterey, CA: Brooks/Cole.

Alexander, J. F., Waldron, H. B., Barton, C., & Mas, C. H. (1989). The minimizing of blaming attributions and behaviors in delinquent families. *Journal of Consulting and Clinical Psychology, 57,* 19–24.

Alexander, J. F., Waldron, H. B., Newberry, A. M., & Liddle, N. (1988). Family approaches to treating delinquents. In E. W. Nunnally, C. S. Chilman, & F. M. Cox (Eds.), *Mental illness, delinquency, addictions, and neglect* (pp. 128–146). Newbury Park, CA: Sage.

Alpern, L., & Lyons-Ruth, K. (1993). Preschool children at social risk: Chronicity and timing of maternal depressive symptoms and child behavior problems at school and at home. *Development and Psychopathology, 5,* 371–387.

Amato, P. R., & Keith, B. (1991). Parental divorce and the well-being of children: A meta analysis. *Psychological Bulletin, 110,* 26–46.

American Psychiatric Association. (1980). *Diagnostic and statistical manual of mental disorders* (3rd ed.). Washington, DC: Author.

American Psychiatric Association. (1987). *Diagnostic and statistical manual of mental disorders* (3rd ed., rev.). Washington, DC: Author.

American Psychiatric Association. (1994). *Diagnostic and statistical manual of mental disorders* (4th ed.). Washington, DC: Author.

Anesko, K. M., & O'Leary, S. G. (1982). The effectiveness of brief parent training for the management of children's homework problems. *Child & Family Behavior Therapy, 4,* 113–126.

Arbuthnot, J., & Gordon, D. A. (1986). Behavioral and cognitive effects of a moral reasoning development intervention for high-risk behavior-disordered adolescents. *Journal of Consulting and Clinical Psychology, 54,* 208–216.

Arnold, D. S., O'Leary, S. G., Wolff, L. S., & Acker, M. M. (1993). The Parenting Scale: A measure of dysfunctional parenting in discipline situations. *Psychological Assessment, 5,* 137–144.

Arnold, J. E., Levine, A. G., & Patterson, G. R. (1975). Changes in sibling behavior following family intervention. *Journal of Consulting and Clinical Psychology, 43,* 683–688.

Atkeson, B. M., & Forehand, R. (1979). Home-based reinforcement programs designed to modify classroom behavior: A review and methodological evaluation. *Psychological Bulletin, 86,* 1298–1308.

Attar, B. K., Guerra, N. G., & Tolan, P. H. (1994). Neighborhood disadvantage, stressful life events, and adjustment in urban elementary-school children. *Journal of Clinical Child Psychology, 23,* 391–400.

Ayllon, T., Garber, S., & Pisor, K. (1975). The elimination of discipline problems through a combined school–home motivational system. *Behavior Therapy, 6,* 616–626.

Baden, A. D., & Howe, G. W. (1992). Mothers' attributions and expectancies regarding their conduct-disordered children. *Journal of Abnormal Child Psychology, 20,* 467–485.

Bailey, J. S., Wolf, M. M., & Phillips, E. L. (1970). Home-based reinforcement and the modification of pre-delinquents' classroom behavior. *Journal of Applied Behavior Analysis, 3,* 223–233.

Bank, L., Marlowe, J. H., Reid, J. B., Patterson, G. R., & Weinrott, M. R. (1991). A comparative evaluation of parent training interventions for families of chronic delinquents. *Journal of Abnormal Child Psychology, 19,* 15–33.

Bardone, A. M., Moffit, T. E., Caspi, A., Dickson, N., & Silva, P. A. (1996). Adult mental health and social outcomes of adolescent girls with depression and Conduct Disorder. *Development and Psychopathology, 8,* 811–829.

Barkley, R. A. (1981). *Hyperactive children: A handbook for diagnosis and treatment.* New York: Guilford Press.

Barkley, R. A., Shelton, T. L., Crosswait, C., Moorehouse, M., Fletcher, K., Barrett, S., Jenkins, L., & Metevia, L. (1996). Preliminary findings of an early intervention program with aggressive hyperactive children. *Annals of the New York Academy of Sciences, 794,* 277–289.

Barrish, H. H., Saunders, M., & Wolf, M. M. (1969). Good Behavior Game: Effects of individual contingencies for group consequences on disruptive behavior in a classroom. *Journal of Applied Behavior Analysis, 2,* 119–124.

Barth, R. P. (1987). Assessment and treatment of stealing. In B. B. Lahey & A. E. Kazdin (Eds.), *Ad-*

vances in clinical child psychology (Vol. 10, pp. 137–170). New York: Plenum Press.

Barton, C., & Alexander, J. F. (1981). Functional Family Therapy. In A. S. Gurman & D. P. Kniskern (Eds.), *Handbook of family therapy* (pp. 403–443). New York: Brunner/Mazel.

Barton, C., Alexander, J. F., Waldron, H., Turner, C. W., & Warburton, J. (1985). Generalizing treatment effects of Functional Family Therapy: Three replications. *American Journal of Family Therapy, 13,* 16–26.

Bates, J. E., Bayles, K., Bennett, D. S., Ridge, B., & Brown, M. M. (1991). Origins of externalizing behavior problems at eight years of age. In D. J. Pepler & K. H. Rubin (Eds.), *The development and treatment of childhood aggression* (pp. 93–120). Hillsdale, NJ: Erlbaum.

Baum, C. G., & Forehand, R. (1981). Long-term follow-up assessment of parent training by use of multiple-outcome measures. *Behavior Therapy, 12,* 643–652.

Baum, C. G., Reyna McGlone, C. L., & Ollendick, T. H. (1986, November). *The efficacy of behavioral parent training: Behavioral parent training plus clinical self-control training, and a modified STEP program with children referred for noncompliance.* Paper presented at the meeting of the Association for Advancement of Behavior Therapy, Chicago.

Beck, A. T., Rush, A. J., Shaw, B. F., & Emery, G. (1979). *Cognitive therapy of depression.* New York: Guilford Press.

Becker, W. C., Madsen, C. H., Arnold, C. R., & Thomas, D. R. (1967). The contingent use of teacher attention and praising in reducing classroom problems. *Journal of Special Education, 1,* 287–307.

Bernal, M. E., Klinnert, M. D., & Schultz, L. A. (1980). Outcome evaluation of behavioral parent training and client-centered parent counseling for children with conduct problems. *Journal of Applied Behavior Analysis, 13,* 677–691.

Berrueta-Clement, J. R., Schweinhart, L. J., Barnett, W. S., Epstein, A. S., & Weikart, D. P. (1984). *Changed lives: The effects of the Perry Preschool Program on youths through age 19.* Ypsilanti, MI: High/Scope Press.

Biederman, J., Baldessarini, R. J., Wright, V., Keenan, K., & Faraone, S. (1993). A double-blind, placebo-controlled study of desipramine in the treatment of ADD: III. Lack of impact of comorbidity and family history factors on clinical response. *Journal of the American Academy of Child and Adolescent Psychiatry, 32,* 199–204.

Bien, N. Z., & Bry, B. H. (1980). An experimentally designed comparison of four intensities of school based prevention programs for adolescents with adjustment problems. *Journal of Community Psychology, 8,* 110–116.

Bierman, K. L. (1983). Cognitive development and clinical interviews with children. In B. B. Lahey &

A. E. Kazdin (Eds.), *Advances in clinical child psychology* (Vol. 6, pp. 217–250). New York: Plenum Press.

Bierman, K. L. (1989). Improving the peer relationships of rejected children. In B. B. Lahey & A. E. Kazdin (Eds.), *Advances in clinical child psychology* (Vol. 12, pp. 53–84). New York: Plenum Press.

Bierman, K. L., Greenberg, M. T., & the Conduct Problems Prevention Research Group. (1996). Social skills training in the Fast Track Program. In R. DeV. Peters & R. J. McMahon (Eds.), *Preventing childhood disorders, substance abuse, and delinquency* (pp. 65–89). Thousand Oaks, CA: Sage.

Bierman, K. L., Miller, C. M., & Staub, S. (1987). Improving the social behavior and peer acceptance of rejected boys: Effects of social skill training. *Journal of Consulting and Clinical Psychology, 55,* 194–200.

Bierman, K. L., & Welsh, J. A. (1997). Social relationship deficits. In E. J. Mash & L. G. Terdal (Eds.), *Assessment of childhood disorders* (3rd ed., pp. 328–365). New York: Guilford Press.

Bird, H. R., & Gould, M. S. (1995). The use of diagnostic instruments and global measures of functioning in child psychiatry epidemiological studies. In F. C. Verhulst & H. M. Koot (Eds.), *The epidemiology of child and adolescent psychopathology* (pp. 86–103). New York: Oxford University Press.

Blechman, E. A. (1981). Toward comprehensive behavioral family intervention: An algorithm for matching families and interventions. *Behavior Modification, 5,* 221–236.

Blechman, E. A. (1996). Coping, competence, and aggression prevention: Part 2. Universal school-based prevention. *Applied & Preventive Psychology, 5,* 19–35.

Blechman, E. A., Dumas, J. E., & Prinz, R. J. (1994). Prosocial coping by youth exposed to violence. *Journal of Child and Adolescent Group Therapy, 4,* 205–227.

Blechman, E. A., Prinz, R. J., & Dumas, J. E. (1995). Coping, competence, and aggression prevention: Part 1. Developmental model. *Applied & Preventive Psychology, 4,* 211–232.

Borduin, C. M., Henggeler, S. W., Blaske, D. M., & Stein, R. (1990). Multisystemic treatment of adolescent sexual offenders. *International Journal of Offender Therapy and Comparative Criminology, 34,* 105–113.

Borduin, C. M., Mann, B. J., Cone, L., Henggeler, S. W., Fucci, B. R., Blaske, D. M., & Williams, R. A. (1995). Multisystemic treatment of serious juvenile offenders: Long-term prevention of criminality and violence. *Journal of Consulting and Clinical Psychology, 63,* 569–578.

Boyle, M. H., Offord, D. R., Racine, Y., Sanford, M., Szatmari, P., Fleming, J. E., & Price-Munn, N. (1993). Evaluation of the Diagnostic Interview for Children and Adolescents for use in general population samples. *Journal of Abnormal Child Psychology, 21,* 663–681.

Bradley, C. (1937). The behavior of children receiving benzedrine. *American Journal of Psychiatry, 94,* 577–585.

Braukmann, C. J., Ramp, K. K., Tigner, D. M., & Wolf, M. M. (1984). The Teaching-Family approach to training group-home parents: Training procedures, validation research, and outcome findings. In R. F. Dangel & R. A. Polster (Eds.), *Parent training: Foundations of research and practice* (pp. 144–161). New York: Guilford Press.

Breen, M. J., & Altepeter, T. S. (1990). *Disruptive behavior disorders in children: Treatment-focused assessment.* New York: Guilford Press.

Breiner, J. L., & Forehand, R. (1981). An assessment of the effects of parent training on clinic-referred children's school behavior. *Behavioral Assessment, 3,* 31–42.

Brestan, E. V., Eyberg, S. M., Boggs, S. R., & Algina, J. (1997). Parent–child interaction therapy: Parents' perceptions of untreated siblings. *Child & Family Behavior Therapy, 19* (3), 13–28.

Brewer, D. D., Hawkins, J. D., Catalano, R. F., & Neckerman, H. J. (1995). Preventing serious, violent, and chronic juvenile offending: A review of evaluations of selected strategies in childhood, adolescence, and the community. In J. C. Howell, B. Krisberg, J. D. Hawkins, & J. J. Wilson (Eds.), *Source book on serious violent, and chronic juvenile offenders* (pp. 61–141). Thousand Oaks, CA: Sage.

Brody, G. H., & Forehand, R. (1985). The efficacy of parent training with maritally distressed and non-distressed mothers: A multimethod assessment. *Behaviour Research and Therapy, 23,* 291–296.

Brooks, R. B., & Snow, D. L. (1972). Two case illustrations of the use of behavior modification techniques in the school setting. *Behavior Therapy, 3,* 100–103.

Brown, P., & Elliot, R. (1965). Control of aggression in a nursery school class. *Journal of Experimental Child Psychology, 2,* 103–107.

Budd, K. S., Liebowitz, J. M., Riner, L. S., Mindell, C., & Goldfarb, A. L. (1981). Home-based treatment of severe disruptive behaviors: A reinforcement package for preschool and kindergarten children. *Behavior Modification, 5,* 273–298.

Budd, K. S., & O'Brien, T. P. (1982). Father involvement in behavioral parent training: An area in need of research. *the Behavior Therapist, 5,* 85–89.

Burns, G. L., & Owen, S. M. (1990). Disruptive behaviors in the classroom: Initial standardization data on a new teacher rating scale. *Journal of Abnormal Child Psychology, 18,* 515–525.

Burns, G. L., & Patterson, D. R. (1990). Conduct problem behaviors in a stratified random sample of children and adolescents: New standardization data on the Eyberg Child Behavior Inventory. *Psychological Assessment, 2,* 391–397.

Burns, G. L., Patterson, D. R., Nussbaum, B. R., & Parker, C. M. (1991). Disruptive behaviors in an outpatient pediatric population: Additional standardization data on the Eyberg Child Behavior Inventory. *Psychological Assessment, 3,* 202–207.

Burns, G. L., Sosna, T. D., & Ladish, C. (1992). Distinction between well-standardized norms and the psychometric properties of a measure: Measurement of disruptive behaviors with the Sutter-Eyberg Student Behavior Inventory. *Child & Family Behavior Therapy, 14,* 43–54.

Burns, G. L., Walsh, J. A., & Owen, S. M. (1995). Twelve-month stability of disruptive classroom behavior as measured by the Sutter–Eyberg Student Behavior Inventory. *Journal of Clinical Child Psychology, 24,* 453–462.

Campbell, M., Adams, P. B., Small, A. M., Kafantaris, V., Silva, R. R., Shell, J., Perry, R., & Overall, J. E. (1995). Lithium in hospitalized aggressive children with Conduct Disorder: A double-blind and placebo-controlled study. *Journal of the American Academy of Child and Adolescent Psychiatry, 34,* 445–453.

Campbell, M., & Cueva, J. E. (1995). Psychopharmacology in child and adolescent psychiatry: A review of the past seven years. Part II. *Journal of the American Academy of Child and Adolescent Psychiatry, 34,* 1262–1272.

Campbell, M., Gonzalez, N. M., & Silva, R. R. (1992). The pharmacologic treatment of conduct disorders and rage outbursts. *Psychiatric Clinics of North America, 15,* 69–85.

Campbell, M., Small, A. M., Green, W. H., Jennings, S. J., Perry, R., Bennett, W. G., & Anderson, L. (1984). Behavioral efficacy of haloperidol and lithium carbonate: A comparison in hospitalized aggressive children with Conduct Disorder. *Archives of General Psychiatry, 41,* 650–656.

Campbell, S. B. (1991). Longitudinal studies of active and aggressive preschoolers: Individual differences in early behavior and in outcome. In D. Cicchetti & S. L. Toth (Eds.), *Rochester Symposium on Developmental Psychopathology: Vol. 2. Internalizing and externalizing expressions of dysfunction* (pp. 57–90). Hillsdale, NJ: Erlbaum.

Campbell, S. B. (1995). Behavior problems in preschool children: A review of recent research. *Journal of Child Psychology and Psychiatry, 36,* 113–149.

Campbell, S. B., & Ewing, L. J. (1990). Follow up of hard to manage preschoolers: Adjustment at age 9 and predictors of continuing symptoms. *Journal of Child Psychology and Psychiatry, 31,* 871–889.

Campis, L. K., Lyman, R. D., & Prentice-Dunn, S. (1986). The Parental Locus of Control Scale: Development and validation. *Journal of Clinical Child Psychology, 15,* 260–267.

Capaldi, D. M. (1991). Co-occurrence of conduct problems and depressive symptoms in early adolescent boys: I. Familial factors and general adjustment at age 6. *Development and Psychopathology, 3,* 277–300.

Capaldi, D. M. (1992). Co-occurrence of conduct problems and depressive symptoms in early adolescent boys: II. A 2-year follow-up at grade 8. *Development and Psychopathology, 4,* 125–144.

Capaldi, D. M., & Patterson, G. R. (1994). Interrelated influences of contextual factors on antisocial behavior in childhood and adolescence for males. In D. C. Fowles, P. Sutker, & S. H. Goodman (Eds.), *Progress in experimental personality and psychopathology research* (pp. 165–198). New York: Springer.

Caspi, A., Henry, B., McGee, R. O., Moffitt, T. E., & Silva, P. A. (1995). Temperamental origins of child and adolescent behavior problems: From age three to fifteen. *Child Development, 66,* 55–68.

Cautela, J. R. (1967). Covert sensitizations. *Psychological Record, 20,* 459–468.

Chamberlain, P. (1990). Comparative evaluation of specialized foster care for seriously delinquent youths: A first step. *Community Alternatives: International Journal of Family Care, 13,* 21–36.

Chamberlain, P. (1994). *Family connections.* Eugene, OR: Castalia.

Chamberlain, P., & Moore, K. J. (in press). Models of community treatment for serious juvenile offenders. In J. Crane (Ed.), *Social programs that really work.* New York: Russell Sage Foundation.

Chamberlain, P., Moreland, S., & Reid, J. B. (1992). Enhanced services and stipends for foster parents: Effects on retention rates and outcomes of children. *Child Welfare, 71,* 387–401.

Chamberlain, P., & Patterson, G. R. (1995). Discipline and child compliance in parenting. In M. H. Bornstein (Ed.), *Handbook of parenting: Vol. 4. Applied and practical parenting* (pp. 205–225). Hillsdale, NJ: Erlbaum.

Chamberlain, P., Patterson, G. R., Reid, J. B., Kavanagh, K., & Forgatch, M. (1984). Observation of client resistance. *Behavior Therapy, 15,* 144–155.

Chamberlain, P., & Reid, J. B. (1987). Parent observation and report of child symptoms. *Behavioral Assessment, 9,* 97–109.

Chamberlain, P., & Reid, J. B. (1991). Using a specialized foster care community treatment model for children and adolescents leaving the state mental health hospital. *Journal of Community Psychology, 19,* 266–276.

Chamberlain, P., & Reid, J. B. (1994). Differences in risk factors and adjustment for male and female delinquents in treatment foster care. *Journal of Child and Family Studies, 3,* 23–39.

Chandler, M., & Moran, T. (1990). Psychopathy and moral development: A comparative study of delinquent and nondelinquent youth. *Development and Psychopathology, 2,* 227–246.

Christian, R. E., Frick, P. J., Hill, N. L., Tyler, L., & Frazer, D. R. (1997). Psychopathy and conduct problems in children: II. Implications for subtyping children with conduct problems. *Journal of the American Academy of Child and Adolescent Psychiatry, 36,* 233–241.

Coie, J. D., & Dodge, K. A. (1998). Aggression and antisocial behavior. In W. Damon (Ed.), *Handbook of child psychology (5th ed.): Vol. 3. Social, emotional, and personality development* (pp. 779–862). New York: Wiley.

Coie, J. D., & Jacobs, M. R. (1993). The role of social context in the prevention of Conduct Disorder. *Development and Psychopathology, 5,* 263–275.

Coie, J. D., & Krehbiel, G. (1984). Effects of academic tutoring on the social status of low-achieving, socially rejected children. *Child Development, 55,* 1465–1478.

Coie, J. D., Lochman, J. E., Terry, R., & Hyman, C. (1992). Predicting early adolescent disorder from childhood aggression and peer rejection. *Journal of Consulting and Clinical Psychology, 60,* 783–792.

Conduct Problems Prevention Research Group. (1992). A developmental and clinical model for the prevention of conduct disorders: The FAST Track Program. *Development and Psychopathology, 4,* 509–527.

Conduct Problems Prevention Research Group. (1997a, April). *Prevention of antisocial behavior: Initial findings from the Fast Track Project.* Symposium presented at the biennial meeting of the Society for Research in Child Development, Washington, DC.

Conduct Problems Prevention Research Group. (1997b, August). Testing developmental theory of antisocial behavior with outcomes from the Fast Track prevention project. In G. R. Patterson (Chair), *Randomized prevention trials as a basis for testing developmental theory.* Symposium presented at the annual meeting of the American Psychological Association, Chicago.

Conners, C. K. (1969). A teacher rating scale for use in drug studies with children. *American Journal of Psychiatry, 126,* 884–888.

Conners, C. K. (1972). Symposium: Behavior modification by drugs. II. Psychological effects of stimulant drugs in children with minimal brain dysfunction. *Pediatrics, 49,* 702–708.

Connor, D. F., & Steingard, R. J. (1996). A clinical approach to the pharmacotherapy of aggression in children. *Annals of the New York Academy of Sciences, 794,* 290–307.

Coplin, J. W., & Houts, A. C. (1991). Father involvement in parent training for oppositional child behavior: Progress or stagnation? *Child & Family Behavior Therapy, 13,* 29–51.

Costello, E. J. (1990). Child psychiatric epidemiology: Implications for clinical research and practice. In B. B. Lahey & A. E. Kazdin (Eds.), *Advances in clinical child psychology* (Vol. 13, pp. 53–90). New York: Plenum Press.

Cox-Jones, C., Lubetsky, M. J., Fultz, S. A., & Kolko, D. J. (1990). Inpatient psychiatric treatment of a young recidivist firesetter. *Journal of the American*

Academy of Child and Adolescent Psychiatry, 29, 936–941.

Craig, W. M., & Pepler, D. J. (1995). Peer processes in bullying and victimization: An observational study. *Exceptionality Education Canada, 5,* 81–95.

Crick, N. R., & Dodge, K. A. (1994). A review and reformulation of social information-processing mechanisms in children's social adjustment. *Psychological Bulletin, 115,* 74–101.

Crick, N. R., & Grotpeter, J. K. (1995). Relational aggression, gender, and social-psychological adjustment. *Child Development, 66,* 710–722.

Crnic, K. A., & Greenberg, M. T. (1990). Minor parenting stresses with young children. *Child Development, 61,* 1628–1637.

Cross Calvert, S., & McMahon, R. J. (1987). The treatment acceptability of a behavioral parent training program and its components. *Behavior Therapy, 18,* 165–179.

Cueva, J. E., Overall, J. E., Small, A. M., Armenteros, J. L., Perry, R., & Campbell, M. (1996). Carbamazepine in aggressive children with Conduct Disorder: A double-blind and placebo-controlled study. *Journal of the American Academy of Child and Adolescent Psychiatry, 35,* 480–490.

Cummings, E. M., & Davies, P. (1994a). *Children and marital conflict: The impact of family dispute and resolution.* New York: Guilford Press.

Cummings, E. M., & Davies, P. T. (1994b). Maternal depression and child development. *Journal of Child Psychology and Psychiatry, 35,* 73–112.

Dadds, M. R., & McHugh, T. A. (1992). Social support and treatment outcome in behavioral family therapy for child conduct problems. *Journal of Consulting and Clinical Psychology, 60,* 252–259.

Dadds, M. R., & Powell, M. B. (1991). The relationship of interparental conflict and global marital adjustment to aggression, anxiety, and immaturity in aggressive and nonclinic children. *Journal of Abnormal Child Psychology, 19,* 553–567.

Dadds, M. R., Sanders, M. R., Behrens, B. C., & James, J. E. (1987). Marital discord and child behavior problems: A description of family interactions during treatment. *Journal of Clinical Child Psychology, 16,* 192–203.

Dadds, M. R., Sanders, M. R., & James, J. E. (1987). The generalization of treatment effects in parent training with multidistressed parents. *Behavioural Psychotherapy, 15,* 289–313.

Dadds, M. R., Schwartz, S., & Sanders, M. R. (1987). Marital discord and treatment outcome in behavioral treatment of child conduct disorders. *Journal of Consulting and Clinical Psychology, 55,* 396–403.

Daly, R. M., Holland, C. J., Forrest, P. A., & Fellbaum, G. A. (1985). Temporal generalization of treatment effects over a three-year period for a parent training program: Directive Parent Counseling (DPC). *Canadian Journal of Behavioural Science, 17,* 379–388.

Darveaux, D. X. (1984). The Good Behavior Game Plus Merit: Controlling disruptive behavior and improving student motivation. *School Psychology Review, 13,* 510–514.

Day, D. M., Bream, L. A., & Pal, A. (1992). Proactive and reactive aggression: An analysis of subtypes based on teacher perceptions. *Journal of Clinical Child Psychology, 21,* 210–217.

Deitz, S. M. (1985). Good Behavior Game. In A. S. Bellack & M. Hersen (Eds.), *Dictionary of behavior therapy techniques* (pp. 131–132). New York: Pergamon Press.

Dinkmeyer, D., & McKay, G. D. (1976). *Systematic training for effective parenting.* Circle Pines, MN: American Guidance Services.

Dishion, T. J., & Andrews, D. W. (1995). Preventing escalation in problem behaviors with high-risk young adolescents: Immediate and 1-year outcomes. *Journal of Consulting and Clinical Psychology, 63,* 538–548.

Dishion, T. J., French, D. C., & Patterson, G. R. (1995). The development and ecology of antisocial behavior. In D. Cicchetti & D. J. Cohen (Eds.), *Developmental psychopathology: Vol. 2. Risk, disorder, and adaptation* (pp. 421–471). New York: Wiley.

Dishion, T. J., Gardner, K., Patterson, G. R., Reid, J. B., Spyrou, S., & Thibodeaux, S. (1984). *The Family Process Code: A multidimensional system for observing family interactions* (Oregon Social Learning Center Technical Report). (Available from Oregon Social Learning Center, 207 E. 5th Avenue, Suite 202, Eugene, OR 97401)

Dishion, T. J., & McMahon, R. J. (in press). Parental monitoring and the prevention of problem behavior: A conceptual and empirical reformulation. In R. S. Ashery (Ed.), *Research meeting on drug abuse prevention through family interventions* (National Institute on Drug Abuse Research Monograph).

Dishion,, T. J., & Patterson, G. R. (1992). Age effects in parent training outcome. *Behavior Therapy, 23,* 719–729.

Dishion, T. J., Patterson, G. R., Stoolmiller, M., & Skinner, M. L. (1991). Family, school, and behavioral antecedents to early adolescent involvement with antisocial peers. *Developmental Psychology, 27,* 172–180.

Dishion, T. J., Reid, J. B., & Patterson, G. R. (1988). Empirical guidelines for a family intervention for adolescent drug use. *Journal of Chemical Dependency Treatment, 1,* 189–224.

Dodge, K. A. (1985). Attributional bias in aggressive children. In P. C. Kendall (Ed.), *Advances in cognitive behavioral research and therapy* (Vol. 4, pp. 73–110). New York: Academic Press.

Dodge, K. A. (1986). A social information-processing model of social competence in children. In M. Perlmutter (Ed.), *Minnesota Symposium on Child Psychology* (Vol. 18, pp. 77–125). Hillsdale, NJ: Erlbaum.

Dodge, K. A. (1991). The structure and function of reactive and proactive aggression. In D. J. Pepler & K. H. Rubin (Eds.), *The development and treatment of childhood aggression* (pp. 201–218). Hillsdale, NJ: Erlbaum.

Dodge, K. A. (1993). The future of research on the treatment of Conduct Disorder. *Development and Psychopathology, 5,* 311–319.

Dodge, K. A., & Coie, J. D. (1987). Social-information-processing factors in reactive and proactive aggression in children's peer groups. *Journal of Personality and Social Psychology, 53,* 1146–1158.

Dodge, K. A., Pettit, G. S., & Bates, J. E. (1994). Socialization mediators of the relation between socioeconomic status and child conduct problems. *Child Development, 65,* 649–665.

Dolan, L. J., Kellam, S. G., Brown, C. H., Werthamer-Larsson, L., Rebok, G. W., Mayer, L. S., Laudolff, J., & Turkkan, J. S. (1993). The short-term impact of two classroom-based preventive interventions on aggressive and shy behaviors and poor achievement. *Journal of Applied Developmental Psychology, 14,* 317–345.

Drotar, D., Stein, R. E. K., & Perrin, E. C. (1995). Methodological issues in using the Child Behavior Checklist and its related instruments in clinical child psychology research. *Journal of Clinical Child Psychology, 24,* 184–192.

Dumas, J. E. (1984a). Child, adult-interactional, and socioeconomic setting events as predictors of parent training outcome. *Education and Treatment of Children, 7,* 351–364.

Dumas, J. E. (1984b). Interactional correlates of treatment outcome in behavioral parent training. *Journal of Consulting and Clinical Psychology, 52,* 946–954.

Dumas, J. E. (1986). Parental perception and treatment outcome in families of aggressive children: A causal model. *Behavior Therapy, 17,* 420–432.

Dumas, J. E. (1989). Treating antisocial behavior in children: Child and family approaches. *Clinical Psychology Review, 9,* 197–222.

Dumas, J. E. (1996). Why was this child referred? Interactional correlates of referral status in families of children with disruptive behavior problems. *Journal of Clinical Child Psychology, 25,* 106–115.

Dumas, J. E., & Albin, J. B. (1986). Parent training outcome: Does active parental involvement matter? *Behaviour Research and Therapy, 24,* 227–230.

Dumas, J. E., & Serketich, W. J. (1994). Maternal depressive symptomatology and child maladjustment: A comparison of three process models. *Behavior Therapy, 25,* 161–181.

Dumas, J. E., & Wahler, R. G. (1983). Predictors of treatment outcome in parent training: Mother insularity and socioeconomic disadvantage. *Behavioral Assessment, 5,* 301–313.

Dumas, J. E., & Wahler, R. G. (1985). Indiscriminate mothering as a contextual factor in aggressive-oppositional child behavior: "Damned if you do and damned if you don't." *Journal of Abnormal Child Psychology, 13,* 1–17.

Duncan, G. J., Brooks-Gunn, J., & Klebanov, P. K. (1994). Economic deprivation and early childhood development. *Child Development, 65,* 296–318.

Dunson, R. M., Hughes, J. N., & Jackson, T. W. (1994). Effect of behavioral consultation on student and teacher behavior. *Journal of School Psychology, 32,* 247–266.

Edelbrock, C. (1985). *Conduct problems in childhood and adolescence: Developmental patterns and progressions.* Unpublished manuscript.

Edelbrock, C., & Costello, A. J. (1988). Structured psychiatric interviews for children. In M. Rutter, A. H. Tuma, & I. S. Lann (Eds.), *Assessment and diagnosis in child psychopathology* (pp. 87–112). New York: Guilford Press.

Edelbrock, C., Costello, A. J., Dulcan, M. K., Kalas, R., & Conover, N. C. (1985). Age differences in the reliability of the psychiatric interview of the child. *Child Development, 56,* 265–275.

Eisenstadt, T. H., Eyberg, S., McNeil, C. B., Newcomb, K., & Funderburk, B. (1993). Parent–child interaction therapy with behavior problem children: Relative effectiveness of two stages and overall treatment outcome. *Journal of Clinical Child Psychology, 22,* 42–51.

Elliott, D. S., Huizinga, D., & Ageton, S. S. (1985). *Explaining delinquency and drug use.* Beverly Hills, CA: Sage.

Embry, L. H. (1984). What to do?: Matching client characteristics and intervention techniques through a prescriptive taxonomic key. In R. F. Dangel & R. A. Polster (Eds.), *Parent training: Foundations of research and practice* (pp. 443–473). New York: Guilford Press.

Eme, R. F., & Kavanaugh, L. (1995). Sex differences in Conduct Disorder. *Journal of Clinical Child Psychology, 24,* 406–426.

Executive Committee of the Council for Children with Behavioral Disorders. (1987). Position paper on definition and identification of students with behavioral disorders. *Behavioral Disorders, 13,* 9–19.

Eyberg, S. M. (1992). Parent and teacher behavior inventories for the assessment of conduct problem behaviors in children. In L. VandeCreek, S. Knapp, & T. L. Jackson (Eds.), *Innovations in clinical practice: A source book* (Vol. 11, pp. 261–270). Sarasota, FL: Professional Resource Press.

Eyberg, S. M., Bessmer, J., Newcomb, K., Edwards, D., & Robinson, E. (1994). *Dyadic Parent–Child Interaction Coding System II: A manual.* Unpublished munuscript, University of Florida, Gainesville.

Eyberg, S. M., Boggs, S. R., & Algina, J. (1995). Parent–child interaction therapy: A psychosocial model for the treatment of young children with conduct problem behavior and their families. *Psychopharmacology Bulletin, 31,* 83–91.

Eyberg, S. M., & Colvin, A. (1994, August). *Restandardization of the Eyberg Child Behavior Inventory.* Paper presented at the annual meeting of the American Psychological Association, Los Angeles.

Eyberg, S. M., & Johnson, S. M. (1974). Multiple assessment of behavior modification with families: Effects of contingency contracting and order of treated problems. *Journal of Consulting and Clinical Psychology, 42,* 594–606.

Eyberg, S. M., & Robinson, E. A. (1982). Parent–child interaction training: Effects on family functioning. *Journal of Clinical Child Psychology, 11,* 130–137.

Fagan, J. (1991). Community-based treatment for mentally disordered juvenile offenders. *Journal of Clinical Child Psychology, 20,* 42–50.

Farrington, D. P. (1986). Age and crime. In M. Tonry & N. Morris (Eds.), *Crime and justice* (Vol. 7, pp. 189–250). Chicago: University of Chicago Press.

Farrington, D. P. (1993). Understanding and preventing bullying. In M. Tonry (Ed.), *Crime and justice: A review of research* (Vol. 17, pp. 381–458). Chicago: University of Chicago Press.

Farrington, D. P. (1995). The development of offending and antisocial behaviour from childhood: Key findings from the Cambridge study in delinquent development. *Journal of Child Psychology and Psychiatry, 36,* 929–964.

Feindler, E. L. (1990). Adolescent anger control: Review and critique. In M. Hersen, R. M. Eisler, & P. M. Miller (Eds.), *Progress in behavior modification* (Vol. 26, pp. 11–59). Newbury Park, CA: Sage.

Feindler, E. L. (1991). Cognitive strategies in anger control interventions for children and adolescents. In P. C. Kendall (Ed.), *Child and adolescent therapy: Cognitive-behavioral procedures* (pp. 66–97). New York: Guilford Press.

Feindler, E. L. (1995). An ideal treatment package for children and adolescents with anger disorders. In H. Kassinove (Ed.), *Anger disorders: Definition, diagnosis, and treatment* (pp. 173–195). Washington, DC: Taylor & Francis.

Feindler, E. L., Ecton, R. B., Kingsley, D., & Dubey, D. R. (1986). Group anger-control training for institutionalized psychiatric male adolescents. *Behavior Therapy, 17,* 109–123.

Feindler, E. L., & Guttman, J. (1994). Cognitive-behavioral anger control training for groups of adolescents: A treatment manual. In C. W. LeCroy (Ed.), *Handbook of child and adolescent treatment manuals* (pp. 170–199). New York: Free Press.

Feindler, E. L., Marriott, S. A., & Iwata, M. (1984). Group anger control training for junior high school delinquents. *Cognitive Therapy and Research, 8,* 299–311.

Fellbaum, G. A., Daly, R. M., Forrest, P., & Holland, C. J. (1985). Community implications of a home-based change program for children. *Journal of Community Psychology, 13,* 67–74.

Ferber, H., Keeley, S. M., & Shemberg, K. M. (1974). Training parents in behavior modification: Outcome of and problems encountered in a program after Patterson's work. *Behavior Therapy, 5,* 415–419.

Fergusson, D. M., & Lynskey, M. T. (1993). The effects of maternal depression on child Conduct Disorder and attention deficit behaviours. *Social Psychiatry and Psychiatric Epidemiology, 28,* 116–123.

Fergusson, D. M., Lynskey, M. T., & Horwood, L. J. (1993). The effect of maternal depression on maternal ratings of child behavior. *Journal of Abnormal Child Psychology, 21,* 245–269.

Fixsen, D. L., & Blase, K. A. (1993). Creating new realities: Program development and dissemination. *Journal of Applied Behavior Analysis, 26,* 597–615.

Fleischman, M. J. (1981). A replication of Patterson's "Intervention for boys with conduct problems." *Journal of Consulting and Clinical Psychology, 49,* 342–351.

Fleischman, M. J., & Szykula, S. A. (1981). A community setting replication of a social learning treatment for aggressive children. *Behavior Therapy, 12,* 115–122.

Forehand, R., & Atkeson, B. M. (1977). Generality of treatment effects with parents as therapists: A review of assessment and implementation procedures. *Behavior Therapy, 8,* 575–593.

Forehand, R., Furey, W. M., & McMahon, R. J. (1984). The role of maternal distress in a parent training program to modify child noncompliance. *Behavioural Psychotherapy, 12,* 93–108.

Forehand, R., Griest, D. L., Wells, K. C., & McMahon, R. J. (1982). Side effects of parent counseling on marital satisfaction. *Journal of Counseling Psychology, 29,* 104–107.

Forehand, R., & Kotchick, B. A. (1996). Cultural diversity: A wake-up call for parent training. *Behavior Therapy, 27,* 187–206.

Forehand, R., Lautenschlager, G. J., Faust, J., & Graziano, W. G. (1986). Parent perceptions and parent–child interactions in clinic-referred children: A preliminary investigation of the effects of maternal depressive moods. *Behaviour Research and Therapy, 24,* 73–75.

Forehand, R., & Long, N. (1988). Outpatient treatment of the acting out child: Procedures, long term follow-up data, and clinical problems. *Advances in Behaviour Research and Therapy, 10,* 129–177.

Forehand, R., & McMahon, R. J. (1981). *Helping the noncompliant child: A clinician's guide to parent training.* New York: Guilford Press.

Forehand, R., Rogers, T., McMahon, R. J., Wells, K. C., & Griest, D. L. (1981). Teaching parents to modify child behavior problems: An examination of some follow-up data. *Journal of Pediatric Psychology, 6,* 313–322.

Forehand, R., Steffe, M. A., Furey, W. A., & Walley, P. B. (1983). Mothers' evaluation of a parent training program completed three and one-half years earlier. *Journal of Behavior Therapy and Experimental Psychiatry, 14,* 339–342.

Forehand, R., Sturgis, E. T., McMahon, R. J., Aguar, D., Green, K., Wells, K., & Breiner, J. (1979). Parent behavioral training to modify child noncompliance: Treatment generalization across time and from home to school. *Behavior Modification, 3,* 3–25.

Forehand, R., Wells, K. C., & Griest, D. L. (1980). An examination of the social validity of a parent training program. *Behavior Therapy, 11,* 488–502.

Forehand, R., & Wierson, M. (1993). The role of developmental factors in planning behavioral interventions for children: Disruptive behavior as an example. *Behavior Therapy, 24,* 117–141.

Forehand, R., Wierson, M., Frame, C. L., Kemptom, T., & Armistead, L. (1991). Juvenile firesetting: A unique syndome or an advanced level of antisocial behavior? *Behaviour Research and Therapy, 29,* 125–128.

Forgatch, M. S. (1991). The clinical science vortex: Developing a theory for antisocial behavior. In D. Pepler & K. H. Rubin (Eds.), *The development and treatment of childhood aggression* (pp. 291–315). Hillsdale, NJ: Erlbaum.

Forgatch, M. S., & Patterson, G. R. (1989). *Parents and adolescents living together. Part 2: Family problem solving.* Eugene, OR: Castalia.

Forgatch, M. S., Patterson, G. R., & Skinner, M. L. (1988). A mediational model for the effect of divorce on antisocial behavior in boys. In E. M. Hetherington & J. D. Arasteh (Eds.), *Impact of divorce, single parenting, and stepparenting on children* (pp. 135–154). Hillsdale, NJ: Erlbaum.

Forgatch, M. S., & Ramsey, E. (1994). Boosting homework: A video tape link between families and schools. *School Psychology Review, 23,* 472–484.

Frick, P. J. (1991). *The Alabama Parenting Questionnaire.* Unpublished rating scale, University of Alabama.

Frick, P. J. (1994). Family dysfunction and the disruptive behavior disorders: A review of recent empirical findings. In T. H. Ollendick & R. J. Prinz (Eds.), *Advances in clinical child psychology* (Vol. 16, pp. 203–226). New York: Plenum Press.

Frick, P. J., & Hare, R. D. (in press). *The Psychopathy Screening Device.* Toronto: Multi-Health Systems.

Frick, P. J., & Jackson, Y. K. (1993). Family functioning and childhood antisocial behavior: Yet another reinterpretation. *Journal of Clinical Child Psychology, 22,* 410–419.

Frick, P. J., Lahey, B. B., Applegate, B., Kerdyck, L., Ollendick, T., Hynd, G. W., Garfinkel, B., Greenhill, L., Biederman, J., Barkley, R. A., McBurnett, K., Newcorn, J., & Waldman, I. (1994). DSM-IV field trials for the disruptive behavior disorders: Symptom utility estimates. *Journal of the American Academy of Child and Adolescent Psychiatry, 33,* 529–539.

Frick, P. J., Lahey, B. B., Loeber, R., Stouthamer-Loeber, M., Christ, M. A. G., & Hanson, K. (1992). Familial risk factors to Oppositional Defiant Disorder and Conduct Disorder: Parental psychopathology and maternal parenting. *Journal of Consulting and Clinical Psychology, 60,* 49–55.

Frick, P. J., O'Brien, B. S., Wootton, J. M., & McBurnett, K. (1994). Psychopathy and conduct problems in children. *Journal of Abnormal Psychology, 103,* 700–707.

Frick, P. J., Van Horn, Y., Lahey, B. B., Christ, M. A. G., Loeber, R., Hart, E. A., Tannenbaum, L., & Hanson, K. (1993). Oppositional Defiant Disorder and Conduct Disorder: A meta-analytic review of factor analyses and cross-validation in a clinic sample. *Clinical Psychology Review, 13,* 319–340.

Funderburk, B. W., & Eyberg, S. M. (1989). Psychometric characteristics of the Sutter–Eyberg Student Behavior Inventory: A school behavior rating scale for use with preschool children. *Behavioral Assessment, 11,* 297–313.

Gadow, K. D. (1991). Clinical issues in child and adolescent psychopharmacology. *Journal of Consulting and Clinical Psychology, 59,* 842–852.

Gadow, K. D., Nolan, E. E., Sverd, J., Sprafkin, J., & Paolicelli, L. (1990). Methylphenidate in aggressive–hyperactive boys: I. Effects on peer aggression in public school settings. *Journal of the American Academy of Child and Adolescent Psychiatry, 29,* 710–718.

Ghaziuddin, N., & Alessi, N. E. (1992). An open clinical trial of trazodone in aggressive children. *Journal of Child and Adolescent Psychopharmacology, 2,* 291–297.

Gibbs, J. C., Arnold, K. D., Ahlborn, H. H., & Cheesman, F. L. (1984). Facilitation of sociomoral reasoning in delinquents. *Journal of Consulting and Clinical Psychology, 52,* 37–45.

Gibbs, J. C., Potter, G. B., Barriga, A. Q., & Liau, A. K. (1996). Developing the helping skills and prosocial motivation of aggressive adolescents in peer group programs. *Aggression and Violent Behavior, 1,* 283–305.

Glick, B., & Goldstein, A. P. (1987). Aggression Replacement Training. *Journal of Counseling and Development, 65,* 356–362.

Goldstein, A. P., & Glick, B. (1994). Aggression Replacement Training: Curriculum and evaluation. *Simulation and Gaming, 25,* 9–26.

Goldstein, A. P., Glick, B., Reiner, S., Zimmerman, D., & Coultry, T. (1986). *Aggression replacement training.* Champaign, IL: Research Press.

Goldstein, A. P., & Pentz, M. A. (1984). Psychological skill training and the aggressive adolescent. *School Psychology Review, 13,* 311–323.

Goldstein, S. (1995). *Understanding and managing children's classroom behavior.* New York: Wiley.

Gordon, D. A., & Arbuthnot, J. (1987). Individual, group, and family interventions. In H. C. Quay (Ed.), *Handbook of juvenile delinquency* (pp. 290–324). New York: Wiley.

Gordon, D. A., Arbuthnot, J., Gustafson, K. E., & McGreen, P. (1988). Home-based behavioral–systems family therapy with disadvantaged juvenile delinquents. *American Journal of Family Therapy, 16*, 243–255.

Gordon, D. A., Graves, K., & Arbuthnot, J. (1995). The effect of Functional Family Therapy for delinquents on adult criminal behavior. *Criminal Justice and Behavior, 22*, 60–73.

Greenberg, M. T., Speltz, M. L., & DeKlyen, M. (1993). The role of attachment in the early development of disruptive behavior problems. *Development and Psychopathology, 5*, 191–213.

Greenberg, M. T., Speltz, M. L., DeKlyen, M., & Endriga, M. C. (1991). Attachment security in preschoolers with and without externalizing behavior problems: A replication. *Development and Psychopathology, 3*, 413–430.

Greenhill, L. L., Solomon, M., Pleak, R., & Ambrosini, P. (1985). Molindone hydrochloride treatment of hospitalized children with Conduct Disorder. *Journal of Clinical Psychiatry, 46*, 20–25.

Greenwood, C. R., Hops, H., Delquadri, J., & Guild, J. (1974). Group contingencies for group consequences in classroom management: A further analysis. *Journal of Applied Behavior Analysis, 7*, 413–425.

Greenwood, C. R., Hops, H., & Walker, H. M. (1977). The durability of student behavior change: A comparative analysis at follow-up. *Behavior Therapy, 8*, 631–638.

Gregg, V., Gibbs, J. C., & Basinger, K. S. (1994). Patterns of delay in male and female delinquents' moral judgment. *Merrill-Palmer Quarterly, 40*, 538–553.

Griest, D. L., Forehand, R., Rogers, T., Breiner, J. L., Furey, W., & Williams, C. A. (1982). Effects of Parent Enhancement Therapy on the treatment outcome and generalization of a parent training program. *Behaviour Research and Therapy, 20*, 429–436.

Griest, D. L., Forehand, R., & Wells, K. C. (1981). Follow-up assessment of parent behavioral training: An analysis of who will participate. *Child Study Journal, 11*, 221–229.

Griest, D. L., & Wells, K. C. (1983). Behavioral family therapy with conduct disorders in children. *Behavior Therapy, 14*, 37–53.

Grizenko, N., Papineau, D., & Sayegh, L. (1993). Effectiveness of a multimodal day treatment program for children with disruptive behavior problems. *Journal of the American Academy of Child and Adolescent Psychiatry, 32*, 127–134.

Guerra, N. G., & Slaby, R. G. (1990). Cognitive mediators of aggression in adolescent offenders: 2. Intervention. *Developmental Psychology, 26*, 269–277.

Guidubaldi, J., & Cleminshaw, H. K. (1985). The development of the Cleminshaw–Guidubaldi Parent Satisfaction Scale. *Journal of Clinical Child Psychology, 14*, 293–298.

Hagino, O. R., Weller, E. B., Weller, R. A., Washing, D., Fristad, M. A., & Kontras, S. B. (1995). Untoward effects of lithium treatment in children aged four through six years. *Journal of the American Academy of Child and Adolescent Psychiatry, 34*, 1584–1590.

Hämäläinen, M., & Pulkkinen, L. (1996). Problem behavior as a precursor of male criminality. *Development and Psychopathology, 8*, 443–455.

Hammond, W. R., & Yung, B. (1993). Psychology's role in the public health response to assaultive violence among young African-American men. *American Psychologist, 48*, 142–154.

Hanf, C. (1969). *A two-stage program for modifying maternal controlling during mother–child (M-C) interaction.* Paper presented at the meeting of the Western Psychological Association, Vancouver, British Columbia.

Hanf, C. (1970). *Shaping mothers to shape their children's behavior.* Unpublished manuscript, University of Oregon Medical School.

Hanf, C., & Kling, J. (1973). *Facilitating parent–child interactions: A two-stage training model.* Unpublished manuscript, University of Oregon Medical School.

Hanson, M., Mackay-Soroka, S., Staley, S., & Poulton, L. (1994). Delinquent firesetters: A comparative study of delinquency and firesetting histories. *Canadian Journal of Psychiatry, 39*, 230–232.

Hawkins, J. D., Catalano, R. F., & Brewer, D. D. (1995). Preventing serious, violent, and chronic juvenile offending: Effective strategies from conception to age 6. In J. C. Howell, B. Krisberg, J. D. Hawkins, & J. J. Wilson (Eds.), *Source book on serious violent, and chronic juvenile offenders* (pp. 47–60). Thousand Oaks, CA: Sage.

Hawkins, J. D., Catalano, R. F., & Miller, J. Y. (1992). Risk and protective factors for alcohol and other drug problems in adolescence and early adulthood: Implications for substance abuse prevention. *Psychological Bulletin, 112*, 64–105.

Hawkins, J. D., Catalano, R. F., Morrison, D. M., O'Donnell, J., Abbott, R. D., & Day, L. E. (1992). The Seattle Social Development Project: Effects of the first four years on protective factors and problem behaviors. In J. McCord & R. E. Tremblay (Eds.), *Preventing antisocial behavior: Interventions from birth through adolescence* (pp. 139–161). New York: Guilford Press.

Hawkins, J. D., Von Cleve, E., & Catalano, R. F. (1991). Reducing early childhood aggression: Results of a primary prevention program. *Journal of the American Academy of Child and Adolescent Psychiatry, 30*, 208–217.

Hawkins, R. P. (1989). The nature and potential of therapeutic foster family care programs. In R. P. Hawkins & J. Breiling (Eds.), *Therapeutic foster care: Critical issues* (pp. 5–36). Washington, DC: Child Welfare League of America.

Hawkins, R. P., Meadowcroft, P., Trout, B. A., & Luster, W. C. (1985). Foster family-based treatment. *Journal of Clinical Child Psychology, 14,* 220–228.

Heath, G. A., Hardesty, V. A., Goldfine, P. E., & Walker, A. M. (1983). Childhood firesetting: An empirical study. *Journal of the American Academy of Child Psychiatry, 22,* 370–374.

Henderson, J. Q. (1981). A behavioral approach to stealing: A proposal for treatment based on ten cases. *Journal of Behavior Therapy and Experimental Psychiatry, 12,* 231–236.

Henderson, J. Q. (1983). Follow-up of stealing behavior in 27 youths after a variety of treatment programs. *Journal of Behavior Therapy and Experimental Psychiatry, 14,* 331–337.

Henggeler, S. W., & Borduin, C. M. (1990). *Family therapy and beyond: A multisystemic approach to treating the behavior problems of children and adolescents.* Pacific Grove, CA: Brooks/Cole.

Henggeler, S. W., Borduin, C. M., Melton, G. B., Mann, B. J., Smith, L., Hall, J. A., Cone, L., & Fuccie, B. R. (1991). Effects of Multisystemic Therapy on drug use and abuse in serious juvenile offenders: A progress report from two outcome studies. *Family Dynamics of Addiction Quarterly, 1,* 40–51.

Henggeler, S. W., Melton, G. B., Brondino, M. J., Scherer, D. G., & Hanley, J. H. (1997). Multisystemic Therapy with violent and chronic juvenile offenders and their families: The role of treatment fidelity in successful dissemination. *Journal of Consulting and Clinical Psychology, 65,* 821–833.

Henggeler, S. W., Melton, G. B., & Smith, L. A. (1992). Family preservation using Multisystemic Therapy: An effective alternative to incarcerating serious juvenile offenders. *Journal of Consulting and Clinical Psychology, 60,* 953–961.

Henggeler, S. W., Melton, G. B., Smith, L. A., Schoenwald, S. K., & Hanley, J. H. (1993). Family preservation using multisystemic treatment: Long-term follow-up to a clinical trial with serious juvenile offenders. *Journal of Child and Family Studies, 4,* 283–293.

Henggeler, S. W., Pickrel, S. G., Brondino, M. J., & Crouch, J. L. (1996). Eliminating (almost) treatment dropout of substance abusing or dependent delinquents through home-based Multisystemic Therapy. *American Journal of Psychiatry, 153,* 427–428.

Henggeler, S. W., Rodick, J. D., Borduin, C. M., Hanson, C. L., Watson, S. M., & Urey, J. R. (1986). Multisystemic treatment of juvenile offenders: Effects on adolescent behavior and family interaction. *Developmental Psychology, 22,* 132–141.

Henggeler, S. W., Schoenwald, S. K., Borduin, C. M., Rowland, M. D., & Cunningham, P. B. (in press). *Multisystemic treatment for antisocial behavior in youth.* New York: Guilford Press.

Herjanic, B., & Reich, W. (1982). Development of a structured psychiatric interview for children: Agreement between child and parent on individual symptoms. *Journal of Abnormal Child Psychology, 10,* 307–324.

Hinshaw, S. P. (1991). Stimulant medication and the treatment of aggression in children with attentional deficits. *Journal of Clinical Child Psychology, 20,* 301–312.

Hinshaw, S. P. (1992). Externalizing behavior problems and academic underachievement in childhood and adolescence: Causal relationships and underlying mechanisms. *Psychological Bulletin, 111,* 127–155.

Hinshaw, S. P., & Anderson, C. A. (1996). Conduct and Oppositional Defiant Disorders. In E. J. Mash & R. A. Barkley (Eds.), *Child psychopathology* (pp. 113–149). New York: Guilford Press.

Hinshaw, S. P., Buhrmester, D., & Heller, T. (1989). Anger control in response to verbal provocation: Effects of stimulant medication for boys with ADHD. *Journal of Abnormal Child Psychology, 17,* 393–407.

Hinshaw, S. P., Heller, T., & McHale, J. P. (1992). Covert antisocial behavior in boys with Attention-Deficit Hyperactivity Disorder: External validation and effects of methylphenidate. *Journal of Consulting and Clinical Psychology, 60,* 274–281.

Hinshaw, S. P., Henker, B., Whalen, C. K., Erhardt, D., & Dunnington, R. E. (1989). Aggressive, prosocial, and nonsocial behavior in hyperactive boys: Dose effects of methylphenidate in naturalistic settings. *Journal of Consulting and Clinical Psychology, 57,* 636–643.

Hinshaw, S. P., Lahey, B. B., & Hart, E. L. (1993). Issues of taxonomy and comorbidity in the development of Conduct Disorder. *Development and Psychopathology, 5,* 31–49.

Hodges, K., & Zeman, J. (1993). Interviewing. In T. H. Ollendick & M. Hersen (Eds.), *Handbook of child and adolescent assessment* (pp. 65–81). Needham Heights, MA: Allyn & Bacon.

Holden, G. W., Lavigne, V. V., & Cameron, A. M. (1990). Probing the continuum of effectiveness in parent training: Characteristics of parents and preschoolers. *Journal of Clinical Child Psychology, 19,* 2–8.

Holleran, P. A., Littman, D. C., Freund, R. D., & Schmaling, K. B. (1982). A signal detection approach to social perception: Identification of negative and positive behaviors by parents of normal and problem children. *Journal of Abnormal Child Psychology, 10,* 547–557.

Hops, H., & Walker, H. M. (1988). *CLASS: Contingencies for Learning Academic and Social Skills.* Seattle, WA: Educational Achievement Systems.

Hops, H., Walker, H. M., Fleischman, D. H., Nagoshi, J. T., Omura, R. T., Skindrud, K., & Taylor, J. (1978). CLASS: A standardized in-class program for acting-out children. II. Field test evaluations. *Journal of Educational Psychology, 70,* 636–644.

Horne, A. M., & Van Dyke, B. (1983). Treatment and maintenance of social learning family therapy. *Behavior Therapy, 14,* 606–613.

Hudson, J., Nutter, R. W., & Galaway, B. (1994). Treatment foster care programs: A review of evaluation research and suggested directions. *Social Work Research, 18,* 198–210.

Huesmann, L. R., Eron, L. D., Lefkowitz, M. M., & Walder, L. O. (1984). Stability of aggression over time and generations. *Developmental Psychology, 20,* 1120–1134.

Hughes, J. N., Grossman, P., & Barker, D. (1990). Teachers' expectancies, participation in consultation, and perceptions of consultant helpfulness. *School Psychology Quarterly, 15,* 167–179.

Humphreys, J., Kopet, T., & Lajoy, R. (1993). Clinical considerations in the treatment of juvenile firesetters. *Clinical Child Psychology Newsletter, 9,* 2–3.

Humphreys, L., Forehand, R., McMahon, R., & Roberts, M. (1978). Parent behavioral training to modify child noncompliance: Effects on untreated siblings. *Journal of Behavior Therapy and Experimental Psychiatry, 9,* 235–238.

Hunt, R. D., Minderaa, R. B., & Cohen, D. J. (1986). The therapeutic effect of clonidine in Attention Deficit Disorder with Hyperactivity: A comparison with placebo and methylphenidate. *Psychopharmacology Bulletin, 22,* 229–236.

Jacob, T., Krahn, G. L., & Leonard, K. (1991). Parent–child interactions in families with alcoholic fathers. *Journal of Consulting and Clinical Psychology, 59,* 176–181.

Jacobson, R. R. (1985). Child firesetters: A clinical investigation. *Journal of Child Psychology and Psychiatry, 26,* 759–768.

Jennings, K. D., Stagg, V., & Connors, R. E. (1991). Social networks and mothers' interactions with their preschool children. *Child Development, 62,* 966–978.

Jensen, P. S., Ryan, N. D., & Prien, R. (1992). Psychopharmacology of child and adolescent Major Depression: Present status and future directions. *Journal of Child and Adolescent Psychopharmacology, 2,* 31–45.

Johnson, D. L., & Walker, T. (1987). Primary prevention of behavior problems in Mexican-American children. *American Journal of Community Psychology, 15,* 375–385.

Johnson, S. M., Bolstad, O. D., & Lobitz, G. K. (1976). Generalization and contrast phenomena in behavior modification with children. In L. A. Hamerlynck, L. C. Handy, & E. J. Mash (Eds.), *Behavior modification and families* (pp. 160–188). New York: Brunner/Mazel.

Johnston, C. (1996). Addressing parent cognitions in interventions with families of disruptive children. In K. S. Dobson & K. D. Craig (Eds.), *Advances in cognitive-behavioral therapy* (pp. 193–209). Thousand Oaks, CA: Sage.

Johnston, C., & Mash, E. J. (1989). A measure of parenting satisfaction and efficacy. *Journal of Clinical Child Psychology, 18,* 167–175.

Jones, R. R. (1974). *"Observation" by telephone: An economical behavior sampling technique* (Oregon Research Institute Technical Report, Vol. 14, No. 1). Eugene: Oregon Research Institute.

Jouriles, E. N., Murphy, C. M., Farris, A. M., Smith, D. A., Richters, J. E., & Waters, E. (1991). Marital adjustment, parental disagreements about child rearing, and behavior problems in boys: Increasing the specificity of the marital assessment. *Child Development, 62,* 1424–1433.

Kafantaris, V., Campbell, M., Padron-Gayol, M. V., Small, A. M., Locascio, J. J., & Rosenberg, C. R. (1992). Carbamazepine in hospitalized aggressive Conduct Disorder children: An open pilot study. *Psychopharmacology Bulletin, 28,* 193–199.

Kahle, A. L., & Kelley, M. L. (1994). Children's homework problems: A comparison of goal setting and parent training. *Behavior Therapy, 25,* 275–290.

Kamphaus, R. W., & Frick, P. J. (1996). *Clinical assessment of child and adolescent personality and behavior.* Needham Heights, MA: Allyn & Bacon.

Katz, L. F., & Gottman, J. M. (1993). Patterns of marital conflict predict children's internalizing and externalizing behavior. *Developmental Psychology, 29,* 940–950.

Kazdin, A. E. (1977a). Assessing the clinical or applied importance of behavior change through social validation. *Behavior Modification, 1,* 427–452.

Kazdin, A. E. (1977b). *The token economy: A review and evaluation.* New York: Plenum Press.

Kazdin, A. E. (1990). Premature termination from treatment among children referred for antisocial behavior. *Journal of Child Psychology and Psychiatry, 31,* 415–425.

Kazdin, A. E. (1995a). Child, parent and family dysfunction as predictors of outcome in cognitive-behavioural treatment of antisocial children. *Behaviour Research and Therapy, 33,* 271–281.

Kazdin, A. E. (1995b). *Conduct disorders in childhood and adolescence* (2nd ed.). Thousand Oaks, CA: Sage.

Kazdin, A. E. (1996a). Combined and multimodal treatments in child and adolescent psychotherapy: Issues, challenges, and research directions. *Clinical Psychology: Science and Practice, 3,* 69–100.

Kazdin, A. E. (1996b). Problem solving and parent management in treating aggressive and antisocial behavior. In E. S. Hibbs & P. S. Jensen (Eds.), *Psychosocial treatments for child and adolescent disorders: Empirically based strategies for clinical practice* (pp. 377–408). Washington, DC: American Psychological Association.

Kazdin, A. E., Bass, D., Siegel, T. C., & Thomas, C. (1989). Cognitive behavioral therapy and relationship therapy in the treatment of children referred for antisocial behavior. *Journal of Consulting and Clinical Psychology, 57,* 522–536.

Kazdin, A. E., Esveldt-Dawson, K., French, N. H., & Unis, A. S. (1987a). Effects of parent management training and problem-solving skills training combined in the treatment of antisocial child behavior. *Journal of the American Academy of Child and Adolescent Psychiatry, 26,* 416–424.

Kazdin, A. E., Esveldt-Dawson, K., French, N. H., & Unis, A. S. (1987b). Problem-solving skills training and relationship therapy in the treatment of antisocial child behavior. *Journal of Consulting and Clinical Psychology, 55,* 76–85.

Kazdin, A. E., Holland, L., & Crowley, M. (1997). Family experience of barriers to treatment and premature termination from child therapy. *Journal of Consulting and Clinical Psychology, 65,* 453–463.

Kazdin, A. E., & Kolko, D. J. (1986). Parent psychopathology and family functioning among childhood firesetters. *Journal of Abnormal Child Psychology, 14,* 315–329.

Kazdin, A. E., Mazurick, J. L., & Bass, D. (1993). Risk for attrition in treatment of antisocial children and families. *Journal of Clinical Child Psychology, 22,* 2–16.

Kazdin, A. E., Mazurick, J. L., & Siegel, T. C. (1994). Treatment outcome among children with externalizing disorder who terminate prematurely versus those who complete psychotherapy. *Journal of the American Academy of Child and Adolescent Psychiatry, 33,* 549–557.

Kazdin, A. E., Siegel, T. C., & Bass, D. (1992). Cognitive problem-solving skills training and parent management training in the treatment of antisocial behavior in children. *Journal of Consulting and Clinical Psychology, 60,* 733–747.

Keith, T. Z. (1982). Time spent on homework and high school grades: A large sample path analysis. *Journal of Educational Psychology, 74,* 248–253.

Kellam, S. G., & Rebok, G. W. (1992). Building developmental and etiological theory through epidemiologically based preventive intervention trials. In J. McCord & R. E. Tremblay (Eds.), *Preventing antisocial behavior: Interventions from birth through adolescence* (pp. 162–191). New York: Guilford Press.

Kellam, S. G., Rebok, G. W., Ialongo, N., & Mayer, L. S. (1994). The course and malleability of aggressive behavior from early first grade into middle school: Results of a developmental epidemiologically based preventive trial. *Journal of Child Psychology and Psychiatry, 35,* 259–281.

Kelley, M. L. (1990). *School–home notes: Promoting children's classroom success.* New York: Guilford Press.

Kemph, J. P., DeVane, C. L., Levin, G. M., Jarecke, R., & Miller, R. L. (1993). Treatment of aggressive children with clonidine: Results of an open pilot study. *Journal of the American Academy of Child and Adolescent Psychiatry, 32,* 577–581.

Kendall, P. C. (1985). Toward a cognitive-behavioral model of child psychopathology and a critique of related interventions. *Journal of Abnormal Psychology, 13,* 357–372.

Kendall, P. C. (1991). Guiding theory for therapy with children and adolescents. In P. C. Kendall (Ed.), *Child and adolescent therapy: Cognitive-behavioral procedures* (pp. 3–22). New York: Guilford Press.

Kendall, P. C., & Braswell, L. (1985). *Cognitive-behavioral therapy for impulsive children.* New York: Guilford Press.

Kendall, P. C., & Braswell, L. (1993). *Cognitive-behavioral therapy for impulsive children* (2nd ed.). New York: Guilford Press.

Kendall, P. C., & MacDonald, J. P. (1993). Cognition in the psychopathology of youth and implications for treatment. In K. S. Dobson & P. C. Kendall (Eds.), *Psychopathology and cognition* (pp. 387–426). San Diego, CA: Academic Press.

Kendall, P. C., Reber, M., McLeer, S., Epps, J., & Ronan, K. R. (1990). Cognitive-behavioral treatment of conduct-disordered children. *Cognitive Therapy and Research, 14,* 279–297.

Kendall, P. C., Ronan, K. R., & Epps, J. (1991). Aggression in children/adolescents: Cognitive-behavioral treatment perspectives. In D. Pepler & K. H. Rubin (Eds.), *The development and treatment of childhood aggression* (pp. 341–360). Hillside, NJ: Erlbaum.

Kendziora, K. T., & O'Leary, S. G. (1992). Dysfunctional parenting as a focus for prevention and treatment of child behavior problems. In T. H. Ollendick & R. J. Prinz (Eds.), *Advances in clinical child psychology* (Vol. 15, pp. 175–206). New York: Plenum Press.

Kirigin, K. A. (1996). Teaching-Family Model of group home treatment of children with severe behavior problems. In M. C. Roberts (Ed.), *Model programs in child and family mental health* (pp. 231–247). Mahwah, NJ: Erlbaum.

Kirigin, K. A., Braukmann, C. J., Atwater, J. D., & Wolf, M. M. (1982). An evaluation of Teaching-Family (Achievement Place) group homes for juvenile offenders. *Journal of Applied Behavior Analysis, 15,* 1–16.

Kirigin, K. A., & Wolf, M. M. (1994, April). *A follow-up evaluation of Teaching-Family Model participants: Implications for treatment technology.* Paper presented at the meeting of the Southwestern Psychological Association, Tulsa, OK.

Klein, N. C., Alexander, J. F., & Parsons, B. V. (1977). Impact of family systems intervention on recidivism and sibling delinquency: A model of primary prevention and program evaluation. *Journal of Consulting and Clinical Psychology, 45,* 469–474.

Klein, R. D. (1979). Modifying academic performance in the grade school classroom. In M. Hersen, R. M. Eisler, & P. M. Miller (Eds.), *Progress in behavior modification* (Vol. 8, pp. 293–321). New York: Academic Press.

Klein, R. G. (1991). Preliminary results: Lithium effects in conduct disorders. In *CME syllabus and proceedings summary, 144th Annual Meeting of the American Psychiatric Association, New Orleans* (pp. 119–120). Washington, DC: American Psychiatric Association.

Klein, R. G., Abikoff, H., Klass, E., Shah, M., & Seese, L. (1994). *Controlled trial of methylphenidate, lithium, and placebo in children and adolescents with conduct disorders.* Paper presented at the meeting of the Society for Research in Child and Adolescent Psychopathology, London.

Kolko, D. J. (1983). Multicomponent parental treatment of firesetting in a six year old boy. *Journal of Behavior Therapy and Experimental Psychiatry, 14,* 349–353.

Kolko, D. J. (1985). Juvenile firesetting: A review and methodological critique. *Clinical Psychology Review, 5,* 345–376.

Kolko, D. J. (1988). Community interventions for childhood firesetters: A comparison of two national programs. *Hospital and Community Psychiatry, 39,* 973–979.

Kolko, D. J. (1996). Education and counseling for child firesetters: A comparison of skills training programs with standard practice. In E. D. Hibbs & P. S. Jensen (Eds.), *Psychosocial treatments for child and adolescent disorders: Empirically based strategies for clinical practice* (pp. 409–433). Washington, DC: American Psychological Association.

Kolko, D. J. (in press). Multimodal partial-day treatment of child antisocial behavior: Service description and multi-level program evaluation. *Continuum: Developments in Ambulatory Mental Health Care.*

Kolko, D. J., & Kazdin, A. E. (1988). Prevalence of firesetting and related behaviors among child psychiatric inpatients. *Journal of Consulting and Clinical Psychology, 56,* 628–630.

Kolko, D. J., & Kazdin, A. E. (1989a). Assessment of dimensions of childhood firesetting among patients and nonpatients: The Firesetting Risk Interview. *Journal of Abnormal Child Psychology, 17,* 157–176.

Kolko, D. J., & Kazdin, A. E. (1989b). The Children's Firesetting Interview with psychiatrically referred and nonreferred children. *Journal of Abnormal Child Psychology, 17,* 609–624.

Kolko, D. J., & Kazdin, A. E. (1991a). Aggression and psychopathology in match-playing and firesetting children: A replication and extension. *Journal of Clinical Child Psychology, 20,* 191–201.

Kolko, D. J., & Kazdin, A. E. (1991b). Motives of childhood firesetters: Firesetting characteristics and psychological correlates. *Journal of Child Psychology and Psychiatry, 32,* 535–550.

Kolko, D. J., Kazdin, A. E., & Meyer, E. C. (1985). Aggression and psychopathology in childhood firesetters: Parent and child reports. *Journal of Consulting and Clinical Psychology, 53,* 377–385.

Kolko, D. J., Loar, L. L., & Sturnick, D. (1990). Inpatient social-cognitive skills training groups with conduct disordered and attention deficit disordered children. *Journal of Child Psychology and Psychiatry, 31,* 737–748.

Kolko, D. J., Watson, S., & Faust, J. (1991). Fire safety/prevention skills training to reduce involvement with fire in young psychiatric inpatients: Preliminary findings. *Behavior Therapy, 22,* 269–284.

Kovacs, M., Paulauskas, S., Gatsonis, C., & Richards, C. (1988). Depressive disorders in childhood. *Journal of Affective Disorders, 15,* 205–217.

Kratzer, L., & Hodgins, S. (1997). Adult outcomes of child conduct problems: A cohort study. *Journal of Abnormal Child Psychology, 25,* 65–81.

Kruesi, M. J. P., & Lelio, D. F. (1996). Disorders of conduct and behavior. In J. M. Wiener (Ed.), *Diagnosis and psychopharmacology of childhood and adolescent disorders* (2nd ed., pp. 401–447). New York: Wiley.

Kuypers, D. S., Becker, W. C., & O'Leary, K. D. (1968). How to make a token system fail. *Exceptional Children, 11,* 101–108.

Lahey, B. B., Applegate, B., Barkley, R. A., Garfinkel, B., McBurnett, K., Kerdyck, L., Greenhill, L., Hynd, G. W., Frick, P. J., Newcorn, J., Biederman, J., Ollendick, T., Hart, E. L., Perez, D., Waldman, I., & Shaffer, D. (1994). DSM-IV field trials for Oppositional Defiant Disorder and Conduct Disorder in children and adolescents. *American Journal of Psychiatry, 151,* 1163–1171.

Lahey, B. B., Gendrich, J. G., Gendrich, S. I., Schnelle, J. F., Gant, D. S., & McNees, M. P. (1977). An evaluation of daily report cards with minimal teacher and parent contacts as an efficient method of classroom intervention. *Behavior Modification, 1,* 381–394.

Lahey, B. B., & Loeber, R. (1994). Framework for a developmental model of Oppositional Defiant Disorder and Conduct Disorder. In D. K. Routh (Ed.), *Disruptive behavior disorders in childhood* (pp. 139–180). New York: Plenum Press.

Lahey, B. B., Loeber, R., Hart, E. L., Frick, P. J., Applegate, B., Zhang, Q., Green, S. M., & Russo, M. F. (1995). Four-year longitudinal study of Conduct Disorder in boys: Patterns and predictors of persistence. *Journal of Abnormal Psychology, 104,* 83–93.

Lally, J. R., Mangione, P. L., Honig, A. S., & Wittner, D. S. (1988, April). More pride, less delinquency: Findings from the ten-year follow-up study of the Syracuse University Family Development Research Program. *Zero to Three, 13–18.*

Le Blanc, M., & Frechette, M. (1989). *Male criminal activity from childhood through youth.* New York: Springer-Verlag.

Leeman, L. W., Gibbs, J. C., & Fuller, D. (1993). Evaluation of a multicomponent group treatment program for juvenile delinquents. *Aggressive Behavior, 19,* 281–292.

Lilienfeld, S. O. (1992). The association between Antisocial Personality and Somatization Disorders: A review and integration of theoretical models. *Clinical Psychology Review, 12,* 641–662.

Lochman, J. E. (1985). Effects of different treatment lengths in cognitive behavioral interventions with aggressive boys. *Child Psychiatry and Human Development, 16,* 45–56.

Lochman, J. E. (1992). Cognitive-behavioral interventions with aggressive boys: Three year follow-up and preventive effects. *Journal of Consulting and Clinical Psychology, 60,* 426–432.

Lochman, J. E., Burch, P. R., Curry, J. F., & Lampron, L. B. (1984). Treatment and generalization effects of cognitive-behavioral and goal-setting interventions with aggressive boys. *Journal of Consulting and Clinical Psychology, 52,* 915–916.

Lochman, J. E., & Curry, J. F. (1986). Effects of social problem-solving training and self-instruction training with aggressive boys. *Journal of Clinical Child Psychology, 15,* 159–164.

Lochman, J. E., & Lampron, L. B. (1988). Cognitive behavioral interventions for aggressive boys: Seven months follow-up effects. *Journal of Child and Adolescent Psychotherapy, 5,* 15–23.

Lochman, J. E., Lampron, L. B., Burch, P. R., & Curry, J. F. (1985). Client characteristics associated with behavior change for treated and untreated aggressive boys. *Journal of Abnormal Child Psychology, 13,* 527–538.

Lochman, J. E., Lampron, L. B., Gemmer, T. C., & Harris, S. R. (1987). Anger coping intervention with aggressive children: A guide to implementation in school settings. In P. A. Keller & S. R. Heyman (Eds.), *Innovations in clinical practice: A source book* (Vol. 6, pp. 339–356). Sarasota, FL: Professional Resource Exchange.

Lochman, J. E., Nelson, W. M., & Sims, J. P. (1981). A cognitive behavioral program for use with aggressive children. *Journal of Clinical Child Psychology, 10,* 146–148.

Lochman, J. E., & Wells, K. C. (1996). A social-cognitive intervention with aggressive children: Prevention effects and contextual implementation issues. In R. D. Peters & R. J. McMahon (Eds.), *Preventing childhood disorders, substance abuse, and delinquency* (pp. 111–143). Thousand Oaks, CA: Sage.

Locke, H. J., & Wallace, K. M. (1959). Short marital adjustment and prediction tests: Their reliability and validity. *Marriage and Family Living, 21,* 251–255.

Loeber, R. (1988). Natural histories of conduct problems, delinquency, and associated substance use: Evidence for developmental progressions. In B. B. Lahey & A. E. Kazdin (Eds.), *Advances in clinical child psychology* (Vol. 11, pp. 73–124). New York: Plenum Press.

Loeber, R., & Dishion, T. S. (1983). Early predictors of male delinquency: A review. *Psychological Bulletin, 94,* 68–99.

Loeber, R., & Keenan, K. (1994). Interaction between Conduct Disorder and its comorbid conditions: Effects of age and gender. *Clinical Psychology Review, 14,* 497–523.

Loeber, R., & Schmaling, K. B. (1985a). Empirical evidence for overt and covert patterns of antisocial conduct problems: A meta-analysis. *Journal of Abnormal Child Psychology, 13,* 337–352.

Loeber, R., & Schmaling, K. B. (1985b). The utility of differentiating between mixed and pure forms of antisocial child behavior. *Journal of Abnormal Child Psychology, 13,* 315–336.

Loeber, R., & Stouthamer-Loeber, M. (1986). Family factors as correlates and predictors of juvenile conduct problems and delinquency. In M. Tonry & N. Morris (Eds.), *Crime and justice* (Vol. 7, pp. 29–149). Chicago: University of Chicago Press.

Loeber, R., Stouthamer-Loeber, M., Van Kammen, W. B., & Farrington, D. P. (1989). Development of a new measure of self-reported antisocial behavior for young children: Prevalence and reliability. In M. W. Klein (Ed.), *Cross national research and self-reported crime and delinquency* (pp. 203–225). Dordrecht, The Netherlands: Kluwer–Nijhoff.

Loeber, R., Weissman, W., & Reid, J. B. (1983). Family interactions of assaultive adolescents, stealers, and nondelinquents. *Journal of Abnormal Child Psychology, 11,* 1–14.

Loeber, R., Wung, P., Keenan, K., Giroux, B., Stouthamer-Loeber, M., Van Kammen, W. B., & Maughan, B. (1993). Developmental pathways in disruptive child behavior. *Development and Psychopathology, 5,* 101–131.

Long, P., Forehand, R., Wierson, M., & Morgan, A. (1994). Does parent training with young noncompliant children have long-term effects? *Behaviour Research and Therapy, 32,* 101–107.

Lyon, G. R. (Ed.). (1994). *Frames of reference for the assessment of learning disabilities: New views on measurement issues.* Baltimore: Paul H. Brookes.

Lyons-Ruth, K. (1996). Attachment relationships among children with aggressive behavior problems: The role of disorganized early attachment patterns. *Journal of Consulting and Clinical Psychology, 64,* 64–73.

Main, M., & Solomon, J. (1990). Procedures for identifying infants as disorganized/disoriented during the Ainsworth Strange Situation. In M. Greenberg, D. Cicchetti, & E. M. Cummings (Eds.), *Attachment in the preschool years: Theory, research and intervention* (pp. 121–160). Chicago: University of Chicago Press.

Martens, B. K., & Hiralall, A. S. (1997). Scripted sequences of teacher interaction. *Behavior Modification, 21,* 308–323.

Mas, C. H., Alexander, J. F., & Barton, C. (1985). Modes of expression in family therapy: A process study of roles and gender. *Journal of Marital and Family Therapy, 11,* 411–415.

Mash, E. J., & Dozois, D. J. A. (1996). Child psychopathology: A developmental-systems perspective.

In E. J. Mash & R. A. Barkley (Eds.), *Child Psychopathology* (pp. 3–60). New York: Guilford Press.

Mash, E. J., & Terdal, L. G. (1997). Assessment of child and family disturbance: A behavioral-systems approach. In E. J. Mash & L. G. Terdal (Eds.), *Assessment of childhood disorders* (3rd ed., pp. 3–68). New York: Guilford Press.

Mattes, J. A. (1990). Comparative effectiveness of carbamazepine and propranolol for rage outbursts. *Journal of Neuropsychiatry and Clinical Neurosciences, 2,* 159–164.

McConaughy, S. H., & Achenbach, T. M. (1994). *Manual for the Semistructured Clinical Interview for Children and Adolescents.* Burlington: University of Vermont, Department of Psychiatry.

McCord, J. (1988). Identifying developmental paradigms leading to alcoholism. *Journal of Studies on Alcohol, 49,* 357–362.

McCord, J., & Tremblay, R. E. (Eds.). (1992). *Preventing antisocial behavior: Interventions from birth through adolescence.* New York: Guilford Press.

McGee, R., Feehan, M., Williams, S., & Anderson, J. (1992). DSM-III disorders from age 11 to age 15 years. *Journal of the American Academy of Child and Adolescent Psychiatry, 31,* 50–59.

McGrath, P., Marshall, P. T., & Prior, K. (1979). A comprehensive treatment program for a firesetting child. *Journal of Behavior Therapy and Experimental Psychiatry, 10,* 69–72.

McMahon, R. J. (1994). Diagnosis, assessment, and treatment of externalizing problems in children: The role of longitudinal data. *Journal of Consulting and Clinical Psychology, 62,* 901–917.

McMahon, R. J., & Estes, A. (1993). *Fast Track parent–child interaction task: Observational data collection manuals.* Unpublished manuscript, University of Washington.

McMahon, R. J., & Estes, A. M. (1997). Conduct problems. In E. J. Mash & L. G. Terdal (Eds.), *Assessment of childhood disorders* (3rd ed., pp. 130–193). New York: Guilford Press.

McMahon, R. J., & Forehand, R. (1983). Consumer satisfaction in behavioral treatment of children: Types, issues, and recommendations. *Behavior Therapy, 14,* 209–225.

McMahon, R. J., & Forehand, R. (1984). Parent training for the noncompliant child: Treatment outcome, generalization, and adjunctive therapy procedures. In R. F. Dangel & R. A. Polster (Eds.), *Parent training: Foundations of research and practice* (pp. 298–328). New York: Guilford Press.

McMahon, R. J., Forehand, R., & Griest, D. L. (1981). Effects of knowledge of social learning principles on enhancing treatment outcome and generalization in a parent training program. *Journal of Consulting and Clinical Psychology, 49,* 526–532.

McMahon, R. J., Forehand, R., Griest, D. L., & Wells, K. C. (1981). Who drops out of treatment during parent behavioral training? *Behavioral Counseling Quarterly, 1,* 79–85.

McMahon, R. J., Forehand, R., & Tiedemann, G. L. (1985, November). *Relative effectiveness of a parent training program with children of different ages.* Paper presented at the meeting of the Association for Advancement of Behavior Therapy, Houston.

McMahon, R. J., Slough, N. M., & the Conduct Problems Prevention Research Group. (1996). Family-based intervention in the Fast Track Program. In R. DeV. Peters & R. J. McMahon (Eds.), *Preventing childhood disorders, substance abuse, and delinquency* (pp. 90–110). Thousand Oaks, CA: Sage.

McMahon, R. J., Tiedemann, G. L., Forehand, R., & Griest, D. L. (1984). Parental satisfaction with parent training to modify child noncompliance. *Behavior Therapy, 15,* 295–303.

McNeil, C. B., Eyberg, S., Eisenstadt, T. H., Newcomb, K., & Funderburk, B. (1991). Parent–child interaction therapy with behavior problem children: Generalization of treatment effects to the school setting. *Journal of Clinical Child Psychology, 20,* 140–151.

Medland, M. B., & Stachnik, T. J. (1972). Good Behavior Game: A replication and systematic analysis. *Journal of Applied Behavior Analysis, 5,* 45–51.

Michelson, L., Mannarino, A. P., Marchione, K. E., Stern, M., Figueroa, J., & Beck, S. (1983). A comparative outcome study of behavioral social-skills training, interpersonal-problem-solving and nondirective control treatments with child psychiatric outpatients. *Behaviour Research and Therapy, 21,* 545–556.

Miczek, K. A., & Barry, H. (1976). Pharmacology of sex and aggression. In S. D. Glick & J. Goldfarb (Eds.), *Behavioral pharmacology* (pp. 176–257). St. Louis, MO: C. V. Mosby.

Middlebrook, J. L., & Forehand, R. (1985). Maternal perceptions of deviance in child behavior as a function of stress and clinic versus nonclinic status of the child: An analogue study. *Behavior Therapy, 16,* 494–502.

Miller, D. L., & Kelley, M. L. (1991). Interventions for improving homework performance: A critical review. *School Psychology Quarterly, 6,* 174–185.

Miller, G. E., & Klungness, L. (1986). Treatment of nonconfrontative stealing in school-age children. *School Psychology Review, 15,* 24–35.

Miller, G. E., & Klungness, L. (1989). Childhood theft: A comprehensive review of assessment and treatment. *School Psychology Review, 18,* 82–97.

Miller, G. E., & Prinz, R. J. (1990). Enhancement of social learning family interventions for childhood Conduct Disorder. *Psychological Bulletin, 108,* 291–307.

Moffitt, T. E. (1990). Juvenile delinquency and Attention Deficit Disorder: Boys' developmental trajectories from age 3 to age 15. *Child Development, 61,* 893–910.

Moffitt, T. E. (1993). "Adolescence-limited" and "life-course-persistent" antisocial behavior: A developmental taxonomy. *Psychological Review, 100,* 674–701.

Moffitt, T. E., Caspi, A., Dickson, N., Silva, P., & Stanton, W. (1996). Childhood-onset versus adolescent-onset antisocial conduct problems in males: Natural history from ages 3 to 18 years. *Development and Psychopathology, 8,* 399–424.

Moore, D., Chamberlain, P., & Mukai, L. (1979). Children at risk for delinquency: A follow-up comparison of aggressive children and children who steal. *Journal of Abnormal Child Psychology, 7,* 345–355.

Morris, S. B., Alexander, J. F., & Waldron, H. (1988). Functional Family Therapy: Issues in clinical practice. In I. R. H. Falloon (Ed.), *Handbook of behavioral family therapy* (pp. 107–127). New York: Guilford Press.

Nelson, C. M., Rutherford, R. B., Center, D. B., & Walker, H. M. (1991). Do public schools have an obligation to serve troubled children and youth? *Exceptional Children, 57,* 406–415.

Nelson, J. R., Smith, D. J., & Dodd, J. (1990). The moral reasoning of juvenile delinquents: A meta analysis. *Journal of Abnormal Child Psychology, 18,* 231–239.

Newberry, A. M., Alexander, J. F., & Turner, C. W. (1991). Gender as a process variable in family therapy. *Journal of Family Psychology, 5,* 158–175.

Novaco, R. W. (1978). Anger and coping with stress: Cognitive-behavioral interventions. In J. P. Foreyt & D. P. Rathjen (Eds.), *Cognitive behavioral therapy: Research and application* (pp. 135–173). New York: Plenum Press.

O'Dell, S. L (1974). Training parents in behavior modification: A review. *Psychological Bulletin, 81,* 418–433.

O'Dell, S. L. (1985). Progress in parent training. In M. Hersen, R. M. Eisler, & P. M. Miller (Eds.), *Progress in behavior modification* (Vol. 9, pp. 57–108). New York: Academic Press.

O'Donnell, J., Hawkins, J. D., Catalano, R. F., Abbott, R. D., & Day, L. E. (1995). Preventing school failure, drug use, and delinquency among low-income children: Long-term intervention in elementary schools. *American Journal of Orthopsychiatry, 65,* 87–100.

Office of Juvenile Justice and Delinquency Prevention. (1996, October). *Second National Training Conference on Strengthening America's Families,* Snowbird, UT.

Offord, D. R., Alder, R. J., & Boyle, M. H. (1986). Prevalence and sociodemographic correlates of Conduct Disorder. *American Journal of Social Psychiatry, 6,* 272–278.

Offord, D. R., Boyle, M. H., Racine, Y. A., Fleming, J. E., Cadman, D. T., Blum, H. M., Byrne, C., Links, P. S., Lipman, E. L., MacMillan, H. L., Grant, N. I. R., Sanford, M. N., Szatmari, P.,

Thomas, H., & Woodward, C. A. (1992). Outcome, prognosis, and risk in a longitudinal follow-up study. *Journal of the American Academy of Child and Adolescent Psychiatry, 31,* 916–923.

O'Leary, K. D., & Drabman, R. (1971). Token reinforcement programs in the classroom: A review. *Psychological Bulletin, 75,* 379–398.

O'Leary, K. D., Becker, W. C., Evans, M. B., & Saudargas, R. A. (1969). A token reinforcement program in a public school: A replication and systematic analysis. *Journal of Applied Behavior Analysis, 2,* 3–13.

O'Leary, K. D., & O'Leary, S. G. (1977). *Classroom management: The successful use of behavior modification* (2nd ed.). New York: Pergamon Press.

Ollendick, T. H., & King, N. J. (1994). Diagnosis, assessment, and treatment of internalizing problems in children: The role of longitudinal data. *Journal of Consulting and Clinical Psychology, 62,* 918–927.

Olweus, D. (1980). Familial and temperamental determinants of aggressive behavior in adolescent boys: A causal analysis. *Developmental Psychology, 16,* 644–660.

Olweus, D. (1990). Bullying among children. In K. Hurrelmann & F. Losel (Eds.), *Health hazards in adolescence: Prevention and intervention in childhood and adolescence* (Vol. 8, pp. 259–297). Berlin: de Gruyter.

Olweus, D. (1991). Bully/victim problems among schoolchildren: Basic facts and effects of a school-based intervention program. In D. J. Pepler & K. H. Rubin (Eds.), *The development and treatment of childhood aggression* (pp. 411–448). Hillsdale, NJ: Erlbaum.

Olweus, D. (1992). Bullying among schoolchildren: Intervention and prevention. In R. Dev. Peters, R. J. McMahon, & V. L. Quinsey (Eds.), *Aggression and violence throughout the lifespan* (pp. 100–125). Newbury Park, CA: Sage.

Olweus, D. (1993). Victimization by peers: Antecedents and long-term outcomes. In K. H. Rubin & J. B. Asendorf (Eds.), *Social withdrawal, inhibition, and shyness in childhood* (pp. 315–341). Hillsdale, NJ: Erlbaum.

Olweus, D. (1996). Bullying at school: Knowledge base and an effective intervention program. *Annals of the New York Academy of Sciences, 794,* 265–276.

Parsons, B. V., & Alexander, J. F. (1973). Short-term family intervention: A therapy outcome study. *Journal of Consulting and Clinical Psychology, 41,* 195–201.

Patterson, G. R. (1974). Interventions for boys with conduct problems: Multiple settings, treatments, and criteria. *Journal of Consulting and Clinical Psychology, 42,* 471–481.

Patterson, G. R. (1975a). *Families: Applications of social learning to family life* (rev. ed.). Champaign, IL: Research Press.

Patterson, G. R. (1975b). *Professional guide for "Families" and "Living with Children."* Champaign, IL: Research Press.

Patterson, G. R. (1976). *Living with children: New methods for parents and teachers* (rev. ed.). Champaign, IL: Research Press.

Patterson, G. R. (1982). *Coercive family process.* Eugene, OR: Castalia.

Patterson, G. R. (1983). Stress: A change agent for family process. In N. Garmezy & M. Rutter (Eds.), *Stress, coping and development in children* (pp. 235–264). New York: McGraw-Hill.

Patterson, G. R., & Bank, L. (1986). Bootstrapping your way in the nomological thicket. *Behavioral Assessment, 8,* 49–73.

Patterson, G. R., & Capaldi, D. M. (1991). Antisocial parents: Unskilled and vulnerable. In P. Cowan & E. M. Hetherington (Eds.), *Family transitions* (pp. 195–218). Hillsdale, NJ: Erlbaum.

Patterson, G. R., Capaldi, D., & Bank, L. (1991). An early starter model for predicting delinquency. In D. J. Pepler & K. H. Rubin (Eds.), *The development and treatment of childhood aggression* (pp. 139–168). Hillsdale, NJ: Erlbaum.

Patterson, G. R., & Chamberlain, P. (1988). Treatment process: A problem at three levels. In L. C. Wynne (Ed.), *The state of the art in family therapy research: Controversies and recommendations* (pp. 189–223). New York: Family Process Press.

Patterson, G. R., & Chamberlain, P. (1994). A functional analysis of resistance during parent training therapy. *Clinical Psychology: Science and Practice, 1,* 53–70.

Patterson, G. R., Chamberlain, P., & Reid, J. B. (1982). A comparative evaluation of a parent training program. *Behavior Therapy, 13,* 638–650.

Patterson, G. R., Cobb, J. A., & Ray, R. S. (1973). A social engineering technology for retraining the families of aggressive boys. In H. E. Adams & I. P. Unikel (Eds.), *Issues and trends in behavior therapy* (pp. 139–210). Springfield, IL: Charles C Thomas.

Patterson, G. R., & Fleischman, M. J. (1979). Maintenance of treatment effects: Some considerations concerning family systems and follow-up data. *Behavior Therapy, 10,* 168–185.

Patterson, G. R., & Forgatch, M. S. (1985). Therapist behavior as a determinant for client noncompliance: A paradox for the behavior modifier. *Journal of Consulting and Clinical Psychology, 53,* 846–851.

Patterson, G. R., & Forgatch, M. S. (1987). *Parents and adolescents living together: Part 1. The basics.* Eugene, OR: Castalia.

Patterson, G. R., & Forgatch, M. S. (1995). Predicting future clinical adjustment from treatment outcome and process variables. *Psychological Assessment, 7,* 275–285.

Patterson, G. R., Ray, R. S., Shaw, D. A., & Cobb, J. A. (1969). *Manual for coding of family interactions* (rev. ed.). New York: Microfiche.

Patterson, G. R., & Reid, J. B. (1973). Intervention for families of aggressive boys: A replication study. *Behaviour Research and Therapy, 11,* 383–394.

Patterson, G. R., Reid, J. B., & Dishion, T. J. (1992). *Antisocial boys.* Eugene, OR: Castalia.

Patterson, G. R., Reid, J. B., Jones, R. R., & Conger, R. E. (1975). *A social learning approach to family intervention: Vol. 1. Families with aggressive children.* Eugene, OR: Castalia.

Peed, S., Roberts, M., & Forehand, R. (1977). Evaluation of the effectiveness of a standardized parent training program in altering the interaction of mothers and their noncompliant children. *Behavior Modification, 1,* 323–350.

Pelham, W. E., & Lang, A. R. (1993). Parental alcohol consumption and deviant child behavior: Laboratory studies of reciprocal effects. *Clinical Psychology Review, 13,* 763–784.

Pepler, D. J., & Craig, W. M. (1995). A peek behind the fence: Naturalistic observations of aggressive children with remote audiovisual recording. *Developmental Psychology, 31,* 548–553.

Pepler, D. J., Craig, W. M., Ziegler, S., & Charach, A. (1993). A school-based antibullying intervention: Preliminary evaluation. In D. Tattum (Ed.), *Understanding and managing bullying* (pp. 76–91). Oxford: Heinemann.

Pepler, D. J., Craig, W. M., Ziegler, S., & Charach, A. (1994). An evaluation of an anti-bullying intervention in Toronto schools. *Canadian Journal of Community Mental Health, 13,* 95–110.

Peters, R. DeV., & McMahon, R. J. (Eds.). (1996). *Preventing childhood disorders, substance abuse, and delinquency.* Thousand Oaks, CA: Sage.

Pfiffner, L. J., & Barkley, R. A. (in press). Treatment of ADHD in school settings. In R. A. Barkley, *ADHD in children and adults: A handbook for diagnosis, assessment, and treatment.* New York: Guilford Press.

Pfiffner, L. J., & O'Leary, S. G. (1987). The efficacy of all-positive management as a function of the prior use of negative consequences. *Journal of Applied Behavior Analysis, 20,* 265–271.

Pfiffner, L. J., Rosen, L. A., & O'Leary, S. G. (1985). The efficacy of an all-positive approach to classroom management. *Journal of Applied Behavior Analysis, 18,* 257–261.

Pigott, H. E., & Heggie, D. L. (1986). Interpreting the conflicting results of individual versus group contingencies in classrooms: The targeted behavior as a mediating variable. *Child & Family Behavior Therapy, 7,* 1–14.

Porter, B., & O'Leary, K. D. (1980). Marital discord and childhood behavior problems. *Journal of Abnormal Child Psychology, 8,* 287–295.

Power, C., Higgins, A., & Kohlberg, L. (1989). *Lawrence Kohlberg's approach to moral education.* New York: Columbia University Press.

Powers, S. W., & Roberts, M. W. (1995). Simulation training with parents of oppositional children: Preliminary findings. *Journal of Clinical Child Psychology, 24,* 89–97.

Presidential Commission on Law Enforcement and the Administration of Justice. (1967). *Task force report: Juvenile delinquency and youth crime.* Washington, DC: U. S. Government Printing Office.

Prinz, R. J., Blechman, E. A., & Dumas, J. E. (1994). An evaluation of peer coping-skills training for childhood aggression. *Journal of Clinical Child Psychology, 23,* 193–203.

Prinz, R. J., & Miller, G. E. (1991). Issues in understanding and treating childhood conduct problems in disadvantaged populations. *Journal of Clinical Child Psychology, 20,* 379–385.

Prinz, R. J., & Miller, G. E. (1994). Family-based treatment for childhood antisocial behavior: Experimental influences on dropout and engagement. *Journal of Consulting and Clinical Psychology, 62,* 645–650.

Prinz, R. J., & Miller, G. E. (1996). Parental engagement in interventions for children at risk for Conduct Disorder. In R. DEV. Peters & R. J. McMahon (Eds.), *Preventing childhood disorders, substance abuse, and delinquency* (pp. 161–183). Thousand Oaks, CA: Sage.

Proctor, M. A., & Morgan, D. (1991). Effectiveness of a response cost raffle procedure on the disruptive classroom behavior of adolescents with behavior problems. *School Psychology Review, 20,* 97–109.

Puig-Antich, J. (1982). Major Depression and Conduct Disorder in prepuberty. *Journal of the American Academy of Child and Adolescent Psychiatry, 21,* 118–128.

Reddy, L. A., & Pfeiffer, S. I. (1997). Effectiveness of treatment foster care with children and adolescents: A review of outcome studies. *Journal of the American Academy of Child and Adolescent Psychiatry, 36,* 581–588.

Reich, W., & Welner, Z. (1988). *Revised version of the Diagnostic Interview for Children and Adolescents (DICA-R).* St. Louis, MO: Department of Psychiatry, Washington University School of Medicine.

Reid, J. B. (Ed.). (1978). *A social learning approach to family intervention: Vol. 2. Observation in home settings.* Eugene, OR: Castalia.

Reid, J. B. (1984, November). Stealing and other clandestine activities among antisocial children. In D. J. Kolko (Chair), *Child antisocial behavior research: Current status and implications.* Symposium conducted at the meeting of the Association for Advancement of Behavior Therapy, Philadelphia.

Reid, J. B. (1987, March). *Therapeutic interventions in the families of aggressive children and adolescents.* Paper presented at the meeting of the Organizzato dalle Cattedre di Psicologia Clinica e delle Teorie di Personalita dell'Universita di Roma, Rome.

Reid, J. B. (1993). Prevention of Conduct Disorder before and after school entry: Relating interventions to developmental findings. *Development and Psychopathology, 5,* 243–262.

Reid, J. B., Baldwin, D. V., Patterson, G. R., & Dishion, T. J. (1988). Observations in the assessment of childhood disorders. In M. Rutter, A. H. Tuma, & I. S. Lann (Eds.), *Assessment and diagnosis in child psychpathology* (pp. 156–195). New York: Guilford Press.

Reid, J. B., Eddy, J. M., Bank, L., & Fetrow, R. (1994, November). *Some preliminary findings from an universal prevention program for Conduct Disorder.* Paper presented at the Fourth National Institute of Mental Health National Conference on Prevention Research, Washington, DC.

Reid, J. B., & Hendricks, A. F. C. J. (1973). A preliminary analysis of the effectiveness of direct home intervention for treatment of pre-delinquent boys who steal. In L. A. Hamerlynck, L. C. Handy, & E. J. Mash (Eds.), *Behavior change: Methodology, concepts, and practice* (pp. 209–220). Champaign, IL: Research Press.

Reid, J. B., Hinojosa Rivera, G., & Lorber, R. (1980). *A social learning approach to the outpatient treatment of children who steal.* Unpublished manuscript, Oregon Social Learning Center, Eugene.

Reis, D. (1975). *Central neurotransmitters in aggressive behaviors: Neural basis of violence and aggression.* St. Louis, MO: Green.

Richters, J. E. (1992). Depressed mothers as informants about their children: A critical review of the evidence for distortion. *Psychological Bulletin, 112,* 485–499.

Riddle, M. A., Nelson, J. C., Kleinman, C. S., Rasmusson, A., Leckman, J. F., King, R. A., & Cohen, D. J. (1991). A case study: Sudden death in children receiving Norpramin. A review of three reported cases and commentary. *Journal of the American Academy of Child and Adolescent Psychiatry, 30,* 104–108.

Rifkin, A., Karajgi, B., Perl, E., Dicker, R., Boppana, V., & Hasan, N. (1989). *Lithium in adolescents with Conduct Disorder.* Paper presented at the Annual New Clinical Drug Evaluation Unit, Key Biscayne, FL.

Robbins, M. S., Alexander, J. F., Newell, R. M., & Turner, C. W. (1996). The immediate effect of reframing on client attitude in family therapy. *Journal of Family Psychology, 10,* 28–34.

Roberts, M. W., Joe, V. C., & Rowe-Hallbert, A. (1992). Oppositional child behavior and parental locus of control. *Journal of Clinical Child Psychology, 21,* 170–177.

Robins, L. N. (1991). Conduct Disorder. *Journal of Child Psychology and Psychiatry, 32,* 193–209.

Rogers, T. R., Forehand, R., Griest, D. L., Wells, K. C., & McMahon, R. J. (1981). Socioeconomic status: Effects on parent and child behaviors and treatment outcome of parent training. *Journal of Clinical Child Psychology, 10,* 98–101.

Rosen, H. S., & Rosen, L. A. (1983). Eliminating stealing: Use of stimulus control with an elementary student. *Behavior Modification, 7,* 56–63.

Rosen, L. A., Gabardi, L., Miller, C. D., & Miller, L. (1990). Home-based treatment of disruptive junior high school students: An analysis of the differential effects of positive and negative consequences. *Behavioral Disorders, 15,* 227–232.

Routh, C. P., Hill, J. W., Steele, H., Elliott, C. E., & Dewey, M. E. (1995). Maternal attachment status, psychosocial stressors and problem behaviour: Follow-up after parent training courses for Conduct Disorder. *Journal of Child Psychology and Psychiatry, 36,* 1179–1198.

Ruma, P. R., Burke, R. V., & Thompson, R. W. (1996). Group parent training: Is it effective for children of all ages? *Behavior Therapy, 27,* 159–169.

Rusby, J. C., Estes, A., & Dishion, T. (1991). *The Interpersonal Process Code (IPC).* Unpublished manuscript, Oregon Social Learning Center, Eugene.

Russo, D. C., Cataldo, M. F., & Cushing, P. J. (1981). Compliance training and behavioral covariation in the treatment of multiple behavior problems. *Journal of Applied Behavior Analysis, 14,* 209–222.

Rutter, M. (1994). Family discord and Conduct Disorder: Cause, consequence, or correlate? *Journal of Family Psychology, 8,* 170–186.

Rutter, M., Harrington, R., Quinton, D., & Pickles, A. (1994). Adult outcome of Conduct Disorder in childhood: Implications for concepts and definitions of patterns of psychopathology. In R. D. Ketterlinus & M. E. Lamb (Eds.), *Adolescent problem behaviors: Issues and research* (pp. 57–80). Hillsdale, NJ: Erlbaum.

Sanders, M. R. (1982). The generalization of parent responding to community settings: The effects of instructions, plus feedback, and self-management training. *Behavioural Psychotherapy, 10,* 273–287.

Sanders, M. R. (1996). New directions in behavioral family intervention with children. In T. H. Ollendick & R. J. Prinz (Eds.), *Advances in clinical child psychology* (Vol. 18, pp. 283–331). New York: Plenum Press.

Sanders, M. R., & Christensen, A. P. (1985). A comparison of the effects of child management and planned activities training in five parenting environments. *Journal of Abnormal Child Psychology, 13,* 101–117.

Sanders, M. R., & Dadds, M. R. (1982). The effects of planned activities and child management procedures in parent training: An analysis of setting generality. *Behavior Therapy, 13,* 452–461.

Sanders, M. R., & Dadds, M. R. (1992). Children's and parents' cognitions about family interaction: An evaluation of video-mediated recall and thought listing procedures in the assessment of conduct-disordered children. *Journal of Clinical Child Psychology, 21,* 371–379.

Sanders, M. R., & Dadds, M. R. (1993). *Behavioral family intervention.* Needham Heights, MA: Allyn & Bacon.

Sanders, M. R., & Glynn, T. (1981). Training parents in behavioral self management: An analysis of generalization and maintenance. *Journal of Applied Behavior Analysis, 14,* 223–237.

Sanders, M. R., & Lawton, J. M. (1993). Discussing assessment findings with families: A guided participation model of information transfer. *Child & Family Behavior Therapy, 15,* 5–35.

Sanson, A., Oberklaid, F., Pedlow, R., & Prior, M. (1991). Risk indicators: Assessment of infancy predictors of pre-school behavioural maladjustment. *Journal of Child Psychology and Psychiatry, 32,* 609–626.

Sarason, I. G., Johnson, J. H., & Siegel, J. M. (1978). Assessing the impact of life changes: Development of the Life Experiences Survey. *Journal of Consulting and Clinical Psychology, 46,* 932–946.

Saunders, J. D., Aasland, O. G., Babor, T. F., de la Fuente, J. R., & Grant, M. (1993). Development of the Alcohol Use Disorders Identification Test (AUDIT): WHO collaborative project on early detection of persons with harmful alcohol consumption—II. *Addiction, 88,* 791–804.

Sayger, T. V., Horne, A. M., & Glaser, B. A. (1993). Marital satisfaction and social learning family therapy for child conduct problems: Generalization of treatment effects. *Journal of Marital and Family Therapy, 19,* 393–402.

Sayger, T. V., Horne, A. M., Walker, J. M., & Passmore, J. L. (1988). Social learning family therapy with aggressive children: Treatment outcome and maintenance. *Journal of Family Psychology, 1,* 261–285.

Schoenwald, S. K., Henggeler, S. W., Pickrel, S. G., & Cunningham, P. B. (1996). Treating seriously troubled youths and families in their contexts: Multisystemic Therapy. In M. C. Roberts (Ed.), *Model programs in child and family mental health* (pp. 317–332). Mahwah, NJ: Erlbaum.

Schumaker, J. B., Hovell, M. F., & Sherman, J. A. (1977). An analysis of daily report cards and parent-managed privileges in the improvement of adolescents' classroom performance. *Journal of Applied Behavior Analysis, 10,* 449–464.

Schweinhart, L. J., Barnes, H. V., & Weikart, D. P. (Eds.). (1993). *Significant benefits: The High/Scope Perry Preschool Study through age 27.* Ypsilanti, MI: High/Scope Press.

Scott, M. J., & Stradling, S. G. (1987). Evaluation of a group programme for parents of problem children. *Behavioural Psychotherapy, 15,* 224–239.

Seitz, V., Rosenbaum, L. K., & Apfel, N. H. (1985). Effects of family support intervention: A ten-year follow-up. *Child Development, 56,* 376–391.

Selzer, M. L., Vinokur, A., & van Rooijen, L. (1975). A self-administered short Michigan Alcoholism Screening Test. *Journal of Studies on Alcohol, 36,* 117–126.

Serbin, L. A., Peters, P. L., McAffer, V. J., & Schwartzman, A. E. (1991). Childhood aggression and withdrawal as predictors of adolescent pregnancy, early parenthood, and environmental risk for the next generation. *Canadian Journal of Behavioural Science, 23,* 318–331.

Serketich, W. J., & Dumas, J. E. (1996). The effectiveness of behavioral parent training to modify antisocial behavior in children: A meta-analysis. *Behavior Therapy, 27,* 171–186.

Seymour, F. W., & Epston, D. (1989). An approach to childhood stealing with evaluation of 45 cases. *Australian and New Zealand Journal of Family Therapy, 10,* 137–143.

Shaffer, D., Fisher, P., Piacentini, J., Schwab-Stone, M., & Wicks, J. (1991). *NIMH Diagnostic Interview Schedule for Children—Version 2.3.* New York: New York State Psychiatric Institute.

Shaffer, D., Schwab-Stone, M., Fisher, P., Cohen, P., Piacentini, J., Davies, M., Conners, C. K., & Regier, D. (1993). The Diagnostic Interview Schedule for Children—Revised version (DISC-R): I. Preparation, field testing, interrater reliability, and acceptability. *Journal of the American Academy of Child and Adolescent Psychiatry, 32,* 643–650.

Sholevar, G. P., & Sholevar, E. H. (1995). Overview. In G. P. Sholevar (Ed.), *Conduct disorders in children and adolescents* (pp. 3–26). Washington, DC: American Psychiatric Press.

Shores, R., Gunter, P., & Jack, S. (1993). Classroom management strategies: Are they setting events for coercion? *Behavioral Disorders, 18,* 92–102.

Skinner, H. A. (1982). The Drug Abuse Screening Test. *Addictive Behaviors, 7,* 363–371.

Slabach, E. H., Morrow, J., & Wachs, T. D. (1991). Questionnaire measurement of infant and child temperament: Current status and future directions. In J. Strelau & A. Angleitner (Eds.), *Explorations in temperament: International perspectives on theory and measurement* (pp. 205–234). New York: Plenum Press.

Smith, P. K., & Sharp, S. (Eds.). (1994a). *School bullying: Insights and perspectives.* London: Routledge.

Smith, P. K., & Sharp, S. (Eds.). (1994b). *Tackling bullying in your school: A practical handbook for teachers.* London: Routledge.

Snyder, J. J. (1991). Discipline as a mediator of the impact of maternal stress and mood on child conduct problems. *Development and Psychopathology, 3,* 263–276.

Snyder, J. J. (1995). Coercion: A two-level theory of antisocial behavior. In W. O'Donohue & L. Krasner (Eds.), *Theories of behavior therapy: Exploring behavior change* (pp. 313–348). Washington, DC: American Psychological Association.

Spanier, G. B. (1976). Measuring dyadic adjustment: New scales for assessing the quality of marriage and similar dyads. *Journal of Marriage and the Family, 38,* 15–28.

Special feature: Rating scales and assessment instruments for use in pediatric psychopharmacology research. (1985). *Psychopharmacology Bulletin, 21*(4).

Speltz, M. L., DeKlyen, M., Greenberg, M. T., & Dryden, M. (1995). Clinic referral for Oppositional Defiant Disorder: Relative significance of attachment and behavioral variables. *Journal of Abnormal Child Psychology, 23,* 487–507.

Speltz, M. L., Greenberg, M. T., & DeKlyen, M. (1990). Attachment in preschoolers with disruptive behavior: A comparison of clinic-referred and nonproblem children. *Development and Psychopathology, 2,* 31–46.

Spence, S. H., & Marzillier, J. S. (1981). Social skills training with adolescent male offenders: II. Short-term, long-term, and generalized effects. *Behaviour Research and Therapy, 19,* 349–368.

Spitzer, A., Webster-Stratton, C., & Hollinsworth, T. (1991). Coping with conduct-problem children: Parents gaining knowledge and control. *Journal of Clinical Child Psychology, 20,* 413–427.

Stanger, C., Achenbach, T. M., & Verhulst, F. C. (1997). Accelerated longitudinal comparisons of aggressive versus delinquent syndromes. *Development and Psychopathology, 9,* 43–58.

Stoewe, J. K., Kruesi, M. J. P., & Lelio, D. F. (1995). Psychopharmacology of aggressive states and features of Conduct Disorder. *Child and Adolescent Psychiatric Clinics of North America, 4,* 359–379.

Stoff, D. M., & Cairns, R. B. (Eds.). (1996). *Aggression and violence: Genetic, neurobiological, and biosocial perspectives.* Mahwah, NJ: Erlbaum.

Stoolmiller, M., Duncan, T. Bank, L., & Patterson, G. R. (1993). Some problems and solutions in the study of change: Significant patterns in client resistance. *Journal of Consulting and Clinical Psychology, 61,* 920–928.

Stouthamer-Loeber, M. (1986). Lying as a problem behavior in children: A review. *Clinical Psychology Review, 6,* 267–289.

Stouthamer-Loeber, M., & Loeber, R. (1986). Boys who lie. *Journal of Abnormal Child Psychology, 14,* 551–564.

Strain, P. S., Lambert, D. L., Kerr, M. M., Stagg, V., & Lenkner, D. A. (1983). Naturalistic assessment of children's compliance to teachers' requests and consequences for compliance. *Journal of Applied Behavior Analysis, 16,* 243–249.

Strain, P. S., Steele, P., Ellis, T., & Timm, M. A. (1982). Long-term effects of oppositional child treatment with mothers as therapists and therapist trainers. *Journal of Applied Behavior Analysis, 15,* 163–169.

Strain, P. S., Young, C. C., & Horowitz, J. (1981). Generalized behavior change during oppositional child training: An examination of child and family demographic variables. *Behavior Modification, 5,* 15–26.

Straus, M. A. (1979). Measuring intrafamily conflict and violence: The Conflict Tactics (CT) Scales. *Journal of Marriage and the Family, 41,* 75–88.

Straus, M. A. (1990). The Conflict Tactics Scales and its critics: An evaluation and new data on validity and reliability. In M. A. Straus & R. J. Gelles (Eds.), *Physical violence in American families: Risk factors and adaptations to violence in 8,145 families* (pp. 49–73). New Brunswick, NJ: Transaction.

Strayhorn, J. M., & Weidman, C. S. (1988). A Parent Practices Scale and its relation to parent and child mental health. *Journal of the American Academy of Child and Adolescent Psychiatry, 27,* 613–618.

Strayhorn, J. M., & Weidman, C. S. (1989). Reduction of attention deficit and internalizing symptoms in preschoolers through parent–child interaction training. *Journal of the American Academy of Child and Adolescent Psychiatry, 28,* 888–896.

Stumpf, J., & Holman, J. (1985). Promoting generalization of appropriate classroom behaviour: A comparison of two strategies. *Behavioural Psychotherapy, 13,* 29–42.

Stumphauzer, J. S. (1976). Elimination of stealing by self-reinforcement of alternative behavior and family contracting. *Journal of Behavior Therapy and Experimental Psychiatry, 7,* 265–268.

Sugai, G., Kameenui, E., & Colvin, G. (1990). *Project PREPARE: Promoting responsible, empirical, and proactive alternatives in regular education for students with behavior disorders* (Grant proposal submitted to Special Projects Competition). Eugene: University of Oregon.

Sugai, G., Kameenui, E., & Colvin, G. (1993). [Project PREPARE: Promoting responsible, empirical, and proactive alternatives in regular education for students with behavior disorders]. Unpublished raw data. University of Oregon, College of Education.

Swanson, J. (1993). Effect of stimulant medication on hyperactive children: A review of reviews. *Exceptional Children, 60,* 154–162.

Switzer, E. B., Deal, T. E., & Bailey, J. S. (1977). The reduction of stealing in second graders using a group contingency. *Journal of Applied Behavior Analysis, 10,* 267–272.

Taplin, P. S., & Reid, J. B. (1977). Changes in parent consequences as a function of family intervention. *Journal of Consulting and Clinical Psychology, 45,* 973–981.

Thompson, R. W., Grow, C. R., Ruma, P. R., Daly, D. L., & Burke, R. V. (1993). Evaluation of a practical parenting program with middle- and low-income families. *Family Relations, 42,* 21–25.

Tingstrom, D. H. (1994). The Good Behavior Game: An investigation of teacher acceptance. *Psychology in the Schools, 31,* 57–65.

Tremblay, R. E., Masse, L. C., Pagani, L., & Vitaro, F. (1996). From childhood physical aggression to adolescent maladjustment. In R. DEV. Peters & R. J. McMahon (Eds.), *Preventing childhood disorders, substance abuse, and delinquency* (pp. 268–299). Thousand Oaks, CA: Sage.

Tremblay, R. E., Pagani-Kurtz, L., Masse, L. C., Vitaro, F., & Pihl, R. O. (1995). A bimodal preventive intervention for disruptive kindergarten boys: Its impact through midadolescence. *Journal of Consulting and Clinical Psychology, 63,* 560–568.

Tremblay, R. E., Vitaro, F., Bertrand, L., LeBlanc, M., Beauchesne, H., Boileau, H., & Lucille, D. (1992).

Parent and child training to prevent early onset of delinquency: The Montreal longitudinal experimental study. In J. McCord & R. E. Tremblay (Eds.), *Preventing antisocial behavior: Interventions from birth through adolescence* (pp. 117–138). New York: Guilford Press.

Turco, T. L., & Elliott, S. N. (1986). Students' acceptability ratings of interventions for classroom misbehaviors: A developmental study of well-behaving and misbehaving youth. *Journal of Psychoeducational Assessment, 4,* 281–289.

U. S. Department of Health, Education, and Welfare, Office of Education. (1977). Education of handicapped children: Implementation of part B of the Education of the Handicapped Act. *Federal Register, 42,* 163.

Vincent, J., Unis, A., & Hardy, J. (1990). Pharmacotherapy of aggression. *Journal of the American Academy of Child and Adolescent Psychiatry, 29,* 839–840.

Vitaro, F., & Tremblay, R. E. (1994). Impact of a prevention program on aggressive children's friendships and social adjustment. *Journal of Abnormal Child Psychology, 22,* 457–475.

Vitiello, B., Behar, D., Hunt, J., Stoff, D., & Ricciuti, A. (1990). Subtyping aggression in children and adolescents. *Journal of Neuropsychiatry, 2,* 189–192.

Vitiello, B., & Stoff, D. M. (1997). Subtypes of aggression and their relevance to child psychiatry. *Journal of the American Academy of Child and Adolescent Psychiatry, 36,* 307–315.

Wahler, R. G. (1975). Some structural aspects of deviant child behavior. *Journal of Applied Behavior Analysis, 8,* 27–42.

Wahler, R. G. (1980). The insular mother: Her problems in parent–child treatment. *Journal of Applied Behavior Analysis, 13,* 207–219.

Wahler, R. G., & Afton, A. D. (1980). Attentional processes in insular and noninsular mothers. *Child Behavior Therapy, 2*(2), 25–41.

Wahler, R. G., Cartor, P. G., Fleischman, J., & Lambert, W. (1993). The impact of synthesis teaching and parent training with mothers of conduct-disordered children. *Journal of Abnormal Child Psychology, 21,* 425–440.

Wahler, R. G., & Cormier, W. H. (1970). The ecological interview: A first step in out-patient child behavior therapy. *Journal of Behavior Therapy and Experimental Psychiatry, 1,* 279–289.

Wahler, R. G., & Dumas, J. E. (1984). Changing the observational coding styles of insular and noninsular mothers: A step toward maintenance of parent training effects. In R. F. Dangel & R. A. Polster (Eds.), *Parent training: Foundations of research and practice* (pp. 379–416). New York: Guilford Press.

Wahler, R. G., & Dumas, J. E. (1989). Attentional problems in dysfunctional mother–child interactions: An interbehavioral model. *Psychological Bulletin, 105,* 116–130.

Wahler, R. G., Leske, G., & Rogers, E. S. (1979). The insular family: A deviance support system for oppositional children. In L. A. Hamerlynck (Ed.), *Behavioral systems for the developmentally disabled: Vol. 1. School and family environments* (pp. 102–127). New York: Brunner/Mazel.

Wahler, R. G., & Sansbury, L. E. (1990). The monitoring skills of troubled mothers: Their problems in defining child deviance. *Journal of Abnormal Child Psychology, 18,* 577–589.

Waldman, I. D., & Lahey, B. B. (1994). Design of the DSM-IV disruptive behavior disorder field trials. *Child and Adolescent Psychiatric Clinics of North America, 3,* 195–208.

Walker, H. M. (1995). *The acting-out child: Coping with classroom disruption* (2nd ed.). Longmont, CO: Sopris West.

Walker, H. M., Block-Pedego, A., Todis, B., & Severson, H. (1991). *School Archival Records Search (SARS): User's guide and technical manual.* Longmont, CO: Sopris West.

Walker, H. M., & Buckley, N. K. (1972). Programming generalization and maintenance of treatment effects across time and across settings. *Journal of Applied Behavior Analysis, 5,* 209–224.

Walker, H. M., Colvin, G., & Ramsey, E. (1995). *Antisocial behavior in school: Strategies and best practices.* Pacific Grove, CA: Brooks/Cole.

Walker, H. M., & Fabre, T. R. (1987). Assessment of behavior disorders in the school setting: Issues, problems, and strategies revisited. In N. G. Haring (Ed.), *Assessing and managing behavior disabilities* (pp. 198–243). Seattle: University of Washington Press.

Walker, H. M., Fonseca Retana, G., & Gersten, R. (1988). Replication of the CLASS program in Costa Rica: Implementation procedures and program outcomes. *Behavior Modification, 12,* 133–154.

Walker, H. M., & Hops, H. (1976). Use of normative peer data as a standard for evaluating classroom treatment effects. *Journal of Applied Behavior Analysis, 9,* 159–168.

Walker, H. M., & Hops, H. (1979). The CLASS program for acting out children: R&D procedures, program outcomes, and implementation issues. *School Psychology Digest, 8,* 370–381.

Walker, H. M., & Hops, H. (1993). *The RECESS program for aggressive children.* Seattle, WA: Educational Achievement Systems.

Walker, H. M., Hops, H., & Fiegenbaum, E. (1976). Deviant classroom behavior as a function of combinations of social and token reinforcement and cost contingency. *Behavior Therapy, 7,* 76–88.

Walker, H. M., Hops, H., & Greenwood, C. R. (1981). RECESS: Research and development of a behavior management package for remediating social aggression in the school setting. In P. S. Strain (Ed.), *The utilization of classroom peers as behavior change agents* (pp. 261–303). New York: Plenum Press.

Walker, H. M., Hops, H., & Greenwood, C. R. (1984). The CORBEH research and development model: Programmatic issues and strategies. In S. C. Paine, G. T. Bellamy, & B. Wilcox (Eds.), *Human services that work: From innovation to clinical practice* (pp. 57–77). Baltimore: Paul H. Brookes.

Walker, H. M., Hops, H., & Greenwood, C. R. (1993). *RECESS: A program for reducing negative–aggressive behavior.* Seattle, WA: Educational Achievement Systems.

Walker, H. M., Hops, H., & Johnson, S. M. (1975). Generalization and maintenance of classroom treatment effects. *Behavior Therapy, 6,* 188–200.

Walker, H. M., Shinn, M. R., O'Neill, R. E., & Ramsey, E. (1987). A longitudinal assessment of the development of antisocial behavior in boys: Rationale, methodology, and first-year results. *RASE: Remedial and Special Education, 8,* 7–16, 27.

Walker, H. M., & Sylwester, R. (1991). Where is school along the path to prison? *Educational Leadership, 49,* 14–16.

Walker, H. M., & Walker, J. E. (1991). *Coping with noncompliance in the classroom: A positive approach for teachers.* Austin, TX: Pro-Ed.

Walker, J. L., Lahey, B. B., Russo, M. F., Frick, P. J., Christ, M. A., McBurnett, K., Loeber, R., Stouthamer-Loeber, M., & Green, S. M. (1991). Anxiety, inhibition, and Conduct Disorder in children: I. Relations to social impairment. *Journal of the American Academy of Child and Adolescent Psychiatry, 30,* 187–191.

Walter, H. I., & Gilmore, S. K. (1973). Placebo versus social learning effects in parent training procedures designed to alter the behavior of aggressive boys. *Behavior Therapy, 4,* 361–377.

Webster-Stratton, C. (1981). Modification of mothers' behaviors and attitudes through a videotape modeling group discussion program. *Behavior Therapy, 12,* 634–642.

Webster-Stratton, C. (1982a). Teaching mothers through videotape modeling to change their children's behavior. *Journal of Pediatric Psychology, 7,* 279–294.

Webster-Stratton, C. (1982b). The long-term effects of a videotape modeling parent-training program: Comparison of immediate and 1-year follow-up results. *Behavior Therapy, 13,* 702–714.

Webster-Stratton, C. (1984). Randomized trial of two parent-training programs for families with conduct-disordered children. *Journal of Consulting and Clinical Psychology, 52,* 666–678.

Webster-Stratton, C. (1989). Systematic comparison of consumer satisfaction of three cost-effective parent training programs for conduct problem children. *Behavior Therapy, 20,* 103–115.

Webster-Stratton, C. (1990a). Long-term follow-up of families with young conduct problem children: From preschool to grade school. *Journal of Clinical Child Psychology, 19,* 144–149.

Webster-Stratton, C. (1990b). Stress: A potential disruptor of parent perceptions and family interactions. *Journal of Clinical Child Psychology, 19,* 302–312.

Webster-Stratton, C. (1994). Advancing videotape parent training: A comparison study. *Journal of Consulting and Clinical Psychology, 62,* 583–593.

Webster-Stratton, C. (1996a). Early intervention with videotape modeling: Programs for families of children with Oppositional Defiant Disorder or Conduct Disorder. In E. S. Hibbs & P. S. Jensen (Eds.), *Psychosocial treatments for child and adolescent disorders: Empirically based strategies for clinical practice* (pp. 435–474). Washington, DC: American Psychological Association.

Webster-Stratton, C. (1996b). Early-onset conduct problems: Does gender make a difference? *Journal of Consulting and Clinical Psychology, 64,* 540–551.

Webster-Stratton, C. (1996c, November). *Preventing conduct problems in Head Start children: Strengthening parenting competencies.* Paper presented at the meeting of the American Public Health Association, New York.

Webster-Stratton, C., & Eyberg, S. M. (1982). Child temperament: Relationship with child behavior problems and parent–child interactions. *Journal of Clinical Child Psychology, 11,* 123–129.

Webster-Stratton, C., & Hammond, M. (1990). Predictors of treatment outcome in parent training for families with conduct problem children. *Behavior Therapy, 21,* 319–337.

Webster-Stratton, C., & Hammond, M. (1997). Treating children with early-onset conduct problems: A comparison of child and parent training interventions. *Journal of Consulting and Clinical Psychology, 65,* 93–109.

Webster-Stratton, C., & Herbert, M. (1993). What really happens in parent training? *Behavior Modification, 17,* 407–456.

Webster-Stratton, C., & Herbert, M. (1994). *Troubled families—Problem children.* Chichester, England: Wiley.

Webster-Stratton, C., Hollinsworth, T., & Kolpacoff, M. (1989). The long-term effectiveness and clinical significance of three cost-effective training programs for families with conduct-problem children. *Journal of Consulting and Clinical Psychology, 57,* 550–553.

Webster-Stratton, C., Kolpacoff, M., & Hollinsworth, T. (1988). Self-administered videotape therapy for families with conduct problem children: Comparison to two other cost effective treatments and a control group. *Journal of Consulting and Clinical Psychology, 56,* 558–566.

Webster-Stratton, C., & Spitzer, A. (1991). Development, reliability, and validity of the Daily Telephone Discipline Interview. *Behavioral Assessment, 13,* 221–239.

Webster-Stratton, C., & Spitzer, A. (1996). Parenting a young child with conduct problems: New insights using qualitative methods. In T. H. Ollendick & R. J. Prinz (Eds.), *Advances in clinical child psychology* (Vol. 18, pp. 1–62). New York: Plenum Press.

Weinrott, M. R., Bauske, B. W., & Patterson, G. R. (1979). Systematic replication of a social learning approach to parent training. In P. O. Sjoden (Ed.), *Trends in behavior therapy* (pp. 331–351). New York: Academic Press.

Weinrott, M. R., Jones, R. R., & Howard, J. R. (1982). Cost-effectiveness of teaching family programs for delinquents: Results of a national evaluation. *Evaluation Review, 6,* 173–201.

Weiss, B., Dodge, K. A., Bates, J. E., & Pettit, G. S. (1992). Some consequences of early harsh discipline: Child aggression and a maladaptive social information-processing style. *Child Development, 63,* 1321–1335.

Weisz, J. R., Walter, B. R., Weiss, B., Fernandez, G. A., & Mikow, V. A. (1990). Arrests among emotionally disturbed violent and assaultive individuals following minimal versus lengthy intervention through North Carolina's Willie M Program. *Journal of Consulting and Clinical Psychology, 58,* 720–728.

Wells, K. C. (1985). Behavioral family therapy. In A. S. Bellack & M. Hersen (Eds.), *Dictionary of behavior therapy techniques* (pp. 25–30). New York: Pergamon Press.

Wells, K. C., & Egan, J. (1988). Social learning and systems family therapy for childhood oppositional disorder: Comparative treatment outcome. *Comprehensive Psychiatry, 29,* 138–146.

Wells, K. C., Forehand, R., & Griest, D. L. (1980). Generality of treatment effects from treated to untreated behaviors resulting from a parent training program. *Journal of Clinical Child Psychology, 9,* 217–219.

Wells, K. C., Griest, D. L., & Forehand, R. (1980). The use of a self-control package to enhance temporal generality of a parent training program. *Behaviour Research and Therapy, 18,* 347–358.

Werry, J. S. (1994). Pharmacotherapy of disruptive behavior disorders. *Child and Adolescent Psychiatric Clinics of North America, 3,* 321–341.

Werry, J. S., & Aman, M. G. (1993). *Practitioner's guide to psychoactive drugs for children and adolescents.* New York: Plenum Press.

Wetzel, R. (1966). Use of behavioral techniques in a case of compulsive stealing. *Journal of Consulting and Clinical Psychology, 30,* 367–374.

Whipple, E. E., Fitzgerald, H. E., & Zucker, R. A. (1995). Parent–child interactions in alcoholic and nonalcoholic families. *American Journal of Orthopsychiatry, 65,* 153–159.

White, J. L., Moffitt, T. E., Caspi, A., Bartusch, D. J., Needles, D., & Stouthamer-Loeber, M. (1994).

Measuring impulsivity and examining its relationship to delinquency. *Journal of Abnormal Psychology, 103,* 1922–1205.

White, M. (1986). Negative explanation, restraint and double description: A template for family therapy. *Family Process, 25,* 169–184.

White, M. A. (1975). Natural rates of teacher approval and disapproval in the classroom. *Journal of Applied Behavior Analysis, 8,* 367–372.

Willie M. v. Hunt et al., 657 F. 2d 55 (1979).

Willner, A. G., Braukmann, C. J., Kirigin, K. A., Fixsen, D. L., Phillips, E. L., & Wolf, M. M. (1977). The training and validation of youth-preferred social behaviors with child care personnel. *Journal of Applied Behavior Analysis, 10,* 219–230.

Willner, A. G., Braukmann, C. J., Kirigin, K. A., & Wolf, M. M. (1978). Achievement Place: A community model for youths in trouble. In D. Marholin (Ed.), *Child behavior therapy* (pp. 239–273). New York: Gardner Press.

Wills, T. A., Schreibman, D., Benson, G., & Vaccaro, D. (1994). Impact of parental substance use on adolescents: A test of a mediational model. *Journal of Pediatric Psychology, 19,* 537–555.

Wiltz, N. A., & Patterson, G. R. (1974). An evaluation of parent training procedures designed to alter inappropriate aggressive behavior of boys. *Behavior Therapy, 5,* 215, 221.

Winett, R. A., & Winkler, R. C. (1972). Current behavior modification in the classroom: Be still, be quiet, be docile. *Journal of Applied Behavior Analysis, 5,* 499–504.

Witt, J. C., Martens, B. K., & Elliott, S. N. (1984). Factors affecting teachers' judgments of the acceptability of behavioral interventions: Time involvement, behavior problem severity, and type of intervention. *Behavior Therapy, 15,* 204–209.

Wolf, M. M., Braukmann, C. J., & Kirigin Ramp, K. A. (1987). Serious delinquent behavior as part of a significantly handicapping condition: Cures and supportive environments. *Journal of Applied Behavior Analysis, 20,* 347–359.

Wolf, M. M., Kirigin, K. A., Fixsen, D. L., Blase, K. A., & Braukmann, C. J. (1995). The Teaching Family Model: A case study in data-based program development and refinement (and dragon wrestling). *Journal of Organizational Behavior Management, 15,* 11–68.

Yoshikawa, H. (1994). Prevention as cumulative protection: Effects of early family support and education on chronic delinquency and its risks. *Psychological Bulletin, 1,* 28–54.

Zahn-Waxler, C. (1993). Warriors and worriers: Gender and psychopathology. *Development and Psychopathology, 5,* 79–89.

Zigler, E., Taussig, C., & Black, K. (1992). Early childhood intervention: A promising preventative for juvenile delinquency. *American Psychologist, 47,* 997–1106.

Zoccolillo, M. (1992). Co-occurrence of Conduct Disorder and its adult outcomes with depressive and anxiety disorders: A review. *Journal of the American Academy of Child and Adolescent Psychiatry, 31,* 547–556.

Zoccolillo, M. (1993). Gender and the development of Conduct Disorder. *Development and Psychopathology, 5,* 65–78.

Zubieta, J., & Alessi, N. (1992). Acute and chronic administration of trazodone in the treatment of disruptive behavior disorders in children. *Journal of Clinical Psychopharmacology, 12,* 346–351.

Zucker, R. A., & Fitzgerald, H. E. (1992). *The Antisocial Behavior Checklist.* (Available from Michigan State University Family Study, Department of Psychology, E. Lansing MI 48824–1117)

PART III

EMOTIONAL AND SOCIAL DISORDERS

CHAPTER 4

Childhood and Adolescent Depression

Alan E. Kazdin
Yale University

Paul L. Marciano
Davidson College

Depression is unique in many ways among the disorders that are studied in developmental psychopathology. Because depression is one of the more thoroughly investigated disorders among adults, an extensive and well-researched array of theoretical models, assessment techniques, and interventions is available to guide research and practice with children and adolescents (e.g., Beckham & Leber, 1995). In addition, aspects of adult depression have drawn attention to the development of the mood disorders in children and adolescents. Depression runs in families, so the children of depressed parents are at risk for the disorder. The study of at-risk children and of parent–child (infant, toddler) interaction patterns among depressed parents has focused attention on the precursors of and processes leading to depression in children. With adult depression research as a guide, research with children and adolescents has accelerated enormously within the past 15 years. Several excellent resources review advances in assessment, diagnosis, epidemiology, and treatment of depression in childhood and adolescence (e.g.,

Hammen, 1991; Harrington, 1993; Reynolds & Johnston, 1994).

The present chapter reviews the advances in treatment and prevention of depression in children and adolescents, with particular emphasis on psychosocial approaches.[1] The chapter describes and evaluates the underpinnings, characteristics, and evidence for several interventions. Relatively few controlled trials are available to evaluate treatment or prevention. Critical issues are raised to place current advances in perspective, to identify lacunae in research, and to point to directions needed to advance clinical research.

CHARACTERISTICS OF DEPRESSION

Depression can be discussed from the perspective of a specific and narrow set of characteristics (symptoms) that individuals present at a given point in time. Yet a broader perspective is needed to capture current findings about depression and its associated features. Depression, from our perspective, consists of a pervasive disorder that encompasses diverse characteristics and domains of functioning well beyond mood-related symptoms. Multiple characteristics of the child, parent, family, and context are likely to reflect dysfunction. We highlight these diverse characteristics of childhood and adolescent depression to provide the context for presenting and evaluating current treatment research.

Diagnosis

In characterizing depression, it is important to distinguish depression as a symptom from depression as a syndrome or disorder. As a symptom, "depression" refers to sad affect and is a common experience of everyday life. As a syndrome or disorder, "depression" refers to a group of symptoms that go together. Sadness may be part of a larger set of symptoms that also includes diminished interest in activities, feelings of worthlessness, sleep disturbances, changes in appetite, and other symptoms.

Several diagnostic systems have emerged to classify disorders. Among the prominent diagnostic systems are the Research Diagnostic Criteria (RDC; Spitzer, Endicott, & Robins, 1978), the 10th revision of the *International Classification of Diseases* (ICD-10; World Health Organization, 1992), and the fourth edition of the *Diagnostic and Statistical Manual of Mental Disorders* (DSM-IV; American Psychiatric Association, 1994). There are differences among the varied diagnostic systems and variations within a given system over time. The DSM is highlighted here because this is the most widely used diagnostic system worldwide (Maser, Kaelber, & Weise, 1991).

The primary category for defining depression as a syndrome in DSM-IV is Major Depressive Disorder. This category refers to dysfunction in which there is a course of one or more Major Depressive Episodes. The criteria for a Major Depressive Episode, on which the diagnosis depends, are presented in Table 4.1. Such an episode requires the presence of five or more of the Criterion A symptoms (one of which is depressed mood or loss of pleasure) for at least 2 weeks. Many of these symptoms appear under many other circumstances and diagnoses. Several of these are highlighted in Table 4.2.

It is important to bear in mind that individual symptoms and several of the symptoms of depression may be present without necessarily signaling Major Depressive Disorder. The focus of

the present chapter is the constellation of depressive symptoms. Our concern here is with youths who experience relatively extreme levels of depressive symptoms as measured by standard questionnaires and inventories, or who meet criteria for Major Depressive Disorder or Dysthymic Disorder as identified through diagnostic interviews. We do not limit our focus to formal diagnosis of depression, because most child and adolescent intervention studies do not report or utilize diagnostic criteria in identifying cases. Moreover, diagnostic criteria are not necessarily the critical cutoff point in defining dysfunction. Youths who fall below current diagnostic criteria (subsyndromal depression) or who no longer meet criteria may still evince impairment in several areas of everyday functioning.

A long-standing issue in diagnosis is whether the criteria for depression for children and adolescents ought to be different from those invoked for adults (e.g., Cytryn & McKnew, 1972; Weinberg, Rutman, Sullivan, Penick, & Dietz, 1973). The DSM criteria, incorporated into standardized diagnostic interviews, can be reliably applied to children, adolescents, and adults. The validity of the criteria has been supported extensively, with both concurrent and predictive correlates, many of which are highlighted in the present discussion. Establishing the validity of one set of criteria (e.g., DSM), of course, does not gainsay the possible validity and utility of other criteria sets as well.

Within DSM-IV, one criterion that varies for depression across the age spectrum relates to irritability (irritable mood). This symptom may be used in place of depressed mood for invoking the diagnostic criteria. Indeed, the majority of depressed youths (over 80%) show irritable mood (Goodyer & Cooper, 1993; Ryan et al., 1987). There has been a continued interest in examining whether core diagnostic features of depression vary over the course of development. Among the differences, depressed adolescents are more likely than children to show more hypersomnia, depressed mood, irritability, hopelessness, anhedonia, and psychomotor retardation, and less exaggerated somatic complaints (e.g., Kashani, Rosenberg, & Reid, 1989; Mitchell, McCauley, Burke, & Moss, 1988; Ryan et al., 1987). Also, suicidal ideations, attempts, and completions are rare in childhood but increase markedly during adolescence (Hawton, 1986). The bases for differences demonstrated to date and the underlying later marital problems, involvement in drugs, delinquency, arrest and criminal conviction, dropping out of

TABLE 4.1. DSM-IV Criteria for Major Depressive Episode

A. Five (or more) of the following symptoms have been present during the same 2-week period and represent a change from previous functioning; at least one of the symptoms is either (1) depressed mood or (2) loss of interest or pleasure.
Note: Do not include symptoms that are clearly due to a general medical condition, or mood-incongruent delusions or hallucinations.
  (1) depressed mood most of the day, nearly every day, as indicated by either subjective report (e.g., feels sad or empty) or observation made by others (e.g., appears tearful). **Note:** In children and adolescents, can be irritable mood.
  (2) markedly diminished interest or pleasure in all, or almost all, activities most of the day, nearly every day (as indicated by either subjective account or observation made by others).
  (3) significant weight loss when not dieting or weight gain (e.g., a change of more than 5% of body weight in a month), or decrease or increase in appetite nearly every day. **Note:** In children, consider failure to make expected weight gains.
  (4) insomnia or hypersomnia nearly every day
  (5) psychomotor agitation or retardation nearly every day (observable by others, not merely subjective feelings of restlessness or being slowed down)
  (6) fatigue or loss of energy nearly every day
  (7) feelings of worthlessness or excessive or inappropriate guilt (which may be delusional) nearly every day (not merely self-reproach or guilt about being sick)
  (8) diminished ability to think or concentrate, or indecisiveness, nearly every day (either by subjective account or as observed by others)
  (9) recurrent thoughts of death (not just fear of dying), recurrent suicidal ideation without a specific plan, or a suicide attempt or a specific plan for committing suicide
B. The symptoms do not meet criteria for a Mixed Episode.
C. The symptoms cause clinically significant distress or impairment in social, occupational, or other important areas of functiong.
D. The symptoms are not due to the direct physiological effects of a substance (e.g., a drug of abuse, a medication) or a general medical condition (e.g., hypothyroidism).
E. The symptoms are not better accounted for by Bereavement, i.e., after the loss of a loved one, the symptoms persist for longer than 2 months or are characterized by marked functional impairment, morbid preoccupation with worthlessness, suicidal ideation, psychotic symptoms, or psychomotor retardation.

Note. From American Psychiatric Association (1994, p. 327). Copyright 1994 by the American Psychiatric Association. Reprinted by permission.

school, and unemployment many similarities among children, adolescents, and adults, and diagnostic criteria (e.g., DSM) can be applied reliably across this spectrum.

Associated Features

Child and Adolescent Characteristics

Youths who meet criteria for one diagnosis often meet criteria for one or more other disorders as well—a phenomenon referred to as "comorbidity." In community studies, comorbidity rates are high among youths who meet criteria for some form of depression (Anderson, Williams, McGee, & Silva, 1987; Angold & Costello, 1993; Goodyer & Cooper, 1993; Kovacs, Feinberg, Crouse-Novak, Paulauskas, & Finkelstein, 1984). Usually 40% to 50% of depressed youths meet criteria for at least one other diagnosis, but rates have approached 80%. The comorbid diagnoses with which depression is associated vary.

Anxiety disorders are relatively common (Brady & Kendall, 1992). The association of anxiety and depression has received special attention, in part because the symptoms overlap, especially in selected measures designed to assess one set of symptoms versus another. Conduct Disorder, Oppositional Defiant Disorder, Attention-deficit/Hyperactivity Disorder, and Substance Abuse are also diagnoses likely to be associated with depression. Comorbidity is unnecessarily restrictive as a way of conceptualizing the characteristics of youths referred for depression. Whether youths meet or do not meet criteria for another disorder is not quite the issue. Clinically depressed youths are likely to show multiple symptoms that extend to other disorders, whether or not they meet criteria for those other disorders. The broad range of symptoms is likely to contribute to overall functioning, treatment strategy, and long-term prognosis.

Apart from disorders and symptoms, dysfunction in other domains is likely to be evident

TABLE 4.2.   Selected DSM-IV Diagnostic Categories Other than Major Depressive Episode That Include Depressive Symptoms

Dysthymic Disorder
Essentially a mood disorder in which many of the symptoms of a Major Depressive Episode are evident in less severe form. The symptoms may be chronic, lasting for at least 1 year in children and adolescents (2 years adults), during which there has been depressed mood most of the day more days than not.

Bipolar I Disorder
A mood disorder in which a Major Depressive Episode is preceded or followed by one or more Manic Episodes (i.e., distinct periods in which there is an unusually elevated, expansive, or irritable mood, along with symptoms such as inflated self-esteem, grandiosity, decreased need for sleep, pressure for speech, flight of ideas, and others). Manic and Major Depressive Episodes may alternate rapidly.

Cyclothymic Disorder
A mood disorder in which some of the symptoms of Major Depressive and Hypomanic Episodes are evident in less severe form. The mood disturbance fluctuates between periods of depressive and hypomanic symptoms. The symptoms must be evident for at least 1 year in children and adolescents (2 years in adults), during which the person has not been symptom-free for more than 2 months at a time.

Separation Anxiety Disorder
Many of the symptoms of depression, such as sadness, excessive worrying, sleep dysfunction, somatic complaints, and social withdrawal, may emerge as part of fear of separation from those to whom the child is attached. In such cases, the symptoms may be clearly associated with the theme of separation. For example, worrying may have a specific focus on worry about being away from the parent. Similarly, somatic complaints may occur in order to enable the child to remain at home or to foster increased attention to the child.

Substance-Induced Mood Disorder
Depressive symptoms are prominent and persistent, but are judged to be the direct physiological consequences of a drug of abuse, medication, or exposure to a toxin. This usually arises in association with intoxication or withdrawal states, but may continue for a period after abstinence from the substance.

Adjustment Disorder with Depressed Mood
Depressive symptoms may emerge as a reaction to an identifiable psychosocial stressor such as divorce of the parents, leaving friends during a move away from home, or serious illness of a parent. In such cases, the symptoms are in temporal proximity to (occur within 3 months of) the stressor. The reaction is viewed as a maladaptive reaction because the person's functioning in everyday life is disrupted or because the symptoms are in excess of a "normal" or usually expected reaction. The symptoms are likely to remit after a period of adjustment with the new circumstances.

Bereavement
Bereavement resembles an Adjustment Disorder in terms of its association with a particular event. However, it is not listed as a disorder, but rather as a "condition that may be a focus of clinical attention." Bereavement is often associated with several depressive symptoms or a full depressive syndrome and temporary impairment in school and social functioning. Yet the reaction is not regarded as clinically significant unless the symptoms remain well beyond a "reasonable" period of adjustment or begin to recur with repeated episodes long after the loss.

and relevant to treatment. First, deficits and distortions of cognitive processes have been found in several studies of depressed youths (see Kaslow, Brown, & Mee, 1994). Some cognitive processes are encompassed by the central or core features (e.g., feelings of worthlessness), and hence are not properly regarded as associated features. Yet a broad range of cognitions have been identified that are well outside the diagnostic criteria that characterize depressed children; these include various manifestations of negative beliefs, attributions of failure, and external locus of control. Second, problems with

social relationships are also common among depressed children and adolescents, including deficiencies in skills of social functioning (e.g., making friends, conversing), deficits in interpersonal problem-solving skills related to social behavior, and poor peer relations (e.g., lower popularity, greater rejection) (see Kaslow et al., 1994). Depressed youths are also more likely to isolate themselves (e.g., play alone, engage in fewer social activities) (e.g., Kazdin, Esveldt-Dawson, Sherick, & Colbus, 1985), which may lead to decreased opportunities for reinforcement from the environment. Third, depressed children are likely to show academic dysfunction, as reflected in poor academic performance and lower levels of grade attainment (e.g., Cole, 1990; Nolen-Hoeksema, Girgus, & Seligman, 1986). Other school-related problems include greater frequency of repetition of a grade, being late and missing (not attending) school, failing to complete homework assignments, and greater dissatisfaction with school, compared with non-depressed peers (Lewinsohn, Roberts, et al., 1994).

As these illustrations convey, the domains of dysfunction of depressed children and adolescents extend well beyond the core symptoms of depression. Although the breadth of dysfunction associated with depression has been elaborated in many studies, the bases for the dysfunction have not been well analyzed. Quite possibly, the many domains of dysfunction are due largely to comorbid conditions that are associated with or follow from the disorder. In such a case, impairment might not be so broad if depression were identified (and treated) early. Even so, from the standpoint of treatment, a presenting case is likely to evince a broad range of symptoms and sources of impairment. The range of features associated with depression has important implications for both assessment and intervention, as discussed later.

Parent, Family, and Contextual Characteristics

Several parent and family characteristics are associated with child and adolescent depression (see Hammen, 1991). Because depression runs in families, identification of a child as depressed means that there is a greater likelihood than population base rates that he or she has a parent who meets diagnostic criteria (current or lifetime) for some form of depression. With a depressed parent, there is also a greater likelihood of marital and family discord and high levels of stress in the home (Beardslee & Wheelock, 1994; Kaslow et al., 1994).

An extensive body of research has focused on depressed mothers and their interactions with their children (see Hammen, 1991). Among the many findings are greater dysphoria, withdrawal, negative verbal and nonverbal behavior, and diminished affect among mothers who are depressed, compared to mothers who are not. These are pertinent findings because youths of these parents are at risk for depression. Studies of youths who are depressed have revealed a range of parent characteristics, including more

negative and punitive behavior directed toward depressed children (compared to their siblings), decreased parental warmth, greater conflict and parental control, less parental support, and more negative and critical evaluation (expressed emotion) (Asarnow, Tompson, Hamilton, Goldstein, & Guthrie, 1994; Kaslow et al., 1994). Depressed adolescents, compared to their nondepressed peers, are more likely to report problems in their family relations, including conflict with parents over a variety of everyday activities (e.g., noise from playing music at home, completing homework) (Lewinsohn, Roberts, et al., 1994). In brief, a depressed child or adolescent is likely to be in a family situation in which there are relatively high levels of stress, nonsupportive interactions, and conflict.

General Comments

The symptoms of depression are obviously critical targets for treatment. At the same time, it is important to bear in mind that depressed children and adolescents are likely to show dysfunction in a broad range of domains. From the standpoint of understanding depression, its correlates, its onset, and its course, many of the characteristics identified in research have not been shown to be related specifically to depression. That is, many of the child, parent, family, and contextual features may reflect more general factors that relate to child psychopathology. In some cases, the factors may emerge as related to depression in part because of comorbidity of other disorders. Consequently, the role of many of the characteristics in relation to the development and course of depression specifically cannot be discerned at this time.

From the standpoint of treatment, significant implications can be drawn. Depression extends well beyond a constellation of defining symptoms. Indeed, we propose that depression ought to be viewed as a child–parent–family–context gestalt. The scope of dysfunction in the child includes multiple domains that cannot be neglected in treatment. The domains may reflect the areas of impairment that led to referral (e.g., school functioning) and that may relate to poor long-term prognosis (e.g., peer rejection). Apart from child domains, parent and family factors may need to be considered in treatment as well.

Prevalence

The prevalence of depression in children and adolescents has been examined in several studies (see Poznanski & Mokros, 1994). Epidemiological studies using DSM criteria (usually DSM-III or DSM-III-R) have examined community samples of youths from ages 4 to 18 (e.g., Bird et al., 1988; Lewinsohn, Hops, Roberts, Seeley, & Andrews, 1993; Reinherz, Giaconia, Lefkowitz, Pakiz, & Frost, 1993). In most of the studies, the prevalence rates for Major Depression vary between 2% and 8%. Dysthymia has been studied less well than Major Depressive Disorder, with estimates ranging from less than 1% up to 9% (e.g., Lewinsohn, Hops, et al., 1993; Polaino-Lorente & Domenech, 1993).

Prevalence rates depend heavily on age and sex. Depression among preschool youths (beginning at age $2\frac{1}{2}$) is quite low, with a rate of less than 1% (Kashani & Carlson, 1987; Kashani & Ray, 1983). Among school-age children, the rate tends to be higher (2%); some evidence suggests that there may be a higher rate of depression for boys than girls (Anderson et al., 1987; Costello et al., 1988; Rutter, 1986). Among adolescents, the prevalence rates tend to be higher (e.g., 2%–8%) for Major Depressive Disorder. Also, there is fairly consistent evidence that the onset of puberty is associated with a greater proportion (e.g., a ratio of approximately 5:1) of depressed females to depressed males. The specific ratio is less well established than is the general finding of a greater proportion of female to male depressed adolescents, and is consistent with the pattern evident in adult depression (Kashani et al., 1987; Lewinsohn, Hops, et al., 1993; McGee, Feehan, Williams, & Anderson, 1992; Rutter, 1986).

It is likely that the prevalence rates underestimate the scope of the problem. We know that many youths who approximate but do not meet criteria for Major Depression (subsyndromal depression) show significant impairment in such domains as social competence, cognitive attributions, coping skills, conflict with parents, and the experience of stressful events. They are also at greater risk than individuals without symptoms for future disorders (e.g., depressive, substance use, or anxiety disorders) (Gotlib, Lewinsohn, & Seeley, 1995; Lewinsohn, Hops, et al., 1993). Thus, meeting diagnostic criteria is not necessarily the point at which significant problems are evident. Also, diagnostic instruments are only one way to operationalize depression. When studied by standardized self-report measures, the rates of depression and impairment are sometimes higher than rates based on diagnostic criteria (see Kazdin, Colbus, & Rodgers,

1987; Roberts, Andrews, Lewinsohn, & Hops, 1990). Finally, rates of depression among children and adolescents appear to be increasing. In studies that follow multiple cohorts of children over time, prevalence rates are higher for more recently born cohorts (Cross-National Collaborative Group, 1992; Lewinsohn, Rohde, Seeley, & Fischer, 1993).

Onset and Course

Most adults report that their first Major Depressive Episode occurred between ages 15 and 19 (Burke, Burke, Regier, & Rae, 1990). Earlier onset (ages 11–14) has been reported as well (Kovacs, Feinberg, Crouse-Novak, Paulauskas, & Finkelstein, 1984; Lewinsohn, Hops, et al., 1993). These estimates are in keeping with prevalence data that show an increase of Major Depressive Disorder during adolescence. Milder versions of depression (Dysthymic Disorder) may have a slightly earlier onset (age 11) (Lewinsohn, Hops, et al., 1993) and serve as a precursor to Major Depression.

For many youths, a Major Depressive Episode is likely to continue for several months. Five to six months has been the most commonly reported duration among community, patient, and at-risk samples (e.g., Kovacs, Feinberg, Crouse-Novak, Paulauskas, Pollock, & Finkelstein, 1984; McCauley et al., 1993; Strober, Lampert, Schmidt, & Morrell, 1993). Rates of recovery from depression are relatively high, with most youths experiencing a significant reduction in depressive symptoms within a year (Goodyer, Germany, Gowrusankur, & Altham, 1991; Keller, Lavori, Beardslee, Wunder, & Ryan, 1991). For example, Kovacs, Feinberg, Crouse-Novak, Paulauskas, Pollock, and Finkelstein (1984) followed patients and showed that 74% of the clinic sample recovered within 1 year after onset and 92% recovered by 2 years. In some studies, recovery from depression includes individuals who continue to show symptoms but at levels considered to be subclinical (e.g., Kovacs, Feinberg, Crouse-Novak, Paulauskas, & Finkelstein, 1984), whereas in other studies the absence of depressive symptoms serves as the criterion (Goodyer et al., 1991). For some youths, depression is chronic and may continue up to 1–2 years, either as a Major Depressive Disorder or as alternating between periods of Major Depression and Dysthymia (Ryan et al., 1987; Sanford et al., 1995; Shain, King, Naylor, & Alessi, 1991). Longer periods of continuous depression are not well studied among children and adolescents.

Although recovery rates are high, so are those for relapse. There is strong evidence that there is continuity in depression, so that the onset of Major Depression Or Dysthymia is a predictor for further episodes. In the longest follow-up study to date, 60% of the children and adolescents identified as depressed were shown to have at least one recurrent episode of Major Depression over the next several years (mean follow-up duration of 18 years) (Harrington, Fudge, Rutter, Pickles, & Hill, 1990, 1991). Depressed youths were at greater risk for a recurrence of depression, when compared to a matched patient sample with other types of dysfunction. The co-occurrence of Major Depression and Dysthymia ("double depression") predicts recurrence and continuation of depression (Asarnow et al., 1988; Kovacs, Feinberg, Crouse-Novak, Paulauskas, Pollock, & Finkelstein, 1984). The presence of depression in the parent and stressors in the home are also risk factors for continued depression (Burge & Hammen, 1991; Hammen, Burge, & Adrian, 1991).

Apart from the course of depression, the short- and long-term prognoses of youths identified as depressed include many untoward outcomes. For example, adolescents who are depressed are at increased risk for later marital problems, involvement in drugs, delinquency, arrest, and criminal conviction, dropping out of school, and unemployment (see Lewinsohn, Roberts, et al., 1994). In general, any comorbid condition (e.g., Conduct Disorder) is likely to increase the risk for long-term difficulties (e.g., subsequent criminality) (Harrington et al., 1991). Consequently, treatment cannot neglect the other conditions with which depression may be associated.

Implications for Treatment

In the past decade in particular, a great deal has been learned about childhood and adolescent depression that has direct relevance for treatment. Among the salient points reviewed previously, depression (broadly defined) is a pervasive disorder insofar as it encompasses a range of child and adolescent domains of functioning, well beyond the defining or core symptoms. Peer and family relations and school functioning are examples of domains that are likely to be impaired. Other symptoms than depression, as reflected in comorbid diagnoses, are likely to be evident and

have their own effects on current impairment and long-term course. Depression (e.g., Major Depressive Disorder, Dysthymic Disorder) is likely to be enduring over the course of development. Although youths are likely to recover from an episode of depression within a year or two, they are also likely to evince continued impairment and dysfunction as well as recurrences of the disorder (Lewinsohn, Roberts, et al., 1994).

The findings from descriptive psychopathology and epidemiology are enormously important in relation to developing and identifying effective interventions. This research provides a framework for designing and evaluating programs that provide care to depressed children. Consequently, we return to many of the issues here in the context of evaluating the effects of current treatments.

ETIOLOGIES OF DEPRESSION

No single cause has been identified that leads to clinical depression. Indeed, the overall term "depression" (mood disorders) refers to a family of disorders; it is likely that the different variations have different, albeit related, causal paths. In addition, within a given type of disorder (e.g., unipolar depression), there may be different paths. There are separate ways to organize the information regarding the factors that lead to depression. Here we highlight models of depression and lines of research they have spawned.

Models of Depression: An Overview

There are multiple conceptual views regarding the factors that lead to depression. The views propose various critical processes and mechanisms involved in the onset and course of depression. The models have been developed and researched in the context of adult depression; extensions to children have been fairly direct in terms of the processes and conceptual views. Broad conceptual approaches (e.g., biological models, cognitive models) have many variations, lines of supportive research, measurement strategies, and emergent issues. The different models are highlighted here to address broader issues about the scope of depression's impact and the implications for its treatment. For further review and discussion of models of depression in relation to children and adolescents, the reader is referred to other sources (Harrington, 1993; Reynolds & Johnston, 1994).

Biological models encompass several areas and findings. Genetic influences have been studied extensively in relation to depression. Among the more reliable findings is that depression runs in families (see Hammen, 1991). Close relatives of persons with Major Depression are more likely to have the disorder than unrelated persons. Findings have been supported in family history, twin, and adoption studies (see Paykel, 1992; Usdin, Asberg, Bertilsson, & Sjoqvist, 1984). The findings do not argue automatically for a single type of influence (e.g., genetic) or for a single direction of the influence (e.g., from parent to child). It is possible that the connection between parent and child depression can be traced to other common contextual influences, such as family adversity and marital discord (Fergusson, Horword, & Lynskey, 1995). At the same time, factors that antedate the child are clear contributors to childhood depression. For example, early (e.g., before the age of 20) onset of depression in the history of the parent greatly increases risk of Major Depression in children and adolescents (see Harrington, 1996). Although depression runs in families, the strength of the association and the mechanisms through which this operates are far from resolved.

Neurobiological studies have focused on a broad array of processes and correlates, including neuroanatomical, neuropsychological, neurochemical, neuroendocrine, and polysomnographic characteristics of depressed children and adolescents (see Emslie, Weinberg, Kennard, & Kowatch, 1994). Various abnormalities have been found in relation to each of these broad domains among depressed children and adolescents, although the findings have been less clear and consistent with youths than they have been with adults. For example, among depressed adults a variety of sleep abnormalities have been found, including delayed sleep onset, decreased sleep efficiency, increased rapid eye movement (REM) during REM sleep periods (REM density), shortened REM latency, and reduced slow-wave (delta) sleep (see Emslie et al., 1994). Some findings (e.g., shortened REM latency) have been found with children as well, but sleep architecture findings have been less clear overall among depressed children and adolescents. Similarly, serotonin, acetylcholine, and dopamine levels in adult depressives have been studied extensively, in part because of their role in the regulation of several domains of functioning related to depression (e.g., sleep regulation, mood, appetite, thought disturbance). Here too,

in part because of the paucity of studies, evidence has not firmly established that child and adolescent characteristics parallel those of adults.

Neurobiological models of depression have received substantial support over the past decade. In particular, there has been growing evidence that the frontal lobe plays a primary role in the regulation of mood and affect (Stuss, Gow, & Hetherington, 1992). For example, recent research has found that infants of depressed mothers exhibit significantly less left frontal electroencephalographic (EEG) activity and higher levels of salivary cortisol as compared to infants of nondepressed mothers (Dawson, Frey, Panagiotides, Osterling, & Hessl, 1997; Hessl et al., 1996). Also, infants exhibiting greater right than left frontal baseline EEG activity experience greater affective distress when separated from their mothers (Davidson & Fox, 1989). These and related findings (see Dawson, Hessl, & Frey, 1994) support a theory of "ontogenetic sculpting" (Kolb, 1989), in which mother–infant interactions alter brain physiology by selectively reinforcing particular neural networks (Edelman, 1987). Mothers who fail to respond adaptively to their infants' affective states may extinguish certain behaviors, and thus fail to reinforce the neural pathways that would aid in affect regulation. Consequently, a dissociation develops between physiological and behavioral systems, for example, although the infant may be physiologically distressed, he or she remains outwardly passive and unresponsive because the infant has not previously been reinforced for such behavior. Although much work remains to be done in this and related fields, including identification of critical time periods for the development of neural networks and possibilities of reversing maladaptive "ontogenetic sculpting," there is little doubt of the neuropsychological, biological, and physiological significance of early mother–child interactions on children's affect regulation.

Cognitive models of depression focus on perceptual and attributional styles and belief systems that may underlie depressive symptoms. Research has advanced in light of early theoretical views focusing on negative cognitions. Beck's (1967) view that depression is associated with negative views about oneself, the future, and the world (the "cognitive triad"), and Seligman's (1975) theory of learned helplessness, stimulated a great deal of work in this area. Over the years, these views have evolved in their own right (e.g., variations in the nature of self-attributions and their perceived specificity and stability) and in relation to other concepts that influence the impact of these cognitions on depression (e.g., stress, self-regulation, vulnerability factors, exposure to negative events in relation to depressogenic attributional style) (see Abramson, Metalsky, & Alloy, 1989; Alloy, 1988). Contemporary work with children and adolescents has identified a variety of negative cognitions, attributions, misperceptions, and deficiencies in problem solving skills associated with depression (see Kaslow et al., 1994). Low levels of self-esteem and perceived competence, high levels of hopelessness and helplessness, and internal attributions of negative events are a few among many thought processes associated with depression in children and adolescents.

Behavioral models have focused on learning, environmental consequences, skills, and behavioral deficits. Symptoms of depression are considered to result from problems in interaction with the environment and deficiencies in responding to environmental stimuli. Early theoretical work in this area (Lewinsohn, 1974) focused on the reduced reinforcement experiences thought to lead to and maintain depression. Treatment approaches derived from the model emphasized the development of pleasant activities to increase reinforcing experiences and interactions with the environment. Social skills deficits (e.g., limited abilities to interact with others) are also included in behavioral approaches; indeed, such deficits may serve as antecedents to reduced pleasant activities within the interpersonal environment.

Interpersonal models are worth distinguishing, although they are often encompassed by behavioral models. Interpersonal treatment approaches emphasize the role of social behavior. The research on parent–child interaction among depressed parents provides support for the view that early parent–child contacts in the home may play a role in increasing vulnerability to depression. Deficits in contact with parents, deficits in parental warmth, and poor attachment bonds are lines of work addressed by this model (see Hammen, 1991).

Socioenvironmental models have focused on stressful life events that may influence the onset or emergence of depression. The significance of stressful events as precursors to depressive symptoms is recognized in everyday life. Bereavement, for example, frequently includes multiple symptoms of depression linked specifically to the death of a loved one. Research with adults (e.g., Paykel, 1992b), children, and adolescents (e.g., Compas, Grant, & Ey, 1994) has supported the role of stressful events in relation to the onset of depressive episodes.

Psychodynamic models focus on the intrapsychic underpinnings of depression and have included models ranging from orthodox psychoanalytic concepts to more revisionist views. At a broad level, central themes have focused on such concepts as ego and superego, narcissism, the need to be loved, and so on (see Bemporad, 1994). Many of these concepts have been less researchable and less well researched than those emanating from other models. Consequently, psychodynamic models have not enjoyed the empirical advances of other models (e.g., biological, cognitive) in relation to childhood and adolescent depression. An important exception is the work of Bowlby (1980) on the role of attachment and child reaction to separation and stressful experiences more generally. The work falls in the tradition of early work on anaclitic depression (Spitz, 1946; Spitz & Wolf, 1946), in which a significant proportion of infants (36%) separated from their mothers showed characteristics of depression (e.g., sadness, withdrawal). Contemporary research has identified insecure attachment patterns that emerge from interactions with depressed parents and place youths at risk for later depression (see Cicchetti, Ganiban, & Barnett, 1991).

Although the majority of paradigms used to conceptualize childhood depression have been downward extensions of adult models, developmentally based models have emerged as well. Among the more well-developed lines of research is the work of Garber and colleagues, who hold the view that children's self-regulation strategies play a central role in overcoming, maintaining, and preventing negative mood states—a view that is receiving theoretical and empirical support (Garber, Braafladt, & Zeman, 1991). From an information-processing perspective, emotion regulation involves a number of identifiable skills: (1) recognizing that changes in affect have occurred and require regulation; (2) accurate interpretation of the event(s) responsible for modifying affect; (3) setting goals to determine the steps necessary to change one's affect; (4) generating appropriate responses to achieve one's goal; (5) evaluation of the expected effectiveness of each response; and (6) the actual implementation of the chosen response. Information-processing models hypothesize that depressed children experience deficits in these skill areas, which make overcoming their negative mood states difficult.

Garber et al. (1991) have conducted several studies examining differences between depressed and nondepressed children, the results of which support an information-processing model. For example, when asked to identify strategies to reduce affective distress, depressed children were more likely than nondepressed children to nominate strategies involving active avoidance and negative behavioral responses (e.g., aggression), whereas nondepressed children were more likely to choose problem-focused and active distraction strategies. Sadly, the negative and aggressive strategies preferred by depressed children may increase their social isolation and exacerbate their distress (Garber et al., 1991). In addition to these response generation deficits, these researchers found that depressed children also experienced deficits at the information evaluation step. Specifically, depressed children were less likely than nondepressed children to believe that their affect could be modified through either self- or mother-generated solutions. Interestingly, another study (Garber et al., 1991) indicated that although depressed mothers produced maladaptive regulation strategies for themselves, they were just as capable as nondepressed mothers of generating effective regulation strategies to help their children's affective distress. Taken together, these findings clearly lend support to an information-processing model and suggest that depressed children experience skill deficits at the strategy generation and evaluation stages during a depressive episode. Longitudinal research is needed to determine whether children experience such deficits during periods of remission. In addition, a fuller understanding of the mechanisms underlying the onset of a depressive episode is necessary before we can effectively use current findings.

As the above-described models convey, depression is multifaceted. Some efforts have been made to address its many facets and to integrate findings generated by the different conceptualizations. For example, some time ago Akiskal (1979) outlined a biobehavioral model of depression, in which genetic predisposition (e.g., decrease in synaptic receptor sensitivity), physiological stressors (e.g., viral infection, hypothyroidism), psychosocial stressors (e.g., object loss), and predispositions (e.g., learned helplessness) were posited to influence biological processes (e.g., neurotransmitters) through a final common pathway in the brain (diencephalon) that mediates mood, arousal, activation, and psychomotor functions. Integrative models sensitize us to the multifaceted nature of depression and begin to suggest possible mechanisms connecting systems that would otherwise be investigated in isolation.

Risk Factors for Onset of Depression

"Risk factors" are characteristics that precede an outcome and are associated with an increase in the likelihood of that outcome over base rates in the general population. Identifying risk factors has important implications for understanding etiology as well as intervention. In relation to etiology, risk factors are precursors and may generate hypotheses about possible mechanisms involved in the onset of a disorder and different paths or progressions leading to the disorder (e.g., different profiles of factors that lead to depression). For example, child gender is a risk factor for depression in adolescence, in light of the increased prevalence of the disorder among females in adolescence (and adulthood). A number of hypotheses have been proffered to explain what mechanisms (e.g., personality styles, coping mechanisms, interaction patterns) might account for sex differences and the varied paths leading to depression (Nolen-Hoeksema & Girgus, 1994). Identifying risk factors and the mechanisms through which they operate also permits early identification of cases (before depression emerges) and of possible areas that might be targeted for intervention to prevent the onset of dysfunction.

Identification of risk factors requires demonstrating the temporal sequence of antecedents and the outcome (e.g., depression). Research on childhood depression is at a relatively early stage in this process. A great deal of work has focused on childhood precursors of adult depression (e.g., related to attachment, loss of a parent) and on characteristics of the offspring of depressed parents (Hammen, 1991). Most work on the characteristics of depression in children and adolescents has focused on concurrent correlates (see Harrington, 1993). That is, children and adolescents are identified as depressed and compared to patient and community controls in relation to some domain of interest (e.g., cognitions, neurotransmitters). This research has elaborated the scope of impairment such youths evince (e.g., cognitive models), as well as mechanisms through which effective treatments (e.g., medication) might operate (e.g., neurotransmitter models) (see Hammen & Rudolf, 1996). As an initial step in identifying key features and possible antecedents to dysfunction, the study of concurrent features can be important. However, much of the correlational research leaves ambiguous whether characteristics implicated in depression are antecedent or subsequent to, or are epiphenomenal, with depression.

Longitudinal research has identified a number of antecedents of depression. Among the more well-demonstrated risk factors for child and adolescent depression are family history (genetic loading) of depression, parent psychopathology (particularly depression of the mother), child gender (females are at greater risk for depression in adolescence), and recent stressful life events (see Hammen, 1991; Harrington, 1993). Although many of these factors increase risk for depression, they are not all specific to depression. For example, children of depressed parents are at risk for Major Depression, but also for a number of other disorders (e.g., substance abuse) (Weissman et al., 1987). Also, teenage mothering is a risk factor for later childhood depression in the offspring (see Kellam, 1990), as well as for impairment and dysfunction in other domains (e.g., antisocial behavior). Consequently, in the process of elaborating risk factors, it will be important to identify their specificity in relation to depression.

"Protective factors" are characteristics that attenuate the likelihood of an outcome among individuals who are at risk for that outcome (Rutter, 1987). Among individuals identified as at risk, many may not show the undesired outcome. Those characteristics that distinguish this latter group are considered as domains that may "protect" the individuals in some way from the onset of the disorder. Factors that attenuate the likelihood of depression among at-risk youths are much less well studied than are risk factors. As an example, interpersonal skills (that elicit positive social responses of others) appear to decrease risk of depression among youths of parents with mood disorders (see Beardslee, Schultz, & Selman, 1987; Hammen, 1991). The specificity of interpersonal skills as a factor to decrease risk for depression, rather than for a variety of other symptom patterns, remains to be demonstrated. More work on both risk and protective factors is critical for elaborating possible factors that are causally related to depressive symptoms (i.e., those factors that, when modified, alter the onset of depressive symptoms).

ASSESSMENT

Assessment Goals and Domains

Assessment of depression in children and adolescents has advanced considerably, as reflected in the availability of a number of measures, diverse methods of assessment, and validation studies with community and clinic samples for many of the measures (see Harrington, 1993; Reynolds, 1994). From the perspective of treatment research, it is useful to delineate four broad domains of assessment that warrant coverage: multiple problem behaviors, depression, depression-related domains, and impairment. The importance of these domains derives from previously reviewed research regarding the scope of dysfunction that is likely to be evident.

Multiple Problem Domains

It is critical to incorporate a broad-based assessment strategy to detail patient dysfunction. "Broad-based assessment" refers here to the use of instruments that sample a wide range of symptoms and problem domains. Psychiatric diagnostic interviews provide one measurement source and are useful for assessing the broad set of symptoms and for delineating comorbid diagnoses. Several diagnostic instruments are available for children (usually beginning at school age) and adolescents, including the Schedule for Affective Disorders and Schizophrenia for School-Age Children (K-SADS), the Diagnostic Interview for Children and Adolescents, the Child Assessment Schedule, and the Diagnostic Interview Schedule for Children (see Edelbrock & Costello, 1988). The measures vary in the nature of the questions (continuous or binary answers for individual symptoms), period over which dysfunction is assessed (current episode, lifetime), intended use (e.g., clinical samples, administered by clinicians; community samples, administered by lay interviewers), and the diagnostic system they cover (e.g., DSM-III-R, DSM-IV). Psychometric properties of individual subsections of diagnostic interviews are not generally well validated as a rule, and better dimensional scales whose reliabilities and validities are more well established are available.

Multiple problem behaviors can also be assessed with dimensional scales. As a familiar example, the Child Behavior Checklist (CBCL;

Achenbach, 1991a) is a parent-completed measure that includes 118 items (each rated on a scale of 0–2). Specific symptom domains (factors) (e.g., Depression, Schizophrenia, Withdrawal, Aggressiveness, Hyperactivity) can be assessed that vary somewhat by age and sex groupings. Also, broad-band scales reflect more general types of behavioral patterns (Internalizing, Externalizing behaviors) and overall dysfunction (Total Behavior Problems). Scales derived on an *a priori* basis and designed to measure social competence (participation in activities, social interaction, progress at school) are included as well. There are teacher and adolescent versions of the scale, referred to as the CBCL Teacher Report Form (Achenbach, 1991b) and Youth Self-Report (Achenbach, 1991c). Each of these scales has been extensively studied, with data from both normative and clinical samples. From the standpoint of treatment, the measures are useful in providing a profile of symptom domains and prosocial functioning, as well as parallel assessment devices from multiple perspectives. Several other scales of dysfunction for children and adolescents exist that rely on parent or teacher ratings (see Barkley, 1988).

Depression

Once a broad measure of dysfunction has been used to sample the range of potential symptoms, it is meaningful to focus more specifically on measures of depression. Many measures of depression have been developed for children and adolescents (Clarizio, 1994; Reynolds, 1994). Among the alternative assessment methods, self-report scales have dominated. Self-report is particularly important in assessing depression, because key symptoms such as sadness, feelings of worthlessness, and loss of interest in activities reflect subjective feelings and self-perceptions. Also, children are often considered to be better sources of information regarding internalizing symptoms than are parents (see Kazdin, 1994).

The most widely used self-report measure is the Children's Depression Inventory (CDI; Kovacs, 1981), which assesses cognitive, affective, and behavioral signs of depression. Children select one of three alternatives that characterize their mood state over the past 2 weeks. For example, for one of the items, children are asked to choose one of following statements: "a. I am sad once in a while," "b. I am sad many times" or "c. I am sad all of the time." The most extreme statement endorsed in each of the 27 items yields a total score for severity of depression.

The CDI has enjoyed widespread use in part because it is an offspring of the Beck Depression Inventory (BDI; Beck, Ward, Mendelson, Mock, & Erbaugh, 1961), the most frequently used inventory to measure depression among adults. Studies of the CDI have evaluated internal consistency, factor structure, test–retest reliability, alternative methods of test administration, gender and age differences, cutoff scores to delineate severe cases of depression, and correlates with other constructs (e.g., self-esteem, hopelessness, and social competence) (see Reynolds, 1994).

Measures completed by significant others are often used to evaluate childhood depression. Ratings by others are important because they are likely to identify symptoms different from those identified by the child. Behavioral correlates of depression (e.g., irritability) and changes in eating and sleep patterns are readily evident to parents and less clearly reported by children. Many of the child self-report measures have also been rephrased so that parents can report on a child's depression. Even if the same measure (e.g., the CDI) is used for the child, it is valuable to include ratings by parents as well. Findings suggest that child and parent ratings of a child's depression show little or no correlation with each other, but that each source of information predicts performance in other domains (see Kazdin, 1994).

Clinicians, teachers, and peers also may provide important information about the child. Clinician ratings can be completed using the Children's Depression Rating Scale (CDRS; Poznanski, Cook, & Carroll, 1979; Poznanski et al., 1984), a measure adapted from the frequently used Hamilton Rating Scale for Depression (HRSD) for adults (Hamilton, 1967). The clinician rates symptom areas of depression based on the child's verbal report and nonverbal behavior (e.g., appearance of sad affect). Ratings by teachers have also been used to assess child depression. Here too, the language of the items is often modified for teachers.

Ratings by peers have taken advantage of the nomination format often used for sociometrics. The Peer Nomination Inventory of Depression (Lefkowitz & Tesiny, 1980) requires children within a group (e.g., a classroom) to nominate others for several specific characteristics. The requirement of having a peer group to provide nominations has limited the use of this measure in clinical settings. Also, the peer nomination format in general raises ethical concerns associated with explicit peer identification of children in relation to negative or undesirable characteristics.

Apart from questionnaires and inventories, direct observations of overt behavior and nonverbal behavior have been assessed and provide another important source of information (Kazdin, Esveldt-Dawson, et al., 1985; Kazdin, Sherick, Esveldt-Dawson, & Rancurello, 1985). In general, observational methods have not been standardized and applied beyond the specific studies of interest. They do, however, convey the utility of developing direct behavioral observational measures that can discriminate depressed and nondepressed patient samples, and their resuls may serve as a dependent measure of treatment outcome.

Depression-Related Constructs

Other measures may be of value because they address specific characteristics of depressive symptoms in greater depth or because they address key areas that are likely to be influenced by depressive symptoms. The range of domains and measures is large, but major candidates for a comprehensive assessment battery can be highlighted.

Low self-esteem or poor evaluations of personal worth are likely to be part of the symptom picture of depression and play a role in alternative models of depression. A self-esteem scale such as the Self-Perception Profile for Children (Harter, 1985) may be useful. This scale assesses self-adequacy and personal competence in five specific domains: Scholastic, Social, Athletic, Physical Appearance, and Behavioral Conduct. A Global Self-Worth scale is also included to measure overall self-esteem.

Perceived control over events is important in cognitive models of depression. In this context, "control" refers to the extent to which an outcome depends on someone's behavior and the perceived competence of the individual to engage in the requisite behaviors (Weisz, Weiss, Wasserman, & Rintoul, 1987). One measure of control is the Multidimensional Measure of Children's Perception of Control (Connell, 1985). The measure examines the extent to which events are perceived as being controlled by the individual, by external sources, or by unknown sources of control. Evidence suggests that depression is related to low perceptions of internal sources of control and high perceptions of unknown sources of control (Weisz et al., 1987).

Related to perceived control, cognitive distortion has been important in behavioral and cognitive views of depression. "Cognitive distortion" refers to negative cognitive "errors"; for example, the individual anticipates outcomes of events to be extremely negative (catastrophizing), assumes that a negative outcome will extend to other situations as well (overgeneralizing), or takes responsibility for negative events (personalizing). To assess these characteristics, the Children's Negative Cognitive Error Questionnaire has been developed (Leitenberg, Yost, & Carroll-Wilson, 1986). The measure includes brief vignettes that cover different types of cognitive distortions in everyday life. Children rate the extent to which each statement reflects their thinking. Cognitive distortion has been shown to relate to children's self-reports of depression, self-esteem, and anxiety.

Generating frequent negative thoughts is another common characteristic of depressed persons. To measure the frequency of automatic negative thoughts with depressed adults, Hollon and Kendall (1980) developed the Automatic Thoughts Questionnaire. This 30-item self-report instrument asks subjects to indicate the frequency with which they experience various automatic negative thoughts; sample items include "I'm no good," "I'm so disappointed with myself," and "I'm a loser," and are scored on a 5-point scale from "never" to "always." This measure has been strongly associated with depressive symptoms in adolescents (Garber, Weiss, & Shanley, 1993) and with the diagnosis of depression in children (Kazdin, 1990; Stark, Humphrey, Laurent, Livingston, & Christopher, 1993).

Helplessness is an attributional style associated with depression, which includes the person's expectation that undesirable events are attributable to internal, stable, and global causes. The Children's Attributional Style Questionnaire has been developed to measure these attributional characteristics among children (Seligman & Peterson, 1986). The measure lists numerous events and asks the child to identify one of two possible causes. The causes among the items vary to encompass different attributional styles, including internal versus external, stable versus unstable, and global versus specific categories. Results suggest that attributional style correlates with depression in children as it does in adults (Seligman & Peterson, 1986).

Hopelessness, or negative expectations toward the future, is especially relevant if there are signs of suicidal attempt or ideation. Hopelessness correlates with suicidal behavior in adults and children (e.g., Beck, Kovacs, & Weissman, 1975; Kazdin, French, Unis, Esveldt-Dawson, & Sherick, 1983). The Hopelessness Scale for Children has been developed to assess whether children view future positive events as likely (Kazdin, Rodgers, & Colbus, 1986). Total scores correlate with depression, suicidal ideation and behavior, and diminished self-esteem, although the relation to suicidal ideation and behavior has not been consistent across studies (e.g., Asarnow, Carlson, & Guthrie, 1987; Asarnow & Guthrie, 1989; Marciano & Kazdin, 1994).

Deficiencies in social behavior are often evident in depression. Social behavior is important to consider also because of the prominent place it has occupied in behavioral and cognitive models. A wide range of social behaviors has been shown to relate to depression among adults, including communication patterns, participation in activities, expressions of affect, eye contact, and others. Relatively few measures are available to assess a wide range of social behaviors in children. An exception is the Matson Evaluation of Social Skills with Youngsters (Matson, Rotatori, & Helsel, 1983). The scale is completed by children or adults and assesses a wide range of children's skills in initiating social interaction, responding to others, making friends, expressing hostility, and others.

Loneliness or perceived isolation from others is related to social behavior and likely to be relevant to depression. An easily completed self-report measure, referred to as the Loneliness Questionnaire, has been developed for school-age children (Asher, Hymel, & Renshaw, 1984; Asher & Wheeler, 1985). The measure includes 16 true–false items in which children evaluate how difficult it is to make friends, how well liked they feel, and whether they have friends to play or to talk with at school. Research has suggested that feelings of loneliness are related to peer rejection (Asher & Wheeler, 1985). The connection between rejection and loneliness raises the prospect of focusing on the peer social network as a means of influencing children's feelings about themselves.

Reinforcing events and activities are relevant for childhood depression, given the behavioral formulation attributing depression in part to a paucity of reinforcing experiences from the environment. Knowledge of these events can be used as a basis for developing specific activities in treatment. Perception of reinforcing events can be measured by the Children's Reinforcement Schedule (Cautela, Cautela, & Esonis, 1983). Separate versions are used for youths of different ages. Youths identify the extent to which they like potentially reinforcing events or activities (on a 3-point scale ranging from "dislike" to "like very much"). Sample items refer to riding a bicycle, traveling to different places, and going to movies. The scales suggest rewarding activities that a child may engage or participate in to reduce depressive symptoms.

The assessment of pleasant and unpleasant activities has also been advanced by development of the Adolescent Activities Checklist (Carey, Kelley, Buss, & Scott, 1986), a self-report scale in which adolescents rate the occurrence and pleasantness of various activities (e.g., watching television, going out to eat). Depressed and nondepressed adolescents (nonclinic sample), identified by scores on the BDI, differed in their ratings of the number of unpleasant activities but not in the number of pleasant activities (Carey et al., 1986). These findings provide a finer-grained analysis of activity patterns associated with depressive symptoms and may direct attention to the appropriate intervention focus.

Life events, or factors in the environment that induce stress, are also relevant for the evaluation of depression. Such events as a recent move, loss of friends, conflict with parents or peers, onset of serious illness or hospitalization, and separation of the parents, may influence the affective symptoms and daily functioning (Compas et al., 1994; Trad, 1987). The magnitude or intensity of an event, the perceived valence of the event, and the number of events within a given period may all be important to understand changes in the youth's behavior. Among alternative measures, the Life Events Record (Coddington, 1972) for children and the Life Events Checklist for older children and adolescents have been especially useful, although a variety of measures are available (see Compas, 1987).

Because depression can influence so many facets of an individual's functioning, many other constructs and measures are relevant as well. Examples include measures related to the family and the context in which the child develops, interpersonal relationships, basic structural and functional aspects of the home, parental dysfunction, school attendance, and academic performance, to mention a few. Given the range of domains and measures that are potentially relevant to childhood depression, researchers must make decisions to delimit the battery.

Impairment

Impairment reflects the extent to which the individual's functioning in everyday life is impeded. Impairment is likely to be related to scope and severity of symptoms. So, for example, severely depressed youths may show both pervasive dysfunction in symptom domains and markedly impaired functioning in everyday life (home, school). However, impairment can be distinguished from symptoms insofar as individuals with similar levels of symptoms (e.g., scores), diagnoses, and patterns of comorbidity are likely to be distinguishable based on their ability to function adaptively. School and academic functioning, peer relations, participation in activities, and health are some of the areas included in impairment.

We know from work highlighted previously that youths who recover from depression and no longer meet diagnostic criteria may continue to show some of the symptoms (Kovacs, Feinberg, Crouse-Novak, Paulauskas, & Finkelstein, 1984). Among the residual characteristics are continuation of internalizing symptoms, emotional reliance (e.g., excessive desire for support and approval from others, anxiety when alone), more stressful life events, and (among adolescents) increased rates of cigarette smoking (Rohde, Lewinsohn, & Seeley, 1994). It is clear from existing research that symptoms are likely to remain among youths considered to be in remission. What is less clear is whether there are any reductions in impairment. Similarly, the impact of treatment on impairment is arguably as important as its impact on primary depressive symptoms. This is particularly relevant to the issue of relapse because impairment is a risk factor for future episodes of depression in adolescents (Lewinsohn, Seeley, Hibbard, Rohde, & Sack, 1996). Thus, assessment batteries designed to measure depression ought to include measures of impairment as well.

As a rule, impairment measures have not been well validated. Among the critical validation studies are those that establish the construct as separate from (i.e., not redundant with) measures of symptoms. The most widely used measure is the Children's Global Assessment Scale (Shaffer et al., 1983), which was derived from the widely used adult Global Assessment Scale (Endicott, Spitzer, Fleiss, & Cohen, 1976). The scale requires a clinical rating on a 100-point scale that combines multiple dimensions (e.g., symptoms, ability to function in different settings). The inclusion of multiple dimensions and

scaling on essentially one item raises conceptual and psychometric issues. A number of other measures are available and are designed in various ways to examine competencies, adaptive functioning, and how the child is doing in various contexts and roles (e.g., peers, school). The Child and Adult Functioning Assessment Scale (Hodges, Bickman, Ring-Kurtz, & Reiter, 1991) and the Social Adjustment Inventory for Children and Adolescents (John, Gammon, Prusoff, & Warner, 1987) are examples.

General Guidelines for Selection of Measures for Treatment Evaluation

No single measure can encompass the multiple facets of dysfunction that depression entails. For the clinician and researcher, it is obvious that assessment of depression ought to include multiple measures that encompass different methods of assessment (e.g., interviews, direct observations), perspectives (e.g., child, parent, teacher), and domains (e.g., affect, cognitions, behavior). Apart from the general advisability of multichannel assessment strategies, specific findings within the area of childhood depression make such strategies particularly advisable. That is, there is significant method variance in the assessment of depression; different methods of assessment may not intercorrelate highly; and measures that do not correlate highly with each other may still reliably predict to different external criteria (e.g., social behavior, suicidal risk) (see Kazdin, 1994; Reynolds, 1994). Based on these considerations, an assessment battery should minimally sample the following:

1. Different sources of information (e.g., the child, parent, teacher).
2. Performance in different settings (e.g., at home and at school).
3. Diverse symptom domains (e.g., depression, symptoms of other disorders).
4. Impairment in everyday functioning.

Evaluation of the child's performance and functioning can be greatly facilitated by using measures with an established normative data base. Normative data, derived from large-scale studies of nonreferred children of different ages, can be very useful in interpreting the scores of individual cases. Normative data are available for very few measures of childhood depression, however. The major exception is the CDI, which now includes several studies with community samples of different age groups (see Reynolds, 1994, for a review). The ability to compare depressed children to same-age and same-sex peers facilitates evaluation of the severity of the problem and/or the magnitude of change over the course of treatment.

It is also useful to select measures with information available on the cutoff scores that define varying degrees or levels of depression. Cutoff scores may be drawn from the normative data to suggest a specific score—for example, the 90th percentile for depression for children of a given age and sex. Cutoff scores can be studied in relation to other measures of impairment as well as long-term course of symptoms. An extreme score on an inventory of depression is not tantamount to a diagnosis of depression according to psychiatric diagnostic criteria (e.g., DSM or RDC). Optimal cutoff scores on various depression scales that maximize classification accuracy have high rates of false positives and false negatives (Kazdin, Colbus, & Rodgers, 1987; Lobovits & Handal, 1985). Thus, identifying an extreme group by means of cutoff scores may be quite useful for research or clinical purposes, but the group so identified differs from those selected through diagnostic procedures. From the standpoint of treatment, one criterion (e.g., diagnosis) is not necessarily superior to another (e.g., cutoff score on a standardized and well-normed measure). Too little research has focused on the implications of using alternative methods of identifying youths and different criteria or scores within a particular method.

Although work on measures of depression has advanced considerably, less attention has been devoted to related domains that we have highlighted (e.g., hopelessness, loneliness, impairment). The validity and utility of these measures at different points in childhood and adolescence, normative data, and possible cutoff scores for varied outcomes have not been well investigated. In relation to treatment, child and adolescent therapy research focuses almost exclusively on measures of symptoms (Kazdin, Bass, Ayers, & Rodgers, 1990), with little attention to other outcome domains likely to influence functioning and long-term prognosis. Development of measures in other domains is an important priority to provide the tools for broader assessment.

TREATMENTS FOR DEPRESSION

There currently exist a variety of psychosocial and psychopharmacological interventions for childhood and adolescent depression. Most of these are derived directly from treatment strategies developed for adults. Unfortunately, only a few controlled outcome studies have evaluated the efficacy of these interventions with children and adolescents.

Cognitive-Behavioral Treatments

Overview

Most psychosocial interventions for depression revolve around the tenets of cognitive-behavioral therapy (CBT). Although "cognitive" and "behavioral" treatments have merged in recent years, they derive from distinguishable (albeit related) theoretical roots. Cognitive approaches for depression stem from the work of Beck (1967), who hypothesized that depressed individuals experience deficits in information processing that lead to and maintain negatively biased views of oneself, the world, and the future. The primary goal of cognitive therapy is to confront, challenge, and modify maladaptive cognitive processes (e.g., negative self-monitoring, short-term focus, excessively high performance standards, failure to self-reinforce, and misattributions).

In contrast, behavioral approaches focus on increasing pleasurable experiences and specific response repertoires (e.g., social skills). Depression is hypothesized to lead to (and be maintained by) a decrease in pleasurable events due to a restricted range of response-contingent reinforcement, fewer available reinforcers, and inadequate social skills (Lewinsohn, 1974). Hence, interventions such as social skills training, which teach children assertiveness, communication, ways of accepting and giving feedback, social problem solving, and conflict resolution, may increase positive interactions with others (e.g., Fine, Forth, Gilbert, & Haley, 1991).

In practice, cognitive and behavioral strategies are integrated into a single treatment package as more adaptive cognitions are hypothesized to lead to more adaptive behavior patterns and vice versa. An example of a broader package is provided in the CBT of Stark and his colleagues, who have completed several studies on the treatment of depressed children. Key characteristics of the treatment are listed in Table 4.3. As evident in the table, the package includes a wide range of activities and techniques (e.g., Stark, Reynolds, & Kaslow, 1987).

Several other techniques are often added to a basic CBT strategy. Although these interventions often serve as ancillary components to CBT, they are sometimes used separately as comparison treatments. Problem-solving interventions, which teach individuals to clarify problem situations and to generate, evaluate, and implement appropriate solutions, have led to reductions in depressive symptoms in adults (Nezu, Nezu, & Perri, 1989) and children (Stark et al., 1987). Therapeutic support can create safe and supportive environments that allow depressed youths to feel connected to and supported by others, and has been an effective treatment for increasing adolescents' self-esteem and in decreasing their depressive symptoms (Fine et al., 1991). Given the anxiety often associated with depression, relaxation training and other anxiety management techniques can be used as well (Kahn, Kehle, Jenson, & Clarke, 1990; Reynolds & Coats, 1986).

Among the most systematic, comprehensive, and well-established programs in the treatment of depression in youths is the Adolescent Coping with Depression Course (CWD-A; Clarke, Lewinsohn, & Hops, 1990), which was modified from the adult version (Lewinsohn, Antonuccio, Steinmetz, & Teri, 1984). The CWD-A is a form of CBT that includes several adjunct treatment techniques and teaches adolescents skills to help control their depression. Key characteristics of the CWD-A are highlighted in Table 4.4. Apart from the core treatment sessions with adolescents, a complementary parent therapy has been developed to help parents support and reinforce their children's treatment. In addition, building upon the adult relapse prevention literature, Lewinsohn and colleagues have recently developed "booster sessions" to bolster the skills taught during treatment (see Lewinsohn, Clarke, & Rohde, 1994; Lewinsohn, Clarke, Rohde, Hops, & Seeley, 1996).

During the first session, adolescents learn that depression results from stressful life events and are provided with a rationale for treatment. Treatment continues with relaxation training through progressive muscle relaxation in an effort to enhance self-efficacy and provide relief quickly. Next, adolescents are taught basic self-change skills, such as self-monitoring and methods for establishing realistic goals. In addition, pleasurable activities and response-contingent reinforcement opportunities from the environment are increased. Subsequent sessions are cognitively oriented and seek to enhance positive thinking by identifying, confronting, and modifying negative cognitions. Although social skills training is integrated throughout the

TABLE 4.3. Outline of Stark's Cognitive-Behavioral Treatment Package

Treatment goals: To change depressed children's thoughts and beliefs at level of core schemas

Treatment characteristics:
  Small group (four or five children)
  24–26 sessions of 45–50 minutes each, over a period of 3½ months
  Therapy twice per week for 8 weeks, once per week thereafter
  Monthly family meetings (1–1½ hours)

Major treatment components:
  Affective education
  Activity scheduling
  Social skills training
  Problem-solving training
  Self-instructional training
  Relaxation training combined with positive imagery
  Cognitive restructuring/cognitive modeling

Key references: Stark et al. (1996); Stark, Reynolds, and Kaslow (1987); Stark, Rouse, and Livingston (1991)

CWD-A, specific sessions teach conversational skills, strategies for making friends, and ways to plan social activities. In addition, general communication, conflict resolution, and negotiation skills are taught. At the end of treatment, two sessions are reserved for skills integration and planning for the future.

Outcome Studies

There are few controlled outcome studies of CBT approaches, even though CBT is the most commonly examined type of procedure. This paucity of studies permits coverage of the individual investigations themselves to reflect, rather than to sample or represent, the literature. This research began with a pioneering study by Butler, Miezitis, Friedman, and Cole (1980), who screened 562 fifth- and sixth-grade children on a self-report depression battery that included multiple measures related to depression (e.g., the CDI, the Piers–Harris Self-Esteem Scale, the Nowicki–Strickland Locus of Control Scale for Children). Students who scored 1.5 standard deviation units above the mean on any two measures, or on the combined total battery, were assigned to one of four conditions: role play, cognitive restructuring, attention placebo, or control. Objectives of the cognitive restructuring included teaching children to recognize irrational and self-deprecating thoughts; to adopt more adaptive interpretations and re-

TABLE 4.4.   Outline of Adolescent Coping with Depression Course

Treatment goals: To provide children with the skills necessary to control their depressed mood

Treatment characteristics:
    Small group (three to eight children)
    16 sessions lasting 2 hours each, over a period of 8 weeks
    Therapy twice per week for 8 weeks (including two joint parent–child sessions)
    "Booster" sessions offered at 4-month intervals over 2-year period
    Parent sessions (one 2-hour session per week for 8 weeks)

Major treatment components:
    Mood monitoring
    Social skills training
    Positive/pleasant activity scheduling
    Relaxation training
    Constructive thinking/cognitive restructuring
    Communication skills training
    Negotiation, conflict resolution, and problem-solving training
    Maintenance training

Key references: Clarke, Lewinsohn, and Hops (1990); Lewinsohn, Clarke, Hops, Rohde, and Andrews (1990); Lewinsohn et al. (1996)

sponses; to enhance listening, social, and problem-solving skills; to increase awareness of their own and others' feelings and thoughts; and to more fully recognize the connection between thoughts and feelings. Children in the attention placebo group were taught to solve problems cooperatively through information-sharing strategies. Control subjects remained in regular classrooms and were unknown to teachers. Treatment sessions were conducted once per week for 10 weeks. Within-group tests from pre- to posttreatment showed that the cognitive restructuring, but not the attention placebo, was associated with improvement. Control subjects showed mixed results, apparently due to the exposure of some subjects to another (uncontrolled) treatment. Unfortunately, no comparisons between the different treatment conditions were made and thus no conclusions regarding their relative efficacy can be drawn.

In the first of two reported studies, Stark et al. (1987), using the CDI, screened 372 children at an elementary school for depressive symptoms. A total of 29 children (43% girls; mean age, 11) who received parental permission and scored 13 or more on a second administration of the CDI were randomly assigned to one of three conditions: self-control, behavioral problem solving,

or a waiting list. Self-control therapy focused on self-monitoring, self-evaluating, self-reward, and developing a more adaptive attributional style. Behavioral problem solving focused on self-monitoring skills, pleasant activity scheduling, sensitivity training, problem solving, and social skills. Twelve treatment sessions were conducted over 5 weeks. Subjects in the waiting list control condition were allowed to participate in any regularly available services and were offered self-control treatment when the first treatment groups finished. Child and parent measures were obtained at pretreatment, posttreatment, and an 8-week follow-up. Results indicated significant reductions in depressive symptoms for "treated" subjects. The only statistically significant difference between any of the three groups was found between the self-control group and the waiting list condition on the CDI. In general, both treatment groups showed improvement at posttreatment with some differences favoring treated rather than control subjects. At follow-up, the control condition was no longer available for comparison purposes.

In a second study, Stark, Rouse, and Livingston (1991) twice screened 700 fourth- to seventh-grade children with the CDI. Twenty-four children reported elevated symptoms of depression and were permitted by their parents to participate in the study. The children were randomly assigned to either a CBT or a traditional counseling condition. The sessions were held in a group format lasting 24 to 26 sessions over a $3\frac{1}{2}$ month period. Individual family meetings were also held monthly. Children in the CBT group learned self-control strategies, as noted previously, as well as social skills training, relaxation training, and cognitive restructuring. The traditional counseling group engaged children in an exercise designed to help them understand their emotions and raise their self-esteem. Depressive symptoms and cognitions were significantly reduced in both groups of children at posttreatment assessment. Children in the CBT group reported significantly fewer depressive cognitions and lower levels of depression than children in the traditional counseling group. These group differences were no longer significant at a 7-month follow-up.

Kahn et al. (1990) using self-report and interview measures, screened 1,293 seventh- and eighth-grade students twice to identify youths (ages 10–14, n = 68) who were moderately to severely depressed. These children were randomly assigned to one of four conditions: CBT, relaxation training, self-modeling therapy, or a waiting list. The CBT was modeled after the CWD-A (Clarke et al., 1990). Youths in the relaxation training condition received training in progressive muscle relaxation. In both conditions, youths met in small groups of two to five for a total of 12 sessions over a 6- to 8-week period. Children in the self-modeling therapy condition received behavioral training (12 individual sessions) that developed overt behaviors incompatible with depression (e.g., positive self-attributions, smiling, and eye contact). In addition, a brief self-modeling video was made depicting each youngster in a nondepressed mood. Each active treatment reduced depressive symptoms in comparison to the control condition at post-treatment and 1-month follow-up. Although treatment groups did not differ significantly from one another, subjects in the CBT group demonstrated more positive treatment effects across all measures. Using clinical cutoff points on the self-report measures of depression, the researchers found that between 70% and 88% of all treated subjects moved from the dysfunctional to functional range on at least one measure, in contrast to only 18% in the waiting-list condition. At the 1-month follow-up, between 59% and 88% of the treated subjects and 19% of controls continued to meet nondepressed criteria on at least one measure.

In a methodologically similar study with an older adolescent population, Reynolds and Coats (1986) recruited and screened 800 adolescents for depressive symptoms. Inclusion criteria required elevated depression scores on multiple measures. Thirty cases (ages 11–19) were randomly assigned to one of three conditions: CBT, relaxation training, and a waiting-list control. One therapist trained in both interventions saw the adolescents in small groups for 10 sessions conducted over 5 weeks. The CBT focused on self-control skills mentioned previously (e.g., self-evaluation, self-reinforcement). Youths receiving relaxation training learned progressive muscle relaxation throughout treatment. At post-treatment, subjects in the two treatment groups scored significantly lower than those in the waiting-list control (delayed-treatment) group on several depression measures. The two active interventions were not significantly different from each other. A 5-week follow-up assessment indicated that youths in the active treatments maintained their decrease in depressive symptoms. At posttreatment, 83% of those in CBT, 75% of those in the relaxation group, and none of the control subjects achieved "normal" functioning

as measured by a BDI score less than 10. At follow-up, all subjects in the active treatment groups met this criterion, in comparison to 44% of those in the control group.

In a clinic-referred sample of adolescents meeting criteria for Major Depressive Disorder or dysthymia, Fine et al. (1991) compared the effectiveness of therapeutic support group and social skills training (ages 13–17, $n = 66$). Forty-one percent of the sample was receiving concurrent psychological treatment at the time of the study. Treatment lasted 12 weeks and was conducted in groups by several different male–female therapy teams. In the support condition, therapists established a secure environment in which adolescents could share common concerns, discuss ways of dealing with difficult situations, and provide one another with support. Therapists sought to enhance individuals' self-concept by pointing out and reinforcing personal strengths. Adolescents in the social skills condition learned a series of skills, including recognition of feelings, assertiveness, communication, ways of accepting and giving feedback, and social problem solving and negotiation. Results indicated a significant decrease in depressive symptoms for youths in both conditions, with slightly greater change favoring the therapeutic support condition. At a 9-month follow-up, there were no significant differences between groups.

Lewinsohn, Clarke, Hops, and Andrews (1990) recruited adolescents meeting diagnostic criteria for major or Intermittent Depressive Disorder (DSM-III or RDC). Subjects (36 females, 23 males; mean age, 16 years) were randomly assigned to one of three treatment conditions: adolescent treatment only, adolescent and parent treatment, or a waiting list. Both treatment groups received the CWD-A, as described earlier. Parents in the adolescent and parent group met for seven 2-hour sessions; they received information regarding their children's treatment and were taught problem solving and conflict resolution skills. Waiting-list cases were informed that they would receive treatment in 7–8 weeks, but were also offered referral to another treatment facility. Assessments were conducted at intake, at posttreatment, and at 1, 6, 12, and 24 months after treatment. According to diagnostic criteria at posttreatment, significantly fewer treated subjects as compared to control subjects continued to meet diagnostic criteria for depression (52.4% of the combined treatment group, 57.1% of the adolescent-only group, and 94.7% of the control group). Furthermore, depression scores on various inventories (BDI and the Center for Epidemiologic Studies Depression Scale [CES-D]) were significantly lower for treated than for control subjects. Treated and control adolescents did not differ on the parent-completed CBCL; however, parents in the parent and adolescent group reported significantly fewer externalizing, internalizing, and depressive symptoms for their children at posttreatment than did parents in the adolescent only group. Adolescents in the two treatment groups did not differ significantly on any self-report measures. Since waiting-list subjects were offered therapy immediately after posttreatment testing, only the two initial treatment groups were compared at follow-up. Furthermore, due to attrition, data from the 12- and 24 month follow-up periods were presented but not analyzed. The 6-month follow-up revealed no differences between the two treatment groups.

A second study evaluating the efficacy of the CWD-A included 96 adolescents who met DSM-III-R criteria for Major Depression or Dysthymia (Lewinsohn, Clarke, & Rohde, 1994). The treatment was similar to the first study, with the addition of an extra week of treatment (two sessions) and follow-up booster sessions. At the end of treatment, subjects were randomly assigned to one of three "booster" conditions. In the first condition, subjects were reassessed and provided booster sessions every 4 months; a second group of subjects received follow-up assessment every 4 months without booster sessions; and in a third condition, adolescents received only two annual assessments. In comparison to waiting-list controls, adolescents in the active treatment conditions reported significant decreases in depressive symptoms. As in the earlier study, no differences were found in the effectiveness of the two treatment groups. Improvement was associated with several subject characteristics: Greater improvement was evident for younger cases, males, and those with greater initial enjoyment and frequency of pleasant activities at pretreatment. Sixty-five percent of teenagers in the adolescent-only condition, 69% of those in the combined treatment group, and 48% in the waiting-list condition no longer met depressive criteria. Relapse rates for recovered adolescents ranged from 9.4% at 1 year posttreatment to 20.4% by the 2-year follow-up. Contrary to expectations, the booster sessions did not appear to affect recovery and relapse ratessignificantly.

In a recent study by Wood, Harrington, and Moore (1996), 53 children who had been re-

ferred from an outpatient clinic to a treatment facility specializing in depression were randomly assigned to either a relaxation treatment ($n = 26$) or a brief (five to eight sessions) form of CBT ($n = 27$). Subjects met criteria (DSM-III-R or RDC) for depression. The CBT included components focused on modifying dysfunctional cognitions, solving social problems, and reducing symptoms associated with depression (e.g., sleep disturbances). CBT was significantly more effective than relaxation training in reducing depressive symptoms. Estimates of clinical significance, derived from questionnaire and diagnostic measures, also favored the CBT group. Treatment differences were no longer evident at 3- and 6-month follow-up assessments, due both to continued improvement by the relaxation group and to a 43% relapse rate within the CBT group.

Overall Evaluation

Overall, these studies indicate that CBT, self-control training, relaxation training, and behavioral problem solving result in significant decreases in depressive symptoms, compared to waiting-list and no-treatment control conditions. Differences in the efficacy of "active" treatments have not generally been found, and when they do exist, they usually disappear by follow-up (e.g., Fine et al., 1991; Stark et al., 1991; Wood et al., 1996). The absence of treatment differences could be due to the brevity (and relatively low doses) of treatment. Small sample sizes and reduced power led to nonsignificant differences even in cases where relatively large effect sizes were evident between treatment groups (e.g., Reynolds & Coats, 1986). The possible high levels of comorbid diagnoses, not considered in the data analyses, may also have increased variation that could compete with detecting differences between treatments.

Among the few available studies, severity of clinical dysfunction has varied widely. Youths in the studies reviewed above ranged from mildly depressed to suicidal; treatment efficacy is likely to vary widely among such populations. Studies did not report the comorbid conditions of their samples, although several mentioned the frequent association of anxiety and conduct problems with depression. Several studies also failed to control for concurrent treatment. Furthermore, for ethical reasons, it was not possible to control for follow-up care, and this could have obscured interpretation of the presence or absence of group differences. For example, in considering the short-lived success of their CBT in comparison to a relaxation control group, Wood et al. (in press) found that a higher percentage of patients in the relaxation group sought additional treatment, resulting, perhaps, in a spurious reduction in relative treatment efficacy for the cognitive-behavioral group. In the end, we have a handful of studies with such diverse populations, treatments, and designs that we are unable to conclude more than the usual chorus: Treatment is more effective than no treatment.

Apart from the generality of the conclusions, there is little in the treatment literature consideration of the significance or role of developmental issues. As our review illustrates, youths from middle childhood through adolescence have been included in several controlled studies. Developmental factors that are known to be related to depression and vary with age (e.g., cognitive processes, peer relations) have not been systematically studied in relation in treatment outcome. Few specific hypotheses about what treatments are likely to be effective at different ages have been proposed or explored in a post hoc fashion. At this point, we do not have developmentally based treatments.

Additional Promising Psychosocial Treatments

Although the currently published outcome literature for the treatment of child and adolescent depression is sparse, this is likely to improve considerably in light of research currently underway. In passing, we mention some other work that has been referred to in various publications. The results are not available at the time of this writing.

Interpersonal Psychotherapy

Interpersonal psychotherapy (IPT) seeks to reduce depressive symptoms by helping individuals to understand current problems within the context of ongoing personal relationships. Techniques commonly taught include self-monitoring of depressive feelings, exploratory questioning, problem clarification, identification of the link between affect and events, and communication skills. Throughout therapy, the client and therapist role-play "real-world" situations, and the therapist provides feedback regarding the patient's interpersonal style. IPT has been effective in treating adult depressives (see Frank & Spanier, 1995). Treatment has been revised for use with depressed adolescents (IPT-A; Moreau, Mufson, Weissman, & Klerman, 1991) and is available in manual form for clinical and re-

search use (Mufson, Moreau, Weissman, & Klerman, 1993). IPT-A has shown promise in reducing depressive symptoms in a 12-week uncontrolled pilot study (Mufson et al., 1994). Specifically, among 12 adolescents meeting DSM-III-R criteria for Major Depression at pretreatment, none met criteria at posttreatment; furthermore, treatment significantly improved subjects' social and global functioning. A randomized, controlled clinical trial is currently underway. Given the effects of IPT with adults, extension of this treatment to adolescents is of considerable interest.

Family Therapy

Family therapy approaches consider maladaptive parent–child interactions as central to the development and maintenance of depressive symptoms in children. As in the first study, results indicated no significant treatment effect at posttreatment or follow-up, furthermore, no treatment effect feedback from and punitive interactions with parents give rise to negative cognitive schema that lead to negative information processing. In light of this view, Stark's group recommends a family therapy approach for the treatment of depression that focuses on modifying maladaptive verbal and behavioral patterns within the family.

Unlike the research support for IPT, only minimal evidence exists supporting the efficacy of family or marital therapy for the treatment of depressed adults (Friedman, 1975; Glick et al., 1985). Furthermore, the only treatment study of depressed youths that included parents was that of Lewinsohn and colleagues (1990), which failed to find a significant difference in posttreatment depressive symptoms between the adolescent-only and combined adolescent plus parent interventions. Nonetheless, the view that child maladjustment is maintained through dysfunctional family relations warrants direct tests in controlled trials.

Interpersonal Family Therapy

Combining the principles of IPT for treating adult depressives with general tenets of family therapy, Kaslow and Racusin (Kaslow & Racusin, 1988; Racusin & Kaslow, 1991) have developed interpersonal family therapy. This treatment for depressed youths integrates family systems theory, cognitive-behavioral psychology, developmental psychopathology, and object relations theory. This model assumes that an improvement in family interactional processes will lead to a corresponding improvement in children's affective, behavioral, cognitive, and interpersonal functioning. To date, outcome studies of this treatment have not been reported.

Pharmacotherapy

Although our emphasis is on psychosocial approaches to treatment, the use of medication cannot be neglected in discussions of interventions for depression. An extensive literature on the effectiveness of medication in double-blind, randomized, controlled trials attests to the effects of medication on depression with adult patients. Major types of medications have included monoamine oxidase inhibitors (e.g., phenelzine) and tricyclics (e.g., imipramine and amitriptyline); more recently, new classes of medications have emerged and are in widespread use (e.g., fluoxetine and sertraline). The effectiveness of medication with adult patients has been reviewed extensively (e.g., Davidson, 1985; Elkins & Rapoport, 1983). Not all studies have shown favorable treatment effects, nor do all patients respond positively. For example, tricyclics have been estimated to be more effective than placebos in approximately 60% to 75% of the studies (see Baldessarini, 1977; Elkins & Rapoport, 1983). However, the literature has gone well beyond establishing global effects for groups that receive active medication or placebo. Selective drug effects have been demonstrated, showing that some subtypes of depression (e.g., bipolar vs. unipolar, primary vs. secondary) are differentially responsive to various medications. Also, other variables (e.g., family history, presence of biological markers) have been identified that predict responsiveness to alternative medications.

Many of the medications for adults have been applied to children. Most of the work to date has been with imipramine and amitriptyline. Uncontrolled trials in the 1960s and 1970s gave way to research with more well-defined samples (in light of more explicit diagnostic criteria), as well as improved methods of monitoring and evaluating medication. As an early example of research with these standards, Puig-Antich and his colleagues demonstrated that imipramine and placebo conditions yielded similar effects in the treatment of depressed children (see Puig-Antich & Weston, 1983). However, significant differences emerged in the medication condition when the group was divided according to median plasma level of imipramine and desipramine (a major metabolite of imipramine). Children with higher levels of medication showed 100% response to treatment, whereas those with lower levels showed only 33% response. These results suggested that treatment effects are dependent upon a steady-state plasma level beyond a particular threshold. A subsequent report of this work continued to show that the plasma levels of these two drugs were related to clinical effects (Puig-Antich et al., 1987).

In the past decade, interest in treating depressed children and adolescents with medication has remained quite high. At the same time, research has not revealed the anticipated advances. The reasons are that there is a relatively high placebo reaction in many studies and the effectiveness of treatment is not that clear (see Ambrosini, Bianchi, Rabinovich, & Elia, 1993; Dujovne, Barnard, & Rapoff, 1995). A few examples convey the focus and findings of the research.

Ryan et al. (1986) treated adolescents ($n = 34$) who met RDC requirements for Major Depressive Disorder. Imipramine was provided for a 6-week period. Fewer than 50% of the cases responded well to the medication. Moreover, symptom reduction was not associated with drug plasma levels. The authors suggested that the high levels of sex hormones during adolescence may interfere with the antidepressant effects of imipramine.

More recently, Hughes et al. (1990) examined the differential effectiveness of imipramine with two groups of children meeting criteria for Major Depression (DSM-III). One group presented with pure depression or depression plus an anxiety disorder, while the other group met criteria for depression plus Conduct Disorder or Oppositional Defiant Disorder. Youths (inpatients, ages 6–12) received either imipramine or placebo. Results indicated that among depressed or depressed and anxious subjects, 57% receiving imipramine (after 6 weeks) were considered "responders," compared to only 20% of children in the placebo group. For those children with concomitant Conduct or Oppositional Defiant Disorder, 33% of imipramine subjects responded by week 6, while twice as many (67%) receiving the placebo were considered responders. These results could explain why previous research (e.g., Ryan et al., 1986) failed to find significant differences between imipramine and placebo response rates with depressed children. Clearly, more studies discriminating between such clinical subgroups will prove instrumental in determining those children for whom pharmacotherapy will be most effective.

In another outcome trial, adolescents (ages 15–19) were randomly assigned to receive desipramine (200 mg daily in divided doses) or placebo for 6 weeks following an initial week of placebo (Kutcher et al., 1994). Assessment of clinical depression was made with the K-SADS, and treatment outcome was determined by scores on the HRSD and BDI. Results indicated no significant differences between treated and control subjects. Furthermore, neither desipramine, its metabolite 2-hydroxy-desipramine, nor their ratio were significantly correlated with treatment outcome. These findings lend no support to the short-term (6-week) use of desipramine with depressed youth.

As a final example, Simeon, Dinicola, Ferguson, and Copping (1990) compared the effectiveness of fluoxetine to placebo among adolescents (ages 13–18) meeting DSM-III criteria for Major Depression. All potential subjects received a 1-week placebo trial in order to eliminate placebo responders. Subsequently, 40 subjects were randomly assigned to a 7-week active treatment or placebo condition. Subjects in the active treatment condition received an initial dose of 20 mg daily that was increased to 40 mg during days 4–7, and then increased again to 60 mg during the second week; individual titration levels were adjusted subsequently throughout the end of the study. Evaluations were conducted at screening, at baseline, and during weekly visits. Although no statistical analyses were presented, the authors reported that symptoms on multiple measures of depression and clinical dysfunction decreased for subjects in both groups over time. In addition, the authors reported that fluoxetine was superior to placebo on all clinical measures except those relating to sleep; however, the differences between the groups were not statistically significant. Follow-up conducted at an average of 24 months after treatment (range 8–46 months) revealed that 10 subjects continued to be depressed and that there were no significant differences between subjects in the two groups. Apart from these illustrations, there are many other controlled trials of medication within the past 10 years that encompass diverse medications (e.g., amitriptyline, desipramine, fluoxetine, and nortriptyline). The reader is referred to more in-depth reviews of

this literature (Harrington, 1993; Johnston & Freuhling, 1994; Sommers-Flanagan & Sommers-Flanagan, 1996).

Research in this area will no doubt accelerate. A few issues may limit the pace of these advances. To begin, the guidelines for administration of medications to children are not as well established as they are with adults. There are significant biological differences between adults and children in such characteristics as drug absorption and metabolism. Much less research is available in general on the pharmacokinetics of medications with children. Also, side effects are a great concern, particularly in young children. Drugs may exert permanent effects on growth, intelligence, and nonsymptomatic behaviors. The impact of medications on developmental changes raises issues not evident with adults. Apart from long-term effects, there are of course more temporary side effects. The severity of these effects can vary widely, from physiological changes undetectable to a child and of unclear or apparently no clinical significance (e.g., increased variability in heart rate or blood pressure), to minor discomfort (e.g., dry mouth), to more severe consequences (e.g., seizures and death). In the case of cyclic antidepressants, side effects (such as dry mouth, sedation, blurred vision, and constipation) are typically relatively minor. However, cardiovascular changes, reduced thresholds for seizures, cardiorespiratory arrest, and fatalities have been reported as well (see Kazdin, Rancurello, & Unis, 1987). Withdrawal of medication may produce side effects as well (e.g., headaches, abdominal pain, vomiting).

At present, however, adverse side effects are not the main issue in relation to medication as a treatment for depression in children and adolescents. The primary concern is the need for demonstrations that medications surpass placebos in randomized controlled trials. Very little work is available with persuasive evidence on this point (Poznanski & Mokros, 1994). Also, as noted earlier, even when symptoms remit, there may remain significant signs of impairment in such domains as social functioning. Our concerns about the failure to integrate developmental issues into outcome studies, mentioned in the context of our review of psychosocial treatments, apply here as well. Developmental issues may be relevant in relation to the varied effects that medications may have (e.g., on sleep) at varied ages, or to the question of whether medications may be more effective at one age or stage of de-velopment rather than another in light of pro-posed biological changes. Further outcome stud-ies and follow-up of cases treated with medication and psychotherapies are likely to in-crease in the next few years. We encourage ex-amination of developmentally based hypotheses to identify moderators of these treatments.

PREVENTION OF DEPRESSION

Generally, it is preferable to prevent the onset of dysfunction rather than to provide treatment once a disorder is present. Several charac-teristics of depression raise the prospect of ef-fective preventive interventions. At-risk youths can be identified based on family genetic predis-position, family-related risk factors (e.g., mater-nal depression), peak periods of incidence (e.g., late childhood/early adolescence), and likely de-velopmental points during which risk increases (e.g., school transitions). The fact that depres-sion is often lifelong increases the significance of early intervention. Perhaps something can be accomplished in childhood that will affect the long-term course. Few studies of prevention of depression in children and adolescents have been reported; we highlight available reports here.

Review of Research

Clarke, Hawkins, Murphy, and Sheeber (1993) reported on two school-based primary preven-tion programs. In the first study, 9th- and 10th-grade students from 25 health classes were ran-domly assigned either to an educational intervention (*n* = 361) or to the "usual" curricu-lum (*n* = 261). Students in the active treatment group received three lectures on the symptoms, causes, and treatment of depression. Although no specific CBT was provided, the curriculum encouraged students to increase their daily pleasant activities. Students completed a depres-sion questionnaire based on the CES-D at pre- and posttreatment, as well as at a 12-week fol-low-up. Analyses indicated that youths in both groups decreased significantly in depressive symptoms; no differences were evident between groups at posttreatment or follow-up. More se-verely depressed boys (but not girls) tended to respond better to treatment than placebo to con-ditions, but the effects were short-lived. The main findings were no differences between in-tervention and nonintervention youths.

A second study by Clarke et al. (1993) com-pared the effectiveness of a behavioral interven-tion (*n* = 190) to a control condition (*n* = 190). Children in the behavioral intervention group re-ceived five consecutive health classes designed to increase the daily rate of their pleasant activi-ties, whereas control subjects received the "usual" health class curriculum. Again, the CES-D was administered at pretreatment, post-treatment, and a 12-week follow-up. As in the first study, results indicated no significant treat-ment effect at posttreatment or follow-up; fur-thermore, no treatment was found for cases with "extreme" scores (CES-D > 23). Based on these discouraging results, the authors suggest that a low rate of pleasant activities may simply be a marker, rather than a cause, of depression. An al-ternative explanation offered was that the pro-gram may not have been sufficiently powerful or may not have been delivered in an effective manner. Both hypotheses seem reasonable.

Clarke et al. (1995) have subsequently en-hanced the quality and increased the power of their intervention. In a recent study, 1,652 ado-lescents were screened in multiple stages to identify youths who experienced depressive symptoms, but did not meet criteria for depres-sion; 150 of these youths (with parental consent) agreed to participate and were assigned ran-domly to a "usual-care" control condition or to a 15-session CBT intervention (three sessions per week for 5 weeks). The active treatment was based upon the CWD-A (Clarke et al., 1990). In order to mirror "real-world" care regularly avail-able, both the control and active treatment groups were allowed to pursue whatever outside sources of care they desired. At posttreatment, assessment data were collected for 125 of the in-itial 150 children; data were available for 120 subjects at a 6-month follow-up, and for 110 children at 12 months. Overall, total incidence of either Major Depression or Dysthymia at fol-low-up was 14.5% for the treated group and 25.7% for the control group—a difference that was statistically significant. This study is note-worthy in several ways, including the use of multistage screening, diagnostic evaluation of the cases, and the inclusion of follow-up.

Jaycox, Reivich, Gillham, and Seligman (1994) reported on prevention of depression in school-age children (10–13 years old). Children were identified based on CDI scores and their report of parental conflict; those relatively high on these measures, rather than showing a par-ticular score (e.g., on the CDI), were included. A total of 143 children were assigned to either one of three active treatment groups ($n = 69$) or to one of two control groups ($n = 74$)—a no-participation group ($n = 50$) or a waiting-list group ($n = 24$). The three treatments offered were cognitive treatment only, social problem-solving skills only, or both. Schools were randomly assigned to conditions. At posttest, no major differences were observed between the three active groups, and they were subsequently collapsed into one treatment group; children from the two control conditions were likewise combined. Results indicated statistical and clinical significance in the relief and prevention of depressive symptoms for those children in the treatment groups, both at the end of treatment and during subsequent 6-month and 2-year follow-ups (Gillham, Reivich, Jaycox, & Seligman, 1995). In fact, differences in depressive symptoms between the two groups grew more discrepant over time, suggesting that treatment immunized children from future depressive episodes (Gillham et al., 1995).

Overall Evaluation

The literature on prevention of depression is much too young to permit firm conclusions to be drawn. The high point is that researchers have focused on preventive efforts. Current work, however preliminary, suggests that CBT-based interventions reduce current levels of depressive symptoms and the risk of future depressive episodes, in comparison to no-treatment or "as-usual" treatment conditions. The lack of specificity among alternative interventions (e.g., Jaycox et al., 1994) and the absence of long-term outcomes suggest some of the research tasks that lie ahead. Examining prevention in the context of prospective, longitudinal studies, where comparisons are available to see how interventions affect the course of depressive symptoms over time among untreated youths, will be invaluable.

CURRENT ISSUES AND LIMITATIONS OF INTERVENTION RESEARCH

At this point in the field, there remains a paucity of randomized controlled trials designed to treat and prevent depression. Exceptions in a few programs of research convey the promise that such trials hold. Among the available studies, a few salient issues emerge that are concerns for the ways in which intervention research is conducted. We focus primarily on treatment issues, in light of our emphasis on the literature reviewed.

Evaluation of Outcome

Our prior discussion has conveyed the importance of broad assessment strategies in evaluating treatment outcome. However, a number of issues that extend beyond the scope of measurement domains and methods are critical to assessing the impact of treatment. Two areas neglected in current research warrant comment.

Magnitude of Therapeutic Change

Treatments have achieved change, but is the change enough to make a difference in the lives of the youths who are treated? "Clinical significance" refers to the extent to which the change in symptoms makes a "real" or important difference to the patients or to others with whom they interact (see Kazdin, 1998). Clinical impairment, discussed previously, is related to clinical significance insofar as impairment reflects functioning in everyday life. Yet clinical significance is usually discussed in relation to the magnitude of change in symptoms on the measures used to evaluate treatment outcome. Clinical significance is important, because it is quite possible for treatment effects to be statistically significant without reflecting changes that have an impact on daily functioning or adjustment.

There are several ways to evaluate clinical significance, including the assessment of whether: (1) symptom levels following treatment are within the normative range for same-age and same-sex peers who function well; (2) significant others in everyday life (e.g., parents, teachers, peers) report a difference in a child's or adolescent's symptoms in daily functioning; and (3) the degree of change (e.g., in standard deviation units) from pre- to posttreatment is large by some commonly accepted criterion (e.g., Jacobson, 1988; Kazdin, 1998). For example, in one of the outcome studies reviewed previously, a measure of clinical significance consisted of the extent to which treated depressed adolescents fell within the nonclinical/nondepressed range on the CDI, two items from a diagnostic interview (K-SADS), and a self-esteem measure (Fine et al., 1991). The CDI results, for which normative data are available, illustrate the findings overall. At a 9-month follow-up assessment, approximately 60% of youths fell within the nonclinical range (about the proportion that would be expected without treatment).

Another way to operationalize clinical significance has been to determine whether individuals continue to meet diagnostic criteria for the disorder at the end of treatment. In such work, youths are selected for inclusion because they meet diagnostic criteria (e.g., RDC or DSM) for some form of depression. Then they are treated and reevaluated at posttreatment on the same diagnostic measures (e.g., Clarke et al., 1992). A clinically significant change is one that reduces the proportion of youths who meet diagnostic criteria after treatment. It is, of course, quite possible that youths will not meet diagnostic criteria for any form of depression (subsyndromal depression) but will still suffer significant impairment in multiple domains (e.g., Gotlib et al., 1995), as discussed previously.

In general, the majority of studies for the treatment of children and adolescents have not examined whether youths have made clinically significant changes (Kazdin et al., 1990). The need to evaluate change among nontreated individuals is particularly important in the context of clinical depression. With the high rates of recovery, we can expect that many untreated children will show significant fluctuations in functioning as part of the episodic nature of the disorder. Whether treatment has contributed to improvement is obviously critical to evaluate.

Beyond the magnitude of change in the usual way, it is important to consider what a clinically important change for different subgroups of depressed youths might look like. For many depressed youths, symptoms may escalate, comorbid diagnoses (e.g., Substance Abuse) may emerge, and family dysfunction may increase. Also, such youths may be at risk for dropping out of school and engaging in antisocial behavior. If treatment were to achieve stability in symptoms and family life and to prevent or delimit future dysfunction, that would be a significant achievement. Thus, clinically significant effects (i.e., whether treatment makes a difference) can have many meanings that are important in the treatment of depression, as well as many other disorders.

Maintenance of Change

In the child and adolescent therapy literature in general, the majority of studies do not include follow-up assessment; among those that do, the median follow-up duration is 5 months (Kazdin et al., 1990). In the general case, evaluation of whether changes are maintained over time is critically important. A number of studies have reported follow-up, usually from several weeks to up to a year, and have shown that the benefits of treatment are continued (e.g., Kahn et al., 1990; Lewinsohn, Rohde, & Seeley, 1994). Much longer follow-up assessments are needed, and the scope of measures to evaluate change ought to be expanded, as discussed previously.

Special follow-up issues can be identified in light of research on characteristics of depression in children and adolescents. As highlighted previously, we know that most youths will recover from their initial depressive episode within several months but will go on to experience further difficulties, including a recurrent depressive episode. For current outcome evaluation, we wish to know whether treatment decreases the duration and severity of the present episode and influences the level and time of recovery, as well as the latency to onset of the next episode. Single-occasion follow-up assessment after treatment can assess many of these characteristics by pointed questions about course and functioning since the termination of treatment. Yet multiple-occasion follow-up assessments are needed to permit analyses (e.g., life tables) that can better describe follow-up course, relapse, and recovery.

In evaluations of the relative merit of different treatments, follow-up data play a critical role. When two (or more) treatments are compared, the treatment that is more (or most) effective immediately after treatment is not always the one that proves to be the most effective treatment in the long run (Kazdin, 1988). Consequently, the conclusions about treatment may vary depending on the timing of outcome assessment. Apart from conclusions about treatment, follow-up may provide important information that permits differentiation among youths. Over time, youths who maintain the benefits of treatment may differ in important ways from those who do not. Understanding who responds and who responds more or less well to a particular treatment can be very helpful for both research and practice. Variation in response to treatment among subgroups can generate hypotheses about what factors contribute to change. Furthermore, this knowledge can be used to match individuals in certain subgroups with particular forms of treatment that may be more effective.

Understanding More about the Interventions

Clearly, the first priority is to identify whether a given intervention achieves change in or prevents child and adolescent dysfunction. Several studies reviewed previously have shown that change can be achieved, if only in the short term. There are limits in the research in relation to understanding how the interventions work and for which individuals they are likely to be effective.

Mechanisms and Processes of Change

Treatments for child and adolescent depression, as currently practiced, are invariably guided by a conceptual model. The models include a theoretical explanation of depression, a rationale for treatment, the processes considered to be essential for change, and the procedures used within the sessions. Obviously, the models are critically important. In current treatment research, however, the models are rarely tested. The proposed processes are not directly assessed or shown to be related to outcome. For example, as we have noted previously, the majority of intervention studies have adopted variants of a CBT model for treating depression. Direct tests of the models would consist of assessing whether processes (cognitions, coping abilities) change and whether these changes are related to improvement in outcome. We do not know of tests where these steps have been completed for treatments of child and adolescent depression.

Outcome differences between two different treatments, not very often achieved in this literature, are taken as tacit support of the models from which the treatments were derived. Yet outcome differences between two treatments could result from variation in the same general characteristic or therapeutic process (e.g., mobilizing hope, generating expectations for change), rather than from treatment-specific processes. Tests of models and processes that underlie change provide the bases for improving treatment. is a pervasive disorder that affects multiple domains in current and future functioning (e.g., family and peer relations, academic functioning) and components of the treatment ought to be modified to improve outcome.

Identifying Who Responds to Treatment

We have known for many years that the critical question of psychotherapy is not what technique is effective, but rather what technique works for whom, under what conditions, as administered by what type of therapists, and so on (Kiesler, 1971). The adult psychotherapy literature has focused on a range of questions to identify factors (e.g., patient, therapist, treatment process) that contribute to outcome. Child and adolescent therapy research has largely neglected the role of child, parent, family, and therapist factors that

may moderate outcome (Kazdin et al., 1990). In the depression intervention research, moderators of treatment outcome have received scant attention.

A few promising leads can be identified. For example, in the program of research on the use of the CWD-A with adolescents, better treatment outcomes were associated with younger cases, males, youths with lower initial levels of depression and anxiety, higher engagement in pleasant activities, and more rational thoughts at pretreatment (see Clarke et al., 1992; Lewinsohn et al., 1996). In addition, Hughes et al. (1990) identified different treatment responses to placebo and imipramine among depressed children with different comorbid clinical profiles (anxiety disorders vs. Conduct Disorder). Exploring multiple factors that relate to outcome, analogous to multiple-risk-factor models, provides an important beginning as a way of matching cases to treatment. Identifying whether some children and adolescents respond to one type of treatment more than another is an important research goal. At this point, the literature cannot speak to this issue. The characteristics that have been studied in relation to treatment outcome (e.g., severity of symptoms, comorbidity, child and family characteristics) have not been examined across different treatments. Consequently, we do not know whether these factors affect responsiveness to any treatment or to particular forms of treatment.

Use of Combined Treatments

There is a keen interest, both in clinical work and in research, in combining treatments (see Kazdin, 1996). The impetus for this stems from the scope of impairment evident in children (e.g., comorbidity, academic dysfunction) and families (e.g., stress, conflict). In the child and adolescent depression interventions reviewed previously, the use of treatment combinations is the rule rather than the exception. For example, in one program the intervention included social skills training, problem-solving skills training, anger control training, relaxation training, scheduling of reinforcing activities, and family therapy (Stark, Rouse, & Kurowski, 1994). Such a combination may be reasonable, based on the wide range of domains likely to be affected by depression. Yet we know very little about the parameters of any of the constituent treatments that influence outcome or the cases to whom the constituent or combined treatment packages are most suitably applied. Combining techniques of which we know relatively little is not a firm base on which to build more effective treatments (Kazdin, 1996).

Many factors in combining treatment affect their likely impact, such as decision rules regarding what treatments to combine, how to combine them (e.g., when, in what order), and how to evaluate their impact. Also, in clinical treatment trials, duration of therapy is fixed or at least finite, so that there is some limit to which modules of varied treatments can be squeezed into the treatment program. Thus, devoting time to delivery of one component treatment invariably involves limiting the time accorded to another component. Weighting the different constituent ingredients in terms of emphasis and actual time without an empirically derived algorithm is easily challenged. An important assumption for combined treatments is that individual treatments are weak and, if combined, should produce additive or synergistic effects. This is a reasonable, even if poorly tested, assumption. An alternative assumption is that the way in which treatment is usually administered, whether as an individual or a combined treatment, inherently limits the likelihood of positive outcome effects—a point discussed further below.

As a general point, combining treatments itself is not likely to be an answer to developing effective treatments, without more thought and evidence about the nature of these combinations. Often treatment combinations are seen as a first line of attack in research. The rationale is that if the broad treatment package has an effect, then further research can dismantle the package (Kazdin, 1988). Yet, even if the package is not effective (or not effective in clinically significant and enduring ways), this may not be a reason to ignore evaluation of the individual components. There is no substitute for understanding individual components of treatment, how they operate, and how they can be maximally deployed to achieve change.

Treatment combinations are also used because of the view that they may not help, but at least are not likely to hurt (i.e., reduce treatment effects). Yet, in other contexts, we know that treatment combinations may not add to individual components and indeed may detract from them. For example, in the treatment of antisocial behavior among adolescents, treatment that combined a parent program and a teen-focused group *increased* behavioral problems and sub-

stance use in comparison to the parent group alone (Dishion & Andrews, 1995). Obviously, one cannot assume that combined treatments will automatically be neutral or better than their constituent treatments.

Important goals of intervention research are to understand the basis for change, to explore alternative models of delivery to improve outcome, and to understand for whom the interventions are effective. These tasks are not incompatible with the use of combined treatments. Yet tests of broad packages without attention to the underpinnings and moderators of change may thwart the long-term goal of developing optimally effective interventions.

Models of Delivering Treatment

In the child and adolescent psychotherapy literature in general, treatment is usually provided for 8–10 weeks (one session per week), after which treatment is terminated (Kazdin et al., 1990). As a rule, the depression treatment research follows the brief and time-limited model of delivering treatment. Obviously, if brief and time-limited treatment is effective, there is no need to raise questions about possible alternatives. Yet, from what is known about the nature and course of depression, more extended and enduring treatments are essential.

To clarify the task of treatment in relation to depression, several different stages or points of change in depression can be delineated. Frank et al. (1991) have presented consensus definitions to convey these different change points in a way that is particularly relevant to the present discussion. Table 4.5 includes these authors' key points and definitions. The current episode of the disorder is the immediate focus of treatment; the goal is to reduce the symptoms and to achieve remission. However, the likelihood of relapse and recurrence of depression prompts one to consider interventions that go beyond reduction of symptoms of the current episode.

In the adult depression literature, considerable attention has been devoted to maintenance therapy—that is, treatment intended to reduce relapse and recurrence of depression (see Frank, Johnson, & Kupfer, 1992). "Maintenance therapy" refers to intervention that is provided after the initial (acute) treatment phase. For example, for adults with recurrent depression, continuation of medication (imipramine) for a period of 3 years after the initial 2-year treatment course

TABLE 4.5. Terms to Characterize Change Points in Depression

Episode: A period of time during which the individual is consistently within the symptomatic range for the disorder and meets diagnostic criteria.

Remission: A period of time in which an improvement is achieved of sufficient magnitude that the individual is no longer fully symptomatic and no longer meets diagnostic criteria for the syndrome. If the individual continues to evince symptoms, this is referred to as a "partial remission"; if the individual is free from symptoms, this is referred to as a "full remission."

Response: Point at which partial remission begins in response to the intervention.

Recovery: A period in which a remission lasts for a specific (or indefinite) period. "Recovery" refers to remission of an episode and not of the disorder.

Relapse: A return of symptoms so that the individual meets diagnostic criteria for an episode of the disorder. "Relapse" is used to refer to a return of the full syndrome while the episode is still ongoing. That is, there may be a period of remission (prior to recovery) during which the full syndrome reemerges.

Recurrence: Appearance of an entirely new episode after there has been a full recovery from the syndrome. The distinction from relapse depends in large part on when in the course the full syndrome emerges.

Note. This material represents consensus definitions. Six terms were considered to be sufficient to characterize relevant change points in the course of unipolar depression, adapted from Frank et al. (1991).

has had a significant prophylactic effect on the recurrence of depression (Frank et al., 1990, 1993; Kupfer et al., 1992). Continuation of full-dose medication (imipramine) was more protective than continuation of half-dose medication and placebo. IPT and cognitive therapy have also been effective in reducing relapse when continued as maintenance strategies after the initial treatment phase (see Frank et al., 1992). As a general conclusion from multiple studies, adults with recurrent depression are very likely to profit from maintenance therapy and to experience much higher rates of relapse without such therapy. A recently reported study with depressed adolescents (9–17 years old) suggested that risk of relapse was reduced with maintenance therapy (CBT) that followed an acute treatment phase (Kroll, Harrington, Jayson, Fraser, & Gowers, 1996). A comparison sample

was selected from a prior study to assess the benefits of maintenance therapy, and hence this was not a randomized trial. Even so, the results were consistent with the larger adult literature on maintenance therapy for depression.

The adult treatment literature on child and adolescent depression continues in the tradition of brief, time-limited therapy. This model of delivering treatment is likely to have limited clinical impact, given the frequency of relapse and recurrence of depression. Two alternative ways of delivering treatment are proposed to increase the likelihood of long-term clinical impact.

The first variation is referred to as a "continued-care model." The model of treatment delivery that may be needed can be likened to the model used in the treatment of diabetes mellitus. With diabetes, ongoing treatment (insulin) is needed to insure that the benefits of treatment are sustained. The benefits of treatment end with discontinuation of treatment. Analogously, in the context of depression, ongoing treatment may be needed. Perhaps after the child or adolescent is referred, treatment should be provided to address the current crises and to have an impact on the youth's functioning at home, at school, and in the community. After improvement is achieved, treatment can be modified rather than terminated. At that point, the child can enter into maintenance therapy—that is, continued treatment, perhaps in varying schedules ("doses") or on a more intermittent basis. This is the model of maintenance therapies already investigated in the context of adult depression (e.g. Frank et al., 1992) and recently pilot-tested with adolescents (Kroll et al., 1996).

Although the rate of recurrence is high, not everyone will have another episode of depression. Consequently, continuation of treatment for everyone may be unnecessary. A second variation of delivering treatment focuses on monitoring cases and then providing treatment as needed. This variation is referred to here as a "dental-care model" to convey a different way of extending treatment. After initial treatment and demonstrated improvement in functioning in everyday life, treatment may be suspended. Beginning at this point, the child's functioning can be monitored regularly (e.g., every 3 months) and systematically (with standardized measures). Treatment can then be provided *pro re nata,* based on the assessment data or emergent issues raised by the family, teachers, or others. The approach resembles the familiar model of dental care in the United States, in which regular checkups are recommended and treatment is provided if and as needed.

With childhood and adolescent depression, we know that recovery rates are high, but that individuals are likely to experience subsequent episodes. Monitoring child functioning and providing maintenance therapy are quite reasonable treatment strategies. Unless alternative models of delivery are considered, current treatments may be quite limited in their long-term effectiveness. Although more effective treatments are sorely needed, the way of delivering currently available treatments ought to be reconsidered. Also, further work is needed to identify and test those at risk for recurrent depression. It may be that high-risk youths can be identified and placed into maintenance therapy (continued-care model), whereas lower-risk youths can be monitored and treated only as needed (the dental-care model).

General Comments

Intervention trials are difficult to mount. The longitudinal nature of the studies, the need for constant monitoring of treatment integrity, the use of control or special treatment conditions for comparison purposes, and the accumulation of sufficient numbers of cases to have sensitive (powerful) tests at posttreatment and follow-up are only some of the challenges. Because such trials are difficult to mount, it is important to maximize the yield of any given trial. To that end, it is important to expand the evaluation of treatment to include multiple domains of functioning, outcome criteria that evaluate the actual impact (clinical significance) of the changes, and both short- and long-term outcome. Direct tests of intervention models and mechanisms of change are no less significant as priorities for research. Treatment advances in the long term depend on understanding how treatment works, in addition to showing that it works. Hypotheses regarding the mechanisms of change can be advanced by studying both intervening processes and individual differences in relation to amenability to change.

CONCLUSIONS

A great deal has been learned about depression in children and adolescents. Within the past 10–15 years, there has been remarkable work that has elaborated the nature of the dysfunction and its concomitant features and clinical course. We have learned that major depression among children and adolescents and is likely to be associated with, as well as to predict, other and is likely to be associated with, as well as to predict, other and is likely to be associated with, as well as to predict, other disorders. The lifelong course of depression and its transmission in families make treatment of special significance.

The prevalence data suggest that large numbers of youths (e.g., 2%–8%) in the general population may meet criteria for depression. We know that many of the youths in need of treatment do not receive care. For example, in the case of depressed adolescents, 70%–80% do not receive treatment (Keller et al., 1991). Furthermore, it is likely that depression is underidentified. In school settings, for example, it is likely that teachers may not view withdrawal and moodiness as possible signs of serious dysfunction. Also, because depression is so often comorbid with externalizing disorders (e.g., Conduct Disorder, Substance Abuse), it is likely to be overshadowed in the clinical picture. Even when systematically assessed and identified, the depression may not receive much explicit attention.

As a related issue, interventions are needed for youths beyond those who may be identified as depressed according to diagnostic criteria. As we have noted earlier, youths with Dysthymia and subsyndromal depression are likely to be impaired and at risk for later Major Depressive Disorder. Attention to such youths in treatment and prevention trials is sorely needed. In addition, youths who are medically ill, particularly those with chronic diseases, are at risk for greater symptoms of depression (e.g., Seigel, Golden, Gough, Lashley, & Sacker, 1990). Thus, focusing on prevalence rates in the general population may underestimate the scope of the problem and the need for treatment trials with varied populations.

It is possible to identify high-risk youths, even though the risk factors for depression in children and adolescents have not been fully elaborated. Depressed parents and families with a history of depression are two risk factors well documented in the literature. More prevention trials with at-risk groups are obvious intervention priorities. There also may be high-risk periods in development that deserve special attention; for example, time of transitions from one school to the next and the onset of adolescence (particularly for girls) are periods associated with stress and increased dysfunction. Both pre-

vention and treatment for youths at these different periods could be very important and informative.

It is prudent to consider depression (broadly
defined) as a recurrent disorder that affects multiple domains of functioning. Current trials focus largely on brief, time-limited treatments.
From the more well-developed outcome literature with adults, several techniques (medication
and psychosocial interventions) have been continued in varying ways for extended periods
(e.g., 3 years) following a treatment phase. The
evidence has been fairly consistent in showing
that there is a prophylactic effect of continued
treatment, as reflected in recurrence of the next
episode. The findings are clear; acting on these
findings and modifying treatment trials are major challenges. Applications of extended treatment in an environment of brief treatments and
managed care raise obvious obstacles. However,
the task is to identify treatments that produce
significant and enduring changes. Longer treatments and treatments followed by maintenance
programs may not be more expensive from a
cost–benefit analysis. Indeed, it is the value of
brief programs that can be called into question.

Multiple lines of work are needed, apart from
identifying treatment and maintenance strategies. Research that identifies who is at risk for
recurrent disorder, or perhaps who is not at risk,
will help serve triage functions for providing
maintenance therapies. We suggested that long-
term therapy is only one alternative to combat
recurrent depression. Systematic monitoring of
youths after treatment should be useful as a basis for identifying when to intervene and for
whom.

Expansion of the settings in which treatment
is provided warrants attention and investigation.
The effective implementation of treatment in
school settings raises promising opportunities
for disseminating interventions more broadly
than traditional clinical services can do. There
are many issues facing adolescents, including
the emergence of at-risk behaviors (e.g., substance use and misuse, sexual activity, antisocial
behavior, academic dysfunction). Providing
comprehensive school-based services has been
suggested as a way to address many domains of
functioning in a way that is acceptable to adolescents themselves (see Lewinsohn, Clarke, &
Rohde, 1994).

At the outset of the chapter, we have under-
scored the scope of domains that depression entails. The pervasive and enduring nature of the
disorder has sweeping implications for the manner in which depression is treated and prevented.
Conceptually, it is important to understand the
ways in which depression unfolds and the sequence leading to impairment in multiple domains. This information has potential for identifying interventions to stop progressions in the
types of dysfunction that such youths evince.
The breadth of impairment ought to influence
evaluation of treatment and preventive efforts as
well. Outcome evaluation must extend well beyond symptom reduction on standardized measures. The outcomes that are evaluated must be
broad and long-term. Our comments have been
directed to examing different models of delivering treatment, investigating the impact of interventions beyond mere symptom reduction, and
asking more analytic questions about the interventions that have begun to emerge.

ACKNOWLEDGMENT

Completion of this chapter was supported by a
Research Scientist Award (No. MH00353) and a
grant (No. MH35408) from the National Institute of Mental Health. Support for this work is
gratefully acknowledged.

NOTE

1. The focus in general terms is on unipolar
depression, rather than bipolar disorders (in
DSM-IV, Bipolar I Disorder, Bipolar II Disorder,
and Cyclothymic Disorder), in which depression
is evident in the context of Manic or Hypomanic
Episodes. Research on bipolar disorders is
sparse with children and adolescents (see
Carlson, 1994).

REFERENCES

Abramson, L. Y., Metalsky, G. I., & Alloy, L. B.
(1989). Hopelessness depression: A theory-based
subtype of depression. *Psychological Review, 96,*
358–372.

Achenbach, T. M. (1991a). *Manual for the Child Behavior Checklist/4–18 and 1991 Profile.* Burlington: University of Vermont, Department of
Psychiatry.

Achenbach, T. M. (1991b). *Manual for the Teacher's
Report Form and 1991 Profile.* Burlington: Univer-
sity of Vermont, Department of Psychiatry.

Achenbach, T. M. (1991c). *Manual for the Youth Self-
Report and 1991 Profile.* Burlington: University of
Vermont, Department of Psychiatry.

Akiskal, H. S. (1979). A biobehavioral approach to depression. In R. A. Depue (Ed.), *The psychobiology of the depressive disorders* (pp. 409–437). New York: Academic Press.

Alloy, L. (Ed.). (1988). *Cognitive processes in depression*. New York: Guilford Press.

Ambrosini, P. J., Bianchi, M. D., Rabinovich, H., & Elia, J. (1993). Antidepressant treatments in children and adolescents: I. Affective disorders. *Journal of the American Academy of Child and Adolescent Psychiatry, 32*, 1–6.

American Psychiatric Association. (1994). *Diagnostic and statistical manual of mental disorders* (4th ed.). Washington, DC: Author.

Anderson, J. C., Williams, S., McGee, R., & Silva, P. A. (1987). The prevalence of DSM-III disorders in pre-adolescent children: Prevalence in a large sample from the general population. *Archives of General Psychiatry, 44*, 69–76.

Angold, A., & Costello, E. J. (1993). Depressive comorbidity in children and adolescents: Empirical, theoretical, and methodological issues. *American Journal of Psychiatry, 150*, 1779–1791.

Asarnow, J. R., Carlson, G. A., & Guthrie, D. (1987). Coping strategies, self-perceptions, hopelessness, and perceived family environments in depressed and suicidal children. *Journal of Consulting and Clinical Psychology, 55*, 361–366.

Asarnow, J. R., Goldstein, J. J., Carlson, G. A., Perdue, S., Bates, S., & Keller, J. (1988). Childhood-onset depressive disorders: A follow-up study of rates of rehospitalization and out-of-home placement among child psychiatric inpatients. *Journal of Affective Disorders, 15*, 245–253.

Asarnow, J. R., & Guthrie, D. (1989). Suicidal behavior, depression, and hopelessness in child psychiatric inpatients: A replication and extension. *Journal of Clinical Child Psychology, 18*, 129–136.

Asarnow, J. R., Tompson, M., Hamilton, E. B., Goldstein, M. J., & Guthrie, D. (1994). Family-expressed emotion, child-onset depression, and child-onset schizophrenia spectrum disorders: Is expressed emotion a nonspecific correlate of child psychopathology or a specific risk factor for depression? *Journal of Abnormal Child Psychology, 22*, 129–146.

Asher, S. R., Hymel, S., & Renshaw, P. D. (1984). Loneliness in children. *Child Development, 55*, 1456–1464.

Asher, S. R., & Wheeler, V. A. (1985). Children's loneliness: A comparison of rejected and neglected peer status. *Journal of Consulting and Clinical Psychology, 53*, 500–505.

Baldessarini, R. J. (1977). *Chemotherapy in psychiatry*. Cambridge, MA: Harvard University Press.

Barkley, R. A. (1988). Child behavior rating scales. In M. Rutter, A. H. Tuma, & I. S. Lann (Eds.), *Assessment and diagnosis in child psychopathology* (pp. 113–155). New York: Guilford Press.

Beardslee, W. R., Schultz, L. H. & Selman, R. L. (1987). Level of social-cognitive development, adaptive functioning, and DSM-III diagnoses in adolescent offspring of parents with affective disorders: Implications of the development of the capacity for mutuality. *Developmental Psychology, 23*, 807–815.

Beardslee, W. R., & Wheelock, I. (1994). Children of parents with affective disorders: Empirical findings and clinical implications. In W. M. Reynolds & H. F. Johnston (Eds.), *Handbook of depression in children and adolescents* (pp. 463–479). New York: Plenum Press.

Beck, A. T. (1967). *Depression: Clinical, experimental, and theoretical aspects*. New York: Harper & Row.

Beck, A. T., Kovacs, M., & Weissman, A. (1975). Hopelessness and suicidal behavior: An overview. *Journal of the American Medical Association, 234*, 1146–1149.

Beck, A. T., Ward, C. H., Mendelson, M., Mock, J., & Erbaugh, J. (1961). An inventory for measuring depression. *Archives of General Psychiatry, 4*, 53–63.

Beckham, E. E., & Leber, W. R. (Eds.). (1995). *Handbook of depression: Treatment, assessment, and research* (2nd ed.). Homewood, IL: Dorsey Press.

Bemporad, J. R. (1994). Dynamic and interpersonal theories of depression. In W. M. Reynolds & H. F. Johnston (Eds.), *Handbook of depression in children and adolescents* (pp. 81–95). New York: Plenum Press.

Bird, H. R., Canino, G., Rubio-Stipec, M., Gould, M. S., Ribera, J., Sesman, M., Woodbury, M., Huertas-Goldman, S., Pagan, A., Sanchez-Lacay, A., & Moscoso, M. (1988). Estimates of the prevalence of childhood maladjustment in a community survey in Puerto Rico. *Archives of General Psychiatry, 45*, 1120–1126.

Bowlby, J. (1980). *Attachment and loss: Vol. 3. Sadness and depression*. New York: Basic Books.

Brady, E. U., & Kendall, P. C. (1992). Comorbidity of anxiety and depression in children and adolescents. *Psychological Bulletin, 111*, 244–255.

Burge, D., & Hammen, C. (1991). Maternal communication: Predictors of outcome at follow-up in a sample of children at high and low risk for depression. *Journal of Abnormal Psychology, 100*, 174–180.

Burke, K. C., Burke, J. D., Regier, D. A., & Rae, D. S. (1990). Age at onset of selected mental disorders in five community populations. *Archives of General Psychiatry, 47*, 511–518.

Butler, L., Miezitis, S., Friedman, R., & Cole, E. (1980). The effect of two school-based intervention programs on depressive symptoms in preadolescents. *American Educational Research Journal, 17*, 111–119.

Carey, M. P., Kelley, M. L., Buss, R. R., & Scott, W. O. N. (1986). Relationship of activity to depression in adolescents: Development of the Adolescent Activities Checklist. *Journal of Consulting and Clinical Psychology, 54*, 320–322.

Carlson, G. A. (1994). Adolescent bipolar disorder: Phenomenology and treatment implications. In W. M. Reynolds & H. F. Johnston (Eds.), *Handbook of depression in children and adolescents* (pp. 41–60). New York: Plenum Press.

Cautela, J. R., Cautela, J., & Esonis, S. (1983). *Forms for behavior analysis with children.* Champaign, IL: Research Press.

Cicchetti, D., Ganiban, J., & Barnett, D. (1991). Contributions from the study of high-risk populations to understanding the development of emotion regulation. In J. Garber & K. A. Dodge (Eds.), *The development of emotion regulation and dysregulation* (pp. 15–48). Cambridge, England: Cambridge University Press.

Clarizio, H. F. (1994). *Assessment and treatment of depression in children and adolescents* (2nd ed.). Brandon, VT: Clinical Psychology.

Clarke, G. N., Hawkins, W., Murphy, M., & Sheeber, L. (1993). School-based primary prevention of depressive symptomatology in adolescents: Findings from two studies. *Journal of Adolescent Research, 8,* 183–204.

Clarke, G. N., Hawkins, W., Murphy, M., Sheeber, L. B., Lewinsohn, P. M., & Seeley, J. R. (1995). Targeted prevention of unipolar depressive disorder in an at-risk sample of high-school adolescents: A randomized trial of a group cognitive intervention. *Journal of the American Academy of Child and Adolescent Psychiatry, 34,* 312–321.

Clarke, G. N., Hops., H., Lewinsohn, P. M., Andrews, J. A., Seeley, J. R., & Williams, J. A. (1992). Cognitive-behavioral group treatment of adolescent depression: Prediction of outcome. *Behavior Therapy, 23,* 341–354.

Clarke, G. N., Lewinsohn, P. M., & Hops, H. (1990). *Adolescent Coping with Depression Course: Leader's manual for adolescent groups.* Eugene, OR: Castalia.

Coddington, R. D. (1972). The significance of life events as etiological factors in the diseases of children: A study of normal population. *Journal of Psychosomatic Research, 16,* 205–213.

Cole, D. A. (1990). The relation of social and academic competence to depressive symptoms in childhood. *Journal of Abnormal Psychology, 99,* 422–429.

Compas, B. E. (1987). Stress and life events during childhood and adolescence. *Clinical Psychology Review, 7,* 275–302.

Compas, B. E., Grant, K. E. & Ey, S. (1994). Psychological stress and child and adolescent depression: Can we be more specific? In W. M. Reynolds & H. F. Johnston (Eds.), *Handbook of depression in children and adolescents* (pp. 509–523). New York: Plenum Press.

Connell, J. P. (1985). A new multidimensional measure of children's perceptions of control. *Child Development, 56,* 1018–1041.

Costello, E. J., Costello, A. J., Edelbrock, C., Burns, B. J., Dulcan, M. K., Brent, D., & Janiszewski, S. (1988). Psychiatric disorders in pediatric primary care. *Archives of General Psychiatry, 45,* 1107–1116.

Cross-National Collaborative Group. (1992). The changing rate of major depression: Cross-national comparisons. *Journal of the American Medical Association, 268,* 3098–3105.

Cytryn, L., & McKnew, D. H. (1972). Proposed classification of childhood depression. *American Journal of Psychiatry, 129,* 149–155.

Davidson, J. (1985). Nonresponse to tricyclic and MAOI drugs: What comes next? In A. Dean (Ed.), *Depression in multidisciplinary perspective* (pp. 173–193). New York: Brunner/Mazel.

Davidson, R. J., & Fox, N. A. (1989). Frontal brain asymmetry predicts infants' response to maternal separation. *Journal of Abnormal Psychology, 98,* 127–131.

Dawson, G., Frey, K., Panagiotides, H., Osterling, J., & Hessl, D. (1997). Infants of depressed mothers exhibit frontal brain activity: A replication and extension of previous findings. *Journal of Child Psychology and Psychiatry, 38,* 79–186.

Dawson, G., Hessl, D., & Frey, K. (1994). Social influences on early developing biological and behavioral systems related to risk for affective disorder. *Development and Psychopathology, 6,* 759–779.

Dishion, T. J., & Andrews, D. W. (1995). Preventing escalation in problem behaviors with high-risk young adolescents: Immediate and 1-year outcomes. *Journal of Consulting and Clinical Psychology, 63,* 538–548.

Dujovne, V. F., Barnard, M. U., & Rapoff, M. A. (1995). Pharmacological and cognitive-behavioral approaches in the treatment of childhood depression. *Clinical Psychology Review, 15,* 589–611.

Edelbrock, C., & Costello, A. J. (1988). Structured psychiatric interviews for children. In M. Rutter, A. H. Tuma, & I. S. Lann (Eds.), *Assessment and diagnosis in child psychopathology* (pp. 87–112). New York: Guilford Press.

Edelman, G. M. (1987). *Neural Darwinism: The theory of neuronal group selection.* New York: Basic Books.

Elkins, R., & Rapoport, J. L. (1983). Psychopharmacology of adult and childhood depression: An overview. In D. P. Cantwell & G. A. Carlson (Eds.), *Affective disorders in childhood and adolescence: An update* (pp. 363–374). New York: Spectrum.

Emslie, G. J., Weinberg, W. A., Kennard, B. D., & Kowatch, R. A. (1994). Neurobiological aspects of depression in children and adolescents. In W. M. Reynolds & H. F. Johnston (Eds.), *Handbook of depression in children and adolescents* (pp. 143–165). New York: Plenum Press.

Endicott, J., Spitzer, R. L., Fleiss, J. L., & Cohen, J. (1976). The Global Assessment Scale. *Archives of General Psychiatry, 33,* 766–771.

Fergusson, D. M., Horwood, L. J., & Lynskey, M. T. (1995). Maternal depressive symptoms and depressive symptoms in adolescents. *Journal of Child Psychology and Psychiatry, 36*, 1161–1178.

Fine, S., Forth, A., Gilbert, M., & Haley, G. (1991). Group therapy for adolescent depressive disorder: A comparison of social skills and therapeutic support. *Journal of the American Academy of Child and Adolescent Psychiatry, 30*, 79–85.

Frank, E., Johnson, S., & Kupfer, D. J. (1992). Psychological treatments in prevention of relapse. In S. A. Montgomery & F. Rouillon (Eds.), *Long-term treatment of depression* (pp. 197–228). Chichester, England: Wiley.

Frank, E., Kupfer, D. J., Perel, J. M., Cornes, C., Jarrett, D. B., Mallinger, A. G., Thase, M. E., McEachran, A. B., & Grochocinski, V. J. (1990). Three-year outcomes for maintenance therapies in recurrent depression. *Archives of General Psychiatry, 47*, 1093–1099.

Frank, E., Kupfer, D. J., Perel, J. M., Cornes, C., Mallinger, A. G., Thase, M. E., McEachran, A. B., & Grochocinski, V. J. (1993). Comparison of full-dose versus half-dose pharmacotherapy in the maintenance treatment of recurrent depression. *Journal of Affective Disorders, 27*, 139–145.

Frank, E., Prien, R. F., Jarrett, R. B., Keller, M. B., Kupfer, D. J., Lavori, P. W., Rush, A. J., & Weissman, M. M. (1991). Conceptualization and rationale for consensus definitions of terms in Major Depressive Disorder: Remission, recovery, relapse, and recurrence. *Archives of General Psychiatry, 48*, 851–855.

Frank, E., & Spanier, C. (1995). Interpersonal psychotherapy for depression: Overview, clinical efficacy, and future directions. *Clinical Psychology: Science and Practice, 2*, 349–369.

Friedman, A. (1975). Interaction of drug therapy with marital therapy in depressed patients. *Archives of General Psychiatry, 36*, 1450–1456.

Garber, J., Braafladt, N., & Zeman, J. (1991). The regulation of sad affect: An information processing perspective. In J. Garber & K. Dodge (Eds.), *The development of emotion regulation and dysregulation* (pp. 208–240). New York: Cambridge University Press.

Garber, J., Weiss, B., & Shanley, N. (1993). Cognitions, depressive symptoms, and development in adolescents. *Journal of Abnormal Psychology, 102*, 47–57.

Gillham, J. E., Reivich, K. J., Jaycox, L. H., & Seligman, M. E. P. (1995). Prevention of depressive symptoms in school children: A two-year follow-up. *Psychological Science, 6*, 343–351.

Glick, I. D., Clarkin, J. E., Spencer, J. H., Haas, G. L., Lewis, A. B., Peyser, J., DeMane, N., Good-Ellis, M., Harris, E., & Lestello, V. (1985). A controlled evaluation of inpatient family interventions: I. Preliminary results of the six-month follow-up. *Archives of General Psychiatry, 42*, 882–886.

Goodyer, I. M., & Cooper, P. (1993). A community study of depression in adolescent girls: II. The clinical features of identified disorder. *British Journal of Psychiatry, 163*, 374–380.

Goodyer, I. M., Germany, E., Gowrusankur, J. & Altham, P. (1991). Social influences on the course of anxious and depressive disorders in school-age children. *British Journal of Psychiatry, 158,* 676–684.

Gotlib, I. H., Lewinsohn, P. M., & Seeley, J. R. (1995). Symptoms versus a diagnosis of depression: Differences in psychosocial functioning. *Journal of Consulting and Clinical Psychology, 63*, 90–100.

Hamilton, M. A. (1967). Development of a rating scale for primary depressive illness. *British Journal of Social and Clinical Psychology, 6*, 278–296.

Hammen, C. (1991). *Depression runs in families: The social context of risk and resilience in children of depressed mothers.* New York: Springer-Verlag.

Hammen, C., Burge, D., & Adrian, C. (1991). Timing of mother and child depression in a longitudinal study of children at risk. *Journal of Consulting and Clinical Psychology, 59,* 341–345.

Hammen, C., & Rudolf, K. D. (1996). Childhood depression. In E. J. Mash & R. A. Barkley (Eds.), *Child psychopathology* (pp. 153–195). New York: Guilford Press.

Harrington, R. (1993). *Depressive disorder in childhood and adolescence.* Chichester, England: Wiley.

Harrington, R. (1996). Family–genetic findings in child and adolescent depressive disorders. *International Review of Psychiatry, 8,* 355–368.

Harrington, R., Fudge, H., Rutter, M., Pickles, A., & Hill, J. (1990). Adult outcomes of childhood and adolescent depression: I. Psychiatric status. *Archives of General Psychiatry, 47,* 465–473.

Harrington, R., Fudge, H., Rutter, M., Pickles, A. & Hill, J. (1991). Adult outcomes of childhood and adolescent depression: II. Links with antisocial disorders. *Journal of the American Academy of Child Psychiatry, 30,* 434–439.

Harter, S. (1985). *Manual for the Self-Perception Profile for Children.* Denver: Author.

Hawton, K. (1986). *Suicide and attempted suicide among children and adolescents.* Beverly Hills, CA: Sage.

Hessl, D., Dawson, G., Frey, K., Panagiotides, H., Self, J., Yamada, E., & Osterling, J. (1996, May). *A longitudinal study of children of depressed mothers: Psychobiological findings related to stress.* Poster session presented at the NIMH Conference for Advancing Research on Developmental Plasticity, Chantilly, VA.

Hodges, K., Bickman, L., Ring-Kurtz, S., & Rieter, M. (1991). Multidimensional measure of level of functioning for children and adolescents. In A. Algarian & R. Freidman (Eds.), *A system of care for children's mental health: Expanding the research base* (pp. 149–154). Tampa, FL: Research and Training Center for Children's Mental Health.

Hollon, S. D., & Kendall, P. C. (1980). Cognitive self-statements in depression: Development of an Automatic Thoughts Questionnaire. *Cognitive Therapy and Research, 4,* 383–397.

Hughes, C. W., Preskorn, S. H., Weller, E., Weller, R., Hassanein, R., & Tucker, S. (1990). The effect of concomitant disorders in childhood depression on predicting treatment response. *Psychopharmacology Bulletin, 26,* 235–238.

Jacobson, N. S. (Ed.). (1988). Defining clinically significant change [Special issue]. *Behavioral Assessment, 10*(2).

Jaycox, L. H., Reivich, K. J., Gillham, J., & Seligman, M. E. P. (1994). Prevention of depressive symptoms in school children. *Behaviour Research and Therapy, 32,* 801–816.

John, K., Gammon, G. D., Prusoff, B. A., & Warner, V. (1987). The Social Adjustment Inventory for Children and Adolescents (SAICA): Testing of a new semistructured interview. *Journal of the American Academy of Child and Adolescent Psychiatry, 26,* 898–911.

Johnston, H. F., & Fruehling, J. J. (1994). Pharmacotherapy for depression in children and adolescents. In W. M. Reynolds & H. F. Johnston (Eds.), *Handbook of depression in children and adolescents* (pp. 365–397). New York: Plenum Press.

Kahn, J. S., Kehle, T. J., Jenson, W. R., & Clarke, E. (1990). Comparison of cognitive-behavioural, relaxation, and self-modeling interventions for depression among middle-school students. *School Psychology Review, 19,* 196–211.

Kashani, J. H., & Carlson, G. A. (1987). Seriously depressed preschoolers. *American Journal of Psychiatry, 144,* 348–350.

Kashani, J. H., Carlson, G. A., Beck, N. C., Hoeper, E. W., Corcoran, C. M., McAllister, J. A., Fallahi, C., Rosenberg, T. K., & Reid, J. C. (1987). Depression, depressive symptoms, and depressed mood among a community sample of adolescents. *American Journal of Psychiatry, 144,* 931–934.

Kashani, J. H., & Ray, J. S. (1983). Depressive related symptoms among preschool-age children in a child development unit. *Child Psychiatry and Human Development, 13,* 233–238.

Kashani, J. H., Rosenberg, T., & Reid, J. (1989). Developmental perspectives in child and adolescent depressive symptoms in a community sample. *American Journal of Psychiatry, 146,* 871–875.

Kaslow, N. J., Brown, R. T., & Mee, L. L. (1994). Cognitive and behavioral correlates of childhood depression: A developmental perspective. In W. M. Reynolds & H. F. Johnston (Eds.), *Handbook of depression in children and adolescents* (pp. 97–121). New York: Plenum Press.

Kaslow, N. J., & Racusin, G. R. (1988). Assessment and treatment of depressed children and their families. *Family Therapy Today, 3,* 39–59.

Kazdin, A. E. (1988). *Child psychotherapy: Developing and identifying effective treatments.* Needham Heights, MA: Allyn & Bacon.

Kazdin, A. E. (1990). Evaluation of the Automatic Thoughts Questionnaire: Negative cognitive processes and depression among children. *Psychological Assessment, 2,* 73–79.

Kazdin, A. E. (1994). Informant variability in the assessment of childhood depression. In W. M. Reynolds & H. F. Johnston (Eds.), *Handbook of depression in children and adolescents* (pp. 249–271). New York: Plenum Press.

Kazdin, A. E. (1996). Combined and multimodal treatments in child and adolescent psychotherapy: Issues, challenges, and research directions. *Clinical Psychology: Science and Practice, 3,* 69–100.

Kazdin, A. E. (1998). *Research design in clinical psychology* (3rd ed.). Needham Heights, MA: Allyn & Bacon.

Kazdin, A. E., Bass, D., Ayers, W. A., & Rodgers, A. (1990). Empirical and clinical focus of child and adolescent psychotherapy research. *Journal of Consulting and Clinical Psychology, 58,* 729–740.

Kazdin, A. E., Colbus, D., & Rodgers, A. (1987). Assessment of depression and diagnosis of depressive disorder among psychiatrically disturbed children. *Journal of Abnormal Child Psychology, 28,* 29–41.

Kazdin, A. E., Esveldt-Dawson, K., Sherick, R. B., & Colbus, D. (1985). Assessment of overt behavior and childhood depression among psychiatrically disturbed children. *Journal of Consulting and Clinical Psychology, 53,* 201–210.

Kazdin, A. E., French, N. H., Unis, A. S., Esveldt-Dawson, K., & Sherick, R. B. (1983). Hopelessness, depression and suicidal intent among psychiatrically disturbed inpatient children. *Journal of Consulting and Clinical Psychology, 51,* 504–510.

Kazdin, A. E., Rancurello, M., & Unis, A. S. (1987). Childhood depression. In G. D. Burrows & J. S. Werry (Eds.), *Advances in human psychopharmacology* (Vol. 4, pp. 1–52). Greenwich, CT: JAI Press.

Kazdin, A. E., Rodgers, A., & Colbus, D. (1986). The Hopelessness Scale for Children: Psychometric characteristics and concurrent validity. *Journal of Consulting and Clinical Psychology, 54,* 241–245.

Kazdin, A. E., Sherick, R. B., Esveldt-Dawson, K., & Rancurello, M. D. (1985). Nonverbal behavior and childhood depression. *Journal of the American Academy of Child Psychiatry, 24,* 303–309.

Kellam, S. G. (1990). Developmental epidemiological framework for family research on depression and aggression. In G. R. Patterson (Ed.), *Depression and aggression in family interaction* (pp. 11–48). Hillsdale, NJ: Erlbaum.

Keller, M. B., Lavori, P. W., Beardslee, W. R., Wunder, J., & Ryan, N. (1991). Depression in children and adolescents: New data on "undertreatment" and a literature review on the efficacy of available treatments. *Journal of Affective Disorders, 21,* 163–171.

Kiesler, D. J. (1971). Experimental designs in psychotherapy research. In A. E. Bergin & S. L. Garfield (Eds.), *Handbook of psychotherapy and behavior change: An empirical analysis* (pp. 36–74). New York: Wiley.

Kolb, B. (1989). Brain development, plasticity, and behavior. *American Psychologist, 44*, 1203–1212.

Kovacs, M. (1981). Rating scales to assess depression in school aged children. *Acta Paedopsychiatrica, 46*, 305–315.

Kovacs, M., Feinberg, T. L., Crouse-Novak, M. A., Paulauskas, S. L., & Finkelstein, R. (1984). Depressive disorders in childhood: I. A longitudinal prospective study of characteristics and recovery. *Archives of General Psychiatry, 41*, 229–237.

Kovacs, M., Feinberg, T. L., Crouse-Novak, M., Paulauskas, S. L., Pollock, M., & Finkelstein, R. (1984). Depressive disorders in childhood: II. A longitudinal study of the risk for a subsequent Major Depression. *Archives of General Psychiatry, 41*, 643–649.

Kroll, L., Harrington, R., Jayson, D., Fraser, J., & Gowers, S. (1996). Pilot study of continuation cognitive-behavioral therapy for Major Depression in adolescent psychiatric patients. *Journal of the American Academy of Child and Adolescent Psychiatry, 35*, 1156–1161.

Kupfer, D. J., Frank, E., Perel, J. M., Cornes, C., Mallinger, A. G., Thase, M. E., McEachran, A. B., & Grochocinski, V. J. (1992). Five-year outcome for maintenance therapies in recurrent depression. *Archives of General Psychiatry, 49*, 769–773.

Kutcher, S., Boulos, C., Ward, B., Marton, P., Simeon, J. S., Ferguson, H. B., Szalai, J., Katic, M., Roberts, N., Dubois, C., & Reed, K. (1994). Response to desipramine treatment in adolescent depression: A fixed-dose, placebo-controlled trial. *Journal of the American Academy of Child and Adolescent Psychiatry, 33*, 686–694.

Lefkowitz, M. M., & Tesiny, E. P. (1980). Assessment of childhood depression. *Journal of Consulting and Clinical Psychology, 48*, 43–50.

Leitenberg, H., Yost, L. W., & Carroll-Wilson, M. (1986). Negative cognitive errors in children: Questionnaire development, normative data, and comparisons between children with and without self-reported symptoms of depression, low self-esteem, and evaluation anxiety. *Journal of Consulting and Clinical Psychology, 54*, 528–536.

Lewinsohn, P. M. (1974). A behavioral approach to depression. In R. J. Friedman & M. M. Katz (Eds.), *The psychology of depression: Contemporary theory and research* (pp. 157–184). Washington, DC: Winston-Wiley.

Lewinsohn, P. M., Antonuccio, D. O., Steinmetz, J., & Teri, L. (1984*). The Coping with Depression Course: A psychoeducational intervention for unipolar depression.* Eugene, OR: Castalia.

Lewinsohn, P. M., Clarke, G. N., Hops, H., & Andrews, J. (1990). Cognitive-behavioral treatment of depressed adolescents. *Behavior Therapy, 21*, 385–401.

Lewinsohn, P. M., Clarke, G. N., & Rohde, P. (1994). Psychological approaches to the treatment of depression in adolescents. In W. M. Reynolds & H. F. Johnston (Eds.), *Handbook of depression in children and adolescents* (pp. 309–344). New York: Plenum Press.

Lewinsohn, P. M., Clarke, G. N., Rohde, P., Hops, H., & Seeley, J. R. (1996). A course in coping: A cognitive-behavioral approach to the treatment of adolescent depression. In E. D. Hibbs & P. Jensen (Eds.), *Psychosocial treatments for child and adolescent disorders: Empirically based strategies for clinical practice* (pp. 109–135). Washington, DC: American Psychological Association.

Lewinsohn, P. M., Hops, H., Roberts, R. E., Seeley, J. R., & Andrews, J. A. (1993). Adolescent psychopathology: I. Prevalence and incidence of depression and other DSM-III-R disorders in high school students. *Journal of Abnormal Psychology, 102*, 133–144.

Lewinsohn, P. M., Roberts, R. E., Seeley, J. R., Rohde, P., Gotlib, I. H., & Hops, H. (1994). Adolescent psychopathology: II. Psychosocial risk factors for depression. *Journal of Abnormal Psychology, 103*, 302–315.

Lewinsohn, P. M., Rohde, P., & Seeley, J. (1994). Psychosocial risk factors for future adolescent suicide attempts. *Journal of Consulting and Clinical Psychology, 62*, 297–305.

Lewinsohn, P., Rohde, P., Seeley, J., & Fischer, S. (1993). Age–cohort changes in the lifetime occurrence of depression and other mental disorders. *Journal of Abnormal Psychology, 102*, 110–120.

Lewinsohn, P. M., Seeley, J. R., Hibbard, J., Rohde, P., & Sack, W. H. (1996). Cross-sectional and prospective relationships between physical morbidities and depression in older adolescents. *Journal of the American Academy of Child and Adolescent Psychiatry, 35*, 1120–1129.

Lobovits, D. A., & Handal, P. J. (1985). Childhood depression: Prevalence using DSM-III criteria and validity of parent and child depression scales. *Journal of Pediatric Psychology, 10*, 45–54.

Marciano, P. L., & Kazdin, A. E. (1994). Self-esteem, depression, hopelessness, and suicidal intent among psychiatrically disturbed inpatient children. *Journal of Clinical Child Psychology, 23*, 151–160.

Maser, J. D., Kaelber, C., & Weise, R. E. (1991). International use and attitudes toward DSM-III and DSM-III-R: Growing consensus in psychiatric classification. *Journal of Abnormal Psychology, 100*, 271–279.

Matson, J. L., Rotatori, A. F., & Helsel, W. J. (1983). Development of a rating scale to measure social skills in children: The Matson Evaluation of Social Skills with Youngsters (MESSY). *Behaviour Research and Therapy, 21*, 335–340.

McCauley, E., Myers, K., Mitchell, J., Calderon, R., Schloredt, K., & Treder, R. (1993). Depression in young people: Initial presentation and clinical course. *Journal of the American Academy of Child and Adolescent Psychiatry, 32*, 714–722.

McGee, R., Feehan, M., Williams, S., & Anderson, J. (1992). DSM-III disorders from age 11 to age 15 years. *Journal of the American Academy of Child and Adolescent Psychiatry, 31*, 50–59.

Mitchell, J., McCauley, E., Burke, P., & Moss, S. J. (1988). Phenomenology of depression in children and adolescents. *Journal of the American Academy of Child Psychiatry, 27,* 12–20.

Moreau, D., Mufson, L., Weissman, M. M., & Klerman, G. L. (1991). Interpersonal psychotherapy for adolescent depression: Description of modification and preliminary application. *Journal of the American Academy of Child and Adolescent Psychiatry, 30*, 642–651.

Mufson, L., Moreau, D., Weissman, M. M., & Klerman, G. L. (1993). *Interpersonal psychotherapy for depressed adolescents.* New York: Guilford Press.

Mufson, L., Moreau, D., Weissman, M. M., Wickramaratne, P., Martin, J., & Samoilov, A. (1994). Modification of interpersonal psychotherapy with depressed adolescents (IPT-A): Phase I and II studies. *Journal of the American Academy of Child and Adolescent Psychiatry, 33*, 695–705.

Nezu, A. M., Nezu, C. M., & Perri, M. G. (1989). *Problem-solving therapy for depression.* New York: Wiley.

Nolen-Hoeksema, S., & Girgus, J. S. (1994). The emergence of gender differences in depression during adolescence. *Psychological Bulletin, 115*, 424–443.

Nolen-Hoeksema, S., Girgus, J. S., & Seligman, M. E. P. (1986). Learned helplessness in children: A longitudinal study of depression, achievement, and explanatory style. *Journal of Personality and Social Psychology, 51*, 435–442.

Paykel, E. S. (Ed.). (1992). *Handbook of affective disorders.* New York: Guilford Press.

Polaino-Lorente, A., & Domenech, E. (1993). Prevalence of childhood depression: Results of the first study in Spain. *Journal of Child Psychology and Psychiatry, 34*, 1007–1117.

Poznanski, E. O., Cook, S. C., & Carroll, B. J. (1979). A depression rating scale for children. *Pediatrics, 64*, 442–450.

Poznanski, E. O., Grossman, J. A., Buchsbaum, Y., Banegas, M., Freeman, L., & Gibbons, R. (1984). Preliminary studies of the reliability and validity of the Children's Depression Rating Scale. *Journal of the American Academy of Child Psychiatry, 23*, 191–197.

Poznanski, E. O., & Mokros, H. B. (1994). Phenomenology and epidemiology of mood disorders in children and adolescents. In W. M. Reynolds & H. F. Johnston (Eds.), *Handbook of depression in children and adolescents* (pp. 19–39). New York: Plenum Press.

Puig-Antich, J., Perel, J., Lupatkin, W., Chambers, W. J., Tabrizi, M. A., King, J., Davies, M., Johnson, R., & Stiller, R. (1987). Imipramine in prepubertal Major Depressive Disorders. *Archives of General Psychiatry, 44*, 81–89.

Puig-Antich, J., & Weston, B. (1983). The diagnosis and treatment of Major Depressive Disorder in childhood. *Annual Review of Medicine, 34*, 231–245.

Racusin, G. R., & Kaslow, N. J. (1991). Assessment and treatment of childhood depression. In P. A. Keller & S. R. Heyman (Eds.), *Innovations in clinical practice: A sourcebook* (Vol. 10, pp. 223–243). Sarasota, FL: Professional Resource Exchange.

Reinherz, H. Z., Giaconia, R. M., Lefkowitz, E. S., Pakiz, B., & Frost, A. K. (1993). Prevalence of psychiatric disorders in a community population of older adolescents. *Journal of the American Academy of Child and Adolescent Psychiatry, 32*, 369–377.

Reynolds, W. M. (1994). Assessment of depression in children and adolescents by self-report questionnaires. In W. M. Reynolds & H. F. Johnston (Eds.), *Handbook of depression in children and adolescents* (pp. 209–233). New York: Plenum Press.

Reynolds, W. M., & Coats, K. I. (1986). A comparison of cognitive-behavioral therapy and relaxation training for the treatment of depression in adolescents. *Journal of Consulting and Clinical Psychology, 54*, 653–660.

Reynolds, W. M., & Johnston, H. F. (Eds.), (1994). *Handbook of depression in children and adolescents.* New York: Plenum Press.

Roberts, R., Andrews, J., Lewinsohn, P., & Hops, H. (1990). Assessment of depression in adolescents using the Center for Epidemiologic Studies Depression Scale. *Psychological Assessment: A Journal of Consulting and Clinical Psychology, 2*, 122–128.

Rohde, P., Lewinsohn, P. M., & Seeley, J. R. (1994). Are adolescents changed by an episode of Major Depression? *Journal of the American Academy of Child and Adolescent Psychiatry, 33*, 1289–1298.

Rutter, M. R. (1986). The developmental psychopathology of depression: Issues and perspectives. In M. Rutter, C. E. Izard, & P. B. Read (Eds.), *Depression in young people: Developmental and clinical perspectives* (pp. 3–30). New York: Guilford Press.

Rutter, M. (1987). Psychosocial resilience and protective mechanisms. *American Journal of Orthopsychiatry, 57*, 316–331.

Ryan, N. D., Puig-Antich, J., Ambrosini, P., Rabinovich, H., Robinson, D., Nelson, B., Iyengar, S., & Twomey, J. (1987). The clinical picture of Major Depression in children and adolescents. *Archives of General Psychiatry, 44*, 854–861.

Ryan, N. D., Puig-Antich, J., Cooper, T., Rabinovich, H., Ambrosini, P., Davies, M., King, J., Torrer, D., & Fried, J. (1986). Imipramine in adolescent Major

Depression: Plasma level and clinical response. *Acta Psychiatrica Scandinavica, 73*, 275–288.

Sanford, M., Szatmari, P., Spinner, M., Munroe-Blum, H., Jamieson, E., Walsh, C., & Jones, D. (1995). Predicting the one year course of adolescent Major Depression. *Journal of the American Academy of Child and Adolescent Psychiatry, 34*, 1618–1628.

Seigel, W. M., Golden, N. H., Gough, J. W., Lashley, M. S., & Sacker, I. M. (1990). Depression, self-esteem, and life events in adolescents with chronic diseases. *Journal of Adolescent Health Care, 11*, 501–504.

Seligman, M. E. P. (1975). *Helplessness: On depression, development and death*. San Francisco: W. H. Freeman.

Seligman, M. E. P., & Peterson, C. (1986). A learned helplessness perspective on childhood depression: Theory and research. In M. Rutter, C. E. Izard, & P. B. Read (Eds.), *Depression in young people: Developmental and clinical perspectives* (pp. 223–249). New York: Guilford Press.

Shaffer, D., Gould, M. S., Brasic, J., Ambrosini, P., Fisher, P., Bird, H., & Aluwahlia, S. (1983). A Children's Global Adjustment Scale (CGAS). *Archives of General Psychiatry, 40*, 1228–1231.

Shain, B. N., King, C. A., Naylor, M., & Alessi, N. (1991). Chronic depression and hospital course in adolescents. *Journal of the American Academy of Child and Adolescent Psychiatry, 30*, 428–433.

Simeon, J. G., Dinicola, V. F., Ferguson, B., & Copping, A. W. (1990). Adolescent depression: A placebo-controlled fluoxetine treatment study and follow-up. *Progress in Neuro-Psychopharmacology and Biological Psychiatry, 14*, 791–795.

Sommers-Flanagan, J., & Sommers-Flanagan, R. (1996). Efficacy of antidepressant medication with depressed youth: What psychologists should know. *Professional Psychology: Research and Practice, 27*, 145–153.

Spitz, R. (1946). Anaclitic depression. *Psychoanalytic Study of the Child, 2*, 113–117.

Spitz, R., & Wolf, K. M. (1946). Anaclitic depression: II. An inquiry into the genesis of psychiatric conditions in early childhood. *Psychoanalytic Study of the Child, 2*, 313–347.

Spitzer, R. L., Endicott, J., & Robins, E. (1978). Research Diagnostic Criteria: Rationale and reliability: *Archives of General Psychiatry, 35*, 773–782.

Stark, K. D., Humphrey, L. L., Laurent, J., Livingston, R., & Christopher, J. (1993). Cognitive, behavioral, and family factors in the differentiation of depressive and anxiety disorders during childhood. *Journal of Consulting and Clinical Psychology, 61*, 878–886.

Stark, K. D., Reynolds, W. M., & Kaslow, N. (1987). A comparison of the relative efficacy of self-control therapy and a behavioral problem-solving therapy for depression in children. *Journal of Abnormal Child Psychology, 15*, 91–113.

Stark, K. D., Rouse, L. W., & Kurowski, C. (1994). Psychological treatment approaches for depression in children. In W. M. Reynolds & H. F. Johnston (Eds.), *Handbook of depression in children and adolescents* (pp. 275–307). New York: Plenum Press.

Stark, K. D., Rouse, L., & Livingston, R. (1991). Treatment of depression during childhood and adolescence: Cognitive behavioral procedures for the individual and family. In P. C. Kendall (Ed.), *Child and adolescent therapy: Cognitive-behavioral procedures* (pp. 165–208). New York: Guilford Press.

Stark, K. D., Swearer, S., Kurowski, C., Sommer, D., & Bowen, B. (1996). Targeting the child and the family: A holistic approach to treating child and adolescent depressive disorders. In E. D. Hibbs & P. Jensen (Eds.), *Psychosocial treatments for child and adolescent disorders: Empirically based strategies for clinical practice* (pp. 207–238). Washington, DC: American Psychological Association.

Strober, M., Lampert, C., Schmidt, S., & Morrell, W. (1993). The course of Major Depressive Disorder in adolescents: Recovery and risk of manic switching in a 24-month prospective, naturalistic follow-up of psychotic and nonpsychotic subtypes. *Journal of the American Academy of Child and Adolescent Psychiatry, 32*, 34–42.

Stuss, D. T., Gow, C. A., & Hetherington, C. R. (1992). "No longer Gage": Frontal lobe dysfunction and emotional changes. *Journal of Consulting and Clinical Psychology, 60*, 349–359.

Trad, P. V. (1987). *Infant and childhood depression: Developmental factors*. New York: Wiley.

Usdin, E., Asberg, M., Bertilsson, L., & Sjoqvist, F. (Eds.). (1984). *Advances in biochemical psychopharmacology: Vol. 39. Frontiers in biochemical and pharmacological research in depression*. New York: Raven Press.

Weinberg, W. A., Rutman, J., Sullivan, L., Penick, E. C., & Dietz, S. G. (1973). Depression in children referred to an education diagnostic center. *Journal of Pediatrics, 83*, 1065–1072.

Weissman, M. M., Gammon, D., John, K., Merikangas, K. R., Warner, V., Prusoff, B. A. & Sholomskas, D. (1987). Children of depressed parents: Increased psychopathology and early onset of Major Depression. *Archives of General Psychiatry, 44*, 847–853.

Weisz, J. R., Weiss, B., Wasserman, A. A., & Rintoul, B. (1987). Control-related beliefs and depression among clinic-referred children and adolescents. *Journal of Abnormal Psychology, 96*, 58–63.

World Health Organization. (1992). *International classification of diseases and health-related problems*. (10th rev.). Geneva: World Health Organization.

Wood, A., Harrington, R., & Moore, A. (1996). Controlled trial of a brief cognitive-behavioral intervention in adolescent patients with depressive disorders. *Journal of Child Psychology and Psychiatry, 37*, 737–746.

CHAPTER 5

Fears and Anxieties

Billy A. Barrios
Stan L. O'Dell
University of Mississippi

Attempts to treat the fears and anxieties of children have played a prominent role in the shaping of the practice of behavior therapy. The school of thought upon which the practice of behavior therapy is founded—behaviorism—owes much of its early survival to Mary Cover Jones's (1924a, 1924b) treatment of young Peter, Bobby, and Vincent's fear of rabbits. The success of her direct conditioning and social imitation treatments provided much-needed early support for the nascent paradigm of behaviorism and its classical conditioning model of emotional disorders (Watson & Rayner, 1920). And the two procedures themselves evolved into what have become two of the most stalwart of all behavioral techniques: systematic desensitization (Wolpe, 1948, 1954, 1958) and modeling (Bandura, 1969, 1971). Interestingly enough, much of the initial evidence establishing the effectiveness and robustness of systematic desensitization and modeling came from the application of these two techniques to the treatment of children's fears and anxieties (e.g., Bandura, Grusec, & Menlove, 1967; Lazarus, 1960; Lazarus & Rachman, 1957; Wolpe, 1958, 1961).

A great many aspects of the current practice of behavior therapy can also be traced back in part, if not in full, to our attempts to treat the fears and anxieties of children. Foremost among these are behavior therapy's interest in self-regulation and verbal mediation (e.g., Kanfer, Karoly, & Newman, 1975), in secondary and primary prevention (e.g., Peterson, Hartmann, & Gelfand, 1980; Poser, 1976), and in psychological reactions to medical illness and medical procedures (e.g., Melamed & Siegel, 1975, 1980). From the aforementioned, it is clear that our efforts to alter the fears and anxieties of children have had considerable influence in defining and advancing the practice of behavior therapy. What is not so clear is whether or not our efforts have led to any appreciable gains in understanding and reducing the fears and anxieties of children. Until recently it appeared that they had not. Indeed, recently it appeared that most of our attempts to change the fears and anxieties of children had been undertaken with the principal purpose of proclaiming or promoting a particular concept or theory or technique, and not of alleviating or remediating a condition of clinical concern.

But, as alluded to above, we have witnessed in the last several years a shift in the view of children's fears and anxieties—from convenient vehicles for promulgating ideas and techniques, to legitimate problem conditions worthy of serious concern and attention (Gittelman, 1986; Johnson & Melamed, 1979; King, Hamilton, & Murphy, 1983; Morris & Kratochwill, 1983a; Ollendick, 1979). As a result, a sizeable literature on the treatment of children's fears and anxieties has been amassed (Bernstein & Borchardt, 1991; Eisen, Kearney, & Schaefer, 1995; Grossman & Hughes, 1992; Kearney & Silverman, 1995; King & Tonge, 1992; Last, 1988; Ollendick, King, & Yule, 1994). In the pages that follow, we summarize the findings from these recent investigations and consolidate them with those from earlier examinations.

Stated in more general terms, the goal of the present chapter is to discuss in depth the subtleties and complexities of the behavioral treatment of children's fears and anxieties. Our discussion revolves around four issues: (1) the question of whether or not to treat the fears and anxieties of children; (2) the identification of a treatment focus, once it has been determined that treatment is warranted; (3) the selection of the most appropriate intervention; and (4) the evaluation of that intervention. Preceding our discussion of each of these issues is a presentation of our working definition of children's fears and anxieties.

TERMINOLOGY, SYMPTOMATOLOGY, AND NOSOLOGY

Definitions

In the child therapy literature and in conversations with child therapists, the following terms are encountered: "fear," "subclinical fear," "clinical fear," "worry," "apprehension," "wariness," "phobia," "phobic reaction," "phobic disorder," "anxiety," "anxiety symptoms," "anxiety state," "anxiety reaction," and "anxiety disorder." The sheer length of this list is dizzying. Far more troubling, however, have been the varied ways in which child therapists have used the various terms. In some instances, the terms have been clearly meant to denote the same phenomenon; in other instances, the terms have been clearly meant to denote different phenomena. In most instances, though, it has been unclear as to whether the terms have been intended to be construed as interchangeable or as independent. As such, we find considerable confusion and controversy surrounding the meaning and utility of the various terms.

All of the terms listed above are founded on the distinction that has been proposed between two of them: "fear" and "anxiety." "Fears" have been defined as complex reactions to perceived threats, with these complex reactions taking the form of escape from or avoidance of the threatening stimuli, subjective feelings of distress in anticipation of or presentation to the threatening stimuli, and physiological changes of discomfort in anticipation of or actual exposure to the threatening stimuli (e.g., Marks, 1969; Morris & Kratochwill, 1983a, 1983b). "Anxieties," on the other hand, have been described as less intense, more diffused patterns of these reactions to stimuli of a less circumscribed, more ambiguous nature (e.g., Jersild, 1954; Johnson & Melamed, 1979). The other terms have been coined to denote variations in the severity, longevity, and complexity of those two general patterns of reactions (e.g., Graziano, DeGiovanni & Garcia, 1979; Miller, Barrett, & Hampe, 1974; Morris, 1980; Poznanski, 1973).

In principle, the positing of different terms for different clinical phenomena may serve a number of valuable functions. For example, the different terms may help predict the most efficacious treatment or the duration needed in order for a particular form of treatment to be efficacious. In practice, however, we see at this time no compelling reason for adopting any of the distinctions that have been proposed among any of the terms. Obvious problems of measurement notwithstanding, the distinctions to date have proven to be of little worth: They have given rise to no new developments in either theory or treatment. As such, we have elected to use the expression "fears and anxieties" in the material that follows and to use the terms "fear" and "anxiety" interchangeably to refer to a complex pattern of motor, subjective, and physiological reactions to a real or imagined threat (e.g., Lang, 1968, 1971, 1984; Rachman, 1977).

Basic to our working definition is potential variation in responding within response categories and across stimulus situations. For example, escape, avoidance, trembling, flailing, crying, clinging, stuttering, swaying, rocking, and nail biting have all been cited as referents or symptoms of the motor component of children's fears and anxieties (e.g., Esveldt-Dawson, Wisner, Unis, Matson, & Kazdin, 1982; Fox & Houston, 1981; Glennon & Weisz, 1978; Katz, Kellerman, & Siegel, 1980; Melamed & Siegel, 1975). Reports of terror, doom, discomfort, impending harm, monsters, and helplessness have all served as referents or symptoms of the subjective component (e.g., Giebenhain & Barrios, 1986; LaGreca, Dandes, Wick, Shaw, & Stone, 1988; Laurent & Stark, 1993; Prins, 1985). And increases in heart rate, pulse volume, respiration, skin conductance, and muscular tension have all served as referents or symptoms for the physiological component (e.g., Beidel, 1988; Beidel, Christ, & Long, 1991; Jay, Ozolins, Elliott, & Caldwell, 1983; Melamed, Yurcheson,

TABLE 5.1. A Partial Listing of the Motoric, Physiological, and Subjective Responses of Children's Fears and Anxieties

Motoric responses	Physiological responses	Subjective responses
Avoidance	Heart rate	Thoughts of being scared
Gratuitous arm, hand, and leg movements	Basal skin response	Thoughts of monsters
	Plamar sweat index	Thoughts of being hurt
Trembling voice	Galvanic skin response	Images of monsters
Crying	Muscle tension	Images of wild animals
Feet shuffling	Skin temperature	Thoughts of danger
Screaming	Respiration	Self-deprecatory thoughts
Nail biting	Palpitation	Self-critical thoughts
Thumb sucking	Breathlessness	Thoughts of inadequacy
Rigid posture	Nausea	Thoughts of incompetence
Eyes shut	Pulse volume	Thoughts of bodily injury
Avoidance of eye contact	Headache	Images of bodily injury
Clenched jaw	Stomach upset	Thoughts racing
Stuttering	Stomachache	Thoughts of imminent death
Physical proximity	Urination	Thoughts of appearing foolish
White knuckles	Defecation	Blanking out
Trembling lip	Vomiting	Thoughts of going crazy
Certain verbalizations[a]	Labored breathing	Difficulty concentrating
Immobility	Blurred vision	Forgetfulness
Swallowing	Numbness	Thoughts of contamination
Twitching	Dizziness	Images of harm to loved ones
Walking rituals	Flushes/chills	Depersonalization

Note. The responses listed here have been documented in the following studies: Ballenger, Carek, Steele, & Cornish-McTighe (1989); Beidel, Christ, & Long (1991); Esveldt-Dawson, Wisner, Unis, Matson, & Kazdin (1982); Garland & Smith (1990); Glennon & Weisz (1978); Hatcher (1989); Hoehn-Saric, Maisami, & Wiegand (1987); Katz, Kellerman, & Siegel (1980); Laurent & Stark (1993); LeBaron & Zeltzer (1984); Lewis & Law (1958); McNamara (1988); Melamed, Hawes, Heiby, & Glick (1975); Melamed & Siegel (1975); Milos & Reiss (1982); Peterson (1987); Rettew, Swedo, Leonard, Lenane, & Rapoport (1992); Ross, Ross, & Evans (1971); Siegel & Peterson (1980); Simpson, Ruzicka, & Thomas (1974); Singer, Ambuel, Wade, & Jaffe (1992); Sonnenberg & Venham (1977); Van Hasselt, Hersen, Bellack, Rosenblum, & Lamparski (1979); Zatz & Chassin (1983). From Barrios & Hartmann (1997). Copyright (1997) by The Guilford Press. Reprinted by permission.

[a]In some cases, the distinction between motor and subjective responses may be difficult to draw. For example, the shouted statement "I am scared!" in response to a large, barking dog is similar to a scream (a motor response) and is, of course, the expression of a thought (a subjective response).

Fleece, Hutcherson, & Hawes, 1978; Van Hasselt, Hersen, Bellack, Rosenblum, & Lamparski, 1979). Table 5.1 offers a long but still partial listing of the various motor, subjective, and physiological symptoms of children's fears and anxieties.

Though diverse, the responses of each component have a shared function or feature. For those of the motor component, it is the feature of performance impairment; for those of the subjective component, it is phenomenological distress; and for those of the physiological component, it is somatovisceral arousal (cf. Lang, 1984; McGlynn & Rose, in press). These three features act as boundaries for the numerous symptoms of children's fears and anxieties and give some semblance of distinctiveness to the response pattern. Because of the latitude of these boundaries, children may differ from one

another in the exact makeup of their fear reactions to a given stimulus situation. For example, one child's fear of attending school may take the form of tantrums and clinging to parents, whereas another child's fear of attending school may take the form of entrance but refusing to participate in any social or evaluative activities (e.g., Kearney & Silverman, 1993). And because of the varying task demands of different stimulus situations, the exact makeup of a given child's fear reactions may vary from one threatening stimulus situation to another. For example, a given child may react to being placed in the dentist's chair by kicking, screaming and gasping for air, and to being called upon in the classroom by trembling, stuttering, and tearing of eyes.

To summarize, our working definition of children's fears and anxieties is that of a complex pattern of motor, subjective, and physiological reactions to a real or imagined threat. Activity within each of the response categories may take many different forms yet remain functionally equivalent. As such, there may be considerable response variation both between and within children—variation from one child to another in the exact expression of the fear and anxiety reactions to the same stimulus; variation within the same child in the exact expression of fear and anxiety reactions to different stimuli.

Classification Schemes

Several different systems for classifying the diverse fears and anxieties of children have appeared over the years. In general, the different systems have tended to be of one of three types: theoretically based, statistically based, or clinically based.[1] Examples of theoretically based taxonomies are those put forth by Hebb (1946), by Seligman (1971), and by Kearney and Silverman (1993). In Hebb's (1946) system, fear and anxiety reactions are grouped according to their presumed etiology: Those thought to be produced by conflicts or sensory deficits form one class of reactions and those thought to be produced by constitutional disturbances or maturational forces form another class of reactions. In Seligman's (1971) system, stimuli of evolutionary significance in the phylogenetic history of the organism are referred to as "prepared," and stimuli of evolutionary insignificance are referred to as "unprepared." Fear and anxiety reactions to prepared stimuli are thought to be easier to learn and harder to unlearn than are fear and anxiety reactions to unprepared stimuli. Examples of prepared stimuli are snakes, spiders, heights, blood, and darkness; examples of unprepared stimuli are flowers, mushrooms, butterflies, and chocolate (Öhman, 1979; Rachman & Seligman, 1976). And in Kearney and Silverman's (1993) system, fears of attending school are classified according to four hypothesized motivating conditions: avoidance of stimuli provoking negative emotions, escape from social-evaluative situations, appeal for attention, and access to positive reinforcement.

A number of the classification schemes are founded on statistical analyses of reports of fears and anxieties by large samples of children and adolescents. The earliest of these factor-analytically derived systems is that of Scherer and Nakamura (1968), in which the fears of children fall into eight categories: failure and criticism; social events; small animals; medical proce-

dures; death; darkness; home and school; and miscellaneous events. Systems developed since then have arrived at similar but shorter lists of categories. Miller, Barrett, Hampe, and Noble (1972b) classify the fears of children into three categories: physical injury, natural events, and psychic stress. Ollendick and associates (Ollendick, 1983, 1987; Ollendick, King, & Frary, 1989; Ollendick, Matson, & Helsel, 1985) classify the fears of children into five categories: failure and criticism; the unknown; minor injury and small animals; danger and death; and medical procedures.

Two better-known statistically derived classification schemes have fears and anxieties as members of a supraordinate class of problem behaviors. In Quay's (1979) system, the problem behaviors of children cluster into four patterns: conduct disorder, anxiety–withdrawal, immaturity, and socialized aggression. Fears and anxieties as defined in this chapter are subsumed by the general pattern of anxiety–withdrawal, which has among its elements anxiousness, fearfulness, shyness, timidity, bashfulness, withdrawal, seclusiveness, social isolation, depression, aloofness, and secretiveness. In Achenbach's (1991a, 1991b, 1991c) system, over 100 different problem behaviors are grouped into eight distinct syndromes: a set of Internalizing disorders, consisting of Withdrawn, Somatic Complaints, Anxious/Depressed, Social Problems, and Thought Problems syndromes; and a set of Externalizing disorders, consisting of the Attention Problems, Delinquent Behavior, and Aggressive Behavior syndromes. A key shared feature of the Internalizing disorders is an excess of anxious behaviors, whereas a key shared feature of the Externalizing disorders is an absence of socially prescribed anxious behaviors.

The clinically based classification systems owe their various groupings to the insights and observations of applied researchers. The most widely advanced, debated, and adopted of these systems are the ones put forth by the American Psychiatric Association (1980, 1987, 1994). Founded on clinical observation, developed by group consensus, and refined by field research, the Association's current system devotes 14 categories to human fears and anxieties. Of these 14 categories, 12 are applicable to the fears and anxieties of children: Separation Anxiety Disorder, Agoraphobia without History of Panic Disorder, Social Phobia, Specific Phobia, Panic Disorder With Agoraphobia, Panic Disorder Without Agorophobia, Obsessive–Compulsive Disorder, Posttraumatic Stress Disorder, Acute Stress Disorder, Generalized Anxiety Disorder, Substance-Induced Anxiety Disorder, and Anxiety Disorder Not Otherwise Specified.

The first four of the disorders are similar in that the child's anxiety in each instance is linked to a discrete stimulus situation, but dissimilar in that in each a different stimulus situation is involved. For Separation Anxiety Disorder (which is actually grouped with the disorders usually first diagnosed in infancy, childhood, or adolescence, rather than with the anxiety disorders per se), the feared situation is separation from home or a significant attachment figure. Excessive anxiety is of at least 4 weeks' duration and takes the form of at least three of the following: unrealistic worry about harm to attachment figure, unrealistic worry about harm to self resulting from separation from this figure, persistent opposition to school attendance, persistent opposition to being home alone, persistent opposition to sleeping or to sleeping away from home, recurrent nightmares involving separation, recurrent physical complaints in anticipation or in the course of separation, and recurrent distress in anticipation or in the course of separation. For Agoraphobia Without History of Panic Disorder, the feared situation is one in which escape might be embarrassing or difficult, or in which assistance might not be forthcoming were incapacitating symptoms to arise. Examples of such situations, which are avoided or endured with pronounced distress or entered only when accompanied by a companion, are crowded stores, elevators, bridges, and buses. And examples of such incapacitating or embarrassing symptoms are dizziness, fainting, heart palpitations, loss of bladder control, and loss of bowel control. For Social Phobia, the feared situation is one or more social activities involving unfamiliar others or possible scrutiny by others. Fear of appearing foolish is of at least 6 months' duration and is evidenced when in the presence of unfamiliar peers and not simply unfamiliar adults. This fear of social or performance situations is distressing or disruptive, and may or may not be recognized by the child as excessive and unreasonable. Examples of such social situations, which are avoided or endured with marked discomfort, are public speaking, speaking to authority figures, initiating conversations, and eating in public places. For Specific Phobia, the feared situation is any circumscribed object or situation other than those heretofore mentioned (e.g., separation from significant other, speaking in the presence of others) and those hereinafter

mentioned (e.g., the objects/situations involved in obsessions or trauma). Fear of these stimuli is disturbing to the child or is interfering with his or her development, and may or may not be recognized by the child as excessive and unreasonable. Examples of such stimuli, which are avoided or endured with marked distress, are animals, water, darkness, heights, loud noises, and medical procedures.

At the heart of the two Panic Disorders is the unexpected occurrence of episodes of intense distress, referred to as Panic Attacks. Such an episode consists of a constellation of four or more cognitive and somatic symptoms (e.g., sweating, pounding heart, rapid breathing, tingling sensations, racing thoughts over losing control) and may or may not be triggered by a situational cue. In Panic Disorder With Agoraphobia, these discrete, recurrent episodes of intense distress are accompanied by an intense fear of situations in which escape might be embarrassing or difficult, or in which assistance might not be forthcoming were debilitating symptoms to arise. In Panic Disorder Without Agoraphobia, no such fear accompanies the discrete recurrent episodes of intense distress.

The six remaining psychiatric categories differ in the degree to which fear and anxiety are associated with specific stimulus cues. In Obsessive–Compulsive Disorder, fear and anxiety are tied to the presence of obsessions (i.e., recurrent repugnant thoughts, images, or impulses) or compulsions (i.e., repetitive but ineffectual behavioral or mental acts). Common themes of obsessions, which exceed the boundaries of ordinary worry and resist suppression, are contamination, doubts, and orderliness. Common examples of compulsions, which are unrealistically aimed at reducing distress or preventing dread, are handwashing, checking, counting, and ordering. The fear and anxiety associated with obsessions and/or compulsions are distressing, time-consuming, and/or interfering with normal development, yet may not be recognized by the child as excessive or unreasonable.

In Posttraumatic Stress Disorder and Acute Stress Disorder anxiety is tied to a catastrophic event that was experienced directly or indirectly and that involved serious actual or threatened harm to self or others. Examples of such terrifying or horrific events are physical attack, sexual assault, natural disaster, kidnapping, and violent automobile accident. The catastrophic event is repeatedly relived through play, dreams, or flashbacks and is accompanied by intense psychological distress or physiological upset. Stimuli associated with the catastrophic event are actively avoided, and general emotional responsiveness is greatly diminished. Marked anxiety associated with the event is also manifested through a heightened state of general arousal (e.g., poor concentration, exaggerated startle response, hypervigilance, sleep disturbances, anger outbursts). This distressing and/or debilitating state of anxiety is of at least 1 months' duration for Posttraumatic Stress Disorder and no greater than 4 weeks' duration for Acute Stress Disorder.

The categories of Substance-Induced Anxiety Disorder and Generalized Anxiety Disorder differ markedly from those previously described. In Substance-Induced Anxiety Disorder, the anxiety symptoms are judged to be due to the direct physiological effects of a substance (such as marijuana, a hallucinogen, an inhalant, or a medication). These anxiety symptoms, though, significantly exceed those typically associated with intoxication or withdrawal and clearly constitute a significant source of distress or impediment to functioning. In Generalized Anxiety Disorder, the anxiety symptoms are not bound to any discernible stimulus situation. Instead, excessive anxiety and persistent worry pervade a wide range of events and activities, from school-related tasks to natural disasters. This excessive anxiety and persistent worry are characteristic of the child's life for the last 6 months and are evidenced by at least one of six symptoms (e.g., restlessness, fatigue, inability to concentrate, sleep disturbances).

The final diagnostic category, Anxiety Disorder Not Otherwise Specified, includes those fear and anxiety reactions that do not fall neatly into any of the 11 aforementioned diagnostic categories. Examples of such reactions are a mixture of significant but not severe anxiety and depressive symptoms, and a pattern of avoidance of social and performance situations stemming from the eating disorder of Anorexia Nervosa.

Summary

Though fundamental to the practice of science, none of the classification systems presented has yet to be shown to be of benefit to us in the practice of behavior therapy as it pertains to the treatment of children's fears and anxieties. For classification to be helpful to us, the various groupings must predict one or more of the following: the scope of the impairments, the most efficacious treatment to employ for those impairments, the duration needed for efficacious treatment, and/or the outcome of treatment. At present, few data exist showing any one of the systems for classifying children's fears and anxieties to be predictive of any one of these relationships (e.g., Bernstein & Garfinkel, 1986; Burke & Silverman, 1987; Jacobs & Nadel, 1985; Morris & Kratochwill, 1983a). With more research, more support for the utility of one or more of the classification schemes may accrue. Until such research is conducted and such support is accrued, the classification systems will continue to offer us little in the way of guidance as to how to treat the fears and anxieties of children.

TO TREAT OR NOT TO TREAT

Fears and anxieties are part and parcel of both childhood and adulthood (see Bauer, 1976; Campbell, 1986; Jersild, 1968; Lewis & Brooks, 1974; Marks, 1987). Some of these reactions are considered adaptive, whereas others are considered maladaptive. In this section we review several of the factors that we might draw upon to determine how maladaptive and in need of treatment a child's fears and anxieties are. Specifically, these factors are the characteristics of the developing child, the characteristics of the fear context, and the characteristics of the family.

Developmental Characteristics

Research spanning some 60 years has repeatedly shown most children as having a great many fears and anxieties. In the classic work by Jersild and Holmes (1935), mothers reported an average of four to five fears for their 2- through 6-year-old children. In a large-scale investigation by Pinter and Lev (1940), 70% of the 540 fifth- and sixth- graders identified themselves as having 10 or more worries. In two separate studies by Pratt (1945), several hundred 4- through 16-year-old children reported an average of five to eight fears. And in the often-cited investigation by Lapouse and Monk (1959), 43% of the mothers of a large sample of 6- through 12-year-olds reported that their children experienced seven or more fears.

Subsequent studies carried out over the last three to four decades have found similar numbers of fears and anxieties for children. For example, in a replication of the Pinter and Lev (1940) study, Orton (1982) obtained comparable numbers of worries among his sample of 645 fifth- and sixth-graders. The Slee and Cross (1989) sample of 1,243 children ranging in age from 4 to 19 years averaged from 8 to 10 intense fears. And the four samples for a series of studies by Ollendick and his associates averaged from 7 to 17 intense fears. In the initial study in this series (Ollendick, 1983), 217 children aged 8 through 11 years reported between 9 and 13 excessive fears. In the next study (Ollendick et al., 1985), 126 children aged 7 through 18 years reported between 11 and 14 intense fears. And in the final two studies (Ollendick & King, 1994; Ollendick et al., 1989), the samples of 1,185 and 648 children ranged in age from 7 to 16 and 12 to 17 years and averaged from 12 to 17 and 7 to 10 pronounced fears, respectively. Several investigations employing smaller samples have obtained estimates similar to those reported above (e.g., Bamber, 1974; Barrios, Replogle, & Anderson-Tisdelle, 1983; Dibrell & Yamamoto, 1988; Eme & Schmidt, 1978; Kirkpatrick, 1984; Maurer, 1965; Nalven, 1970; Scherer & Nakamura, 1968).

Recent investigations have also shown specific types and clusters of anxiety symptoms to be quite common among children of all ages. For example, Beidel et al. (1991) interviewed 76 children aged 8 through 13 for the presence or absence of 16 different somatic symptoms of anxiety (e.g., chest pains, dizziness, sweating, headaches). The percentage of children endorsing the presence of any given symptom ranged from 10% to 70%, and the total number of symptoms endorsed as present by the children averaged from three to seven. Bell-Dolan, Last & Strauss (1990) interviewed 62 "never psychiatrically ill" children for the presence–absence of 90 different anxiety symptoms. Seventeen of the symptoms were reported as present by at least 10% of these 5- through 18-year-olds. And in their two community-wide studies of the prevalence of anxiety symptoms and clusters of anxiety symptoms, Kashani and Orvaschel (1988, 1990) interviewed over 350 children and their parents. In the first of these studies, over 17% of their sample of 14-, 15-, and 16-year-olds were judged to have sufficient numbers of anxiety symptoms to warrant concern. And in the second of these studies, 21% of their sample of 8-, 12-, and 17-year-olds were judged to have sufficient numbers of such symptoms to warrant concern.

With increasing age, there appear to be changes in the foci, frequency, and form of the fears and anxieties of children. The prominent fears and anxieties for young infants differ from those for young children, which in turn differ from those for older children. This shift in the targets of fears and anxieties continues through adolescence into adulthood. For young infants, the situations most commonly feared are heights, loss of support, and sudden, intense events such as loud noises (Ball & Tronick, 1971; Bronson, 1972; Jersild, 1954; Jersild & Holmes, 1935). For 1-, 2-, and 3-year-olds, the typical fear objects are strangers, loud noises, separation from caretakers, novel stimuli, and toileting activities (Jersild & Holmes, 1935; Miller et al., 1974). With preschoolers and first-graders, fears and anxieties have as their major foci animals, darkness, parental separation and abandonment, supernatural beings such as monsters and ghosts, and natural occurrences such as thunder and lightning (Bauer, 1976; Jersild & Holmes, 1935; Lapouse & Monk, 1959; Maurer, 1965; Poznanski, 1973; Pratt, 1945; Slee & Cross, 1989). Older elementary school children also fear natural phenomena such as earthquakes, tornadoes, thunder, and lightning, but most of their fears center around school-, health-, and home-related events. Among the school events that trouble children of this age group are test-taking, poor grades, rejection by classmates, and reprimand by the principal; among the health events are physical injury and illness, death, and medical procedures; and among the home events are parental conflicts and parental punishment (Angelino, Dollins, & Mech, 1956; Croake & Knox, 1973; Eme & Schmidt, 1978; Lapouse & Monk, 1959; Nalven, 1970; Ollendick, 1983; Orton, 1982; Pinter & Lev, 1940; Scherer & Nakamura, 1968). With adolescents, fears and anxieties tend to be related to school events, physical illness, and personal adequacy. Also appearing as sources of great concern and worry are economic, political, and sexual matters (Allan & Hodgson, 1968; Angelino et al., 1956; Herbertt & Innes, 1979; Kirkpatrick, 1984; Maurer, 1965; Ollendick & King, 1994; Pratt, 1945; Slee & Cross, 1989; Winker, 1949).[2]

With increasing age, there also appears to be a decrease in the sheer number of fears and anxieties. For example, Holmes (1935) observed the reactions of 2- through 5-year-olds to strangers, darkness, and the like, and noted that the younger the child, the greater the number of fears displayed. Similar age trends have been reported by MacFarlane, Allen, and Honzik (1954) for 3- through 14-year-olds, by Bauer (1976) for 4- through 12-year-olds; by Maurer (1965) for 5-through 14-year-olds; by Barrios et al. (1983) for 5- through 16-year-olds; by Lapouse and Monk (1959) for 6- through 12-year-olds; and by Bamber (1974) for 12- through 18-year-old boys. More recent studies surveying greater numbers of children and age groups have likewise noted fewer fears for older children (e.g., Dong, Yang, & Ollendick, 1994; Gullone & King, 1992; Ollendick & King, 1994; Ollendick et al., 1985, 1989; Slee & Cross, 1989).[3]

With increasing age may also come changes in the exact form that a fear reaction to a particular stimulus situation takes. For example, in their reaction to separation from an attachment figure, young children express their distress through nightmares and overt opposition, whereas old children do so through complaints of physical ailments on days of school/separation (Francis, Last, & Strauss, 1987). Young children and older children also differ in their expression of pervasive or generalized anxiety, with older children reporting greater numbers of anxiety symptoms and greater amounts of worry over the appropriateness of past behavior than younger children (Strauss, Lease, Last, & Francis, 1988). And with respect to the specific anxiety symptom of worry, older children are more varied and elaborate in this type of response to a wide range of stimulus situations than are younger children (Vasey, Crnic, & Carter, 1994). Changes in the symptom constellations of other specific anxiety reactions have been noted, but have not yet been well delineated (e.g., Rettew, Swedo, Leonard, Lenane, & Rapoport, 1992).

The fears and anxieties of children tend to vary not only with age but also with gender, ethnic affiliation, and socioeconomic status. At every age across the span of childhood, girls tend to report greater numbers of anxiety symptoms and greater numbers of fear reactions than boys do (e.g., Bamber, 1974; Croake, 1969; Croake & Knox, 1973; Gullone & King, 1992; Kashani & Orvaschel, 1988, 1990; King, Ollier, et al., 1989; Kirkpatrick, 1984; Ollendick, 1983; Ollendick et al., 1985; Pratt, 1945; Ryall & Dietiker, 1979; Scherer & Nakamura, 1968; Spence & McCathie, 1993). Furthermore, girls tend to differ from boys in the types of fears and anxieties they experience, with fears of animals and physical illness and injury being more common among girls than boys, and fears of economic and academic failure being more common among boys than girls (e.g., Bamber, 1974;

Kirkpatrick, 1984; Ollendick, 1983; Orton, 1982; Pinter & Lev, 1940; Pratt, 1945; Scherer & Nakamura, 1968; Winker, 1949).[4]

Long overlooked, differences in the fears and anxieties of children of different ethnic groups have begun to be noted. The studies conducted to date point to greater numbers of fears and anxieties and anxiety symptoms among African American children than among European American children (Kashani & Orvaschel, 1988; Lapouse & Monk, 1959; Last & Perrin, 1993). They also suggest differences between these two children groups in terms of the exact expression of their fear reactions to test-taking situations, with European American children displaying more pronounced physiological upset and African American children displaying more collateral fears of social situations (Beidel, Turner, & Trager, 1994). Other groups of children have been found to differ from children of mainstream Western cultures in terms of the types of fears and anxieties experienced. For example, Caribbean children report more intense fears of nature (e.g., darkness, animals) than do mainstream Western children (Payne, 1988), and Chinese children report more intense fears of social-evaluative situations (e.g., failing a test, getting poor grades) than do Western children (Dong et al., 1994).

With respect to socioeconomic status, children from low-income families tend to be similar to children from middle-income families in the numbers of fears and anxieties, but dissimilar in the targets of those fears and anxieties (Richman, Stevenson, & Graham, 1982). Though both groups of children fear small animals, lower-income children tend to be frightened of rats and roaches, whereas middle-income children tend to be frightened of poisonous insects. The same appears to be true of the two groups' fears of economic misfortune, with lower-income children tending to be anxious about necessity items and middle-income children tending to be anxious about less essential items (e.g., Angelino et al., 1956; Nalven, 1970; Pinter & Lev, 1940; Pratt, 1945; Simon & Ward, 1974).[5]

Over the years, numerous and sundry problem behaviors have been observed in conjunction with child cases of fears and anxieties (cf. Graziano, DeGiovanni, & Garcia, 1979; Morris & Kratochwill, 1983a). For example, Poznanski (1973) noted the following among 18 children aged 4 through 12 suffering from excessive fears: hyperactivity, encopresis, enuresis, obesity, overdependency, nightmares, somatic complaints, learning difficulties, obsessive–compulsive tendencies, and bed sharing. From this list, and similar lengthier ones compiled by other child therapists, have emerged three types of problem behaviors with consistent ties to the fears and anxieties of children. The first of these is other intense fear reactions. In other words, with the appearance of one severe fear reaction comes the increased likelihood of the occurrence of another severe fear reaction. For non-referred children suffering from an extreme fear of one type of situation, the probability of their suffering from an extreme fear of another type of situation has been estimated to be approximately .40 (Kashani & Orvaschel, 1988, 1990). For clinic-referred children, this probability has been estimated to be between .41 and .96, with the exact probability dependent upon the nature of the principal situation feared (Francis, Last, & Strauss, 1992; Last, Perrin, Hersen, & Kazdin, 1992; Last, Strauss, & Francis, 1987). In examining the co-occurrence of severe fears, child therapists have also sought to identify what types of fear reactions tend to occur in concert with one another. For children fearful of separation from an attachment figure, there appears to be a heightened chance of also being fearful of physical ailments and natural events; for children fearful of social and evaluative situations, there is a heightened chance of also being troubled by a wide range of nonperformance situations; and for children plagued by periodic Panic Attacks, there is a heightened chance of also being tormented by unrealistic worries concerning past, present, and future events (Francis et al., 1992; Last et al., 1992).

Another problem condition that has frequently been found to accompany the fears and anxieties of children is the mood disturbance of depression (cf. Brady & Kendall, 1992). Among nonreferred children reporting extreme levels of anxiety, the likelihood of a given child's also reporting extreme levels of depression has been established to range from as low as .16 (Anderson, Williams, McGee, & Silva, 1987) to as high as .33 (Kashani & Orvaschel, 1988, 1990). Much higher estimates for the occurrence of an accompanying depressive condition have been put forth for clinic-referred children, with the lowest figure being that of .25 (Last et al., 1992) and the highest figure being .81 (Bernstein & Garfinkel, 1986). The occurrence of an accompanying depressive condition has not been linked to any specific type or types of anxiety

reactions, as some researchers have noted high rates of depression among children fearful of separation from significant attachment figures (Bernstein, 1991; Kovacs, Gatsonis, Paulauskas, & Richards, 1989; Mitchell, McCauley, Burke, & Moss, 1988), whereas others have noted high rates of depression among children fearful of social-evaluative situations (Last et al., 1992). A consistent picture has begun to emerge with respect to the specific type of children most likely to display coexisting anxiety and depressive reactions—that is children who are advanced in age, extreme in levels of disturbance, and encumbered with multiple fears (Bernstein, 1991; Strauss et al., 1988). The limited data on the chronology of anxiety and depressive symptoms suggest that the former symptons often predate the latter, and thus that anxiety may be a harbinger of a severe mood disturbance (Hershberg, Carlson, Cantwell, & Strober, 1982; Kovacs et al., 1989; Stavrakaki, Vargo, Boodoosingh, & Roberts, 1987). Though extremely tentative, this temporal relationship between anxiety and depression has obvious implications for early treatment and treatment evaluation—two matters that are taken up in later sections of the chapter.

Certain disruptive behaviors have also been found to occur in conjunction with the fears and anxieties of children with a certain degree of regularity. Among nonreferred children evidencing severe anxiety, marked problems in concentration and frequent episodes of acting out have been observed (Kashani & Orvaschel, 1990). Among clinic-referred samples reporting severe anxiety, one or more of three disruptive behavior patterns (Attention-Deficit/Hyperactivity Disorder, Conduct Disorder, and Oppositional Defiant Disorder) have been detected in 8% to 28% of the children (Last et al., 1992; Strauss et al., 1988). Intensive studies of these three disorders provide additional support for reliable, moderate ties to the fears and anxieties of children (e.g., Anderson et al., 1987; Bird, Canino, & Rubio-Stipec, 1988; Livingston, Dykman, & Ackerman, 1990; Woolston et al., 1989).

As findings on the persistence of children's fears and anxieties have accrued, so have doubts as to these fears and anxieties being short-lived. Much of the early research shows the fears and anxieties of children to be fairly fleeting, whereas much of the recent research shows them to be far more enduring. For example, three studies in the 1930s all reported the life span of most childhood fears to be no greater than 12 weeks. Three-fourths of the fears of Jersild and

Holmes's (1935) 2- through 5-year-olds had vanished by the end of the 3-week assessment period. Virtually all of the fears of Slater's (1939) 2- and 3-year-olds had abated by the end of 4 weeks. And over one-half of the fears of Hagman's (1932) child subjects had disappeared by the end of 3 months.

Two important series of studies in the early 1970s reinforced this initial view of children's fears and anxieties as transient: the epidemiological research of Agras and his colleagues (Agras, Chapin, & Oliveau, 1972; Agras, Sylvester, & Oliveau, 1969) and the treatment outcome research of Miller and his colleagues (Hampe, Noble, Miller, & Barrett, 1973; Miller, Barrett, Hampe, & Noble, 1972a). Specifically, Agras and his colleagues questioned adult phobics as to the origins of their fears, and tracked 10 child and adolescent phobics over a 5-year period. Few of the adult phobics traced their fears back to childhood (Agras et al., 1969), and none of the child and adolescent phobics reported being very fearful at the 5-year follow-up (Agras et al., 1972). Miller and his colleagues assigned 67 phobic children to 8 weeks of reciprocal inhibition therapy, psychotherapy, or no treatment. At 6 weeks posttreatment, all groups including the control condition evidenced significant reductions in phobic behavior (Miller et al., 1972a). At 2 years posttreatment, 80% of the children were symptom-free, with only 7% of the children continuing to be very fearful (Hampe et al., 1973). The findings as a whole led to the bold conclusion that "the lifespan of phobias in children appears to be somewhere between two weeks and two years, with most phobias dissipating within one year of onset" (Hampe et al., 1973, p. 452).

More recent studies portray the fears and anxieties of children as being much more persistent. For example, the reports of fears and anxieties on the part of Eme and Schmidt's (1978) fourth graders were remarkably stable over a 1-year period, in terms of both their absolute numbers and their targets of distress. So too have been the reports of children's fears and anxieties gathered over lesser intervals of time, such as 1 week (Gullone & King, 1992; Ollendick, 1983; Ryall & Dietiker, 1979), 1 month (Barrios et al., 1983; McCathie & Spence, 1991), 2 months (Kendall, 1994), and 6 months (Dong et al., 1994).

The few studies that have carried out formal assessments over intervals greater than one year also show the fears and anxieties of children to be fairly stable in nature. In their 2-year study of the fears of a sample of 94 children aged 7- to 10 years, Spence and McCathie (1993) obtained moderate stability coefficients for the various age groups and for the sample as a whole. And in their 2- to 16-year follow-up of 79 children suffering from severe obsessions and compulsions, Rettew et al. (1992) noted strikingly similar numbers of anxiety symptoms across the broad time span.

Recent studies of the age of onset of adults' fears and anxieties offer further support for a view of the fears and anxieties of children as that of far from fleeting. Unlike the adult phobics questioned in the early Agras et al. (1969) study, many of the anxious adults questioned in more recent investigations have traced the origin of their fears to childhood (e.g., Burke, Burke, Regier, & Rae, 1990; Öst, 1987, 1991; Reich, 1986; Thyer, Parrish, Curtis, Nesse, & Camerson, 1985). For example, approximately 33% of the anxious adults examined by Black (1974) cited their obsessions and compulsions as having their onset before the age of 15. And in a large epidemiological study of dental fear, Milgrom, Foset, Melnick, and Weinstein (1988) identified 67% of their adult respondents as having acquired their fear reaction in early childhood and an additional 18% as having acquired their fear reaction during adolescence.

Be they persistent or evanescent, the critical question surrounding the fears and anxieties of children is whether or not they are serious enough to warrant our concern. For years, the prevailing view has been that they are not. To be exact, the long-standing view of the severity of children's fears has been that of a J-shaped distribution curve, with numerous reports of modest to mild reactions and occasional reports of moderate to extreme reactions (Miller et al., 1973; Ollendick & Francis, 1988). This sanguine picture of the fears and anxieties of children appears to have arisen in part from the few early epidemiological studies on their incidence and persistence (e.g., Agras et al., 1972; Rutter, Tizard, & Whitmore, 1970) and in part from the few published surveys of their referrals for treatment. As mentioned earlier, these early epidemiological studies characterized the severe fears of children as being both scarce and short-lived. And as for the few published surveys of clinics and therapists, they revealed few referrals of anxious and fearful children to treatment agencies—a finding suggesting that the fears and anxieties of these children might not be particularly bothersome to the children or to their parents or to their teachers. For example, of 239 consecutive cases referred to the Maudsley Hospital Children's Department, only 10 were for fear reactions (Graham, 1964). Of 547 cases referred to 19 child behavior therapists during a 6-month period, only 7% were for specific fear-related conditions (Graziano & DeGiovanni, 1979). And of all the child cases referred for psychological treatment prior to 1980, it is estimated that only 3% to 4% were for fears and anxieties (Johnson & Melamed, 1979).

Findings from more recent epidemiological studies and pertinent surveys give us cause for much greater concern with regard to the seriousness of children's fears and anxieties. As mentioned earlier, 17% to 21% of the children in Kashani and Orvaschel's (1988, 1990) two community-wide studies were judged to have sufficient numbers of anxiety symptoms to warrant concern. Also noteworthy is the finding that nearly half of these children were judged as sufficiently fearful to warrant their designation as "clinical cases." Comparable percentages of "severe cases" of fears and anxieties have been obtained in other large-scale investigations (e.g., Anderson et al., 1987; Costello, 1989; McGee et al., 1990). Even investigations employing stringent multistage screening procedures have identified heightened levels of anxiety among an alarmingly large number of children (Laurent, Hadler, & Stark, 1994; Whitaker et al., 1990).

Other recent findings indicate that these distressing fears and anxieties of children may also be significantly interfering with children's orderly pursuit of personal and social goals and rewards (e.g., McCathie & Spence, 1991; Ollendick & King, 1994). For example, Ollendick and King (1994) questioned 648 youths aged 12- to 17 about the extent to which their fears prevented them from participating in desired or required activities. Over 60% of the youths reported high levels of daily interference due to their many fears and anxieties; an additional 26% of the youths reported moderate levels of daily interference.

It should also be pointed out that despite the infrequency with which parents in past years sought treatment services for their children's fears and anxieties, the availability of such services has increased steadily over the last 10 years. For example, most pediatric hospitals in the United States currently offer some form of intervention to alleviate the fears and worries of children undergoing diagnostic and medical procedures (Eland & Anderson, 1977; Peterson & Harbeck, 1988; Peterson & Ridley-Johnson,

1980). The same is true of clinics specializing in the treatment of debilitating fears and anxieties. Most such clinics now have units devoted to the treatment of the fears of children, in addition to those devoted to the treatment of adults' fears. There are three obvious reasons for this proliferation of treatment services. One is the fact that when programs for reducing the fears and anxieties of children are offered, adults make very good use of these programs (e.g., Albano, 1996; Giebenhain, 1985; Peterson & Shigetomi, 1981). A second reason is that theorists are now seeing children's fears and anxieties as far more insidious and deleterious than previously thought (e.g., Albano, Chorpita, & Barlow, 1996; Jacobs & Nadel, 1985). And a third reason is that large numbers of child therapists are apparently giving some credence to the findings from the more recent epidemiological studies and surveys (e.g., Albano, 1996). As a consequence of these and other unidentified forces, the fears and anxieties of children are now being more assiduously studied and aggressively treated than ever (Bernstein & Borchardt, 1991; Kendall et al., 1992; Last, 1988). All of this suggests to us that we would be unwise to dismiss outright the fears and anxieties of children as trivial and harmless.

In sum, fears and anxieties are quite common among children of all ages. They tend to vary in their exact expression as a function of age; in their exact number as a function of age and gender; and in their exact foci as a function of age, gender, ethnic affiliation, and socioeconomic status. The appearance of a severe fear reaction to one type of stimulus situation tends to be accompanied by a severe fear of another type of situation, a mood disturbance of depression, and a select subset of disruptive behaviors. How persistent and how serious the many fears and anxieties are have yet to be well established. Long thought of as short-lived and innocuous, children's many fears and anxieties have begun revealing themselves as being much more enduring and debilitating. Given this changing picture of the course and seriousness of children's fears and anxieties, the most cautious approach would be to treat all presenting cases. This may not, however, be the most judicious and efficacious tack to take with a given child. Stimulus and familial considerations may advise a slightly different course of action, such as that of refraining from treating the child, or treating a family member other than the fearful child. The nature and implications of these two classes of considerations are discussed below.

Characteristics of the Fear Context

Earlier, we have defined "fears and anxieties" as collections of reactions to a perceived threat. Given this definition, the objective dangers posed by the stimulus situation are critical in determining whether or not a child's fear reactions constitute a problem, and, in turn, in determining whether or not a child's fear reactions warrant treatment. Perceptions of threat and responses of alarm that are in accord with the objective menace of the stimulus situation are seen as rational and adaptive; those that are in discord with the objective menace of the stimulus situation are seen as irrational and maladaptive (e.g., Marks, 1969; Miller et al., 1974; Ollendick & Francis, 1988).

Because this question involves a developing child, it is perhaps best that a developmental perspective be taken to judge the degree of mismatch between the perceived and actual dangers presented by the feared situation (Cicchetti, 1984, 1993). Children of different ages have different processes of reasoning and different repertoires of skills. It stands to reason, then, that the same stimulus situation may hold very different demands and threats for children of very different ages. Estimation of a stimulus situation's objective danger should therefore be carried out from the vantage point of the developing child, and not from the vantage point of the mature adult (e.g., parent, therapist). More to the point, this estimation of threat should be carried out from the perspective of the normative child for the age group in question. And this age-specific threat should serve as the backdrop against which the rationality–irrationality of the child's perceptions of threat and the adaptiveness–maladaptiveness of the child's responses of alarm are appraised.[6]

Characteristics of the Family

The fears and anxieties of family members are also a factor in whether or not to treat the fears and anxieties of a given child. Of the many studies that have examined the relationship between maternal anxiety and child anxiety, the vast majority have found considerable correspondence between the two (e.g., Bernstein & Garfinkel, 1988; Frick, Silverthorn, & Evans, 1994; Last, Hersen, Kazdin, Francis, & Grubb, 1987; Muris, Steerneman, Merkelbach, & Meesters, 1996; Peterson & Brownlee-Dufeck, 1984; Winer, 1982). A portion of this evidence for a positive correlation between the fear reactions of the mother and the fear reactions of the child comes from treatment outcome studies. In several instances, incidental or intentional treatment of mothers' fears occurred in conjunction with programmed treatment of their children's fears. And in those instances, fluctuations in the mothers' fear reactions were found to mirror the changes in their children's fear reactions.

For example, Peterson and Shigetomi (1981) trained fearful children in the use of several techniques for coping with anxiety and pain. Among the techniques taught were comforting self-talk, cue-controlled relaxation, and pleasant imagery. Though the mothers of the children did not themselves receive any instructions in the use of coping techniques, they did actively assist in the training of their children in the use of these techniques. That is, the mothers coached the children in proper execution of the skills, monitored the children's practice of the skills, and prompted the children as to when to draw upon the skills. As an "unexpected" outcome, the mothers reported reductions in their own anxiety and increments in their own self-confidence, and these changes paralleled the changes observed in their children's reactions to the feared situation. In a systematic replication of the Peterson and Shigetomi (1981) study, Zastowny, Kirschenbaum, and Meng (1981) had mothers undergo treatment for their own anxiety in addition to assisting in the treatment of their children's anxiety. Again, decrements in the children's fear reactions to the target situation were accompanied by decrements in the mothers' fear reactions to the same situation.

Though less researched than maternal anxiety, sibling anxiety has also been linked to the fears and anxieties of young children (Bernstein & Garfinkel, 1988; Winer, 1982). Observing an older sibling receiving treatment for his or her fears and anxieties has been shown to have a beneficial effect on the fears and anxieties of the younger brother or sister (e.g., Ghose, Giddon, Shiere, & Fogels, 1969). Having siblings accompany a child into a feared situation has also been shown to decrease the child's anxiety with respect to that situation (e.g., Hawley, McCorkle, Witteman, & Van Ostenberg, 1974). And having siblings who have had repeated, presumably unpleasant experiences with a particular stimulus has been found to increase the likelihood of a child's developing a fear reaction to the same stimulus (e.g., Bailey, Talbot, & Taylor, 1973).

Combined, these findings suggest that mothers and siblings exert considerable influence over the fears and anxieties of children. Furthermore, these findings imply that in certain cases it may be more expedient and permanent to treat the fears and anxieties of the mother and the siblings than to treat the fears and anxieties of the identified child directly (e.g., Klesges, Malott, & Ugland, 1984). Such treatment of maternal and sibling anxiety may eliminate the need for treatment of the identified child's anxiety, or may serve as a precondition to efficacious and enduring treatment of the identified child's anxiety.[7]

TREATMENT FOCUS AND DEVELOPMENT

Once we have judged the fears and anxieties of a child to be problematic, our next task is to specify the focus and nature of our treatment. We do so by drawing upon our theory of children's fears and anxieties. Theory highlights for us the mechanisms that may be responsible for the origin and maintenance of fears and anxieties, and intimates to us the actions that may alter these mechanisms for the better. There is, however, no one behavioral theory of children's fears and anxieties. There are, in fact, many different accounts of the acquisition and perpetuation of children's fears and anxieties, all of which have emanated from the behavioral paradigm. In this section, we describe the seven most prominent of these behavioral theories.[8]

Respondent Conditioning Theory

According to the original formulation by Watson and Morgan (1917), fears and anxieties are acquired by means of Pavlovian conditioning. An unconditioned stimulus that reliably evokes the unconditioned response of fear follows in close proximity a conditioned stimulus that initially does not evoke such a response. Upon repeated pairings, the conditioned stimulus alone comes to elicit fear. Stimuli to which fear is displayed but for which there have been no direct pairings with an unconditioned stimulus are explained by the principle of stimulus generalization.

Though the demonstrations of fear induction through classical conditioning are numerous, so too are the criticisms of the respondent conditioning theory (e.g., Delprato & McGlynn, 1984; Eysenck, 1968, 1976; Rachman, 1977, 1978). Several attempts to replicate Watson and

Rayner's (1920) results have failed to do so when objects other than a white rat have been used as conditioned stimuli (e.g., Bregman, 1934; English, 1929; Valentine, 1930). These studies, along with more recent ones (e.g., Öhman, 1979), call into question the theory's equipotentiality premise—the premise that all neutral stimuli have an equal probability of becoming feared objects via respondent conditioning. Available data clearly show that this is not the case.

Other data pose other problems for the respondent conditioning theory. For example, according to the theory, trauma (e.g., the unconditioned stimulus) is crucial to the establishment of a fear reaction. In many cases of fears and anxieties, however, the individuals report no recollection whatsoever of a trauma (e.g., Rachman, 1977; Rimm, Janda, Lancaster, Nahl, & Ditmar, 1977). Moreover, the distribution of common fears and anxieties among children and adults is contrary to what one would predict from the theory (Rachman, 1977). Children have more traumatic interactions with needles, fire, and tricycles than they do with darkness, dogs, and imaginary creatures; yet fears of the latter are far more prevalent than fears of the former.

The respondent conditioning theory is also at a loss to explain how children develop fears and anxieties without directly encountering the conditioned and unconditioned stimuli. The theory deems such direct exposure necessary for the formulation of a fear reaction, but there is considerable evidence that simply observing another display a fear reaction may lead to the development of a fear reaction (e.g., Bandura, 1969, 1977b; Rachman, 1977). Finally, persistence of fear reactions poses yet another problem for the respondent conditioning theory. According to the theory, there should be a gradual diminution of the fear response to the repeated presentation of the conditioned stimulus in the absence of the unconditioned stimulus. From our discussion of the temporal stability of children's fears and anxieties, it is clear that not all fear reactions diminish upon repeated presentations of the conditioned stimulus without the unconditioned stimulus.

Though now much maligned, the respondent conditioning theory did stimulate our earliest efforts at the treatment of children's fears and anxieties (Jones, 1924a, 1924b; Wolpe, 1958). And these early efforts did lead to the formation of the therapeutic procedure known as systematic desensitization (Wolpe, 1961)—a procedure that for many years was the treatment of choice for maladaptive fears and anxieties.

Revised Respondent Conditioning Theories

The respondent conditioning theory of fears and anxieties has undergone a number of revisions in order to overcome the weaknesses just described. The most notable of these are the revised formulations of Rachman (1977, 1990, 1991) and Seligman (1970, 1971). In Rachman's (1977, 1990, 1991) revision of the model, there are three possible routes by which fears and anxieties can be acquired: respondent conditioning, modeling, and verbal instruction. The model does away with the equipotentiality premise and inserts in its place the notion of hereditary determinants of fear—the notion that some stimuli are more biologically predisposed to becoming fear objects than are others.

This notion that different stimuli have different potential as fear objects is the cornerstone of Seligman's (1970, 1971) revised respondent conditioning model, preparedness theory. According to preparedness theory, fears and anxieties both to stimuli of evolutionary significance and to those of evolutionary insignificance are acquired by the same general process of respondent conditioning. The two classes of fear reactions are thought to differ, though, in the speed with which they are acquired and the speed with which they are extinguished. Fear reactions to stimuli of evolutionary significance presumably are more easily established, severe, enduring, and resistant to treatment than are fear reactions to stimuli of evolutionary insignificance.

Though preparedness theory offers us an explanation for the unusual distribution of children's fears and anxieties, it has few clinical and experimental data to offer us in support of its major propositions. The work of Öhman and his colleagues (Fredrikson, Hugdahl, & Öhman, 1977; Hugdahl & Öhman, 1977; Öhman, Erikson, & Olofsson, 1975; Öhman, Erixon, & Lofberg, 1975; Öhman, Fredrikson, Hugdahl, & Rimmö, 1976) is a case in point. Pictures of snakes, spiders, mushrooms, and flowers are paired with electric shocks. Conditioned responses to the snakes and spiders develop more quickly and extinguish more slowly than conditioned responses to the mushrooms and flowers. Proponents of the theory attribute the differential rates of acquisition and extinction to differences in biological preparedness. In the phylogenetic history of humans, snakes and spiders were of greater evolutionary significance than mushrooms and flowers; therefore, we humans are more prepared to fear snakes and spiders than we are to fear mushrooms and flowers. The flaw in this line of reasoning, and thus in this line of evidence, is that it is not at all clear which stimuli should be thought of as biologically prepared and which as neutral (Delprato, 1980; McNally, 1995). For those stimuli thought to be biologically prepared, the clinical data are not at all in line with the theory's predictions (DeSilva, Rachman, & Seligman, 1977; McNally, 1987; Rachman & Seligman, 1976). Fear reactions to stimuli thought to be biologically prepared do not appear to be any more severe, enduring, or intractable than fear reactions to stimuli thought to be neutral.

Two-Factor Theory

Classical two-factor theory posits both respondent and instrumental conditioning in the origin and maintenance of fears and anxieties (Mowrer, 1939, 1947, 1960). Respondent conditioning is involved in the acquisition of fears and anxieties; instrumental conditioning is involved in their maintenance. Neutral objects and events are paired with an unconditioned stimulus, whereupon the neutral stimuli alone come to evoke visceral arousal (i.e., a fear response). This fear response gives rise to the instrumental behavior of avoidance, which leads to a reduction in visceral arousal, thereby reinforcing the act of avoidance and enhancing the probability of its recurrence.

Classical two-factor theory has had considerable impact on the practice of behavior therapy vis-à-vis fears and anxieties. This impact notwithstanding, it has come under a great deal of criticism through the years (e.g., Bandura, 1969; Rachman, 1976; Seligman & Johnston, 1973). The most pertinent of these criticisms centers around the presumed role that fear plays in mediating avoidance and that fear reduction plays in reinforcing avoidance. From the theory, it follows that fear is necessary for the instigation of avoidance, and that fear reduction is necessary for the acquisition and perpetuation of avoidance. However, numerous findings call into question this hypothesized relationship between fear and avoidance behavior (see Bandura, 1969; Delprato & McGlynn, 1984). It has been demonstrated repeatedly that avoidance behavior can be acquired in the absence of fear (e.g., Auld, 1951; Wenzel & Jeffrey, 1967; Wynne & Soloman, 1955); that avoidance behavior can persist in the face of diminished respondent fear (e.g., Black, 1958; Brush, 1957; Solomon, Kamin, & Wynne, 1953); and that avoidance behavior can decrease in the face of undiminished respondent fear (e.g., Leitenberg, Agras, Butz, & Wincze, 1971).

Approach–Withdrawal Theory

To overcome the shortcomings described above, classical two-factor theory has undergone several revisions. Delprato and McGlynn (1984) have organized these various revisions into a loose conceptual framework, which they call approach–withdrawal theory. The theory is in essence a compilation of the views of such behavior theorists as D'Amato (1970), Denny (1971, 1976), Dinsmoor (1954, 1977), Gray (1971), Hernnstein (1969), Keehn (1966), and Schoenfeld (1950).

According to approach–withdrawal theory, fear acquisition begins with the pairing of a neutral stimulus and an unconditioned stimulus. During early trials, there is escape or withdrawal from the aversive stimulus. Upon repeated trials, the offset of the unconditioned stimulus is followed by a state of relaxation or relief, along with approach to a nonaversive area. Through backchaining, approach to the nonaversive area comes to occur before the onset of the unconditioned stimulus; thus, we have the establishment of avoidance behavior. The neutral or conditioned stimulus does not evoke fear, but instead functions as a cue for relaxation and approach behavior. When extinction is instituted (i.e., nonpresentation of the unconditioned stimulus), relaxation backchains to the conditioned stimulus, whereupon it competes with withdrawal and culminates in the elimination of the avoidance response (Delprato & McGlynn, 1984).

In approach–withdrawal theory, we have a solution to the dilemma of the persistence of avoidance behavior in the face of diminished respondent fear. Avoidance behavior is not seen as being maintained by fear reduction (as it is in classical two-factor theory), but is seen as being maintained by relaxation and approach, which are conceptualized as response-contingent safety cues. The presence or absence of respondent fear is therefore inconsequential to the occurrence or nonoccurrence of avoidance, for it is contingent approach to safety that sustains the avoidance response (Delprato & McGlynn, 1984; Denny, 1971).

An important aspect of approach–withdrawal theory is the prominence it assigns to positive reinforcement in the acquisition and maintenance of fears and anxieties. Orthodox respondent conditioning theory, revised respondent conditioning theories, and two-factor theory ascribe no such role to positive reinforcement. For years, though, our clinical observations have been telling us that in some instances of fears and anxieties, operant factors have been at work (e.g., Lazarus, Davison, & Polefka, 1965). In approach–withdrawal theory, we finally have a well-formulated model of fears and anxieties that recognizes their contribution. In other words, we now have a well-formulated model that promotes the application of contingency management procedures in the treatment of children's fears and anxieties.

Self-Efficacy Theory

According to Bandura (1977a, 1978, 1982), all fear and anxiety reactions are mediated by a central cognitive construct-self-efficacy expectations, or the conviction that one can interact adaptively with the feared object. These expectations emanate from four types of experiences: personal encounters with the target stimulus, vicarious encounters with the target stimulus, somatovisceral arousal experiences during encounters with the target stimulus, and verbal persuasion (Bandura, 1977a, 1978).

Perceptions of self-efficacy are thought to dictate the exact expression of fear and anxiety. The stronger the perceptions of self-efficacy, the less subjective distress, performance impairment, and autonomic agitation vis-à-vis the feared object. The stronger the perceptions of self-efficacy, the greater the perseverance and coping in the face of obstacles vis-à-vis the feared object. And the stronger the perceptions of self-efficacy, the greater the generalization of adaptive behavior to objects and situations beyond the feared object and feared situation (Bandura, 1977a, 1978).

Within this framework, treatment takes the form of modifying the fearful child's self-efficacy expectations. There are four general strategies for altering these expectations: performance accomplishments, vicarious experiences, emotional arousal techniques, and verbal exhortation (Bandura, 1977a). Performance-based treatments are presumed to be the most effective of the four strategies, for they are presumed to provide the most veridical information regarding performance capabilities. The other three strategies provide less dependable information regarding performance capabilities; therefore, they are less effective in altering perceptions of self-efficacy, which in turn makes them less effective in altering the fears and anxieties of children.

Bioinformational Theory

Lang's (1977, 1979, 1984) bioinformational theory of emotion also has fear being mediated by a cognitive construct—an affective image. The image is composed of stimulus, response, and semantic propositions. Stimulus propositions are units of information concerning the features of the feared object or event; response propositions are units of information concerning the subjective, motor, and physiological components of the fear reaction; and semantic propositions are units of information concerning the meaning embodied in the stimulus–response sequence. When accessed and activated from the long-term store, the affective image dictates the exact form the fear reaction takes.

From the perspective of bioinformational theory, the treatment of fears and anxieties is a two-stage process: evocation of the affective image, followed by reorganization of its propositional network. The affective image may be evoked through either *in vivo* or *in vitro* exposure to the feared stimulus. Once accessed from the long-term store, the image becomes amenable to change. It is at this point where the fear reaction too becomes amenable to change, for it is the affective image that mediates the expression of the fear reaction. The propositional network or the image is altered by providing new and more adaptive information regarding the properties of the feared stimulus, the responses to this stimulus, and the meaning of these responses to the stimulus. This new stimulus, response, and semantic information may be presented through any one of several different media or combinations of media. Among these are physiological feedback, verbal instruction, and kinesthetic feedback from direct and vicarious encounters with the feared stimulus.

Atop this theoretical foundation, Foa and Kozak (1986) have erected a promising framework for the treatment of fears and anxieties through the use of exposure-based procedures. Useful guidelines are offered with respect to the procedural features: evocative medium, content of evocative information, degree of attention, and duration of exposure. Conditions interfering with effective exposure-based treatment are also identified (e.g., cognitive avoidance, depression).

Integrative Model

Drawing upon his extensive experience as a clinical researcher and practitioner, Barlow (1988) has proposed an integrative framework for understanding and treating the maladaptive fears and anxieties of adults and children. Within this framework, maladaptive fears and anxieties arise from the interaction of three major sets of forces: biological vulnerabilities, which predispose the individual to heightened sensitivity and heightened responsivity to novel or stressful stimuli; negative life events, which may be experienced directly or vicariously; and psychological vulnerabilities, which include a limited sense of personal control, a restricted attention focus, and a marked propensity for catastrophizing.

Given this view of fears and anxieties as resulting from a combination of behavioral action potentials and maladaptive cognitive processes, the model cites three elements as necessary for successful treatment. The first of these is the acquisition of new action tendencies toward the feared stimulus—action tendencies to replace the existing behavioral response (e.g., flight, avoidance) that is neurologically encoded. The second is the formation of a perception of personal mastery and control over the threat associated with the feared stimulus. And the third is the redirection of attention away from internal cues that distract the individual from external cues helpful in managing the stimulus situation. Other suggested targets for intervention are the reduction of exaggerated or apprehensive cognitions, the reduction of elevated physiological responding, the development of coping skills, and the enhancement of social support.

Summary

At present, no one behavioral theory of children's fears and anxieties has emerged as dominant. In large part this is because no one behavioral theory has been able to account for the emerging picture of the ecosystem of the fearful and anxious child. It is an ecosystem for which the following have been tentatively identified: genetic and familial patterns, mother–child interaction patterns, parenting style, and information-seeking and -processing style. A number of twin and family studies point to a genetic component in the development of children's fears and anxieties (Carey & Gottesman, 1981; Weissman, 1985, 1993). The twin studies conducted to date show significantly higher concordance rates of anxiety disorders among monozygotic twins than among dizygotic twins (e.g., Slater & Shields, 1969; Torgersen, 1978, 1983, 1985, 1993). And the family studies conducted to date show a high degree of association between the anxiety disorders of children and those of their parents (e.g., Cohen, Badal, Kilpatrick, Reed, & White, 1951; Crowe, Noyes, Pauls, & Slymen, 1983; Last, Hersen, Kazdin, Orvaschel, & Perrin, 1991; Noyes, Clancy, Crowe, Hoenk, & Slymen, 1978; Weissman, Leckman, Merikangas, Gammon, & Prusoff, 1984).

Studies of the family interaction patterns of anxious and fearful children show the mothers to be overprotective and restrictive in their general dealings with the children (e.g., Bernstein & Garfinkel, 1988; Brown, 1979; Kagan & Moss, 1962; LaFrenière & Dumas, 1992; Lewis & Michalson, 1983; Messer & Beidel, 1994), the parents to be overly lax and inconsistent in their general disciplining of the children (e.g., Allan & Hodgson, 1968; Sarnat, Peri, Nitzan, & Perlberg, 1972; Venham, Murray, & Gaulin-Kremer, 1979), and the parents to be agitated and inept in their handling of childhood crisis situations (e.g., Blount, Sturges, & Powers, 1990; Kashani et al., 1990; Melamed & Siegel, 1985; Robinson, 1978).

Considerable research also points to a well-defined behavioral disposition and a preferred social information processing style on the part of fearful and anxious children. The former is expressed as the consistent display of upset and withdrawal vis-à-vis novel or unfamiliar situations (e.g., Kagan, Reznick, Clarke, Snidman, & Garcia-Coll, 1984; Rosenbaum et al., 1992). And the latter is expressed as a marked preference for information avoidance as opposed to information seeking vis-à-vis the environment (e.g., Burstein & Meichenbaum, 1979; Knight et al., 1979; Unger, 1982).

None of the behavioral theories described here adequately incorporate these genetic, family, and dispositional variables into their accounts of the development of children's fears and anxieties. They may need to do so in order for us to achieve a fuller and richer understanding of the development and maintenance of children's fears and anxieties. They are, however, the theories that have given rise to an abundant supply of treatments. In the next section, we review the particulars and potency of each of these treatments.

BEHAVIORAL TREATMENTS

Our coverage of the major behavioral interventions for children's fears and anxieties begins with a description of each of the treatments, followed by a review of the research on the effectiveness of the procedure. Though not comprehensive, our review of the research literature does span the years 1924 to 1996 and does draw from over 50 professional journals and books. A summary listing of the major treatment groupings and their major elements is provided in Table 5.2.

Systematic Desensitization and Its Variants

As a treatment for children's fears and anxieties, systematic desensitization consists of three basic steps: (1) The child is trained in deep muscle relaxation; (2) the child rank-orders from least distressing to most distressing several situations involving the feared stimulus; and (3) the child imagines each one of the situations while in a relaxed state (see Hatzenbuehler & Schroeder, 1978; Morris & Kratochwill, 1983a, 1983b). This pairing of a state antagonistic to anxiety (i.e., relaxation) with imaginal representations of the feared stimulus begins with the least distressing situation and ends with the most distressing one. Progression from one hierarchy scene to another occurs when the child is able to imagine the feared situation and remain relatively calm.

Many variations of this basic procedure have been employed in the treatment of children's fears and anxieties. Game playing, storytelling, feeding, maternal contact, therapist contact, and anger have all been used in the place of relaxation as the anxiety-antagonistic state. Slides, photographs, and toys of the feared stimulus have all been used in the place of imaginal representations of the feared stimulus. Whenever the actual feared stimulus has been used rather than some substitute, the treatment has been referred to as "*in vivo* desensitization." And whenever the imaginal scenario of the child confronting the feared stimulus has included support from the child's favorite superhero, the treatment has been referred to as "emotive imagery" (e.g., Lazarus & Abramovitz, 1962).

Table 5.3 in the Appendix to this chapter presents a summary of the procedures and findings of 44 studies that have investigated the effectiveness of desensitization and its variants. Collectively, over 600 children were treated for over 16

TABLE 5.2.   Six Major Groupings of Behavioral Treatments for Children's Fears and Anxieties

Treatment category	Techniques included	General description
Desensitization	Imaginal desensitization *In vivo* desensitization Emotive imagery Self-control desensitization	An anxiety-antagonistic state is paired with representations of the feared stimulus in a graduated, systematic fashion.
Prolonged exposure	Imaginal flooding *In vivo* flooding Reinforced practice Response prevention Implosion	Intense, extended exposure to representations of the feared stimulus is carried out.
Modeling	Live modeling Symbolic modeling Covert modeling Participant modeling	Opportunities to observe another person interacting adaptively with the feared stimulus are provided.
Contingency management	Shaping Negative reinforcement Time out Response cost	A reward is provided for interacting with the feared stimulus, or a reward is rescinded for refusing to interact with the feared stimulus, or both.
Self-management	Self-monitoring Self-instructional training Thought stopping Cue-controlled relaxation Pleasant imagery	Adaptive ways of appraising an upcoming feared situation, viewing an ongoing feared situation, and/or responding physiologically to a feared situation are taught.
Combined treatments	All of the above	Some combination of the five procedures above is offered.

different types of fears and anxiety reactions. The children ranged in age from 11½ months to 20 years, and the fear reactions ranged in duration from 2 weeks to 9 years. Among the most frequently treated fears and anxieties were those related to school, nighttime, small animals, separation, and test taking.

The vast majority of the studies had as their focus the effects of either systematic desensitization or *in vivo* desensitization; a small number of the studies had as their focus the effects of either emotive imagery or some combination of systematic desensitization, *in vivo* desensitization, and other behavioral treatments. Uncontrolled case studies outnumbered true experiments by nearly 3:1. Both types of investigations, though, consistently found systematic desensitization and its variants to be highly effective in reducing the fears and anxieties of children. These positive effects were evidenced across all three components of the fear reactions—subjective, motor, and physiological—and were maintained across intervals ranging in duration from 3 months to 2 years. Though limited, some evidence was also obtained for the

generalization of these positive effects to other settings and other problem behaviors (e.g., enuresis).

Prolonged Exposure and Its Variants

In prolonged exposure treatments, the child is asked from the outset to confront a threatening version of the feared stimulus, either real or imagined. This immediate, intense, and extended exposure to the feared stimulus may take one of four forms: imaginal flooding, *in vivo* flooding, implosion, and reinforced practice. In imaginal flooding, the child first constructs a list of situations involving the feared stimulus and rank-orders these situations from least distressing to most distressing. Beginning with an intermediate scene, the child imagines each situation, leading up to and including the most distressing one. For each situation, the child continues imagining the scene until he or she is no longer frightened of it. Successive scenes are handled in an identical fashion (e.g., Hersen, 1968; Saigh, 1986, 1987). Very similar in format to imaginal flooding, *in vivo* flooding has the child construct a hierarchy of anxiety-eliciting situations involving the feared stimulus, select a situation at an intermediate point in the hierarchy, and confront the situation and all successive situations in the hierarchy in a systematic fashion. Most critical is that these situations the child confronts are not images, photographs, or slides, but actual ones involving the actual feared stimulus (e.g., Kandel, Ayllon, & Rosenbaum, 1977; Kolko, 1984; Menzies & Clarke, 1993).

Of the two remaining prolonged exposure techniques, one (implosion) makes use of images of the feared stimulus; the other (reinforced practice) makes use of authentic versions of the feared stimulus. In implosion, the child imagines an unrealistic yet nevertheless horrific scenario involving the feared stimulus. The scenario is imagined again and again until the child ceases to be perturbed by it (e.g., Ollendick & Gruen, 1972; Smith & Sharpe, 1970). In reinforced practice, the child is rewarded for remaining in the presence of the feared stimulus for progressively longer periods of time. Initially, the child remains in the presence of the feared stimulus only for as long as is tolerable. Once this tolerance threshold is determined, the child is rewarded for remaining progressively longer in the presence of the feared stimulus (e.g., Leitenberg & Callahan, 1973; Luiselli, 1978).

When the anxious child is suffering from obsessions and accompanying compulsions, a technique known as response prevention is almost invariably employed in conjunction with one of the aforementioned exposure procedures (March, 1995). Essentially, the technique calls either for the child to refrain voluntarily from displaying the ritualistic behaviors or for the treatment staff to restrain the child physically from engaging in the ritualistic behaviors (e.g., Bolton & Turner, 1984; Zikis, 1983). With either variation, the intent is the same—to block the avoidance behaviors until anxiety dissipates (Dar & Greist, 1992).

Table 5.4 in the Appendix presents a summary of the procedures and findings of 21 studies that have examined the effectiveness of the various prolonged exposure treatments. Across all studies, over 120 children were treated for over 13 different types of fears and anxieties. The children ranged in age from 3 to 16 years, and their fears ranged in duration from 2 weeks to 10 years. Of the different types of fears and anxieties targeted, the most frequently treated were those related to school, physical harm, and contamination.

The vast majority of the studies had as their focus the therapeutic effects of imaginal and *in vivo* flooding. Though few of the studies were true experiments, nearly all found the four exposure treatments effective in reducing the fears and anxieties of children. Evidence of effectiveness was found across all three components of the fear reaction; evidence of maintenance of treatment benefits was found across intervals ranging from 1 month to 8 years; and evidence of generalization of these benefits was found across untreated settings and untreated behaviors.

Modeling and Its Variants

All forms of modeling therapies for children's fears and anxieties call for the observation of another person interacting adaptively with the feared stimulus (cf. Morris & Kratochwill, 1983a, 1983b). They differ from one another primarily in the directness of these observations and the rehearsal of the responses depicted in the observations. In live modeling, the fearful child directly observes a child or an adult interacting appropriately with the feared stimulus (e.g., Jones, 1924b; Ritter, 1968; White & Davis, 1974). In symbolic modeling, the fearful child observes a filmed or slide presentation of a child or an adult interacting appropriately with the feared stimulus (e.g., Bandura & Menlove, 1968; Ginther & Roberts, 1982; Hill, Liebert, & Mott, 1968; Melamed & Siegel, 1975). In covert modeling, the fearful child imagines a child or an adult interacting appropriately with the feared stimulus (e.g., Chertock & Bornstein, 1979). And in participant modeling, the fearful child first observes (either directly or indirectly) adaptive responding toward the feared stimulus, then practices duplicating those adaptive responses. This practice in adaptive responding is typically supplemented with guided instruction, support, and feedback from the therapist (e.g., Bandura, Blanchard, & Ritter, 1969; Lewis, 1974; Matson, 1983).

Each of the four major types of modeling therapies has a number of subtypes based upon the nature and number of models employed. The single-model subtype makes use of only one child or adult in its demonstration of adaptive behavior toward the feared stimulus; the multiple-models subtype uses several different children or adults (e.g., Bandura & Menlove, 1968). In the similar-model(s) subtype, the fearful child observes a child or children of like age, gender, and race, whereas in the dissimilar-model(s) subtype, the fearful child observes a person or persons of discrepant age, gender, or race (e.g., Weissbrod & Bryan, 1973). The mastery-model(s) subtype has a person fearlessly interacting with the feared stimulus, whereas the coping-model(s) subtype has a person uneasily but successfully interacting with the feared stimulus (e.g., Klorman, Hilpert, Michael, LaGana, & Sveen, 1980; Kornhaber & Schroeder, 1975). Combinations of these six subtypes make up still other subtypes for each of the four major modeling treatments.

Table 5.5 in the Appendix provides a listing of the features and findings of 34 studies that have examined the effectiveness of modeling treatments for children's fears and anxieties. As a whole, the studies treated over 1,300 children suffering from 11 different types of fears and anxieties. The children ranged in age from $1\frac{3}{4}$ years to 17 years, and the anxiety reactions ranged in duration from several days to 16 months. Most common among the 11 different types of fears treated were those associated with small animals, dental procedures, and medical procedures.

Approximately 50% of the studies had as their focus the effects of symbolic modeling, 20% the effects of participant modeling, and 30% the relative effects of two or more of the different modeling therapies. Virtually all of the studies employed experimental designs in their tests of the effects of the modeling therapies, and virtually all of the studies found the modeling therapies to be highly effective in reducing the fears and anxieties of children. Reductions were evidenced across all three of the components of the fear state, across settings not targeted in treatment, and across problem behaviors not addressed in treatment. Maintenance of these reductions was evidenced across intervals ranging from 5 months to 1 year.

When compared to the control conditions of no treatment and an attention placebo, the modeling treatments proved to be consistently more effective. And when compared to one another, the treatment of participant modeling proved to be consistently more effective than live, symbolic, and covert modeling. Few consistent findings, however, emerged from the comparisons among the six principal subtypes.

Several of the studies looked at the role that several child and parental characteristics may play in mediating treatment outcome. Two variables that were found to bear no relationship to treatment outcomes were the therapeutic expectancies of the child (Mann, 1972) and the gender of the child (Bandura & Menlove, 1968; Ginther & Roberts, 1982; Ritter, 1968; Roberts, Wurtle, Boone, Ginther, & Elkins, 1981). Five variables that were found to bear a relationship to treatment outcome were the age of the child, the self-control of the child, the defensiveness of the child, the similarity of the child to the model, and the anxiety of the parent toward the feared stimulus. Specifically, the older the child, the more likely the child was to benefit from treatment (e.g., Gilbert et al., 1982; Melamed & Siegel, 1975; Peterson, Schultheis, Ridley-Johnson, Miller, & Tracy, 1984). The child high in self-control and low in defensiveness was also more likely to benefit from treatment than the child low in self-control and high in defensiveness (Klingman, Melamed, Cuthbert, & Hermecz, 1984). The more closely the child resembled the model in terms of age, fear level, and previous experience with the feared stimulus, the greater the probability of a positive treatment outcome (e.g., Klingman et al., 1984; Kornhaber & Schroeder, 1975; Melamed, Meyer, Gee, & Soule, 1976; Melamed et al., 1978). Finally, the less fearful the parent was toward the stimulus the child feared, the more likely the child was to benefit from modeling therapy (Peterson et al., 1984).

Information on these and other mediators of treatment outcome is most pertinent to the task of treatment selection. Choosing the optimum treatment for a given fearful child should be based upon such information, along with information on other conceptual and practical considerations. Precisely how these various bodies of information are assimilated, integrated, and utilized is discussed in a later section on treatment selection.

Contingency Management

Treatment of children's fears and anxieties by contingency management calls for the manipulation of the external events that follow the children's reactions. This manipulation of environmental consequences has taken many different forms (cf. Gelfand, 1978; Morris & Kratochwill, 1983a; Richards & Siegel, 1978). In some instances, the child has received a reward for interacting with the feared stimulus; in others, the child has had a reward rescinded for refusing to interact with the feared stimulus; and in still others, the child has been subjected to some combination of the two (e.g., Ayllon, Smith, & Rogers, 1970; Boer & Sipprelle, 1970). On some occasions, rewards have been dispensed for progressively bolder steps toward the feared stimulus; on other occasions, penalties have been imposed for failing to take such bold steps; and on still other occasions, some combination of the two sets of contingencies has been applied (e.g., Luiselli, 1978).

Table 5.6 in the Appendix offers a summary of the features and findings of the 19 studies that have examined the effectiveness of contingency management procedures. Across all studies, 59 children were treated for 10 different types of fear and anxiety reactions. The children ranged in age from 3 to 15 years, and the fears ranged in duration from 1 month to 5 years. Of the 10 different types of fears and anxieties treated, the most common were those in regard to school and social situations.

Virtually all of the 19 studies had as their focus the therapeutic effects of contingency management per se, with the sole exception having as its focus the relative therapeutic effects of two different types of contingency management procedures. Approximately half of the studies were controlled in nature, and almost all of the studies reported successful fear reduction through contingency management treatments. Reductions were evidenced across subjective, motor, and physiological fear responses, and these reductions were evidenced across nontreated settings and nontreated fear stimuli. Maintenance of these reductions was evidenced across intervals ranging from 1 month to 1 year.

Self-Management

In self-management treatments for children's fears and anxieties, the focus is on manipulation of the children's subjective and physiological reactions to the feared stimuli (cf. Melamed, Klingman, & Siegel, 1984; Morris & Kratochwill, 1983a). To manipulate the children's subjective reactions to the feared stimuli, the children are taught adaptive ways of appraising an upcoming feared situation, adaptive ways of thinking about an ongoing feared situation, or both (e.g., Fox & Houston, 1981; Peterson & Shigetomi, 1981). Adaptive ways of appraising an upcoming feared situation generally consist of viewing and construing the situation as less threatening; adaptive ways of thinking about an ongoing fear situation usually consist of saying to oneself that one can effectively handle the situation. To manipulate the children's physiological reactions to the feared stimuli, the children are typically instructed in deep muscle relaxation, creative visualization, or both (e.g.,

Bankart & Bankart, 1983; Peterson & Shigetomi, 1981). The training in deep muscle relaxation generally entails learning how to relax one's muscles on cue; the training in creative visualization usually involves learning how to conjure up images of peacefulness and tranquility.[9]

To date, 19 studies have examined the effects of self-management treatments for children's fears and anxieties. A summary of their major features and findings is presented in Table 5.7 in the Appendix. Together, the studies examined over 600 children and 11 different fears. The children ranged in age from $2\frac{1}{2}$ years to 16 years, and the fears ranged in duration from 2 weeks to 3 years. The most common types of fears addressed were those of darkness, dental procedures, and test taking. Experimental designs were used in 15 of the 19 studies, with the majority of the studies finding the self-management treatments superior to no treatment or an attention placebo. This superiority was evidenced across all three fear response components and was maintained across intervals ranging from 1 week to 3 years in length. In a few of these studies, the spread of these treatment benefits to untreated problem behaviors and to untreated settings was also observed (Eisen & Silverman, 1991; Kanfer et al., 1975).

Several of the studies tested the validity of a number of the child and parental variables thought to be possible mediators of treatment outcome. Among the child variables tested, no support was obtained for either age or gender as a mediator of treatment outcome (Nocella & Kaplan, 1982; Rosenfarb & Hayes, 1984; Siegel & Peterson, 1980). Support was, however, obtained for the variables of defensiveness and trait anxiety. As expected, the more defensive the child was, the less the child was found to benefit from self-management treatment (Fox & Houston, 1981). Not expected, though, was the finding that the higher the trait anxiety of the child, the less the child profited from self-management treatment (Fox & Houston, 1981). The sole parental variable examined was that of maternal anxiety toward the stimulus feared by the child, and it was found to bear a negative relationship to treatment outcome (Peterson & Shigetomi, 1981).

Combined Treatments

Various combinations of the aforementioned five procedures have been used to treat the fears and anxieties of children. These combined interventions differ from one another in the number of techniques included and the order in which the techniques are implemented. Examples of two-, three-, and four-technique combinations are described in the paragraphs below.

An example of a two-technique combined intervention is Graziano and associates' home-based program for nighttime fears (Graziano & Mooney, 1980; Graziano, Mooney, Huber, & Ignasiak, 1979). Mixing elements of self-management with contingency management, the program first calls for training in deep muscle relaxation, pleasant imagery, and courageous self-talk. Children practice each of the three self-control skills each night at bedtime and are rewarded by their parents for how well they perform the skills. Another example of a two-technique combined intervention is Esveldt-Dawson et al. (1982) performance-based program for fear of school and/or strangers. Mixing elements of modeling with contingency management, the program begins with verbal instruction and then moves to actual demonstration in adaptive ways of interacting with the feared stimulus. The children practice duplicating the modeled events and are systematically rewarded for closer approximations to criterion performance.

Three examples of three-technique combined interventions are the programs developed by Miller et al. (1972a); by Jay, Elliot, Ozolins, Olson, and Pruitt (1985); and by Barlow and Seidner (1983). Desensitization, modeling, and contingency management are combined in the first two programs; desensitization, prolonged exposure, and self-management are the components of the third program. The Miller et al. (1972a) program first has parents dispensing rewards for nonfearful responding, then has the child undergoing imaginal desensitization and participant modeling. A slightly different sequencing of these procedures is involved in the Jay et al. (1985) program, where the child is initially trained in emotive imagery, subsequently exposed to a modeling film, and eventually reinforced for courageous behavior while in the actual stimulus situation. In the Barlow and Seidner (1983) program, children frightened of being alone or away from home first receive training in relaxation-based panic management techniques, and then receive instruction in adaptive ways of appraising and behaving in the feared situation. Finally, they venture out into the feared situation for progressively longer periods of time.

Two examples of four-technique combined interventions are the program developed by MacDonald (1975) for the treatment of a fear of

small animals and the program developed by Kendall (1994) for the treatment of an assortment of fears and anxieties. In her treatment of an 11-year-old boy's long-standing fear of dogs, MacDonald (1975) employed two variants of desensitization: one in which the relaxed state was paired with images of the feared object, and one in which the relaxed state was paired with photographs of the feared object. To these two variants of desensitization, she added components of participant modeling, prolonged *in vivo* exposure, and contingency management. And for the final portion of the program, she had the parents rewarding progressively less fearful contact with dogs.

In his treatment of children frightened of separation from significant attachment figures, interaction with similar-age others, or nonspecific social situations, Kendall (1994) instructed children in a variety of techniques across the course of 16 sessions. Initial meetings were devoted to somatic training—teaching the children to discriminate anxious bodily reactions from nonanxious responses and training the children in deep muscle relaxation. The next block of meetings focused on self-instructional training—providing the children with a host of cognitive strategies, such as coping self-talk, verbal self-direction, self-evaluation, and self-reward. The remaining sessions involved graduated imaginal and *in vivo* exposure to the various stressful situations, with the therapist modeling and encouraging the use of the various somatic and cognitive strategies throughout these encounters. Across the course of the weekly sessions, the children were also assigned homework tasks calling for practice in the aforementioned coping techniques and were systematically rewarded for completeing these tasks.

Table 5.8 in the Appendix summarizes the procedures and findings from the 40 studies that have examined the effectiveness of 15 different combined treatments for children's fears and anxieties. Across all studies, over 700 children ranging in age from 3 to 17 years were treated for over 20 different types of fears and anxieties ranging in duration from 2 weeks to 11 years. Of the different types of fear and anxiety reactions treated, the most common were those toward school-related events, darkness, and social situations. Approximately three-fourths of the studies addressed the effects of two-technique treatments, with the remaining one-fourth examining the effects of three- and four-technique interventions.

Virtually all of the 40 investigations, 23 of which were controlled experiments and 17 of which were uncontrolled case reports, found substantial reductions in fear responding with the various compound interventions. These reductions in responding were evidenced across the subjective, motoric, and physiological symptoms of fear and were maintained across intervals ranging from 6 weeks to 4 years. Spread of these treatment benefits was observed across nontreated settings, nontreated fears, and nontreated problem behaviors.

In the many comparisons carried out between combined treatments and no treatment and between combined treatments and attention placebos, only one study failed to find the combined treatments superior to the two control conditions (i.e., Mayer et al., 1971). In the few comparisons carried out between combined treatments and single-technique treatments, the combined interventions tended to be more effective than the single-technique treatments in terms of both immediate and long-term benefits (Miller & Kassinove, 1978; O'Connor, 1972; Williams & Jones, 1989). And in the only study to compare the effects of one combined intervention to those of another, the two treatments were found to be equivalent (Miller & Kassinove, 1978).

Only a few studies looked at the role that certain child and parental variables might play in mediating treatment outcome. Of the child variables examined, no support was obtained for gender, intelligence, socioeconomic status, and fear duration as mediators of treatment outcome; some support was obtained for the variable of age, with the younger the child, the greater the benefits from treatment (Miller et al., 1972a). Such support was also obtained for the parental variables of motivation and involvement. The more highly motivated and involved the parent, the more positively the child benefited from the intervention (Kendall, 1994; Miller et al., 1972a).

Summary

Though differences in methods and measures make cross-study comparisons among the different treatment procedures difficult, a few general statements can be offered. All six treatment procedures produced significant reductions in a variety of children's fears and anxieties, with these reductions being evidenced across the subjective, motor, and physiological components of the different fear and anxiety reactions. The reliability with which these significant reductions

were achieved (and thus with which they can be expected when these interventions are used) was greater for the subjective and motor responses than for the physiological responses, as too few studies included an assessment of the latter dimension.

Of the studies that carried out some type of follow-up assessment, a 1-year maintenance of the aforementioned treatment effects was observed for modeling and contingency management, a 2-year maintenance of effects for desensitization, a 3-year maintenance of effects for self-management, a 4-year maintenance of effects for combined interventions, and an 8-year maintenance of effects for prolonged exposure. Inequivalence in the length of these follow-up assessments precludes any statements about the equivalence or inequivalence among the treatments. Longer follow-ups may quite possibly have revealed continued maintenance of benefits for each of the treatments and thus established comparability among the treatments in terms of these effects. Of the few studies that examined the spread of treatment effects to untreated settings, untreated fears, and/or untreated problem behaviors, such generalization was observed for all of the procedures. But, as noted for the reliability with which reductions in the physiological symptoms of children's fears and anxieties have been achieved, the reliability with which these maintenance and generalization effects have been achieved is also in question because of the small number of studies including such assessments.

Though all of the procedures have been applied in the treatment of a wide range of fears and anxieties, the procedures do differ in the types of fears and anxieties to which they have been predominantly applied. Desensitization treatments have been used primarily with children frightened of small animals, prolonged exposure treatments with children plagued by obsessions and compulsions, modeling treatments with children faced with stressful medical procedures, and self-management treatments with children fearful of nighttime and test-taking situations. Both contingency management and combined treatments have been employed mainly with children frightened of school-related events and social situations. As will be revealed in the material that follows, the reason why these certain types of fears and anxieties have tended to be treated with certain types of interventions appears to be a practical and not an empirical one.

Very different treatment durations were also reported for the six different procedures—a finding leading us to believe that the different procedures may require different lengths of time to achieve their respective effects. The self-management and modeling treatments tended to be of relatively brief duration; the prolonged exposure treatments of moderate duration; and the contingency management, desensitization, and combined treatments of extended duration. We should note, though, that a wide range of durations was reported for each of the six procedures. Applications of the modeling treatments ranged in duration from 6 minutes to 20 days; the self-management treatments, from 15 minutes to 15 weeks; and the prolonged exposure treatments, from 3 days to 12 weeks. For the remaining procedures of contingency management, desensitization, and combined techniques, treatment extended in some cases for as long as 17, 6, and 18 months, respectively.

Only a dozen or so studies directly compared the effects of the six treatment procedures to one another. Few in number, the studies varied in the treatments they compared, the types of children they treated, the fears they treated, and the methods they used to assess those fears. Thus, little can be concluded from these treatment comparisons. If we can conclude anything from these various studies, it is that more treatment may not necessarily mean better treatment. That is, more treatment (i.e., a combined intervention) does not necessarily lead to changes beyond those achieved through less treatment (i.e., any of the single-technique interventions). This is, of course, a contention that is very much open to doubt and that will continue to be so until treatment comparison studies of a more standardized nature are conducted.[10]

In concluding, we should note that behavioral treatments are not the only treatments available for use with fearful and anxious children. Psychoanalytic, systems, and pharmacological interventions have been and continue to be viable treatment alternatives (e.g., Barker, 1984; Bernstein, 1994; Bolton, 1994; Dalton, 1983; Elmhirst, 1985; Herbert, 1984; Rapoport, Swedo, & Leonard, 1992). Data on the effectiveness of these approaches are, however, quite equivocal as well as quite scarce. For example, one search for systematic pharmacological trials for childhood fears and anxieties yielded only 13 controlled studies (Allen, Leonard, & Swedo, 1995). And the findings from these controlled studies, along with those from open trials and case reports, yielded only at best a mixed picture for the efficacy of a host of medications (e.g., tricyclic antidepressants, benzodiazepines, serotonin reuptake inhibitors, monoamine oxidase inhibitors). Clearly, much more research is needed before a verdict can be reached on the effectiveness of pharmacological (as well as psychoanalytic and systems) treatments for children's fears and anxieties.[11] Such research will certainly differ from research on the effectiveness of behavioral treatments for children's fears and anxieties along certain dimensions, but will parallel behavioral research along other dimensions. The section below on treatment evaluation should therefore be of interest to both behavioral and nonbehavioral readers.

TREATMENT SELECTION

Given the number of potentially successful interventions and their variations, the issue of treatment selection emerges. Of course, in the few previously discussed areas where evidence of differential effectiveness exists, this information must be weighed heavily. In addition, how the treatment will be evaluated must be considered; for example, whether the targeted change is primarily motor, subjective or physiological could alter the type of intervention selected. Although there is as yet little empirical guidance, thoughtful consideration of the match between treatments and other factors should assist in the decision process.

As with any clinical intervention, a large number of factors may potentially interact with treatment selection. The following section briefly discusses the use of each of the six previously described techniques in conjunction with four additional factors: the nature of the fear and its stimulus; the characteristics of the child and parent; cost-effectiveness; and ethical considerations.

Systematic Desensitization

Systematic desensitization seems especially applicable when the fear is symbolic (such as fear of nuclear war), or when *in vivo* exposure to the feared stimulus is readily available and approachable in stages (such as fear of large dogs). Not all types of fears, however, can be easily translated into a hierarchy. Fears that do not easily lend themselves to segmentation (such as fears of test taking and speaking before a group) may require more challenging and more costly approaches to setting up effective hierarchies.

Imagery and relaxation may require skills beyond those possessed by young children. Motivation and cooperation of the child and parent may have to be high for this technique. When imaginal exposure is sufficient, systematic desensitization would seem to be relatively cost-effective. Perhaps most important, the use of a gradual hierarchy reduces the risk of ethical problems when compared to more intense exposure or possibly coercive contingency management techniques.

Prolonged Exposure

In instances where a hierarchy is impractical, prolonged exposure may be applicable. Also, when treatment time must be reduced to the absolute minimum, this method could be indicated. When, for example, a child must undergo an emergency medical procedure, treatment time may be minimal. Both children and parents may, however, have strong feelings about cooperating with the higher levels of anxiety associated with prolonged exposure treatments. Thus, their attitudes and opinions may have to be considered (Gelfand, 1978; Graziano, DeGiovanni, & Garcia, 1979; March, 1995). The biggest problems with this technique are probably ethical ones when the treatment is chosen by the parent or therapist on behalf of the child. Some parents advocate "sink or swim" approaches to dealing with their children's fears. It would seem, however, that a child has a right to a treatment that involves the least possible discomfort. The fact that escape must be eliminated also presents ethical problems.

Modeling

Modeling appears to have wide applicability, particularly with older children (Melamed et al., 1984). Its use does present some problems, however. Although the therapist, parent, or sibling may serve as a model, their validity in the eyes of the child may be limited. The presentation of convincing models dealing with fears similar to those of the child may be difficult and costly. When this technique can be used, however, it seems likely to have high face validity, to be acceptable to both the child and parent, and to present few ethical problems.

Contingency Management

The introduction of reinforcers and/or punishers into the treatment would seem to offer a variety

of risks and advantages. They would seem most applicable when the fear stimulus and the fear response of interest are overt in nature. With imaginal stimuli or subjective responses, contingencies could promote false reporting by the child. Certainly, when the child's motivation to face the feared situation is low, contingencies could be extremely helpful. If we assume that higher motivation might facilitate treatment, contingencies could increase cost-effectiveness.

Sometimes parents have strong negative reactions to some reinforcers and punishers. These reactions could be particularly intense if there is also parental hesitancy to "push" the child into anxiety-provoking situations. Perhaps the most difficult aspect of contingency management, then, is that of its potential ethical problems. For example, offering strong reinforcers could encourage the child to experience more anxiety during treatment than is warranted. Ethical problems in the use of punishment seem obvious. Although few therapists might advocate the use of punishment to motivate a child to face a feared stimulus, they must deal with the fact that some parents do.

Self-Management

Self-management would seen to have few drawbacks and many advantages, at least with older children. It should be applicable whether the fear stimulus is real or imaginal and should allow *in vivo* application. Also, there should be few objections by the child or parent to its use and few ethical problems. However, depending on the type of self-management employed, the child will have to possess abilities involving abstraction, intellect, memory, data recording, and so on. Also, the work of Melamed and Peterson suggests that children high in the dispositional characteristic of self-control and low in defensiveness are most likely to benefit (Klingman et al., 1984; Peterson & Tobler, 1984).

Combined Treatments

As treatments are combined, the relevant factors just described will, of course, all have to be considered.

Interactions with Other Treatments

The selection of the primary treatment method for fear and anxiety reduction will also have to consider a variety of factors that may interact with any child and family intervention. One primary dimension is whether the intervention will require more general treatment of the child or parent. For example, the parent may provide secondary gains for many fears, and these must be eliminated for successful treatment. Eliminating secondary gains may interact with maintenance effects when contingency management or even other techniques are employed. Also, the treatments described above do not deal with the elimination of recurrent causes of fears, such as parents who teach "neurotic styles" of functioning. How the selection of treatment techniques will interact with these complex individual and family factors is beyond the scope of this chapter and our knowledge. Be that as it may, the clinician must attempt to deal with these issues in a thoughtful manner.

TREATMENT EVALUATION

Evaluating the effectiveness of a treatment for children's fears and anxieties is every bit as complex as selecting a treatment. Multiple considerations enter into an overall evaluation of the treatment's worth. In this section, we discuss what is entailed in an assessment of the integrity, benefits, and costs of an intervention, and what is included in a determination of an intervention's effectiveness as a treatment for children's fears and anxieties.

Treatment Integrity

Before we ascertain the costs and benefits associated with a particular treatment, we must first ascertain whether or not the treatment has indeed been implemented. That is, we must first assess the integrity of the treatment—the degree to which the treatment has been delivered as intended (Yeaton & Sechrest, 1981). As noted earlier, all treatments for children's fears and anxieties come with a protocol. The protocol specifies each of the tasks the therapist, the child, and (in some instances) the parent or teacher must perform in order for the treatment to be operative. Given the disagreements that exist in definition, classification, and explanation of children's fears and anxieties, one would expect to find widespread disagreement over the protocols' particulars. However, just the opposite is true: There is really little disagreement over what concrete, molar acts are needed for a treatment to be operative.

On the surface, then, assessing the integrity of a treatment is a rather straightforward affair. The actions of the therapist, the child, and (in some instances) the parent or the teacher are all monitored for their accordance with what the treatment protocol asks of each of them. For some interventions, the integrity of treatment hinges almost entirely upon the actions of one of these four persons: the therapist, child, parent, or teacher. For example, in contingency management the child is either rewarded for progressive approach toward the feared object, punished for continued avoidance of the feared object, or both. The therapist, parent, or teacher is the person typically assigned to monitor the child's behavior and to dispense the rewards, punishers, or both accordingly. Failure to carry out this assignment faithfully will result in a corrupted version of the treatment. Another intervention whose integrity rests primarily upon the actions of a single person is the participant modeling treatment developed by Melamed and associates (Klingman et al., 1984). According to its protocol, the child watches a film of a peer demonstrating various breathing and imagery techniques for coping with dental-related fear and anxiety. Time is allotted after each demonstration for the child to practice the technique. If the child neither views the modeling film nor practices the coping techniques during the designated times, a tainted version of the treatment has been administered.

The integrity of most of our treatments for children's fears and anxieties centers on the combined actions of the therapist, the child, and (in some instances) the parent or teacher. For example, in imaginal desensitization, the therapist's duties are to instruct the child in deep muscle relaxation techniques, to construct from the child's list of anxiety-provoking situations an anxiety hierarchy, to present each hierarchy scene to the child while he or she is in a relaxed state, and to present each anxiety-provoking scene upon mastery of the anxiety-provoking scene immediately below it in the hierarchy. For the child, the duties of imaginal desensitization are to follow the therapist's instructions to tense and relax various muscles, to compile a list of situations involving the feared stimulus, to rank-order the situations in terms of the fear they engender, to imagine each scene with great vividness while in a relaxed state, and to cease imagining the scene upon disruption of the relaxed state. For the treatment to be faithfully implemented, the therapist and the child must faithfully carry out their respective duties.

An example of an intervention whose integrity lies in the collective hands of the therapist, the child, and the parent is the self-control treatment developed by Peterson and associates (e.g., Peterson & Shigetomi, 1981; Siegel & Peterson, 1980, 1981). According to its protocol, the therapist has the assignment of demonstrating various techniques for coping with anxiety and alerting the child and the parent as to when it may be advantageous to use the techniques. The parent has the assignment of getting the child to practice the techniques and prompting the child as to when it is fitting to use the techniques. And the child has the assignment of simply complying with these parental instructions. If all three parties dutifully carry out their assignments, then it is safe to say that the treatment has been carried out as intended.[12]

Though an assessment of treatment integrity is integral to an evaluation of treatment effectiveness, we know of only two studies to date that have conducted such an assessment (Kane & Kendall, 1989; Kendall, 1994).[13] From our vantage point, there appear to be two major reasons for our continuing failure to monitor the fidelity of our treatments for children's fears and anxieties. One is the historically crude and confused state of our assessment of the effects of our treatments—a matter discussed at greater length elsewhere. And the other is the scarcity of instruments for measuring the integrity of our treatments. The two reasons are, of course, interrelated. Increased sensitivity to the inadequacies of our assessment of treatment outcome has prompted increased attention to and efforts at developing sound and sensitive measures of treatment outcome (Barrios & Hartmann, 1988, 1997; Barrios, Hartmann, & Shigetomi, 1981; Barrios & Shigetomi, 1985). Devoting more and more attention and energy to the development of sound measures of treatment outcome has left us with less and less attention and energy to devote to the development of sound measures of treatment integrity. We believe that we have now made sufficient advances in the former to warrant a shift in our efforts to the latter. And we are of the hope that such a shift takes place soon, so that we may begin more systematic evaluation and cultivation of our treatments for children's fears and anxieties.

Treatment Benefits

The benefits of treatment can be examined from one or more of the following three perspectives: the impact of treatment on the problem condition per se, on other immediate problem conditions, and on projected problem conditions. The former perspective focuses on the localized effects of treatment; the two latter perspectives focus on the generalized effects of treatment. Current thinking is that both types of perspectives are needed for a thorough analysis of the benefits of any treatment (e.g., Mash & Terdal, 1977; Stokes & Baer, 1977; Yates, 1981).

Problem Condition

Earlier we have noted that children's fears and anxieties are seen as complex patterns of subjective, motor, and physiological responses. Given this conceptualization, assessment of children's fears and anxieties entails the measurement of multiple responses within and across the subjective, motor, and physiological response components (Barrios & Hartmann, 1988, 1997; Barrios & Shigetomi, 1985). Measurement of only a single response within each of the components or of multiple responses within only one of the components offers an incomplete picture of the fear pattern, and thus constitutes an inadequate assessment of the problem condition. What is needed, then, for an adequate assessment of treatment impact on the problem condition is the measurement of multiple responses within and across the multiple response components.

Also needed for an adequate assessment of the effects of treatment on the fear reaction per se is the measurement of that reaction across different settings and different time periods. Measurement across different settings allows for estimation of the benefits of treatment across different representations and presentations of the feared stimulus. Measurement across different time periods allows for estimation of the persistence of the benefits of treatment. Combined, the measurement of the fear reaction's complex response pattern and the measurement of that reaction across different settings and time periods make for a thorough assessment of treatment impact on the problem condition.

To date, the vast majority of our assessments have been less than thorough. Only 14 of the 177 outcome studies reviewed in the previous section monitored activity from all three of the response systems.[14] As such, these studies merit special mention. One is the treatment of a multi-phobic child by Van Hasselt et al. (1979). Frightened by blood, heights, and school exams, the child received desensitization treatment for each of his fears. To assess the effects of desensitization, Van Hasselt and his associates collected measures of the child's subjective, motor, and physiological reactions to each stimulus. For the feared stimulus of blood, degree of approach to a blood-soaked pillowcase served as a measure of motor responding; self-rating of discomfort during approach served as the measure of subjective responding; and heart rate and finger pulse volume during approach served as the measures of physiological responding. For heights, degree of ascent up a stepladder served as the measure of motor responding; self-rating of discomfort during ascent served as the measure of subjective responding; and heart rate upon ascent served as the measure of physiological responding. For school exams, trials to errorless performance on a memory task served as the measure of motor responding; self-ratings of discomfort during the memory task served as the measure of subjective responding; and heart rate and finger pulse volume during the memory task served as the measures of physiological responding.

Many of the remaining triple-response-system assessments have been carried out by either Melamed's or Peterson's research team. In their systematic studies of the effects of modeling treatments on children's fears of medical and dental procedures, Melamed and her associates gather several self-ratings of the children's discomfort during the procedures, observe the children's overt behavior during the procedure for several signs of anxiety, and monitor several of the children's physiological responses to the procedures (Klingman et al., 1984; Melamed et al., 1976; Melamed & Siegel, 1975). In their systematic studies of the effects of self-control treatments on children's fears of medical and dental procedures, Peterson and her associates survey a very similar set of subjective, motoric, and physiological responses through use of a similar set of methods (Peterson & Shigetomi, 1981; Siegel & Peterson, 1980, 1981).

As noted earlier, a thorough assessment of the localized effects of treatment calls not only for the measurement of the multiple components of fear, but also for the measurement of multiple responses within each of the components of fear. Few studies have followed this second directive. Most studies have limited their assessment of the subjective, motor, or physiological components of fear to a single response. Such studies tell us little about the benefits of treatment for the sundry responses within a single component of fear. However, a handful of studies have measured two or more responses from one or more of the response systems, and these studies likewise deserve mention. Some of them have already been described—the investigation by Van Hasselt et al. (1979); the investigations by Melamed and her associates (Klingman et al., 1984; Melamed et al, 1976, 1978; Melamed & Siegel, 1975); and the investigations by Peterson and her associates (Peterson et al., 1984; Peterson & Shigetomi, 1981; Siegel & Peterson, 1980, 1981). One study that heretofore has not been described in this context is the treatment of a multiphobic child by Esveldt-Dawson et al. (1982). In their assessment of the child's fear of school situations and strangers, Esveldt-Dawson and her associates observed the child for a host of motor signs of anxiety. Among the behaviors observed were eye contact, giggling, furrowing of the brow, grimacing, voice volume, speech fluency, and body posture. By tracking a host of responses rather than a single response, Esveldt-Dawson and her associates were better able to gauge the impact of their treatment on the motoric component of the child's fear reactions.

Two other guidelines for a thorough assessment of treatment impact on the problem condition are the measurement of responding to the feared stimulus across different settings and across different follow-up periods. To date, far more studies have complied with the second guideline than with the first. Two of the few studies that did assess the persistence of treatment benefits across variations in the testing situations are the investigations by Kanfer et al. (1975) and by Murphy and Bootzin (1973). Kanfer and his associates looked at the effects of their self-management treatment across two testing situations. The two testing situations were similar in that they both involved the presentation of the feared stimulus of darkness, but were dissimilar in that they utilized different modes of presentation. For one of the testings, the child was seated alone in a room with a device to control room illumination at his side. Left in total darkness, the child increased the lighting whenever he became uncomfortable. Time spent in total darkness was recorded. For the other testing, the child was again seated alone in a room with a device for controlling room illumination at his side. Left in a fully illuminated room, the child decreased the lighting to the lowest level he could tolerate. Degree of illumination was recorded. Murphy and Bootzin (1973) also carried out two assessments of the effects of their participant modeling treatment for fear of snakes. In one of the testings, the child approached and handled the snake. In the other testing, the child remained stationary while the snake was brought to him. In both situations, the degree of proximity to and contact with the snake was recorded.

Other Problem Conditions

Another element of a comprehensive assessment of the benefits of treatment is an assessment of the spread of treatment effects to untreated problem conditions. These untreated problem conditions may take the form of other fears and anxieties on the part of the child; other, nonfear-related disturbances on the part of the child; fears and anxieties on the part of peers and family members; or non-fear-related disturbances on the part of peers and family members. Of the four types of problem conditions, the two most frequently inspected have been those of the treated child. Among the non-targeted fears and anxieties of the treated child that have been assessed are those to specific and nonspecific stimuli (i.e., generalized anxiety). And among the nonfear-related problems of the treated child that have been assessed are depressed mood, disruptive behaviors, poor peer relations, poor family relations, and poor academic performance (e.g., Albano, Marten et al., 1995; Ayllon et al., 1970; Barlow & Seidner, 1983; Kendall, 1994; LeUnes & Siemsglusz, 1977; Ollendick, 1995; Sanders & Jones, 1990).

The anxieties and nonfear-related troubles of the treated child's peers, siblings, and parents make up the other two types of problem conditions. In their investigation of their treatment for agoraphobia, Barlow and Seidner (1983) examined the parents' interactions with the children, along with the children's reactions to being alone and out of the home. This broadened assessment of treatment effects allowed Barlow and Seidner (1983) to check for improvements in parental behavior concomitant with improvements in children's approach behavior.

Projected Problem Conditions

The final element in a comprehensive assessment of treatment benefits is an assessment of the treatment's impact on projected problem conditions. This is, in essence, an assessment of the preventive effects of treatment. Of the many different problem conditions a treatment for children's fears and anxieties could possibly prevent, the most likely candidates are the future fears and anxieties of the children. They are therefore the problem conditions of primary interest to us in our examination of a treatment's preventive capabilities.

Though preventive research itself is a difficult undertaking (e.g., Gelfand & Hartmann, 1977; Roberts & Peterson, 1984), assessment of the preventive effects of our treatments for children's fears and anxieties need not be. Developmental data show the fears and anxieties of children of different ages to cluster around different stimuli. The common fear stimuli of each of the different age groups have been presented in an earlier section of this chapter. This breakdown of fear stimuli by age group can guide us in our assessment of the preventive effects of our treatments for children's fears and anxieties (Barrios & Shigetomi, 1980; King et al., 1983).

To date, no study has employed this strategy in its assessment of the preventive effects of a treatment for children's fears and anxieties. In fact, no study to date has examined the preventive effects of any of our treatments for children's fears and anxieties—certainly not the long-range, preventive effects we are referring to here. This gap in our assessment practices is one that obviously needs to be filled.

Treatment Costs

All treatments for children's fears and anxieties involve certain costs, most of which are borne by the child, the parent, and the therapist. In general, the costs are of two types: financial and psychological. For the child, the financial costs of the treatment are almost always negligible, since it is almost always the parent who pays the fee for treatment services. The same cannot be said of the psychological costs of treatment for the child. All of our treatments for children's fears and anxieties call for enduring some discomfort, be it subjective, physiological, or both; thus, all of our treatments involve some psychological costs for the child. For some of our treatments, such as desensitization and modeling, the amount of discomfort the child is asked to tolerate may be minimal; for other treatments, such as prolonged exposure and contingency management, the amount of discomfort may be substantial.

Another possible psychological cost to the child as a result of treatment is the stigmatization that accompanies being singled out as a child with a problem. This stigmatization may take the form of social rejection, social ridicule, or both. For some of our treatments, such as desensitization and prolonged exposure, it may be very obvious that the child is being singled out as having a problem; for other treatments, such as group-administered modeling and self-management, it may not be so obvious. Treatments may differ, then, in terms of this particular psychological price that the child may be called upon to pay.

The treatment of children's fears and anxieties also involves certain costs—financial and psychological—for the parent and the therapist. For example, financially, the parent must part with some of his or her income to cover the fee for treatment services.[15] And psychologically, the parent may incur some loss in the quality of his or her life as a result of participating in the treatment of the child. The therapist too sustains certain financial and psychological losses in treating the fears and anxieties of children. For example, in devoting time and energy to the treatment of a child's fears and anxieties, a therapist may have less time and energy to devote to more lucrative activities or to other professional and personal pursuits.

At its simplest, the evaluation of treatment effectiveness is seen as a comparison of treatment benefits to treatments costs. To date, no study has performed such a comparison, for to date no study has assessed the costs of treatment. There appear to be two reasons for not doing so. One is the more pressing need to upgrade our assessment of the benefits of treatment (e.g., Barrios & Hartmann, 1988; Barrios et al., 1981; Barrios & Shigetomi, 1985). Obviously, before we assess the costs of treatment, we had better be reasonably certain about the benefits of treatment. Most of our energies and efforts have gone toward achieving this certainty. The second reason is our unfamiliarity with the notion of treatment cost—its conceptualization and its assessment (Yates, 1985). Most of us are unacquainted with the different perspectives from which costs can be defined, the different methods by which costs can be assessed, and the different procedures by which costs and benefits can be compared. An assignment for the immediate future is for us to become better acquainted with the formulation and measurement of the concept of treatment costs.

Summary

Treatment evaluation is integral to our comprehension and remediation of children's fears and anxieties. Conscientious and meticulous evaluation of the effectiveness of our treatments provides us with insights into which of our theories of children's fears and anxieties would be best to develop and which would be best to discard, as well as similar insights about the treatments themselves. Unfortunately, our evaluation of our treatments has been neither conscientious nor meticulous. Only recently have we begun to broaden our assessment of the fear condition such that it coincides with how we conceptualize the construct. Still awaiting us are the development of methods for assessing the integrity, the long-term benefits, and the costs of our treatments. Advances in our understanding and treating of fears and anxieties will also depend upon our attending to several other matters. In the chapter's final section, we discuss these matters.

SUMMARY AND RECOMMENDATIONS

Our review of behavioral treatments for children's fears and anxieties reveals that we suffer from no shortage of techniques. We do, however, suffer from a shortage of guidelines and models that would facilitate advancements in our understanding and treatment of children's fears and anxieties. In the paragraphs that follow, we describe the particulars of our situation and offer some possible remedies.[16]

First and foremost, we lack a consensually agreed upon precise definition of "fear and anxiety." Heretofore we have defined "fear and anxiety" as a complex pattern of subjective, motor, and physiological responses. We have not, however, delineated the specific subjective, motor, and physiological responses that constitute the pattern. Consequently, many different combinations of responses to the same stimulus have shared the same "fear and anxiety" label. This liberal use of the label has enabled us to amass a sizeable literature on children's fears and anxieties, but has disabled us from clarifying what is meant by the label. For us to systematically study the pattern of children's fears and anxieties, we must first specify the exact content and configuration of the response pattern. In other words, we must render our current vague definition of children's fears and anxieties more explicit.[17]

Related to this need for a more explicit response definition of children's fears and anxieties is the need for more explicit criteria for problematic fears and anxieties. Our long-standing practice has been to judge a child's fears and anxieties as problematic if the child's parent, teacher, or some other significant adult has judged the responding to be problematic. This has been a most unproductive practice. It has led to great variability in the types of responding designated as maladaptive and to little clarity in what constitutes maladaptive responding. For us to reliably identify fears and anxieties as problematic, we need operational definitions of problem fears and anxieties. The diagnostic criteria set forth by the American Psychiatric Association (1994) for 14 specific fears and anxieties are examples of such operational definitions, which many in the field have enthusiastically embraced. We may not, however, wish to use these criteria to identify the problem fears and anxieties of children. We may instead wish to use criteria that are more quantitative in nature—that specify the exact form and frequency of responding for children of varying ages and that have empirical ties to designated levels of interference with or impairments in functioning. Such diagnostic criteria would be more consistent with the behavioral-developmental perspective advocated here and elsewhere (e.g., Barrios & Hartmann, 1988, 1997; Campbell, 1986; Cicchetti, 1993). And such diagnostic criteria may be devised through expansion of the methodology developed by Ollendick and King (1994).

Given the complex nature of children's fears and anxieties, we can address the pattern from any number of different directions. We can direct our treatment efforts at the responding of the subjective component, the motor component, the physiological component, or some combination of the three. We can direct our treatment efforts at the level of the fearful child or at the level of the family system of which the fearful child is an element. Our task is to select the optimum level at which to intervene and the optimum targets at which to aim our treatment efforts. We look to both theory and data for help in performing this task. Contemporary behavioral theories of children's fears and anxieties have not been of much help, though, in carrying out the task of target behavior selection (Barrios & Hartmann, 1988; Barrios et al., 1981). For the most part, the theories offer few insights into the direction of influence from one element of the family system to another, or from one component of the fear pattern to another. For our purposes, we need behavioral theories that are truly developmental in nature (e.g., Barrios & Hartman, 1988; Campbell, 1986). We need theories that specify the role parents and siblings play in the origin, maintenance, and modification of a child's fears and anxieties; we also need theories specifying the role that responding in one component of the fear pattern plays in the instigation, perpetuation, and modification of respond-

ing in the other two components of the fear pattern.[18]

Aside from theory, we can draw upon data to guide us in the selection of a target behavior. Data that would be of most help to us would be those on the interrelationships among the three components of the fear state—the degree of association among the three types of responding at any given point in time (i.e., concordance), and the rate of change among the fear responding as a function of treatment (i.e., synchrony). Such data on the concordance and synchrony among the fear responses of adults are quite plentiful (e.g., Agras & Jacobs, 1981; Hodgson & Rachman, 1974; Rachman & Hodgson, 1974; Taylor & Agras, 1981; Vermilyea, Boice, & Barlow, 1984). Such data, though, are quite scarce for the fear responses of children (Barrios & Shigetomi, 1985). For target behavior selection in our treatment of children's fears and anxieties to be in any sense empirically based, we need more estimates of concordance and synchrony.

We are of the opinion, then, that having formal models for target behavior selection—be they theoretical or empirical in nature—is far preferable to having no such formal models. And we are of the same opinion regarding formal models for treatment selection. Rather than continuing our long-standing practice of selecting a treatment for children's fears and anxieties largely on the basis of personal preference, we may wish to adopt and examine one of the four models we have available to us at this time. Two of these have arisen from the literature on children's fears and anxieties, and two from the literature on adults' fears and anxieties. One of the former is the requisite-matching model described in this chapter and in greater detail elsewhere (Barrios & Hartmann, 1988). The other is the motivation-matching model developed by Kearney and Silverman (1990a) for the treatment of school refusal. In their model, there are four categories of hypothesized variables maintaining the problem condition and there are four prescribed interventions for remediating the problem condition—one for each of the four sources of motivation. In the profile-matching model, treatment is chosen on the basis of the profile of subjective, motor, and physiological responses (Heimberg, Gansler, Dodge, & Becker, 1987; Jerremalm, Jansson, & Öst, 1986; Öst, Jerremalm & Johansson, 1981; Schwartz, Davidson, & Goleman, 1978; Trower, Yardley, Bryant, & Shaw, 1978). For example, for a fear profile in which subjective responses are predominant, the model advises us to apply a treatment whose predominant focus is the subjective component; and for a fear profile in which motor responses are predominant, the model advises us to apply a treatment whose predominant focus is the motor component. For each possible profile of subjective, motor, and physiological responses, the model offers similar advice. Also from the literature on the fears and anxieties of adults is the treatment selection model put forth by Barlow (1988). For each of the specific types of anxieties listed in the American Psychiatric Association's (1987, 1994) classification system, Barlow's model recommends the implementation of a specific type of intervention. All of the recommendations emanate directly from the author's explanatory accounts and the field's empirical examinations of the various anxiety conditions.[19]

Perhaps more pressing than the need for formal models for target behavior and treatment selection is the need for formal models for treatment evaluation. To date, our efforts at evaluation have been largely haphazard: We have been incomplete and inconsistent in our assessment of the costs and benefits of our treatments, and we have been divided in our efforts to amass a solid data base. A more unified front is obviously needed in regard to treatment evaluation. For there to be a consolidated approach to treatment evaluation, we must agree on three items (Mash, 1985). First, we must agree on the relevant dimensions that make up the concepts of treatment costs and treatment benefits. Second, we must develop sound measures for each of the relevant dimensions and agree to employ the measures in our studies of treatment effectiveness. And third, we must agree on a set of rules for integration of the data on costs and benefits. Arriving at some consensus on all three of these items will provide us with a coherent framework for assessing the worth of our treatments.

The keen interest now shown in children's fears and anxieties clearly differs from the interest shown in the past. Previously, children's fears and anxieties were seen as convenient vehicles for testing the validity of our theories and techniques; as such, the performance patterns were secondary to our interest in our theories and techniques. Today, children's fears and anxieties occupy a more prominent role. They are seen as problem conditions worthy of our attention and concern; as such, there is now a concerted effort to develop powerful programs for the prevention and remediation of children's fears and anxieties. For such efforts to prove successful, it is clear that we must become more systematic and assiduous in our pursuits. Our hope is that this chapter has provided us with sufficient direction and motivation to take those steps—steps that will lead us to a more satisfying understanding and treatment of children's fears and anxieties.

ACKNOWLEDGMENT

Portions of the present material appeared in a companion chapter on the behavioral assessment of children's fears and anxieties (Barrios & Hartmann, 1997). Copyright 1997 by The Guilford Press. Used by permission.

NOTES

1. We trust that the reader recognizes that our assignation of any given classification system as theoretically, statistically, or clinically based is one of degree, as more than one of these processes is involved in the creation of any taxonomy.

2. We should note that some investigators have found good agreement among children of varying ages in terms of the types of objects, activities, and situations they fear most. For example, Ollendick et al. (1985) found near-perfect overlap in the 10 most common fears reported by 7- to 9-year-olds, 10- to 12-year-olds, 13- to 15-year-olds, and 16- to 18-year olds. The eight fears cited by all four age groups were: not being able to breathe, a burglar breaking into the house, fire, being struck by a vehicle, death or dead people, bomb attacks or being invaded, looking foolish, and getting poor grades. And in a more recent study employing similar methodology, Gullone and King (1992) found perfect agreement in the 10 most common fears indicated by their three age groups of 7- to 10-year-olds, 11- to 14-year-olds, and 15- to 18-year olds. These 10 shared fears were AIDS, someone in the family dying, not being able to breathe, being threatened with a gun, taking dangerous drugs, being kidnapped, dying, nuclear war, murderers, and sharks. Though held in common, the 10 fears did differ in their exact rank ordering from age group to age group—a finding suggesting the existence of a cluster of fears that is consistent in its makeup across the ages of childhood, but that varies in the prominence of the individual constituent fears according to the exact age of the child.

3. Some studies have found no appreciable decline in the numbers of fears and anxieties with increasing age (e.g., Angelino et al., 1956; Angelino

& Shedd, 1953; Croake & Knox, 1973; Dunlop, 1952; Maurer, 1965; Morgan, 1959; Ollendick, 1983; Ollendick, Yule, & Ollier, 1991; Ryall & Dietiker, 1979). These studies differ from those cited above in that they have tended to survey a much more narrow range of age groups—a tendency that may have precluded them from detecting a general drop in the number of fears and anxieties experienced across the span of childhood.

4. A few studies have failed to find differences between girls and boys in the number of anxiety symptoms displayed (Last, Perrin, Hersen, & Kazdin, 1992; Zohar et al., 1992), the number of fears and anxieties reported (Angelino et al., 1956; Eme & Schmidt, 1978; Maurer, 1965; Nalven, 1970), and the types of fears and anxieties experienced (Gullone & King, 1992; King, Ollier, et al., 1989; Ollendick et al., 1985, 1989). Such studies are at present not numerous enough to challenge the general trends reported above.

5. Apart from these somewhat predictable differences, investigators have yet to find strong and reliable relationships between socioeconomic status and numbers of anxiety symptoms or between socioeconomic status and intensity of anxiety reactions to such common stimulus situations as separation from an attachment figure and school attendance (e.g., Kashani & Orvaschel, 1988, 1990).

6. For a more detailed discussion of the intricacies and difficulties in determining the problem status of a child's fear reaction, please see Barrios and Hartmann (1997).

7. Long ignored, paternal anxiety has been a focus of a few recent investigations and has been found to correspond with child anxiety (Last, Hersen, Kazdin, Orvaschel, & Perrin, 1991; Messer & Beidel, 1994). We trust that further research will delineate the exact role that paternal anxiety plays in the development and maintenance of children's fears and anxieties—and, in doing so, will define for us how much attention we should accord to paternal anxiety in the assessment and treatment of children's fears and anxieties.

8. In highlighting the theories that have been most influential in spawning or promoting the currently available behavioral treatments for children's fears and anxieties, we in no way wish to minimize the contributions that other theorists have made in advancing our understanding of the development of fears and anxieties. For example, Gray (1987) has directed our attention to established and hypothesized relationships between the biological structures of the behavioral inhibition and septohippocampal systems and the clinical phenomena of panic and situational and generalized anxiety.

Kagan (1994) has alerted us to the role that temperament—specifically, the tendency of "behavioral inhibition to the unfamiliar"—may play in precipitating certain childhood anxieties. And Reiss (1987, 1991) has introduced to us a promising individual difference or mediating variable in the acquisition and exacerbation of fears–"anxiety sensitivity," the fear of anxiety-related sensations.

9. We have classified the technique of thought stopping as a self-management procedure, as the focus of this technique is the alteration of the subjective or cognitive dimension of an anxiety reaction. In standard form, the technique calls for the child to conjure up a negative thought associated with the feared situation and for the therapist to interrupt this train of thought by shouting "Stop!" Upon several repetitions of this sequence, the child assumes the role of the therapist and interrupts his or her own train of thought through the shouting of "Stop!" This shouting is subsequently replaced with a subvocalizing of the word, followed by an imagining of a pleasant scene (e.g., Ownby, 1983).

10. Though the contention that more treatment leads to better outcome has yet to be proven, the trend in recent years has been toward the development and employment of more and more complex interventions. Should this trend continue, the task facing child therapists will be that of "dismantling" these elaborate interventions—determining which of the elements of these elaborate interventions are essential and which are extraneous (e.g., Kazdin, 1987; Kendall, 1994; March, 1995).

11. We should note that investigators of pharmacological treatments for children's fears and anxieties face formidable obstacles that investigators of nonpharmacological treatments do not (Allen et al., 1995). Among these are high material costs and liability concerns, low numbers of interested and trained fellow scientists, and high demands for assurances of minimal risks and considerable benefits with treatment. We suspect that these barriers along with the requirements that come with increasing experimental rigor, have discouraged systematic study of drug treatments for children's fears and anxieties. We also suspect that the disappointing findings described above have had a hand in discouraging research. The situation, however, should not be seen as completely bleak, as the findings have not been altogether disappointing for all drug treatments. Double-blind studies have found both clomipramine and fluoxetine useful in reducing obsessions and compulsions (De Vaugh-Geiss et al., 1992; Flament et al., 1985; Leonard et al., 1989; Riddle et al., 1992); open trials have found busiprone successful in treating

symptoms of generalized anxiety (Kranzler, 1988; Kutcher, Reiter, Gardner, & Klein, 1992); and early reports from a double-blind study have found clonazepam helpful in decreasing the frequency and intensity of Panic Attacks (Kutcher et al., 1992). Data of these sorts encourage investigators to persist in their search for effective pharmacological treatments for children's fears and anxieties.

12. Examples of more recently developed interventions in which therapist, child, and parent are all called upon to play active roles are those of Albano and her associates (Albano, Knox, & Barlow, 1995; Albano, Marten, Holt, Heimberg, & Barlow, 1995) and Kendall et al. (1992).

13. These two studies (Kane & Kendall, 1989; Kendall, 1994) are noteworthy in two respects: They are the sole investigations to include an assessment of treatment integrity, and they are fine illustrations of the complexities involved in the assessment of treatment integrity. Through the use of audiotaped recordings of the sessions, the degree to which therapists adhered to the treatment protocol was directly assessed. Indirect assessment of each child's participation in and each parent's collaboration with treatment was carried out through use of a homework recording booklet with the former and a rating of involvement with the latter.

14. The subjective, motoric, and physiological symptoms of children's fears and anxieties can be measured through a multitude of methods, with the multitude of methods varying in the directness and immediacy with which the symptoms are assessed (Barrios, 1988; Barrios & Hartmann, 1997; Cone, 1979). That being the case, included in this set of 14 studies that monitored activity from all three of the response systems are 3 that assessed physiological symptoms through the method of self-report (Kane & Kendall, 1989; Kendall, 1994; Ollendick, 1995). The remaining 11 studies all assessed physiological responses through the use of direct mechanical recording devices.

15. In these times of exorbitant health care costs, the true bearer of these treatment costs will in most cases be some third-party payer (e.g., insurance company, government agency, employer). And, to be sure, these third-party payers are most concerned with the financial costs associated with the various treatment options—so much so that child clinicians are increasingly concerned that matters of treatment costs will be accorded greater importance than matters of treatment benefits in the prescription and evaluation of services. For an enlightened discussion of how we child therapists might approach this new participant in the assessment, treatment selection, and treatment evaluation process, please see Mash and Hunsley (1993).

16. We, of course, echo the recommendations put forth by several astute commentators in the field (e.g., Albano & Chorpita, 1995; Bernstein & Borchardt, 1991; March, 1995; Moreau & Weissman, 1992; Ollendick & Francis, 1988; Saigh, 1992; Silverman & Kearney, 1991; Wolff & Rapoport, 1988). Among the most pressing of these are the need for the following: measurement of multiple responses through multiple methods; inclusion of appropriate control conditions; assessment of the maintenance and generalization of treatment gains across varying lengths of time; comparative studies of the relative merits of the various behavioral interventions; controlled trials comparing behavioral interventions to alternative treatments; component analyses of the various compound interventions; and identification of mediators and predictors of treatment outcome. Rather than devote the concluding section of this chapter to a restatement of these recommendations, we have elected to discuss several fundamental matters that underlie the skillful implementation of them.

17. We are not so naive as to think that we will arrive at a monolithic definition for children's fears and anxieties. Instead, we foresee ourselves formulating several specific response definitions for the several commonly noted fear situations, with each definition being fashioned according to stimulus and developmental considerations.

18. Recently proposed transactional models of emotional disorders (e.g., Blount, Davis, Powers, & Roberts, 1991; LaFrenière & Dumas, 1992; Melamed, 1993) may help to meet these needs of ours, as they have already met with some success in isolating child characteristics, caregiver characteristics, and child–caregiver interactions related to certain children's fears and anxieties. The generality of these relationships and the validity of other hypothesized relationships await our examination.

19. Examining the merits of these models for treatment selection will be a challenging affair. For example, the requisite-matching model provides no guidelines for deciding when a treatment requisite has been met; the profile-matching model provides no guidelines for deciding between treatments with the same predominant focus; and the template of the motivation-matching model has yet to be applied to fears and anxieties other then those related to the school situation. As significant as these obstacles appear to be, they pale in comparison to the shortcomings of a purely idiosyncratic approach to treatment selection. Such an approach defies speci-

fication. If we are unable to specify the way in which we choose a treatment for children's fears and anxieties, we are unable to evaluate and refine our selection process. It is for these reasons that we recommend the adoption of a more formalized approach to treatment selection.

REFERENCES

Achenbach, T. M. (1991a). *Manual for the Child Behavior Checklist/4–18 and 1991 Profile*. Burlington: University of Vermont, Department of Psychiatry.

Achenbach, T. M. (1991b). *Manual for the Teacher's Report Form and 1991 Profile*. Burlington: University of Vermont, Department of Psychiatry.

Achenbach, T. M. (1991c). *Manual for the Youth Self-Report and 1991 Profile*. Burlington, VT: University of Vermont Department of Psychiatry.

Agras, W. S., Chapin, H. N., & Oliveau, D. C. (1972). The natural history of phobia. *Archives of General Psychiatry, 26*, 315–317.

Agras, W. S., & Jacobs, R. G. (1981). Phobia: Nature and measurement. In M. Mavissakalian & D. H. Barlow (Eds.), *Phobia: Psychological and pharmacological treatment* (pp. 35–62). New York: Guilford Press.

Agras, W. S., Sylvester, D., & Oliveau, D. C. (1969). The epidemiology of common fears and phobias. *Comprehensive Psychiatry, 10*, 151–156.

Albano, A. M. (1996, January). *Cognitive–behavioral treatment of panic disorders and interactions with pharmacology*. Workshop presented at the University of Mississippi.

Albano, A. M., & Chorpita, B. F. (1995). Treatment of anxiety disorders of childhood. *Psychiatric Clinics of North America, 18*, 767–784.

Albano, A. M., & Chorpita, B. F., & Barlow, D. H. (1996). Anxiety disorders. In E. J. Mash & R. A. Barkley (Eds.), *Child psychopathology* (pp. 196–241). New York: Guilford Press.

Albano, A. M., Knox, L. S., & Barlow, D. H. (1995). Obsessive–compulsive disorder. In A. R. Eisen, C. A. Kearney, & C. E. Shaefer (Eds.), *Clinical handbook of anxiety disorders in children and adolescents* (pp. 282–316). Northvale, NJ: Jason Aronson.

Albano, A. M., Marten, P. A., Holt, C. S., Heimberg, R. G., & Barlow, D. H. (1995). Cognitive-behavioral group treatment for Social Phobia in adolescents: A preliminary study. *Journal of Nervous and Mental Disease, 183*, 649–656.

Allan, T. K., & Hodgson, E. W. (1968). The use of personality measurements as a determinant of patient cooperation in an orthodontic practice. *American Journal of Orthodontics, 54*, 433–440.

Allen, A. J., Leonard, H., & Swedo, S. E. (1995). Current knowledge of medications for the treatment of childhood anxiety disorders. *Journal of the American Academy of Child and Adolescent Psychiatry, 34*, 976–986.

Allen, K., Hart, B., Buell, S., Harris, R., & Wolf, M. (1964). Effects of social reinforcement on isolate behavior of a nursery school child. *Child Development, 35*, 511–518.

American Psychiatric Association. (1980). *Diagnostic and statistical manual of mental disorders* (3rd ed.). Washington, DC: Author.

American Psychiatric Association. (1987). *Diagnostic and statistical manual of mental disorders* (3rd ed., rev.). Washington, DC: Author.

American Psychiatric Association. (1994). *Diagnostic and statistical manual of mental disorders* (4th ed.). Washington, DC: Author.

Anderson, J. C., Williams, S., McGee, R., & Silva, P. A. (1987). DSM-III disorders in preadolescent children. *Archives of General Psychiatry, 44*, 69–76.

Andrews, W. R. (1971). Behavioral and client-centered counseling of high school underachievers. *Journal of Counseling Psychology, 18*, 93–96.

Angelino, H., Dollins, J., & Mech, E. V. (1956). Trends in the "fears and worries" of school children as related to socio-economic status and age. *Journal of Genetic Psychology, 89*, 263–276.

Angelino, H., & Shedd, C. (1953). Shifts in the content of fears and worries relative to chronological age. *Proceedings of the Oklahoma Academy of Science, 34*, 180–186.

Auld, F. (1951). The effects of tetraethylammonium on a habit motivated by fear. *Journal of Comparative and Physiological Psychology, 44*, 565–574.

Ayllon, T., Smith, D., & Rogers, M. (1970). Behavioral management of school phobia. *Journal of Behavior Therapy and Experimental Psychiatry, 1*, 125–138.

Bailey, P. M., Talbot, A., & Taylor, P. P. (1973). A comparison of maternal anxiety levels with anxiety levels manifested in child dental patients. *Journal of Dentistry for Children, 40*, 277–284.

Ball, W., & Tronick, E. (1971). Infant responses to impending collision: Optical and real. *Science, 171*, 818–820.

Ballenger, J. C., Carek, D. J., Steele, J. J., & Cornish-McTighe, D. (1989). Three cases of Panic Disorder with agoraphobia in children. *American Journal of Psychiatry, 146*, 922–924.

Bamber, J. H. (1974). The fears of adolescents. *Journal of Genetic Psychology, 125*, 127–140.

Bandura, A. (1969). *Principles of behavior modification*. New York: Holt, Rinehart & Winston.

Bandura, A. (Ed.). (1971). *Psychological modeling: Conflicting theories*. Chicago: Aldine-Atherton.

Bandura, A. (1977a). Self-efficacy: Toward a unifying theory of behavioral change. *Psychological Review, 84*, 191–215.

Bandura, A. (1977b). *Social learning theory*. Englewood Cliffs, NJ: Prentice-Hall.

Bandura, A. (1978). Reflections on self-efficacy. *Advances in Behaviour Research and Therapy, 1,* 237–269.

Bandura, A. (1982). Self-efficacy mechanism in human agency. *American Psychologist, 37,* 122–147.

Bandura, A., Blanchard, E. B., & Ritter, B. (1969). Relative efficacy of desensitization and modeling approaches for inducing behavioral, affective, and attitudinal changes. *Journal of Personality and Social Psychology, 13,* 173–199.

Bandura, A., Grusec, E., & Menlove, F. L. (1967). Vicarious extinction of avoidance behavior. *Journal of Personality and Social Psychology, 5,* 16–23.

Bandura, A., & Menlove, F. (1968). Factors determining vicarious extinction of avoidance behavior through symbolic modeling. *Journal of Personality and Social Psychology, 8,* 99–108.

Bankart, C. P., & Bankart, B. B. (1983). The use of song lyrics to alleviate a child's fears. *Child and Family Behavior Therapy, 5,* 81–83.

Barabasz, A. (1973). Group desensitization of test anxiety in elementary schools. *Journal of Psychology, 83,* 295–301.

Barker, P. (1984). Family dysfunction and anxiety in children. In V. P. Varma (Ed.,), *Anxiety in children* (pp. 89–104). London: Croom Helm.

Barlow, D. H. (1988). *Anxiety and its disorders: The nature and treatment of anxiety and panic.* New York: Guilford Press.

Barlow, D. H., & Seidner, A. L. (1983). Treatment of adolescent agoraphobics: Effects on parent-adolescent relations. *Behaviour Research and Therapy, 21,* 519–526.

Barrios, B. A. (1988). On the changing nature of behavioral assessment. In A. S. Bellack & M. Hersen (Eds.), *Behavioral assessment: A practical handbook* (3rd ed., pp. 3–41). Elmsford, NY: Pergamon Press.

Barrios, B. A., & Hartmann, D. P. (1997). Anxieties and fears. In E. J. Mash & L. G. Terdal (Eds.), *Assessment of childhood disorders* (3rd ed., pp. 230–327). New York: Guilford Press.

Barrios, B. A., & Hartmann, D. P. (1988). Fears and anxieties. In E. J. Mash & L. G. Terdal (Eds.), *Behavioral assessment of childhood disorders* (2nd ed., pp. 196–264). New York: Guilford Press.

Barrios, B. A., Hartmann, D. P., & Shigetomi, C. (1981). Fears and anxieties in children. In E. J. Mash & L. G. Terdal (Eds.), *Behavioral assessment of childhood disorders* (pp. 259–304). New York: Guilford Press.

Barrios, B. A., Replogle, W., & Anderson-Tisdelle, D. (1983, December). *Multisystem–unimethod analysis of children's fears.* Paper presented at the meeting of the Association for Advancement of Behavior Therapy, Washington, D. C.

Barrios, B. A., & Shigetomi, C. (1980). Coping skills training: Potential for prevention of fears and anxieties. *Behavior Therapy, 11,* 431–439.

Barrios, B. A., & Shigetomi, C. (1985). Assessment of children's fears: A critical review. In T. R. Kra-

tochwill (Ed.), *Advances in school psychology.* (Vol. 4, pp. 89–132). Hillsdale, N. J.: Erlbaum.

Bauer, D. D. (1968). A case of desensitization and tutoring therapy. *Exceptional Child, 34,* 386–387.

Bauer, D. H. (1976). An exploratory study of developmental changes in children's fears. *Journal of Child Psychology and Psychiatry, 17,* 69–74.

Beidel, D. C. (1988). Psychophysiological assessment of anxious emotional states in children. *Journal of Abnormal Psychology, 97,* 80–82.

Beidel, D. C., Christ, M. A. G., & Long, P. J. (1991). Somatic complaints in anxious children. *Journal of Abnormal Child Psychology, 19,* 659–670.

Beidel, D. C., Turner, M. W., & Trager, K. N. (1994). Test anxiety and childhood anxiety disorders in African American and White school children. *Journal of Anxiety Disorders, 8,* 169–179.

Bell-Dolan, D. J., Last, C. G., & Strauss, C. C. (1990). Symptoms of anxiety disorders in normal children. *Journal of the American Academy of Child and Adolescent Psychiatry, 29,* 759–765.

Bentler, P. M. (1962). An infant's phobia treated with reciprocal inhibition therapy. *Journal of Child Psychology and Psychiatry, 3,* 185–189.

Bernstein, G. A. (1991). Comorbidity and severity of anxiety and depressive disorders in a clinic sample. *Journal of the American Academy of Child and Adolescent Psychiatry, 30,* 43–50.

Bernstein, G. A. (1994). Pharmacological interventions. In T. H. Ollendick, N. J. King, & W. Yule (Eds.), *International handbook of phobic and anxiety disorders in children and adolescents* (pp. 439–451). New York: Plenum Press.

Bernstein, G. A., & Borchardt, C. M. (1991). Anxiety disorders of childhood and adolescence: A critical review. *Journal of the American Academy of Child and Adolescent Psychiatry, 30,* 519–532.

Bernstein, G. A., & Garfinkel, B. D. (1986). School phobia: The overlap of affective and anxiety disorders. *Journal of the American Academy of Child Psychiatry, 2,* 325–241.

Bernstein, G. A., & Garfinkel, B. D. (1988). Pedigrees, functioning, and psychopathology in families of school phobic children. *American Journal of Psychiatry, 145,* 70–74.

Bird, H. R., Canino, G., & Rubio-Stipec, M. (1988). Estimates of the prevalence of childhood maladjustment in a community survey in Puerto Rico. *Archives of General Psychiatry, 45,* 1120–1126.

Black, A. H. (1958). The extinction of avoidance under curare. *Journal of Comparative and Physiological Psychology, 51,* 519–524.

Black, A. (1974). The natural history of obsessional neurosis. In H. R. Beech (Ed.), *Obsessional states,* (pp. 3–32). London: Methuen.

Blagg, N. R., & Yule, W. (1984). The behavioral treatment of school-refusal: A comparative study. *Behaviour Research and Therapy, 22,* 119–127.

Blount, R. L., Davis, N., Powers, S. W., & Roberts, M. C. (1991). The influence of environmental factors and coping style on children's coping and distress. *Clinical Psychology Review, 11*, 93–116.

Blount, R. L., Sturges, J. W., & Powers, S. W. (1990). Analysis of child and adult behavioral variations by phase of medical procedure. *Behavior Therapy, 21*, 33–48.

Boer, A. P., & Sipprelle, C. N. (1970). Elimination of avoidance behavior in the clinic and its transfer to the normal environment. *Journal of Behavior Therapy and Experimental Psychiatry, 1*, 169–174.

Bolton, D. (1994). Family systems interventions. In T. H. Ollendick, N. J. King, & W. Yule (Eds.), *International handbook of phobic and anxiety disorders in children and adolescents* (pp. 397–414). New York: Plenum Press.

Bolton, D., & Turner, D. (1984). Obsessive-compulsive neurosis with conduct disorder in adolescence: A report of two cases. *Journal of Child Psychology and Psychiatry, 25*, 133–139.

Bornstein, P. H., & Knapp, M. (1981). Self-control desensitization with a multi-phobic boy: A multiple baseline design. *Journal of Behavior Therapy and Experimental Psychiatry, 12*, 281–285.

Boyd, L. T. (1980). Emotive imagery in the behavioral management of adolescent school phobia: A case approach. *School Psychology Digest, 9*, 186–189.

Brady, E. U., & Kendall, P. C. (1992). Comorbidity of anxiety and depression in children and adolescents. *Psychological Bulletin, 111*, 244–255.

Bregman, E. O. (1934). An attempt to modify the emotional attitudes of infants by the conditioned response technique. *Journal of Genetic Psychology, 45*, 169–198.

Bronson, G. W. (1972). Infants' reactions to unfamiliar persons and novel objects. *Monographs of the Society for Research in Child Development, 37* (3, Serial No. 148).

Brown, R. (1979). Beyond separation. In D. Hall & M. Stacey (Eds.), *Beyond Separation*. London: Routledge & Kegan Paul.

Brown, R. E., Copeland, R. E., & Hall, R. V. (1974). School phobia: Effects of behavior modification treatment applied by an elementary school principal. *Child Study Journal, 4*, 125–133.

Brush, F. R. (1957). The effects of shock intensity on the acquisition and extinction of an avoidance response in dogs. *Journal of Comparative and Physiological Psychology, 50*, 547–552.

Buell, J., Stoddard, P., Harris, F. R., & Baer, D. M. (1968). Collateral social development accompanying reinforcement of outdoor play in a preschool child. *Journal of Applied Behavior Analysis, 1*, 167–173.

Burke, A. E., & Silverman, W. K. (1987). The prescriptive treatment of school refusal. *Clinical Psychology Review, 7*, 353–362.

Burke, K. C., Burke, J. D., Regier, D. A., & Rae, D. S. (1990). Age at onset of selected mental disorders in five community populations. *Archives of General Psychiatry, 47*, 511–518.

Burstein, S., & Meichenbaum, D. (1979). The work of worrying in children undergoing surgery. *Journal of Abnormal Child Psychology, 7*, 121–132.

Campbell III, L. M. (1973). A variation of thought-stopping in a twelve-year-old boy: A case report. *Journal of Behavior Therapy and Experimental Psychiatry, 4*, 69–70.

Campbell, S. B. (1986). Developmental issues. In R. Gittelman (Ed.), *Anxiety disorders of childhood* (pp. 24–57). New York: Guilford Press.

Carey, G., & Gottesman, I. I. (1981). Twin and family studies of anxiety, phobic, and obsessive disorders. In D. F. Klein & J. G. Rabkin (Eds.), *Anxiety: New research and changing concepts* (pp. 117–136). New York: Raven Press.

Cavior, N., & Deutsch, A. M. (1975). Systematic desensitization to reduce dream-induced anxiety. *Journal of Nervous and Mental Disease, 161*, 433–435.

Chapel, J. L. (1967). Treatment of a case of school phobia by reciprocal inhibition. *Canadian Psychiatric Association Journal, 12*, 25–28.

Chertock, S. L., & Bornstein, P. H. (1979). Covert modeling treatment of children's dental fears. *Child Behavior Therapy, 1*, 249–255.

Cicchetti, D. (1984). The emergence of developmental psychopathology. *Child Development, 55*, 1–7.

Cicchetti, D. (1993). Developmental psychopathology: Reactions, reflections, projections. *Developmental Review, 13*, 471–502.

Clark, D. A., Sugrin, I., & Bolton, D. (1982). Primary obsessional slowness: A nursing treatment programme with a 13-year-old male adolescent. *Behaviour Research and Therapy, 20*, 289–292.

Clement, P. W., & Milne, D. C. (1967). Group play therapy and tangible reinforcers used to modify the behavior of 8-year-old boys. *Behaviour Research and Therapy, 5*, 301–312.

Cohen, M. E., Badal, D. W., Kilpatrick, A., Reed, E. W., & White, P. D. (1951). The high familial prevalence of neurocirculatory asthenia (anxiety neurosis, effort syndrome). *American Journal of Human Genetics, 3*, 126–158.

Cone, J. D. (1979). Confounded comparisons in triple response mode assessment research. *Behavioral Assessment, 1*, 85–95.

Costello, E. J. (1989). Child psychiatric disorders and their comorbidity in a primary care pediatric sample. *Journal of the American Academy of Child and Adolescent Psychiatry, 28*, 851–855.

Coyle, P. J. (1968). The systematic desensitization of reading anxiety: A case study. *Psychology in the School, 5*, 140–141.

Cradock, C., Cotler, S., & Jason, L. A. (1978). Primary prevention: Immunization of children for speech anxiety. *Cognitive Therapy and Research, 2*, 389–396.

Cretekos, C. J. G. (1977). Some techniques in rehabilitating the school-phobic adolescent. *Adolescence, 12*, 237–246.

Croake, J. W. (1969). Fears of Children. *Human Development, 12*, 239–247.

Croake, J. W., & Knox, F. H. (1973). The changing nature of children's fears. *Child Study Journal, 3*, 91–105.

Croghan, L. M. (1981). Conceptualizing the critical elements in a rapid desensitization to school anxiety: A case study. *Journal of Pediatric Psychology, 6*, 165–170.

Croghan, L., & Musante, G. J. (1975). The elimination of a boy's high-building phobia by *in vivo* desensitization and game playing. *Journal of Behavior Therapy and Experimental Psychiatry, 6*, 87–88.

Crowe, R. R., Noyes, R., Pauls, D. L., & Slymen, D. (1983). A family study of panic disorder. *Archives of General Psychiatry, 44*, 933–937.

Dahlquist, L. M., Gil, K. M., Armstrong, F. D., Ginsberg, M., & Jones, B. (1985). Behavioral management of children's distress during chemotherapy. *Journal of Behavior Therapy and Experimental Psychiatry, 16*, 325–329.

Dalton, P. (1983). Family treatment of an obsessive-compulsive child: A case report. *Family Process, 22*, 99–108.

D'Amato, M. R. (1970). *Experimental psychology: Methodology, psychophysics, and learning.* New York: McGraw-Hill.

Dar, R., & Greist, J. (1992). Behavior therapy for obsessive-compulsive disorder. *Psychiatric Clinics of North America, 15*, 885–894.

Davis, A. F., Rosenthal, T. L., & Kelley, J. E. (1981). Actual fear cues, prompt therapy, and rationale enhance participant modeling with adolescents. *Behavior Therapy, 12*, 536–542.

Deffenbacher, J. L., & Kemper, C. C. (1974). Counseling test-anxious sixth graders. *Elementary School Guidance and Counseling, 21*, 23–29.

Delprato, D. J. (1980). Hereditary determinants of fears and phobias: A critical review. *Behavior Therapy, 11*, 79–103.

Delprato, D. J., & McGlynn, F. D. (1984). Behavioral theories of anxiety disorders. In S. M. Turner (Ed.), *Behavioral treatment of anxiety disorders* (pp. 63–122). New York: Plenum.

Denny, M. R. (1971). Relaxation theory and experiments. In F. R. Brush (Ed.), *Aversive conditioning and learning* (pp. 235–296). New York: Academic Press.

Denny, M. R. (1976). Post-aversion relief and relaxation and their implications for behavior therapy. *Journal of Behavior Therapy and Experimental Psychiatry, 7*, 315–321.

DeSilva, P., Rachman, S., & Seligman, M. E. P. (1977). Prepared phobias and obsessions: Therapeutic outcome. *Behaviour Research and Therapy, 15*, 65–77.

De Vaugh-Geiss, J., Moroz, G., Biederman, J., Cantwell, D., Fontaine, R., Greist, J. H., Reichler, R., Katz, R., & Landau, P. (1992). Clomipramine hydrochloride in childhood and adolescent obsessive-compulsive disorder-A multicenter trial. *Journal of the American Academy of Child and Adolescent Psychiatry, 31*, 45–49.

Dibrell, L. L., & Yamamoto, K. (1988). In their own words: Concerns of young children. *Child Psychiatry and Human Development, 19*, 14–25.

DiNardo, P. A., & DiNardo, P. (1981). Self-control desensitization in the treatment of a childhood phobia. *The Behavior Therapist, 4*, 15–16.

Dinsmoor, J. A. (1954). Punishment: I. The avoidance hypothesis. *Psychological Review, 61*, 34–46.

Dinsmoor, J. A. (1977). Escape, avoidance, punishment: Where do we stand? *Journal of the Experimental Analysis of Behavior, 28*, 83–95.

Doleys, D. M., & Williams, S. C. (1977). The use of natural consequences and a makeup period to eliminate school-phobic behavior: A case study. *Journal of School Psychology, 15*, 44–50.

Dong, Q., Yang, B., & Ollendick, T. H. (1994). Fears in Chinese children and adolescents and their relations to anxiety and depression. *Journal of Child Psychology and Psychiatry, 35*, 351–363.

Doyal, G. T., & Friedman, R. J. (1974). Anxiety in children: Some observations for the school psychologist. *Psychology in the Schools, 11*, 161–164.

Dunlop, G. (1952). *Certain aspects of children's fears.* Unpublished master's thesis, University of North Carolina, Raleigh.

Eisen, A. R., Kearney, C. A., & Schaefer, C. E. (Eds.). (1995). *Clinical handbook of anxiety disorders in children and adolescents.* Northvale, NJ: Jason Aronson.

Eisen, A. R., & Silverman, W. K. (1991). Treatment of an adolescent with bowel movement phobia using self-control therapy. *Journal of Behavior and Experimental Psychiatry, 22*, 45–51.

Eland, J. M., & Anderson, J. E. (1977). The experience of pain in children. In A. Jacox (Ed.), *Pain: A source book for nurses and other health professionals* (pp. 68–87). Boston: Little, Brown.

Elmhirst, S. I. (1984). A psychoanalytic approach to anxiety in childhood. In V. P. Varma (Ed.), *Anxiety in children* (pp. 1–14). London: Croom Helm.

Eme, R., & Schmidt, D. (1978). The stability of children's fears. *Child Development, 49*, 1277–1279.

English, H. B. (1929). Three cases of the "conditioned fear response." *Journal of Abnormal and Social Psychology, 24*, 221–225.

Esveldt-Dawson, K., Wisner, K. L., Unis, A. S., Matson, J. L., & Kazdin, A. E. (1982). Treatment of phobias in a hospitalized child. *Journal of Behavior Therapy and Experimental Psychiatry, 13*, 77–83.

Evers, W. L., & Schwarz, J. C. (1973). Modifying social withdrawal in preschoolers: The effects of filmed modeling and teacher praise. *Journal of Abnormal Child Psychology, 1*, 248–256.

Eysenck, H. J. (1968). A theory of the incubation of anxiety/fear responses. *Behaviour Research and Therapy, 6*, 309–321.

Eysenck, H. J. (1976). The learning theory model of neurosis: A new approach. *Behaviour Research and Therapy, 14*, 251–267.

Faust, J., & Melamed, B. G. (1984). Influence of arousal, previous experience, and age on surgery preparation of same day of surgery and in-hospital pediatric patients. *Journal of Consulting and Clinical Psychology, 52*, 359–365.

Faust, J., Olson R., & Rodriguez, H. (1991). Same-day surgery preparation: Reduction of pediatric patient arousal and distress through participant modeling. *Journal of Consulting and Clinical Psychology, 59*, 475–478.

Flament, M. F., Rapoport, J. L., Berg, C. J., Sceery, W., Kilts, C., Mellström, B., & Linnoila, M. (1985). Clomipramine treatment of childhood obsessive–compulsive disorder. A double-blind controlled study. *Archives of General Psychiatry, 42,* 977–983.

Foa, E. B., & Kozak, M. J. (1986). Emotional processing of fear: Exposure to corrective information. *Psychological Bulletin, 99*, 20–35.

Fox, J. E., & Houston, B. K. (1981). Efficacy of self-instructional training for reducing children's anxiety in evaluative situation. *Behaviour Research and Therapy, 19*, 509–515.

Francis, G., Last, C. G., & Strauss, C. C, (1987). Expression of separation anxiety disorder: The roles of age and gender. *Child Psychiatry and Human Development, 18*, 82–89.

Francis, G., Last, C. G., & Strauss, C. C, (1992). Avoidant disorder and social phobia in children and adolescents. *Journal of the American Academy of Child and Adolescent Psychiatry, 31*, 1086–1089.

Franco, D. P., Christoff, K. A., Crimmins, D. E., & Kelly, J. A. (1983). Social skills training for an extremely shy young adolescent: An empirical case study. *Behavior Therapy, 14*, 568–575.

Fredrikson, M., Hugdahl, K., & Öhman, A. (1977). Electrodermal conditioning to potentially phobic stimuli in male and female subjects. *Biological Psychology, 4*, 305–314.

Freeman, B. J., Roy, R. R., & Hemmick, S. (1976). Extinction of a phobia of physical examination in a seven-year-old mentally retarded boy: A case study. *Behaviour Research and Therapy, 14*, 63–64.

Frick, P. J., Silverthorn, P., & Evans, C. (1994). Assessment of childhood anxiety using structured interviews: Patterns of agreement among informants and association with maternal anxiety. *Psychological Assessment, 6*, 372–379.

Friedman, A. G., & Ollendick, T. H. (1989) Treatment programs for severe night-time fears: A methodological note. *Journal of Behavior Therapy and Experimental Psychiatry, 20*, 171–178.

Friedmann, C. T. H., & Silvers, F. M. (1977). A multimodality approach to inpatient treatment of obsessive-compulsive disorder. *American Journal of Psychotherapy, 31*, 456–465.

Garland, E. J., & Smith, D. H. (1990). Panic disorder on a child psychiatric consultation service. *Journal of the American Academy of Child and Adolescent Psychiatry, 29*, 785–788.

Garvey, W. P., & Hegrenes, J. R. (1966). Desensitization techniques in the treatment of school phobia. *American Journal of Orthopsychiatry, 36*, 147–152.

Gelfand, D. M. (1978). Behavioral treatment of avoidance, social withdrawal and negative emotional states. In D. D. Wolman, J. Egan, & A. O. Ross (Eds.), *Handbook of treatment of mental disorders in childhood and adolescence* (pp. 132–159). Englewood Cliffs, NJ: Prentice-Hall.

Gelfand, D. M., & Hartmann, D. P. (1977). The prevention of childhood behavior disorders. In B. B. Lahey & A. E. Kazdin (Eds.), *Advances in clinical child psychology* (Vol. 1, pp. 362–396). New York: Plenum Press.

Genshaft, J. L. (1982). The use of cognitive behavior therapy for reducing math anxiety. *School Psychology Review, 11*, 32–34.

Genshaft, J. L., & Hirt, M. L. (1980). The effectiveness of self-instructional training to enhance math achievement in women. *Cognitive Therapy and Research, 4*, 91–97.

Ghose, L. J., Giddon, D. B., Shiere, F. R., & Fogels, H. R. (1969). Evaluation of sibling support. *Journal of Dentistry for Children, 36*, 35–40.

Giebenhain, J. E. (1985). *Multi-channel assessment of children's fears of the dark.* Unpublished doctoral dissertation, University of Mississippi, Oxford, MS.

Giebenhain, J. E., & Barrios, B. A. (1986, November). *Multi-channel assessment of children's fears.* Paper presented at the meeting of the Association for Advancement of Behavior Therapy, Chicago.

Giebenhain, J. E., & O'Dell, S. L. (1984). Evaluation of a parent-training manual for reducing children's fear of the dark. *Journal of Applied Behavior Analysis, 17*, 121–125.

Gilbert, B. O., Johnson, S. B., Spiller, R., McCallum, M., Silverstein, J. H., & Rosenbloom, A. (1982). The effects of a peer-modeling film on children learning to self-inject insulin. *Behavior Therapy, 13*, 186–193.

Ginther, L. J., & Roberts, M. C. (1982). A test of mastery versus coping modeling on the reduction of children's dental fears. *Child and Family Behavior Therapy, 4*, 41–52.

Gittelman, R. (Ed.). (1986). *Anxiety disorders of childhood.* New York: Guilford Press.

Glennon, B., & Weisz, J. R. (1978). An observational approach to the assessment of anxiety in young children. *Journal of Consulting and Clinical Psychology, 46*, 1246–1257.

Graham, P. (1964). *Controlled trial of behavior therapy vs. Conventional therapy: A pilot study.* Unpublished doctoral dissertation, University of London.

Gray, J. A. (1971). *The psychology of fear and stress.* New York: McGraw-Hill.

Gray, J. A. (1987). *The psychology of fear and stress* (2nd ed.). Cambridge, England: Cambridge University Press.

Graziano, A. M., & DeGiovanni, I. S. (1979). The clinical significance of childhood phobias: A note on the proportion of child-clinical referrals for the treatment of children's fears. *Behaviour Research and Therapy, 17,* 161–162.

Graziano, A. M., & DeGiovanni, I. S., & Garcia, K. A. (1979). Behavioral treatment of children's fears: A review. *Psychological Bulletin, 86,* 804–830.

Graziano, A. M., & Mooney, K. C. (1980). Family self-control instruction for children's nighttime fear reduction. *Journal of Consulting and Clinical Psychology, 48,* 206–213.

Graziano, A. M., & Mooney, K. C. (1982). Behavioral treatment of "nightfears" in children: Maintenance of improvement at 2½- to 3-year follow-up. *Journal of Consulting and Clinical Psychology, 50,* 598–599.

Graziano, A. M., Mooney, K. C., Huber, C., & Ignasiak, D. (1979). Self-control instructions for children's fear reduction. *Journal of Behavior Therapy and Experimental Psychiatry, 10.* 221–227.

Grindler, M. (1988). Effects of cognitive monitoring strategies on the test anxieties of elementary students. *Psychology in the Schools, 25,* 428–436.

Grossman, P. B., & Hughes, J. N. (1992). Self-control interventions with internalizing disorders: A review and analysis. *School Psychology Review, 21,* 229–245.

Gullone, E., & King, N. J. (1992). Psychometric evaluation of a Revised Fear Survey Schedule for Children and Adolescents. *Journal of Child Psychology and Psychiatry, 33,* 987–998.

Hagman, E. R. (1932). A study of fears of children of preschool age. *Journal of Experimental Education, 1,* 110–130.

Hampe, E., Noble, H., Miller, L. C., & Barrett, C. L. (1973). Phobic children one and two years post-treatment. *Journal of Abnormal Psychology, 82,* 446–453.

Handler, L. (1972). The amelioration of nightmares in children. *Psychotherapy: Theory, Research, and Practice, 9,* 54–56.

Harris, K. R., & Brown, R. D., (1982). Cognitive behavior modification and informed teacher treatments for shy children. *Journal of Experimental Education, 50,* 137–143.

Hatcher, S. (1989). A case of doll phobia. *British Journal of Psychiatry, 155,* 255–257.

Hatzenbuehler, L. C., & Schroeder, H. E. (1978). Desensitization procedures in the treatment of childhood disorders. *Psychological Bulletin, 85,* 831–844.

Hawley, B. P., McCorkle, A. D., Witteman, J. K., & Van Ostenberg, P. (1974). The first dental visit for children from low socioeconomic families. *Journal of Dentistry for Children, 41,* 376–381.

Hebb, D. O. (1946). On the nature of fear. *Psychological Review, 53,* 259–276.

Heimberg, R. G, Gansler, D., Dodge, C. S., & Becker, R. E. (1987). Convergent and discriminant validity of the Cognitive-Somatic Anxiety Questionnaire in a social phobic population. *Behavioral Assessment, 9,* 379–388.

Herbert, M. (1984). Psychological treatment of childhood neuroses. In V. P. Varma (Ed.), *Anxiety in children* (pp. 172–193). London: Croom Helm.

Herbertt, R. M., & Innes, J. M. (1979). Familiarization and preparatory information in the reduction of anxiety in child dental patients. *Journal of Dentistry for Children, 46,* 319–323.

Herrnstein, R. J. (1969). Method and theory in the study of avoidance, *Psychological Review, 76,* 49–69.

Hersen, M. (1968). Treatment of a compulsive and phobic disorder through a total behavior therapy program: A case study. *Psychotherapy: Theory, Research, and Practice, 5,* 220–225.

Hersen, M. (1970). Behavior modification approach to a school-phobia case. *Journal of Clinical Psychology, 26,* 128–132.

Hershberg, S. G., Carlson, G. A., Cantwell, D. P., & Strober, M. (1982). Anxiety and depressive disorders in psychiatrically disturbed children. *Journal of Clinical Psychiatry, 43,* 358–361.

Hill, J. H., Liebert, R. M., & Mott, D. E. W. (1968). Vicarious extinction of avoidance behavior through films: An initial test. *Psychological Reports, 22,* 192.

Hodgson, R., & Rachman, S. (1974). Desynchrony in measures of fear: II. *Behaviour Research and Therapy, 12,* 319–326.

Hoehn-Saric, E., Maisami, M., & Weigand, D. (1987). Measurement of anxiety in children and adolescents using semi-structured interviews. *Journal of the American Academy of Child and Adolescent Psychiatry, 26,* 541–545.

Holmes, F. B. (1935). An experimental study of the fears of young children. In A. T. Jersild & F. B. Holmes (Eds.), *Children's fears* (Child Development Monograph No. 20, pp. 167–296). New York: Columbia University Press.

Holmes, F. B. (1936). An experimental investigation of a method of overcoming children's fears. *Child Development, 7,* 6–30.

Hugdahl, K., Fredrikson, M., & Öhman, A. (1977). "Preparedness" and "arousability" as determinants of electrodermal conditioning. *Behaviour Research and Therapy, 15,* 345–353.

Hugdahl, K., & Öhman, A. (1977). Effects of instructions on acquisition and extinction of electrodermal responses to fear relevant stimuli. *Journal of Experimental Psychology: Human Learning and Memory, 3,* 608–618.

Jackson, D. A., & Wallace, R. F. (1974). The modification and generalization of voice loudness in a fifteen-year-old retarded girl. *Journal of Applied Behavior Analysis, 7,* 461–471.

Jackson, H. J., & King, N. J. (1981). The emotive imagery treatment of a child's trauma-induced phobia.

Journal of Behavior Therapy and Experimental Psychiatry, 12, 325–328.

Jacobs, W. J., & Nadel, L. (1985). Stress-induced recovery of fears and phobias. *Psychological Review, 92*, 512–531.

Jay, S. M., Elliott, C. H., Ozolins, M., Olson, R. A., & Pruitt, S. D. (1985). Behavioural management of children's distress during painful medical procedures. *Behaviour Research and Therapy, 23*, 513–520.

Jay, S. M., Ozolins, M., Elliott, C., & Caldwell, S. (1983). Assessment of children's distress during painful medical procedures. *Journal of Health Psychology, 2*, 133–147.

Jerremalm, A., Jansson, K., & Öst, L. G. (1986). Cognitive and physiological reactivity and the effects of different behavioral methods in the treatment of social phobia. *Behaviour Research and Therapy, 24*, 171–180.

Jersild, A. T. (1954). Emotional development. In L. Carmichael (Ed.), *Manual of child psychology* (2nd ed., pp. 833–917). New York: Wiley.

Jersild, A. T. (1968). *Child psychology* (6th ed.). Englewood Cliffs, NJ: Prentice-Hall.

Jersild, A. T., & Holmes, F. (Eds.). (1935). *Children's fears* (Child Development Monograph No. 20). New York: Columbia University Press.

Johnson, S. B., & Melamed, B. G. (1979). The assessment and treatment of children's fears. In B. B. Lahey & A. E. Kazdin (Eds.), *Advances in clinical child psychology* (Vol. 2, pp. 107–139). New York: Plenum Press.

Johnson, T., Tyler, V., Thompson, R., & Jones, E. (1971). Systematic desensitization and assertive training in the treatment of speech anxiety in middle-school students. *Psychology in the Schools, 8*, 263–267.

Jones, M. C. (1924a). The elimination of children's fears. *Journal of Experimental Psychology, 1*, 383–390.

Jones, M. C. (1924b). A laboratory study of fear: The case of Peter. *Pedagogical Seminar, 31*, 308–315.

Jones, R. T., Ollendick, T. H., McLaughlin, K. J., & Williams, C. E. (1989). Elaborative and behavioral rehearsal in the acquisition of fire emergency skills and the reduction of fear of fire. *Behavior Therapy, 20*, 93–101.

Kagan, J. (1994). *Galen's prophecy: Temperament in human nature*. New York: Basic Books.

Kagan, J., & Moss, H. A. (1962). *Birth to maturity*. New York: Wiley.

Kagan, J., Reznick, J. S., Clarke, C. Snidman, N., & Garcia-Coll, C. (1984). Behavioral inhibition to the unfamiliar. *Child Development, 55*, 2212–2225.

Kandal, H. J., Ayllon, T., & Rosenbaum, M. S. (1977). Flooding or systematic exposure in the treatment of extreme social withdrawal in children. *Journal of Behavior Therapy and Experimental Psychiatry, 8*, 75–81.

Kane, M. T., & Kendall, P. C. (1989). Anxiety disorders in children: A multiple-baseline evaluation of a cognitive-behavioral treatment. *Behavior Therapy, 20*, 499–508.

Kanfer, F. H., Karoly, P., & Newman, A. (1975). Reduction of children's fear of the dark by confidence-related and situational threat-related verbal cues. *Journal of Consulting and Clinical Psychology, 43*, 251–258.

Kashani, J. H., & Orvaschel, H. (1988). Anxiety disorders in mid-adolescence: A community sample. *American Journal of Psychiatry, 145*, 960–964.

Kashani, J. H., & Orvaschel, H. (1990). A community study of anxiety in children and adolescents. *American Journal of Psychiatry, 147*, 313–318.

Kashani, J. H., Vaidya, A. F., Soltys, S. M., Dandoy, A. C., Katz, L. M., & Reid, J. C. (1990). Correlates of anxiety in psychiatrically hospitalized children and their parents. *American Journal of Psychiatry, 147*, 319–323.

Katz, E. R., Kellerman, J., & Siegel, S. E. (1980). Behavioral distress in children with cancer undergoing medical procedures: Developmental considerations. *Journal of Consulting and Clinical Psychology, 48*, 356–365.

Kazdin, A. E. (1987). The evaluation of psychotherapy: Research design and methodology. In S. L. Garfield & A. E. Bergin (Eds.), *Handbook of psychotherapy and behavior change: An empirical analysis* (3rd ed., pp. 25–68). New York: Wiley.

Kearney, C. A., & Silverman, W. K. (1990a). A preliminary analysis of a functional model of assessment and treatment for school refusal behavior. *Behavior Modification, 14*, 340–366.

Kearney, C. A., & Silverman, W. K. (1990b). Treatment of an adolescent with obsessive-compulsive disorder by an alternating response prevention and cognition therapy: An empirical analysis. *Journal of Behavior Therapy and Experimental Psychiatry, 21*, 39–47.

Kearney, C. A., & Silverman, W. K. (1993). Measuring the function of school refusal behavior: The School Refusal Assessment Scale. *Journal of Consulting and Clinical Psychology, 22*, 85–96.

Kearney, C. A., & Silverman, W. K. (1995). Anxiety disorders. In V. B. Van Hasselt & M. Hersen (Eds.), *Handbook of adolescent psychopathology: A guide to diagnosis and treatment* (pp. 435–464). Lexington, MA: Lexington Books.

Keehn, J. D. (1966). Avoidance responses as discriminated operants. *British Journal of Psychology, 57*, 375–389.

Keller, M. F., & Carlson, P. M. (1974). The use of symbolic modeling to promote social skills in preschool children with low levels of social responsiveness. *Child Development, 45*, 912–919.

Kellerman, J. (1980). Rapid treatment of nocturnal anxiety in children. *Journal of Behavior Therapy and Experimental Psychiatry, 11*, 9–11.

Kelley, C. K. (1976). Play desensitization of fear of darkness in preschool children. *Behaviour Research and Therapy, 14*, 79–81.

Kendall, P. C. (1994). Treating anxiety disorders in children: Results of a randomized clinical trial. *Journal of Consulting and Clinical Psychology, 62,* 100–110.

Kendall, P. C., Chansky, T. E., Kane, M. T., Kim, R., Kortlander, E., Ronan, K. R., Sessa, F. M., & Sigueland, L. (1992). *Anxiety disorders in youth: Cognitive behavioral interventions.* Needham, MA: Allyn and Bacon.

Kennedy, W. A. (1965). School phobia: Rapid treatment of fifty cases. *Journal of Abnormal Psychology, 70,* 285–289.

King, N. J., Cranston, F., & Josephs, A. (1989). Emotive imagery and children's nighttime fears: A multiple baseline design evaluation. *Journal of Behavior Therapy and Experimental Psychiatry, 20,* 125–135.

King, N. J., Hamilton, D. I., & Murphy, G. C. (1983). The prevention of children's maladaptive fears. *Child and Family Behavior Therapy, 5,* 43–57.

King, N. J., Ollier, K., Iacuone, R., Schuster, S., Bays, K., Gullone, E., & Ollendick, T. H. (1989). Fears of children and adolescents: A cross-sectional Australian study using the Revised-Fear Survey Schedule for Children. *Journal of Child Psychology and Psychiatry, 30,* 775–784.

King, N. J., & Tonge, B. J. (1992). Treatment of childhood anxiety disorders using behavior therapy and pharmacotherapy. *Australian & New Zealand Journal of Psychiatry, 26,* 644–651.

Kirkpatrick, D. R. (1984). Age, gender and patterns of common intense fears among adults. *Behaviour Research and Therapy, 22,* 141–150.

Kissel, S. (1972). Systematic desensitization therapy with children: A case study and some suggested modifications. *Professional Psychology, 3,* 164–168.

Klesges, R. C., Malott, J. M., & Ugland, M. (1984). The effects of graded exposure and parental modeling on the dental phobias of a four-year-old girl and her mother. *Journal of Behavior Therapy and Experimental Psychiatry, 15,* 161–164.

Klingman, A., Melamed, B. G., Cuthbert, M. I., & Hermecz, D. A. (1984). Effects of participant modeling on information acquisition and skill utilization. *Journal of Consulting and Clinical Psychology, 52,* 414–422.

Klorman, R., Hilpert, P. L., Michael, R., LaGana, C., & Sveen, O. B. (1980). Effects of coping and mastery modeling on experienced and inexperienced pedodontic patients' disruptiveness. *Behavior Therapy, 11,* 156–168.

Knight, R., Atkins, A., Eagle, C., Evans, N., Finklestein, J. W., Fukushima, D., Katz, J., & Weimer, H. (1979). Psychological stress, ego defenses, and cortisol productions in children hospitalized for elective surgery. *Psychosomatic Medicine, 41,* 40–49.

Knox, L. S., Albano, A. M., & Barlow, D. H. (1996). Parental involvement in the treatment of childhood obsessive-compulsive disorder: A multiple-baseline examination incorporating parents. *Behavior Therapy, 27,* 93–114.

Kolko, D. J. (1984). Paradoxical instruction in the elimination of avoidance behavior in an agoraphobic girl. *Journal of Behavior Therapy and Experimental Psychiatry, 15,* 51–58.

Kolko, D. J., Ayllon, T., & Torrence, C. (1987). Positive practice routines in overcoming resistance to the treatment of school phobia: A case study with follow-up. *Journal of Behavior Therapy and Experimental Psychiatry, 18,* 249–257.

Kondas, O. (1967). Reduction of examination anxiety and "stage-fright" by group desensitization and relaxation. *Behaviour Research and Therapy, 5,* 275–281.

Kornhaber, R. C., & Schroeder, H. E. (1975). Importance of model similarity on extinction of avoidance behavior in children. *Journal of Consulting and Clinical Psychology, 43,* 601–607.

Kovacs, M., Gatsonis, C., Paulauskas, S. L., & Richards, C. (1989). Depressive disorders in childhood: A longitudinal study of comorbidity with and risk for anxiety disorders. *Archives of General Psychiatry, 46,* 776–782.

Kranzler, H. R. (1988). Case study: Use of busiprone in an adolescent with overanxious disorder. *Journal of the American Academy of Child and Adolescent Psychiatry, 27,* 739–790.

Kuroda, J. (1969). Elimination of children's fears of animals by the method of experimental desensitization: A application of learning theory to child psychology. *Psychologia: An International Journal of Psychology in the Orient, 12,* 161–165.

Kutcher, S. P., Reiter, S., Gardner, D. M., & Klein, R. G. (1992). The pharmacotherapy of anxiety disorders in children and adolescents. *Pediatric Clinics of North America, 15,* 41-67.

LaFreniére, P. J., & Dumas, J. E. (1992). A transactional analysis of early childhood anxiety and social withdrawal. *Development and Psychopathology, 4,* 385–402.

LaGreca, A. M., Dandes, S. K., Wick, P., Shaw, K., & Stone, W. L. (1988). Development of the Social Anxiety Scale for Children: Reliability and concurrent validity. *Journal of Consulting and Clinical Psychology, 17,* 84–91.

Lang, P. J. (1968). Fear reduction and fear behaviors. In. J. M. Shlien (Ed.), *Research in psychotherapy* (Vol. 3, pp. 90–103). Washington, DC: American Psychological Association.

Lang, P. J. (1971). The application of psychophysiological methods to the study of psychotherapy and behavior modification. In A. E. Bergin & S. L. Garfield (Eds.), *Handbook of psychotherapy and behavior change* (pp. 75–125). New York: Wiley.

Lang, P. J. (1977). Fear imagery: An information processing analysis. *Behavior Therapy, 8,* 862–886.

Lang, P. J. (1979). A bio-informational theory of emotional imagery. *Psychophysiology, 16,* 495–512.

Lang, P. J. (1984). Cognition in emotion: Concept and action. In C. E. Izard, J. Kagan, & R. B. Zajonc

(Eds.), *Emotions, cognition, and behavior* (pp. 192–228). New York: Cambridge University Press.

Lapouse, R., & Monk, M. A. (1959). Fears and worries in a representative sample of children. *American Journal of Orthopsychiatry, 29*, 223–248.

Last, C. G. (Ed.). (1988). Childhood anxiety disorders [Special issue]. *Behavior Modification, 12* (2).

Last, C. G., Hersen, M., Kazdin, A. E., Francis, G., & Grubb, H. J. (1987). Psychiatric illness in the mothers of anxious children. *American Journal of Psychiatry, 144*, 1580–1583.

Last, C. G., Hersen, M., Kazdin, A. E., Orvaschel, H., & Perrin, S. (1991). Anxiety disorders in children and their families. *Archives of General Psychiatry, 48*, 928–934.

Last, C. G., & Perrin, S. (1993). Anxiety disorders in African-American and white children. *Journal of Abnormal Child Psychology, 21*, 153–164.

Last, C. G., Perrin, S., Hersen, M., & Kazdin, A. E. (1992). DSM-III-R anxiety disorders in children: Sociodemographic and clinical characteristics. *Journal of the American Academy of Child and Adolescent Psychiatry, 31*, 1070–1076.

Last, C. G., Strauss, C. C., & Francis, G. (1987). Comorbidity among childhood anxiety disorders. *Journal of Nervous and Mental Disease, 175*, 726–730.

Laurent, J., Hadler, J. R., & Stark, K. D. (1994). A multiple-stage screening procedure for the identification of childhood anxiety disorders. *School Psychology Quarterly, 9*, 239–255.

Laurent, J., & Stark, K. D. (1993). Testing the cognitive content-specificity hypothesis with anxious and depressed youngsters. *Journal of Abnormal Psychology, 102*, 226–237.

Laxer, M., Quarter, J., Kooman, A., & Walker, K. (1969). Systematic desensitization and relaxation of high test-anxious secondary school students. *Journal of Counseling Psychology, 16*, 446–451.

Laxer, M., & Walker, K. (1970). Counterconditioning versus relaxation in the desensitization of test anxiety. *Journal of Counseling Psychology, 17*, 431–436.

Lazarus, A. A. (1960). The elimination of children's phobias by deconditioning. In H. J. Eysenck (Ed.), *Behavior therapy and the neuroses* (pp. 114–122). New York: Pergamon Press.

Lazarus, A. A., & Abramovitz, A. (1962). The use of emotive imagery in the treatment of children's phobias. *Journal of Mental Science, 108*, 191–195.

Lazarus, A. A., Davison, G. C., & Polefka, D. A. (1965). Classical and operant factors in the treatment of a school phobia. *Journal of Abnormal Psychology, 70*, 225–229.

Lazarus, A. A., & Rachman, S. (1957). The use of systematic desensitization in psychotherapy. *South African Medical Journal, 31*, 334–337.

Leal, L. L., Baxter, E. G., Martin, J., & Marx, R. W. (1981). Cognitive modification and systematic desensitization with test anxious high school students. *Journal of Counseling Psychology, 28*, 525–528.

LeBaron, S., & Zeltzer, L. (1984). Assessment of acute pain and anxiety in children and adolescents by self-reports, observer reports, and a behavior checklist. *Journal of Consulting and Clinical Psychology, 52*, 729–738.

Leitenberg, H., Agras, S., Butz, R., & Wincze, J. (1971). Relationship between heart rate and behavioral change during the treatment of phobias. *Journal of Abnormal Psychology, 78*, 59–68.

Leitenberg, H., & Callahan, E. J. (1973). Reinforced practice and education of different kinds of fears in adults and children. *Behaviour Research and Therapy, 11*, 19–30.

Leonard, H. L., Swedo, S. E., Rapoport, J. L., Koby, E. V., Lenane, M. C., Cheslow, D. L., & Hamburger, M. A. (1989). Treatment of obsessive-compulsive disorder with clomipramine and desipramine in children and adolescents: A double-blind crossover comparison. *Archives of General Psychiatry, 46*, 1088–1092.

LeUnes, A., & Siemsglusz, S. (1977). Paraprofessional treatment of school phobia in a young adolescent girl. *Adolescence, 12*, 115–121.

Lewis, M., & Brooks, J. (1974). Self, others, and fear: Infants' reactions to people. In M. Lewis & L. A. Rosenblum (Eds.), *The origins of fear* (pp. 195–228). New York: Wiley.

Lewis, M., & Michalson, L. (1982). The measurement of emotional state. In C. E. Izard (Ed.), *Measuring emotions in infants and children* (pp. 178–207). London: Cambridge University Press.

Lewis, S. (1974). A comparison of behavior therapy techniques in the reduction of fearful avoidant behavior. *Behavior Therapy, 5*, 648–655.

Lewis, T. M., & Law, D. B (1958). Investigation of certain autonomic responses of children to a specific dental stress. *Journal of the American Dental Association, 57*, 769–777.

Linscheid, T. R., Tarnowski, K. J., Rasnake, L. K., & Brams, J. S. (1987). Behavioral treatment of food refusal in a child with short-gut syndrome. *Journal of Pediatric Psychology, 12*, 451–459.

Little, S., & Jackson, B. (1974). The treatment of test anxiety through attentional and relaxation training. *Psychotherapy: Theory, Research, and Practice, 11*, 175–178.

Livingston, R. L., Dykman, R. A., & Ackerman, P. T. (1990). The frequency and significance of additional self reported psychiatric diagnoses in children with attention deficit disorder. *Journal of Abnormal Child Psychology, 18*, 465–478.

Luiselli, J. K. (1978). Treatment of an autistic child's fear of riding a school bus through exposure and reinforcement. *Journal of Behavior Therapy and Experimental Psychiatry, 9*, 169–172.

Lyon, L. W. (1983). A behavioral treatment of compulsive lip-biting. *Journal of Behavior Therapy and Experimental Psychiatry, 14*, 275–276.

MacDonald, M. L. (1975). Multiple impact behavior therapy in a child's dog phobia. *Journal of Behav-*

ior Therapy and Experimental Psychiatry, 6, 317–322.

MacFarlane, J., Allen, L., & Honzik, M. (1954). *A developmental study of the behavior problems of normal children between twenty-one months and fourteen years.* Berkeley: University of California Press.

Mann, J. (1972). Vicarious desensitization of test anxiety through observation of videotaped treatment. *Journal of Counseling Psychology, 19,* 1–7.

Mann, J., & Rosenthal, T. L. (1969). Vicarious and direct counterconditioning of test anxiety through individual and group desensitization. *Behaviour Research and Therapy, 7,* 359–367.

March, J. S. (1995). Cognitive-behavioral psychotherapy for children and adolescents with OCD: A review and recommendations for treatment. *Journal of the American Academy of Child and Adolescent Psychiatry, 34,* 7–18.

Marks, I. M. (1969). *Fears and phobias.* New York: Academic Press.

Marks, I. M. (1987). *Fears, phobias, and rituals.* Oxford: Oxford University Press.

Mash, E. J. (1985). Some comments on target selection in behavior therapy. *Behavioral Assessment, 7,* 63–78.

Mash, E. J., & Hunsley, J. (1993). Behavior therapy and managed mental health care: Integrating effectiveness and economics in mental health practice. *Behavior Therapy, 24,* 67–90.

Mash, E. J., & Terdal, L. G. (1977). After the dance is over: Some issues and suggestions for follow-up assessment in behavior therapy. *Psychological Reports, 41,* 1287–1308.

Matson, J. L. (1981). Assessment and treatment of clinical fears in mentally retarded children. *Journal of Applied Behavior Analysis, 14,* 287–294.

Matson, J. L. (1983). Exploration of phobic behavior in a small child. *Journal of Behavior Therapy and Experimental Psychiatry, 14,* 257–260.

Maurer, A. (1965). What children fear. *Journal of Genetic Psychology, 106,* 265–277.

Mayer, G. E., Beggs, D. L., Fjellstedt, N., Forhetz, J., Nighswander, J. K., & Richards, R. (1971). The use of public commitment and counseling with elementary school children: An evaluation. *Elementary School Guidance and Counseling, 5,* 22–34.

McCathie, H., & Spence, S. H., (1991). What is the Revised Fear Survey Schedule for Children measuring? *Behaviour Research and Therapy, 29,* 495–502.

McGee, R., Feehan, M., Williams, S., Partiridge, F., Silva, P. A., & Kelly, J. (1990). DSM-III disorders in a large sample of adolescents. *Journal of the American Academy of Child and Adolescent Psychiatry, 29,* 611–619.

McGlynn, F. D., & Rose, M. P. (in press). Assessment of anxiety and fear. In M. Hersen & A. S. Bellack (Eds.), *Behavioral assessment: A practical handbook* (4th ed.). New York: Pergamon Press.

McNally, R. J. (1987). Preparedness and phobias: A review. *Psychological Bulletin, 101,* 283–303.

McNally, R. J. (1995). Preparedness, phobias, and the Panglossian paradigm. *Behavioral and Brain Sciences, 18,* 303–304.

McNamara, E. (1988). The self-management of school phobia: A case study. *Behavioural Psychotherapy, 16,* 217–229.

Melamed, B. G. (1993). Putting the family back in the child. *Behaviour Research and Therapy, 31,* 239–248.

Melamed, B. G., Hawes, R. R., Heiby, E., & Glick, J. (1975). Use of filmed modeling to reduce uncooperative behavior of children dental treatment. *Journal of Dental Research, 54,* 797–801.

Melamed, B. G., Klingman, A., & Siegel, L. J. (1984). Childhood stress and anxiety: Individualizing cognitive behavioral strategies in the reduction of medical and dental stress. In A. W. Meyers & W. E. Craighead (Eds.), *Cognitive behavior therapy with children* (pp. 289–314). New York: Plenum Press.

Melamed, B. G., Meyer, R., Gee, C., & Soule, L. (1976). The influence of time and type of preparation on children's adjustment of hospitalization. *Journal of Pediatric Psychology, 1,* 31–37.

Melamed, B. G., & Siegel, L. J. (1975). Reductions of anxiety in children facing hospitalization and surgery by use of filmed modeling. *Journal of Consulting and Clinical Psychology, 43,* 511–521.

Melamed, B. G., & Siegel, L. J. (1980). *Behavioral medicine.* New York: Springer.

Melamed, B. G., & Siegel, L. J. (1985). Children's reactions to medical stressors: An ecological approach to the study of anxiety. In A. H. Tuma & J. Maser (Eds.), *Anxiety and the anxiety disorders* (pp. 369–388). Hillsdale, NJ: Erlbaum.

Melamed, B. G., Yurcheson, R., Fleece, E. L., Hutcherson, S., & Hawes, R. (1978). Effects of film modeling on the reduction of anxiety-related behaviors in individuals varying in level or previous experience in the stress situation. *Journal of Consulting and Clinical Psychology, 46,* 1357–1367.

Menzies, R. G., & Clarke, J. C. (1993). A comparison of *in vivo* and vicarious exposure in the treatment of childhood water phobia. *Behaviour Research and Therapy, 31,* 9–15.

Messer, S. C., & Beidel, D. C. (1994). Psychosocial correlates of childhood anxiety disorders. *Journal of the American Academy of Child and Adolescent Psychiatry, 33,* 975–983.

Milgrom, P., Foset, L., Melnick, S., & Weinstein, P. (1988). The prevalence and practice management consequences of dental fear in a major US city. *Journal of the American Dental Association, 116,* 641–647.

Miller, L. C., Barrett, C. L., & Hampe, E. (1974). Phobias of childhood in a prescientific era. In S. Davids (Ed.), *Child personality and psychopathology* (pp. 89–134). New York: Wiley.

Miller, L. C., Barrett, C. L., Hampe, E., & Noble, H. (1972a). Comparison of reciprocal inhibition psychotherapy and waiting list control for phobic children. *Journal of Abnormal Psychology, 79,* 269–279.

Miller, L. C., Barrett, C. L., Hampe, E., & Noble, H. (1972b). Factor structure of childhood fears. *Journal of Consulting and Clinical Psychology, 39,* 264–268.

Miller, N., & Kassinove, H. (1978). Effects of lecture, rehearsal, written homework, and IQ on the efficacy of a rational-emotive school mental health program. *Journal of Community Psychology, 6,* 366–373.

Miller, P. M. (1972). The use of visual imagery and muscle relaxation in the counterconditioning of a phobic child: A case study. *Journal of Nervous and Mental Disease, 154,* 457–460.

Milos, M. E., & Reiss, S. (1982). Effects of three play conditions on separation anxiety in young children. *Journal of Consulting and Clinical Psychology, 50,* 389–395.

Mitchell, J., McCauley, E., Burke, P. M., & Moss, S. J. (1988). Phenomenology of depression in children and adolescents. *Journal of the American Academy of Child and Adolescent Psychiatry, 27,* 12–20.

Montenegro, H. (1968). Severe separation anxiety in two preschool children successfully treated by reciprocal inhibition. *Journal of Child Psychology and Psychiatry, 9,* 93–103.

Moreau, D., & Weissman, M. M. (1992). Panic disorder in children and adolescents: A review. *American Journal of Psychiatry, 149,* 1306–1314.

Morelli, G. (1983). Adolescent compulsion: A case study involving cognitive-behavioral treatment. *Psychological Reports, 53,* 519–522.

Morgan, G. A. V. (1959). Children who refuse to go to school. *Medical Officer, 102,* 221–224.

Morris, R. J. (1980). Fear reduction methods. In F. H. Kanfer & A. P. Goldstein (Eds.), *Helping people change* (2nd ed., pp. 248–293). New York: Pergamon Press.

Morris, R. J., & Kratochwill, T. R. (1983a). Childhood fears and phobias. In R. J. Morris & T. R. Kratochwill (Eds.), *The practice of child therapy* (pp. 53–85). New York: Pergamon Press.

Morris, R. J., & Kratochwill, T. R. (1983b). *The practice of child therapy* New York: Pergamon Press.

Morris, R. J., & Kratochwill, T. R. (1983c). *Treating children's fears and phobias: A behavioral approach.* New York: Pergamon Press.

Mowrer, O. H. (1939). A stimulus-response analysis of anxiety and its role as a reinforcing agent. *Psychological Review, 46,* 553–565.

Mowrer, O. H. (1947). On the dual nature of learning: A reinterpretation of "conditioning" and "problem solving." *Harvard Educational Review, 17,* 102–148.

Mowrer, O. H. (1960). *Learning theory and behavior.* New York: Wiley.

Muller, S. D., & Madsen, C. H. (1970). Group desensitization for "anxious" children with reading problems. *Psychology in the Schools, 7,* 184–189.

Muris, P., Steerneman, P., Merckelbach, H., & Meesters, C. (1996). Parental modeling and fearfulness in middle childhood. *Behaviour Research and Therapy, 34,* 265–268.

Murphy, C. M., & Bootzin, R. R. (1973). Active and passive participation in the contact desensitization of snake fear in children. *Behavior Therapy, 4,* 203–211.

Nalven, F. B. (1970). Manifest fears and worries of ghetto vs. middle-class suburban children. *Psychological Reports, 27,* 285–286.

Neisworth, J. T., Madle, R. A., & Goeke, K. E. (1975). "Errorless" elimination of separation anxiety: A case study. *Journal of Behavior Therapy and Experimental Psychiatry, 6,* 79–82.

Ney, P. G. (1967). Combined therapies in a family group. *Canadian Psychiatric Association Journal, 12,* 379–385.

Ney, P. G. (1968). Combined psychotherapy and deconditioning of a child's phobia. *Canadian Psychiatric Association Journal, 13,* 293–294.

Nicolau, R., Toro, J., & Prado, C. P. (1991). Behavioral treatment of a case of psychogenic urinary retention. *Journal of Behavior Therapy and Experimental Psychiatry, 22,* 63–68..

Nocella, J., & Kaplan, R. M. (1982). Training children to cope with dental treatment. *Journal of Pediatric Psychology, 7,* 175–178.

Noyes, R., Clancy, J., Crowe, R., Hoenk, R. P., & Slymen, D. J. (1978). The familial prevalence of anxiety neurosis. *Archives of General Psychiatry, 35,* 1057–1074.

Obler, M., & Terwilliger, R. F. (1970). Pilot study on the effectiveness of systematic desensitization with neurologically impaired children with phobic disorders. *Journal of Consulting and Clinical Psychology, 34,* 314–318.

O'Connor, R. D. (1972). Relative efficacy of modeling, shaping, and the combined procedures for modification of social withdrawal. *Journal of Abnormal Psychology, 79,* 327–334.

Öhman, A. (1979). Fear relevance, autonomic conditioning, and phobias: A laboratory model. In P. O. Sjödén, S. Bates, & W. S. Dockens III (Eds.), *Trends in behavior therapy* (pp. 107–133). New York: Academic Press.

Öhman, A., Eriksson, A., & Olofsson, C. (1975). One-trial learning and superior resistance to extinction of autonomic responses conditioned to potentially phobic stimuli. *Journal of Comparative and Physiological Psychology, 88,* 619–627.

Öhman, A., Erixon, G., & Löfberg, I. (1975). Phobias and preparedness: Phobic versus neutral pictures as conditioned stimuli for human autonomic responses. *Journal of Abnormal Psychology, 84,* 41–45.

Öhman, A., Fredrikson, M., Hugdahl, K., & Rimmö, D. (1976). The premis of equipotentiality in human classical conditioning: Conditioned electrodermal responses to potentially phobic stimuli. *Journal of Experimental Psychology: General, 105,* 331–337.

Ollendick, T. H. (1979). Fear reduction techniques with children. In M. Hersen, R. M. Eisler, & P. M. Miller (Eds.), *Progress in behavior modification* (Vol. 8, pp. 127–168). New York: Academic Press.

Ollendick, T. H. (1983). Reliability and validity of the Revised Fear Survey Schedule for Children (FSSC-R). *Behaviour Research and Therapy, 21,* 685–692.

Ollendick, T. H. (1987). The Fear Survey Schedule for Children—Revised. In M. Hersen & A. S. Bellack (Eds.), *Dictionary of behavioral assessment techniques.* (pp. 118–120). New York: Pergamon Press.

Ollendick, T. H. (1995). Cognitive behavioral treatment of panic disorder with agoraphobia in adolescents: A multiple baseline design analysis. *Behavior Therapy, 26,* 517–532.

Ollendick, T. H., & Francis, G. (1988). Behavioral assessment and treatment of childhood phobias. *Behavior Modification, 12,* 165–204.

Ollendick, T. H., & Gruen, G. E. (1972). Treatment of a bodily injury phobia with implosive therapy. *Journal of Consulting and Clinical Psychology, 38,* 389–393.

Ollendick, T. H., Hagopian, L. P., & Huntzinger, R. M. (1991). Cognitive-behavior therapy with nighttime fearful children. *Journal of Behavior Therapy and Experimental Psychiatry, 22,* 113–121.

Ollendick, T. H., & King, N. J. (1994). Fears and their level of interference in adolescents. *Behaviour Research and Therapy, 32,* 635–638.

Ollendick, T. H., & King, N. J., & Frary, R. B. (1989). Fears in children and adolescents: Reliability and generalizability across gender, age, and nationality. *Behaviour Research and Therapy, 27,* 19–26.

Ollendick, T. H., King, N. J., & Yule, W. (Eds.). (1994). *International handbook of phobic and anxiety disorders in children and adolescents.* New York: Plenum Press.

Ollendick, T. H., Matson, J. L., & Helsel, W. J. (1985). Fears in children and adolescents: Normative data. *Behaviour Research and Therapy, 23,* 465–467.

Ollendick, T. H., Yule, W., & Ollier, K. (1991). Fears in British children and their relationship to manifest anxiety and depression. *Journal of Child Psychology and Psychiatry, 32,* 321–331.

O'Reilly, P. P. (1971). Desensitization of fire bell phobia. *Journal of School Psychology, 9,* 55–57.

Orton, G. L. (1982). A comparative study of children's worries. *Journal of Psychology, 100,* 153–162.

Öst, L. G. (1987). Age of onset in different phobias. *Journal of Abnormal Psychology, 46,* 223–229.

Öst, L. G. (1991). Acquisition of blood and injection phobia and anxiety response patterns in clinical patients. *Behaviour Research and Therapy, 29,* 323–332.

Öst, L. G., Jerremalm, A., & Johansson, J. (1981). Individual response patterns and the effects of different behavioral methods in the treatment of social phobia. *Behaviour Research and Therapy, 19,* 1–16.

Ownby, R. L. (1983). A cognitive behavioral intervention with a thirteen-year-old boy. *Psychology in the Schools, 20,* 219–222.

Parish, T. S., Buntman, A. D., & Buntman, S. R. (1976). Effect of counterconditioning on test anxiety as indicated by digit span performance. *Journal of Educational Psychology, 68,* 297–299.

Patterson, G. R. (1965). A learning theory approach to the treatment of the school phobic child. In L. P. Ullman & L. Krasner (Eds.), *Case studies in behavior modification* (pp. 279–285). New York: Holt, Rinehart & Winston.

Payne, M. A. (1988). Adolescent fears: Some Caribbean findings. *Journal of Youth and Adolescence, 17,* 255–266.

Peterson, L. (1987). Not safe at home: Behavioral treatment of a child's fear of being at home alone. *Journal of Behavior Therapy and Experimental Psychiatry, 18,* 381–385.

Peterson, L., & Brownlee-Duffeck, M. (1984). Prevention of anxiety and pain due to medical and dental procedures. In M. C. Roberts & L. Peterson (Eds.), *Prevention of problems in childhood: Psychological research and application* (pp. 267–308). New York: Wiley.

Peterson, L., Hartmann, D. P., & Gelfand, D. M. (1980). Prevention of child behavior disorders: A lifestyle change for child psychologists. In P. Davidson & S. Davidson (Eds.), *Behavior medicine: Changing health lifestyles.* (pp. 195–221). New York: Brunner/Mazel.

Peterson, L., & Harbeck, C. (1988). *The pediatric psychologist: Issues in professional development and practice.* Champaign, IL: Research Press.

Peterson, L., & Ridley-Johnson, R. (1980). Pediatric hospital response to survey on prehospital preparation for children. *Journal of Pediatric Psychology, 5,* 1–7.

Peterson, L., Schultheis, K., Ridley-Johnson, R., Miller, D. J., & Tracy, K. (1984). Comparison of three modeling procedures on the presurgical and postsurgical reactions of children. *Behavior Therapy, 15,* 197–203.

Peterson, L., & Shigetomi, C. (1981). The use of coping techniques in minimizing anxiety in hospitalized children. *Behavior Therapy, 12,* 1–14.

Peterson, L., & Toler, S. M. (1984). Self-regulated presurgical preparation for children. In B. Stabler (chair), *Biobehavioral management of illness in children.* Symposium conducted at the meeting of the American Psychological Association, Toronto.

Phillips, D., & Wolpe, S. (1981). Multiple behavioral techniques in severe separation anxiety of a twelve-year-old. *Journal of Behavior Therapy and Experimental Psychiatry, 12,* 329–332.

Pinter, R., & Lev, J. (1940). Worries of school children. *Journal of Genetic Psychology, 56,* 67–76.

Pomerantz, P. B., Peterson, N. T., Marholin, D., & Stern, S. (1977). The *in vivo* elimination of a child's water phobia by a paraprofessional at home. *Jour-*

nal of Behavior Therapy and Experimental Psychiatry, 8, 417–421.

Poser, E. G. (1976). Strategies for behavioral prevention. In P. O. Davidson (Eds), *The behavioral management of anxiety, depression and pain* (pp. 35–53). New York: Brunner/Mazel.

Poznanski, E. (1973). Children with excessive fears. *American Journal of Orthopsychiatry, 43,* 438–439.

Pratt, K. C. (1945). A study of the "fears" of rural children. *Journal of Genetic Psychology, 67,* 179–194.

Prins, P. J. M. (1985). Self-speech and self-regulation of high- and low-anxious children in the dental situation: An interview study. *Behaviour Research and Therapy, 23,* 641–650.

Quay, H. C. (1979). Classification. In H. C. Quay & J. S. Werry (Eds.), *Psychopathological disorders of childhood* (2nd ed., pp. 1–42). New York: Wiley.

Queiroz, L. O. S., Mota, M. A., Madi, M. B. B. P., Sossai, D. L., & Boren, J. J. (1981). A functional analysis of obsessive-compulsive problems with related therapeutic procedures. *Behaviour Research and Therapy, 19,* 377–388.

Rachman, S. J. (1976). The passing of the two-stage theory of fear and avoidance: Fresh possibilities. *Behaviour Research and Therapy, 14,* 125–131.

Rachman, S. J. (1977). The conditioning theory of fear-acquisition. A critical examination. *Behaviour Research and Therapy, 15,* 375–387.

Rachman, S. J. (1978). *Fear and courage.* San Francisco: W. H. Freeman.

Rachman, S. J. (1990). The determinants and treatment of simple phobias. *Advances in Behaviour Research and Therapy, 12,,* 1–30.

Rachman, S. J. (1991). Neoconditioning and the classical theory of fear acquisition. *Clinical Psychology Review, 11,* 115–173.

Rachman, S., & Hodgson, R. (1974). Synchrony and desynchrony in fear and avoidance. *Behaviour Research and Therapy, 12,* 311–318.

Rachman, S. J., & Seligman, M. E. P. (1976). Unprepared phobias: "Be prepared." *Behaviour Research and Therapy, 14,* 333–338.

Rainwater, N., Sweet, A. A., Elliot, L., Bowers, M., McNeil, J., & Stump, N. (1988). Systematic desensitization in the treatment of needle phobias for children with diabetes. *Child and Family Behavior Therapy, 10,* 19–31.

Rapoport, J. L., Swedo, S. E., & Leonard, H. L. (1992). Childhood obsessive compulsive disorder. *Journal of Clinical Psychiatry, 53* (Supplement), 6–11.

Raskind, L. T., & Nagle, R. J. (1980). Modeling effects on the intelligence test performance of test-anxious children. *Psychology in the Schools, 17,* 351–355.

Reich, J. (1986). The epidemiology of anxiety. *Journal of Nervous and Mental Disease, 174,* 129–135.

Reiss, S. (1987). Theoretical perspectives on the fear of anxiety. *Clinical Psychological Review, 7,* 141–153.

Reiss, S. (1991). Expectancy theory of fear, anxiety, and panic. *Clinical Psychology Review, 11,* 141–153.

Rettew, D. C., Swedo, S. E., Leonard, H. L., Lenane, M. C., & Rapoport, J. L. (1992). Obsessions and compulsions across time in 79 children and adolescents with obsessive-compulsive disorder. *Journal of the American Academy of Child and Adolescent Psychiatry, 31,* 1050–1056.

Ribordy, S. C., Tracy, R. J., & Bernotas, T. D. (1981). The effects of an attentional training procedure on the performance of high and low test-anxious children. *Cognitive Therapy and Research, 5,* 19–28.

Richards, C. S., & Siegel, L. J. (1978). Behavioral treatment of anxiety states and avoidance behaviors in children. In D. Marholin II (Ed.), *Child behavior therapy* (pp. 274–338). New York: Gardner Press.

Richman, N., Stevenson, J., & Graham, P. (1982). Prevalence of behavior problems in 3-year-old children: An epidemiological study in a London borough. *Journal of Child Psychology and Psychiatry, 16,* 272–287.

Riddle, M. A., Scahill, L., King, R. A., Hardin, M. T., Andeson, G. M., Ort, S. I., Smith, J. C., Leckman, J. F., & Cohen, D. J. (1992). Double-blind crossover trial of fluoxetine and placebo in children and adolescents with obsessive-compulsive disorder. *Journal of the American Academy of Child and Adolescent Psychiatry, 31,* 1062–1069.

Rimm, D. C., Janda, L. H., Lancaster, D. W., Nahl, M., & Ditmar, K. (1977). An exploratory investigation of the origin and maintenance of phobias. *Behaviour Research and Therapy, 15,* 231–238.

Ritter, B. (1968). The group treatment of children's snake phobias using vicarious and contact desensitization procedures. *Behaviour Research and Therapy, 6,* 1–6.

Ritter, B. (1969). Treatment of acrophobia with contact desensitization. *Behaviour Research and Therapy, 7,* 41–46.

Roberts, M. C., & Peterson, L. (184). Prevention models: Theoretical and practical implications. In M. C. Roberts & L. Peterson (Eds.), *Prevention of problems in childhood: Psychological research and applications* (pp. 1–39). New York: Wiley.

Roberts, M. C., Wurtle, S. K., Boone, R. R., Ginther, L. J., & Elkins, P. D. (1981). Reductions of medical fears by use of modeling: A preventive application in a general population of children. *Journal of Pediatric Psychology, 6,* 293–300.

Robinson, C. M. (1978). Developmental counseling approach to death and dying education. *Elementary School Guidance and Counseling, 12,* 178–187.

Rosenbaum, J. F., Biederman, J., Boldue, E. A., Hirshfeld, D. R., Faraone, S. V., & Kagan, J. (1992). Comorbidity of parental anxiety disorders as risk for childhood-onset anxiety in inhibited children. *American Journal of Psychiatry, 149*, 475–481.

Rosenfarb, I., & Hayes, S. C. (1984). Social standard setting: the Achilles heel of informational accounts of therapeutic change. *Behavior Therapy, 15*, 515–528.

Ross, D. M., Ross, S. A., & Evans, T. A. (1971). The modification of extreme social withdrawal by modeling with guided participation. *Journal of Behavior Therapy and Experimental Psychiatry, 2*, 273–279.

Rutter, M., Tizard, J., & Whitmore, K. (1970). *Education, health and behavior.* New York: Wiley.

Ryall, M. R., & Dietiker, K. E. (1979). Reliability and clinical validity of the Children's Fear Survey Schedule. *Journal of Behavior Therapy and Experimental Psychiatry, 10*, 303–310.

Saigh, P. A. (1986). *In vitro* flooding in the treatment of a six-year-old boy's posttraumatic stress disorder. *Behaviour Research and Therapy, 24*, 685–688.

Saigh, P. A. (1987). *In vitro* flooding of a posttraumatic stress disorder. *School Psychology Review, 16*, 203–211.

Saigh, P. A. (1992). The behavioral treatment of child and adolescent posttraumatic stress disorder. *Advances in Behaviour Research and Therapy, 14*, 247–275.

Sanders, M. R., & Jones, L. (1990). Behavioural treatment of injection, dental and medical phobias in adolescents: A case study. *Behavioural Psychotherapy, 18*, 311–316.

Sarnet, H., Peri, J. N., Nitzan, E., & Perlberg, A. (1972). Factors which influence cooperation between dentist and child. *Journal of Dental Education, 36*, 9–15.

Scherer, M. W., & Nakamura, C. Y. (1968). A fear survey schedule for children (FSS-FC): A factor analytic comparison with manifest anxiety (CMAS). *Behaviour Research and Therapy, 6*, 173–182.

Schoenfeld, W. N. (1950). An experimental approach to anxiety, escape, and avoidance behavior. In P. H. Hoch & J. Zubin (Eds.), *Anxiety.* (pp. 70–99). New York: Grune & Stratton.

Schwartz, G. E., Davidson, R. J., & Goleman, D. J. (1978). Patterning of cognitive and somatic processes in the self-regulation of anxiety: Effects of meditation versus exercise. *Psychosomatic Medicine, 40*, 321–328.

Seligman, M. E. P. (1970). On the generality of the laws of learning. *Psychological Review, 77*, 406–413.

Seligman, M. E. P. (1971). Phobias and preparedness. *Behavior Therapy, 2*, 307–320.

Seligman, M. E. P., & Johnston, J. C. (1973). A cognitive theory of avoidance learning. In F. J. McGuigan & D. B. Lumsden (Eds.), *Contemporary approaches to conditioning and learning* (pp. 69–110). Washington, DC: V. H. Winston.

Sheslow, D. V., Bondy, A. S., & Nelson, R. O. (1982). A comparison of graduated exposure, verbal coping skills, and their combination on the treatment of children's fear of the dark. *Child and Family Behavior Therapy, 4*, 33–45.

Siegel, L. J., & Peterson, L. (1980). Stress reduction in young dental patients through coping skills and sensory information. *Journal of Consulting and Clinical Psychology, 48*, 785–787.

Siegel, L. J., & Peterson, L. (1981). Maintenance effects of coping skills and sensory information on young children's response to repeated dental procedures. *Behavior Therapy, 12*, 530–535.

Silverman, W. K., & Kearney, C. A. (1991). The nature and treatment of childhood anxiety. *Educational Psychology Review, 3*, 335–361.

Simon, A., & Ward, L. (1974). Variables influencing the sources, frequency, and intensity of worry in secondary school pupils. *British Journal of Social and Clinical Psychology, 13*, 391–396.

Simpson, W. J., Ruzicka, R. L., & Thomas, N. R. (1974). Physiologic responses of children to initial dental experience. *Journal of Dentistry for Children, 41*, 465–470.

Singer, L. T., Ambuel, B., Wade, S., & Jaffe, A. C. (1992). Cognitive behavioral treatment of health-impairing food phobias in children. *Journal of the American Academy of Child and Adolescent Psychiatry, 31*, 847–852.

Slater, E. (1939). Responses to a nursery school situation of 40 children. *Society for Research in Child Development Monograph, 11* (No. 4).

Slater, E., & Shields, J. (1969). Genetical aspects of anxiety. *British Journal of Psychiatry, 3*, 62–71.

Slee, P. T., & Cross, D. G. (1989). Living in the nuclear age: an Australian study of children's and adolescent's fears. *Child Psychiatry and Human Development, 19*, 270–278.

Smith, R. E., & Sharpe, T. M., (1970). Treatment of a school phobia with implosive therapy. *Journal of Consulting and Clinical Psychology, 35*, 239–243.

Solomon, R. L., Kamin, L. J., & Wynne, L. C. (1953). Traumatic avoidance learning: The outcomes of several extinction procedures with dogs. *Journal of Abnormal and Social Psychology, 48*, 291–302.

Sonnenberg, E., & Venham, L. (1977). Human figure drawing as a measure of the child's response to dental visits. *Journal of Dentistry for Children, 44*, 438–442.

Spence, S. H., & McCathie, H. (1993). The stability of fears in children: A two-year prospective study. *Journal of Child Psychology and Psychiatry, 34*, 579–585.

Screenivasan, U., Manocha, S. N., & Jain, V. K. (1979). Treatment of severe dog phobia in childhood by flooding: A case report. *Journal of Child Psychology and Psychiatry, 20*, 255–260.

Stanley, L. (1980). Treatment of ritualistic behaviour in an eight-year-old girl by response prevention: A case report. *Journal of Child Psychology and Psychiatry, 21*, 85–90.

Stavrakaki, C., Vargo, B., Boodoosingh, L., & Roberts, N. (1987). The relationship between anxiety and depression in children: Rating scales and clinical variables. *Canadian Journal of Psychiatry, 32*, 433–439.

Stokes, T. F., & Baer, D. M. (1977). An implicit technology of generalization. *Journal of Applied Behavior Analysis, 10*, 349–367.

Strauss, C. C., Lease, C. A., Last, C. G., & Francis, G. (1988). Overanxious disorder: An examination of developmental difference. *Journal of Abnormal Child Psychology, 16*, 433–443.

Tahmisian, J. A., & McReynolds, W. T. (1971). Use of parents as behavioral engineers in the treatment of a school-phobic girl. *Journal of Counseling Psychology, 18*, 225–228.

Tasto, D. L. (1969). Systematic desensitization, muscle relaxation and visual imagery in the counterconditioning of a four-year-old phobic child. *Behaviour Research and Therapy, 7*, 409–411.

Taylor, C. B., & Agras, W. S. (1981). Assessment of phobia. In D. H. Barlow (Ed.), *Behavioral assessment of adult disorders* (pp. 181–208). New York: Guilford Press.

Thyer, B. A., Parrish, R. T., Curtis, G. C., Nesse, R. M., & Camerson, O. G. (1985). Ages of onset of DSM-III anxiety disorders *Comprehensive Psychiatry, 26*, 113–122.

Torgerson, S. (1978). The contribution of twin studies to psychiatric nosology. In W. E. Nance (Ed.), *Twin research: Part A, Psychology and methodology* (pp. 125–130). New York: Alan R. Liss.

Torgerson, S. (1983). Genetic factors in anxiety disorders. *Archives of General Psychiatry, 40*, 1085–1089.

Torgerson, S. (1985). Hereditary differentiation of anxiety and affective neurosis. *British Journal of Psychiatry, 146*, 530–534.

Torgerson, S. (1993). Relationship between adult and childhood anxiety disorders: Genetic hypothesis. In C. G. Last (Ed.), *Anxiety across the lifespan: A developmental perspective* (pp. 113–127). New York: Springer.

Trower, P., Yardley, K., Bryant, B., & Shaw, P. (1978). The treatment of social failure: A comparison of anxiety-reduction and skills acquisition procedures on two social problems. *Behavior Modification, 2*, 41–60.

Ultee, C. A., Griffioen, D., & Schellekens, J. (1982). The reduction of anxiety in children: A comparison of the effects of 'systematic desensitization *in vitro*' and 'systematic desensitization *in vivo*'. *Behaviour Research and Therapy, 20*, 61–67.

Unger, M. (1982). *Defensiveness in children as it influences acquisition of fear-relevant information.* Unpublished master's thesis, University of Florida.

Valentine, C. W. (1930). The innate bases of fear. *Journal of Genetic Psychology, 37*, 394–420.

Van der Ploeg, H. M. (1975). Treatment of frequency of urination by stories competing with anxiety. *Journal of Behavior Therapy and Experimental Psychiatry, 6*, 165–166.

Van der Ploeg-Stapert, J. D., & Van der Ploeg, H. M. (1986). Behavioral group treatment of test anxiety: An evaluation study. *Journal of Behavior Therapy and Experimental Psychiatry, 17*, 255–259.

Van Hasselt, V. B., Hersen, M., Bellack, A. S., Rosenblum, N. D., & Lamparski, D. (1979). Tripartite assessment to the effects of systematic desensitization in a multi-phobic child: An experimental analysis. *Journal of Behavior Therapy and Experimental Psychiatry, 10*, 51–55.

Vasey, M. W., Crnic, K. A., & Carter, W. G. (1994). Worry in childhood: A developmental perspective. *Cognitive Therapy and Research, 18*, 529–549.

Venham, L. L., Murray, P., & Gaulin-Kremer, E. (1979). Child-rearing variables affecting the preschool child's response to dental stress. *Journal of Dental Research, 58*, 2042–2045.

Vermilyea, J., Boice, R., & Barlow, D. H. (1984). Rachman and Hodgson (1974) A decade later: How do desynchronous response systems relate to the treatment of agoraphobia? *Behaviour Research and Therapy, 22*, 615–621.

Watson, J. B., & Morgan, J. J. B. (1917). Emotional reactions and psychological experimentation. *American Journal of Psychology, 28*, 163–174.

Watson, J. B., & Rayner, P. (1920). Conditioned emotional reactions. *Journal of Experimental Psychology, 3*, 1–14.

Weiner, I. B. (1967). Behavior therapy in obsessive-compulsive neurosis: Treatment of an adolescent boy. *Psychotherapy: Theory, Research, and Practice, 4*, 27–29.

Weissbrod, C. W., & Bryan, J. H. (1973). Filmed treatment as an effective fear-reduction technique. *Journal of Abnormal Child Psychology, 1*, 196–201.

Weissman, M. M. (1985). The epidemiology of anxiety disorders: Rates, risks, and familial patterns. In A. H. Tuma & J. D. Maser (Eds.), *Anxiety and the anxiety disorders* (pp. 275–296). Hillsdale, NJ: Erlbaum.

Weissman, M. M. (1992). Family genetic studies of panic disorder. *Journal of Psychiatric Research,*

Weissman, M. M., Leckman, J. F., Merikangas, K. R., Gammon, G. D., & Prusoff, B. A. (1984). Depression and anxiety disorders in parents and children. *Archives of General Psychiatry, 41*, 845–852.

Wenzel, B. M., & Jeffrey, D. W. (1967). The effect of immunosympathectomy on the behavior of mice in aversive situations. *Physiology and Behavior, 2*, 193–201.

Whitaker, A., Johnson, J., Shaffer, D., Rapoport, J. L., Kalikow, K., Walsh, T., Davies, M., Braiman, S., & Dolinsky, A. (1990). Uncommon troubles in young people: Prevalence estimates of selected psychiatric disorders in a nonreferred adolescent population. *Archives of General Psychiatry, 47*, 487–496.

White, W. C., Jr., & Davis, M. T. (1974). Vicarious extinction of phobic behavior in early childhood. *Journal of Abnormal Child Psychology, 2*, 25–32.

Williams, C. E., & Jones, R. T. (1989). Impact of self-instructions on response maintenance and children's fear of fire. *Journal of Clinical Child Psychology, 18,* 84–89.

Willmuth, M. E. (1988). Cognitive-behavioral and insight-oriented psychotherapy of an eleven-year-old boy with obsessive-compulsive disorder. *American Journal of Psychotherapy, 42,* 472–478.

Wilson, N. H., & Rotter, J. D. (1986). Anxiety management training and study skills counseling for students on self-esteem and test anxiety and performance. *The School Counselor, 9,* 18–31.

Winer, G. A. (1982). A review and analysis of children's fearful behavior in dental settings. *Child Development, 53,* 1111–1133.

Winker, J. B. (1949). Age trends and sex differences in the wishes, identification, activities and fears of children. *Child Development, 20,* 191–196.

Wolff, R., & Rapoport, J. (1988). Behavioral treatment of childhood obsessive-compulsive disorder. *Behavior Modification, 12,* 252–266.

Wolpe, J. (1948). *An approach to the problem of neurosis based on the conditioned response.* Unpublished doctoral dissertation, University of Witwatersand, South Africa.

Wolpe, J. (1954). Reciprocal inhibition as the main basis of psychotherapeutic effects. *Archives of Neurology and Psychiatry, 72,* 205–226.

Wolpe, J. (1958). *Psychotherapy by reciprocal inhibition.* Stanford, CA: Stanford University Press.

Wolpe, J. (1961). The systematic desensitization treatment of neuroses. *Journal of Nervous and Mental Disease, 132,* 189–203.

Woolston, J. L., Rosenthal, S. L., Riddle, M. A., Sparrow, S. S., Cicchetti, D., & Zimmerman, L. D. (1989). Childhood comorbidity of anxiety/affective disorders and behavior disorders. *Journal of the American Academy of Child and Adolescent Psychiatry, 28,* 707–713.

Word, P., & Rozynko, V. (1974). Behavior therapy of an eleven-year-old girl with reading problems. *Journal of Learning Disabilities, 7,* 551–554.

Wynne, L. C., & Solomon, R. L (1955). Traumatic avoidance learning: Acquisition and extinction in dogs deprived of normal peripheral autonomic function. *Genetic Psychology Monographs, 52,* 241–284.

Yates, A. J. (1981). Behavior therapy: Past, present, future—imperfect? *Clinical Psychology Review, 1,* 269–291.

Yates, B. T. (1985). Cost-effectiveness analysis and cost-benefit analysis: An introduction. *Behavioral Assessment, 7,* 207–234.

Yeaton, W. H., & Sechrest, L. (1981). Critical dimensions in the choice and maintenance of successful treatments: Strength, integrity, and effectiveness. *Journal of Consulting and Clinical Psychology, 49,* 156–167.

Yule, W., Sacks, B., & Hersov, L. (1974). Successful flooding treatment of a noise phobia in an 11-year-old. *Journal of Behavior Therapy and Experimental Psychiatry, 5,* 209–211.

Zastowny, T. R., Kirschenbaum, D. S., & Meng, A. L. (November 1981). *Coping skills training for children: Effects on distress before, during, and after hospitalization for surgery.* Paper presented at the meeting of the Association for Advancement of Behavior Therapy, Toronto.

Zatz, S., & Chassin, L. (1983). Cognitions of test-anxious children. *Journal of Consulting and Clinical Psychology, 51,* 526–534.

Zikis, P. (1983). Treatment of an 11-year-old obsessive-compulsive ritualizer and tiquer girl with *in vivo* exposure and response prevention. *Behavioral Psychotherapy, 11,* 75–81.

Zohar, A. H., Ratzoni, G., Pauls, D. L., Apter, A., Bleich, A., Kron, S., Rappaport, M., Weizman, A., & Cohen, D. J. (1992). An epidemiological study of obsessive-compulsive disorder and related disorders in Israeli adolescents. *Journal of the American Academy of Child and Adolescent Psychiatry, 31,* 1057–1061.

APPENDIX: SUMMARIES OF STUDIES ON THE BEHAVIORAL TREATMENT OF CHILDREN'S FEARS AND ANXIETIES

TABLE 5.3. A Summary of Desensitization Treatments for Children's Fears and Anxieties

Author(s)	Feared stimulus	Subjects	Research design	Treatment	Outcome
Barabasz (1973)	Test taking	5th- and 6th-graders (n = 87)	Experiment	Children assigned to one of two conditions: imaginal desensitization (5 sessions) or no treatment.	At posttest, desensitization superior to no treatment in terms of physiological and motor responses.
Bentler (1962)	Water	11½-mo-old with fear duration of approximately 2 wk	Case study	*In vivo* desensitization with game playing and maternal contact as the anxiety-antagonistic response. Treatment administered by the mother over a period of 1 mo.	At posttreatment, significant reductions in motor responses. At 6-mo follow-up, maintenance of treatment gains.
Bornstein & Knapp (1981)	Separation, travel, illness	12-yr-old male with fear duration of 2 yr	Multiple-baseline	Self-control imaginal desensitization administered for 4 days for each stimulus.	At posttreatment, significant reductions in subjective responses. Generalization of treatment gains to new settings and maintenance of treatment gains at 1-yr follow-up.
Cavior & Deutsch (1975)	Nighttime, nightmares	16-yr-old male with fear duration of 1 yr	Case study	Imaginal desensitization with relaxation as the anxiety-antagonistic response administered for 3 sessions.	At posttreatment, significant reductions in subjective and physiological responses. Generalization of treatment gains to new behaviors (social interaction) and maintenance of treatment gains at 6-mo follow-up.
Chapel (1967)	School	11-yr-old	Case study	Imaginal desensitization.	At posttreatment, significant reductions in fear.
Coyle (1968)	School, reading	14-yr-old female	Case study	Imaginal desensitization followed by *in vivo* desensitization, for a total of 11 sessions.	At posttreatment, significant reductions in motor responses. Maintenance of treatment gains at 3-mo follow-up.
Croghan (1981)	School	17-yr-old male with fear duration of 5 yr	Case study	Imaginal desensitization with relaxation as the anxiety-antagonistic response administered for 6 sessions.	At posttreatment, significant reductions in subjective responses. Maintenance of treatment gains at 1-yr follow-up.

(continued)

TABLE 5.3.   (*continued*)

Author(s)	Feared stimulus	Subjects	Research design	Treatment	Outcome
Croghan & Musante (1975)	Heights	7-yr-old male with fear duration of 6 mo	Case study	*In vivo* desensitization with game playing as the anxiety-antagonistic response administered for 6 sessions.	At posttreatment, significant reductions in motor responses. Generalization of treatment gains in other stimuli and maintenance of treatment gains at 1-yr follow-up.
Deffen-bacher & Kemper (1974)	Test taking	11 male and 10 female 6th-graders	Experiment	Children were assigned to one of two conditions: imaginal desensitization or no-treatment. Imaginal desensitization was conducted in small groups in weekly 45-min sessions spanning a 7-wk period.	At posttreatment, desensitization superior to control condition on the performance measure.
DiNardo & DiNardo (1981)	Contamina-tion	9-yr-old male with fear duration of 8 mo	Case study	Self-control imaginal desensitization administered for 14 sessions.	At posttreatment, significant reductions in motor responses. Maintenance of treatment gains at 1-yr follow-up.
Doyal & Friedman (1974)	Test taking	5th-grade female	Case study	Imaginal desensitization with relaxation as the anxiety-antagonistic response administered for 10 sessions.	At posttreatment, significant reductions in subjective responses. Maintenance of treatment gains at 6-mo follow-up.
Freeman, Roy, & Hemmick (1976)	Physical exam	7-yr-old retarded male with fear duration > 2 wk	Case study	*In vivo* desensitization with social contact as the anxiety-antagonistic response administered for 11 sessions.	At posttreatment, significant reductions in motor responses. Generalization of treatment gains to other stimuli.
Garvey & Hegrenes (1966)	School	10-yr-old male with fear duration > 6 mo	Case study	*In vivo* desensitization with therapist contact as the anxiety-antagonistic response administered for 20 days.	At posttreatment, significant reductions in motor responses. Maintenance of treatment gains at 2-yr follow-up.
Jackson & King (1981)	Darkness, noises	5-yr-old male with fear duration > 1 mo	Time series	Emotive imagery administered for 4 sessions.	At posttreatment, significant reductions in subjective and motor responses. Maintenance of treatment gains at 18-mo follow-up.

(*continued*)

TABLE 5.3. (*continued*)

Author(s)	Feared stimulus	Subjects	Research design	Treatment	Outcome
Jones (1924a)	Small animal	2¾-yr-old male	Case study	*In vivo* desensitization.	At posttreatment, significant reductions in subjective and motor responses. Generalization of treatment gains to other stimuli.
Kellerman (1980)	Nighttime	5-yr-old male with fear duration > 1 mo	Case study	*In vitro* and *in vivo* desensitization with anger as the anxiety-antagonistic response.	At posttreatment, significant reductions in motor responses. Maintenance of treatment gains at 24-mo follow-up.
	Separation, school, darkness	8-yr-old female	Case study	*In vitro* and *in vivo* desensitization with anger as the anxiety-antagonistic response.	At posttreatment, significant fear reduction. Maintenance of treatment gains at 16-mo follow-up.
	Darkness	13-yr-old female with fear duration of 5 yr	Case study	*In vitro* and *in vivo* desensitization with variety of behaviors as the anxiety-antagonistic response.	At posttreatment, significant fear reduction. Maintenance of treatment gains at 9-mo follow-up.
Kelley (1976)	Darkness	4- and 5-yr-olds ($n = 40$)	Experiment	Children assigned to one of five conditions: *in vitro* desensitization, *in vitro* desensitization with noncontingent tangible reward, *in vitro* desensitization with contingent tangible reward, attention placebo, or no treatment. Treatment administered weekly over a 3-wk period.	At posttreatment, no group differences in motor and subjective responses.
King, Cranston, & Josephs (1989)	Darkness	6-yr-old male, 8-yr-old female, and 11-yr-old female with fear history ranging from 7 mo to several years	Multiple-baseline across subjects	Emotive imagery administered over 6–13 sessions (30 min each).	With the institution of treatment, improvements in performance measures for two of the three children. No noticeable change in self-ratings of distress for any of the children, as ratings for all children were minimal for the baseline assessment.

(*continued*)

TABLE 5.3.   (*continued*)

Author(s)	Feared stimulus	Subjects	Research design	Treatment	Outcome
Kissel (1972)	Small animal	11-yr-old female with fear duration of 9 yr	Case study	Imaginal and *in vitro* desensitization with therapist contact as the anxiety-antagonistic response administered for 6 sessions.	At posttreatment, significant reductions in motor responses.
Kondas (1967)	Public Speaking	11- through 15-yr-olds (*n* = 23)	Experiment	Children assigned to one of four conditions: imaginal desensitization (12 sessions), autogenetic training (7 sessions), imaginal desensitization without relaxation (4 sessions), or no treatment.	At posttreatment, all three treatments superior to no treatment in terms of subjective responses, with imaginal desensitization superior to the other three conditions in terms of physiological responses. At 5-mo follow-up, maintenance of subjective treatment gains for imaginal desensitization with and without relaxation.
Kuroda (1969)	Small animals	3- and 4-yr-olds	Experiment	Children assigned to one of two conditions: *in vivo* desensitization with game playing as the anxiety-antagonistic response or no treatment.	At posttreatment, *in vivo* desensitization superior to no treatment in terms of motor responses.
Laxer, Quarter, Kooman, & Walker (1969)	Test taking	9th-through 12th-graders (*n* = 89)	Experiment	Children assigned to one of three conditions: imaginal desensitization (30 sessions), relaxation (30 sessions), or no treatment.	At posttreatment, no group differences in terms of subjective and motor responses. Relaxation superior to no treatment in terms of responses to other stimuli.
Laxer & Walker (1970)	Test taking	Secondary school students (*n* = 110)	Experiment	Children assigned to one of six conditions: imaginal desensitization, relaxation, rehearsal, relaxation plus prolonged exposure, attention placebo, or no treatment. Treatment administered for 20 sessions.	At posttreatment, imaginal desensitization and relaxation superior to no treatment in terms of subjective responses. No group differences in terms of motor responses and fear responses to other stimuli.

(*continued*)

TABLE 5.3. (*continued*)

Author(s)	Feared stimulus	Subjects	Research design	Treatment	Outcome
Lazarus (1960)	Vehicles	8-yr-old male with fear duration of 2 yr	Case study	Imaginal and *in vivo* desensitization with eating as the anxiety-antagonistic response administered over a period of 6 wk.	At posttreatment, significant reductions in motor responses. Generalization of treatment gains to other settings.
	Separation	9-yr-old female with fear duration of 4 mo.	Case study	Imaginal desensitization administered for 5 sessions.	At posttreatment, significant reductions in motor responses. Generalization of treatment gains to other settings and maintenance of gains at 15-mo follow-up.
	Small animals	3-yr-old male with fear duration of 5 mo	Case study	Drug-assisted, *in vivo* desensitization administered over a 5-wk period.	At posttreatment, significant reductions in motor responses. Maintenance of treatment gains at 1-yr follow-up.
Lazarus & Abramovitz (1962)	Small animals	14-yr-old male with fear duration of 3 yr	Case study	Emotive imagery administered for 5 sessions.	At posttreatment, significant reductions in subjective responses. Maintenance of treatment gains at 1-yr follow-up.
	Darkness	10-yr-old male with fear duration of 1 yr	Case study	Emotive imagery administered for 3 sessions.	At posttreatment, significant reductions in subjective responses. Maintenance of treatment gains at 11-mo follow-up.
	School	8-yr-old female	Case study	Emotive imagery administered for 4 sessions.	At posttreatment, significant reductions in motor responses. Generalization of treatment gains to other problem behaviors (enuresis).
Lazarus & Rachman (1957)	Hospital	14-yr-old male with fear duration of 4 yr	Case study	Imaginal desensitization administered for 10 sessions.	At posttreatment, significant reductions in motor responses. Maintenance of treatment gains at 3-mo follow-up.
LeUnes & Siems-glusz (1977)	School	14-yr-old female with fear duration > 3 mo	Case study	*In vivo* desensitization with therapist contact as the anxiety-antagonistic response. Treatment administered by a paraprofessional over a 10-wk period.	At posttreatment, significant reductions in motor responses. Generalization of treatment gains to new behaviors (social interaction).

(*continued*)

TABLE 5.3. (*continued*)

Author(s)	Feared stimulus	Subjects	Research design	Treatment	Outcome
Mann & Rosenthal (1969)	Test taking	39 female and 32 male 12- through 14-yr-olds	Experiment	Children assigned to one of six conditions: individual imaginal desensitization, individual vicarious desensitization, group imaginal desensitization, group vicarious desensitization with individual model, group vicarious desensitization with group model, or no treatment. Treatment ranged from 6 to 8 sessions.	At posttreatment, no group differences in terms of subjective and motor responses.
Miller (1972)	Separation, death, school	10-yr-old female with fear duration > 8 wk	Case study	For fear of separation, imaginal desensitization administered over 12-wk period. For fear of dying, *in vivo* flooding administered after imaginal and *in vivo* desensitization proved unsuccessful. For fear of school, imaginal and *in vivo* desensitization administered.	At posttreatment, significant reductions in subjective and motor responses. Generalization of treatment gains to other problem behaviors (enuresis) and maintenance of treatment gains at 18-mo follow-up.
Montenegro (1968)	Separation	6-yr-old male with fear duration > 1 yr	Case study	*In vivo* desensitization with eating as the anxiety-antagonistic response administered for 10 sessions.	At posttreatment, significant reductions in subjective and motor responses. Maintenance of treatment gains at 10-mo follow-up.
	Separation	3-yr-old female with fear duration > 4 mo	Case study	*In vivo* desensitization with eating as the anxiety-antagonistic response, supplemented by a parent- and therapist-administered contingency management program. Treatment administered for 16 sessions.	At posttreatment, significant reductions in subjective and motor responses. Maintenance of treatment gains at 18-mo follow-up.

(*continued*)

TABLE 5.3. (*continued*)

Author(s)	Feared stimulus	Subjects	Research design	Treatment	Outcome
Muller & Madsen (1970)	School, reading	16 males and 12 females with average age 12 yr, 8 mo	Experiment	Children assigned to one of three conditions: imaginal desensitization (13 sessions) followed by *in vivo* desensitization (7 sessions), attention placebo (20 sessions), or no treatment.	At posttreatment, desensitization and attention placebo superior to no treatment in terms of subjective responses. No group differences in terms of motor responses. Generalization of subjective treatment gains to new stimuli for desensitization and placebo conditions.
Ney (1967)	School	13-yr-old	Case study	Imaginal desensitization.	At posttreatment, significant fear reduction.
Ney (1968)	Small animals	4-yr-old	Case study	*In vivo* desensitization.	At posttreatment, significant reductions in motor responses.
O'Reilly (1971)	Noise	6-yr-old female with fear duration of 3 yr	Case study	*In vivo* desensitization with game playing and story telling as the anxiety-antagonistic response.	At posttreatment, significant reductions in motor responses.
Parish, Buntman, & Buntman (1976)	Test taking	39 males and 36 females ranging in age from 9 to 13 yr	Experiment	Children assigned to one of three conditions: *in vitro* desensitization with saying positive words as the anxiety-antagonistic response (4 sessions), attention placebo (4 sessions), or no treatment.	At posttreatment, *in vitro* desensitization superior to attention placebo and no treatment in terms of motor responses.
Phillips & Wolpe (1981)	Separation	12-yr-old male with fear duration of 2 yr	Case study	*In vivo* and imaginal desensitization administered for 88 sessions.	At posttreatment, significant reductions in subjective and motor responses. Maintenance of treatment gains at 2-yr follow-up.
Rainwater et al., (1988)	Needles	13 males and 12 females, ranging in age from 7 to 20 yr	Case study	Weekly sessions of imaginal and *in vivo* desensitization were carried out on an individual basis. Average number of sessions required for completion of treatment was 3.	At posttreatment, over 90% of the children displayed criterion performance and reported minimal anxiety. These treatment gains were maintained at 1-yr follow-up.

(*continued*)

TABLE 5.3. (*continued*)

Author(s)	Feared stimulus	Subjects	Research design	Treatment	Outcome
Tasto (1969)	Noise	4-yr-old male	Case study	*In vivo* desensitization administered after imaginal desensitization proved unsuccessful. Treatment administered by parent for a total of 6 sessions.	At posttreatment, significant reductions in motor responses. Maintenance of treatment gains at 4-mo follow-up.
Ultee, Griffioen, & Schelle-kens (1982)	Water	12 males and 12 females ranging in age from 5 to 10 yr	Experiment	Children assigned to one of three conditions: *in vivo* desensitization (8 sessions), imaginal desensitization (4 sessions) plus *in vivo* desensitization (4 sessions), or no treatment.	At posttreatment, *in vivo* desensitization superior to imaginal plus *in vivo* desensitization and no treatment in terms of motor responses.
van der Ploeg (1975)	School	14-yr-old male	Case study	Imaginal desensitization with story telling as the anxiety-antagonistic response administered for 15 sessions, supplemented with *in vivo* desensitization.	At posttreatment, significant reductions in subjective and motor responses. Maintenance of treatment gains at 18-mo follow-up.
Van Hasselt, Hersen, Bellack, Rosenblum & Lampar-ski (1979)	Blood, heights, test taking	11-yr-old male with fear duration > 3 yr	Multiple-baseline	Imaginal desensitization administered over 16 wk.	At posttreatment, significant reductions in subjective and motor responses. No reductions in physiological responses. Generalization of treatment gains to new settings and maintenance of treatment gains at 6-mo follow-up.
Wolpe (1958)	Social situations	11-yr-old male	Case study	Imaginal desensitization administered for 8 sessions.	At posttreatment, significant fear reduction.
Wolpe (1961)	Social situations	Child of unknown age and gender	Case study	Imaginal desensitization.	At posttreatment, significant fear reduction.
		13-yr-old male	Case study	Imaginal desensitization.	At posttreatment, no fear reduction.
Word & Rozynko (1974)	School, reading	11-yr-old female	Case study	Imaginal desensitization administered for 9 sessions.	At posttreatment, significant reductions in subjective and motor responses. Maintenance of treatment gains at 1-yr follow-up.

TABLE 5.4. A Summary of Prolonged Exposure Treatments for Children's Fears and Anxieties

Author(s)	Feared stimulus	Subjects	Research design	Treatment	Outcome
Bolton & Turner (1984)	Contamination with associated compulsive washing.	14-yr-old male with a 5-yr history; 14-yr-old male with a 1-yr history	Case study	For one child, an initial unsuccessful program of exposure plus response prevention, followed by a contingency management program to reduce disruptive behavior. For the other child, a program of exposure plus response prevention (combined with pharmacotherapy), administered over 4 wk and totaling over 100 hr.	For one child, increments in disruptive behaviors and no decrements in anxious behaviors. For the other child, treatment resulted in decrements in both anxious and disruptive behaviors, which were maintained at 12-mo follow-up.
Hatcher (1989)	Doll	14-yr-old male with a fear duration of 10 yr	Case study	Graded exposure administered for 12 weekly sessions (30 min each), supplemented with homework assignments calling for self-imposed exposure to the feared stimulus.	At posttreatment, marked reduction in subjective distress and behavioral avoidance. Treatment gains maintained at 10-mo follow-up.
Hersen (1968)	School, physical illness	12-yr-old male	Case study	Imaginal and *in vivo* flooding administered for 9 sessions, supplemented by contingency management program administered by parent.	At posttreatment, significant reductions in subjective and motor responses. Generalization of treatment gains to new behaviors and maintenance of treatment gains at 6-mo follow-up.
Johnson, Tyler, Thompson, & Jones (1971)	Public speaking	6th- through 8th-graders (*n* = 24)	Experiment	Children assigned to one of three conditions: reinforced practice (9 sessions), imaginal desensitization (9 sessions), or no treatment.	At posttreatment, reinforced practice and imaginal desensitization superior to no treatment in terms of subjective responses.
Jones (1924b)	Small animals	3-yr-old	Case study	*In vivo* flooding	At posttreatment, significant reductions in motor responses.
Kandal, Ayllon, & Rosenbaum (1977)	Social situations	4-yr-old male with fear duration > 2 wk	Multiple-baseline	*In vivo* flooding administered for 11 sessions.	At posttreatment, significant reductions in subjective and motor responses. Maintenance of treatment gains at 5-mo follow-up.

(*continued*)

TABLE 5.4.   (*continued*)

Author(s)	Feared stimulus	Subjects	Research design	Treatment	Outcome
	Social situations	8-yr-old male with fear duration > 3 yr	Multiple-baseline	*In vivo* flooding (1 session) followed by graduated *in vivo* exposure (11 sessions).	At posttreatment, significant reductions in motor responses. Maintenance of treatment gains at 9-mo follow-up.
Kennedy (1965)	School	25 males and females ranging in age from 4 to 16 yr	Case study	Prolonged exposure administered by the parent for an average period of 3 days.	At posttreatment, significant reductions in motor responses. Maintenance of treatment gains at 8-yr follow-up.
Knox, Albano, & Barlow (1996)	Monsters, contamination, loss of possessions, harm to others, along with associated rituals	1 white female and 3 white males ranging in age from 8 to 13 yr and in fear duration from 6 mo to 4 yr	Multiple-baseline across subjects	A 4-wk treatment program of therapist- and parent-assisted graduated *in vivo* and imaginal exposure plus response prevention, administered sequentially across 4 children. For each week, 3 sessions of approximately 90-min duration conducted. Treatment followed by 6 maintenance sessions carried out over 8 wk.	Reductions in subjective distress and compulsive rituals occurred with the introduction of parental involvement in the treatment. Maintenance of these gains for most of the subjects at 3- and 12-mo follow-ups. Generalization of benefits to untreated anxiety conditions and depressed mood.
Kolko (1984)	Being alone, physical injury	16-yr-old female with fear duration > 6 mo	Case study	Graduated *in vivo* exposure administered over a period of 3 wk.	At posttreatment, significant reductions in subjective and motor responses. Maintenance of treatment gains at 9-mo follow-up.
Leitenberg & Callahan (1973)	Darkness	8 females and 6 males ranging in age from 5 to 6 yr	Experiment	Children assigned to one of two conditions: reinforced practice (8 sessions) or no treatment.	At posttreatment, reinforced practice superior to no treatment in terms of motor responses.
Luiselli (1978)	Vehicles	7-yr-old male with fear duration of 6 mo	Case study	Reinforced practice administered for 9 sessions.	At posttreatment, significant reductions in motor responses. Maintenance of treatment gains at 1-mo follow-up.

(*continued*)

TABLE 5.4. (*continued*)

Author(s)	Feared stimulus	Subjects	Research design	Treatment	Outcome
Menzies & Clarke (1993)	Water	31 males and 17 females ranging in age from 3 to 8 yr	Experiment	Children assigned to one of four conditions: graduated *in vivo* exposure, live modeling, live modeling plus graduated *in vivo* exposure, or no treatment. Treatment consisted of 3 weekly sessions (30-min each).	At posttreatment, graduated *in vivo* exposure and live modeling plus graduated *in vivo* exposure superior to live modeling and no treatment on all behavioral and subjective measures. No differences among the three treatment groups on generalization of performance to a new setting. At 12-wk follow-up, maintenance of treatment gains better for the live modeling plus graduated *in vivo* exposure condition than for the graduated *in vivo* exposure condition.
Ollendick & Gruen (1972)	Physical injury	8-yr-old male with fear duration of 3 yr	Case study	Implosion administered for 2 sessions.	At posttreatment, significant reductions in motor responses. Maintenance of treatment gains at 3-mo follow-up.
Saigh (1986)	Multiple (related to trauma)	6-yr-old male with fear duration of 25 mo	Multiple-baseline across stimuli	Imaginal flooding administered sequentially across four stimulus situations, for a total of 11 sessions (40-min each)	With the advent of treatment, significant reductions in subjective and behavioral distress. Maintenance of treatment gains at 6-mo follow-up.
Saigh (1987)	War-related trauma	10-yr-old female with a fear duration of greater than 3 yr	Multiple-baseline across stimuli	Approximately 1-hr sessions of imaginal flooding were conducted twice a week for 4 wk.	Systematic reductions in subjective distress and avoidance with the sequential application of treatment. Maintenance of these gains at 6-mo follow-up and spread of these benefits to other problem conditions.

(*continued*)

TABLE 5.4.   (*continued*)

Author(s)	Feared stimulus	Subjects	Research design	Treatment	Outcome
Smith & Sharpe (1970)	School	13-yr-old male with fear duration of 60 days	Case study	Implosion administered for 6 sessions.	At posttreatment, significant reductions in subjective, motor, and physiological responses. Generalization of treatment gains to new settings. Maintenance of treatment gains at 13-wk follow-up and generalization of gains to other feared stimuli and other problem behaviors (peer relations, academic performance).
Screeni-vasan, Manocha, & Jain (1979)	Dog	11-yr-old female with fear duration of 5 yr	Case study	Following unsuccessful systematic desensitization treatment, 6 1-hr sessions of *in vivo* flooding conducted over a 10-day period.	At posttreatment, successful approach and adaptive interaction observed, minimal subjective distress reported. Maintenance of treatment gains at 12- and 24-wk follow-ups.
Stanley (1980)	Checking rituals associated with bedroom and dressing	8-yr-old female with an approx-imately 6 mo history of ritualistic behavior	Case study	A program of response prevention implemented by the child's parents over a 3-wk period.	With the application of treatment, complete elimination of ritualistic behaviors along with all subjective distress. No evidence of symptom substitution. Evidence of generalization across situations and behaviors. Maintenance of these beneficial effects at 1-yr follow-up.
Weiner (1967)	Unspecified, with associated washing, dressing, reading, writing, and order rituals	15-yr-old male with a recent onset of compulsive rituals	Case study	A self-administered program of graduated exposure, response prevention, and response substitution carried out over the course of 8 weekly sessions.	Marked reductions in subjective distress and ritualistic behaviors with the application of treatment. Maintenance of these treatment gains and improvements in general areas of functioning (e.g., academic work, eating habits) at 7-mo follow-up.

(*continued*)

TABLE 5.4. (*continued*)

Author(s)	Feared stimulus	Subjects	Research design	Treatment	Outcome
Yule, Sacks, & Hersov (1974)	Noises	9-yr-old male	Case study	*In vivo* flooding administered (2 sessions) after *in vivo* desensitization (22 sessions) proved only partially successful.	At posttreatment, significant reductions in subjective and motor responses. Maintenance of treatment gains at 25-mo follow-up.
Zikis (1983)	Interference with rituals	11-yr-old female with a 6-yr history of compulsive rituals	Case study	Two sessions of therapist-administered *in vivo* exposure plus response prevention (total of 60 min) combined with daily parent-and self-administered sessions of *in vivo* exposure plus response prevention (total of 39 hr over a 5-wk period).	After 3 wk of treatment, no reported or observed displays of rituals. Maintenance of treatment gains at 12, 16, 23, 32, 43, and 52 weeks of follow-up.

TABLE 5.5.   A Summary of Modeling Treatments for Children's Fears and Anxieties

Author(s)	Feared stimulus	Subjects	Research design	Treatment	Outcome
Bandura, Blanchard, & Ritter (1969)	Small animals	Unknown number of 13- through 17-yr-olds	Experiment	Children assigned to one of four conditions: participant modeling (2 hr), symbolic modeling (2 hr), imaginal desensitization (4 hr), or no treatment.	At posttreatment, all three treatments superior to no treatment in terms of subjective, motor, and physiological responses. Participant modeling superior to imaginal desensitization in terms of subjective and motor responses. Symbolic modeling superior to imaginal desensitization in terms of subjective and physiological responses. Generalization of treatment gains to other fear stimuli for participant modeling and symbolic modeling. Generalization of treatment gains to new settings and maintenance of treatment gains at 1-mo follow-up.
Bandura & Menlove (1968)	Small animals	32 females and 16 males ranging in age from 3 to 5 yr	Experiment	Children assigned to one of three conditions: filmed modeling of single mastery model, filmed modeling of multiple mastery models, or attention placebo. Treatment films were 6 min in length and shown 4 times.	At posttreatment, no group differences in terms of motor responses. At 1-mo follow-up, filmed modeling of multiple mastery models superior to filmed modeling of single mastery model and attention placebo. Generalization of treatment gains to other fear stimuli.
Chertock & Bornstein (1979)	Dental treatment	Unknown number of 5- through 13-yr-olds	Experiment	Children assigned to one of three conditions: covert modeling with coping model, covert modeling with mastery model, or prolonged imaginal exposure.	At posttreatment, no group differences in terms of subjective and motor responses.

(continued)

TABLE 5.5. (*continued*)

Author(s)	Feared stimulus	Subjects	Research design	Treatment	Outcome
Clark, Sugrin, & Bolton (1982)	Making mistakes, with associated obsessional slowness	13-yr-old male with a 16-mo history	Multiple-baseline across behaviors	Multiple target behaviors were treated by means of a participant modeling program or a prompting, pacing, and shaping program. The participant modeling program consisted of live demonstration, guided practice, verbal instruction, and encouragement (and on occasion, response prevention); treatment averaged 4–5 sessions per wk over 3–5 wk. The prompting, pacing, and shaping program also on occasion included response prevention; treatment averaged 3–5 sessions per wk over 2–4 wk.	Both treatments produced improvements in target behaviors, with participant modeling proving to be slightly more effective than prompting, pacing, and shaping. These benefits were short-lived, as rapid decay in treatment effects occurred upon termination of each program.
Davis, Rosenthal, & Kelley (1981)	Small animals	91 females ranging in age from 13 to 18 yr	Experiment	Children assigned to 1 of 12 variants of participant modeling. The treatments varied in terms of the immediacy of therapy (immediate vs. delayed), the types of treatment stimuli (*in vivo* vs. *in vitro*), and the type of rationale (rationale vs. no rationale). Treatment duration was 3 hr.	At posttreatment and 3-wk follow-up, immediate participant modeling with *in vivo* stimuli and rationale superior to others in terms of subjective and motor responses.
Evers & Schwarz (1973)	Social situations	8 males and 5 females ranging in age from 2 to 4 yr	Experiment	Children assigned to one of two conditions: filmed modeling (23 min in length) or filmed modeling (23 min in length) plus teacher-administered contingency management (2 days).	At posttreatment, both treatments equally effective in reducing motor responses. Maintenance of treatment gain at 4-wk follow-up.
Faust & Melamed (1984)	Medical treatment	4-through 17-yr-olds (*n* = 66)	Experiment	Children assigned to one of two conditions: filmed modeling (10 min in length) or attention placebo.	At posttreatment, filmed modeling superior to attention placebo in terms of motor responses.

(*continued*)

TABLE 5.5.   (*continued*)

Author(s)	Feared stimulus	Subjects	Research design	Treatment	Outcome
Faust, Olson, & Rodriguez (1991)	Medical procedures	26 children ranging in age from 4 to 10 yr	Experiment	Children assigned to one of three conditions: a participant modeling film viewed with their mothers (10-min duration), a participant modeling film viewed alone (10-min duration), or an information control film viewed alone (10-min duration).	At posttreatment, participant modeling film viewed alone resulted in greater reductions in heart rate and sweating than did the two other conditions. Both modeling conditions evidenced less behavioral distress than the control condition did.
Gilbert et al. (1982)	Medical treatment	15 females and 13 males ranging in age from 6 to 9 yr	Experiment	Children assigned to one of two conditions: filmed modeling (7 min in length) or attention placebo.	At posttreatment, no group differences in terms of subjective, motor, and physiological responses.
Ginther & Roberts (1982)	Dental treatment	33 females and 27 males ranging in age from 4 to 12 yr	Experiment	Children assigned to one of three conditions: symbolic modeling with mastery model, symbolic modeling with coping model, or no treatment. Modeling treatments were 10 min in duration.	At posttreatment, no group differences in terms of subjective and motor responses to targeted and nontargeted stimuli.
Hill, Liebert & Mott (1968)	Small animals	18 male preschoolers	Experiment	Children assigned to one of two conditions: filmed modeling with mastery model (11 min in length) or attention placebo.	At posttreatment, modeling superior to attention placebo in terms of motor responses.
Holmes (1936)	Darkness	14 children ranging in age from 39 to 54 mo	Case study	Participant modeling administered for 3 to 6 sessions.	At posttreatment, significant reductions in motor responses for 13 of the 14 children.
Jones (1924a, 1924b)	Small animals	30-mo-old male	Case study	Live modeling.	At posttreatment, significant fear reduction.
	Small animals	21-mo-old male	Case study	Participant modeling.	At posttreatment, significant fear reduction.

(*continued*)

TABLE 5.5. (*continued*)

Author(s)	Feared stimulus	Subjects	Research design	Treatment	Outcome
Jones, Ollendick, McLaughlin, & Williams (1989)	Fire	3rd-graders (*n* = 46)	Experiment	Children assigned to one of three conditions: participant modeling, participant modeling with elaborative verbal rehearsal, or no treatment. Training sessions were conducted in small groups over three consecutive days and lasted approximately 60 min each.	At posttreatment, both modeling conditions superior to no treatment on performance measures. Modeling with elaborative rehearsal superior to modeling alone and no-treatment in terms of measures of subjective distress.
Keller & Carlson (1974)	Social situations	3- to 10-yr-olds (*n* = 19)	Experiment	Children assigned to one of two conditions: filmed modeling (4 min in length and shown 4 times) or attention placebo.	At posttreatment, filmed modeling superior to attention placebo in terms of motor responses. Maintenance of treatment gains at 3-wk follow-up.
Klesges, Malott, & Ugland (1984)	Dental treatment	4-yr-old female with fear duration of 1 yr	Case study	Filmed modeling plus participant modeling with the mother serving as the coping model. Treatment was administered for 6 sessions.	At posttreatment, significant reductions in subjective and motor responses. Maintenance of treatment gains at 6-mo follow-up.
Klingman, Melamed, Cuthbert, & Hermecz (1984)	Dental treatment	20 males and 18 females ranging in age from 8 to 13 yr	Experiment	Children assigned to one of two conditions: participant modeling (17 min in duration) or filmed modeling (17 min in length).	At posttreatment, participant modeling superior to filmed modeling in terms of subjective, motor, and physiological responses. Generalization of treatment gains to other stimuli and behaviors greater for participant modeling.
Klorman, Hilpert, Michael, LaGana, & Sveen (1980)	Dental treatment	34 males and 26 females ranging in age from 3 to 14 yr	Experiment	Children assigned to one of three conditions: filmed modeling with coping model (10 min in length), filmed modeling with mastery model (10 min in length), or attention placebo.	At posttreatment, no group differences in terms of motor responses.

(*continued*)

TABLE 5.5. (*continued*)

Author(s)	Feared stimulus	Subjects	Research design	Treatment	Outcome
	Dental treatment	26 females and 20 males ranging in age from 4 to 13 yr	Experiment	Children assigned to one of three conditions: filmed modeling with coping model (10 min in length), filmed modeling with mastery model (10 min in length), or attention placebo.	At posttreatment, no group differences in terms of motor responses.
	Dental treatment	17 males and 13 females ranging in age from 4 to 12 yr	Experiment	Children assigned to one of three conditions: filmed modeling with coping model (10 min in length), filmed modeling with mastery model (10 min in length), or attention placebo.	At posttreatment, both modeling treatments superior to attention placebo in terms of motor responses.
Kornhaber & Schroeder (1975)	Small animals	50 female 2nd- and 3rd-graders	Experiment	Children assigned to one of five conditions: filmed modeling with adult mastery model, filmed modeling with child mastery model, filmed modeling with child coping model, filmed modeling with adult coping model, or no treatment. All filmed modeling treatments were 6–7 min in duration.	At posttreatment, filmed modeling with child models superior to other conditions in terms of motor response. Filmed modeling with child coping model superior to no treatment and filmed modeling with adult mastery model in terms of subjective responses.
Lewis (1974)	Water	40 males ranging in age from 5 to 12 yr	Experiment	Children assigned to one of four conditions: participant modeling (18 min in length), filmed modeling (8 min in length), rehearsal, or attention placebo.	At posttreatment, all treatments superior to attention placebo in terms of motor responses. Participant modeling superior to filmed modeling and rehearsal; rehearsal superior to filmed modeling. Generalization of treatment gains to new settings and maintenance of gains at 5-day follow-up.

(*continued*)

TABLE 5.5. (*continued*)

Author(s)	Feared stimulus	Subjects	Research design	Treatment	Outcome
Mann (1972)	Test taking	7th- and 8th-graders (*n* = 80)	Experiment	Children assigned to one of four conditions: filmed modeling with instructions to imitate, filmed modeling with instructions not to imitate, partial modeling film with instructions not to imitate, or no treatment. Treatment administered for 6 sessions.	At posttreatment, all three modeling treatments superior to no treatment in terms of subjective and motor responses. Maintenance of treatment gains at 4-wk follow-up.
Matson (1981)	Social situations	3 females ranging in age from 8 to 10 yr, with fear duration > 6 mo	Multiple-baseline	Participant modeling administered by the parent over a period of 20 days.	At posttreatment, significant reductions in subjective and motor responses. Maintenance of treatment gains at 6-mo follow-up.
Matson (1983)	Small animals	3-yr-old female with fear duration > 6 mo	Multiple-baseline	Participant modeling administered by the parent for a total of 22 sessions.	At posttreatment, significant reductions in subjective and motor responses. Maintenance of treatment gains at 1-yr follow-up.
Melamed, Meyer, Gee, & Soule (1976)	Medical treatment	4- through 12-yr-olds (*n* = 48)	Experiment	Children assigned to one of four conditions: preoperative filmed modeling 1 wk in advance with full preparation, preoperative filmed modeling 1 wk in advance with minimal preparation, preoperative filmed modeling same day with full preparation, or preoperative filmed modeling same day with minimal preparation. Modeling film had a coping model and was 16 min long.	At posttreatment, all four treatments produced significant reductions in subjective, motor, and physiological responses. Generalization of treatment gains to other fear stimuli.

(*continued*)

TABLE 5.5.   *(continued)*

Author(s)	Feared stimulus	Subjects	Research design	Treatment	Outcome
Melamed & Siegel (1975)	Hospital	4- through 12-yr-olds (*n* = 60)	Experiment	Children assigned to one of two conditions: filmed modeling with a coping model (16 min in length) of attention placebo.	At posttreatment, filmed modeling superior to attention placebo in terms of subjective, motor, and physiological responses. Generalization of treatment gains to other fear stimuli.
Melamed, Yurcheson, Fleece, Hutcherson, & Hawes (1978)	Dental treatment	4- through 12-yr-olds (*n* = 80)	Experiment	Children assigned to one of five conditions: lengthy modeling film of coping model (10 min), lengthy information film (10 min), brief modeling film of coping model (4 min), or attention placebo.	At posttreatment, both modeling films superior to other conditions in terms of subjective and motor responses.
Murphy & Bootzin (1973)	Small animals	1st- through 3rd-graders (*n* = 67)	Experiment	Children assigned to one of three conditions: active participant modeling, passive participant modeling, or no treatment. Treatment duration averaged 2 sessions.	At posttreatment, both participant modeling treatments superior to no treatment in terms of motor responses.
Peterson, Schultheis, Ridley-Johnson, Miller, & Tracy (1984)	Medical treatment	2- through 11-yr-olds (*n* = 44)	Experiment	Children assigned to one of four conditions: local modeling film (50 min in length), commercial modeling film (50 min in length), symbolic modeling (50 min in length), or information.	At posttreatment, all three modeling treatments superior to information in terms of motor responses. No group differences in term of subjective responses.
Raskind & Nagle (1980)	Test taking	48 white males and 48 white females, ranging in age from 9 to 11 yr	Experiment	Children assigned to one of three conditions: a 10-min film of a coping model, a 10-min film of a supported model, or a 10-min control film.	No significant differences among the three conditions on the performance measure.

(continued)

TABLE 5.5. (*continued*)

Author(s)	Feared stimulus	Subjects	Research design	Treatment	Outcome
Ritter (1968)	Small animals	28 females and 16 males ranging in age from 5 to 11 yr	Experiment	Children assigned to one of three conditions: participant modeling (3 sessions), live modeling (3 sessions), or no treatment.	At posttreatment, both modeling conditions superior to no treatment in terms of motor responses. Participant modeling superior to live modeling. No group differences in terms of subjective responses to targeted and nontargeted stimuli
Ritter (1969)	Heights	Unknown number of 14- through 18-yr-olds	Experiment	Children assigned to one of three conditions: participant modeling with physical support, participant modeling, or live modeling: All treatments administered in 1 session.	At posttreatment, both participant modeling conditions superior to live modeling in terms of motor responses. Participant modeling with physical support superior to participant modeling, No group differences in terms of subjective responses.
Roberts, Wurtele, Boone, Ginther, & Elkins (1981)	Hospital	7- through 12-yr-olds (*n* = 36)	Experiment	Children assigned to one of two conditions: symbolic modeling with coping model (30 min in duration) or attention placebo.	At posttreatment, modeling superior to attention placebo in terms of subjective responses. Maintenance of treatment gains at 2-wk follow-up. No group differences in responses to nontargeted stimuli.
Weissbrod & Bryan (1973)	Small animals	25 male 4th- and 5th graders	Experiment	Children assigned to one of five conditions: filmed modeling with same-age model and actual feared stimulus, filmed modeling with same-age model and replica of feared stimulus, filmed modeling with younger model and actual feared stimulus, filmed modeling with younger model and replica of feared stimulus, or attention placebo. Each modeling film 2 min in length and shown 4 times.	At posttreatment, all modeling treatments superior to attention placebo in terms of motor responses. Modeling treatments with actual feared stimulus superior to modeling treatments with replica of feared stimulus. Maintenance of treatment gains at 2-wk follow-up.

(*continued*)

TABLE 5.6.   A Summary of Contingency Management Treatments for Children's Fears and Anxieties

Author(s)	Feared stimulus	Subjects	Research design	Treatment	Outcome
Allen, Hart, Buell, Harris, & Wolf (1964)	Social situations	4-yr-old male	Reversal design	Contingency management program administered by teacher for 14 days.	At posttreatment, significant reductions in motor responses maintenance of treatment gains at 26-day follow-up.
Ayllon, Smith, & Rogers (1970)	School	8-yr-old female with fear duration of 1 yr	Case study	Shaping program for school attendance plus home-based motivational program for child and mother. Program administered by mother for 1 mo.	At posttreatment, significant reductions in motor responses. Generalization of treatment gains to other problem behaviors (somatic complaints, academic performance, classroom behavior) and maintenance of treatment gains at 9-mo follow-up.
Boer & Sipprelle (1970)	Food	4-yr-old female with fear duration of 6 mo	Case study	Shaping program for the eating of solid foods administered for 7 sessions.	At posttreatment, significant reductions in motor responses. Generalization of treatment gains to other settings and fear stimuli and maintenance of treatment gains at 13-mo follow-up.
Brown, Copeland, & Hall (1974)	School	11-yr-old male with fear duration of 2 yr	Changing-criterion	Shaping program administered by principal for 17 days.	At posttreatment, significant reductions in motor responses. Maintenance of treatment gains at 1-yr follow-up.
Buell, Stoddard, Harris, & Baer (1968)	Social situations	3-yr-old female with fear duration ≥ 1 mo	Reversal	Contingency management program administered by teacher for 36 days.	At posttreatment, significant reductions in motor responses. Generalization of treatment gains to other social behaviors.
Clement & Milne (1967)	Social situations	11 males ranging in age from 8 to 9 yr	Experiment	Children assigned to one of three conditions: contingency management with tangible reward (14 sessions), contingency management with social reward (14 sessions), or no treatment.	At posttreatment, contingency management with tangible reward superior to other two conditions in terms of motor responses. No group differences in terms of subjective responses.
Cretekos (1977)	School	Male aged 13 yr, 10 mo, with fear duration of 5 yr	Case study	Teacher-assisted contract for school attendance implemented for 6 wk.	At posttreatment, significant reductions in motor and physiological responses.

(continued)

TABLE 5.6   (*continued*)

Author(s)	Feared stimulus	Subjects	Research design	Treatment	Outcome
Doleys & Williams (1977)	School	7-yr-old female with fear duration ≥ 2 yr	Case study	Teacher- and parent-assisted contingency management program administered for 16 days.	At posttreatment, significant reductions in motor responses. Maintenance of treatment gains at 4-mo follow-up.
Hersen (1970)	School	12-yr-old male	Case study	Teacher- and parent-assisted contingency management program administered for 15 wk.	At posttreatment, significant reductions in motor responses. Maintenance of treatment gains at 6-mo follow-up.
Holmes (1936)	Heights	39-mo-old female, 51-mo-old male	Case study	Contingency management program administered for 9 to 11 sessions.	At posttreatment, significant reductions in motor responses for one of the two children.
Jackson & Wallace (1974)	Social situations	15-yr-old female with fear duration ≥ 3 mo	Reversal	Teacher-assisted contingency management program administered for 100 days.	At posttreatment, significant reductions in motor responses. No generalization of treatment gains to new settings.
Kolko, Ayllon, & Torrence (1987)	School	6-yr-old white female	Case study	Negative reinforcement contingencies for classroom attendance instituted and applied for a 4-wk period.	Marked improvement in classroom attendance, social interaction, and academic performance with the institution of contingencies. Maintenance of these treatment gains at 1-yr follow-up.
Linscheid, Tarnowski, Rasnake, & Brams (1987)	Food	6-yr-old male	Multiple-baseline/changing criterion	A program of contingent reinforcement and brief time out introduced sequentially across a variety of food items. Criterion intake for each food item was increased systematically. Program was administered over the course of a 60-day hospital stay and continued at home upon discharge.	Systematic increases in food intake with the introduction of behavioral contingencies. Continuation of treatment gains upon discharge from the hospital and the implementation of the program at home. Enhancement of treatment gains at 6-mo follow-up.

(*continued*)

TABLE 5.6.   *(continued)*

Author(s)	Feared stimulus	Subjects	Research design	Treatment	Outcome
Morelli (1983)	unspecified, with compulsive tapping	13-yr-old male with a 3-yr history of ritualistic behaviors	Case study	A 3-wk contingency management program of positive social reinforcement for appropriate motor behavior, carried out by the mother. Institution of the contingency management program was preceded by cognitive therapy for the mother to reduce her anger associated with her child's compulsive behaviors, and by intensive instruction in contingency management (this preliminary phase lasted 8 wk).	Marked reduction in compulsive behavior with the introduction of treatment. No displays of the rituals at 9-mo follow-up.
Neisworth, Madle, & Goeke (1975)	Separation	4-yr-old female with fear duration of 1 yr	Case study	Shaping and fading program administered for 7 sessions.	At posttreatment, significant reductions in motor responses. Maintenance of treatment gains at 6-mo follow-up.
Obler & Terwilliger (1970)	Vehicles, small animals	7-through 12-yr-olds (*n* = 30)	Experiment	Children assigned to one of two conditions: shaping program (10 sessions) or no treatment.	At posttreatment, shaping program superior to no treatment in terms of motor responses.
Patterson (1965)	School	7-yr-old male with fear duration ≥ 2 yr	Case study	Teacher- and parent-assisted shaping program administered for 23 sessions.	At posttreatment, significant reductions in motor responses. Maintenance of treatment gains at 3-mo follow-up.
Queiroz, Mota, Madi, Sossai, & Boren (1981)	Multiple (e.g., bedroom), along with rituals	12-yr-old female	Case study	Contingency management program for approach and adaptive behavior carried out over a 17-mo period.	At posttreatment, complete absence of avoidance and ritualistic behaviors along with appearance of adaptive behaviors. Maintenance of treatment gains at 1-yr follow-up.
Tahmisian & McReynolds (1971)	School	13-yr-old female with fear duration ≥ 1 yr	Case study	Parent-administered contingency management program carried out for 3 wk after imaginal desensitization proved unsuccessful.	At posttreatment, significant reductions in subjective and motor responses. Maintenance of treatment gains at 4-wk follow-up.

TABLE 5.7. A Summary of Self-Management Treatments for Children's Fears and Anxieties

Author(s)	Feared stimulus	Subjects	Research design	Treatment	Outcome
Bankart & Bankart (1983)	School	9-yr-old male with fear duration of 2 wk	Case study	Program of self-monitoring and coping self-talk administered for 2–3 days.	At posttreatment, significant reductions in motor responses. Maintenance of treatment gains at 2-yr follow-up.
Campbell (1973)	Ruminations about death	12-yr-old male with a 9-mo history	Case study	Four weekly treatment sessions of thought-stopping were conducted.	Immediate reductions in the frequency of ruminations upon initiation of treatment; complete elimination upon the 4th wk of treatment. Maintenance of benefits at 3-yr follow-up, along with generalization of effects to other problem behaviors.
Cradock, Cotler, & Jason (1978)	Public speaking	14-yr-old females ($n = 40$)	Experiment	Children assigned to one of three conditions: self-control (6 sessions), imaginal desensitization (6 sessions), or no treatment.	At posttreatment, self-control and imaginal desensitization superior to no treatment in terms of subjective responses. Self-control superior to imaginal desensitization. No group differences in terms of motor responses.
Dahlquist, Gil, Armstrong, Ginsberg, & Jones (1985)	Medical procedure	11-yr-old male, 13-yr-old female, and 13-yr-old male	Multiple-baseline across subjects	Coping skills program of cue-controlled relaxation, controlled breathing, pleasant imagery, and positive self-talk administered sequentially across the three children.	Following intervention, marked decreases in behavioral and subjective measures of distress. Only parent ratings of children's distress failed to drop in accord with treatment.
Eisen & Silverman (1991)	Bowel movement	15-yr-old male with a fear duration of 3 yr	Case study	A 14-wk program of coping self-talk and imagery in conjunction with role plays and a graduated series of imaginal and *in vivo* fear-related scenes.	At posttreatment, substantial improvement on all subjective, motoric, and physiological measures. Parental ratings of interference with adaptive functioning also indicated marked improvement. Enhancement of treatment gains and evidence of generalized effects (increase in self-concept and positive mood, decrease in behavioral problems) at 6-mo follow-up.

(continued)

TABLE 5.7.   (*continued*)

Author(s)	Feared stimulus	Subjects	Research design	Treatment	Outcome
Fox & Houston (1981)	Public Speaking	33 female and 23 male 4th-graders	Experiment	Children assigned to one of three conditions: coping self-talk (1 session), attention placebo (1 session), or no treatment.	At posttreatment, attention placebo and no treatment superior to coping self-talk in terms of subjective responses.
Genshaft (1982)	Math	7th-grade females (*n* = 36)	Experiment	Children assigned to one of three conditions: self-instructional training plus tutoring, tutoring only, or no treatment. The first two conditions consisted of 2 sessions (approximately 1 hr each) per wk for 8 wk.	At posttreatment, the self-instructional training plus tutoring condition superior to the other two conditions on both subjective and performance measures.
Genshaft & Hirt (1980)	Math	7th-grade white females (*n* = 36)	Experiment	Children assigned to one of three conditions: self-instructional training plus tutoring (twice-weekly 40-min sessions for 8 wk), tutoring (twice-weekly 40-min sessions for 8 wk), or no treatment.	At posttreatment, self-instructional training plus tutoring superior to tutoring only and no treatment on math performance measure. Both self-instructional training and tutoring superior to no-treatment on attitudinal measure of math and science activities.
Grindler (1988)	Test taking	66 black and white male and female 4th- and 5th-graders	Experiment	Children assigned to one of two conditions: self-instructional training or attention control; for each condition, twice-weekly 40-min sessions conducted over 4 consecutive wk.	At posttreatment and 6-wk follow-up, no differences between the two conditions on subjective and behavioral measures.
Kanfer, Karoly, & Newman (1975)	Darkness	30 males and 15 females ranging in age from 5 to 6 yr	Experiment	Children assigned to one of three conditions: coping self-talk, information, or attention placebo. All conditions administered for 1 session.	At posttreatment, coping self-talk superior to information and attention placebo in terms of motor response. Information superior to attention placebo. Generalization of treatment gains to other settings.

(*continued*)

TABLE 5.7. (*continued*)

Author(s)	Feared stimulus	Subjects	Research design	Treatment	Outcome
Leal, Baxter, Martin, & Marx (1981)	Test taking	10th-graders (*n* = 30)	Experiment	Children assigned to one of three conditions: self-instructional training (6 weekly sessions of 1 hr each), systematic desensitization (6 weekly sessions of 1 hr each), or no treatment.	At posttreatment, systematic desensitization slightly superior to self-instructional training and no-treatment on the performance measure; self-instructional training clearly superior to systematic desensitization and no-treatment on the subjective measure.
Nocella & Kaplan (1982)	Dental treatment	5- through 13-yr-olds (*n* = 30)	Experiment	Children assigned to one of three conditions: self-management program of relaxation and coping self-talk (1 session), attention placebo (1 session), or no treatment.	At posttreatment, self-management superior to attention placebo and no treatment in terms of motor response.
Ownby (1983)	Contamination (along with compulsive hand-washing and cleaning rituals)	13-yr-old male with 3-mo history	Case study	A self-management program of self-monitoring and thought stopping, presented over 3 sessions (30 min each) and implemented over a 3-wk period. A 12-wk maintenance phase followed in which weekly 15-min reviews of progress were conducted and thought stopping was continued but self-recording was discontinued.	Marked reductions in the frequency of hand-washing across the course of the treatment. Maintenance of treatment gains at 6- and 18-mo follow-up assessments. Generalization of benefits to new behaviors and settings.
Peterson & Shigetomi (1981)	Hospital	35 females and 31 males ranging in age from 2 to 10 yr	Experiment	Children assigned to one of five conditions: parent-assisted coping skills training, filmed modeling with a mastery model, coping skills training plus filmed modeling, information, or attention placebo. All conditions administered for 1 session.	At posttreatment, coping skills training and coping skills training plus modeling superior to filmed modeling in terms of motor responses. No group differences in terms of subjective and physiological responses.

(*continued*)

TABLE 5.7.   (*continued*)

Author(s)	Feared stimulus	Subjects	Research design	Treatment	Outcome
Ribordy, Tracy, & Bernotas (1981)	Test taking	48 children ranging in age from 9 to 12 yr and of various ethnic and racial backgrounds	Experiment	Children assigned to one of three conditions: attentional training (1 session), attention placebo (1 session), or no treatment.	At posttreatment, attentional superior to attention placebo and no treatment on the target performance measure. No differences among the conditions on a generalization performance measure.
Rosenfarb & Hayes (1984)	Darkness	19 males and 19 females ranging in age from 5 to 6 yr	Experiment	Children assigned to one of six conditions: program of coping self-talk administered in private, program of coping self-talk administered in public, modeling film shown in private, modeling film shown in public, attention placebo, or placebo film. All conditions administered for 1 session.	At posttreatment, coping self-talk administered in public and modeling film shown in public superior to other four conditions in terms of motor responses.
Sheslow, Bondy, & Nelson (1982)	Darkness	16 females and 16 males ranging in age from 4 to 5 yr	Experiment	Children assigned to one of four conditions: coping self-talk, *in vivo* desensitization, coping self-talk plus *in vivo* desensitization, or attention placebo.	At posttreatment, *in vivo* desensitization and coping self-talk plus *in vivo* desensitization superior to coping self-talk and attention placebo in terms of motor responses. No group differences in terms of subjective responses.

(*continued*)

TABLE 5.7. (*continued*)

Author(s)	Feared stimulus	Subjects	Research design	Treatment	Outcome
Siegel & Peterson (1980, 1981)	Dental treatment	42 children ranging in age from 42 to 71 mo	Experiment	Children assigned to one of three conditions: coping skills training, information, or attention placebo.	At posttreatment, coping skills training and information superior to attention placebo in terms of motor and physiological responses. No group differences in terms of subjective responses. At 1-wk follow-up, coping skills training and information superior to attention placebo in terms of motor responses. Information superior to coping skills training and attention placebo in terms of physiological response. No group differences in terms of subjective responses.
Wilson & Rotter (1986)	Test taking	6th- and 7th-graders ($n = 54$; 44% female, 56% male; 89% black, 11% white)	Experiment	Children assigned to one of five conditions: anxiety management training, study skills, anxiety management training plus study skills, attention placebo, or no treatment. The first four conditions consisted of twice-weekly 45-min sessions for 3 consecutive wk.	At posttreatment and 2-mo follow-up, the three treatment conditions of anxiety management training, study skills, and their combination superior to the two control conditions on the subjective but not performance measure of test anxiety. No significant differences among the three treatment conditions at either of the assessments.

TABLE 5.8.   A Summary of Combined Treatments for Children's Fears and Anxieties

Author(s)	Feared stimulus	Subjects	Research design	Treatment	Outcome
Albano, Marten, Holt, Heimberg, & Barlow (1995)	Social	3 white males and 2 white females, ranging in age from 12 to 17 yr	Case study	A combined intervention consisting of self-management training, modeling, and *in vivo* exposure, carried out in a group format over 16 weekly sessions (90 min each). Parents participated in 4 of the sessions and assisted the children in completing the recording procedures and practice exercises.	At posttreatment, significant reductions in subjective and behavioral distress and depressed mood for most of the subjects. No noticeable change in physiological upset. Similar pattern of findings at 3-, 6-, and 12-mo follow-up assessments, along with marked improvement in untreated fears and anxieties.
Andrews (1971)	Test taking	48 male 10th- and 11th-graders	Experiment	Children assigned to one of three conditions: combined treatment of imaginal desensitization and contingency management, client-centered treatment, or no treatment. Treatments administered for 10 sessions.	At posttreatment, combined treatment superior to client-centered and no treatment in terms of subjective responses. No group differences in terms of motor responses.
Barlow & Seidner (1983)	Being alone	2 females and 1 male ranging in age from 15 to 17 yr; fear duration ranging from 14 mo to 4 yr	Case study	Parent-assisted combined treatment of desensitization, self-management, and prolonged exposure administered for 10 sessions.	At posttreatment, significant reductions in subjective and motor responses for two of the three children. Generalization of treatment gains to other problem behaviors (family relations) and maintenance of treatment gains at 6-mo follow-up.
Bauer (1968)	Mathematics	7th-grade male	Case study	Combined treatment of imaginal desensitization and modeling administered over a period of 4 mo.	At posttreatment, significant reductions in motor responses.

(*continued*)

TABLE 5.8. (*continued*)

Author(s)	Feared stimulus	Subjects	Research design	Treatment	Outcome
Blagg & Yule (1984)	School	33 males and 33 females ranging in age from 11 to 16 yr, with fear duration ≥ 3 days	Experiment with nonrandom assignment	Children assigned to one of three conditions: combined treatment of parent-assisted contingency management and *in vivo* flooding (average duration of 2½ wk), inpatient hospitalization (average duration of 45 wk), or home tutoring and psychotherapy (average duration of 72 wk).	At posttreatment, combined treatment superior to hospitalization and home tutoring in terms of motor responses. Generalization of treatment gains to other fear stimuli and other problem behaviors (extroversion and neuroticism) and maintenance of treatment gains at follow-up of 3 yr, 10 mo.
Boyd (1980)	School	16-yr-old male with fear duration ≥ 3 wk	Case study	Combined treatment of emotive imagery and contingency management administered over a 3-wk period.	At posttreatment, significant reductions in motor responses.
Esveldt-Dawson, Wisner, Unis, Matson, & Kazdin (1982)	School, strangers	12-yr-old female	Multiple-baseline	Combined treatment of participant modeling and contingency management administered for 20 sessions.	At posttreatment, significant reductions in subjective and motor responses. Generalization of treatment gains to new settings and other fear stimuli and maintenance of treatment gains at 21-wk follow-up.
Franco, Christoff, Crimmins, & Kelly (1983)	Social situations	14-yr-old male	Multiple-baseline	Combined treatment of participant modeling and contingency management administered weekly for 49 wk.	At posttreatment, significant reductions in subjective and motor responses. Maintenance of treatment gains at 3-mo follow-up.
Friedman & Ollendick (1989)	Darkness	5 males and 1 female, ranging in age from 7 to 10 yr and in fear duration from 8 mo to 6 yr	Multiple-baseline across subjects	A 5-wk multicomponent program consisting of relaxation training, self-instructional training, and contingency management, administered sequentially across two groups of children.	Parental ratings of behavior revealed substantial improvement for all children. Not all of these gains could be attributed to the intervention, as those children with extended baselines evidenced some improvement prior to the introduction of treatment. Maintenance of these benefits at 2-wk follow-up.

(*continued*)

TABLE 5.8.   (*continued*)

Author(s)	Feared stimulus	Subjects	Research design	Treatment	Outcome
Friedmann & Silvers (1977)	Leaving home, counting rituals	18-yr-old white male with a 2-yr history	Case study	A 13-wk inpatient treatment program of milieu therapy, family therapy, insight-oriented therapy, thought stopping, assertion therapy and contingency management.	Upon discharge from the hospital program, marked reduction in obsessive–compulsive behaviors. Maintenance of treatment gains at $2\frac{1}{2}$-yr follow-up, with generalization of benefits to other anxiety conditions and problem behaviors.
Giebenhain & O'Dell (1984)	Darkness	4 males and 2 females ranging in age from 3 to 11 yr, with fear duration $\geq$ 1 yr	Multiple-baseline	Parent-administered combined treatment of self-management and contingency management carried out for 2 wk.	At posttreatment, significant reductions in motor responses. No changes in subjective responses. Maintenance of treatment gains at 12-mo follow-up.
Graziano & Mooney (1980, 1982)	Darkness	18 males and 15 females ranging in age from 6 to $13\frac{1}{2}$ yr, with fear duration from $1\frac{1}{2}$ to $10\frac{1}{4}$ yr	Experiment	Children assigned to one of two conditions: parent-assisted combined treatment of self-management and contingency management (3-wk duration) or no treatment.	At posttreatment, combined treatment superior to no treatment in terms of motor responses. Maintenance of treatment gains at 3-yr follow-up.
Graziano, Mooney, Huber, & Ignasiak (1979)	Darkness	5 males and 2 females ranging in age from $8\frac{1}{2}$ to $12\frac{3}{4}$ yr, with fear duration from 3 to 6 yr	Case study	Parent-assisted combined treatment of self-management and contingency management administered over a period of 3 to 19 wk.	At posttreatment, significant reductions in subjective and motor responses. Maintenance of treatment gains at 1-yr follow-up.
Handler (1972)	Nightmares	11-yr-old male	Case study	Combined treatment of imaginal flooding and participant modeling administered for 2 sessions.	At posttreatment, significant reductions in motor responses. Maintenance of treatment gains at 6-mo follow-up.

(*continued*)

TABLE 5.8. (*continued*)

Author(s)	Feared stimulus	Subjects	Research design	Treatment	Outcome
Harris & Brown (1982)	Social, public speaking	4th-, 5th-, and 6th-graders (*n* = 109)	Experiment	Children randomly assigned to one of three conditions: a combined behavioral treatment, a classroom teacher knowledgeable in techniques for reducing social fears, and a no-treatment control. The combined treatment consisted of self-instructional training and imaginal desensitization; treatment was carried out in groups of 6 to 10 by four therapists for a total of 10 sessions (45 min each) spanning a 5-wk period.	At posttreatment, combined intervention was superior to knowledgeable-teacher and no-treatment control conditions on a measure of subjective distress; this superiority evidenced across all grade levels.
Jay, Elliott, Ozolins, Olson, & Pruitt (1985)	Medical procedure	3 females and 2 males, ranging in age from $3\frac{1}{2}$ to 7 yr	Multiple-baseline across subjects	An intervention consisting of breathing exercises, emotive imagery, filmed modeling, behavioral rehearsal, and contingency management, administered sequentially across subjects. The complete procedure lasted approximately 45 min.	Behavioral ratings indicated a reduction in distress following intervention.
Kane & Kendall (1989)	Generalized	1 male and 3 females, ranging in age from 9 to 13 yr	Multiple-baseline across subjects	A multifaceted treatment program consisting of coping skills training, self-instructional training, modeling, graduated exposure, and contingency management, administered sequentially across subjects. Twice weekly sessions of (1 hr each) were conducted for a total of 16–20 sessions.	Parental and child reports indicated reductions in subjective, motoric, and physiological distress with the advent of treatment. Maintenance of treatment gains at 3- to 6-mo follow-up for only two of the four children.

(*continued*)

TABLE 5.8.   (*continued*)

Author(s)	Feared stimulus	Subjects	Research design	Treatment	Outcome
Kearney & Silverman (1990a)	Bats	14-yr-old white male	Alternating treatments	Response prevention and cognitive therapy, administered on alternating weeks over a 12-wk period. For each week, two treatment sessions (30-45 min each) were conducted.	At posttreatment, marked improvement on all self-report and observational measures. Response prevention superior to cognitive therapy on some of the subjective and behavioral measures, inferior to cognitive therapy on others. Maintenance of treatment gains at 6-mo follow-up.
Kearney & Silverman (1990b)	School	5 white males and 2 white females, averaging $12\frac{1}{2}$ yr in age and less than 1 yr in fear duration	Case study	Based on an assessment of motivating factors, children received one of three interventions: desensitization, self-management plus participant modeling, or contingency management.	At posttreatment, 6 of 7 children attending school on a full-time basis and experiencing minimal subjective distress. Collateral subjective and behavioral improvements consistent with identified motivating factors. Maintenance of nearly all treatment gains at 6-mo follow-up.
Kendall (1994)	Unfamiliar persons, separation from attachment figure, or non-specific in natue	9- to 13-yr-olds ($n = 47$), with 60% males, and 40% females, 76% white and 24% black	Experiment	Children assigned to one of two conditions: cognitive-behavioral therapy or 8-wk waiting-list control. Cognitive-behavioral therapy consisted of relaxation training, coping self-talk, modeling, imaginal rehearsal, *in vivo* exposure, and contingent reinforcement. Individual treatment ranged in duration from 16 to 20 weekly sessions (50–60 min each) and included regular homework assignments. Treatment was provided by seven different therapists and monitored for adherence to protocol.	At posttreatment, cognitive-behavioral condition superior waiting-list control condition on all but one of the multiple subjective, motoric, and physiological response measures gathered through multiple methods (i.e., self-report, parental report, teacher report, direct observation). Generalization of treatment gains to other problem behaviors (i.e., depression) and maintenance of treatment gains at 1-yr follow-up.

(*continued*)

TABLE 5.8. *(continued)*

Author(s)	Feared stimulus	Subjects	Research design	Treatment	Outcome
Lazarus, Davison, & Polefka (1965)	School	9-yr-old male with fear duration ≥ 4 yr	Case study	Combined treatment of *in vivo* desensitization, emotive imagery, and contingency management administered over a period of $4\frac{1}{2}$ mo.	At posttreatment, significant reductions in motor responses. Generalization of treatment gains to other problem behaviors (family relations) and maintenance of treatment gains at 10-mo follow-up.
Little & Jackson (1974)	Test taking	19 males and 18 females, average age of 12 yr	Experiment	Children assigned to one of five conditions: attentional training, relaxation training, attentional plus relaxation training, placebo control, or no treatment. The first four conditions consisted of hourly meetings twice a wk for 3 wk. Attentional training called for viewing modeling tapes of children coping with testing situations, working samples of various academic tasks, and receiving periodic prompting to focus attention on the task.	At posttreatment, attentional plus relaxation training superior to all other conditions in reducing subjective distress. All four conditions superior to no-treatment on performance measures.
Lyon (1983)	Unspecified, with compulsive lip biting	12-yr-old male with over 6-yr history	Case study	A combined treatment program consisting of self-monitoring, aversive response substitution, and cue-controlled relaxation, administered over a 5-wk period.	Complete elimination of the compulsive behavior upon 5 weeks of treatment, with no recurrences reported at 7-mo follow-up.
MacDonald (1975)	Small animals	11-yr-old male with fear duration of 8 yr	Case study	Parent-assisted combined treatment of desensitization, participant modeling, prolonged exposure, and contingency management, administered for 16 sessions.	At posttreatment, significant reductions in subjective and motor responses. Generalization of treatment gains to other fear stimuli and maintenance of treatment gains at 2-yr follow-up.

(continued)

TABLE 5.8. (*continued*)

Author(s)	Feared stimulus	Subjects	Research design	Treatment	Outcome
Mayer et al. (1971)	School, test taking	5th- and 6th-graders (*n* = 54)	Experiment	Children assigned to one of five conditions: combined treatment of public self-management and contingency management, combined treatment of private self-management and contingency management, instruction, waiting list, or no treatment. Combined treatments administered weekly for 12 wk.	At posttreatment, no group differences in terms of subjective responses.
McNamara (1988)	School	12-yr-old female with fear duration of less than 1 yr	Case study	A program of self-monitoring, stress inoculation, imaginal rehearsal, and *in vivo* desensitization, carried out over the course of approximately 10 sessions (30 min to 1 hr each).	With the institution of treatment, marked improvement on subjective and behavioral measures.
Miller, Barrett, Hampe, & Noble (1972b)	Varied from child to child; most common were school and darkness	37 males and females ranging in age from 6 to 15 yr	Experiment	Children assigned to one of three conditions: combined treatment of desensitization, modeling and contingency management; psychotherapy; or no treatment. Treatment administered for 24 sessions.	At posttreatment, combined treatment and psychotherapy superior to no treatment in terms of motor responses. Generalization of treatment gains to other fear stimuli and maintenance of treatment gains at 14-wk follow-up.
Miller & Kassinove (1978)	Generalized	4th-graders (*n* = 96)	Experiment	Children assigned to one of four conditions: self-management, self-management plus participant modeling, self-management plus participant modeling plus homework, or no treatment. Treatment administered daily for 12 wk.	At posttreatment, self-management plus participant modeling with and without homework superior to no treatment in terms of subjective responses.
Nicolau, Toro, & Prado (1991)	Micturition, with associated rituals	13-yr-old female with an 11-yr history	Case study	A combined treatment program of self-monitoring imaginal and *in vivo* desensitization, response prevention, and parent-assisted contingency management, carried out over a 7-wk period.	Marked reduction in avoidance behavior and compulsive rituals with the application of treatment. Maintenance of treatment gains at 2-yr follow-up.

(*continued*)

TABLE 5.8. (*continued*)

Author(s)	Feared stimulus	Subjects	Research design	Treatment	Outcome
O'Connor (1972)	Social situations	33 children	Experiment	Children assigned to one of four conditions: filmed modeling (23 min in length), filmed modeling plus contingency management, contingency management plus control film, or attention placebo. Contingency management treatments administered over a 2-wk period.	At posttreatment, all three treatments superior to attention placebo in terms of motor responses. Maintenance of treatment gains for two modeling treatments at 6-wk follow-up.
Ollendick (1995)	Public places (in connection with panic)	3 white females and 1 white male, ranging in age from 13 to 17 yr and in fear duration from 6 mo to 6 yr	Multiple-baseline across subjects	A cognitive-behavioral program consisting of progressive muscle relaxation, breathing retraining, cue-controlled relaxation, applied relaxation, self-instructional training, and *in vivo* exposure, administered sequentially across subjects. Treatment ranged in duration from 6 to 9 wk, with brief maintenance sessions conducted 2 wk and 1 mo posttreatment.	Systematic reductions in subjective, physiological, and behavioral indices of anxiety with the application of treatment. Generalization of therapeutic benefits to other anxiety reactions and problem conditions (i.e., depression). Maintenance of treatment and generalization effects at 6-mo follow-up.
Ollendick, Hagopian, & Huntzinger (1991)	Darkness	10-yr-old white female with fear duration of 3 mo and 8-yr-old white female with fear duration of 7 mo	Multiple-baseline across subjects	An intervention of self-management training and self-management plus contingency management, applied sequentially with each child and across the two children. The self-management portion of the intervention consisted of 6 weekly sessions (50 min each); the additional contingency management component involved 8–12 weekly sessions (30-50 min each).	With the introduction of the contingency management component, the intervention led to improvement on subjective and behavioral measures of distress. Generalization of therapeutic effects to other anxiety reactions (i.e., separation anxiety). Maintenance of these treatment gains at 1- to 2-yr follow-up.
Peterson (1987)	Separation	8-yr-old white female with fear duration of approximately 1 yr	Case study	A program of relaxation training, self-instruction, distracting activities, and reinforced practice, carried out over the course of 8 weekly sessions (1 hr each).	At posttreatment, sizeable improvement on subjective and behavioral measures. Maintenance of treatment gains at 1- to 2-yr follow-up.

(*continued*)

TABLE 5.8.   (*continued*)

Author(s)	Feared stimulus	Subjects	Research design	Treatment	Outcome
Pomerantz, Peterson, Marholin, & Stern (1977)	Water	4-yr-old male	Case study	Parent-administered program of contingency management and participant modeling. Treatment carried out for 11 sessions.	At posttreatment, significant reductions in motor responses. Maintenance of treatment gains at 6-mo follow-up.
Queiroz, Mota, Madi, Sossai, & Boren (1981)	Multiple (e.g., dark, thunder, being alone), along with rituals	9-yr-old male	Case study	Over an 18-mo period, a program of contingency management and *in vivo* desensitization.	Marked behavioral improvements with consistent application of the treatment procedure.
Sanders & Jones (1990)	Multiple (i.e., injections, medical procedure)	13-yr-old female with fear duration of approximately 8 mo	Multiple-baseline across stimuli	A multifaceted treatment consisting of coping skills training, imaginal desensitization, *in vivo* desensitization, and participant modeling, administered sequentially across feared stimuli. A total of 20 sessions carried out.	Reductions in subjective and behavioral distress with the introduction of treatment. Evidence of generalization of treatment effects across situations and problem behaviors (i.e., Conduct Disorder). Maintenance of these therapeutic benefits at 9-mo follow-up.
Singer, Ambuel, Wade, & Jaffe (1992)	Food	3 males, 6 to 8 yr old, with a fear history of 4 wk to 5 yr	Multiple-baseline/ changing-criterion	Combined intervention of contingency management, systematic desensitization, and cognitive restructuring, administered over the course of 16 to 60 days.	Changes in eating behavior in accord with sequential application of treatment. Generalization of therapeutic benefits to different food items and meal situations. Maintenance of therapeutic benefits at 5-mo to 2-yr follow-up.
van der Ploeg-Stapert & van der Ploeg (1986)	Test taking	68 males and females, averaging 14 yr of age	Experiment	Children assigned to one of two conditions: a multifaceted program consisting of relaxation, study skills, rational–emotive training, and parental support (9 weekly sessions of 90 min each) or no treatment.	At posttreatment, multifaceted program superior to no treatment on all self-report measures of subjective and physiological anxiety. At 3-mo follow-up, enhancement of treatment gains on self-report and performance measures.

(continued)

TABLE 5.8. (*continued*)

Author(s)	Feared stimulus	Subjects	Research design	Treatment	Outcome
Williams & Jones (1989)	Fire	26 females and 22 males, ranging in age from $7\frac{1}{2}$ to $10\frac{1}{2}$ yr	Experiment	Children assigned to one of four conditions: participant modeling, participant modeling plus self-instructional training, attention control, or no treatment. For the three intervention conditions, 3 sessions (50 to 60 min each) were conducted over 3 consecutive days.	At posttreatment, two modeling conditions superior to attention control and no treatment on the motor performance measure. No differences among the groups on any of the measures of subjective distress. Maintenance of the performance gains at 5-mo follow-up, with participant modeling plus self-instructional training evidencing greater maintenance than participant modeling alone.
Willmuth (1988)	Harm to family members, with associated compulsive rituals	11-yr-old male with a 2- to 3-wk history	Case study	A program of self-monitoring and parent-supervised response prevention and contingency management, was carried out over a 5-mo period. Treatment supplemented with insight-oriented psychotherapy.	At posttreatment, child reported being free of bothersome thoughts regarding family members and refrained from exhibition of the ritualistic behaviors. Treatment gains maintained at 3-, 12-, and 18-mo follow-ups.

CHAPTER 6

Problems in Social Relationships

Steven A. McFadyen-Ketchum
Kenneth A. Dodge
Vanderbilt University

Historically, treatment of the problems of being unable to get along socially with other persons has not held a place of high esteem in American psychiatry and psychology. Certainly, in contrast with exotic disorders such as autism and Tourette syndrome, social incompetence has been viewed as commonplace and nonscientific. The mental health profession has often abdicated responsibility for resolving these problems to popular writers, moral educators, and hucksters. Likewise, the educational system has not seen fit to place children's social skills on its priority list. Yet there is abundant evidence to indicate that positive social relationships, especially with peers, are necessary requisites for mental health and educational success (see Kupersmidt, Coie, & Dodge, 1990, and Parker & Asher, 1987, for reviews), and that negative relationships with peers, parents, and others are associated with long-term negative outcomes, including substance misuse and interpersonal violence (Kupersmidt et al., 1990; Patterson, Reid, & Dishion, 1992; Pepler & Slaby, 1994). With the advent of behavioral interventions and social skills training programs designed to improve peer relationships, and stimulant medication interventions with hyperactive children designed to decrease behaviors that interfere with social relationships, this evidence has begun to have an impact on mental health and educational systems. These programs have flourished in the last 20 years, along with research evaluating their efficacy. Recently, adjunctive social system interventions, primarily within the family, have been found to improve the immediate and long-term outcomes of these programs greatly (Kazdin, 1995). The goals of this chapter are to describe some of these behavioral, social skills, and stimulant medication interventions for preschool and young school-age children and their adjunctive use with family interventions; to evaluate the scientific merit of these interventions; and to guide further inquiry in this area.

THE RATIONALE FOR FOCUSING ON SOCIAL RELATIONSHIP PROBLEMS IN CHILDREN

In order to provide a context for this review, the rationale for focusing on social relationship problems in children is briefly described. The rekindling of interest in social competence ("*re*kindling," because initial interest dates back at least to the days of ancient Greeks such as Demosthenes and Socrates; McFall & Dodge, 1982) came with the finding that measures of social competence are predictive of positive adjustment following psychiatric hospitalization. For example, Zigler and Phillips (1961) found that simple measures of competence such as marital and occupational status could be used to predict outcome in psychiatric patients. Jacobs, Muller, Anderson, and Skinner (1973) found that psychiatric patients who had positive social relationships (contrasted with those who did not) were relatively likely to respond favorably to treatment in a psychiatric ward and to fare well following release from the hospital. The consensus of these findings was that social competence indicators were positively correlated with favorable prognoses. Roff (1963) took this work a step further by demonstrating that measures of social interactions in childhood, especially with peers, were predictive of psychological maladjustment in later life. Children who had difficulty in getting along with peers at age 8 were at increased risk for bad-conduct discharges from military service 10–15 years later and for psychoses in young adulthood.

Since then, the predictive relation between early social relationship problems and later maladjustment has been replicated in a variety of studies—with follow-back and follow-up designs; with measures of early peer relationships ranging from sociometrics (Cowen, Pederson, Babigian, Izzo, & Trost, 1973) to ratings made from child guidance clinic data (Robins, 1966); and with a surprising variety of maladjustment outcomes. These outcomes include general measures of externalizing and internalizing (or neurotic) behavior (Coie, Terry, Lenox, Lochman, & Hyman, 1995; Kupersmidt et al., 1990; and Parker & Asher, 1987), as well as general psychiatric impairment and problems in life functioning (Farrington, 1991; Kupersmidt et al., 1990; Parker & Asher, 1987). More specific outcome measures include physical and verbal aggression (Dodge, 1993a), truancy and school dropout (Coie et al., 1995; Kupersmidt et al., 1990; Parker & Asher, 1987), juvenile and adult criminality (Kupersmidt et al., 1990; Parker & Asher, 1987), sexual promiscuity (Tremblay, 1991), schizophrenia (Kupersmidt et al., 1990; Parker & Asher, 1987), suicide (Shaffer, 1974; Stengel, 1971), and illicit drug use and alcoholism (Farrington, 1991; Kandel, 1982; Parker & Asher, 1987).

With the publication of Parker and Asher's (1987) and Kupersmidt et al.'s (1990) comprehensive reviews of these findings, clearly demonstrating the robustness of the relation between early childhood peer relationship problems and

later-life problems, the focus of empirical inquiry shifted toward attempts to explain this relation. Parker and Asher (1987) presented two models. According to the first of these, peer rejection may play a causal role, along with deviant behavior, in the development of maladjusted outcomes. Negative reactions of peers may, for example, serve to convince children that others are not to be trusted, thus producing aggressive or withdrawn responses (see also Dodge, 1993b). Parker and Asher's (1987) second model maintains that peer rejection plays no direct causal role, functioning incidentally to child deviance, and serving as a marker useful in identifying children at risk for later maladjustment, but playing no real part in its development. Peers may, for example, react negatively to children but provoke no subsequent changes in their cognitions or behavior.

Dodge (1993b) has conducted one of the few empirical tests comparing these models. Essentially, if the causal rather than the incidental model is correct, it follows that the relation between early peer rejection and later maladjustment is not merely due to the common effect of early child deviance on these variables—in other words, that peer rejection and child deviance play incremental roles in the development of later-life problems (see Baron & Kenny, 1986). Dodge (1993b) was able to demonstrate this effect using longitudinal data from a large ($n = 585$) community sample collected to study children's social development. By regressing a measure of third grade aggression on kindergarten peer rejection after first controlling for kindergarten aggression, Dodge (1993b) showed that the variance accounted for by peer rejection remained statistically significant. Though by itself this finding does not prove a causal role for peer rejection, it could not have happened had the incidental model been correct. Dodge (1993b) was also able to show that early aggression and peer rejection interact to account for later aggression, with high-aggression-rejected children (both boys and girls) showing the highest levels of third-grade aggression. This additional finding is important because it is consistent with a view of social rejection that incorporates child temperament as an additional explanatory variable. In this case, measures of problematic temperament (e.g., resistance to control or reactivity; Rothbart & Bates, 1997) are represented by an early measure of aggressive and disruptive behavior. Taken together, these findings demonstrate that it is not sufficient to think of maladjusted development as stemming from either child deviance or peer rejection. Rather, both must be taken into account.

Children with poor peer relationships are not only at risk for later aggressive behavior and the many other later-life problems mentioned above; they are also known to be concurrently likely to have difficulties in academic performance at school (Kohn, 1977; Coie & Koeppl, 1990), and to be overrepresented in referrals to child guidance clinics (Kupersmidt et al., 1990; Richters & Cicchetti, 1993). In addition, even though a child's level of social competence is not usually the primary focus of psychological and psychiatric inquiry, deficient peer relationships are a common feature of a number of child psychological disorders, including Attention-Deficit/Hyperactivity Disorder (ADHD), Oppositional Defiant Disorder (ODD), and Conduct Disorder (CD)(see American Psychiatric Association, 1994, and Dodge, 1989). Even those socially rejected children who are not identified as having psychiatric problems are likely to report high levels of personal unhappiness and loneliness (Asher, Parkhurst, Hymel, & Williams, 1990). At least half of rejected children are unable to resolve their difficulties on their own and remain socially rejected over several years (Coie & Dodge, 1983). Given the pervasiveness of these problems, it is perplexing why parents and professionals do not typically refer rejected children for psychological intervention.

IDENTIFYING CHILDREN WITH PROBLEMS IN SOCIAL RELATIONSHIPS

Because the literature on social competence has origins in so many areas of research, there are few agreed-upon criteria for identifying the child who is experiencing problems in social relationships. Information about these problems has come from many sources, including teachers, parents, peers, adult observers and the children themselves (Asher & Coie, 1990). Estimates about the magnitude of these problems also vary. Peer informant data indicate that from 6% to 11% of all children in the third through sixth grades of elementary schools have not even a single friend in their classrooms (Asher, 1990; Hymel & Asher, 1977). The rate of friendlessness is slightly higher among boys than among girls, but this difference has not held up across all studies (Asher & Hymel,

1981; French & Tyne, 1982). About 12% of the children meet criteria as socially rejected (Coie, Dodge, & Coppotelli, 1982). These criteria include relatively few peer nominations of a child as being liked and many nominations as being disliked.

At least four different sources of information have been used to diagnose problems in peer relations. At the most general level, teachers or other adults who are familiar with a child's behavior (such as parents) have simply nominated children who are having difficulties relating to peers. This is the most common route to identification, as demonstrated in the process of referral to child guidance and mental health clinics. Parents often refer their children for "behavior problems," which include an array of problems with compliance, aggression, and negative affect; however, the primary reason for referral is rarely an explicit focus on social incompetence (Kazdin, 1995). Children's social behavior has been evaluated more systematically through structured measures such as the Child Behavior Checklist (Achenbach, 1991a, 1991b), the Social Behavior Questionnaire (Tremblay et al., 1991), the Social Interaction Rating Scale (Hops, Walker, & Greenwood, 1979), and the Social Behavior Rating Scale (Greenwood, Walker, Todd, & Hops, 1979). These measures have been used to identify general problems in peer relations, as well as specific types of problem behaviors such as aggression, hyperactivity, and withdrawal. The validity of these measures has been demonstrated by their positive correlations with other assessments of peer relationship problems, including direct observations and referrals to mental health clinics. It is assumed that adults who know a child well are in a position to understand that child's social interactions with peers. However, a large portion of the peer culture is hidden from adults (Youniss, 1981), and adults' assessments may be biased by the child's academic performance or conduct toward adults (Coie, Dodge, & Kupersmidt, 1990). The validity of adult rating instruments has proven far greater for general identification of problem children than for the identification of specific types of problems (for a review, see Hops & Greenwood, 1988).

A second source of information has been the peer group. Sociometric nominations as being liked or disliked have been used to identify three different groups of socially maladjusted children (Coie et al., 1982; Newcomb, Bukowski, & Pattee, 1993). The "socially rejected" child is identified as being liked by few or no peers, as well as being disliked by many peers. The "socially neglected" child is liked by few peers as well, but is not highly disliked. The "controversial" child, on the other hand, is highly liked as well as highly disliked. All three groups may be targets for intervention, although longitudinal data have demonstrated that the low status of rejected children is more stable across 5 years than is the low status of neglected and controversial children (Coie & Dodge, 1983). In addition, the rejected child is clearly at risk for juvenile delinquency and school dropout, whereas the risk status of neglected and controversial children is less clear (Kupersmidt et al., 1990). Validity of the construct of rejected status has been demonstrated in a number of other ways, in addition to the predictive evidence concerning maladaptive outcomes. A high proportion of rejected children are known to behave deviantly toward peers, including high levels of aggression and other inappropriate behaviors (Coie et al., 1990; Newcomb et al., 1993). They lack a variety of social-cognitive skills (Dodge & Feldman, 1990), and they report high levels of loneliness (Asher et al., 1990). The rejected child is thus clearly a target for intervention aimed at improving social competence.

It is tempting to equate peer status groupings with particular psychiatric disorders. Rejected children are known to display (as a group) high rates of aggressive behavior, and neglected children have been thought of as shy and perhaps anxious; these conceptualizations suggest links to externalizing problems such as ADHD, ODD, and CD and to internalizing problems such as anxiety or depressive disorders, respectively (see Dodge, 1993 a). The evidence suggests that these links are premature, however. Whereas externalizing children are known to be likely to be socially rejected, a sizeable portion of rejected children show other patterns of behavior (Coie et al., 1990; Hinshaw, 1994) including hyperactivity accompanied by social withdrawal and lack of aggression (Hinshaw & Melnick, 1995). Likewise, neglected children are a heterogeneous group, with few coherent patterns that characterize the entire group. Indeed, neglected status and internalizing behaviors (including social withdrawal) have not shown the predictive patterns to later psychopathology that were once thought likely. Instead, externalizing behavior, especially interpersonal aggression, has emerged as the primary childhood behavioral marker of later maladjustment (Hinshaw & Mel-

nick, 1995; Kupersmidt et al., 1990; Richters & Cicchetti, 1993; Coie, 1990; Parker & Asher, 1987).

A third source of information used to identify socially incompetent children has been direct observation by adults. Unfortunately, because aggressive behaviors occur relatively infrequently and because adult observation is experienced as intrusive by older children, most observational studies have been conducted with children 8 years old and younger (Coie et al., 1990). For the most part, these studies reveal that cooperative play and rule following is associated with popular peer status, whereas disruptive and aggressive interactions and rule violations are associated with peer rejection (Coie, Dodge, & Kupersmidt, 1990). An important finding in studies using contrived play group designs is that rejection develops very quickly among unacquainted peers, emerging by the end of the third play session (Coie & Kupersmidt, 1983; Dodge, 1983), or even sooner in the case of highly aggressive boys diagnosed also as having ADHD (Hinshaw & Melnick, 1995). Such rejection is associated primarily with aggression and rule violation and with the failure to use prosocial behaviors (Boivin, Dodge, & Coie, 1994).

A fourth method of identifying socially maladaptive children has been self-report. Asher and Wheeler (1985) have developed a measure of reported loneliness and have found that about 10% of elementary school children report themselves to be unusually lonely. This measure has correlated highly with self-referrals for counseling (Williams, 1986).

IDENTIFYING TARGETS FOR INTERVENTION

Few of the procedures for identifying socially maladaptive children are fully helpful in identifying the behavioral patterns related to social maladaptation as they occur in the natural environment, and none are adequate for understanding the development of the etiology of these problems. Even though a theory of social incompetence would seem to be prerequisite for the development of treatments for these children, many interventions have proceeded without a systematic understanding of the nature of these problems. Often the goals of intervention are determined intuitively by their face validity; for example, it is assumed that increased interaction (e.g., O'Connor, 1969) or improved role taking (e.g., Chandler, Greenspan, & Barenboim, 1974) might improve children's status with peers. The goals (and techniques) therefore have varied widely across studies, making comparisons and the systematic development of theory difficult.

Several investigators have begun taking a more systematic approach, however. Beginning with the work of Goldfried and D'Zurilla (1969), theorists have argued that the process of identifying a socially incompetent individual begins with the judgment made by one person about another. Usually the judge is an expert (such as a teacher or a clinician). The four sources listed above for identification of socially incompetent children (i.e., adults who know the children, peers, impartial adults engaging in direct observation, and the children themselves) are four kinds of judges. This judgment process is distinguished from the identification of behavioral qualities that have led others to make a judgment of incompetence. Behavioral performance qualities thus constitute a second aspect of the theory.

Many behaviorally oriented investigators have gone about evaluating behavioral performance by counting the frequencies of various behaviors displayed by competent and incompetent children (Kelly, 1982). Those behaviors that incompetent children fail to display at adequate rates are called "behavioral deficits," whereas those behaviors that are overrepresented are called "behavioral excesses." This is the rationale for targeting the rate of social interaction as a key behavior (e.g., Furman, Rahe, & Hartup, 1979). Of course, the validity of this procedure requires that the targeted behavior actually correlates with the judges' ratings of overall competence. Unfortunately, this empirical step is often bypassed. In fact, because rate of interaction does not correlate well with peers' sociometric evaluations, the empirical basis for targeting it as a focus of intervention is questionable (Asher & Hymel, 1981; see also Coie, 1990). High rates of aggression, on the other hand, are clearly related to teachers', parents', and peers' evaluations, and are thus appropriate candidates for targeting (Coie et al., 1990). Other behaviors have also shown positive associations with judgments of social competence and are thus appropriate foci for intervention: social initiations (Gottman, 1977); group entry bids (Putallaz & Wasserman, 1989); asking and answering questions (Gottman, Gonso, & Schuler, 1976); greet-

ing peers (LaGreca & Santogrossi, 1980); task participation and rule following (Coie et al., 1990; Hymel & Asher, 1977); cooperation and sharing (Coie et al., 1990; McFadyen-Ketchum, 1991); and praise to peers (LaGreca & Mesibov, 1979).

Because the behavioral correlates of competence judgments are likely to vary across age, sex, and subcultural groups, and depend on the behavioral norms of such groups (Boivin et al., 1995; Wright, Giammarino, & Parad, 1986), the approach of identifying specific behaviors that correlate with judgments of social competence is a tedious task. Another major problem has been the failure to take into account the ecological system and context in which these behaviors occur. For example, Dodge, Coie, and Brakke (1983) found that social initiations were positively correlated with positive peer status on the playground and negatively correlated with studies in the classroom work setting for elementary-school-age children. Obviously, the task demands of the playground and work settings differ, and success in each setting requires responsiveness to these task demands. Analyses of these tasks will determine what behavioral patterns (not only frequencies, but also styles and sequences) are associated with success at the task. These patterns can then be targeted for intervention.

This approach was taken in the creative work by Gottman (1983), who analyzed components of 5-year-old children's conversation during the critical task of friendship formation. He identified six behavioral patterns that empirically differentiated successful from unsuccessful outcomes (the outcomes being judgments by peers that a child was liked). These included the extent to which children (1) communicated clearly and in connected ways; (2) exchanged information; (3) established common play activities with their partners; (4) explored similarities and differences; (5) resolved conflicts; and (6) disclosed private information. Parker and Gottman (1985) recognized that a correlation between these patterns and successful outcomes would not necessarily indicate that these patterns were responsible for outcomes, so they ingeniously manipulated these six patterns experimentally (through a talking doll that played with children). They presented children with dolls that either displayed or did not display these patterns. Indeed, children liked the "socially competent" dolls much more than the "incompetent" dolls. These six behavioral patterns are thus em-

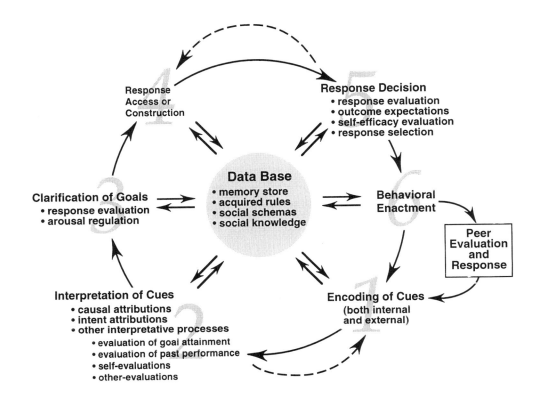

FIGURE 6.1. A reformulated social information-processing model of children's social adjustment. Adapted from the conceptualization by Crick and Dodge (1994). Copyright 1994 by the American Psychological Association. Adapted by permission.

pirically based candidates for targeting in intervention aimed at improving children's friendship-making success.

The task-analytic approach holds great promise for the field. However, there is danger in arbitrarily (nonempirically) identifying which tasks are "critical," in the same way that it has been argued that critical behaviors should not be identified arbitrarily. Goldfried and D'Zurilla (1969) and McFall (1982) have suggested procedures for systematically identifying the critical tasks for particular populations, so that social competence can be assessed within those task areas. The procedures include the following steps: (1) identifying the most relevant life tasks for a population by soliciting nominations from members of that population and "experts" who are knowledgeable about this population; (2) conducting a task analysis of successful and unsuccessful behaviors at each task; (3) obtaining

a representative sample of an individual's performance at the task; (4) establishing task-specific criteria for evaluating performance; (5) evaluating the actual performance; and (6) interpreting the evaluation results. Freedman, Rosenthal, Donahoe, Schlundt, and McFall (1978) have used these steps to identify critical situations for adolescent boys (e.g., confrontations with adult authorities, peer pressure, and academic failure situations), and they have found that juvenile delinquent boys performed less adequately in these situations than did socially competent boys. Dodge, McClaskey, and Feldman (1985) have used a similar procedure with elementary-school-age children, as has McFadyen-Ketchum (1991) with preschool-age children.

McFadyen-Ketchum (1991) found that potentially conflictual interactions involving the use of play objects (e.g., disagreements over who would have possession of a desirable toy) were particularly salient for young children, and that the highest levels of aggression and other disruptive behaviors occurred in such situations in day care and preschool settings (see also Shantz, 1987; Shantz & Hartup, 1992). According to teacher judges who had worked with target children for at least 3 months, physical and verbal aggression (e.g., grabbing, hitting, and yelling) and other forms of disruptive behavior (e.g., jumping in the area where others were playing) were unlikely to resolve conflicts, but cooperation (e.g., offering the other child an alternative toy), making use of teacher help, and assertion (e.g., asking the other child to wait for a short time before surrendering the desired toy) did serve to resolve disagreements and maintain ongoing play.

Once children are identified by judges as having problems in social relations, and once the particular deficient behavioral responses to specific tasks are identified, many clinicians are ready to attempt to train more competent behavioral responses. Reinforcement-oriented interventions are characterized by their focus at this level (Kelly, 1982). However, for complex patterns (e.g., exploring similarities and differences with a peer), simple reinforcement of a desired behavior may not be effective, because the necessary behavior is not yet in the child's repertoire. Several theorists (e.g., Dodge, 1986; Mize & Ladd, 1990; McFall, 1982) have recognized that these complex behaviors occur as a function of component cognitive processes, such as the child's ability to recognize another's thoughts and to anticipate the consequences of certain behaviors. These cognitive processes thus constitute yet another level at which intervention might be targeted. Dodge (1986, 1993a) has proposed a model of five social information-processing steps that are crucial for socially competent performance of most tasks (see also Rubin & Krasnor, 1986). These steps include (1) observation and encoding of ongoing peer behavior during interaction; (2) interpretation of the behavior (e.g., attributions about peer intentions); (3) memory search to access ways to respond; (4) response evaluation and choice of a preferable response; and (5) enactment of the chosen response. Crick and Dodge (1994) have since expanded this model by emphasizing the role of prior learning and ongoing representation as processes that inform a child's store of memories (or data bank) that is drawn on in an interactive way during ongoing interactions, and by

adding a sixth step (goal setting) preceding the memory search step. Crick and Dodge's expanded model is illustrated in Figure 6.1.

A large body of evidence has accumulated to indicate that these social-cognitive skills are indeed related to behavioral patterns and to positive judgments by others. For example, at the encoding step, socially incompetent children are less attentive to relevant social cues than are their more competent peers (Dodge, Pettit, McClaskey, & Brown, 1986; Dodge & Price, 1994; Dodge & Tomlin, 1987). At the interpretation step, socially rejected and aggressive children are inaccurate in detecting peer intention cues (Dodge, Murphy, & Buchsbaum, 1984; Waldman, 1996) and biased toward hostile interpretations of peer intentions (Dodge, 1980; McFadyen-Ketchum, 1993; Slaby & Guerra, 1988; Waldman, 1996). At the goal clarification step, children who are well adjusted tend to select relationship-enhancing goals (e.g., providing assistance to peers), whereas aggressive and/or rejected children tend to construct goals that are damaging to relationships (e.g., winning at all costs or getting even; Melnick & Hinshaw, 1996; Taylor & Asher, 1989). In addition, socially incompetent children compared to competent children access fewer competent responses in conflict situations with peers (Pettit, Dodge, & Brown, 1988; Quiggle, Garber, Panak, & Dodge, 1992), anticipate more positive outcomes for incompetent responses (e.g., aggression; Perry, Perry, & Rasmussen, 1986; Crick & Ladd, 1990; Dodge & Price, 1994), and enact competent responses with less skill (Dodge et al., 1985; Dodge & Price, 1994).

A general model of the assessment and treatment of social incompetence thus includes at least three levels of assessment: the evaluation of judgments about a child's competence (made by an "expert"); the identification of problematic social tasks and behaviors for the child; and the identification of social-cognitive skill deficits that may be related to the ineffective performance of those tasks. It also includes interventions that correspond to these three levels of assessment. Because the goal in most cases is to improve the judgments that others make, interventions have differing requirements to prove their efficacy. Interventions aimed at changing a child's behavioral patterns (including those that are entirely medicinal) must demonstrate that the patterns do change and that the judgments of others change in a corresponding fashion. Interventions aimed at training social-cognitive skills must demonstrate that these skills do indeed improve, that skill enhancement leads to changes in behavioral patterns, and that behavioral changes lead to improvement in judgments by others.

In addition, even when these stringent requirements are met, it is not enough to assume that procedures that work for a particular population will work for all populations. For example, the bulk of research on the behavioral correlates of peer rejection has been conducted with elementary-school-age and preadolescent boys (Dodge & Feldman, 1990). These findings inform much (though not all) of the research reviewed in this chapter. At this writing, though investigators like Crick and her colleagues have begun expanding our understanding of the role of relational aggression (e.g., spreading rumors) in the social development of girls (Crick, 1995; Crick & Grotpeter, 1995), not a great deal is known about the determinants of psychopathological development for girls (see, e.g., McFadyen-Ketchum, Bates, Dodge, & Pettit, 1996; Zahn-Waxler, 1993) or about treatments that would maximize positive outcomes for girls (see Arnold, 1995; Maccoby, 1990; Webster-Stratton, 1996; Zoccolillo, 1993; Zahn-Waxler, 1993). Age-related differences are also of concern. Findings with young children, including those reviewed here, tend to support the finding for older children that overt physical and verbal aggression ought to be a primary focus of intervention (Hinshaw & Melnick, 1995; Reid, 1993). However, the forms that aggressive behavior takes vary widely across development, starting with temper tantrums and noncompliance with parental requests in preschool (both boys and girls), progressing through fighting and property destruction (mostly boys) and starting rumors (mostly girls) in elementary school, and appearing as assault and serious vandalism (mostly boys) and shoplifting (mostly girls) in adolescence (see Hinshaw, Lahey, & Hart, 1993; Reid, 1993; Zoccolillo, 1993; Zahn-Waxler, 1993). Finally, the social context in which social relationships develop also plays a role. Boivin et al. (1995), for example, found that the normative level of aggression within peer groups plays a role in how readily members of those groups become rejected (see also Dodge, 1997). The issues, then, of age, sex, and contextual factors in social development clearly require careful empirical inquiry, much of which has not yet been carried out. Finally, research has been conducted on a number of other issues that are beyond the scope of the present chapter. Principal among these are emotion regulation and temperament (see, e.g., Garber & Dodge, 1991; Dodge, 1997; Eisenberg et al., 1993; Hinshaw & Melnick, 1995). The focus, then, in the present chapter is on the work that has been done. It should nevertheless be borne in mind that the present treatment is to some extent incomplete.

BEHAVIORAL INTERVENTIONS

Most child-oriented interventions have been focused on either training social-cognitive skills or altering specific behavioral patterns. The techniques that have been used in the latter case are the ones familiar to any behavioral clinician (see also the section on stimulant medications and ADHD, later in this chapter): positive reinforcement, punishment, modeling, shaping, instruction, rehearsal, feedback, and so on (Ladd & Mize, 1983). Given the focus on behavioral change, interventions using these techniques have not generally been concerned with changing global aspects of children's peer status, but rather have targeted specific behaviors for enhancement or extinction, for example—increasing the rate of positive social contact and cooperation, and decreasing the rate of aggression and disruption.

Enhancing Specific Prosocial Behaviors

Walker, Hops, Greenwood, and Todd (1979), for example, used adult praise and tokens to enhance three types of social behavior in withdrawn children. The targeted behaviors were initiating interactions, responding to peers, and extending the chain of interaction. Similar contingencies of reinforcement have been used to increase the frequency of cooperative interactions in aggressive children (Brown & Elliot, 1965; Hart, Reynolds, Baer, Brawley, & Harris, 1968). Behavioral interventions have proven to be effective with children diagnosed with ADHD as well (Barkley, 1989 and Chapter 2, this volume; Carlson, Pelham, Milich & Dixon, 1992; Pelham, et al., 1993).

However, there are problems with these studies and with the use of contingent reinforcement in general. Though positive effects are achieved during intervention, behavioral changes do not reach normative levels, do not persist once treatment is terminated, and do not readily generalize to new settings (Ladd & Mize, 1983; Weiss & Hechtman, 1993). Even when specific techniques to achieve generalization are used, such as fading (Timm, Strain, & Eller, 1979), booster training sessions (Paine et al., 1982), the use of peers as change agents (Strain, Shores, & Timm, 1977), and the use of group contingencies (Weinrott, Corson, & Wilchesky, 1979), evidence for generalization has been lacking (Greenwood & Hops, 1981). In addition, the administration of specific reinforcements by an adult has proved to be intrusive. Reinforcement by a teacher following an initial positive social behavior by a child may disrupt the ongoing social interchange among children and may actually be harmful to the peer interaction (Walker et al., 1979).

Inhibition of Aggressive Behaviors

Various punishment techniques have been employed to inhibit aggressive and disruptive behaviors, which contribute to some children's poor peer relations (Coie, 1990; Newcomb et al., 1993; Reid, 1993). Overt punishments, such as reprimands and physical strikes, have not proven very effective (see Kazdin, 1985). When used in combination with verbal instruction and positive reinforcement of prosocial behaviors, however, reprimands have proven effective in decreasing aggression (Bierman, Miller, & Stabb, 1987). Time out from reinforcement opportunities has also been used effectively to reduce aggressive behavior (Drabman & Spitalnik, 1973). However, as with positive reinforcement of prosocial behavior, lack of cross-setting generalization and poor maintenance of effects over time have been noted with these procedures (Bierman et al., 1987; Kazdin, 1985). In addition, there is little evidence that inhibiting aggressive behaviors will enhance positive peer relationships (Kazdin, 1985).

Conclusions

The success that clinical researchers have obtained in altering specific behaviors in children for at least a short period of time in a particular setting is remarkable. Though not theoretically complex, positive reinforcement and punishment techniques are noteworthy in their power to alter behaviors. However, the problems of cross-setting generalization and maintenance over time, and the fact that behavioral procedures

have failed to produce actual improvement in a child's peer relationships, force us to agree with Kazdin (1995; see also Barkley, 1989 and Chapter 2, this volume; Ladd & Mize, 1983; Weiss & Hechtman, 1993) that operant procedures used alone have been generally ineffective in changing either the social behavior of socially rejected children or peer judgments about them.

Several specific factors are likely to account for these failures. First, the selection of interactive tasks and of behaviors for modification has often been made without empirical justification. Second, even when behaviors have been targeted on an empirical basis, the application of empirical findings regarding a *group* of children will apply only loosely to individuals within that group. For example, rejected children have been found as a group to display disruptive and ineffective strategies when initiating play with peers, but not all rejected children display this pattern (Dodge, Schlundt, Schocken, & Delugach, 1983; Hinshaw & Melnick, 1995). Aggressive behavior is a good case in point. Though it is true that a great many studies have identified aggression as a correlate of peer rejection, in some groups of children aggression is a normative behavior that is not associated with rejection (Boivin et al., 1995). Therefore, targeting initiation behavior or aggression in an intervention for rejected children is appropriate for only a portion of such children. Very few researchers have matched the treatment to specific characteristics of the children with whom they are intervening.

Third, the behavioral approaches have failed to focus on component skills that may be responsible for specific behavior patterns. The general information-processing model of social competence described above (Crick & Dodge, 1994) suggests that social-cognitive skills are requisites of competent social behavior. Because behavioral interventions are environmental manipulations, their impact on variables that are internal to a child is probably minimal. Social-cognitive skills, on the other hand, are taught in such a way that a child's way of thinking about himself or herself and about ways of responding to others is changed. Skills acquired by the child in this way can be remembered and carried into new situations. Thus, long-term effects and cross-situational generalization can be achieved. This premise, in combination with the operant conditioning techniques already described, has been the basis of a group of interventions called "social-cognitive skills training."

SOCIAL-COGNITIVE SKILLS TRAINING INTERVENTIONS

Social-cognitive skills training procedures have origins in the work conducted over 50 years ago by Chittendon (1942). She taught children to display specific social behaviors (taking turns, sharing, and playing together) through skits enacted with dolls; more importantly, she taught them how to recognize specific social goals and situations prior to teaching them the actual behaviors to display in these situations. Goal recognition is a social cognitive skill. Her results were impressive, in that children exhibited less "dominative behavior" (as aggression and disruption were called at the time) and more cooperative behavior in their classrooms, with changes in dominative behavior lasting at the 1-month follow-up.

All social-cognitive skills training interventions are oriented toward enhancing one or more cognitive skills that are theoretically and/or empirically related to effective social behavior. The model of social information processing described earlier in this chapter (Crick & Dodge, 1994) suggests that the following skills are candidates for intervention: (1) selective attention to relevant social cues and ability to resist distraction by irrelevant cues; (2) the accurate interpretation of social situations and others' intentions; (3) appropriate goal selection and orientation; (4) the generation of appropriate behavioral responses to specific situations; (5) the anticipation of outcomes of one's behavior; (6) the skillful enactment of behavioral strategies; and, finally, the monitoring and adjustment of one's own behavior according to environmental demands. The monitoring skill includes a child's ability to notice peer responses to his or her just-enacted behavior and represents a feedback loop to Step 1 (observation and encoding of ongoing peer behavior) in Crick and Dodge's (1994) six-step scheme. Thus, each step contributes uniquely to behavioral competence in interacting with peers (Dodge & Price, 1994), and a child skilled in all six steps plus the monitoring skill is able to adjust to multiple peers, across situations and time.

Ladd and Mize (1983) identified three kinds of skills closely allied to Crick and Dodge's (1994) scheme that are most often the focus of intervention: (1) knowledge of specific behavioral strategies and the contexts in which those strategies should be used; (2) the ability to convert knowledge of social strategies into skillful social behaviors in interactions with peers; and (3) the ability to evaluate one's own performance and adjust it according to environmental demands. These three skills are similar to the last three information-processing steps, and the feedback loop to Step 1, identified by the Crick and Dodge (1994) model. Ladd and Mize (1983) noted that, in general, those programs that emphasize all three skill areas have been the most successful in leading to improvements in peer relations. Three different traditions epitomize work in this area: social problem-solving training, anger coping training, and coaching.

Social Problem-Solving Training

Spivack and Shure (1974) have developed the most widely used program for teaching young children social problem-solving skills. Their program for preschool children consists of 46 daily lessons that are oriented toward teaching children to generate novel and competent solutions to interpersonal dilemmas. In recent years this technique has been developed further and applied to the behavioral problems of older, conduct-disordered children. Whereas Spivack and Shure (see Shure, 1980) emphasized a dialoguing process that allowed children to develop their own behavioral solutions, whether competent or not, with the understanding that children would gradually select those that were the most successful in achieving positive interactions with peers, current applications emphasize the shaping of competent responses through corrective feedback and operant conditioning (see Kazdin, Bass, Siegel, & Thomas, 1989, and Kazdin, Siegel, & Bass, 1992 for examples).

Kazdin (1995) has recently reviewed intervention research based on social problem-solving procedures carried out with impulsive, aggressive, and conduct-disordered children (for detailed reviews, see Baer & Nietzel, 1991, and Durlak, Fuhrman, & Lampman, 1991). Though few have included all six of the steps posited by Crick and Dodge (1994) or the three skills identified by Ladd and Mize (1983), these interventions have led to reductions in aggressive and disruptive behaviors at home, at school, and in the community, with gains lasting up to 1 year. These interventions include work with community samples as well as with clinically referred children. Though these findings are encouraging, questions remain. The principal difficulty is that the magnitude of child behavior change is relatively small, with many treated children remaining outside the range of normative functioning. Moreover, though both cognitive processes and social behaviors have been shown to change, these changes are not always correlated with each other; thus, the basis for the demonstrated gains remains unclear (Kazdin, 1995). Finally, interventions with children who are themselves high-risk (e.g., both peer-rejected and aggressive) or who live in high-risk families (e.g., presence of parental psychopathology) have resulted in fewer gains than have interventions with other children (Bierman et al., 1987; Kazdin et al., 1992).

Anger Coping Training

In the social problem-solving interventions discussed above, the contribution of emotion, particularly anger and its association with aggression (Dodge, 1991), is conspicuously unaddressed factor (Gottman, 1986). However, Lochman and his colleagues have developed and evaluated components of an anger coping program for aggressive boys (Lochman, 1985; Lochman, Burch, Curry, & Lampron, 1984; Lochman, Lampron, Burch, & Curry, 1985). This program integrates training in the interpretation of problems and in the inhibition of impulsive and angry responding with the traditional social problem-solving training programs and behavioral interventions already discussed. The basis of the anger coping component is the work of Novaco (1978) on anger control. In its most recent form (Lochman, Coie, Underwood, & Terry, 1993), a combination of individual interventions (26 lasting 30 minutes each) and small-group intervention (8 sessions) was conducted at school with 52 fourth-grade children. Separate sessions are devoted to social problem solving, positive play training, group entry skill training (see also Putallaz, 1989, for a discussion of successful and unsuccessful group entry behaviors), and dealing effectively with negative feelings. The sessions focused on seven goals: (1) establishing behavior management within groups through rules and contingent reinforcements; (2) teaching children to use self-talk to inhibit impulsive behavior; (3) teaching children to identify problems and interpret social cues accurately; (4) encouraging children to generate alternative solutions and to consider the consequences of the solutions to interpersonal problems; (5) helping children learn to control physiological arousal when angry through imitation of effective control displayed on videotapes; (6) helping children plan and make their own videotape of effective anger control and problem solving; and (7) dialoguing, discussion, role playing, and goal setting in order to encourage generalization of learned skills to classroom settings. Postintervention and 1-year follow-up data indicate that children who were identified in a fourth-grade intervention as both aggressive and rejected showed the greatest gains. Specifically, these students achieved significant reductions in aggression and social rejection, compared to a randomly assigned control group. This finding is of particular importance, given the failure of social problem-solving interventions without the anger control component to gain lasting effects with these same children (Bierman et al., 1987); thus, the Lochman et al. program represents an important advance.

Coaching

According to Ladd and Mize (1983), few interventions have emphasized all three of the training components that they see as essential aspects of a successful program (i.e., skill knowledge, skill performance, and maintenance generalization of performance). Those interventions that do emphasize all of these components are called "coaching programs." The term has been selected carefully, for it implies that the coach nurtures, tutors, and mentors the child's skill development. It also emphasizes the skill-enhancing aspect of the intervention.

The fundamental aspects of coaching have been outlined by McFall (1976) and systematized by Oden and Asher (1977), who evaluated it in a five-session controlled study with unpopular third- and fourth-graders. In their program, they focused on four behavioral areas that have been found to be critical to social acceptance (participation, cooperation, communication, and validation/support). During each of the first two sessions, children were instructed in each of these four areas (to teach skill knowledge); they practiced performance of these skills in an interaction with a classmate; they reviewed their performance with their coach; and they were encouraged to try out these skills in their classrooms (to foster generalization). Even though these four steps characterize many social problem-solving and behavioral interventions, the coaching procedure is unique in several respects. Most importantly, the coach emphasizes social skills concepts, rather than discrete behaviors. The coach follows a five-step procedure during the instruction of each concept that demonstrates this emphasis. These five steps are as follows: (1) The child is asked to define the concept (e.g., participation); (2) the child is asked to give examples of the concept; (3) the child is asked to give examples of the antithesis of the concept; (4) the child is asked for more examples and is asked to elaborate these ideas; and (5) the coach then provides additional exemplars (a "conversation" occurs; see McFadyen-Ketchum, 1993, for a discussion). The child is thus undergoing concept learning, rather than the acquisition of discrete behavior in the absence of a context. A second feature of this procedure is the nature of the relationship between the coach and the child. The coach is a knowledgeable helper who has a script to follow, but who also attends to the child's particular assets and deficits. Another feature is that different classmate peers serve as partners during the practice, so that the child will be exposed to a variety of classmates, but also so that the classmates will get to see the child behave in a prosocially oriented way. In the last three sessions, coaches focus the child's learning in those areas where the child requires special help, thus accommodating individual differences in skill deficits.

In the Oden and Asher (1977) intervention, coached children's gains in positive peer ratings from pre- to posttreatment were greater than those of control children. These gains were maintained over a 1-year follow-up period but were not associated with detectable changes in peer-interactive behavior. In a second study following essentially the same procedure but methodologically restructured to focus on specific behavioral deficiencies in the intervention group, Ladd (1981) was able to detect gains both in peer ratings and in two of the three targeted behaviors (asking questions, leading, and offering support to peers). This latter finding adds support to the hypothesis that behavior change brought about through the treatment process leads to changes in peer ratings.

Since then, Mize and Ladd (1990) have replicated the coaching intervention with preschool children. Using essentially the same approach described above, and focusing on four key social behaviors relevant to preschool children (i.e., leading, asking questions, commenting on ongoing play, and supporting peers), coaching was conducted with children who were either rejected or neglected by peers and who also showed behavioral deficits (high levels of aggression or low levels of the four targeted behaviors). Sociodramatic play (guided by coaches using hand puppets) was adopted as an intervention device that would evoke cognitive and be-

havioral rehearsal of these behaviors, and an elaborate fading procedure was used to enhance transfer from the training room to the classroom. Subsequent classroom observation revealed that intervention children more than doubled their use of the targeted behavioral skills in interactions with peers, whereas control children showed a slight decrease. In addition, these behavioral changes were reflected in corresponding changes in the strategies intervention children recommended during social knowledge interviews for use in hypothetical dilemmas. The correlation between composite measures of changes in social cognition and behavior was .34, supporting the hypothesis that the behavior changes were brought about by cognitive changes induced by intervention. Importantly, behavior changes were also associated with improvements in sociometric ratings ($r = .28$), which were maintained at a 1-month follow-up.

Conclusions

By focusing on the underlying cognitive processes that are hypothesized to be responsible for competent behavior, social-cognitive skills training procedures have attempted to enhance both temporal and situational generalization of the effects found in behavioral interventions. Descriptive and experimental studies have shown that numerous social information-processing skills are in fact related to positive peer status, so the skills training procedures have focused on teaching children these skills. These efforts have been successful. A large number of studies has shown positive effects at posttesting, and the potential for lasting effects that generalize to novel situations is obviously much greater for social-cognitive skills training approaches than for the behavioral approaches. This is to be expected. Because many socially rejected children are raised in environments in which deviant behaviors are modeled and reinforced (Pettit et al., 1988), short-term behavioral interventions conducted in entirely different environments are not likely to yield lasting and generalized effects. In contrast, the skills training approaches are directed at the acquisition of social cognitions that presumably guide behavioral performance across all situations, rendering maintenance of effects and generalization more likely.

This is intriguing theory, and the findings are encouraging. However, the limits of these approaches are obvious. Treatment effects, though statistically significant, are clinically small. Kazdin's (1995) review, for example, points out that even though behavioral and cognitive change occurs, most treated children remain outside the range of normal functioning for same-age and same-sex peers. This may be because there is often no change in peer acceptance, even though positive changes in behavioral performance are achieved (Bierman et al., 1987). Thus, the role of the peer group in these interventions has not been resolved. Second, even though the theoretical model guiding this work posits a link between a child's skills deficits and his or her peer acceptance, few attempts have been made to match interventions to specific assessments of individual children's needs. Third, little evidence has been reported that supports the theoretical model of social-cognitive skills as a mechanism of competent behavior and as a mediator of peer acceptance. That is, with the exception of the work of Mize and Ladd (1990) reported above, few attempts have been made to link changes in skills directly to changes in behavior and peer acceptance. Clearly, more work is needed in this area. Finally, the durability of effects for these treatments has so far extended no further than 1 year. It will be necessary to show much longer periods of positive follow-up data before these interventions can be thought of as fully successful.

STIMULANT MEDICATION AND ATTENTION-DEFICIT/ HYPERACTIVITY DISORDER

In addition to behavioral and social-cognitive interventions, stimulant medications for children diagnosed with ADHD represent a third approach to the treatment of social relationship problems. Indeed, ADHD-diagnosed children (especially boys showing high levels of comorbid aggression) frequently show the very cognitive and behavioral deficits that are most often associated with peer rejection and the long-term problematic outcomes mentioned earlier in this chapter (Hinshaw & Melnick, 1995; Pelham et al., 1991; see also Hinshaw, 1994, for a discussion of behavioral heterogeneity in ADHD).

Findings

Referring again to the Crick & Dodge (1994) model of social interaction presented earlier, we find from ADHD research that diagnosed children show deficits in encoding social cues (e.g., overattending to peer negative behavior and failure to notice nonnegative behavior; Milich &

Dodge, 1984; Whalen, Henker, & Granger, 1990), in interpreting social cues (e.g., inferring hostile intentions in peers; Milich & Dodge, 1984), in goal clarification (e.g., favoring troublemaking and rule-breaking goals; Melnick & Hinshaw, 1996), in response access and decision (e.g., viewing aggression as an effective response to provocation; Milich & Dodge, 1984), and in behavioral enactment (e.g., showing high levels of controlling behavior, aggression, and anger as well as stealing and cheating; Cunningham, Siegel, & Offord, 1985; Hinshaw, Heller, & McHale, 1992; Hinshaw & Melnick, 1995; Madan-Swain & Zental, 1990; Pelham et al., 1991). In addition, ADHD diagnosed children fail to take responsibility for the negative impact of these deficits (Hoza, Pelham, Milich, Pillow, & McBride, 1993). In return, peers perceive children with ADHD as aggressive and intrusive (Hinshaw & Melnick, 1995; Whalen, Henker, Castro, & Granger, 1987) and respond by moving away (Cunningham et al., 1985), by increasing the frequency of negative behaviors (e.g., grabbing, hitting, and derogatory statements), by decreasing the frequency of problem-solving behaviors (Madan-Swain & Zental, 1990), and by rapidly forming judgments of rejection (among unfamiliar children, this can occur within just a few hours; Bickett & Milich, 1990; Erhardt & Hinshaw, 1994; Hinshaw & Melnick, 1995; Pelham & Bender, 1982).

Stimulant intervention (primarily methylphenidate) has in some respects reversed these negative effects and in others has failed to produce hoped-for positive effects, especially in the long term (Hinshaw, 1994; Weiss & Hechtman, 1993). Stimulants have shown a very high success rate (about 90%; Hinshaw, 1994) in the short-term increase of attending behaviors (Murphy, Pelham, & Lang, 1992) and decrease of disruptive behaviors, including physical and verbal aggression and stealing, without significant decreases in prosocial behaviors (see Hinshaw, 1994, for a review; see also Cunningham et al., 1985; Gadow et al., 1990; Gadow, Paolicelli, Nolan, & Schwartz, 1992; Gittelman & Kanner, 1986; Granger, Whalen, & Henker, 1993; Hinshaw, Henker, Whalen, Erhardt, & Dunnington, 1989; Hinshaw et al., 1992; Hinshaw & Melnick, 1995; Pelham & Bender, 1982; Whalen, Henker, Castro, & Granger, 1987). It is particularly important to note that in ADHD-diagnosed children, stimulant medication intervention reliably lowers the frequency of these problematic behaviors to levels similar to those of normally developing peers (Hinshaw et al.,

1989; Hinshaw, 1991). Peers have responded by remaining in contact and by using lower levels of controlling and negative behavior (Cunningham, Siegel, & Offord, 1991; Gadow et al., 1992). However, stimulants have been less successful in the social cognitive domain, and have had little impact on peer judgments. Consistent with the finding of Milich & Dodge (1984) that ADHD-diagnosed children tend to view peers in a hostile light, stimulant treatment does not decrease their attention to the negative behavior of peers (Whalen et al., 1990), nor does it decrease the tendency to deny responsibility for social difficulties (Pelham et al., 1993). Finally, even when medicated, hyperactive children continue to be rejected by peers at higher levels than their more normative peers are (Pelham & Bender, 1982; Whalen et al., 1989; see also Hinshaw & Melnick, 1995). In addition, the evidence to date is that stimulant medication treatment, though showing the short-term gains for ADHD children listed above, fails to bring about long-term gains in social adjustment (Hinshaw, 1994; Weiss & Hechtman, 1993).

Conclusions

It is clear that impressive gains in behavioral normalization for ADHD-diagnosed children have been achieved through the use of stimulant medications. However, as with the behavioral and social-cognitive interventions discussed earlier, serious limitations remain. Principal among these is the failure of medications to achieve positive changes in the way ADHD-diagnosed children view peers and in the concomitant failure to evoke normative levels of acceptance from peers. Given the evidence that hostile attributions are associated with peer rejection (Crick & Dodge, 1994) and that rejection is linked with long-term negative outcomes (Kupersmidt et al., 1990; Parker & Asher, 1987), it is not surprising that short-term behavioral gains have not translated into long-term gains. However, there may be another reason for this failure. As mentioned above, peer rejection occurs very quickly—usually within the first day of interaction among unacquainted peers, and sometimes much faster (Hinshaw & Melnick, 1995). A review of the present corpus of ADHD literature reveals no study that has applied medication intervention before peer judgments have had a chance to form. In all the unacquainted-peer studies known to us, children were allowed to interact for several days before stimulant medication trials were begun. Therefore, it remains possible that short-term gains

both in ADHD-diagnosed children's cognitions about peers and in peer's acceptance of ADHD-diagnosed children (and subsequent longer-term gains in positive adjustment) could be achieved if medications were begun before the children met each other. This is, of course, only a hypothesis that remains to be tested. However, its importance lies in drawing empirical attention to the potentially powerful causal role of peer rejection (for a detailed discussion, see Dodge, 1993b). If it is early and quick-forming rejection that drives the system of child cognitions and behaviors discussed thus far in this chapter, then it becomes easy to understand why behavioral, social-cognitive, and stimulant medication interventions have largely failed to prevent the development of negative later-life outcomes. All three of these interventions focus entirely on troubled children and not on peers (or, for that matter, on other important social partners such as parents and teachers). Therefore, it may be that peers, parents, and teachers as well as troubled children ought to be the foci of intervention (see Conduct Problems Prevention Research Group [CPPRG], 1992). No intervention program known to us following the three intervention traditions discussed thus far has made this effort. However, family- and school-based interventions have. These are discussed next.

THE RATIONALE FOR FOCUSING ON PROBLEMATIC SOCIAL RELATIONSHIPS IN THE FAMILY AND THE SCHOOL

We have reviewed the three major types of interventions that have been traditionally aimed at improving children's social relationships: behavioral interventions, social-cognitive skills training, and the use of stimulant medications. All have focused interventive efforts directly on troubled children. However, investigators within these traditions have repeatedly noted the difficulties of intervening with children whose families are in severe disarray (for reviews; see Barkley, 1990; Kazdin, 1995; and Patterson et al., 1992). Thus, in recent years intervention efforts have also been aimed at the families of children—particularly at the types of parent–child interactions that could cause children to have difficulties in the social domain. Some of these interventions have added schools so that teachers and peers can be included as well.

This emphasis makes sense if a causal role is assumed for parent–child interactions (supplemented by teacher and peer interactions) in the development of deviant child behavior, social cognitions, and subsequent peer rejection and long-term problematic outcomes. For example, it may be that intrusive and coercive parent–child interactions at home produce or exacerbate child aggression, hyperactivity, and other dysfunctional behaviors (Barkley, 1990; Jacobvitz & Sroufe, 1987; Patterson et al., 1992), which in turn produce rejection by peers in settings outside the home (Bierman & Wargo, 1995; Coie, 1990). Indeed, experiments aimed at replacing coercive parenting with affection and nonrestrictive control have achieved reductions in child aggression and hyperactivity that persist for up to 8 years (Johnson, Kahn, & Devila, 1976; Johnson & Walker, 1987; Yoshikawa, 1994), and longitudinal studies of unacquainted peers clearly show that peer rejection occurs very quickly for children who use high levels of these problematic behaviors during play (Boivin et al., 1995; Coie & Kupersmidt, 1983; Dodge, 1983; Erhardt & Hinshaw, 1994; Putallaz, 1983). It is also possible, of course, that parental behavior and child deviance play incremental roles in the production of children's social dysfunction (Bell & Chapman, 1986; Lytton, 1990). A recent review conducted by Yoshikawa (1994) of intervention studies with long-term outcome data showed that interventions focusing both on parent–child interactions at home and on teacher–child and peer–child interactions at preschool produced the greatest long-term gains, including gains in behavioral domains relevant to peer acceptance and rejection (e.g., decreased fighting, hyperactivity, lying, and cheating). In either case, parent–child interactions appear to play a role in the development of problematic child behavior and subsequent peer rejection. Thus, we now turn to studies of parent–child and parent–child–school interventions for for children's social problems.

FAMILY AND SCHOOL-BASED INTERVENTIONS

Parent Management Training

The work of Patterson and his colleagues at the Oregon Social Learning Center (OSLC) has been seminal in charting the role of parenting in child behavioral outcomes (Patterson, 1982; Patterson et al., 1992). Essentially, Patterson posits an unintentional behavioral conditioning paradigm involving children and their primary caregivers (usually mothers), which begins to operate early in a child's social development. According to Patterson (1982; Patterson et al., 1992), when mothers initially respond to the oppositional behaviors produced by most children at about the age of 2 years with negative prohibitions (harsh verbalizations and/or harsh physical control), but then back down when children offer resistance (as many toddlers do), they negatively reinforce child oppositional behavior. That is, the children (and the mothers) escape from the negative interchanges when the mothers back down, thus making it more likely that the children will resist (and the mother will back down) on subsequent occasions. Over time, children graduate from relatively innocuous oppositional behaviors to the use of aggressive and other disruptive behaviors, thus learning that the best way to deal with interpersonal conflict is through the use of such behaviors. Detailed observations of mother–child interactions conducted by Snyder and his colleagues (Snyder & Patterson, 1986, 1995; Snyder, Edwards, McGraw, Kilgore, & Holton, 1994) have supported this hypothesis. Patterson (1982; Patterson et al., 1992) has further hypothesized that the use of aggression and other socially dysfunctional behaviors eventually generalizes to peers.

Parent management training, then, has been aimed at replacing these negative parent–child interchanges with more positive interactions, so that children will learn to use positive ways to deal with others (for reviews see Dumas, 1989; McMahon & Wells, 1989 and Chapter 3, this volume; and Kazdin, 1987). As mentioned above, when combined with behavioral and skills acquisition interventions with children conducted in preschool settings, the results have been impressive. Yoshikawa's (1994) review included a large number of early intervention studies with young children (from birth to 5 years of age) of low socioeconomic status (SES). Both mothers and children (along with teachers and peers; see especially Johnson et al., 1976) were taught positive ways of interacting in frequent, programmatic interventions extending over a period of at least 2 years. Mothers and fathers were also taught adult-level positive problem-solving skills. Long-term results (more than 2 years) showed decreases for treatment children compared to control peers in subsequent child delinquency, fighting, hyperactivity, lying, and cheating, as well as increases in teacher ratings of social-emotional development. As young adults, these children showed higher levels of employment and lower levels of dependence on welfare. One particularly successful program (Weikart &

Schweinhart, 1992) also showed decreases in school dropout for both males and females, and fewer pregnancies and births in female participants. The decreases in problematic social behavior, school dropout, and pregnancy, and the increases in social-emotional standing, indicate that children's acceptance by peers probably improved as well (though peer acceptance was not directly assessed). These findings are particularly impressive in that the follow-ups were conducted over the course of 5 to 14 years.

Yoshikawa's (1994) review also reveals that similar interventions conducted only with mothers (or, alternatively, only with children, failed to produce comparable results). This is strong evidence that intervention, at least in the case of preschool-age children, should be carried out with both parents and children, and probably with peers and teachers as well. However, except for brief descriptions of efforts to replace coercive parental control measures with affection and nonrestrictive control, none of the successful parent–child studies described in detail exactly what was done with children or with parents, so it remains unclear why intervention children performed better than their peers.

Tremblay et al. (1992) have recently completed a successful intervention with low-SES children based on the OSLC model for parent intervention (Patterson et al., 1992) and a social skills training/coaching model for child intervention. This study provided a relatively complete description of interventions and their effects on child social behavior, as well as the sorts of parental behaviors with children and child behaviors with peers that bring about these positive changes. Parents were taught a series of five key skills: (1) monitoring their children's behavior so that they would know precisely where to aim their interventive efforts; (2) using positive reinforcement for prosocial behavior; (3) using effective, nonabusive punishments for aggressive and disruptive behavior; (4) managing family crises; and (5) learning how to use what they had learned in settings outside the home (generalization). Via coaching, peer modeling, self-instructions, behavioral rehearsal, and reinforcement contingencies, all in the company of actual peers, children were taught social-cognitive skills. These skills included paying attention to ongoing peer behavior, following rules, dealing effectively with anger, and dealing with peer rejection and teasing. Treatment in the Tremblay et al. (1992) study lasted 2 years (from age 7 to age 9). Subsequently, teacher, peer, mother, and subject ratings were collected yearly

for 3 years. Compared to control peers, treatment children showed lower levels of teacher-rated fighting (by age 12), higher levels of school achievement, and higher levels of overall teacher- and peer-rated adjustment. There was also less self-reported delinquent behavior in the treatment group.

Another successful intervention with preschool and young school-age children, conducted with middle-class families to increase child compliance with adult requests, was completed by Forehand and McMahon (1981; see also an application of these procedures to children of preschool age who were diagnosed with ADHD—Pisterman et al., 1989). Their work, like that of the studies reviewed by Yoshikawa (1994), has the strength of showing long-term positive outcomes lasting up to 14 years (Forehand & Long, 1988; Long, Forehand, Wierson, & Morgan, in press), and has the added advantage of providing particularly thorough descriptions of interventions. These descriptions are too detailed to present here and are described only in truncated form. Essentially, investigators used the behavioral and social-cognitive interventions described earlier to intervene directly with the children. At the same time, investigators taught parents to be precise observers of children's behavior, and coached parents in the skills of behavioral and cognitive intervention. Directed readings and homework assignments regarding behavior management principles, childproofing the home, and developing realistic expectations of children were presented. Then parenting skills were taught via modeling, role playing, and *in vivo* rehearsal: how to attend to appropriate behavior while ignoring inappropriate behavior, how to present clearly worded and appropriate commands, and how to use time out when children failed to comply. Thus, intervention was carried out in a very programmatic fashion, as in the Tremblay et al. (1992) study and the studies reviewed by Yoshikawa (1994), it was also applied over extended periods of time, thereby providing both children and parents with plenty of practice. As a result, treatment parents compared to control parents showed a marked increase in clearly worded commands, a decrease in vague and inappropriate commands, and increases in consistent reinforcement of children's compliant behavior and positive interactions. These gains produced companion gains in children's behavior. Treatment children compared to controls showed increases in compliance to appropriate parental commands. In addition, long-term follow-up demonstrated no differences between treatment children's use of interpersonal aggression and that of a normally developing comparison group (Forehand & Long, 1988).

Webster-Stratton (1993, 1996, 1997) has also carried out interventions with parents and their young children (preschool and early school age), with the added advantage that teacher-provided measures of school social behavior were collected. Like Tremblay et al. (1992), Webster-Stratton has used parent management training based on the OSLC model, and has also used the behaviorally specific interventions developed by Forehand and McMahon (1981). Moreover, as in the successful studies reviewed by Yoshikawa (1994), she has added skill training regarding adult-level personal issues of importance to parents, as well as interventions intended to improve relations between parents and teachers. This last component includes anger management, coping with depression, ways to get and give support, and problem-solving strategies between adults. A unique feature of this program is the use of videotapes and group instruction to present information about effective parent–child interactions based on Bandura's modeling theory (Bandura, 1986).

Results are promising. Parents have been successful in reducing children's level of aggression at home by 20% to 60% (Webster-Stratton, 1993, 1997), and situational generalization (from clinic to home) and temporal generalization (1 to 4 years) have been achieved (Webster-Stratton, 1993). What is particularly important about this research is that evidence of positive changes in children's social cognitions and behavior toward peers has been found, though these gains are largely confined to home settings (Webster-Stratton, 1997). However, Webster-Stratton (1996) has recently completed a study using independent teacher reports that also shows generalization of positive behavioral changes to school settings, persisting for a period of up to 2 years. These changes (for both boys and girls) include decreases in hyperactivity, aggression, and internalizing behavior. Pfiffner and McBurnett (in press) have also recently completed work of a similar type, showing treatment-setting-to-school generalization for children diagnosed with ADHD. Evidence of generalization was strongest for the combined parent and child intervention.

Kazdin et al. (1992) have carried out interventions similar to those described above with parents and slightly older children (aged 7 to 13 years) and with much the same results, though follow-up has been extended at last report to

only 1 year. Children who received social skills training (including practice with real-life peers) and whose parents also received parent management training showed the greatest gains, including decreases in the types of problem behaviors at both home and school that have been shown by play group research (Coie & Kupersmidt, 1983; Dodge, 1983; Hinshaw & Melnick, 1995; Putallaz, 1983) and sociometric research (Bierman et al., 1987; Erhardt & Hinshaw, 1994) to be associated with peer rejection. Of most importance, these decreases were large enough to bring treated children within the range of their normally developing peers at posttreatment and became even larger by the 1-year follow-up.

A School-Based Program

The present discussion would be incomplete without mentioning the school-based work of Dan Olweus (1991, 1993, 1994). Though his effort has focused primarily on schools and on teachers and peers, he has also included parents. Consistent with the idea that child-only interventions have limited long-term impact, Olweus has successfully intervened via school-system-wide programs. The emphasis has been on bullying. However, as Olweus (1991, 1993, 1994) reports, the most recalcitrant bullies are those who show the very cognitions (e.g., viewing aggression as a desirable response, failing to see themselves as responsible for problems) and behaviors (e.g. aggression, anger, and hyperactivity) that have been discussed earlier as contributing heavily to peer rejection. Also, like highly aggressive children (Coie et al., 1990) and ADHD-diagnosed children (Hinshaw & Melnick, 1995; Klein & Mannuzza, 1991), bullies (especially boys) are likely to experience the serious lifelong problems mentioned at the beginning of this chapter (Olweus, 1991, 1993, 1994).

Olweus's program begins by collecting information about bullying events and behavior from students and teachers in each school within the system that has been chosen for intervention. This information serves to establish baseline measures of problematic behaviors that are to be decreased, the conditions under which they occur, and the characteristics of both bullies and victims. In Norway and Sweden, where most of his work has been done up to this time, Olweus (1994) has found that the preponderance of bullying occurs at school and that about 7% of elementary school and young adolescent children can be described as bullies (remaining at about 10% for boys from grade 2 to grade 9, and decreasing from 5% to 2% for girls). He has also found (Olweus, 1994) that the prevalence rate of being bullied stays relatively constant across class size, but varies systematically with sex and grade (more boys than girls; decreasing from 17% of all children in grade 2 to 5% in grade 9). In addition to the usual cognitions and problematic behaviors toward peers, Olweus (1994) has found that bullying is also associated with aggression toward adults (both teachers and parents) and is particularly characteristic of boys who are stronger than other boys and who show early forms of difficult temperament (e.g., hotheadedness). Consistent with the research on parenting presented above, Olweus (1994) has also found that bullying is associated with mothers who are uninvolved and fail to show warmth toward their children, who fail to set limits regarding aggression, and who use coercive, power-assertive child-rearing methods.

Once the school-based information has been gathered, it is shared with teachers and parents; a school conference day is held to review the findings and make decisions about how to proceed in each school as a whole, and also within each classroom and with individual students. Teachers are free to modify the program to fit their classroom situation, but several basic principles are always followed at the school level. Since most bullying at school occurs at times and in settings where teachers are scarce (recess, lunchtime, restrooms; Olweus, 1991, 1993), and since stronger (often older) students usually bully weaker students, a supervision plan is formulated designating which teachers will be present at those times and places; younger students are separated from older students; and teachers are empowered to intervene quickly and decisively when bullying occurs. A copy of this plan (and any attending details that pertain to the particular school) is sent home so that parents are aware of the decisions that have been taken. Then, when bullying occurs, sanctions are imposed (e.g., being required to have a serious, nonhostile talk with the principal), and information about the bully is shared with other teachers and with the child's parents. In addition to these measures, an attitude of warmth toward and interest in all students (including bullies) is encouraged; attractive outdoor equipment that invites positive play (instead of conflict) is provided; teachers involve both bullies and victimized and neglected children in activities that include the more popular students; and informal opportunities to comment on positive aspects of each student are taken advantage of. Parents are also encouraged to contact teachers by telephone or in person if they have concerns about their children, and teachers receive encouragement and support in small informal groups that meet regularly to maintain an ongoing discussion about ways to improve the effectiveness of their efforts.

Intervention is also carried out at the individual classroom level. Teachers engage students in conversations about class rules designed to decrease bullying. Again, teachers are free to make modifications to fit their individual classrooms, but several basic rules always apply. These are stated in concrete, definitive language: Bullying/aggression will not be tolerated (i.e., the teacher will intervene and students will tell the teacher when they witness bullying); students who are bullied will immediately be helped by the teacher and by other students (e.g., if the teacher does not see the bullying, students will tell him or her); and students who are easily left out will be actively included in all activities. Teachers maintain an atmosphere of warmth and praise, strive to include all students in the life of the classroom, and impose nonhostile sanctions when bullying occurs that focus entirely on problematic behavior rather than on the person. In this way all children simultaneously receive positive messages about their value to the class and to the school, and, when necessary, negative messages about problematic behavior (Olweus, 1994). More individualized steps are taken with particularly recalcitrant bullies. This can include removing a bully from the school. In this way it is made very clear to everyone what sort of behavior is problematic and how seriously the rules designed to decrease bullying are being taken (Olweus, 1993).

The results of this program are encouraging. Student reports collected over the course of the first 2 years of intervention showed significant declines in the occurence of bullying among both boys and girls, with greater declines after the second year than the first. By the end of the second year, the number of students reporting being bullied or bullying others dropped by 50% compared to the original baseline data. There was also no increase in bullying outside of school. In addition, there were decreases in vandalism, theft, and truancy, and an increase in student satisfaction with school life.

Conclusions

What is impressive about the results of the parent–child and parent–child–school intervention studies reviewed here is that in addition to evidence of long-term gains that apply to both low- and middle- SES families, the immediate posttreatment effects of these studies are generally stronger than those achieved with child-only or parent-only approaches. Of particular clinical importance is the success of these programs in bringing levels of interpersonal problems within the behavioral limits shown by normally developing peers (Kazdin, 1995).

However, there are also limitations in this research as it presently stands. Data remain limited regarding changes in child social cognitions and behaviors, as well as subsequent peer judgments of treated versus control children. Therefore, at this point, even though the results of some of the social-cognitive training studies and the most recent study by Webster-Stratton (1997) support these effects, it is not yet established that children treated through combined parent–child or teacher–parent–child interventions learn to think about themselves, their behavior toward others, and the behavior of others toward them in new and more positive ways (see Kazdin, 1995). Also, it has to be assumed that this new way of thinking (if it really does occur reliably) in turn guides social behavior, decreasing aggression, hyperactivity, and other forms of dysfunctional responses, and increasing cooperation, listening, the use of positive affect, and other forms of positive responses. The final assumption is that these behavioral changes produce a more positive view of treated children by peers and other social partners. As a result, though we now know that treatments focusing on parents, schools, and children do work to bring about positive changes in children's social behavior, the details about how and why they work and about their impact on other people remain unclear.

Olweus's (1991, 1993, 1994) work is a good case in point. Significant reductions in bullying/aggression were achieved, but data regarding the source of this change (presumably via cognitive changes within individual children) were not obtained, nor were follow-up data obtained to test whether or not aggression levels would remain low following treatment in the absence of continued teacher–peer–parent intervention. Actually, there are some other school-based data, collected by Charles Cunningham and his colleagues working with elementary-school-age children in Canada (though this group uses an entirely peer-mediated intervention; Cunningham et al., in press), indicating that such effects

may be temporary. A particular strength of this research was the use of direct observations of playground bullying/aggression to determine treatment effects. Like Olweus (1994), Cunningham et al. found that recess (with teachers absent) provided a setting for high levels of bullying. When pairs of trained peer mediators were placed on the playground, levels of direct physical aggression were found to drop immediately by 50% (compared to nontreatment baseline) and to remain at that level over the course of 2 school years. However, this effect applied only as long as the peer mediators were present. In one school, the number of mediators was inadvertently allowed to drop to minimal levels; on 2-year follow up, it was found in this school that the level of playground aggression had returned to the baseline level. When extra mediators were added, the aggression level again dropped immediately to 50% of baseline. These findings strongly suggest that the effect of decreased aggression was due entirely to the immediate demand characteristics of the intervention, rather than to any enduring effect on children's cognitions and behavioral habits. Finally, in both the Olweus and Cunningham et al. studies, no cross-setting data were collected to see whether effects would generalize from school to home.

So it remains the case that the only programs presenting evidence of long-term (more than 2 years) posttreatment and cross-setting (home and school) effectiveness in reducing problematic social behavior are those that intervene with parents and children in the home, and also with children and peers in the school (i.e., Tremblay et al., 1992; Yoshikawa, 1994). All the other programs known to us (i.e., child-only, parent-only, and school-based programs) have not yet presented evidence supporting generilization either longer than 2-years or across settings. These differential generalization effects are probably due to differences in the scope of interventions (CPPRG, 1992; Dumas, 1989; Kazdin, 1987). Interventions that target more people in the child's social world, and that target broader domains of child behavior as well as social cognitions, appear to produce more enduring effects.

Thus, the study of children's social problems is left with two important unanswered questions: (1) Is it possible to achieve long-term prevention of social problems through the use of comprehensive programs utilizing a full range of interventive elements identified by the behavioral, social-cognitive, family, and school intervention research reviewed above? (2) When preventive effects are achieved, especially in peer interactions, do social-cognitive changes in children's understanding of how to interact with others account for them? The answers to these questions have great practical and scientific significance, because even the most successful interventions described above leave some children unaffected. Until a great deal more is understood about the causal processes involved and practical ways to bring about change in these processes, many children will remain unhelped. Accordingly, one ongoing effort to provide data that will help answer these questions is now described as "postcript" to this discussion.

Postscript: The FAST Track Program

The FAST Track Program (CPPRG, 1992) has two primary components and corresponding research samples of young children. Data collection for a large, normative, longitudinal sample ($n = 387$) was begun in 1992 to assess the role played by social-interactive and social-cognitive variables in the development of adaptive and maladaptive outcomes. At the same time, data collection for an experimental intervention study ($n = 900$, collected in three annual cohorts) was begun to assess the efficacy of a comprehensive intervention in preventing maladaptive development. Data collection for both samples was begun just prior to children's entry into first grade. At that time, 12,000 boys and girls from impoverished backgrounds were screened to identify 900 children who were at high risk for later CD. Identification was based on a combination of behavior problems at school and at home. The 900 high-risk children were then randomly assigned to receive intervention or not. It is beyond the scope of the present chapter to describe these samples and the data collection fully. Therefore, given the focus on the prevention of social problems in young children, the present description is limited to an overview of the ongoing clinical intervention being conducted with half of the high-risk sample (see also CPPRG, 1992).

As a program of intervention, the FAST Track Program has been designed to incorporate the successful features of the programs already discussed (as well as educational interventions that have not been reviewed here), with the goal of preventing the development of CD in a sample of high-risk, low-SES children. The rationale is simple: Given that treatment components showing some success have already been identified, it should be possible to maximize success by combining these components. Accordingly, FAST Track intervention is conducted with parents, their preschool-age children, and the children's schools. This intervention program is being carried out over the course of 12 years, from grades 1 through 12. Though the specific content of component interventions will change over time to match the developmental needs of the children as they age, the goals of intervention will remain the same. Currently, all FAST Track children are in their early school years; therefore, only the treatment components designed for young children are described.

Treatment goals for parents include the development of positive social-learning-based parenting skills and the development of positive family–school relationships. These goals will be accomplished through group and individual treatment sessions aimed at (1) teaching the use of anger control (Lochman's model) and enhancing family organization and a sense of personal empowerment (see CPPRG, 1992); (2) teaching the use of appropriate behavioral interventions and disciplinary practices to reduce children's disordered behavior at home (Forehand & McMahon's and Webster-Stratton's models), and (3) teaching means to foster children's learning as they enter elementary school (e.g., creating a structured learning environment in the home; see Burgoyne, Hawkins, & Catalano, 1991). Goals for children include the reduction of disruptive behavior in the school setting, improvments in social-cognitive skills and peer interactions, and gains in educational attainment (especially reading). These goals will be accomplished through (1) classroom intervention to increase child self control (see CPPRG, 1992, Kusche & Greenberg, in press), as well as clear teacher communication and reinforcement of positive child behavior (Forehand & McMahon's model); (2) a combined program of social skills training (guided by Crick & Dodge's model; see also Bierman et al., 1987), anger control (Lochman's model), and coaching (Ladd & Mize's model); and (3) academic tutoring in phonics-oriented reading skills (see Wallach & Wallach, 1976, and also CPPRG, 1992). Academic tutoring will be conducted partly in the presence of parents to enhance the parent's awareness of the children's real academic needs. All of these treatment components will be conducted in an integrated fashion in schools where all the children are eligible. It is hoped that in this way each component can be used to enhance the effectiveness of all other components, and that a higher probability of treatment success will result.

The evaluation of FAST Track will include assessments of the effectiveness of each component of intervention in achieving proximal gains in targeted domains, as well as an assessment of the effectiveness of the integrated full program in achieving long-term prevention of CD in adolescence. Initial evaluation reports have shown that the comprehensive program has been effective in achieving proximal gains in social-cognitive skills and peer social acceptance in elementary school (CPPRG, 1993). Future analyses will be conducted to determine whether gains in proximal domains will lead to and mediate intervention effects on long-term outcomes.

FINAL COMMENT

In spite of their checkered status in psychiatric history, problems in social relationships have emerged as central to the development of psychopathology, and interventions to foster positive social relationships have taken center stage in modern prevention research. Theories of the roles that family processes, social information-processing patterns, and social behavior play in the development of problems in social relationships have been formulated and are being tested through longitudinal inquiry. A technology for successful intervention in family processes, social cognition, and social behavior is forthcoming. The next step in clinical research will be the test of whether the integration of intervention components in a comprehensive package will result in children's development of positive social relationships, and, in turn, in the prevention of psychopathology. This test will have the added virtue of informing theory regarding the development, function, and effects of problems in children's social relationships.

REFERENCES

Achenbach, T. M. (1991a). *Manual for the Child Behavior Checklist/4–18 and 1991 Profile*. Burlington: University of Vermont, Department of Psychiatry.

Achenbach, T. M. (1991b). *Manual for the Teacher's Report Form and 1991 Profile*. Burlington: University of Vermont, Department of Psychiatry.

American Psychiatric Association. (1994). *Diagnostic and statistical manual of mental disorders* (4th ed.). Washington, DC: Author.

Arnold, L. E. (1995). Sex differences in ADHD: Conference summary. *Journal of Abnormal Child Psychology, 24*, 555–569.

Asher, S. R. (1990). Recent advances in the study of peer rejection. In S. R. Asher & J. D. Coie (Eds.), *Peer rejection in childhood* (pp. 3–14). New York: Cambridge University Press.

Asher, S. R., & Coie, J. D. (Eds.). (1990). *Peer rejection in childhood*. New York: Cambridge.

Asher, S. R., & Hymel, S. (1981). Children's social competence in peer relations: Sociometric and behavioral assessment. In J. D. Wine & M. D. Smye (Eds.), *Social competence* (pp. 125–157). New York: Guilford Press.

Asher, S. R., Parkhurst, J. T., Hymel, S., & Williams, G. A. (1990). Peer rejection and loneliness in childhood. In S. R. Asher & J. D. Coie (Eds.), *Peer rejection in childhood* (pp. 253–273). New York: Cambridge University Press.

Asher, S. R., & Wheeler, V. (1985). Children's loneliness: A comparison of rejected and neglected peer status. *Journal of Consulting and Clinical Psychology, 53*, 500–505.

Baer, R. A., & Nietzel, M. T. (1991). Cognitive and behavioral treatment of impulsivity in children: A meta-analytic review of the outcome literature. *Journal of Clinical Child Psychology, 20,* 400–412.

Bandura, A. (1986). *Social foundations of thought and action: A social cognitive theory*. Englewood Cliffs, NJ: Prentice-Hall.

Barkley, R. A. (1989). Attention-Deficit/Hyperactivity Disorder. In E. J. Mash & R. A. Barkley (Eds.), *Treatment of childhood disorders* (pp. 39–72). New York: Guilford Press.

Barkley, R. A. (1990) *Attention-Deficit Hyperactivity Disorder: A handbook for diagnosis and treatment*. New York: Guilford Press.

Baron, R. M., & Kenny, D. A. (1986). The moderator–mediator variable distinction in social psychological research: Conceptual, strategic, and statistical considerations. *Journal of Personality and Social Psychology, 51*, 1173–1182.

Bell, R. Q., & Chapman, M. (1986). Child effects in studies using experimental or brief longitudinal approaches to socialization. *Developmental Psychology, 22*, 595–603.

Bickett, L., & Milich, R. (1990). First impressions formed of boys with Attention Deficit Disorder. *Journal of Learning Disabilities, 23*, 253–259.

Bierman, K. L., Miller, C. L., & Stabb, S. D. (1987). Improving the social behavior and peer acceptance of rejected boys: Effects of social skill training with instructions and prohibitions. *Journal of Consulting and Clinical Psychology, 55*, 194–200.

Bierman, K. L., & Wargo, J. B. (1995). Predicting the longitudinal course associated with aggressive–rejected, aggressive (nonrejected), and rejected (nonaggressive) status. *Development and Psychopathology, 7*, 669–682.

Boivin, M., Dodge, K. A., & Coie, J. D. (1995). Individual–group behavioral similarity and peer status in experimental play groups of boys: The social misfit revisited. *Journal of Personality and Social Psychology, 69*, 269–279.

Brown, P., & Elliot, R. (1965). Control of aggression in a nursery school class. *Journal of Experimental Child Psychology, 2*, 103–107.

Burgoyne, K., Hawkins, D., & Catalano, R. (1991). *How to help your child succeed in school.* Seattle, WA: Developmental Research and Programs.

Carlson, C. L., Pelham, W. E., Milich, R., & Dixon, J. (1992). Single and combined effects of methylphenidate and behavior therapy on the classroom performance of children with Attention Deficit-Hyperactivity Disorder. *Journal of Abnormal Child Psychology, 20*, 213–232.

Chandler, M. J., Greenspan, S., & Barenboim, C. (1974). Assessment and training of role-taking and referential communication skills in institutionalized emotionally disturbed children. *Developmental Psychology, 10*, 546–553.

Chittendon, G. F. (1942). An experimental study in measuring and modifying assertive behavior in young children. *Monographs of the Society for Research in Child Development, 7* (Issue No. 31).

Coie, J. D. (1990). Toward a theory of peer rejection. In S. R. Asher & J. D. Coie (Eds.), *Peer rejection in childhood* (pp. 3–14). New York: Cambridge University Press.

Coie, J. D., & Dodge, K. A. (1983). Continuity of children's social status: A five-year longitudinal study. *Merrill–Palmer Quarterly, 29*, 261–282.

Coie, J. D., Dodge, K. A., & Coppotelli, H. (1982). Dimensions and types of social status: A cross-age perspective. *Developmental Psychology, 18*, 557–570.

Coie, J. D., Dodge, K. A., & Kupersmidt, J. B. (1990). Peer group behavior and social status. In S. R. Asher & J. D. Coie (Eds.), *Peer rejection in childhood* (pp. 17–59). New York: Cambridge University Press.

Coie, J. D., & Koeppl, G. K. (1990). Adapting intervention to the problems of aggressive and disruptive rejected children. In S. R. Asher & J. D. Coie (Eds.), *Peer rejection in childhood* (pp. 309–337). New York: Cambridge University Press.

Coie, J. D., & Kupersmidt, J. B. (1983). A behavioral analysis of emerging social status in boys' groups. *Child Development, 54*, 1400–1416.

Coie, J. D., Terry, R., Lenox, K., Lochman, J., & Hyman, C. (1995). Childhood peer rejection and aggression as predictors of stable patterns of adolescent disorder. *Development and Psychopathology, 7*, 697–713.

Conduct Problems Prevention Research Group (CPPRG). (1992). A developmental and clinical model for the prevention of Conduct Disorder: The FAST Track Program. *Development and Psychopathology, 4*, 509–528.

Conduct Problems Prevention Research Group (CPPRG). (1993, March). *An initial evaluation of the FAST Track Program.* Paper presented at the bi-

ennial meeting of the Society for Research in Child Development, New Orleans.

Cowen, E. L., Pederson, A., Babigian, H., Izzo, L. D., & Trost, M. A. (1973). Long-term follow-up of early detected vulnerable children. *Journal of Consulting and Clinical Psychology, 41*, 438–446.

Crick, N. R. (1995). Relational aggression: The role of intent attributions, feelings of distress, and provocation type. *Development and Psychopathology, 7*, 313–322.

Crick, N. R., & Dodge, K. A. (1994). A review and reformulation of social information-processing mechanisms in children's social adjustment. *Psychological Bulletin, 115*(1), 74–101.

Crick, N. R., & Grotpeter, J. K. (1995). Relational aggression, gender, and social-psychological adjustment. *Child Development, 66*, 710–722.

Crick, N. R., & Ladd, G. W. (1990). Children's perceptions of the outcomes of aggressive strategies: Do the ends justify being mean? *Developmental Psychology, 29*, 244–254.

Cunningham, C. E., Cunningham, L. J., Martorelli, V., Tran, A., Young, J., & Zacharias, R. (1997). *The effects of primary division, student-mediated conflict resolution programs on playground agression.* Unpublished manuscript.

Cunningham, C. E., Siegel, L. S., & Offord, D. R. (1985). A developmental dose–response analysis of the effects of methylphenidate on the peer interactions of attention deficit disordered boys. *Journal of Child Psychology and Psychiatry, 26*, 955–971.

Cunningham, C. E., Siegel, L. S., & Offord, D. R. (1991). A dose-response analysis of the effects of methylphenidate on the peer interactions and simulated classroom performance of ADD children with and without conduct problems. *Journal of Child Psychology and Psychiatry, 32*, 439–452.

Dodge, K. A. (1980). Social cognition and children's aggressive behavior. *Child Development, 51*, 162–170.

Dodge, K. A. (1983). Behavioral antecedents of peer social status. *Child Development, 54*, 1386–1399.

Dodge, K. A. (1986). A social information processing model of social competence in children. In M. Perlmutter (Ed.), *Minnesota Symposium on Child Psychology* (Vol. 18, pp. 77–125). Hillsdale, NJ: Erlbaum.

Dodge, K. A. (1989). Problems in social relationships. In E. J. Mash & R. A. Barkley (Eds.), *Treatment of childhood disorders* (pp. 222–244). New York: Guilford Press.

Dodge, K. A. (1991). Emotion and social information processing. In J. Garber & K. A. Dodge (Eds.), *The development of emotion regulation* (pp. 159–181). New York: Cambridge University Press.

Dodge, K. A. (1993a). Social-cognitive mechanisms in the development of Conduct Disorder and depression. *Annual Review of Psychology, 44*, 559–584.

Dodge, K. A. (1993b, March). *Social information processing and peer rejection factors in the devel-*

opment of behavior problems in children. Paper presented at the biennial meeting of the Society for Research in Child Development, New Orleans.

Dodge, K. A. (1997). *A biopsychosocial model of the development of chronic conduct problems in adolescence*. Manuscript submitted for publication.

Dodge, K. A., Coie, J. D., & Brakke, N. P. (1983). Behavior patterns of socially rejected and neglected preadolescents: The roles of social approach and aggression. *Journal of Abnormal Child Psychology*, *10*, 389–410.

Dodge, K. A., & Feldman, E. (1990). Issues in social cognition and sociometric status. In S. R. Asher & J. D. Coie (Eds.), *Peer rejection in childhood* (pp. 119–155). New York: Cambridge University Press.

Dodge, K. A., McClaskey, C. L., & Feldman, E. (1985). Situational approach to the assessment of social competence in children. *Journal of Consulting and Clinical Psychology*, *53*, 344–353.

Dodge, K. A., Murphy, R. R., & Buchsbaum, K. (1984). The assessment of intention-cue detection skills in children: Implications for developmental psychopathology. *Child Development*, *55*, 163–173.

Dodge, K. A., Pettit, G. S., McClaskey, C. L., & Brown, M. M. (1986). Social competence in children. *Monographs of the Society for Research in Child Development*, *51*(2, Serial No. 213).

Dodge, K. A., & Price, J. M. (1994). On the relation between social information processing and socially competent behavior in early school-aged children. *Child Development*, *65*, 1385–1397.

Dodge, K. A., Schlundt, D. C., Schocken, I., & Delugach, J. D. (1983). Social competence and children's social status: The role of peer group entry strategies. *Merrill–Palmer Quarterly*, *29*, 309–336.

Dodge, K. A., & Tomlin, A. (1987). Cue-utilization as a mechanism of attributional bias in aggressive children. *Social Cognition*, *5*, 280–300.

Drabman, R., & Spitalnik, R. (1973). Social isolation as a punishment procedure: A controlled study, *Journal of Experimental Psychology*, *16*, 236–249.

Dumas, J. E. (1989). Treating antisocial behavior in children: Child and family approaches. *Clinical Psychology Review*, *9*, 197–222.

Durlak, J. A., Fuhrman, T., & Lampman, C. (1991). Effectiveness of cognitive-behavioral therapy for maladapting children: A meta-analysis. *Psychological Bulletin*, *110*, 204–214.

Eisenberg, N., Fabes, R. A., Bernzweig, M. K., Poulin, R., & Hanish, L. (1993). The relations of emotionality and regulation to preschoolers' social skills and sociometric status. *Child Development*, *64*, 1418–1438.

Erhardt, D., & Hinshaw, S. P. (1994). Initial sociometric impressions of hyperactive and comparison boys: Predictions from social behaviors and from nonbehavioral variables. *Journal of Consulting and Clinical Psychology*, *62*, 833–842.

Farrington, D. P. (1991). Childhood aggression and adult violence: Early precursors and later life outcomes. In D. J. Pepler & K. H. Rubin (Eds.), *The development and treatment of childhood aggression* (pp. 5–30). Hillsdale, NJ: Erlbaum.

Forehand, R., & Long, N. (1988). Outpatient treatment of the acting out child: Procedures, long term follow-up data, and clinical problems. *Advances in Behaviour Research and Therapy*, *10*, 129–177.

Forehand, R., & McMahon, R. J. (1981). *Helping the noncompliant child: A clinician's guide to parent training*. New York: Guilford Press.

French, D. C., & Tyne, T. F. (1982). The identification and treatment of children with peer-relationship difficulties. In J. P. Curran & P. M. Monti (Eds.), *Social skills training: A practical handbook for assessment and treatment* (pp. 280–312). New York: Guilford Press.

Freedman, B. J., Rosenthal, L., Donahoe, C. P., Jr., Schlundt, D. G., & McFall, R. M. (1978). A social-behavioral analysis of skill deficits in delinquent and nondelinquent adolescent boys. *Journal of Consulting and Clinical Psychology*, *46*, 1448–1462.

Furman, W., Rahe, D. F., & Hartup, W. W. (1970). Rehabilitation of socially withdrawn preschool children through mixed-age socialization. *Child Development*, *50*, 915–922.

Gadow, K. D., Nolan, E. E., Sverd, J., Sprafkin, J., & Paolicelli, L. (1990). Methylphenidate in aggressive hyperactive boys: I. Effects on peer aggression in public school settings. *Journal of the American Academy of Child and Adolescent Psychiatry*, *29*, 710–718.

Gadow, K. D., Paolicelli, L. M., Nolan, E. E., Schwartz, J., Sprafkin, J., & Sverd, J. (1992). Methylphenidate in aggressive hyperactive boys: II. Indirect effects of medication treatment on peer behavior. *Journal of Child and Adolescent Psychopharmacology*, *2*, 49–61.

Garber, J., & Dodge, K. A. (Eds.). (1991). *The development of emotion regulation and dysfunction*. New York: Cambridge University Press.

Gittelman, R., & Kanner, A. (1986). Psychopharmacotherapy. In H. C. Quay & J. Werry (Eds.), *Psychopathological disorders of childhood* (3rd. ed., pp. 455–494). New York: Wiley.

Goldfried, M. R., & D'Zurilla, T. J. (1969). A behavioral-analytic model for assessing competence. In C. D. Spielberger (Ed.), *Current topics in clinical and community psychology* (Vol. 1, pp. 151–196). New York: Academic Press.

Gottman, J. (1977). The effects of a modeling film on social isolation in preschool children: A methodological investigation. *Journal of Abnormal Child Psychology*, *5*, 69–78.

Gottman, J. (1983). How children become friends. *Monographs of the Society for Research in Child Development*, *48* (3, Serial No. 201).

Gottman, J. (1986). Merging social cognition and social behavior: Commentary. *Monographs of the So-*

ciety for Research in Child Development, 51(2, Serial No. 213), 81–85.

Gottman, J., Gonso, J., & Schuler, P. (1976). Teaching social skills to isolated children. *Journal of Abnormal Child Psychology, 4*, 179–197.

Granger, D. A., Whalen, C. K., & Henker, B. (1993). Perceptions of methylphenidate effects on hyperactive children's peer interactions. *Journal of Abnormal Child Psychology, 21*, 535–549.

Greenwood, C. R., & Hops, H. (1981). Group oriented contingencies and peer behavior change. In P. Strain (Ed.), *The utlization of classroom peers as behavior change agents* (pp. 189–259). New York: Plenum Press.

Greenwood, C. R., Walker, H. M., Todd, N. M., & Hops, H. (1979). Selecting a cost-effective screening measure for the assessment of preschool social withdrawal. *Journal of Applied Behavior Analysis, 12*, 639–652.

Hart, B. M., Reynolds, N. J., Baer, D. M., Brawley, E. R., & Harris, F. R. (1968). Effects of contingent and noncontingent social reinforcement on the cooperative play of a preschool child. *Journal of Applied Behavior Analysis, 1*, 73–76.

Hinshaw, S. P. (1991). Stimulant medication and the treatment of aggressive children with attentional deficits. *Journal of Clinical Child Psychology, 20*, 301–312.

Hinshaw, S. P. (1994). *Attention deficits and hyperactivity in children*. Thousand Oaks, CA: Sage.

Hinshaw, S. P., Heller, T., & McHale, J. P. (1992). Covert antisocial behavior in boys with Attention-Deficit Hyperactivity Disorder: External validation and effects of methylphenidate. *Journal of Consulting and Clinical Psychology, 60*, 274–281.

Hinshaw, S. P., Henker, B., Whalen, C. K., Erhardt, D, & Dunnington, R. E. (1989). Aggressive, prosocial, and nonsocial behavior in hyperactive boys: Dose effects of methylphenidate in naturalistic settings. *Journal of Consulting and Clinical Psychology, 57*, 636–643.

Hinshaw, S. P., Lahey, B. J., & Hart, E. L. (1993). Issues of taxonomy and comorbidity in the development of conduct disroder. *Development and Psychopathology, 5*, 31–49.

Hinshaw, S. P., & Melnick, S. M. (1995). Peer relationshipts in boys with Attention-Deficit Hyperactivity Disorder with and without comorbid aggression. *Development and Psychopathology, 7*, 627–647.

Hops, H., & Greenwood, C. R. (1988). Social skills deficits. In E. J. Mash & L. G. Terdal (Eds.), *Behavioral assessment of childhood disorders* (2nd ed., pp. 263–316). New York: Guilford Press.

Hops, H., Walker, H. M., & Greenwood, C. R. (1979). PEERS: A program for remediating social withdrawal in school. In L. A. Hamerlynck (Ed.), *Behavioral systems for the developmentally disabled in school and home environments* (pp. 48–88). New York: Brunner/Mazel.

Hoza, B., Pelham, W. E., Milich, R., Pillow, D., & McBride, K. (1993). The self-perceptions and attributions of attention deficit hyperactivity disordered and nonreferred boys. *Journal of Abnormal Child Psychology, 21*, 271–286.

Hymel, S., & Asher, S. R. (1977, April). *Assessment and training of isolated children's social skills*. Paper presented at the biennial meeting of the Society of Research in Child Development, New Orleans. (ERIC document Reproduction Service No. ED 136 930)

Jacobs, M. A., Muller, J. J., Anderson, J., & Skinner, J. R. (1973). Prediction of improvement in coping with pathology in hospitalized psychiatric patients: A replication study. *Journal of Consulting and Clinical Psychology, 40*, 343–349.

Jacobvitz, D., & Sroufe, L. A. (1987). The early caregiver–child relationship and Attention-Deficit Disorder with Hyperactivity in kindergarten: A prospective study. *Child Development, 58*, 1488–1495.

Johnson, D. L., Kahn, A. J., & Devila, R. (1976). *Houston Parent–Child Development Center, Final Report*. Houston, TX: Houston Parent–Child Development Centers. (ERIC Document Reproduction Service No. Ed. 194 538)

Johnson, D. L., & Walker, T. (1987). Primary prevention of behavior problems in Mexican-American children. *American Journal of Community Psychology, 15*, 375–385.

Kandel, D. B. (1982). Epidemiological and psychosocial perspectives in adolescent drug abuse. *Journal of the American Academy of Child Psychiatry, 21*, 328–347.

Kazdin, A. E. (1985). *Treatment of antisocial behavior in children*. Homewood, IL: Dorsey Press.

Kazdin, A. E. (1987). Treatment of antisocial behavior in children: Current status and future directions. *Psychological Bulletin, 102*(2), 187–203.

Kazdin, A. E. (1995). *Conduct disorders in childhood and adolescence* (2nd ed.). Thousand Oaks, CA: Sage.

Kazdin, A. E., Bass, D., Siegel, T., & Thomas, C. (1989). Cognitive-behavioral treatment and relationship therapy in the treatment of children referred for antisocial behavior. *Journal of Consulting and Clinical Psychology, 57*, 522–535.

Kazdin, A. E., Siegel, T., & Bass, D. (1992). Cognitive problem-solving skills training and parent management training in the treatment of antisocial behavior in children. *Journal of Consulting and Clinical Psychology, 60*, 733–747.

Kelly, J. A. (1982). *Social-skills training: A practical guide for interventions*. New York: Springer.

Klein, R. G., & Mannuzza, S. (1991). Long-term outcome of hyperactive children: A review. *Journal of the American Academy of Child and Adolescent Psychiatry, 30*, 383–387.

Kohn, M. (1977). *Social competence, symptoms, and underachievement in childhood: A longitudinal perspective*. Washington, DC: Winston.

Kupersmidt, J. B., Coie, J. D., & Dodge, K. A. (1990).
The role of peer relationships in the development
of disorder. In S. R. Asher & J. D. Coie (Eds.), *Peer
rejection in childhood* (pp. 274–308). New York:
Cambridge University Press.

Kusche, C. E., & Greenberg, M. T. (in press). *The
PATHS Curriculum*. Seattle, WA: EXCEL.

Ladd, G. W. (1981). Effectiveness of a social learning
method for enhancing children's social interactions
and peer acceptance. *Child Development, 52,* 171–
178

Ladd, G. W., & Mize, J. (1983). A cognitive–social
learning model of social skill training. *Psychological Review, 90,* 127–157.

LaGreca, A. M., & Mesibov, G. B. (1979). Social
skills intervention with learning disabled children:
Selecting skills and implementing training. *Journal
of Clinical Child Psychology, 8,* 234–241.

LaGreca, A. M., & Santogrossi, D. A. (1980). Social
skills training with elementary school students: A
behavioral group approach. *Journal of Consulting
and Clinical Psychology, 48,* 220–227.

Lochman, J. E. (1985). Effects of different treatment
lengths in cognitive behavioral interventions with
aggressive boys. *Child Psychiatry and Human Development, 16,* 45–56.

Lochman, J. E., Burch, P. R., Curry, J. F., & Lampron,
L. B. (1984). Treatment and generalization effects
of cognitive-behavioral and goal-setting interventions with aggressive boys. *Journal of Consulting
and Clinical Psychology, 52,* 915–916.

Lochman, J. E., Coie, J. D., Underwood, M. K., &
Terry, R. (1993). Effectiveness of a social relations
intervention program for aggressive and nonaggressive, rejected children. *Journal of Consulting
and Clinical Psychology, 61,* 1053–1058.

Lochman, J. E., Lampron, L. B., Burch, P. R., &
Curry, J. F. (1985). Client characteristics associated
with behavior change of treated and untreated aggressive boys. *Journal of Abnormal Child Psychology, 13,* 527–538.

Long, P., Forehand, R., Wierson, M., & Morgan, A. (in
press). Moving into adulthood: Does parent training with young noncompliant children have long
term effects? *Behaviour Research and Therapy.*

Lytton, H. (1990). Child and parent effects in boys'
Conduct Disorder: A reinterpretation. *Developmental Psychology, 26,* 683–697.

Maccoby, E. E. (1990). Gender and relationships: A
developmental account. *American Psychologist,
45,* 513–520.

Madan-Swain, A., & Zental, S. S. (1990). Behavioral
comparisons of liked and disliked hyperactive children in play contexts and the behavioral accommodations by their classmates. *Journal of Consulting
and Clinical Psychology, 58,* 197–209.

McFadyen-Ketchum, S. A. (1991, April). *A situational assessment of age and gender differences in
the social competence of preschool children.* Poster
presented at the biennial meeting of the Society for
Research in Child Development, Seattle, WA.

McFadyen-Ketchum, S. A. (1997, April). Change in
aggression: Identifying children at risk and causes
of interpersonal violence. In R. Tremblay (Chair),
*Modeling development patterns of antisocial be-
havior.* Symposium at the biennial meeting of the
Society for Research in Child Development, Washington, DC.

McFadyen-Ketchum, S. A. (1993, March). *Learning
to interact competently with preschool peers: The
contribution of mother–child conversations at
home.* (Chair), Symposium presented at the biennial meeting of the Society for Research in Child
Development, New Orleans, LA.

McFadyen-Ketchum, S. A., Bates, J. E., Dodge, K. A.,
and Pettit, G. S. (1996). Patterns of change in early
childhood aggressive–disruptive behavior: Gender
differences in predictions from early coercive and
affectionate mother–child interactions. *Child Development, 67,* 2417–2433.

McFall, R. M., (1976). *Behavioral training: A skill acquisition approach to clinical problems.* Morris-
town, NJ: General Learning Press.

McFall, R. M. (1982). A review and reformulation of
the concept of social skills. *Behavioral Assessment,
4,* 1–33.

McFall, R. M., & Dodge, K. A. (1982). Self-management and interpersonal social skills. In P. Karoly &
F. H. Kanfer (Eds.), *Self-management and behavior
change: From theory to practice,* (pp. 353–392).
New York: Pergamon Press.

McMahon, R. J., & Wells, K. C. (1989). Conduct disorder. In E. J. Mash & R. A. Barkley (Eds.), *Treatment of childhood disorders* (pp. 73–134). New
York: Guilford Press.

Melnick, S. M., & Hinshaw, S. P. (1996). What they
want and what they get: The social goals of boys
with ADHD and comparison boys. *Journal of Abnormal Child Psychology, 24,* 169–185.

Milich, R., & Dodge, K. A. (1984). Social information processing in child psychiatric populations.
Journal of Abnormal Child Psychology, 12, 471–
490.

Mize, J., & Ladd, G. W. (1990). Toward the development of successful social skills training for preschool children. In S. R. Asher & J. D. Coie (Eds.),
Peer rejection in childhood (pp. 274–308). New
York: Cambridge University Press.

Murphy, D. A., Pelham, W. E., & Lang, A. R. (1992).
Aggression in boys with Attention Deficit-Hyperactivity Disorder: Methylphenidate effects on naturalistically observed aggression, response to
provocation, and social information processing.
Journal of Abnormal Child Psychology, 20, 451–
466.

Newcomb, A. F., Bukowski, W. M., & Pattee, L.
(1993). Children's peer relations: A meta-analytic
review of popular, rejected, neglected, controversial, and average sociometric status. *Psychological
Bulletin, 113*(1), 99–128.

Novaco, R. W. (1978). Anger and coping with stress:
Cognitive behavioral intervention. In J. P. Foreyt &

D. P. Rathjen (Eds.), *Cognitive behavioral therapy: Research and application* (pp. 135–173). New York: Plenum Press.

O'Connor, R. D. (1969). Modification of social withdrawal through symbolic modeling. *Journal of Applied Behavior Analysis, 2,* 15–22.

Oden, S. L., & Asher, S. R. (1977). Coaching children in social skills for friendship making. *Child Development, 48,* 495–506.

Olweus, D. (1991). Bully/victim problems among school children: Basic facts and effects of a school based intervention program. In D. Pepler & K. Rubin (Eds.), *The development and treatment of childhood aggression* (pp. 411–488). Hillsdale, NJ: Erlbaum.

Olweus, D. (1993). *Bullying in school: What we know and what we can do.* Oxford: Blackwell.

Olweus, D. (1994). Annotation: Bullying at school: Basic facts and effects of a school based intervention program. *Journal of Child Psychology and Psychiatry, 35,* 1171–1190.

Paine, S. C., Hops, H., Walker, H. M., Greenwood, C. R., Fleishman, D. H., & Guild, J. J. (1982). Repeated treatment effects: A study of maintaining behavior change in socially withdrawn children. *Behavior Modification, 6,* 171–199.

Parker, R. D., & Asher, S. R. (1987). Peer acceptance and later personal adjustment: Are low-accepted children at risk? *Psychological Bulletin, 102,* 357–389.

Parker, R. D., & Gottman, J. M. (1985, April). *Making friends with an extraterrestrial: Conversational skills and friendship formation in young children.* Paper presented at the biennial meeting of the Society for Research in Child Development, Toronto.

Patterson, G. R. (1982). *Coercive family process.* Eugene, OR: Castalia.

Patterson, G. R., Reid, J. B., & Dishion, T. J. (1992). *Antisocial boys.* Eugene, OR: Castalia.

Pelham, W. E., & Bender, M. E. (1982). Peer relationships in hyperactive children: Description and treatment. In K. Gadow & I. Bialer (Eds.), *Advances in learning and behavioral disabilities* (Vol. 1, pp. 365–436). Greenwich, CT: JAI Press.

Pelham, W. E., Carlson, C. L., Sams, S. E., Vallano, G., Dixon, M. J., & Hoza, B. (1993). Separate and combined effects of methylphenidate and behavior modification on the classroom behavior and academic performance of ADHD boys: Group effects and individual differences. *Journal of Consulting and Clinical Psychology, 60,* 506–515.

Pelham, W. E., Milich, R., Cummings, E. M., Murphy, D. A., Schaughency, E. A., & Greiner, A. R. (1991). Effects of background anger, provocation, and methylphenidate on emotional arousal and aggressive responding in attention-deficit hyperactivity disordered boys with and without concurrent aggressiveness. *Journal of Abnormal Child Psychology, 19,* 407–426.

Pelham, W. E., Murphy, D. A., Vannatta, K., Milich, R., Licht, R. G., Gragy, E. M. Greenslade, K. E.,

Greirer, A. R., & Vodde-Hamilton, M. (1993). Methylphenidate and attributions in boys with Attention-Deficit Hyperactivity Disorder. *Annual Progress in Child Psychiatry and Child Development,* 242–265.

Pepler, D. J., & Slaby, R. G. (1994). Theoretical and developmental perspectives on youth and violence. In L. D. Eron, J. H. Gentry, & P. Schlegel (Eds.), *Reason to hope: A psychological perspective on violence and youth.* Washington, DC: American Psychological Association.

Perry, D. G., Perry, L. C., & Rasmussen, P. (1986). Cognitive social learning mediators of aggression. *Child Development, 57,* 700–711.

Pettit, G. S., Dodge, K. A., & Brown, M. M. (1988). Early family experience, social problem solving patterns, and children's social competence. *Child Development, 59,* 107–120.

Pfiffner, L. J., & McBurnett, K. (in press). Social skills training with parent generalization: Treatment effects for children with ADD/ADHD. *Journal of Consulting and Clinical Psychology.*

Pisterman, S., McGrath, P., Firestone, P., Goodman, J. T., Webster, I., & Mallory, R. (1989). Outcome of parent-mediated treatment of preschoolers with Attention Deficit Disorder with Hyperactivity. *Journal of Consulting and Clinical Psychology, 57,* 628–635.

Putallaz, M. (1983). Predicting children's sociometric status from their behavior. *Child Development, 54,* 1417–1426.

Putallaz, M. (1989). Children's naturalistic entry behavior and sociometric status: A developmental perspective. *Developmental Psychology, 25,* 297–305.

Putallaz, M., & Wasserman, A. (1989). Children's naturalistic entry behavior and sociometric status: A developmental perspective. *Developmental Psychology, 25,* 297–305.

Quiggle, N., Garber, J., Panak, W., & Dodge, K. A. (1992). Social-information processing in aggressive and depressed children. *Child Development, 63,* 1305–1320.

Reid, J. B. (1993). Prevention of Conduct Disorder before and after school entry: Relating interventions to developmental findings. *Development and Psychopathology, 5,* 243–262.

Richters, J. E., & Cicchetti, D. (Eds.). (1993). Toward a developmental perspective on Conduct Disorder [Special Issue]. *Development and Psychopathology, 5*(1–2).

Robins, L. N. (1966). *Deviant children grown up.* Baltimore: Williams & Wilkins.

Roff, M. (1963). Childhood social interactions and young psychosis. *Journal of Clinical Psychology, 19,* 152–157.

Rothbart, M. K., & Bates, J. E. (1998). Temperament. In N. Eisenberg (Vol. Ed.), *Handbook of child psychology: Vol. 3. Social, emotional, and personality development* (5th ed.). New York: Wiley.

Rubin, K. H., & Krasnor, L. R. (1986). Social-cognitive and social-behavioral perspectives on problem solving. In M. Perlmutter (Ed.), *Minnesota Symposium on Child Psychology* (Vol. 18, pp. 1–65). Hillsdale, NJ: Erlbaum.

Shaffer, D. (1974). Suicide in childhood and early adolescence. *Journal of Child Psychology and Psychiatry, 15,* 275–291.

Shantz, C. U. (1987). Conflicts between children. *Child Development, 58,* 283–305.

Shantz, C. U., & Hartup, W. (1992). *Conflict in child and adolescent development.* New York: Cambridge University Press.

Shure, M. B. (1980). Real-life problem solving for parents and children: An approach to social competence. In D. P. Rathjen & J. P. Foreyt (Eds.), *Social competence: Interventions for children and adults* (pp. 54–68). New York: Pergamon Press.

Slaby, R. G., & Guerra, N. G. (1988). Cognitive mediators of aggression in adolescent offenders: 1. Assessment. *Developmental Psychology, 24,* 580–588.

Snyder, J., Edwards, P., McGraw, K., Kilgore, K., & Holton, A. (1994). Escalation and reinforcement in mother-child conflict: Social processes associated with physical aggression. *Development and Psychopathology, 6,* 305–321.

Snyder, J., & Patterson, G. R. (1986). The effects of consequences on patterns of social interaction: A quasi-experimental approach to reinforcement in natural interaction. *Child Development, 57,* 1257–1268.

Snyder, J., & Patterson, G. R. (1995). Individual differences in social aggression: A test of a reinforcement model of socialization in the natural environment. *Behavior Therapy, 26,* 371–391.

Spivack, G., & Shure, M. B. (1974). *Social adjustment of young children: A cognitive approach to solving real-life problems.* San Francisco: Jossey-Bass.

Stengel, E. (1971). *Suicide and attempted suicide.* Harmondsworth, England: Penguin.

Strain, P. S., Shores, R. E., & Timm, M. A. (1977). Effects of peer social initiations on the behavior of withdrawn preschool children. *Journal of Applied Behavior Analysis, 10,* 189–198.

Taylor, A. R., & Asher, S. R. (1989). *Children's goals in game playing situations.* Unpublished manuscript.

Timm, M. A., Strain, P. S., & Eller, P. H. (1979). Effects of systematic response dependent fading and thinning procedures on the maintenance of child–child interaction. *Journal of Applied Behavior Analysis, 12,* 208–228.

Tremblay, R. E. (1991). Aggression, prosocial behavior, and gender: Three magic words, but no magic wand. In D. J. Pepler & K. H. Rubin (Eds.), *The development and treatment of childhood aggression* (pp. 71–78). Hillsdale, NJ: Erlbaum.

Tremblay, R. E., Loeber, R., Gagnon, C., Charlebois, P., Larivee, S., & LeBlanc, M. (1991). Disruptive boys with stable and unstable high fighting behavior patterns during junior elementary school. *Journal of Abnormal Child Psychology, 19,* 285–300.

Tremblay, R. E., Vitaro, F., Bertrand, L., LeBlanc, M., Beauchesne, H., Boileau, H., & David, L. (1992). Parent and child training to prevent early onset of delinquency: The Montreal longitudinal study. In J. McCord & R. E. Tremblay (Eds.), *Preventing antisocial behavior: Interventions from birth through adolescence* (pp. 117–138). New York: Guilford Press.

Waldman, I. D. (1996). Aggressive boys' hostile perceptual and response biases: The role of attention and impulsivity. *Child Development, 67,* 1015–1033.

Walker, H. M., Hops, H., Greenwood, C. R., & Todd, N. (1979). Differential effects of reinforcing topographic components of free play social interaction: Analysis and direct replication. *Behavior Modification, 3,* 291–321.

Wallach, M. A., & Wallach, L. (1976). *Teaching all children to read.* Chicago: University of Chicago Press.

Webster-Stratton, C. (1993). Strategies for helping early school-aged children with Oppositional Defiant and Conduct Disorders: The importance of home–school partnerships. *School Psychology Review, 22,* 437–457.

Webster-Stratton, C. (1996). Early-onset conduct problems: Does gender make a difference? Journal of *Consulting and Clinical Psychology, 64,* 540–551.

Webster-Stratton, C. (1997). Treating children with early-onset conduct problems: A comparison of child and parent training interventions. *Journal of Consulting and Clinical Psychology, 65,* 93–109.

Weikart, D., & Schweinhart, L. J. (1992). High/Scope preschool program outcomes. In J. McCord & R. E. Tremblay (Eds.), *Preventing antisocial behavior: Interventions from birth through adolescence* (pp. 67–86). New York: Guilford Press.

Weinrott, M. R., Corson, L. A., & Wilchesky, M. (1979). Teacher mediated treatment of social withdrawal. *Behavior Therapy, 10,* 281–294.

Weiss, G., & Hechtman, L. T. (1993). *Hyperactive children grown up* (2nd ed.). New York: Guilford Press.

Whalen, C. K., Henker, R., Buhrmeister, D., Hinshaw, S. P., Huber, A., & Laski, K. (1989). Does stimulant medication improve the peer status of hyperactive children? *Journal of Consulting and Clinical Psychology, 57,* 545–549.

Whalen, C. K., Henker, B., Castro, J., & Granger, D. (1987). Peer perceptions of hyperactivity and medication effects. *Child Development, 58,* 816–828.

Whalen, C. K., Henker, B., & Granger, D. (1990). Social judgment processes in hyperactive boys: Effects of methylphenidate and comparisons with normal peers. *Journal of Abnormal Child Psychology, 18,* 297–316.

Williams, G. (1986, November). *Advances in identifying subgroups of rejected and neglected children.*

Paper presented at the meeting of the Merrill–Palmer Society, Detroit.

Wright, J. C., Giammarino, M., & Parad, H. W. (1986). Social status in small groups: Individual–group similarity and the social "misfit." *Journal of Personality and Social Psychology, 50,* 523–536.

Yoshikawa, H. (1994). Prevention as cumulative protection: Effects of early family support and education on chronic delinquency and its risks. *Psychological Bulletin, 115*(1), 28–54.

Youniss, J. (1981). *Parents and peers in social development.* New York: Appleton-Century-Crofts.

Zahn-Waxler, C. (1993). Warriors and worriers: Gender and psychopathology. *Development and Psychopathology, 5,* 79–89.

Zigler, E., & Phillips, L. (1961). Social competence and outcome in psychiatric disorder. *Journal of Abnormal and Social Psychology, 63,* 264–271.

Zoccolillo, M. (1993). Gender and development of Conduct Disorder. *Development and Psychopathology, 5,* 65–78.

PART IV

DEVELOPMENTAL DISORDERS

CHAPTER 7

Mental Retardation

Benjamin L. Handen

University of Pittsburgh Medical Center
Western Psychiatric Institute and Clinic

There is a considerable history of educational and psychological treatment interventions for children and adults with mental retardation. In modern times, such attempts can be dated back to the work of Edouard Seguin in 19th-century France, who led a movement emphasizing that individuals with a variety of handicapping conditions could be taught if provided appropriate training. This movement soon took root in the United States, beginning in the middle of the 19th century. As a result, a number of schools for children and adults with mental retardation were established. These early institutions were based on the principle of "moral education," which assumed that through education, individuals with mental retardation could be elevated to a level of normal human existence. However, within a few decades it became apparent that this experiment had been a failure and that only a small percentage of individuals with mental retardation were able to return successfully to society and independent living situations. Gradually, institutions began to change in character, serving less of an educational and more of a custodial purpose as a means of protecting individuals with mental retardation from society (Wolfensberger, 1969).

A century later, we once again find ourselves in a period when there is considerable optimism regarding treatment options for individuals with mental retardation. The deinstitutionalization movement of the 1960s; the court cases and the passing of state and federal mandates for the provision of services to preschoolers and school-age children with mental retardation in the 1970s and 1980s; and the inclusion movement of the 1990s have all brought about impressive change in the service delivery system for this population. There are a wide range of areas in which treatment efforts may now be focused. Some interventions are directed toward the child, while others emphasize the provision of services to families or teachers of children with mental retardation. The present chapter addresses a number of specific types of child-focused interventions, including educational efforts, skill development (e.g., social skills, communication skills), management of behavior problems (including specific interventions and treatments for behavioral problems that tend to be specific to children with mental retardation), and psychopharmacological interventions. In addition, parent training and community-based interventions are covered. Finally, the chapter examines a selected group of nontraditional interventions.

DEFINITION AND CLASSIFICATION OF MENTAL RETARDATION

"Mental retardation" refers to a particular state of functioning beginning prior to age 18 in which limitations in intelligence coexist with deficits in adaptive skills (American Association on Mental Retardation [AAMR], 1992). However, this definition has been revised a number of times during the past few decades, in response to our changing understanding of the disorder and to various consumer, professional, political, and social forces. For example, in 1959 the American Assocation on Mental Deficiency (AAMD), as the AAMR was then called, specified that individuals with IQ scores one standard deviation or more below the mean of 100 were to be considered to have mental retardation (Heber, 1959). Because most IQ tests have a mean of 100 and a standard deviation of 15–16 points, this affected a significant portion of the U. S. adult and child population (up to 16%, or 32 million people). In 1973, the cutoff point was changed to two standard deviations below the mean (IQ below 70), thereby lowering the incidence of mental retardation to about 3%, or 6 million individuals (Grossman, 1973). A 1983 revision of the AAMD definition provided greater clarity for clinicians working in the field: "Mental retardation refers to significantly subaverage intellectual functioning resulting in or associated with impairments in adaptive behavior and manifested during the developmental period" (Grossman, 1983, p. 11). Three specific factors were involved in this definition: (1) an IQ score below 70, (2) associated adaptive deficits, and (3) the occurrence of deficits prior to age 18. This definition was not without some controversy, however, due to disagreement among professionals regarding both the definition of adaptive behavior as well as how to assess it (Zigler & Hodapp, 1986).

In 1992, the AAMR proposed and adopted this new definition of mental retardation:

Mental retardation refers to substantial limitations in present functioning. It is characterized by significantly subaverage intellectual functioning, existing concurrently with related limitations in two or more of the following applicable adaptive skills areas: communication,

self-care, home living, social skills, community use, self-direction, health and safety, functional academics, leisure, and work. Mental retardation manifests before age 18. (AAMR, 1992, p. 5)

Four assumptions were considered essential to the application of this definition:

1. Valid assessment considers cultural and linguistic diversity as well as differences in communication and behavioral factors;
2. The existence of limitations in adaptive skills occurs within the context of community environments typical of the individual's age peers and is indexed to the person's individualized needs for supports;
3. Specific adaptive limitations often coexist with strengths in other adaptive skills or other personal capabilities; and
4. With appropriate supports over a sustained period, the life functioning of the person with mental retardation will generally improve. (AAMR, 1992, p. 5)

Three aspects of this new definition remain controversial. First, the IQ range has once again been changed, to include individuals with an IQ standard score of approximately 70–75 or below. Second, there is a requirement that up to 10 areas of adaptive functioning be assessed; yet there are still no agreed-upon parameters for assessing adaptive behavior in a number of these areas (MacMillan, Gresham, & Siperstein, 1995). Finally, the AAMR has eliminated the previously used classification system, which divides individuals with mental retardation into four categories based upon level of cognitive functioning. This change is discussed below.

A number of classification systems have been developed for individuals with mental retardation during the past few decades. Such systems are needed because of the heterogeneity of this population. They serve as a means of distinguishing among subgroups, which enables clinicians to determine the level and intensity of required services and to examine long-term prognosis and treatment outcome. The two most common classification systems involve division by either functional ability or etiology. There are three commonly used classification systems based upon functional ability. One is based upon the 1973 and 1983 AAMD definitions of mental retardation, which divided severity of disability into four categories (mild, moderate, severe, and profound). This classification system continues to be widely accepted and used; for example, the American Psychiatric Association (APA, 1994) has retained these four categories of cognitive functioning to categorize individuals with Mental Retardation in the most recent revision of the *Diagnostic and Statistical Manual of Mental Disorders* DSM-IV). Individuals who function within the mild range of mental retardation constitute approximately 89% of those diagnosed with mental retardation. This group has also been classified within many educational systems as "educable mentally retarded" (EMR). Individuals with moderate mental retardation account for approximately 6% of those with mental retardation. Within many educational systems this group has been labeled as "trainable mentally retarded" (TMR). Individuals with severe mental retardation make up approximately 3.5% of the population of children and adults with mental retardation. Finally, fewer than 1.5% of children and adults with mental retardation fall in the category of profound mental retardation.

In the 1992 revision of its classification system, the AAMR placed individuals with mental retardation along a continuum of needed levels of support (i.e., intermittent, limited, extensive, and pervasive). For example, an individual with mental retardation may be described as "a 10-year-old female with mental retardation who requires limited supports in self-care and extensive supports in communication." Although it might be assumed that a child diagnosed with mild mental retardation will require intermittent supports in most areas, this is not necessarily true. For example, a child with an IQ of 65 may require no assistance in self-care and only intermittent supports in social skills, but because of a severe expressive language disorder may require extensive supports in communication. Such functional descriptions are designed to assist clinicians and educators to plan for an individual's service needs.

Finally, educators have developed their own classification system for purposes of program placement. Terms such as EMR (children functioning in the mild range of mental retardation) or TMR (children functioning within the moderate range of mental retardation) have been used for a number of years. Yet, with the growing trend toward inclusionary practices, these labels provide little guidance for classroom placement. Instead, districts may gradually move toward more functional descriptors of a child's needs as placement becomes less often based upon level of cognitive functioning. Instead, appropriate

services follow the child, who may be served in any number of settings (including regular education classrooms). It is important that clinicians who assess and treat children with mental retardation understand the different classification systems in order to communicate with professionals from a range of disciplines. Table 7.1 contrasts the three most commonly used classification systems.

An alternative classification system divides individuals into categories based upon etiology. It has been generally accepted that between 25% and 50% of individuals with mental retardation have an organic etiology for their cognitive and adaptive skills deficits (see Zigler & Hodapp, 1986). The remaining group of individuals is assumed to have mental retardation stemming from psychosocial or familial factors. However, the AAMR (1992) publication on the definition and classification of mental retardation suggests that this two-factor classification system is no longer appropriate. First, as Masland (1988) argues, the fact that there is no known cause for the presence of mental retardation does not necessarily mean that a organic etiological explanation does not exist. It may be that our knowledge and technology are not yet advanced enough to detect many of the causes of mental retardation. For example, it was not until 1969 that fragile-X syndrome was discovered (Lubbs, 1969). This syndrome may account for a considerable number of males with mental retardation and is caused by what appears to be a pinching of the tips of the long arm of the X chromosome. Just as recently, there has been a greater appreciation of the potential adverse effects of lead poisoning, even at subclinical levels. Raloff (1982) estimates that as many as 20% of inner-city minority preschoolers may have cognitive or learning deficits due to lead intake. Second, McLaren and Bryson (1987) conducted a review of 13 epidemiological studies and found that in approximately 50% of cases of mental retardation, there were multiple possible causal factors, some of which might be considered familial and others organic. Therefore, the AAMR (1992, p. 71) proposed a multifactorial approach to etiology involving the following four categories:

1. Biomedical: factors that relate to biologic processes, such as genetic disorders or nutrition.
2. Social: factors that relate to social and family interaction, such as stimulation and adult responsiveness.

TABLE 7.1.   Classification of Mental Retardation

Level of mental retardation (APA, 1994)	Educational classification	Support required (AAMR, 1992)[a]	IQ range	Percentage of persons with MR
Mild	Educable	Intermittent	55–69	89.0
Moderate	Trainable	Limited	40–55	6.0
Severe	Severe or trainable (dependent)	Extensive	25–39	3.5
Profound	Profound or custodial	Pervasive	< 25	1.5

[a]Intensities of support do not necessarily correlate directly with other classification systems. For example, although an individual with mild mental retardation is likely to require intermittent support in many areas, specific areas of strength may require no support, and specific areas of weakness may require limited or extensive support.

Note. Adapted from Sattler (1988, p. 648). Copyright 1988 by Jerome M. Sattler, Publisher. Adapted by permission.

3. Behavioral: factors that relate to potentially causal behaviors, such as dangerous (injurious) activities or maternal substance abuse.
4. Educational: factors that relate to the availability of educational supports that promote mental development and the development of adaptive skills.

PSYCHIATRIC DISORDERS IN CHILDREN WITH MENTAL RETARDATION

It is estimated that between 20% and 35% of noninstitutionalized children and adults with mental retardation have psychiatric diagnoses or behavior problems (Parsons, May, & Menolascino, 1984). Such estimates are even greater for those residing in residential settings, ranging up to 59% of this population (Hill & Bruininks, 1984). Various factors appear to affect prevalence estimates, including gender (Koller, Richardson, Katz, & McLaren, 1983), age (Jacobson, 1982), level of mental retardation (Koller et al., 1983), and psychiatric diagnostic criteria (Fraser, Leudar, Gray, & Campbell, 1986). Among children and adolescents with mental retardation, rates of behavior problems and/or psychiatric disorders have been found to be four to five times those of typically developing children and adolescents (Rutter, Graham, & Yule, 1970; Koller et al., 1983). Common maladaptive behaviors have been reported to include disruptive behavior, injury to self, injury to others, damage to property, and breaking of rules (Hill & Bruininks, 1984). Jacobson (1982) surveyed over 30,000 individuals with mental retardation residing in New York State to document the extent of behavior problems; 8,784 of these individuals were under the age of 21. Table 7.2 provides a summary of the overall rates of behavior problems from the Jacobson survey, based upon age and cognitive functioning level. In general, there appears to be an increase in the percentage of children and adolescents with mental retardation and behavior problems as children age and cognitive levels decrease (i.e., those with lower IQs have a greater percentage of behavior problems). The only exception to this finding involves children and adolescents functioning within the profound range of mental retardation.

Children with mental retardation experience the full range of psychiatric disorders (Eaton & Menolascino, 1982). For example, it is estimated that between 9% and 18% of children with mental retardation meet diagnostic criteria for Attention-Deficit/Hyperactivity Disorder (ADHD) (Ando & Yoshimura, 1978; Epstein, Cullinan, & Gadow, 1986; Jacobson, 1982)—three to four times the prevalence rate in typically developing children. By contrast, little is known about the rate of depression in children and adolescents with mental retardation. In a 1971 study of all persons with mental retardation in a South London district, none of the 140 children and adolescents (15 years of age or less) with IQs less than 50 met diagnostic criteria for an affective disorder (Corbett, 1979). Conversely, in a study of children with mental retardation admitted to inpatient psychiatric settings, up to 8% were diagnosed with a depressive disorder (Matson, Barrett, & Helsel, 1988). Diagnosis of psychiatric disorders in children and adolescents with mental retardation often requires that the clinician rely on observable behavior rather than self-report (MacLean, 1993).

TABLE 7.2. Percentage of Behavior Problems by Age and Level of Functioning

Cognitive level	Age	*n* (cases)	Percentage with behavior problems
Mild mental retardation	0–12	708	40%
Mild mental retardation	13–21	818	55%
Moderate mental retardation	0–12	640	47%
Moderate mental retardation	13–21	1,163	60%
Severe mental retardation	0–12	652	54%
Severe mental retardation	13–21	1,208	65%
Profound mental retardation	0–12	1,056	38%
Profound mental retardation	13–21	2,539	57%

Note. From Jacobson (1982, p. 129). Copyright 1982 by Pergamon Press, Ltd. Reprinted by permission.

In general it is accepted that diagnostic criteria for psychiatric disorders, such as those found in DSM-IV (APA, 1994), can be reasonably applied to children and adolescents functioning at or above the mild range of mental retardation (IQs above 50). However, these criteria may be less appropriate or useful for those functioning below that level (MacLean, 1993).

A number of diagnoses or conditions are often associated with specific maladaptive behaviors. For example, children with fragile-X syndrome typically function in the mild to moderate range of mental retardation and often exhibit attentional deficits, hyperactivity, hand flapping, hand biting, perseverative speech, preoccupation with inanimate objects, shyness, and poor social interaction (Hagerman & Sobesky, 1989). Lesch–Nyhan syndrome is often associated with severe self-injury (Nyhan, 1976), whereas children with Prader–Willi syndrome have an abnormality in the hypothalamic region of the brain, resulting in insatiable overeating (Reber, 1992). Rett's Disorder is typically characterized by regression in skills following a normal early course of development and the subsequent appearance of stereotyped hand movements (APA, 1994). Children with Autistic Disorder often engage in a range of maladaptive behaviors, such as stereotyped and repetitive motor mannerisms (e.g., hand or finger flapping), impairments in social interactions, and deficits in communication (e.g., delayed expressive language development, stereotyped and repetitive use of language)(APA, 1994). The presence of specific maladaptive behaviors during an assessment may suggest that a particular disorder or syndrome be considered. In addition, knowledge of such disorders and any associated behavioral deficits and excesses can greatly in-

form the development of an appropriate treatment plan.

EDUCATIONAL SERVICES

The most common treatment interventions offered to children with mental retardation are school-based educational services. Toward this end, an important group of laws has been enacted guaranteeing education for children with mental retardation. Perhaps the most important piece of federal legislation was Public Law 94–142, which was enacted in 1975 and stressed the concepts of "normalization" and "least restrictive environment." Later laws, such as Public Law 99–457, which was enacted in 1986, recognized the need for comprehensive early intervention services and enhanced educational services for infants and young children with disabilities (including mental retardation). More recently still, there has been a growing movement to include children with mental retardation in our schools and communities (the Individuals with Disabilities Education Act of 1991; see Schive, 1995). This is exemplified by the inclusion of children with mental retardation full-time in classrooms with typically developing peers. Given that school-based services clearly represent the most intensive and extended treatment interventions for children with mental retardation, it is reasonable to ask whether such services are indeed effective.

Early Intervention

Children with mental retardation generally follow a developmental pattern similar to that of their typically developing peers. However, the rate and limits of a child's development will be based upon a range of factors, including the severity of the handicapping condition, family support, and type of programming offered (Guralnick & Bricker, 1987). A small group of early studies documented that the provision of educational services prior to age six might have a significant impact upon both the rate and limits of development in children with mental retardation. For example, Skeels (1966) reported the results of a 30-year follow-up of two groups of institutionalized infants—one group was removed from an orphanage at 18 months of age and transferred to an institution where they were cared for by a group of women with mental retardation, and the other group remained in the orphanage, where they received little stimulation. The children in the two groups were comparable, with cognitive functioning ranging from mental retardation to the low-average range of intelligence. At 2-year follow-ups, the children raised in the institution had gained an average of 28 IQ points while those remaining in the orphanage had lost an average of 26 IQ points (Skodak & Skeels, 1949). At 30-year follow-up, the 13 individuals in the "treatment" group were all self-supporting and living in the community, with a 12th-grade median educational level. Eight of the 12 "control" individuals remained institutionalized (one had died), with a 3rd-grade median educational level. Although this study has significant methodological weaknesses, such as the comparability of the two groups and the attribution of the significant differences between them to early experiences (Ramey & Baker-Ward, 1982), it provided compelling documentation of the ability to affect the rate of development positively.

A study by Kirk (1958) compared the progress of 81 preschoolers with mental retardation (IQs from 45 to 80) who were assigned to one of four interventions: a community-based preschool program, an institutional preschool program, community living with no services, and institutionalization with no services. Both groups who attended preschool programs outperformed their peers on a range of developmental measures. However, these differences failed to be observed at a 1-year follow-up after the first year of elementary school.

The typical early intervention program uses a developmental model to guide educational objectives in conjunction with a behavioral teaching technology. The service delivery models fall into three categories: home-based, center-based, or a combination of the two. According to Gu-

ralnick and Bricker (1987), although there is an extensive literature on early intervention, interpreting the efficacy of these services is difficult because of numerous methodological problems. First is the problem of creating homogeneous groupings of children with mental retardation. Only the literatures on children with Down syndrome and with Autistic Disorder (see Newsom, Chapter 8, this volume) have been able to address this issue. Otherwise, groups studied encompass a wide range of disorders across all levels of mental retardation. Second, many studies have lacked independent staff members to assess and observe children, have failed to demonstrate interrater reliability, have neglected to use tools sensitive to and standardized for children with mental retardation, and have failed to establish clear criteria for inclusion of children. Third, random assignment to a treatment or control group has been the exception, as there have been ethical issues in withholding services to children with developmental disabilities.

The interpretation of the findings of this literature must be tempered with an understanding of these methodological limitations. In their review of this literature, Guralnick and Bricker (1987) divide studies into those focusing on children with Down syndrome and those studying preschoolers with other biologically based delays. The findings of the research on preschoolers with Down syndrome are impressive, especially in view of earlier work, which has clearly documented that although gradual improvement in cognitive development occurs, the rate of development among children with Down syndrome slows progressively over time. Consequently, infants with Down syndrome evidence a considerable overlap in developmental functioning with typically developing infants, but experience a general decline on measures of cognitive functioning through early childhood (Carr, 1975; Morgan, 1979).

The results of work evaluating the efficacy of early intervention in children with Down syndrome strongly suggest that this decline in cognitive functioning can be reduced or entirely eliminated. Such results have been obtained not only in less well-controlled studies (e.g., Kysela, Hillyard, McDonald, & Ahlsten-Taylor, 1981), in which only pre- and posttreatment measures were used, but in a number of studies in which control groups were utilized (e.g., Connolly, Morgan, Russell, & Richardson, 1980; Rynders & Horrobin, 1980; Aronson & Fallstrom, 1977). Similar results have been noted in other developmental domains, but the results have been less consistent across studies and not as robust. Less is known, however, about the length of time early intervention should be provided or the age at which such services should first be offered. For example, Aronson and Fallstrom (1977) found fewer differences between their treatment and control groups at a 1-year follow-up than at the conclusion of their initial intervention. Conversely, Connolly, Morgan, and Russell (1984) documented continued gains at a 4-year follow-up in a group of children who had received early intervention services prior to age 3. Clunies-Ross (1979) found that children who received services earlier obtained higher scores on developmental measures. However, a number of methodological issues (e.g., a correlation between the provision of earlier services and parental motivation) make it difficult to draw conclusions about the issue of timing (Guralnick & Bricker, 1987).

In contrast to the research in early intervention services among children with Down syndrome, the work conducted among children with other biologically based delays is less compelling (Guralnick & Bricker, 1987). The vast majority of studies have utilized basic pre- and posttreatment measures without a control group. The few studies that were reasonably well controlled documented only modest gains in developmental measures. For example, Goodman, Cecil, and Barker (1984) reported a mean increase of 7 points on standardized intelligence tests in their treatment group versus the control group. A prospective study conducted by Moxley-Haegert and Serbin (1983) examined the effectiveness of a parent education program. After 1 month of treatment, the treatment group had made significant gains over a control group on the Bayley Scales of Infant Development Motor scale (but not on the mental scale)—gains that were maintained at a 1-year follow-up. Guralnick and Bricker (1987) emphasize that the small number of children participating in many of these studies did not allow for the separate analysis of such factors as cognitive functioning level. For example, though gains were documented among children with severe or profound mental retardation, such gains were proportionally small (e.g., Bricker & Down, 1980; Sandow, Clarke, Cox, & Stewart, 1981). In addition, gains in curriculum-based skills did not necessarily generalize to measures of general cognitive development (Moxley-Haegert & Serbin, 1983; Revill & Blunden, 1979).

It is also felt that changes on curriculum-based measures or general cognitive assessment tools often fail to provide a thorough picture of the positive effects of early intervention efforts. For example, few studies address gains in such areas as social competence, emotional stability, parent–child relationships, or overall family functioning and stress. Dunst and his colleagues have examined the efficacy of family-oriented early intervention services in a number of such collateral areas (e.g., Dunst, Trivette, & Jodry, in press). These areas are addressed below under "Community-Based Interventions."

Primary and Secondary School Education

Once children with mental retardation reach school age, various placement options are often available. The most restrictive settings include residential treatment, private programs, and center-based programs (entire schools devoted to serving children with special needs). Less restrictive options begin with special education classes, which are located within a regular school but provide few or no opportunities for children with mental retardation to interact with typically developing peers. In many settings, children with special needs are integrated (or mainstreamed) into nonacademic classes such as gym, art, music, and homeroom, where academic demands are at a minimum. More recently, the inclusion movement's emphasis on placing children with special needs in a regular classroom for all subject areas has gained support. Any required ancillary services are provided in the classroom, and the classroom teacher is provided with consultation in adapting the curriculum for each child with special needs.

The goals of inclusion go beyond addressing academic skills. For example, it is hoped that the inclusion of children with special needs will improve levels of acceptance for such children in the community, and that typically developing peers will be more open to supporting policies that welcome individuals with various handicapping conditions into the workplace, churches, and neighborhoods. There is certainly ample evidence that individuals with severe handicaps can learn to do meaningful work in their communities, such as working in offices or for industry. For example, Brown (1995) describes a program in Madison, Wisconsin, in which funds for sheltered workshops were successfully transferred to support the placement of young adults with mental retardation in meaningful jobs in the community. The role of the schools was to provide on-the-job training during the final years of educational training. Brown's work illustrates that prior thinking regarding the abilities of individuals with mental retardation must constantly be challenged.

Hocutt (1996) has reviewed close to 100 papers that have examined the effectiveness of special education during the past 25 years, including studies comparing various placement options. The review covers a range of diagnostic categories, including learning disabilities, emotional/behavioral disorders, sensory impairments, and mental retardation. Hocutt concludes that much of the research on special education efficacy has significant methodological problems (e.g., small sample sizes, nonrandom assignment, inappropriate dependent measures). In addition, many of the studies that have been used to criticize traditional special education in favor of more inclusive education models are based on outdated research. For example, Carlberg and Kavale (1980) conducted a frequently cited meta-analysis of 50 studies comparing general versus special education placement. Overall, they found better outcome in general education classrooms for students with mild mental retardation. Yet considerable changes in the definition of EMR have occurred during the past three decades, bringing into question the generalizability of studies conducted prior to 1980 to today's special education students.

A later and more extensive study of students with mild mental retardation found classroom success to be predicted by such factors as the active involvement of students in teacher-directed and supervised instruction, and the use of cooperative learning approaches (in which children with delays were involved in frequent interactions with typically developing peers)(Kaufman, Agard, & Semmel, 1985). Conversely, academic success for typically developing students was best predicted by family background (e.g., parents' education, socioeconomic status). A further examination of more recent research suggests that the characteristics of the most effective educational interventions include intensive and reasonably individualized instruction, along with frequent monitoring of student progress. Most of these interventions require considerable resources, such as smaller class sizes, consultation, increased teacher planning time, the addition of teacher aides in the classroom, and intensive training. Overall, this research suggests that instruction, rather than placement, is the critical factor in both academic

and social success for special education students. In other words, what occurs in a particular academic setting may be more important than the setting itself. Hocutt (1996) concludes that the research to date fails to support inclusion as a model for all students with disabilities. However, if provided with adequate resources, schools should be better able to instruct a growing number of special education students within the general education classrooms.

SKILLS DEVELOPMENT: TECHNIQUES FOR PROGRAMMED INSTRUCTION

One helpful way to understand many of the behavior problems observed in children and adults with mental retardation is to view these as specific skills deficits. In fact, a primary focus of positive programming during the past decade has been on the need to include the teaching of communication and other skills to individuals with severe behavior problems as a primary component of any intervention plans (e.g., Donnellan, LaVigna, Negri-Shoeltz, & Fasbender, 1988). For example, a classic study by Carr and Durand (1985) demonstrated the power of teaching functional communication skills to a group of adolescents who exhibited aggression and self-injurious behavior (SIB). A functional analysis of these behaviors found that aggression and SIB served to communicate the desire to terminate or avoid tasks, and that they occurred most often during periods of low adult attention and high task difficulty. The adolescents were taught either to say, "I don't understand," if an error was made during a difficult task, or to ask, "Am I doing good work?" during easier tasks. The rates of aggression and SIB were functionally related to the use of these new communicative skills.

The teaching of new skills—whether they be basic academic concepts, self-help skills, social skills, or communication skills—requires considerable precision. Children and adolescents with mental retardation must learn in small, incremental steps. As such, an entire technology of instruction has been developed to teach new behaviors, to bring behaviors under stimulus control, and to promote generalization. Below is only a brief overview of these techniques. The reader is referred to texts such as that by Sulzer-Azaroff and Mayer (1991), or chapters such as the one by Huguenin, Weidenman, and Mulick

(1991), for greater detail on programmed instruction.

A principle common to all of the following procedures is that of "errorless learning" in which the learner experiences a minimum of errors. For children with mental retardation this can be particularly important, as these children often have long histories of failure and may tend to give up easily when faced with challenging tasks (e.g., Carr & Durand, 1985). In addition, stimulus control procedures are important tools when working with children with mental retardation; this population is felt to be more likely to respond to irrelevant stimuli than their typically developing peers, because of a tendency to attend to fewer aspects of the environment (Zeaman & House, 1963).

Shaping

Shaping involves the teaching of a new behavior via reinforcement of successive approximations of the target behavior. Such behaviors either do not exist in the child's repertoire or occur so infrequently that there are few opportunities to reinforce the behavior (Sulzer-Azaroff & Mayer, 1991). For example, this technique has been used to teach dressing skills (Watson & Uzzell, 1980), social skills (Foxx, McMorrow, Bittle, & Ness, 1986), conversational skills (Minkin et al., 1976) and feeding skills (Riordan, Iwata, Finney, Wohl, & Stanley, 1984) to individuals with mental retardation.

Shaping requires that the instructor start with an existing skill or behavior and gradually reinforce closer approximations to the desired outcome. For example, a child may at first be reinforced for saying any sound when asked whether he or she wants to eat. Later, only the sound "eee" is accepted; finally, "eat" is required before a meal is served. Shaping has also been used with children with histories of food refusal who are initially required to eat a single bite. Over time, the requirement is gradually increased (two bites, three bites, etc.) until any entire meal is offered to the child (Handen, Mandell, & Russo, 1986). Shaping has been used to address behavior problems as well. For example, we (Handen, Apolito, & Seltzer, 1984) used a changing-criterion design to decrease repetitive speech in an autistic adolescent. The adolescent was initially reinforced even if relatively high rates of repetitive speech occurred. Over time, the incidents of repetitive speech permitted to earn reinforcers were gradually decreased until a rate of zero per day was attained.

Task Analysis

Task analysis is the breaking down of a complex skill or sequence of behaviors into its component behaviors (Sulzer-Azaroff & Mayer, 1991). Each component is listed in the order of occurrence. For example, the following is a 10-step task analysis for putting on a shirt:

1. Sit on chair.
2. Place flattened-out shirt on lap.
3. Make sure side with label is on top.
4. Grasp bottom of shirt with both hands.
5. Pull shirt over head.
6. Push head through appropriate hole.
7. Push right arm through appropriate hole.
8. Push left arm through appropriate hole.
9. Grasp bottom of shirt with both hands.
10. Pull shirt down.

Each analysis must be tailored to the individual child, based upon his or her own skill level. In other words, if a particular step is too difficult for a child, the instructor may need to break the steps down into smaller components; steps that are too easy may be combined with other steps. Skills can also be broken down into more basic components, often in a developmental sequence. For example, the Carolina Curriculum for Preschoolers with Special Needs (Johnson-Martin, Attermeier, & Hacker, 1990) provides curriculum sequences in a range of development areas, such as attention and memory, size and number concepts, and receptive language skills. Several published assessment tools and curricula provide task analyses for teaching a range of skills, including self-help and community living skills (e.g., Cooke, Apollini, & Sundberg, 1981; Cuvo, 1978; Popovich, 1981; Slentz, Close, Benz, & Taylor, 1982), preschool or preacademic skills (e.g., Johnson-Martin et al., 1990), and vocational and prevocational skills (Gold, 1980).

Chaining

Once a task analysis has been developed, the individual steps are taught by means of chaining, in which the components of a task analysis are combined into a sequence. Tasks are typically taught in either a forward method (forward chaining), a backward method (backward chaining), or a concurrent method (teaching all steps simultaneously). The various methods refer to which step is to be taught first. For example, teaching a child to put on a shirt (see the sample task analysis above) is easiest if backward chaining is used. The instructor places the shirt over the child's head, puts the child's arms in the sleeves, and then teaches the child to pull the shirt down. Once this step is mastered, the next prior step can be taught. Backward chaining takes advantage of two behavioral concepts: those of the conditioned reinforcer and the discriminative stimulus. As completion of the target step is frequently paired with a reinforcer such as praise or food, the step itself may become a conditioned reinforcer. Consequently, completion of one step may be reinforced by completion of the subsequent step (e.g., because pulling the shirt down is consistently followed by praise and a hug, completion of this step eventually takes on reinforcing properties and serves to reinforce completion of the previous step in the chain). Similarly, the frequent pairing of steps that lead to reinforcement may result in one step's becoming a discriminative stimulus for the subsequent step. In other words, it becomes a signal for the step to follow.

Prompting and Fading

Prompting and fading have been used to teach a wide range of skills and concepts to children and adults with mental retardation, including academic skills (e.g., Reese, 1971), self-help skills (e.g., Freagon & Rotatori, 1982), athletic skills (e.g., Luyben, Funk, Morgan, Clark, & Delulio, 1986), and social skills (e.g., Odom, Chandler, Ostrosky, McConnell, & Reaney, 1992). The first step is to bring the target behavior under stimulus control of the prompt. For example, a child can be taught to point reliably to the letter A when the instructor does so, in order for the child to begin to learn letter recognition skills. Many types of prompts are available to the instructor, including physical guidance, pointing, modeling, verbal cues, and visual cues (stimulus shaping). Physical guidance involves guiding the individual's hands to complete a task or step of a task (e.g., physically guiding a child to turn off the water as the last step of a handwashing task analysis). Pointing prompts are often seen as less intensive or intrusive than the provision of physical guidance. For example, the instructor may point to the color red in order to prompt the child to do so as well. Verbal cues, in which the instructor provides a simple instruction to prompt the task or step (e.g., "Pull down your

shirt," "Turn off the water") may be among the least intensive prompts. Other prompts, such as visual cues, do not necessarily require that an instructor be present. For example, a stove can be color-coded so that the burners and associated knobs match, in order to make it easier for an individual to turn on the correct burner.

Once a target behavior is under stimulus control, systematic elimination of the prompt can begin. Fading is a technique frequently used for this purpose. For example, Young, West, Howard, and Whitney (1986) used a fading procedure called "graduated guidance" (initially providing physical guidance, and gradually fading guidance with lessened pressure or changing the locus of guidance) to teach independent dressing to developmentally disabled children. Piazza and Fisher (1991) successfully used fading to address sleep problems in four children with developmental disabilities. First, a baseline was obtained to identify the exact time of sleep onset. Then bedtime was reestablished using the time of sleep onset plus 30 minutes (i.e., if a child typically fell asleep at 10:00 P.M., the new bedtime would be 10:30 P.M.). Then the established bedtime was gradually advanced until an acceptable time for sleep onset was obtained. Another example of eliminating prompts is a technique called "graduated prompting." This involves using progressively more intrusive prompts as needed, starting with the least intrusive (e.g., verbal prompts) and subsequently moving to more intrusive prompts (e.g., modeling/pointing and physical guidance). For example, Freagon and Rotatori (1982) used such a three-step graduated prompting strategy to teach toothbrushing and handwashing to group home residents. Residents were initially prompted with a verbal prompt (e.g., "pick up the toothbrush") and given a few seconds to respond. Correct responding was praised, while nonresponding resulted in a combination of a verbal and gestural prompt. Finally, physical assistance was provided if needed.

An additional technique for decreasing a child's dependence upon prompts is called "stimulus delay" (Touchette, 1971). In stimulus delay, the prompt or cue remains unchanged in its intensity, but is delayed in time as the child begins to anticipate the prompt and correctly responds. For example, Zane, Handen, Mason, and Geffin (1984) taught four adults with mental retardation to identify international community symbols (e.g., the international symbol for "toilet"). Initially, when a set of five symbols was placed before a subject, the examiner said,

"Point to _____" while simultaneously pointing to the correct symbol. Once the subject was consistently responding correctly, a 1-second delay was placed between the statement "Point to _____" and the pointing prompt. As the subject learned that he or she could be reinforced for either waiting for the pointing prompt or correctly anticipating the prompt and pointing prior to the examiner, the length of the delay was gradually increased up to 5 seconds. Acquisition occurred when a subject consistently and correctly anticipated the examiner's pointing prompt. Stimulus delay has been used to teach a wide range of skills, including assembling bicycle brakes, bedmaking, instruction following, and color discrimination. A review of this literature (Handen & Zane, 1987) provides a summary of procedural variations used with stimulus delay, as well as recommendations regarding which procedures appear to be most successful for working with children with mental retardation.

Generalization

Programming for generalization is a major focus of programmed instruction, as research indicates that both children and adults with mental retardation often have difficulty demonstrating acquired skills outside of the instructional setting. For example, Garcia, Bullet, and Rust (1977) taught two children with mental retardation to use sentences containing five-word chains and to describe a series of pictures. However, these newly acquired skills did not transfer to other settings until they were specifically trained across all environments. Similarly, Bruder (1986) taught parents of toddlers at risk for developmental delays a set of behavioral techniques with which to instruct their children. The parents were found to make best use of those skills that were trained in more than one setting.

Sulzer-Azaroff and Mayer (1991) suggest a number of ways to promote generalization. One option is modifying behaviors sequentially. This involves specifically teaching target behaviors across environments (e.g., home, school, and community) and individuals (e.g., teachers, peers, and parents). A second option is training to naturally supportive conditions—that is, teaching behaviors that are likely to be supported in the natural environment. For example, Haring, Roger, Lee, Breen, and Gaylord-Ross (1986) taught three moderately handicapped children conversational skills by first interviewing typically developing peers to identify age-appropri-

ate conversational patterns. This resulted in more effective generalization than had been documented by other investigators. Another option is to insure the training of sufficient exemplars. This simply involves providing instruction in as many settings or situations as possible, or with as many different people as possible, to promote generalization. Training loosely—in other words, being less precise regarding how stimuli are presented and which correct responses are allowed—is still another way to promote generalization. For example, a teacher may intentionally request a response in different ways (e.g., "What's your name?", "Tell me your name," "Who are you?") or reinforce a variety of correct answers (e.g., "My name is John," "I'm John"). The method of "incidental teaching" utilizes the concept of training loosely by using natural, unplanned opportunities to teach new skills. For example, McGee, Krantz, and McClannahan (1985) found that preschoolers with autism were able to generalize their use of prepositions if training occurred whenever children spontaneously asked for an item and were subsequently prompted to use prepositions.

Using indiscriminable antecedent and consequential contingencies promotes generalization, because individuals are unable to discriminate the contingencies in effect. For example, Baer, Williams, Osnes, and Stokes (1985) describe promoting play activities with a preschooler. Initially, the child was reinforced for saying that she was going to play with one of three target toys, but play increased only temporarily. Subsequently, the child was reinforced only for playing with one of the toys after saying she would. Not only did play increase for the three target toys, but play increased for nontarget toys as well (generalization) despite the fact that the child continued to be reinforced only for stating her intent to play with nontarget toys (not for actually playing with them). Finally, programming common stimuli encourages generalization by using stimuli or cues in the training setting that are similar to those in the real world. For example, Aeschleman and Schladenhauffen (1984) taught shopping skills in a simulated grocery store to adolescents with severe mental retardation. The adolescents were able to maintain their acquired skills in the community.

TEACHING SELF-HELP SKILLS

The teaching of self-help skills is of primary importance for teachers, clinicians, and families of children with mental retardation. The acquisition of such skills significantly increases an individual's independence and allows for greater involvement in the community. For example, toilet training is often a prerequisite for enrollment in a number of school- and community-based programs. Greater independence in the home may lessen family stress and the amount of one-to-one time required by the child with mental retardation. The development of more advanced self-help skills, such as the ability to shop for food, follow a recipe, or balance a checkbook, may play a significant role in determining the type of independent living situation options made available to an individual.

Behavioral techniques have been used for a number of years to teach basic skills such as toileting, feeding, personal hygiene, and dressing. There is a wealth of published research demonstrating the efficacy of such procedures in this area (see Reid, Wilson, & Faw, 1991). Many of the techniques used in the instruction of self-help skills are covered above in the section on programmed instruction.

Toilet Training

A number of interventions have been developed to address toilet training in children and adults with mental retardation during the past three decades. The basic characteristics of most behavioral toileting programs include (1) keeping a toileting chart; (2) toileting at scheduled times on a consistent basis, once baseline data have been obtained; (3) providing reinforcement for successful voiding and being "dry"; and, in some cases, 4) providing specific consequences following accidents. In addition, behavioral toileting programs have focused on teaching the natural sequence of toileting behaviors (e.g., pulling pants down, sitting on the toilet, voiding, pulling pants up, flushing).

A toileting manual written for parents of children with mental retardation (Baker, Brightman, Heifetz, & Murphy, 1977) incorporates most of these principles. The initial step is to take a 1- to 2-week toileting baseline to determine the most likely times when a child's bladder will be full and voiding will occur. From these data, appropriate times to prompt a child to use the toilet can be determined. Placing the child on the toilet when the bladder is full increases the likelihood that successful voiding will occur and that the child will learn to associate bladder fullness with using the toilet. Adjustments to the toileting schedule can be made, based upon data from an ongoing toileting chart. Immediate reinforcement of successful voiding is also provided. Figure 7.1 is a sample toileting chart from Baker et al. (1977). Empirical support for behavioral toileting programs is also provided by Mahoney, Van Wagenen, and Meyerson (1971) and Van Wagenen, Meyerson, Kerr, and Mahoney (1969).

One particularly well-known toilet training program, developed by Azrin and Foxx (1971), uses more intensive training procedures with children and adults with mental retardation. This approach involves a number of components, some similar to those of Mahoney et al. (1971) and Van Wagenen et al. (1969): (1) reinforcement of appropriate voiding; (2) punishment for voiding accidents (e.g., verbal reprimands, having the individual change his or her soiled clothes and mop the floor); (3) use of automatic urine detection alarms; (4) encouragement of increased drinking of liquids to increase frequency of voiding; and (5) teaching of toilet-related skills. Azrin and Foxx (1971) successfully used this method to toilet-train nine individuals with mental retardation (with IQs ranging from 7 to 45) in an average of 6 days with 8 hours of training per day. Azrin, Sneed, and Foxx (1973) developed a similar rapid method of treating bedwetting in individuals with mental retardation, using a bedwetting alarm, overcorrection, and reinforcement.

Others have used various combinations of the components described above to toilet-train children with mental retardation. For example, Richmond (1983) used praise and favorite liquids to reinforce being dry and voiding appropriately along with reprimands following accidents, to toilet-train developmentally delayed preschoolers. Hobbs and Peck (1985) demonstrated the effectiveness of reinforcement alone to toilet-train individuals with profound mental retardation. Finally, Friman and Vallmer (1995) demonstrated that a bedwetting alarm could be successfully used during the day to treat diurnal enuresis.

Self-Feeding

Behavioral interventions have also been used with considerable success to address self-feeding, including the acquisition of appropriate feeding skills, elimination of inappropriate mealtime behaviors, and managing of food refusal. Feeding is an area of critical importance, both as an important developmental step toward independence and as a means of maintaining proper nutrition and growth.

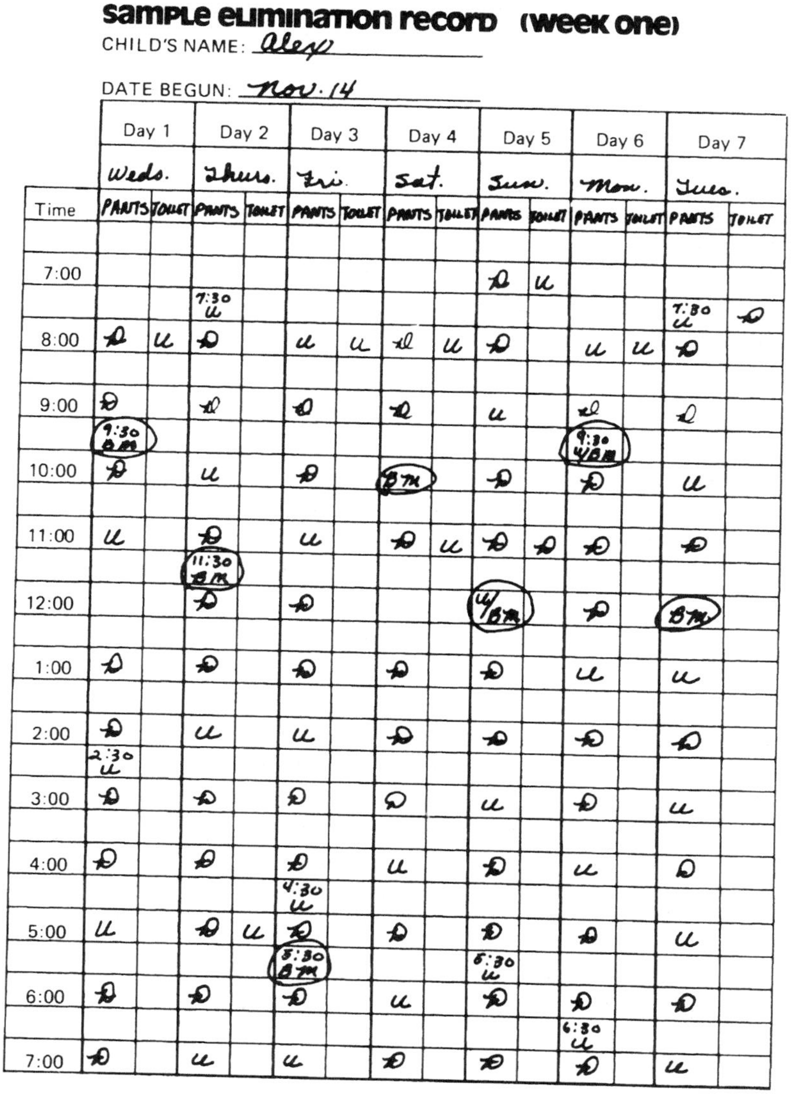

sample elimination record (week one)

CHILD'S NAME: _Alex_

DATE BEGUN: _Nov. 14_

Time	Day 1 Weds. PANTS	TOILET	Day 2 Thurs. PANTS	TOILET	Day 3 Fri. PANTS	TOILET	Day 4 Sat. PANTS	TOILET	Day 5 Sun. PANTS	TOILET	Day 6 Mon. PANTS	TOILET	Day 7 Tues. PANTS	TOILET
7:00			7:30 u						D	u	7:30 u			D
8:00	D	u	D		u	u	D	u	D		u	u	D	
9:00	D		D		D		D		u		D		D	
	9:30 BM										9:30 U BM			
10:00	D		u		D		BM		D		D		u	
11:00	u		D		u		D	u	D	D	D		D	
			11:30 BM											
12:00			D		D				U BM		D		BM	
1:00	D		D		D		D		D		u		u	
2:00	D		u		u		D		D		D		D	
	2:30 u													
3:00	D		D		D		D		u		D		u	
4:00	D		D		D		u		D		u		D	
					4:30 u									
5:00	u		D	u	D		D		D		D		u	
					5:30 BM				5:30 u					
6:00	D		D		D		u		D		D		D	
											6:30 u			
7:00	D		u		u		D		D		D		u	

FIGURE 7.1. Toilet-training chart. From Baker, Brightman, Heifetz, and Murphy (1977, p. 15). Copyright 1977 by Research Press. Reprinted by permission.

The teaching of skills related to self-feeding has typically involved programmed instruction techniques. First, each specific skill (e.g., using a spoon, wiping with a napkin, cutting with a knife) is task-analyzed (Sulzer-Azaroff & Mayer, 1991) into its basic component steps. The following is a typical task analysis for using a spoon:

1. Pick up spoon in hand.
2. Scoop food.
3. Bring spoon to mouth.
4. Open mouth and place spoon in mouth.
5. Remove spoon from mouth.
6. Place spoon on table.

Then the components are taught by means of either backward or forward chaining (see the section above on programmed instruction). In other words, the child is guided through the steps, and either the first step (forward chaining) or the last step (backward chaining) is the initial skill to be taught. Finally, various prompting techniques (e.g., physical assistance, gestural cues, and verbal cues) are provided and then faded in a systematic manner when needed. Empirical support for the effectiveness of such interventions with children and adults with mental retardation is provided by a number of researchers (e.g., Berkowitz, Sherry, & Davis, 1971; Matson, Ollendick, & Adkins, 1980; O'Brien, Bugle, & Azrin, 1972; Song & Gandhi, 1974).

In addition to teaching basic self-feeding skills, research has supported the use of behavioral interventions to address inappropriate mealtime behaviors, such as food stealing (Barton, Guess, Garcia, & Baer, 1970), rapid food ingestion (Favell, McGimsey, & Jones, 1980), and vomiting (Babbitt et al., 1994). Interventions to maintain appropriate mealtime behavior have ranged from the removal of food (O'Brien & Azrin, 1972), the use of time out (Plummer, Baer, & LeBlanc, 1977), and verbal reprimands (O'Brien & Azrin, 1972) to differential reinforcement of appropriate mealtime behavior (Favell et al., 1980). Teaching specific mealtime skills has also received considerable attention in the literature, including training adults with mental retardation to prepare meals independently (Sanders & Parr, 1989) and to order food in restaurants (Marholin, O'Toole, Touchette, Berger, & Doyle, 1979).

Finally, some children with mental retardation, especially those with accompanying medical complications, have difficulty with oral intake. For example, some such children have been fed for extended periods with gastrointestinal tubes or intravenously. We (Handen et al., 1986) describe the use of behavioral techniques such as reinforcement and shaping to induce oral feeding in hospitalized children, many of whom had developmental disabilities. The procedure involved requiring the initial intake of only small amounts of food (followed by reinforcement) and gradually increasing intake requirements in small steps across time. Subsequent work in this area has been conducted by other researchers (e.g., Babbitt et al., 1994) to address such issues as limited food preferences, dependence upon non-oral feeding methods, food refusal, gagging and vomiting, and difficulty eating more textured foods.

Dressing and Grooming Skills

Less research has been conducted with dressing and grooming skills than in the areas of toileting and feeding (Reid et al., 1991). Task analyses, forward and backward chaining, and prompting hierarchies have been used successfully to teach basic skill of dressing and grooming (e.g., Doleys, Stacy, & Knowles, 1981; Horner & Keilitz, 1975). A review of this area by Reid (1982) suggests five areas of focus for future research: (1) the development of interventions to teach more complex behaviors (e.g., selecting clothing on the basis of color standards, function, and weather); (2) the development of methods to teach individuals with both mental retardation and physical handicaps; (3) the development of intensive training programs; (4) the development of methods to train caregivers to carry out the teaching of self-help skills; and (5) issues of social validation (i.e., what to teach individuals with mental retardation in regard to clothing fashion). Finally, issues of generalization must be addressed to insure that acquired skills are performed at the appropriate time and setting.

Social Skills

Social skills deficits are often identified as important treatment targets for both children and adults with mental retardation. The development of appropriate social skills is necessary for fostering friendships within the community, and, later on, for succeeding in competitive or semicompetitive employment. Social skills cover a wide range, from maintaining eye contact when speaking with others, using language, and sharing toys to more complex skills such as problem solving and entering groups.

Early research among individuals with mental retardation tended to utilize operant techniques to increase basic components of social behavior. For example, Whitman, Mercurio, and Caponigri (1970) used food and praise to increase the participation of two children with severe mental retardation in play sessions. Reinforcement, modeling, and prompting have been used to increase more complex behaviors such as conversational skills in individuals with mental retardation (e.g., Barton, 1973; Hansen, St. Lawrence, & Christoff, 1989). Typically developing peers have been successfully used to prompt social interactions in children with disabilities (e.g., Odom et al., 1992). Other researchers have examined the specific effects of various environments on promoting appropriate social behavior in children with mental retardation. For example, Chandler, Fowler, and Lubbeck (1992) found differential rates of social interactions of preschoolers with special needs to be based upon such variables as type of activity, type and rate of teacher prompting, and group composition. Finally, a number of social skills curricula are available to teach social skills to individuals with mental retardation (e.g., McClennen, Hoekstra, & Bryan, 1980).

BEHAVIOR PROBLEM MANAGEMENT

Behavioral interventions have a long history of use in children and adults with mental retardation. Applied behavior analysis techniques have been successfully implemented to treat a range of maladaptive behaviors (including aggression, SIB, and feeding problems), as well as to improve behaviors (such as work completion, remaining in seat, and the use of alternative forms of communication). The proper use of a behavioral intervention program first requires an appropriate baseline and/or functional analysis of the behavior. Once this is accomplished, the treatment program can be developed based upon the findings of these initial observations. Such a program should include (1) methods to prevent maladaptive behavior from occurring, or antecedent control; (2) alternative behaviors to teach or reinforce; and (3) consequences designed to decrease the rate of the maladaptive behavior.

Collecting Baseline Data

Various methods are available for collecting baseline data prior to implementing a program for behavior change. The easiest method is simply recording the frequency of the target behavior (i.e., counting the number of occurrences of the event). For example, Kern, Mauk, Marder, and Mace (1995) examined the functional relationship between breath holding and various situations (e.g., being placed alone in a room, during play, being provided with adult attention) in a child with severe mental retardation and Cornelia de Lange syndrome. The dependent measure was simply the number of breath-holding episodes counted during each 10-minute observation period. Other examples might be recording the number of aggressive acts during the school day or the number of times a student used inappropriate language (e.g., swore). A second option is recording the duration of an event. This may be useful when a clinician is observing behaviors such as remaining in seat or playing appropriately: The clinician simply records the total time a child engages in the target behavior during the observation period. A more complex

observational strategy is the recording of event sequences—that is, the scoring of ongoing sequences of behavioral events, such as might occur during a mother–child interaction. Such data provide information on interactional patterns of behavior that can be used in treatment. For example, we (Caro-Martinez, Lurier, & Handen, 1994) observed two groups of mothers and their developmentally delayed preschoolers (a group with behaviors suggestive of ADHD, and a group of controls) during a clinic task in which each mother asked her child to comply with 10 requests. Delayed preschoolers in the control group were significantly more compliant than those in the ADHD group; as a result, mothers in the control group used significantly more praise and less physical assistance.

Still another option for examining the relationship between the target behavior and the environment is to conduct a functional assessment. This may involve collecting data over a period of a few days or weeks (depending upon the rate of the behavior of interest). When the target behavior occurs, information on possible antecedents (e.g., date, time, who was involved, what was occurring at the time), a description of the behavior, the consequences (i.e., how the behavior was managed), along with the possible function of the behavior are recorded. With these data, the clinician begins to develop hypotheses as to the function of the behavior. Behavior analysts have typically divided the functions of maladaptive behavior into five categories: task avoidance, attention seeking, sensory, desiring something, and a combination of functions. Therefore, an important aspect of a functional analysis is to determine the actual function of the behavior.

One example is illustrated by Cooper et al. (1992), who used a functional assessment model to evaluate 10 children with behavior problems during a single outpatient visit. Each child was observed in five different situations: free play, a difficult academic task (which was not preferred by the child), an easy academic task (which was highly preferred by the child), parent attention during the condition among these three on which the child performed best alone, and a teacher attention condition. For 8 of the 10 children, clear patterns of performance occurred, resulting in specifically tailored treatment recommendations based upon assessment results. Figure 7.2 shows the percentage of intervals of both appropriate and off-task behavior as a function of the level of task difficulty and interest for one subject, Kurt, in the Cooper et al. study.

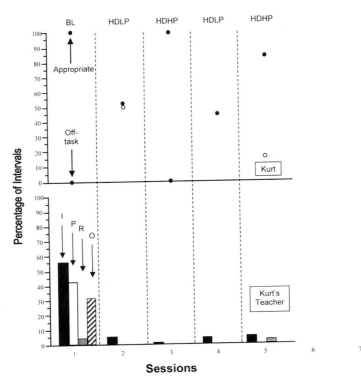

FIGURE 7.2.   Percentage of occurrence of child behaviors (appropriate and off-task) and teacher behaviors (I, instructions; P, praise, R, reprimands; O, other interactions) across conditions (BL, baseline/free-play; HDLP, high-demand/low-preference; HDHP, high-demand/high-preference). From Cooper (1992). Copyright 1992 by the Society for the Experimental Analysis of Behavior, Inc. Reprinted by permission.

Every behavioral treatment plan can be considered a single-subject experimental design. For example, once such a plan has been implemented, it will be important to continue to obtain data on the frequency or duration of the target behavior in order to assess program efficacy. At the very least, the plan should involve an AB design, which allows the clinician to examine behavior both prior to and following the intervention. However, a number of alternative and more powerful single-subject designs allow the clinician to demonstrate a functional relationship between the intervention and target behavior.

Sulzer-Azaroff and Mayer (1991) describe a number of single-subject designs for behavior change programs. The most basic design is a withdrawal or ABAB design; this simply involves returning to baseline conditions (A) after implementing a behavioral procedure (B). Experimental control of the procedure is demonstrated when the behavior returns to baseline levels when the procedure is withdrawn and changes again when the behavioral procedure is reinstituted. One disadvantage of such a design is that a clinician may not wish to return to baseline conditions after obtaining a significant decrease in such behaviors as SIB or aggression.

A second design option is a multiple-baseline design. This can be conducted across behaviors, settings, or individuals. For example, data are obtained on a target behavior across a number of individuals. A behavioral program is implemented for only a single child while data continue to be collected on the others. Experimental control is demonstrated if the behavior changes for the targeted child but not for the remaining individuals. The intervention is subsequently implemented for each succeeding child, while baseline conditions remain in effect for the others. For example, Durand and Carr (1992) compared the ability of time out and functional communication training to decrease challenging behaviors (e.g., aggression, oppositionalism, tantrums, and property destruction) in a group of 12 children with developmental disabilities. Figure 7.3 illustrates the multiple-baseline de-

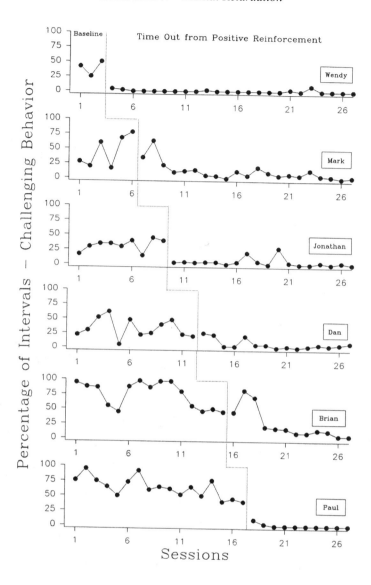

FIGURE 7.3. Challenging behavior for each of the participants in the time-out group as a function of the intervention. From Durand and Carr (1992, p. 787). Copyright 1992 by the Society for the Experimental Analysis of Behavior, Inc. Reprinted by permission.

sign across the six children in the time-out group.

A third option is a changing-criterion design. This involves using graduated steps to change the criterion for delivering consequences until the desired change in the target behavior is obtained. Experimental control is demonstrated when the behavior matches the set criterion level. In an example described earlier (Handen et al., 1984), a changing-criterion design was

used to decrease repetitive speech in an autistic adolescent. The adolescent was initially reinforced even if relatively high rates of repetitive speech occurred. Over time, the incidents of repetitive speech permitted to earn reinforcers were gradually decreased until a rate of zero per day was attained.

Finally, an alternating-treatment design allows experimental control to be demonstrated by alternately employing two or more different interventions with the same child. For example, Singh, Beale, and Dawson (1981) compared the relative effectiveness of a short-duration (3-second or 1-minute) and a long-duration (3-minute) facial screening intervention on the rate of SIB in an adolescent with mental retardation. The three different interventions were applied concurrently; they were randomly alternated between sessions on a daily basis. It was found that the 1-minute intervention was most effective in reducing SIB.

Techniques for Increasing Behaviors

The most effective means of increasing or strengthening appropriate behavior is the use of positive reinforcement. This involves the presentation of a stimulus (e.g., praise, food) contingent upon the occurrence of the target behavior, which results in an increase in the rate of that behavior. Identifying appropriate reinforcers for children with mental retardation can often be challenging. This is because naturally occurring reinforcers, such as positive feedback from others, smiles, or pleasure felt upon completing a challenging task, are not necessarily motivating to all children with mental retardation. In addition, some children with mental retardation have not been exposed to a wide range of potential reinforcers because of their limited experiences in the community or with peers.

A number of researchers have developed systems for identifying potential reinforcers for children with mental retardation. For example, Green et al. (1988) compared staff opinion and the systematic assessment of preferences in individuals with profound mental retardation. Similarly, Pace, Ivancic, Edwards, Iwata, and Page (1985) described a systematic method of assessing reinforcer value in individuals with profound mental retardation; the potential reinforcers they examined included hugs, verbal interactions, liquids, a vibrator, music, a light board, a fan, and a heating pad. Additional methods of identifying potential reinforcers include talking with individuals who know a child best, such as family members or teachers. Finally, one may simply observe a child for a period of time to identify his or her high-probability behaviors. Premack (1959) demonstrated that behaviors in which an individual freely engaged might be effectively used to reinforce low-rate behaviors. Using the "Premack principle," one may find unlikely options—such as being allowed to engage in self-stimulatory behaviors or simply being left alone—that may serve as potential reinforcers for a child.

Reinforcers are either unconditioned/primary or conditioned/secondary reinforcers. Primary reinforcers, such as food or liquids, are naturally effective reinforcers. Secondary reinforcers require an individual to learn that a given stimulus has reinforcing properties. This typically occurs as the child interacts with his or her environment. However, in working with children with mental retardation, the clinician may need to start with a primary reinforcer in order to begin to increase desired behaviors. When the primary reinforcers are frequently paired with other stimuli (e.g., praise, hugs), the latter assume reinforcing properties as well.

Reinforcers are often divided into a number of categories: edible reinforcers (food, liquids), social reinforcers (praise, hugs), tangible reinforcers (toys, prizes), activity reinforcers (playing a game, listening to music), and generalized reinforcers (tokens, money). Generalized reinforcers, such as tokens, can be extremely effective with children with mental retardation. These become conditioned reinforcers through their frequent pairing with other established reinforcers. Tokens are effective because they allow a child both to delay reinforcement and to choose from a range of potential reinforcers. For example, it may not be feasible for a child to earn time playing a computer game after completing a single task. However, awarding the child a token serves to reinforce task completion and allows the child to delay exchanging the token for a reinforcer until later in the day (e.g., when a total of 10 tokens have been earned). The use of generalized reinforcers also eliminates problems with satiation (a child's tiring of a particular reinforcer), in that a wide variety of reinforcing items can be purchased.

A number of guidelines may help to increase reinforcement effectiveness. The first is that a reinforcer should be appropriate. In other words, a clinician should establish that the chosen consequence is reinforcing to a child and that it matches the behavioral requirement. For example, just because a child finds breaks reinforcing, providing a 15-minute break following only 5 minutes of work is probably not an appropriate match between the behavior required and the reinforcer. Second, a primary reinforcer should always be paired with other naturally occurring events or stimuli to develop secondary or learned reinforcers (e.g., edible reinforcers should be paired with praise). When teaching a new behavior, a clinician should initially provide reinforcement immediately following the behavior. For example, if a child is being taught to look at staff members when prompted, "Look at me," reinforcement should immediately follow the making of eye contact. This serves to strengthen the association between the desired behavior and the reinforcer, and also prevents nontarget behaviors from being inadvertently reinforced. Naturally occurring reinforcers should also be used whenever possible. For example, if a child is being taught to ask for juice, juice should be the reinforcer. A continuous-reinforcement schedule (reinforcement of every occurrence of the target behavior) should be used initially to establish a new behavior. For example, if a child is being taught to hang up his or her coat upon arrival in the classroom, this should be praised each time the behavior occurs. Once a behavior is established, an intermittent-reinforcement schedule can be introduced.

It has generally been accepted that the use of extrinsic reinforcement tends to reduce task interest and creativity, as well as to undermine intrinsic motivation (Eisenberger & Cameron, 1996). Consequently, many teacher training materials and business publications specifically recommend against the use of reward or incentive systems (e.g., Kohn, 1993; Tagano, Moran, & Sawyers, 1991). Yet, in a recent review of this issue, Eisenberger and Cameron (1996) found that the detrimental effects of reinforcement occur only under specific conditions that can easily be remedied. Their analysis of the literature on reinforcement suggests that it is important for reinforcement to be based upon task completion or the meeting of a certain level of quality. Studies in which reinforcement has had decremental effects on subsequent performance have typically involved a single presentation of reinforcement (independent of performance), followed by a period of time in which reinforcement is withheld. Subsequent performance is then found to decrease, relative to that of individuals who were not reinforced initially for their performance. However, such situations are not typical of true-life learning experiences, in which individuals often perform tasks repeatedly and are reinforced repeatedly prior to the termination of reward. In such cases, little if any decrement in performance is noted. Similar results have been noted in research on creativity, where such behavior can either be enhanced or thwarted, depending upon how reinforcement is administered (see Eisenberger & Selbst, 1994).

Finally, negative reinforcement can also result in an increase in behavior. Whereas positive reinforcement involves consequences that motivate and keep individuals going, negative reinforcers are those that individuals attempt to avoid or escape (e.g., pain, reprimands, discomfort). The use of negative reinforcement is different from punishment. In punishment, an aversive or unpleasant event follows the occurrence of the target behavior and results in a *decrease* in the rate of that behavior. Conversely, negative reinforcement involves reducing or removing a negative event following the occurrence of the target behavior, resulting in an *increase* in the rate of that behavior. For example, Iwata, Dorsey, Slifer, Bauman, and Richman (1994) have found that some children with mental retardation engage in SIB to avoid or escape from adult demands. The demands are reduced or terminated when SIB occurs, thereby negatively reinforcing this behavior. Similarly, Carr, Newsom, and Binkoff (1980) demonstrated that two children with mental retardation were able to decrease demands placed upon them by engaging in aggressive behavior (staff had negatively reinforced aggression). A parent who nags her daughter until she cleans her room is also using negative reinforcement. Sulzer-Azaroff and Mayer (1991) caution that the use of negative reinforcement to change behavior involves a number of risks because aversive stimuli are used. This may include the appearance of escape behaviors (e.g., a child avoids going to class) or aggression. Consequently, they recommend that positive reinforcement be used except in rare instances.

Techniques for Reducing Behaviors

Behavior modification is generally known for its ability to reduce or eliminate maladaptive behaviors. During the past 15–20 years, local, state, and federal guidelines regarding the implementation of such techniques have been developed. Most guidelines specifically allow the use of the majority of behavioral interventions described below. However, programs intended both to increase and to decrease specific behaviors must often be submitted to and approved by an internal review committee, and ongoing documentation, data keeping, and periodic review are required. For example, the state of Pennsylvania and most other states provide specific guidelines for the use of restrictive interventions in such settings as sheltered workshops and community residences (e.g., Pennsylvania Department of Public Welfare, 1995b). Such guidelines promote the use of least restrictive interventions prior to that of more restrictive programs. Any program that restricts clients' access to reinforcers, whether it be a complex token economy system or the use of a simple contingency (e.g., telling clients that they must finish their dinner in order to watch TV) may require a written protocol and committee approval under some guidelines.

There has also been a strong movement to promote only positive interventions in work with children with mental retardation (e.g., Donnellan et al., 1988; Horner et al., 1990). Such a position has stirred considerable controversy among professionals (see Horner et al., 1990). At the extreme may be issues related to the use of controversial interventions, such as electric shock to treat life-threatening conditions (e.g., severe SIB; Linscheid, Iwata, Ricketts, Williams, & Giffin, 1990). On the other end of the continuum are issues related to the appropriateness of such interventions as time out or response cost, which are considered to be aversive or restrictive interventions by some groups. The interventions described below are presented in order of what is generally considered increasing restrictiveness (Sulzer-Azaroff & Mayer, 1991).

Differential Reinforcement

Differential reinforcement involves reinforcing a range of alternative behaviors. There are two types: differential reinforcement of incompatible behaviors (DRI) and differential reinforcement of other behaviors (DRO). Implementing DRI requires that a clinician identify a behavior or class of behaviors incompatible with the target behavior the clinician is attempting to decrease. For example, we (Miltenberger, Handen, & Capriotti, 1987) used a range of interventions, including DRI, to treat hand stereotypies in a child with mental retardation. In this study, behaviors incompatible with stereotypy (e.g., keeping hands down, using hands to play with toys) were specifically reinforced.

DRO has also been called "differential reinforcement of zero rates of behavior." It differs somewhat from DRI, in that reinforcement is given following a period of *time* in which a specific behavior has not occurred. Reinforcement is not based on the occurrence of a specific behavior, as in DRI. DRO can be useful in decreasing highly disruptive or interfering behaviors. For example, Luiselli and Reisman (1980) describe the use of DRO to decrease inappropriate

sounds and aggression in three children with mental retardation by reinforcing the children if the target behaviors did not occur.

The advantages of differential reinforcement procedures are that they are constructive, benign, and acceptable, and can result in lasting change (Sulzer-Azaroff & Mayer, 1991). To insure the effectiveness of DRI, Sulzer-Azaroff and Mayer recommend that the clinician identify behaviors that are *clearly* incompatible with the target behavior (e.g., shaking hands is incompatible with hugging). In addition, it is best to select behaviors to reinforce that are already well established in the child's repertoire. Behaviors selected for reinforcement should also be likely to be supported in the natural environment (e.g., talking nicely will be more likely to result in attention from others) and should serve the same functions as the target behavior. For example, Carr and Durand (1985) found that four children engaged in behaviors such as aggression, tantrums, and SIB when given difficult tasks and minimal adult attention. The children were subsequently taught to ask for help as a means of gaining adult attention in such situations, resulting in significant decreases in maladaptive behaviors. DRO's effectiveness can be enhanced by maximizing the opportunities for reinforcement (e.g., if self-stimulatory behaviors occur every 3 minutes, the DRO schedule should start at about 2 minutes) and only gradually adjusting the schedule of reinforcement once gains are made (Sulzer-Azaroff & Mayer, 1991).

Differential reinforcement procedures also have a number of potential disadvantages. First, the effects may be delayed, requiring that other interventions be used in combination with DRI/ DRO to deal with occurrences of the targeted undesirable behavior. For example, reinforcing appropriate use of hands for a child who is aggressive may also require that time out be used following incidents of hitting. DRO requires that those implementing the program continue to watch for maladaptive behaviors; it is also possible that other maladaptive behaviors will be inadvertently reinforced.

Extinction

Extinction involves withholding reinforcement following a behavior that was previously reinforced (Sulzer-Azaroff & Mayer, 1991). To implement an extinction program, the most important step is to identify what is presently maintaining the target behavior. For example, we (Handen et al., 1986) have found that children with feeding problems often engage in such behaviors as crying, spitting out food, or pushing food away when presented with food during meals. If food presentation is discontinued following such behaviors, termination of demands to eat is probably helping to maintain these behaviors. Similarly, Iwata et al. (1994) have found that some children who exhibit SIB do so to gain adult attention. Consequently, when an adult leaves the child alone, SIB increases and is reinforced when the adult returns and attends to the child.

Extinction results in a gradual reduction in behavior, but the reduction is often long-lasting. It is most effective when used in combination with positive reinforcement. For example, Reese, Howard, and Rosenberger (1974) found that reinforcing alternative responses in combination with extinction for incorrect responses resulted in fewer errors than did extinction alone in a group of men with mental retardation. In clinical settings, extinction is often referred to as "planned ignoring." However, planned ignoring can only be an effective form of extinction if adult attention is determined to be the source of reinforcement for the target behavior. Sulzer-Azaroff and Mayer (1991) cite a number of potential disadvantages to the use of extinction. The first is the fact that its effects are delayed; this could result in extinction's being an inappropriate intervention for such behaviors as running into the street or exposing oneself in public. The second potential disadvantage is the frequent appearance of an "extinction burst." In other words, when a behavior is initially placed on extinction, it typically becomes worse (e.g., the child who whines when not getting his or her way is likely to whine more when parents first stop responding to this behavior). Again, this property makes extinction an inappropriate intervention for behaviors that may reach dangerous levels. There is also some evidence that the use of extinction can induce aggression (Skinner, 1953). Finally, extinction may be difficult to implement in situations in which the clinician cannot control the source of reinforcement. For example, adults may ignore a child who swears, but peers may continue to respond, thereby helping to reinforce and maintain the behavior.

Response Cost

Response cost involves the loss of a reinforcer contingent upon the target response. Because it is an aversive procedure, such a program must be consistent with regulatory law and may need to be approved by an institutional review committee. Response cost is different from punishment, in that punishment involves presenting an aversive consequence contingent upon a specific behavior, whereas response cost involves removal of a reinforcer following the target behavior (e.g., loss of a privilege such as watching television due to an episode of aggression). Response cost can also be used as part of a token economy system, wherein a child is fined points or tokens contingent upon a target behavior. For example, Burchard and Barrera (1972) demonstrated that fines as part of a token economy system reduced swearing, property destruction, and aggression in five of six adolescents with mental retardation as effectively as the use of time out did.

The advantages of response cost, according to Sulzer-Azaroff and Mayer (1991), are a strong and rapid reduction in behavior, convenience, and possible long-lasting effects. Despite such advantages, there are a number of potential problems with the use of this procedure. First, the very ease of its use makes it more likely that response cost will be abused. For example, it can be used too often and penalties can be too harsh if the program is not well monitored. Once a child loses too many points or privileges, he or she may have little incentive to try to earn points or privileges back. In addition, as with any aversive intervention, such programs may result in aggression or escape. For example, a child may increase levels of maladaptive behavior in response to being fined, or may avoid situations in which a fine might be levied. It is important when implementing response cost to combine such an intervention with a reinforcement program. For example, Sanok and Striefel (1979) successfully treated a child with elective mutism by reinforcing appropriate verbal responses with a penny and praise, along with fining the child a penny for nonverbal responses. Finally, Sulzer-Azaroff and Mayer (1991) suggest that children have a reserve of points before fines are implemented and that the magnitude of the fines be determined empirically. In other words, the behavior should be monitored under different cost magnitudes until the desired reduction in behavior is obtained.

Time Out

Time out involves limiting access to sources of reinforcement for a specified period of time contingent upon a target behavior (Sulzer-Azaroff & Mayer, 1991). It differs from response cost because reinforcement is removed for a period of time rather than by a specified amount (e.g., 2 tokens). For time out to be used effectively, the clinician must control all potential sources of reinforcement. For example, time out may be inappropriate for many children who engage in high rates of self-stimulatory behavior or SIB, because these children are less likely to find removal from an activity and/or attention aversive. Similarly, adult attention should be limited during the time-out period.

Sulzer-Azaroff and Mayer (1991) suggest that the duration of time out be kept relatively short (e.g., 5–10 minutes). Studies that have compared differential durations of time out have found periods of 5 minutes or less to be as effective for most children as 15- to 30-minute periods (Kendall, Nay, & Jeffers, 1975; White, Nielsen, & Johnson, 1972). In addition, a study by Mace, Page, Ivancic, and O'Brien (1986) found time out to be just as effective whether children were required to sit quietly at the end of the time-out period or simply allowed to return to the group at the conclusion of time out, regardless of their behavior. Finally, as with all other procedures designed to reduce behavior, time out is most effective when combined with other reinforcement interventions.

Time out has been most often associated with the removal of a child from the group to a separate time-out room or a time-out area within a room. However, there are many variations of time out that can be just as effective. Nelson and Rutherford (1983) describe the use of planned ignoring, in which an adult simply drops his or her head and remains motionless for a few seconds following a maladaptive response. For example, a teacher can use a 10-second planned ignoring response whenever a student starts to engage in inappropriate speech (e.g., laughing, swearing). Another variation, called "contingent observation," involves removing the child only a few feet from the area for time out so that he or she can observe activities but not participate. Finally, Foxx and Shapiro (1978) describe the use of a time-out ribbon with a group of students with severe mental retardation. Students lost the ribbon for a few minutes following the occurrence of specific maladaptive behaviors. Reinforcers such as treats and praise were only given to students who were wearing their ribbons. One common rule of thumb is to use 1 minute for each year of age (e.g., placing a 5-year-old in time out for 5 minutes).

Sulzer-Azaroff and Mayer (1991) suggest that the main advantage of time out is its ability to reduce behavior. Another advantage for families is its utility (i.e., a child can be placed in a time-out chair in most settings—at home, at a rela-

tive's house, in a store). Despite this, there are a number of disadvantages to the use of time out. Sulzer-Azaroff and Mayer (1991) suggest that time out has the potential for abuse and may lead to the suppression of other, appropriate behaviors. Moreover, when a child is in time out there is a loss of learning time (especially opportunities to be reinforced for engaging in appropriate behaviors). Time out is also not universally effective. For example, Doleys, Wells, Hobbs, Roberts, and Cartelli (1976) found time out to be less effective than social punishment (i.e., scolding) in improving rates of compliance in a group of children with mental retardation. Similarly, Solnick, Rincover, and Peterson (1977) found time out to be ineffective at eliminating tantrums in a 6-year-old girl with autism, because the child simply engaged in stereotypic behaviors during the time-out period. In the same study, time out failed to decrease spitting and SIB in a 16-year-old with mental retardation until the non-time-out environment was "enriched" (i.e., highly desirable activities were placed in the classroom so that time out resulted in a loss of access to these materials). One might hypothesize that time out for noncompliance could also be ineffective because one might actually reinforce noncompliant behavior by allowing a child to escape from a demand situation. However, we (Handen, Parrish, McClung, Kerwin, & Evans, 1992) compared time out and guided compliance (physically assisting a child to comply with a request) as treatments for noncompliance in preschoolers with developmental disabilities. Time out was found to be the most effective intervention as long as a child was returned to the demand situation immediately after the time-out period.

The most significant disadvantages of time out are the legal restrictions and public concerns regarding its use. For example, the *Wyatt v. Stickney* (1972) decision specifically prohibits the use of seclusion with individuals with mental retardation, but allows for professionally supervised time-out as part of a behavior shaping-program. Various settings and jurisdictions have specific policies regarding the use of time out. As with all behavioral interventions, the clinician will need to be aware of the regulations that apply to his or her particular region and facility.

Restrictive Interventions

Interventions such as overcorrection and positive practice have been used with considerable success to treat such behaviors as SIB and stereotypies in children and adults with mental retardation (Foxx & Azrin, 1972, 1973). These interventions are aversive procedures that are designed both to decrease the rate of maladaptive behavior and to increase appropriate behavior. Overcorrection involves restoring the environment or conditions to the same state as existed prior to the maladaptive behavior, or an improved state. For example, if a child draws on a classroom wall, he or she is required to clean off the wall. Positive practice, by contrast, involves, repeatedly practicing an acceptable alternative behavior (Sulzer-Azaroff & Mayer, 1991). For example, Foxx and Azrin (1973) used positive practice to successfully decrease head weaving in a child with mental retardation. Overcorrection was not felt to be appropriate, since no damage to the environment resulted. However, the child was instructed to practice moving her head in one of three positions (up, down, or straight), and assisted to hold her head in each position for 15 seconds. The entire procedure required 5 minutes. Overcorrection and positive practice have also been used as consequences for toileting accidents with individuals with mental retardation (Azrin & Foxx, 1971). In this case, the individuals had to clean up the area, wash any soiled clothing, shower, and put on clean clothes. An additional, more restrictive procedure is called "facial screening," which involves covering a child's eyes with a cloth or hand for 5 to 15 seconds contingent upon maladaptive behavior. This procedure has been used successfully to decrease SIB (e.g., Winston, Singh, & Dawson, 1984) and stereotypies (e.g., McGonigle, Duncan, Cordisco, & Barrett, 1982). As with all other aversive procedures, the above restrictive interventions must be combined with reinforcement of appropriate behaviors, and there are likely to be regulations regarding their use (Sulzer-Azaroff & Mayer, 1991).

BEHAVIOR PROBLEMS SPECIFIC TO MENTAL RETARDATION

A number of behavior problems tend to be specific to individuals with mental retardation. SIB and stereotypies are perhaps the best-known and most researched of these behaviors, and they are specifically discussed in this section.

Knowledge about the assessment and treatment of SIB and stereotypies is extremely important for any clinician working with children with mental retardation. Estimates of the incidence of SIB range from 0% to 74% of institu-

tionalized populations, with higher rates occurring among individuals functioning within the severe to profound ranges of mental retardation (see Johnson & Day, 1992). Rates are considerably less in community-based facilities, ranging from 17% to 20% (Eyman & Call, 1977). Stereotyped behaviors tend to occur among individuals with mental retardation, autism, or blindness. Among children with mental retardation, rates appear to be highest for those functioning in the severe (8.7%) or profound (10.4%) ranges of mental retardation versus a rate of 1.9% among children and adolescents with mild mental retardation (Jacobson, 1982). Children and adolescents living in community settings evidenced lower reported rates of stereotyped behaviors than those in developmental centers (Jacobson, 1982). The terms "self-injury" and "stereotyped behavior" are often confused and have frequently been interchanged (Schroeder, 1991). However, they refer to two separate entities, which may well have their bases in different biological mechanisms (Schroeder, 1991).

SIB is behavior that produces physical injury to the individual's own body (Tate & Baroff, 1966). Such behaviors often include head banging, self-biting, self-hitting, hair pulling, eye poking, pica, and chronic rumination. Rates may range from a few times to thousands of times a day. Conversely, stereotypies, or self-stimulatory behaviors, are highly consistent and repetitious motor or posturing responses that are excessive in rate, frequency, and/or amplitude and that do not appear to possess any adaptive significance (Baumeister, 1978). Such behaviors typically include hand flapping, rocking, and twirling objects. Stereotypies may often be developmentally appropriate (e.g., rocking or banging of objects by infants). A stereotypic behavior is only deemed a problem when it occurs for extended periods, is no longer age-appropriate, and interferes with the individual's ability to learn or be engaged with his or her environment (Berkson, 1987).

The etiology and treatment of SIB and stereotypies differ considerably. There are a few known syndromes in which a high incidence of SIB has been noted. For example, Lesch–Nyhan syndrome (Lesch & Nyhan, 1964) is a sex-linked disorder of purine metabolism in which individuals engage in severe self-mutilation (e.g., self-biting). The extent of SIB appears to be unrelated to cognitive functioning levels (Nyhan, 1976). This relationship between SIB and a biochemical defect is of considerable importance in furthering our understanding of both neurobiology and SIB. Self-injury has also been noted in a number of other genetic disorders, although at rates significantly lower than that of Lesch–Nyhan syndrome; these include the Cornelia de Lange, Rett, Tourette, and fragile-X syndromes. However, no causal links between these disorders and SIB has been found. SIB is also reported to occur in children with autism.

Neurobiological studies, most of which have been conducted with animals, have suggested some possible models for the occurrence of SIB. For example, preliminary results suggest that dopamine depletion in the basal ganglia or an imbalance in neurotransmitter function in brain dopamine pathways, due to aberrant perinatal development may lead to SIB in children with Lesch–Nyhan syndrome (for a review, see Schroeder, Breese, & Mueller, 1990). Other work has been conducted to investigate the endogenous opioid peptide hypothesis (Sandman et al., 1983), in which beta-endorphin levels are thought to increase with the occurrence of SIB. Consequently, the pain threshold is elevated and tolerance for SIB raised, resulting in the conceptualization of SIB as an addictive behavior. It is hoped that such neurobiological research will eventually lead to pharmacological interventions directly based upon neurobiological theory (see the section below on psychopharmacological treatment).

The recent use of functional analysis for the assessment of SIB has led to specific treatment interventions. Functional analysis posits that SIB is maintained (and possibly developed) by environmental contingencies. For example, Iwata et al. (1994) used this model to better understand variables associated with SIB in nine children with developmental disabilities. During an extended baseline period, children were repeatedly observed for 15-minute blocks of time. Each child was exposed to four different experimental conditions: social disapproval for SIB; planned ignoring during academic demands, in which the clinician turned away for 30 seconds following SIB (with praise given for task completion); planned ignoring during a no-demand play situation; and an alone condition. Six of nine subjects exhibited higher levels of SIB under specific stimulus conditions, suggesting that within-subject variability was a function of features of the environment. Figure 7.4 illustrates the percentage of 10-second intervals in which SIB was observed for four subjects. These findings have implications for the selection of appropriate treatment interventions.

Many different interventions have been used to treat SIB. Schroeder (1991) divides the most efficacious interventions into three categories: behavior-enhancing, behavior-reducing, and pharmacological interventions. Several behavior-enhancing interventions, such as DRO, DRI, and skills acquisition, have been described earlier. However, they are typically used in combination with behavior-reducing interventions (e.g., extinction, time out), making it difficult to assess the relative efficacy of any single behavior-enhancing component (Schroeder, 1991). A second category of behavior-enhancing interventions is called "stimulus-based treatments." These are described in detail by Carr, Taylor, Carlson, and Robinson (1989) and involve making changes in the range of possible stimuli associated with SIB. For example, the difficulty of work tasks, the number of transitions, or noise levels may be reduced if these are associated with increased rates of SIB. Finally, as a last resort, protective equipment (e.g., helmet, mitts, arm splints) and/or simply blocking an individual from engaging in SIB may have to be used to reduce SIB while more positive behavior-enhancing interventions are implemented or to allow for extinction of SIB to occur. For example, Luiselli (1991) described the use of padded mittens to allow for sensory extinction in an 18-year-old woman with mental retardation who engaged in eye pressing. Over a 60-day period, the mittens were gradually faded to latex gloves and then completely eliminated (see Figure 7.5). Similarly, Pace, Iwata, Edwards, and McCosh (1986) used inflatable air splints to prevent a 15-year-old adolescent with mental retardation from scratching skin from behind his ears. During treatment sessions, adult praise and touch were provided for playing with toys. Over time, the air pressure in the splints was gradually decreased (a fading procedure) while the absence of SIB was maintained.

Behavior-reducing interventions have been thoroughly studied and have also been discussed earlier. Interventions such as facial screening (see review by Rojahn & Marshburn, 1992) and overcorrection (see review by Van Houten, Rolider, & Houlihan, 1992) have been shown to be successful in reducing SIB in children and adults with mental retardation in a number of studies. For example, Gross, Farrar, and Liner (1982) compared facial screening and overcorrection for treating hair pulling in a preschooler with mental retardation. Both procedures included the use of high-density DRO. Results indicated that whereas overcorrection/DRO led to

FUNCTIONAL ANALYSIS OF SELF-INJURY

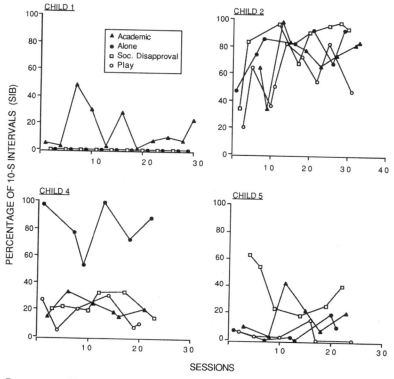

FIGURE 7.4.   Percentage of intervals of self-injury for subjects 1, 2, 4, and 5 across sessions and experimental conditions. From Iwata, Dorsey, Slifer, Bauman, and Richman (1994, p. 205). Copyright 1994 by the Society for the Experimental Analysis of Behavior, Inc. Reprinted by permission.

a considerable decrease in hair pulling, facial screening/DRO resulted in an immediate elimination of the target behavior. Other, more restrictive aversive interventions have also been used to treat SIB, including water mist (e.g., Dorsey, Iwata, Ong, & McSween, 1980) and electric shock (e.g., Linscheid et al., 1990). With the growing interest in the functional analysis of SIB, the choice of treatment should be based, at least in part, on the assessment results. For example, if a child is found to engage in SIB primarily as a means to avoid or escape task demands, interventions might include adjusting the difficulty of task demands, teaching the child an alternative way to communicate his or her desire not to do the task (e.g., Carr & Durand, 1985), as well as a procedure such as overcorrection, which requires that the child comply with a given task demand (e.g., Van Houten et al., 1992). The final form of intervention, psychopharmacological treatment, has proven helpful in some cases and is discussed in a later section of this chapter.

The hypothesized etiology of stereotyped behavior is similar to that of SIB. Schroeder (1991) divides the theories into those that see stereotypic behavior driven by endogenous or internal factors and those that propose more environmental variables. Although these two types of theories are not necessarily mutually exclusive, the former would suggest that such behaviors are highly resistant to change by modification of external stimuli. Conversely, theories suggesting that stereotypic behavior may be maintained by perceptual reinforcement would lead to the assumption that such behaviors can be decreased or eliminated by external contingencies. As with SIB, interventions include those that enhance nonstereotypic behaviors and those that seek to reduce these behaviors. For example, Haring and Kennedy (1990) successfully used tokens to reinforce on-task behavior and omission of stereotypic behavior (DRO) in severely disturbed children. The use of overcorrection to decrease head weaving in a child with mental retardation (Azrin & Foxx, 1973) has

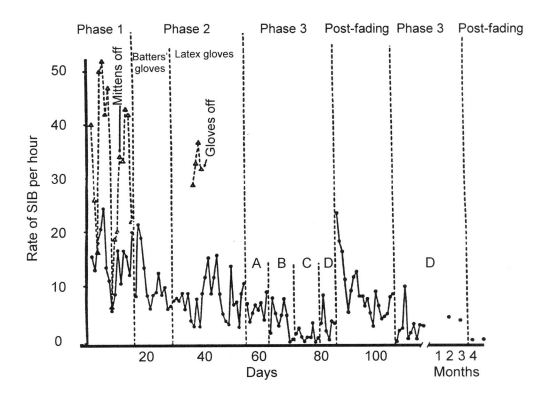

FIGURE 7.5.   Rate of SIB (eye pressing) per hour. Large padded mittens employed during Phase 1 were faded to latex gloves (Phase 2), which were gradually eliminated across four steps (A–D during Phase 3). From Luiselli (1991, p. 316). Copyright 1991 by Behavioral Residential Treatment. Reprinted by permission.

been previously described. Barrett, Matson, Shapiro, and Ollendick (1981) compared facial screening and DRO to treat stereotypic behavior in two children with mental retardation. They found DRO alone to be unsatisfactory, whereas facial screening was effective in reducing the target behaviors. Other investigators have used combinations of positive reinforcement and decelerative interventions. For example, we (Miltenberger et al., 1987) combined positive reinforcement (DRI) and facial screening to decrease stereotypic behavior in a child with severe mental retardation. Although behavioral interventions have been used successfully to reduce stereotypic behavior in children with mental retardation, some medications have also proven useful and are described below.

PSYCHOPHARMACOLOGICAL TREATMENT

There is a long tradition of prescribing psychotropic medications for children and adults with

mental retardation. As with individuals without mental retardation, such medications are used to treat specific symptoms; they are not prescribed to treat mental retardation per se. With the deinstitutionalization movement in the 1960s, a major effort was begun to significantly decrease the use of medication among children and adults with mental retardation. Yet surveys conducted as recently as 1985 have documented that up to 44% of individuals residing in institutions continue to be prescribed medication for behavior control (Hill, Balow, & Bruininks, 1985). Studies have also documented that 25%–40% of community residents with mental retardation continue to be placed on medication for behavior control, and that within the public school setting, 7%–15% of children with mental retardation are prescribed such medications (Cullinan, Gadow, & Epstein, 1987; Gadow & Kalachnik, 1981; Hill et al., 1985; Martin & Agran, 1985). Overall, medication use continues to be most pronounced in institutions and tends to decrease as settings become less restrictive. Similarly, medication is prescribed most often for children and adults who are functioning within the severe to profound ranges of mental retardation, with an inverse relationship between frequency of use and level of cognitive functioning.

The clinician has an important role to play in the use of medication among children with mental retardation in both the home and school settings. First, observation and description of behavior can assist in the diagnosis of a disorder and determination of possible drug intervention. Second, the clinician can do much to determine the efficacy of medication and to monitor possible adverse side effects through observation and documentation of behavior. Another potential role is to monitor adverse affects on learning and cognition. Finally, the clinician must serve as a resource for the development of nonpharmacological interventions, which must accompany the use of most medications if an effective and comprehensive treatment program is to be implemented. Such interventions have been presented in some detail in the preceding sections.

Table 7.3 provides a summary of six general drug classes (stimulants, neuroleptics, anticonvulsants, antihistamines, sedatives, anxiolytics and antimanics, antidepressants, and other drugs), along with their indications for use in children. Below is a brief overview of the research on the use of these classes for children with mental retardation. For each class, information is presented on efficacy, effects on learning and cognition, and side effects.

Stimulant Medication

Stimulant medication is typically prescribed for the treatment of ADHD, a disorder that affects 9%–18% of children with mental retardation (Ando & Yoshimura, 1978; Epstein, et al., 1986; Jacobson, 1982). Among children with mild to moderate mental retardation, stimulants are the most commonly prescribed medication for behavior control. Recent research on the efficacy of stimulants such as methylphenidate in children with mental retardation has involved well-controlled studies, typically including the use of double-blind, placebo-controlled designs. Such studies have documented positive drug response rates of 62%–70% (Aman, Marks, Turbott, Wilsher, & Merry, 1991; Handen, Breaux, Gosling, Ploof, & Feldman, 1990; Handen, Breaux, et al., 1992)—rates only slightly lower than those for typically developing children with ADHD. However, there is little evidence to support the efficacy of stimulants in children functioning within the severe to profound ranges of mental retardation (Aman et al., 1991). Moreover, there is some evidence that children with mental retardation may experience an unusually high rate of adverse side effects, such as motor tics and social withdrawal (Handen, Feldman, Gosling, Breaux, & McAuliffe, 1991). Finally, although stimulant medication may result in gains in attention span and on-task behavior among children with mental retardation, learning deficits will not necessarily be addressed. Other, education-based interventions may need to be provided (Handen, McAuliffe, & Caro-Martinez, 1996).

Neuroleptics

Recent prevalence studies estimate that neuroleptics are prescribed to approximately 30% of institutionalized individuals with mental retardation (Hill et al., 1985), 20% of children with severe to profound mental retardation (Gadow & Poling, 1988), and 2%–4% of school-age children with mild to moderate mental retardation in public school settings (Gadow & Poling, 1988). Despite such a high rate of use in this population, little research on the efficacy of neuroleptic drugs among children with mental retardation has been conducted during the past two decades. Much of the available work has involved small sample sizes, is of poor methodological quality, and has involved subjects whose diagnoses have been poorly described. Additionally, much of this research has tended to focus on adult populations. The findings of such studies are not necessarily generalizable to children or adolescents with mental retardation (Campbell et al., 1993). Neuroleptics have generally been prescribed for management of aggression, hyperactivity, SIB, stereotypies, and antisocial behaviors. There is some evidence of differential effectiveness among neuroleptics in children with mental retardation. For example, there is questionable evidence supporting the efficacy of chlorpromazine in children with mental retardation (see review by Aman & Singh, 1991), and some research suggests that this drug may actually increase inappropriate behaviors or adversely affect cognitive functioning (Aman, White, & Field, 1984; Marholin, Touchette, & Stewart, 1979; Moore, 1960). Conversely, there is sound evidence that thioridazine can contribute to the control of such behaviors as hyperactivity, aggression, SIB, and stereotypies among children with mental retardation (see review by Aman & Singh, 1980).

Haloperidol is less sedating than thioridazine, which may cause fewer adverse cognitive ef-

TABLE 7.3.   Selected Pharmacological Agents Used with Children

Drug class	Examples (brand names)	Indications
Stimulants	Methylphenidate (Ritalin) Dextroamphetamine (Dexedrine) Pemoline (Cylert)	ADHD
Neuroleptics	Chlorpromazine (Thorazine) Thioridazine (Mellaril) Haloperidol (Haldol)[a] Clozapine (Clozaril) Risperidone (Risperidol)	Psychosis, mania, and aggression [a]Haloperidol is also used to treat Tourette syndrome
Anticonvulsants	Clonazepam (Klonopin) Phenobarbital Phenytoin (Dilantin)	Seizure disorders
	Carbamazepine (Tegretol) Valproic acid (Depakene) Divalproex sodium (Depakote)	Seizure disorders and bipolar disorder

Anxiolytics and sedatives	Antihistamines
	    Diphenhydramine (Benadryl)
	    Hydroxyzine (Atarax)
		Sleep disorders

	Anxiolytics
	    Chlordiazepoxide (Librium)
	    Diazepam (Valium)
	    Lorazepan (Ativan)
	    Alprazolam (Xanax)
	    Traizolam (Halcion)
		Sleep disorders, excited/aggressive states, anxiety disorders

	Atypical Anxiolytics Buspirone (Buspar)	Overanxious, avoidant and phobic disorders
Antidepressants and antimanics	Monoamine oxidase inhibitors	Depression; rarely used in children

	Tricyclics
	    Imipramine (Tofranil)
	    Clomipramine (Anafranil)
	    Desipramine (Norpramin)
	    Nortriptyline (Pamelor)
		Depression and bedwetting
		Depression, bedwetting
		Depression, ADHD
		Depression

	Selective serotonin reuptake inhibitors
	    Fluoxetine (Prozac)
	    Sertraline (Zoloft)
	    Paroxetine (Paxil)
	    Fluvoxamine (Luvox)
		Depression
		Obsessive–compulsive disorder

	Antimanics
	    Lithium (Eskalith)
	    Valproic acid (Depakene)
	    Divalproex sodium (Depakote)
	    Carbamazepine (Tegretol)
		Bipolar disorder
		Bipolar disorder, seizures

Other drugs	Clonidine (Catapres) Naltrexone (Revia) Fenfluramine (Pondimin)	ADHD, Tourette syndrome Self-injury ADHD, autism

[a]Not often used with children.

fects. Some recent research has documented the efficacy of this drug in controlling maladaptive behavior. For example, Aman, Teehan, White, Turbott, and Vaithianathan (1989) found a 23% reduction in stereotypies among a group of adolescents and adults with severe to profound mental retardation. Some newer, atypical neuroleptics, such as risperidone, appear to have fewer extrapyramidal symptoms than the classic neuroleptics and have shown some potential promise in the treatment of hyperactivity, aggression, oppositional behavior, and SIB in children with mental retardation and/or autism (Hardan, Johnson, Johnson, & Hrecznyj, 1996).

Most studies documenting negative effects of neuroleptics on learning involved the use of chlorpromazine, a drug with considerable sedating effects (see review by Aman & Singh, 1991). Conversely, studies involving the use of less sedating neuroleptics such as haloperidol have documented gains in learning among children with mental retardation (e.g., Anderson et al., 1984). Aman and Singh (1991) suggest that the effects of neuroleptics on learning are probably based on a number of factors, such as dosage, the particular drug used, and the degree to which target behaviors have interfered with performance.

Finally, in addition to sedation, potential adverse side effects of neuroleptics include dry mouth, blurred vision, urinary retention, abdominal pain, postural hypotension, and tardive dyskinesia. The latter is a movement disorder that is most common among individuals who have received large doses of neuroleptics for extended periods and may not be evident until the discontinuation of medication. It is of particular concern because the effects are irreversible (i.e., they continue or worsen after drug termination) in a substantial number of individuals.

Anticonvulsants

Between 12% and 16% of preschoolers and school-age children with moderate mental retardation are prescribed anticonvulsant drugs (Gadow & Kalachnik, 1981). About 2% of these children take these medications for both seizure control and behavioral concerns (Gadow & Kalachnik, 1981). Although few data are available on the prevalence of anticonvulsant drug therapy among children with mild mental retardation, studies of early childhood special education programs found anticonvulsants to be

prescribed in 6.6% of students (Gadow, 1977). Some studies which have examined the effects of anticonvulsants on behavior; however, most early research prior to the 1980s was poorly controlled or anecdotal (see Aman, 1983). Among children with mental retardation, studies that have examined the use of these medications for behavior control have had equivocal results (e.g., Goldberg & Kurland, 1970; Reid, Naylor, & Kay, 1981). Consequently, there is little support for the use of anticonvulsant drugs to control behavior in children with mental retardation (Aman & Singh, 1991). Finally, there is evidence that anticonvulsant drugs can adversely affect learning, cognition, motor functioning, and behavior (see review by Aman & Singh, 1991).

Anxiolytics

Antianxiety drugs, such as benzodiazepines, are prescribed for 4%–6% of individuals with mental retardation residing in the community (Hill et al., 1985). There are few studies on the ability of this class of drugs to control acting-out behavior in children with mental retardation (see review by Aman & Singh, 1991). Adverse side effects are likely to include depression of learning performance, drowsiness and sedation, increased irritability, and hyperactivity (see Handen, 1993; Werry & Aman, 1993). Anxiolytics have typically been prescribed to treat sleep disorders, excited/aggressive states, and anxiety disorders in children. The most common reasons for the use of sedatives such as diphenhydramine and hydroxyzine in children is to treat sleep disorders.

Antidepressants and Antimanics

Antidepressants are prescribed to fewer than 2% of adults and children with mental retardation (Hill et al., 1985). Most commonly this class of drugs is used for behavior control; there is little research on the efficacy of antidepressants for the treatment of depression among individuals with mental retardation (Gualtieri & Hawk, 1982). Antidepressant drugs can be divided into three categories: monoamine oxidase inhibitors (MAOIs), tricyclics (e.g., imipramine, desipramine), and selective serotonin reuptake inhibitors (e.g., fluoxetine, sertraline).

Most of the research with MAOIs and individuals with mental retardation was conducted over two decades ago, and most of this work was methodologically unsound. This class of drugs is now rarely used in pediatric populations because of its dangerous side effects (see Aman & Singh, 1991). There are few, if any, studies of the efficacy of tricyclic antidepressants for behavior control in children with mental retardation. Studies in adults with mental retardation are equivocal, with some showing positive findings (e.g., Field, Aman, White, & Vaithianathan, 1986), and others documenting a worsening of such behaviors as irritability, social withdrawal, and activity level (Aman, White, Vaithianathan, & Teehan, 1986). Difficulties in diagnosing depression in individuals with mental retardation (especially those functioning in the severe and profound ranges of mental retardation) make this literature a challenge to interpret. Tricyclics such as imipramine have a long history of use in treating nocturnal enuresis in typically developing children, but may be less efficacious in children with mental retardation (Blackwell & Currah, 1973). Desipramine has been found to be useful in treating ADHD in typically developing children (e.g., Biederman, Baldessarini, Wright, Knee, & Harmatz, 1989), but has not been studied in a controlled fashion in children with mental retardation. Finally, clomipramine has been used in the treatment of OCD and SIB in some children and adults with autism and/or pervasive developmental disorders (Gordon et al., 1992; McDougle et al., 1992).

Although studies involving the use of selective serotonin reuptake inhibitors such as fluoxetine are now appearing frequently in the literature, little information is available on children with mental retardation. Only a few studies have examined the efficacy of fluoxetine in older adolescents and adults with mental retardation (see review by Bregman, 1996). Most involved individuals functioning within the severe and profound ranges of mental retardation and targeted both depression and SIB. Although positive results are reported for most subjects (e.g., Bodfish & Madison, 1993; Markowitz, 1992; Ricketts et al., 1993), few of these studies were well controlled and many are case reports or open trials involving small groups of subjects. There is little available information on the effects of antidepressants on cognitive functioning and learning for children with mental retardation.

Finally, antimanics such as lithium carbonate, which have a long history as successful treatments for bipolar disorders, have been prescribed to treat aggression, overactivity, SIB, and affective disorders in individuals with mental retardation. For example, Dostal and Zvolsky (1970) documented a 53% reduction in aggression and 43% reduction in activity level in a group of 14 adolescents with severe mental retardation treated with lithium. However, lithium is not recommended for children under the age of 12 because of a lack of research in this area (Physicians' Desk Reference, 1995). Carbamazepine, an anticonvulsant, has also been used as a mood stabilizer in children (Stromgrew & Boller, 1985). More recently, the anticonvulsants valproic acid and divalproex sodium have been approved for the treatment of bipolar disorder. However, there is little information available on the efficacy of the latter two medications for the treatment of bipolar disorder among children and adults with mental retardation.

PARENT TRAINING

Parent training has become a well-accepted component of most treatment plans for children with mental retardation and other developmental disabilities (Harris, Alessandri, & Gill, 1991). In fact, a number of studies have demonstrated that parent-based treatment interventions can be superior to clinic-based treatment alone (e.g., Koegel, Schreibman, Britten, Burke, & O'Neill, 1982). Researchers in the field have demonstrated that parents can be trained in a wide range of behavioral interventions, including time out, positive reinforcement, token economies, and skill acquisition (see review by Harris et al., 1991). A number of highly structured parent training books and curriculums have also been field-tested and published during the past two decades. These include the skills training series for children with special needs by Baker, Brightman, Heifetz, and Murphy, (1976, 1977), covering such areas as teaching self-help skills, enhancing language skills, toilet training, and managing behavior problems. Similarly, Harris (1983) has described a 15-session parent training program covering such topics as social learning theory, data collection, reinforcement, punishment, chaining, fading, prompting, language stimulation and development, and generalization and maintenance of acquired skills.

A number of different approaches to parent training are available to the clinician. First, parents can be taught to manage behavior problems specific to their child's individual needs. Conversely, parents can be instructed via a general course or curriculum that covers a range of basic topics relevant to most families with children with mental retardation (e.g., reinforcement principles, behavior problem management, skills teaching). Finally, the question of whether to provide individual or group instruction must be considered. For example, there is some available literature documenting the efficacy of parent training within a group setting (e.g., Harris, 1983). However, in some cases, individualized instruction may be more appropriate. Clark and Baker (1983) identified a number of risk factors for parents who tended to do poorly with group instruction, including lower socioeconomic status, less experience with behavior modification techniques, and anticipation of greater problems in teaching their children. Conversely, parents who had intact marriages and who had made prior efforts to teach their children were more likely to have completed the group parent training course and to report successful outcomes.

The issue of maintenance and generalization remains a significant concern with most parent training interventions. Follow-up studies suggest that a majority of families discontinue the use of behavioral interventions and teaching over time. For example, Harris (1986) conducted a 4- to 7-year follow-up of children with autism who had participated in a parent training program. Fewer than half of the parents indicated that they were still using formal behavioral interventions with their children. Similar results were reported by Holmes, Hemsley, Rickett, and Likierman (1982) in their work with families of children with autism. In a study involving parents of children with mental retardation, Baker, Heifetz, and Murphy (1980) reported that most families had ceased formal teaching efforts at a 1-year follow-up. Obstacles included time constraints, the children's limited ability to learn, and lack of professional support. In their review of this literature, Harris et al. (1991) suggest that clinicians should not expect families to continue to implement behavioral interventions without ongoing professional support.

Parent training advocates have focused upon two somewhat different instructional methods: discrete-trial learning and incidental teaching. The former method has a longer history, dating back to work conducted with children with autism in the 1970s (e.g., Koegel, Russo, & Rincover, 1977). Typically, it involves teaching parents to obtain their child's attention; to provide simple, clear commands; to allow time for the child to respond; to provide appropriate levels of prompting (e.g., gestural cues, physical guidance); and to use appropriate consequences following the child's response. The pace of the lesson is typically controlled by the adult. The child is seated in an area where distractions are minimized, and the specific tasks are adult-selected. More recently, discrete-trial training has gained some notoriety through Lovaas's training program for children with autism and pervasive developmental disabilities (Lovaas, 1993; McEachin, Smith, & Lovaas, 1993). The McEachin et al. (1993) paper describes long-term outcome following intensive in-home treatment of preschoolers with autism; gains have been encouraging for a number of subjects involved in this research. This method of discrete-trial training has also been packaged and offered to families by a number of for-profit organizations.

The second instructional method, incidental teaching, has also received considerable attention in the literature (e.g., McGee et al., 1985). This less formal teaching approach involves using most interactions with children as opportunities for learning. Incidental teaching is characterized by (1) teaching in response to child initiations (e.g., a child approaches an adult to request or gesture for a preferred item); (2) teaching in the context of other activities (e.g., teaching during a play activity or a transition between activities); (3) teaching tasks selected by the child (e.g., if the child wants a specific toy, that is the task); and (4) not relying on standard prompting strategies, but varying prompts based upon the child's initial responses. In one of the few investigations comparing these two instructional methods (McGee et al., 1985), children with autism were taught expressive use of prepositions via both discrete-trial training and incidental teaching. Results indicated that incidental teaching promoted greater generalization and more spontaneous use of prepositions than did discrete-trial training.

COMMUNITY-BASED INTERVENTIONS

Family-centered assessment and intervention (Dunst, Trivette, & Deal, 1994) have recently come to be recognized as playing an important role in serving the needs of children with special needs and their families. This assessment and treatment model encompasses three goals: (1) identifying family needs, priorities, or concerns; (2) locating the formal and informal resources for meeting the needs; and (3) helping families identify their strengths and capabilities, and use these to procure resources in ways that strengthen family functioning (Hobbs et al., 1984). Family-centered or community-based resources offer a direct contrast to a professional-service-based resources model, which has historically been provided by agencies and school systems. The latter model is defined as "a specific or particular activity employed by a professional or professional agency for rendering help or assistance to an individual or group, such as occupational therapy or special instruction" (Trivette, Dunst, & Deal, in press, p. 75). Conversely, community-based resources are defined as "the full range of possible types of community help or assistance that might be mobilized and used to meet the needs of an individual or group" (Trivette et al., 1997, p. 76). Such an approach emphasizes using multiple sources of informal and formal community resources to address the needs of a child and his or her family, rather than relying on professional assistance.

According to Trivette et al. (1997), the professional-service-based model has a number of inherent weaknesses. For example, this model tends to be self-limiting because it is defined by what professionals do and is professionally centered. A second weakness is that this model is based upon providing limited resources only to the most needy families, as determined by professionals. Finally, this model often limits the use of richer and more diverse informal services and support networks which are available in the community.

The community-based resources model is supported by a growing body of empirical evidence. Three studies conducted by Dunst and his colleagues support the benefits of community-based practices over professional-service-based interventions in terms of their impact on families. For example, Dunst, Trivette, Starnes, Hamby, and Gordon (1993) conducted extensive case studies of the characteristics and effects of various types of practices employed by human service agencies in their work with a group of 22 families. The families were asked to rate their reactions or feelings to various practices, as well as to rate the treatment outcome (on a 5-point scale) for both professional-service-based and resource-based practices. Findings indicated that

practices deemed community-based were associated with significantly more positive outcomes than were professional-service-based models. A second study (Dunst, 1991) compared professional-service-based (formalized respite care) and community-based (collaborative efforts to identify a range of community-based child care options) early intervention programming with 30 families that had been randomly assigned to one of these two possible treatments. Results indicated that the resource-based approach demonstrated significantly greater change than did the professional-service-based model on measures of the number of individuals who provided child care, successful attempts to obtain child care, perceived control over obtaining child care, and overall satisfaction with child care. Finally, 1,300 parents of children participating in early intervention programs were requested to rate the extent to which service practices emphasized community resources, the level of progress their children made, and the extent to which parents felt in control over the kinds of services and activities provided (Trivette et al., 1997). Results indicated significantly higher ratings of child progress and parental control when practices were resource-based rather than professional-service-based.

Twelve specific categories of community-based resources are listed below (Dunst, Trivette, & Deal, 1988):

- Economic resources
- Physical and environmental resources
- Food and clothing resources
- Medical and dental care resources
- Employment and vocational resources
- Transportation and communication resources
- Adult education and enrichment resources
- Child education and intervention resources
- Child care resources
- Recreational resources
- Emotional resources
- Cultural and social resources

For instance, specific examples of recreational resources include story times at a local library, classes at the YMCA/YWCA or community center, play groups, and children's programs offered at churches. Trivette et al. (in press) describe a number of steps for assessing community-based resources. The first is to identify a family's needs, concerns, and priorities. Next, one must assist the family to identify resources for meeting each of these needs. This can best be accomplished through the development of a community network map, which identifies individuals who and institutions that come in contact with the family, and other resources that might be tapped to address family concerns. Trivette et al. (in press) recommend that resources available to address each concern be mapped separately, so as to insure that this process remain focused.

ALTERNATIVE OR NONTRADITIONAL INTERVENTIONS

A number of alternative or nontraditional therapies have claimed to treat a range of symptoms associated with mental retardation. Such interventions have not typically been subjected to rigorous scientific investigation; the claims for them are based instead upon subjective reports or case reports from only a few children or adults. In fact, some of these therapies have no scientific basis whatever. Van Dyke (1995, p. 300) recommends that families ask themselves seven questions when considering the risks and benefits of using alternative or nontraditional interventions. These are adapted here as follows:

1. Has your child's doctor or therapist provided written, convincing, easily understood information about research documenting the benefits of the therapy?
2. What are the possible risks of the procedure or therapy?
3. Do the benefits outweigh the risks?
4. Do you and your child want the therapies?
5. What kind of follow-up care is needed? How will your child be monitored? Who will monitor the child and how often will he or she be seen?
6. What are the long-term results? How are these documented?
7. What are the costs? Will insurance cover all or part of them?

Some of the more common alternative or nontraditional treatment options are presented below.

Cell Therapy

Cell therapy dates back to the 1960s and involves the use of injections containing freeze-dried animal cells. It was hypothesized that the injection of fetal cells might lead to improved brain growth (see review by Van Dyke, 1995). Proponents of this treatment cite gains on measures of IQ, motor, speech and social skills, as well as increased height, head circumference, and brain size, in children with Down syndrome. Typically, cell therapy may be combined with other treatments (e.g., vitamin or mineral therapy). However, research has provided little evidence to support it. In fact, Van Dyke (1995) suggests that cell therapy is not without certain risks, especially anaphylactic shock if the child is allergic to the injected material.

Vitamin Therapy

Harrell, Capp, Davis, Peerless, and Ravitz (1981) reported dramatic improvement (increases of up to 16 IQ points) in a group of children with mental retardation who had been given large doses of a vitamin/mineral formula in combination with thyroid supplementation (called the Bronson GTC3 formula). Subsequent research failed to replicate these earlier results (see review by Aman & Singh, 1988). There are a number of potential risks involved in the use of megavitamin therapies, including toxicity of vitamins if taken in large doses over extended periods; liver problems, nausea, vomiting, growth impairment, increased intracranial pressure, anaphylactic shock, and death with large doses of vitamin A; weakness, fatigue, headaches, vomiting, diarrhea, growth problems, and kidney problems with large doses of vitamin D; and liver problems with large doses of vitamin E.

Growth Hormone

With the recent availability of synthetic human growth hormone, some preliminary studies have suggested that synthetic growth hormone might promote growth if initiated at an early age, especially for children with Down syndrome (see Van Dyke, 1995). However, data in support of this therapy are preliminary at best, and risks such as increased rates of leukemia remain a concern.

Zinc/Selenium Supplements

Zinc and selenium are trace elements that affect the functioning of enzymes. In addition, zinc has beneficial effects on white blood cells, immunity, and metabolism. According to Van Dyke (1995), some preliminary studies have suggested that zinc and selenium (in combination with a dietary supplement) may improve immune system functioning and growth in children with Down syndrome. However, these data are extremely preliminary, and the available research has not been conducted in a controlled manner.

Dimethyl Sulfoxide

Dimethyl sulfoxide is a solvent that has been touted as improving cognitive functioning in children with Down syndrome. However, studies of it have failed to support such claims (Van Dyke, 1995).

Piracetam

Piracetam, a new drug structurally similar to a neurotransmitter, has been hypothesized to improve learning and memory. Although studies of adults with Alzheimer's disease and children with learning disabilities have suggested potential benefits, no research has been conducted in individuals with mental retardation (see review by Van Dyke, 1995).

Vitamin B$_6$ and 5-Hydroxytryptophan

Studies have documented that individuals with Down syndrome are deficient in both vitamin B$_6$ (pyridoxine) and 5-hydroxytryptophan (a serotonin precursor) by comparison with controls (Coleman et al., 1985; Pueschel, Reed, Cronk, & Goldstein, 1980). Both Coleman et al. (1985) and Pueschel et al. (1980) hypothesized that pyridoxine might increase serotonin levels in this population. The latter research group conducted a 3-year double-blind study comparing the effects of placebo, megadoses of pyridoxine, 5-hydroxytryptophan, and a pyridoxine–5-hydroxytryptophan combination in children with Down syndrome. Although increased end products of serotonin metabolism were documented in 40% of subjects, no gains were noted in adaptive measures and language development. Similarly, a 3-year study comparing pyridoxine and placebo in a group of infants with Down syndrome was conducted by Coleman et al. (1985). Although clinical and adaptive measures showed no effects, significant gains on measures of social functioning were found at the 3-year follow-up. However, approximately 5% of individuals taking pyridoxine reported side effects, including vomiting, abdominal pain, photosensitive blisters, and motor and sensory polyneuropathy. In their review of this literature, Aman and Singh (1988) conclude that research results have failed to provide evidence that vitamin B$_6$ produces useful clinical changes in children with Down syndrome.

Folic Acid

Folic acid, a vitamin, is the parent compound for a group of naturally occurring molecules called "folates." Individuals who have folate deficiencies may evidence a range of psychiatric symptoms. Administration of folic acid to adults with psychiatric disorders was reported to produce improvements in mood, drive, and sociability (Abou-Saleh & Coppen, 1986). In 1977, it was serendipitously found that the frequency of expression of fragile sites on human chromosomes grown in vitro was increased by culture media that were folate-deficient (see review by Aman & Kern, 1990–91). This led to the hypothesis that administration of folic acid might improve functioning in children diagnosed with fragile-X syndrome. As noted earlier in the chapter, this syndrome is a genetic disorder in which fragile sites are found on a significant proportion of the X chromosomes of cells grown in tissue culture (Turner & Jacobs, 1983). Behaviorally, individuals with fragile-X syndrome often exhibit overactivity, inattention, and behaviors similar to those of children and adults with autism (e.g., SIB and stereotypic behavior) (Hagerman, McBogg, & Hagerman, 1983); cognitive functioning ranges from profound to mild mental retardation. Aman and Kern (1990–91) reviewed the literature on folic acid efficacy in individuals with fragile-X syndrome and mental retardation, and concluded that although the research is incomplete, there are indications that prepubertal children may evidence improved behavioral and cognitive functioning with this treatment. However, there is not enough evidence to evaluate the potential efficacy of folic acid treatment for children with mental retardation alone.

Patterning

Patterning is derived from the work of Doman and Delacato (Delacato, 1966), which is based upon the assumption that a child must pass through the proper developmental sequence of stages of motor ability, language, visual, auditory, and other sensory to attain proper neurological organization. Patterning involves having an adult passively move a child's limbs in order first to initiate primitive newborn patterns and then to progress gradually through developmentally appropriate movement patterns (see review by Van Dyke, 1995). The therapy program requires a number of hours daily and considerable commitment by families and their social support networks. There is no research evidence documenting either short- or long-term results of patterning, leading organizations such as the American Academy of Pediatrics (1982) to express concern about this form of treatment (Gallico & Lewis, 1992).

Sensory Integration

Sensory integration is a treatment approach designed to address perceptual problems (Ayres, 1972). The theory behind it is that the ability of the cortex to respond to auditory and visual stimuli depends upon the organization of the stimuli in the brainstem (Gallico & Lewis, 1992, p. 380). To improve brainstem functioning, the child is given activities to improve balance and fine motor coordination. To date, there are few well-controlled studies providing evidence that sensory integration is helpful for children with mental retardation or other learning disorders (see Golden, 1984).

Facilitated Communication

Facilitated communication (FC) is a process by which a "facilitator" assists an individual with impaired communication skills to use a keyboard to communicate with others. This is typically accomplished by physically supporting the hand or arm of the individual. Initially developed by Rosemary Crossley in Australia, FC was introduced in the United States in 1989 by Douglas Biklen of Syracuse University (see Biklen, 1990), and quickly gained a strong following. Facilitators frequently reported that individuals previously thought to be severely or profoundly retarded and/or diagnosed with autism could communicate complex thoughts and feelings via FC. Subsequently, there were a number of high-profile cases concerning alleged abuse of individuals with mental retardation by family members or caregivers in which the allegations of abuse were made via FC (Hostler et al., 1993).

As with many new techniques or movements, the number of adherents initially grew at an impressive rate. Proponents of FC offered workshops in many sections of the country. A number of FC newsletters were also published to disseminate and share information. Changes in special education policy and service provision were made as well. For example, the General Assembly of Virginia mandated FC for use with handicapped individuals throughout the state. Despite the early enthusiasm of the proponents of FC, controlled research data began to tell a different story. Of 26 controlled studies involving 218 subjects, only 2 studies (and a total of 4 subjects) have shown any evidence of individuals' communicating via FC (Jacobson, 1993). Consequently, many professional organizations, including the AAMR, the APA, and the American Psychological Association have cautioned that FC should not be used to make any important decisions relevant to the individual being facilitated without clear, objective evidence as to the authorship of such messages.

FUTURE DIRECTIONS

A number of compelling issues face the field of mental retardation during the coming few years and into the new millennium. Hodapp and Dykens (1994) discuss five current issues and future challenges facing the field of mental retardation: definitional issues, the need for improved service delivery, joining the cultures of behavioral research (etiology-based research culture versus those using level of impairment approaches, such as psychologists and special educators), dual diagnosis, and changing populations with mental retardation. To this list should probably be added novel treatments, medication efficacy, prevention, ethical concerns, and political and social trends affecting service delivery. It is important for professionals within the field to be aware of how each of these issues may affect their work. Some of these issues are discussed below.

Definition of Mental Retardation

The field of mental retardation is continuing to struggle with issues relating to the very definition of mental retardation. As noted earlier, the 1992 revision of the AAMR definition has raised the IQ range for mental retardation from below 70 to "below 70 or 75," and also requires deficits in 2 of 10 adaptive functioning domains. This new definition has not been fully accepted by all professional associations, school districts, or states. For example, the American Psychological Association's Division 33 (Mental Retardation) has rejected this definition (Jacobson & Mulick, 1993), while the APA (1994) has chosen to accept the adaptive functioning provision of the AAMR definition but has retained the IQ cutoff of 70. Various school districts continue to use IQ cutoffs ranging from 70 to 79 for placement in special education eligibility. As Hodapp and Dykens (1996) suggest, this ongoing debate illustrates the many constituencies involved in the field of mental retardation, including individuals with mental retardation themselves, their families, professionals, and local, state, and federal agencies.

Trends in Service Delivery Systems and Funding

Perhaps the most important future direction involves service delivery systems themselves. The trend toward inclusion of students with mental retardation in classrooms with typically developing peers will continue to grow. A greater number of special education teachers will therefore work in an itinerant model, providing services to students in their regular classrooms, teaching in teams with regular education colleagues, and offering consultation. In fact, a number of universities (e.g., Duquesne University, Pittsburgh, PA) have begun to require that students in training for regular education also be trained as special education teachers. This reflects the need for all teachers to be skilled at instructing children with a wide range of abilities. We may soon see state teacher certification requirements reflecting this philosophy of inclusion. Inclusion efforts, which have shown growing promise among preschool and elementary school classrooms, will need to be expanded to serve middle- and high-school-age students. As the end of a decade of serious inclusion efforts approaches, the field may need to step back, examine its many successes as well as failures, and make any needed adaptations in this approach.

Statewide service provision models have also been developed in a number of areas and may continue to expand. Perhaps the best-known is the TEACCH model for children with autism, developed at the University of North Carolina in 1976, which has gradually been extended to the entire state (Schopler, Mesibov, & Hearsey, 1995). More recently, Delaware has implemented a statewide program for all children with a diagnosis of autism, including early intervention, inclusionary services, and vocational training (Delaware Department of Education, 1991).

Efforts will also continue to be made to provide a greater continuum of care for individuals living in their communities who have dual diagnoses of mental retardation and emotional/behavioral disorders. With support from the federal government, states have improved their efforts to coordinate and serve children and adolescents with severe emotional problems, including children with mental retardation and psychiatric disorders. For example, in 1984, Congress appropriated funds for the states to develop a comprehensive mental health service system for children and adolescents. The Child and Adolescent Service System Program (CASSP), was designed to help children and adolescents receive needed mental health services. CASSP's core principles emphasize the need for services to be child-centered, family-focused, community-based, multisystem (services planned in collaboration with all involved agencies), culturally competent (services recognize and respect attitudes, beliefs, and customs characteristic of each child's ethnic group), and least restrictive/least intrusive (Pennsylvania Department of Public Welfare, 1995a). Adherence to these principles has resulted in improved community- and family-based services. Despite such improvements in service delivery and coordination, many states have decreased their financial support for special education and mental health services. This has strained educational budgets and required districts to make hard choices regarding how the remaining funds will be allocated. Mental health care providers are facing similar problems .

Although some states no longer provide institutional care for individuals with mental retardation, as a result of major gains in deinstitutionalization and community placement (e.g., Vermont, New Hampshire, Maine, and Rhode Island), others continue to provide custodial care in congregate settings. Those remaining in state developmental centers (who are mostly adults) often have greater medical and psychiatric needs than individuals living in the community. Providing community-based services for this population is the current and growing challenge for the field. In some states, parent and family groups have been at odds regarding the continued need for large institutions to serve individuals with significant medical or behavioral needs. This has resulted in battles for limited financial resources (e.g., Pennsylvania House Bill 1000, 1995).

In addition, service providers are being challenged to provide meaningful employment opportunities for individuals with mental retardation, beyond traditional efforts for training in such areas as food service and janitorial work. Service providers will also be asked to rethink their roles vis-à-vis their "clients." For example, the 1990 passage of the Americans with Disabilities Act, a Civil Rights Act for People with Disabilities, has strengthened the voice of people with disabilities in advocating for themselves, directing their services, and gaining physical access to public spaces. Therefore, agencies will be called upon to be more responsive to the people they serve.

Changing Populations

Hodapp and Dykens (1996) provide data on the growing population of children with developmental disabilities as a result of alcohol and/or drug use among pregnant mothers, cases of lead poisoning in children, and the rise in the pediatric AIDS population. Such disabilities are often also associated with maternal undernutrition during the prenatal period, inadequate prenatal care, and the possible presence of hepatitis or sexually transmitted diseases (Conlon, 1992). Research indicates that all of these factors may be related to low birth weights, microcephaly, and cognitive and/or learning deficits (Conlon, 1992; Needleman et al., 1990). It remains unclear to what extent these groups of children will represent a greater portion of individuals with mental retardation, as interventions such as improved in utero genetic diagnosis and gene therapies cure or lessen the effects of a range of conditions presently associated with mental retardation. In addition, with improved medical services and technology, we are seeing increased life expectancy for individuals with mental retardation; thus, there is a growing

subspecialization in the area of geriatric services.

Prevention

Prevention efforts are typically categorized as primary, secondary, or tertiary. Primary interventions focus upon preventing health problems that can lead to mental retardation; examples include providing good prenatal care, routine health care, accident prevention, removing lead paint from houses, and so on. (Kasten & Coury, 1991). Secondary interventions are attempts to correct situations tht are likely to lead to mental retardation, such as amniocentesis and genetic counseling, newborn screening for phenylketonuria (and subsequent treatment if required), surgical placement of a shunt to treat hydrocephaly, and treatment for congenital hypothyroidism (Kasten & Coury, 1991). In addition, such programs as Head Start and other efforts to prevent developmental delays fall into the category of secondary prevention. Finally, tertiary prevention involves treatment of already existing mental retardation. This might include chelation therapy for a child with lead poisoning or vitamin B_6 for a child with Down syndrome.

It is likely that continuing gains will be made in all areas of prevention. For example, research continues to identify genetic causes for mental retardation that were previously thought to be familial (e.g., fragile-X syndrome). We can expect to see additional discoveries in the future. Similarly, we are beginning to learn more about the potential adverse affects of environmental toxins (e.g., lead, asbestos). As states enact laws to promote the use of seat belts, bicycle helmets, and other safety devices we will also witness a decrease in the number of head injuries and resulting cognitive impairments in children.

Novel Treatments and Approaches

The promulgation of new treatments for mental retardation and associated psychiatric disorders will continue. Interest in treatments such as patterning during the 1960s and 1970s has been replaced by interest in FC and new treatments for motor disorders in the 1990s. Many of these treatments have limited research support, but will gain popularity nonetheless among families of individuals with mental retardation, as well as among private and public agencies. There is also a growing movement to promote the use of "positive approaches" with individuals with mental retardation (e.g., Lovett, 1996). The proponents of such approaches tend to reject more traditional behavioral interventions, which are seen as coercive in nature. Similarly, the traditional habilitation model tends to be rejected (especially for adults), with greater emphasis on providing those supports needed for an individual to function as successfully as possible in the community. This includes developing community ties, social supports, and informal community networks. As discussed earlier, many states have developed treatment guidelines that severely limit the use of more traditional behavioral interventions. It will be important for professionals in the field to understand these interventions and trends in service philosophy. Such an understanding will allow clinicians to have meaningful and helpful discussions with families regarding the possible benefits and risks of various treatment options. It will also be essential in order for clinicians to develop and implement treatment plans consistent with the prevailing philosophies of the agencies or schools in which children or adolescents are served.

Medication Efficacy

As discussed in an earlier section, we know relatively little about many of the medications used to treat both children and adults with mental retardation. This is due both to an earlier, mistaken belief that individuals with mental retardation are less likely to have psychiatric disorders, and to the fact that children and adults with mental retardation have tended to be excluded in many medication efficacy studies. With the growing acceptance that individuals with mental retardation can have the full range of psychiatric disorders and may actually be at greater risk than the general population for behavioral/emotional problems, we have begun to see an increase in drug studies with this population.

Ethical Concerns

Batshaw and Perret (1992) note that a number of ethical dilemmas face health care professionals working with individuals with developmental disabilities. Many of these dilemmas have resulted from the availability of more complex technology, which provides earlier information regarding the status of a fetus, as well as the ability to keep infants alive despite significant and often life-threatening physical defects. Important questions include the following:

1. Should screening and prenatal diagnosis be performed on women who are genetically at-risk of having children with severe disabilities?,
2. If so, should their fetuses be aborted? Are there instances in which medical care can ethically be withheld from a newborn infant with a disability?,
3. Is it ethical to perform experimental research on children with disabilities?,
4. Is it ethical to use infants who have ultimately fatal birth defects as organ donors?, and
5. Should young adults with mental retardation have full sexual rights? (Batshaw & Perret, 1992, p. 547)

In addition, does an adolescent or adult with mental retardation have the right to refuse medical or psychiatric care? Can such an individual be denied medical treatment (e.g., transplants or other life-saving procedures) because of an assumed poorer "quality of life"? What rights do adolescents and adults with mental retardation have to determine where they will live and work? And should individuals with mental retardation be allowed to be parents? Many of these ethical issues are based upon the assumption that individuals with mental retardation are "different" and of lesser value than the general population. Moreover, these issues have typically been discussed without the direct participation of people with mental retardation.

CONCLUSION

The field of mental retardation has witnessed a significant change in its service delivery system during the past few decades. Along with this change has come the development of a wide range of treatment interventions. Although some of these have been controversial, many have a strong empirical base to support their clinical efficacy. The majority of treatment interventions have been directed toward children, but some have emphasized the provision of services to families and/or teachers of children with mental retardation. The present chapter has presented information on a range of child-focused interventions (e.g., educational efforts, skill development, behavior problem management, psychopharmacological interventions), as well as parent training, community-based interventions, and nontraditional treatments. This chapter's approach to the treatment of behavior problems in children with mental retardation has been to address the development of appropriate communication, social, and self-help skills, along with the elimination of maladaptive behaviors and the reinforcement of alternative, appropriate behaviors. The needs to conduct a thorough functional assessment prior to treatment, to implement empirically based interventions, to use single-subject designs to demonstrate clinical efficacy, and to program for generalization have also been emphasized. Finally, the appropriateness of adjunct treatments, such as pharmacotherapy, has also been discussed. It is only through a carefully considered combination of a range of resources and interventions that the needs of children with mental retardation and their families can be met.

REFERENCES

Abou-Saleh, H. T., & Coppen, A. (1986). Psychiatric progress: The biology of folate in depression. Implications for nutritional hypotheses of the psychoses. *Journal of Psychiatric Research, 20,* 91–101.

Aeschleman, S., & Schladenhauffen, J. (1984). Acquisition, generalization and maintenance of grocery shopping skills by severely mentally retarded adolescents. *Applied Research in Mental Retardation, 5,* 145–258.

Aman, M. G. (1983). Psychoactive drugs in mental retardation. In J. L. Matson & F. Andrasik (Eds.), *Treatment issues and innovations in mental retardation* (pp. 455–513). New York: Plenum Press.

Aman, M. G., & Kern, R. A. (1990–91). The efficacy of folic acid in fragile-X syndrome and other developmental disabilities. *Journal of Child and Adolescent Psychopharmacology, 1,* 285–295.

Aman, M. G., Marks, R. E., Turbott, S. H., Wilsher, C. P., & Merry, S. N. (1991). Clinical effects of methylphenidate and thioridazine in intellectually subaverage children. *Journal of the American Academy of Child and Adolescent Psychiatry, 30,* 246–256.

Aman, M. G., & Singh, N. N. (1980). The usefulness of thioridazine for treating childhood disorders: Fact or folklore? *American Journal of Mental Deficiency, 84,* 331–338.

Aman, M. G., & Singh, N. N. (1988). Vitamin, mineral, and dietary treatments. In M. G. Aman & N. N. Singh (Eds.), *Psychopharmacology of the developmental disabilities* (pp. 168–196). New York: Springer-Verlag.

Aman, M. G., & Singh, N. N. (1991). Pharmacological intervention. In J. L. Matson & J. H. Mulick (Eds.), *Handbook of mental retardation* (2nd ed., pp. 347–372). New York: Pergamon Press.

Aman, M. G., Teehan, C. J., White, A. J., Turbott, S. H., & Vaithianathan, C. (1989). Haloperidol treatment with chronically medicated residents: Dose effects on clinical behavior and reinforcement contingencies. *American Journal of Mental Retardation, 93,* 452–460.

Aman, M. G., White, A. J., & Field, C. J. (1984). Chlorpromazine effects on stereotypic and conditioned behavior: A pilot study. *Journal of Mental Deficiency Research, 28,* 253–260.

Aman, M. G., White, A. J., Vaithianathan, D., & Teehan, C. J. (1986). Preliminary study of imipramine in profoundly retarded residents. *Journal of Autism and Developmental Disorders, 16,* 263–273.

American Academy of Pediatrics. (1982). The Doman–Delacato treatment of neurologically handicapped children. *Pediatrics, 70,* 810–812.

American Association on Mental Retardation (AAMR). (1992). *Mental retardation: Definition, classification, and systems of supports* (9th ed.). Washington, DC: Author.

American Psychiatric Association (APA). (1994). *Diagnostic and statistical manual of mental disorders* (4th ed.). Washington, DC: Author.

Anderson, L. T., Campbell, M., Grega, D. M., Perry, R., Small, A. M., & Green, W. H. (1984). Haloperidol in the treatment of infantile autism: Effects on learning and behavioral symptoms. *American Journal of Psychiatry, 141,* 1195–1202.

Ando, H., & Yoshimura, I. (1978). Prevalence of maladaptive behavior in retarded children as a function of IQ and age. *Journal of Abnormal Child Psychology, 6,* 345–349.

Aronson, M., & Fallstrom, K. (1977). Immediate and long-term effects of developmental training in children with Down's syndrome. *Developmental Medicine and Child Neurology, 19,* 489–494.

Ayres, A. J. (1972). Improving academic scores through sensory integration. *Journal of Learning Disabilities, 5,* 338–343.

Azrin, N. H., & Foxx, R. M. (1971). A rapid method of toilet training the institutionalized retarded. *Journal of Applied Behavior Analysis, 4,* 89–99.

Azrin, N. H., Sneed, T., & Foxx, R. M. (1973). Dry bed: A rapid method of eliminating bedwetting (enuresis) of the retarded. *Behaviour Research and Therapy, 11,* 427–434.

Babbitt, R. L., Hoch, T. A., Coe, D. A., Cataldo, M. F., Kelly, K. J., Stackhouse, C., & Perman, J. A. (1994). Behavioral assessment and treatment of pediatric feeding disorders. *Journal of Developmental and Behavioral Pediatrics, 15,* 278–291.

Baer, D. M., Williams, J., Osnes, P., & Stokes, T. (1985). Generalized verbal control and correspondence training. *Behavior Modification, 9,* 477–489.

Baker, B. L., Brightman, A. J., Heifetz, L. J., & Murphy, D. M. (1976). *Behavior problems: A skills training series for children with special needs.* Champaign, IL: Research Press.

Baker, B. L., Brightman, A. J., Heifetz, L. J., & Murphy, D. M. (1977). *Toilet training: A skills training series for children with special needs.* Champaign, IL: Research Press.

Baker, B. L., Heifetz, L. J., & Murphy, M. D. (1980). Behavioral training for parents of mentally retarded children: One-year follow-up. *American Journal of Mental Deficiency, 85,* 31–38.

Barrett, R. P., Matson, J. L., Shapiro, E. S., & Ollendick, T. H. (1981). A comparison of punishment and DRO procedures for treating stereotypic behavior of mentally retarded children. *Applied Research in Mental Retardation, 2,* 247–256.

Barton, E. S. (1973). Operant conditioning of appropriate and inappropriate social speech in the profoundly retarded. *Journal of Mental Deficiency Research, 17,* 183–191.

Barton, E. S., Guess, D., Garcia, E., & Baer, D. M. (1970). Improvement of retardates' mealtime behaviors by timeout procedures using multiple baseline techniques. *Journal of Applied Behavior Analysis, 3,* 77–84.

Batshaw, M. L., & Perret, Y. M. (1992). Some ethical dilemmas. In M. L. Batshaw & Y. M. Perret (Eds.), *Children with disabilities: A medical primer* (3rd ed., pp. 547–561). Baltimore: Paul H. Brookes.

Baumeister, A. A. (1978). Origins and control of stereotyped movements. In C. E. Meyer (Ed.), *Quality of life in severely and profoundly mentally retarded people: Research foundations for improvement* (AAMD Monograph No. 3.). Washington, DC: American Assocation on Mental Deficiency.

Berkowitz, S., Sherry, P., & Davis, B. (1971). Teaching self-feeding skills to profound retardates using reinforcement and fading procedures. *Behavior Therapy, 2,* 62–67.

Berkson, G. (1987, August). *Three approaches to an understanding of abnormal stereotyped behaviors.* Paper presented at the 95th Annual Convention of the American Psychological Association, New York.

Biederman, J., Baldessarini, R. J., Wright, V., Knee, D., & Harmatz, J. S. (1989). A double-blind placebo controlled study of desipramine in the treatment of ADD: I. Efficacy. *Journal of the American Academy of Child and Adolescent Psychiatry, 28,* 777–784.

Biklen, D. (1990). Communication unbound: Autism and praxis. *Harvard Educational Review, 60,* 291–314.

Blackwell, B., & Currah, J. (1973). The psychopharmacology of nocturnal enuresis. In I. Kolvin, R. McKeith, & S. Meadow (Eds.), *Bladder control and enuresis* (pp. 231–257). London: Heinemann.

Bodfish, J. W., & Madison, J. T. (1993). Diagnosis and fluoxatine treatment of compulsive behavior disorder of adults with mental retardation. *American Journal on Mental Retardation, 98,* 360–367.

Bregman, J. D. (1996). Mental retardation: Pharmacologic interventions. *Child and Adolescent Psychiatric Clinics of North America, 5,* 853–879.

Bricker, D. D., & Down, M. G. (1980). Early intervention with the young severely handicapped child. *Journal of the Association for the Severely Handicapped, 5,* 130–142.

Brown, L. (1995, February). *Transition issues for people with disabilities.* Talk presented at the Allegheny County Intermediate Unit, Pittsburgh.

Bruder, M. B. (1986). Acquisition and generalization of teaching techniques: A study with parents of toddlers. *Behavior Modification, 10,* 391–414.

Burchard, J. D., & Barrera, F. (1972). An analysis of timeout and response cost in a programmed environment. *Journal of Applied Behavior Analysis, 5,* 271–282.

Campbell, M., Gonzalez, N. M., Ernst, M., Silva, R. R., & Werry, J. S. (1993). Antipsychotics (neuroleptics). In J. S. Werry & M. G. Aman (Eds.), *Practitioner's guide to psychoactive drugs for children and adolescents* (pp. 269–296). New York: Plenum Medical Book Company.

Carlberg, C., & Kavale, K. (1980). The efficacy of special versus regular class placement for excecptional children: A meta-analysis. *Journal of Special Education, 14,* 295–309.

Caro-Martinez, L., Lurier, A., & Handen, B. L. (1994, October). *Developmentally disabled preschoolers with and without attention deficit hyperactivity disorder: A comparison study.* Paper presented at the Conference on Children and Adolescents with Emotional or Behavioral Disorders, Virginia Beach, VA.

Carr, E. G., & Durand, M. (1985). Reducing behavior problems through functional communication training. *Journal of Applied Behavior Analysis, 18,* 111–126.

Carr, E. G., Newsom, C. D., & Binkoff, J. A. (1980). Escape as a factor in the aggressive behavior of two retarded children. *Journal of Applied Behavior Analysis, 13,* 101–117.

Carr, E. G., Taylor, J. C., Carlson, J. I., & Robinson, S. (1989, September). *Reinforcement and stimulus-based treatments for severe behavior problems in developmental disabilities.* Paper presented at the Consensus Development Conference on Destructive Behavior, National Institutes of Health, Bethesda, MD.

Carr, J., (1975). *Young children with Down's syndrome.* London: Butterworth.

Pennsylvania Department of Public Welfare. (1995a). *Pennsylvania Child and Adolescent Service System Program (CASSP): A comprehensive mental health service system for children, adolescents and their families* [Pamphlet]. Harrisburg: Author.

Chandler, L. K., Fowler, S. A., & Lubbeck, R. C. (1992). An analysis of the effects of multiple setting events on the social behavior of preschool children with special needs. *Journal of Applied Behavior Analysis, 25,* 249–263.

Clark, D. B., & Baker, B. L. (1983). Predicting outcome in parent training. *Journal of Consulting and Clinical Psychology, 51,* 309–311.

Clunies-Ross, G. G. (1979). Accelerating the development of Down's syndrome infants and young children. *Journal of Special Education, 13,* 169–177.

Coleman, M., Sobel, S., Bhagaven, H. N., Coursin, D., Marquardt, A., Guay, M., & Hunt, C. (1985). A double blind study of vitamin B6 in Down's syndrome infants: Part I. Clinical and biochemical results. *Journal of Mental Deficiency Research, 29,* 233–240.

Conlon, C. J. (1992). New threats to development: Alcohol, cocaine, and AIDS. In M. L. Batshaw & Y. M. Perret (Eds.), *Children with disabilities: A medical primer* (3rd ed., pp. 111–136). Baltimore: Paul H. Brookes.

Connolly, B., Morgan, S., & Russell, F. F. (1984). Evaluation of children with Down syndrome who participated in an early intervention program: Second follow-up study. *Physical Therapy, 64,* 1515–1519.

Connolly, B., Morgan, S., Russell, F. F., & Richardson, B. (1980). Early intervention with Down syndrome children: Follow-up report. *Physical Therapy, 60,* 1405–1408.

Cooke, T., Apollini, T., & Sundberg, D. (1981). *Early independence: A developmental curriculum.* Bellevue, WA: Edmark.

Cooper, L., Wacker, D., Thursby, E., Plagmann, L., Harding, J., Millard, T., & Derby, M. (1992). Analysis of the effects of task preferences, task demands, and adult attention on child behavior in outpatient and classroom settings. *Journal of Applied Behavior Analysis, 25,* 823–840.

Corbett, J. A. (1979). Psychiatric morbidity and mental retardation. In F. E. James & R. P. Snaith (Eds.), *Psychiatric illness and mental handicap* (pp. 11–25). London: Gaskell.

Cullinan, D., Gadow, K. D., & Epstein, M. H. (1987). Psychotropic drug treatment among learning disabled, educable mentally retarded, and seriously emotionally disturbed students. *Journal of Abnormal Child Psychology, 15,* 469–477.

Cuvo, A. J. (1978). Validating task analyses of community living skills. *Vocational Evaluation and Work Adjustment Bulletin, 11,* 13–21.

Delacato, C. H. (1966). *Neurological organization and reading.* Springfield, IL: Charles C Thomas.

Delaware State Department of Education. (1991). *Delaware administrative manual: Programs for exceptional children.* Dover: Author.

Doleys, D. M., Stacy, D., & Knowles, S. (1981). Modification of grooming behavior in adult retarded. *Behavior Modification, 5,* 119–128.

Doleys, D. M., Wells, K. C., Hobbs, S. A., Roberts, M. W., & Cartelli, L. M. (1976). The effects of social punishment on noncompliance: A comparison with timeout and positive practice. *Journal of Applied Behavior Analysis, 9,* 471–482.

Donnellan, A. M., LaVigna, G. G., Negri-Shoeltz, N., & Fassbender, L. L. (1988). *Progress without punishment: Effective approaches for learners with behavior problems.* New York: Teachers College Press.

Dorsey, M. F., Iwata, B. A., Ong, P., & McSween, T. E. (1980). Treatment of self-injurious behavior using a water mist: Initial response suppression and generalization. *Journal of Applied Behavior Analysis, 13,* 343–353.

Dostal, T., & Zvolsky, P. (1970). Antiaggressive effects of lithium salts in severely mentally retarded adolescents. *International Pharmacopsychiatry, 5,* 203–207.

Dunst, C. J. (1991, February). *Empowering families: Principles and outcomes.* Paper presented at the 4th Annual Research Conference, "A System of Care of Children's Mental Health: Expanding the Research Base," Tampa, FL.

Dunst, C. J., Trivette, C. M., & Deal, A. G. (1988). *Enabling and empowering families: Principles and guidelines for practice.* Cambridge, MA: Brookline Books.

Dunst, C. J., Trivette, C. M., & Deal, A. G. (1994). *Supporting and strengthening families: Methods, strategies and practices* (Vol. 1). Cambridge, MA: Brookline Books.

Dunst, C. J., Trivette, C. M., & Jodry, W. (in press). Influences of social support on children with disabilities and their families. In J. M. Guralnick (Ed.), *The effectiveness of early intervention: Directions for second generation research.* Baltimore: Paul H. Brookes.

Dunst, C. J., Trivette, C. M., Starnes, A. L., Hamby, D. W., & Gordon, N. J. (1993). *Building and evaluating family support initiatives: A national study of programs for persons with developmental disabilities.* Baltimore: Paul H. Brookes.

Durand, V. M., & Carr, E. G. (1992). An analysis of maintenance following functional communication training. *Journal of Applied Behavior Analysis, 25,* 777–794.

Eaton, I., & Menolascino, F. (1982). Psychiatric disorder in the mentally retarded: Types, problems, and challenges. *American Journal of Mental Deficiency, 139,* 1297–1303.

Eisenberger, R., & Cameron, J. (1996). Detrimental effects of reward: Reality or myth? *American Psychologist, 51,* 1153–1166.

Eisenberger, R., & Selbst, M. (1994). Does reward increase or decrease creativity? *Journal of Personality and Social Psychology, 49,* 520–528.

Epstein, M. H., Cullinan, D., & Gadow, K. (1986). Teacher ratings of hyperactivity in learning-disabled, emotionally disturbed, and mentally retarded children. *Journal of Special Education, 22,* 219–229.

Eyman, R. K., & Call, T. (1977). Maladaptive behavior and community placement of mentally retarded persons. *American Journal of Mental Deficiency, 82,* 137–144.

Favell, J., McGimsey, J., & Jones, M. (1980). Rapid eating in the retarded: Reduction by nonaversive procedures. *Behavior Modification, 4,* 481–492.

Field, C. J., Aman, M. G., White, A. J., & Vaithiana-than, C. (1986). A single-subject study of imi-pramine in a mentally retarded woman with depressive symptoms. *Journal of Mental Deficiency Research, 30,* 191–198.

Foxx, R. M., & Azrin, N. H. (1972). Restitution: A method of eliminating aggressive–disruptive be-haviour of retarded and brain damaged patients. *Behaviour Research and Therapy, 10,* 15–27.

Foxx, R. M., & Azrin, N. H. (1973). The elimination of autistic self-stimulatory behavior by overcorrec-tion. *Journal of Applied Behavior Analysis, 6,* 1–14.

Foxx, R. M., McMorrow, M., Bittle, R., & Ness, J. (1986). An analysis of social skills generalization in two natural settings. *Journal of Applied Behavior Analysis, 19,* 299–305.

Foxx, R. M., & Shapiro, S. T. (1978). The timeout rib-bon: A nonexclusionary timeout procedure. *Jour-nal of Applied Behavior Analysis, 11,* 125–136.

Fraser, W., Leudar, I., Gray, J., & Campbell, I. (1986). Psychiatric and behaviour disturbance in mental handicap. *Journal of Mental Deficiency Research, 30,* 49–57.

Freagon, S., & Rotatori, A. F. (1982). Comparing natu-ral and artificial environments in training self-care skills to group home residents. *Journal of the Asso-ciation for the Severely Handicapped, 7,* 73–86.

Friman, P. C., & Vallmer, D. (1995). Successful use of the nocturnal urine alarm for diurnal enuresis. *Journal of Applied Behavior Analysis, 28,* 89–90.

Gadow, K. D. (1977). *Psychotropic and antiepileptic drug treatment with children in early childhood special education.* Champaign: University of Illi-nois, Institute for Child Behavior and Develop-ment. (ERIC Document Reproduction Service No. ED 162 294).

Gadow, K. D., & Kalachnik, J. (1981). Prevalence and pattern of drug treatment for behavior and seizure disorders of TMR students. *American Journal of Mental Deficiency, 85,* 588–595.

Gadow, K. D., & Poling, A. G. (1988). *Pharma-cotherapy and mental retardation.* Boston: College Hill Press.

Gallico, R., & Lewis, M. E. B. (1992). Learning dis-abilities. In M. L. Batshaw & Y. M. Perret (Eds.), *Children with disabilities: A medical primer* (3rd ed., pp. 365–385). Baltimore: Paul H. Brookes.

Garcia, E. E., Bullet, J., & Rust, F. P. (1977). An ex-perimental analysis of language training generali-zation across classroom and home. *Behavior Modification, 1,* 531–550.

Gold, M. (1980). *Try another way training manual.* Champaign, IL: Research Press.

Goldberg, J. B., & Kurland, A. A. (1970). Dilantin treatment of hospitalized cultural-familial retarda-tion. *Journal of Nervous and Mental Disease, 150,* 133–137.

Golden, G. S. (1984). Symposium on learning disor-ders: Controversial therapies. *Pediatric Clinics of North America, 31,* 459–469.

Goodman, J. F., Cecil, H. S., & Barker, W. F. (1984). Early intervention with retarded children: Some encouraging results. *Developmental Medicine and Child Neurology, 26,* 47–55.

Gordon, C. T., Rapoport, J. L., Hamburger, S. D., State, R., & Mannheim, G. (1992). Differential re-sponse of seven subjects with autistic disorder to clomipramine and desipramine. *American Journal of Psychiatry, 149,* 363–366.

Green, C. W., Reid, D. H., White, L. K., Halford, R. C., Brittain, D. P., & Gardner, S. M. (1988). Identi-fying reinforcers for persons with profound handi-caps: Staff opinion versus systematic assessment of preferences. *Journal of Applied Behavior Analysis, 21,* 31–43.

Gross, A. M., Farrar, M. J., & Liner, D. (1982). Re-duction of trichotillomania in a retarded cere-bral palsied child using overcorrection, facial screening, and differential reinforcement of other behavior. *Education and Treatment of Children, 5,* 133–140.

Grossman, J. J. (Ed.). (1973). *Manual on terminology and classification in mental retardation.* Washing-ton, DC: American Association on Mental Defi-ciency Special Publication series no. 2.

Grossman, J. J. (Ed.). (1983). *Classification in mental retardation.* Washington, DC: American Associa-tion on Mental Deficiency.

Gualtieri, C. T., & Hawk, B. (1982). Antidepressant and antimanic drugs. In S. I. Breuning & A. D. Pol-ing (Eds.), *Drugs and mental retardation* (pp. 215–234). Springfield, IL: Charles C Thomas.

Guralnick, M. J., & Bricker, D. (1987). Cognitive and general developmental delays. In M. J. Guralnick & F. C. Bennett (Eds.), *The effectiveness of early in-tervention for at-risk and handicapped children* (pp. 115–168). Orlando, FL: Academic Press.

Hagerman, R. J., McBogg, P., & Hagerman, P. J. (1983). The fragile X syndrome: History, diagno-sis, and treatment. *Journal of Developmental and Behavioral Pediatrics, 4,* 122–130.

Hagerman, R. J., & Sobesky, W. E. (1989). Psychopa-thology in fragile X syndrome. *American Journal of Orthopsychiatry, 59,* 142–152.

Handen, B. L. (1993). Pharmacotherapy in mental re-tardation and autism. *School Psychology Review, 22,* 162–183.

Handen, B. L., Apolito, P. M., & Seltzer, G. B. (1984). Use of DRL to decrease repetitive speech in an autistic adolescent. *Journal of Behavior Therapy and Experimental Psychiatry, 15,* 359–364.

Handen, B. L., Breaux, A. M., Gosling, A., Ploof, D. L., & Feldman, H. (1990). Efficacy of Ritalin among mentally retarded children with ADHD. *Pe-diatrics, 86,* 922–930.

Handen, B. L., Breaux, A. M., Janosky, J., McAuliffe, S., Feldman, H., & Gosling, A. (1992). Effects and non-effects of methylphenidate in children with mental retardation and ADHD. *Journal of the American Academy of Child and Adolescent Psy-chiatry, 31,* 455–461.

Handen, B. L., Feldman, H., Gosling, A., Breaux, A. M., & McAuliffe, S. (1991). Adverse side effects of Ritalin among mentally retarded children with ADHD. *Journal of the American Academy of Child and Adolescent Psychiatry, 30*(2), 241–245.

Handen, B. L., Mandell, F., & Russo, D. C. (1986). Feeding induction in children who refuse to eat. *American Journal of Diseases of Children, 140,* 52–54.

Handen, B. L., McAuliffe, S., & Caro-Martinez, L. (1996). Learning effects of methylphenidate in children with mental retardation. *Journal of Developmental and Physical Disabilities, 8,* 335–346.

Handen, B. L., Parrish, J. M., McClung, T. J., Kerwin, M. E., & Evans, L. D. (1992). Using guided compliance versus time out to promote child compliance: A preliminary comparative analysis in an analogue context. *Research in Developmental Disabilities, 13,* 159–170.

Handen, B. L., & Zane, T. (1987). Delayed prompting: A review of procedural variations and results. *Research in Developmental Disabilities, 8,* 307–330.

Hansen, D. J., St. Lawrence, J. S., & Christoff, K. A. (1989). Group conversational-skills training with inpatient children and adolescents. *Behavior Modification, 13,* 4–31.

Hardan, A., Johnson, K., Johnson, C., & Hrecznyj, B. (1996). Risperidone treatment of children and adolescents with developmental disorders. *Journal of the American Academy of Child and Adolescent Psychiatry, 35,* 1551–1556.

Haring, T. G., & Kennedy, C. H. (1990). Contextual control of problem behavior in students with severe disabilities. *Journal of Applied Behavior Analysis, 23,* 235–243.

Haring, T. G., Roger, B., Lee, M., Breen, C., & Gaylord-Ross, R. (1986). Teaching social language to moderately handicapped students. *Journal of Applied Behavior Analysis, 19,* 159–171.

Harrell, R. F., Capp, R. H., Davis, D. R., Peerless, J., & Ravitz, L. R. (1981). Can nutritional supplements help mentally retarded children?: An exploratory study. *Proceedings of the National Academy of Sciences USA, 78,* 574–578.

Harris, S. L. (1983). *Families of the developmentally disabled: A guide to behavioral intervention.* New York: Pergamon Press.

Harris, S. L. (1986). Parents as teachers: A four to seven year follow up of parents of children with autism. *Child and Family Behavior Therapy, 8,* 39–47.

Harris, S. L., Alessandri, M., & Gill, M. J. (1991). Training parents of developmentally disabled children. In J. L. Matson & J. A. Mulick (Eds.), *Handbook of mental retardation* (2nd ed., pp. 373–381). New York: Pergamon Press.

Heber, R. (1959). A manual on terminology and classification in mental retardation (rev. ed.). *American Journal of Mental Deficiency, 56*(Monograph Suppl.).

Hill, B. K., Balow, E. A., & Bruininks, R. H. (1985). A national study of prescribed drugs in institutions and community residential facilities for mentally retarded people. *Psychopharmacology Bulletin, 21,* 279–284.

Hill, B. K., & Bruininks, R. (1984). Maladaptive behavior of mentally retarded individuals in residential facilities. *American Journal of Mental Deficiency, 88,* 380–387.

Hobbs, N., Dokecki, P., Hoover-Dempsey, K., Moroney, R., Shayne, M., & Weeks, K. (1984). *Strengthening families.* San Francisco: Jossey-Bass.

Hobbs, T., & Peck, C. (1985). Toilet training people with profound mental retardation: A cost effective procedure for large residential settings. *Behavioral Engineering, 9,* 50–57.

Hocutt, A. M. (1996). Effectiveness of special education: Is placement the critical factor? *The Future of Children, 6,* 77–102.

Hodapp, R. M., & Dykens, E. M. (1994). Mental retardation's two cultures of behavioral research. *American Journal of Mental Retardation, 98,* 675–687.

Holmes, N., Hemsley, R., Rickett, J., & Likierman, H. (1982). Parents as cotherapists: Their perceptions of a home-based behavioral treatment for autistic children. *Journal of Autism and Developmental Disorders, 12,* 331–342.

Horner, R. H., Dunlap, G., Koegel, R. L., Carr, E. G., Sailor, W., Anderson, J., Albin, R. W., & O'Neill, R. E. (1990). Toward a technology of "nonaversive" behavioral support. *Journal of the Association for Persons with Severe Handicaps, 15,* 125–132.

Horner, R. H., & Keilitz, I. (1975). Training mentally retarded adolescents to brush their teeth. *Journal of Applied Behavior Analysis, 8,* 301–309.

Hostler, S. L., Allaire, J. H., & Christoph, R. A. (1993). Childhood sexual abuse reported by facilitated communication. *Pediatrics, 91,* 1190–1192.

Huguenin, N., Weidenman, L., & Mulick, J. A. (1991). Programmed instruction. In J. L. Matson & J. A. Mulick (Eds.), *Handbook of mental retardation* (2nd ed., pp. 451–467). New York: Pergamon Press.

Iwata, B., Dorsey, M., Slifer, K, Bauman, K., & Richman, G. (1994). Toward a functional analysis of self-injury. *Journal of Applied Behavior Analysis, 27,* 197–210.

Jacobson, J. W. (1982). Problem behavior and psychiatric impairment within a developmentally disabled population: I. Behavior frequency. *Applied Research in Mental Retardation, 3,* 121–139.

Jacobson, J. W. (1993, August). *Facilitated communication: Don't look at the man behind the curtain.* Symposium presented at the 112th Annual Convention of the American Psychiatric Association, Toronto.

Jacobson, J. W., & Mulick, J. (1992). A new definition of mental retardation or a new definition of practice? *Psychology in Mental Retardation and Developmental Disabilities, 18,* 9–14.

Johnson, W. L., & Day, R. M. (1992). The incidence and prevalence of self-injurious behavior. In J. K. Luiselli, J. L. Matson, & N. N. Singh (Eds.), *Self-injurious behavior: Analysis, assessment, and treatment* (pp. 21–58). New York: Springer-Verlag.

Johnson-Martin, N., Attermeier, S., & Hacker, B. (1990). *The Carolina Curriculum for Preschoolers with Special Needs*. Baltimore: Paul H. Brookes.

Kasten, E. F., & Coury, D. L. (1991). Health policy and prevention of mental retardation. In J. L. Matson & J. A. Mulick (Eds.), *Handbook of mental retardation* (2nd ed., pp. 336–344). New York: Pergamon Press.

Kaufman, M., Agard, T. A., & Semmel, M. I. (1985). *Mainstreaming learners and their environment*. Cambridge, MA: Brookline Books.

Kendall, P. C., Nay, W. R., & Jeffers, J. (1975). Timeout duration and contrast effects: A systematic evaluation of a successive treatments design. *Behavior Therapy, 6*, 609–615.

Kern, L., Mauk, J., Marder, T., & Mace, F. C. (1995). Functional analysis and intervention for breath holding. *Journal of Applied Behavior Analysis, 28*, 339–340.

Kirk, S. A. (1958). *Early education of the mentally retarded*. Urbana: University of Illinois Press.

Koegel, R. L., Russo, D. C., & Rincover, A. (1977). Assessing and training teachers in the generalized use of behavior modification with autistic children. *Journal of Applied Behavior Analysis, 10*, 197–205.

Koegel, R. L., Schreibman, L., Britten, K., Burke, J., & O'Neill, R. (1982). A comparison of parent training to direct child treatment. In R. L. Koegel, A. Rincover, & A. L. Egel (Eds.), *Educating and understanding the autistic child* (pp. 260–279). San Diego, CA: College Hill Press.

Kohn, A. (1993). *Punished by rewards*. Boston: Houghton Mifflin.

Koller, H., Richardson, S., Katz, M., & McLaren, J. (1983). Behavior disturbance since childhood among 5-year birth cohort of all mentally retarded young adults in a city. *American Journal of Mental Deficiency, 87*, 386–395.

Kysela, G., Hillyard, A., McDonald, L., & Ahlsten-Taylor, J. (1981). Early intervention: Design and evaluation. In R. L. Schiefelbusch & D. D. Bricker (Eds.), *Language intervention series: Vol. 6. Early language: Acquisition and intervention* (pp. 341–388). Baltimore: University Park Press.

Lesch, M., & Nyhan, W. (1964). A familial disorder of uric acid metabolism and central nervous system function. *American Journal of Medicine, 36*, 561–570.

Linscheid, T., Iwata, B., Ricketts, R. W., Williams, D. E., & Giffin, J. C. (1990). Clinical evaluation of the Self-Injurious Behavior Inhibiting System (SIBIS). *Journal of Applied Behavior Analysis, 23*, 53–78.

Lovaas, O. I. (1993). The development of a treatment–research project for developmentally disabled and autistic children. *Journal of Applied Behavior Analysis, 26*, 617–630.

Lovett, H. (1996). *Learning to listen: Positive approaches and people with difficult behavior*. Baltimore: Paul H. Brookes.

Lubbs, H. A. (1969). A marker-X chromosome. *American Journal of Human Genetics, 21*, 231–244.

Luiselli, J. K. (1991). Application of protective equipment and equipment-fading for the treatment of self-injurious behavior in a pediatric nursing-care resident. *Behavioral Residential Treatment, 6*, 311–319.

Luiselli, J. K., & Reisman, J. (1980). Some variations in the use of differential reinforcement procedures with mentally retarded children in specialized treatment settings. *Applied Research in Mental Retardation, 1*, 277–288.

Luyben, P. D., Funk, D. M., Morgan, J. K., Clark, K. A., & Delulio, D. W. (1986). Team sports for the severely retarded: Training a side-of-the-foot soccer pass using a maximum-to-minimum prompt reduction strategy. *Journal of Applied Behavior Analysis, 19*, 431–436.

Mace, F. C., Page, T. J., Ivancic, M. T., & O'Brien, S. (1986). Effectiveness of brief time-out with and without contingent delay: A comparative analysis. *Journal of Applied Behavior Analysis, 19*, 79–86.

MacLean, W. E., Jr. (1993). Overview. In J. L. Matson & R. P. Barrett (Eds.), *Psychopathology in the mentally retarded* (2nd ed., pp. 1–14). Needham Heights, MA: Allyn & Bacon.

MacMillan, D. L., Gresham, F. M., & Siperstein, G. N. (1995). Heightened concerns over the 1992 AAMR definition: Advocacy versus precision. *American Journal of Mental Retardation, 100*, 87–97.

Mahoney, K., Van Wagenen, R. K., & Meyerson, L. (1971). Toilet training of normal and retarded children. *Journal of Applied Behavior Analysis, 4*, 173–181.

Marholin, D., O'Toole, K. M., Touchette, P. E., Berger, P. L., & Doyle, D. A. (1979). "I'll have a Big Mac, large fries, large Coke, and apple pie . . ." or teaching adaptive community skills. *Behavior Therapy, 10*, 236–248.

Marholin, D., Touchette, P. E., & Stewart, R. M. (1979). Withdrawal of chronic chlorpromazine medication: An experimental analysis. *Journal of Applied Behavior Analysis, 12*, 159–171.

Markowitz, P. I. (1992). Effects of fluoxetine on self-injurious behavior in the developmentally disabled: A preliminary study. *Journal of Clinical Psychopharmacology, 12*, 27–31.

Martin, J. E., & Agran, M. (1985). Psychotropic and anticonvulsant drug use by mentally retarded adults across community residential and vocational placements. *Applied Research in Mental Retardation, 6*, 33–49.

Masland, R. H. (1988). *Career research award address*. Paper presented at the annual meeting of the

American Academy of Mental Retardation, Washington, DC.

Matson, J. L., Barrett, R. P., & Helsel, W. J. (1988). Depression in mentally retarded children. *Research in Developmental Disabilities*, 9, 39–46.

Matson, J. L., Ollendick, T., & Adkins, J. (1980). A comprehensive dining program for mentally retarded adults. *Behaviour Research and Therapy*, 18, 107–112.

McClennen, S. E., Hoekstra, R. R., & Bryan, J. E. (1980). *Social skills for adults with severe retardation*. Champaign, IL: Research Press.

McDougle, C. J., Price, L. H., Volkmar, F. R., Goodman, W., Ward-O'Brien, D., Nielson, M., Bregman, J., & Cohen, D. (1992). Clomipramine in autism: Preliminary evidence of efficacy. *Journal of the American Academy of Child and Adolescent Psychiatry, 31*, 746–750.

McEachin, J. J., Smith, T., & Lovaas, O. I. (1993). Long-term outcome for children with autism who received early intensive behavioral treatment. *American Journal of Mental Retardation*, 97, 359–372.

McGee, G. G., Krantz, P. J., & McClannahan, L. E. (1985). The facilitative effects of incidental teaching on preposition use by autistic children. *Journal of Applied Behavior Analysis*, 18, 17–31.

McGonigle, J. J., Duncan, D. V., Cordisco, L., & Barrett, R. P. (1982). Visual screening: An alternative method for reducing stereotypic behavior. *Journal of Applied Behavior Analysis*, 15, 461–467.

McLaren, J., & Bryson, S. E. (1987). Review of recent epidemiological studies of mental retardation: Prevalence, associated disorders, and etiology. *American Journal of Mental Retardation*, 92, 243–254.

Miltenberger, R. G., Handen, B. L., & Capriotti, R. (1987). Physical restraint, visual screening and DRI in the treatment of stereotypy. *Scandinavian Journal of Behavior Therapy*, 16, 51–57.

Minkin, N., Braukmann, C., Minkin, B., Timbers, G., Timbers, B., Fixsen, D., Phillips, E., & Wolf, M. M. (1976). The social validation and training of conversational skills. *Journal of Applied Behavior Analysis*, 9, 127–139.

Moore, J. W. (1960). The effects of a tranquilizer (Thorazine) on the intelligence and achievement of educable mentally retarded women. *Dissertation Abstracts*, 20, 3200.

Morgan, S. B. (1979). Development and distribution of intellectual and adaptive skills in Down syndrome children: Implications for early intervention. *Mental Retardation*, 17, 247–249.

Moxley-Haegert, L., & Serbin, L. A. (1983). Developmental education for parents of delayed infants: Effects on parental motivation and children's development. *Child Development, 54*, 1324–1331.

Needleman, H. L., Schell, A., Bellinger, D., Leviton, A., & Allfred, E. N. (1990). The long-term effects of exposure to low doses of lead in childhood: An 11-year follow-up report. *New England Journal of Medicine, 322*, 83–88.

Nelson, C. M., & Rutherford, R. B. (1983). Timeout revisited: Guidelines for its use in special education. *Exceptional Education Quarterly, 3*, 56–67.

Nonaversive behavioral support [special issue]. (1990). *Journal of the Association for Persons with Severe Handicaps, 15,* 125–249.

Nyhan, W. (1976). Behavior in the Lesch–Nyhan syndrome. *Journal of Autism and Childhood Schizophrenia, 6*, 235–252.

O'Brien, F., & Azrin, N. H. (1972). Developing proper mealtime behaviors of the institutionalized retarded. *Journal of Applied Behavior Analysis, 5*, 389–399.

O'Brien, F., Bugle, C., & Azrin, N. H. (1972). Training and maintaining a retarded child's proper eating. *Journal of Applied Behavior Analysis, 5*, 67–72.

Odom, S. L., Chandler, L. K., Ostrosky, M., McConnell, S. R., & Reaney, S. (1992). Fading teacher prompts from peer initiation interventions for young children with disabilities. *Journal of Applied Behavior Analysis, 25*, 307–317.

Pace, G. M., Ivancic, M. T., Edwards, G. L., Iwata, B. A., & Page, T. J. (1985). Assessment of stimulus preference and reinforcer value with profoundly retarded individuals. *Journal of Applied Behavior Analysis, 18*, 249–255.

Pace, G. M., Iwata, B. A., Edwards, G. L., & McCosh, K. C. (1986). Stimulus fading and transfer in treatment of self-restraint and self-injurious behavior. *Journal of Applied Behavior Analysis, 19*, 381–389.

Parsons, J. A., May, J. G., & Menolascino, F. J. (1984). The nature and incidence of mental illness in mentally retarded individuals. In F. J. Menolascino & J. A. Stark (Eds.), *Handbook of mental illness in the mentally retarded* (pp. 3–44). New York: Plenum Press.

Pennsylvania Department of Public Welfare. (1995b, July 17). *Licensing inspection instrument for community homes for individuals with mental retardation* (Regulations, Chapter 6400). Harrisburg: Author.

Pennsylvania House Bill 1000, Committee on Health and Human Services (amending the act of October 20, 1966; 3rd Sp. Sess., P. L. 96, No. 6) (March 13, 1995).

Physicians' Desk Reference. (1995). Oradell, NJ: Medical Economics.

Piazza, C., & Fisher, W. (1991). A faded bedtime with response cost protocol for treatment of multiple sleep problems in children. *Journal of Applied Behavior Analysis, 24*, 129–140.

Plummer, S., Baer, D. M., & LeBlanc, J. (1977). Functional considerations in the use of procedural timeout and an effective alternative. *Journal of Applied Behavior Analysis, 10*, 689–705.

Popovich, D. (1981). *A prescriptive behavioral checklist for the severely and profoundly retarded* (Vol. 3). Baltimore: University Park Press.

Premack, D. (1959). Toward empirical behavior laws: I. Positive reinforcement. *Psychological Review, 66,* 219–233.

Pueschel, S. M., Reed, R. B., Cronk, C. E., & Goldstein, B. I. (1980). 5-Hydroxytryptophan and pyridoxine: Their effects in young children with Down's syndrome. *American Journal of Diseases of Children, 134,* 838–844.

Raloff, J. (1982). Childhood lead: Worrisome national levels. *Science News, 121,* 88.

Ramey, C., & Baker-Ward, L. (1982). Psychosocial intervention for infants with Down syndrome: A controlled trial. *Pediatrics, 65,* 463–468.

Reber, M. (1992). Dual diagnosis: Psychiatric disorders and mental retardation. In M. L. Batshaw & Y. M. Perret (Eds.), *Children with disabilities: A medical primer* (3rd ed., pp. 421–440). Baltimore: Paul H. Brookes.

Reese, R. P. (1971). *Skills training for the special child* [Film]. (Available from Behavioral Films, 202 West St., Granby, MA 01033)

Reese, E. P., Howard, J., & Rosenberger, P. (1974, August). *A comparison of three reinforcement procedures in assessing visual capacities of profoundly retarded individuals.* Paper presented at the meeting of the American Psychological Association, New Orleans.

Reid, A. H., Naylor, G. J., & Kay, D. S. (1981). A double-blind placebo controlled, crossover trial of carbamazepine in overactive, severely mentally handicapped patients. *Psychological Medicine, 11,* 109–113.

Reid, D. H. (1982). Trends and issues in behavioral research on training feeding and dressing skills. In J. L. Matson & F. Andrasik (Eds.), *Treatment issues and innovations in mental retardation* (pp. 213–240). New York: Plenum Press.

Reid, D. H., Wilson, P., & Faw, G. (1991). Teaching self-help skills. In J. L. Matson & J. A. Mulick (Eds.), *Handbook of mental retardation* (2nd ed., pp. 436–450). New York: Pergamon Press.

Revill, S., & Blunden, R. (1979). A home training service for preschool developmentally handicapped children. *Behaviour Research and Therapy, 17,* 207–214.

Richmond, G. (1983). Shaping bowel and bladder continence in developmentally retarded preschool children. *Journal of Autism and Developmental Disabilities, 13,* 197–204.

Ricketts, R. W., Goza, A. B., Ellis, C. R., Singh, Y. N., Singh, N. N., & Cooke, J. C. (1993). Fluoxetine treatment of severe self-injury in young adults with mental retardation. *Journal of the American Academy of Child and Adolescent Psychiatry, 32,* 865–869.

Riordan, M. M., Iwata, B. A., Finney, J. W., Wohl, M. K., & Stanley, A. E. (1984). Behavioral assessment and treatment of chronic food refusal in handicapped children. *Journal of Applied Behavior Analysis, 17,* 327–341.

Rojahn, J., & Marshburn, E. (1992). Facial screening and visual occlusion. In J. K. Luiselli, J. L. Matson, & N. N. Singh (Eds.), *Self-injurious behavior: Analysis, assessment, and treatment* (pp. 200–234). New York: Springer-Verlag.

Rutter, M., Graham, P., & Yule, W. (1970). *A neuropsychiatric study in childhood.* London: Spastics International.

Rynders, J. E., & Horrobin, J. M. (1980). Educational provisions for young children with Down's syndrome. In J. Gottlieb (Ed.), *Educating mentally retarded persons in the mainstream* (pp. 109–147). Baltimore: University Park Press.

Sanders, M. R., & Parr, J. M. (1989). Training developmentally disabled adults in independent meal preparation. *Behavior Modification, 13,* 168–191.

Sandman, C. A., Datta, P., Barron-Quinn, J., Hoehler, F., Williams, C., & Swanson, J. (1983). Naloxone attenuates self-abusive behavior in developmentally disabled clients. *Applied Research in Mental Retardation, 3,* 5–11.

Sandow, S. A., Clarke, A., Cox, M., & Stewart, F. (1981). Home intervention with parents of severely subnormal pre-school children: A final report. *Child: Care, Health and Development, 7,* 135–144.

Sanok, R. L., & Striefel, S. (1979). Elective mutism: Generalization of verbal responding across people and settings. *Behavior Therapy, 10,* 357–371.

Sattler, J. M. (1988). *Assessment of children* (3rd ed.). San Diego, CA: Jerome M. Sattler, Publisher.

Schive, K. (1995, September). In defense of educational choice. *Exceptional Parent,* pp. 50–52.

Schopler, E., Mesibov, G. B., & Hearsey, K. (1995). Structured teaching in the TEACCH system. In E. Schopler & G. B. Mesibov (Eds.), *Learning and cognition in autism* (pp. 243–268). New York: Plenum Press.

Schroeder, S. R. (1991). Self-injury and stereotypy. In J. L. Matson & J. A. Mulick (Eds.), *Handbook of mental retardation* (2nd ed., pp. 382–396). New York: Pergamon Press.

Schroeder, S. R., Breese, G. R., & Mueller, R. A. (1990). Dopaminergic mechanisms in self-injurious behavior. In D. K. Routh & M. Wolraich (Eds.), *Advances in developmental and behavioral pediatrics* (Vol. 9, pp. 181–198). Greenwich, CT: JAI Press.

Singh, N. N., Beale, I. L., & Dawson, M. J. (1981). Duration of facial screening and suppression of self-injurious behavior: Analysis using an alternating treatments design. *Behavioral Assessment, 3,* 411–420.

Skeels, H. M. (1966). Adult status of children with contrasting early life experiences: A follow-up study. *Monographs of the Society for Research in Child Development, 31*(3, Serial No. 105).

Skinner, B. F. (1953). *Science and human behavior.* New York: Macmillan.

Skodak, M., & Skeels, H. (1949). A final follow-up study of one hundred adopted children. *Journal of Genetic Psychology, 74,* 84–125.

Slentz, K., Close, D., Benz, M., & Taylor, V. (1982). *Community Living Assessment and Teaching System (CLATS): Self-care curriculum.* Omro, WI: Conover.

Solnick, J. V., Rincover, A., & Peterson, C. R. (1977). Some determinants of the reinforcing and punishing effects of time-out. *Journal of Applied Behavior Analysis, 10,* 415–424.

Song, A., & Gandhi, R. (1974). An analysis of behavior during the acquisition and maintenance phases of self-spoon feeding skills of profound retardates. *Mental Retardation, 12,* 25–28.

Sovner, R., Fox, C. J., Lowry, M. J., & Lowry, M. A. (1993) Fluoxetine treatment of depression and associated self-injury in 2 adults with mental retardation. *Journal of Intellectual Disabilities Research, 37,* 301–311.

Stromgrew, L. S., & Boller, S. (1985). Carbamazepine in treatment and prophylaxix of manic-depressive disorder. *Psychiatry Development, 4,* 349–367.

Sulzer-Azaroff, B., & Mayer, R. G. (1991). *Behavior analysis for lasting change.* New York: Holt, Rinehart & Winston.

Tagano, D. W., Moran, D. J., III, & Sawyers, J. K. (1991). *Creativity in early childhood classrooms.* Washington DC: National Education Association.

Tate, B. G., & Baroff, G. S. (1996). Aversive control of self-injurious behaviour in a psychotic boy. *Behaviour Research and Therapy, 4,* 281–287.

Touchette, P. E. (1971). Transfer of stimulus control: Measuring the moment of transfer. *Journal of the Experimental Analysis of Behavior, 15,* 347–354.

Trivette, C. M., Dunst, C. J., & Deal, A. G. (in press). Resource-based early intervention practices. In S. K. Thurman, J. R. Cronwell, & S. R. Gottwald (Eds.), *The contexts of early intervention: Systems and settings* (pp. 73–92). Baltimore: Paul H. Brookes.

Turner, G., & Jacobs, P. (1983). Marker (X): Linked mental retardation. *Advances in Human Genetics, 13,* 83–112.

Van Dyke, D. C. (1995). Alternative and unconventional therapies in children with Down syndrome. In D. C. Van Dyke, P. Mattheis, S. S. Eberly, & J. Williams (Eds.), *Medical and surgical care for children with down syndrome: A guide for parents* (pp. 289–302). Bethesda, MD: Woodrine House.

Van Houten, R., Rolider, A., & Houlihan, M. (1992). Treatments of self-injury based on teaching compliance and/or brief physical restraint. In J. K. Luiselli, J. L. Matson, & N. N. Singh (Eds.), *Self-injurious behavior: Analysis, assessment, and treatment* (pp. 181–199). New York: Springer-Verlag.

Van Wagenen, R. K., Meyerson, L., Kerr, N. J., & Mahoney, K. (1969). Field trials of a new procedure for toilet training. *Journal of Experimental Child Psychology, 8,* 147–159.

Watson, L. S., & Uzzell, R. (1980). Teaching self-help skills, grooming skills, and utensil feeding skills to the mentally retarded. In J. L. Matson & J. R. McCartney (Eds.), *Handbook of behavior modification with the mentally retarded* (pp. 151–176). New York: Plenum Press.

Werry, J. S., & Aman, M. G. (1993). Anxiolytics, sedatives, and miscellaneous drugs. In J. S. Werry & M. G. Aman (Eds.), *Practitioner's guide to psychoactive drugs for children and adolescents* (pp. 391–415). New York: Plenum Medical Book Company.

White, G. D., Nielsen, G., & Johnson, S. M. (1972). Timeout duration and the suppression of deviant behavior in children. *Journal of Applied Behavior Analysis, 5,* 111–120.

Whitman, T. L., Mercurio, J. R., & Caponigri, V. (1970). Development of social responses in two severely retarded children. *Journal of Applied Behavior Analysis, 3,* 133–138.

Winston, A. S., Singh, N. N., & Dawson, M. J. (1984). Effects of facial screening and blindfold on self-injurious behavior. *Applied Research in Mental Retardation, 5,* 29–42.

Wolfensberger, W. (1969). The origin and nature of our institutional models. In R. B. Kugel & W. Wolfensberger (Eds.), *Changing patterns in residential services for the mentally retarded* (pp. 59–171). Washington, DC: U. S. Government Printing Office.

Wyatt v. Stickney, 344 F. Supp. 373, 387 (M. D. Ala. 1972).

Young, K. R., West, R. P., Howard, V. F., & Whitney, R. (1986). Acquisition, fluency training, generalization, and maintenance of dressing skills of two developmentally disabled children. *Education and Treatment of Children, 9,* 16–29.

Zeaman, D., & House, B. J. (1963). The role of attention in retardate discrimination learning. In N. R. Ellis (Ed.), *Handbook of mental deficiency* (pp. 159–223). New York: McGraw-Hill.

Zane, T. Z., Handen, B. L., Mason, S. A., & Geffin, C. (1984). Teaching symbol identification: A comparison of standard prompting and intervening response procedures. *Analysis and Intervention in Developmental Disabilities, 4,* 367–377.

Zigler, E., & Hodapp, R. M. (1986). *Understanding mental retardation.* New York: Cambridge University Press.

CHAPTER 8

Autistic Disorder

Crighton Newsom
Southwest Ohio Developmental Center

Children with Autistic Disorder present a constellation of severe problems that are usually evident by early childhood. The most definitive characteristic is an extreme failure in socialization: Autistic children show little interest in other human beings, including the other members of their own families, and are quite content to remain alone for long periods of time. A second area of obvious deficiency is language. Up to half of such children do not speak more than a few words or use gestures; instead, they show only primitive communicative acts, such as taking an adult by the hand to the door to have it opened or throwing tantrums to get an adult to stop making a demand. The other half have some meaningful speech, but will also frequently echo the words or phrases of others without understanding them. Third, these children exhibit a very limited, rigid behavioral repertoire, largely dominated by self-isolation, idiosyncratic preoccupations, stereotyped routines, and (often) disruptive and self-injurious behaviors. At the same time, motor development is often normal or only mildly delayed. Most autistic children are found to be mentally retarded when assessed with intelligence tests and adaptive behavior scales, showing considerable scatter across cognitive and developmental domains. A few children show some advanced "splinter" skills within a circumscribed area, such as music, numbers, or reading. Not surprisingly, such children have proved sufficiently challenging, both clinically and theoretically, to have attracted considerable attention from researchers and practitioners in all the helping professions.

HISTORY

There are a few scattered reports of apparently autistic children in the 19th century, including the famous case of the Wild Boy of Aveyron (Itard, 1801/1962). However, such children were usually not distinguished from mentally retarded children. In the early decades of the 20th century, investigators began to make finer discriminations among children with severe deviations in development, identifying and describing children who regressed after a period of normal development (Heller, 1908/1954) and children who seemed to have schizophrenia of early onset (Bender, 1942; Potter, 1933). During the 1940s and 1950s, various schizophrenia-like syndromes were described by Gesell and Amatruda (1941), Kanner (1943), Asperger (1944/1991), Bergman and Escalona (1949), Rank and McNaughton (1950), and Mahler (1952). Only Kanner's syndrome attracted sustained attention and endured, although interest in Heller's and

Asperger's syndromes has revived recently, as indicated later in the section on diagnosis.

The endurance of Kanner's (1943) syndrome can be attributed to several factors. These include his prestigious position as head of child psychiatry at Johns Hopkins and his authorship of the standard text in the field for several decades. Furthermore, his description of his first 11 autistic patients was unusually detailed and comprehensive. Perhaps most important, the disorder itself—describing children who lack a characteristic so fundamental as human attachment—is inherently compelling not only to scientists and clinicians but also to the general public, as evidenced in frequent mass media presentations. The main features of Kanner's syndrome include extreme self-isolation, obsessive insistence on the "preservation of sameness," either muteness or noncommunicative speech with echolalia, pronoun reversal, and idiosyncratic, "metaphorical" usages, excellent rote memory, literal thought processes, normal physical development, and apparently normal intellectual potential. Kanner believed that the condition was due to some innate inability to establish social relationships and named the syndrome "early infantile autism" (Kanner, 1949)

Infantile autism soon became a popular and overextended diagnosis (Kanner, 1965). During the 1950s, most clinicians ignored Kanner's initial observation that the appearance of autism in early infancy seemed to point to innate causal factors. Instead, they offered thoroughgoing psychoanalytic theories attributing causation to parental psychopathology and harmful rearing practices. Treatment prescriptions included separation of the child from the parents, play therapy, and milieu therapy, combined with long-term psychotherapy for the child and the parents (e.g., Bettelheim, 1956; Despert, 1951; Mahler, 1952; Rank & McNaughton, 1950; Szurek, 1956). However, the psychoanalytic approach proved to be a theoretical and clinical dead end (Bartak & Rutter, 1973; Kanner, 1969; Rimland, 1964)—a classic case of the risks of error and even harm inherent in informal observation of limited samples, unsupported by systematic study. Other, more scientific investigators continued to pursue the possibility of physiological causes and attempted to establish some organization among autism and other conditions believed to be variants of childhood schizophrenia (Bender, 1955; Eisenberg, 1956; Fish, 1957). These efforts set the stage for the current era.

During the 1960s, several lines of research and treatment that are still prominent were established. Basic facts about the actual characteristics of autistic children were gathered in epidemiological and medical studies (Lotter, 1966; Rutter & Lockyer, 1967; Schain & Yannet, 1960). These studies showed that most autistic children were in fact also mentally retarded, that they came from all social classes, and that a small but significant percentage had signs of neurological impairment. Other research began to identify deficits in basic perceptual, cognitive, and linguistic processes, again indicating the likelihood of some type of neurological dysfunction (Hermelin & O'Connor, 1964; Pronovost, Wakstein, & Wakstein, 1966; Tubbs, 1966). Objective studies of parents failed to find evidence of significant psychopathology or harmful rearing practices (Pitfield & Oppenheim, 1964; Rimland, 1964; Rutter & Brown, 1966). Finally, behavioral clinical researchers found that some of the problems of autistic children that were most intractable to psychodynamic therapies, such as social deficits, language abnormalities, and maladaptive behaviors, were amenable to procedures derived from operant learning theory (Ferster, 1961; Hewett, 1965; Lovaas, Berberich, Perloff, & Schaeffer, 1966; Lovaas, Freitag, Gold, & Kassorla, 1965; Risley & Wolf, 1967). The data emerging from these and many other studies forced a complete reconceptualization of the problem of autism. Rutter (1988) summarized the shift from a psychodynamic to a developmental perspective by stating, "Autistic children have not withdrawn from reality because of mental illness; rather, they have failed fully to enter reality because of a widespread and serious disturbance in the developmental process" (p. 265).

Accompanying this shift in perspective has been a substantial growth of research from the early 1970s through the present on virtually every topic that is or might be relevant to understanding and treating children with autism, representing fields ranging from genetics to national educational policy. Figure 8.1 shows the acceleration in the growth of research on autism over the last two decades—an acceleration so sharp that research on autism now surpasses that on mental retardation. Indeed, Rutter and Schopler's (1987) observation a decade ago that autism is probably the best studied of all childhood disorders remains true today. Consequently, this chapter can only sample a very large literature.

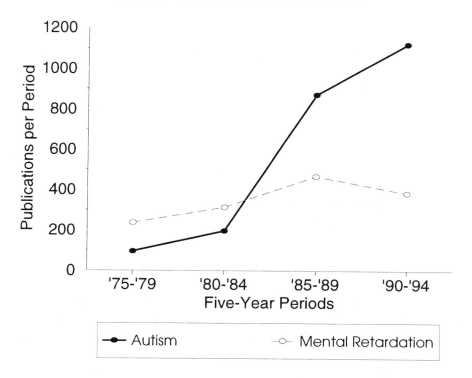

FIGURE 8.1. Number of references in the PsycINFO data base for autism (filled circles) and mental retardation (open circles) for consecutive 5-year periods.

NATURE AND DIAGNOSIS

At a descriptive level, children with autism and other pervasive developmental disorders, known collectively as the "autistic spectrum" (Wing & Attwood, 1987), can be located within a hypothetical continuum of pervasiveness and severity of disability (Cohen, Paul, & Volkmar, 1986). At the most pervasive end of the continuum fall profoundly retarded, multihandicapped children, who exhibit a fairly uniform pattern of profound impairments across the domains of intellectual, adaptive, social, language, and motor functioning. At the least pervasive end of the continuum lie children with specific developmental disorders, characterized by relatively mild impairments in only one domain. Children classified as having a pervasive developmental disorder fall between these two extremes, showing an uneven pattern of impairments across several domains. Autism is thus best conceptualized as a disorder of multiple primary deficits (Goodman, 1989). Such an approach suggests that some combination of deficits is specific to autism and universal among autistic individuals (Ozonoff, Pennington, & Rogers, 1991). One such com-

plex model (Waterhouse, Fein, & Modahl, 1996) is described later; however, much more research is needed to determine what configuration of deficits is both specific and universal.

Diagnostic Criteria

The current diagnostic criteria for Autistic Disorder in the Diagnostic and Statistical Manual of Mental Disorders (DSM-IV; American Psychiatric Association [APA], 1994) follow Wing's (1991) concept of autism as a disorder of socialization, communication, and imagination (Table 8.1). The list of characteristics in Table 8.1 is not a revision of the DSM-III-R criteria, but a somewhat shortened version of the criteria in the International Classification of Diseases, 10th revision (ICD-10; World Health Organization, 1992). This approach was taken because the DSM-III-R criteria were found to be overly broad, resulting in too many false positives, especially among individuals with severe mental retardation (Volkmar, Bregman, Cohen, & Cicchetti, 1988). The ICD-10 criteria had the best combination of sensitivity (the proportion of true cases meeting the criteria) and specificity

TABLE 8.1. DSM-IV Diagnostic Criteria for Autistic Disorder

A. A total of six (or more) items from (1), (2), and (3), with at least two from (1) and one each from (2) and (3):
  (1) qualitative impairment in social interaction, as manifested by at least two of the following:
    (a) marked impairment in the use of multiple nonverbal behaviors such as eye-to-eye gaze, facial expression, body postures, and gestures to regulate social interaction
    (b) failure to develop peer relationships appropriate to developmental level
    (c) a lack of spontaneous seeking to share enjoyment, interests, or achievements with other people (e.g., by a lack of showing, bringing, or pointing out objects of interest)
    (d) lack of social or emotional reciprocity
  (2) qualitative impairments in communication as manifested by at least one of the following:
    (a) delay in, or total lack of, the development of spoken language (not accompanied by an attempt to compensate through alternative modes of communication such as gesture or mime)
    (b) in individuals with adequate speech, marked impairment in the ability to initiate or sustain a conversation with others
    (c) stereotyped and repetitive use of language or idiosyncratic language
    (d) lack of varied, spontaneous make-believe play or social imitative play appropriate to developmental level
  (3) restricted repetitive and stereotyped patterns of behavior, interests, and activities, as manifested by at least one of the following:
    (a) encompassing preoccupation with one or more stereotyped and restricted patterns of interest that is abnormal either in intensity or focus
    (b) apparently inflexible adherence to specific, nonfunctional routines or rituals
    (c) stereotyped and repetitive motor mannerisms (e.g., hand or finger flapping or twisting, or complex whole-body movements)
    (d) persistent preoccupation with parts of objects
B. Delays or abnormal functioning in at least one of the following areas, with onset prior to age 3 years:
  (1) social interaction
  (2) language as used in social communication
  (3) symbolic or imaginative play
C. The disturbance is not better accounted for by Rett's Disorder or Childhood Disintegrative Disorder.

Note. From American Psychiatric Association (1994, pp. 70–71). Copyright 1994 by the American Psychiatric Association. Reprinted by permission.

(the proportion of true noncases failing to meet the criteria), as well as the highest level of agreement with clinicians' diagnoses, in comparison with DSM-III and DSM-III-R (Volkmar et al., 1994). The main shortcoming of the DSM-IV criteria is that, like previous versions, they relegate sensory and perceptual abnormalities (hyper- or hypo-sensitivity to sounds, lights, textures, or odors, high pain threshold, overselective attention, impaired shifting of attention, cross-modal integration impairments) to the status of associated features. This conflicts with the belief of many in the field that such abnormalities are cardinal symptoms (e.g., Burke, 1991; Courchesne et al., 1994; Dawson & Lewy, 1989; Lovaas, Koegel, & Schreibman, 1979; Ornitz, 1989; Waterhouse, 1988).

When one is making diagnostic distinctions between autistic and other developmentally disabled children, the focus is on the quality of the children's social functioning (item A1 in Table 8.1). The level of social functioning must be below the overall developmental level or mental age (MA) for children to be diagnosed as autistic (Rutter, 1985). At the low end of the intelligence continuum, the social deficits of autistic children can be difficult to distinguish from those of severely and profoundly retarded children. Usually, however, even a child with profound retardation will show simple social behaviors such as eye contact, smiling, and social approach that are commensurate with his or her MA (Wing, 1981a). In practice, one can compare a child's tested MA on an intelligence test with his or her age-equivalent scores on the Socialization subdomains (Interpersonal Relationships, Play and Leisure Time, Coping Skills) of the Vineland Adaptive Behavior Scales (Sparrow, Balla, & Cicchetti, 1984). Autistic children score at a significantly lower level in the Socialization subdomains than their overall MAs would predict (Volkmar et al., 1987; Klin, Volkmar, & Sparrow, 1992).

Among normally intelligent and mildly retarded children, it can be difficult to distinguish between autistic children and children with Asperger's Disorder (APA, 1994; Wing, 1991), Schizoid and Schizotypal Personality Disorders (APA, 1994; Wolff & Barlow, 1979), and Schizophrenia in childhood (Asarnow, 1994). In general, autistic children differ from such children by (1) having a lower overall level of cognitive functioning, academic achievement, and language development (Sparrow et al., 1986; Wing, 1981a, 1981b; Wing & Gould, 1979); (2) showing somewhat better motor coordination (Sparrow et al., 1986; Wing, 1981b); and (3) showing earlier onset and more severe social and language deficits than children with schizophrenia, as well as lacking the hallucinations and delusions the latter children develop in later childhood (Asarnow, 1994; Kolvin, Ounsted, Humphrey, & McNay, 1971). It should be noted, however, that it is still not clear where and how sharply the lines should be drawn between these groups (Cohen et al., 1986; Frith, 1991; Petty, Ornitz, Michelman, & Zimmerman, 1984).

The differential diagnosis requires attention to the three other categories in the subsection of DSM-IV entitled "Pervasive Developmental Disorders." Rett's Disorder (Hagberg, 1995; Perry, Sarlo-McGarvey, & Haddad, 1991) describes children who begin to exhibit several specific deficits after 6–12 months of normal development. Head growth decelerates, gross motor skills deteriorate, and there is a loss of interest in the environment. Between 12 and 36 months, there is rapid developmental regression and a loss of purposeful hand movements, with the development of stereotypical hand-wringing movements. Rett's Disorder occurs only in girls in its classic form, but some male variants have been reported (Christen & Hanefeld, 1995). Childhood Disintegrative Disorder (formerly Heller's disease) describes children who show a profound regression in language, self-care skills, and sociability following 2–4 years of normal development; it is usually traceable to some kind of neurological deterioration (Rutter, 1985). Asperger's Disorder applies to children who show the same kinds of social impairments and restricted, stereotyped interests as autistic children, but not the language impairments. Indeed, there is some controversy over the need for thinking of these children as anything but autistic children with normal intelligence (DeLong & Dwyer, 1988; Szatmari, Tuff, Finlayson, & Bartolucci, 1990; Volkmar, Paul, & Cohen, 1985). They are extremely egocentric, socially inept, and preoccupied with some highly abstract, circumscribed interest. Their speech is noticeably odd, and they typically ramble on at great length about topics

of interest only to themselves. Pervasive Developmental Disorder Not Otherwise Specified is a remainder category for children who show pervasive impairments but do not fully meet the criteria of one of the other categories.

The diagnostic criteria listed in Table 8.1 are stated with sufficient clarity to permit accurate diagnosis in most cases if used carefully. Elaborations, clinical presentations, and diagnostic guidelines are provided in other sources (e.g., Newsom & Hovanitz, 1997, which also reviews formal diagnostic instruments; APA, 1994; Schreibman, 1988; Frith, 1989). In the present context, it is more useful to have some acquaintance with current theories in each domain of the "autistic triad": abnormalities in socialization, in communication, and in patterns of interests and activities.

Theories of Autistic Dysfunction

Theories of Social Impairment

Echoing Kanner, some theorists have proposed that the asociality of autistic children results from more fundamental affective deficits. Studies have shown that autistic children are less able than matched retarded children to attend to and to recognize affective stimuli, such as facial expressions and emotional verbalizations (Hobson, 1986; Hobson, Ouston, & Lee, 1988), or to express emotions and affective states (Snow, Hertzig, & Shapiro, 1987). Integrating such findings with theoretical treatments of the normal development of self-concepts, Hobson (1990, 1993) has traced asociality to an incomplete self-concept—one that is unable to relate to the social as well as the physical environment, or to others' emotional attitudes as well as their actions. Accordingly, children with autism can perceive and understand the inanimate world but have a biologically based impairment in perceiving and responding to the affective expressions and emotional behaviors of others (Hobson, 1990). Hobson suggests that the autistic child's failure to develop an "interpersonal" self in parallel with the "ecological," or object-oriented, self explains some characteristic phenomena. These children's lack of appreciation of the psychological dimension of other people accounts for their not sharing experiences with others, not engaging in joint attention strategies, and not imitating others (Curcio, 1978; Dawson & Adams, 1984; Landry & Loveland, 1988). Their lack of understanding of people as agents results in actions directed at the body parts of people rather than the people themselves, as when an autistic child attacks the hand that restrains him or her instead of protesting to the restraining person or places someone's hand on a doorknob to get the door opened (Carr & Kemp, 1989; Kanner, 1943).

Baron-Cohen, Leslie, and Frith (1985) have proposed that the social unrelatedness of autistic children results from their lack of a "theory of mind"—the ability to attribute mental states (knowledge, intentions, beliefs, feelings) to oneself and others. Baron-Cohen and his colleagues have used tasks normally mastered by 4 years of age to conduct a series of studies of the ability of high-functioning autistic children to infer what someone else knows or expects, to distinguish between mental and physical events, and to distinguish between appearances and reality. They have shown that most autistic children with MAs well above 4 years fail such tasks, while nearly all normal and retarded controls with even lower MAs succeed (Baron-Cohen, 1989a, 1989b; Baron-Cohen et al., 1985; Baron-Cohen, Leslie, & Frith, 1986; Leslie & Frith, 1988; Perner, Frith, Leslie, & Leekam, 1989; Sodian & Frith, 1992). Those autistic children who do pass tasks requiring first-order belief attributions (e.g., "Mary thinks the marble is in the basket") typically fail tasks involving second-order attributions ("Mary thinks that John thinks . . .") (Baron-Cohen, 1989a; Ozonoff et al., 1991). Frith (1989) proposes that the lack of a theory of mind explains several findings regarding social deficits in autistic children. The absence of attempts to establish shared attention through protodeclarative gestures can be explained by an inability to consider others as having interests that might be similar to the children's own. Deviant eye contact can be attributed to the children's failure to learn that gaze is used to signal particular mental states. Lack of genuine empathic contact occurs because the children are unable to "read" others' thoughts, needs, and feelings in social interchanges. Leslie and Frith (1990) argue that lack of a theory of mind is due to an earlier failure to develop "metarepresentations," or thoughts about one's own and others' thoughts—an ability that normally emerges in the second year of life. The basic deficit in autism is thus believed to be a cognitive deficit, not an affective one.

Finally, Mundy (1995) hypothesizes that brain mechanisms that regulate self-initiated social approach behaviors—specifically, joint attention bids—are impaired in autistic children. Deficits in joint attention discriminate autistic from other developmentally disabled children (Lewy & Dawson, 1992) and are correlated with severity of symptom presentation and subsequent language development (Mundy, Sigman, & Kasari, 1990). An autistic child's lack of social approach behaviors precludes crucial intersubjective experiences with others and the associated social information and feedback necessary to the development of social-cognitive skills. Therefore, the child fails to develop the full array of social-cognitive capacities required for adaptive social interactions.

Theories of Communication Deficit

Peters (1983) has proposed that normal children's strategies of language acquisition lie on a continuum from "gestalt" to "analytic." The former strategy involves reliance on formulaic language (imitations and routines) that are reproduced as single units, with no analysis of their linguistic structure and little or no comprehension of the utterances themselves. The latter strategy involves the use of forms that are generated on the basis of linguistic rules, with greater comprehension of structure and meaning. Prizant and Schuler (Prizant, 1983; Prizant & Schuler, 1987) have extended Peters's theory to autism, suggesting that the predominance of echolalia in autistic children's early speech is evidence that they lie at the gestalt end of the continuum. They memorize and repeat language "chunks" (immediate and delayed echolalia), and only later segment and analyze these forms to develop a more rule-governed system. This gestalt approach to language learning derives from a general cognitive style of holistic, gestalt processing, as seen in relative strengths in reproduction of melodic patterns, construction of visual–spatial arrays of objects, and solution of puzzles, form boards, and block design tasks. Such a strategy is inefficient when applied to language, which accounts for the delays and slowness of language acquisition in autistic children (Prizant & Schuler, 1987).

Tager-Flusberg (1989) notes that from the earliest stages of communicative development, autistic children show profound deficits in social communication behaviors, especially joint attention, informing, and initiating. As language develops, there is an asynchrony between form and function, such that syntactic and lexical aspects are typically in advance of pragmatic functioning. Even in linguistically advanced autistic children, who have mastered word order and have large vocabularies, many pragmatic functions of language are deficient, including limited sharing of information, idiosyncratic us-ages, problems with speaker–listener relations, and difficulties in initiating and maintaining topics and taking turns in conversations. Tager-Flusberg (1989) argues that the common ele-ment in all the communicative functions with which autistic children have difficulty is failure to understand that language can be used to in-form and influence others—a failure that may reflect the underlying cognitive deficit identi-fied by Baron-Cohen et al. (1985) as the lack of a theory of mind.

Theories of Repetitive, Stereotyped Behaviors

Lewis and Baumeister (1982) argue that stereo-typies are high-frequency biobehavioral rhythms controlled by neural oscillators, or "pacemak-ers," in the brain that can function in the absence of sensory feedback. Evidence from a wealth of neurochemistry studies reviewed by Lewis and Baumeister (1982) suggests that the emergence of stereotypies in humans could result from a dysfunction in the nigro-striatal dopamine tract in the basal ganglia, which regulates responsive-ness to stimulation and sensorimotor integra-tion. A deficiency in dopamine results in dopamine receptor supersensitivity, a compensa-tory increase in the sensitivity of postsynaptic dopamine receptors. In recent studies by Lewis and his colleagues, there is evidence for a defi-ciency in dopamine in developmentally disabled individuals who engage in stereotypies relative to those who do not (Bodfish, Powell, Golden, & Lewis, 1995; Lewis et al., 1996).

Lovaas, Newsom, and Hickman (1987) and Rincover (1978) accord a central role to sen-sory feedback in their developmental–operant theories of stereotyped behaviors. Such "self-stimulatory" behaviors are viewed as persisting elaborations of the normal repetitive behaviors of infancy (Thelen, 1979) that continue beyond infancy in autistic children due to failure to acquire more mature behaviors that could re-place them. Stereotyped behaviors derive their strength from the automatic reinforcing effects of the sensory or perceptual feedback that they produce (Rincover, Cook, Peoples, & Packard, 1979). The sensory/perceptual reinforcers may be enteroceptive (e.g., vestibular stimulation from body rocking or spinning), exteroceptive (e.g., the visual pattern of objects in a row from object lining), or a combination of the two (e.g., kinesthetic and visual stimulation from hand flapping or string twirling). Over the course of

long-term intensive treatment, developmentally lower stereotypies (such as rocking and hand flapping) change to developmentally higher ones (preoccupations with numbers or timeta-bles, delayed echolalia of certain words or phrases, repeated assembly and disassembly of puzzles) (Epstein, Taubman, & Lovaas, 1985).

A multistage theory of stereotypies has been offered by Guess and Carr (1991). At Level I, common in normal infants and profoundly re-tarded children, stereotypies constitute a bio-logically determined behavior state. At Level II, stereotypies are homeostatic responses to envi-ronmental under- or over-stimulation, serving to regulate arousal at an optimal level. The transi-tion from Level I to Level II occurs when a child becomes less state-dependent and more aware of and aroused by environmental events. In Level III, stereotypies and repetitive self-injurious be-haviors are instrumental behaviors, controlled by conditioned positive and negative reinforcers (Durand & Carr, 1987; Carr, 1977). Transitions from Level II to Level III may reflect emerging socially based motivational needs and a more re-sponsive social milieu.

Although the foregoing ideas represent major trends in contemporary theorizing about the main characteristics of autism, it is important to note that each has significant weaknesses and limitations not discussed here. Furthermore, there are serious gaps of greater or lesser magni-tude between each theory and actual clinical practice at the present time. Nevertheless, this sampling does give an indication of the vitality and variety of theoretical approaches being brought to bear on the difficult problems that autism presents.

Prevalence and Sex Ratio

Wing (1993) reviewed 16 epidemiological stud-ies conducted over the past 30 years in various countries and found prevalence rates ranging from 3.3 to 16 per 10,000 children. The wide variation in rates was due to differing diagnostic criteria and case-finding methods. The only two studies conducted in the United States have re-ported rates of 3.3 per 10,000 in North Dakota (Burd, Fisher, & Kerbeshian, 1987) and 3.6 per 10,000 in Utah (Ritvo et al., 1989). The ratio of males to females is about 4:1 (Lord, Schopler, & Revicki, 1982). Although girls are affected at a lower rate than boys, they tend to be more se-verely cognitively disabled than boys, for reasons that are presumably genetic in origin but remain obscure (Lord et al., 1982).

Etiology

The complexity of neuroanatomical and neurochemical systems, and the subtlety of the processes involved, have made the task of charting the biological substrate of autism profoundly difficult. It has been estimated that a definite cause can be identified in only 5%–10% of cases (Rutter, Bailey, Bolton, & Le Couteur, 1994).

Evidence for the heritability of autism comes from twin and family studies. In twin studies, high rates of concordance for autism are found in identical pairs, and low rates are found in fraternal pairs (Bailey et al., 1995). Studies of families have indicated that 3%–5% of the siblings of autistic children are also autistic and 8% of the extended families include another member who is autistic (Baird & August, 1985; Smalley & Collins, 1996). Family studies also reveal an increased prevalence of mental retardation and specific cognitive disabilities in the siblings of autistic children. This suggests that what is inherited is a polygenic disorder that increases the liability for all cognitive impairments, including autism (Bailey et al., 1995; Baird & August, 1985; Bolton et al., 1994).

How the genetic abnormalities are expressed in brain dysfunction is slowly coming into focus. Evidence of deficits in executive function, joint attention, emotion perception, and theory of mind point to frontal and midbrain impairment (Hughes & Russell, 1993; McEvoy, Rogers, & Pennington, 1993; Mundy, 1995; Ozonoff et al., 1991). Consistent findings from autopsy and neuroimaging studies include an increase in brain weight, delayed maturation of the frontal cortex, truncated dendritic tree development of neurons in the limbic system, and a decrease in the number of Purkinje cells in the cerebellum (Bauman & Kemper, 1985; Courchesne et al., 1994; Zilbovicius et al., 1995).

The most comprehensive neurophysiological model of autism presented so far is that of Waterhouse et al. (1996). They hypothesize that four key dysfunctions based on overlapping neural systems can account for the characteristic behaviors of autism. The first dysfunction is "canalesthesia," or the fragmentation of cross-modal information processing and memories, due to excessive cell-packing density in the hip-

pocampal system. The second dysfunction is impaired assignment of the affective, reinforcing significance of stimuli, due to an abnormal amygdala. The third dysfunction is asociality, due to aberrant functioning of the neuropeptide systems involving oxytocin, vasopressin, and endogenous opioids, along with abnormal functioning of the serotonin system. The final dysfunction is extended selective attention, including excessively focused attention and delayed shifting of attention, resulting from abnormal temporal and parietal association areas. A simplified diagram of the interaction among the systems appears in Figure 8.2. As the figure shows, Waterhouse et al. (1996) view brainstem and cerebellum abnormalities as associated but noncausal factors (right side of Figure 8.2). Frontal lobe dysfunction is viewed as a consequence of aberrant input from the amygdala, the hippocampus, and temporal and parietal cortices (left side of Figure 8.2). The Waterhouse et al. (1996) model is admittedly speculative, but it does have the significant virtue of integrating many findings regarding specific dysfunctions in several neurological systems to a greater degree than any other current theories.

Prognosis and Course

Predictions of outcome are hazardous at best with such a heterogeneous population, especially when children are very young. In the absence of early, intensive intervention, only 1%–2% of autistic individuals became "normal" in the sense that there is little difference between them and children who have never been diagnosed as autistic. About 10% have what is often considered to be a "good" outcome; that is, they achieve adequate functioning in language and/or social behavior and make satisfactory progress in school or work, but usually retain obvious peculiarities of speech or personality. Another 20% have "fair" outcomes, or continue to make social and educational progress in spite of a significant handicap, such as impoverished speech. About 70% have "poor" or "very poor" outcomes, with very limited progress in all areas and major remaining handicaps (DeMyer et al., 1973; Eisenberg, 1956; Gillberg & Steffenburg, 1987; Lotter, 1974; Rutter, Greenfeld, & Lockyer, 1967).

Studies of adolescents and adults have shown that there are exacerbations of symptoms (hyperactivity, self-injury, compulsivity) in about 35% of cases and epilepsy in 20%–30% during puberty or early adolescence (Deykin

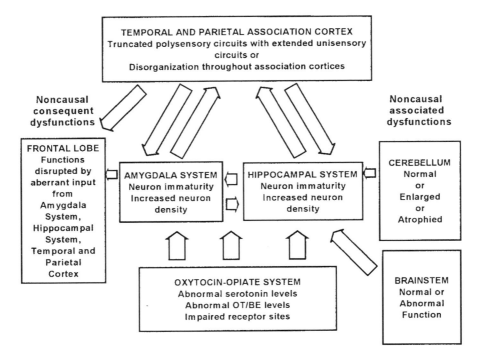

FIGURE 8.2.   Diagram of the model of the four proposed core neural dysfunctions in autism proposed by Waterhouse et al. (1996). OT, oxytocin; BE, beta-endorphin. From Waterhouse, Fein, and Modahl (1996, p. 460). Copyright 1996 by the American Psychological Association. Reprinted by permission.

& MacMahon, 1979; Gillberg & Steffenburg, 1987). In later adolescence and adulthood, abnormalities such as stereotyped motor movements, flat affect, generalized anxiety, and social improprieties are frequently observed even in high-functioning individuals (Rumsey, Rapoport, & Sceery, 1985). Loneliness, social ineptitude, and employment are acute problems. Adaptive behavior remains at or below mental age (Paul, Harcherik, Volkmar, & Cohen, 1985; Rumsey et al., 1985). Complex obsessive–compulsive rituals may develop and speech may resemble that of schizophrenics by including idiosyncratic usages, perseveration, excessive concreteness, monotonous tone, repetitive questioning, and talking to oneself (Paul, 1987; Rumsey et al., 1985). However, the hallucinations and delusions of schizophrenia are lacking. More relevant alternative diagnoses would include anxiety disorders and Schizoid and Obsessive–Compulsive Personality Disorders (Rumsey et al., 1985).

The practical usefulness of the foregoing outcome findings for making individual predictions is unknown. On one hand, the recent emergence and gradual dissemination of effective early intervention programs, community-referenced

educational curricula, supported employment opportunities, and varied community living options invite considerable optimism (Dawson & Osterling, 1996; Harris & Handleman, 1994; Koegel & Koegel, 1995; Kozloff, 1994; McEachin, Smith, & Lovaas, 1993; Simeonsson, Olley, & Rosenthal, 1987). On the other hand, these new developments are still not widely available, and there are disturbing findings, such as those showing minimal or no increase in the IQs of autistic children in ordinary special education programs (Freeman, Ritvo, Needleman, & Yokota, 1985; Lord & Schopler, 1989; Eaves & Ho, 1996). Green et al. (1986) found that in the "average" special education classroom (of 43 studied) for severely handicapped children, the children were on task less than half of the designated instructional time, and almost two-thirds of their on-task time involved nonfunctional tasks (i.e., tasks that did not involve natural materials and/or age-appropriate skills). Such an environment would seem to stand little chance of making much difference in the outcomes described above.

The most general conclusion that emerges from both the outcome studies mentioned above and the early intervention studies to be described later is that autistic children can be roughly divided into two large groups based on measured intelligence (recognizing the hazards of making any predictions from intelligence tests in early childhood) (Lotter, 1974; Lovaas & Smith, 1988; Rutter, 1988). The first group is composed of those in the severely and profoundly retarded ranges of intelligence; the second, of those in the moderately retarded through normal ranges. The prognosis for most children in the first group remains limited at the present time, with most individuals requiring supervised living and work arrangements throughout life. The appropriate treatment strategy for children in this group emphasizes the acquisition of behaviors that will make the children's lives less difficult than they would otherwise be and allow them to function as independently as possible. The main objectives include self-care skills, a reasonable degree of compliance with instructions and simple rules, basic social and affective behaviors, communication of needs and wants, appropriate play, and the reduction of harmful behaviors. In later childhood and adolescence, a steadily increasing emphasis on domestic living skills and work-related skills is most appropriate in preparation for supervised living and work environments. In working with the parents of such a child, the clinician must walk the narrow path between undue pessimism and unwarranted optimism. Communications that focus excessive attention on the child's deficiencies, or that, on the other hand, raise expectations for dramatic improvement, are to be avoided. The main jobs are to teach the parents how to teach basic skills, how to control inappropriate behaviors, and how to solve the inevitable problems that arise within the family and between the family and educational and other service providers. Equally important is the informal modeling of the celebration of progress, however slow and incremental at times, and the simple enjoyment of the child's unique and attractive characteristics.

For the second group of children, those in the moderately retarded to normal ranges, outcome is dependent not only on intelligence but also on when treatment begins and how intensive it is. As might be expected, this group accounts for those who achieve normal or near-normal outcomes (DeMyer et al., 1973; Freeman et al., 1985; Lovaas & Smith, 1988; McEachin et al., 1993; Rutter et al., 1967). The general treatment strategy for young autistic children in this group should therefore assume the nature of a "total push" approach, in which time is of the essence

in order to take maximum advantage of the plasticity of neurological and behavioral processes early in life. In practice, this entails 30–40 hours a week of one-to-one behavioral intervention, supervised by clinicians with expertise in applied behavior analysis as used with autistic children (Green, 1996; Lovaas, 1987; Perry, Cohen, & DeCarlo, 1995; McEachin et al., 1993). In addition to the objectives just mentioned for lower-functioning children, there are major emphases on fluent verbal language, age-appropriate social interactions with normal peers, and behaviors and skills expected in normal preschool and elementary classrooms (Harris & Handleman, 1994; Lovaas, 1981, 1996; Lovaas & Smith, 1988). Extensive parent training and support are crucial and should be made available to every family willing and able to mount a comprehensive in-home treatment program.

INITIAL TREATMENT

There are three main tasks at the beginning of treatment. First, the teacher (of whatever title—classroom teacher, parent, clinician, or therapist) begins by building rapport with the child. Second, the teacher addresses certain basic skills that are prerequisites to more complex behaviors. These "learning readiness" skills include sitting in a chair, coming to the teacher when called, attending to the teacher (making eye contact), and looking at and manipulating task materials (Lovaas & Buch, 1997). Concurrently, behaviors that interfere with learning, such as tantrums, aggression, and noncompliance, are minimized. These last two treatment objectives occur in parallel because they are interdependent: Initial teaching efforts will not progress very far unless some control of disruptive behaviors is accomplished, and the reduction of disruptive behaviors requires the strengthening of alternative behaviors if it is to endure. Conceptually, initial treatment programs establish some basic rules of social interaction, the neglect of which will result in disruptions and delays in all subsequent treatment efforts.

Learning readiness training and early behavior management efforts also seem to have more subtle but equally important effects on both the child and the teacher. For the child, initial treatment programs establish adults as sources of consistent positive and negative consequences, often for the first time in the child's life. They also teach the child how to learn from the social environment by introducing very clear stimulus-response–consequence instructional cycles (discrete trials) as the basic framework of many future teaching interactions. For the teacher, especially if he or she is a parent, initial treatment programs provide some satisfaction and self-confidence in being able to influence the child in positive ways; these feelings do much to alleviate feelings of inadequacy (Lovaas, 1981; Maurice, 1996; Schreibman, Koegel, Mills, & Burke, 1984).

Building Rapport

Some simple procedures not unlike those used with other child clinical populations are useful for increasing basic social behaviors and establishing a rudimentary level of rapport early in treatment. DeMyer and Ferster (1962) had teachers begin working with autistic children by participating in their ongoing activities, both to habituate the children to physical closeness and to identify potential social and activity reinforcers, which were then used to strengthen simple social, affectionate, and play behaviors. Subsequent studies have included some aspects of this approach. One technique is simply to imitate the child's toy manipulations. Doing so results in increased eye contact, touches, and vocalizations directed at the teacher (Dawson & Adams, 1984; Tiegerman & Primavera, 1981, 1984). Another technique is to prompt the child to engage in play with a preferred toy, as determined by prior assessment of the amount of time the child spends playing with various toys. Play with preferred toys is accompanied by decreased social avoidance behavior (e.g., gaze aversion, head hanging, moving away) in comparison to play with nonpreferred toys (Koegel, Dyer, & Bell, 1987).

Rapport-building activities are not something done at the beginning of treatment and then dropped, but are continued and elaborated throughout treatment. Carr et al. (1994) suggest that after an initial level of positive interaction is achieved, further efforts should focus on making oneself a signal for simple communication by approaching the child and waiting expectantly for him or her to make a request in some fashion, prompting it if necessary, and immediately responding to it. Later, it is worthwhile to help the child become more attractive to others by teaching personal hygiene, grooming, and dressing skills, and to help the child to become more likeable by teaching him or her to participate successfully in activities enjoyed by other family members, such as dining out, exercise, or listening to music.

Teaching Attention

Basic procedures for teaching appropriate sitting in a chair, coming when called, and attending to the teacher and to task materials begin during the first hour of treatment and are presented in Lovaas (1981), Lovaas and Buch (1997), and Kozloff (1974). Procedures for teaching visual attention can serve here as a good example of how such skills are taught.

With autistic children who already make at least some spontaneous eye contact, it may be sufficient to use differential reinforcement to increase the rate of eye contact, providing praise and/or edibles when it occurs and ignoring its nonoccurrence (Brooks, Morrow, & Gray, 1968; McConnell, 1967). In many autistic children, however, the rate of eye contact is negligible, and it rarely occurs on request. Therefore, eye contact is usually taught through discrete-trial procedures after the child has been taught the prerequisite behaviors of sitting quietly with hands down. Discrete-trial training (Koegel, Russo, Rincover, & Schreibman, 1982; Lovaas, 1981) is a fundamental teaching methodology employed in one form or another in virtually every early training activity with autistic children. Its value lies in its parsing of the continuous flow of ordinary adult–child interactions into highly distinctive (discrete) events that are more easily discriminated by the child. The essential components of each training trial are the following:

1. The teacher presents a brief, salient stimulus (instruction or question).
2. The instruction is accompanied by a prompt (assistance that insures a correct response) if the child needs one to execute the response correctly. This is an optional component that, if used, is faded as soon as the child begins to respond correctly on his or her own.
3. The child responds correctly or incorrectly.
4. The teacher provides an appropriate consequence (reinforces correct responses; ignores or corrects incorrect responses). One commonly used error correction strategy is the "No, No, Prompt" approach. The child is told "No" in a neutral tone of voice for the first and

second incorrect responses, then prompted to make the correct response on the next trial.

5. There is a brief intertrial interval before the next stimulus is presented, in order to insure that it has a salient onset.

Eye contact training illustrates the use of these components very clearly. The teacher starts a trial by saying "Look," then prompts the child to look by holding an edible reward near the bridge of his or her (the teacher's) nose or beside one eye. Because of the natural variability in the child's eye movements, the child's gaze will move from the edible to the teacher's face, and he or she is rewarded at that moment. Over trials the edible as a prompt is faded (gradually moved farther away from the teacher's face), to shift stimulus control of eye contact from the prompt to the teacher's instruction. Alternatively, instead of fading the prompt spatially, the teacher can delay its presentation for increasing durations after the command. The objective is simply to establish 2–3 seconds of eye contact on request at a fairly reliable level, such as 80% of requests. Two or three seconds are sufficient for the child to attend to the teacher's next verbalization or model; there is no need to teach the child to stare for long durations (Mirenda, Donnellan, & Yoder, 1983).

Once eye contact begins to occur reliably in one-to-one training sessions, it is generalized across persons and settings through "incidental teaching" (Hart & Risley, 1975) to make it a functional social and educational skill. At home, the child is required to make eye contact during interactions with parents and siblings just before being allowed access to naturally occurring reinforcers, such as opening the refrigerator door, turning on the television, or going outside (Kozloff, 1974; Lovaas, 1981). Similarly, in subsequent teaching programs, the child is required to look at the teacher's hand and body movements during motor imitation training, at the teacher's mouth or hands during spoken or signed communication training, and at objects or pictures during discrimination tasks.

Management of Mild Problem Behaviors

Interfering behaviors encountered early in treatment with young autistic children typically include tantrums, throwing or destroying objects, aggression, and self-injury. Such behaviors are very common early in treatment because the children are learning to respond reliably to demands for the first time in their lives. Lovaas and Buch (1997) note that in their clinical experience, aggressive behavior during the first hour of treatment seems to be predictive of future success in treatment, whereas indifference or obliviousness suggests a less favorable prognosis.

One useful approach to treatment is suggested by the fact that autistic children are frequently described as negativistic or "noncompliant" in teaching situations (Volkmar, 1986). Defining the problem of disruptive behavior as noncompliance leads to procedures that attempt to reduce disruptive behaviors indirectly by strengthening compliance as a class of appropriate alternative behaviors (Craighead, O'Leary, & Allen, 1973; Striefel, Wetherby, & Karlan, 1978). Russo, Cataldo, and Cushing (1981) conducted compliance training with developmentally disabled children by presenting one of three simple commands ("Come here," "Sit down," "Stand up"), along with an appropriate gesture, every 30–45 seconds during 10-minute sessions. If the children complied with the instruction within 5 seconds, they received a hug, praise, and an edible reward. Noncompliance and disruptive behaviors were ignored. With unusually disruptive children, it is more effective to physically prompt the children through the behavior than to ignore noncompliance (Neef, Shafer, Egel, Cataldo, & Parrish, 1983; Parrish, Cataldo, Kolko, Neef, & Egel, 1986). The Russo et al. (1981) procedure not only increased the children's rates of compliance, but also resulted in substantial reductions of their disruptive behaviors, such as self-injury, aggression, and inappropriate crying. Replications and extensions of this finding have established that compliant behaviors and disruptive behaviors are inversely related response classes; strengthening one class of behaviors reduces the other class (Neef et al., 1983; Parrish et al., 1986).

Another effective approach to dealing with noncompliance is the "behavioral momentum" technique of Mace et al. (1988). This technique takes advantage of the tendency of behavior to persist for a while following a change in stimuli. The teacher first presents a series of three or four instructions that the child is highly likely to carry out ("high-probability" instructions), then presents the problematic, "low-probability" instruction. For example, the teacher may say, "Give me five," "Shake my hand," "Give me a hug," then say, "Put away your toys." The antecedent presentation of high-probability instructions at a fairly rapid rate with immediate reinforcement for compliance appears to generalize to the subsequent low-probability instruction (Mace et al., 1988).

An understanding of a common motivation for disruptive behaviors in teaching situations has facilitated the development of additional treatments. Several studies (Carr & Durand, 1985a; Carr & Newsom, 1985; Carr, Newsom, & Binkoff, 1976, 1980; Weeks & Gaylord-Ross, 1981) have shown that tantrums, aggression, and self-injury are far more likely to occur when demands (instructions, requests, questions) are presented to autistic children than when no demands are made, and that disruptive behaviors often cease abruptly when a clear signal is given that no more demands will be made. These findings can be explained by Patterson's (1976) coercion hypothesis of the development of disruptive behavior in conduct-disordered children. Patterson found that high levels of disruptive behaviors in such children often follow parents' commands and cease when the children's disruptive behaviors result in the termination of commands. Over a period of time, the children repeat or escalate the intensity of their disruptive (coercive) behaviors because these are strengthened through negative reinforcement (the termination of an aversive stimulus—in this case, the parents' commands). Similarly, with autistic children, teachers' instructions can function as aversive stimuli, which the children try to escape by engaging in disruptive behaviors. If the teachers do stop their instructions whenever the children are disruptive, the disruptive behaviors are strengthened through negative reinforcement. This scenario is especially likely with young autistic children, who may have had no history with the relatively high rates of demands that normally occur in one-to-one teaching situations.

The conceptualization of disruptive behaviors as avoidance or escape behaviors maintained by negative reinforcement helps to generate interventions for reducing coercive interactions (Carr & Newsom, 1985). First, any operation that serves to attenuate the aversive properties of a teaching situation should result in a decrease of problem behaviors. The aversiveness of the demands in the teaching situation can be attenuated by creating a "positive context" of engaging, playful social interaction between demand presentations; by providing frequent breaks; and by using highly preferred foods, toys, and sensory stimuli as reinforcers (Carr & Newsom, 1985; Carr et al., 1976, 1980; Rincover & Newsom, 1985).

A second intervention suggested by an escape conceptualization involves a variant of extinction and is similar to the compliance training procedure described above (Russo et al., 1981). If the disruptive behavior has been maintained by the negative reinforcement of successful escape, then it follows that if a child is not permitted to escape following the disruptive behavior, the behavior should become nonfunctional and decrease. Escape extinction can be arranged by "working through" the child's disruptive behavior—that is, continuing to present demands and prompts at a steady pace regardless, of the child's behavior (Carr et al., 1980; Plummer, Baer, & LeBlanc, 1977). A corollary of the escape hypothesis is that any treatment procedure that allows escape to occur contingent upon a disruptive behavior is contraindicated. Time out can worsen escape-motivated problem behaviors by negatively reinforcing them (Carr et al., 1980).

The acquisition of learning readiness skills can last from an hour to a few weeks of daily sessions, depending on a child's level of functioning, the extent of disruptive behaviors, and the teacher's skill. Certainly, by the end of the first month all children should be reliably sitting in a chair for 15–20 minutes at a time, looking at the teacher on request, following a few simple instructions, and displaying little or no disruptive behavior. Subsequent training is devoted primarily to early social and communicative behaviors, as described in the next two sections; however, self-care skills and independent play must also be addressed in order to help the children become more independent and to improve their ability to function appropriately during free time.

SOCIAL BEHAVIOR

Imitation and Observational Learning

The fundamental importance of imitation in learning and socialization was stated years ago by Bandura (1962), who noted that the acquisition of complex acts such as social and linguistic behaviors would be extremely time-consuming and difficult if each of the components of such behaviors had to be learned individually and then chained together. This argument acquires special force in work with autistic children. If shaping and prompting were the only techniques available for teaching such children, the extent of their progress would be severely limited, simply as a function of the limited amount of time available for teaching countless individual behaviors and combining them into meaningful sequences and patterns of complex behaviors. The importance of imitation in the acquisition of social behaviors by autistic children is highlighted by the finding that imitative ability correlates more highly with other social behaviors than do intelligence and chronological age (Dawson & Adams, 1984).

Imitation is normally taught through discrete-trial procedures (Hingtgen, Coulter, & Churchill, 1967; Lovaas, Freitas, Nelson, & Whalen, 1967; Young, Krantz, McClannahan, & Poulson, 1994). It is usually best to begin by using objects and toys that are easy for a child to manipulate appropriately and whose manipulation is functional in producing an effect on the environment. DeMyer et al. (1972) found that autistic children were more successful at imitating behaviors that lay below their tested MAs and that involved object manipulation (e.g., stacking blocks, banging a spoon, covering a doll) than they were at imitating behaviors that were at or above their MAs and that involved only body movements (e.g., hopping on one foot, clapping). Object-related behaviors are easier to imitate because the object used on each trial remains in view as a prompt for the appropriate imitative manipulation. Further, Guess, Keogh, and Baer (1977) found that object manipulations producing an immediate effect were learned more rapidly than similar movements with no obvious functionality. For example, squeezing a plastic bottle of liquid into a pan was acquired sooner than squeezing an empty bottle. During the initial imitation training trials, most autistic children must be manually prompted to reproduce the teacher's model. Subsequently, the major problem in imitation training becomes that of fading the prompt. Various ways of fading the prompt can be attempted, such as (1) gradually reducing the force of the prompt (Baer, Peterson, & Sherman, 1967; Furnell & Thomas, 1981; Metz, 1965); (2) moving its location up the child's arm away from the hand in small increments (Striefel & Wetherby, 1973); or (3) delaying the prompt after the teacher's model for progressively increasing durations in 1-second steps (Handen & Zane, 1987; Striefel, Bryan, & Aikins, 1974).

A different approach to teaching imitation is Keogh, Guess, and Baer's (1977) Fast Motor Imitation Program (published in Baer, 1978), which is especially suitable for lower-functioning children. The initial behavioral models include highly effective visual prompts for imitation: The teacher offers the child something he or she wants (e.g., candy) with a straight-ahead arm movement, and the child takes the candy with a reaching response that closely resembles the teacher's model. Manual prompting and its attendant prompt-fading difficulties are thus avoided from the outset of training. Over trials, the teacher's arm movements are varied from left to right and from high to low, and the candy is hidden in a closed hand. Further steps add standing up, stepping left and right, and manipulating objects. The success of this innovative procedure with individuals who have failed to learn through other imitation training procedures (Baer, 1978) may be due to a number of features, including (1) beginning with a response (reaching) that is already in the child's repertoire; (2) the use of a "within-stimulus" prompt (the edible in the teacher's hand; cf. Schreibman, 1975); (3) the direct relationship between the response and the acquisition of the reinforcer (Koegel & Williams, 1980); and (4) the ease with which the edible as a prompt can be removed without loss of the behavior.

After the child has acquired several imitative behaviors, new behaviors modeled by the teacher will be learned in progressively fewer trials, eventually requiring only one demonstration (Baer et al., 1967; Lovaas et al., 1967; Metz, 1965). When the child begins to imitate novel behaviors on their first presentation by the teacher, training focuses on making imitation durable (resistant to extinction) and generalizing imitation to other situations and persons (Bucher & Bowman, 1974; Furnell & Thomas, 1981; Kozloff, 1974). At the same time, the behaviors to be imitated are increasingly refined to include oral–motor movements and sounds as a prerequisite to speech (Lovaas, 1977, 1981).

The generalization of imitation across persons leads to the procedures used to study observational or "vicarious" learning in normal children (Bandura, 1969). In most studies of observational learning, autistic children have learned social, language, or academic skills by observing a peer model who already performs the skill competently. Training in observational learning is usually conducted by having a normal peer confederate (or another autistic child who already knows the target behavior) sit next to the autistic child, model a behavior that has been instructed by the teacher, and receive a reward while the autistic child watches. The autistic child is then given an opportunity to perform the same behavior, to determine whether observational learning has occurred. Outside of structured classroom settings, another effective approach involves a "follow-the-leader" format, in which an autistic child is taught to attend to and imitate the actions of a peer-leader, who models a number of play activities in sequence (Carr & Darcy, 1990). Behaviors taught through observational learning procedures have included appropriate toy play (Carr & Darcy, 1990; Tryon & Keane, 1986), beginning academic skills (Egel, Richman, & Koegel, 1981), simple vocational workshop skills (Brown & Holvoet, 1982), and expressive language skills (Charlop, Schreibman, & Tryon, 1983; Coleman & Stedman, 1974; Ihrig & Wolchik, 1988).

Expressing Affection

Teaching an autistic child to express affection in simple ways enables him or her to reciprocate the affection received from parents, siblings, teachers, and peers, and is therefore a behavior that should be taught as early as possible. Initially, the child can be taught to give a hug or a kiss on request through manual prompting and edible reinforcement procedures (Lovaas, 1981). At a more advanced level, a hug can become a discriminative stimulus for verbalizations of affection (e.g., "I like you" for teachers and classmates; "I love you" for family members). Charlop and Walsh (1986) showed that such sentences could be taught through verbal modeling immediately after a hug and maintained as the verbal model was gradually delayed. The sentences generalized across relevant persons and settings, but, appropriately, not to strangers.

Nordquist, Twardosz, and McEvoy (1982) and McEvoy et al. (1988) investigated procedures designed for a school setting that incorporated discriminative stimulus training as part of an effort to make peers' and teachers' behaviors effective social reinforcers for autistic children. The Nordquist et al. (1982) procedure consisted of two phases. In the first phase, "affection activities," one autistic child was grouped with five or six nonhandicapped children and two teachers. The activities emphasized expressing affection by smiling, hugging, tickling, and patting. A different set of nonhandicapped children participated each day to promote generalization. In the second phase, "incidental teaching," whenever one of the autistic children wanted something during the school day, he or she had to find a nonhandicapped peer and interact with the peer briefly in order to obtain the object or to

join the activity. For example, if the autistic child wanted to swing, he or she had to find a nonhandicapped child and ask the child to push or ride with him or her on the swing. Note that this type of incidental teaching constituted discriminative stimulus training: The autistic children had to attend to peers to obtain reinforcement. Both of the subjects of this study, who rarely interacted with peers during baseline observations, showed increased social interactions and participation in activities after affection activities were introduced, and still greater increases when the incidental-teaching requirement was added.

Autistic adolescents were taught to display appropriate affective verbal and facial responses through the use of a large number of scenarios for each of several common situations by Gena, Krantz, McClannahan, and Poulson (1996). The scenarios consisted of brief statements or questions presented by the therapist. For example, in teaching the adolescent to show sympathy, the therapist would say, "I have a terrible headache," and exhibit a serious facial expression. A correct response by the adolescent would be to direct eye gaze toward the therapist and state a sympathetic response ("I'm sorry to hear that") while maintaining a serious facial expression. Other affective categories trained were talking about favorite things, laughing about absurdities, showing appreciation, and indicating dislike. After acquisition, the appropriate affective displays generalized to novel adults in different settings and showed maintenance over time. Gena et al. (1996) noted that token reinforcement and error correction procedures were rapidly effective in training affective responses, but that shaping affect to approximate the participants' own spontaneous affective displays required further training.

Social Play and Social Skills Groups

Several studies have shown that solitary play can be taught through observational learning procedures (Lovaas et al., 1967; Tryon & Keane, 1986), through self-reinforcement procedures (Stahmer & Schreibman, 1992), and through prompting and reinforcement with either edibles or the intrinsic sensory reinforcers available in some toys (Eason, White, & Newsom, 1982; Koegel, Firestone, Kramme, & Dunlap, 1974; Rincover et al., 1979; Santarcangelo, Dyer, & Luce, 1987). Although such procedures are effective in teaching independent play behaviors and are therefore valuable early in treatment, the acquisition of such behaviors is not typically followed by spontaneous social play among autistic children or between autistic children and normal peers (Romanczyk, Diament, Goren, Trunell, & Harris, 1975). Therefore, additional procedures are employed to teach social play.

In their study of social play, Romanczyk et al. (1975) taught autistic children to engage in social toy play with their autistic peers in classroom play groups. Every 30 seconds, two of the children were rewarded with edibles and praise if they were playing with a peer. If a child was not playing socially, he or she was placed next to another child, and a hand was placed on the toy the other child was playing with. After social play had increased to a high level, the prompts were faded by decreasing their frequency over eight sessions. The main advantage of the Romanczyk et al. (1975) procedure is that it can be used in group situations, without extensive one-to-one intervention.

Pretend play is a key deficit in autistic children that is believed to indicate mental representational impairments (Leslie, 1987). Goldstein and Cisar (1992) used scripts to teach social pretend play to autistic preschoolers and their classmates. The children were organized in triads consisting of one autistic child and two normal peers. Each triad was taught to act out each of three different scripts describing typical interactions in a pet shop, magic show, and carnival. After training, the autistic children showed increased use of the verbal and social behaviors of the scripts during pretend play, as well as increased social behaviors not related to the scripts.

As part of their systematic program of research on procedures to improve classroom instructional methods for autistic and other handicapped children, Kamps and her colleagues have studied procedures that improve social interaction as well as academic learning (Kamps et al., 1992; Kamps, Barbetta, Leonard, & Delquadri, 1994; Dugan et al., 1995). Kamps et al. (1992) investigated the use of social skills training in groups to facilitate social interactions between autistic 7-year-olds and their nonhandicapped peers in an integrated first-grade classroom. Training occurred during the first 10 minutes of 20-minute play groups held four times weekly. Specific skills were selected from published social skills curricula and included initiating and maintaining interactions, giving and accepting compliments, taking turns and sharing, helping others and asking for help, and including others

in activities. The autistic children showed increases in both the frequency and duration of appropriate social interactions. In other studies in integrated classrooms, classwide peer tutoring (Kamps et al., 1994) and cooperative learning groups (Dugan et al., 1995) resulted in increased social interaction between autistic children and their nonhandicapped peers.

Although the lack of a theory of mind has been prominent recently in explanations of the social deficiencies of autistic children (Baron-Cohen, Tager-Flusberg, & Cohen, 1993; Frith, 1989), only one study so far has examined the effects of improvements in theory of mind performance on social behavior. Ozonoff and Miller (1995) conducted weekly social skills training sessions for a group of normally intelligent autistic adolescents. Modeling, role playing, and feedback were used to teach the understanding of states of knowledge, belief, deception, and intention in the context of perspective-taking and false-belief tasks like those used to test for theory-of-mind deficits. Games, parties, and field trips were used to generalize the concepts taught in the group setting. Post-tests on standard theory-of-mind tasks showed considerable improvement over pretest scores, and were also superior to the pre-and posttest scores of a no-treatment control group. There were, however, no changes on a standardized assessment of social skills, the Social Skills Rating System (SSRS; Gresham & Elliott, 1990)—perhaps because the SSRS focuses on basic interaction and conversation skills, and not the perspective-taking skills acquired in theory-of-mind training (Ozonoff & Miller, 1995). It remains to be seen whether or not more extensive remediation of theory of mind deficits can have an impact on social behavior in natural environments.

Peer-Mediated Interventions

The most common strategy for remediating the asociality of autistic children involves teaching normal or mildly handicapped peers to engage in appropriate social interactions with them (Strain & Odom, 1986). A practical reason for this approach is that the use of peer mediators can extend social interventions to multiple children concurrently once the peers are trained (Strain, 1980). A second reason—one that becomes increasingly important as more autistic children are educated in integrated classrooms—is that generalization and maintenance of social skills will be more likely if normal peers in such settings are involved in the intervention (Stokes & Baer, 1977). Research has shown that the mere exposure of handicapped children to normal peers through integrated classroom placements does not result in significant observational learning by the handicapped children (Guralnick, 1976; Snyder, Apolloni, & Cooke, 1977).

Peer Initiation Procedures

The peer initiation procedure that has received the most study is that introduced by Strain, Shores, and their colleagues (Strain, 1977; Strain, Shores, & Timm, 1977). Several preliminary sessions are devoted to training a peer confederate to initiate toy play interactions. The teacher plays the role of an autistic child and uses instructions, modeling, and praise to teach the peer. On half the trials, the teacher complies with the peer's toy play initiations; on the other half, the teacher ignores the initiations in order to prepare the child for behaviors likely to occur with the autistic child. The peer is taught to persist until the teacher finally complies (Odom, Hoyson, Jamieson, & Strain, 1985; Ragland, Kerr, & Strain, 1978; Strain, 1983; Strain, Kerr, & Ragland, 1979). In some studies, practice with an autistic child while the teacher provides instructions and feedback to the peer is also a component of training (e.g., Odom & Strain, 1986; Shafer, Egel, & Neef, 1984). The content of the training has varied across studies. In a useful, highly empirical approach to content selection, Goldstein, Kaczmarek, Pennington, and Shafer (1992) based the content of peer training on previous research by Ferrel (1990), which identified specific types of interactions that were most likely to evoke a response in handicapped as well as normal children. They taught 3- to 5-year-old peers to engage in the following strategies: establishing mutual attention, commenting about ongoing activities, and acknowledging the partner's responses.

The initial studies of the peer initiation model with autistic children showed that the procedure was rapidly effective in bringing about increases in their social play (Ragland et al., 1978; Strain et al., 1979). In these initial studies, however, little generalization of social interaction occurred in settings where the peers did not initiate interactions. Therefore, subsequent research has addressed procedural variables that might enhance generalization.

Generalization is more likely in settings that include nonhandicapped peers than in segregated settings. Strain (1983) exposed four autistic children to the peer initiation procedure; generalization of their social interactions was assessed under segregated or integrated conditions. Generalization of social interaction occurred only in the integrated sessions. Additional data indicated that the normal peers both initiated interactions with the autistic children and responded positively to their initiations far more frequently than did the handicapped peers. In the segregated setting, the autistic children's social behaviors underwent extinction.

Another factor improving generalization is more realistic training. Instead of having a peer work with an adult in a role-playing format during training, Shafer et al. (1984) and Brady, Shores, McEvoy, Ellis, and Fox (1987) taught the peer to interact directly with an autistic child. In the Shafer et al. (1984) study, for example, the experimenter first modeled toy play interactions with the autistic child while the peer watched, then coached the peer while the peer interacted with the autistic child. Three of the four autistic children in the study showed large increases in social behavior directed toward peer trainers, and two showed increased social behavior toward untrained peers.

A comprehensive approach to promoting generalization is the social support network model developed by Haring and Breen (1992). These investigators enlisted groups of four or five nonhandicapped peers in a junior high school to prompt and reinforce social interactions in two moderately retarded, socially withdrawn adolescent boys, one of whom was autistic. The peers participated in weekly meetings to assess each week's interactions during breaks between classes and lunch periods, and to develop strategies for improving the target children's interactions in the coming week. The investigators' role was largely limited to facilitating the group meetings and teaching some appropriate social responses to the handicapped boys. Both boys showed increased frequencies of appropriate social interactions across the school day, and additional measures showed increased unprompted interactions outside of school and improved attitudes and ratings of friendship toward the boys by their peers.

Teaching Autistic Children to Initiate Interactions

The studies reviewed above, as well as more recent studies (e.g., Roeyers, 1996; Schleien, Mustonen, & Rynders, 1995) indicate that autistic children's social interactions are composed almost entirely of responses to peers' initiations. Some investigators have addressed the problem of teaching autistic children to initiate appropriate interactions and thus not to be so dependent on peers' initiations.

Oke and Schreibman (1990) compared the effects of peer initiation training with those of training a high-functioning autistic boy to initiate play interactions with the same peers. A unique feature of this study was the use of videotaped examples of successful versus unsuccessful initiation strategies in teaching the peers and the autistic boy to initiate play interactions. The autistic boy's initiations were more frequent after he was taught to initiate than during peer initiation sessions.

Because many autistic persons have limited language for elaborating interactions, Brady et al. (1984) and Gaylord-Ross, Haring, Breen, and Pitts-Conway (1984) adopted the strategy of structuring social interactions around leisure objects that could be shared with nonhandicapped peers in a context of brief verbal exchanges. This strategy of letting the objects carry the burden of the interaction was enhanced by selecting items that would be interesting to the normal peers, such as hand-held video games, an earphone radio, and a pack of gum. In the Gaylord-Ross et al. (1984) study, a training script was devised for each item; each script included phrases and sentences for each component (initiation, elaboration, and termination) of the interaction. Training sessions continued until each of two autistic boys had been exposed sequentially to six different peers as multiple exemplars of the normal students at the school. A stringent evaluation of the training was conducted by measuring the number and durations of social interactions initiated by the autistic boys toward naive peers in the school courtyard during daily breaks. Both participants showed large increases in these measures of generalized social interaction over baseline conditions. Training scripts and sequentially introduced normal peers were also employed by Breen, Haring, Pitts-Conway, and Gaylord-Ross (1985) to teach four autistic adolescents to engage in appropriate social interactions during breaks at job sites.

Another approach to increasing an autistic child's self-initiations is to teach peers to respond appropriately to initiations before prompting the autistic child to initiate (Odom & Strain, 1986). Zanolli, Daggett, and Adams (1996) initially taught peers to respond positively to initiations by two preschool autistic peers, then conducted "priming" sessions with the autistic children just prior to play sessions. In priming sessions, the autistic children were prompted to look at a peer, smile, touch the peer's hand, and make a verbal request. Both participants showed trained and untrained spontaneous initiations in the play sessions.

Sibling-Mediated Procedures

In some families with autistic children, there are siblings who are willing to become peer trainers if given the opportunity. As Schreibman, O'Neill, and Koegel (1983) noted, siblings can play an important role as facilitation agents for an autistic child's social interactions with other children in the neighborhood, and can also provide continuity between school and home for educational programs. James and Egel (1986) developed a procedure for training siblings of severely retarded children to teach social play (a procedure that is directly applicable to families with autistic children). Each of three siblings first observed the experimenter while she modeled instructions, prompts, and praise with the handicapped child. Then the sibling practiced with the child and received feedback from the experimenter. To increase the probability of social initiations by the handicapped children, the siblings also received training in incidental teaching. Through modeling and role playing, each sibling learned to withhold a desired toy until the handicapped child requested it and to prompt a request if necessary. These procedures resulted in increased reciprocal social play interactions in three normal–handicapped sibling dyads, which were maintained over a 6-month follow-up period.

A note of caution should be considered in working with the siblings of autistic children. Although our experience has been that siblings usually respond very positively to the opportunity to learn better ways of interacting with their autistic siblings, some siblings perceive themselves as having greater caretaking and supervision responsibilities than children whose siblings are not handicapped. Therefore, sibling training programs should be designed with attention to the need to avoid adding to that burden (James & Egel, 1986). Helpful in this regard are negotiating schedules with the sibling to avoid conflicts with other activities, and letting the sibling establish some of the treatment priorities based on his or her own problems in living with the autistic sibling.

This review of strategies for addressing the social unrelatedness of autistic children shows that social behavior can be taught and improved through appropriate teaching methods. Although a promising start has been made, the social domain is large and complex, and is extensively interwoven with the domains of language and affect. Therefore, more extensive improvements in social functioning will require attention to behaviors in all three domains concurrently. Moreover, the attainment of a significant level of social competence and fluency seems to require the ability to use learned social skills discriminatively and flexibly according to specific social contexts (Frith, 1989). The development of this ability will probably entail complex treatment strategies that include both direct training in key skills (e.g., observational learning) and the extensive involvement of peers as trainers and models in a variety of settings from an early age (Lovaas & Smith, 1988).

COMMUNICATION

The three major strategies for establishing a basic repertoire of functional language are operant training in spoken language (Guess, Sailor, & Baer, 1978; Lovaas, 1977, 1981); sign language training (Carr, Binkoff, Kologinsky, & Eddy, 1978; Schaeffer, 1980); and the use of pictures, communication boards, speech output devices, and other "augmentative" communication devices (Alpert, 1980; Bondy & Frost, 1994). The operant speech training procedures commonly used to establish an initial repertoire of expressive and receptive verbal labels are described in some detail, to indicate the general approach used to establish functional communication in nonverbal and minimally verbal children. Sign language training, the question of whether to use speech training or sign training, and the controversial topic of facilitated communication are more briefly discussed.

Operant Training in Spoken Language

In operant spoken-language training, the teaching of expressive speech is usually preceded by training in receptive labeling and accompanied by speech imitation training as needed.

Receptive Labeling

It is usually most effective to begin receptive training with highly preferred foods, toys, and other objects that lend themselves to repeated presentations. The teacher begins by presenting the item (e.g., a cup of juice) and telling the child, "Juice" (later varied as "Get juice," "Drink juice," "Where's the juice?," etc., as the child is able to deal with more complex instructions). If the child touches or picks up the cup of juice, he or she is rewarded with a sip of the juice and the teacher's praise. If the child does not respond, the teacher provides an imitative prompt (picks up the cup) or a manual prompt (moves the child's hand to the cup). The stimulus item is removed for a brief intertrial interval, then presented again with the same command. The prompt is faded over trials, until the child responds reliably to the spoken command. Next, a second item (e.g., a preferred toy) is taught the same way, with praise and a few seconds of play with the toy being the reinforcement. After the child responds correctly and reliably to each item presented alone, the two items are presented simultaneously on each trial. The teacher names one or the other item in random order across trials and rewards the child for touching the named item on each trial.

The literature on discrimination training with developmentally disabled children indicates the value of employing the following procedural variables in teaching receptive discriminations:

1. The child's correct responses should secure a reward naturally related to the response, rather than an unrelated reward (Janssen & Guess, 1978; Koegel & Williams, 1980; Williams, Koegel, & Egel, 1981). For example, in the description above, the child's correct response to "Juice" results in drinking a sip of the juice, and the response to the name of the toy terminates in playing with the toy. If such response–reinforcer relationships cannot be arranged (e.g., tasks involving nonconsumable or nonmanipulable items), and arbitrary reinforcers such as edibles must be used, each training object should be associated with a different, specific reinforcer (Litt & Schreibman, 1982).

2. Intertrial intervals should be kept relatively brief (1–4 seconds) in order to minimize forgetting and distracting behaviors (Dunlap, Dyer, & Koegel, 1983; Koegel, Dunlap, & Dyer, 1980).

3. Trials should continue at a steady pace in spite of mildly disruptive behaviors. Stopping trials when such behaviors occur allows the child to escape the task momentarily, which can strengthen disruptive behaviors through the negative reinforcement of escaping from or delaying the task (Carr & Newsom, 1985; Plummer et al., 1977).

4. Already mastered "maintenance" tasks should be interspersed on trials between trials with acquisition tasks, with no reinforcement or praise only for correct responding on maintenance trials (Charlop, Kurtz, & Milstein, 1992; Dunlap, 1984).

Various prompting and prompt-fading procedures can be tried to bring the child's responses under discriminative instructional control:

1. Modeling the correct response with an identical set of objects just before the child responds, then fading the model across trials (Lovaas, 1981; Zane, Handen, Mason, & Geffin, 1984).
2. Pointing to the correct object immediately after the instruction early in training, then fading the prompt by delaying its presentation in 1-second increments after the instruction (Godby, Gast, & Wolery, 1987; Striefel et al., 1974).
3. Maximizing acoustic differences between the two words by prolonging one of the words, repeating it, or saying it more loudly, then gradually fading out the emphasis (Striefel et al., 1978; Striefel & Wetherby, 1973; Witt & Wacker, 1981).
4. Requiring the child to wait for 3–5 seconds after the instruction before making a response (Dyer, Christian, & Luce, 1982), or to verbalize the critical cue in the teacher's instruction before responding (Koegel, Dunlap, Richman, & Dyer, 1981).

Once the child has learned five or six words, two types of generalization training are begun (Lovaas, 1981). First, different exemplars of each object are used to teach the child to generalize within classes of objects while maintaining discriminations between classes of objects, or simple concepts. Second, the child is taught to identify the objects in different settings and with different individuals. Frequently throughout the day, other teachers, parents, and siblings require the child to "get" or "find" or "show me" the objects he or she has just learned to identify. Such specific training in generalization across multiple settings and persons is crucial to making language functional for autistic children, as they typically fail to generalize (Rincover & Koegel, 1975) or maintain (Koegel & Rincover, 1977) newly acquired behaviors without it.

Expressive Speech

When the child has learned to identify about 10 objects receptively, expressive training with the same objects begins in a paradigm of successive discrimination training (Lovaas, 1981). The teacher places the first object on the table and, when the child looks at it, says its name as a verbal prompt for the child to name it. If the child has difficulty with speech imitation, procedures like those described in Guess et al. (1978) or Lovaas (1977, 1981) should be used. Over trials the verbal prompt is faded by reducing its volume and/or delaying its presentation, in order to shift stimulus control from the teacher's verbal model to the sight of the object. The name of a second object is taught in the same way. Then the two objects are presented in random order across trials until the child is able to name each object correctly without prompting on several consecutive trials. In subsequent training, the name of each new object is first taught in isolation; then trials with the new object are intermixed with trials with the previously trained objects for discrimination training. As is the case with receptive labeling, acquisition of each new expressive label after the first three or four is positively accelerated, but the rate of acquisition is highly variable across children (Lovaas, 1977).

Once the child has learned to name several items, basic requests (e.g., "I want _____," "Gimme _____") and answers to simple questions (e.g., "What's this?") are taught, so as to make the newly acquired labels more useful in ordinary spoken interactions.

After requests have been taught through imitation, the teacher's model can be faded by delaying its presentation to shift control of the child's sentence from the model to the sight of the object, in order to make the child's requests more spontaneous (Charlop, Schreibman, & Thibodeau, 1985). The reason for teaching basic request forms early in training is that they facilitate generalization by allowing the child to use language to obtain reinforcers in the natural environment. Thus, requests are more immediately and generally functional for an autistic child than are descriptive statements, because the latter are largely maintained by social attention—a very weak reinforcer for autistic children early in treatment (Goetz, Schuler, & Sailor, 1979).

Generalization training begins when the child has mastered about six labels, and it is again concerned with generalization within classes of similar items and with functional usage of the labels in natural settings (Lovaas, 1981). Special efforts to promote generalization across environments are necessary, because the tight control over attention and responding that is often required to teach beginning speech seems to combine with the overly selective attention that is characteristic of most autistic children (Lovaas et al., 1979) to result in their frequent failure to generalize speech to settings and persons not involved in the original training (Handleman, 1979; Harris, 1975; Rincover & Koegel, 1975). The main strategy for promoting generalized speech usage is to insure that the child's spoken language is immediately functional in producing frequent and varied reinforcing effects in everyday environments. This is accomplished by conducting brief teaching interactions requiring the child to use words to obtain natural reinforcers and to complete daily routines. The result has been the development of a group of procedures known collectively as "milieu teaching" or "incidental teaching" after the name of the first of these procedures to be studied (Hart & Risley, 1975, 1982).

Incidental Teaching

Incidental-teaching procedures vary in detail and specific purpose, but they share four features that distinguish them from the discrete-trial language training procedures just described.

1. Discrete-trial training is a massed-trials approach controlled and paced by the teacher; incidental-teaching episodes consist of only one trial or a few trials at a time, which are usually initiated by the child.
2. Discrete-trial training occurs in time-limited, one-to-one sessions away from distractions; incidental teaching occurs intermittently throughout the day in naturalistic, everyday environments.
3. In discrete-trial training, the training stimuli are often teacher-selected objects, and the reinforcers may be arbitrary events such as food and praise; in incidental teaching, the training stimuli are child-selected items, and the reinforcer is access to the item.
4. With autistic children, discrete-trial methods are typically employed to teach new language *forms;* incidental-teaching procedures are employed to teach new language *functions*—that is, to help the child use language forms to influence others or to elaborate acquired forms in order to communicate better (Carr, 1985; McGee, Krantz, & McClannahan, 1985).

One of the most frequently used incidental-teaching techniques is the time delay procedure (Halle, Marshall, & Spradlin, 1979; Halle, Baer, & Spradlin, 1981), designed to shift stimulus control from the teacher's prompts to environmental cues. The time delay procedure can be used whenever the child needs assistance or wants an item. Instead of instructing or modeling an appropriate response, the teacher looks at the child and waits expectantly, either for gradually increasing durations across trials (e.g., 2, 4, 6, etc., seconds) or for a fixed duration on each trial (e.g., 10 seconds). If the child makes an appropriate response during the delay, it is reinforced with assistance or the desired item. If an incorrect response or no response occurs, the teacher models the word or phrase and reinforces the child's correct imitation. With more advanced children, a general request for the appropriate response can be made ("You need to tell me what you want"). The delay procedure teaches the child to respond to nonverbal cues: To determine what verbalization is appropriate to the situation, the child must attend to cues in the environment (e.g., a desired object, the start of an activity, the teacher's arrival with cups of juice) in addition to the teacher. Eventually, the objects and events are themselves sufficient to cue appropriate speech. The variety and extent of the child's language learning depend on the teacher's skill in providing appropriate prompts and in maximizing the frequency of incidental-teaching interactions (Halle, 1982). To increase the frequency of opportunities, the teacher places desired materials out of reach on a shelf but in sight of the child, and keeps the incidental teaching interactions brief and comfortable for the child (Hart & Risley, 1982).

Modifications of incidental-teaching procedures indicate that they can be used to teach initial speech skills as well as to generalize existing skills. McGee, Krantz, Mason, and McClannahan (1983) taught receptive labels to autistic adolescents living in a group home by conducting a few training trials at the start of each of the tasks of a lunch-making routine. Prior to beginning each task in the routine (e.g., making sandwiches, preparing snacks, bagging the items), the adolescent was requested to hand the teacher one of the items used in the task from an array of five objects on the kitchen counter. Completion of the receptive labeling tasks for a set of objects enabled the adolescent to proceed with the corresponding lunch preparation activity. The procedure resulted in rapid acquisition of receptive labels that had not been learned when access to the lunch preparation items was noncontingent. Similarly, Leung (1994) taught spontaneous requests to autistic boys in five to nine sessions, using time delay procedures with the pieces of multicomponent toys. A variation of the McGee et al. (1983) procedure is the "behavior chain interruption" procedure, in which a training trial is inserted into the middle of a regularly occurring chain of behaviors in the child's daily life (e.g., making toast, removing and hanging up a coat, brushing teeth) (Goetz, Gee, & Sailor, 1985). At a predetermined step in the chain, the child is interrupted and has to make an appropriate request for an item in order to continue the chain. This procedure effectively promotes spontaneous speech, because it takes advantage of an autistic child's strong motivation to complete a well-established routine once having started it.

Koegel, O'Dell, and Koegel (1987) presented a procedure that involves the one-to-one sessions typical of the discrete-trial format, yet loosens the structure of such training through the use of incidental-teaching techniques in order to operationalize some correlates of normal speech acquisition. These include turn taking; the speaker–listener exchanges occurring in normal communication; shared control; the sharing of attention, materials, and tasks; and natural consequences for speaking, such as access to desired objects or events. Koegel, O'Dell, and Koegel (1987) called their procedure a "Natural Language Teaching Paradigm"; it consisted of the following techniques, used with two mute autistic children in a clinic setting:

1. Instead of the teacher's selecting the training objects (toys) arbitrarily, the child selected one from a pool of objects by looking at, touching, or pointing at the object.
2. Instead of drilling the child on one object in massed trials until mastery, the teacher changed the object whenever the child selected a different object.
3. Instructing the child to label the object was replaced by the teacher's playing with the object and modeling its name; if the child failed to imitate, the teacher simply played with the object and modeled its name again.
4. Any spoken response, not just a correct response or an approximation, was reinforced.
5. Reinforcement consisted of praise and the opportunity to play with the object instead of praise and edibles.

Both of the children studied by Koegel, O'Dell, and Koegel (1987) showed substantial increases in imitation, spontaneous vocalizations, and generalized imitation. Laski, Charlop, and Schreibman (1988) showed that parents could be successfully taught to use procedures like those used by Koegel, O'Dell, and Koegel (1987), with corresponding increases in their children's imitations and answers to questions. The main value of the procedure seemed to be its ability to increase the frequency of existing speech, although the investigators noted anecdotally that novel words and phrases also occurred. These studies show that developmental concepts can serve a heuristic role in suggesting some novel arrangements of behavioral variables. However, few studies of the Natural Language Paradigm have been published, and there is the risk that making training too much like everyday interactions may simply recreate situations exactly like those in which autistic children fail to learn (Smith, 1993).

Subsequent language training depends on the outcome of the attempt to establish spoken language. Young children who acquire labeling should receive further training that is informed by knowledge of normal development. Training in early semantic relationships focuses on possessives ("Billy's coat," "my car"), locatives ("on the plate"), noun–action phrases ("Mommy sits"), and action–object phrases ("drink juice"). Early morpheme rules include the "-s" suffix for plurals and possessives, and the present progressive and past tenses ("-ing," "-ed") (Howlin & Rutter, 1987; Lovaas, 1977). Examples of the advanced language skills taught to autistic children include the use of prepositions and pronouns (Lovaas, 1977; McGee et al., 1985; Sailor & Taman, 1972), speaking in compound sentences (Stevens-Long & Rasmussen, 1974), answering "yes" and "no" appropriately (Hung, 1980; Neef, Walters, & Egel, 1984), asking questions and seeking information (Hung, 1977; Taylor & Harris, 1995), recalling past events (Lovaas, 1977), making spontaneous requests (Charlop et al., 1985), reducing excessive echolalia (McMorrow, Foxx, Faw, & Bittle, 1987; Schreibman & Carr, 1978), and engaging in conversations (Dyer & Luce, 1996; Freeman & Dake, 1996; Lovaas, 1977; Haring, Roger, Lee, Breen, & Gaylord-Ross, 1986).

An innovative example of teaching autistic children to converse with each other was provided by Krantz and McClannahan (1993). They used scripts to teach a group of verbal autistic children who were able to read to converse with each other during art activities without teacher prompts. Each child started with a written instruction to "Do art and talk a lot," as well as a list of 10 statements and questions to say during the art activity (e.g., "John, what did you do on Friday?" "Max, what color do you have?"). Over sessions, the words in the scripts were gradually removed. The children continued to talk to each other, taking turns and staying on topic, without interrupting each other.

In very general terms, the outcomes that can be expected from operant speech training with autistic children appear to depend primarily on each child's initial language level. Howlin (1981) reviewed 70 studies published between 1964 and 1980, involving 125 cases. Children initially using single words were divided about equally between those using single words spontaneously (52%) and those developing spontaneous phrase speech (48%). The best outcomes occurred with initially echolalic children; over 83% of these children advanced to appropriate, spontaneous phrase speech.

Sign Language Training

The basic techniques for teaching signing are similar to those used to teach speech. A typical program for teaching initial receptive sign labeling through simultaneous sign–speech communication training is that developed by Carr and Dores (1981). The teacher starts with two objects on the table and signs the name of one of the objects while simultaneously saying its name. Correct responses (touching the named object) are reinforced with praise and edibles. The positions of the objects on the table, and the names signed and spoken by the teacher, vary randomly across trials. Training continues until the child is able to respond correctly to both of the teachers sign–word stimuli during randomly intermixed trials. One new object is added each time the child masters the current words. Prompting and fading procedures like those described earlier in connection with receptive speech are used if needed.

If the child fails to learn receptive discriminations with training like that described by Carr and Dores (1981), certain modifications studied by Pridal (1982) have been found to be helpful with severely and profoundly retarded autistic children. Pridal (1982) found that learning is greatly enhanced when (1) the initial signs are iconic—that is, they consist of movements like those normally used to manipulate the object; (2) the teacher simply signs the name of the object, without simultaneously saying its name; (3) the child is required to imitate (rehearse) the teacher's sign before touching one of the objects;

(4) the objects used in initial training are limited to those found in preliminary assessments to be highly reinforcing; and (5) the reinforcer for identifying the correct object is a few seconds of play with it.

Expressive signing is also taught through procedures like those used in operant speech training (Carr et al., 1978). The efficiency of learning will be enhanced if the teacher minimizes any hand-related self-stimulatory behaviors before beginning sign training, so that it is easy to tell when the child makes the correct sign or a close approximation. It is also very helpful if the child has acquired generalized motor imitation, as modeling is the primary teaching technique. Even so, manual prompts may still be necessary to refine the topographies of the child's signs, so that they more closely resemble the signs being taught (Carr, 1981).

An alternative to the procedures developed by Carr and his colleagues for teaching initial expressive signs has been described by Schaeffer (1980). Although the procedure has not been evaluated as rigorously as that of Carr et al. (1978), it is interesting because it is reminiscent of the behavior chain interruption strategy (Goetz et al., 1985) described in the section on incidental teaching. The teacher begins by holding out a desired edible and waiting. When the child reaches for the food, the teacher catches the hand and moves it into position to make the sign for the edible, molds the hand and moves it through the sign, and only then gives the child the edible. The teacher's manual prompts are gradually faded over many trials, until the child makes the sign independently. Subsequent signs can be taught similarly by interrupting reaching for other reinforcers.

After the child can reliably use signs to label about 10 reinforcing objects and events, phrases (Carr, Kologinsky, & Leff-Simon, 1987) and spontaneous usage (Carr & Kologinsky, 1983) are taught and generalized.

Speech Training or Sign Training?

The emergence of sign training as a major alternative to speech training for autistic children has resulted in the need to consider both strategies in planning communication interventions. Unfortunately, there are no brief assessment procedures that will allow us to match clients with intervention strategies with any degree of certainty about the outcome. Spoken language is the norm for communication in society, and its acquisition will insure the widest possible audience both within and outside of treatment settings—a factor important in generalization and maintenance. Therefore, most clinicians retain a preference for speech training and make the decision in accordance with the child's performance during a trial of speech training.

A difficulty with the performance-based approach is that objective criteria for judging whether or not a child's progress is "too slow" are not yet available. However, some clinical rules of thumb can be applied. On the basis of his experience with many autistic children, Lovaas (1981) has observed that if a child is over 6 years of age when treatment starts, vocalizes only simple vowel sounds and no difficult consonants (e.g., K, Q, L), and fails to learn to imitate at least five sounds during the first 3 months of treatment, further progress in speech training will continue to be slow, and consideration should be given to sign training. Carr (1981), in addition, notes that there are some autistic children who acquire fairly good receptive language but whose spoken articulation remains so poor that no one can understand them; hence, expressive sign training may be appropriate for them.

One way of making the performance-based approach to assessment more efficient is to conduct speech and simultaneous communication training concurrently, in an alternating-treatments design (Barlow & Hayes, 1979). The child is exposed to both a speech training session and a simultaneous sign–speech communication session each day for 3–4 weeks. The training modality that produces the more rapid rate of acquisition of words then becomes the treatment method used in subsequent training (Barrera, Lobato-Barrera, & Sulzer-Azaroff, 1980; Barrera & Sulzer-Azaroff, 1983; Brady & Smouse, 1978; Schaeffer, Kollinzas, Musil, & McDowell, 1977).

The ideal alternative to the performance-based approach would be a relatively brief assessment based on the child's presenting behaviors, in order to predict which training modality will ultimately produce the best outcome. Some potential predictor variables that may become a part of a more efficient assessment procedure are gradually being identified. For example, the predictive value of speech imitation has been established experimentally by Carr and his associates (Carr & Dores, 1981; Carr, Pridal, & Dores, 1984). Carr et al. (1984) found that mute children who were "good" speech imitators (i.e.,

could imitate 74% or more of a list of 50 simple consonant–vowel sounds) later learned to respond correctly to receptive discrimination tasks whether they were given speech-only training or sign-only training, whereas children who were "poor" imitators (imitated 20% or fewer of the sounds) learned the discriminations with sign training but not with speech training. Remington and Clarke (1983) replicated these findings with expressive labeling tasks.

Finally, the decision about which communication training approach to use should always be subject to change. The child's progress as determined by regular, objective assessments should indicate whether the child should continue to receive the type of training he or she is currently receiving or should be exposed to another approach. If both speech and sign language training efforts fail, efforts should shift to another augmentative system that permits practical communication, such as picture boards or cards (Alpert, 1980; Bondy & Frost, 1994; McDonald, 1980; Shane, 1981). The Picture Exchange Communication System of Bondy and Frost (1994), in which the child hands the teacher a picture of a desired item to request it, is especially useful with lower-functioning children because it does not require the imitation of complex hand movements or verbalizations. It is becoming a popular alternative to sign language training because, by relying on pictures, it does not require others in the child's environment to know a new form of language.

Facilitated Communication

Difficult problems are a magnet for unproven therapies, and this is especially true in the case of autism. Although we cannot address all those now practiced (see Smith, 1996, for a recent review), we briefly discuss facilitated communication because of its prevalence and controversial nature. Facilitated communication is a method of providing manual assistance to a child by lightly holding the child's wrist or arm while he or she types or points to letters on a keyboard or alphabet board. The physical support is purportedly not intended to prompt specific responses, but to help stabilize the arm, to help the child maintain focus, and to provide emotional support and encouragement. Support is supposed to be faded eventually, but in practice it goes on indefinitely. The procedure was developed by a special educator in Australia (Crossley & McDonald, 1980), initially for motorically impaired children; it was then publicized in the United States as a method for revealing "unexpected literacy" far beyond measured ability in nonverbal autistic and retarded individuals (Biklen, 1990). While being facilitated, such individuals appeared to produce phrases and sentences describing complex memories and feelings, correct answers to difficult academic problems, and other advanced language skills. Only a few uncontrolled, qualitative research studies and anecdotal observations were offered in its support. Objective, controlled research has overwhelmingly shown that facilitated communication is simply not valid communication by the person being facilitated (for reviews, see Delmolino & Romanczyk, 1995; Eberlin, McConnachie, Ibel, & Volpe, 1993; Green, 1994; Jacobson & Mulick, 1994; Jacobson, Mulick, & Schwartz, 1995; Shane, 1994). As Spitz (1996) stated, "Indeed, I believe it is safe to say that never in the history of psychology and education has there been so sizable a body of research in which the results have been so absolutely conclusive, in this case that it is the facilitator and not the client who is doing the communicating" (p. 97).

Is it conceivable that a child with autism and severe retardation could learn to type a few words independently while being facilitated? Certainly; almost any prompting strategy, by whatever name and rationale, will work some of the time with some individuals. But then the question becomes, Is this the most effective and efficient way to teach communication, based on available research? The answer here is clearly No. Perhaps the most interesting questions about facilitated communication are these: Why did it achieve such widespread popularity, and how could facilitators be so unaware of their own role in guiding the participants' responses? Regarding the first question, relative effort is obviously involved: It is far easier to prompt apparent communicative responses than it is to do the arduous work of operant speech or sign language training. Furthermore, Jacobson and Mulick (1994) have suggested that some well-established cognitive factors are involved in the intellectual acceptance of facilitated communication, such as misperception and misinterpretation of incomplete data and biased evaluation of ambiguous data. It is important to avoid an exclusive emphasis on the negative aspects of the presence of a handicapped child on the family that At the larger social level, Jacobson et al. (1994, 1995) note that many service providers in developmental disabilities have insufficient scientific education to evaluate new technologies, and that many academic supporters of facilitated communication have adopted a postmodernist, antiscientific philosophical stance toward research. Facilitators' unawareness of their role in guiding communications may be due to their making the attributional error of ascribing the facilitated individuals' behavior to internal rather than external factors.

In view of the points made above, facilitated communication should be treated as an experimental undertaking that is subject to the same informed consent and human rights committee review procedures as other experimental procedures. Appropriate procedures for objectively evaluating facilitated communication in individual cases have been presented by Jacobson and Mulick (1994) and Meinhold, Teodoru, and Koch (1993).

WORKING WITH FAMILIES

Historically, behavioral interventions with the families of autistic children were motivated primarily by the parents' requests for help in dealing with disruptive and dangerous behaviors occurring in the home (e.g., Risley, 1968; Wetzel, Baker, Roney, & Martin, 1966). Somewhat later, it became apparent that language and other behaviors established so laboriously in clinics would not generalize to the home unless parents were taught to use the same behavioral techniques (Kozloff, 1973; Lovaas, Koegel, Simmons, & Long, 1973). Another motivation for professional intervention is that of helping the family to cope with the additional stress imposed on the family as a system by the presence of a severely handicapped child (Harris, 1983; Donnellan & Mirenda, 1984; Kozloff, 1979, 1994). Most recently, some families with young autistic children are seeking professional help in setting up in-home intensive treatment programs modeled after that of Lovaas's (1987, 1996) early intervention project.

Parent Training

Although training programs for the parents of autistic children differ considerably in methods and scope, they usually involve some combination of the following elements: lectures, readings, practice with feedback, tests for mastery of didactic materials, home visits for consultations and demonstrations of treatment techniques, telephone consultations, and follow-up contacts.

The content of a typical parent training course includes simple data recording, functional analysis of behaviors, and elementary behavior modification principles (e.g., reinforcement, shaping, prompting, fading, chaining, generalization, and maintenance). Usually included are specific methods for teaching such skills as eye contact, imitation, speech, play, and self-care skills. Parent training programs often include group discussion sessions to deal with practical problems in the home and school, to share information about medical providers willing to work with handicapped children, and to arrange needed services such as respite care or brief residential treatment (e.g., Harris, 1983; Koegel & Koegel, 1995; Kozloff, 1994).

Representative studies of the effects of parent training programs for families of autistic children indicate some of the advantages of parent training as well as some of the unsolved problems in this area. Harris and her colleagues have provided 10-week training courses for small groups of parents for many years, in connection with their educational program at Rutgers (Harris, 1983; Harris & Boyle, 1985). In studies of some of these groups, there were significant improvements in the parents' behavior modification skills and in the children's language, with initially verbal children progressing to a greater extent than initially mute children (Harris, Wolchik, & Milch, 1982). In a multiple-regression analysis of parental predictors of change in children, Milch (1983) found that the parents' skillfulness at two behavioral techniques—shaping and recognition of the need for prompts—were predictive of the child's progress in language. In addition, the number of behavior management and academic programs the parents had in effect, and the number of hours that both mother and father spent working with the child, were predictive of the child's progress at a 3-month follow-up (Milch, 1983). In a 4- to 7-year follow-up with 30 families, Harris (1986) found that parents whose children were in behaviorally oriented educational programs were more likely to continue to use behavior modification techniques than parents whose children attended schools that were not behavioral.

In London, Howlin and her colleagues conducted a home-based parent training program for 16 families of high-functioning autistic boys (mean age of 6 years) whose nonverbal IQs ranged from 60 to over 120 (mean IQ of 87) (Howlin & Rutter, 1987). Treatment extended over an 18-month period, with two matched control groups whose members were provided outpatient treatment "relatively infrequently" for 6 and 18 months, respectively. The parents of the experimental group were visited by psychologists for 2–3 hours weekly or biweekly during the first 6 months and monthly during the last 12 months. Mothers were individually trained to teach basic language skills and to manage behavior problems in their autistic children. Counseling on various practical problems and family stresses was provided as needed, and occasional respite services were provided. Some of the main findings at 18 months were the following:

1. Children in the treatment group showed significantly fewer problem behaviors (tantrums, aggression, and eating, sleeping, and toileting problems) and ritualistic or obsessional behaviors.
2. The treatment group showed significantly more social responsiveness to parents, other adults, and peers, and a developmentally higher level of simple play with objects (including pretend play), but not more imaginative play or self-initiated interactive play with peers.
3. Analyses of audiotapes of the children's speech showed that the treatment group children were significantly superior to their matched controls in quantity and communicativeness of speech, but were not significantly different in linguistic level.
4. There were no significant differences in IQ, which actually declined a few points in both groups. At age 18, one of the treatment group children was in a private, regular school; all the others were in segregated residential placements or lived at home and attended segregated schools or sheltered workshops. Among the controls at age 21, one had a regular job while living at home; the rest were in residential placements or attended segregated schools or workshops.

These negative results regarding IQ and placements are particularly disappointing, given the high mean intelligence level of the sample. Although only post hoc speculation about why the treatment group failed to achieve a better long-term outcome is possible, three factors seem important in the light of current knowledge. First, only two of the treatment group children were still very young (under 4 years of age) when treatment began. Second, the intervention was deliberately not very intensive; only 20–30 minutes a day (about 2.5 hours a week) were spent in structured one-to-one teaching sessions. Third, the investigators had no control over what happened in the homes between their weekly visits or in the special education classes most of the children attended. The relevance of these factors will become apparent when intensive early intervention programs are described later.

In summary, parent training programs clearly have beneficial and worthwhile effects on both parents and their autistic children, and they are generally well received by parents. In the absence of contingencies from outside the home, however, it appears that most parents eventually drop structured teaching sessions for one reason or another, such as illness, employment, other demands on their time, and the needs of other family members (Harris, 1986; Holmes, Hemsley, Rickett, & Likierman, 1982). In spite of this, the children appear to maintain their gains for at least a year (Harris, Wolchik, & Weitz, 1981), apparently because parents continue to use some reinforcement and behavior management techniques informally. The long-term outcome of the traditional parent training and consultation approach in terms of an autistic individual's residential situation and employment, however, may not be appreciably altered (Howlin & Rutter, 1987). This conclusion reflects not a weakness of parent training efforts so much as an indication of the need for a more comprehensive intervention in such a serious disorder, as described later in the section on early intervention.

Parent Counseling

In addition to teaching parents better ways of interacting with their autistic children, work with families typically entails providing guidance and assistance in dealing with various other problems related to living with severely handicapped children (DeMyer, 1979; Donnellan & Mirenda, 1984; Harris, 1983; Kozloff, 1994; Schopler & Mesibov, 1984). Empirical studies have shown greater perceived parenting stress in the parents of autistic children than in those of mentally retarded and normal children, but this stress can be moderated by acquiring practical teaching and behavior management skills and by recruiting social support (Birnbrauer & Leach, 1993; Bristol & Schopler, 1983; Holroyd & McArthur, 1976; Wolf, Noh, Fisman, & Speechley, 1989).

Harris (1983) has provided a useful discussion of the difficulties most families face and productive ways of helping them deal with pragmatic, emotional, and interpersonal problems.

Pragmatic Problems

The pragmatic problems confronting parents often arise from a lack of community resources, difficulty in locating appropriate services, and similar concerns. Some of the more common issues are dealing with school systems not committed to providing optimal educational services to autistic children, finding health service providers who are able and willing to work with a handicapped child, managing finances to cope with extra expenses, finding free time away from the daily demands of rearing an autistic child, and making a decision about residential care as an autistic adolescent grows older. In this area, the clinician's experience in the community can be invaluable if it includes knowledge of (1) the ways in which particular school systems operate; (2) contact persons for support networks, such as parents' associations; (3) capable health care providers, lawyers, and financial planners; (4) sources of respite care; and (5) the available alternatives among residential care providers, and their relative quality in meeting the needs of autistic adults. For parents conducting early intervention programs in their homes, assistance in finding students to work as therapists is extremely helpful.

Emotional Problems

Problems such as depression, guilt, anger, and feelings of inadequacy affect all parents of autistic children to a greater or lesser degree at various times (DeMyer, 1979; Harris, 1983). Such problems require careful assessment to determine their seriousness and source. The main question is whether they are normal reactions to living with a very difficult child or are reactions to something else, such as marital, work-related, or other problems. An estimate of severity and chronicity is necessary to decide whether supportive counseling should be followed with a recommendation for more specific therapy.

Interpersonal Problems

The presence of an autistic child inevitably has an impact on the entire family system. As a consequence, the parents may have problems involving lack of mutual support, withdrawal from family involvement, sexual difficulties, and other issues (DeMyer, 1979; Harris, 1983). Problems involving normal siblings can include the siblings' feeling resentment or embarrassment about the autistic sibling, not being allowed to go places or do things because the autistic sibling cannot participate, being given too much responsibility for the care of the autistic sibling (or too little guidance in how to interact appropriately with the sibling), and not receiving a fair share of the parents' attention (Harris, 1994; McHale, Simeonsson, & Sloan, 1984). Grandparents, friends, colleagues at work, and even strangers encountered in the community can create problems with unsolicited advice and criticism. Helping families to cope with such problems may well involve several different levels of intervention, which again should flow from an adequate assessment of the nature and scope of the difficulties. The possibility that relatively simple interventions can have important extra benefits should not be overlooked. For example, in the area of sibling relationships, Schreibman et al. (1983) found that teaching normal siblings how to teach play skills to their autistic siblings led to measurable improvements in the normal siblings' attitudes and feelings toward their autistic brothers or sisters.

It is important to avoid an exclusive emphasis on the negative aspects of the presence of a handicapped child on the family (which are stressed in many studies), and to keep in mind that even a very difficult child can make some important positive contributions, such as helping the parents to learn love, patience, acceptance, and discriminations between the important and trivial aspects of life (Turnbull, Blue-Banning, Behr, & Kerns, 1986). Bristol (1984) has identified successful coping strategies used by parents of autistic children that should be encouraged. The strategies ranked as most important by the parents fell into the following categories: (1) helping the child by learning effective teaching and behavior management skills; (2) controlling the meaning of the child's disability by endowing it with a higher significance through religious faith or through positive comparisons with the "worse" past and the "better" present; (3) seeking and receiving the spouse's or partner's support; (4) focusing on the relationships and needs within the family; and (5) self-development through the cultivation of interests and activities not directly related to the autistic child.

As an autistic child grows through adolescence and enters adulthood, the focus needs to shift from training and counseling to creating a social network of support that extends beyond the family. One promising model for doing so is the Group Action Planning model of Turnbull and Turnbull (1996). An "action group" consists of the autistic individual, family members, friends, teachers or job coaches, community citizens, and professionals having a strong commitment to helping the individual succeed in living as normal a life as possible. Regular meetings are held in which the desires of the individual set the agenda and creative problem solving is used to address goals in each major life domain: family, friendships, supported living, education and work, and community participation.

Finally, the clinician should be aware that many families are beginning to find extrafamilial support on the Internet. There are a number of on-line sources of information and mailing lists devoted to autism, and some families use these regularly to share ideas and resources and to provide mutual emotional support.

EARLY INTERVENTION

The logic of early intervention with autistic children is based on the well-known observation that considerable neurological development continues for years after birth (Jacobson, 1978). The brain can exhibit considerable plasticity in overcoming early insults, and the development of cortical synaptic connections in the young child is influenced by the timing and quality of early experience (Huttenlocher, 1988). Directly relevant are scattered reports of recovery to normal levels of intellectual, linguistic, social, and educational or vocational functioning in individual cases of children who were clearly autistic when very young (DeMyer et al., 1973; Kanner, 1973; Rimland, 1964; Gajzago & Prior, 1974). Such reports encourage the idea that more autistic children might attain a good long-term outcome if appropriate treatment were provided early enough and intensively enough.

Preschool Programs

Most early intervention occurs in preschool classroom programs based in universities, private educational organizations, and public schools (Dawson & Osterling, 1996; Harris & Handleman, 1994). Dawson and Osterling (1996) have reviewed the reports of the better-known model preschool programs for children with autism and find six common elements among them. The first element is a curriculum that emphasizes attention, imitation, language, play, and social skills. A behavioral or developmental–behavioral approach is the most common orientation to curriculum implementation. The second element is the provision of intensive one-to-one and small-group instruction, which is subsequently faded to more natural classroom conditions to enhance generalization and maintenance. Most model programs also feature integrated classrooms in order to promote social development through planned interactions with normal peers. Third, most programs are highly structured in terms of the organization of the environment and the daily routine. Fourth, behavior management is addressed through functional analysis and the teaching of appropriate alternative behaviors. Fifth, substantial effort is devoted to preparing each child and the receiving teachers for the transition to a kindergarten or first-grade classroom. Sixth, parent training is offered along with in-home consultations and treatment.

Overall, most autistic children in model preschool programs show substantial gains on standardized test scores, and about 50% achieve placements in public schools (Dawson & Osterling, 1996). Although these results are far better than those seen in average special education programs (Eaves & Ho, 1996; Freeman et al., 1985; Lord & Schopler, 1989), it is difficult to evaluate the 50% figure. Published reports have often not spelled out in detail whether or not supports (e.g., a classroom aide or frequent teacher consultations) were required to establish and maintain the placements, nor is it always clear whether the placements were in regular or special education classrooms. Furthermore, most published reports fail to mention comparisons with any control groups, leaving unclear the degree to which public school placements were determined more by the attitudes and policies of local school districts regarding inclusion than by the children's prior participation or nonparticipation in a model preschool program.

Although the data on outcomes are incomplete, the data on developmental progress in children in behavioral preschool programs do show that most make impressive gains in language, overall developmental rate, and reduction of autistic symptomatology (Harris & Handleman, 1994). These accomplishments are important and occur in spite of the limitations inherent in classrooms, such as limited time for one-to-one teaching, a relatively short instructional day, and few opportunities for teaching and generalization in the home and community. Another

model of service delivery that overcomes these problems is behavioral treatment in the home by well-trained and supported parents and their therapy aides. The most successful example of this approach is the Early Intervention Project at the University of California at Los Angeles (UCLA).

The UCLA Early Intervention Project

In the early 1970s, Lovaas began treating very young autistic children (under 4 years of age) by teaching the parents to be the primary therapists, with the direction and help of graduate and undergraduate students who worked along with them in the homes (Lovaas, 1987, 1996; Lovaas & Smith, 1988). The children in the intensive treatment group (Experimental Group) of 19 children received at least 40 hours a week of one-to-one instruction. The children in a control group of 19 children (Control Group 1), who could not be served by the UCLA staff due to an insufficient number of uncommitted staff members at the time of referral, attended special education classes and received 10 or fewer hours a week of one-to-one instruction. A second, no-contact control group (Control Group 2) consisted of 21 children from a larger group being followed at the UCLA Medical School during the same time period in a long-term study of cognitive and language characteristics (Freeman et al., 1985). Most of these children also attended preschool special education classes. The Experimental Group mean deviation IQ was 53, the Control Group 1 mean was 46, and the Control Group 2 mean was 59 (Lovaas, 1987; McEachin et al., 1993).

Treatment was conducted for at least 2 years, and longer for some children who needed more help. During the first year, the parents were trained in an apprenticeship model, working with experienced graduate students for a minimum of 10 hours a week in the home. Undergraduate students worked with each child in the home for about 30 hours a week. The program for the Experimental Group was that described in Lovaas (1981). The first phase of treatment was devoted to teaching imitation, toy play, self-help skills, and affectionate behaviors. Aggressive, self-stimulatory, and self-injurious behaviors were eliminated through reinforcement of appropriate alternative behaviors, extinction, timeout, and mild punishment.

The second phase emphasized expressive speech and complex language, interactive play with peers, and closely supervised exposures to

Classroom Placements

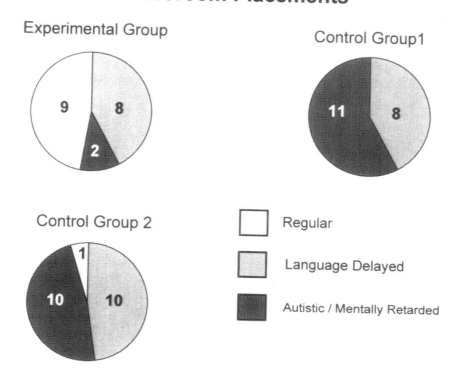

FIGURE 8.3. Classroom placements of children in the Experimental and Control Groups in the UCLA early intervention studies. Shown are numbers of children in each type of classroom placement at mean age 7 years. "Regular" refers to a regular class in a public school without support; "Language Delayed" refers to a special education class for children with language delays or aphasia; "Autistic/Mentally Retarded" refers to a special education class for children with autism and/or mental retardation. The data are from Lovaas (1987).

normal preschool settings. The third phase focused on teaching observational learning, classroom skills, cause–effect relationships, and social rules. When the children were old enough for kindergarten, as many as possible were placed in regular kindergartens in public schools, with the autism diagnosis not mentioned to avoid placement in a special education program. After kindergarten, placement was left up to school personnel.

The first outcome data were obtained when the children were 7 years old (Lovaas, 1987). Figure 8.3 shows the distribution of educational placements, and Figure 8.4 shows the changes in IQs, for the three groups of children. Of the 19 Experimental Group subjects, 9 (47%) were found to be educationally and intellectually normal: They had successfully completed the regular first-grade class without support, had been recommended for promotion by their teachers to a regular second-grade class, and scored at or above average on standardized IQ tests. The

mean IQs of these best-outcome children increased 37 points, from 70 to 107. Overall, the 19 Experimental Group children showed a 30-point increase in mean IQ from 53 to 83. In contrast, none of the children in Control Group 1 obtained a regular class placement, and their IQs increased only minimally (from 46 to 52). Similarly, only one of the children in Control Group 2 achieved a regular classroom placement, and the mean IQ remained unchanged (59 at 3 years, 58 at 7 years). The outcomes for the children in the control groups probably mirror those in special education programs almost anywhere. For example, Lord and Schopler (1989) found that the mean IQ of 72 children in the statewide TEACHH program in North Carolina changed minimally from 57 at age 3 to 64 at age 7.

McEachin et al. (1993) conducted a long-term follow-up of the Experimental Group children when their average age was 13, and compared them with the Control Group 1 children on measures of intelligence, adaptive behavior, and

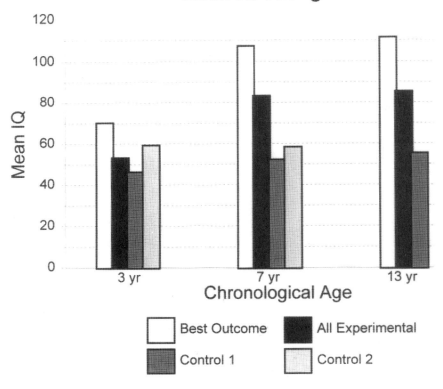

FIGURE 8.4.   Measured intelligence of children in the Experimental and Control Groups in the UCLA early intervention studies. The black bars represent all Experimental Group children combined; the white bars represent the subset of the Experimental Group with the best outcomes. The two types of gray bars represent the Control Groups. Control Group 2 was lost to follow-up after the assessment of 7-year-olds. The data are from Lovaas (1987) and McEachin, Smith, and Lovaas (1993).

personality. In the Experimental Group, 1 of the best-outcome group of 9 children had been moved from a regular to a special education class and 1 of the other 10 children had moved from special to regular education, leaving the overall proportion of children in regular education at 47%. The mean deviation IQ of the entire Experimental Group was 85, and it was 111 for the best-outcome subgroup (Figure 8.4). When compared with normal children with no history of behavior disorder, eight of the nine best-outcome children showed no significant differences from the normal controls on independently administered intelligence, adaptive behavior, and personality scales. Residual deficits in language use or social behavior in some of the children were minor and not noticeable to school personnel. In Control Group 1, none of the 19 children were in a regular class, as had been true at the age 7 follow-up, and the mean IQ was 55. These findings of no significant improvement in IQ in

Control Group 1 again resemble those in other studies of older children receiving conventional special education: Eaves and Ho (1996) reported that mean Verbal and Performance IQs (58 and 63, respectively) did not change from age 7 to age 11 in 76 autistic and other pervasively disordered children.

Independent, partial replications of the UCLA studies have reported impressive, if not always as dramatic, results for young autistic children receiving about 20 hours a week of behavioral treatment (Green, 1996; Rogers, 1996). A prospective study at Murdoch University in Western Australia (Birnbrauer & Leach, 1993) and a retrospective study at the University of California at San Francisco (Sheinkopf & Siegel, 1998) showed gains in IQ into the normal range and improvements in language and adaptive behavior skills, along with decreases in problem behaviors, in about 45% of the children involved in home programs. In nonexperimental studies,

Groden, Domingue, Chesnick, Groden, and Baron (1983) describe a case of recovery to normal intelligence and school placement in a child who began intensive behavioral treatment at 2 years of age. Perry, Cohen, and DeCarlo (1995) and Maurice (1993) describe two autistic children in the same family who, after receiving intensive behavioral treatment over 2 years, were judged by independent professionals to have recovered from autism.

In the aggregate, the findings of intensive early intervention programs conducted in model preschool programs and in homes justify the following conclusions. Measured intelligence in autistic children can be significantly increased instead of remaining stable, as is usually found, and 30%–50% of autistic children can succeed in regular classes at age-appropriate grade levels in public schools (Anderson, Campbell, & Cannon, 1994; Fenske, Zalenski, Krantz, & McClannahan, 1985; McClannahan & Krantz, 1994; Lovaas, 1987; McEachin et al., 1993; Strain & Cordisco, 1994), again contrary to the usual findings (Eaves & Ho, 1996; Freeman et al., 1985; Howlin & Rutter, 1987; Lord & Schopler, 1989). For these outcomes to occur, the following conditions seem to be necessary: (1) The child is functioning in the moderately retarded or higher ranges of intelligence, and does not have a progressive neurological condition, such as Rett's Disorder (T. Smith, Klevstrand, & Lovaas, 1995); (2) treatment begins at an early age, ideally before 30 months; (3) the treatment is behaviorally oriented and intensive, in terms of 30–40 hours per week of high-quality one-to-one instruction and a high level of involvement by well-trained and supported parents; and (4) the treatment is supervised by a professional with considerable experience in the application of behavioral methods to autistic children.

Since the publication of Maurice's (1993) book describing the recovery of her two autistic children through behavioral early intervention, there has been a rapid increase in demand for this approach by parents of young children. Many parents seek professional assistance in mounting comprehensive "ABA/DTT" (applied behavior analysis/discrete-trials training) programs in their homes, modeled after the UCLA program. This need has created a demand for expertise in behavioral instructional methods, behavior management, and curriculum design for young autistic children. There is also an increased demand for legal expertise in obtaining the necessary funding from school districts to hire therapists for this unique form of "home

schooling." Clinicians lacking these highly specialized skills should refer parents to the following World Wide Web site for the names of some organizations and professionals providing such services: http://pages.prodigy.net/damian-porcari/recovery.htm.

ANALYSIS AND TREATMENT OF PROBLEM BEHAVIORS

Problem behaviors commonly observed in autistic children include tantrums, self-injury, aggression, and repetitive, stereotyped (self-stimulatory) behaviors. Such behaviors can be characterized in several ways. At a descriptive, pragmatic level, they are behavioral excesses that are problematic because their high rate and/or high intensity produce disruptive and harmful effects on a child's immediate social or physical environment and often on the child himself or herself. Even behaviors that are not physically harmful to the child or others, such as stereotyped behaviors, may be psychologically harmful to the child because they interfere with learning and stigmatize the child in the community (Koegel & Covert, 1972; Runco, Charlop, & Schreibman, 1986). From a developmental–behavioral perspective, problem behaviors are continuations and elaborations of infantile behaviors that persist because the learning of more adaptive behaviors fails to occur in developmentally disabled children (Lovaas et al., 1987). Many problem behaviors can be cast metaphorically as primitive communicative acts serving social functions for an autistic child, such as seeking attention or requesting escape from demands (Carr et al., 1994; Carr & Durand, 1985b; Donnellan, Mirenda, Mesaros, & Fassbender, 1984; Durand, 1990). This perspective leads to an emphasis on function over form, in which the relationship of problem behaviors to environmental events is more important than the topographies of specific behaviors. Greater research attention to the motivation of problem behaviors has led to a conspicuous shift in most quarters away from punishment-oriented interventions to skill- and communication-building approaches based on detailed individual assessments of the functional connections between the behaviors and their contexts (e.g., Carr, Robinson, & Palumbo, 1990; Durand, 1990; Gardner & Sovner, 1994; Koegel, Koegel, & Dunlap, 1996; Vollmer, Marcus, Ringdahl, & Roane, 1995).

Some of the variables implicated by research on problem behaviors in autistic children are or-

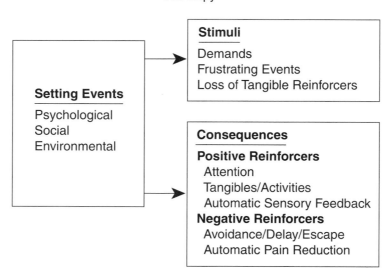

FIGURE 8.5.   A schematic model organizing selected classes of variables influencing problem behaviors.

ganized in the heuristic model of Figure 8.5. First come the "predisposing factors," or subject characteristics, that are inherent in the disorder and set the stage for difficulties in adapting to increasingly complex environments as the child grows older. For example, the delayed cognitive development of most autistic children presumably renders many everyday situations incomprehensible and possibly threatening; functional language deficits make it impossible to assert oneself appropriately, to report anxiety, discomfort, or pain, or to make easily understood requests (Carr, Reeve, & Magito-McLaughlin, 1996); asociality results in disregard of social cues and insensitivity to social reinforcers (Howlin, 1986; Klin, 1991), and high levels of stereotypy preempt attention to much of the physical and social environment (Koegel & Covert, 1972; Lovaas, Litrownik, & Mann, 1971).

"Setting events" are relatively global prior changes in the internal or external environment that interact with subsequent events to alter their impact on behavior (Horner, Vaughn, Day, & Ard, 1996; Michael, 1982; Wahler & Fox, 1981). Physiological setting events include painful or uncomfortable internal states, such as fatigue, hunger, illness, ear infections, toothaches, sei-

zures, menses, mood, allergies, constipation, and pharmacological effects of drugs (Carr & Smith, 1995; Carr et al., 1996; Durand, 1982; Gedye, 1989; Gunsett, Mulick, Fernald, & Martin, 1989; Kennedy & Meyer, 1996; Wacker, Harding, et al., 1996). Social setting events include unpleasant interactions earlier in the day, the presence of certain other people in the environment (Taylor & Carr, 1992; Taylor, Ekdahl, Romanczyk, & Miller, 1994; Touchette, McDonald, & Langer, 1985), and extinction of appropriate behaviors (Carr & Durand, 1985a; Lovaas et al., 1965). Environmental setting events include crowded settings (McAfee, 1987), settings barren of play and educational materials (Horner, 1980), a daily routine that lacks predictability and opportunities to make choices (Brown, 1991; Flannery & Horner, 1994; Lalli, Casey, Goh, & Merlino, 1994), and novel and long-duration tasks (Charlop, 1986; Mace, Browder, & Lin, 1987; R. G. Smith, Iwata, Goh, & Shore, 1995).

"Stimuli" are discrete antecedents that occur immediately before problem behavior episodes and can be shown to exert stimulus control over them. These include demands (requests, instructions, prompts, and interruptions) (Carr &

TABLE 8.2. Protocol for In-Home Assessment and Treatment of Problem Behavior

Method	Purpose
Phase 1: Descriptive assessment	
Scatterplot[a]	Identify times of the day associated with problem behavior
A-B-C assessment[b]	Identify naturally occurring events associated with behavior
Parent interview	Identify primary behavior concerns and events associated with behavior
Activity selection	Categorize toys and activities across structural variables
Preference assessment	Identify potential reinforcers
Phase 2: Structural analysis	
Structural analysis[c]	Identify antecedent events that set the occasion for behavior
Phase 3: Functional analysis	
Functional analysis[d]	Identify maintaining events for behavior
Phase 4: Treatment and follow-up	
Treatment probes	Analyze treatment effects across intervention sessions and generalization conditions
Brief functional analysis	Analyze durability of maintaining events over time
Parent checklist	Address correspondence of treatment probes to parent reports of child behavior
Treatment acceptability	Assess general acceptability of treatment, parent perceptions of treatment effectiveness, and any negative side effects

Note. From Wacker, Peck, Derby, Berg, and Harding (1996, p. 55). Copyright 1996 by Paul H. Brookes. Reprinted by permission.
[a]From Touchette, MacDonald, and Langer (1985).
[b]From Bijou, Peterson, and Ault (1968).
[c]From Carr and Durand (1985a).
[d]From Iwata, Dorsey, Slifer, Bauman, and Richman (1982).
[e]From Reimers and Wacker (1988).

Durand, 1985a; Carr & Newsom, 1985; Carr et al., 1976, 1980; Durand & Crimmins, 1987, 1988; Iwata, Dorsey, Slifer, Bauman, & Richman, 1982; Iwata, Pace, Cowdery, Kalsher, & Cataldo, 1990; R. G. Smith et al., 1995; Weeks & Gaylord-Ross, 1981; Zarcone, Iwata, Smith, Mazaleski, & Lerman, 1994); frustrating events, or denial of access to reinforcing objects and activities (Edelson, Taubman, & Lovaas, 1983); and loss of tangible reinforcers (Durand & Crimmins, 1988; Edelson et al., 1983; Lovaas et al., 1965).

"Consequences" are the relatively immediate effects of problem behaviors that function as positive or negative reinforcers. Positive reinforcers include attention (Carr & McDowell, 1980; Iwata et al., 1982; Lovaas et al., 1965; Lovaas & Simmons, 1969); tangibles and activities, such as food, toys, other objects, and access to preferred activities (Durand & Crimmins, 1988); and automatic sensory feedback intrinsic to the performance of the act, such as that accompanying stereotypy, noise making, property destruc-

tion, and some self-injury (Favell, McGimsey, & Schell, 1982; Lovaas et al., 1987; Rincover & Devany, 1982). Examples of negative reinforcers include avoidance or delay of and escape from subjectively aversive demands, tasks, and settings (Bird, Dores, Moniz, & Robinson, 1989; Carr & Durand, 1985a; Carr & Newsom, 1985; Carr et al., 1976, 1980; Durand & Crimmins, 1987, 1988; Iwata et al., 1982; Iwata, Vollmer, & Zarcone, 1990; Lalli, Casey, & Kates, 1995; Weeks & Gaylord-Ross, 1981) and behaviors that produce automatic pain reduction or distraction (Carr & Smith, 1995; Gunsett et al., 1989).

The variables listed in Figure 8.5 are only a representative, nonexhaustive set of those studied to date. Others will undoubtedly be identified in future research. Moreover, the problem behaviors of individual children will prove to be influenced by idiosyncratic factors not listed here but often discoverable through appropriate functional analysis procedures (e.g., Carr et al., 1994; Iwata, Vollmer, & Zarcone, 1990; Pyles & Bailey, 1990; Wacker, Peck, Derby, Berg, &

Harding, 1996). Functional analysis is currently in a stage of rapid development, and various approaches are evident in the relevant literature. One good example of state-of-the-art assessment and treatment for the problem behaviors of autistic children is described in the remainder of this section.

Wacker, Peck, et al. (1996) have developed a comprehensive approach in work with young autistic children in their homes. Their protocol is shown in Table 8.2.

Phase 1: Descriptive assessment. The first phase is concerned with identifying events associated with problem behaviors. Parents are asked to record their child's behavior for at least a week by indicating the frequency of problem behaviors during 30-minute intervals throughout the day on a scatterplot like that described by Touchette et al. (1985). In addition, the parents write a brief description of the events that precede the behavior, the specific behavior, and their response to the behavior in an A-B-C format (Bijou, Peterson, & Ault, 1969). Then the results of the scatterplot and A-B-C recordings are reviewed with the parents in an interview intended to elicit the parents' priorities and to develop preliminary hypotheses about events controlling the child's behaviors. Next, an assessment to select activities and toys to use in subsequent analyses and to employ as reinforcers in treatment are identified by having the parents go through the child's toys and categorize them as high or low in child preference, difficulty level, and amount of parent attention associated with playing with them. This is followed by a brief preference assessment, in which the child is given free access to toys while the duration of time spent playing with each toy is recorded.

Phase 2: Structural analysis. The second phase is conducted to identify more precisely the antecedent stimuli that set the occasion for problem behavior (Axelrod, 1987; Carr & Durand, 1985a). During 5- to 10-minute sessions, one variable (e.g., demand level—high or low) is varied while others (e.g., continuous attention and preferred task) are held constant. These results are compared with those from sessions in which a second variable (e.g., task preference: preferred—nonpreferred) is varied while demand level and attention are held constant, and so on.

Phase 3: Functional analysis. A functional analysis (Iwata et al., 1982) is conducted to test hypotheses regarding the consequences believed to maintain problem behaviors. A free-play control session is conducted first: The child has access to preferred toys with no demands being made and noncontingent parent attention. In alternating sessions, consequences for problem behavior (e.g., contingent attention or contingent escape from a nonpreferred task) are arranged to determine their ability to maintain the behavior.

Phase 4: Treatment and follow-up. Based on the results of the information derived from the first three phases, an intervention package is designed and put into effect. It usually involves functional communication training (Carr & Durand, 1985a) to give the child appropriate alternative behaviors for obtaining the reinforcement previously available for problem behaviors, along with consequences such as extinction, redirection, guided compliance, or timeout for problem behaviors (Steege, Wacker, Berg, Cigrand, & Cooper, 1989; Fisher et al., 1993; Wacker et al., 1990). Weekly follow-up assessment procedures are used to evaluate treatment outcomes and the durability of the initial assessment results. Treatment probes are conducted by the clinicians to assess their continued effectiveness and generalization. Brief functional assessment sessions are conducted to determine whether the maintaining variables persist over time. Parents complete a simple checklist developed by Cooper et al. (1992) to rate the child's behavior during the week. Checklist results are compared to direct observation data, to determine their correspondence with the clinicians' observations and resolve any differences. Finally, parents complete the Treatment Acceptability Rating Form (Reimers & Wacker, 1988), which assesses the parents' understanding of the treatment, their perceptions of treatment effectiveness, and side effects of treatment.

An illustrative example of the use of the Wacker, Peck et al. (1996) protocol is provided in their case presentation of a young autistic boy:[1]

Nile was a 3-year-old boy who was nonverbal and had been diagnosed with developmental delay and autism. Whenever family members attempted to interact with him, he engaged in severe aggression (e.g., biting, pinching, scratching others), self-injury (e.g., biting, hitting himself, head banging), and tantrums (e.g., screaming, destroying toys).

We began our assessment by directly observing Nile's behavior under various antecedent conditions (e.g., high vs. low attention, high vs. low demand tasks, high vs. low preference tasks). Although Nile engaged in some inappropriate behavior during all conditions, he consistently exhibited the most problematic behavior when he was required to perform demanding tasks, which for him even included requests to play. This was consistent with his parents' reports to us and led to the hypothesis that Nile's inappropriate behavior was maintained by negative reinforcement.

Next, we conducted a functional analysis to verify that escape from demanding tasks served to increase, or reinforce, Nile's inappropriate behavior. During the functional analysis, we alternated conditions in which no demands were placed on Nile (parallel play with his mom) with conditions in which he was required to complete a demanding task (play a certain way) but was allowed to briefly escape the task contingent on inappropriate behavior. Inappropriate behavior increased during sessions in which he was allowed to escape demanding tasks; however, once the task demands were removed, inappropriate behavior decreased immediately. This confirmed our hypothesis of negative reinforcement.

The functional communication training package involved teaching Nile to request breaks from demanding tasks by signing "done." The package consisted of three major components: 1) providing breaks from demanding tasks contingent on signing, 2) withholding reinforcement (continuing the activities) contingent on inappropriate behavior, and 3) pairing positive parent attention with access to reinforcement. During treatment, Nile was prompted by his mother (and later by his brother and father) to complete part of a play activity. As soon as he complied with one step of the activity, Nile was prompted to sign "done." If Nile signed "done," the task was removed, and he was allowed to take a break. On his breaks, Nile's parents shadowed him and played with him, but they did not attempt to direct him to other activities. Our hope was that, over time, social interactions with his family would become reinforcing rather than aversive to him. After his break, Nile was required to complete another step of the task and to sign "done." If he engaged in inappropriate behavior at any time, he was not allowed to take a break; instead, he was required to continue working on the task.

Over time, we gradually increased the amount of time he stayed on task prior to requesting a break. After approximately 3 months,

Nile began to sign "done" independently and even began to verbalize "done." Within 6 months, a marked decrease in inappropriate behavior occurred, and, equally important, he began to play with family members and to verbalize other words. (pp. 63–64)

Wacker, Peck, et al. (1996) reported that after their approach was used with 13 children for at least 6 months, 10 showed reductions in problem behavior of at least 90%, and 12 displayed the anticipated increases in social collateral behavior.

CONCLUSIONS

A few general conclusions emerge from this review of some aspects of current behavioral approaches to the treatment of children with autism.

1. The many different procedures described in this chapter indicate a significant increase in the complexity of the behavioral treatment of children with autism from its beginnings in the mid-1960s. As a result, considerable specialized training in applied behavior analysis is essential to clinical effectiveness (Carr & Carlson, 1993; Lovaas, 1996; Lovaas & Buch, 1997; Shook & Favell, 1996). The increase in complexity of teaching procedures is largely due to an increase in the range and complexity of (a) the behaviors addressed (e.g., social play and peer interactions, functional language, age-appropriate academic skills); (b) the instructional formats in which the procedures are are used (naturalistic and incidental-teaching arrangements, in addition to formal discrete-trial sessions); and (c) the situations in which these procedures are applied (homes, classrooms, playgrounds, and other community settings, in addition to laboratories and clinics). The increased complexity of behavior management procedures results from the accrual of a base of knowledge about the causes of problem behaviors through the use of functional analysis methods, permitting the application of multicomponent, hypothesis-driven strategies instead of trial-and-error approaches (Carr & Carlson, 1993; Repp, Felce, & Barton, 1988; Iwata, Vollmer, & Zarcone, 1990).

2. The most distinctive characteristic of autistic children, their asociality, can be addressed in meaningful ways at various levels of intervention. The more extensive gains require changes in a child's social environment, as well as direct treatment of specific social deficits.

The involvement of normal peers in integrated settings appears to be essential to the maintenance and elaboration of age-appropriate social behaviors. Unfortunately, society's typical service delivery models (segregated classrooms, group homes, and developmental centers) have yet to incorporate many changes that would facilitate social development (Sailor, 1996). Particularly disturbing is the failure of most public school preschool programs to incorporate up-to-date, empirically based methods that offer the greatest hope in early intervention. However, models of service delivery are subject to selection by consequences, just as species, individual behaviors, and cultural practices are (Skinner, 1981). We can therefore expect that most existing models will eventually change to resemble behavioral home-based (Maurice, Green, & Luce, 1996) and school-based programs (Harris & Handleman, 1994) more closely. Some parents who are unable to wait for institutional evolution because their children need intensive treatment now are already going beyond existing special education models and are establishing community-based early intervention organizations in several cities (Huff, 1996).

3.   Work with an autistic child and his or her family frequently presents the challenge of balancing one's efforts among the child, the rest of the family system, and outside stressors. At different times the priorities change, necessitating considerable sensitivity and flexibility. Interestingly, intensive home-based programs tend to improve family interaction and reduce stress instead of the opposite. Lovaas and Smith (1988) noted that when several volunteer students were provided for the autistic child in each family they worked with, the parents had many additional hours a week available to take care of other family members and to attend to personal needs. Birnbrauer and Leach (1993) found that parents implementing an intensive home-based early intervention program showed a substantially greater decrease in perceived stress than did the parents of control children. Over time, significant sources of stress often shift from the autistic child to problems outside the family, such as those posed by intransigent school districts or insurance companies. Practical knowledge of the relevant systems with which parents must deal is invaluable.

4.   The behavioral approach to the treatment of autistic children must be considered one of the triumphs of modern psychology. Few approaches with any clinical population, and no other approaches with this population, come close to matching its accumulation of experimental knowledge over several decades; its diligent, programmatic development of increasingly effective treatment procedures; and its proven success in improving the clients' condition—sometimes dramatically so. Behavioral intervention can reach a considerable distance down the developmental continuum and achieve some remarkably beneficial results. That noted, much cause for humility remains. It seems that to bring about recovery to normal or near-normal functioning, behavioral treatment needs some help from nature in the form of a central nervous system still open to major modifications via sufficiently intensive and well-timed interventions. A medical analogy is apt: The successful treatment of most diseases requires help from nature in the form of a reasonably healthy immune system. Much remains to be learned before we are in a position to offer hope for global improvement in older and lower-functioning children. However, it is also true that this conclusion tells us more about the current state of our knowledge than about preordained limits on the children's progress. Advances in our understanding of behavioral and neurological processes show no signs of slowing down, indicating the likelihood of significant changes in work with autistic children in the future. The overriding message of this chapter is that there is much that can be done now for every child.

NOTE

1.   The case of Nile, from Wacker, Peck, et al. (1996), is reprinted by permission of Paul H. Brookes.

REFERENCES

Alpert, C. (1980). Procedures for determining the optimal nonspeech mode with the autistic child. In R. L. Schiefelbusch (Ed.), *Nonspeech language and communication* (pp. 389–420). Baltimore: University Park Press.

American Psychiatric Association. (1994). *Diagnostic and statistical manual of mental disorders* (4th ed.). Washington, DC: Author.

Anderson, S. R., Campbell, S., & Cannon, B. O. (1994). The May Center for Early Childhood Education. In S. L. Harris & J. S. Handleman (Eds.), *Preschool education programs for children with autism* (pp. 15–36). Austin, TX: Pro-Ed.

Asarnow, J. R. (1994). Annotation: Childhood-onset schizophrenia. *Journal of Child Psychology and Psychiatry, 35,* 1345–1371.

Asperger, H. (1991). 'Autistic psychopathy' in childhood (U. Frith, Trans.). In U. Frith, (Ed.), *Autism and Asperger syndrome* (pp. 37–92). Cambridge, England: Cambridge University Press. (Original work published 1944)

Axelrod, S. (1987). Functional and structural analyses of behavior: Approaches leading to reduced use of punishment procedures? *Research in Developmental Disabilities, 8,* 165–178.

Baer, D. M. (1978). The behavioral analysis of trouble. In K. E. Allen, V. A. Holm, & R. L. Schiefelbusch (Eds.), *Early intervention: A team approach* (pp. 57–93). Baltimore: University Park Press.

Baer, D. M., Peterson, R. F., & Sherman, J. A. (1967). The development of imitation by reinforcing behavioral similarity to a model. *Journal of the Experimental Analysis of Behavior, 10,* 405–416.

Bailey, A., LeCouteur, A., Gottesman, L., Bolton, P., Simonoff, E., Yuzda, E., & Rutter, M. (1995). Autism as a strongly genetic disorder: Evidence from a British twin study. *Psychological Medicine, 25,* 63–77.

Baird, T. D., & August, G. J. (1985). Family heterogeneity in infantile autism. *Journal of Autism and Developmental Disorders, 15,* 315–321.

Bandura, A. (1962). Social learning through imitation. In M. R. Jones (Ed.), *Nebraska Symposium on Motivation* (Vol. 10, pp. 211–269). Lincoln: University of Nebraska Press.

Bandura, A. (1969). *Principles of behavior modification.* New York: Holt, Rinehart & Winston.

Barlow, D., & Hayes, S. (1979). Alternating treatment designs: One strategy for comparing the effects of two treatments in a single subject. *Journal of Applied Behavior Analysis, 12,* 199–210.

Baron-Cohen, S. (1989a). The autistic child's "theory of mind": A case of specific developmental delay. *Journal of Child Psychology and Psychiatry, 30,* 285–297.

Baron-Cohen, S. (1989b). Are autistic children "behaviorists"? An examination of their mental–physical and appearance–reality distinctions. *Journal of Autism and Developmental Disorders, 19,* 579–600.

Baron-Cohen, S., Leslie, A. M., & Frith, U. (1985). Does the autistic child have a "theory of mind"? *Cognition, 21,* 37–46.

Baron-Cohen, S., Leslie, A. M., & Frith, U. (1986). Mechanical, behavioral, and intentional understanding of picture stories in autistic children. *British Journal of Developmental Psychology, 4,* 113–125.

Baron-Cohen, S., Tager-Flusberg, H., & Cohen, D. J. (Eds.). (1993). *Understanding other minds: Perspectives from autism.* Oxford: Oxford University Press.

Barrera, R. D., Lobato-Barrera, D., & Sulzer-Azaroff, B. (1980). A simultaneous treatment comparison of three expressive language training programs with a mute autistic child. *Journal of Autism and Developmental Disorders, 10,* 21–37.

Barrera, R. D., & Sulzer-Azaroff, B. (1983). An alternating treatment comparison of oral and total communication training programs with echolalic autistic children. *Journal of Applied Behavior Analysis, 16,* 379–394.

Bartak, L., & Rutter, M. (1973). Special educational treatment of autistic children: A comparative study. I. Design of study and characteristics of units. *Journal of Child Psychology and Psychiatry, 14,* 161–179.

Bauman, M. L., & Kemper, T. L. (1985). Histoanatomic observations of the brain in early infantile autism. *Neurology, 35,* 866–874.

Bender, L. (1942). Childhood schizophrenia. *The Nervous Child, 1,* 138–140.

Bender, L. (1955). Twenty years of clinical research on schizophrenic children with special reference to those under six years of age. In G. Caplan (Ed.), *Emotional problems of early childhood* (pp. 503–515). New York: Basic Books.

Bergman, P., & Escalona, S. K. (1949). Unusual sensitivities in very young children. *Psychoanalytic Study of the Child, 3–4,* 333–352.

Bettelheim, B. (1956). Schizophrenia as a reaction to extreme situations. *American Journal of Orthopsychiatry, 26,* 507–518.

Bijou, S. W., Peterson, R. F., & Ault, M. H. (1968). A method to integrate descriptive and experimental field studies at the level of data and empirical concepts. *Journal of Applied Behavior Analysis, 1,* 175–191.

Biklen, D. (1990). Communication unbound: Autism and praxis. *Harvard Educational Review, 60,* 291–314.

Bird, F., Dores, P. A., Moniz, D., & Robinson, J. (1989). Reducing severe aggressive and self-injurious behaviors with functional communication training. *American Journal on Mental Retardation, 94,* 37–48.

Birnbrauer, J. S., & Leach, D. J. (1993). The Murdoch early intervention program after two years. *Behaviour Change, 10,* 63–74.

Bodfish, J. W., Powell, S. B., Golden, R. N., & Lewis, M. H. (1995). Blink rate as an index of dopamine function in adults with mental retardation and repetitive behavior disorders. *American Journal on Mental Retardation, 99,* 335–344.

Bolton, P., MacDonald, H., Pickles, A., Rios, P., Goode, S., Crowson, M., Bailey, A., & Rutter, M. (1994). A case–control family history study of autism. *Journal of Child Psychology and Psychiatry, 35,* 877–900.

Bondy, A. S., & Frost, L. A. (1994). The Delaware autistic program. In S. L. Harris & J. S. Handleman (Eds.), *Preschool education programs for children with autism* (pp. 37–54). Austin, TX: Pro-Ed.

Brady, D. O., & Smouse, A. D. (1978). A simultaneous comparison of three methods for language training with an autistic child: An experimental single case analysis. *Journal of Autism and Childhood Schizophrenia, 8,* 271–279.

Brady, M. P., Shores, R. E., Gunter, P., McEvoy, M. A., Fox, J. J., & White, C. (1984). Generalization of an adolescent's social interaction behavior via multiple peers in a classroom setting. *Journal of the Association for Persons with Severe Handicaps, 9,* 278–286.

Brady, M. P., Shores, R. E., McEvoy, M. A., Ellis, D., & Fox, J. J. (1987). Increasing social interactions of severely handicapped autistic children. *Journal of Autism and Developmental Disorders, 17,* 375–390.

Breen, C., Haring, T., Pitts-Conway, V., & Gaylord-Ross, R. (1985). The training and generalization of social interaction during breaktime at two job sites in the natural environment. *Journal of the Association for Persons with Severe Handicaps, 10,* 41–50.

Bristol, M. M. (1984). Family resources and successful adaptation to autistic children. In E. Schopler & G. B. Mesibov (Eds.), *The effects of autism on the family* (pp. 289–310). New York: Plenum Press.

Bristol, M. M., & Schopler, E. (1983). Stress and coping in families of autistic adolescents. In E. Schopler & G. B. Mesibov (Eds.), *Autism in adolescents and adults* (pp. 251–278). New York: Plenum Press.

Brooks, B. D., Morrow, J. E., & Gray, W. F. (1968). Reduction of autistic gaze aversion by reinforcement of visual attention responses. *Journal of Special Education, 2,* 307–309.

Brown, F. (1991). Creative daily scheduling: A nonintrusive approach to challenging behaviors in community residences. *Journal of The Association for Person with Severe Handicaps, 16,* 75–84.

Brown, F., & Holvoet, J. (1982). Effect of systematic peer interaction on the incidental learning of two severely handicapped students. *Journal of the Association for the Severely Handicapped, 7,* 19–28.

Bucher, B., & Bowman, E. A. (1974). The effects of a discriminative cue and an incompatible activity on generalized imitation. *Journal of Experimental Child Psychology, 18,* 22–33.

Burd, L., Fisher, W., & Kerbeshian, J. (1987). A prevalence study of pervasive developmental disorders in North Dakota. *Journal of the American Academy of Child and Adolescent Psychiatry, 26,* 704–710.

Burke, J. C. (1991). Some developmental implications of a disturbance in responding to complex environmental stimuli. *American Journal on Mental Retardation, 96,* 37–52.

Carr, E. G. (1977). The motivation of self-injurious behavior: A review of some hypotheses. *Psychological Bulletin, 84,* 800–816.

Carr, E. G. (1981). Sign language. In O. I. Lovaas (Ed.), *Teaching developmentally disabled children* (pp. 153–161). Austin, TX: Pro-Ed.

Carr, E. G. (1985). Behavioral approaches to language and communication. In E. Schopler & G. B. Mesibov (Eds.), *Communication problems in autism* (pp. 37–57). New York: Plenum Press.

Carr, E. G., Binkoff, J. A., Kologinsky, E., & Eddy, M. (1978). Acquisition of sign language by autistic children: I. Expressive labelling. *Journal of Applied Behavior Analysis, 11,* 489–501.

Carr, E. G., & Carlson, J. I. (1993). Reduction of severe behavior problems in the community using a multicomponent treatment approach. *Journal of Applied Behavior Analysis, 26,* 157–172.

Carr, E. G., & Darcy, M. (1990). Setting generality of peer modeling in children with autism. *Journal of Autism and Developmental Disorders, 20,* 45–59.

Carr, E. G., & Dores, P. A. (1981). Patterns of language acquisition following simultaneous communication with autistic children. *Analysis and Intervention in Developmental Disabilities, 1,* 347–361.

Carr, E. G., & Durand, V. M. (1985a). Reducing behavior problems through functional communication training. *Journal of Applied Behavior Analysis, 18,* 111–126.

Carr, E. G., & Durand, V. M. (1985b). The social-communicative basis of severe behavior problems in children. In S. Reiss & R. Bootzin (Eds.), *Theoretical issues in behavior therapy* (pp. 219–254). New York: Academic Press.

Carr, E. G., & Kemp, D. C. (1989). Functional equivalence of autistic leading and communicative pointing: Analysis and treatment. *Journal of Autism and Developmental Disorders, 19,* 561–578.

Carr, E. G., & Kologinsky, E. (1983). Acquisition of sign language by autistic children: II. Spontaneity and generalization effects. *Journal of Applied Behavior Analysis, 16,* 297–314.

Carr, E. G., Kologinsky, E., & Leff-Simon, S. (1987). Acquisition of sign language by autistic children: III. Generalized descriptive phrases. Journal of *Autism and Developmental Disorders, 17,* 217–229.

Carr, E. G., Levin, L., McConnachie, G., Carlson, J. I., Kemp, D. C., & Smith, C. E. (1994). *Communication-based intervention for problem behavior.* Baltimore: Paul H. Brookes.

Carr, E. G., & McDowell, J. J. (1980). Social control of self-injurious behavior of organic etiology. *Behavior Therapy, 11,* 402–409.

Carr, E. G., & Newsom, C. (1985). Demand-related tantrums: Conceptualization and treatment. *Behavior Modification, 9,* 403–426.

Carr, E. G., Newsom, C. D., & Binkoff, J. A. (1976). Stimulus control of self-destructive behavior in a psychotic child. *Journal of Abnormal Child Psychology, 4,* 139–153.

Carr, E. G., Newsom, C. D., & Binkoff, J. A. (1980). Escape as a factor in the aggressive behavior of two retarded children. *Journal of Applied Behavior Analysis, 13,* 101–117.

Carr, E. G., Pridal, C., & Dores, P. A. (1984). Speech versus sign comprehension in autistic children: Analysis and prediction. *Journal of Experimental Child Psychology, 37,* 587–597.

Carr, E. G., Reeve, C. E., & Magito-McLaughlin, D. (1996). Contextual influences on problem behavior in people with developmental disabilities. In L. K. Koegel, R. L. Koegel, & G. Dunlap (Eds.), *Positive behavioral support: Including people with difficult behavior in the community* (pp. 403–423). Baltimore: Paul H. Brookes.

Carr, E. G., Robinson, S., & Palumbo, L. W. (1990). The wrong issue: Aversive vs. nonaversive treatment. The right issue: Functional vs. nonfunctional treatment. In A. C. Repp & N. N. Singh (Eds.), *Perspectives on the use of nonaversive and aversive interventions for persons with developmental disabilities* (pp. 361–371). Sycamore, IL: Sycamore.

Carr, E. G., & Smith, C. E. (1995). Biological setting events for self-injury. *Mental Retardation and Developmental Disabilities Research Reviews, 1,* 94–98.

Charlop, M. H. (1986). Setting effects on the occurrence of autistic children's immediate echolalia. *Journal of Autism and Developmental Disorders, 16,* 473–483.

Charlop, M. H., Kurtz, P. F., & Milstein, J. P. (1992). Too much reinforcement, too little behavior: Assessing task interspersal procedures in conjunction with different reinforcement schedules with autistic children. *Journal of Applied Behavior Analysis, 25,* 795–808.

Charlop, M. H., Schreibman, L., & Thibodeau, M. G. (1985). Increasing spontaneous verbal responding in autistic children using a time delay procedure. *Journal of Applied Behavior Analysis, 18,* 155–166.

Charlop, M. H., Schreibman, L., & Tryon, A. S. (1983). Learning through observation: The effects of peer modeling on acquisition and generalization in autistic children. *Journal of Abnormal Child Psychology, 11,* 355–366.

Charlop, M. H., & Walsh, M. E. (1986). Increasing autistic children's spontaneous verbalizations of affection: An assessment of time delay and peer modeling procedures. *Journal of Applied Behavior Analysis, 19,* 307–314.

Christen, H. J., & Hanefeld, F. (1995). Male Rett variant. *Neuropediatrics, 26,* 81–82.

Cohen, D. J., Paul, R., & Volkmar, F. R. (1986). Issues in the classification of pervasive and other developmental disorders: Toward DSM-IV. *Journal of the American Academy of Child Psychiatry, 25,* 213–220.

Coleman, S. C., & Stedman, J. M. (1974). Use of a peer model in language training in an echolalic child. *Journal of Behavior Therapy and Experimental Psychiatry, 5,* 275–279.

Cooper, L. J., Wacker, D. P., Thursby, D., Plagmann, L. A., Harding, J., & Derby, K. M. (1992). Analysis of the effects of task preferences, task demands, and adult attention on child behavior in outpatient and classroom settings. *Journal of Applied Behavior Analysis, 25,* 823–840.

Courchesne, E., Townsend, J., Akshoomoff, N. A., Saitoh, O., Yeung-Courchesne, R., Lincoln, A. J., James, H. E., Haas, R. H., Schreibman, L., & Lau, L. (1994). Impairment in shifting attention in autistic and cerebellar patients. *Behavioral Neuroscience, 108,* 848–865.

Craighead, W. E., O'Leary, K. D., & Allen, J. S. (1973). Teaching and generalization of instruction-following in an "autistic" child. *Journal of Behavior Therapy and Experimental Psychiatry, 4,* 171–176.

Crossley, R., & McDonald, A. (1980). *Annie's coming out.* Harmondsworth, England: Penguin Books.

Curcio, F. (1978). Sensorimotor functioning and communication in mute autistic children. *Journal of Autism and Childhood Schizophrenia, 8,* 281–292.

Dawson, G., & Adams, A. (1984). Imitation and social responsiveness in autistic children. *Journal of Abnormal Child Psychology, 12,* 209–226.

Dawson, G., & Lewy, A. (1989). Arousal, attention, and the socioemotional impairments of individuals with autism. In G. Dawson (Ed.), *Autism: Nature, diagnosis, and treatment* (pp. 49–74). New York: Guilford Press.

Dawson, G., & Osterling, J. (1996). Early intervention in autism: Effectiveness and common elements of current approaches. In M. J. Guralnick (Ed.), *The effectiveness of early intervention* (pp. 307–326). Baltimore: Paul H. Brookes.

DeLong, G. R., & Dwyer, J. T. (1988). Correlation of family history with specific autistic subgroups: Asperger's syndrome and bipolar affective disease. *Journal of Autism and Developmental Disorders, 18,* 593–600.

Delmolino, L. M., & Romanczyk, R. G. (1995). Facilitated communication: A critical review. *The Behavior Therapist, 18,* 27–30.

DeMyer, M. K. (1979). *Parents and children in autism.* Washington, DC: V. H. Winston.

DeMyer, M. K., Alpern, G. D., Barton, S., DeMyer, W. E., Churchill, D. W., Hingtgen, J. N., Bryson, C. Q., Pontius, W., & Kimberlin, C. (1972). Imitation in autistic, early schizophrenic, and non-psychotic subnormal children. *Journal of Autism and Childhood Schizophrenia, 2,* 264–287.

DeMyer, M. K., Barton, S., DeMyer, W. E., Norton, J. A., Allen, J., & Steele, R. (1973). Prognosis in autism: A follow-up study. *Journal of Autism and Childhood Schizophrenia, 3,* 199–246.

DeMyer, M. K., & Ferster, C. B. (1962). Teaching new social behavior to schizophrenic children. *Journal of the American Academy of Child Psychiatry, 1,* 443–461.

Despert, J. L. (1951). Some considerations relating to the genesis of autistic behavior in children. *American Journal of Orthopsychiatry, 21,* 335–350.

Deykin, E. Y., & MacMahon, B. (1979). The incidence of seizures among children with autistic symptoms. *American Journal of Psychiatry, 136,* 1310–1312.

Donnellan, A. M., & Mirenda, P. L. (1984). Issues related to professional involvement with families of individuals with autism and other severe handicaps. *Journal of the Association for the Severely Handicapped, 9,* 16–25.

Donnellan, A. M., Mirenda, P. L., Mesaros, R. A., & Fassbender, L. L. (1984). Analyzing the communicative functions of aberrant behavior. *Journal of the Association for Persons with Severe Handicaps, 9,* 201–212.

Dugan, E., Kamps, D., Leonard, B., Watkins, N., Rheinberger, A., & Stackhaus, J. (1995). Effects of cooperative learning groups during social studies for students with autism and fourth-grade peers. *Journal of Applied Behavior Analysis, 28,* 175–188.

Dunlap, G. (1984). The influence of task variation and maintenance tasks on the learning and affect of autistic children. *Journal of Experimental Child Psychology, 37,* 41–46.

Dunlap, G., Dyer, K., & Koegel, R. L. (1983). Autistic self-stimulation and intertrial interval duration. *American Journal of Mental Deficiency, 2,* 194–202.

Durand, V. M. (1982). A behavioral/pharmacological intervention for the treatment of severe self-injurious behavior. *Journal of Autism and Developmental Disorders, 12,* 243–251.

Durand, V. M. (1990). *Severe behavior problems: A functional communication training approach.* New York: Guilford Press.

Durand, V. M., & Carr, E. G. (1987). Social influences on "self-stimulatory" behavior: Analysis and treatment application. *Journal of Applied Behavior Analysis, 20,* 119–132.

Durand, V. M., & Crimmins, D. B. (1987). Assessment and treatment of psychotic speech in an autistic child. *Journal of Autism and Developmental Disorders, 17,* 17–28.

Durand, V. M., & Crimmins, D. B. (1988). Identifying the variables maintaining self-injurious behavior. *Journal of Autism and Developmental Disorders, 18,* 99–117.

Dyer, K., Christian, W. P., & Luce, S. C. (1982). The role of response delay in improving the discrimination performance of autistic children. *Journal of Applied Behavior Analysis, 15,* 231–240.

Dyer, K., & Luce, S. C. (1996). *Teaching practical communication skills.* Washington, DC: American Association on Mental Retardation.

Eason, L. J., White, M. J., & Newsom, C. (1982). Generalized reduction of self-stimulatory behavior: An effect of teaching appropriate play to autistic children. *Analysis and Intervention in Developmental Disabilities, 2,* 157–169.

Eaves, L. C., & Ho, H. H. (1996). Brief report: Stability and change in cognitive and behavioral characteristics of autism through childhood. *Journal of Autism and Developmental Disorders, 26,* 557–569.

Eberlin, M., McConnachie, G., Ibel, S., & Volpe, L. (1993). Facilitated communication: A failure to replicate the phenomenon. *Journal of Autism and Developmental Disorders, 23,* 507–530.

Edelson, S. M., Taubman, M. T., & Lovaas, O. I. (1983). Some social contexts of self-destructive behavior. *Journal of Abnormal Child Psychology, 11,* 299–312.

Egel, A. L., Richman, G. S., & Koegel, R. L. (1981). Normal peer models and autistic children's learning. *Journal of Applied Behavior Analysis, 14,* 3–12.

Eisenberg, L. (1956). The autistic child in adolescence. *American Journal of Psychiatry, 112,* 607–613.

Epstein, L. J., Taubman, M. T., & Lovaas, O. I. (1985). Changes in self-stimulatory behaviors with treatment. *Journal of Abnormal Child Psychology, 13,* 281–294.

Favell, J. E., McGimsey, J. F., & Schell, R. M. (1982). Treatment of self-injury by providing alternate sensory activities. *Analysis and Intervention in Developmental Disabilities, 2,* 83–104.

Fenske, E. C., Zalenski, S., Krantz, P. J., & McClannahan, L. E. (1985). Age at intervention and treatment outcome for autistic children in a comprehensive intervention program. *Analysis and Intervention in Developmental Disabilities, 5,* 49–58.

Ferrel, D. R. (1990). *Communicative interaction between handicapped and nonhandicapped preschool children: Identifying facilitative strategies.* Unpublished doctoral dissertation, University of Pittsburgh.

Ferster, C. B. (1961). Positive reinforcement and behavioral deficits in autistic children. *Child Development, 32,* 437–456.

Fish, B. (1957). The detection of schizophrenia in infancy. *Journal of Nervous and Mental Disease, 125,* 1–24.

Fisher, W., Piazza, C., Cataldo, M. F., Harrell, R., Jefferson, G., & Conner, R. (1993). Functional communication training with and without extinction and punishment. *Journal of Applied Behavior Analysis, 26,* 23–36.

Flannery, K. B., & Horner, R. H. (1994). The relationship between predictability and problem behavior for students with severe disabilities. *Journal of Behavioral Education, 4,* 157–176.

Freeman, B. J., Ritvo, E. R., Needleman, R., & Yokota, A. (1985). The stability of cognitive and linguistic parameters in autism: A five-year prospective study. *Journal of the American Academy of Child Psychiatry, 24,* 459–464.

Freeman, S., & Dake, L. (1996). *Teach me language: A language manual for children with autism, As-*

perger's syndrome, and related developmental disorders. Langley, British Columbia, Canada: SKF Books.

Frith, U. (1989). *Autism: Explaining the enigma.* Cambridge, MA: Blackwell.

Frith, U. (Ed.). (1991). *Autism and Asperger syndrome.* Cambridge, England: Cambridge University Press.

Furnell, J. R. G., & Thomas, G. V. (1981). Intermittent reinforcement of imitation in subnormal children: Effect on resistance to extinction. *Behavior Analysis Letters, 1,* 117–122.

Gajzago, C., & Prior, M. (1974). Two cases of "recovery" in Kanner syndrome. *Archives of General Psychiatry, 31,* 264–268.

Gardner, W. I., & Sovner, R. (1994). *Self-injurious behaviors: Diagnosis and treatment.* Willow Street, PA: VIDA.

Gaylord-Ross, R. J., Haring, T. G., Breen, C., & Pitts-Conway, V. (1984). The training and generalization of social interaction skills with autistic youth. *Journal of Applied Behavior Analysis, 17,* 229–247.

Gedye, A. (1989). Extreme self-injury attributed to frontal lobe seizures. *American Journal on Mental Retardation, 94,* 20–26.

Gena, A., Krantz, P. J., McClannahan, L. E., & Poulson, C. L. (1996). Training and generalization of affective behavior displayed by youth with autism. *Journal of Applied Behavior Analysis, 29,* 291–304.

Gesell, A., & Amatruda, C. S. (1941). *Developmental diagnosis.* New York: Harper.

Gillberg, C., & Steffenburg, S. (1987). Outcome and prognostic factors in infantile autism and similar conditions: A population-based study of 46 cases followed through puberty. *Journal of Autism and Developmental Disorders, 17,* 273–287.

Godby, S., Gast, D. L., & Wolery, M. (1987). A comparison of time delay and system of least prompts in teaching object identification. *Research in Developmental Disabilities, 8,* 283–306.

Goetz, L., Gee, K., & Sailor, W. (1985). Using a behavior chain interruption strategy to teach communication skills to students with severe disabilities. *Journal of the Association for Persons with Severe Handicaps, 10,* 21–30.

Goetz, L., Schuler, A., & Sailor, W. (1979). Teaching functional speech to the severely handicapped: Current issues. *Journal of Autism and Developmental Disorders, 9,* 325–343.

Goldstein, H., & Cisar, C. L. (1992). Promoting interaction during sociodramatic play: Teaching scripts to typical preschoolers and classmates with disabilities. *Journal of Applied Behavior Analysis, 25,* 265–280.

Goldstein, H., Kaczmarek, L., Pennington, R., & Shafer, K. (1992). Peer-mediated intervention: Attending to, commenting on, and acknowledging the behavior of preschoolers with autism. *Journal of Applied Behavior Analysis, 25,* 289–305.

Goodman, R. (1989). Infantile autism: A syndrome of multiple primary deficits? *Journal of Autism and Developmental Disorders, 19,* 409–424.

Green, C. W., Reid, D. H., McCarn, J. E., Schepis, M. M., Phillips, J. F., & Parsons, M. B. (1986). Naturalistic observations of classrooms serving severely handicapped persons: Establishing evaluative norms. *Applied Research in Mental Retardation, 7,* 37–50.

Green, G. (1994). The quality of the evidence. In H. C. Shane (Ed.), *Facilitated communication: The clinical and social phenomenon* (pp. 157–226). San Diego, CA: Singular Press.

Green, G. (1996). Early behavioral intervention for autism: What does research tell us? In C. Maurice, G. Green, & S. C. Luce (Eds.), *Behavioral intervention for young children with autism* (pp. 29–44). Austin, TX: Pro-Ed.

Gresham, F. M., & Elliott, S. N. (1990). *Social Skills Rating System.* Circle Pines, MN: American Guidance Service.

Groden, G., Domingue, D., Chesnick, M., Groden, J., & Baron, G. (1983). Early intervention with autistic children: A case presentation with pre-program, program and follow-up data. *Psychological Reports, 53,* 715–722.

Guess, D., & Carr, E. (1991). Emergence and maintenance of stereotypy and self-injury. *American Journal on Mental Retardation, 96,* 299–319.

Guess, D., Keogh, W., & Baer, D. (1977). *Imitation training for difficult to teach severely handicapped children: An analysis of new procedures.* Topeka: Kansas Department of Social and Rehabilitation Services.

Guess, D., Sailor, W., & Baer, D. (1978). *Functional speech and language training for the severely handicapped.* Lawrence, KS: H & H Enterprises.

Gunsett, R. P., Mulick, J. A., Fernald, W. B., & Martin, J. L. (1989). Brief report: Indications for medical screening prior to behavioral programming for severely and profoundly mentally retarded clients. *Journal of Autism and Developmental Disorders, 19,* 167–172.

Guralnick, M. J. (1976). The value of integrating handicapped and non-handicapped preschool children. *American Journal of Orthopsychiatry, 42,* 236–245.

Hagberg, B. (1995). Clinical delineation of Rett syndrome variants. *Neuropediatrics, 26,* 62.

Halle, J. W. (1982). Teaching functional language to the handicapped: An integrative model of natural environment teaching techniques. *The Journal of the Association for the Severely Handicapped, 7,* 29–37.

Halle, J. W., Baer, D. M., & Spradlin, J. E. (1981). Teachers' generalized use of delay as a stimulus control procedure to increase language use in handicapped children. *Journal of Applied Behavior Analysis, 14,* 389–409.

Halle, J. W., Marshall, A., & Spradlin, J. E. (1979). Time delay: A technique to increase language use and facilitate generalization in retarded children. *Journal of Applied Behavior Analysis, 12,* 431–439.

Handen, B. L., & Zane, T. (1987). Delayed prompting: A review of procedural variations and results. *Research in Developmental Disabilities, 8,* 307–330.

Handleman, J. S. (1979). Generalization by autistic-type children of verbal responses across settings. *Journal of Applied Behavior Analysis, 12,* 273–282.

Haring, T. G., & Breen, C. G. (1992). A peer-mediated social network intervention to enhance the social integration of persons with moderate and severe disabilities. *Journal of Applied Behavior Analysis, 25,* 319–131.

Haring, T. G., Roger, B., Lee, M., Breen, C., & Gaylord-Ross, R. (1986). Teaching social language to moderately handicapped students. *Journal of Applied Behavior Analysis, 19,* 159–171.

Harris, S. L. (1975). Teaching language to nonverbal children—with emphasis on problems of generalization. *Psychological Bulletin, 82,* 565–580.

Harris, S. L. (1983). *Families of the developmentally disabled: A guide to behavioral intervention.* New York: Pergamon Press.

Harris, S. L. (1986). Brief report: A 4- to 7-year questionnaire follow-up of participants in a training program for parents of autistic children. *Journal of Autism and Developmental Disorders, 16,* 377–383.

Harris, S. L. (1994). *Siblings of children with autism: Guide for families.* Bethesda, MD: Woodbine House.

Harris, S. L., & Boyle, T. D. (1985). Parents as language trainers of children with autism. In E. Schopler & G. B. Mesibov (Eds.), *Communication problems in autism* (pp. 207–227). New York: Plenum Press.

Harris, S. L., & Handleman, J. S. (Eds.). (1994). *Preschool education programs for children with autism.* Austin, TX: Pro-Ed.

Harris, S. L., Wolchik, S. A., & Milch, R. E. (1982). Changing the speech of autistic children and their parents. *Child and Family Behavior Therapy, 4,* 151–173.

Harris, S. L., Wolchik, S. A., & Weitz, S. (1981). The acquisition of language skills by autistic children: Can parents do the job? *Journal of Autism and Developmental Disorders, 11,* 373–384.

Hart, B., & Risley, T. R. (1975). Incidental teaching of language in the preschool. *Journal of Applied Behavior Analysis, 8,* 411–420.

Hart, B., & Risley, T. R. (1982). *How to use incidental teaching for elaborating language.* Lawrence, KS: H & H Enterprises.

Heller, T. (1954). About dementia infantilis (W. Hulse, Trans.). *Journal of Nervous and Mental Disease, 119,* 610–616. (Original work published 1908)

Hermelin, B., & O'Connor, N. (1964). Effects of sensory input and sensory dominance on severely disturbed children and on subnormal controls. *British Journal of Psychology, 55,* 201–206.

Hewett, F. M. (1965). Teaching speech to an autistic child through operant conditioning. *American Journal of Orthopsychiatry, 35,* 927–936.

Hingtgen, J. N., Coulter, S. K., & Churchill, D. W. (1967). Intensive reinforcement of imitative behavior in mute autistic children. *Archives of General Psychiatry, 17,* 36–43.

Hobson, R. P. (1986). The autistic child's appraisal of expressions of emotion. *Journal of Child Psychology and Psychiatry, 27,* 321–342.

Hobson, R. P. (1990). On the origins of self and the case of autism. *Development and Psychopathology, 2,* 163–191.

Hobson, R. P. (1993). *Autism and the development of mind.* Hillsdale, NJ: Erlbaum.

Hobson, R. P., Ouston, J., & Lee, A. (1988). What's in a face?: The case of autism. *British Journal of Psychology, 79,* 441–453.

Holmes, N., Hemsley, R., Rickett, J., & Likierman, H. (1982). Parents as cotherapists: Their perceptions of a home-based behavioral treatment for autistic children. *Journal of Autism and Developmental Disorders, 12,* 331–342.

Holroyd, J., & McArthur, D. (1976). Mental retardation and stress on the parents: A contrast between Down syndrome and childhood autism. *American Journal of Mental Deficiency, 80,* 431–436.

Horner, R. D. (1980). The effects of an environmental "enrichment" program on the behavior of institutionalized profoundly retarded children. *Journal of Applied Behavior Analysis, 13,* 473–491.

Horner, R. H., Vaughn, B. J., Day, H. M., & Ard, W. R. (1996). The relationship between setting events and problem behavior. In L. K. Koegel, R. L. Koegel, & G. Dunlap (Eds.), *Positive behavioral support: Including people with difficult behavior in the community* (pp. 381–402). Baltimore: Paul H. Brookes.

Howlin, P. A. (1981). The effectiveness of operant language training with autistic children. *Journal of Autism and Developmental Disorders, 11,* 89–105.

Howlin, P. A. (1986). An overview of social behavior in autism. In E. Schopler & G. B. Mesibov (Eds.), *Social behavior in autism* (pp. 103–131). New York: Plenum Press.

Howlin, P. A., & Rutter, M. (1987). *Treatment of autistic children.* New York: Wiley.

Huff, R. C. (1996). Community-based early intervention for children with autism. In C. Maurice, G. Green, & S. C. Luce (Eds.), *Behavioral intervention for young children with autism* (pp. 251–266). Austin, TX: Pro-Ed.

Hughes, C. H., & Russell, J. (1993). Autistic children's difficulty with mental disengagement from an object: Its implications for theories of autism. *Developmental Psychology, 29,* 498–510.

Hung, D. W. (1977). Generalization of "curiosity" questioning behavior in autistic children. *Journal of Behavior Therapy and Experimental Psychiatry, 8,* 237–245.

Hung, D. W. (1980). Training and generalization of yes and no as mands in two autistic children. *Journal of Autism and Developmental Disorders, 10,* 139–152.

Huttenlocher, P. R. (1988). Developmental neurobiology: Current and future challenges. In F. J. Menolascino & J. A. Stark (Eds.), *Preventive and curative intervention in mental retardation* (pp. 101–111). Baltimore: Paul H. Brookes.

Ihrig, K., & Wolchik, S. A. (1988). Peer versus adult models in autistic children's learning: Acquisition, generalization, and maintenance. *Journal of Autism and Developmental Disorders, 18,* 67–79.

Itard, J. M. G. (1962). *The wild boy of Aveyron* (G. Humphrey & M. Humphrey, Trans.). New York: Appleton-Century-Crofts. (Original work published 1801)

Iwata, B. A., Dorsey, M. F., Slifer, K. J., Bauman, K. E., & Richman, G. S. (1982). Toward a functional analysis of self-injury. *Analysis and Intervention in Developmental Disabilities, 2,* 3–20.

Iwata, B. A., Pace, G. M., Kalsher, M. J., Cowdery, G. E., & Cataldo, M. F. (1990). Experimental analysis and extinction of self-injurious escape behavior. *Journal of Applied Behavior Analysis, 23,* 11–27.

Iwata, B. A., Vollmer, T. R., & Zarcone, J. R. (1990). The experimental (functional) analysis of behavior disorders: Methodology, applications, and limitations. In A. C. Repp & N. N. Singh (Eds.), *Perspectives on the use of nonaversive and aversive interventions for persons with developmental disabilities* (pp. 301–330). Sycamore, IL: Sycamore.

Jacobson, J. W., Eberlin, M., Mulick, J. A., Schwartz, A. A., Szempruch, J., & Wheeler, D. L. (1994). Autism, facilitated communication, and future directions. In J. L. Matson (Ed.), *Autism in children and adults* (pp. 59–83). Pacific Grove, CA: Brooks/Cole.

Jacobson, J. W., & Mulick, J. A. (1994). Facilitated communication: Better education through applied ideology. *Journal of Behavioral Education, 4,* 95–107.

Jacobson, J. W., Mulick, J. A., & Schwartz, A. A. (1995). A history of facilitated communication: Science, pseudoscience, and antiscience. *American Psychologist, 50,* 750–765.

Jacobson, M. A. (1978). *Developmental neurobiology* (2nd ed.). New York: Plenum Press.

James, S. D., & Egel, A. L. (1986). A direct prompting strategy for increasing reciprocal interactions between handicapped and nonhandicapped siblings. *Journal of Applied Behavior Analysis, 19,* 173–186.

Janssen, C., & Guess, D. (1978). Use of function as a consequence in training receptive labeling to severely and profoundly retarded individuals. *AAESPH Review, 3,* 246–258.

Kamps, D. M., Barbetta, P. M., Leonard, B. R., & Delquadri, J. (1994). Classwide peer tutoring: An integration strategy to improve reading skills and promote peer interactions among students with autism and general education peers. *Journal of Applied Behavior Analysis, 27,* 49–61.

Kamps, D. M., Leonard, B. R., Vernon, S., Dugan, E. P., Delquadri, J. C., Gershon, B., Wade, L., & Folk, L. (1992). Teaching social skills to students with autism to increase peer interactions in an integrated first-grade classroom. *Journal of Applied Behavior Analysis, 25,* 281–288.

Kanner, L. (1943). Autistic disturbances of affective contact. *The Nervous Child, 2,* 181–197.

Kanner, L. (1949). Problems of nosology and psychodynamics in early infantile autism. *American Journal of Orthopsychiatry, 19,* 416–426.

Kanner, L. (1965). Infantile autism and the schizophrenias. *Behavioral Science, 10,* 412–420.

Kanner, L. (1969). The children haven't read those books. *Acta Paedopsychiatrica, 36,* 2–11.

Kanner, L. (1973). How far can autistic children go in matters of social adaptation? In L. Kanner (Ed.), *Childhood psychosis: Initial studies and new insights* (pp. 189–213). Washington, DC: V. H. Winston.

Kennedy, C. H., & Meyer, K. A. (1996). Sleep deprivation, allergy symptoms, and negatively reinforced problem behavior. *Journal of Applied Behavior Analysis, 29,* 133–135.

Keogh, B., Guess, D., & Baer, D. (1977). *Fast Motor Imitation Program.* Lawrence: University of Kansas, Department of Human Development and Family Life.

Klin, A. (1991). Young autistic children's listening preferences in regard to speech: A possible characterization of the symptom of social withdrawal. *Journal of Autism and Developmental Disabilities, 21,* 29–42.

Klin, A., Volkmar, F. R., & Sparrow, S. S. (1992). Autistic social dysfunction: Some limitations of the theory of mind hypothesis. *Journal of Child Psychology and Psychiatry, 33,* 861–876.

Koegel, R. L., & Covert, A. (1972). The relationship of self-stimulation to learning in autistic children. *Journal of Applied Behavior Analysis, 5,* 381–388.

Koegel, R. L., Dunlap, G., & Dyer, K. (1980). Intertrial interval duration and learning in autistic children. *Journal of Applied Behavior Analysis, 13,* 91–99.

Koegel, R. L., Dunlap, G., Richman, G. S., & Dyer, K. (1981). The use of specific orienting cues for teaching discrimination tasks. *Analysis and Intervention in Developmental Disabilities, 1,* 187–198.

Koegel, R. L., Dyer, K., & Bell, L. K. (1987). The influence of child-preferred activities on autistic children's social behavior. *Journal of Applied Behavior Analysis, 20,* 243–252.

Koegel, R. L., Firestone, P. B., Kramme, K. W., & Dunlap, G. (1974). Increasing spontaneous play by suppressing self-stimulation in autistic children. *Journal of Applied Behavior Analysis, 7,* 521–528.

Koegel, R. L., & Koegel, L. K. (Eds.). (1995). *Teaching children with autism: Strategies for initiating*

positive interactions and improving learning opportunities. Baltimore: Paul H. Brookes.

Koegel, R. L., Koegel, L. K., & Dunlap, G. (1996).
*Positive behavioral support: Including people with
difficult behavior in the community.* Baltimore:
Paul H. Brookes.

Koegel, R. L., O'Dell, M. C., & Koegel, L. K. (1987).
A natural language teaching paradigm for nonverbal autistic children. *Journal of Autism and Developmental Disorders, 17,* 187–200.

Koegel, R. L., & Rincover, A. (1977). Research on the
difference between generalization and maintenance
in extra-therapy responding. *Journal of Applied Behavior Analysis, 10,* 1–12.

Koegel, R. L., Russo, D. C., Rincover, A., & Schreibman, L. (1982). Assessing and training teachers. In
R. L. Koegel, A. Rincover, & A. L. Egel (Eds.),
Educating and understanding autistic children (pp.
178–202). San Diego, CA: College-Hill Press.

Koegel, R. L., & Williams, J. A. (1980). Direct versus
indirect response-reinforcer relationships in teaching autistic children. *Journal of Abnormal Child
Psychology, 8,* 537–547.

Kolvin, I., Ounsted, C., Humphrey, M., & McNay, A.
(1971). Studies in the childhood psychoses: II. The
phenomenology of childhood psychoses. *British
Journal of Psychiatry, 118,* 385–395.

Kozloff, M. A. (1973). *Reaching the autistic child: A
parent training program.* Champaign, IL: Research
Press.

Kozloff, M. A. (1974). *Educating children with learning and behavior problems.* New York: Wiley.

Kozloff, M. A. (1979). *A program for families of children with learning and behavior problems.* New
York: Wiley.

Kozloff, M. A. (1994). *Improving educational outcomes for children with disabilities: Principles for
assessment, program planning, and evaluation.*
Baltimore: Paul H. Brookes.

Krantz, P. J., & McClannahan, L. E. (1993). Teaching
children with autism to initiate to peers: Effects of
a script-fading procedure. *Journal of Applied Behavior Analysis, 26,* 121–132.

Lalli, J. S., Casey, S., Goh, H., & Merlino, J. (1994).
Treatment of escape-maintained aberrant behavior
with escape extinction and predictable routines.
Journal of Applied Behavior Analysis, 27, 705–
714.

Lalli, J. S., Casey, S., & Kates, K. (1995). Reducing
escape behavior and increasing task completion
with functional communication training, extinction, and response chaining. *Journal of Applied Behavior Analysis, 28,* 261–268.

Landry, S., & Loveland, K. A. (1988). Communicative behaviors in autism and developmental language delay. *Journal of Child Psychology and
Psychiatry, 29,* 621–634.

Laski, K. E., Charlop, M. H., & Schreibman, L.
(1988). Training parents to use the natural language
paradigm to increase their autistic children's

speech. *Journal of Applied Behavior Analysis, 21,*
391–400.

Leslie, A. M. (1987). Pretense and representation:
The origins of "theory of mind." *Psychological Review, 94,* 412–426.

Leslie, A. M., & Frith, U. (1988). Autistic children's
understanding of seeing, knowing and believing.
British Journal of Developmental Psychology, 4,
315–324.

Leslie, A. M., & Frith, U. (1990). Prospects for a cognitive neuropsychology of autism: Hobson's
choice. *Psychological Review, 97,* 122–131.

Leung, J. (1994). Teaching spontaneous requests to
children with autism using a time delay procedure
with multi-component toys. *Journal of Behavioral
Education, 4,* 21–31.

Lewis, M. H., & Baumeister, A. A. (1982). Stereo-
typed mannerisms in mentally retarded persons:
Animal models and theoretical analyses. In N. R.
Ellis (Ed.), *International review of research in
mental retardation* (Vol. 11, pp. 123–161). New
York: Academic Press.

Lewis, M. H., Bodfish, J. W., Powell, S. B., Wiest, K.,
Darling, M., & Golden, R. N. (1996). Plasma HVA
in adults with mental retardation and stereotyped
behavior: Biochemical evidence for a dopamine
deficiency model. *American Journal of Mental Deficiency, 100,* 413–427.

Lewy, A., & Dawson, G. (1992). Social stimulation
and joint attention deficits of young autistic children. *Journal of Abnormal Child Psychology, 20,*
555–566.

Litt, M. D., & Schreibman, L. (1982). Stimulus-spe-
cific reinforcement in the acquisition of receptive
labels by autistic children. *Analysis and Intervention in Developmental Disabilities, 1,* 171–186.

Lord, C., & Schopler, E. (1989). The role of age at assessment, developmental level, and test in the stability of intelligence scores in young autistic
children. *Journal of Autism and Developmental
Disorders, 19,* 483–499.

Lord, C., Schopler, E., & Revicki, D. (1982). Sex differences in autism. *Journal of Autism and Developmental Disorders, 12,* 317–330.

Lotter, V. (1966). Epidemiology of autistic conditions
in young children. I. Prevalence. *Social Psychiatry,
1,* 124–137.

Lotter, V. (1974). Social adjustment and placement of
autistic children in Middlesex: A follow-up. *Journal of Autism and Childhood Schizophrenia, 4,* 11–
32.

Lovaas, O. I. (1977). *The autistic child: Language development through behavior modification.* New
York: Irvington.

Lovaas, O. I. (1981). *Teaching developmentally disabled children.* Austin, TX: Pro-Ed.

Lovaas, O. I. (1987). Behavioral treatment and normal educational and intellectual functioning in
young autistic children. *Journal of Consulting and
Clinical Psychology, 55,* 3–9.

Lovaas, O. I. (1996). The UCLA Young Autism model of service delivery. In C. Maurice, G. Green, & S. C. Luce (Eds.), *Behavioral intervention for young children with autism* (pp. 241–248). Austin, TX: Pro-Ed.

Lovaas, O. I., Berberich, J. P., Perloff, B. F., & Schaefer, B. (1966). Acquisition of imitative speech by schizophrenic children. *Science, 151,* 705–707.

Lovaas, O. I., & Buch, G. (1997). Intensive behavioral intervention with young autistic children. In N. N. Singh (Ed.), *Prevention and treatment of severe behavior problems* (pp. 61–86). Pacific Grove, CA: Brooks/Cole.

Lovaas, O. I., Freitag, G., Gold, V. J., & Kassorla, I. C. (1965). Experimental studies in childhood schizophrenia: Analysis of self-destructive behavior. *Journal of Experimental Child Psychology, 2,* 67–84.

Lovaas, O. I., Freitas, L., Nelson, K., & Whalen, C. (1967). The establishment of imitation and its use for the development of complex behavior in schizophrenic children. *Behaviour Research and Therapy, 5,* 171–181.

Lovaas, O. I., Koegel, R. L., & Schreibman, L. (1979). Stimulus overselectivity in autism: A review of research. *Psychological Bulletin, 86,* 1236–1254.

Lovaas, O. I., Koegel, R. L., Simmons, J. Q., & Long, J. S. (1973). Some generalization and follow-up measures on autistic children in behavior therapy. *Journal of Applied Behavior Analysis, 6,* 131–166.

Lovaas, O. I., Litrownik, A., & Mann, R. (1971). Response latencies to auditory stimuli in autistic children engaged in self-stimulatory behaviour. *Behaviour Research and Therapy, 9,* 39–49.

Lovaas, O. I., Newsom, C., & Hickman, C. (1987). Self-stimulatory behavior and perceptual reinforcement. *Journal of Applied Behavior Analysis, 20,* 45–68.

Lovaas, O. I., & Simmons, J. Q. (1969). Manipulation of self-destruction in three retarded children. *Journal of Applied Behavior Analysis, 2,* 143–157.

Lovaas, O. I., & Smith, T. (1988). Intensive behavioral treatment for young autistic children. In B. B. Lahey & A. E. Kazdin (Eds.), *Advances in clinical child psychology* (Vol. 11, pp. 285–324). New York: Plenum Press.

Mace, F. C., Browder, D. M., & Lin, Y. (1987). Analysis of demand conditions associated with stereotypy. *Journal of Behavior Therapy and Experimental Psychiatry, 18,* 25–31.

Mace, F. C., Hock, M. L., Lalli, J. S., West, B. J., Belfiore, P., Pinter, E., & Brown, D. K. (1988). Behavioral momentum in the treatment of noncompliance. *Journal of Applied Behavior Analysis, 21,* 123–141.

Mahler, M. S. (1952). On child psychosis and schizophrenia: Autistic and symbiotic infantile psychoses. *Psychoanalytic Study of the Child, 7,* 286–305.

Maurice, C. (1993). *Let me hear your voice: A family's triumph over autism.* New York: Knopf.

Maurice, C. (1996). Why this manual? In C. Maurice, G. Green, & S. C. Luce (Eds.), *Behavioral intervention for young children with autism* (pp. 3–12). Austin, TX: Pro-Ed.

Maurice, C., Green, G., & Luce, S. C. (Eds.). (1996). *Behavioral intervention for young children with autism.* Austin, TX: Pro-Ed.

McAfee, J. K. (1987). Classroom density and the aggressive behavior of handicapped children. *Education and Treatment of Children, 10,* 134–145.

McClannahan, L. E., & Krantz, P. J. (1994). The Princeton Child Development Institute. In S. L. Harris & J. S. Handleman (Eds.), *Preschool education programs for children with autism* (pp. 107–126). Austin, TX: Pro-Ed.

McConnell, O. L. (1967). Control of eye contact in an autistic child. *Journal of Child Psychology and Psychiatry, 8,* 249–255.

McDonald, E. T. (1980). Early identification and treatment of children at risk for speech development. In R. L. Schiefelbusch (Ed.), *Nonspeech language and communication* (pp. 49–79). Baltimore: University Park Press.

McEachin, J. J., Smith, T., & Lovaas, O. I. (1993). Long-term outcome for children with autism who received early intensive behavioral treatment. *American Journal on Mental Retardation, 97,* 359–372.

McEvoy, M. A., Nordquist, V. M., Twardosz, S., Heckaman, K. A., Wehby, J. H., & Denny, R. K. (1988). Promoting autistic children's peer interaction in an integrated early childhood setting using affection activities. *Journal of Applied Behavior Analysis, 21,* 193–200.

McEvoy, R., Rogers, S., & Pennington, R. (1993). Executive function and social communication deficits in young autistic children. *Journal of Child Psychology and Psychiatry, 34,* 563–578.

McGee, G. G., Krantz, P. J., Mason, D., & McClannahan, L. E. (1983). A modified incidental-teaching procedure for autistic youth: Acquisition and generalization of receptive object labels. *Journal of Applied Behavior Analysis, 16,* 329–338.

McGee, G. G., Krantz, P. J., & McClannahan, L. E. (1985). The facilitative effects of incidental teaching on preposition use by autistic children. *Journal of Applied Behavior Analysis, 18,* 17–31.

McHale, S. M., Simeonsson, R. J., & Sloan, J. L. (1984). Children with handicapped brothers and sisters. In E. Schopler & G. B. Mesibov (Eds.), *The effects of autism on the family* (pp. 327–342). New York: Plenum Press.

McMorrow, M. J., Foxx, R. M., Faw, G. D., & Bittle, R. G. (1987). Cues–pause–point language training: Teaching echolalics functional use of their verbal labeling repertoires. *Journal of Applied Behavior Analysis, 20,* 11–22.

Meinhold, P., Teodoru, J., & Koch, E. (1993, August). *Clinical method for testing claims of facilitated communication.* Paper presented at the Annual

Convention of the American Psychological Association, Toronto.

Metz, J. R. (1965). Conditioning generalized imitation in autistic children. *Journal of Experimental Child Psychology, 2,* 389–399.

Michael, J. (1982). Distinguishing between the discriminative and motivational functions of stimuli. *Journal of the Experimental Analysis of Behavior, 37,* 149–155.

Milch, R. E. (1983). *A comparison of 10 and 20 week behavioral training programs for parents of autistic children.* Unpublished doctoral dissertation, Rutgers University.

Mirenda, P. L., Donnellan, A. M., & Yoder, D. E. (1983). Gaze behavior: A new look at an old problem. *Journal of Autism and Developmental Disorders, 13,* 397–409.

Mundy, P. (1995). Joint attention and social-emotional approach behavior in children with autism. *Development and Psychopathology, 7,* 63–82.

Mundy, P., Sigman, M., & Kasari, C. (1990). A longitudinal study of joint attention and language development in autistic children. *Journal of Autism and Developmental Disorders, 20,* 115–128.

Neef, N. A., Shafer, M. S., Egel, A. L., Cataldo, M. F., & Parrish, J. M. (1983). The class specific effects of compliance training with "do" and "don't" requests: Analogue analysis and classroom application. *Journal of Applied Behavior Analysis, 16,* 81–99.

Neef, N. A., Walters, J., & Egel, A. L. (1984). Establishing generative yes/no responses in developmentally disabled children. *Journal of Applied Behavior Analysis, 17,* 453–460.

Newsom, C., & Hovanitz, C. A. (1997). Autism. In E. J. Mash & L. G. Terdal (Eds.), *Assessment of childhood disorders* (3rd ed., pp. 408–452). New York: Guilford Press.

Nordquist, V. M., Twardosz, S., & McEvoy, M. A. (1982, November). *A naturalistic approach to the problem of establishing social reinforcers in autistic children.* Paper presented at the convention of the Association for Advancement of Behavior Therapy, Los Angeles.

Odom, S. L., Hoyson, M., Jamieson, B., & Strain, P. S. (1985). Increasing handicapped preschoolers' peer social interactions: Cross-setting and component analysis. *Journal of Applied Behavior Analysis, 18,* 3–16.

Odom, S. L., & Strain, P. S. (1986). A comparison of peer-initiation and teacher-antecedent interventions for promoting reciprocal social interaction of autistic preschoolers. *Journal of Applied Behavior Analysis, 19,* 59–71.

Oke, N. J., & Schreibman, L. (1990). Training social initiations to a high-functioning autistic child: Assessment of collateral behavior change and generalization in a case study. *Journal of Autism and Developmental Disorders, 20,* 479–497.

Ornitz, E. M. (1989). Autism at the interface between sensory and information processing. In G. Dawson (Ed.), *Autism: Nature, diagnosis, and treatment* (pp. 174–207). New York: Guilford Press.

Owens, R. E., & House, L. I. (1984). Decision-making processes in augmentative communication. *Journal of Speech and Hearing Disorders, 49,* 18–25.

Ozonoff, S. & Miller, J. N. (1995). Teaching theory of mind: A new approach to social skills training for individuals with autism. *Journal of Autism and Developmental Disorders, 25,* 415–433.

Ozonoff, S., Pennington, B. F., & Rogers, S. J. (1991). Executive function deficits in high-functioning autistic individuals: Relationship to theory of mind. *Journal of Child Psychology and Psychiatry, 32,* 1081–1105.

Parrish, J. M., Cataldo, M. F., Kolko, D. J., Neef, N. A., & Egel, A. L. (1986). Experimental analysis of response covariation among compliant and inappropriate behaviors. *Journal of Applied Behavior Analysis., 19,* 241–254.

Patterson, G. R. (1976). The aggressive child: Victim and architect of a coercive system. In E. J. Mash, L. A. Hamerlynck, & L. C. Handy (Eds.), *Behavior modification and families* (pp. 267–316). New York: Brunner/Mazel.

Paul, R. (1987). Nautral history. In D. J. Cohen & A. M. Donnellan (Eds.), *Handbook of autism and pervasive developmental disorders* (pp. 121–147). New York: Wiley.

Paul, R., Harcherik, D., Volkmar, F. R., & Cohen, D. J. (1985, October). *Adaptive behavioral outcomes in severe disorders of language acquisition.* Paper presented at the meeting of the American Academy of Child Psychiatry, San Antonio, TX.

Perner, J., Frith, U., Leslie, A. M., & Leekam, S. (1989). Exploration of the autistic child's theory of mind: Knowledge, belief, and communication. *Child Development, 60,* 689–700.

Perry, A., Sarlo-McGarvey, N., & Haddad, C. (1991). Brief report: Cognitive and adaptive functioning in 28 girls with Rett Syndrome. *Journal of Autism and Developmental Disorders, 21,* 551–556.

Perry, R., Cohen, I., & DeCarlo, R. (1995). Case study: Deterioration, autism, and recovery in two siblings. *Journal of the American Academy of Child Psychiatry, 34,* 232–237.

Peters, A. (1983). *The units of language acquisition.* London: Cambridge University Press.

Petty, L., Ornitz, E. M., Michelman, J. D., & Zimmerman, E. G. (1984). Autistic children who later become schizophrenic. *Archives of General Psychiatry, 41,* 129–135.

Pitfield, M., & Oppenheim, A. M. (1964). Child rearing attitudes of mothers of psychotic children. *Journal of Child Psychology and Psychiatry, 5,* 51–57.

Plummer, S., Baer, D. M., & LeBlanc, J. M. (1977). Functional considerations in the use of procedural timeout and an effective alternative. *Journal of Applied Behavior Analysis, 10,* 689–706.

Potter, H. W. (1933). Schizophrenia in children. *American Journal of Psychiatry, 89,* 1253–1270.

Pridal, C. G. (1982, May). Teaching sign language to low-functioning autistic children. Paper presented at the conference of the Association for Behavior Analysis, Milwaukee.

Prizant, B. (1983). Language acquisition and communicative behavior in autism: Toward an understanding of the "whole" of it. *Journal of Speech and Hearing Disorders, 48,* 296–307.

Prizant, B., & Schuler, A. L. (1987). Facilitating communication: Theoretical foundations. In D. J. Cohen & A. M. Donnellan (Eds.), *Handbook of autism and pervasive developmental disorders* (pp. 289–300). New York: Wiley.

Pronovost, W., Wakstein, M. P., & Wakstein, D. J. (1966). A longitudinal study of speech behaviour and language comprehension of fourteen children diagnosed as atypical or autistic. *Exceptional Children, 33,* 19–26.

Pyles, D. A. M., & Bailey, J. S. (1990). Diagnosing severe behavior problems. In A. C. Repp & N. N. Singh (Eds.), *Perspectives on the use of nonaversive and aversive interventions for persons with developmental disabilities* (pp. 382–401). Sycamore, IL: Sycamore Publishing.

Ragland, E. U., Kerr, M. M., & Strain, P. S. (1978). Behavior of withdrawn autistic children: Effects of peer social initiations. *Behavior Modification, 2,* 565–578.

Rank, B., & McNaughton, D. (1950). A clinical contribution to early ego development. *Psychoanalytic Study of the Child, 5,* 53–65.

Reimers, T., & Wacker, D. (1988). Parents' ratings of the acceptability of behavioral treatment recommendations made in an outpatient clinic: A preliminary analysis of the influence of treatment effectiveness. *Behavioral Disorders, 14,* 7–15.

Remington, B., & Clarke, S. (1983). Acquisition of expressive signing by autistic children: An evaluation of the relative effects of simultaneous communication and sign-alone training. *Journal of Applied Behavior Analysis, 16,* 315–328.

Repp, A. C., Felce, D., & Barton, L. E. (1988). Basing the treatment of stereotypic and self-injurious behaviors on hypotheses of their causes. *Journal of Applied Behavior Analysis, 21,* 281–289.

Rimland, B. (1964). *Infantile autism.* New York: Appleton-Century-Crofts.

Rincover, A. (1978). Sensory extinction: A procedure for eliminating self-stimulatory behavior in psychotic children. *Journal of Abnormal Child Psychology, 6,* 299–310.

Rincover, A., Cook, R., Peoples, A., & Packard, D. (1979). Using sensory extinction and sensory reinforcement principles for programming multiple adaptive behavior change. *Journal of Applied Behavior Analysis, 12,* 221–233.

Rincover, A., & Devany, J. (1982). The application of sensory extinction procedures to self-injury. *Analysis and Intervention in Developmental Disabilities, 2,* 67–81.

Rincover, A., & Koegel, R. L. (1975). Setting generality and stimulus control in autistic children. *Journal of Applied Behavior Analysis, 8,* 235–246.

Rincover, A., & Newsom, C. D. (1985). The relative motivational properties of sensory and edible reinforcers in teaching autistic children. *Journal of Applied Behavior Analysis, 18,* 237–248.

Risley, T. R. (1968). The effects and side effects of punishing the autistic behaviors of a deviant child. *Journal of Applied Behavior Analysis, 1,* 21–34.

Risley, T. R., & Wolf, M. (1967). Establishing functional speech in echolalic children. *Behaviour Research and Therapy, 5,* 73–88.

Ritvo, E. R., Freeman, B. J., Pingree, C., Mason-Brothers, A. Jorde, L., Jenson, W. R., McMahon, W. M., Peterson, P. B., Mo, A., & Ritvo, A. (1989) The UCLA–University of Utah epidemiological study of autism: Prevalence. *American Journal of Psychiatry, 146,* 194–245.

Roeyers, H. (1996). The influence of nonhandicapped peers on the social interactions of children with a pervasive developmental disorder. *Journal of Autism and Developmental Disorders, 26,* 303–320.

Rogers, S. J. (1996). Brief report: Early intervention in autism. *Journal of Autism and Developmental Disorders, 26,* 243–246.

Romanczyk, R. G., Diament, C., Goren, E. R., Trunell, G., & Harris, S. L. (1975). Increasing isolate and social play in severely disturbed children: Intervention and postintervention effectiveness. *Journal of Autism and Childhood Schizophrenia , 5,* 57–70.

Rumsey, J. M., Rapoport, J. L., & Sceery, W. R. (1985). Autistic children as adults: Psychiatric, social, and behavioral outcomes. *Journal of the American Academy of Child Psychiatry, 24,* 465–473.

Runco, M. A., Charlop, M. H., & Schreibman, L. (1986). The occurrence of autistic children's self-stimulation as a function of familiar versus unfamiliar stimulus conditions. *Journal of Autism and Developmental Disorders, 16,* 31–44.

Russo, D. C., Cataldo, M. F., & Cushing, P. J. (1981). Compliance training and behavioral covariation in the treatment of multiple behavior problems. *Journal of Applied Behavior Analysis, 14,* 209–222.

Rutter, M. (1985). Infantile autism and other pervasive developmental disorders. In M. Rutter & L. Hersov (Eds.), *Child and adolescent psychiatry* (2nd ed., pp. 545–566). Oxford: Blackwell.

Rutter, M. (1988). Biological basis of autism: Implications for intervention. In F. J. Menolascino & J. A. Stark (Eds.), *Preventive and curative intervention in mental retardation* (pp. 265–294). Baltimore: Paul R. Brookes.

Rutter, M., Bailey, A., Bolton, P., & Le Couteur, A. (1994). Autism and known medical conditions: Myth and substance. *Journal of Child Psychology and Psychiatry, 35,* 311–322.

Rutter, M., & Brown, G. (1966). The reliability and validity of measures of family life and relationships in families containing a psychiatric patient. *Social Psychiatry, 1,* 38–53.

Rutter, M., Greenfeld, D., & Lockyer, L. (1967). A five to fifteen year follow-up study of infantile psychosis. II. Social and behavioral outcome. *British Journal of Psychiatry, 113,* 1183–1199.

Rutter, M., & Lockyer, L. (1967). A five to fifteen year follow-up study of infantile psychosis. I. Description of sample. *British Journal of Psychiatry, 113,* 1169–1182.

Rutter, M. & Schopler, E. (1987). Autism and pervasive developmental disorders: Concepts and diagnostic issues. *Journal of Autism and Developmental Disorders, 17,* 159–186.

Sailor, W. (1996). New structures and systems change for comprehensive positive behavioral support. In L. K. Koegel, R. L. Koegel, & G. Dunlap (Eds.), *Positive behavioral support: Including people with difficult behavior in the community* (pp. 163–206). Baltimore: Paul H. Brookes.

Sailor, W., & Taman, T. (1972). Stimulus factors in the training of prepositional usage in three autistic children. *Journal of Applied Behavior Analysis, 5,* 183–190.

Santarcangelo, S., Dyer, K., & Luce, S. C. (1987). Generalized reduction of disruptive behavior in unsupervised settings through specific toy training. *Journal of the Association for Persons with Severe Handicaps, 12,* 38–44.

Schaeffer, B. (1980). Spontaneous language through signed speech. In R. L. Schiefelbusch (Ed.), *Nonspeech language and communication* (pp. 421–446). Baltimore: University Park Press.

Schaeffer, B, Kollinzas, G., Musil, A., & McDowell, P. (1977). Spontaneous verbal language for autistic children through signed speech. *Sign Language Studies, 17,* 287–328.

Schain, R. J., & Yannet, H. (1960). Infantile autism: An analysis of 50 cases and a consideration of certain neurophysiologic concepts. *Journal of Pediatrics, 57,* 560–567.

Schleien, S. J., Mustonen, T., & Rynders, J. E. (1995). Participation of children with autism and nondisabled peers in a cooperatively structured community art program. *Journal of Autism and Developmental Disorders, 25,* 397–413.

Schopler, E., & Mesibov, G. B. (1984). *The effects of autism on the family.* New York: Plenum.

Schreibman, L. (1975). Effects of within-stimulus and extra-stimulus prompting on discrimination learning in autistic children. *Journal of Applied Behavior Analysis, 8,* 91–112.

Schreibman, L. (1988). *Autism.* Newbury Park, CA: Sage.

Schreibman, L., & Carr, E. G. (1978). Elimination of echolalic responding to questions through the training of a generalized verbal response. *Journal of Applied Behavior analysis, 11,* 453–463.

Schriebman, L., Koegel, R.L., Mills, D.L., & Burke, J.C. (1984). Training parent–child interactions. In E. Schopler & G. Mesibov (Eds.), *The effects of autism on the family* (pp. 187–205). New York: Plenum Press.

Schreibman, L., O'Neill, R. E., & Koegel, R. L. (1983). Behavioral training for siblings of autistic children. *Journal of Applied Behavior Analysis, 16,* 129–138.

Shafer, M. S., Egel, A. L., & Neef, N. A. (1984). Training mildly handicapped peers to facilitate changes in the social interaction skills of autistic children. *Journal of Applied Behavior Analysis, 17,* 461–476.

Shane, H. C. (1981). Decision-making in early augmentative communication system use. In R. L. Schiefelbusch & D. D. Bricker (Eds.), *Early language: Acquisition* (pp. 389–425). Baltimore: University Park Press.

Shane, H. C. (1994). *Facilitated communication: The clinical and social phenomenon.* San Diego: Singular Press.

Sheinkopf, S. J., & Siegel, B. (in press). Home based behavioral treatment of young children with autism. *Journal of Autism and Developmental Disorders, 28,* 15–23.

Shook, G. L., & Favell, J. E. (1996). Identifying qualified professionals in behavior analysis. In C. Maurice, G. Green, & S. C. Luce (Eds.), *Behavioral intervention for young children with autism* (pp. 221–229). Austin, TX: Pro-Ed.

Sigman, M., & Ungerer, J. (1981). Sensorimotor skills and language comprehension in autistic children. *Journal of Abnormal Child Psychology, 9,* 149–165.

Simeonsson, R. J., Olley, J. G., & Rosenthal, S. L. (1987). Early intervention for children with autism. In M. J. Guralnick & F. C. Bennett (Eds.), *The effectiveness of early intervention for at-risk and handicapped children* (pp. 275–296). New York: Academic Press.

Skinner, B. F. (1981). Selection by consequences. *Science, 213,* 501–504.

Smalley, S. L., & Collins, F. (1996). Brief Report: Genetic, prenatal, and immunologic factors. *Journal of Autism and Developmental Disorders, 26,* 195–198.

Smith, R. G., Iwata, B. A., Goh, H. L., & Shore, B. A. (1995). Analysis of establishing operations for self-injury maintained by escape. *Journal of Applied Behavior Analysis, 2–8,* 515–535.

Smith, T. (1993). Autism. In T. R. Giles (Ed.), *Effective psychotherapies* (pp. 107–133). New York: Plenum.

Smith, T. (1996). Are other treatments effective? In C. Maurice, G. Green, & S. C. Luce (Eds.), *Behavioral intervention for young children with autism* (pp. 45–59). Austin, TX: Pro-Ed.

Smith, T., Klevstrand, M., & Lovaas, O. I. (1995). Behavioral treatment of Rett's Disorder: Ineffectiveness in three cases. *American Journal on Mental Retardation, 100,* 317–322.

Snow, M., Hertzig, M., & Shapiro, T. (1987). Expressions of emotion in young autistic children. *Journal of the American Academy of Child and Adolescent Psychiatry, 26,* 836–838.

Snyder, L., Apolloni, T., & Cooke, T. (1977). Integrated settings at the early childhood level: The role of nonretarded peers. *Exceptional Children, 43,* 262–269.

Sodian, B., & Frith, U. (1992). Deception and sabotage in autistic, retarded, and normal children. *Journal of Child Psychology and Psychiatry, 33,* 591–606.

Sparrow, S., Balla, D., & Cicchetti, D. (1984). *Vineland Adaptive Behavior Scales.* Circle Pines, MN: American Guidance Service.

Sparrow, S. S., Rescorla, L. A., Provence, S., Condon, S. O., Goudreau, D., & Cicchetti, D. V. (1986). Follow-up of "atypical" children: A brief report. *Journal of the American Academy of Child Psychiatry, 25,* 181–185.

Spitz, H. H. (1996). Comment on Donnellan's review of Shane's (1994) Facilitated Communication: The Clinical and Social Phenomenon. *American Journal on Mental Retardation, 101,* 96–100.

Stahmer, A. C., & Schreibman, L. (1992,). Teaching children with autism appropriate play in unsupervised environments using a self-management treatment package. *Journal of Applied Behavior Analysis, 25,* 447–459.

Steege, M. W., Wacker, D. P., Berg, W. K., Cigrand, K. K., & Cooper, L. J. (1989). The use of behavioral assessment to prescribe and evaluate treatments for severely handicapped children. *Journal of Applied Behavior Analysis, 22,* 23–33.

Stevens-Long, J., & Rasmussen, M. (1974). The acquisition of simple and compound sentence structure in an autistic child. *Journal of Applied Behavior Analysis, 7,* 473–479.

Stokes, T. F., & Baer, D. M. (1977). An implicit technology of generalization. *Journal of Applied Behavior Analysis, 10,* 349–367.

Strain, P. S. (1977). Effects of peer social initiations on withdrawn preschool children: Some training and generalizion effects. *Journal of Abnormal Child Psvchology, 5,* 445–455.

Strain, P. S. (1980). Social behavior programming with severely handicapped and autistic children. In B. Wilcox & A. Thompson (Eds.), *Critical issues in educating autistic children and youth* (pp. 179–206). Washington: U. S. Department of Education, office of Special Education.

Strain, P. S. (1983). Generalization of autistic children's social behavior change: Effects of developmentally integrated and segregated settings. *Analysis and Intervention in Developmental Disabilities, 3,* 23–34.

Strain, P. S., & Cordisco, L. K. (1994). LEAP Preschool. In S. L. Harris & J. S. Handleman (Eds.), *Preschool education for children with autism* (pp. 225–244). Austin, TX: Pro-Ed.

Strain, P. S., Hoyson, M. H., & Jamieson, B. J. (1985). Normally developing preschoolers as intervention agents for autistic-like children: Effects on class deportment and social interactions. *Journal of the Division for Early Childhood, 9,* 105–115.

Strain, P. S., Kerr, M. M., & Ragland, E. U. (1979). Effects of peer-mediated social initiations and prompting/reinforcement procedures on the social behavior of autistic children. *Journal of Autism and Developmental Disorders, 9,* 41–54.

Strain, P. S., & Odom, S. L. (1986). Peer-social initiations: Effective intervention for social skills development of exceptional children. *Exceptional Children, 52,* 543–552.

Strain, P. S., Shores, R. E., & Tino, M. A. (1977). Effects of peer initiations on the social behavior of withdrawn preschool children. *Journal of Applied Behavior Analysis, 10,* 289–298.

Striefel, S., Bryan, K. S., & Aikins, D. A. (1974). Transfer of stimulus control from motor to verbal stimuli. *Journal of Applied Behavior Analysis, 7,* 123–135.

Striefel, S., & Wetherby, B. (1973). Instruction-following behavior of a retarded child and its controlling stimuli. *Journal of Applied Behavior Analysis, 6,* 663–670.

Striefel, S., Wetherby, B., & Karlan, G. (1978). Developing generalized instruction-following behavior in severely retarded people. In C. E. Meyers (Ed.), *Quality of life in severely and profoundly mentally retarded people* (pp. 267–326). Washington: American Association on Mental Deficiency.

Szatmari, P., Tuff, L., Finlayson, A. J., & Bartolucci, G. (1990). Asperger's syndrome and autism: Neurocognitive aspects. *Journal of the American Academy of Child and Adolescent Psychiatry, 29,* 130–136.

Szurek, S. A. (1956). Psychotic episodes and psychotic maldevelopment. *American Journal of Orthopedic Psychiatry, 26,* 519–543.

Tager-Flusberg, H. (1989). A psycholinguistic perspective on language development in the autistic child. In G. Dawson (Ed.), *Autism: Nature, diagnosis, and treatment* (pp. 92–115). New York: Guilford.

Taylor, B., & Harris, S. L. (1995). Teaching children with autism to seek information: Acquisition of novel information and generalization of responding. *Journal of Applied Behavior Analysis, 28,* 3–14.

Taylor, J., & Carr, E. G. (1992). Severe problem behaviors related to social interaction: I. Attention seeking and social avoidance. *Behavior Modification, 16,* 305–335.

Taylor, J., Ekdahl, M., Romanczyk, R. G., & Miller, M. (1994). Escape behavior in task situations: Task versus social antecedents. *Journal of Autism and Developmental Disorders, 24,* 331–344.

Thelen, E. (1979). Rhythmical stereotypies in normal human infants. *Animal Behavior, 27,* 699–715.

Tiegerman, E., & Primavera, L. (1981). Object manipulation: An interactional strategy with autistic children. *Journal of Autism and Developmental Disorders, 11,* 427–438.

Tiegerinan, E., & Primavera, L. H. (1984). Imitating the autistic child: Facilitating communicative gaze behavior. *Journal of Autism and Developmental Disorders, 14,* 27–38.

Touchette, P. E., MacDonald, R. F., & Langer, S. N. (1985). A scatter plot for identifying stimulus control of problem behavior. *Journal of Applied Behavior Analysis, 18,* 343–351.

Tryon, A. S., & Keane, S. P. (1986). Promoting imitative play through generalized observational learning in autisticlike children. *Journal of Abnormal Child Psychology, 14,* 537–549.

Tubbs, V. K. (1966). Types of linguistic disability in psychotic children. *Journal of Mental Deficiency Research, 10,* 230–240.

Turnbull, A. P., Blue-Banning, M., Behr, S., & Kerns, G. (1986). Family research and intervention: A value and ethical examination. In P. R. Dokecki & R. M. Zaner (Eds.), *Ethics of dealing with persons with severe handicaps* (pp. 119–140). Baltimore: Paul H. Brookes.

Turnbull, A. P., & Turnbull, H. R. (1996). Group action planning as a strategy for providing comprehensive family support. In L. K. Koegel, R. L. Koegel, & G. Dunlap (Eds.), *Positive behavioral support: Including people with difficult behavior in the community* (pp. 99–114). Baltimore: Paul H. Brookes.

Volkmar, F. R. (1986). Compliance, noncompliance, and negativism. In E. Schopler & G. B. Mesibov (Eds.), *Social behavior in autism* (pp. 171–188). New York: Plenum Press.

Volkmar, F. R., Bregman, J., Cohen, D. J., & Cicchetti, D. V. (1988). DSM-III and DSM-III-R diagnosis of autism. *American Journal of Psychiatry, 145,* 1404–1408.

Volkmar, F. R., Klin, A., Siegel, B., Szatmari, P., Lord, C., Campbell, M., Freeman, B. J., Cicchetti, D. V., Rutter, M., Kline, W., Buitelaar, J., Hattab, Y., Fombonne, E., Fuentes, J., Werry, J., Stone, W., Kerbeshian, J., Hoshino, Y., Bregman, J., Loveland, K., Szymanski, L., & Towbin, K. (1994). Field trial for Autistic Disorder in DSM-IV. *American Journal of Psychiatry, 151,* 1361–1367.

Volkmar, F. R., Paul, R., & Cohen, D. J. (1985). The use of "Asperger's syndrome." *Journal of Autism and Developmental Disorders, 15,* 437–439.

Volkmar, F. R., Sparrow, S. S., Goudreau, D., Cicchetti, D. V., Paul, R., & Cohen, D. J. (1987). Social deficits in autism: An operational approach using the Vineland Adaptive Behavior Scales. *Journal of the American Academy of Child and Adolescent Psychiatry, 26,* 156–161.

Vollmer, T. R., Marcus, B. A., Ringdahl, J. E., & Roane, H. S. (1995). Progressing from brief assess-

ments to extended experimental analyses in the evaluation of aberrant behavior. *Journal of Applied Behavior Analysis, 28,* 561–576.

Wacker, D. P., Harding, J., Cooper, L. J., Derby, K. M., Peck, S., Asmus, J., Berg, W. K., & Brown, K. A. (1996). The effects of meal schedule and quantity on problematic behavior. *Journal of Applied Behavior Analysis, 29,* 79–87.

Wacker, D. P., Peck, S., Derby, K. M., Berg, W., & Harding, J. (1996). Developing long-term reciprocal interactions between parents and their young children with problematic behavior. In L. K. Koegel, R. L. Koegel, & G. Dunlap (Eds.), *Positive behavioral support: Including people with difficult behavior in the community* (pp. 51–80). Baltimore: Paul H. Brookes.

Wacker, D. P., Steege, M. W., Northup, J., Sasso, G., Berg, W., Reimers, T., Cooper, L., Cigrand, K., & Donn, L. (1990). A component analysis of functional communication training across three topographies of severe behavior problems. *Journal of Applied Behavior Analysis, 23,* 417–429.

Wahler, R. G., & Fox, J. J. (1981). Setting events in applied behavior analysis: Toward a conceptual and methodological expansion. *Journal of Applied Behavior Analysis, 14,* 327–338.

Waterhouse, L. (1988). Speculations on the neuroanatomical substrate of special talents. In L. Obler & D. Fein (Eds.), *The exceptional brain* (pp. 493–512). New York: Guilford Press.

Waterhouse, L., Fein, D., & Modahl, C. (1996). Neurofunctional mechanisms in autism. *Psychological Review, 103,* 457–489.

Weeks, M., & Gaylord-Ross, R. (1981). Task difficulty and aberrant behavior in severely handicapped students. *Journal of Applied Behavior Analysis, 14,* 449–463.

Wetzel, R. J., Baker, J., Roney, M., & Martin, M. (1966). An operant analysis of child–family interaction: Outpatient treatment of autistic behaviour. *Behaviour Research and Therapy, 4,* 169–177.

Williams, J. A., Koegel, R. L., & Egel, A. L. (1981). Response–reinforcer relationships and improved learning in autistic children. *Journal of Applied Behavior Analysis, 14,* 53–60.

Wing, L. (1981a). Language, social, and cognitive impairments in autism and severe mental retardation. *Journal of Autism and Developmental Disorders, 11,* 31–44.

Wing, L. (1981b). Asperger's syndrome: A clinical account. *Psychological Medicine, 11,* 115–129.

Wing, L. (1991). The relationship between Asperger's syndrome and Kanner's autism. In U. Frith (Ed.), *Autism and Asperger syndrome* (pp. 93–121). New York: Cambridge University Press.

Wing, L. (1993). The definition and prevalence of autism: A review. *European Child and Adolescent Psychiatry, 2,* 61–74.

Wing, L., & Attwood, A. (1987). Syndromes of autism and atypical development. In D. J. Cohen & A. M. Donnellan (Eds.), *Handbook of autism and pervasive developmental disorders* (pp. 3–19). New York: Wiley.

Wing, L., & Gould, J. (1979). Severe impairments of social interaction and associated abnormalities in children: Epidemiology and classification. *Journal of Autism and Developmental Disorders, 9,* 11–29.

Witt, J. C., & Wacker, D. P. (1981). Teaching children to respond to auditory directives: An evaluation of two procedures. *Behavior Research of Severe Developmental Disabilities, 2,* 175–189.

Wolf, L. C., Noh, S., Fisman, S. N., & Speechley, M. (1989). Brief report: Psychological effects of parenting stress on parents of autistic children. *Journal of Autism and Developmental Disorders, 19,* 157–166.

Wolff, S., & Barlow, A. (1979). Schizoid personality in childhood: A comparative study of schizoid, autistic and normal children. *Journal of Child Psychology and Psychiatry, 20,* 29–46.

World Health Organization. (1992). *The ICD-10 classification of mental and behavioral disorders: Clinical descriptions and diagnostic guidelines.* Geneva: Author.

Young, J. M., Krantz, P. J., McClannahan, L. E., & Poulson, C. L. (1994). Generalized imitation and response-class formation in children with autism. *Journal of Applied Behavior Analysis, 27,* 685–698.

Zane, T., Handen, B. L., Mason, S. A., & Geffin, C. (1984). Teaching symbol identification: A comparison between standard prompting and intervening response procedures. *Analysis and Intervention in Developmental Disabilities, 4,* 367–377.

Zanolli, K., Daggett, J., & Adams, T. (1996). Teaching preschool age autistic children to make spontaneous initiations to peers using priming. *Journal of Autism and Developmental Disorders, 26,* 407–422.

Zarcone, J. R., Iwata, B. A., Smith, R. G., Mazaleski, J. L., & Lerman, D. C. (1994). Reemergence and extinction of self-injurious escape behavior during stimulus (instructional) fading. *Journal of Applied Behavior Analysis, 27,* 307–316.

Zilbovicius, M., Garreau, B., Samson, Y., Remy, P., Barthelemy, C., Syrota, A., & Lelord, G. (1995). Delayed maturation of frontal cortex in childhood autism. *American Journal of Psychiatry, 152,* 248–252.

CHAPTER 9

Learning Disabilities

G. Reid Lyon

National Institute of Child Health and Human Development
National Institutes of Health

Laurie E. Cutting

Johns Hopkins University School of Medicine

An extraordinarily complex task confronting researchers, clinicians, and teachers is to identify and understand the instructional factors and decisions that should be considered when teaching children with learning disabilities (LDs). Frequently, youngsters with LDs do not process information in a manner that allows them to profit from typical classroom instruction, even though the children are as intelligent as their classmates and have, at least initially, similar opportunities to learn. As such, the importance of instruction and treatment is central to the concept of LDs as handicapping conditions. Clearly, from a clinical standpoint, the ecological and clinical validity of the diagnosis of an LD is linked directly to its ability to inform treatment and instructional decisions. Within this context, the primary goal of this chapter is to identify and discuss what we believe are critical issues in the treatment of LDs.

Before we embark upon this examination, several themes that guide the organization of this chapter should be summarized. First, the construct of LDs and the many definitions that serve as conceptual frameworks for the diagnosis and treatment of LDs continue to be frequently misunderstood. Indeed, even a cursory

perusal of the literature relevant to the history and current status of LDs reveals that the field has been, and continues to be, beset by pervasive disagreements about the definition of LDs, diagnostic criteria, assessment practices, treatment procedures, and educational policies (Lyon, 1996a). During the past decade, and particularly within the past 5 years, substantial progress has been made in developing a reliable and valid classification system for at least some specific types of LDs (e.g., reading disability) (Lyon, 1995a, 1996a, 1996b). To understand advances in the treatment of LDs, one must understand the field's struggle for a scientific foundation. Accordingly, a section of this chapter addresses the field's transition from clinical intuition to clinical science.

Second, in order to fully understand the diversity of treatment concepts and methods for each type of LD, one must appreciate that they emanate from a wide range of frameworks, models, and theories. Specifically, issues relevant to the purposes of treatment, to the ways in which assessments should be conducted and related to treatment, and to the validity of different treatment protocols can be best addressed by identifying the historical and contemporary models and theories that guide instructional decision making for individuals with LDs (Lyon & Moats, 1988). Thus, in a subsequent section of the chapter we focus on selected schools of thought that serve as a basis for contemporary treatment methods.

Third, the conduct of treatment research with individuals with LDs is both complex and extremely labor-intensive. Within the context of this complexity, several factors have consistently impeded attempts to study the effectiveness and the efficacy of different interventions in a well-controlled manner. For future research and treatment efforts to be as productive and informative as possible, these factors need to be specifically identified and discussed. Thus, a section of this chapter is devoted to methodological limitations that have reduced the value of intervention research.

Fourth, LDs are not a single disorder; rather, they constitute a general category of disabilities in a number of specific domains. Thus, for clarity, we have elected to examine research relevant to the prevention and/or remediation of disabilities in three domains—reading, written language, and mathematics—and have organized the remainder of the chapter for this purpose. These domains have been selected both because of their prominence in current definitions of LDs, and because many children and adults are identified as having LDs due to unexpected underachievement or atypical development in these areas.

Finally, some caveats are in order. Given the enormous volume and complexity of literature on topics associated with treatment and instruction, our review of relevant research is necessarily selective rather than exhaustive. For example, given space limitations, it was not possible to address research related to intervention for disorders of attention or for social and emotional difficulties—areas of development that are clearly problematic for many children with LDs. (In any case, these types of problems are discussed in other chapters of this book.) Moreover, although various theoretical and conceptual models related to treatment are reviewed, as are specific treatment methods, we do not view the work emanating from these different sources and perspectives as necessarily contradictory. Rather, thoughtful integration of cognitive/linguistic, behavioral/task-analytic, neuropsychological, and constructivist perspectives, for instance, could ultimately result in efficacious treatment for individuals with different types of LDs. Lastly, the literature is replete with claims for instructional and treatment methods that are based upon subjective, nonreplicated clinical reports, testimonial information, and anecdotal statements. For purposes of brevity and clarity, we have limited our discussion to methods and approaches that have some empirical basis. However, the reader should note that wide variation exists among studies of the different treatment/teaching methods we have selected for discussion.

HISTORY OF THE FIELD: THE PASSAGE FROM CLINICAL INTUITION TO CLINICAL SCIENCE

Since its recognition as a federally designated handicapping condition in 1968, the field of learning disabilities now represents approximately one-half of all children receiving special education nationally (U. S. Department of Education, 1989). Yet LDs have traditionally been among the least understood and most debated disabling conditions that affect children (Lyon, 1996a; Moats & Lyon, 1993).

Again, by way of background, LDs are not a single disorder but a general category composed of specific disabilities. These are usually organized into seven areas: (1) receptive language (listening), (2) expressive language (speaking), (3) basic reading skills (decoding and word recognition), (4) reading comprehension, (5) written expression, (6) arithmetic calculation, and (7) mathematics reasoning. These separate types of LDs frequently co-occur with one another, and also with deficits in social skills, emotional disorders, and disorders of attention. The reader should note that LDs are not synonymous with reading disability (dyslexia), although they are frequently misinterpreted as such (Lyon, 1995a). However, most of the available information concerning LDs relates to reading disabilities (Lyon, 1996a, 1996b), and the majority of children with LDs have their primary deficits in reading (Lerner, 1989).

The field of LDs was not born primarily of scientific inquiry, but developed over time to meet the clinical and educational needs of children that were not being addressed by existing policies and programs (see Lyon, 1996a, 1996b; Moats & Lyon, 1993). Specifically, the study of LDs was initiated because of the practical need (1) to understand individual differences among children and adults who displayed *specific* deficits in spoken and written language while maintaining integrity in general intellectual functioning; and (2) to provide services to students who were not being adequately served by the general educational system (Moats & Lyon, 1993; Zigmond, 1993; Torgesen, 1991).

In the early 1960s, special education services were simply not provided to children who manifested learning difficulties but who were average or above in general intellectual abilities. These children did not manifest behaviors or characteristics typically associated with mentally retarded, emotionally disturbed, physically impaired, visually impaired, or hearing-impaired individuals. Thus they were overlooked or excluded from basic special educational services. Because of this void, parents and educators, under the leadership of Samuel Kirk, established the Association for Children with Learning Disabilities (ACLD) and convened its first meeting in Chicago in 1963. At this meeting, a rigorous advocacy agenda was developed to promote recognition of LDs as handicapping conditions. At the same time, a clinical and scientific focus was identified that reflected the views of several disciplines with a tradition of interest in learning problems—neurology, psychology, remedial education, and speech–language pathology. Pioneers within each of these disciplines promoted theories of disability, designed tests presumed to measure information-processing dysfunctions, and developed remedial techniques that were appealing because they were logically designed to address deficits in learning (Moats & Lyon, 1993; Torgesen, 1991).

The field progressed rapidly through many developmental stages after the initial formal recognition of LDs as handicapping conditions in 1968. These historical trends and stages have been summarized in several sources (Doris, 1993; Hallahan & Cruickshank, 1973; Kavale & Forness, 1985; Myers & Hammill, 1990), and these should be consulted for more comprehensive reviews. In brief, the diagnostic concept of LDs gained significant momentum during the 1970s and 1980s. The proliferation of children diagnosed as having LDs during these two decades was related to multiple factors. First, it was clear that many children had difficulties in learning to read, to write, and to understand and apply mathematics concepts at a rate or in a manner commensurate with age and grade expectations. Thus the newly developed category provided such youngsters a clinical "home" and eligibility for special education services. Second, it became clear that receiving a diagnosis of an LD on the basis of deficits in a specific area

of academic achievement did not imply low intelligence, behavioral difficulties, or sensory handicaps. On the contrary, children with LDs manifest difficulties in learning *despite* having average to above-average intelligence, and they typically also have intact vision, hearing, and emotional status. Within this context, the fact that children with LDs display normal intelligence gave parents and teachers hope that difficulties in learning to read, write, calculate, or reason mathematically could be surmounted if only the right arrangement of instructional conditions and settings could be identified. Third, it emerged that an LD label is not a stigmatizing one. Parents and teachers were (and are) certainly more comfortable with the term than with etiologically based labels such as "brain injury," "minimal brain dysfunction," or "perceptual handicap" (see Lyon, 1996a).

The fact that LDs were initially and formally identified as handicapping conditions on the basis of advocacy rather than systematic scientific inquiry is certainly not uncommon in the domains of psychology, medicine, education, or public policy. In fact, in the United States the majority of scientific advances are typically stimulated by vocal critics of the educational or medical status quo. Indeed, it is rare that a psychological condition, disease, or educational problem is afforded attention until political forces are mobilized by parents, patients, or victims expressing their concerns about the quality of life to their elected officials. Clearly this was the case in the field of LDs, where parents and child advocates successfully lobbied Congress to enact legislation in 1970 via the Education of the Handicapped Act (P. L. 91–230), which authorized funds for research and training programs to address the needs of children with specific LDs (Doris, 1993).

DEFINITIONAL ISSUES

A fundamental historical assumption underlying the construct of LDs is that the academic difficulties manifested by individuals with LDs are *unexpected*, given the often recognized disparity between such difficulties and other factors (such as relatively robust intellectual capabilities, opportunities to learn, and freedom from extreme social disadvantage or emotional disturbance). In addition, traditional definitions of LDs provide statements that emphasize what the condition is not, rather than what it is. For example, the statutory definition of LDs contained in the

Individuals with Disabilities Education Act (IDEA) of 1991 is as follows:

> The term "specific learning disability" means a disorder in one or more of the basic psychological processes involved in understanding or in using language, spoken or written, which may manifest itself in an imperfect ability to listen, speak, read, write, spell, or to do mathematical calculations. The term includes such conditions as perceptual handicaps, brain injury, minimal brain dysfunction, dyslexia, and developmental aphasia. The term does not include children who have learning disabilities which are primarily the result of visual, hearing, or motor handicaps, or mental retardation, or emotional disturbance, or of environmental, cultural, or economic disadvantage. (§ 300)

As can be seen, an important part of the definition of LDs under the IDEA is its use of exclusionary language. Specifically, LDs cannot be attributed primarily to mental retardation, emotional disturbance, cultural differences, or environmental or economic disadvantage. This aspect of the definition clearly reflects the historical underpinnings of the category that were discussed earlier. Thus, the concept of LDs that is embedded in federal law focuses on the notion of a discrepancy between a child's academic achievement and his or her capacity and opportunity to learn. More succinctly, Zigmond (1993) notes that typical definitions of "learning disabilities reflect unexpected learning problems in a seemingly capable child" (p. 254).

Despite the significant role that a definition should play in the scientific and clinical understanding of LDs, the federal definition currently encased in law is far too vague and ambiguous, from a classification perspective, to provide clear guidance for clinical and research practices (Fletcher & Morris, 1986; Lyon, 1996a). As can be seen above, the definition fails to provide *specific* and objective guidelines and inclusionary criteria for distinguishing individuals with LDs from those with other primary handicaps or generalized learning difficulties (for discussions of this issue see Lyon, 1996a, 1996b; Moats & Lyon, 1993). Recent attempts to tighten the definition have not fared appreciably better, as can be seen in the revised definition produced by the National Joint Committee on Learning Disabilities (NJCLD, 1988):

> Learning disabilities is a general term that refers to a heterogeneous group of disorders manifested by significant difficulties in the acquisition and use of listening, speaking, reading, writing, reasoning, or mathematical abilities. These disorders are intrinsic to the individual, presumed to be due to central nervous system dysfunction, and may occur across the life span. Problems in self-regulatory behaviors, social perception, and social interaction may exist with learning disabilities but do not by themselves constitute a learning disability. Although learning disabilities may occur concomitantly with other handicapping conditions (for example, sensory impairment, mental retardation, serious emotional disturbance) or with extrinsic influences (such as cultural differences, insufficient or inappropriate instruction), they are not the result of those conditions or influences. (p. 1)

On the positive side, the NJCLD definition reflects consensus on the concept of LDs in clinical, educational, and political arenas; it eliminates the word "children"; and it adopts a life span perspective that is more consistent with the wide age range of individuals in need of identification and services in adulthood and in occupational/vocational settings (Hammill, 1990). Unfortunately, this revised definition falls short of providing consistent inclusionary criteria for classification.

The negative consequences of inadequate definitions are serious. Clinically, the criteria for assigning support services for individuals with LDs are typically not clear or justified by research findings; this situation leads to numerous inequities in who does and who does not receive specialized services and programs. Similarly, vague descriptions of the nature of LDs provided in current definitions fail to provide guidance about which specific cognitive and academic skills are impaired and require remedial attention. Unfortunately, the lack of emphasis in current definitions on the salience of specific academic, cognitive, and information-processing skills necessary for learning contributes to inadequate training for professionals concerned with children's school performance (see Moats, 1994a; Moats & Lyon, 1996).

Concerns about the limitations of these types of omnibus exclusionary definitions have prompted many scholars to call for a moratorium on the development of broad definitions, at least for research purposes. For example, Stanovich (1993) has stated the following:

> Scientific investigations of some generically defined entity called "learning disability" simply

makes little sense given what we already know about heterogeneity across various learning domains. Research investigations must define groups specifically in terms of the domain of deficit (reading disability, arithmetic disability. (p. 273)

In line with this suggestion, recent attempts to develop definitions for specific types of LDs have been made. For example, a working group composed of clinicians and scientists from universities within the United States and Canada, representatives from the Orton Dyslexia Society, and representatives from the National Institute of Child Health and Human Development (NICHD) recently constructed a new definition of dyslexia (reading disability) that attempts to reduce the exclusionary language inherent in all definitions of LDs and dyslexia, and to define dyslexia using the most current and valid research evidence available at this time:

> Dyslexia is one of several distinct learning disabilities. It is a specific language-based disorder of constitutional origin characterized by difficulties in single word decoding, usually reflecting insufficient phonological processing. These difficulties in single word decoding are often unexpected in relation to age and other cognitive and academic abilities; they are not the result of generalized developmental disability or sensory impairment. Dyslexia is manifest by variable difficulty with different forms of language, often including, in addition to problems with reading, a conspicuous problem with acquiring proficiency in writing and spelling. (Lyon, 1995a, p. 9)

The construction of this new definition provides an example of how research can inform policy and practice, and provides one example of how the field of LDs is beginning to move from a context of clinical intuition toward one of clinical science. Note that in contrast to the general definitions of LDs, the Orton research-based definition is composed of specific, data-based, *inclusionary* statements that can be operationalized.

It goes without saying that the field of LDs is a long way away from constructing inclusionary definitions for the different types of academic disabilities that are included in typical general exclusionary definitions, such as the first two definitions given above. The domain-specific definition developed for dyslexia (reading disability)—the most prevalent type of the different

LDs—represents a first attempt at constructing a classification system that identifies different types of LDs as well as the distinctions and interrelationships among these types and other developmental disorders (Lyon, 1995a, 1996a).

Despite the lengthy time that it has taken the scientific community to generate more parsimonious research-based definitions and coherent classification systems for specific types of LDs, a number of conceptual approaches for treatment, intervention, and remediation have emerged from the clinical community over the past 25 years. These are reviewed in the next section.

CONCEPTUAL APPROACHES TO THE TREATMENT OF LEARNING DISABILITIES

The types of instructional treatment methods that are applied to individuals with LDs are influenced significantly by the conceptual approach or model that is used to formulate the rationale, purposes, and outcomes of the treatment. Researchers and clinicians differ in their views with respect to such approaches. For example, if one believes that specific academic deficits are a function of aberrant neural processing of information, then the treatment method might target the hypothesized underlying neurological substrate responsible for the deficits, in the hope that improvements in neural processing will result in improvements in the academic behavior. On the other hand, if one minimizes the role of the nervous system in understanding learning deficits, then the academic behavior itself becomes the target for treatment. Obviously, these are overly simplistic examples of complex approaches, but they indicate how approaches to treatment are influenced by conceptual and/or theoretical points of view. In point of fact, different conceptual approaches to the treatment of individuals with LDs are more easily discussed at a general level, but lose their explanatory power when one attempts to employ them to generate specific instructional methods (see Lyon & Moats, 1988).

Historical Treatment Perspectives

When LDs were first recognized in the early 1960s as handicapping conditions, and the field of LDs became a category of special education, the treatment approaches prominent at that time were reflected in three conceptual models (Bateman, 1965; Hallahan, Kauffman, & Lloyd, 1996): (1) the medical or etiological model; (2) the psychoeducational or diagnostic–remedial model; and (3) the behavioral or task-analytic model (Figure 9.1).

The Medical or Etiological Model

Medically oriented approaches viewed LDs as overt symptoms of underlying biological pathology. The inferred pathology was conceptualized by different theorists as affecting, for example, language development, perceptual systems, perceptual–motor organization, and ocular–motor functioning (see Mann, 1979, for a review). For example, deficits in oral language could be described as a primary language disorder due to organic impairment resulting from putative anoxia. Recommended treatment might involve patterning exercises to "stimulate" brain regions thought to subserve the language process in question.

It is difficult, if not impossible, to find evidence (beyond testimonials and anecdotal reports) to support the assumptions, treatment methods, and stated outcomes associated with these early medical or etiological approaches (Lyon & Moats, 1988). Given the noticeable lack of validity for such methods, the use of medical or etiological approaches to guide treatment has declined substantially over the years.

The Psychoeducational or Diagnostic–Remedial Model

In the main, proponents of psychoeducational models of LDs interpreted academic deficits as reflecting aberrations in the ability to perceive, integrate, and remember auditory and visual information, associated with the development of listening, speaking, reading, and writing behaviors (Frostig, 1967; Kirk & Kirk, 1971). Assessment procedures were developed to identify specific strengths and weaknesses in auditory and visual processes hypothesized to be related to academic functioning, and this information was considered in the process known as "clinical teaching." In contrast to the medical model, the psychoeducational approach advocated teaching academic skills as well as information-processing abilities (not underlying biological processes), by taking into account the student's modality preferences or areas of information-processing strength (visual, auditory, and/or kinesthetic), the nature of the content to be learned (verbal or nonverbal), and the response required (oral or written).

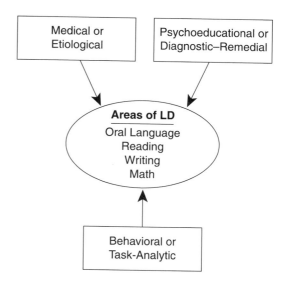

FIGURE 9.1. Historical approaches to the treatment of LDs.

Psychoeducational or diagnostic–remedial approaches have not received a great deal of support in the scientific literature (Lyon & Moats, 1988). There is little evidence that such approaches have incorporated the essential elements of learning, and the notions of modality preferences and learning styles have been reported to be conceptually and empirically weak (Foorman, 1995; Liberman & Shankweiler, 1985). In addition, many of the assessment measures designed to evaluate auditory and visual processing characteristics and other learning styles were flawed with respect to reliability and validity, and were related only minimally to academic content (Coles, 1978). It is possible that, given time, reformulations of psychoeducational models will inspire confidence in their use in determining what and how to teach individuals with LDs.

The Behavioral or Task-Analytic Model

In significant contrast to medical and psychoeducational models and approaches, behavioral approaches have conceptualized LDs as resulting from a mismatch between enabling behaviors and the characteristics of the academic task (Lyon & Moats, 1988). There is no assumption of underlying pathology or information-processing deficiency. Instead, assessment and instructional activities are directed toward evaluating academic skill deficits and modifying them with techniques derived from learning theory. The major assumption guiding this approach is that academic content consists of skill hierarchies, and that complex academic behaviors such as reading, writing, and mathematics can be task-analyzed into component subskills. Direct instruction is then applied to insure that all prerequisite subskills are mastered and the target behaviors taught.

Reviews of the effectiveness of behavioral interventions with individuals with LDs have generally indicated favorable results with respect to increasing attentional and academic skills (see Gadow, Torgesen, & Dahlem, 1985). However, there has been some concern that academic skills acquired through the application of behavioral procedures do not generalize to contexts not incorporated in the training paradigm, and that some behavioral interventions are neither practical nor cost-effective (Myers & Hammill, 1990). In addition, as Torgesen (1986) has pointed out, early behavioral models have typically provided no conceptual framework for the ultimate understanding of individual differences in cognitive processing or neurological functioning, and this could limit our ultimate understanding of why certain teaching procedures succeed or fail with particular learners.

As we discuss next, these three historical approaches to the assessment and treatment of children with LDs have, despite their stated shortcomings, contributed substantially to the intervention models that are in use today. This is particularly true of behavioral approaches to intervention, which continue to demonstrate efficacy with specific types of academic deficits.

Contemporary Perspectives

A review of the current literature relevant to the treatment of LDs indicates that a number of approaches have evolved to guide instruction. The approaches include cognitive, cognitive-behavioral, task-analytic, neuropsychological, and constructivist models (Figure 9.2). As Hallahan et al. (1996) have pointed out, the theoretical roots and emphases of these models often overlap, and they are distinguished only by their relative degree of attention to various factors.

Cognitive Models

The cognitive models that serve as frameworks for treatment and intervention today are descendants of the psychoeducational models discussed earlier. Cognitive models typically emphasize the processes involved in human thinking and are frequently referred to as "infor-

mation-processing models" (Hallahan et al., 1996). Whereas the earlier psychoeducational models focused on the reception, perception, integration, and expression of information, contemporary cognitive models address specific information-processing abilities related to such domains as memory (e.g., rehearsal), thinking (e.g., metacognition), and more specific skills (e.g., the role of phonological awareness in the development of basic reading skills).

Cognitive models are typically derived from cognitive and developmental psychology, and their views of LDs suggest that instruction should be directed toward enabling students to exercise self-conscious, deliberate, and strategically applied efforts when learning academic content (Brown & Campione, 1986). With respect to teaching an individual with an LD problem-solving behaviors, assessment procedures are designed to determine whether the student can analyze the nature of the problem, relate the nature of the problem to previous experience, devise a strategic plan for operating on the information, and monitor and adjust performance (Flavell, 1979; Hallahan et al., 1996). Instructional emphasis is then directed toward (1) increasing the learner's awareness of task demands, (2) teaching the student to employ appropriate strategies to facilitate task completion, and (3) teaching the student to monitor the success of the strategy (Lyon & Moats, 1988).

Support for the application of cognitive (e.g., metacognitive) principles to the assessment and instruction of problem-solving behaviors has accrued from studies that have characterized individuals with LDs as failing to enlist efficient, task-appropriate strategies and to orchestrate their use (Palinscar & Brown, 1987). For example, Torgesen (1987) found that poor readers were less likely than good readers to spontaneously use organization and memory strategies to aid in the grouping and subsequent recall of pictorial stimuli. However, following direct instruction in the use of categorization as a mnemonic aid, differences in recall between the groups were erased.

Similar procedures to teach students with LDs how to use existing academic skills in a strategically optimal manner, so that content information can be acquired, manipulated, stored, retrieved, and expressed, have been applied to instructional situations involving thinking and organizational skills (Borkowski & Burke, 1996; Graham & Harris, 1996), reading comprehension (Palinscar & Brown, 1987), arithmetic problem solving (Cawley & Miller, 1986); writ-

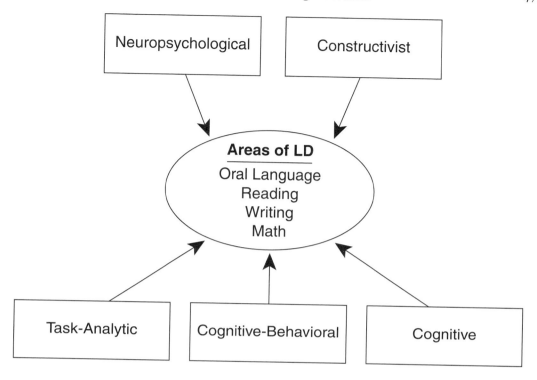

FIGURE 9.2. Current approaches to the treatment of LDs.

ten language skills (Englert, Hiebert, & Stewart, 1986; Graham & Harris, 1996), memory skills (Brown, 1975), and study skills (Wong, 1986).

A more narrow conceptualization and application of a cognitive model can be seen in studies on cognitive/linguistic factors in skill acquisition. In the main, these studies have employed language-based models, which are used primarily to conceptualize the nature of linguistic deficits associated with reading, writing, and spelling disorders (Blachman, 1991; Catts, 1986; Liberman, 1992; Liberman & Shankweiler, 1985; Lyon, 1995b; Moats, 1994b; Stanovich, 1992). More specifically, deficiencies in phonological coding and short-term memory for linguistic material have been causally linked to poor reading decoding, poor spelling, word retrieval problems, and reading comprehension difficulties (Adams, 1990; Shankweiler & Liberman, 1989; Share & Stanovich, 1995; Vellutino, Scanlon, & Tanzman, 1994). The major deficiency associated with poor reading, according to this conceptual model, is neither auditory, visual, nor kinesthetic; it is a linguistic deficit that interferes with the reader's ability to grasp the concept that words have parts (phonemes,

syllables, and morphemes), and that these are parts represented by the abstract alphabetical code.

In turn, this point of view has provided a rationale for the language-based curriculum that teaches listening, speaking, reading, and writing skills in a logical, sequential, explicit, and multisensory manner, regardless of the learner's general cognitive profile (Farnham-Diggory, 1986). More specifically, students are taught to analyze the sound structure of words, to associate and use sound–symbol relations, to generate inflections and derivational forms of words, to create syntactic transformations, and to analyze text structure (Lyon & Moats, 1988; Moats & Lyon, 1996). Intervention approaches based upon this type of cognitive/linguistic conceptualization have received a good deal of support in the research literature, particularly with respect to beginning reading development. The more current work in this area is summarized in a later section of the chapter.

Cognitive-Behavioral Models

As the name suggests, cognitive-behavioral models integrate the empirical principles of behavioral approaches with the notion that affective and cognitive states influence behavior as well. In contrast to traditional radical behavioral approaches, this view includes mental activities in the active determination of behavior. In addition, unlike the strictly cognitive approaches, cognitive-behavioral models recognize the considerable influence of contingencies of reinforcement on learning (Hallahan et al., 1996). A critical concept in the development of cognitive-behavioral approaches to intervention is "reciprocal determinism"—that is, the idea that behavior, environmental events, and internal variables such as thoughts and feeling interact with and influence one another. Within this context, the application of behavioral principles to modify external behavior is a legitimate intervention method, as is the application of strategies to alter cognitive processing and metacognitive behavior (see Meichenbaum, 1977).

In contrast to strict cognitive approaches to intervention, cognitive-behavioral interventions emphasize actively involving students in learning, particularly with respect to monitoring and directing their thinking and then measuring the outcomes of the intervention in an objective manner (Borkowski & Burke, 1996; Hallahan et al., 1996). Thus, in teaching a student word attack and word recognition skills, the student not only is exposed to the specific subskills involved, but also is taught a strategy for applying these skills to the reading process (for additional examples, see Braswell & Kendall, 1988; Whitman, Burgio, & Johnson, 1984).

A strong argument for utilizing cognitive-behavioral approaches with individuals with LDs is that multicomponent, integrative interventions are necessary to address interrelated problems of an affective, behavioral, and cognitive nature. An excellent example of such an integrated model is "self-regulated strategy development" (SRSD; see Graham & Harris, 1996), which was designed to help students (1) master higher-level cognitive processes and strategies underlying effective performance on a variety of academic tasks; (2) develop autonomous, reflective, self-regulated use of these processes and strategies; and (3) form positive attitudes about themselves and their academic capabilities. According to Graham and Harris (1996), students learn specific strategies for successfully engaging in academic tasks, in conjunction with procedures for applying and regulating the use of these strategies in the tasks, and for modifying undesirable behaviors such as impulsivity that may interfere with performance. SRSD has been employed ef-

fectively to teach strategies and self-regulation procedures in reading and mathematics (Bednarczyk & Harris, 1992; Case, Harris, & Graham, 1992), as well as writing (Graham & Harris, 1996).

Task-Analytic Models

Interventions that are guided by a task-analytic perspective have a rich theoretical and experimental history. In essence, task-analytic models place the student's actions and the environment foremost, and deemphasize underlying causal mechanisms or thought processes. Functionally, task-analytic models require that an operational learning objective first be specified, followed by a detailed description and sequencing of the specific steps necessary to achieve the objective (Hallahan et al., 1996). A number of different theories of learning have contributed to the design and implementation of task-analytic models, with stimulus control factors being emphasized by researchers studying concept learning (Carnine, Silbert, & Kameenui, 1990; Engelmann & Carnine, 1982), and reinforcement contingencies being emphasized by radical behaviorists (Bijou, 1970; Lovitt, 1967; Skinner, 1968).

Many of the intervention concepts inherent within task-analytic models are exemplified within the context of direct instruction (Rosenshine & Stevens, 1986). In the main, direct instruction consists of nine teaching functions: (1) a review of prerequisite learning; (2) a short statement of goals at the beginning of the lesson; (3) a presentation of new concepts and material in small steps, with student practice after each step; (4) the provision of clear and detailed instructions and explanations; (5) the provision of a high level of practice for all students; (6) a continual checking of student understanding of concepts through responses to teacher questions; (7) the explicit guidance of students during initial practice; (8) the provision of systematic feedback and corrections; and (9) the provision of explicit instruction and practice for seatwork exercises. Where necessary, it also includes (10) the monitoring of students during seatwork.

These direct-instruction teaching functions have been expanded and elaborated by Englemann and his colleagues at the University of Oregon (Carnine, 1980; Englemann & Carnine, 1982; Gersten, White, Falco, & Carnine, 1982). Specifically, although the Oregon group's approach is similar to that of Rosenshine and Stevens (1986) with respect to placing a strong emphasis on the teacher's behavior in the form of explicit correction, reinforcement, and provision of practice opportunities for students, Englemann and his colleagues also stress the logical analysis of the instructional communication between the teacher and the student. A central feature of this logical analysis is that instruction should provide the opportunity for only one interpretation of the concept that has been presented ("faultless instruction"). As Engelmann and Carnine (1982) have noted, if the instructional presentation fosters more than one interpretation, some students will learn the wrong one and thus prolong or inhibit learning of the correct concept. Within the teaching lesson itself, the interaction between teachers and students is structured by having lessons presented according to field-tested scripts. In the typical lesson, a teacher works with a small group of students. The teacher asks questions of the students at a rate as high as 10–12 per minute, and the students answer chorally, with the teacher then providing reinforcement or corrective feedback depending upon the accuracy of student answers.

Although the instructional principles associated with direct instruction and other task-analytic methods have been criticized because of the extensive structure provided by the teacher, the effectiveness of such methods has clearly been demonstrated both with normally achieving students (Carnine, 1980) and with students with LDs (Gersten et al., 1982). When compared to students receiving instruction via standard classroom practices, students in groups provided direct instruction typically outperform controls by at least three-fourths of a standard deviation (White, 1988).

Neuropsychological Models

Neuropsychological approaches to the instruction of individuals with LDs incorporate assessment and remediation concepts from both traditional medical and psychoeducational theories and models; they thus share some of these models' shortcomings, particularly with respect to the reliability and construct validity of assessment procedures (Brown & Campione, 1986; Lyon & Moats, 1988; Taylor, 1983) and to ecological validity (Lyon & Moats, 1988). We consider neuropsychological models to be variants of medical models, in that they stress the role of neurobiology in learning. We are addressing neuropsychological models separately in this chapter because they are chronologically more current than traditional medical models and because they emphasize remediation of the academic learning deficiencies. Neuropsychological approaches have proliferated in the last decade, commensurate with advances in the basic neurosciences.

In general, neuropsychological models and theories of LDs conceptualize learning strengths and weaknesses as manifestation of efficient and inefficient brain regions or systems (Fisk & Rourke, 1983; Obrzut & Hynd, 1983; Rourke, 1991, 1995). Within this context, instruction is designed so that intact neural systems will be exploited in bypassing the areas of dysfunction. For example, a number of researchers (see Kirby & Robinson, 1987) have extended theoretical concepts relevant to cerebral asymmetry and hemispheric specialization to explain both the information-processing and response characteristics of children with LDs. Others (see Fletcher & Morris, 1986; Lyon & Flynn, 1991) have hypothesized that LDs can result from a number of independent neurobehavioral deficiencies in information processing, thus underscoring the need to identify LD subtypes and subtype-specific interventions. Within these approaches, neuropsychological aptitudes such as simultaneous and sequential processing, linguistic (phonological, semantic, syntactic) processing, and visual–spatial reasoning capacities are considered when direct instruction of academic skills is undertaken.

Evidence to support the clinical efficacy and scientific validity of these neuropsychological approaches remains sparse. Lyon and his colleagues (see Lyon, 1985; Lyon, Moats, & Flynn, 1988) have adduced preliminary data suggesting that LDs subtypes, identified on the basis of subtype members' performance on neuropsychological tasks, differ significantly with respect to response to reading instruction. However, Lyon (1996a) and Newby and Lyon (1991) have cautioned against the overinterpretation of these data and have provided a number of guidelines for research on teaching methods for various subtypes.

Bakker and his associates (see Bakker, 1984; Bakker & Vinke, 1985) have replicated experiments wherein hemisphere-specific stimulation increased the reading capabilities of two subtypes of dyslexic children. Although Bakker's data provide some support for the practice of classifying LDs by processing subtype, the results of these experiments should be interpreted with caution. Dyslexic subjects in the Bakker and Vinke (1985) study were inadequately described with respect to marker variables, were drawn from a low-IQ school-identified population, and were not well differentiated with regard to subtypes. Furthermore, procedures with known reliability constraints (dichotic listening paradigms and patterns of oral reading errors) were used to form subtypes, which places in question the internal validity of this type of classification (Lyon & Risucci, 1988).

Despite some strides in the use of neuropsychological theories and models to guide instruction for the learning disabled, it appears premature to accept, without qualification, the validity of such practices. The valid measurement of neuropsychological aptitudes for instruction is in an embryonic stage, making the prediction of various forms of treatment extremely difficult.

Constructivist Models

Constructivist models rely heavily on the work of Piaget (see, e.g., Piaget & Inhelder, 1969) and stress, with respect to intervention and treatment, the "holistic" presentation of material to the student. A clear philosophical characteristic of constructivist models is their rejection of behavioral and task-analytic principles (Hallahan et al., 1996). Constructivists argue that academic material that is analyzed into constituent objectives is meaningless to students. The holistic perspective espoused in constructivist models is captured in this statement by Poplin (1988):

> Structuralist philosophy, constructivist theory, and holistic beliefs define the learning enterprise in opposition to reductionist behavioral learning theory and suggest that the task of schools is to help students develop new meanings in response to new experiences rather than to learn the meanings others have created. This change in the very definition of learning reveals principles of learning that beg consideration in designing classroom instruction. (p. 401)

In a more specific vein, Poplin (1988) has outlined 14 holistic/constructivist principles that should guide instruction. Some of these principles are as follows: New experiences are integrated into the whole spiral of knowledge, so that new pieces of knowledge, the new meanings, are much larger than the sum of their parts; the learner is always learning, and the process of self-regulation, not reinforcement theory, determines best when, what, and how things are learned; instruction is best derived from student interest and talent, not from deficits or curriculum materials; the assessment of student development, interests, and involvement is more important to teachers than is student performance

on reductionist subskills and subprocesses; problems in learning are the result of interactions of personalities, interests, development expectations, and previous experiences; and passion, trust, and interest are paramount—subjectivity surrounding learning, and cognitive processes, are only part of the picture.

In a review of the literature relevant to constructivist models, several themes can be observed with respect to the application of such models to teaching. These themes include (1) teacher empowerment; (2) child-centered instruction; (3) the integration of listening, speaking, reading, and writing with the student's interests and background; (4) a disavowal of the value of teaching subskills; and (5) a view that children are naturally predisposed to learning and that instruction provides activities (in the broadest sense) to facilitate the learner's ability to construct meaning from experience (see Reid & Hresko, 1981).

It is difficult to obtain objective, empirical data to support the general philosophy undergirding constructivist models or the importance and validity of the specific themes addressed here. Just as constructivist theorists eschew data-driven, behavioral approaches, they also appear uncomfortable with the assessment of efficacy through standard experimental designs. Thus, the actual power of instructional procedures based upon constructivist tenets has not been well established, at least in traditional ways. However, case studies and anecdotal reports are numerous.

Perhaps the best-known application of constructivist models to guide instruction is in the area of reading, where "whole-language" approaches have gained prominence. Until recently, formal experimental studies of the effects of whole-language approaches, particularly on the reading performance of individuals with LDs, have been rare. However, in the past four years, the NICHD has supported a number of investigations to assess the effects of several instructional methods, some of which are based upon a whole-language philosophy. The findings from these studies are reviewed later in the chapter.

Some Conclusions about Conceptual Models and Approaches to Treatment

The conceptual models discussed here have been summarized briefly, and the limited nature of the discussion has prevented us from including all of the fine points that characterize the different perspectives. However this discussion has made it clear that the models differ with respect to whether instruction should proceed from specific subskills to the general or vice versa; whether a highly structured or an unstructured type of instruction is advocated; whether the teaching strategies recommended are specific or more general in nature; and whether the effects of particular methods should be directly and explicitly evaluated or inferred from general student performance. Clearly, these differences are frequently fueled by strong philosophical debates, which typically are not greatly informed by research. It is also clear, as we discuss later in the chapter, that conceptual models based upon well-established principles of learning (e.g., cognitive, cognitive-behavioral, and behavioral/task-analytic approaches) are significantly more efficacious for individual with LDs than are approaches emphasizing assessment and teaching practices that are limited in content ecological validity (neuropsychological and constructivist approaches). It is also clear that in practice a combination of these modes is frequently employed, with the finer distinctions blurred by the dynamic nature of the intervention/treatment process.

METHODOLOGICAL LIMITATIONS OF RESEARCH ON THE TREATMENT OF LEARNING DISABILITIES

A review of the literature related both to LDs as a general category and to domain-specific LDs (e.g., dyslexia) indicates that until recently no single teaching method, treatment intervention, or combination of methods has been found to yield clinically significant, long-term gains (Lyon, 1996a; Lyon & Flynn, 1991; Lyon & Moats, 1997, 1988). This does not mean that such gains have not been produced; it means only that they have been hard to identify for a variety or methodological reasons. Specifically, over the years several factors have contributed to limitations in documenting treatment efficacy for underachieving children, including children with LDs. An understanding of these factors is critical to an accurate analysis of existing treatment approaches, and should be considered in the design of intervention studies (see Lyon & Moats, 1997). These factors are reviewed here.

First, many studies addressing the efficacy of different treatment intervention methods have studied heterogeneous groups of children with LDs who are identified by vague and inconsistent criteria and who demonstrate unaccounted-for differences in demographic features (e.g., socioeconomic status, race, ethnicity, number of parents, etc.), in number and severity of behavioral and academic disabilities, and in the co-morbidity of these disabilities (Morris et al., 1994). As such, not only have replication efforts been impeded, but it has been difficult to determine specific treatment effects and outcomes due to the influence of uncontrolled variables. Moreover, this lack of clarity about children's demographic, academic, behavioral, and information-processing characteristics has made it difficult to identify which intervention methods are most efficacious for which particular children and under what specific ecological (contextual) conditions (Lyon, 1987; 1996a; Lyon & Moats, 1997).

Second, many studies of how children with LDs respond to teaching methods and approaches have employed procedures that are poorly described and defined. For instance, few intervention studies critically describe how and why intervention/task stimuli are represented to the children. In addition, the type of response that the procedure requires of a child is rarely defined in detail. For example, in intervention studies involving reading disorders, few studies have provided sufficiently detailed answers to the following questions (Johnson, 1994): What is the nature of the structure of the spoken and written language used in the teaching methodology? What is the nature of the vocabulary? Is the vocabulary controlled? Are the sequence of phonological representations controlled? On what basis were the words to be read in the intervention phase selected? Do the word stimuli possess a consistent phoneme–grapheme relationship? How many meaningful nouns and verbs are used? Is the sentence structure similar to the child's oral language? What is the nature of the content of the reading material used in the intervention?

Third, intervention studies using methods or approaches that consist of several treatment components or procedures rarely report which component or procedure, or which combination or sequence of procedures, is most critical to promoting gains in learning (Zigmond, 1994). In addition, few studies address the interaction among teaching method, content acquisition, stage of development, and learner characteristics. Likewise, intervention studies employing multimodal methods frequently fail to identify how and why different interventions are selected, or what roles different interventions play in achieving treatment gains. This information is critical, because some children with LDs may require a more intensive emphasis, a different sequence, or a longer duration of exposure to and teaching on particular components of the intervention program (Lyon & Moats, 1997).

Fourth, the majority of intervention studies conducted with children with LDs have been relatively brief in duration (Berninger, 1994a, 1994b; Lyon & Moats, 1997, 1988). Thus, when limited effects of a method or intervention are reported, it is not clear whether the limited efficacy is due to the intervention itself or to the fact that it was employed for a duration that was too short to promote long-term change, no matter how robust the intervention. Moreover, it is likely that even the most powerful interventions may not result in measurable effects if traditional pretest–posttest designs are employed and only two measurement points are sampled. One reason why this may be the case is related to the fact that difference scores are confounded by regression toward the mean. Measurement methods must be able to assess both the rate *and* degree of change over time, and to be able to predict the slope and intercept of individual growth curves with multiple measures, including type of intervention, individual-difference variables, ecological variables, and the like (Francis et al., 1994; Lyon & Moats, 1997; Shaywitz & Shaywitz, 1994).

Fifth, many studies assessing the efficacy of different interventions may have been confounded by the effects of previous and concurrent interventions (Lyon & Flynn, 1989). It is unclear whether a history of a particular type of intervention significantly influences response to an ongoing intervention. Likewise, it is not well understood whether concurrent interventions or methods being used in either regular or special class settings influence response to ongoing experimental interventions. These issues must be addressed, in order to separate specific treatment effects from additive practice or inhibitory effects produced by previous or concurrent interventions.

Sixth, a significant number of treatment studies involving children with LDs have not separated specific treatment effects from clinician or teacher effects. That is, limited attention has been paid to delineating those teacher and contextual variables (e.g., teacher experience, teacher training, teacher–student relationship, etc.) that influence change within any treatment program (Lyon & Moats, 1997, 1988).

Seventh, it is not clear from the existing intervention literature whether gains in academic skills developed under highly controlled intervention conditions generalize to less controlled naturalistic settings (Lyon, 1996a; Lyon & Moats, 1997). For example, follow-up studies of treatment benefits have typically shown a decrease in intervention gains, particularly when measurements are taken in settings that differ from those employed in the original intervention trials (Lyon & Moats, 1997).

Eighth, it is rare that intervention studies analyze the degree of teacher fidelity with respect to the administration of the method or methods (Berninger, 1994a, 1994b). This is unfortunate, given that even teachers who are trained in similar ways have been found to deviate significantly from their application of a method once in the experimental setting (Lovett, 1991).

Taken individually or in combination, the methodological artifacts described here can limit the interpretability of an intervention study or can undermine confidence in a particular intervention method. Over the past few years, a number of NICHD-funded reading intervention studies have attempted to account for, and address, a number of these factors.

DOMAIN-SPECIFIC INTERVENTION METHODS: A SELECTIVE REVIEW

Limited space does not permit a comprehensive review of all treatment and teaching methods employed with children who manifest difficulties in learning to read, write, and carry out mathematical operations. Thus, the following sections are devoted to reviewing some the most highly researched intervention methods for deficits within these academic domains. Readers should also note that a number of treatment programs have been developed to enhance the memory skills (e.g., Tarver, Hallahan, Kaufman, & Ball, 1976), metacognitive abilities (Borkowski, 1992; Borkowski & Burke, 1996; Case et al., 1992; Flavell, 1979; Graham & Harris, 1996), attentional skills (Hall, Lund, & Jackson, 1968; Hallahan, Kneedler, & Lloyd, 1993; Hallahan, Lloyd, Kosiwicz, Kaufman, & Graves, 1979; Keogh & Margolis, 1976), and social behavior (Dunlap et al., 1994) of children with LDs. These references should be perused for specific examples of intervention programs in these domains. In addition, readers are referred to Lyon (1996a) for a review of literature related to etiologies, epidemiology, developmental course, and common comorbidities for reading, written language, and mathematics disorders.

Interventions for Deficits in Reading Skills

Of all the LDs, reading disabilities are the most common, affecting 60% to 80% of children receiving special education services for LDs (Lerner, 1989). In addition, reading disabilities significantly impede the development of many academic skills and the acquisition of content knowledge. Writing ability; the development of mathematical reasoning skills; and knowledge about science, social studies, English, and the like are all critically dependent upon fluent decoding and comprehension of the written word. Moreover, children with specific LDs in reading are at substantial risk for poor adolescent and adult outcomes. Seventy-five percent of children with disabilities in reading who are not identified until the third grade continue to have reading problems through high school (Shaywitz & Shaywitz, 1994)

Because of the significantly deleterious effect that reading disabilities have on educational, social, and occupational well-being, a substantial amount of research in the area of prevention and remediation of reading problems has taken place in the last decade. This research, and the specific teaching methods and approaches that have been studied, are described here within four categories: (1) methods and procedures designed to prevent reading disabilities; (2) early intervention methods and procedures; (3) reading remediation methods and procedures; and (4) specific methods and procedures to enhance reading comprehension skills.

Prevention of Reading Disabilities

Studies designed to assess the capability of specific approaches to prevent reading disabilities have accumulated in recent years, because of the increased ability to predict which children will develop such difficulties as they enter and proceed through school (see Torgesen, Wagner, & Rashotte, 1994a). In the main, this enhanced predictive ability has emerged from research that has demonstrated (1) that most reading difficulties are the result of deficits in word recognition (Bruck, 1990; Perfetti, 1985; Stanovich, 1991); (2) that problems in word recognition are themselves the result of deficits in phonological awareness, or the ability to notice, think about,

or manipulate sounds in words (Adams, 1990; Brady & Shankweiler, 1991; Liberman & Shankweiler, 1991); and (3) that poor reading can be predicted during kindergarten and first grade by analyzing children's performance on measures assessing phonological awareness and other types of phonological processing such as phonological memory and lexical access (Torgesen et al., 1994a).

The most recent and comprehensive prevention studies have been supported by the NICHD within the National Institutes of Health as part of a large treatment initiative for reading disabilities (see Lyon, 1995b). One study is underway at the University of Houston under the direction of Dr. Barbara Foorman, and one is being conducted at Florida State University under the leadership of Dr. Joseph Torgesen. These investigations, which are in progress at this time, are summarized next, followed by a discussion of the Syracuse University prevention studies (Blachman, 1991; Blachman, Ball, Black, & Tangel, 1994).

The Houston Model Kindergarten Project (Foorman, Francis, Beeler, Winikates, & Fletcher, 1997) is designed to prevent reading problems by incorporating 15 minutes of daily phonological awareness activities into the kindergarten curriculum of two schools. The training activities are based on the English translation of the Lundberg, Frost, and Petersen (1988) program used in Sweden and Denmark. The activities consist of games in the areas of listening, rhyming, identifying sentences and words, and manipulating syllables and phonemes. The activities involving syllables, initial sounds, and phonemes consist of analyzing words into the relevant constituent parts, as well as synthesizing (i.e., blending) the parts back into the whole word. For instance, in a training activity for initial sounds, a child may analyze "sand" into "s-and" and then synthesize it into "sand" again. At the phoneme level, the analysis of "s-a-n-d" is represented by the use of colored blocks.

The prevention program is being provided to 100 kindergarten children, and their development in phonological and early reading skills is being assessed at the ends of grades 1–3. Eighty-one children in traditional kindergarten settings are serving as control students. Data following the first 2 years of this 5-year study indicate that children receiving the Lundborg et al. (1988) activities on a daily basis significantly outperformed control children on tasks assessing letter identification, phonemic analysis, and single-word reading (see Foorman, Francis, Shaywitz, Shaywitz, & Fletcher, in press).

The Florida State Prevention Study (Torgesen, Wagner, Rashotte, Alexander, & Conway, 1997) is a 5-year longitudinal study that is nearing completion. Children were selected for participation in the study in the first semester of kindergarten, based upon their scores on a test of letter name knowledge and a measure of phonological awareness that has been demonstrated to accurately identify children at risk for early reading difficulties (Torgesen et al., 1994a). Logistic-regression procedures were used to identify children's reading skill levels by the second grade. Youngsters with IQs below 75 were excluded from the sample.

The 180 children in the final prevention sample were randomly assigned to four treatment conditions: (1) phonological awareness training plus synthetic phonics (PASP) instruction embedded within real-word reading and spelling activities (embedded phonics); (2) phonics instruction embedded with real-word reading and spelling activities; (3) a regular kindergarten/classroom support group receiving individual instruction to support the goals of the regular classroom program; and (4) a no-treatment control group. Children in each treatment condition are provided with 80 minutes of one-on-one instruction each week during kindergarten and the first grade (see Torgesen et al., 1997, for a discussion of this study).

Data analyzed during December of the second grade following 2 years of prevention activities indicated that the PASP program was related to significantly higher gains in alphabetic reading skills (decoding) and spelling than were the embedded-phonics and the regular-classroom-based treatments. Children in the embedded-phonics and regular-classroom intervention groups outperformed no-treatment control youngsters. Children in all three treatment groups performed equally well on measures of single-word reading, indicating that enhanced preventative instruction is beneficial, no matter what the training format is. It remains to be seen whether the different treatment conditions will produce differential outcomes in reading comprehension and in all reading skills over a 5-year period.

The Syracuse University studies (see Blachman et al., 1994) have demonstrated that explicit instruction in phonological awareness during kindergarten has significant positive effects on reading development during the first grade.

Within this context, Blachman and her colleagues have shown that proper instruction carried out by informed teachers can prevent reading failure both for children with inherent LDs in basic reading skills and for children whose lack of exposure to "language-rich" environments and language development activities during the first 5 years of life places them at risk for reading deficits.

Specifically, in a series of studies (Blachman et al., 1994; Tangel & Blachman, 1995), the Syracuse researchers exposed 84 low-income, inner-city kindergarten children to 11 weeks of intensive instruction, with one teacher instructing a small group of four to five students in several aspects of phonological awareness for 20 minutes per day. At the end of the 11 weeks, children receiving the intensive phonological treatment significantly outperformed control children on tasks assessing the ability to read phonetically regular words and related tasks. A follow-up study conducted in February and May of the first-grade year showed that these gains were maintained if the first-grade curriculum contained the same emphasis on phonological skill development and on the relation of these skills to decoding, word recognition, and textual reading.

In summary, research programs designed to develop and implement preventative programs for children at risk for reading disabilities are being carried out in several areas of the United States. The most effective programs appear to be those that incorporate explicit phonological awareness training, and that insure that phonological skills are applied directly to decoding, word recognition, and text comprehension activities. Within this context, they primarily reflect elements of the cognitive, cognitive-behavioral, and task-analytic intervention models discussed earlier. All of the prevention research programs discussed here are ongoing, and the maintenance and generalization of gains in pre-reading and early reading skills to later reading behavior are not yet fully understood. It is clear, however, that the phonologically based prevention activities are helpful to at-risk children and may play a significant role in reducing the negative effects of reading disabilities.

Early Intervention Reading Programs

By way of background, it is important for readers to note that there are enduring controversies about the nature of beginning reading instruction, and particularly beginning reading instruction for children with LDs. Early intervention programs are typically aligned with one of two perspectives: the code-emphasis approach and the whole-language (or literature-based) approach. Although the substantial debates between proponents of these two perspectives have been comprehensively summarized elsewhere (Foorman, 1995; Mather, 1992), each perspective is briefly described here.

Proponents of code-emphasis approaches to beginning reading and early intervention are based upon the notion that the ability to decode and recognize words accurately and fluently is essential to reading comprehension and developing an interest in reading (Hallahan et al., 1996). Intervention methods that are informed by a code-emphasis perspective are clearly derived from cognitive, cognitive-behavioral, and task-analytic intervention models. A major focus is on the provision of direct instruction, to help the child develop an understanding of all the main sound–symbol relationships (both vowel and consonant) and the application of phonics skills to the reading of new and/or unfamiliar words. Code-emphasis methodologists believe that specific instruction in word structure in decontextualized frameworks is often necessary and facilitates reading acquisition (Mather, 1992). More recently, an additional emphasis has been placed on the development of specific cognitive/linguistic skills (phonemic awareness) that serve as prerequisites to decoding and word recognition skills. For children whose reading difficulties are characterized by slow, labored, and incorrect decoding and pronunciation of words, a code-emphasis approach is viewed as essential. For example, Stanovich (1994) has stated:

> Reading for meaning [comprehension] is greatly hindered when children are having too much trouble with word recognition. When word recognition processes demand too much cognitive capacity, fewer cognitive resources are left to allocate to higher level processes of text integration and comprehension.

Research conducted on the effectiveness of code-emphasis approaches for students with LDs shows substantial support for this perspective. For example, Stein and Goldman (1980), Carnine (1977), and Carnine et al. (1990) have reported that DISTAR Reading (a program with a code-emphasis approach) and other methods of direct instruction in phonics concepts signifi-

cantly increased the basic reading and reading comprehension skills of young readers with LDs. Likewise, Williams (1980) found that The ABDs of Reading, a program based upon code-emphasis principles, was highly effective for children with LDs.

In marked contrast to the code-emphasis perspective, proponents of whole-language approaches feel that decontextualized instruction in sound–symbol relationships (phonics) disrupts the reading process; they strongly oppose direct instruction in decoding, and object to teaching practices that fragment the language arts into hierarchies of discrete skills (Goodman, 1986). Within a whole-language orientation, the understanding of meaning is the focus of instruction in reading and writing. As such, whole, meaningful texts are used—not isolated words, sounds, or vocabulary-controlled studies (Mather, 1992). The underlying belief is that children, even those with reading problems, will learn the language rules essential for reading naturally without explicit instruction. Within this context, the whole-language perspective on beginning reading and early intervention derives from constructivist approaches to instruction.

One difficulty in analyzing research on whole-language approaches is that they are typically not well defined (Foorman, 1995; Hallanan et al., 1996). In the main, however, evidence in support of whole-language instruction is meager. Stahl and Miller (1989), in a comprehensive review of 51 studies of whole-language instruction, reported that such approaches are no more effective than the basal programs with which they were compared. These negative findings are certainly related to a good deal of recent research, which shows that even good readers do not come to the reading task in a natural way and do require an understanding of the alphabetical principle and the application of phonics rules. Moreover, success in a whole-language reading program requires retention of words and natural acquisition of letter–sound relationships—skills that are markedly and frequently deficient in individuals with LDs (Lyon, 1995a). Readers are referred to Foorman (1995) and Mather (1992) for recent reviews of this evidence.

In a recent series of early intervention studies, Foorman et al. (1997) contrasted the effects of code-emphasis and whole-language approaches for reading-disabled children receiving Chapter 1 services in the first and second grades. All children ($n = 357$) were reading below the 25th percentile on standardized measures of reading achievement. The children were taught by one of three approaches: (1) a direct-instruction curriculum (Open Court's [1995] Collection for Young Scholars), which provided instruction in phonemic awareness, sound–symbol relationships, blending of sounds, writing, and reading in text; (2) an embedded-phonics program (Hiebert et al., 1992), which emphasized the learning of phonics concepts within the context of whole words; and (3) a whole-language curriculum, which stressed contextual reading, responses to literature, writing, spelling, and phonics in context, integration of reading, writing, listening, and speaking, and no decontextualized instruction in phonemic awareness or phonics. All children received the same amount of time in the respective programs, with comparable student–teacher ratios.

Growth curve analyses were conducted on measures of phonological awareness, word reading, and spelling administered at four time points between September and April. The results of these analyses showed that students in the direct-instruction group improved at a faster rate than whole-language students, and had significantly higher April scores in word reading, phonological processing, and spelling. The means for embedded-phonics students were between those of the other two groups. A significantly higher percentage of students in the whole-language and embedded-phonics groups than in the direct-instruction group showed little improvement in word reading over the year. In addition, Foorman et al. (1997) found that the relationship between phonological analysis and word reading was stronger for direct-instruction students than for whole-language students; the authors interpreted this finding as suggesting that the effects of direct instruction on word reading stemmed from its effects on phonological awareness. In summary, the Foorman et al. (1997) data indicate that for children whose reading is markedly below age and grade expectations, a direct-instruction code-emphasis early intervention program—one that incorporates and balances the explicit and systematic teaching of phonological awareness, phonics, and textual reading skills—is superior to early intervention methods based upon whole-language principles.

A popular early intervention program for first-grade children reading in the lower 20% of their class is Reading Recovery (RR; Clay, 1987, 1993). As Foorman (1995) has pointed out, RR shares a number of characteristics with whole-language-based approaches. Both approaches use only whole books, and they both stress that basic decoding and phonics skills should be taught in the context of real reading and writing activities, not in isolation. In addition, both approaches teach the child to employ multiple strategies (use of context clues, word attack, etc.) to identify words, and not to focus on only one strategy. However, in contrast to the child-centered whole-language philosophy, RR places the responsibility for selecting the reading materials on the teacher rather than the child, and also emphasizes mastery of the material. In essence, RR stresses the need to screen children for reading difficulties early in the first grade, and to provide intensive one-to-one tutorial instruction that emphasizes reading familiar text, writing words in a manner that encourages the induction of phonemic awareness and sound–symbol relationships, and integrating reading and writing activities.

A comprehensive review of the effectiveness studies conducted to date with RR has indicated that the program does result in substantial gains in reading for approximately 70% of the children enrolled (Shanahan & Barr, 1995). However, it should be noted that many of the studies reviewed were methodologically flawed. What seems clear is that readers with LDs may not profit from the RR program as much as other poor readers, primarily because the RR program does not stress the explicit teaching of phonemic awareness in the context of reading; in RR, phonemic awareness and sound–symbol relationships are taught in the context of spelling and writing activities. For instance, Iverson and Tunmer (1993) compared the reading growth of children enrolled in the standard RR program with children enrolled in a modified RR program supplemented with direct instruction in phonemic awareness in the context of reading. Although both RR groups significantly outperformed control children on a variety of reading measures, children in the modified RR program progressed significantly faster than those in the standard program. The reader is referred to the review of research on RR by Shanahan and Barr (1995) for a comprehensive summary of studies to date and an analysis of the cost-effectiveness of the RR program.

In summary, the data seem clear in indicating that early intervention programs that stress direct and explicit instruction in phonemic awareness, phonics, and contextual reading are substantially more effective than programs that deemphasize the learning of reading subskills and favor instead an emphasis on context and meaning. The data are also clear in demonstrating that early intervention has a more substantial and lasting effect on reading development than does later remediation.

Reading Remediation Programs

Unfortunately, not all children with reading disabilities have the benefit of appropriate prevention and intervention programs. In fact, the majority of such youngsters are not identified for special education services until the late second-grade or third-grade year. Even more unfortunate is the finding that severe reading disabilities diagnosed after age 8 are refractory to treatment (Fletcher & Foorman, 1994). Little has changed in the past 25 years. For instance, a survey by Strag (1972) found that "when the diagnosis of dyslexia was made in the first two grades of school nearly 82 percent of the students could be brought up to their normal classroom work, while only 46 percent of the dyslexic problems identified in the third grade were remediated and only 10 to 15 percent of those observed in grades five to seven could be helped when the diagnosis of learning problems was made at those grade levels" (p. 52). More recent longitudinal studies have supported this conclusion: Shaywitz, Fletcher, and Shaywitz (1994) have reported that approximately 74% of children identified as reading-disabled in the third grade continue to manifest reading difficulties through their high school years, despite the fact that many have received special education. Although remediation programs applied at later elementary grades do not net the same improvement as early intervention programs, gains in reading skills are possible if the remediation is directly related to the content deficiencies, the teacher is well trained, and both the intensity and duration of the remediation are sufficient.

Historically, remediation approaches used with disabled readers are multisensory in nature, are provided in an individualized fashion, and are used to develop spelling and writing skills as well as reading skills. Examples of these types of methods are the Fernald approach (Fernald, 1943) and the Orton–Gillingham approach (Gillingham & Stillman, 1965). The Fernald approach incorporates principles of language experience and whole-word (not whole-language) instruction in the teaching format. In essence, the reading material to be learned is provided by the students through the dictation of their own stories. Fernald (1943) argued that this type of approach could help to overcome the negative feelings that many children have because of their prolonged difficulties in learning to read. From these stories, the students select words that they wish to learn and work directly on them, repeatedly saying and tracing the words until they can be written from memory. Words that are mastered are kept in a file, and the words are used to generate additional reading material. The Fernald approach emphasizes learning words as wholes and discourages teaching students how to "sound out" new words. Given what is now known about the importance of decoding skills in the learning-to-read process, it is not surprising that the Fernald method has not been substantiated by research evidence (Myers, 1978).

In contrast, multisensory synthetic phonic methods such as those recommended in the Orton–Gillingham approach have received recent research support, particularly when they are combined with explicit phonemic awareness training. In essence, the standard Orton–Gillingham approach, also known as an alphabetical phonics method, requires the student to learn associations between letters and sounds that are required in reading, spelling, and writing tasks. Children are taught to see a letter (visual), hear its sound (auditory), say its sound (auditory), trace the letter (tactile), and write the letter (kinesthetic). When the first 10 letter–sound associations have been mastered, work on blending letters into words is initiated. Words mastered are eventually inserted into sentences and passages to promote textual reading and reading comprehension.

Although the standard Orton–Gillingham approach has received little research support (Hallahan et al., 1996), recent studies that combine this approach with methods to enhance phonemic awareness have demonstrated some effectiveness with learning-disabled readers. For example, Torgesen et al. (1997b) combined the synthetic phonics techniques described here with a program designed to stimulate phonemic awareness through the use of concrete manipulatives (colored blocks) and to help children discover the articulatory positions and movements associated with different phonemes. The phonemic awareness activities were based solely on the Auditory Discrimination in Depth program, developed by Patricia and Charles Lindamood (Lindamood & Lindamood, 1975). This combined program was provided to third-grade students who had been identified as learning-disabled by school officials. Torgesen et al. (1997b) found that children receiving this combined instruction made significant gains in both word attack skills and word recognition skills over a 1-year period. In another study using the same combined approach, Alexander, Anderson, Heilman, Voeller, and Torgesen (1991) provided 65 hours of phonemic awareness and synthetic phonics training to 65 severely dyslexic children. This intensive treatment approach improved the reading skills of the children from an average initial reading score of 77 to an average of 98.4 (mean = 1000) on a measure of alphabetical reading skills.

A number of behaviorally based corrective reading programs and instructional techniques have been applied with older poor readers in classroom settings. Borrowing directly from direct-instruction principles, Englemann, Becker, Hanner, and Johnson (1978) developed the Corrective Reading Program. In this task-analytic program, both decoding and comprehension skills are developed in a systematic, sequential, and carefully paced manner. Specifically, the program includes scripted daily lessons to teach the skills required for fluent and accurate decoding. In addition, questioning strategies are taught to enhance comprehension. Research with the Corrective Reading Program has shown significant positive effects with learning-disabled readers at the older age ranges (Polloway, Epstein, Polloway, Patton, & Ball, 1986).

Cognitive and constructivist approaches to intervention have also guided the development of a number of strong intervention programs for learning-disabled readers. For instance, a method called "reciprocal teaching" (Palinscar & Klenk, 1992) stresses the importance of providing instruction within a social context, of initially providing supports (prompts) to help students perform activities, and of having students demonstrate developing competence by explaining to fellow students how to arrive at a reading solution. Palinscar and Klenk (1992) have described reciprocal teaching in this manner:

Reciprocal teaching . . . refers to an instructional procedure that takes place in a collaborative learning group and features guided practice in the flexible application of four concrete strategies to the task of text comprehension: questioning, summarizing, clarifying, and predicting. The teacher and group of students take turns leading discussions regarding the content of the text they are jointly attempting to understand. (p. 213)

In summary, similar to the results obtained in the early intervention studies, gains in reading skill development can be achieved at later ages if the remediation programs provide intensive systematic instruction in a range of skills to include phonemic awareness, phonics, and textual reading. Importantly, the remediation must be strategic, systematic, and carefully designed, and it should be based on treatment principles that recognize and balance the importance of both code instruction and the appreciation of meaning.

Interventions for Deficits in Reading Comprehension

Although difficulties with decoding inevitably have an impact on reading comprehension, there are other causes for comprehension deficiencies. Garner, Alexander, and Hare(1991) cite five possible causes for comprehension failure, aside from difficulty with decoding: confusion about task demands, meager domain knowledge, weak comprehension monitoring, low self-esteem, and low interest. Many of the intervention methods described below address how to remediate these causes of reading failure. The reader should note that since the preceding sections have addressed interventions for decoding difficulties, this section concentrates on methods that improve reading comprehension when a decoding deficit is not the primary deficit in reading.

Reading comprehension intervention is often classified into two different types of instruction: "specific skills instruction" and "strategy instruction" (Clark & Uhry, 1995). As the name suggests, specific skills instruction focuses on teaching specific skills that can be applied to texts, such as vocabulary instruction, finding the main idea, making inferences, and finding facts. Vocabulary instruction can be taught through either definitional approaches or contextual approaches to learning vocabulary (see Carlisle, 1993, for a discussion). Skills such as finding the main idea and making inferences can be taught by reading short passages and answering questions. One example of a program that focuses on teaching children how to find the main idea in stories and how to make complex inferences is the Barnell Loft Specific Skills Series (Barnell, 1982). Another program that teaches these specific skills is a computer program called the Reading Comprehension System (Control Data Corporation, 1980), which presents passages of varying levels of difficulty to the child. After reading each passage, the child is then asked questions about word meanings, syntax, word relationships, and inferences. The program provides feedback to the student and has the student continue at each level until mastery is achieved. The Reading Comprehension System has been shown to be effective; Boettcher (1983) found that students made significant gains on the California Achievement Tests after 9 weeks of instruction, 45 minutes per week, with this system. Despite the success of specific skills instruction, Clark and Uhry (1995) note that it has been criticized for being vague (e.g., what is a "main idea"?) (Maria, 1987) and for involving too many exercises that resemble testing more than teaching (Durkin, 1978–1979).

In contrast to specific skills instruction, which involves a "passively learned set of routines," strategy instruction is "viewed as cognitive processes requiring decision making and critical thinking" (Clark & Uhry, 1995, p. 107). Strategy instruction in reading comprehension is an outgrowth of several cognitive psychology theories and concepts, notably schemas, metacognition, and mediated learning. For example, schemas involve the idea that a reader brings certain psychological frameworks, or "mental schemas," to a text. During reading, in order for the reader to comprehend, facts must be added or adjusted to the reader's mental schema. The study of metacognition has also had considerable influence on reading comprehension research. It has been found that "good readers who possess metacognitive skills in reading are aware of the purpose of reading and differentiate between task demands. They actively seek to clarify the purposes or task demands through self-questioning prior to reading the given materials . . . [and] evaluate their own comprehension of materials read" (Wong, 1991, pp. 239–40). Research has shown that readers who have deficits in comprehension lack these metacognitive skills (Baker & Brown, 1984a, 1984b; Wong, 1985). Finally, the concept of mediated learning, which involves the effects of student–teacher interactions on children's later ability to solve problems independently, has also influenced reading comprehension theory and instruction. For example, Katherine Maria (1990) conceptualizes reading instruction as an interaction among reader, text, and teacher. The reader brings decoding ability, oral vocabulary, and background knowledge to the text. The text is no longer perceived as having a single meaning for all students. Rather, meaning is constructed through this interaction. The teacher is viewed as a manager and facilitator who provides direct instruction in strategies, but who also encourages independence (Clark & Uhry, 1995).

Other intervention methods based on these types of cognitive strategies have been developed to teach reading comprehension. For example, as discussed earlier, Palinscar and Brown (1983, 1985) have developed a teaching method called "reciprocal teaching" that has been found to enhance reading comprehension skills. In addition, Pressley and his colleagues have developed an intervention to increase reading comprehension skills, called transactional strategies, that is based upon Vygotskian concepts (Pressley et al., 1991). In this method of instruction, students are "provided with direct instruction in a number of comprehension strategies and are encouraged to talk about and choose a strategy for understanding what they read . . . students are provided with positive instruction when a strategy is successful" (Clark & Uhry, 1995, p. 111). Instruction also involves teachers modeling different comprehension strategies. Teacher feedback has indicated an enthusiastic response to the transactional teaching method.

Bos and Anders (1990) have developed an interactive teaching model, which is similar to Pressley et al.'s (1991) transactional teaching method, and is also based upon Vygotskian principles. This model incorporates six teaching–learning characteristics: (1) activating prior knowledge; (2) integrating new knowledge with old knowledge; (3) cooperative knowledge sharing and learning; (4) predicting, justifying, and confirming concepts and text meaning; (5) predicting, justifying, and confirming relationships among concepts; and (6) purposeful learning. Initially, a teacher models these strategies for the students, but gradually moves away from being an instructor to being more of a facilitator. Results of two studies indicated that these strategies allow students to learn a substantial amount from texts (Anders et al., 1990; Bos & Reyes, 1989). However, interviews with students indicated that they gained procedural knowledge of the strategies, but not conditional knowledge of them.

Although the specific skill training and strategy instruction methods have some similarities, it has been found that the most effective instruction for children with reading comprehension disabilities involves direct instruction, multiple opportunities for instruction, and carefully sequenced lessons (Clark & Uhry, 1995). Strategies based upon cognitive concepts (i.e., strategy instruction) appear to be the most effective methods of intervention for reading comprehension, and have provided the best results to date for improving disabled readers' comprehension.

Interventions for Deficits in Written Language Skills

Interventions for LDs that affect handwriting, spelling, and written composition have been developed but not studied as extensively as those for reading disabilities. The relative paucity of intervention research in the area of written language is due in part to the complexity of the multiple linguistic tasks that must be negotiated in the writing process. Consider that in expressing oneself in writing, one has to formulate the ideas to be expressed, organize and sequence them in a coherent fashion, produce the ideas in a syntactically correct format, spell the words correctly, and produce the content legibly via motor response. Furthermore, once one gains competence in these foundation skills, they must be integrated within a broader cognitive system that superimposes organizational strategies on issues of genre structure, text coherence and cohesion, and sense of audience. Given the number of variables that could be studied in research on written language intervention, it is not surprising that investigations have focused on only parts of the process.

Interventions for Deficits in Handwriting

Handwriting is composed of a set of complex behaviors that are developed over a period of time. Difficulties in both printing and cursive writing stem from a number of factors including motor deficits, visual–motor coordination problems, visual memory deficits, and reading disabilities. The term "dysgraphia" has been used historically to refer to a difficulty in transducing visual information to the motor system (Johnson & Myklebust, 1967) that manifests itself in an inability to copy. Bain (1991) has observed that students with handwriting difficulties have four characteristics that appear in contiguity: (1) unconventional grip; (2) fingers very near the pencil point; (3) difficulty in erasing; and (4) trouble with letter alignment.

Intervention methods for writing difficulties have traditionally been based upon clinical observation and clinical models. Johnson and Myklebust (1967) conducted a substantial amount of clinical research involving written language disorders, including handwriting deficits. From their research, they developed a comprehensive task-analytic model for the treatment of handwriting difficulties. Another method for the remediation of written language deficits is the Gillingham and Stillman (1965) approach. This is a clinically based method used by many teachers working with learning-disabled students and is characterized by the following: (1) The teacher models a large letter on the blackboard, writing and saying the name; (2) the student traces the letter while saying the name (this tracing stage continues until the student is secure with both the letter formation and the name); (3) the student copies the letter while saying the name; and (4) the student writes the letter from memory while saying the name.

In addition to these types of multisensory intervention methods, some studies have assessed the utility of improving handwriting by teaching children to verbally guide themselves through the process (Hayes & Flower, 1980). For example, when making the lowercase letter m, a child is taught to say, "First, I make a short stick, then I make one hhuuummmp, two hhhuuummmps. There, that's an m" (Hallahan et al., 1996, p. 267). Other techniques are based upon more elaborate cognitive-behavioral models, such as self-instruction (Graham, 1982) and self-recording.

One popular approach to help students compensate for handwriting difficulties involves the use of computers and keyboarding skills. However, although many students report that they prefer to use computers rather than to write by hand, the results of several studies indicate that keyboarding is of little genuine help if a student does not have an understanding of computer use (Hallahan et al., 1996).

Interventions for Deficits in Spelling

The English spelling system, or orthography, is an alphabetical system in which phonemic units (speech sounds) are represented by graphemes (letters or letter combinations) (Bailet, 1991). For both children and primary-grade teachers, this fundamental relationship between spoken and written language is the most important aspect underlying literacy development. Spelling disabilities are ubiquitous among individuals with LDs and frequently co-occur with disorders of oral language, reading, motor skills, and attention (Moats, 1994b). Spelling is never mastered by most individuals with reading disabilities, who after appropriate intervention can usually improve their decoding skills, but typically continue to be poor spellers (Bruck, 1987). This finding, as well as the number of people who read well but spell poorly (Frith, 1980), suggests that reading and spelling are to some extent dissociated and that theoretical models of one skill will not necessarily explain the other (Moats, 1994b).

However, as in reading, phonemic awareness training procedures that provide concrete visual materials for students to manipulate, in parallel with auditory input, appear to be effective in improving spelling abilities (Bradley & Bryant, 1985). These types of methods are probably successful for at least two reasons (Bailet, 1991). First, they provide a concrete, visual means of representing abstract spoken phonemes. Second, they provide children with an opportunity for physically manipulating chips or plastic letters to match their spoken counterparts, rather than requiring mental manipulation. A good example of this type of program for spelling is the Lindamoods' Auditory Discrimination in Depth program, mentioned earlier in connection with reading remediation (Lindamood & Lindamood, 1975). This program provides intensive work on phonemic segmentation and requires students to learn to identify and classify sounds, represent sound segments and syllables using colored blocks, and to associate phonemes with graphemes.

In addition to the Orton–Gillingham and Fernald multisensory methods to improve reading and spelling (also described earlier), a number of behavioral/task-analytic interventions have been applied to improve spelling behavior in children with LDs. For example, Lovitt, Guppy, and Blattner (1969) found that free time contingent upon improved spelling accuracy had positive effects on spelling performance. In addition, Gerber (1986) and Kauffman, Hallahan, Haas, Brame, and Boren (1978) reported that imitating students' spelling errors and then requiring the children to write the words correctly boosted performance significantly. Readers are referred to McNaughton, Hughes, and Clark (1994) for a relatively recent review of behavioral interventions for spelling difficulties.

As they have in the remediation of handwriting deficits, computers have begun to play a role in interventions for spelling difficulties. For example, MacArthur, Haynes, Malouf, and Harris (1990) found that computer-assisted spelling practice produced more academic engagement and better spelling achievement than traditional practice with pencil and paper. Likewise, Stevens, Blackhurst, and Slaton (1991) found that microcomputer presentation of a behavioral spelling program substantially increased student performance.

Interventions for Deficits in Written Composition and Expression

The ability to produce one's thoughts in writing is a complex form of communication requiring a number of cognitive abilities. In producing a written composition, the student must simultaneously attend to the subject, the text, and the reader. Deficits in oral language and reading are often precursors to difficulties in the writing process, and attention and memory play critical roles as well (Gregg, 1991).

As simple as it sounds, some researchers (e.g., Kraetsch, 1981) have found that increased writing practice can be a significant force in improving written composition. In more detailed interventions, methods that require students to take two related sentences and write them as one (sentence combining) have produced significant gains in written composition (O'Hare, 1973). More recently, story grammar techniques have been studied in relation to written composition and expression (Hallahan et al., 1996). "Story grammar" involves teaching students to employ a strategic outline to insure that the necessary components are present in their compositions (Graves, Montague, & Wong, 1989; Montague & Graves, 1993).

A number of cognitive-behavioral intervention techniques have been employed to increase composition skills. For example, Graham and Harris (1996) discuss the use of SRSD (mentioned earlier in the discussion of cognitive-behavioral models) in helping students master the higher-level cognitive processes involved in written composition, and in helping them develop the self-regulated use of these processes. Using SRSD, Graham and Harris stimulated significant gains in learning-disabled children's length and quality of story writing (Graham & Harris, 1993), and found that such gains were maintained over time and generalized across settings and persons (Graham, Harris, MacArthur, & Schwartz, 1991). Readers are referred to Hallahan et al. (1996) for additional examples of cognitive-behavioral methods for written composition.

MacArthur (1988) has reported that the use of computers can enhance the remediation of students' written language composition skills. Students appear to enjoy composing on the computer in contrast to producing stories via handwriting. However, as with the use of computers in any intervention setting, the student must be comfortable with the operation and limitations of the computer.

In summary, there are many intervention methods for the remediation of deficits in handwriting, spelling, and written composition. As in other content areas, clinicians and teachers must be aware that written language is an extremely complex domain, requiring the integration of oral language, written language, cognitive, and motor skills. Within this context, a combination of the different intervention methods discussed in this section is likely to net the greatest improvements in the writing skills of children with LDs.

Interventions for Deficits in Arithmetic and Mathematics Skills

In general, children who manifest LDs in mathematics typically display deficits in arithmetic calculation and/or mathematics reasoning skills (Lyon, 1996a). Fleishner (1994) has reported that mathematics LDs often co-occur with deficits in reading, writing, and/or oral language. However, she and others make the point that when comorbidity occurs to this degree, an LD in mathematics should not be construed as a selective impairment, but rather as a feature of a generalized problem (Feagans & McKinney, 1981; Fleishner & Frank, 1979). As is the case for interventions in written language, solid research in the treatment of mathematics disorders is just beginning to emerge. A major difficulty in diagnosing LDs in mathematics is that in mathematics, more than in any other content area, learning is tied closely to the teacher's knowledge and preparation in the teaching of math skills.

Difficulties in developing arithmetic calculation skills are frequently linked to difficulties in writing numerals and mathematical symbols correctly, recalling the meanings of symbols and answers to basic facts, counting, and following the steps in a multistep algorithm (Glennon & Cruickshank, 1981). In turn, the ability to reason mathematically in the context of word problems is negatively influenced by the presence of extraneous information, complex syntactic structures, change in numbers and types of nouns used, and the use of certain verbs (Blankenship & Lovitt, 1976; Hallahan et al., 1996).

As with instructions in other content areas, the teaching of arithmetic and mathematics skills has the following characteristics: (1) The instruction takes place in groups; (2) it is teacher-directed; (3) it is academically focused; and (4) it is individualized for each student in the group (Stevens & Rosenshine, 1981). Some basal or developmental programs used for children with LDs have many of these characteristics. For example, Connecting Math Concepts (Englemann, Carnine, Englemann, & Kelly, 1991) is a basal program based upon a behavioral/task-analytic model that is frequently used for primary- and elementary-age students with LDs. This program grew out of the DISTAR Arithmetic program, also developed by Englemann (Englemann & Carnine, 1975). Both programs contain highly structured lessons involving frequent teacher questions and student answers. A number of studies have demonstrated the efficacy of Connecting Math Concepts and DISTAR Arithmetic with learning-disabled children (Carnine, 1991). For example, Wellington (1994) found that the DISTAR Arithmetic program significantly enhanced both computational skills and problem-solving skills in students with LDs.

A number of specialized intervention programs have also been developed for children with LDs (Hallahan et al., 1996). One such program is Structural Arithmetic, developed by Stern and Stern (1971). This program is designed to help children in kindergarten through the third grade better understand numeration and relationships between numbers. Different-colored blocks and sticks represent numbers from 1 to 10. Numerical relationships are represented to the students through combinations of these manipulatives. Similarly, Project Math (Cawley et al., 1976) is designed to help learning-disabled students from kindergarten through the sixth grade discover meaningful principles underlying mathematics. Specifically, six highly structured "strands" are used to teach patterns, sets, numbers, fractions, geometry, and measurement concepts. These concepts are made more meaningful to the students by integrating them with the students' daily experiences and by individualizing the instruction. Field tests of Project MATH have demonstrated positive results (see Cawley, Fitzmaurice, Shaw, Kahn, & Bates, 1978).

In addition to basal programs and specialized instructional programs, a number of teaching techniques have been shown to be useful in helping children with LDs develop arithmetic and mathematics concepts. For example, Rivera and Smith (1987), summarizing research on the value of modeling in teaching computational skills, found teacher demonstrations of calculation algorithms and higher-level procedural steps to be effective in increasing both computational and problem-solving behaviors in students. In addition, Lloyd and his colleagues (Cullinan, Lloyd, & Epstein, 1981; Lloyd, 1980) have tested the value of strategy training with children who are deficient in math skills. In this type of training, a task analysis of the relevant cognitive operation is demonstrated and explained to the students. When students have mastered the component skills, strategies are provided that help the students integrate the steps and apply them in different problem-solving contexts. Finally, cognitive-behavioral models of intervention have given rise to the development of self-instructional strategy techniques to help guide students with LDs through a variety of problem-solving contexts (Hallahan et al., 1996). A key component in this type of technique is to teach a student first to verbalize the steps that should be used in solving a particular mathematics problem. Once the student has mastered the application of the problem-solving algorithm, the student is taught to instruct himself or herself, but using subvocal directions. This type of technique has been shown to be useful with both elementary-age students (Lovitt & Curtiss, 1968) and adolescents (Seabaugh & Schumaker, 1993).

In summary, although deficits in arithmetic and mathematics reasoning abilities are common among individuals with LDs, research-based interventions are just beginning to emerge. In the main, the most useful treatment methods and techniques have evolved from cognitive and behavioral models of intervention. It should also be pointed out that children with mathematics-based LDs are extremely vulnerable to the negative effects of limited teacher experience and the improper application of pedagogical principles.

SUMMARY AND CONCLUSIONS

The road to establishing the efficacy of treatment approaches and methods designed for children with LDs is a long one. Until the past decade, little progress had been made in developing an understanding of the core clinical and diagnostic features of each of the major LD types, and even this understanding is not equally robust for all types of LDs. The lion's share of our current knowledge about children's difficulties in learning academic concepts resides in the area of reading development in general and basic reading skills in particular. A substantial number of converging studies strongly support the hypothesis that difficulties in learning to read are highly related to linguistic deficits in the phonological processing area. These findings have provided a foundation for the development and experimental test of treatment modalities that target the linguistic deficiencies as well as the basic reading skill deficits. From this work, the data are clear that for a reading-disabled individual to gain access to print, the individual must receive a balanced intervention program composed of direct and explicit instruction in phonemic awareness; a systematic generalization of this learning to the learning of sound–symbol relationships (phonics); and many opportunities to practice these coding skills within the context of reading meaningful, interesting, and controlled texts. The sooner in a child's school career that this can take place, the better.

Our current knowledge of what works best for children with deficits in written language and mathematics is less well developed. This is due in part to the fact that we simply know less about the etiological factors that presage these difficulties, the core cognitive deficits that define the disorders, and the developmental courses associated with these types of LDs.

It goes without saying that a substantial increase in intervention research for different types of well-defined lLDs will have to occur if children are to receive the best treatment that we can offer. To provide a full understanding of the many factors that will influence a youngster's response to treatment, such research must be primarily longitudinal and long-term in design. Although this type of research is time-consuming and expensive, it is probably the only way to identify clearly which teaching approaches or combination of teaching approaches have the highest probability of success with which children, at which age, in which setting, and with which types of teachers.

REFERENCES

Adams, M. J. (1990). *Beginning to read: Thinking and learning about print.* Cambridge, MA: MIT Press.

Alexander, A., Anderson, H., Heilman, P. C., Voeller, K., & Torgesen, J. K. (1991). Phonological awareness training and remediation of analytic decoding deficits in a group of severe dyslexics. *Annals of Dyslexia, 41,* 193–206.

Anders, P. L., Bos, C. S., Scanlon, D., Gallego, M., Duran, G. Z., & Reyes, E. (1990). *Facilitating content learning through interactive strategy instruction with middle school learning disabled students.* Unpublished raw data.

Bain, A. M. (1991). Handwriting disorders. In A. M. Bain, L. L. Bailet, & L. C. Moats (Eds.), *Written language disorders: Theory into practice* (pp. 43–64). Austin, TX: Pro-Ed.

Bailet, L. L. (1991). Development and disorders of spelling in the beginning school years. In A. M. Bain, L. L. Bailet, & L. C. Moats (Eds.), *Written language disorders: Theory into practice* (pp. 1–22). Austin, TX: Pro-Ed.

Baker, L., & Brown, A. L. (1984a). Cognitive monitoring in reading. In P. D. Pearson (Ed.), *Understanding reading comprehension* (pp. 21–44). Newark, DE: International Reading Association.

Baker, L., & Brown, A. L. (1984b). Metacognitive skills in reading. In P. D. Pearson (Ed.), *Handbook of reading research* (pp. 126–140). New York: Longman.

Bakker, D. J. (1984). The brain as a dependent variable. *Journal of Clinical Neuropsychology, 6,* 1–16.

Bakker, D. J., & Vinke, J. (1985). Effects of hemispheric-specific stimulation on brain activity and reading in dyslexics. *Journal of Clinical Neuropsychology, 7,* 505–525.

Bateman, B. (1967). An educator's view of a diagnostic approach to learning disorders. In J. Hellmuth (Ed.), *Learning disorders* (Vol. 1, pp. 219–239). Seattle, WA: Special Child Publications.

Bednarczyk, D., & Harris, K. R. (1992). [Raw grammar to improve reading comprehension]. Unpublished raw data.

Berninger, V. W. (1994a). Future directions for research on writing disabilities: Integrating endogenous and exogenous variables. In G. R. Lyon (Ed.), *Frames of reference for the assessment of learning disabilities: New views on measurement issues* (pp. 419–440). Baltimore: Paul H. Brookes.

Bermomger. V. W. (1994b). *Reading and writing acquisition: A developmental neuropsychological perspective.* Dubuque, IA: Brown and Benchmark.

Bijou, S. (1970). What psychology has to offer education—now. *Journal of Applied Behavior Analysis, 3,* 65–71.

Blachman, B. A. (1991). Getting ready to read. In J. F. Kavanagh (Ed.), *The language continuum: From infancy to literacy* (pp. 41–62). Parkton, MD: York Press.

Blachman, B. A., Ball, E. W., Black, R. S., & Tangel, D. M. (1994). Kindergarten teachers develop phoneme awareness in low-income, inner-city classrooms: Does it make a difference? *Reading and Writing: An Interdisciplinary Journal, 6,* 1–18.

Blankenship, C., & Lovitt, T. C. (1976). Story problems: Merely confusing or downright befuddling? *Journal for Research in Mathematics Education, 7,* 290–298.

Boettcher, J. V. (1983). Computer-based education: Classroom application and benefits for the learning disabled. *Annals of Dyslexia, 33,* 203–221.

Borkowski, J. G. (1992). Metacognitive theory: A framework for teaching literacy, writing, and math skills. *Journal of Learning Disabilities, 25,* 253–257.

Borkowski, J. G., & Burke, J. E. (1996). Theories, models, and measurements of executive functioning: An information processing perspective. In G. R. Lyon & N. A. Kransnegor (Eds.), *Attention, Memory and Executive Functioning* (pp. 235–278). Baltimore, MD: Paul H. Brookes.

Bos, C. S., & Anders, P. L. (1990). Interactive teaching and learning: Instructional practices for teaching content and strategic knowledge. In T. E. Scruggs & B. Y. L. Wong (Eds.), *Intervention research in learning disabilities* (pp. 161–185). New York: Springer-Verlag.

Bos, C. S., & Reyes, E. (1989). *Knowledge, use, and control of interactive cognitive strategy for learning form content area texts.* Paper presented at the annual meeting of the National Reading Conference.

Brady, S. A., & Shankweiler, D. P. (Eds.). (1991). *Phonological processes in literacy.* Hillsdale, NJ: Erlbaum.

Bradley, L., & Bryant, R. (1985). *Rhyme and reason in reading and spelling* (International Academy for Research in Learning Disabilities, Monograph Series No. 1). Ann Arbor: University of Michigan Press.

Braswell, L., & Kendall, P. C. (1988). Cognitive-behavioral methods with children. In K. S. Dobson (Ed.), *Handbook of cognitive-behavioral therapies* (pp. 167–213). New York: Guilford Press.

Brown, A. L. (1975). The development of memory: Knowing, knowing about knowing, and knowing how to know. In H. W. Reese (Ed.), *Advances in child development and behavior* (Vol. 10, pp. 102–149). New York: Academic Press.

Brown, A. L., & Campione, J. (1986). Psychological theory and the study of learning disabilities. *American Psychologist, 41,* 14–21.

Bruck, M. (1987). The adult outcomes of children with learning disabilities. *Annals of Dyslexia, 37,* 252–263.

Bruck, M. (1990). Word-recognition skills of adults with childhood diagnoses of dyslexia. *Developmental Psychology, 26,* 439–454.

Carlisle, J. F. (1993). Selecting approaches to vocabulary instruction for the reading disabled. *Learning Disabilities Research and Practice, 8,* 97–105.

Carnine, D. W. (1977). Phonics versus look–say: Transfer to new words. *Reading Teacher, 30,* 636–640.

Carnine, D. W. (1980). Preteaching versus concurrent teaching on the component skills of a multiplication problem-solving strategy. *Journal for Research in Mathematics Education, 11,* 37–379.

Carnine, D. W. (1991). Increasing the amount and quality of learning through direct instruction: Implications for mathematics. In J. W. Lloyd, N. N. Singh, & A. C. Repp (Eds.), *The regular education initiative: Alternative perspectives on concepts, is-*

sues, and models (pp. 163–175). Sycamore, IL: Sycamore.

Carnine, D. W., Silbert, J., & Kameenui, E. J. (1990). *Direct instruction: Reading* (2nd ed.). Columbus, OH: Merrill.

Case, L. P., Harris, K. R., & Graham, S. (1992). Improving the mathematical problem-solving skills of students with learning disabilities: Self-regulated strategy development. *Journal of Special Education, 26*(1), 1–19.

Catts, H. (1986). Speech production/phonological deficits in reading-disordered children. *Journal of Learning Disabilities, 19,* 504–508.

Cawley, J. F., Fitzmaurice, A. M., Goodstein, H. A., Lepore, A. V., Sedlak, R., & Althause, V. (1976). *Project MATH.* Tulsa, OK: Educational Development Corporation.

Cawley, J. F., Fitzmaurice, A. M., Shaw, R., Kahn, H., & Bates, H., III. (1978). Mathematics and learning disabled youth: The upper grade levels. *Learning Disability Quarterly, 1*(4), 37–52.

Cawley, J. F., & Miller, J. H. (1986). Selected views on metacognition, arithmetic problem-solving, and learning disabilities. *Learning Disabilities Focus, 2,* 36–48.

Clark, D. B., & Uhry, J. K. (1995). *Dyslexia: Theory and practice of remedial instruction.* Baltimore, MD: York Press.

Clay, M. (1985). *The early detection of reading difficulties* (3rd ed.). Portsmouth, NH: Heinemann.

Clay, M. (1993). *An observation survey of early literacy achievement.* Portsmouth, NH: Heinemann.

Coles, G. S. (1978). The learning-disabilities test battery: Empirical and social issues. *Harvard Educational Review, 48,* 313–340.

Control Data Corporation. (1980). *The Reading Comprehensive System.* Chicago: Author.

Cullinan, D., Lloyd, J., & Epstein, M. H. (1981). Strategy training: A structured approach to arithmetic instruction. *Exceptional Education Quarterly, 2*(1), 41–49.

Dole, J. A., Duffy, G. G., Roehler, L. R., & Pearson, P. D. (1991). Moving from the old to the new: Research on reading comprehension instruction. *Review of Education Research, 61,* 239–264.

Doris, J. L. (1993). Defining learning disabilities: A history of the search for consensus. In G. R. Lyon, D. B. Gray, J. F. Kavanagh, & N. A. Krasnegor (Eds.), *Better understanding learning disabilities: New views from research and their implications for education and public policies* (pp. 97–116). Baltimore: Paul H. Brookes.

Dunlap, G., dePerczel, M., Clarke, S., Wilson, D., Wright, S., White, R., & Gomez, A. (1994). Choice making to promote adaptive behavior for students with emotional and behavioral challenges. *Journal of Applied Behavior Analysis, 27,* 505–518.

Durkin, D. (1978–79). What classroom observations reveal about reading comprehension instruction. *Reading Research Quarterly, 14,* 481–533.

Engelmann, S., Becker, W. C., Hanner, S., & Johnson, G. (1978). *Corrective Reading Program: Series guide.* Chicago: Science Research Associates.

Engelmann, S., & Carnine, D. W. (1975). *DISTAR arithmetic I* (2nd ed.). Chicago: Science Research Associates.

Engelmann, S., & Carnine, D. W. (1982). *Theory of instruction: Principles and applications.* New York: Irvington.

Engelmann, S., Carnine, D. W., Engelmann, O., & Kelly, B. (1991). *Connecting Math Concepts.* Chicago: Science Research Associates.

Englert, C. S., Hiebert, E. H., & Stewart, S. R. (1986). Spelling unfamiliar words by an analogy strategy. *Journal of Special Education, 19,* 291–306.

Farnham-Diggory, S. (1986). Commentary: Time, now, for a little serious complexity. In S. P. Cici (Ed.), *Handbook of cognitive, social, and neuropsychological aspects of learning disabilities* (Vol. 1, pp. 123–158). Hillsdale, NJ: Erlbaum.

Feagans, L., & McKinney, J. D. (1981). The pattern of exceptionality across domains of learning disabled children. *Journal of Applied Developmental Psychology, 1,* 313–328.

Fernald, G. (1943). *Remedial techniques in basic school subjects.* New York: McGraw-Hill.

Fisk, J. L., & Rourke, B. P. (1983). Neuropsychological subtyping of learning disabled children: History, methods, implications. *Journal of Learning Disabilities, 16,* 529–531.

Flavell, J. H. (1979). Metacognition and cognitive monitoring: A new area of cognitive developmental inquiry. *American Psychologist, 34,* 906–911.

Fleishner, J. E. (1994). Diagnosis and assessment of mathematics learning disabilities. In G. R. Lyon (Ed.), *Frames of reference for the assessment of learning disabilities: New views on measurement issues* (pp. 441–458). Baltimore: Paul H. Brookes.

Fleishner, J. E., & Frank, B. (1979). Visual–spatial ability and mathematics achievement in learning disabled and normal boys. *Focus on Learning Problems in Mathematics, 1,* 7–22.

Fletcher, J. M., & Foorman, B. R. (1994). Issues in definition and measurement of learning disabilities: The need for early intervention. In G. R. Lyon (Ed.), *Frames of reference for the assessment of learning disabilities: New views on measurement issues* (pp. 185–200). Baltimore: Paul H. Brookes.

Fletcher, J. M., & Morris, R. (1986). Classification of disabled learners: Beyond exclusionary definitions. In S. J. Cici (Ed.), *Handbook of cognitive, social, and neuropsychological aspects of learning disabilities* (Vol. 1 pp. 55–80). Hillsdale, NJ: Erlbaum.

Foorman, B. R. (1995). Research on the "great debate": Code-oriented versus whole language approaches to reading instruction. *School Psychology Review, 24,* 376–392.

Foorman, B. R., Francis, D. J., Beeler, T., Winikates, D., & Fletcher, J. M. (1997). Early interventions for children with reading problems: Study designs and preliminary findings. *Learning Disabilities: A Multidisciplinary Journal, 8,* 63–72.

Foorman, B. R., Francis, D. J., Shaywitz, S. E., Shaywitz, B. A., & Fletcher, J. M. (in press). The case for early reading intervention. In B. Blachman (Ed.), *Foundations of reading acquisition and dyslexia.* Mahwah, NJ: Erlbaum.

Francis, D. J., Shaywitz, S. E., Steubing, K. K., Shaywitz, B. A., & Fletcher, J. M. (1994). Measurement of change: Assessing behavior over time and within a developmental framework. In G. R. Lyon (Ed.), *Frames of reference for the assessment of learning disabilities: New views on measurement issues* (pp. 29–68). Baltimore: Paul H. Brookes.

Frith, U. (Ed.). (1980). *Cognitive processes in spelling.* New York: Academic Press.

Frostig, M. (1967). Education of children with learning disabilities. In E. C. Frierson & W. B. Barbe (Eds.), *Educating children with learning disabilities* (pp. 387–398). New York: Appleton-Century-Crofts.

Gadow, K., Torgesen, J. K., & Dahlem, W. E. (1985). Learning disabilities. In M. Herson, V. B. Hanslet, & J. L. Matson (Eds.), *Behavior therapy for the developmentally and physically disabled: A handbook* (pp. 310–351). New York: Academic Press.

Garner, R., Alexander, P. A., & Hare, V. C. (1991). Reading comprehension failure in children. In B. Y. L. Wong (Ed.), *Learning about learning disabilities* (pp. 283–307). San Diego, CA: Academic Press.

Gerber, M. M. (1986). Generalization of spelling strategies by LD students as a result of contingent imitation/modeling and mastery criteria. *Journal of Learning Disabilities, 19,* 530–537.

Gersten, R. M., White, W. A., Falco, R., & Carnine, D. (1982). Teaching basic discriminations to handicapped and non-handicapped individuals through a dynamic presentation of instructional stimuli. *Analysis and Intervention in Developmental Disabilities, 2,* 305–317.

Gillingham, A., & Stillman, B. (1965). *Remedial training for children with specific disability in reading, spelling and penmanship* (7th ed.). Cambridge, MA: Educators Publishing Service.

Glennon, V. J., & Cruickshank, W. M. (1981). Teaching mathematics to children and youth with perceptual and cognitive deficits. In V. J. Glennon (Ed.), *The mathematical education of exceptional children and youth: An interdisciplinary approach* (pp. 50–94). Reston, VA: National Council of Teachers of Mathematics.

Goodman, K. S.(1986). *What's whole in whole language?* Portsmouth, NH: Heinemann.

Graham, S. (1982). Composition research and practice: A unified approach. *Focus on Exceptional Children, 14,* 1–16.

Graham, S., & Harris, K. (1993). Self-regulated strategy development: Helping students with learning problems develop as writers. *Elementary School Journal, 94,* 169–181.

Graham, S., & Harris, K. (1996). Addressing problems in attention, memory, and executive function. In G. R. Lyon & N. A. Krasnegor (Eds.), *Attention, memory, and executive function* (pp. 349–366). Baltimore: Paul H. Brookes.

Graham, S., Harris, K., MacArthur, C., & Schwartz, S. (1991). Writing and writing instruction with students with learning disabilities: A review of a program of research. *Learning Disability Quarterly, 14,* 89–114.

Graves, A., Montague, M., & Wong, B. Y. (1989, April). *The effects of procedural facilitation on story composition of learning disabled students.* Paper presented at the annual meeting of the American Educational Research Association, San Francisco.

Gregg, N. (1991). Disorders of written expression. In A. Bain, L. Bailet, & L. Moats (Eds.), *Written language disorders: Theory into practice* (pp. 65–97). Austin, TX: Pro-Ed.

Hall, R. V., Lund, D., & Jackson, D. (1968). Effects of teacher attention on study behavior. *Journal of Applied Behavior Analysis, 1,* 1–12.

Hallahan, D. P., & Cruickshank, W. M. (1973). *Psychoeducational foundations of learning disabilities.* Englewood Cliffs, NJ: Prentice-Hall.

Hallahan, D. P., Kauffman, J., & Lloyd, J. (1996). *Introduction to learning disabilities.* Needham Heights, MA: Allyn & Bacon.

Hallahan, D. P., Kneedler, R. D., & Lloyd, J. W. (1993). Cognitive behavior modification techniques for learning disabled children: Self-instruction and self-monitoring. In J. D. McKinney & L. Feagans (Eds.), *Current topics in learning disabilities* (Vol. 1, pp. 207–244). Norwood, NJ: Ablex.

Hallahan, D. P., Lloyd, J. W., Kosiwicz, J. M., & Graves, A. W. (1979). Self-monitoring of attention as a treatment for a learning disabled boy's off-task behavior. *Learning Disability Quarterly, 2,* 24–32.

Hammill, D. D. (1990). On defining learning disabilities: An emerging consensus. *Journal of Learning Disabilities, 23,* 74–84.

Hammill, D. D., Leigh, J. E., McNutt, G., & Larsen, S. C. (1981). A new definition of learning disabilities. *Learning Disabilities Quarterly, 4,* 336–342.

Hayes, J. R., & Flower, L. S. (1980). Identifying the organization of the writing process. In L. W. Gregg & E. R. Steinbery (Eds.), *Cognitive processes in writing* (pp. 3–30). Hillsdale, NJ: Erlbaum.

Hiebert, E. H., Colt, J. M., Catto, S. L., & Gury, E. C. (1992). Reading and writing of first grade students in a restructured Chapter 1 program. *American Educational Research Journal, 29,* 545–572.

Individuals with Disabilities Act of 1990 (IDEA), PL 101-476 (October 30, 1990). 20 U.S.C. SS 1400 et seq. *U.S. Statutes at Large, 104,* 1103–1151.

Individuals with Disabilities Education Act (IDEA), 34, C.F. R. § 300 (1991).

Iverson, S., & Tunmer, W. (1993). Phonological processing skills and the Reading Recovery program. *Journal of Educational Psychology, 85,* 112–120.

Johnson, D. J., & Myklebust, H. (1967). *Learning disabilities.* New York: Grune & Stratton.

Johnson, D. J. (1994). Measurement of listening and speaking. In G. R. Lyon (Ed.), *Frames of reference for the assessment of learning disabilities: New views on measurement issues* (pp. 201–227). Baltimore: Paul H. Brookes

Kauffman, J. M. Hallahan, D. P., Haas, K., Brame, T., & Boren, R.(1978). Imitating children's errors to improve their spelling performance. *Journal of Learning Disabilities, 11,* 217–222.

Kavale, K., & Forness, S. (1985). *The science of learning disabilities.* San Diego, CA: College-Hill Press.

Keogh, B. K., & Margolis, J. (1976). Learn to labor and wait: Attentional problems of children with learning disabilities. *Journal of Learning Disabilities, 9,* 176–286.

Kirby, J. R., & Robinson, G. L. (1987). Simultaneous and successive processing in reading disabled children. *Journal of Learning Disabilities, 20,* 243–252.

Kirk, S. A., & Kirk, W. D. (1971). *Psycholinguistic learning disabilities: Diagnosis and remediation.* Chicago: University of Chicago Press.

Kraetsch, G. A. (1981). The effects of oral instructions and training on the expansion of written language. *Learning Disability Quarterly, 4,* 82–90.

Lerner, J. W. (1989). Educational interventions in learning disabilities. *Journal of the American Academy of Child and Adolescent Psychiatry, 28,* 326–331.

Liberman, I. Y. (1992). The relation of speech to reading and writing. In R. Frost & L. Katz (Eds.), *Orthography, phonology, morphology, and meaning* (pp. 167–188). New York: Elsevier.

Liberman, I. Y., & Shankweiler, D. (1985). Phonology and the problems of learning to read and write. *Remedial and Special Education, 6,* 8–17.

Liberman, I. Y., & Shankweiler, D. (1991). Phonology and beginning reading: A tutorial. In L. Rieben & C. A. Perfetti (Eds.), *Learning to read: Basic research and its implications* (pp. 3–17). Hillsdale, NJ: Erlbaum.

Lindamood, C., & Lindamood, P. (1975). *Augitory discrimination in depth.* Austin, TX: Pro-Ed.

Lloyd, J. W. (1980). Academic instruction and cognitive-behavior modification. *Exceptional Education Quarterly, 1,* 53–63.

Lovett, M. W. (1991). Reading, writing, and remediation: Perspectives on the dyslexic learning disability from remedial outcome data. *Learning and Individual Differences, 3,* 295–305.

Lovitt, T. C. (1967). Assessment of children with learning disabilities. *Exceptional Children, 34,* 233–239.

Lovitt, T. C., & Curtiss, K. A. (1968). Effects of manipulating an antecedent event on mathematics response rate. *Journal of Applied Behavior Analysis, 1,* 329–333.

Lovitt, T. C., Guppy, T. E., & Blattner, J. E. (1969). The use of a free time contingency with fourth graders to increase spelling accuracy. *Behaviour Research and Therapy, 7,* 151–156.

Lundberg, I., Frost, J., & Peterson, O. (1988). Effects of an extensive program for stimulating phonological awareness in preschool children. *Reading Research Quarterly, 23,* 263–284.

Lyon, G. R. (1985). Identification and remediation of learning disability subtypes. *Learning Disability Focus, 1,* 21–35.

Lyon, G. R. (1987). Learning disabilities research: False starts and broken promises. In S. Vaughn & C. Bos (Eds.), *Research in learning disabilities: Issues and future directions* (pp. 69–85). San Diego, CA: College-Hill Press.

Lyon, G. R. (1995a). Toward a definition of dyslexia. *Annals of Dyslexia, 45,* 3–30.

Lyon, G. R. (1995b). Research initiatives and discoveries in learning disabilities. *Journal of Child Neurology, 120,* 57–51.

Lyon, G. R. (1996a). Learning disabilities. In E. Mash & R. Barkley (Eds.), *Child psychopathology* (pp. 390–435). New York: Guilford Press.

Lyon, G. R. (1996b). Learning disabilities: Past, present, and future perspectives. *The Future of Children, 6,* 24–46.

Lyon, G. R., & Flynn, J. M. (1991). Assessing subtypes of learning disabilities. In H. L. Swanson (Ed.), *Handbook on the assessment of learning disabilities: Theory, research, and practice* (pp. 59–74). Austin, TX: Pro-Ed.

Lyon, G. R., & Moats, L. C. (1988). Critical issues in the instruction of the leaning disabled. *Journal of Consulting and Clinical Psychology, 56,* 830–835.

Lyon, G. R., & Moats, L. C. (1997). Critical conceptual and methodological considerations in reading intervention research. *Journal of Learning Disabilities 30,* 578–588.

Lyon, G. R., Moats, L. C., & Flynn, J. M. (1988). From assessment to treatment: Linkages to interventions with children. In M. Tramontana & S. Hooper (Eds.), *Assessment issues in child neuropsychology* (pp. 182–210). New York: Plenum Press.

Lyon, G. R., & Risucci, D. (1988). Issues in the classification of learning disabilities. In K. Kavale (Ed.), *Learning disabilities: State of the art and practice* (pp. 48–61). San Diego: College-Hill.

MacArthur, C. A. (1988). The impact of computers on the writing process. Special Issue: Research and instruction in written language. *Exceptional Children, 54,* 536–542.

MacArthur, C. A., Haynes, J. A., Malouf, D. B., & Harris, K. (1990). Computer assisted instruction with learning-disabled students: Achievement, engagement, and other factors that influence achievement. *Journal of Educational Computing Research, 6,* 311–328.

Mann, L. (1979). *On the trail of process.* New York: Grune & Stratton.

Maria, K. (1987). A new look at comprehension instruction for reading disabled readers. *Annals of Dyslexia, 37,* 264–278.

Maria, K. (1990). *Reading comprehension issue instruction: Issues and strategies*. Parkton, MD: York Press.

Mather, N. (1992). Whole language reading instruction for students with learning disabilities: Caught in the crossfire. *Learning Disabilities Research and Practice, 7*, 87–95.

McNaughton, D., Hughes, C. A., & Clark, K. (1994). Spelling instruction for students with learning disabilities: Implications for research and practice. *Learning Disability Quarterly, 17*, 169–185.

Meichenbaum, D. (1977). *Cognitive behavior modification*. New York: Plenum Press.

Moats, L. C. (1994a). The missing foundation in teacher education: Knowledge of the structure of spoken and written language. *Annals of Dyslexia, 44*, 81–102.

Moats, L. C. (1994b). Honing the concepts of listening and speaking: A prerequisite to the valid measurement of language behavior in children. In G. R. Lyon (Ed.), *Frames of reference for the assessment of learning disabilities: New views on measurement issues* (pp. 229–241). Baltimore: Paul H. Brookes.

Moats, L. C., & Lyon, G. R. (1993). Learning disabilities in the United States: Advocacy, science, and the future of the field. *Journal of Learning Disabilities, 26*, 282–294.

Moats, L. C., & Lyon, G. R. (1996). Wanted: Teachers with knowledge of language. *Topics in Language Disorders, 16*, 73–86.

Montague, M., & Graves, A. (1993). Improving students' story writing. *Teaching Exceptional Children, 25*, 36–37.

Morris, R., Lyon, G. R., Alexander, D., Gray, D., Kavanagh, J., Rourke, B., & Swanson, H. (1994). Proposed guidelines and criteria for describing samples of persons with learning disabilities. *Learning Disability Quarterly, 17*, 106–109.

Myers, C. A. (1978). Reviewing the literature on Fernald's technique of remedial reading. *Reading Teacher, 31*, 614–619.

Myers, P., & Hammill, D. D. (1990). *Learning disabilities: Basic concepts, assessment practices, and instructional strategies*. Austin, TX: Pro-Ed.

National Joint Committee on Learning Disabilities. (1988). Letter to NJCLD member organizations.

Newby, R. F., & Lyon, G. R. (1991). Neuropsychological subtypes of learning disabilities. In J. E. Obrzut & G. W. Hynd (Eds.), *Neuropsychological foundations of learning disabilities: A handbook of issues, methods, and practice* (pp. 355–385). New York: Academic Press.

Obrzut, J. E., & Hynd, G. W. (1983). The neurobiological and neurophysiological foundations of learning disabilities. *Journal of Learning Disabilities, 16*, 515–520.

O'Hare, F. (1973). *Sentence-combining: Improving student writing without formal grammar instruction*. Urbana, IL: National Council of Teachers of English.

Open Court Reading (1995). *Collections for young scholars*. Peru, IL: SRA/McGraw Hill.

Palinscar, A., & Brown, A. (1983). *Reciprocal teaching of comprehension-monitoring activities* (Technical Report No. 269). Urbana, IL: The University of Illinois, Center for the Study of Reading.

Palinscar, A., & Brown, A. (1985). Reciprocal teaching: A means to a meaningful end. In J. Osborn, P. T. Wilson, & R. C. Anderson (Eds.), *Reading education: Foundations for a literate America* (pp. 66–87). Lexington, MA: D.C. Heath.

Palinscar, A. S., & Brown, D. A. (1987). Enhancing instructional time through attention to metacognition. *Journal of Learning Disabilities, 20*, 66–75.

Palinscar, A. S., & Klenk, L. (1992). Fostering literacy learning in supportive contexts. *Journal of Learning Disabilities, 25*, 211–225.

Perfetti, C. A. (1985), *Reading skill*. Hillsdale, NJ: Erlbaum.

Piaget, J., & Inhelder, B. (1969). *Memory and intelligence*. New York: Basic Books.

Polloway, E. J., Epstein, M. H., Polloway, C., Patton, J., & Ball, D. (1986). Corrective Reading Program: An analysis of effectiveness with learning disabled and mentally retarded students. *Remedial and Special Education, 7*, 41–47.

Poplin, M. S. (1988). Holistic/constructivist principles of the teaching/learning process: Implications for the field of learning disabilities. *Journal of Learning Disabilities, 21*, 401–416.

Pressley, M., Gaskins, I. W., Cunicelli, E. A., Burdick, N. J., Schaub-Matt, M., Lee, D. S., & Powell, N. (1991). Strategy instruction at Benchmark School: A faculty interview study. *Learning Disability Quarterly, 14*, 19–48.

Reid, D. K., & Hresko, W. P. (1981). *A cognitive approach to learning disabilities*. New York: McGraw-Hill.

Rivera, D., & Smith, D. D. (1987). Influence of modeling on acquisition and maintenance of computational skills: A summary of research findings from three sites. *Learning Disability Quarterly, 10*, 69–80.

Rourke, B. P. (Ed.). (1991). *Neuropsychological validation of learning disability subtypes*. New York: Guilford Press.

Rourke, B. P. (Ed.). (1995). *Syndrome of nonverbal learning disabilities: Neurodevelopmental manifestations*. New York: Guilford Press.

Rosenshine, B., & Stevens, R. (1986). Teaching functions. In M. C. Wittrock (Ed.), *Handbook of research on teaching* (3rd ed., pp. 376–391). New York: Macmillan.

Seabaugh, G. O., & Schumaker, J. B. (1993). The effects of self-regulation training on the academic productivity of secondary students with learning problems. *Journal of Behavioral Education, 4*, 109–133.

Shankweiler, D., & Liberman, I. Y. (1989). *Phonology and reading disability*. Ann Arbor: University of Michigan Press.

Shanahan, T., & Barr, R. (1995). Reading Recovery: An independent evaluation of the effects of an early instructional intervention for at-risk learners. *Reading Research Quarterly, 30,* 958–996.

Share, D., & Stanovich, K. (1995). Cognitive processes in early reading development: Accommodating individual differences into a model of acquisition. *Issues in Education: Contributions to Educational Psychology, 1,* 1–57.

Shaywitz, B. A., & Shaywitz, S. E. (1994). Measuring and analyzing change. In G. R. Lyon (Ed.), *Frames of reference for the assessment of learning disabilities: New views on Measurement issues* (pp. 29–58). Baltimore: Paul H. Brookes.

Shaywitz, S. E., Fletcher, J. M., & Shaywitz, B. A. (1994). Issues in the definition and classification of Attention Deficit Disorder. *Topics in Language Disorders, 14,* 1–25.

Skinner, B. F. (1968). *The technology of teaching.* New York: Appleton-Century-Crofts.

Stahl, S. A., & Miller, P. D. (1989). Whole language and language experience approaches for beginning reading: A quantitative research synthesis. *Review of Education Research, 59,* 87–116.

Stanovich, K. E. (1991). Discrepancy definitions of reading disability: Has intelligence led us astray? *Reading Research Quarterly, 26,* 7–29.

Stanovich, K. E. (1992). Speculations on the causes and consequences of individual differences in early reading acquisition. In P. Gough, L. Ehri, & R. Trieman (Eds.), *Reading acquisition* (pp. 307–342). Hillsdale, NJ: Erlbaum.

Stanovich, K. (1993). The construct validity of discrepancy definition of reading disabilities. In G. R. Lyon, D. B. Gray, J. F. Kavanaugh, & N. A. Krasnegor (Eds.), *Better understanding learning disabilities: New views from research and their implications for education and public policies,* (pp. 273–307). Baltimore: Paul H. Brookes.

Stanovich, K. E. (1994). Romance and reality. *The Reading Teacher, 47,* 280–291.

Stein, C. L. E., & Goldman, J. (1980). Beginning reading instruction for children with minimal brain dysfunction. *Journal of Learning Disabilities, 13,* 219–222.

Stern, C. A., & Stern, M. B. (1971). *Children discover arithmetic: An introduction to Structural Arithmetic* (rev. ed.). New York: Harper & Row.

Stevens, K. B., Blackhurst, A. E., & Slaton, D. D.(1991). Teaching memorized spelling with a microcomputer: Time delay and computer-assisted instruction. *Journal of Applied Behavior Analysis, 24,* 153–160.

Stevens, R., & Rosenshine, B. (1981). Advances in research on teaching. *Exceptional Education Quarterly, 2*(1), 1–9.

Tangel, D. M., & Blachman, B. A. (1995). Effect of phoneme awareness instruction on kindergarten children's invented spelling. *Journal of Reading Behavior, 24,* 233–261.

Tarver, S. G., Hallahan, D. P., Kauffman, J. M., & Ball, D. W. (1976). Verbal rehearsal and selective attention in children with learning disabilities: A developmental lag. *Journal of Experimental Child Psychology, 22,* 375–385.

Taylor, E. (1983). Measurement issues and approaches. In M. Rutter (Ed.), *Developmental neuropsychiatry* (pp. 239–258). New York: Guilford Press.

Torgesen, J. K. (1986). Learning disabilities theory: Its current state and future prospects. *Journal of Learning Disabilities, 19,* 399–407.

Torgesen, J. K. (1987). Thinking about the future by distinguishing between issues that have answers and those that do not. In S. T. Vaughn & C. S. Bos, (Eds.), *Issues and future directions for research in learning disabilities* (pp. 55–64). San Diego, CA: College-Hill Press.

Torgesen, J. K. (1991). Learning disabilities: Historical and conceptual issues. In B. Wong (Ed.), *Learning about learning disabilities* (pp. 3–39). San Diego, CA: Academic Press.

Torgesen, J. K., Wagner, R. K., & Rashotte, C. A. (1994a). Longitudinal studies of phonological awareness training on word learning in kindergarten children. *Journal of Educational Psychology, 84,* 364–370.

Torgesen, J. K., Wagner, R. K., & Rashotte, C. A. (1994b). Longitudinal studies of phonological processing and reading. *Journal of Learning Disabilities, 27,* 276–286.

Torgesen, J. K., Wagner, R. K., Rashotte, C. A., & Conway, T. (1997). Preventative and remedial interventions for children with severe reading disabilities. *Learning Disabilities: A Multidisciplinary Journal, 8,* 51–62.

U.S. Department of Education. (1989a). *To assure the free appropriate public education of all children with disabilities: Thirteenth annual report to Congress.* Washington, DC: U.S. Government Printing Office.

U.S. Department of Education. (1989b). *To assure the free appropriate public education of all handicapped children: Eleventh report to Congress on the implementation of the Education of the Handicapped Act.* Washington, DC: Department of Education.

Vellutino, F. R., Scanlon, D. M., & Tanzman, M. S. (1994). Components of reading ability: Issues and problems in operationalizing word identification, phonological coding, and orthographic coding. In G. R. Lyon (Ed.), *Frames of reference for the assessment of learning disabilities: New views on measurement issues* (pp. 279–329). Baltimore: Paul H. Brookes.

Wagner, R. K., Torgesen, J. D., & Rashotte, C. A. (1994). Development of reading-related phonological processing abilities: New evidence of bidirectional causality from a latent variable longitudinal study. *Developmental Psychology, 30,* 73–87.

White, W. A. T. (1988). A meta-analysis of the effects of direct instruction in special education. *Education and Treatment of Children, 11,* 364–374.

Whitman, T., Burgio, L., & Johnson, M. B. (1984). Cognitive behavioral interventions with mentally retarded children. In A. W. Meyers & W. E. Craighead (Eds.), *Cognitive behavior therapy with children* (pp. 193–227). New York: Plenum Press.

Williams, J. P. (1980). Teaching decoding with an emphasis on phoneme analysis and phoneme blending. *Journal of Educational Psychology, 72,* 1–15.

Wong, B. Y. L. (1985). Issues in cognitive-behavior interventions in academic skill areas. *Journal of Abnormal Child Psychology, 13,* 425–442.

Wong, B. Y. L. (1986). Metacognition and special education: A review of a view. *Journal of Special Education, 20,* 9–29.

Wong, B. Y. L. (1991). The Relevance of Metacognition to Learning Disabilities. In B. Y. L. Wong (Ed.), *Learning about learning disabilities* (pp. 231–258). San Diego, CA: Academic Press.

Zigmond, N. (1993). Learning disabilities from an educational perspective. In G. R. Lyon, D. B. Gray, J. F. Kavanagh, & N. A. Krasnegor (Eds.), *Better understanding learning disabilities: New views from research and their implications for education and public policies* (pp. 251–272). Baltimore: Paul H. Brookes.

Zigmond, N. (1994, July). *Acquisition of reading in children with severe LD* (Application No. PHS/NICHD R01). Grant application submitted to the National Institute of Child and Human Development, Bethesda, MD.

PART V

CHILDREN AT RISK

CHAPTER 10

Child Physical Abuse
and Neglect

Sandra T. Azar
Clark University

David A. Wolfe
University of Western Ontario

The scope of the problem of child maltreatment has grown enormously since Kempe and his colleagues wrote their seminal paper on the battered child syndrome in the early 1960s (Kempe, Silverman, Steele, Droegemueller, & Silver, 1962). In fact, in its major reports to the nation, the U.S. Advisory Board on Child Abuse and Neglect (USABCAN, 1990, 1993) found the problem to be so enormous and serious, and the failure of the system designed to deal with the problem so catastrophic, that they compared the crisis to a national emergency. Sadly, the number of children reported as abused and neglected in the United States doubled from 1.4 million children in 1986 to 2.8 million in 1993 (Sedlack & Broadhurst, 1996).

During its early stages, the child abuse field focused on identification of cases and developing legal strategies for dealing with perpetration and protecting children. This required attention to physical consequences to a greater extent than to psychological harm. Whereas research on the psychological impact of abuse and neglect on children's social, emotional, and behavioral out-

comes has progressed steadily over the past decade (Wolfe & McEachran, 1997), this progress has not been matched by similar advances in treatment. In this chapter we outline many of the critical issues that have arisen in the child abuse and neglect treatment field over the past decade, and offer suggestions for advancing clinical practice and research.

As a result of intensive research on the effects of child maltreatment, its developmental impact is becoming more clearly understood. The growing interest of behavioral scientists in the plight of maltreated children has also helped to identify the inadequacies in the lives of these children—such as the lack of a stable home environment, of positive interactions with adults and siblings, and of opportunities for learning prosocial behavior—that often coexist with maltreatment and potentiate its impact (Aber & Cicchetti, 1984; Azar, Barnes, & Twentyman, 1988; Wolfe, 1987).

This chapter begins with an overview of the child, parent, and family factors that are believed to cause or result from child maltreatment (the term "maltreatment" is used to refer to physical abuse and to physical and emotional neglect; the more specific terms are used when referring to each specific type). A conceptual framework is presented to offer a theoretical basis for understanding the development of abusive and neglectful behavior over time, and to assist treatment planners in the recognition of major family "symptoms" that foretell greater risk of maltreatment. This framework is accompanied by an assessment overview that focuses on the general needs of the family and the specific needs of the parent and child. Treatment methods that have shown promise or have received empirical support with maltreating families are then discussed in detail. Although our understanding of the impact of maltreatment on children has progressed tremendously (Wekerle & Wolfe, 1996), strategies for combating it remain stagnant (Becker et al., 1995; National Research Council, 1993; Wolfe & Wekerle, 1993). In particular, studies of treatment outcomes with abused and neglected children have been few and far between (Azar & Bober, in press; Fantuzzo, 1990).

We emphasize the use of behavioral and cognitive-behavioral approaches with maltreating families, because these methods have received the most empirical support and clinical detail. We also outline special issues and precautions that have emerged from treatment efforts with this population. Where applicable, new directions in treatment and prevention are also discussed, with the intention that these promising approaches will receive further expansion and research.

DEFINITION AND SCOPE

Conceptual Definition

A parent who abuses a child is often viewed by community members as being quite different or distinct from nonabusive parents. That is, abusive behavior is so inconceivable to many individuals that a false dichotomy surfaces inadvertently to separate and define "abusive" parents in relation to "normal" parents. However, such a clear distinction between abusive and nonabusive parents does not readily appear if one looks at the different styles of parenting in each community. A parent's behavior toward his or her offspring may change dramatically at any given moment in response to child- or situationally-related demands, and at times this behavior includes negative interactions. What most often distinguishes parents who have been reported

for abuse from socioeconomically matched parents who have not, however, is the chronic and escalating pattern of conflict between the parent and child, culminating in more and more serious harm over time (Knutson & Bower, 1994). In addition, what may make this pattern most detrimental to children's outcomes is that it takes place in the absence of compensatory factors (e.g., positive interactions, a strong social support network), some of which are crucial in facilitating children's social, cognitive, and emotional development.

Rather than viewing child abuse and neglect as phenomena that are distinct and separate from other parental actions, therefore, the present approach to conceptualizing these problems focuses on a continuum model of parenting behavior (see Bell & Harper, 1977; Wolfe, 1991). At one extreme of the continuum are those practices considered to be most harmful and inappropriate (such as striking the child with a dangerous object, burns, physical and emotional rejection, etc.), and at the other extreme are methods that promote the child's social, emotional, and intellectual development. From this perspective, child abuse and neglect can be defined, for treatment purposes, in terms of the *degree to which a parent uses aversive or inappropriate control strategies with his or her child and/or fails to provide minimal standards of caregiving and nurturance* (Wolfe, 1987). Child abuse, accordingly, is not viewed as being necessarily a symptom of an undefined personality disorder, but rather is conceptualized as the hypothetical extreme of aversive control to which a parent will go during interactions with his or her child without exercising restraint. The psychological mechanisms associated with such lack of control (e.g., thought processes, emotional responses) have received greater attention in recent studies, which have begun to clarify the extent to which abusive behavior is a function of characteristics of the individual (e.g., personality disturbance, cognitive styles, neurological problems) and situational factors that foster such behavior (e.g., aversive child behavior, marital conflict, unmanageable stress).

The previous definition of child abuse and neglect for treatment-planning purposes does not imply that the consequences to the child are not serious; abusive acts were responsible for over 1,000 child deaths in 1993 alone (NCCAN, 1994). Rather, this viewpoint intends to draw attention toward those aspects of abuse that resemble "typical" parenting methods except in terms of their severity. Furthermore, this definition highlights not only the physically harmful methods that a parent might use, but also those methods that may be inadequate to meet the child's needs, such as a lack of physical attention or praise, or unclear directives from the parent (Azar, 1986, 1989a).

This view of child maltreatment as an extreme disturbance of child rearing, therefore, emphasizes the nature of the socialization process (i.e., cultural values, overly rigid and inflexible parent–child role schemas, and norms) that permits the use of violence as a means of interpersonal control and problem solving. Maltreating families are ones in which the usual balances between reward and punishment and between discipline and affection have broken down, and where there are failures in the contingency between parent and child behavior (e.g., maternal negative responses to prosocial child behavior; Cerezo, D'Ocon, & Dolz, 1996). As a result, developmental accomplishments and progression often fall behind. Thus, abusive and neglectful families have ceased to function as facilitators of children's social and cognitive development and to promote healthy socialization (Maccoby & Martin, 1983).

Incidence and Profile of Child Abuse and Neglect

The number of children who are officially reported to child protection agencies because of child abuse and neglect has climbed each year, with a 331% increase in reporting rates over the last decade and a half (NCCAN, 1994). The third National Incidence Study (NIS), conducted in 1993, estimated that almost 3 million incidents of child maltreatment occurred during that year (Sedlak & Broadhurst, 1996). NIS estimates are derived from official reports of abuse and neglect, as well as a nationally representative sample of professionals who come in contact with maltreated children in a variety of settings. Maltreatment situations are classified into four major types: physical abuse, child neglect, sexual abuse, and emotional abuse. With the exception of physical abuse, each of these categories is broken down further into subtypes.

To account for the fact that maltreatment affects children regardless of actual physical injuries, the NIS definitions of maltreatment allow for two different sets of definitional standards: the "harm standard," whereby children have suffered demonstrable harm as a result of maltreatment; and the "endangerment standard," which includes all of the harm standard children, but

adds those who have not yet been harmed by maltreatment but who have experienced maltreatment that puts them in danger of being harmed. Approximately three times as many children are endangered as are harmed. Based on the endangerment standard, the total incidence of all forms of maltreatment in 1993 was 42 children out of every 1,000 in the United States—a figure that had doubled since the previous survey was conducted in 1986.

The profile of the characteristics of maltreatment has remained constant in recent years. Child neglect continued to be the most common form of maltreatment in 1993, with almost 30 children out of every 1,000 in the United States (70% of cases) becoming victims of physical, emotional, or educational neglect in that year. All forms of abuse affected another 18 per 1,000, or 43% of cases overall (due to overlap, these percentages summed to more than 100%). Specifically, physical abuse accounted for 22%, sexual abuse for 11%, and emotional abuse for 19% of maltreatment incidents (again, with overlap in reports). Sexual abuse reports and substantiated cases rose dramatically in the 1980s, but have leveled off more recently (Sedlack & Broadhurst, 1996).

Although child maltreatment occurs at all ages, younger children are more likely to be reported for physical neglect, latency-age children for emotional neglect (such as witnessing spousal abuse), and teens for physical abuse. Sexual abuse, in contrast, is relatively constant from age 3 on, which attests to children's vulnerability from early preschool years throughout childhood (Sedlack & Broadhurst, 1996). Gender differences in maltreatment rates are generally insignificant, with the important exception of specific types of abuse. Girls are 25% more likely to be victims of any form of abuse than boys (20.2 females vs. 16.1 males per 1,000 in the general U. S. population), which essentially reflects the fact that their risk of sexual abuse is nearly three times that of boys (6.8 vs 2.3 males per 1,000).

A sociodemographic profile of families reported for child abuse and neglect illuminates many of the cultural and social forces that determine child-rearing methods and that at the same time may contribute to family discord and violence. Although maltreatment occurs in all socioeconomic groups, clinical reports, surveys, and official statistics consistently find that it is most likely to happen among the poor or disadvantaged (Gelles, 1983; Sedlack & Broadhurst, 1996). Studies of the representativeness of epidemiological data indicate that this finding does not appear to be a bias in reporting, especially since it has consistently emerged over the last 20 years of data gathering (Pelton, 1994). For example, the incidence rate for overall maltreatment rises from 42 to 99 per 1,000 children among those from the poorest families (i.e., those with an income of <$15,000 per year). This rate is 3 times greater than that of children from moderate-income families ($15,000–<$30,000 per year), and 25 times higher than that of children from families in the highest income bracket (>$30,000 per year). Similarly, the relationship of family structure to maltreatment deserves consideration. Children living in single-parent homes are at significantly greater risk of both physical abuse and neglect, and those living in father-only homes are almost twice as likely to be physically abused as those living with mothers alone (Sedlak & Broadhurst, 1996).

Perpetrator characteristics are also relevant to treatment approaches, given that few fathers or father figures have been involved in treatment evaluation studies involving this population. A child's birth parents are, for the most part, the perpetrators of all forms of child maltreatment (79.2%; NCCAN, 1994). There are important exceptions, however, as well as key gender differences in the nature of abuse or neglect. Nearly one-half of sexually abused children in the NCCAN (1994) study were abused by persons other than parents or parent figures (compared to only a fraction in other categories). Consistent with the fact that mothers and mother substitutes tend to be the primary caretakers, 87% of all neglected children and 93% of physically neglected children suffered at the hands of female perpetrators. In contrast, abused children in all categories were more often maltreated by males: 67% of all abused children, 89% of sexually abused, 63% of emotionally abused, and 58% of physically abused children were maltreated by males. (Note: In this chapter, we will concentrate on physical abuse and physical and emotional neglect. For a full discussion of the important topic of child sexual abuse, see V. V. Wolfe, Chapter 11, this volume.)

THEORETICAL–CONCEPTUAL FORMULATIONS

Distinctions between different theoretical formulations of child abuse and neglect have become less clear in recent years, which may re-flect the fact that they share important commonalities and do not necessarily represent radically opposed viewpoints of maltreating parents (Wolfe, 1985). Almost all theoretical work in the area has focused on physical abuse, so our discussion of theories regarding neglect is thereby limited (see Wekerle & Wolfe, 1996, and Azar, Povilaitis, Lauretti, & Pouquette, 1997, for further details).

The three major models of child abuse that were developed throughout the 1970s (i.e., the psychopathological, sociocultural, and social-interactional models) all reflect attempts to understand individual characteristics of abusive parents in relation to prior experience and current demands. One distinction that can be inferred from these explanations, however, is the amount of emphasis each model places on the parent as the principal cause of abuse, as opposed to situational circumstances or the broader sociocultural milieu (Azar, 1991a; Belsky, 1980).

The major theories of child abuse focus primarily on explanations as to *why* a parent might abuse a child, and *how* family process can develop into violent interactions (see Azar, 1991a; Azar, Povilaitis, Lauretti, & Pouwuette, 1997; Wekerle & Wolfe, 1996). Although it is beyond the scope of this chapter to expound on these theories, three tenets can be summarized to form a foundation for the discussion that follows.

The first of these tenets relates to the importance of recognizing and studying the *context* of maltreatment, such as the nature of family life, environmental stressors affecting the family, and sociodemographic factors. The context of child maltreatment, as argued by sociocultural theorists, is described typically as being one of social and economic family deprivation. Such deprivation may be the force that transforms predisposed, high-risk parents into abusive or neglectful parents (see Garbarino & Stocking, 1980). The greater degree of stress in the social environment of the abusive parent increases the probability that family violence will surface as an attempt to gain control or cope with irritating, stressful events. In the case of neglect, stress may be so great as to cause parents to withdraw entirely from their parenting responsibilities as an avoidant coping strategy. According to this perspective, child maltreatment is not an isolated social phenomenon or a personality defect of the parent per se; rather, this view maintains that "normal" parents may be socialized into harmful child care practices through the interaction of cultural, community, and familial influences (Belsky, 1980; Parke, 1977). This tenet is supported by studies indicating that, for example, socioeconomic factors (e.g., unemployment, restricted educational and occupational opportunities, poor housing) account for a large proportion of the variance in rates of child abuse and neglect reports (Garbarino, 1976; Gil, 1970). The context of maltreatment emerges as a critical factor in determining treatment goals and directions, as discussed later in this chapter.

The second major tenet drawn from child abuse theories relates to the social-interactional *process* that is ongoing between parent and child (within the context of the family and larger social structure). This process resembles similar processes that occur in normal and in clinically distressed parent–child relationships, such as the reciprocation of aversive behavior, reinforcement of inappropriate behavior, ineffective use of punishment, and conditioned emotional arousal. This interactional process approaches the etiology and maintenance of abuse in terms of the dynamic interplay between individual, family, and social factors in relation to both past (e.g., previous abuse as a child in the parent's history) and present (e.g., a demanding child) events that shape the parent–child relationship. Although parental characteristics are considered important determinants of an abusive episode, the emphasis is mostly upon the *processes* that define the relationship between the parent and child. It should be pointed out that these processes are not limited only to observable behaviors, such as parental criticisms, child behavior problems, yelling, or displays of anger and aggression. The relevance of cognitive and affective processes, such as intelligence, attitudes, expectations regarding children's behavior, problem-solving capacities, attributions for behavior, depression and anger, also emerges in studies of how abusive parents process the stressful aspects of their environment.

The third tenet to be incorporated into the current model concerns the learning-based explanations for aggressive behavior that are implicit in the two previous explanations. Particularly relevant to an understanding of the escalation from punishment to abuse are the psychological processes linking mood states and emotional arousal to the disinhibition of aggression.

It comes as no surprise that an individual's behavior can be greatly influenced by his or her mood and/or relative state of quiescence versus arousal. What is most salient to the study of child abuse, however, is the recognition that negative experiences with intimate others can have affective "tags" when stored in memory (Bower, 1981). When these experiences are recalled at some later point in time, the recollection of the actual event may bias or overshadow the person's mood at the time. Thus, a parent's previous mood of distress and anger toward others or the child may be recalled by the child's current expression or behavior, even though it is not necessarily provocative. In turn, this association between mood and memory can lead to an overgeneralized (i.e., more angry, more aggressive) response by the parent. Presumably, the adult is responding to cues that have been previously associated with frustration and anger, and consequently the adult's behavior toward the child may be potentiated by these conditioning experiences (Berkowitz, 1983; Vasta, 1982). Recent cognitive formulations have also emphasized the role that stable, maladaptive, preexisting relational schemas and scripts play in triggering an abusive episode (Azar, 1986, 1989a, 1997). That is, the abusive parent's schemas for the parent's and child's roles are overly rigid and inappropriate, such that the realities of parenting constantly violate them and produce distress.

The person's level of arousal and his or her beliefs about the *source* of this arousal play a critical role in determining the actual expression of aggression. An abusive parent, for example, may have been angered and aroused (i.e., hyper-alert, tense, anxious, in a state of emotional re-activity) by a previous encounter with someone (an employer, neighbor, motorist, etc.), which lowers his or her threshold for anger and aggression with others (e.g., family members). These feelings of anger create a need for justification, such as blaming others for causing him or her to feel angry, upset, and bothered, which in return encourages further anger and aggression (Averill, 1983). Because of the child's availability and lower-status position, he or she becomes a likely target for this blaming process. The resulting anger and arousal interferes with rational problem solving, such that the parent's awareness of the outcome of his or her actions is diminished and the disciplinary behaviors come under control of emotional and reflexive factors (Vasta, 1982). In this state, the physical punishment may be prolonged, and the act itself can become invigorating or cathartic (see Zillman, 1979). Cognitive formulations have also argued for preexisting skill deficits (e.g., generally poor problem-solving capacities) that increase the probability of heightened frustration and of the parent's information-processing capacities' narrowing under conditions of situational and child-rearing stress

(Azar, 1989a, 1997; Milner, 1993). In addition, over time, the blaming of the child may solidify into an attributional bias, such that even nonintentional aversive child behavior becomes cause for an excessive negative retaliation.

How parents gradually acquire the preconditions that lead to the rather sudden onset of an abusive episode or to chronic rejection and neglect remains a critical concern to treatment planning. Different approaches to intervention may be more relevant at different stages in the development of the preconditions of maltreatment.

The role of information-processing disturbances has been highlighted in recent studies (see Azar & Twentyman, 1986; Azar, 1989a, 1997; Milner, 1993), which attempt to explain the full breadth of disturbed transactions in abusive and neglectful families beyond those involving child noncompliance. These views propose that parents may misperceive or mislabel typical child behavior in ways that lead to developmentally maladaptive responses (e.g., neglectful behavior), as well as to greater frustration and aggression. One possibility is that parents at risk for abusive and neglectful behavior have disturbed schemas regarding the role of parents in children's lives, as well as appropriate behaviors to expect from children. For example, some abusive and neglectful parents view children as having the perspective-taking capacities of adults; therefore, parents see them as able to understand from a young age what their parents are thinking and feeling, and to adjust their behavior accordingly. Children inevitably violate these unrealistic standards, and this results in tension in the family system. Such schemas also lead parents to fail to respond in appropriate ways regarding the developmental needs of children. Parents may make less use of explanation, because they believe that children "know" what they are doing or what is expected of them. Even when a child is behaving appropriately, a parent may believe that he or she is being noncompliant. Because such parents misperceive the meaning of child behavior, their children's needs for information, stimulation, and basic care and monitoring are less likely to be met, resulting in potential neglect situations (e.g., the parents' leaving young children alone in an apartment with the belief that they can handle such situations). Over time, because children fail to live up to such parental standards and to behave as parents believe children "should," children may be seen as intentionally withholding appropriate responses and resisting the parents' efforts. Par-

ents may attribute such behavior to children's "disposition," which strengthens their expectations for further misbehavior. Negative self-attributions may result (e.g., "I'm a lousy mother. Other mothers can get their kids to do these things"), leaving parents with a lowered sense of self-efficacy in their role as parents and making the tasks involved less rewarding. Parents may consequently avoid attempts to address their children's needs. At other times they may take actions to teach or discipline their children, but because their responses are coercive and they do not facilitate the children's emotional, social, and behavioral development.

Research work has begun to document the existence of such cognitive disturbances and to link them to parental responses. Abusive and at-risk parents, for example, have been shown to have higher levels of unrealistic expectations regarding both the social-cognitive and physical care capacities of children (e.g., beliefs that a 3-year-old can comfort them when they are upset, that a 4-year-old can pick out the right clothing for the weather, or that a teenager can help patch up their marital problems) (Azar, Robinson, Hekimian, & Twentyman, 1984; Azar & Rohrbeck, 1986). Child-abusing parents have also shown a negative attributional bias in interpreting child behavior in a few studies (Azar, 1989a; Larrance & Twentyman, 1983). Unrealistic expectations and negative intent attributions to children have both been linked to higher levels of punishment assigned to aversive child behavior and lower use of explanation (a more adaptive parenting strategy) (Azar, 1991a, 1991b; Barnes & Azar, 1990). These cognitive factors have also been linked to social workers' ratings of family dysfunction and child jeopardy, as well as to lower parental empathy (Azar, 1989b). Finally, Miller and Azar (1996) showed that mothers at risk for child abuse displayed a more generalized attributional bias, making more internal attributions for negative outcomes for others as well as themselves. The finding that child-abusing parents appear to assign more responsibility to their children for negative outcomes (e.g., the children are intentionally misbehaving or "out to get" the parents; Larrance & Twentyman, 1983) is particularly important, in light of evidence suggesting that the extent to which children are held responsible for negative behavior influences the severity of punishment deemed appropriate by parents (Dix, Ruble, & Zambarano, 1989). Thus, such attributions would heighten the probability that children will be harshly treated.

The task of professionals dealing with such distressed families is to interrupt these processes and to intervene in such a way as to restore the families' ability to cope with external demands and provide for the developmental and socialization needs of their children. Cognitive and behavioral assessment and intervention approaches show much promise in assisting in this task.

TREATMENT ISSUES WITH MALTREATING FAMILIES

Early methods of treatment for physical abuse (e.g., lay counseling, psychotherapy, and provisions of support services) were too narrow in scope to produce changes in the disturbed family interaction patterns that are central to child abuse and neglect. By the late 1970s, national evaluation studies indicated high recidivism rates both during and after treatment (Cohn, 1979; Herrenkohl, Herrenkohl, Egolf, & Seech, 1979), which prompted strategies that targeted child-rearing attitudes, skill deficiencies, and anger control. Intervention techniques for the kinds of deficits exhibited by physically abusive families were modified for this population on the basis of well-developed behavioral training methods, such as child management skills training, stress and anger management training, and cognitive restructuring approaches (Dangel & Polster, 1984; McMahon & Forehand, 1984; Novaco, 1975).

Approaches based on social learning theory are well suited to address characteristics of abusive and neglectful parents that often impede treatment efforts. Maltreating parents are often lower in intellectual functioning and education than nonmaltreating parents are (Schilling & Schinke, 1984), and typically have fewer economic and social resources available. Behavioral approaches are more effective than insight-oriented approaches with less sophisticated clients because they are concrete and problem-focused (Foxx, McMorrow, & Mennemeier, 1984; Foxx, McMorrow, & Schloss, 1983; Kazdin & Polster, 1973), and match the clients' expectations that psychological treatments should be prescriptive, like medical treatments (Aronson & Overall, 1966; Lorion, 1978). Finally, behavioral approaches may be perceived as more "educational" in nature; this is less threatening to abusive and neglectful parents, who may worry that they are seen as "crazy" and/or may lack motivation for long-term insight-oriented therapies.

Though all of these reasons make behavioral strategies attractive for treating abuse and neglect, there are some limitations in the use of these approaches as well. First, some maltreating parents suffer from long-standing personality disorders or severe disturbances (e.g., psychosis) that may require long-term psychiatric and pharmacological interventions. Such approaches may precede or replace behavioral treatment when necessary. Second, the involvement of the legal system may interfere with clients' motivation (e.g., they may fear that the observations required in such treatment may be used against them). More attention is given to this problem later in the chapter.

A third limitation in using behavioral methods is related to the requirement that parents practice new parenting strategies with their children, which may not be possible if children are in foster care and parents have limited visitation. Role playing and special supervised visitation arrangements may be viable interim solutions to this problem. Fourth, behavioral approaches with family members may be inadequate to modify the families' lack of social and economic resources, which may require collaborative efforts with social service agencies for vocational training and other programs.

Finally, a more general and less easily resolved limitation to the application of behavioral techniques with maltreating families has to do with the state of our understanding of child maltreatment as a "behavioral" problem. Although progress has occurred in our empirical knowledge base in the last decade, the building of this data base has continued to be slow (Azar, Fantuzzo, & Twentyman, 1984; National Research Council, 1993). Behavioral interventions require a clear, empirically grounded understanding of the topography of the disorder to be treated (i.e., the antecedents and consequences that elicit and maintain the behavior). Some of the most relevant dimensions to be assessed and then targeted in treatment may still be unknown. These issues are addressed throughout the remainder of this chapter.

ASSESSMENT ISSUES

The causes and outcomes of child maltreatment are entwined with parents' childhood and early adult history, child-rearing skills, stressful events, and social relationships, and the features of children, among other factors. In view of the complexity of this problem, behavioral assessment and treatment of abusive and neglectful families must be approached as a multistage process. Assessment typically begins with impressionistic data from reporting and referral sources, and then narrows toward the evaluation of more specific intervention needs. In addition, several aspects of assessing, as well as of treating, abusive and neglectful families are unique (Wolfe & McEachran, 1997); these aspects are highlighted in this section and the one that follows.

Developing an Assessment Strategy

Assessment of a family typically begins by consulting with the family's social worker to review the allegations, evidence, proceedings, and decisions that affect the evaluation, leading to the formulation of appropriate assessment questions. The social worker's perspective on the family should be carefully outlined, as well as preliminary goals that have been prepared with the family. Following this initial consultation, several intermediate goals must be met prior to making case management decisions and initiating intervention with a maltreating family. These goals include two general concerns requiring initial screening and attention: (1) determining danger and risk to the child, and (2) identifying general strengths and problem areas of the family system. These are followed by more specific goals: (3) identifying parental needs vis-à-vis child-rearing demands, and (4) identifying child needs.

This assessment strategy has been summarized in Table 10.1, which specifies the purpose of assessment in view of decisions that must be made and precautions that must be heeded. In reference to the first two general assessment concerns (see above), the examiner often must first address the degree of dangerousness or risk to the child that currently exists in the family, in order to assist the child protection agency and/or courts in deciding on apprehension and alternative placement of the child versus having the child remain in his or her own home. Although violence prediction is controversial, evaluating level of risk may have some utility (Grisso & Appelbaum, 1992). This overriding concern of child protection is typically approached in conjunction with other community professionals involved with the family (e.g., physicians, social workers, public health nurses), although the psychologist's role is critical in identifying the major strengths and problem areas of the family system that guide the decision for child place-

ment. An interview with the parent(s) can begin to establish the significance of different etiological factors, such as parental background, the couple relationship, perceived areas of stress and support, and psychiatric or physical symptomatology that may have a bearing on a parent's behavior toward the child.

Assessment findings that have more specific relevance to behavioral treatment emerge during the detailed identification of parental and child needs (see Table 10.1). At this point the examiner is concerned with identification or development of possible treatment alternatives for the family; this requires more specialized assessment instruments and skills, as discussed below. It should be noted that materials collected may ultimately serve legal purposes (e.g., in hearings concerning the termination of parental rights, establishing parental lack of progress in treatment), and therefore evaluators must have specific knowledge of legal criteria and measurement issues (Azar, Benjet, Furmann, & Cavallaro, 1995). Further details concerning assessment of maltreated children and their families are provided in Wolfe and McEachran (1997).

Assessing Parental Responses to Child-Rearing Demands

Child maltreatment is strongly linked to events that involve the child in some manner, despite the formidable influence of parental background, psychological functioning, and situational stressors (Wolfe, 1985). Therefore, the following assessment overview of the parent's typical daily behavior with his or her child includes self-report and observational procedures in reference to situations that may lead to parent–child conflict and maladaptive caretaking responses. This strategy involves an analysis of idiosyncratic cognitions, arousal patterns, fluctuations in mood and affect, and characteristic response styles during everyday child-rearing situations.

Parenting involves considerable cognitive activity. Parents must balance long- and short-term socialization goals and must make continuous judgments regarding the meaning of child behavior, its causes, and whether intervention is required. This is especially true before the child has language. As noted earlier, there is some evidence of bias in these interpretive processes in abusive and neglectful parents (Azar, 1989b, 1997; Crittenden, 1993). These disturbances can occur at the precue level (e.g., preexisting expectancies regarding child behavior), in the as-

TABLE 10.1. Child Abuse and Neglect Assessment Strategy: An Overview

Purpose	Pending decisions	Precautions
A. Determining dangerousness and risk to the child in cases of detected or undetected maltreatment	Apprehension of child Alternative placement of child	Removing and returning child to family is highly stressful Initial impression of family may be distorted

B. Identifying general strengths and problem areas of the family system
  Family background
  Marital relationship
  Perceived areas of stress and supports
  Symptomatology
	Identification of major factors (antecedents, consequences, and individual characteristics) suspected to be operative within the family
	Directions for protective services, supports, additional community services
		Involvement of too many professionals may overwhelm family
		"Crises" that family members report may change dramatically
		Parent–child problems may be embedded in chronic family problems (e.g., financial; marital) that resist change

C. Identification of parental needs vis-à-vis child-rearing demands
  Child-rearing methods and skills
  Anger and arousal toward child
  Perceptions and expectations of children
	Behavioral intervention planning and establishing priority of needs	Parental behavior toward child may be a function of both proximal (e.g., child behavior) and distal (e.g., job stress) events
		Numerous treatment interferences must be identified (e.g., resistance, socioeconomic status, marital problems)

D. Identification of child needs
  Child behavior problems with family members
  Child adaptive abilities and cognitive and emotional development
	Referral to school-based intervention
	Behavioral interventions (e.g., parent training)
	Returning child to family
		Unclear or delayed expression of symptom/impairments
		Child's behavior may be partially a function of recent family separation and change

Note. From Wolfe and McEachran (1997). Copyright 1997 by The Guilford Press. Reprinted by permission.

signment of causality after a child cue has been labeled as noncompliance (e.g., negative dispositional attributions), or in the active selection of responses (e.g., problem-solving capacities). Assessment, therefore, should include what a parent thinks is normal child behavior and the "typical" meaning the parent assigns to a child's responses. For example, the Parent Opinion Questionnaire assesses parental unrealistic expectations regarding appropriate behavior in children that may lead to anger and frustration, as well as developmentally inappropriate responses,; it distinguishes abusive and neglectful mothers from controls (Azar, Robinson, et al., 1984; Azar & Rohrbeck, 1986). The Adult/Adolescent Parenting Inventory (Bavolek, 1984) has been used to measure parenting attitudes in four areas: parental expectations of the child; empathy toward the child's needs; belief in the value of physical punishment; and parent–child role reversal. Parents should also be questioned regarding their assignment of causality for aversive child behavior, which may provide evidence

of attributional biases that may need to be addressed in anger management work and that may interfere with parents' engaging in child management strategies. For example, it will be difficult for parents to remain calm if they believe that their child is "out to get" them. Thought-listing strategies can also be helpful to solicit cognitions (Interpersonal Process Recall; Elliott, 1986). Table 10.2 lists common narratives suggesting cognitive problems.

In addition to parental cognitions, a parent's emotional reactivity or displeasure in response to aversive environmental demands merits careful attention, because of the role it is believed to play as a mediator of anger and aggression (Averill, 1983; Berkowitz, 1983; Wolfe, 1985). Although maltreating parents may be unwilling to acknowledge the full extent of their culpability, they are often willing to describe their feelings of anger and irritation that they believe are "provoked" by their children or by family events. As well, they are more willing to describe their feelings of anger and "loss of control" if provided with distinctive cues or examples, such as interacting with their children in a high-conflict situation or discussing a recent conflict (e.g., Koverola, Elliot-Faust, & Wolfe, 1984). Therefore, feelings of anger, tension, and frustration can be identified most readily by asking parents to provide recent examples of irritating child behaviors, the circumstances in which these occurred, how they felt and interpreted the situation, and how they reacted. Similarly, mood and affect disturbances (e.g., depression, anxiety, agitation) that precede or follow parent–child conflicts can be assessed in the context of the clinical interview or through standardized tests, such as the Minnesota Multiphasic Personality Inventory—2 (Butcher, Dahlstrom, Graham, Tellegen, & Krammer, 1989), the Symptom Checklist—90 (Derogatis, 1983), or the Child Abuse Potential Inventory (CAPI; Milner, 1986).

Alternatively, self-monitoring of annoyance, anger, or similar feelings that lead to conflict with the child can be achieved by using an "anger diary" (Wolfe, Kaufman, Aragona, & Sandler, 1981), in which the parent records his or her feelings of anger or frustration in response to incidents of child misbehavior, or by having the parent review videotapes from previous parent–child interactions in the clinic and identify changes in affect and/or irritation during an ongoing, realistic interchange with the child. The latter is clinically useful for assessing each parent's distinctive pattern of emotional arousal and cognitive attributions in reference to typical situations involving his or her own child, especially if the child is young and behaves spontaneously during clinic observations. Moreover, parents' review of videotaped interactions with their own children can be a valuable introduction to behavioral intervention, whereby parents are put in the role of observers and problem solvers in reference to their own situation. From a clinical perspective, this approach is usually well received and very productive in enlisting cooperation and identifying important issues.

Assessment of child-rearing methods that a parent uses on a daily basis with his or her child is critical for developing behavioral treatment objectives. Such assessment is aimed at determining the frequency and quality of parenting methods that favor the child's social and cognitive development, as well as identifying the functional relationships between parent and child behavior. This task can be approached in several ways, including both self-report and observational strategies. The CAPI (Milner, 1986)

has been specifically designed to measure problem areas related to parental and family background (such as those identified above) that are associated with an increased probability of abuse. The Abuse scale consists of six factor subscales: Distress, Rigidity, Unhappiness, Problems with Child and Self, Problems with Family, and Problems with Others. In addition, there is a Lie scale that indicates the degree of deceptive responding (e.g., "I love all children"). In addition to assessing personality and situational factors that may lead to aggressive responses, parental knowledge and skill concerning ways to promote healthy child development can be approached through specific skill measures, such as the Parental Problem-Solving Measure (Hanson, Pallotta, Christopher, Conaway, & Lundquist, 1995).

Observations of parent–child transactions are invaluable for revealing the nature and quality of the parent–child relationship. Abusive and neglectful parents differ from nonmaltreating parents in the quality of interactions with their infants, preschoolers, and school-age children, lending support for the significance of this method (Wolfe, 1985). In particular, maltreating parents are less interactive and less positive toward their children (Bousha & Twentyman, 1984; Burgess & Conger, 1978); they fail to modify their behavior in response to the children's needs; and they are more inclined to make inappropriate demands of young children (Crittenden, 1982; Trickett & Kuczynski, 1986). Such insensitive caregiving can have a far-reaching negative impact upon children's development, and may account for many of the disturbances found among maltreated children (Azar et al., 1988; Azar & Bober, in press).

Several observational systems exist for assessing interactions between members of aggressive families (see Wolfe & McEachran, 1997). When a family is observed either in the home or the clinic, major child-rearing dimensions that may require intervention can be assessed, such as verbal and physical positive behaviors, criticisms, commands, and verbal and physical negative behaviors. Moreover, aspects of the affective "delivery" of these behaviors can be determined firsthand, such as using appropriate voice tone, orienting the child to the task, using age-appropriate language and directions, and showing interest in the child's response. Along with all these categories of behaviors, failures in the contingency between parent and child behaviors have also been suggested as distinguishing aspects of abusive families' transactions; these

TABLE 10.2. Phrases in Parents' Narratives That May Signal the Need for Cognitive Work

Phrase	Sample statements	Distorted underlying assumption/expectation/ cognitive problem
"He/she knows . . ."	"He knew I was tired." "He knows his father had a bad day." "She knows I don't let her do that."	Assumption of mind reading
A string of personality-based comments	"He's a sneak." "She's selfish."	Stable, negative internal attributions
Evidence of a power struggle	"She thinks she's boss!" "I can't let her get away with this!" "He thinks he can put one over on me!"	Low self-efficacy
Overly personalized explanations of causality with strong language	"He knew it would get to me." "He knew people were watching, and he did it anyway." "She was trying to destroy me."	Misattributions
Self-deprecatory statements	"He must think I'm stupid." "She must really think I'm dumb!"	Negative self-schema
Explanations that are similar to descriptions of others in the parent's life	"He's just like his father—no good!" "She looks at me just like my mother did when I did something wrong." "When she does that, she reminds me of me."	Discrimination failure

include maternal negative responses to prosocial child behavior and inappropriate responses to child deviant behavior (Cerezo et al., 1996).

Neglect-related issues deserve special consideration, although few measures are available. Family resource scales exist (Dunst, 1986; Magura & Moses, 1986), as well as scales for rating home cleanliness (Rosenfield-Schlicter, Sarber, Bueno, Greene, & Lutzker, 1983; Watson-Perczel, Lutzker, Green, & McGimpsey, 1988), safety (e.g., Tertinger, Greene, & Lutzker, 1984), and provision of health care (Magura & Moses, 1986). Skills-oriented assessment in areas relevant to neglect may also be useful to adapt for use with neglectful parents, such as abilities to recognize and act on medical problems (Delgado & Lutzker, 1985), and emergency response skills (e.g., ability to respond effectively to a grease fire; Tymchuk, 1992). Although such assessment strategies require further development, they may prove useful to guide intervention directions with neglectful families.

Importantly, careful consideration should be given to cultural differences and child-rearing practices (Azar & Benjet, 1994). For example,

high levels of parental control may be seen negatively in one culture, but may be seen as signs of caring and stability in another (Thompson, 1994). Knowledge of the culture may also influence an evaluator's interpretation of social cues. For example, a child's turning his or her eyes downward when speaking to an adult family member may be mistakenly seen as fear, when it may in fact represent a sign of respect. An evaluator should make efforts to become knowledgeable about the culture of a family; these can often begin by consulting with a colleague or seeking input from community members.

Assessing the Needs of the Child

An investigation of a maltreated child's development and social behavior across settings is often necessary to determine his or her current needs, since maltreated children may display a wide range of behavioral and emotional symptomatology that varies according to their development. Although abused children are seldom found to display problem behaviors indicative of a clinical disorder (Azar & Bober, in press;

Wolfe & Mosk, 1983), they are often described by their parents and teachers as being extremely difficult and annoying. These problems have been traced to the beginning of the parent–child relationship, in which an early "mismatch" between parental expectations and infant development creates friction and discord. In response, maltreated children show a wide range of developmental changes and deviations (Cicchetti & Lynch, 1995), so their treatment needs must be sensitive to the ongoing circumstances (e.g., exposure to other forms of family violence, foster placement) that work in combination either to attenuate the effects of powerful traumatic events or to turn a minor developmental crisis into a major impairment (Azar & Bober, in press; Lipsett, 1983). The physical consequences of maltreatment (e.g., neurological damage due to head injuries, anemia due to poor nutrition) also need to be considered therapeutically in terms of links to psychological outcomes (e.g., embarrassment due to disfiguring scars, which increase the child's social distance from peers) and in terms of the child's ability to deal with therapeutic intervention itself (e.g., attentional problems) (Azar, Breton, & Miller, 1998).

Disturbances in social, intellectual, and socioemotional realms are seen in maltreated children throughout each phase of their development. Early disruptions in the relationship between parents and their infants have been shown to result in both anxious and disorganized attachment patterns (e.g., clinging, rigidity, withdrawal). Findings from prospective studies have linked such early attachment problems to patterns of declining developmental abilities over the first 2 years of life (e.g., speech and language, social interaction; Egeland & Farber, 1984; Egeland & Sroufe, 1981) and vulnerability to failure in later developmental areas that rely to some extent on early attachment success (Aber & Allen, 1987).

Abused preschool children show developmental delays related to their ability to discriminate emotions in others (Frodi & Smetana, 1984; Camras, Ribordy, Spaccarelli, & Stefani, 1986) and to their moral and social judgment (e.g., their ability to judge allocation of resources and fairness of rules; Smetana, Kelly, & Twentyman, 1984). They have been shown to be more difficult to manage and to have more marked developmental delays in language, self-control, and peer interactions than nonclinic samples of children. Heightened aggressiveness and hostility toward others (especially authority figures), as well as angry outbursts with little or no provocation, continue to be prominent behavioral characteristics of younger abused children (Kolko, 1992; Wolfe, in press). Such children are more prone to engaging in power struggles and counteracting peer aggression with aggression or resistance, rather than distress (Howes & Eldredge, 1985).

In contrast, neglected preschoolers appear more socially avoidant (Hoffman-Plotkin & Twentyman, 1984), show evidence of lacking empathy (George & Main, 1979), and seem to have more difficulty dealing with challenging tasks or interpersonal situations, compared to either abused or normal children (Egeland, Sroufe, & Erickson, 1983). Parent, teacher, and child report measures of behavior problems (e.g., destructiveness, fighting with siblings) have consistently indicated that the abused school-age child is perceived as more difficult to manage, less socially mature, and less capable of developing trust with others (Herrenkohl, Herrenkohl, Toedter, & Yanushefski, 1984; Kinard, 1980; Salzinger, Kaplan, Pelcovitz, Samit, & Kreiger, 1984; Wolfe & Mosk, 1983). Crittenden (1992), on the other hand, found that neglected preschool and school-age children tended to remain isolated during opportunities for free play with other children. Neglected school-age children, compared to nonmaltreated children, have been found to be more passive, to display fewer overtures of affection, and to produce less frequent initiations of play behavior in interactions with their mothers (Bousha & Twentyman, 1984; Crittenden, 1992).

Studies of physically abused school children concur with those of younger children, finding that such children often have significant learning and motivational problems at school, as well as a higher rate of aggressive and destructive behavior. Peer acceptance and reciprocity play a critical role in providing children with the social experiences and social support they require in order to learn to adapt successfully to a wide range of situations—not only in the behavioral domain, but in the areas of socioemotional and cognitive development as well. Not surprisingly, the social competence of children who have been maltreated shows impairment as they enter unfamiliar peer and school situations (Feldman et al., 1995). A recent study of the social relationships of physically abused 8- to 12-year-old children (Salzinger, Feldman, Hammer, & Rosario, 1993) found them to be at increased risk for lower social status (especially peer rejection) in the classroom, and to be perceived by their classmates as demonstrating more negative and fewer positive social behaviors. Such rejection by peers is a concern, in that it is the strongest predictor of school dropout and delinquency in adolescence, is associated with aggression, and has shown stability over time. Similar negative interactional patterns between abused children and their parents (e.g., yelling, hitting, and destructiveness) have been observed (Bousha & Twentyman, 1984; Lorber, Felton, & Reid, 1984; Reid, Taplin, & Lorber, 1981).

Abused and neglected children appear to suffer from many academic, cognitive, and language delays during both the preschool and school-age years (Eckenrode, Laird, & Doris, 1993; Fox, Long, & Langlois, 1988; Wodarski, Kurtz, Gaudin, & Howing, 1990). Neglected children are particularly at an increased risk for displaying deficits on measures of language ability and intelligence (Crouch & Milner, 1993). Salzinger et al. (1984) found that both abused children ($n = 30$) and neglected children ($n = 26$) performed at 2 years below grade level in verbal and math abilities compared to non-maltreated children ($n = 480$), with approximately one-third of the maltreated children failing one or more subjects and/or being placed in a special classroom.

Socioemotional problems have also been observed. Increasing evidence points to the association between maltreatment (especially physical abuse) and depressed symptomatology, even when socioeconomic status is controlled for (Allen & Tarnowski, 1989; Downey & Walker, 1992; Kaufman, 1991; Kinard, 1995; Toth, Manly, & Cicchetti, 1992). Physically abused children also demonstrate lower levels of self-esteem on self-report measures (Allen & Tarnowski, 1989; Kinard, 1982), as well as parent report measures (Kaufman & Cicchetti, 1989). There is some evidence of Posttraumatic Stress Disorder (PTSD) symptoms in physically abused children, although these seem less prominent than in sexually abused children (Deblinger, McLear, Atkins, Ralphe, & Foa, 1989; Pelcovitz et al., 1994).

Although maltreated adolescents have been seldom studied, some evidence for problems in this period has emerged as well. For example, studies of chronically abused children who have reached adolescence have confirmed a correlational relationship between abuse and juvenile crime that exceeds the variance accounted for by family socioeconomic factors alone (Lewis, Shanok, Pincus, & Glaser, 1979; Tarter, Hegedus, Winsten, & Alterman, 1984). More-

over, youths from violent and neglectful families begin social dating with inappropriate expectations about relationships. Girls as well as boys who grew up in violent homes report more violence—especially verbal abuse and threats—toward their dating partners as well as toward themselves (Wolfe, Wekerle, Reitzel-Jaffe, & Lefebvre, 1998). Dating violence and a past history of family violence are strong prerelationship predictors of intimate violence in early adulthood and marriage (Murphy, Meyer, & O'Leary, 1994; O'Leary, Malone, & Tyree, 1994). Maltreated children, therefore, are at increased risk of transforming verbally abusive behaviors into an early patterning of a violent dynamic in intimate partnerships.

Clinical assessment of the child must take into consideration the parent's subjective perceptions of the child, as well as other sources of objective information regarding the child's behavior and development (e.g., self-report, reports of significant others such as teachers and social workers, and behavioral observations in the home or school). Major assessment questions can be formulated around two primary concerns: (1) child behavior problems with family members, and (2) child adaptive abilities (social, cognitive, academic, and emotional development). With older children (over age 6), self-reported symptoms, social capacities, fears, and self-concept may also be assessed for treatment purposes. Since the needs of abused and neglected children are extensive, a broad-spectrum screening that includes clinical interviews and traditional global screening devices can be used to begin the process, followed by a more targeted assessment to follow up on specific problems related to the child's unique history.

Several well-validated and clinically useful parental report instruments for assessing a child's development and behavior, such as the Child Behavior Checklist (Achenbach, 1991), are available as starting points for intervention planning. Such instruments permit the clinician to obtain a broad spectrum of information as to the parent's perception of problem areas in the parent–child relationship; parents are usually quite willing to provide this information, since they feel that their behavior stems directly from their children's difficulties. Because of a maltreating parent's potential to distort the level of a child's aversive behavior, ancillary reports from other adults who know the child are crucial (e.g., foster parents, social workers, school teachers). These reports also provide information regarding the child's adjustment in other settings. The child's adaptive abilities, in addition, can be initially screened through parental report instruments or interviews to determine the level of performance that the child has mastered in important developmental areas (e.g., speech, social interactions, self-care, etc.), with more thorough assessment in areas where disturbances are uncovered.

Child self-report can also assist the examiner in understanding the child's overall functioning and can provide insight into current fears or anxieties, which may be quite disruptive. A semistructured child interview provides a good beginning point for eliciting a child's feelings and perceptions about the family. This interview should address what has happened to the child, his or her feelings about these events, his or her perceptions of blame and responsibility, and his or her view of the future, along with related topics of school and family interests, dislikes, and concerns. In one study involving 160 maltreated youths, McGee, Wolfe, and Olson (1995) found that the majority viewed the offenders as the major causes of their maltreatment; however, for physical and emotional abuse, one-third of the sample identified their own misbehavior as the major cause for what happened. This finding underscores the importance of assessing children's attributions for maltreatment, both for targeting self-blame statements as well as the underlying belief that they could have prevented such acts and are somewhat to blame.

A child's crisis adjustment is very important for deciding immediate treatment directions. Following the interview, a short battery of tests can be given to assess the child's fear and anxiety (e.g., the Fear Survey Schedule for Children, Ollendick, 1978; the Children's Manifest Anxiety Scale—Revised, Reynolds & Richmond, 1978), unhappiness and depression (e.g., the Children's Depression Inventory, Kovacs, 1994), and attitudes toward other family members, especially parents (e.g., the Parent Perception Inventory, Hazzard, Christensen, & Margolin, 1983). Observations (during interviews) can also be useful. The interviewer should be sensitive to verbal and somatic indices of anxiety or negative affect (e.g., poor eye contact, twitching movements, long silences, sadness) and should make every attempt to determine the origins or reference for such emotions, which are often linked to foster care placement, uncertainty over family reunion, and/or fear of further maltreatment. Other instruments that might be utilized to assess trauma include the PTSD Reaction Index (Pynoos et al., 1987) or the Child Dissociative Checklist (Bernstein & Putnam, 1986). Instruments specifically designed to assess the issues over which family conflict arises with adolescents may also be useful for this age group and may provide situations for use in discussing negotiation skills and communication (see also Foster & Robins, Chapter 12, this volume).

A common assessment strategy for understanding a child's expression and recognition of emotions, as well as his or her interpersonal behavior, involves parent–child or peer interactions (Feshbach, 1989). Haskett and Kistner (1991), in their study of peer interactions of preschool-age abused children, observed children during three 10-minute free-play sessions across three different mornings. Quality of social behaviors was indexed by the number of initiations of positive interaction (i.e., social initiation and peer reciprocation) and the occurrence of aggression (both instrumental and hostile), negative verbalization, and rough play. Abused children initiated fewer positive interactions with peers and exhibited a higher proportion of negative behavior than the comparison children; moreover, peers were less likely to reciprocate the initiations of the abused children, although they approached these children just as often as other peers. Assessment of adolescents' behavior with peers and dating partners may also be warranted. These dimensions are of particular importance for this age group, because maltreated children are at an increased risk of becoming victims or victimizers during the formation of intimate relationships in early to middle adolescence (Wolfe, Wekerle, & Scott, 1997). The Conflict in Relationships questionnaire (Wolfe, Reitzel-Jaffe, Gough, & Wekerle, 1994) was developed specifically to serve as a measure of positive and negative conflict resolution in reference to dating situations.

Determining Treatment Priorities

Once a child's abilities and needs are assessed, findings can be integrated with those of the parent's report and observations of current behavior to establish treatment priorities. First and foremost, the feasibility of the parent and child's remaining together must be decided, and then treatment recommendations to support the family unit must be formulated. The most specific question is clearly the potential for future violence or continued neglect on the parent's part. As noted earlier, there is a large literature debating the merits of psychologists' making violence predictions (Brody, 1990; Cocozza & Steadman,

1978; Ennis & Litwack, 1974; Monahan, 1981; Stone, 1975). Grisso and Appelbaum (1992) have argued that mental health professionals are able to make level-of-risk statements, but not dichotomous-risk ones. That is, risk statements can be made that involve probability for a given type or class of individuals of which the individual is a member. These can only be made, in their view, if certain criteria are met: (1) when the group about which one is making a prediction is clearly defined; (2) when the setting of the individual has limited parameters (e.g., a hospital ward, a minimum-security prison), and (3) when the time frame of prediction is short. This suggests that risk assessment must be an ongoing task in treatment. Kolko (1996a) describes the use of weekly self-reports of behavioral risk indicators in treatment, which may assist the therapist in determining therapeutic responses and which may be useful in such ongoing monitoring. Risk assessment methods that have been developed by child welfare agencies may also be useful (American Public Welfare Association, 1988).

The second step in the treatment plan is typically to establish a timetable and hierarchy of priorities for addressing the major parental and child needs revealed by the assessment. The order in which targets are addressed must be carefully considered with maltreating families. For example, teaching a parent to ignore a child's tantrums may place the child at higher risk if the parent does not yet have well-established ways for dealing with the child's increased attempts to gain attention. The following is a point summary of empirical and clinical findings concerning individual and family characteristics of child maltreatment; the list reflects the principal issues that warrant assessment and treatment consideration for this population (Wolfe & Wekerle, 1993).

Child Intervention Needs
1. Deficits in social sensitivity and relationship development (these include problems with attachment formation, the development of empathy, interpersonal trust, and affective expression).
2. Deficits in cognitive, language, and moral development (these refer to poor social judgment, communication skills, and school performance in particular).
3. Problems with self-control and aggression.
4. Concerns about health, safety, and protection from harm.

Parent Intervention Needs
1. Symptoms of emotional distress, learning impairments, and personality deficits that limit adult adjustment and coping.
2. Emotional arousal and reactivity to child provocation, and poor control of anger and hostility.
3. Inadequate and inappropriate methods of teaching, discipline, and child stimulation.
4. Perceptions and expectations of children, reflected by rigid and limited beliefs about child rearing and by negative biases.
5. Negative lifestyle and habits related to the use of alcohol or drugs, prostitution, and subcultural peer groups, which interfere with the parent–child relationship and parental problem-solving capacities.

Family/Situational Intervention Needs
1. Couple discord and/or coercive family interactions, and/or (for mothers) a history of violent male partners.
2. Chronic economic problems and associated socioeconomic stressors.
3. Social isolation and the inability to establish meaningful social supports.

SPECIAL TREATMENT CONSIDERATIONS

Before we discuss applications of behavioral techniques to the treatment of child abuse and neglect, a number of more general concerns that are relevant to any treatment approach to these problems need to be addressed. These concerns fall under three general headings: the characteristics of maltreating parents, the characteristics of their children, and contextual factors that influence the development of therapeutic relationships.

Characteristics of Maltreating Parents

Abusive parents typically do not identify themselves as having a problem and are not self-referred for treatment (Azar & Twentyman, 1986; Conger, 1982). Because most families commonly use corporal punishment as a means of controlling child behavior, some parents may believe (falsely) that society places no bounds or restraints on such techniques. Because of ambiguity or subcultural differences in where such limits may exist despite legal sanctions, maltreating parents may not accept their designation as violating community standards in this respect (Conger, 1982).

This fundamental disagreement between society's judgment and that of a maltreating parent is important to keep in mind as the therapist approaches treatment. There is often some element of coercion or involuntariness involved; as a result, resistance to treatment is usually high, and motivation for change is often an issue. This fact is reflected in the high treatment dropout rates found among abuse cases, ranging from 32% to 87% (Reid, 1985; Wolfe, Aragona, Kaufman, & Sandler, 1980). This issue often needs to be resolved before treatment can effectively begin. One solution is to help the family reframe the problem in terms of day-to-day difficulties that a parent can identify. "Child noncompliance," "poor ability to deal with stress," "vocational difficulties," and "lack of supports" may all be more easily accepted problem definitions than "abuse or neglect" for such parents. A therapist's openness to such redefinitions and acceptance of the parent's way of seeing the problem is crucial to reducing resistance, for two reasons. First, it may reduce the parent's fear of being evaluated and labeled as a "bad" parent by the therapist. Being labeled as a person who "has trouble handling children" or as someone who is "very lonely" (e.g., without social supports) or "stressed" may be easier for the parent to accept. Second, such redefinitions may serve to differentiate the therapist from the referral source (e.g., child protective services or courts), whom the parent may see as the "cause" of the family's trouble.

In developing this reformulation, the therapist must take care not to collude with the client's assertion that no problem exists. A delicate balance must be achieved. For some clients, the only problem definition that they are initially willing to accept is that they are "in trouble" and that the therapist may help them to learn ways to interact with their children that will assist them in getting "out of trouble." Lack of compliance with treatment may still occur despite such reformulations. Many maltreating families lead chaotic lifestyles, and competing life crises may interfere with participation in treatment (e.g., eviction, domestic violence, and legal troubles; Justice & Justice, 1976). The requirements of treatment may be one of the few stresses that they put aside. The use of lay therapists as ad-

junct treatment agents has been seen as essential to produce treatment compliance, by helping the family members to deal with these life problems and reduce some of their ambient stress levels (Kempe & Helfer, 1972).

Incentives to improve participation and attendance have been cited by behaviorally oriented clinicians as being important with these families (Azar & Twentyman, 1986; Conger, 1982; Wolfe, Kaufman, Aragona, & Sandler, 1981), but typical behavioral methods for increasing participation may not work with this population. The fact that many do not have telephones, for example, precludes the widespread use of telephone prompts, shown to improve attendance in parent training with other clients (Ayllon & Roberts, 1975). Initial monetary deposits, another commonly used technique (Hagen, Foreyt, & Durham, 1976), may represent a hardship for such families. More appropriate strategies include use of tangible incentives for attendance (e.g., movie tickets) (Ambrose, Hazzard, & Haworth, 1980) and provision of transportation and babysitting (Azar & Twentyman, 1986). Behavioral contracts with clear objectives have also been used successfully (Gambrill, 1983; Wolfe, Kaufman, Aragona, & Sandler, 1981). Court ordering of treatment attendance has produced gains in completion of treatment by the parents (Wolfe et al., 1980); however, few child maltreatment cases become involved in the criminal justice system (as opposed to child welfare), and court-ordered treatment can have undesirable side effects. Emphasizing a more positive approach, Conger (1982) suggests that a behavior therapist may contract with a parent to act as his or her advocate with the protective service agency or with the court if certain objectives are met, such as treatment attendance and acquisition of specific skills (Doctor & Singer, 1978).

The effectiveness of these suggestions for improving treatment compliance has not been tested empirically. Although such incentives and assistance for complying with treatment may produce better attendance at sessions, they do not insure that clients will make the personal investment in treatment that is required to make lasting behavioral changes. For example, a mother who had been court-ordered to complete a behavioral parent training group run by one of the authors conscientiously *attended* every session, but spent her time looking out the window each session and did not participate in group discussions.

The social isolation and poor relationship histories of the maltreating parent are final factors that need to be addressed as the therapeutic relationship begins. Wahler and his colleagues have shown that a combination of social isolation and socioeconomic disadvantage reduces the probability that parent–child interactions changes will occur, and also limits their generalization over time (Wahler, 1980). Because of poor relationship skills, a parent may also act inappropriately toward the therapist (e.g., testing limits, making excessive demands, being overly dependent, etc.). In the initial stages of treatment, the therapist may need to define clearly the parameters of the relationship, and along the way inform the parent as to what is expected in such relationships. Studies of therapy preparation techniques with disadvantaged clients indicate that such efforts improve success (Heitler, 1973, 1976). This process can also be an important source of role modeling for relationship-building skills.

Characteristics of Abused and Neglected Children

Specific treatment considerations involving the maltreated child have received little attention in the behavioral literature. In addition, treatment efforts to date have primarily focused on families of preschool-age or elementary-school-age children; little mention has been made of work with families of toddlers or adolescents. This is noteworthy, given that the most dangerous period for abuse occurs between the ages of 3 months and 3 years (Gambrill, 1983), with the vast majority of deaths due to abuse occurring before age 5. As well, recent reports suggest that a second peak in incidence rates occurs in adolescence (Farber & Joseph, 1985), although abuse during this period may go unreported (Burgdorf, 1988).

The characteristics of these younger and older age groups of abused children may explain their absence in the behavioral treatment literature. The participation of young abused infants or toddlers in treatment may be limited because of developmental considerations, and priority may be given to parental behavior changes. When an abuse report involves a child in this age group, treatment commonly focuses on changing a parent's negative responses to normal developmental behavior, such as crying (e.g., Sandford & Tustin, 1974). In addition, given the greater vulnerability of this younger age group, interven-

tion is more likely to include placement outside of the home; if abuse or neglect is severe, parental rights to the child may be terminated.

The lack of treatment studies regarding abused and neglected adolescents focuses on different concerns. For this older age group, the consequences of maltreatment most often surface as disruptive behaviors, such as running away (Farber, McCord, Kinast, & Baum-Faulkner, 1984) and delinquency (Lewis et al., 1979), and such behaviors have probably overshadowed parental abuse or neglect as a focus of treatment. There also may be a bias toward seeing adolescents as participants in family violence (i.e., they may hit back) and not as victims (Azar, 1991b). Clearly, additional investigations need to be conducted to address the behavioral treatment needs of younger and older groups of maltreated children.

Behavioral treatment efforts can involve preschool-age or elementary-school-age children in two ways: They may participate in parent–child interaction training, or may be treated in other settings, such as the day care center or school. With some exceptions (Azar et al., 1998; Haskett & Myers, 1994; Kolko, 1996b; Urquiza & McNeil, 1996), only the former approach has been discussed in detail. Although many of the issues that need to be considered in treating maltreated children are no different from those typical of behavioral child treatment in general, child maltreatment cases have unique features that need to be addressed. The majority of these issues have to do with the unusual experiences of these children in their relationships with caretakers. Psychological maltreatment (e.g., exploitation, humiliation, etc.), which often accompanies abuse or neglect, gives rise to a number of common themes in therapy to which therapists need to be sensitive. These include issues of trust, anticipation of rejection, feelings of loss, and fear.

First, abused children may approach interactions with the therapist and other adults fearfully (Mann & McDermott, 1983). Hypervigilance has been commonly noted in such children when they encounter a new adult (Martin & Beezley, 1976), especially if the abuse was very recent. Therefore, developing trust may be the initial task of intervention work (Galdston, 1979). Such children, for example, may require greater control over what happens in treatment sessions, or may become anxious if left alone in a room with a therapist or other adult. Keeping the door open or allowing children to leave sessions when they choose may be important in building a therapeutic relationship.

As previously noted, an abused child may exhibit aggressive behavior either during work with the child alone or in the presence of the parent. In such circumstances, the therapist's calm handling of the behavior is crucial to provide the child with a different experience (e.g., a desensitizing experience), as well as to model appropriate caretaking responses for the parent. Given the possibility that a parent may feel inadequate or be dogmatic about his or her parenting, care must be taken not to undermine the parent's role with the child during work with the dyad.

A third area of concern in undertaking treatment involving a maltreated child is how much faith to put in the child's reports of home interactions. Children in such families have learned not to report difficulties. Previous disclosures, for example, may have resulted in foster care placement—an event that a maltreated child may have perceived as punishment for "telling." The child may have also encountered further abuse by the parent, if no actions were taken. The child's readiness and comfort for sharing information regarding home interactions should determine how much is asked of him or her in this regard. If disclosures of abuse or neglect are made, the child needs to be prepared for the actions that might be taken. This should be done at a level that is developmentally appropriate.

Observations of parent–child interactions also need to be approached with caution. In our work, abusive parents sometimes threaten or bribe their children to perform in a particular way during observational sessions, prior to arriving at the clinic for a session. A therapist must be alert to the stress that such observations place on a family and, ultimately, on the child. For example, the therapist's presence in the home may intensify parental responses to child noncompliance (e.g., a parent may feel that the child is purposefully trying to make him or her "look bad"). The negative consequences may not be evident while the therapist is present, but only erupt once he or she has left. Care needs to be taken to provide a "cooling-down" period in which any residual parental anger can be discussed and resolved. Such protections are essential to insure the safety of the child throughout the intervention. Therapy will be of little use if the child must continue to devote energy to concerns about harm. If the child remains in parental custody, concurrent work with parents should be required. Concurrent work with foster or adoptive parents may also be useful during the course of individual work with maltreated children, to help foster parents cope with the children's response to their past maltreatment (Azar & Bober, in press). In addition, sometimes children who have sustained physical abuse or been subjected to chronic neglect will have developmental impairments, such as attentional and/or language disorders. In such instances, therapists may need to make adaptations, such as simplifying their language in presenting new skills, breaking down complex tasks into smaller pieces, providing written as well as oral instructions, and providing controlled outlets for activity (e.g., greater use of role plays and other activities).

Contextual Factors Affecting the Therapeutic Relationship

The last areas of concern in approaching treatment with abusive and neglectful families relate to the development of a therapeutic relationship. The nature of child maltreatment and the referral source introduce a number of factors not present in most therapy situations. First and foremost, behavior therapists may have personal reactions to the serious injury and neglect of children, which, depending upon their intensity, may interfere with their ability to work effectively with offenders. Steele (1975) notes two reactions of therapists: (1) denial, or (2) a surge of anger and an urge to scold the parents. Obviously, both reactions can be destructive to establishing a therapeutic relationship. The assumptions underlying the behavioral approach may inhibit such reactions, since abusive and neglectful behaviors are viewed as environmentally determined (e.g., learned) and are not viewed as something "intrinsically bad" about the parents.

Referral of an abusive family by social service agencies or the court system often can result in a different kind of role strain for the behavior therapist. Two conflicting goals present themselves in the course of such treatment—therapeutic intervention with the family versus physical protection of the child. Training for accomplishing the latter is often lacking in a therapist's preparation and experience. Moreover, actions taken to accomplish protection for the child may negatively affect the family's chance of success in treatment. There is no easy solution to this conflict; rather, it requires cooperative effort with social service agencies that have responsibility for child protection (see Wolfe, Kaufman, et al., 1981a).

Another area where role strain occurs is in the area of client confidentiality. Given the figures cited earlier indicating a high rate of recidivism *during* treatment, the probability of the need to report maltreatment is high. This legal requirement should be discussed at the outset with parents (Azar & Twentyman, 1986) and this discussion can be resurrected if it becomes necessary to report. Clearly, though this precaution does not entirely alleviate the obstacles to maintaining a therapeutic relationship with such clients if reporting occurs, at the very least it defines overtly for the clients the limitations of confidentiality.

If reporting becomes necessary, following certain steps may be helpful to minimize the effects on the relationship. If possible, a report should not be made without first informing the client. An offer should be made to the client to make the report himself or herself or with the therapist's assistance, rather than the therapist's making it alone. These steps may reduce some of the anger at being "betrayed" and may act as a positive element in therapy. In making a self-referral, the client is also taking the first step toward acknowledging a problem, which may motivate change (Prochaska, DiClemente, & Norcross, 1992). Follow-up with the client in dealing with the authorities can also act to enhance the therapeutic relationship; that is, the first time such a report was made the client had to go through the process alone, and now he or she has the therapist to help. In addition, such self-referral is often viewed as a hopeful sign by authorities, and in less serious cases it may actually lessen the repercussions of having reoffended.

Court involvement can hamper assessment and treatment, because full disclosure of assessment findings and treatment progress is required. Clients need to be made aware that this will take place at the beginning of treatment, and the content of any written report should be discussed with them whenever feasible. Such behavior on the therapist's part will help to differentiate the therapist's role from that of the "authorities" and may facilitate cooperation.

The fact that a maltreating parent is often "pushed" into treatment can also result in conflicting agendas. The parent and the therapist may differ in their goals for treatment. The parent's position may be "I want to get the social service agency off my back, so I'll come to ses-

sions, but don't expect me to do anything." Here, the therapist needs to make his or her own position and the goals of intervention clear, and to work out a compromise with the client that is within the bounds of treatment. Written contracts with the family, discussed earlier, may be useful in this regard to spell out clearly expectations.

The social service agency's and the therapist's agendas may also conflict. The agency's goal in seeking treatment for the family may be to demonstrate that the agency has tried every possible alternative for reuniting the family before starting proceedings for permanent removal of the child, whereas the therapist's assumption may be that he or she is working to reunite the family (of course, the reverse situation can also occur). Again, goals must be clearly specified before treatment proceeds.

Working with children may result in agenda conflict as well. Children may want to return to their maltreating parents, and the therapist may be given the task of dealing with such children's behavioral problems in adjusting to permanent removal. Conversely, children may wish to remain with their foster families, and the therapist may be asked to help them adjust to being returned home. These conflicting agendas can produce role strain on the individuals involved. At the outset of therapy, therefore, the goals of the referral source, the family, the child, and the therapist need to be expressed and agreed upon.

Two final areas have to do with the value system of the therapist. First, the maltreating parent and the therapist may come from different racial/ethnic backgrounds or social strata. Since "good parenting" can be thought of as a relativistic goal, therapists must be careful not to generalize their own personal views on parenting to the families they are asked to treat (Azar, 1996). A culturally relativistic point of view, which attempts to define treatment goals in relation to cultural, community, and personal expectations and capabilities, has been advocated in the literature (Azar & Benjet, 1994). Second, unrealistic expectations by the therapist and the family of what progress will be made should be anticipated. Highly stressed and disadvantaged families are slow to make detectable changes and require much patience. Such families may also expect all their problems to be handled by the therapist. Even with the elimination of maltreatment, parents in such families may still not be "ideal" parents or even "ideal" clients. A goal that may be the most realistic is to help them to become *adequate* parents.

Each of these areas must be considered as the therapist begins treating an abusive or neglectful parent and his or her family, as well as during the course of treatment. Failure to address each of these issues carefully may limit the progress that might be achieved through use of a behavioral approach.

TREATMENT DECISIONS RELATED TO CLIENTS, FORMAT, AND SUPPORT PERSONNEL

Parent versus Child Focus

Treatments of child abuse and neglect via behavioral strategies have included a number of different cognitive and behavioral targets. Treatment outcome studies have been carried out with individual parents, children, parent–child dyads, families, and parent groups, in both clinic and in home settings. Most studies have treated maternal caregivers. The bulk of this work has focused on changing parent–child interaction patterns through the use of training in child management skills, role playing, and feedback. In addition to attempts to change parent–child interactions directly, other efforts have been aimed at broad-spectrum skill deficits associated with the occurrence of maltreatment. These have included systematic desensitization to increase tolerance for aversive child behavior, stress management and anger control training, and cognitive restructuring of distorted interpretations of child behavior. Neglect has also been targeted (e.g., home safety, home hygiene, budgeting, etc.), and combinations of these approaches have been utilized. A few studies have tailored programs to the individual needs of clients, selecting as targets unique antecedent conditions specific to the parents involved (e.g., marital discord, migraines, alcohol use, etc.). Other potential targets have been discussed in descriptive reports of behavioral programs, such as vocational assistance (Justice & Justice, 1978; Lutzker & Rice, 1984), but empirical work has not yet documented the success of such targets.

As noted earlier, parental treatment has clearly been predominant in efforts to date, despite the occurrence of child behavioral and developmental problems resulting from parental inadequacies. The only child behavior that has been addressed with any frequency in the litera-

ture is noncompliance, but even this behavior has been approached through parent training. A number of reasons exist for this emphasis on parental treatment as the method of choice for intervention work, even where child disturbances are evident. Child behavior therapy in general has turned to parent training as the method of choice for intervention work, based on the assumption that parents constitute a "continuous treatment resource" who are the most powerful agents in a child's environment (Johnson & Katz, 1973). Furthermore, in the general clinical child population, the use of such training has been shown to be highly effective in producing favorable changes in child behavior across a number of problem areas (Gordon & Davidson, 1981; O'Dell, 1974), and similar findings have been reported with abusive populations (Crozier & Katz, 1979). Furthermore, parent training may be more effective than individual child treatment for socioeconomically disadvantaged families (Love, Kaswan, & Bugenthal, 1972).

Despite the emphasis on parent treatment in the literature, some recent work has suggested the use of dyadic therapy, in which children and parents are coached through interactions to promote a more positive relationship (Urquiza & McNeil, 1996). Parallel treatment, in which parents and elementary-school-age children have received comparable interventions, has also been attempted (Kolko, 1996b).

Treatment focusing on the child and his or her difficulties should also be carefully considered. As discussed earlier, maltreated children have been shown to exhibit a wide range of behavioral and emotional problems. This maladaptive behavior has also been shown to extend beyond the home setting to include interactions with others (e.g., foster care parents, teachers, peers, etc.; George & Main, 1979; Hoffman-Plotkin & Twentyman, 1984; Reidy, 1977), and it may continue to be maintained in these settings despite changes in the family. Training efforts may need to be conducted in each of these settings to enhance the changes produced at home. Because of the heterogeneity of behavioral problems exhibited by maltreated children, one standard approach cannot be outlined.

Content, Format, and Setting

The decision as to whether the abusing or neglectful parent, the couple (if one exists), the parent–child dyad, or the child should be treated, as well as decisions about the structure and content of that treatment, should be made according to the specific needs of the family. Although parent training is the most commonly used strategy, this approach may not be the treatment of choice if parental or child characteristics or aspects of the family's situation indicate that child-rearing problems are not the biggest source of difficulty. An issue that arises during assessment is whether the child or children are actually exhibiting deviant behavior that warrants change, or whether the problem is primarily due to inappropriate expectations on the part of the parent(s). In the latter case, a cognitive-behavioral strategy to deal with such inappropriate perceptions may be the starting point of treatment (see following discussion).

It may also be decided that other significant parent-related problems need to be handled before changes in parent–child interactions are attempted. For example, a parent who has a significant alcohol problem may require treatment prior to working on parent–child interactional problems, since attempts to produce parenting changes may be doomed to failure due to the effects of alcoholism. Extreme marital conflict is another factor associated with maltreatment (Berger, 1980) that may have its own effects on child outcome (Rosenbaum & O'Leary, 1981; Jouriles, Murphy, & O'Leary, 1989; Wolfe, Jaffe, Wilson, & Zak, 1985). Such relationship problems may preclude the parents' working together in a collaborative manner, and may therefore mean that a lower priority must be placed at first on parent training. Similarly, if parents' stress level is high and resources are so low that they are incapable of altering their social environment, then the effectiveness of parent training strategies will also be severely limited unless support services can be provided (Azar, Ferguson, & Twentyman, 1992; Gordon & Davidson, 1981). Finally, intrapersonal difficulties, such as severe depression, may limit parents' ability to benefit from parent training (Miller, 1975). In each of these scenarios, other problem areas may require treatment either before or simultaneously with behavioral interventions for parent–child problems. Despite these other treatment needs, however, it is important to reaffirm that in the majority of cases, treatment of abusive or neglectful families must focus on the parent–child relationship and its context (e.g., the family, financial limits, alcohol usage, etc.).

If parent training is to be utilized, a decision needs to be made as to whether a parent will be seen individually or with other parents in a group. If parental deficit areas are highly specific, or a parent is too low-functioning or socially avoidant to benefit from material presented in a group session, individual treatment may be preferred. Although no study has compared individual to group behavioral treatment with maltreating parents, an extensive general psychotherapy literature has made such comparisons. Group treatment, for the most part, has been favored in such studies (Bedner & Kaul, 1978).

The use of groups in modifying parental behavior has a number of advantages (Rose, 1969): exposing parents to a wider range of target behaviors and intervention strategies; providing role models and reinforcers of change in parenting behavior (Arnold, 1978), breaking up the social isolation of maltreating parents and providing a place where social skills can informally be attained (Salzinger, Kaplan, & Artemyeff, 1983); and allowing greater efficiency in terms of staff time (Rinn, Vernon, & Wise, 1975; Rose, 1969). Several investigators who have used groups with child maltreaters have encouraged the formation of relationships between group members by having them exchange phone numbers and providing refreshments or lunch outside of the session to promote social interactions (Azar, 1984; Barth, Blythe, Schinke, Stevens, & Schilling, 1983).

Both individual and group parent training have been used with maltreating parents, and some researchers have used a combination of both methods. For example, Wolfe, Sandler, and Kaufman (1981) and Azar and Twentyman (1984; Azar, 1989b, 1997) combined group parenting sessions with weekly individual home visits. The role of the home visitor was to promote generalization of the gains made during group sessions and to provide extra practice in the trained techniques. Both studies provide sound arguments, and supportive results, for combining individual and group training.

In addition to decisions regarding the structure of treatment, the choice of setting must also be made. Three different settings have been used with abusive families in research efforts to date: (1) the standard clinic office or educational group; (2) a controlled learning environment in the clinic; and (3) the home. As before, a combination of these settings has often been utilized (e.g., group didactic training and home practice sessions, or individual office discussions followed by practice in a structured laboratory analogue situation). The controlled learning environment can be equipped with a one-way mirror and bug-in-the-ear transmitter device to guide parents through interactions with their children. Such a guided approach has been shown to produce rapid behavioral change with other clinical populations, and in two case studies involving an abusive mother (Crimmins, Bradlyn, St. Lawrence, & Kelly, 1984; Wolfe et al., 1982). This mode of treatment is especially suited for parents who need concrete demonstrations and feedback, but clearly requires extensive therapist time and effort to promote generalization to the home. Unfortunately, systematic, empirically based guidelines are not yet available on the impact of these structural and setting variables (Gordon & Davidson, 1981).

The Use of Lay Therapists and Support Services as an Adjunct to Treatment

"Lay therapists" or family support volunteers are commonly used in community-based therapies for child abuse and neglect (see Kempe & Helfer, 1972). These adjunct workers assist with day-to-day crises while the family is in treatment. The goal of their work has been to allow the therapist more opportunity to focus on therapeutic issues, and to help reduce the family stress level enough to allow parents to work on therapeutic issues as well. The presence of a volunteer or "home aide" has also been assumed to help provide a social support network for parents and to model social skills informally (Kempe & Helfer, 1972).

Other support services have also been provided to maltreating parents while they were involved in treatment, such as home maker services, day care, respite care, and hot lines. Again, the goal of each of these services has been to reduce the family stress level to the point where the parents can work on behavioral changes. Behavioral methods designed to mobilize or modify supports available to parents are used commonly in the child welfare system. One study with neglectful parents (Gaudin, Wodarski, Arkinson, & Avery, 1990) attempted to decrease neglect through strengthening informal support networks, using personal networking, linking volunteers with families, employing neighborhood helpers, and providing social skills training. The findings were encouraging, although design limitations restrict conclusions.

Although support services may be beneficial to these families, how such services interact with other forms of treatment needs to be considered. The use of such services, for example, may influence clients' attributions for changes produced in treatment; therefore, support services need to be provided without encouraging a sense of dependency in family members. Support workers need to be carefully trained to provide a structured learning atmosphere with the goal of increasing the family's effectiveness and operation. For instance, if a parent is having trouble with a landlord, the support worker might help the parent generate alternative solutions to the problem, have the parent decide on one alternative, role-play the response, and then have the parent deal with the problem himself or herself. Such a process would promote skills that could be utilized by the parent in future encounters with life stressors, whereas the worker's talking to the landlord for the family would resolve only the immediate difficulty. Support workers in the traditional literature have more often provided the latter function. In brief, support workers and services may be useful in facilitating treatment effects in behavioral interventions, although empirical work is needed to test their utility and effectiveness.

SPECIFIC TREATMENT METHODS FOR MALTREATING FAMILIES

Once the decisions about treatment target areas, structure, and format have been made, the choice of specific intervention methods remains. A limited number of standard cognitive and behavioral methods have been employed with child maltreaters to date, such as behavioral rehearsal, cognitive restructuring, feedback, skills training (e.g., parent training, anger and self-control training, and stress management training) and treatment of antecedent conditions. In addition to programs that focus on just one of these skill areas, several treatment programs have utilized a package approach that works on a number of target areas simultaneously. In many cases, however, the techniques being employed have been modified to meet the special needs of maltreating families. Therefore, each of these commonly used methods is discussed with specific consideration to their application with maltreating families (Wolfe & Werkele, 1993). Several single-case and group studies involving behavioral efforts with child maltreaters have appeared in the literature. In addition, there have been four comparative treatment studies (Azar & Twentyman, 1984; Brunk, Henggeler, &

Whelan, 1987; Egan, 1983; Kolko, 1996b). Methods that hold promise but have not been fully evaluated are also mentioned, in anticipation that future efforts will be directed toward these areas (e.g., specific child treatments, behavioral consultation, home visitation).

Parent-Focused Treatment

Modeling and Behavioral Rehearsal

Modeling and role playing of newly acquired behaviors are probably the most common components in behavioral treatments of child abuse or neglect, and in parent training in particular (see Denicola & Sandler, 1980; Smith, 1984; Wolfe, Kaufman, et al., 1981). These techniques have been demonstrated to be quite effective in producing changes in interpersonal interactions (Eisler, Hersen, & Agras, 1973; Twentyman & McFall, 1975). Maltreating parents' feelings of inadequacy regarding their parenting behavior or general interpersonal skills may make them more reluctant than most clients to undertake role playing. Presenting a clear rationale is especially crucial with this population. Therapist modeling of "role-playing" behavior initially may also be useful in reducing parents' anxiety. An early program developed by Barth et al. (1983) demonstrated how parents might gradually be worked into role playing. Examples of desirable child management approaches were first presented via videotape, followed by therapist modeling of the behaviors. Finally, parents were provided with scripts to follow in their initial role-play attempts, and they were praised for their effort. Such careful shaping of behavior is often necessary with this population of parents to facilitate involvement and behavior change.

In group interventions, asking other parents to act out particular parents' situations or to act as coaches in a role play may also reduce the pressure in using such a technique. A danger of using role plays with this population, however, is that on occasion inappropriate parental responses (e.g., coercive responses) may be volunteered by group members during "coaching." Therapists must be careful to deal with such responses immediately; otherwise, parents are likely to incorporate such negative responses into their repertoire.

Feedback

An important component of role playing is the provision of feedback. Again, careful attention needs to be paid to the manner in which feedback is provided with this population. Given the nature of interactions within abusive families, parents are accustomed to giving and receiving negative feedback. If the therapist's approach to feedback is perceived as negative or harsh, parents have less opportunity to learn or benefit from their experience. In addition, maltreating parents are often sensitive to any comments about their child-rearing methods, and may leave treatment if sessions are too critical.

The feedback process during a role play helps refine parents' response toward the desired goal behavior; more importantly, it models for them a different way of responding when faced with needing to correct the behavior of another. It is especially important, therefore, that feedback be presented in as positive a manner as possible (e.g., what a parent is doing right, not wrong). Initially, the frequency of praise for attempting or acquiring new parenting behaviors must be higher than with other populations, and/or commensurate with each parent's preference for certain forms of praise (e.g., some parents prefer quiet recognition, and others prefer a lot of attention and fanfare). The therapist can also model acceptance of negative feedback by describing instances of self-criticism.

Cognitive Restructuring

Cognitive restructuring is a method of addressing irrational or dysfunctional beliefs that may lead to inappropriate responses (e.g., misattributions, distorted beliefs, unrealistic expectancies) (Azar, 1984, 1986, 1997; Azar & Twentyman, 1986). Recent evidence has supported the idea that child abusers possess cognitive styles and belief systems that could play such a mediational role. For example, abusers have been shown to ascribe greater negative intentionality to their children's behavior than do normal parents, even when that behavior is within developmental norms (Larrance & Twentyman, 1983; Plotkin, 1983), and to have more unrealistic expectations of what is appropriate to expect in children's behavior (Azar, Robinson, et al., 1984; Azar & Rohrbeck, 1986). Such appraisals can lead to an increased probability of aggression (Averill, 1983), as well as parenting responses that may be less facilitating of children's developments (e.g., unrealistic expectations have been linked to less use of explanation; Barnes & Azar, 1990).

Cognitive restructuring involves, first of all, clients' recognition that their thoughts about situations and others affect their behavior. Once this relationship is acknowledged, clients are required to generate their own "personalized cognitions" about situations that are problematic. An example is a father's interpretation of his 2-year-old's unwillingness to go take a nap as an active attempt to devalue him as a parent (e.g., "He must think I'm really stupid"), rather than typical 2-year-old behavior. Those cognitions are then challenged by the therapist, and an attempt is made to replace them with ones that are more appropriate (e.g., "Here we go again—I've just got to be patient"). Generating such "personalized" cognitions may be very difficult for maltreating parents. Role-playing problematic situations can help them to identify their dysfunctional thoughts *in vivo*. Imagery techniques have also been used (Azar, 1984). Extremely stressful situations, for example, can be described in which a potentially triggering child event is introduced. An example of such a vignette is the following:

> Your landlord just came by and said that he is evicting you. Your welfare check that was due yesterday still hasn't arrived, and you and your boyfriend had a bad fight last night. You have on your new white dress that you saved for weeks to buy and your child comes up to you and despite telling him to be careful, he spills his Kool-Aid all over it. (Azar, 1984, p. 166)

Once the client has successfully imagined this situation (or a self-generated problem situation), questioning can take place regarding what the parent would be saying to himself or herself at that moment, and how these statements would affect his or her actions. Dramatizations of examples clients spontaneously provide can be particularly useful. Questioning can start with what a parent is feeling. Once a feeling is stated, the parent can then be asked how the child's behavior made him or her feel, or what the parent expected of the child in this situation. It is also helpful to ask the parent whether other people besides the child make him or her feel the same way. One mother, for example, found conflict with her 3-year-old very difficult to take and perceived him as intentionally trying to make her feel "stupid." When she was asked about others in her life, it became clear that the child's father, her ex-boyfriend, used to belittle her in conflict situations, and that the boy looked very much like his father.

In building a rationale for going through this exercise, it is important for therapists to model the process by sharing their own examples

where cognitions resulted in responses that were inappropriate. The exact process of rational re-evaluation can then be modeled, with alternative cognitive statements generated as solutions. If clients still have difficulty generating cognitions, therapists may need to provide examples. Scripts that include such cognitive statements may also be helpful to provide material for cognitive training (Barth et al., 1983). In group treatment, exercises designed to generate parents' ideas regarding their definitions of "good" parenting or a "good" child can also elicit what may be considered overly idealized parental expectations regarding themselves and those around them (Azar, 1984).

Once such statements and belief systems are identified, challenging them can be undertaken. Parents can be questioned as to whether such self-statements help or hinder their job as parents (e.g., allow them to act as good teachers to their children). Beliefs regarding the similarity of children's understanding and ability to those of adults can also be disputed by using concrete demonstrations. For example, with parents of preschoolers, Piagetian conservation tasks can be shown in a group situation as concrete evidence that children do not think in the same way that adults do. The faulty belief systems and inappropriate self-statements can then be replaced with ones like these: "He's only 2," "He doesn't know any better," "It may feel like I can't take any more, but I can handle it. She's only a child. She doesn't know what I've been through today," or "It was an accident. Kids do these things."

The Use of Resources and Technology

Each of the methods described above may be augmented by the use of other resources and technology, such as concrete demonstrations of appropriate child-rearing methods. For instance, coaching can be carried out through the use of a bug-in-the-ear transmitter and a one-way mirror. Such training allows for prompting, shaping, and reinforcement of new responses as they happen, which may be more powerful training methods than demonstration alone.

Videotaped observations of staged parenting situations (Barth et al., 1983) and of the clients and their children (Wolfe & Manion, 1984) may make therapist suggestions more salient to maltreating parents. Videotaped modeling has been used successfully as part of parent training with other populations (Webster-Stratton, 1984, 1994). Over the course of treatment, previous parent–child tapes can be replayed to illustrate to the clients progress made, and also to note how a relapse might appear.

Board games to train social skills among adults with mental retardation (Foxx et al., 1983) have been adapted for use with low-functioning maltreating parents (Fantuzzo, Wray, Hall, Goins, & Azar, 1986). Using a common board game, Sorry, parents make moves on the board dependent upon their responses to various parenting and social problem situations. More elaborate responses to situations are gradually shaped and socially reinforced. In group programs, films may also be useful adjuncts to provide material for discussion. Commercially produced parenting films and audiotapes are available illustrating behavioral techniques, as well as the handling of general parenting and child development issues.

Skills Training

Skills training has been utilized with child maltreaters in three general areas: parent training, anger control, and stress management. Work in each area may be broad, going beyond parent–child relationships to include more general social skills training. In each case, standardized training packages developed for other populations have been employed, with modifications carried out to meet the specific needs of this population.

Parent Training. Child management skills training has been described in detail in the literature. Standard parent training packages typically include (1) teaching parents to track child problem behaviors that they have selected, (2) education in techniques based on social learning theory, such as the identification of antecedents and the use of reinforcement, extinction, time out, and punishment to change behavior (usually presented didactically); and (3) home application of techniques. Record keeping (e.g., charting of child behavior) is often required, and reading often supplements didactic presentations.

The most basic of issues in undertaking parent training with maltreating parents (especially abusive ones) is their willingness to give up physical forms of punishment and to utilize more positive means of control. Even if a parent is willing to attempt a different approach, attending to the child's good behavior takes time to produce results, and the parent may become frustrated. Rather than completely removing the parent's only means of control, the therapist can establish a contractual agreement with the parent at the outset of such training to practice a non-physical form of punishment for a specified period of time, thus allowing for a gradual shift in behavior (Wolfe, Kaufman, et al., 1981).

The requirements of standard training packages may also be difficult for the typical maltreating parent. A parent's chaotic lifestyle, for example, may interfere with the consistent collection of data usually required in such programs, making simplification of data collection procedures necessary. Collecting data for a single day or afternoon, rather than a week, may be more practical with such families. With some parents, verbally reviewing over the phone what occurred in a given day may be the only way to collect such information consistently.

Training parents in the use of reinforcement and punishment techniques may also present problems. Parents' own state of economic and emotional deprivation, for example, may interfere with their use of reinforcement with their children. A clinical example of this occurred in a case where a child's bedwetting was the target of intervention. This behavior resulted in the mother's becoming angry and at times aggressive. When a reinforcement procedure was worked out with the family, it quickly became clear that despite the initial success of the program, the maltreating mother was sabotaging it by failing to maintain its consistent use. It was only after a parental reward (i.e., special attention from her spouse) was systematically introduced contingent on her carrying out the program that progress could be made. High levels of therapist encouragement are also needed initially to motivate such a parent to try the new techniques.

Even if a parent reports active use of the new techniques and desired improvement in a child's behavior, observation of the parent's application of the methods is needed. Manipulative behavior on the part of parents often occurs because of their legal status or because of a sincere desire to "please" the therapist.

Particular dangers exist in training abusive parents in behavioral punishment strategies. Because of the inappropriate judgment of such parents, there is a greater potential for misuse of techniques. "Time-out" procedures, such as placing a child in his or her own room for misbehavior, need to be carefully reviewed and rehearsed with parents; otherwise, they may proceed to lock children in closets or other closed spaces. "Grandma's rule" (e.g., "If you do *X,* then *Y* will happen"; Becker, 1971) can easily be twisted into a new form of parental tyranny unless extreme caution is used in training. The types of behavior most appropriate for targeting with this technique should be carefully specified with each client. Extinction (e.g., ignoring of negative child behavior), another common behavioral method, can also have negative side effects, because it usually results in an increase in a child's aversive behavior before a reduction occurs. Clients should be warned that this may take place, and cognitive coping strategies should be provided to get them through this stressful period (e.g., they can be told to *interpret* this increase as a sign of success).

Single-case studies involving child management training with abusive parents, in which role modeling, rehearsal, and feedback were combined with bibliotherapy, have shown increases in positive parental behavior and decreases in negative behavior (Denicola & Sandler, 1980; Sandler, Van Dercar, & Milhoan, 1978; Wolfe & Sandler, 1981). Positive "spillover" in prosocial child behavior was also observed, as well as maintenance of effects over periods ranging from 1 to 7 months. Wolfe et al. (1982) and Crimmins et al. (1984) showed similar effects when these techniques were combined with the use of a radio transmitter to coach abusive and neglectful mothers who were cognitively limited in live interactions with their children.

Overall, parent training efforts have shown success in changing interaction patterns in the abusing and neglectful parents studied. In addition, some limited data have suggested maintenance over time. Although this approach holds promise, limitations of the outcome studies exist. Clients often either have been court-ordered into treatment or have been under some threat of losing custody of their children. As well, treatment has been provided in the home by highly trained professionals (e.g., graduate students, psychologists). These parameters are not typical of most treatment settings, raising questions as to whether the methods would work under different circumstances. Finally, with some notable exceptions (Kolko, 1996b; Wolfe, Sandler, & Kaufman, 1981), recidivism data have not been reported. Without this most crucial of outcome information, it is difficult to assess the usefulness of the techniques.

Anger Control Strategies.   Along with parenting skills training, instruction in self-control and anger control strategies is useful with abusive parents, given their heightened arousal and poor ability to cope with stress. Cognitive and behavioral techniques have been used with other populations to reduce anger and to increase coping ability (Novaco, 1975). Such techniques have obvious applicability to this population (Azar & Twentyman, 1984; Barth et al., 1983; Nomellini & Katz, 1983; Wolfe, Sandler, & Kaufman, 1981). The most common strategies include the following components: (1) early detection of physiological and cognitive cues associated with anger arousal; (2) replacing anger-producing thoughts with more appropriate cognitions; and (3) developing self-control skills to modulate the expression of anger in anger-eliciting situations.

Nomellini and Katz (1983) used these techniques in a set of three case studies. Treatment took place in parents' homes for six to eight 90-minute sessions, and outcome data included home observations, pre–post scores on the Novaco Anger Scale, and self-monitoring of "angry urges" by the parents. During and after treatment, parents showed significant reductions in aversive behavior and "angry urges," as well as substantial decreases on the Anger Scale. Maintenance of effects were shown over follow-up periods ranging from 2 to 6 months. Recidivism data were not obtained, however, and corresponding changes in positive behavior were small. In another study focusing on self-control, Barth et al. (1983) made extensive use of role playing with and without scripts and coaching. Parents were also instructed to reward themselves when they carried out the procedures at home. After eight group sessions, the treated parents showed significantly greater improvement in behavioral and cognitive responses during a role play and in response to videotaped situations than an untreated control group did. Positive changes were also found on paper-and-pencil measures of nervousness, calmness, and irritability. Unfortunately, the sources of subjects for the two groups differed (e.g., the treated parents were referred by child protective services, while the controls were recruited from a well-baby clinic program), raising questions regarding comparability of the two groups. Despite this drawback, the study provides examples of innovative self-control techniques that can be employed with child-maltreating parents.

In addition to cognitive techniques, a few single-case design studies have incorporated systematic desensitization, in which progressive muscle relaxation techniques are trained and hierarchies of aversive child behavior are created (Gilbert, 1976; Koverola et al., 1984; Sanders, 1978; Sandford & Tustin, 1974). One of these studies incorporated help from the adult partner or spouse to reinforce new responses shown by the target parent and to increase generalization (Gilbert, 1976). Generally, these studies have supported the usefulness of desensitization with abusive parents for reducing their intolerance for aversive or stressful child behavior, and in one case for increasing a mother's positive contact with her child (Gilbert, 1976). Maintenance of behavioral effects has been satisfactory, although recidivism data are scarce. Koverola et al. (1984), however, found that interruptions caused by the many life stresses experienced by an abusive mother resulted in a return to pretreatment functioning during follow-up. Such intervening factors, typical in such families, may interfere with this coping and relaxation intervention. Again, though these single-case design studies show promise, effectiveness needs to be demonstrated across a broader spectrum of parents.

A word of caution in using anger control techniques as the only form of treatment is also in order. There is evidence to suggest that training in control of anger may not be sufficient to change an abusive parent's behavior toward a child (Egan, 1983). Specifically, a parent may be less likely to engage in aggressive responses with a child, but this does not mean that the parent will respond in appropriate or optimal ways to the child's behavior. Over time, the child management situation may deteriorate to the point where the anger control techniques are insufficient to prevent abuse from occurring.

Stress Reduction Strategies.   Stress reduction techniques are a third skill training approach employed with abusive parents. This type of training, like anger control, is usually included as part of a larger package of treatment. Training typically includes instruction in relaxation techniques and cognitive-behavioral methods of reducing stress. Parents are trained to recognize how the negative ways they interpret situations lead them to become stressed, and to substitute stress-reducing self-statements for negative ones. They are also trained to perform actions to reduce their stress level (e.g., leave the situation, seek outside advice, increase resources). Parents may be required to read written material on stress reduction techniques between treatment sessions, and to keep notebooks on class material and do homework assignments (Egan, 1983). Parents have also been provided with relaxation tapes to practice this strategy between

sessions (Wolfe, Sandler, & Kaufman, 1981). Since general coping abilities in this population may be low, a broad range of situations—parenting as well as nonparenting—need to be included for maximum benefit.

Stress reduction techniques and anger control training are subject to many of the same problems as parenting skills training (e.g., lack of client sophistication, manipulation, etc.), and modifications of presentation may be needed, depending upon the characteristics of the individuals being served. Training in the home may also be a crucial factor in the success of these approaches (Wolfe, Kaufman, et al., 1981).

Treatment of Antecedents of Abuse and Strategies for Addressing Neglect-Related Issues

Along with addressing parental skills and cognitive processes related to maltreatment, some work has been directed to stressful antecedent conditions that might set up situations where maltreatment is more likely. Outcome studies have tailored their treatment to specific and most relevant needs of the families. Multiple targets, including depression, marital discord, migraine headaches, and vocational goals, are typically chosen (Campbell, O'Brien, Bickett, & Lutzker, 1983; Conger, Lahey, & Smith, 1981; Justice & Justice, 1978). Marital treatment, for example, has included use of the behavioral techniques outlined by Jacobson (1978) and of reciprocity counseling procedures (Azrin, Naster, & Jones, 1973). Unfortunately, these studies, though promising, are also limited by design weaknesses (e.g., small sample sizes or lack of a control group).

Neglect-related issues have been addressed by behavioral interventions, but to a very limited extent. Strategies include teaching parents home safety skills to "childproof" their homes (Tertinger et al., 1984), meal planning and budgeting to improve the nutrition provided to children (Sarber, Halasz, Messmer, Bickett, & Lutzker, 1983), symptom recognition skills to improve parents' ability to identify illness in their children and to make appropriate responses (Delgado & Lutzker, 1985), emergency skills (Tymchuk, 1992), and home cleanliness (Watson-Perczel et al., 1988). Because neglect affects more children and may have more far-reaching consequences than other forms of maltreatment (Dubowitz, 1991), expansion of methods for this population is sorely needed.

Multicomponent Treatment Approaches

Behavioral efforts have evaluated the impact of multicomponent (package) approaches to treatment, given the complexity of factors leading to maltreatment. Packages can also be delivered in group formats by agencies that serve families, thereby meeting the differing needs of a larger number of families at one time. Social services agencies usually have limited resources available, and the development of effective packages may have utility. Furthermore, the urgency of the problem often requires immediate changes in a family, and lengthy assessment periods to determine specific target areas are not always possible.

Several treatment studies have shown how a multicomponent approach may be successfully applied. Wolfe, Sandler, and Kaufman (1981) used a group treatment format that emphasized several behavioral methods in their competency-based program for abusive parents. Individual home-based sessions served as adjuncts to group training sessions. Eight abusive families referred by child protective services were provided with eight sessions of group training, while another eight abusive families received the usual level of monitoring provided by the referring agency. Training focused on child management skills and anger control, as taught via didactic instruction, problem solving, role modeling, rehearsal, self-control training, and in-home implementation. During observations of parent–child interactions in the home, treated subjects were found to use appropriate child management procedures (e.g., positive reinforcement, effective punishment and commands) significantly more than waiting-list controls did. This difference was maintained at a 1-year follow-up, and the treated group was found to have no recurrences of abuse at that time (one abuse report occurred in the control group).

Two large-scale programs that are based on social learning theory and that operate in the community with large numbers of maltreating clients have also been evaluated. Project 12-Ways, a large treatment program operating in a primarily rural area of Illinois, uses a variety of behavioral techniques to deal with child maltreatment (Lutzker & Rice, 1984). In-home services (treatment and training) are provided to families referred to the project by child protective services. Areas of treatment include parent–child training, stress reduction, self-control training, social support, assertiveness training, use of leisure time, health maintenance and nutrition, home safety, job placement, marital discord counseling, alcoholism referral, and money management. Selection of treatment provided is based on individual case needs. To evaluate the efficacy of the program, 50 abusive and neglectful families were randomly selected from 150 families served in 1 year of the program's operation. A comparison group of families was also selected from the same referral sources as the treated families. The families in both groups had at least one previous incident of abuse or neglect. The names of treated families were matched against state registry data of incidents of abuse and neglect to determine reincidence, both during treatment and after services were terminated; data for control families were also obtained. Results indicated that the program was successful in reducing multiple incidences of maltreatment in participating families relative to the control group, but overall recidivism rates were unaffected. Because of the variations in the specific treatments offered each individual family, solid conclusions regarding the effectiveness of any one type of treatment are difficult to make from the results of this study.

In two interesting community studies, Szykula and Fleischman (1985) demonstrated the impact that social-learning-theory-based intervention programs might have on out-of-home placement of abused and neglected children. The families treated in the two studies were referred by state child protective services and were selected because they were considered at risk for protective placement of their children outside the home due to abuse. Families all had children between the ages of 3 and 12 years of age; they were described as primarily white and of lower socioeconomic status, and about 50% of the parents were single. The treatment package included methods based on social learning theory: training parents in the tracking of problem behavior; the use of reinforcement and time-out procedures to modify behavior; problem solving, and cognitive self-control training to deal with anger, guilt, depression, and anxiety. Phone supervision of assignments was also employed. Each family received 15 to 25 hours of treatment-oriented contact time. The investigators found that there was an 85% drop in out-of-home placements during the program's operation, but that placements rebounded to previous levels during a 9-month break in the program.

Out-of-home placements for reasons other than abuse showed no change over the entire period of study. There was also no recidivism for abuse among treated families during treatment and at a 1-year follow-up (unfortunately the number of families involved was not reported). A noteworthy aspect of this program was that it used bachelor's- and master's-level caseworkers as treatment agents, providing a better demonstration of the utility of such techniques in typical treatment settings.

Szykula and Fleischman's (1985) second study used an experimental design with 48 abusive families and the same treatment package described above, with out-of-home placement again used as the outcome measure. Families were first divided into two levels of severity, "less difficult" and "more difficult," based on review of each family's social history and case file. Less difficult cases ($n = 26$) had fewer than three reports of abuse, had no serious difficulty with housing or transportation, and had a child's conduct identified as a major problem. More difficult cases ($n = 22$) had three or more reports of abuse, had serious problems with unemployment, had consistent transportation and housing difficulties, and had been identified as having major problems outside of a parent's relationship with a child (e.g., frequent fights with boyfriends or extended family, extreme feelings of anger and/or depression, and frequent difficulties with others in their community). Families within each difficulty level were randomly assigned to either the treatment package or a control condition that received standard social services (ranging from limited supervision to other forms of therapy available in the community). Outcome data indicated that the treatment package was most successful in reducing out-of-home placement for the less difficult group (1 of 13 of the treated families vs. 5 of 13 of the controls), but not for the more difficult group (7 of 11 of the treated families vs. 5 of 11 of the controls). In their conclusions, the researchers point out that the success rates for the first study may have been due to differential referrals of less difficult cases. Their findings also show a need for refining methods to discriminate between those families who will or will not benefit from social-learning-theory-based treatments.

These studies suggest the viability of programmatic application of social-learning-theory-based interventions for child maltreatment. Findings suggest that they may be effective in reducing the incidence of maltreatment and out-of-home placement of children for a broader range of maltreating families. Packages also may allow the widespread dissemination of such methods. However, because of the use of multiple components, the specific methods responsible for their effectiveness await further determination.

Comparative Treatment Effectiveness

Four studies have evaluated differential treatment effectiveness in order to specify methods that are most beneficial with this population. Comparisons involved different types of behavioral treatments (Egan, 1983); different forms of cognitive-behavioral treatment versus an insight-oriented intervention (Azar & Twentyman, 1984); systemic treatment versus social-learning-theory-based treatment (Brunk et al., 1987); and, most recently, cognitive-behavioral treatment versus family therapy (Kolko, 1996b).

Egan (1983) compared the impact of two behavioral strategies, using four study conditions: stress management training only ($n = 11$), child management only ($n = 11$), a combination of stress management and child management training ($n = 9$), and a waiting-list control group that received only social service monitoring ($n = 10$). Evaluation was conducted via paper-and-pencil measures of affect associated with life changes and perceptions of family cohesion and conflict, observations of parent–child interaction patterns, and parental report of child management strategies in hypothetical child-rearing situations. Treatment took place weekly over a 6-week period, and evaluations were done prior to families' beginning treatment and at termination. Waiting-list controls received evaluations 6 weeks apart. The results indicated some differential treatment effects: Stress management training led to changes in the feelings of parents, and child management training produced changes in specific child management skills.

A second comparative treatment study involved abusive and neglectful parents with children between the ages of 3 and 5 years (Azar & Twentyman, 1984). The effectiveness of a cognitive-behavioral package was compared to that of an insight-oriented approach using a short-term (10-week) group treatment format. The cognitive-behavioral package included (1) child management skills training, (2) cognitive restructuring, (3) stress management and anger control training, and (4) communications skills training.

Four study conditions were used: (1) cognitive-behavioral group treatment with weekly home visits designed to promote generalization of treatment effects ($n = 13$); (2) cognitive-behavioral group treatment with weekly supportive home visits to control for the extra attention received in a home visit ($n = 16$); (3) insight-oriented group treatment with weekly supportive home visits ($n = 14$); and (4) a waiting-list control group that received the normal services provided by the local child protective services ($n = 16$). Home visitors were trained university undergraduates.

Evaluations of the abusive and neglectful mothers were carried out prior to the beginning of treatment, at termination, and at a 2-month follow-up. Outcome measures included behavioral observations in the home and in the laboratory; paper-and-pencil measures of parental knowledge of child development, problem-solving ability, and unrealistic expectations of appropriate child behavior; and caseworker reports of parenting problems. Although differences were found between the two forms of cognitive-behavioral treatment on some of the paper-and-pencil and behavioral measures at posttreatment and follow-up, no differential treatment effects were found at posttest or at the 2-month follow-up. Significant differences between treatment (i.e., all treatments) and no treatment did occur at posttreatment on caseworker reports of parenting problems and at posttreatment and follow-up on maternal behavior in the home. A 1-year follow-up of the three treated conditions indicated no recidivism for the cognitive- behavioral group with generalization training (0 of 13 cases), but 37.5% reincidence (6 of 16 cases) for the cognitive-behavioral training without the generalization training and 21.4% reincidence (3 out of 14 cases) for the insight-oriented group.

Brunk et al. (1987) compared a systemic approach delivered individually to a social-learning-theory-based group package. Both treatments involved $1\frac{1}{2}$-hour sessions for an 8-week period. The parent training was carried out in a clinic setting and modeled after that of Wolfe, Kaufman, et al. (1981), described earlier. The multisystemic therapy for most families took place in the home; content varied depending upon family needs, but included reframing, joining, and prescribed tasks. Marital issues were discussed in some families, and most parents received parent education aimed at more effective child management strategies and more appropri-

ate expectations for children. Interestingly, work was also done with some parents on their relationships with extended family members and with social agencies, and with children on peer relationships. Results favored the multisystemic therapy for restructuring parent–child relationships, whereas parent training decreased parents' social problems. The researchers speculated that the latter finding was due to the effect of group participation on social isolation, although the lack of a control condition and differences in formats and settings make firm conclusions difficult. Arguably, the multisystemic approach may have been more effective because it worked on changing cognitive distortions and relationship skills across multiple relationships.

Kolko (1996b) randomly assigned 55 physically abusive families either to individual child and parent cognitive-behavioral therapy or to family therapy, and had a comparison group that received routine community services. This study is interesting in that children received social-learning-theory-based treatment paralleling that of parents. Measures of child, parent, and family dysfunction and adjustment were collected from both participants. In the cognitive-behavioral condition, children and parents received separate therapists who implemented parallel protocols based on social learning theory principles designed to address their cognitive, affective, and behavioral repertoires. Treatment was aimed at teaching intrapersonal and interpersonal skills. For children, it involved reviewing their perspectives on family stressors and violence and training in coping and self-control skills (e.g., safety and support planning, relaxation). Parents also reviewed their perspectives on violence and physical punishment, attributional style and expectations, self-control (e.g., anger control, cognitive coping), and contingency management (e.g., attention, reinforcement, time out). The family therapy condition also had a social learning theory base. The protocol was designed to enhance family functioning and relationships (Alexander & Parsons, 1982; Robin & Foster, 1989), to increase cooperation and motivation of all family members by promoting an understanding of coercive behavior, and to teach positive communication skills and problem solving. The control condition received typical child protective services (e.g., support groups, homemaking, home-based services).

Although all treatment groups showed improvement over time, the cognitive-behavioral therapy and family therapy groups were associated with improvements in parent-reported child-to-parent violence and child externalizing behaviors, parental distress and abuse risk, and family conflict and cohesion. No differences were found between cognitive-behavioral and family therapy on consumer satisfaction or maltreatment risk at termination. Only one family in both of these two groups showed another incident of maltreatment over a 1-year period, whereas in the community group there were three such cases. This study had a large number of measures relative to the number of subjects treated, again making conclusions tentative. In addition, both treatment conditions included cognitive elements (e.g., work on attributions in cognitive-behavioral therapy and problem-solving training in family therapy), so it cannot be determined whether the treatments were significantly different to produce differential treatment results.

Overall, the effectiveness of behavioral approaches in the treatment of maltreating parents, especially physical abusers, is supported by these single- and multicomponent studies. Although the question of differential effectiveness of behavioral versus other treatments is equivocal, the combination of behavioral group training with active home training seems effective at reducing recidivism. Future efforts need to use larger sample sizes to permit a test of what treatment works best for which type of client.

Child-Focused Treatments

Studies involving specific treatments for abused or neglected children are uncommon. Our discussion focuses primarily on the special issues and adaptations required to work with this population. Types of treatments that have been used with abuse and neglect victims include therapeutic day care and foster care to provide safety and fostering of developmental skills (Culp, Heide, & Richardson, 1987; Ayoub, 1991), behavioral skills training (e.g., social skills; Fantuzzo et al., 1988), and initial efforts to address PTSD symptoms (Deblinger, McLeer, & Henry, 1990). We discuss these methods in reference to four major categories of intervention: removal of a child from the home, developmental stimulation work, behavioral consultation, and studies aimed at treating trauma symptoms with children with other forms of maltreatment (which may be applicable to abused children as well).

Foster Care Placement and Day Care

Since its recognition as a major social problem, the most commonly used "intervention" for abused and neglected children has been to remove them from their homes. Two types of removal have occurred: foster care placement outside the home for a specified period of time, or day care placement for a limited number of hours each day. Foster care placement was originally advocated as a means of dealing with child maltreatment for two reasons. First, it was assumed to remove the child from harm and provide a stable and therapeutic environment. Second, it was also believed to provide a brief time for the family to undergo rehabilitation before the child was returned.

Foster care placement has, however, recently come under criticism for economic and social reasons. Child welfare services were originally designed for short-term evaluation and placement, with the hope that children would soon be returned home or adopted. But for many it has become a purgatory (B. Azar, 1995). In any given year, more than 500,000 U. S. children reside in foster care (Morganthau et al., 1994), with infants, toddlers, and preschoolers making up the fastest-growing percentage of new placements. Although foster care is intended to be short-term, fewer than 40% of children under 10 years of age who remain in care longer than 2 years will ever return home, and 60% of children born to parents with substance use problems and discharged from the hospital to foster care are still there 3 years later (B. Azar, 1995). The shortage of trained foster parents results in shifting children from one home to the next and often in separating siblings (Shealy, 1995).

Even though the child welfare system has been the main line of defense in assisting child victims of abuse and neglect (as well as related family crises) for almost a century, we know very little about the effectiveness of this system (Thompson & Wilcox, 1995). Accordingly, it is no secret that child welfare systems in North America are considered failures. The performance of the U.S. system was evaluated by the U.S. Advisory Board on Child Abuse and Neglect (1990), which concluded that there were emergency needs in every part of the system.

A final criticism involves the assumption that rehabilitation of a parent is occurring while a child is in placement. Early reports indicated that only limited treatment services were typically provided to parents (Mass & Engler, 1959; Stone, 1969), and treatment deliverers still tend to be inadequately trained and to carry heavy caseloads, making intervention spotty (Williams, 1983). In addition, parental contact with a child in foster care may be quite limited. Lack of contact may make return of the child home and unification of the family after foster placement a difficult transition for both parent and child. Children who have spent most of their lives in foster placement, after much court litigation, are being returned to parents they hardly know.

Research on the impact of foster placement is limited, and much of it is flawed methodologically, making it difficult to reach definitive conclusions on its effects. Some work suggests that those children showing the poorest outcomes as adults (e.g., incarceration) following foster care also had shown poor adjustment prior to foster placement (Widom, 1991). On the other hand, foster care itself has been blamed for long-term negative outcomes in adulthood, such as higher levels of homelessness (Mangine, Royse, Wieche, & Nietzel, 1990). In one study that controlled for poverty, effects of foster placement were found over and above those associated with economic deprivation (e.g., an external attributional style, higher peer rejection; McIntyre, Launsbury, Bernton, & Steel, 1988). These diverse outcomes in relation to foster care may vary with the age of the child (Hurwitz, Simms, & Farrington, 1994; Rutter, 1989).

As an alternative to foster placement, day care is often used, at least for the young child. Clinical reports have described research day care programs specifically designed to deal with maltreated children (Martin, 1976). Such specially designed programs are rare, and more often than not such children are placed in day care settings with nonmaltreated children without modifications to programming. Nevertheless, a few therapeutic day care centers have arisen, aimed at more than providing the child with a safe place during the day and relief of stress for the parent. These settings provide opportunities for maltreated children to develop and sustain basic trust in others, to have positive social interactions with peers, and to explore alternative affective and behavioral responses through activities (Ayoub, 1991). Key to such settings is the ongoing modeling of nonviolent conflict resolution by staff members. Evaluations have shown improved performance by participants on developmental standardized tests (Culp, Heide, & Richardson, 1987; Culp, Richardson, & Heide,

1987; Parish, Meyers, Brandner, & Templin, 1985). There is also some indirect evidence that the social interactions of abused preschoolers improve with such interventions (Howes & Espinosa, 1985)

Although the effects of day care programs may be positive, difficulties may also arise. Observational studies in such centers indicate that staff members may be unprepared to handle these children's emotional and behavioral difficulties. In addition, when exposed to an environment where the caretakers are more flexible and show higher levels of attention than those found in their own home, the maltreated children may behave differently at home: They may become more demanding of attention and less compliant, as well as showing a preference for the day care staff. These new behaviors may be perceived negatively by the parents and, paradoxically, may increase child abuse risk. One solution may be to integrate parents into the day care program in some way, which can be accomplished by prearranged observation sessions of the program or actual involvement of the parents in classroom activities. In such centers, parents can take part in classroom activities and attend supportive or educational groups with other parents (Ayoub, 1991; Crittenden, 1983). With their permission, they can also be videotaped while interacting with teachers and children. Later, these videotapes can be used as a source of group discussion with staff members or with outside consultants (Ayoub, 1991). Such informal instruction can be a valuable adjunct to treatment of such parents.

One study on the impact of day care on child placement suggests that without modifications, the typical programs provided may indeed have a negative impact. Crittenden (1983) followed 22 children for 4 years after protective day care was sought. In 9 cases adequate day care could not be arranged (e.g., because of lack of transportation, unavailability of openings, and insufficient funds). Although no differences between the two groups were found at the time of referral in development, home environment, and maternal attachment, at a 1-year follow-up the day care group surprisingly showed higher rates of out-of-home placement (13 of 13 for the day care group vs. 6 of 9 for the group not receiving day care). At a 4-year follow-up, no differences occurred in placement figures for the two groups. Since this study did not use random assignment, its results must be viewed with caution, because the two groups may have differed in some systematic way. It does, however, raise questions regarding the assumption that day care will have a positive impact.

Stimulation Training

Because of the nature of interactions within abusive and neglectful families (e.g., low levels of parent–child interaction), developmental delays are often noted among maltreated children. These developmental delays and the associated lowered responsivity may further exacerbate disturbed family functioning (e.g., interaction with a delayed and unresponsive child is less reinforcing to the parent; Azar, 1986). Interventions, therefore, might be undertaken that increase the parent's stimulation of and sensitivity toward the child (Wolfe, 1991).

A large literature exists describing programs designed to intervene with infants and young children whose environments are thought to provide inadequate resources for facilitating growth and development. The earliest of this work was conducted with infants and young children subjected to the understimulating environments of institutional care (e.g., orphanage residents). This early work stimulated large-scale efforts to increase the cognitive and social stimulation provided to children at risk because of the deprivation associated with poverty, such as Head Start programs. Although there is still much debate about the effectiveness of these efforts, there is some agreement regarding the positive impact of those programs that have targeted changes in parents' behavior. Programs to teach parents ways to promote child development and language skills have resulted in positive child outcomes (Karnes, Teska, Hodgins, & Badger, 1970; Levinstein, 1969).

These interventions may benefit maltreating families as well. Wolfe and his colleagues (Wolfe & Manion, 1984; Wolfe, Edwards, Manion, & Koverola, 1988) described a competency-based stimulation program for parents at risk for abuse, and suggested that such training be aimed at increasing the positive nature of parent–child interactions (e.g., positive physical contact, positive child experiences, nonaversive control). Parents are shown through modeling, role playing, and feedback how to engage in daily activities with their children that serve to strengthen the children's areas of deficiency and to promote adaptive functioning. The activities they suggest are behaviorally specific and include developmentally appropriate language abilities (e.g., eye contact, responding to simple sounds or phrases, producing sounds, etc.) and social interaction abilities (e.g., following directions, engaging in play with parents, expressing affection and needs).

Field, Widmayer, Stringer, and Ignatoff (1980), using a similar intervention with African American adolescent mothers, showed that it is very effective in producing developmental gains in children. Play behavior may be a particularly important behavior to teach abusive parents, in that low levels of this behavior have been associated with at-risk, "difficult" child status (Field, 1979). Work on facilitating such behavior has been incorporated into behavioral parent training programs (Eyberg & Boggs, 1989) and used with abusive parents and their preschool children in a recent study (Urquiza & McNeil, 1996). Further empirical work is needed to explore the effectiveness of stimulation programs with abusive parents (see Wekerle & Wolfe, 1993, and Wolfe & Wekerle, 1993, for additional comments regarding early intervention programs for maltreated and high-risk children).

Behavioral Consultation with Day Care, School, and Foster Care Settings

While efforts are being directed at improving interactions in the home, inappropriate child behaviors that were acquired from an abusive or neglectful environment may be maintained by caretakers' reactions in other settings. Behavioral consultation to staff members in these other settings may be important to help support the changes made at home by parents and to facilitate the overall adjustment of children. Unfortunately, such consultation has not been discussed in the literature.

Reward programs to reduce aggressive behavior in school settings have been undertaken with other populations by teachers and other staff members, and such programs may also be useful for aggressive abused children. Day care staff members, for example, may be trained in the use of reinforcement, and reward aggressive children for periods when they are behaving in a nonaggressive or prosocial way. In this manner, the staff can also be shown how to implement time-out procedures in a way that is best suited to the needs of the children and the skills being taught to the parents at home.

Socially withdrawn behavior has also been handled via behavioral techniques, such as peer prompting of social initiations (Strain, Shores, & Timm, 1977; Strain & Timm, 1974). In three intervention studies using such techniques with child victims of maltreatment, Fantuzzo and his associates (Fantuzzo, Stovall, Stovall, Hightower, & Goins, 1987; Fantuzzo et al., 1988; Davis &

Fantuzzo, 1989) found that positive, prosocial responses and initiations improved for withdrawn maltreated children as a function of peer- and adult-mediated play sessions conducted in a playroom setting. It is noteworthy, however, that maltreated children who tended to be aggressive showed an increase in negative behaviors in response to peer-initiated social interaction, and thus may have required more adult contact (Davis & Fantuzzo, 1989), whereas withdrawn maltreated children were more responsive to peer-initiated strategies. Similarly, Fantuzzo et al. (1988) discovered that withdrawn neglected children actually responded more favorably to peer-initiated social interaction, but decreased their social behavior in response to adult initiations.

Interventions Aimed at Trauma Symptoms

Symptoms of PTSD and stress management problems can occur among victims of physical and sexual abuse, although the incidence of PTSD appears to be lower among physically abused than among sexually abused children (Pelcovitz et al., 1994; Wolfe, Sas, & Wekerle, 1994). The chronicity of the abuse and related stressors (e.g., number of out-of-home placements, need for hospitalization, etc.) have a bearing on how a child may adapt in both the short and long term (Famularo, Kinscherff, & Fenton, 1990; Terr, 1991). Many abused children are the victims of a series of traumas rather than a single traumatic event. Also, unlike other kinds of trauma that children experience, abuse victims may not only lack the support of loved ones in coping with the trauma; the loved ones may in fact be the perpetrators. This fact may engender greater withdrawal and mistrust in abused children relative to other victims of trauma.

Lipovksy (1991) emphasizes four goals for the treatment of children and adolescents with PTSD: education, facilitation of emotional expression, anxiety control, and controlled exposure to memories of the event. Clinicians may find that pursuit of some of these goals may be enhanced by group treatment, whereas others may be best attempted in individual work. In an individual setting, therapists must be sensitive to the possibility that abuse victims may be too fearful to confide quickly in an adult (Aber & Allen, 1987; Steward, Farquhar, Dicharry, Glick, & Martin, 1986). Exposure to memories of the abusive event through play therapy techniques or imaginal exposure, however, may be best accomplished in an individual setting, because it is more difficult to monitor the child and control

the emotional dynamics involved in a group setting. In contrast, education goals, which emphasize teaching children about normal reactions to stress and general coping strategies (Lipovsky, 1991), may be facilitated by a group. Seeing that other abused children share similar symptoms and concerns, for example, may help to "destigmatize" the experience. However, the clinician must be careful to monitor individual reactions, for what may be an innocuous topic of discussion for one child may bring back painful memories of abuse for another.

With some exceptions, outcome studies for treatment of PTSD-related symptoms have largely focused upon adults, and they have been criticized for lack of adherence to experimental design (e.g., random assignment to treatment condition; McFarlane, 1989). Controlled exposure techniques have been used successfully to alleviate trauma due to other types of stressors in adults (McMillan, 1991; Richards & Rose, 1991) and children (Jones & Peterson, 1993). Anxiety management interventions such as biofeedback (Peniston, 1986) has also been used successfully with adults. Such approaches have begun to be adapted successfully for use with child sexual abuse victims and may have utility for victims of physical abuse as well. Deblinger, McLear, and Henry (1990) reduced PTSD-related symptoms among sexually abused children with a treatment package that included gradual exposure, modeling, education, coping, and prevention skills training. Nonoffending parents received cognitive-behavioral coping strategies concurrently, to help them respond appropriately to their children's behavioral difficulties and emotional symptoms. Treatment produced reductions in PTSD symptoms with this population, paving the way for its application with children from other backgrounds of maltreatment.

Summary of Treatment Methods

The absence of child-focused treatment outcome research continues to be striking. Further work needs to be directed toward gathering information on how best to deal with a maltreated child's problems, as well as to enhance family functioning enough to insure his or her safety and continued growth. In teaching new child-rearing skills to maltreating parents, a therapist must be aware of the contextual factors that interact with the family's acquisition of new parenting methods, as well as the potential misuse of the material presented. Consistent monitoring of information the parents have acquired during sessions needs to be done, and careful evaluations of parental use of techniques carried out if failures occur. Regrettably, the modifications needed for work with these families have not received much attention in the literature. Finally, there is a pressing need to develop methods for assisting children with histories of physical and emotional abuse and neglect. Stimulation training, behavioral consultations, and stress management/coping are promising approaches.

CONCLUSIONS AND FUTURE DIRECTIONS

In the decade prior to the first edition of this volume, behavioral approaches to treating child abuse and neglect developed quickly. This work, however, has slowed considerably in the last decade as more attention was directed at understanding developmental outcomes among abused and neglected children, and the impact of other forms of violence affecting children (e.g., exposure to domestic violence, sexual abuse). Behavioral and cognitive-behavioral approaches show real promise as effective means of changing interaction patterns within families. To date, most of this work has focused on changing the parents' behavior. Large-scale efforts to validate their effectiveness with larger samples are needed, as is work identifying the families for whom these strategies are most useful. Particularly important would be further development of interventions aimed at families where the children are infants or adolescents. Over the last decade, interventions aimed at treating the psychological effects of abuse or neglect upon children have shown promise, and such work clearly needs to continue.

Prevention and early intervention using social-learning-theory-based methods is an important area for research at all levels of causation (Wekerle & Wolfe, 1993). At a societal level, mass media campaigns are emerging as a universal way of enhancing parenting skills, based on various behavioral and family systems strategies (Sanders, 1996). At the community and school levels, increased awareness of risk indicators allows for early identification of individuals at risk of child maltreatment, and services can be offered without coercion or labeling. Mothers and fathers can be offered assistance during pregnancy, or provided with education and skills training related to child development during high school. Adolescents who have experi-

rienced negative parental role models, or who have other special needs related to cognitive or behavioral abilities, can be offered preventive preparenting training programs (Azar, 1991b), as well as ones focused on general relationship skills (Wolfe, Wekerle, & Scott, 1997).

At the individual level, need for support, instruction, and resource linkage among new parents is best met by a personalized outreach strategy, such as home visitation. This approach is illustrated by the Prenatal/Early Infancy Project of Olds and colleagues (Olds, Henderson, Chamberlin, & Tatelbaum, 1986; Olds, Henderson, & Kitzman, 1994; Olds et al., 1997), which began in the late 1970s. This team targets first-time parents with one or more child maltreatment risk factors, such as teen parents, single parents, and low-income families. Child care services and pre- and postnatal nurse home visits are offered to establish resource linkages and provide child development education. Notably, individuals receiving this intervention are viewed in terms of their strengths and abilities rather than their deficits, which translates into an empowerment strategy. Women are assisted in understanding and meeting their own needs and those of their newborn children, and are taught skills necessary to enhance this relationship as well as their own self-development.

The encouraging findings from this prospective prevention program support these methods of influencing major psychological determinants of healthy parent–child relationships. Relative to controls, mothers receiving the program have developed or changed their understanding of child health and development, their expectations for their own development, and their self-efficacy. Therapeutic alliances are also formed with the mother and other family members during pregnancy, so that when family stressors become significant, family members can be linked with needed health and human services (e.g., families are assisted in locating financial aid, subsidized housing, family counseling, nutritional supplementation, clothing and furniture, and proper medical care). This program is underway at three U.S. sites, and a variation of the program is underway in Canada. Encouragingly, a 15-year follow-up with 324 mothers and 315 of their firstborn adolescents has revealed that this program of prenatal and early childhood home visitation by nurses can reduce subsequent pregnancies, use of welfare, child maltreatment, and criminal behavior among low-income mothers and children (Olds et al., 1997). These findings offer convincing opportunities to prevent maltreatment and related social and family problems on the basis of early intervention services. Clearly, efforts to enhance positive experiences at an early stage in the development of the parent–child relationship hold considerable promise for the prevention of child maltreatment and its consequences.

REFERENCES

Aber, J. L., & Allen, J. P. (1987). The effects of maltreatment on young children's socio-emotional development. *Developmental Psychology, 23,* 406–414.

Aber, J. L., & Cicchetti, D. (1984). The socio-emotional development of maltreated children: An empirical and theoretical analysis. In H. Fitzgerald, B. Lester, & M. Yogman (Eds.), *Theory and research in behavioral pediatrics* (Vol. 2, pp. 147–205). New York: Plenum Press.

Achenbach, T. M. (1991). *Manual for the Child Behavior Checklist/4–18 and 1991 Profile.* Burlington: University of Vermont, Department of Psychiatry .

Alexander, J., & Parsons, B. (1982). *Functional family therapy.* Monterey, CA: Brooks/Cole.

Allen, D. M., & Tarnowski, K. J. (1989). Depressive characteristics of physically abused children. *Journal of Abnormal Child Psychology, 17,* 1–11.

Ambrose, S., Hazzard, A., & Haworth, J. (1980). Cognitive-behavioral parenting groups for abusive families. *Child Abuse and Neglect, 4,* 119–125.

American Public Welfare Association. (1988). *Second national roundtable on CPS risk assessment.* Washington, DC: Author.

Arnold, E. L. (1978). *Helping parents help their children.* New York: Brunner/Mazel.

Aronson, H., & Overall, B. (1966). Treatment expectations of parents in two social classes. *Social Work, 11,* 35–41.

Averill, J. R. (1983). Studies on anger and aggression: Implications for theories of emotion. *American Psychologist, 38,* 1145–1160.

Ayllon, T., & Roberts, M. D. (1975). Mothers as educators for their children. In T. Thompson & W. S. Dockens (Eds.), *Applications of behavior modification* (pp. 107–137). New York: Academic Press.

Ayoub, C. (1991). Physical violence and preschoolers: The use of therapeutic day care in the treatment of physically abused children and children from violent families. *The Advisor, 4,* 1–18.

Azar, B. (1995, September). Foster care has bleak history. *APA Monitor,* p. 8.

Azar, S. T. (1984). *An evaluation of the effectiveness of cognitive behavioral versus insight oriented mothers groups with child maltreaters.* Unpublished doctoral dissertation, University of Rochester.

Azar, S. T. (1986). A framework for understanding child maltreatment: An integration of cognitive behavioral and developmental perspectives. *Canadian Journal of Behavioral Science, 18,* 340–355.

Azar, S. T. (1989a). Training parents of abused children. In C. E. Schaefer & J. M. Briesmeister (Eds.), *Handbook of parent training* (pp. 414–441). New York: Wiley .

Azar, S. T. (1989b, November). *Unrealistic expectations and attributions of negative intent among teenage mothers at risk for child maltreatment: The validity of a cognitive view of parenting.* Poster presented at the annual meeting of the Association for Advancement of Behavior Therapy, Washington, DC.

Azar, S. T. (1991a). Models of physical child abuse: A metatheoretical analysis. *Criminal Justice and Behavior, 18,* 30–46.

Azar, S. T. (1991b, April). *Concern about the physical abuse of adolescents: A case of neglect.* Paper presented at the annual meeting of the Eastern Psychological Association, New York.

Azar, S. T. (1996). Cognitive restructuring of professionals' schema regarding women parenting in poverty. *Women and Therapy, 18,* 149–163.

Azar, S. T. (1997). A cognitive behavioral approach to understanding and treating parents who physically abuse their children. In D. Wolf & R. McMahon (Eds.), *Child abuse: New directions in prevention and treatment across the life span* (pp. 78–100). Thousand Oaks, CA: Sage.

Azar, S. T., Barnes, K. T., & Twentyman, C. T. (1988). Developmental outcomes in physically abused children: Consequences of parental abuse or the effects of a more general breakdown in caregiving behaviors? *The Behavior Therapist, 11,* 27–32.

Azar, S. T., & Benjet, C. L. (1994). A cognitive perspective on ethnicity, race and termination of parental rights. *Law and Human Behavior, 18,* 249–268.

Azar, S. T., Benjet, C., Fuhrmann, G., & Cavallaro, L. (1995). Termination of parental rights: Can behavioral research help Solomon? *Behavior Therapy, 26,* 599–623.

Azar, S. T., & Bober, S. L. (in press). Developmental outcomes in abused children: The result of a breakdown in socialization environment. In W. Silverman & T. Ollendick (Eds.), *Group intervention in the school and the community* (pp. 376–400). Needham Heights, MA: Allyn & Bacon.

Azar, S. T., Breton, S. J., & Miller, L. P. (1998). Cognitive behavioral group work and physical child abuse: Intervention and prevention. In K. C. Stoiber & T. Kratochwill (Eds.), *Group intervention in the school and the community* (pp. 376–400). Needham Heights, MA: Allyn & Bacon.

Azar, S. T., Fantuzzo, J., & Twentyman, C. T. (1984). An applied behavioural approach to child maltreatment: Back to basics. *Advances in Behaviour Research and Therapy, 6,* 6–11.

Azar, S. T., Ferguson, E., & Twentyman, C. T. (1992). Social competence. In P. H. Wilson (Ed.), *Principles and practice of relapse prevention* (pp. 329–348). New York: Guilford Press.

Azar, S. T., Povilaitis, T., Lauretti, A., & Poquette, C. (1997). Theory in child abuse. In J. Lutzker (Ed.), *Child abuse: A handbook of theory, research and treatment* (pp. 3–30). New York: Plenum Press.

Azar, S. T., Robinson, D. R., Hekimian, E., & Twentyman, C. T. (1984). Unrealistic expectations and problem solving ability in maltreating and comparison mothers. *Journal of Consulting and Clinical Psychology, 52,* 687–691.

Azar, S. T., & Rohrbeck, C. A. (1986). Child abuse and unrealistic expectations: Further validation of the Parent Opinion Questionnaire. *Journal of Consulting and Clinical Psychology, 54,* 867–868.

Azar, S. T., & Twentyman, C. T. (1984, November). *An evaluation of the effectiveness of behaviorally versus insight oriented group treatments with maltreating mothers.* Paper presented at the annual meeting of the Association for Advancement of Behavior Therapy, Philadelphia.

Azar, S. T., & Twentyman, C. T. (1986). Cognitive-behavioral perspectives on the assessment and treatment of child abuse. In P. C. Kendall (Ed.), *Advances in cognitive-behavioral research and therapy* (Vol. 5, pp. 237–267). New York: Academic Press.

Azrin, H. N., Naster, B. J., & Jones, R. (1973). Reciprocal counseling: A rapid learning based procedure for marital counseling. *Behaviour Research and Therapy, 11,* 365–383.

Barnes, K. T., & Azar, S. T. (1990, August). *Maternal expectations and attributions in discipline situations: A test of a cognitive model of parenting.* Poster presented at the annual meeting of the American Psychological Association, Boston.

Barth, R. P., Blythe, B. J., Schinke, S. P., Stevens, P., & Schilling, R. F. (1983). Self-control training with maltreating parents. *Child Welfare, 62,* 313–324.

Bavolek, S. J. (1984). *Handbook of the Adult/Adolescent-Parenting Inventory.* Park City, UT: Family Development Resources.

Becker, W. C. (1971). *Parents are teachers.* Champaign, IL: Research Press.

Becker, J. V., Alpert, J. L., BigFoot, D. S., Bonner, B. L., Geddie, L. F., Henggeler, S. W., Kaufman, K. L., & Walker, C. E. (1995). Empirical research on child abuse treatment: Report by the Child Abuse and Neglect Treatment Working Group, American Psychological Association. *Journal of Clinical Child Psychology, 24,* 23–46.

Bedner, R. L., & Kaul, T. J. (1978). Experiential group research: Current perspectives. In S. L. Garfield & A. E. Bergin (Eds.), *Handbook of psychotherapy and behavior change: An empirical analysis* (2nd ed., pp. 769–815). New York: Wiley.

Bell, R. Q., & Harper, L. (1977). *Child effects on adults.* Hillsdale, NJ: Erlbaum.

Belsky, J. (1980). Child maltreatment: An ecological integration. *American Psychologist, 35,* 320–335.

Berger, A. (1980). The child abusing family: Part I. Methodological issues and parent-related characteristics of abusing families. *American Journal of Family Therapy, 8,* 53–66.

Berkowitz, L. (1983). Aversively stimulated aggression: Some parallels and differences in research with animals and humans. *Amercian Psychologist, 38,* 1135–1144.

Bernstein, E. M., & Putnam, F. W. (1986). Development, reliability, and validity of a dissociation scale. *Journal of Nervous and Mental Disease, 174,* 725–735.

Bousha, D., & Twentyman, C. T. (1984). Abusing, neglectful and comparison mother–child interactional style. *Journal of Abnormal Psychology, 93,* 106–114.

Bower, G. H. (1981). Mood and memory. *American Psychologist, 36,* 129–148.

Brody, B. (1990). Prediction of dangerousness in different contexts. In R. Rosner & R. Weinstock (Eds.), *Ethical practice in psychiatry and the law* (pp. 185–196). New York: Plenum Press.

Brunk, M., Henggeler, S. W., & Whelan, J. P. (1987). Comparison of multisystemic therapy and parent training in the brief treatment of child abuse and neglect. *Journal of Consulting and Clinical Psychology, 55,* 171–178.

Burgdorf, K. (1988). *Study of national incidence and prevalence of child abuse and neglect.* Washington, DC: National Center on Child Abuse and Neglect.

Burgess, R. L., & Conger, R. D. (1978). Family interaction in abusive, neglectful and normal families. *Child Development, 49,* 1163–1173.

Butcher, J. N., Dahlstrom, W. G., Graham, J. R., Tellegen, A., & Krammer, B. (1989). *Minnesota Multiphasic Personality, Inventory—2 (MMPI-2): Manual for administration and scoring.* Minneapolis: University of Minnesota Press.

Campbell, R. V., O'Brien, S., Bickett, A. D., & Lutzker, J. R. (1983). In-home parent training of migraine headaches and marital counselling as an ecobehavioral approach to prevent child abuse. *Journal of Behavior Therapy and Experimental Psychiatry, 14,* 147–154.

Camras, L. A., Ribordy, S., Spaccarelli, S., & Stefani, R. (1986, August). *Emotion recognition and production by abused children and mothers.* Paper presented at the annual meeting of the American Psychological Association, Washington, DC.

Cerezo, M. A., D'Ocon, A., & Dolz, L. (1996). Mother–child interactive patterns in abusive families versus non-abusive families: An observational study. *Child Abuse and Neglect, 20,* 573–587.

Cicchetti, D., & Lynch, M. (1995). Failures in the expectable environment and their impact on individual development: The case of child maltreatment. In D. Cicchetti & D. J. Cohen (Eds.), *Developmen-*

tal psychopathology: Vol. 2. Risk, disorder, and adaptation (pp. 32–71). New York: Wiley.

Cocozza, J., & Steadman, H. (1978). Prediction in psychiatry: An example of misplaced confidence in experts. *Social Problems, 25,* 265–276.

Cohn, A. H. (1979). Essential elements of successful child abuse and neglect treatment. *Child Abuse and Neglect, 3,* 491–496.

Conger, R. D. (1982). Behavioral intervention for child abuse. *The Behavior Therapist, 5,* 49–53.

Conger, R. D., Lahey, B. B., & Smith, S. S. (1981, July). *An intervention program for child abuse: Modifying maternal depression and behavior.* Paper presented at the Family Violence Research Conference, University of New Hampshire, Durham, NH.

Crimmins, D. B., Bradlyn, A. S., St. Lawrence, J. S., & Kelly, J. (1984). A training technique for improving the parent–child interaction skills of an abusive–neglectful mother. *Child Abuse and Neglect, 8,* 533–539.

Crittenden, P. M. (1982). Abusing, neglecting, problematic, and adequate dyads: Differentiating by patterns of interaction. *Merrill–Palmer Quarterly, 27,* 201–218.

Crittenden, P. M. (1983). The effects of mandatory protective daycare on mutual attachment in maltreating mother–infant dyads. *Child Abuse and Neglect, 3,* 297–300.

Crittenden, P. M. (1992). Treatment of anxious attachment in infancy and early childhood. *Developmental Psychopathology, 4,* 575–602.

Crittenden, P. M. (1993). An information processing perspective on the behavior of neglectful parents. *Criminal Justice and Behavior, 20,* 27–48.

Crouch, J. L., & Milner, J. S. (1993). Effects of child neglect on children. *Criminal Justice and Behavior, 20,* 49–65.

Crozier, J., & Katz, R. C. (1979). Social learning theory treatment of child abuse. *Journal of Behavior Therapy and Psychiatry, 10,* 213–220.

Culp, R. E., Heide, J. S., & Richardson, M. T. (1987). Maltreated children's developmental scores: Treatment versus nontreatment. *Child Abuse and Neglect, 11,* 29–34.

Culp, R. E., Richardson, M. T., & Heide, J. S. (1987). Differential development progress of maltreated children in day treatment. *Social Work, 32,* 497–499.

Dangel, R. F., & Polster, R. A. (Eds.). (1984). *Parent training: Foundations of research and practice.* New York: Guilford Press.

Davis, S., & Fantuzzo, J. W. (1989). The effects of adult and peer social initiations on social behavior of withdrawn and aggressive maltreated preschool children. *Journal of Family Violence, 4,* 227–248.

Deblinger, E., McLear, S. V., Atkins, M. S., Ralphe, D., & Foa, E. (1989). Post-traumatic stress in sexually abused, physically abused, and nonabused children. *Child Abuse and Neglect, 13,* 403–408.

Deblinger, E., McLeer, S. V., & Henry, D. (1990). Cognitive behavioral treatment for sexually abused children suffering from post traumatic stress: Preliminary findings. *Journal of the American Academy of Child and Adolescent Psychiatry, 29,* 747–752.

Delgado, A. E., & Lutzker, J. R. (1985, November). *Training parents to identify and report their children's illness.* Paper presented at the annual convention of the Association for Advancement of Behavior Therapy, Houston, TX.

Denicola, J., & Sandler, J. (1980). Training abusive parents in cognitive behavioral techniques. *Behavior Therapy, 11,* 263–270.

Derogatis, L. R. (1983). *SCL-90 administration, scoring, and procedures manual—II.* Towson, MD: Clinical Psychometric Research.

Dix, T. H., Ruble, D. N., & Zambarano, R. J. (1989). Mothers' implicit theories of discipline: Child effects, parent effects, and the attribution process. *Child Development, 60,* 1373–1391.

Doctor, R. M., & Singer, E. M. (1978). Behavioral intervention strategies with child abusive parents: A home intervention program. *Child Abuse and Neglect, 2,* 57–68.

Downey, G., & Walker, E. (1992). Distinguishing family-level and child-level influences on the development of depression and aggression in children at risk. *Development and Psychopathology, 4,* 81–95.

Dubowitz, H. (1991). The impact of child maltreatment on health. In R. H. Starr & D. A. Wolfe (Eds.), *The effects of child abuse and neglect* (pp. 278–294). New York: Guilford Press.

Dunst, C. H. (1986). *Family resources, personal well-being, and early intervention.* Unpublished manuscript, Family Infant and Preschool Program, Western Carolina Center, Morganton, NC.

Eckenrode, J., Laird, M., & Doris, J. (1993). School performance and disciplinary problems among abused and neglected children. *Developmental Psychology, 29,* 53–62.

Egan, K. (1983). Stress managment and child management with abusive parents. *Journal of Clinical Child Psychology, 12,* 292–299.

Egeland, B., & Farber, E. A. (1984). Infant–mother attachment: Factors related to its development and changes over time. *Child Development, 55,* 753–771.

Egeland, B., & Sroufe, L. A. (1981). Attachment and early maltreatment. *Child Development, 52,* 44–52.

Egeland, B., Sroufe, A., & Erickson, M. (1983). The developmental consequence of different patterns of maltreatment. *Child Abuse and Neglect, 7,* 459–469.

Eisler, R. M., Hersen, M., & Agras, W. S. (1973). Effects of videotape and instructional feedback on nonverbal marital interactions: An analogue study. *Behavior Therapy, 4,* 551–558.

Elliott, R. (1986). Interpersonal process recall (IPR) as a psychotherapy process research method. In L.

S. Greenberg & W. M. Pinsof (Eds.), *The psychotherapeutic process: A research handbook* (pp. 503–527). New York: Guilford Press.

Ennis, B., & Litwack, T. (1974). Psychiatry and the presumption of expertise. Flipping coins in the courtroom. *California Law Review, 62,* 693–752.

Eyberg, S., & Boggs, S. T. (1989). Parent training for oppositional defiant preschoolers. In C. E. Schaefer & J. M. Friesmeister (Eds.), *Handbook of parent training: Parents as co-therapists for children's behavior problems* (pp. 105–132). New York: Wiley.

Famularo, R., Kinscherff, R., & Fenton, T. (1990). Symptom differences in acute and chronic presentation of childhood Post-Traumatic Stress Disorder. *Child Abuse and Neglect, 14,* 439–444.

Fantuzzo, J. W. (1990). Behavioral treatment of the victims of child abuse and neglect. *Behavior Modification, 14,* 316–339.

Fantuzzo, J. W., Jurecic, L., Stovall, A., Hightower, A. D., Goins, C., & Schachtel, D. (1988). Effects of adult and peer social initiations on the social behavior of withdrawn, maltreated preschool children. *Journal of Consulting and Clinical Psychology, 56,* 34–39.

Fantuzzo, J. W., Stovall, A., Schachtel, D., Goins, C., & Hall, R. (1987). The effects of peer social initiations on the social behavior of withdrawn maltreated preschool children. *Journal of Behavior Therapy and Experimental Psychiatry, 18,* 357–363.

Fantuzzo, J. W., Wray, L., Hall, R., Goins, C., & Azar, S. T. (1986). Parent and social skills training for mentally retarded mothers identified as child maltreaters. *American Journal of Mental Deficiency, 91,* 135–140.

Farber, E. D., & Joseph, J. A. (1985). The maltreated adolescent: Patterns of physical abuse. *Child Abuse and Neglect, 8,* 295–299.

Farber, E., McCord, D., Kinast, C., & Baum-Faulkner, D. (1984). Violence in families of adolescent runaways. *Child Abuse and Neglect, 8,* 295–299.

Feldman, R. S., Salzinger, S., Rosario, M., Alvarado, L., Caraballo, L., & Hammer, M. (1995). Parent, teacher, and peer ratings of physically abused and nonmaltreated children's behavior. *Journal of Abnormal Child Psychology, 23,* 317–334.

Feshbach, N. D. (1989). The construct of empathy and the phenomenon of physical maltreatment of children. In D. Cicchetti & V. Carlson (Eds.), *Child maltreatment: Theory and research on the causes and consequences of child abuse and neglect* (pp. 349–373). New York: Cambridge University Press.

Field, T. (1979). Games people play with normal and high risk infants. *Child Psychiatry and Human Development, 10,* 41–48.

Field, T., Widmayer, S. M., Stringer, S., & Ignatoff, E. (1980). Teenage, lower class, black mothers and their preterm infants: An intervention and development follow-up. *Child Development, 51,* 426–436.

Fox, L., Long, S. H., & Langlois, A. (1988). Patterns of language comprehension deficit in abused and neglected children. *Journal of Speech and Hearing Disorders, 53,* 239–244.

Foxx, R. M., McMorrow, M. J., & Mennemeier, M. (1984). Teaching social/vocational skills to retarded adults with a modified table game: An analysis of generalization. *Journal of Applied Behavior Analysis, 17,* 343–352.

Foxx, R. M., McMorrow, M. J., & Schloss, C. (1983). Stacking the deck: Teaching social skills to retarded adults with a modified table game. *Journal of Applied Behavior Analysis, 16,* 157–170.

Frodi, A., & Smetana, J. (1984). Abused, neglected, and nonmaltreated preschoolers' ability to discriminate emotions in others: The effects of IP. *Child Abuse and Neglect, 8,* 459–465.

Galdston, R. (1979). Preventing the abuse of little children. In D. G. Gil (Ed.), *Child abuse and violence* (pp. 340–353). New York: Academic Press.

Gambrill, E. D. (1983). Behavioral intervention with child abuse and neglect. In M. Hersen, R. M. Eisler, & P. M. Miller (Eds.), *Progress in behavior modification* (Vol. 17, pp. 1–56). New York: Academic Press.

Garbarino, J. (1976). A preliminary study of some ecological correlates of child abuse: The impact of socioeconomic stress on mothers. *Child Development, 47,* 178–185.

Garbarino, J., & Stocking, S. H. (1980). *Protecting children from abuse and neglect.* San Francisco: Jossey-Bass.

Gaudin, J. M., Jr., Wodarski, J. S., Arkinson, M. K., & Avery, I. S. (1990). Remedying child neglect: Effectiveness of social network interventions. *Journal of Applied Sciences, 15,* 97–123.

Gelles, R. J. (1983). An exchange/social control theory. In D. Finkelhor, R. J. Gelles, G. T. Hotaling, & M. A. Strauss (Eds.), *The dark side of families* (pp. 151–165). Beverly Hills, CA: Sage.

George, C., & Main, M. (1979). Social interactions of young abused children: Approach, avoidance and aggression. *Child Development, 50,* 306–318.

Gil, D. G. (1970). *Violence against children: Physical child abuse in the United States.* Cambridge, MA: Harvard University Press.

Gilbert, M. R. (1976). Behavioral approach to the treatment of child abuse. *Nursing Times, 72,* 140–143.

Gordon, S. B., & Davidson, N. (1981). Behavioral parent training. In A. F. Gurman & D. P. Kniskern (Eds.), *Handbook of family therapy* (pp. 517–555). New York: Bruner/Mazel.

Grisso, T., & Appelbaum, P. S. (1992). Is it unethical to offer predictions of future violence? *Law and Human Behavior, 16,* 621–633.

Hagen, R. L., Foreyt, J. P., & Durham, T. W. (1976). The dropout problem: Reducing attrition in obesity research. *Behavior Therapy, 7,* 463–471.

Hanson, D. J., Pallotta, G. M., Christopher, J. S., Conaway, R. L., & Lundquist, L. M. (1995). The Parental Problem-Solving Measure: Further evaluation with maltreating and non-maltreating parents. *Journal of Family Violence*, *10*, 319–336.

Haskett, M. E., & Kistner, J. A. (1991). Social interactions and peer perceptions of young physically abused children. *Child Development*, *62*, 979–990.

Haskett, M. E., & Myers, L. W. (1994, August). *The Parent–Child Problem-Solving Program: A description and qualitative assessment.* Paper presented at the annual meeting of the American Psychological Association, Los Angeles.

Hazzard, A., Christensen, A., & Margolin, G. (1983). Children's perception of parental behaviors. *Journal of Abnormal Child Psychology*, *11*, 49–59.

Heitler, J. B. (1973). Preparation of lower-class patients for expressive group psychotherapy. *Journal of Consulting and Clinical Psychology*, *41*, 251–260.

Heitler, J. B. (1976). Preparatory techniques in initiating expressive psychotherapy with lower-class unsophisticated patients. *Psychological Bulletin*, *83*, 339–352.

Herrenkohl, E. C., Herrenkohl, R. C., Toedter, L., & Yanushefski, A. M. (1984). Parent–child interactions in abusive and non-abusive families. *Journal of the American Academy of Child Psychiatry*, *23*, 641–648.

Herrenkohl, R. C., Herrenkohl, E. C., Egolf, B., & Seech, M. (1979). The repetition of child abuse: How frequently does it occur? *Child Abuse and Neglect*, *3*, 67–72.

Hoffman-Plotkin, D., & Twentyman, C. T. (1984). A multimodal assessment of behavioral and cognitive deficits in abused and neglected preschoolers. *Child Development*, *55*, 794–802.

Howes, C., & Eldredge, R. (1985). Responses of abused, neglected, and non-maltreated children to the behaviors of their peers. *Journal of Applied Developmental Psychology*, *6*, 261–270.

Howes, C., & Espinosa, M. P. (1985). The consequences of child abuse for the formation of relationships with peers. *Child Abuse and Neglect*, *9*, 397–404.

Hurwitz, S. M., Simms, M. D., & Farrington, R. (1994). Impact of developmental problems on young children's exits from foster care. *Journal of Developmental and Behavioral Pediatrics*, *15*, 105–110.

Jacobson, N. S. (1978). Specific and nonspecific factors in the effectiveness of a behavioral approach to the treatment of a marital discord. *Journal of Consulting and Clinical Psychology*, *45*, 92–100.

Johnson, C. A., & Katz, C. (1973). Using parents as change agents for their children. *Journal of Applied Behavior Analysis*, *14*, 131–200.

Jones, R. W., & Peterson, L. W. (1993). Post-Traumatic Stress Disorder in a child following an automobile accident. *Journal of Family Practice*, *36*, 223–225.

Jouriles, E. N., Murphy, T., & O'Leary, K. D. (1989). Interspousal aggression, marital discord, and child problems. *Journal of Consulting and Clinical Psychology*, *57*, 453–455.

Justice, B., & Justice, R. (1978). Evaluating outcome of group therapy for abusing parents. *Corrective and Social Psychiatry and Journal of Behavioral Technology*, *14*, 45–49.

Justice, R., & Justice, B. (1976). *The abusing family.* New York: Human Sciences Press.

Karnes, M. B., Teska, J. A., Hodgins, A. S., & Badger, I. D. (1970). Educational intervention at home by mothers of disadvantaged infants. *Child Development*, *41*, 925–935.

Kaufman, J. (1991). Depressive disorders in maltreated children. *Journal of the American Academy of Child and Adolescent Psychiatry*, *30*, 257–265.

Kaufman, J., & Cicchetti, D. (1989). The effects of maltreatment on school-aged children's socio-emotional development: Assessments in a day-camp setting. *Developmental Psychology*, *25*, 516–524.

Kazdin, A. E., & Polster, R. (1973). Intermittent token reinforcement and response maintenance in extinction. *Behavior Therapy*, *4*, 386–391.

Kempe, C. H., & Helfer, R. E. (1972). *Helping the battered child and his family.* Philadelphia: Lippincott.

Kempe, C. H., Silverman, F. N., Steele, B. F., Droegenmueller, W., & Silver, H. K. (1962). The battered child syndrome. *Journal of the American Medical Association*, *181*, 17–24.

Kinard, E. M. (1980). Emotional development in physically abused children. *American Journal of Orthopsychiatry*, *50*, 686–696.

Kinard, E. M. (1982). Experiencing child abuse: Effects on emotional adjustment. *American Journal of Orthopsychiatry*, *52*, 82–91.

Kinard, E. M. (1995). Perceived social support and competence in abused children: A longitudinal perspective. *Journal of Family Violence*, *10*, 73–98.

Knutson, J. F., & Bower, M. E. (1994). Physically abusive parenting as an escalated aggressive response. In M. Potegal & J. F. Knutson (Eds.), *The dynamics of aggression: Biological and social processes in dyads and groups* (pp. 195–225). Hillsdale, NJ: Erlbaum.

Kolko, D. J. (1992). Characteristics of child victims of physical violence: Research findings and clinical implications. *Journal of Interpersonal Violence*, *7*, 244–276.

Kolko, D. J. (1996a). Clinical monitoring of treatment course in child physical abuse: Child and parent reports. *Child Abuse and Neglect*, *20*, 23–43.

Kolko, D. J. (1996b). Individual cognitive behavioral treatment and family therapy for physically abused children and their offending parents: A comparison of clinical outcomes. *Child Maltreatment*, *1*, 322–342.

Kovacs, M. (1994). *Children's Depression Inventory Manual.* Toronto: Mental Health System.

Koverola, C., Elliot-Faust, O., & Wolfe, D. A. (1984). Clinical issues in the behavioral treatment of a child abusive mother experiencing multiple life stressors. *Journal of Clinical Child Psychology, 13,* 187–191.

Larrance, D. L., & Twentyman, C. T. (1983). Maternal attributions in child abuse. *Journal of Abnormal Psychology, 92,* 449–457.

Levinstein, P. (1969, April). *Cognitive growth in pre-schoolers through stimulation of verbal interaction with mothers.* Paper presented at the annual meeting of the American Orthopsychiatry Association, New York.

Lewis, D. O., Shanok, S. S., Pincus, J. H., & Glaser, G. H. (1979). Violent juvenile delinquents: Psychiatric, neurological, psychological, and abuse factors. *Journal of American Academy of Child Psychiatry, 18,* 307–319.

Lipovsky, J. A. (1991). Posttraumatic Stress Disorder in children. *Family and Community Health, 14,* 42–51.

Lipsett, L. (1983). Stress in infancy: Toward understanding the origins of coping behavior. In N. Garmezy & M. Rutter (Eds.), *Stress, coping, and development in children* (pp. 161–190). New York: McGraw-Hill.

Lorber, R., Felton, D. K., & Reid, J. (1984). A social learning approach to the reduction of coercive processes in child abusive families: A molecular analysis. *Advances in Behaviour Research and Therapy, 6,* 29–45.

Lorion, R. P. (1978). Research on psychotherapy and behavior change with the disadvantaged. In S. L. Garfield & A. E. Bergin (Eds.), *Handbook of psychotherapy and behavior change: An empirical analysis* (2nd ed., pp. 903–938). New York: Wiley.

Love, L. R., Kaswan, J., & Bugenthal, D. (1972). Differential effectiveness of three clinical interventions for different socioeconomic groupings. *Journal of Consulting and Clinical Psychology, 39,* 347–360.

Lutzker, J., & Rice, J. M. (1984). Project 12-Ways: Measuring outcome of a large in-home service for treatment and prevention of child abuse and neglect. *Child Abuse and Neglect, 8,* 519–524.

Maccoby, E. E., & Martin, J. A. (1983). Socialization in the context of the family: Parent–child interaction. In E. M. Hetherington (Vol. Ed.), *Handbook of child psychology* (4th ed.): Vol. 4. *Socialization, personality, and social development* (pp. 1–101). New York: Wiley.

Magura, S., & Moses, B. S. (1986). *Outcome measures for child welfare services: Theory and applications.* Washington, DC: Child Welfare League of America.

Mangine, S., Royse, D., Wieche, V., & Nietzel, M. (1990). Homelessness among adults raised as foster children. *Psychological Reports, 67,* 739–745.

Mann, E., & McDermott, J. F. (1983). Play therapy for victims of child abuse and neglect. In C. E. Schaefer & K. J. O'Connor (Eds.), *Handbook of play therapy* (pp. 283–307). New York: Wiley.

Martin, H. P. (1976). *The abused child: A multidisciplinary approach to developmental issues and treatment.* Cambridge, MA: Ballinger.

Martin, H. P., & Beezley, P. (1976). Behavioral observations of abused children. *Developmental Medicine and Child Neurology, 19,* 373–387.

Mass, H. S., & Engler, R. (1959). *Children in need of parents.* New York: Columbia University Press.

McFarlane, A. C. (1989). The treatment of Post-Traumatic Stress Disorder. *British Journal of Medical Psychology, 62,* 81–90.

McGee, R., Wolfe, D. A., & Olson, J. (1995, June). *Why me? A content analysis of adolescents' causal attributions for their maltreatment experiences.* Paper presented at the meeting of the Canadian Psychological Association, Charlottetown, Prince Edward Island.

McIntyre, A., Launsbury, K., Bernton, D., & Steel, H. (1988). Psychosocial characteristics of foster children. *Journal of Applied Developmental Psychology, 9,* 125–137.

McMahon, R. J., & Forehand, R. (1984). Parent training for the noncompliant child: Treatment outcome, generalization, and adjunctive therapy procedures. In R. F. Dangel & R. A. Polster (Eds.), *Parent training: Foundations of research and practice* (pp. 298–328). New York: Guilford Press.

McMillan, T. M. (1991). Post-Traumatic Stress Disorder and severe head injury. *British Journal of Psychiatry, 159,* 431–433.

Miller, W. H. (1975). *Systematic parent training.* Champaign, IL: Research Press.

Miller, L. R., & Azar, S. T. (1996). The pervasiveness of maladaptive attributions in mothers at-risk for child abuse. *Family Violence and Sexual Assault Bulletin, 12,* 31–37.

Milner, J. S. (1986). *The Child Abuse Potential Inventory: Manual* (2nd ed.). Webster, NC: Psytec.

Milner, J. S. (1993). Social information processing and physical child abuse. *Clinical Psychology Review, 13,* 275–294.

Monahan, J. (1981). *The clinical prediction of violence.* Rockville, MD: National Institute of Mental Health.

Morgenthau, T., Springen, K., Smith, V. E., Rosenberg, D., Beale, G., Bogert, C., Gegax, T. T., & Joseph, N. (1994, December 12). The orphanage. *Newsweek,* pp. 28–32.

Murphy, C. M., Meyer, S., & O'Leary, K. D. (1994). Dependency characteristics of partner assaultive men. *Journal of Abnormal Psychology, 103,* 729–735.

National Center on Child Abuse and Neglect (NCCAN). (1994). *Child maltreatment 1992: Reports from the states to the National Center on Child Abuse and Neglect.* Washington, DC: U. S. Government Printing Office.

National Research Council. (1993). *Understanding child abuse and neglect.* Washington, DC: National Academy Press.

Nomellini, S., & Katz, R. C. (1983). Effects of anger control training on abusive parents. *Cognitive Therapy and Research, 7*, 57–68.

Novaco, R. W. (1975). *Anger control: The development and evaluation of an experimental treatment.* Lexington, MA: Lexington Books.

O'Dell, S. (1974). Training parents in behavior modification: A review. *Psychological Bulletin, 81*, 418–433.

Olds, D., Eckenrode, J., Henderson, C. R., Kitzman, H., Powers, J., Cole, R., Sidora, K., Morris, P., & Pettit, L. (1997). Long-term effects of home visitation on maternal life course, child abuse and neglect, and children's arrests: 15-year follow-up of a randomized trial. *Journal of the American Medical Association, 278*(8), 637–643.

Olds, D., Henderson, C. R., Chamberlin, R., & Tatelbaum, R. (1986). Preventing child abuse and neglect: A randomized trial of nurse home visitation. *Pediatrics, 78*, 65–78.

Olds, D., Henderson, C. R., & Kitzman, H. (1994). Does prenatal and infancy nurse home visitation have enduring effects on qualities of parental care giving and child health at 25 to 50 months of life? *Pediatrics, 93*, 89–98.

O'Leary, K. D., Malone, J., & Tyree, A. (1994). Physical aggression in early marriage: Prerelationship and relationship effects. *Journal of Consulting and Clinical Psychology, 62*, 594–602.

Ollendick, T. H. (1978). Reliability and validity of the Revised Fear Survey Schedule for Children (FSSC-R). *Behaviour Research and Therapy, 21*, 685–692.

Parish, R. A., Meyers, P. A., Brandner, A., & Templin, K. H. (1985). Developmental milestones of abused children and their improvement with a family oriented approach to treatment. *Child Abuse and Neglect, 9*, 245–250.

Parke, R. D. (1977). Socialization into child abuse: A social interactional perspective. In J. L. Tapp & F. J. Levine (Eds.), *Law, justice and the individual in society: Psychological and legal issues* (pp. 183–199). New York: Holt, Rinehart & Winston.

Pelcovitz, D., Kaplan, S., Goldenberg, B., Mandel, F., Lehane, J., & Guarrera, J. (1994). Post-Traumatic Stress Disorder in physically abused adolescents. *Journal of the American Academy of Child and Adolescent Psychiatry, 33*(3), 305–312.

Pelton, L. H. (1994). The role of material factors in child abuse and neglect. In G. B. Melton & F. D. Barry (Eds.), *Protecting children from abuse and neglect: Foundations for a new national strategy* (pp. 131–181). New York: Guilford Press.

Peniston, E. G. (1986). EMG biofeedback-assisted desensitization treatment for Vietnam combat veterans' post-traumatic stress disorder. *Clinical Biofeedback and Health an International Journal, 9*, 35–41.

Plotkin, R. (1983). *Cognitive mediation in disciplinary action among mothers who have abused or neglected their children: Dispositional and environmental factors.* Unpublished doctoral dissertation, University of Rochester.

Prochaska, J., DiClemente, C., & Norcross, J. (1992). In search of how people change. *American Psychologist, 47*, 1102–1114.

Pynoos, R. S., Frederick, C., Nader, K., Arroyo, W., Steinberg, A., Eth, S., Nunez, F., & Fairbanks, L. (1987). Life threat and posttraumatic stress in school-age children. *Archives of General Psychiatry, 44*, 1057–1063.

Reid, J. B. (1985). Behavioral approaches to intervention and assessment with child abusive families. In P. H. Bornstein & A. Kazdin (Eds.), *Handbook of clinical behavior therapy with children* (pp. 772–802). Homewood, IL: Dorsey Press.

Reid, J. B., Taplin, P., & Lorber, R. (1981). A social interactional approach to the treatment of abusive families. In R. B. Stuart (Ed.), *Violent behavior: Social learning approaches to prediction, management, and treatment* (pp. 83–101). New York: Brunner/Mazel.

Reidy, T. J. (1977). The aggressive characteristics of abused and neglected children. *Journal of Clinical Psychology, 33*, 1140–1145.

Reynolds, C. R., & Richmond, B. O. (1978). What I think and feel: A revised measure of children's mainfest anxiety. *Journal of Abnormal Psychology, 6*, 271–280.

Richards, D. A., & Rose, J. S. (1991). Exposure therapy for Post-Traumatic Stress Disorder: Four case studies. *British Journal of Psychiatry, 158*, 836–840.

Rinn, R. C., Vernon, J. C., & Wise, M. J. (1975). Training parents of behavior-disordered children in groups: A three years' program evaluation. *Behavior Therapy, 6*, 378–387.

Robin, A. L., & Foster, S. L. (1989). *Negotiating parent–adolescent conflict: A behavioral–family systems approach.* New York: Guilford Press.

Rose, D. (1969). A behavioral approach to the group treatment of parents. *Social Work, 14*, 12–29.

Rosenbaum, A., & O'Leary, K. D. (1981). Children: The unintended victims of marital violence. *American Journal of Orthopsychiatry, 51*, 692–699.

Rosenfield-Schlicter, M. D., Sarber, R. E., Bueno, G., Greene, B. F., & Lutzker, J. (1983). Maintaining accountability for an ecobehavioral treatment of one aspect of child neglect: Personal cleanliness. *Education and Treatment of Children, 6*, 153–164.

Rutter, M. (1989). Intergenerational continuities and discontinuities in serious parenting difficulties. In D. Cicchetti & V. Carlson (Eds.), *Child maltreatment: Theory and research on the causes and consequences of child abuse and neglect* (pp. 317–348). New York: Cambridge University Press.

Salzinger, S., Feldman, R. S., Hammer, M., & Rosario, M. (1993). The effects of physical abuse on children's social relationships. *Child Development, 64*, 169–187.

Salzinger, S., Kaplan, S., & Artemyeff, C. (1983). Mothers' personal social networks and child maltreatment. *Journal of Abnormal Psychology, 92,* 68–72.

Salzinger, S., Kaplan, S., Pelcovitz, D., Samit, C., & Kreiger, R. (1984). Parent and teacher assessment of children's behavior in child maltreating families. *Journal of the American Academy of Child Psychiatry, 23,* 458–464.

Sanders, M. (1996, November). *A media strategy for promoting parenting skills.* Paper presented at the annual meeting of the Association for Advancement of Behavior Therapy, New York.

Sanders, W. (1978). Systematic desensitization in the treatment of child abuse. *American Journal of Psychiatry, 135,* 483–484.

Sandford, D. A., & Tustin, R. D. (1974). Behavioral treatment of parental assault on a child. *New Zealand Psychologist, 2,* 76–82.

Sandler, J., Van Dercar, C., & Milhoan, M. (1978). Training child abusers in the use of positive reinforcement practices. *Behaviour Research and Therapy, 16,* 169–175.

Sarber, R. E., Halasz, M. M., Messmer, M. C., Bickett, A. D., & Lutzker, J. R. (1983). Teaching menu planning and grocery shopping skills to a mentally retarded mother. *Mental Retardation, 21,* 101–106.

Schilling, R. F., & Schinke, S. P. (1984). Maltreatment and mental retardation. *Perspectives and Progress in Mental Retardation, 1,* 11–22.

Sedlak, A. J., & Broadhurst, D. D. (1996). *Third national incidence study of child abuse and neglect.* Washington, DC: U.S. Government Printing Office.

Shealy, C. N. (1995). From Boys Town to Oliver Twist: Separating fact from fiction in welfare reform and out-of-home placement of children and youth. *American Psychologist, 50,* 565–580.

Smetana, J., Kelly, M., & Twentyman, C. (1984). Abused, neglected, and nonmaltreated children's conceptions of moral and social-conventional transgressions. *Child Development, 55,* 277–287.

Smith, J. E. (1984). Non-accidental injury to children: I. A review of behavioral interventions. *Behaviour Research and Therapy, 22,* 331–347.

Steele, B. F. (1975). Working with abusive parents: A psychiatric view. *Children Today, 4,* 3–5.

Steward, M. S., Farquhar, L. C., Dicharry, D. C., Glick, D. R., & Martin, P. W. (1986). Group therapy: A treatment of choice for young victims of child abuse. *International Journal of Group Psychotherapy, 36,* 261–277.

Stone, A. (1975). *Mental health and law: A system in transition.* Rockville, MD: National Institute of Mental Health.

Stone, H. D. (1969). *Reflections on foster care: A report of a national survey of attitudes and practice.* New York: Child Welfare League.

Strain, P. S., Shores, R. E., & Timm, M. A. (1977). Effects of peer social initiations on the behavior of withdrawn preschool children. *Journal of Applied Behavior Analysis, 10,* 289–298.

Strain, P. S., & Timm, M. A. (1974). An experimental analysis of social interaction between a behaviorally disordered preschool child and her classroom peers. *Journal of Applied Behavior Analysis, 7,* 583–590.

Szykula, S. A., & Fleischman, M. J. (1985). Reducing out-of-home placements of abused children: Two controlled studies. *Child Abuse and Neglect, 9,* 277–284.

Tarter, R. E., Hegedus, A. E., Winsten, N. E., & Alterman, A. I. (1984). Neuropsychological, personality, and familial characteristics of physically abused delinquents. *Journal of the American Academy of Child and Adolescent Psychiatry, 23,* 668–674.

Terr, L. (1991). Childhood traumas: An outline and overview. *American Journal of Psychiatry, 148,* 10–20.

Tertinger, D. A., Greene, B. F., & Lutzker, J. R. (1984). Home safety: Development and validation of one component of an ecobehavioral treatment program for abused and neglected children. *Journal of Applied Behavior Analysis, 17,* 150–174.

Thompson, R. A. (1994). Social support and the prevention of child maltreatment. In G. B. Melton & F. D. Barry (Eds.), *Protecting children from abuse and neglect: Foundations for a new national strategy* (pp. 40–130). New York: Guilford Press.

Thompson, R. A., & Wilcox, B. L. (1995). Child maltreatment research: Federal support and policy issues. *American Psychologist, 50,* 789–793.

Toth, S. L., Manly, J. T., & Cicchetti, D. (1992). Child maltreatment and vulnerability to depression. *Development and Psychopathology, 14,* 97–112.

Trickett, P. K., & Kuczynski, L. (1986). Children's misbehaviors and parental discipline strategies in abusive and nonabusive families. *Developmental Psychology, 22,* 115–123.

Twentyman, C. T., & McFall, R. M. (1975). Behavioral training of social skills in shy males. *Journal of Consulting and Clinical Psychology, 43,* 384–395.

Tymchuk, A. J. (1992). Predicting adequacy of parenting by people with mental retardation. *Child Abuse and Neglect, 16,* 165–178.

Urquiza, A. J., & McNeil, C. B. (1996). Parent–child interaction therapy: An intensive dyadic intervention for physically abusive families. *Child Maltreatment, 1,* 134–144.

U.S. Advisory Board on Child Abuse and Neglect (USABCAN). (1990). *Child abuse and neglect: Critical first steps in response to a national emergency.* Washington, DC: U.S. Government Printing Office.

U. S. Advisory Board on Child Abuse and Neglect (USABCAN). (1993). *Neighbors helping neighbors: A new national strategy for the protection of children.* Washington, DC: U.S. Government Printing Office.

Vasta, R. (1982). Physical child abuse: A dual component analysis. *Developmental Review, 2*, 164–170.

Wahler, R. G. (1980). The insular mother: Her problems in parental reinforcement control. *Journal of Applied Behavior Analysis, 2*, 159–170.

Watson-Perczel, M., Lutzker, J. R., Greene, B. F., & McGimpsey, B. J. (1988). Assessment and modification of home cleanliness among families adjudicated for child neglect. *Behavior Modification, 12*, 57–87.

Webster-Stratton, C. (1984). Randomized trial of two parent training programs for families with conduct-disordered children. *Journal of Consulting and Clinical Psychology, 52*, 666–678.

Webster-Stratton, C. (1994). Advancing videotape parent training: A comparison study. *Journal of Consulting and Clinical Psychology, 62,* 299–315.

Wekerle, C., & Wolfe, D. A. (1993). Prevention of child physical abuse and neglect: Promising new directions. *Clinical Psychology Review, 13,* 501–540.

Wekerle, C., & Wolfe, D. A. (1996). Child maltreatment. In E. J. Mash & R. Barkley (Eds.), *Child psychopathology* (pp. 492–537). New York: Guilford Press.

Widom, C. S. (1991). Role of placement experience in mediating the criminal consequences of early childhood victimization. *American Journal of Orthopsychiatry, 61*, 195–209.

Williams, G. (1983). Child abuse reconsidered. The urgency of authentic prevention. *Journal of Clinical Child Psychology, 12*, 312–319.

Wodarski, J. S., Kurtz, P. D., Gaudin, J. M., & Howing, P. T. (1990). Maltreatment and the school-aged child: Major academic, socioemotional, and adaptive outcomes. *Social Work, 35*, 506–513.

Wolfe, D. A. (1985). Child-abusive parents: An empirical review and analysis. *Psychological Bulletin, 97*, 462–482.

Wolfe, D. A. (1987). *Child abuse: Implications for child development and psychopathology.* Newbury Park, CA: Sage.

Wolfe, D. A. (1991). *Preventing physical and emotional abuse of children.* New York: Guilford Press.

Wolfe, D. A. (in press). *Child abuse: Implications for child development and psychopathology* (2nd ed.). Thousand Oaks, CA: Sage.

Wolfe, D. A., Aragona, J., Kaufman, K., & Sandler, J. (1980). The importance of adjudication in the treatment of child abuse: Some preliminary findings. *Child Abuse and Neglect, 4*, 127–135.

Wolfe, D. A., Edwards, B., Manion, I., & Koverola, C. (1988). Early intervention for child abuse and neglect: A preliminary investigation. *Journal of Consulting and Clinical Psychology, 56,* 40–47.

Wolfe, D. A., Jaffe, P., Wilson, S. K., & Zak, L. (1985). Children of battered women: The relation of child behavior to family violence and maternal stress. *Journal of Consulting and Clinical Psychology, 53*, 657–665.

Wolfe, D. A., Kaufman, D., Aragona, J., & Sandler, J. (1981). *The child management program for abusive parents.* Winter Park, FL: Anna.

Wolfe, D. A., & Manion, I. G. (1984). Impediments to child abuse prevention: Issues and directions. *Advances in Behaviour Research and Therapy, 6,* 47–62.

Wolfe, D. A., & McEachran, A. (1997). Child physical abuse and neglect. In E. J. Mash & L. Terdal (Eds.), *Assessment of childhood disorders* (3rd ed., pp. 523–568). New York: Guilford Press.

Wolfe, D. A., & Mosk, M. D. (1983). Behavioral comparisons of children from abusive and distressed families. *Journal of Consulting and Clinical Psychology, 51*, 702–708.

Wolfe, D. A., Reitzel-Jaffe, D., Gough, R., & Wekerle, C. (1994). *The Conflicts in Relationships: Measuring physical and sexual coercion among youth.* (Available from the Youth Relationships Project, Department of Psychology, University of Western Ontario, London, Ontario, N6A 5C2, Canada)

Wolfe, D. A., & Sandler, J. (1981). Training abusive parents in effective child management. *Behavior Modification, 5*, 320–335.

Wolfe, D. A., Sandler, J., & Kaufman, K. (1981). A competency-based parent training program for abusive parents. *Journal of Consulting and Clinical Psychology, 49*, 633–640.

Wolfe, D. A., Sas, L., & Wekerle, C. (1994). Factors associated with the development of Posttraumatic Stress Disorder among child victims of sexual abuse. *Child Abuse and Neglect, 18*, 37–50.

Wolfe, D. A., St. Lawrence, J., Graves, K., Brehony, K., Bradlyn, D., & Kelly, J. (1982). Intensive behavioral parent training for a child abusive mother. *Behavior Therapy, 13*, 438–451.

Wolfe, D. A., & Wekerle, C. (1993). Treatment strategies for child physical abuse and neglect: A critical progress report. *Clinical Psychology Review, 13*, 473–500.

Wolfe, D. A., Wekerle, C., Reitzel-Jaffe, D., & Lefebvre, L. (1998). Factors associated with abusive relationships among maltreated and non-maltreated youth. *Development and Psychopathology, 10*, 61–86.

Wolfe, D. A., Wekerle, C., & Scott, K. (1997). *Empowering youth to promote nonviolence: Issues and solutions.* Thousand Oaks, CA: Sage.

Zillman, D. (1979). *Hostility and aggression.* Hillsdale, NJ: Erlbaum.

CHAPTER 11

Child Sexual Abuse

Vicky Veitch Wolfe

London Health Sciences Centre,
London, Ontario, Canada

During the past two decades, North Americans have dramatically increased their awareness of the extent of child sexual abuse and the serious consequences of such abuse for its victims, their families, and our culture. Mental health professionals have responded to this increasingly evident problem by providing prevention and intervention services to children and their families through the mass media, the schools, the legal system, and child protective service agencies, as well as through more traditional venues such as mental health clinics and hospitals. The response has addressed prevention needs at all levels: primary, secondary, and tertiary. Primary prevention efforts have targeted schools and at-risk populations to educate children about the risks of sexual abuse and about avenues for empowering themselves if they are approached by sexually opportunistic individuals. Secondary prevention efforts have focused on reducing "system-induced stress" when sexually abused children face the legal system. Tertiary care interventions are designed to ameliorate abuse-related sequelae and to reduce the probability of long-term effects.

Mental health inroads into developing effective prevention and intervention efforts have been remarkable, given the fact that issues related to sexual abuse have only received serious attention by mental health researchers during the past 20 years; however, this chapter highlights the need for further conceptual development and more sophisticated treatment outcome research. This chapter is organized according to primary, secondary, and tertiary interventions, with an emphasis on goal-oriented and abuse-specific interventions. At the primary prevention level, basic questions about school- and parent-based personal safety skill training are addressed, including children's knowledge about personal safety training, effectiveness of various training approaches with different age and sex groups, and concerns about possible negative effects of personal safety training. At the secondary prevention level, efforts toward easing children's path through the legal system are reviewed, with emphasis on both protective and empowering strategies. At the tertiary care level, interventions directed toward ameliorating the short- and long-term effects of sexual abuse are reviewed, with an emphasis on strategies that directly address symptoms known to characterize victims of such abuse: trauma symptoms and sexuality problems. The chapter concludes with an overview of our progress in the areas of prevention and intervention, and identifies areas in need of further development.

EPIDEMIOLOGY

"Child sexual abuse" is generally defined as any sexual experience between a child and someone at least 5 years older, or an adolescent and someone at least 10 years older (Finkelhor, 1979). Most definitions of sexual abuse also include cases where the offender used coercion or force or abused authority, regardless of the age difference between victim and offender. Some definitions of sexual abuse require evidence of coercion, force, or abuse of authority for adolescents, even when age differences reach 10 years or more. Epidemiological studies estimate that 27% of females and 16% of males experience at least one episode of sexual abuse during their childhood or adolescence (Timnick, 1985; Finkelhor, Hotaling, Lewis, & Smith, 1990). Abusive acts vary from relatively minor events (e.g., invitations for sexual behavior or touching of clothed genitals) to very serious forms of abuse. However, at least two-thirds of abuse cases involve either serious (e.g., digital penetration) or very serious acts (e.g., vaginal, anal, or oral intercourse; Russell, 1983). The majority of abuse is perpetrated by individuals outside the family; however, girls are more likely to be abused by family members, with approximately 5% of females reporting abuse by a father figure (Russell, 1984).

Early retrospective surveys of adults who were abused as children reveal that only 3% to 6% of those abused ever reported their abuse during their childhood (Russell, 1983; Timnick, 1985). However, because of mandated reporting legislation and public awareness campaigns, reports of sexual abuse have increased dramatically. Finkelhor (1994), comparing conservative estimates of prevalence to known estimates of incidence, calculated disclosure rates in the early 1990s at approximately 30%. Perhaps as a result of more recent prevention and intervention efforts, some epidemiological studies suggest that sexual abuse prevalence rates may be declining (Bagley, 1988; Finkelhor et al., 1990; Finkelhor & Dziuba-Leatherman, 1994).

PRIMARY PREVENTION AND PROMOTION OF EARLY DISCLOSURE

School-Based Personal Safety Training

Schools have traditionally taught personal safety skills to children; however, with the growing recognition of childhood sexual abuse, school-based personal safety programs grew in prevalence and scope in the 1980s, increasingly focusing on the prevention of sexual abuse (Wurtele & Miller-Perrin, 1992). A relatively recent U. S. national survey of 2,000 children between the ages of 10 and 16 revealed that 67% of children had participated in a school-based abuse or victimization prevention program at some time (Finkelhor & Dziuba-Leatherman, 1995).

School-based personal safety programs vary in many ways, but all have a central theme: Sexual abuse can be prevented if children recognize inappropriate adult behavior, resist inducements, react quickly to leave the situation, and tell someone about the incident (Conte, Rosen, & Saperstein, 1986). School-based prevention programs have been used with children of all grades, including children in day care and kindergarten. Programs differ in format and style, ranging from 1 to 12 or more sessions, and utilizing books and workbooks, films, live theatre, classroom discussion, role plays and enactments, and/or parental involvement (Conte et al., 1986). Program content also varies, with some programs specifically addressing sexual abuse prevention and other programs addressing a wider array of prevention topics (e.g., prevention of physical assault by classroom bullies). Most sexual abuse prevention programs include such concepts as body ownership, the touch continuum, secrets, acting on one's own intuition, saying "No," and locating helpful people to tell. However, programs differ in the extent to which they explicitly address the sexual nature of abuse. Some programs focus on self-esteem and self-protection, avoiding direct discussion of sexuality issues out of concern of introducing children to sexuality prematurely. However, direct, explicit instruction about the sexual aspects of sexual abuse are advocated by some, since self-protection requires that children be able to recognize abusive situations (Finkelhor, 1986). Since at least 90% of abuse is perpetrated by individuals who are well known to the victims, some experts advocate that personal safety programs highlight this fact and teach children how to recognize and debunk the lies, manipulations, and forms of coercion that are used to gain children's compliance and secrecy (Berliner, 1984; Conte et al., 1986).

Evaluation of school-based personal safety training involves several issues (Kolko, 1988; Miller-Perrin & Wurtele, 1986; O'Donohue, Geer, & Elliot, 1992; Wolfe, 1990): (1) Do children gain new personal safety knowledge and skills, and do they retain their knowledge and skills over time? (2) Are some strategies more effective than others for teaching personal safety skills? (3) Are there negative effects of school-based personal safety training programs? (4) Do personal safety training programs increase rates of either actual or fabricated abuse allegations? Each of these issues is reviewed below.

Do Children Learn New Information and Skills, and Retain These Skills over Time?

Before evaluating the effectiveness of personal safety skill programs, investigators should consider children's pretraining knowledge and skills. Pre- and posttraining evaluations reveal that most children have some basic information about sexual abuse before training. Most elementary-school-age children know that they should seek help if approached sexually (D.A. Wolfe, MacPherson, Blount, & Wolfe, 1986), that it is unsafe to get into a car with a stranger, that it is wrong for an adult to touch their private parts, and that it is wrong for anyone to tell them not to tell their parents about something the children did with that person (Sigurdson, Strang, & Doig, 1987).

Pretraining knowledge and misinformation vary with age, however. Wurtele and Miller-Perrin (1987) found that younger children (mean age = 6.1 years) had trouble defining sexual abuse, whereas most older children (mean age = 11.3 years) accurately included sexual contact in their definitions of sexual abuse. Most children believed that perpetrators tend to be males and saw victims as primarily females; however, younger boys tended to view victims as either males or females. Older children believed that perpetrators are mostly adolescents or adults, while younger children saw perpetrators as closer in age to themselves. Older children recognized that most perpetrators are known to their victims, while younger children tended to believe that perpetrators are strangers. Older children tended to see perpetrators as deviant or "crazy," and many children believed that sexual abuse involves serious physical aggression. Approximately 20% of children, regardless of age, could not think of ways to protect themselves against sexual abuse. When children did offer suggestions, saying "no," getting away, and telling someone were the most common ones.

Despite the fact that most children have some knowledge of personal safety concepts prior to training, most pre–post evaluations of personal safety skill training programs find

that trained children demonstrate statistically significant increases in knowledge, compared with no-training control groups (Conte, Rosen, Saperstein, & Shermack, 1985; Harvey, Forehand, Brown, & Holmes, 1988; Kolko, Moser, Litz, & Hughes, 1987; Liang, Bogat, & McGrath, 1993; Nemerofsky, Carran, & Rosenberg, 1994; Saslawsky & Wurtele, 1986; Wurtele, 1990; Wurtele, Gillispie, Currier, & Franklin, 1992). Having information about sexual abuse is not necessarily the same as having the skills to protect oneself, however. Skill acquisition has been assessed in several different ways: asking questions about how they would respond in different abusive situations (Berrick, 1988; Kleemeier, Webb, Hazzard, & Pohl, 1988; Saslawsky & Wurtele, 1986); assessing verbal and behavioral responses to role-play procedures (Miltenberger & Thiesse-Duffy, 1988); and in vivo tests of resistance to inappropriate requests by adults (Fryer, Kraizer, & Miyoshi, 1987a, 1987b).

The most commonly used knowledge and skill acquisition instrument is the *What If Situations Test* (WIST; Saslawsky & Wurtele, 1986). The WIST involves four vignettes describing potential encounters with adults who make sexual advances toward children. Questions are then asked to determine whether a child (1) recognizes the inappropriateness of the situation; (2) indicates that he or she would verbally refuse the advance; (3) describe a response in which he or she would leave the situation; and (4) list the names of those whom he or she would tell about what happened. Fryer et al. (1987a, 1987b) tested skill acquisition and utilization by having a "stranger" ask each child to assist him by accompanying him to his car. Although these *in vivo* strategies may more closely resemble "real-life" generalization of personal safety skills, ethical concerns limit the utility of such strategies on a routine basis. While most studies show increased personal safety knowledge following prevention programs, evaluation programs are less consistent in demonstrating actual skill acquisition. Stilwell, Lutzker, and Greene (1988) found no improvement in behavioral scores following personal safety training, despite improvement in verbal responses; however, several other programs have demonstrated both knowledge and skill acquisition (Miltenberger & Thiesse-Duffy, 1988; Harvey et al., 1988; Saslawsky & Wurtele, 1986).

Most studies show greater gains in knowledge and skill for older children than for younger children (Conte et al., 1985; Saslawsky & Wurtele, 1986; Wurtele, Saslawsky, Miller, Marrs, & Britcher, 1986). As well, younger children appear to retain less information over time than older children do. Borkin and Frank (1986) found that only 4% of 3-year-olds and 43% of 4-year-olds correctly recalled at least one safety rule at a 4- to 6-week follow-up assessment. Miltenberger and Thiesse-Duffy (1988) found that 6- and 7-year-olds maintained personal safety information over a 2-month follow-up period; however, 4- and 5-year olds did not. Nemerofsky et al. (1994), using the WIST, found that younger children retained less information than older children when assessed at a 6-week follow-up: 3-year-olds missed 41% of items, 4-year-olds missed 27%, 5-year-olds missed 19%, and 6-year-olds missed 14%. In contrast, some studies have demonstrated significant improvements in knowledge and skill acquisition that were retained at follow-ups ranging from 3 to 12 weeks (Harvey et al., 1988; Saslawsky & Wurtele, 1986). Fryer et al. (1987a, 1987b), using the *in vivo* assessment strategy described earlier (i.e., each child was asked by a "stranger" to accompany him to his car), found that 79% of trained children refused to accompany the stranger, compared with 53% of children who had not received training. When the skill acquisition test was repeated 6 months later, the majority of trained children continued to refuse to accompany the stranger.

Regardless of age, children learn and retain some skills more readily than others. Plummer (1984) found that children generally retained such concepts as that some promises should be broken (such as a promise not to tell), that abusers can be people they know, and that children should not blame themselves if abused. Several studies have demonstrated that children have greater difficulty learning and retaining abstract prevention concepts as compared to more concrete information (Conte et al., 1985; Wurtele, Kast, Miller-Perrin, & Kondrick, 1989). Wurtele et al. (1989) found that children had difficulty understanding such concepts as "trusting one's intuition," as compared to more concrete information (e.g., as defining abuse by specific actions). Oldfield, Hays, and Megel (1996) found that children in grades 1–6, after viewing the film *Touch*, were more likely to give incorrect answers to questions related to the concept of "stranger" and the concept that abuse can be perpetrated by trusted adults, including family members.

Are Some Teaching Strategies More Effective Than Others?

In line with the fact that abstract concepts are more difficult for children to grasp, programs that focus on concrete concepts and involve modeling and behavioral rehearsal appear to be the most effective in assuring knowledge and skill acquisition and retention over time. Wurtele et al. (1989) showed that preschoolers had more difficulty learning about inappropriate touches when a "feelings-based" ("Trust your instincts") training approach was compared to a behavioral skills training approach ("Inappropriate touches are . . . "). Poche, Yoder, and Miltenberger (1988) found that children who had participated in a videotape program with behavioral rehearsal were less likely to agree to accompany a stranger (as part of an *in vivo* skill test) than were children who had participated in a standard safety program. Behavioral rehearsal appears to be particularly essential to effective training. Wurtele et al. (1986) compared the effectiveness of various educational approaches for teaching personal safety skills to children. These approaches included (1) a filmed program, *Touch*; (2) a behavioral skills training program in which modeling, behavioral rehearsal, and social reinforcement were used; (3) a combination of the two; and (4) a no-training presentation. Behavioral skills training, alone or in combination with the film, was more effective than either the film alone or the control presentation with regard to both knowledge and skill acquisition. These gains were maintained at a 3-month follow-up. Finkelhor and Dziuba-Leatherman (1995), in their national survey of children, found that those children whose training included a behavioral rehearsal component were more likely to report having used their skills in a "real-life" situation.

Recently, personal safety skill training has begun to include parents in the training process, and have demonstrated that parents can add substantially to the learning process. Wurtele, Kast, and Melzer (1992) compared skill acquisition of Head Start children across four conditions: teacher-trained, parent-trained, parent- and teacher-trained, and an attention control group. Children in all three trained groups demonstrated more knowledge and skill than the attention control group did. Children who received training from their parents showed greater improvements in their ability to recognize inappropriate touch requests and in their personal safety skills than did children taught only by their teachers.

In addition to variations in training strategy, program effectiveness has been related to a number of child characteristics. As already noted, age is a very important variable to consider in evaluating the effectiveness of training approaches. Though young children may perform more poorly on outcome evaluations as compared to older children, younger children tend to rate programs as more helpful and report that personal safety skill training programs contain more new information (Finkelhor & Dziuba-Leatherman, 1995). Girls tend to find school-based programs more interesting, more helpful, and full of more new information than boys do (Finkelhor & Dziuba-Leatherman, 1995). Changing the training format may help make the subject more interesting to boys. Garbarino (1987) evaluated the effectiveness of two Spiderman comic book presentations of sexual abuse information; one comic portrayed a boy who had been sexually abused by a teenage babysitter, and the other portrayed a girl who had been sexually abused by her father. The girl ran away from home when her mother did not believe her allegations. Despite matching the sex of the victim to the reader, Garbarino (1987) found that girls were less interested in the Spiderman presentation than were boys. Girls also reported more fear and anxiety after reading the comic than boys did, perhaps since the comic portrayed a more negative scenario for the girl victim than for the boy victim.

Fryer et al. (1987a) found that children who had a more positive self-concept prior to training were more likely to utilize their skills in the *in vivo* assessment of skill acquisition. These results suggest that children must feel confident and assertive before they can muster the courage to say "no" to an adult.

Do Programs Create Undue Fear and Worry among Participants?

Concerns have been voiced that school-based personal safety programs may have negative effects on children by creating undue fear and anxiety among them, contributing to their distrust of adults, and negatively affecting their attitudes toward sex. Programs that have addressed these issues have generally shown small increases in program-related fears and worries (Binder & McNiel, 1987; Garbarino, 1987; Miltenberger & Thiesse-Duffy, 1988). From their national survey of children and parents,

Finkelhor and Dziuba-Leatherman (1995) found that 8% of children said they worried "a lot" and 53% said they worried "a little" following school-based personal safety programs. Further more, 16% of parents reported they had noticed an increase in their children's fear of adults. Children who are young, are black, and come from homes of lower socioeconomic status (SES) tend to report more program-related fears and worries (Finkelhor & Dziuba-Leatherman, 1995; Miller-Perrin & Wurtele, 1986). Interestingly, Finkelhor and Dziuba-Leatherman (1995) point out that children who are vulnerable to program-related fears and worries are also the ones who rate the programs most highly (young, black, and lower-SES). In a multivariate analysis, reporting "worrying" as a result of a program was the most powerful predictor of rating the program as "helpful." Finkelhor and Dziuba-Leatherman (1995) point out that fear and anxiety may actually be adaptive responses since the children are learning about a true danger. Nevertheless, it is important that children perceive that the skills acquired as a result of training are effective in helping them cope should they be faced with a sexually abusive situation; otherwise, they may feel less able to cope with these new fears. Binder and McNiel (1987) found that children reported feeling safer and more confident in their ability to protect themselves following personal safety training. Other positive psychological effects have been noted as well. Binder and McNiel (1987) found that personal safety training resulted in more communication between children and their parents regarding sexuality issues. Plummer (1984) found that personal safety training did not increase children's negative perceptions of sexuality; in fact, prior to training, 15.9% of children felt that all sexual touches were negative, whereas after training that percentage dropped to 10%.

Do Programs Increase Rates of Either Actual or Fabricated Abuse Allegations?

School-based personal safety programs have two ultimate goals: (1) that children recognize potentially abusive situations and react in a way that enables them to avoid the abuse; and (2) that children report inappropriate sexual advances to a responsible adult as soon as possible, whether or not an actual offense occurs. With regard to the former, Finkelhor and Dziuba-Leatherman (1995) found that many children reported using skills they learned as a result of personal safety training: 25% said they had used the information from the program to help a friend; 5% said they had told an adult "no" as a result of what they had learned; and 14% said they had told an adult about something, based upon what they had learned from their program. Children who had participated in programs that included behavioral rehearsal and parent involvement were more likely to report using their skills in "real life." Girls and younger children were the most likely to report using the skills they learned from personal safety training.

Several studies have demonstrated increases in rates of reporting abuse following school-based personal safety training. Oldfield et al. (1996) evaluated Project Trust, an elementary-school-based victimization prevention program based upon the film *Touch,* with a large sample ($n = 1,269$) of children in grades 1–6. The group that received training had a higher incidence of first-time reports of maltreatment than that of the group that did not receive training. All maltreatment reports were independently verified, quelling concerns that abuse prevention program might encourage false allegations of maltreatment (Goldstein, Freud, & Solnit, 1979). Kolko et al. (1987) compared children who had participated in the Red Flag/Green Flag prevention program with no-training controls. Six months later, 20 children in the experimental condition had reported inappropriate touching, whereas no children in the control group reported abuse.

Parent-Based Personal Safety Training

Although it is clear that prevention programs are primarily oriented toward elementary- school-age children, it is also becoming apparent that parental involvement or supplemental parental training can increase a program's effectiveness, particularly for young children. Parental involvement is important both because most programs require parental consent for a child's participation, and because parents can reinforce prevention concepts and skills, answer questions, and correct children's misperceptions. To avoid confusing children, it is important that parents and schools teach similar concepts. Involving parents in the educational process also reduces secrecy in regard to the topic of sexual abuse and stimulates parent–child discussions of sexuality in general. Many parents express desires to be involved in prevention efforts with

their children (Elrod & Rubin, 1993; Wurtele, 1993; Wurtele, Kvaternick, & Franklin, 1992).

Without some level of professional support and/or training, a high percentage of parents either do not talk to their children about sexual abuse or fail to include important prevention information in their discussions. Finkelhor (1986) found that only 29% of parents said they had discussed sexual abuse with their children. Public awareness has probably resulted in more parent-based prevention work. In a more recent survey, Wurtele, Kvaternick, and Franklin (1992) found that 59% of parents said they had discussed sexual abuse with their preschoolers, on average 5.4 times. Nevertheless, parents tend to "water down" prevention information (Elrod & Rubin, 1993; Wurtele, Kvaternick, & Franklin, 1992). Wurtele, Kvaternick, and Franklin (1992) found that most parents warned their children about strangers; however, substantially fewer warned their children about known adults (61%), teens (52%), relatives (35%), parents (21.5%), or siblings (19%). Parents also tend to wait until children are about 9 years of age (Elrod & Rubin, 1993; Finkelhor, 1986); however, some studies estimate that in at least one-third of abuse cases, the abuse starts prior to that age.

If parents are to be involved in prevention programs, they themselves need to be educated. However, parent education programs, especially those addressing sexual abuse, are typically poorly attended (Berrick, 1988). Parents appear to learn little from these programs and report discussing few sexual abuse topics or active prevention strategies with their children following training. To address this issue, Elrod and Rubin (1993) surveyed parents and found that they most desired information on the following topics: (1) how to identify abuse, (2) how to react to signs of abuse, and (3) how to get accurate information from a child without creating false allegations. Parents also wanted to know how to talk to their children about sex and sexual abuse in developmentally sensitive ways that would not scare them.

Wurtele and her colleagues have demonstrated that both middle- and lower-SES parents can effectively teach preschoolers the skills necessary to recognize and respond to inappropriate sexual gestures (Wurtele, Currier, Gillispie, & Franklin, 1991; Wurtele, Gillispie, et al., 1992; Wurtele et al., 1992). However, parents of preschool children often require ongoing consultation and encouragement by professionals if they are to complete instruction (Wurtele, 1993).

Abuse Disclosure

Despite widespread efforts to prevent sexual abuse and encourage early disclosure, it is clear that some children do not disclose their abuse. As noted earlier, researchers' best estimates are that 30% of sexually abused children disclose their abuse during their childhood (Finkelhor, 1994). Although this is a great improvement over the past, the likelihood that 70% of abused children go undetected is quite concerning. For those who do not immediately report their abuse, 44% will be repeatedly abused by the same perpetrators (Sas, Cunningham, Hurley, Dick, & Farnsworth, 1995). Of further concern is the probability that the more seriously abused children are the ones who go undetected. The longer abuse persists, the greater the likelihood that a child will never disclose the abuse (Sas et al., 1995). Sas et al. (1995) found that children were less likely to disclose sexual abuse immediately if the perpetrators were family members, were alcoholics, were emotionally close to the children, had "groomed" the children prior to the abuse, or had used force. Retrospective studies of disclosure rates indicate that several variables impede a child's ability to disclose: perception that a parent will not believe them, concerns about personal safety, fear of the effect on the family, fear of blame and punishment, loyalty to perpetrator, shame, and helplessness (Roesler & Wind, 1994).

Sas et al. (1995) found that children who immediately reported their abuse stated their reasons as follows: prior education, a desire to protect self and others, a wish for retaliation, and a desire to talk to someone about "something unusual that happened." Sas et al. (1995) asked children about how prevention programs affected their decisions to disclose. On the positive side, at least some of the children who disclosed immediately reported that "prior education" had played a role in their decision to disclose. Half of the children recalled participating in prevention programs prior to the first episode of abuse; however, only 7% reported that abuse prevention programs had helped or "partially helped" them make their disclosure. Of the 524 sexually abused children interviewed, 25 indicated that following the onset of their abuse they participated in a sexual abuse prevention program, but still did not disclose. When the children were asked how prevention programs could be improved, the following suggestions were made: Start at an early grade; be specific; be realistic; don't be preachy; explain why it is important for children to tell; explain what happens after disclosure; have someone other than a teacher do the training; stress to children that abuse is not their fault; stress that the offender will be punished; provide one-to-one lessons rather than just in groups; and train teachers how to respond to disclosures.

Summary of the Primary Prevention Literature

Primary prevention studies suggest several guidelines for school-based personal safety skill programs: (1) Program content should focus on concrete concepts and use active training methods, such as modeling and behavioral rehearsal; (2) parents should have opportunities to be involved in the training process; (3) schools should start training during the kindergarten and early elementary grades, and should repeat training regularly to insure that younger children do not forget personal safety skills; and (4) programs should adjust content to make programs more interesting for different age groups and for both boys and girls. Group school-based programs may be less effective in encouraging disclosures by children who are abused by family members or those abused by same-sex perpetrators, particularly children who have been abused repeatedly. Prevention programs are unlikely to deal with those issues directly. However, given the prevalence of abuse by family members and by same-sex perpetrators, prevention curricula should develop strategies for addressing these issues directly and in detail without creating undue distrust of family members or undue alarm about same-sex sexual contacts.

SECONDARY PREVENTION: REDUCING SYSTEM-INDUCED TRAUMA

Criminal Prosecution of Child Sexual Abuse Cases

Once sexual abuse has been disclosed and verified by police, questions about criminal prosecution arise. Prosecution of offenders serves several societal and social functions (Wolfe, Sas, & Wilson, 1987). First, prosecution provides a clear motivation for the offender to stop the abuse and insures protection for that child, as well as other children. Second, rates of prosecution reflect the community's norm that such behavior is considered morally and legally wrong, and that violation of sexual abuse laws will not be tolerated (Bulkley, 1982; Finkelhor, Gomes-Schwartz, & Horowitz, 1984). Third, treatment programs for offenders have recognized the importance of working closely with the criminal justice system, in order to improve the probability that the perpetrator will become engaged in therapy (Barbaree & Marshall, 1991). Fourth, if courtroom procedures are handled appropriately and if a child is adequately prepared (Stern, 1993), involvement with the criminal justice system can be therapeutic for the child, because it can help him or her gain a sense of mastery over the victimization experience (Sas, Hurley, Austin, & Wolfe, 1991; Sas, Hurley, Hatch, Malla, & Dick, 1993). Nonetheless, many verified cases of abuse go unprosecuted, for two primary reasons: (1) concerns about the effects of prosecution on the mental health of the child, and (2) concerns that the child will not be able to provide credible evidence.

Finkelhor (1983) estimated that criminal action occurred in approximately 24% of U. S. cases, with considerable variation across states. More recent analyses suggest higher rates of prosecution, ranging from 37% of cases in Alberta, Canada (Stephens, Grinnell, Thomlison, & Krysik, 1991) to 50% of cases in Cook County, Illinois (Martone, Jaudes, & Cavins, 1996). Though prosecution rates appear to be increasing, only 3–4% of sexually abused children known to official agencies ever testify in criminal trials (Saunders, Kilpatrick, Resnick, Hanson, & Lipovsky, 1992). Even among those cases referred for prosecution, only 11%–17% of child victims ever end up testifying in a criminal trial, primarily because many accused offenders eventually plead guilty. Nonetheless, approximately 50% of cases referred for prosecution require that the children testify at some legal proceeding, such as a preliminary hearing (Goodman et al., 1992).

Courtroom testimony can be quite stressful; 74.3% of parents and 63.7% of children who testify in court describe it as a negative experience (Lipovsky, Tidwell, Kilpatrick, Saunders, & Dawson, 1991). Up to 30% of cases result in acquittal, which can have negative mental health effects on the child victims (Sas et al., 1995). Following children throughout the prosecution process, Sas et al. (1991) reported that 5% dropped out of school, 6% reported suicidal ideation or made a suicide attempt that led to hospitalization, and 15% reported feeling estranged from extended family members who supported the accused. Prior to testifying, children identify a number of fears, including fears of the testimony itself, the defense attorney, and seeing the defendant; after testifying, children report that the most distressing aspects were seeing the defendant and not having their parents in the courtroom (Goodman et al., 1992). Children also fear that the defendant will retaliate and that they will not be believed.

Despite their court-related fears and anxieties, many children feel relieved after testifying in court, with subsequent reductions in anxiety and depressive symptoms (Goodman et al., 1992). Children's adjustment following court proceedings appears to relate to three factors (Goodman et al., 1992; Runyan, Everson, Edelson, Hunter, & Coulter, 1988): testifying in multiple, prolonged, or delayed proceedings; harsh direct examination or cross-examination; and maternal support or lack of it. Nonetheless, there is little evidence that participating in legal proceedings results in long-term adjustment problems, although it may delay psychological recovery from the abuse (Goodman et al., 1992; Lipovsky, 1992). In fact, some evidence suggests that children can benefit from the experience. Sas et al. (1995) found that 85% of children who provided courtroom testimony were positive about their involvement and reported no regrets; only 9% harbored regrets. Ninety-one percent of victims said they would advise a friend to tell the police if a similar incident occurred; 84% said they would call the police if they were abused again; and 80% said that if they were abused again, they would want the case prosecuted.

Courtroom and Legal System Accommodations for Children

As noted earlier, many cases of child sexual abuse go unprosecuted because of concerns about the negative effect of a court appearance on a child and concerns that the child will not be able to provide accurate, credible testimony. These issues are closely intertwined, since court-related stress can have a negative impact on a child's ability to provide accurate evidence (Saywitz & Nathanson, 1993) and can negatively affect jurors' perceptions of a child's credibility (Leippe, Manion, & Romanczyk, 1992; Wells, Tuttle, & Luus, 1989). Likewise, a child's mental health can be negatively affected by an acquittal in a trial for which he or she served as a witness (Goodman et al., 1992; Sas et al., 1993). Interventions to assist child witnesses fall into two categories: "protective" and "empowering" (Davies & Westcott, 1995). Protective interventions are those designed to alter the system in a way that reduces stress (e.g., testifying via closed-circuit television [CCTV], allowing hearsay evidence), whereas empowering interventions teach children about the court process and assist them in overcoming court-related anxieties.

Protective Courtroom Alterations and Strategies: Use of CCTV

As noted earlier, children often identify testifying in the presence of the accused as one of their strongest fears prior to going to court; after court, children often identify seeing the offender as one of the most stressful aspects of their testimony (Goodman et al., 1992; Whitcomb, Shapiro, & Stellwagen, 1985). To relieve children of the stress of direct confrontation with the accused, courts have allowed children to testify either with a screen that blocks the child's view of the defendant (but allows the defendant to view the child) or via CCTV. Of the two options, CCTV is the more popular strategy, since it appears to be more effective in reducing child-related stress. Typically, the child testifies in a room adjacent to the main courtroom, and the testimony is simultaneously viewed in the courtroom via a television monitor. Often arrangements are made for two-way communication, so that the child can view the courtroom as the court views the child.

CCTV, and other strategies that protect the child from direct confrontation with the accused, have been challenged as an infringement upon the accused's right to "face-to-face" confrontation with the accuser, which is guaranteed by the "confrontation clause" of the Sixth Amendment to the U. S. Constitution. The confrontation clause has the following purposes: It (1) insures that the witness provides testimony under oath; (2) requires that the witness submit to cross-examination; and (3) permits the "trier of fact" to observe the demeanor of the witness while he or she is testifying in the presence of the defendant, in order to assess the witness's credibility (Bulkley, 1988). Two issues have been debated with regard to the application of the confrontation clause with child witnesses (Gordon, 1992): (1) Does the term "confront" require an actual face-to-face encounter? (2) Does potential emotional trauma to a witness qualify as sufficient ground for an exception to the usual courtroom practice of having a witness testify in the presence of the accused?

Two recent U.S. Supreme Court decisions have addressed these issues (Gordon, 1992). In the case Coy v. Iowa (1988), the U. S. Supreme Court ruled that the confrontation clause gives defendants the right to confront all witnesses face-to-face, and that exceptions to that right should be allowed only in cases when necessary to further an important public policy and only where the reliability of the testimony is otherwise assured. In a subsequent case, *Maryland v. Craig* (1990), the U. S. Supreme Court ruled that the right to face-to-face confrontation is not absolute, and ruled that CCTV for child witnesses is permissible because the state has a compelling interest in protecting child witnesses from emotional harm. However, the court also ruled that decisions to use CCTV must be made on a "case-by-case" basis, with the goal of protecting the welfare of a "particular" child. Furthermore, the court ruled that the reason for CCTV was due to the potential harm from testifying in the presence of the accused, not simply because the child feared testifying in court.

As of 1992, 32 states had enacted statutes that authorized judges to allow child witnesses to testify via CCTV (Whitcomb, 1992). However, use of CCTV in the United States has been rare (California Attorney General's Office, 1988). Aside from the restriction that CCTV be used only under special circumstances, prosecutors generally prefer child witnesses to testify directly in the courtroom in the presence of the defendant, because such testimony is considered to have a greater emotional impact on the trier of fact (Toby, Goodman, Batterman-Faunce, Orcutt, & Sachsenmaier, 1995). However, the assumptions behind decisions to use or not to use CCTV have largely gone untested. The utility of this technology must be evaluated by three standards (Toby et al., 1995): (1) reduced child stress, (2) enhanced accuracy of testimony, and (3) enhanced credibility in the view of the trier of fact.

Because of legal and ethical constraints, it has been difficult to evaluate the effectiveness of CCTV in the US. Several countries are more liberal in the use of CCTV. In England, the need for protective measures of child witnesses is assumed (Davies & Westcott, 1995). The 1988 Criminal Justice Act in Great Britain legalized two-way CCTV for children under the age of 15 in cases of sexual or physical assault; in 1991, the use of CCTV was extended to teens under the age of 18 in cases of sexual assault. On the other hand, in Canberra, Australia, CCTV was introduced on an experimental basis, with decisions to use CCTV made by the presiding judge (Cashmore, 1992).

Two quasi-experimental studies have attempted to evaluate the effectiveness of CCTV—one in England (Davies & Noon, 1991) and the other in Canberra, Australia (Cashmore, 1992). Neither evaluation involved randomized assignment to comparison groups; however, both evaluations included control groups of children who provided testimony in open court (each study drew its control sample from a geographical area different from that of its CCTV group). Davies and Noon's (1991) English CCTV sample was compared with a Scottish open-court sample that was considerably different from the CCTV group; the Scottish sample included more boys and included more cases of physical abuse rather than sexual assault. The Canberra CCTV sample was compared with a New South Wales open-court sample that was similar with regard to the age of the victims and the severity of sexual assaults. Cashmore (1992) also evaluated a local control group of children who provided testimony in open court; unfortunately, the local open-court control group was significantly older than the CCTV group.

In both of these studies, court personnel (judges, prosecutors, defense attorneys, court clerks) were surveyed regarding their opinions about CCTV; as well, evaluations were conducted to determine whether children performed better with CCTV. In both studies, the opinions of court personnel were overwhelmingly positive. Neither study found substantial differences in satisfaction ratings between prosecutors and defense attorneys. In fact, in Cashmore's (1992) study, defense attorneys reported that a major advantage of CCTV was that the children were more composed and could therefore be questioned more rigorously with less risk of an emotional breakdown. Davies and Noon (1991) found that nearly half of the court professionals surveyed indicated that children who provided testimony via CCTV seemed less stressed than children who testified in open court; furthermore, 20% felt that children provided more information when interviewed via CCTV.

Davies and Noon (1991) found that the English children who used CCTV were seen as less unhappy, more forthcoming, more audible, and more resistant to leading questions than the Scottish children who testified in open court. Cashmore (1992) found that CCTV users were rated as less anxious in giving their testimony

than either of the control groups. Cashmore (1992) compared children who wanted to use CCTV but were denied its use with children who wanted CCTV and were granted its use. The deprived group was rated as more unhappy and as having poorer concentration during the examination by the prosecutor, and as more unhappy, less cooperative, and as providing fewer details during the examination by the defense. Despite being offered the use of CCTV, some children in Cashmore's study chose to testify in open court. No differences were found between the children who declined CCTV and their peers who used CCTV, suggesting that children who do not opt for CCTV when it is available tend to do fine without it.

Courtrooms do not make good experimental laboratories, since random assignment is not possible and since it is difficult to evaluate such factors as the accuracy of a child's testimony when the exact details of the incident in question are not known. As such, experimental studies that standardize the event about which the child "testifies" and that allow for random group assignment are particularly useful for evaluating the effects of specific court or courtroom procedures (e.g., open court vs. CCTV; availability vs. absence of support person) on various outcomes (e.g., child stress, accuracy of testimony, and juror's perceptions of the child as credible). Experimental studies have demonstrated that testifying in an open-court atmosphere is related to greater anxiety than is testifying in a smaller private room with or without CCTV (Hill & Hill, 1987; Saywitz & Nathanson, 1993). Furthermore, heightened anxiety during courtroom testimony has been related to more errors of omission (i.e., providing less information) and commission (i.e., less resistance to leading questions; Saywitz & Nathanson, 1993), particularly with younger children (Toby et al., 1995).

Other experimental studies have demonstrated the effects of confronting the accused on the accuracy and completeness of children's testimony. Peters (1990) conducted an experiment in which children witnessed a theft; during the course of the theft, the thief told each child to keep the theft a secret. Half the children were interviewed in the presence of the thief, while half were interviewed without the thief present. Only 5% of children interviewed in the presence of the thief were immediately truthful, whereas 28% of the children interviewed without the thief present were truthful. Later, when home with their parents, many of the children disclosed the theft; however, children interviewed in the thief-absent condition were four times more likely to tell their parents about the theft than those children who had been in the thief-present interview. Many of the children cited the fact that the thief had told them not to tell as their reason for not telling about the thief.

CCTV may assist jurors to focus on the relevant aspects of a child's testimony, rather than the child's courtroom anxiety. Swim, Borgida, and McCoy (1992) found in a mock-trial situation that jurors remembered more of the testimony when the child testified via CCTV than when the child testified in open court. However, Toby et al. (1995) found that mock jurors had more negative views of children who testified by CCTV than of children who testified in open court. Despite jurors' perceptions that children who testified by CCTV were less stressed than children who testified in open court, jurors rated children who provided CCTV testimony as less believable, less accurate, more likely to have made up the story, less able to discern fact from fantasy, less attractive, less intelligent, and less confident. Interestingly, there were no differences in jurors' abilities to discern the accuracy of children's testimony when children testified via CCTV versus open court. In fact, there was no relationship between jurors' ratings of children's believability and perceptions of the defendants' guilt.

Improved Interviewing Strategies and Use of Hearsay Evidence

In many legal jurisdictions, cases that involve young victims (often under the age of 7) are not prosecuted due to concerns that the children will not make adequate witnesses (Finkelhor, 1983). Often young children are not capable of providing the detailed information about a specific event that is necessary to gain a conviction in criminal court (Goodman, Hirschman, Hepps, & Rudy, 1991; Saywitz, Goodman, Nicholas, & Moan, 1991). Furthermore, though both young and old witnesses are susceptible to memory distortions resulting from a number of causes (e.g., suggestion from others, retroactive interference, autosuggestion, or confabulation), there is some evidence that these types of problems are more prevalent among young children (Ceci & Bruck, 1993; Goodman, Bottoms, Shaver, & Quas, 1995). Although interviewer contamination can be minimized by relying on open-ended questions, younger children tend to reveal detailed information only when probed with specific and direct forms of questioning (Saywitz et al., 1991).

Saywitz (1995) noted that children's ability to provide testimony would be likely to improve if questioners closely matched their vocabulary to the children's ability. Many children do not understand many of the terms that are often used in court (e.g., "charges," "allegations," "defendant," "minor"). Whereas older children are often aware that they do not know the meaning of words, young children unknowingly make auditory discrimination errors (e.g., "jewelry" for "jury") or homonym errors (e.g., "court" is assumed to mean a place to play basketball). Saywitz (1995) has made several suggestions for questioning young children: using monosyllabic words; using proper names instead of pronouns; using the names of items or places instead of referents such as "this," "that," "here," or "there"; using simple grammar and sentence structure; using active rather than passive voice; avoiding questions that require a child to assume the perspective of another person; and making clear transitions when changing one's line of questioning.

Despite improved questioning strategies, young children may simply be unable to provide clear testimony within the confines of a courtroom atmosphere. If a case is to be prosecuted, hearsay evidence may be necessary. "Hearsay statements" are statements made outside of court; as such, they are not subject to cross-examination and are therefore, according to the Sixth Amendment, not admissible in criminal court. There are two requirements for hearsay statements to be admissible into evidence (Gordon, 1992): (1) The declarant must be unavailable to testify (e.g., deceased or unwilling to testify); and (2) there must be some compelling evidence to the "almost certain" reliability of the statement, either through a recognized exception (e.g., a dying declaration) or through circumstances surrounding the making of the statement that support their reliability. Many child sexual abuse victims are perceived as either too young or too emotionally vulnerable to testify in court, and therefore are not allowed to give evidence in criminal court. However, in less stressful circumstances (e.g., an investigative interview or in a disclosure to a parent), such children may have made statements that appear to be reliable; therefore, those statements may be eligible to be entered as evidence in criminal trials as hearsay evidence.

The issue of hearsay in child sexual abuse cases was addressed by the U. S. Supreme Court in the case of *Idaho v. Wright* (1990). This case involved a child who was deemed too immature to testify in court; however, the child had made incriminating statements to a pediatrician, which were allowed in the lower court as an exception to the hearsay prohibition. Although the Supreme Court ruled that the child's statements were not sufficiently reliable to be submitted as evidence for the case of *Idaho v. Wright*, it did not dismiss the possibility of allowing evidence in similar cases, especially if a child makes statements spontaneously or repeatedly and if the statements are accompanied by other factors suggesting reliability, such as mental state, use of terminology unexpected for a child of similar age, or lack of motive to fabricate. The Supreme Court, however, refused to specify criteria necessary for ruling when hearsay evidence may be admissible, leaving cases that use hearsay open for appeal.

Empowering Courtroom Strategies

Court Preparation Programs. Court preparation programs (also known as victim/witness assistance programs) generally share similar goals and training components (Davies & Westcott, 1995). Most programs include an educational component that teaches children about the courtroom, court process, and people in the courtroom. Children also learn the meaning of taking the oath, the importance of telling the truth, and ways to respond to unfair or unclear questioning tactics. Court-related fears and anxieties are often explored, and some programs have included court-related desensitization and stress management procedures. For example, Sas et al. (1991) combined several strategies to help children prepare psychologically for court: (1) deep breathing and deep muscle relaxation exercises to manage stress; (2) development of court-related fear hierarchies, with related systematic desensitization to address court-related fears and anxieties; and (3) cognitive restructuring and empowerment exercises to enhance motivation and confidence for courtroom testimony. The latter strategy involved having the children make lists that outlined their personal strengths, reviewed their positive reasons for attending court, and reinforced the concept that each child was part of the prosecution team.

A number of teaching resources have been developed to assist with court preparation, including activity booklets (e.g., Ontario Ministry of the Attorney General, 1989) and videotapes (e.g., Canadian Department of Justice, 1992; Spectrum South Productions, 1989). Doll-size courtrooms, court-related puppets and clothing,

and visits to the courtroom facilitate both the educational and desensitization processes. Some programs are conducted in group format (Sisterman Keeney, Amacher, & Kastanaskis, 1992), whereas other programs utilize an individualized approach (Sas et al., 1991). All programs avoid direct discussion of the particular details of a child's case, in order to avoid allegations of coaching (Davies & Westcott, 1995).

Most court preparation programs provide a victim advocate who acts as a liaison between the prosecutor's office and the victim and the victim's family. Regular contact between the prosecutor's office and the family has been related to reduced parental distress, which in turn probably reduces child anxiety (Lipovsky et al., 1991). Vertical management of prosecution (e.g., assigning one prosecutor to follow child sexual abuse cases from the point of laying the charge throughout the trial and sentencing) can facilitate communication and positive relationships between victim advocates and victims' families (Lipovsky & Stern, 1997). A victim advocate often attends court with a child to serve as a support, since parents who may be called as a witness are often not allowed in the courtroom when their child testifies. Some evidence indicates that making a support person available to a child witness can lead to more accurate testimony (Moston & Engelberg, 1992).

Evaluations of courtroom preparation programs have been limited, primarily due to difficulties in maintaining sufficient control over legal proceedings to allow for an adequate evaluation. A notable exception is the Child Witness Program in Ontario. Sas et al. (1991, 1993) compared a basic (education and support) court preparation program with an enhanced (education, support, and stress management) program. Pre–post testing demonstrated significant improvement court-related knowledge following training. Unfortunately, the groups differed: The enhanced treatment group included children who were more seriously abused, children who were abused more often, and children who experienced more pretrial treatment delays. Comparison of the two groups did not reveal significant differences with regard to reduction of depressive symptoms (both groups improved over time); however, both general and abuse-related fears improved more for the children who participated in the enhanced program. Courtroom observations did not reveal significant differences between groups, but the measures used may have lacked sensitivity to treatment outcome. Although police officers did not rate the two groups differently with regard to courtroom performance, prosecutors rated the behavior of the children in the enhanced program as significantly superior to that of the children in the basic program.

Teaching Children to Resist Suggestion and Facilitating More Complete Testimony. As noted earlier, experimental studies provide a more controllable environment for evaluating the various components of court preparation programs. Saywitz and her colleagues (Saywitz, Snyder, & Lamphear, 1996; Saywitz & Moan-Hardie, 1994; Saywitz & Nathanson, 1993) have evaluated two procedures that may prove helpful in preparing children to provide complete and accurate information in court: (1) teaching children to resist suggestive questions, and (2) teaching children to elaborate on their accounts of events.

To teach resistance to suggestive questions, children were read a story about a child who went along with the suggestions of people who put their hopes or guesses into their questions (Saywitz & Moan-Hardie, 1994). The unanticipated negative results of the child character's acquiescence were highlighted in the story, and the character eventually learned the benefits of telling the truth even in the face of suggestive questions by authority figures. Child participants were then taught a stepwise strategy for responding to leading questions: (1) Stop and think about questions about memory; (2) mentally replay the event and compare their memory with the "guess" put into the leading question; (3) answer the question, or say "I don't know" or "I don't remember"; and (4) use motivational self-statements to promote confidence and assertiveness ("I knew there would be questions like this" and "I won't go along"). The response strategy was practiced with feedback in mock interrogations about previously reviewed videos. In posttesting, as compared with a control group, the trained group made 26% fewer errors in response to misleading questions.

One reason why young children may not provide sufficient detail to open-ended questioning is that they have yet to develop a cognitive framework that assists them in remembering to tell the full content of their story. A technique called "narrative elaboration" teaches children how to organize the elements of an event into five forensically relevant, theoretically driven categories (participants, setting, actions, conver-

sations/affect, and consequences). Each category is represented by a simple drawing on a card. Children are taught to use the categories and cards as mnemonic devices during questioning. Prior to questioning about the abuse episode, children practice using the narrative elaboration procedure to recall videotaped vignettes, using the cards to remind themselves to report as much as possible about each category. When children are questioned about the event under investigation, they are first asked for free recall (i.e., "What happened?"). Then they are given the cards and told to elaborate on their initial narrative by using the cards to trigger retrieval of any additional information ("Does this picture remind you to tell anything else?"). Saywitz and Snyder (1996) compared children trained in the narrative elaboration technique with children instructed to be accurate and with a control group of children. Children in the narrative elaboration condition demonstrated a 53% improvement over the control group with regard to the amount of detail included in their story. Even young children in the training condition outperformed older children in the control groups.

Summary of Secondary Prevention Strategies

Criminal prosecution plays a pivotal role in societal efforts to reduce child sexual abuse. To accommodate the special challenges of prosecuting cases with children as witnesses, secondary prevention efforts have included both protective measures (i.e., broadening hearsay exceptions for young children, educating the court about developmentally sensitive questioning for young children, and use of CCTV) and empowerment strategies (i.e., court preparation, stress management, teaching children how to avoid suggestive lines of questioning). CCTV has created the most controversy for the legal system, but also holds the greatest potential for reducing court-related distress among child witnesses. Evidence further suggests that reductions in court-related stress may reduce errors of omission and commission in children's testimony. Though legal in many states, CCTV is rarely used in the US because of two factors: (1) concerns that convictions may be overturned on appeal, and (2) concerns that children may be perceived by jurors less favorably if they testify via CCTV than if they testify in the open courtroom. Some research does indicate that children who testify via CCTV are perceived less favorably than children who testify in open court; however, there is no evidence that jurors' decisions to acquit or convict are related to use of CCTV.

Alternatively, empowering efforts have demonstrated significant advances in preparing children to provide courtroom testimony. Court preparation procedures have primarily focused on teaching children about courtroom procedures and teaching them stress management skills. More recent advances also include strategies for assisting children to avoid the pitfalls for suggestive questioning and to elaborate on the details of their abuse story.

TERTIARY PREVENTION AND CARE

Sexual Abuse Sequelae: An Overview

Recent literature reviews (Kendall-Tackett, Williams, & Finkelhor, 1993; Wolfe & Birt, 1997) highlight three major findings regarding sexual abuse sequelae: (1) Sexually abused children display and report more internalizing and externalizing adjustment problems than their non-abused peers; (2) sexually abused children display a broad range of behavioral and emotional problems, some linked to their sexual abuse experience and others apparently linked to familial and other environmental circumstances; and (3) two problem areas—Posttraumatic Stress Disorder (PTSD) symptoms and sexuality problems—are disproportionately prevalent in sexually abused children as compared to appropriate comparison groups (e.g., clinic-referred nonabused children). Kendall-Tackett et al. (1993) found that 20%–50% of children appear to be symptom-free at the time they are assessed. However, at least 30% show clinically significant problems within the first several months following disclosure (Wolfe, Gentile, & Wolfe, 1989). Several classes of factors mediate the impact of sexual abuse: severity and course of the abuse, premorbid child characteristics, family functioning, and community supports and stressors (Wolfe & Wolfe, 1988; Wolfe & Birt, 1997).

PTSD Conceptualizations of Sexual Abuse Sequelae

The PTSD literature provides an important framework for conceptualizing sexual abuse sequelae. Briefly, PTSD diagnostic criteria include (1) an experience of an event posing serious threat, to which the individual responds with great helplessness, fear, or horror; (2) three sets of symptoms, including reexperiencing aspects of the abuse (e.g., nightmares, intrusive thoughts), avoidance strategies that serve as a means of escape from trauma-related stimuli, and persistent, increased autonomic arousal (particularly when the person is faced with trauma-related stimuli or memories of the trauma); and (3) duration of symptoms for at least 1 month following the traumatic event and symptoms resulting in clinically meaningful distress or functional impairment. Recent diagnostic revisions for PTSD in the Diagnostic and Statistical Manual of Mental Disorders, fourth edition (DSM-IV; American Psychiatric Association, 1994) support consideration of PTSD as a diagnosis for some child sexual abuse victims. The DSM-IV notes specifically that child sexual abuse can be considered traumatic, by including in the definition of trauma "developmentally inappropriate sexual experiences without threatened or actual violence or injury" (p. 424).

Research with child sexual abuse victims has documented relatively high rates of PTSD symptoms via a number of assessment strategies, including parent reports (Wells, McCann, Adams, Voris, & Ensign, 1995; Wolfe et al., 1989; Wolfe, Wolfe, Michienzi, Sirles, & Evans, 1992), child reports (Friedrich, Jaworski, Hexschl, & Bengston, in press; Ligezinska et al., 1996; Pirrelo, 1994; Wolfe et al., 1989; D.A. Wolfe, Sas, & Wekerle, 1994), social worker checklists (Conte & Schuerman, 1987; Mennen & Meadows, 1993), chart reviews (Kiser, Heston, Millsap, & Pruitt, 1991), and professional evaluations (Livingston, Lawson, & Jones, 1993; McLeer, Deblinger, Atkins, & Ralphe, 1988; McLeer, Deblinger, Henry, & Orvaschel, 1992). Between 49% and 57% of sexual abuse victims meet DSM-III-R or DSM-IV criteria for PTSD (Kendall-Tackett et al., 1993; Pirrelo, 1994; D.A. Wolfe et al., 1994). Abuse severity has been linked to the severity of PTSD symptomatology, including intrusive thoughts, general and abuse-related fears, negative attitudes toward sex, and feelings of vulnerability to further abuse (Kiser et al., 1991; D.A. Wolfe et al., 1994; Wolfe, 1993; Wolfe et al., 1989). Coercion and force have also been related to trauma responses (Basta & Peterson, 1990; Elwell & Ephross, 1987). Children who experience both sexual and physical abuse appear to be at particular risk for PTSD (Kiser et al., 1991). Several studies have also linked severity of PTSD symptoms to social support (Kiser et al., 1991;

McLeer et al., 1992; Pirrelo, 1994) and attributional style (Taska & Feiring; 1995; Wolfe, 1993; Wolfe et al., 1989).

*Conceptual Models to Account
for Specific PTSD Criteria*

Reexperiencing Symptoms. The DSM-IV (American Psychiatric Association, 1994) requires one or more of the following symptoms for an individual to meet the criteria for the reexperiencing dimension of PTSD: (1) recurring intrusive, upsetting recollections of the event (images, thoughts, perceptions); (2) recurring upsetting dreams of the event; (3) feeling or acting as though the event is happening again (reliving the event, hallucinations, illusions, dissociative flashbacks); (4) severe psychological distress at exposure to cues (internal or external) that resemble or represent aspects of the traumatic event; and (5) physiological reactions on exposure to cues (internal or external) that resemble or represent aspects of the event. Young children may differ from older children and adults in the manifestation of these symptoms. Young children may express their trauma-related intrusive thoughts through thematic, repetitive play. Young children may complain of frightening dreams, but may be unable to describe or recognize the content of the dream as trauma-related. Finally, rather than describing flashbacks, young children may relive their trauma through specific reenactments of it (American Psychiatric Association, 1994).

Cognitive conceptualizations may explain the psychological function of PTSD reexperiencing symptoms. Silver, Boone, and Stones (1983) speculated that reexperiencing symptoms are traumatized individuals' attempts "make meaning" of their experiences. Janoff-Bulman (1989) suggested that reexperiencing symptoms reflect the accommodation process that occurs when individuals attempt to assimilate a traumatic event into their preexisting schemas, which conceptualized the world as safe, orderly, and meaningful. For children, reexperiencing symptoms may reflect their need to understand the traumatic event or may indicate that the children are missing information that may help them "make meaning" of the trauma. As an analogy, children may experience their abuse as a puzzle that has many missing pieces or pieces that do not fit together. Once their puzzle is "put together," their reexperiencing symptoms are likely to stop. For young children, the pieces of the puzzle may be simple and few; however, for the developmentally immature, those pieces may be quite chal-

lenging. These puzzle pieces may include questions such as "Am I safe?," "Will my parents protect me?," or "Why did he hurt me?" Young children may have great difficulty understanding that an abuser could have been "fun and nice" but also scary and hurtful. As children mature and are able to recognize the complexity of the abuse situation, reexperiencing symptoms may reemerge and encompass new concepts (e.g., attributions of responsibility, feelings of guilt, and difficulties assimilating conflicting information and loyalties about the offender).

Fears and Avoidance. DSM-IV diagnostic criteria for PTSD require the presence of three or more of the following avoidance symptoms: (1) attempts to avoid feelings, thoughts, or talk related to the trauma; (2) attempts to avoid people, places, or activities that bring back recollections of the trauma; (3) inability to remember a major aspect of the trauma; (4) notably decreased participation or interest in meaningful activities; (5) feelings of separation or estrangement from others; (6) restricted range of emotions (e.g., inability to feel love); and (7) a sense of a truncated future. Children may have difficulty describing some of these symptoms or may be unaware that their behavior is "avoidant." Most PTSD scholars recognize a changing pattern of PTSD symptoms over time related to avoidance symptomatology. Horowitz (1993) noted a vacillation between reexperiencing symptoms and avoidance. Wolfe (1990b) noted that abuse-related fears and reexperiencing symptoms tended to dissipate over the course of the first year following abuse disclosure; however, at the same time, avoidance symptoms increased. This inverse pattern suggests that children learn to avoid trauma stimuli in response to abuse-related fears and reexperiencing symptoms, and that these strategies can be intermittently effective in warding off recurrence of those symptoms.

Berliner and Wheeler (1987) used Mowrer's (1960) two-factor theory (classical and instrumental conditioning) to conceptualize the persistent symptoms of anxiety and avoidance frequently observed in victims. That is, fear and anxiety are classically conditioned during the abuse to previously neutral stimuli (conditioned stimuli) that were present during the abuse through pairing with abuse characteristics (unconditioned stimuli). During the abuse, the child may have experienced extreme fear accompanied by physiological reactivity (unconditioned response); conditions associated with the abuse (e.g., darkness, bedtime, male caretakers) may subsequently evoke high levels of fear and physiological reactivity in the absence of abuse (conditioned responses). The principles of stimulus generalization and higher-order conditioning may account for the generalization of fear and anxiety to other related stimuli. Avoidance behaviors are instrumentally maintained through negative reinforcement because avoidance and escape behaviors result in a reduction in the classically conditioned responses.

Physiological Hyperarousal. The DSM-IV requires two or more of the following symptoms of persistently increased arousal to meet diagnostic criteria for PTSD: (1) trouble going to sleep or staying asleep; (2) irritability or angry outbursts; (3) trouble concentrating; (4) hypervigilance; and (5) excessive startle response. With adult PTSD sufferers, considerable research has been amassed indicating long-term alterations in neural processes (Charney, Deutch, Southwick, & Krystal, 1995), particularly with regard to increased physiological reactivity to stressful events as compared to non-PTSD sufferers. There is some evidence of a dose–response effect; that is, individuals who experienced more intense or more frequent exposure to traumatic events tend to show correlated increases in physiological reactivity when faced with ordinary stressors (Southwick, Yehuda, & Morgan, 1995). Charney et al. (1995) have equated PTSD to a chronic illness, and suggested that the pathophysiology of PTSD should be viewed as a "continuously evolving neural process" (p. 28).

Perry, Pollard, Blakley, Baker, and Vigilante (1996) suggest that infants and young children, whose brains are still developing, are particularly vulnerable to long-term alterations of neural processes following trauma. During a traumatic event, norepinephrine excites the sympathetic nervous system, resulting in increased heart rate, blood pressure, respiration, release of stored sugar, and sense of hypervigilance (i.e., a "fight-or-flight" response). Repetitive neural activation through further traumatic experiences or through PTSD reexperiencing symptoms can "kindle" neural pathways, leading to sensitization—a process in which decreasingly intense external stimuli are required to evoke neural activation. As it can for adults, intense or repetitive trauma can lead for children to increased physiological arousal in response to everyday stressors. Essentially, the neural processing changes may lead children to be stuck in a perpetual state of fear, charac-

terized by hyperreactivity and emotional sensitivity. Such children can move easily from mild anxiety to feeling threatened and terrorized. It is possible that these changes in physiological reactivity create changes similar to those of Attention-Deficit/Hyperactivity-Disorder. Glod and Teicher (1996) found that physically and sexually abused children with PTSD displayed activity patterns similar to those of children with Attention-Deficit/Hyperactivity Disorder (based upon motion-logger actigraphs). These activity patterns were most prevalent for children who experienced abuse during the very early years of their childhood.

Type II PTSD Conceptualizations

Finkelhor (1990) has criticized the PTSD perspective as too narrow in describing sexual abuse sequelae and as failing to account for cognitive issues resulting from abuse. Trauma conceptualizations from Terr (1987) and cognitive conceptualizations from Peterson and Seligman (1983), as well as the theories of Janoff-Bulman (1989) and Silver et al. (1983) (described earlier), provide bases for expanding the PTSD model to account for the cognitive issues that often result from sexual abuse (and other traumas).

Terr (1987) recognized that child sexual abuse differs from many forms of trauma in that it is often repeated over long periods of time in secret, thereby requiring victims to adapt to their abusive situation via strategies that are either developmentally or psychologically inappropriate or damaging, particularly when these strategies are generalized beyond the abusive situation. Terr included as examples of these adaptations psychogenic numbing and dissociation, substance use problems, rage, mistrust, interpersonal relationship problems, suicidal ideation, and "unremitting sadness." Terr (1987, 1991) has proposed a dual classification for patients suffering from trauma-related disorders. Type I disorders follow exposure to a single traumatic event, whereas Type II disorders result from multiple or long-standing experiences with extreme stress (e.g., sexual abuse). Although Type I and Type II PTSD patients experience similar symptoms, Type II patients are thought to develop the abnormal coping strategies and psychological symptoms described above, which are eventually incorporated into the patients' personality style.

The revised learned helplessness model addresses cognitive changes related to uncontrollable experiences such as sexual abuse. Children attribute causes to events on the basis of three dimensions (internal–external, stable–unstable, and global–specific; Seligman et al., 1984). Individuals tend to base their causal attributions on situational factors; however, when causation is ambiguous, individuals attribute causation in their own idiosyncratic style. A self-enhancing attributional style (similar to the more familiar notion of optimism) is characterized by internal, stable, global attributions about positive events and by external, unstable, specific attributions about negative events; it is related to positive self-esteem and resistance to depression. A self-deprecatory attributional style (similar to pessimism) is characterized by external, unstable, specific attributions about positive events and internal, stable, global attributions about negative events; it is related to poor self-concept and depressive symptomatology (Seligman et al., 1984). Peterson and Seligman (1983) suggested that individual differences in attributional style are shaped by life events, but also affect reactions to life events. Thus, as negative life events "pile up," an individual's attributional style is likely to change, and such changes may affect the ways the individual copes with subsequent life events (e.g., the person may respond with learned helplessness even when events are controllable).

My colleagues and I (Wolfe & Birt, 1995; Wolfe & Gentile, 1992) have elaborated on these models, using a cognitive-behavioral framework. The severity of sexual abuse (level of sexual intrusiveness, use of coercion/force) is thought to relate to DSM-IV-defined PTSD symptoms, whereas the course of abuse (duration and frequency of abuse, relationship between child and perpetrator) is thought to relate to dysfunctional cognitive processes and dysfunctional coping, as represented by (1) learned helplessness and depression; (2) dissociation; (3) excessive emotionality and passivity when coping with day-to-day and trauma-related stressors; and (4) excessive, poorly managed responses to anger-provoking situations. The literature supporting the concept of Type II trauma and associated symptomatology is described below.

Depression and Suicidal Ideation and Behavior. It is becoming increasingly clear that a relatively high number of sexually abused children display depressive symptoms (Ligezinska et al., 1996; Lipovsky, Saunders, & Murphy, 1989; Wolfe, 1993), particularly among children referred for clinical services (Edwall, Hoffman,

& Harrison, 1989; Famularo, Kinscherff, & Fenton, 1990; Inderbitzen-Pisaruk, Sawchuck, & Hoier, 1992; Koverola, Pound, Heger, & Lytle, 1993; Lanktree, Briere, & Zaidi, 1991; Sansonnet-Hayden, Haley, Marriage, & Fine, 1987; Wozencraft, Wagner, & Pellegrin, 1991). Several studies support the idea that depressive and suicidal symptoms are more prevalent among sexually abused children who have experienced Type II forms of trauma (repetitive abuse over longer periods of time by a familial perpetrator; Brant, King, Olson, Ghaziuddin, & Naylor, 1996; Bryant & Range, 1996; Kiser et al., 1991; Sas et al., 1993; Wolfe, 1990a). Caution should be used, however, in interpreting these results, and particularly in evaluating suggestions that trauma victims' depressive symptoms are of similar etiology to or require similar treatment as more "classical" cases of childhood depression. There appears to be high comorbidity of PTSD and depressive symptoms among sexual abuse victims (Brant et al., 1996), which may be related to a number of issues. First, childhood affective states are not readily discernible (Wolfe et al., 1989), and elevations on measures of depression may simply reflect an increase in global negative affect. Furthermore, Terr (1991) suggests an important difference between the "futurelessness" of depressed and traumatized individuals. For traumatized children, "the future is a landscape filled with crags, pits, and monsters," while for the depressed, "the future is a bleak, featureless landscape stretched out to infinity" (Terr, 1991, p. 14).

Dissociation. DSM-IV (American Psychiatric Association, 1994) defines the essential feature of dissociative disorders as a failure to integrate cognitive functions associated with consciousness, identity, memory, or perception of the environment. Memory dysfunctions include deficits in retrieval of knowledge across behavioral states, deficits in retrieval of autobiographic memory, difficulties discerning actual events from events experienced vicariously through dreams, reading, or conversation, and intermittent and disruptive intrusion of traumatic memories into awareness (Putnam, 1994). Disturbances of identity may be manifested as depersonalization and different "personalities," which Putnam (1994) redefines as "narrow ranges of functioning and affect that are best conceptualized as discrete behavioral states" (p. 252). Dissociative patients may feel controlled by a force within themselves, over which they have little or no control.

Terr (1991) has conceptualized dissociation as a coping strategy used to reduce overwhelming anxiety in situations of extreme stress. Some suspect that children have a greater (or even innate) capacity to dissociate, which dissipates as more effective coping strategies develop. However, when intensively or repeatedly traumatized, young children may rely upon their dissociative capacities as a coping strategy, such that dissociative responses are negatively reinforced and therefore maintained as automatic reactions to stressful situations; they may become similar to habits.

Although the onset of dissociative disorders is believed to occur in early childhood, dissociative disorders are rarely diagnosed in children, perhaps due to the subtleties of childhood dissociative symptoms (Kluft, 1985; McElroy, 1992). Children's dissociative symptoms are often attributed to other causes. For instance, trance-like behaviors may be misdiagnosed as truancy, conduct problems, or moodiness (Coons, 1986; McElroy, 1992). Some dissociative symptoms, such as imaginary friends, can be interpreted as normal (McElroy, 1992). Often dissociation goes undiagnosed, either because dissociative symptoms are not evident at the time of assessment (Johnson, 1987; Kluft, 1985) or because other diagnoses are given, such as PTSD, Major Depression, Schizophrenia, or Borderline Personality Disorder (Coons, Bowman, & Milstein, 1988; Coons, Bowman, Pellow, & Schneider, 1989; Ogata et al., 1990).

Perry et al. (1996) have described a dissociative continuum as an alternative to the hyperarousal continuum (described earlier). When faced with a traumatic situation, an infant or child initially responds by crying in order to gain assistance from a caretaker. If crying fails to rescue the child from the trauma, the child may move from the hyperarousal continuum to the dissociative continuum, which may include a "freeze" or "surrender" response. Psychobiologists speculate that females and children are more likely to react in a dissociative manner to trauma, since dissociative rather than hyperarousal responses are more likely to result in survival for those who are physically weaker than their attackers (the primary enemies during prehistoric times were big cats and human males). Perry et al. (1996) speculate that the more immobile, helpless, and powerless an individual feels, the more likely he or she is to utilize dissociative responses. As the kindling process does in the case of hyperarousal, the frequency of dissociative experiences may pre-

dispose a child to the development of a dissociative disorder, whereby dissociative responses are triggered by lower-grade stressors.

Several investigations have revealed relatively high rates of both parent-reported and child-reported dissociative symptoms among sexually abused children as compared to nonabused, non-clinic-referred children (Birt, DiMito, & Wolfe, 1995; Malinosky-Rummell & Hoier, 1991; Putnam, Helmers, Horowitz, & Trickett, 1995). In contrast, Friedrich et al. (in press) found no differences in dissociation between sexually abused and nonabused adolescent psychiatric patients. The differences between studies may be due to the fact that measures of childhood dissociation are in their initial stages of psychometric evaluation, and have yet to show evidence of both concurrent and discriminative validity. We (Birt et al., 1995) found that children were more likely to report using dissociative coping strategies during their abuse when the abuse involved more serious sexual acts or higher levels of coercion and force. However, supporting the Type II notion linking dissociation with repetitive abuse, children who were repeatedly abused were more likely to display dissociative symptoms on a day-to-day basis. Likewise, Malinosky-Rummell and Hoier (1991) found that self-reports and parent reports of dissociative strategies were predicted by the number of sexually abusive incidents experienced by a child. Friedrich et al. (in press) also found that child-reported and parent-reported child dissociation among adolescent psychiatric patients was positively related to severity and duration of abuse, as well as to a child's age and gender (older girls reported more dissociative symptoms).

Coping Style. "Coping" has generally been defined as "any and all responses made by an individual who encounters a potentially harmful outcome" (Silver & Wortman, 1980, p. 281). Coping is generally dichotomized into bipolar dimensions, such as approach versus avoidance or problem-focused versus emotion-focused coping. No one coping strategy is effective in all situations, and effective coping may depend upon selecting the strategies that are most effective in terms of the controllability of the situation. When a stressor is controllable, strategies intended to alter the situation have been associated with lower levels of distress and fewer negative emotions (Hubert, Jay, Saltoun, & Hayes, 1988; Hyson, 1983). However, when a person is faced with uncontrollable stressors, coping strategies that reduce emotional distress or avoid the stressor appear to be most effective (Altshuler & Ruble, 1989; Band & Weisz, 1988; Spirito, Stark, & Williams, 1988).

Children's decisions to report the onset of sexual abuse appear to have more to do with premorbid child characteristics such as coping style than with anything about the abuse (Love, Jackson, & Long, 1990). When confronted with a sexual abuse situation, a child may perceive the situation as controllable and act to stop the abuse, either by refusing to participate or by telling someone about the abuse after the first episode. However, if the child perceives the situation as uncontrollable, he or she may seek avenues to reduce distress, such as distancing, repression, or avoidance. Emotional reactions such as anger and hostility may be redirected toward "safer" others, such as peers, siblings, or nonoffending parents. Once the abuse is disclosed or terminated, the child may continue to cope with abuse-related sequelae via avoidant strategies or strategies designed to escape emotional distress.

Johnson and Kenkel (1991) found a significant connection between emotional distress and two coping strategies among child sexual abuse victims: wishful thinking and tension reduction (which was defined as responding to stress by eating, drinking, using drugs, and having sex). Unfortunately, as is true with much of the coping-based literature, it is difficult to tell whether high distress led to the use of these strategies, or whether the use of these strategies was partially responsible for the maintenance of high levels of distress. DiLillo, Long, and Russell (1994) examined retrospective reports of childhood coping among intra- and extrafamilial sexual abuse survivors. As compared to extrafamilial victims, intrafamilial victims reported using both more emotion-focused and more problem-focused coping. As in the Johnson and Kenkel (1991) study, intrafamilial victims were more likely to use wishful thinking, as well as self-isolation and self-blame. If we assume that intrafamilial abuse is more stressful than extrafamilial abuse, this study sheds light on the chicken–egg question; that is, it appears that the more stressful the situation, the more likely victims are to employ all forms of coping.

Anger. Anger management problems have historically been linked to conduct problems, family disruption and discord, and poor parental child management skills. Anger problems are often anecdotally reported by clinicians working with sexually abused children, and research has

demonstrated relatively high rates of externalizing behavior problems among such children when compared to nonclinic control samples. The question arises as to whether anger management problems among sexually abused children are related to the sexual abuse, or to familial factors that often occur concomitantly with sexual abuse, such as family discord and other forms of maltreatment (physical and emotional abuse, neglect, or exposure to family violence). We (Birt & Wolfe,1995) found that parents of sexually abused children reported relatively high rates of aggressive behaviors in the children. However, in multiple-regression analyses, children's perceptions of family functioning accounted for more variance in the anger measures than did aspects of the abuse (which also added significantly to the variance). Contrary to the Type I–Type II notion that anger problems may emanate from chronic abuse, the study found that anger problems were more closely linked with Type I abuse severity. Interestingly, sexual abuse victims who also experienced emotional maltreatment reported the highest levels of anger when faced with common childhood stressors. However, sexual abuse victims who also experienced physical abuse were reported by their parents to display the highest levels of aggression.

Other research also links anger problems with Type I PTSD. Steiner, Garcia, and Matthews (1997) found relatively high rates of PTSD among incarcerated juvenile delinquents; the majority of traumatizing events were related to family-based violence. Delinquents with PTSD showed difficulties with restraint, impulse control, and suppression of aggression. As well, they tended to rely on such defenses as projection, somatization, conversion, dissociation, and withdrawal.

Factors That Mediate the Severity of PTSD Symptoms

Attributional Style. Attributional style may explain the linkages among sexual abuse, PTSD, depressive symptoms, and coping style. Attributional style has been closely linked to child depressive symptoms, both in general and clinical populations of children (Joiner & Wagner, 1995) and among sexually abused children (Morrow, 1991; Wolfe, 1993; Wolfe et al., 1989). My colleagues and I (Wolfe, 1993; Wolfe et al., 1989) demonstrated links between general attributional style and abuse-specific attributions and PTSD symptoms following abuse disclosure and at 3- and 9-month follow-ups. Optimism, or positive attributions for positive events, seemed to facilitate resilience, in that PTSD avoidance was less prevalent among more optimistic children. Both general and abuse-specific pessimistic attributions (i.e., internal, global, and stable attributions about negative events; abuse-specific attributions such as seeing the world as dangerous, feeling vulnerable to further abuse, abuse-related self-blame, guilt, or shame) appear to be associated with PTSD symptoms (Taska & Feiring, 1995; Wolfe et al., 1989). Conceptually, attributional style may be linked to coping style. Optimistic attributions may be linked to active coping, whereas pessimistic attributions may be linked with passive and/or avoidant coping.

Social Support. PTSD is often linked with the availability of social support (Foy, Sipprelle, Rueger, & Caroll, 1984). Kiser et al. (1991) found that the families of PTSD-positive sexually abused children were more likely than the families of PTSD-negative sexually abused children to be judged by clinicians as dysfunctional. PTSD appears to be more common among incestuously abused children, particularly when the offender was a parental figure (McLeer et al., 1992; Pirrelo, 1994). Treatment outcome appears to be related to family support and family functioning. Merrick, Allen, and Crase (1994) found that treatment outcome was related to support by a nonoffending caretaker and to family involvement in therapy.

Sexuality Problems

Unlike most of the other problems associated with childhood sexual abuse, childhood sexuality problems have not been identified by the DSM-IV as constituting a disorder. Little is known about childhood sexuality, so it is difficult to draw the line between what is considered normal childhood sexual behavior and sexual behavior that is dysfunctional, age-inappropriate, or coercive. Recent surveys of sexuality in children under age 12 indicate that some sexual behaviors are fairly common, such as masturbation; however, more serious sexual behaviors, such as aggressive sexuality, attempts to engage others in sexual behavior, and behaviors that appear to be imitations of adult sexual activity (e.g., oral–genital contact, masturbating with objects, inserting objects into genitalia, simulated sexual intercourse) are quite rare. Fewer than 2% of parents or day care providers noted those behaviors for individual children (Friedrich, Grambsch, Broughton, Kuiper, & Beilke,

1991; Lindblad, Gustafsson, Larsson, & Lundin, 1995). By contrast, up to 41% of sexually abused children display sexual behavior problems (Kendall-Tackett et al., 1993; Tharinger, 1990). Adams, McClellan, Douglass, McCurry, and Storch (1995) found that 82% of sexually abused children and adolescents treated at a day and residential psychiatric hospital exhibited significant sexual problems. Three types of sexual problems were identified: (1) hypersexual (excessive flirtatiousness, inappropriate touching); (2) exposing (e.g., public masturbation, self-exposing); and (3) victimizing (molestation, incest, rape). Sexually abused children who exhibited exposing and/or victimizing behaviors were more likely to have been physically abused in addition to their sexual abuse. Sexually abused girls who exhibited hypersexual behaviors were likely to have a PTSD diagnosis. In a related study, McClellan et al. (1996) found that onset of sexual abuse at an early age was the strongest predictor of all types of inappropriate sexual behavior.

Johnson and Feldmeth (1993) have categorized children's sexual problems along a continuum: (1) normal sexual exploration, (2) sexual reactivity, (3) noncoercive sexual behavior with other children, and (4) molestation of other children. Normal sexual exploration is characterized as relatively infrequent and primarily oriented toward self-education or genital/bathroom humor. Sexually reactive children are described as overly focused on sexuality, with relatively frequent and compulsive masturbation and autoerotic behaviors. Children who engage other children in noncoercive sexual behavior are described as having several goals—sexual arousal, relating to peers, and/or coping with stress.

Johnson and Feldmeth (1993) have described children who molest other children as impulsive, compulsive, and aggressive. These children are described as having poor interpersonal skills, in that they have few friends and few interests, lack empathy for others, and have additional behavioral problems. Etiological factors include a history of sexual abuse, emotional abuse, and severe and unpredictable punishments; a sexually stimulating environment; and exposure to family violence (Friedrich & Luecke, 1988; Johnson, 1988, 1989). Children who molest are described as selecting highly vulnerable victims, including infants, young children, and handicapped children. Horton, Hogan, and Cruise (1995) found that sexually abused children who molested other children, as compared to sexually abused children who did not go on to molest others, had experienced more long-term abuse and the abuse tended to be more serious. Many of the children who went on to molest other children had experienced other forms of maltreatment, including neglect and physical abuse. Finally, Rasmussen, Burton, and Christopherson (1992) have noted five possible precursors to sexual offending by young children: prior traumatization, inadequate social skills, lack of social intimacy, impulsiveness, and poor parental monitoring or supervision.

As adolescents, sexual abuse victims are at significant risk for early initial forays into sexuality and earlier consensual sexual intercourse (Wyatt, 1985). Up to 66% of pregnant teens report a history of childhood sexual abuse (Boyer & Fine, 1991; Gershenson et al., 1989). Approximately 60% of prostitutes report a history of childhood sexual abuse prior to entering prostitution; 73% of prostitutes indicate that they began their prostituting while they were still minors (Fraser, 1985). Furthermore, a history of sexual abuse has been related to unsafe sexual decision making and poor HIV-preventive communication skills (Brown, Kessel, Lourie, Ford, & Lipsitt, 1997).

Tharinger (1990) has highlighted several theoretical models that help to understand the development of inappropriate sexual behavior among sexually abused children. Yates (1982) has suggested that sexual abuse may prematurely eroticize children, who must then cope with sexual impulses for which they have no appropriate outlet. Social learning theory suggests that sexually abused children learn their sexual roles and sexual behaviors through the sexually abusive relationship; that is, they learn to use sexuality to gain affection and acceptance, or learn to appease others through sex to avoid other forms of abuse or maltreatment (Tharinger, 1990). Trauma theory suggests that sexual behavior by sexually abused children may be a reenactment of their abuse experiences, which in turn may be an attempt to gain mastery over the abuse experiences.

From a developmental perspective, premature introduction to sexuality may disrupt children's psychosexual development by thrusting them into their phallic stage without prior accomplishment of earlier developmental tasks, which serve as the foundation for understanding and managing the complexity characteristic of interpersonal sexual relationships (Tharinger, 1990). For example, latency-age emphasis on skill building and personal accomplishment may be thwarted by an overwhelming preoccupation with sexuality. In fact, several studies have documented relatively low scores for sexually abused children on the Social Competence domain of the Child Behavior Checklist (CBCL) (Wolfe et al., 1989).

Treatment of Sexual Abuse Victims and Their Families: An Overview

Areas to Be Addressed in Treatment and in Treatment Research

Most longitudinal studies of sexual abuse victims demonstrate significant abatement of symptoms over time (Kendall-Tackett et al., 1993; Oates, O'Toole, Lynch, Stern, & Cooney, 1994; Sas et al., 1993). However, these trends toward symptom abatement appear to stop as time passes. In their 5-year follow-up of an Australian sample of sexually abused children, Tebbutt, Swanston, Oates, and O'Toole (1997) found no symptom abatement between their 18-month and 5-year follow-up periods. Despite general improvement in symptomatology, a high percentage of sexually abused children continue to show clinically significant symptoms at various assessment points during their childhood (Oates et al., 1994) and into adulthood (Jumper, 1995; Neumann, Hauskamp, Pollock, & Briere, 1996). Furthermore, between 10% and 33% of sexually abused children show more symptoms over time, including some children who were symptom-free at the initial assessment (Kendall-Tackett et al., 1993; Oates et al., 1994). Chronicity of abuse appears to be the only abuse-related variable that consistently relates to duration of symptoms (Famularo et al., 1990; Oates et al., 1994; Wolfe, 1990b). Maternal support and maternal coping have also been related to duration of symptomatology (Everson, Hunter, Runyan, Edelsohn, & Coulter, 1989; Goodman et al., 1992). Involvement in therapy does not necessarily relate to symptom abatement (Oates et al., 1994). However, abuse-specific treatment programs show evidence of treatment-related symptom reductions (Kendall-Tackett et al., 1993; Finkelhor & Berliner, 1995).

These longitudinal findings, combined with research on abuse sequelae, highlight the need for sexual abuse treatment and outcome studies of such treatment to assure the following three characteristics (Beutler, Williams, & Zetzer, 1994; Finkelhor & Berliner, 1995):

1. The treatment protocol should address symptoms known to relate to sexual abuse (i.e.,

PTSD or sexuality problems) or factors known to exacerbate or attenuate sexual abuse sequelae (i.e., social support/family dysfunction or attributional issues).

2. Participants in treatment research must show clinically significant abuse-related symptoms which are quantified through psychometrically sound assessment tools.

3. The research design must include random assignment to appropriate comparison groups to control for the passage of time and placebo effects. Because of ethical concerns about withholding treatment, random assignment to community "standard" treatments (e.g., nondirective play therapy or standard group therapy for children) is recommended.

Developing a Treatment Plan

Sexually abused children are often referred for treatment simply because of their abuse history, because their caregivers expect that the abuse caused psychological damage or because they hope to prevent problems "down the road." However, sexual abuse is an event, not a psychological disorder (Berliner, 1996); therefore; the treatment needs of individual children vary widely. Adequate assessment is required to assure that a treatment plan matches a child's needs. Although the issue of matching presenting problems to type of intervention appears to be fundamental to effective mental health interventions, a surprising number of sexual abuse treatment outcome evaluation programs have failed to match presenting problems with the intervention offered (Beutler et al., 1994; Finkelhor & Berliner, 1995). The problem is magnified in clinical service programs. A survey of programs offering services to sexually abused children and their families revealed that fewer than half utilized standardized or program-specific assessment tools on a regular basis, and that even fewer programs (26%) integrated assessment into the therapeutic process at points before, during, and after treatment (Keller, Cicchinelli, & Gardner, 1989).

Given the wide array of symptoms linked to sexual abuse, the assessment process should be thorough (multimethod, multisymptom, and multi-informant). Assessment strategies should include parent and child reports (and school reports when available). When observational assessments (observations of family interaction, of play during nondirective play therapy sessions, and of behaviors and conversational content during interviews and art sessions) are possible, they can facilitate the interpretation of more

standardized assessments (Crittenden, 1996). The assessment protocol should include measures that tap both global (general personality and behavioral problems) and abuse-specific (PTSD Types I and II; sexuality problems) adjustment problems. The assessment process should also explore known mediators of abuse-related sequelae (abuse severity and course, general and abuse-specific attributional style, and family functioning). A full exploration of assessment issues is beyond the scope of this chapter; the interested reader should consult Wolfe and Birt (1997).

Such a complex and heterogeneous assessment battery requires a strategy for making therapeutic decisions. That is, how does one translate assessment results into treatment goals and objectives? Figure 11.1 in the Appendix to this chapter presents a checklist developed for use in our clinic to assist in individualizing treatment plans, based upon the taking of a thorough history and completion of the assessment battery described in Wolfe and Birt (1997). Figure 11.2, also in the Appendix, presents a second checklist designed to address family issues that are often present in cases of child sexual abuse; it includes problems that affect many families (level of family structure, cohesiveness, adaptability) and problems that are specifically related to sexual abuse (i.e., issues related to paternal or sibling incest).

Because of the heterogeneity of problems presented by sexually abused children, no single therapeutic approach will be effective with any particular child or family. Most clinical services for sexually abused children are offered through either mental health or hospital-based clinics (36%) or through social service or child protective service agencies (34%) (Keller et al., 1989). Most clinical programs offer a variety of therapeutic modalities, including individual counseling (93%), family counseling (90%), dyad counseling (e.g., mother–daughter; 75%) group therapy (84%), and support groups (70%). Over half of programs offer individual, family, dyadic, and group therapy to their clients; another 31% offer some combination of individual therapy and group or family therapy. Programs tend to offer a mix of services and to utilize a variety of therapeutic orientations and techniques. At least half of the programs surveyed by Keller et al. (1989) offered the following: insight therapy, play therapy, behavior modification, art therapy, and a number of education approaches (e.g., psychoeducation, heterosocial skills training, and cognitive restructuring).

Because of the heterogeneous needs of sexually abused children and their families, a "modular" treatment approach may be the most effective strategy for developing individualized treatment plans and for evaluating therapeutic effectiveness. That is, specific programs and techniques need to be developed and evaluated that address the particular abuse-specific sequelae exhibited by particular children. Clinicians can then prioritize treatment goals and can systematically utilize proven interventions in a goal-oriented fashion. Particular abuse-specific goals should be established and monitored on a regular basis. Friedrich (1996) describes a goal attainment process that allows for continuous monitoring of therapeutic progress. Goals are individually established, with acceptable and desirable outcomes denoted. Alternatively, clinicians can monitor treatment outcome and make treatment-related decisions by regularly completing checklists of abuse-related treatment goals, such as those presented in Figures 11.1 and 11.2 (in the appendix at the end of this chapter).

Interventions Addressing Abuse-Specific Sequelae

Interventions Directed toward Reducing Reexperiencing Symptoms

In line with cognitive theories, the remedy for reexperiencing symptoms may be for a child to talk about the trauma so that he or she can "make sense" of the abuse experiences. Two problems arise in setting this as a goal in therapy. First, many child victims are seen for therapy simultaneously with legal proceedings. Many children have never fully disclosed their abuse, and information revealed in therapy may require further disclosure through legal channels. If a child will be a witness in a criminal proceeding, great caution and careful documentation are needed to assure that processes designed to help a child "make meaning" of his or her experiences do not in some way "lead" further disclosures (i.e., disclosures following leading statements or questions) or add suggestions to the child's story. Careful communication between the therapist and prosecutor may assure that the process of treatment does not interfere with prosecution.

The second problem with therapy geared toward "making meaning" relates to the second set of criteria for PTSD, avoidance symptoms. Most children find talking about their past abuse experiences stressful and are quite skillful at

avoiding activities that require them to remember or discuss their abuse openly. In fact, avoidance is the likely key to why trauma victims fail to process the emotional aspects of their trauma adequately. Foa and Riggs (1993) note that fear-related aspects of trauma memories tend to be more disorganized than other memories, which probably affects a victim's ability to process fear-related information. Perhaps fear-related memories elicit avoidance responses to such an extent that the victim never fully thinks through the entire sequence of his or her memories of the trauma.

Highly avoidant children may need to be "eased" into discussions of the abuse once they feel more comfortable with their therapists. Most therapies for sexually abused children include avenues for expressing trauma-related feelings and thoughts through nonverbal means, such as play, art, and/or drama. Considerable debate has developed regarding the advantages of traditional nondirective play therapy and more directive, goal-oriented play approaches (Rasmussen & Cunningham, 1995). Nondirective play therapy provides a warm, supportive environment for children to resolve their own problems with minimal direction from therapists. Nondirective therapy helps build therapist–child rapport and allows a child to use play as a medium of expression. The primary disadvantage of this approach lies with the assumption that sexually abused children can "make meaning" of their abuse without external interventions or "corrections." Terr (1981) has noted that traumatized children may repeatedly reenact trauma-related themes without apparent resolution. Interpretations and/or corrections are seen as necessary for the child to progress and move forward.

For example, for a child who repeatedly reenacts themes of vulnerability, a therapist might add to the play—themes of external protection (e.g., the mother arrives in time to foil an abuse attempt) or themes of self-efficacy (e.g., the child manages to divert the abuser's attention while the child dials 911 to report abusive behavior). Some traumatized children may be so avoidant of trauma-related issues that they limit their play to highly structured activities that allow little self-expression. Thus, the children have little opportunity to explore their experiences via play environment. A more directive play therapist might create an environment for such a child that encourages exploration of abuse-related issues, perhaps through games or activities that address abuse issues directly. Rasmussen and Cunningham (1995) note several other factors that may inhibit sexually abused children from working on their traumas via nondirective play therapy: demands for secrecy by an offender; lack of assertiveness or a belief that children should not talk to adults about sexual abuse; a desire to please the therapist and therefore not to talk about negative life events; and cognitive misattributions or distortions (e.g., children's beliefs that they did something wrong or that an offender will know what happens in the playroom setting).

As an alternative, the play environment can be used to help children understand their abuse via planned activities and experiences. Educational materials can be helpful in assisting children to make meaning of their abuse. The movie *Good Things Can Still Happen* (National Film Board of Canada, 1992) is an entertaining and insightful film designed to help children understand the linkage between symptoms and past abuse. Cunningham and MacFarlane (1991) have developed a number of activities suitable for working individually with children in a structured playroom atmosphere, including a PTSD workbook that involves information, art activities, self expression, and coping activities. The Rainbow Game (Rainbow House, Children's Resources Center, 1989) is a board game that includes a number of psychological techniques of self-expression and desensitization (e.g., word association, thematic apperception cards); it also prompts children to solve problems related to uncomfortable situations that place them at risk for abuse, or family- and peer-related problems. Davis and Sparks (1988) developed a series of therapeutic stories that can be used to introduce such concepts as trauma, empowerment, and healing, as well as issues of secrecy and disclosure.

Eventually, it is important that children be able to talk about their abuse experiences with their therapists. However, young children may not be used to providing details in their narratives about life events, or may minimize the sexual aspects of their story (Saywitz et al., 1991). Saywitz's narrative elaboration procedure (Saywitz & Nathanson, 1993) may be helpful in assisting children to understand their abuse by providing children with cues for information they can include in their story, without being suggestive. Friedrich (1990) described a Traumatic Events Interview process drawn from the work of Eth and Pynoos (1985). The interview includes three stages: (1) initial interventions that establish the framework for obtaining more in-

formation later (e.g., letting a child know that the therapist has talked with other children who have had similar experiences, creating an expectation that the events need to be described, asking the child to tell the story through drawing); (2) revivification (e.g., beginning to discuss the details of the abuse, talking about feeling overwhelmed by emotions, reviewing sensory experiences, identifying the worst moment, inquiring about dreams related to the abuse, and trying to "make meaning" of why it happened) and (3) tying up loose ends (e.g., summarizing what has been discussed, emphasizing the normality and understandability of the child's responses, complimenting the child on his or her ability to articulate the story and on aspects of the story that reflect bravery or wisdom, discussing dialectical feelings such as fear vs. anger and feeling relieved vs. feeling guilt, and discussing what the child has learned about himself or herself and the abuse as a result of the interview).

Rothbaum and Foa (1996) suggest that adult victims derive long-term benefits from therapies that involve prolonged exposure, in part because the process permits a reevaluation of the meaning represented in the memory. Furthermore, repeatedly recalling the memory makes it possible to give structure and organization to the memory. A study by DiSavino et al. (1993) provided some evidence to support this idea, in that narratives about trauma showed improved organization after prolonged exposure, and this improvement corresponded to reductions in PTSD symptoms.

Interventions Directed toward Reducing Fears and Avoidance

Several researchers have applied the two-factor model to explain some of the symptomatology resulting from adult sexual assaults (Holmes & St. Lawrence, 1983; Kilpatrick, Veronen, & Resnick, 1979) and adult PTSD sufferers (Foa, Steketee, & Rothbaum, 1989). From this model, it would follow that repeated presentation of the conditioned stimuli (e.g., dark, bedtime, male caretakers) without escape would eventually weaken the association between the conditioned stimuli and the conditioned responses. Research with a number of different types of traumas has demonstrated that exposure to memories of the trauma is probably the essential element of effective PTSD treatments (van der Kolk, McFarlane, & van der Hart, 1996). Cognitive therapy, systematic desensitization, and stress inoculation have all been demonstrated to be effective with adult trauma victims. Even the controversial technique of eye movement desensitization and reprocessing (Shapiro, 1995) includes elements of exposure. The patient is told to maintain an image of the original traumatic experience and to evoke the feelings associated with the event while simultaneously engaging in an eye movement technique.

Deblinger and Heflin (1996) describe the use of a "gradual exposure" intervention that combines the elements of systematic desensitization and prolonged exposure. Children are encouraged to confront feared stimuli, including their thoughts and memories of the abuse, in a graduated fashion. Children are initially encouraged to endure low-level anxiety-provoking stimuli before moving on to confront more distressing stimuli. Children are provided alternative methods for confronting and addressing abuse-related issues, including openly discussing the abuse, reading, doll play, drawing, writing, poetry, and singing. A therapist may begin discussing abuse-related issues by reviewing factual information regarding sexual abuse, such as prevalence and information about sexual abuse and sexual offenders. Children are later encouraged to describe their least distressing abuse-related memories, followed by increasingly stressful aspects of the abuse. By the end of treatment, the children are expected to confront abuse reminders and discuss abuse-related memories without experiencing significant distress. Deblinger, Lippmann, and Steer (1996) evaluated the effectiveness of the gradual exposure component of a sexual abuse treatment program. Compared to a community control group, and to a comparison group of children whose mothers received training, children who participated in the graduated exposure treatment displayed fewer parent-reported and child-reported PTSD symptoms at the end of treatment.

In a similar study, Berliner and Saunders (1996) described a group treatment program that incorporated gradual exposure with stress inoculation training. Children in the experimental group were taught several issues related to fear and danger: (1) Fear is an the automatic response to danger; (2) danger is experienced through three channels (thinking, feeling, and doing); (3) scared feelings can occur even when there is no apparent danger; and (4) reminders of abuse experiences can trigger fear responses. Children were taught progressive relaxation and given a relaxation tape for practice at home. Children were taught two coping strategies for

use when they experienced fear: the quieting reflex and thought stopping. These skills were practiced in sessions, and children were encouraged to use them during the intervals between group sessions. During the gradual exposure sessions, children were taught the concept of habituation ("If you talk about a bad experience a lot in a safe situation, after a while it doesn't feel so bad to remember it"). Children then drew pictures of their abuse experiences. As well, each child was encouraged to describe the abuse activities openly with the group, along with abuse-related thoughts and feelings. Children were encouraged to use stress inoculation strategies when describing their abuse experiences. Children were also encouraged to support each other and to remind each other to use their stress inoculation strategies. Although the children displayed pre–post improvements on several measures related to PTSD (abuse-related fears, physiological anxiety), the children in the experimental treatment group did not differ significantly from a matched comparison group of children who participated in a group that did not include the gradual exposure and stress inoculation components. Examination of pretest measures revealed that many of the children in both groups were not displaying clinically significant symptomatology; therefore, both groups probably improved simply as a result of the passage of time and as a result of the supportive nature and exposure to abuse-related issues in both groups.

Both the Deblinger et al. (1996) and the Berliner and Saunders (1996) programs focused on latency-age children. Cohen and Mannarino (1996b) evaluated an abuse-specific treatment program for preschoolers. Treatment programs that specifically address the issues of preschoolers are particularly important for two reasons: (1) approximately one-third of sexual abuse cases involve a child under age 6; and (2) preschoolers, as compared to adolescents and children, tend to show a higher prevalence of sexually inappropriate behavior (Friedrich, Urquiza, & Beilke, 1986) and greater fears and anxieties (Wolfe et al., 1989). Because of these victims' young age, nonoffending parents need to play an central role in their treatment. The Cohen and Mannarino program, called the Cognitive Behavioral Treatment for Sexual Abuse Program (CBT-SAP), provides individual therapy to a child and a nonoffending parent. Fear and anxiety are addressed in both the child's and the parent's therapy. The program for parents also includes the following components: attributions of responsibility, emotional support, behavior management, legal issues, and coping with one's own past abuse. The children's program also includes the following components: personal safety skill training, feelings about the offender, regressive behaviors, and inappropriate sexual behaviors. Intervention strategies include cognitive reframing, thought stopping, positive imagery, contingency management, and problem solving.

Pre–post comparisons of treatment efficacy, compared with a nonspecific therapy approach, demonstrated superior effectiveness of the CBT-SAP on the following variables: the CBCL Internalizing and Externalizing scales, the Child Sexual Behavior Inventory (CSBI), and the Weekly Behavior Record (21 common preschool behavior problems). For the CSBI and the CBCL, preintervention mean problem scores all fell into the clinical range; at postintervention evaluation, all scores from the CBT-SAP group averaged in the nonclinical range. Unfortunately, because the program includes a number of strategies designed to address a number of abuse-related symptoms, it is difficult to link specific treatment effects with specific treatment components. Follow-up studies evaluating effectiveness of specific components will be very important.

Interventions Directed toward Reducing Physiological Hyperarousal

Alterations to neural processes may account for concerns that PTSD anxieties may be particularly resistant to extinction. Nonetheless, some treatment outcome studies with adult combat veterans have demonstrated reductions in physiological reactivity as a result of exposure-based cognitive-behavioral treatments (Boudewyns & Hyer, 1990; Bowen & Lambert, 1986). Adult patients with PTSD are particularly likely to misuse drugs and alcohol, perhaps in an attempt to self-medicate their physiological symptoms (Davidson & van der Kolk, 1996); therefore, it is possible that child sexual abuse victims, particularly those who experience long-term abuse, are at high risk for misusing drugs and alcohol as adolescents. In fact, a high percentage of adolescents presenting to residential substance use programs have a history of childhood sexual abuse (71% to 90% of females and 42% of males; Rohsenow, Corbett, & Devine, 1988).

As a remedy to these psychophysiological effects, psychopharmacological approaches have been used both independently and as an adjunct to psychotherapeutic treatment approaches for PTSD. Davidson and van der Kolk (1996), in their review of psychopharmacological approaches, have suggested different approaches for acute versus chronic PTSD patients. Drugs that decrease autonomic arousal, such as benzodiazepines or clonidine, are seen as most effective for acute PTSD patients, with the goal to prevent "kindling" of the trauma (the resulting physiological effects of kindling) by controlling nightmares and intrusive symptoms. Fluoxetine and tricyclic antidepressants are considered more effective for individuals with well-established, chronic PTSD. Only one drug, propranolol, a beta-adrenergic blocker, has been evaluated with children. Famularo, Kinscherff, and Fenton (1988) reported use of propranolol with child victims of physical and/or sexual abuse, and noted improvements of symptoms related to hypervigilance and hyperarousal. Terr (1997) described using propranolol as an adjunct to systematic desensitization for a young trauma victim. Harmon and Riggs (1996) described using clonidine to treat PTSD symptoms among traumatized preschool children. Positive effects were noted for aggression, impulsivity, emotional lability, hyperarousal, hypervigilance, generalized anxiety, oppositionality, insomnia, and nightmares.

Nonpharamacological efforts have also been used to reduce hyperarousal. Both the Berliner and Saunders (1996) and the Deblinger and Heflin (1996) programs utilized relaxation training and other anxiety reduction techniques. Friedrich (1995) highlighted several general principles helpful in reducing dysregulation in the process of individual, group, and family therapy: creating a sense of safety; reducing arousal and agitation (through regular routines and rituals); and helping children learn and abide by interpersonal boundaries, which are often forgotten when children become overaroused. Thus far, however, no research has examined physiological reactivity with regard to treatment outcome.

Friedrich (1996) has suggested that physiological hyperarousal may inhibit development of normal affect regulation. Katz and Gottman (1991) have described the development of emotion regulation among children in terms of increasing ability to cope with arousal through (1) inhibiting inappropriate behavior related to strong affect; (2) self-soothing in response to physiological arousal; (3) focusing attention despite physiological arousal; and (4) organizing the self in order to attain external goals. Interventions that address these developmental milestones may be particularly effective in helping traumatized children overcome affect-driven difficulties.

Interventions Addressing Dissociative Tendencies

The first clinical issues for treating dissociation is recognizing it, since dissociative processes are not easily identified among children, as noted earlier. Elsewhere (Wolfe & Birt, 1997), parent and child report strategies for assessing dissociation are described; however, these measures are relatively new and have not yet demonstrated discriminant validity via comparisons between traumatized children and other clinic-referred populations. Friedrich (1990) found that the Rorschach test was valuable in identifying dissociative processes on a case-by-case basis. Dissociative children may present themselves as relatively well-functioning on self-report questionnaires; however, when faced with more ambiguous stimuli, their defenses may weaken and therefore permit more spontaneous responding. The format of the Rorschach may allow examiners to witness dissociative phenomena in action, in that respondents are first asked to describe what they see and are later asked to describe aspects of the card accounted for their perceptions. Friedrich (1990) described several cases in which children either deteriorated as the cards became more complex and colorful, or denied their earlier responses (particularly responses that involved either sexuality or mutilation).

Although dissociation may serve an adaptive function during the traumatic experience, generalization of dissociative symptoms outside of the abusive situations can seriously affect a child's ability to function interpersonally and academically. In my own limited experience with dissociative children, triggers for dissociative behaviors tend to be ordinary stressors, such as interpersonal or familial stressors, academic pressures, or boredom. Dissociative tendencies are quite notable when children are in the classroom, and may take the form of dawdling, procrastination, passive noncompliance, and intellectual slowness.

The conceptualization that dissociation may be practiced repeatedly during successive abuse experiences suggests that dissociation may well be treated as a habit disorder. Components of treatments of habit disorders include increasing one's awareness of the habit, self- or other-monitoring, and developing of an alternative or competing response (Azrin & Nunn, 1973). Gil (1991) and James (1989) describe similar strategies for addressing dissociative behaviors. They recommend helping a child gain an awareness of his or her dissociative behavior by providing a label that the child and therapist can use to communicate about the dissociation. The child is then helped to identify situations when he or she dissociates and to develop alternative responses. Gil (1991) suggests that therapist in the playroom environment ask the child to act "as if" he or she is dissociating, which allows the therapist to gain an understanding of the child's dissociative behavior.

Collaborative work with teachers and caregivers is essential, since children are unlikely to exhibit dissociative behaviors during structured therapy sessions. Teachers and caregivers can be taught to label the dissociative behaviors for these children and to provide positive instruction and rewards for "on-task" or alternative behaviors. Because of the "habitual" nature of dissociative behaviors, problems may recur during times of stress, and "booster sessions" may be required to assure that the habit does not recur.

Interventions Addressing Sexuality Problems

Sexually reactive children are most likely to be referred for treatment by concerned caregivers. On the other hand, children who engage other children in sexual behavior, coerced or not, are often referred by a child protective services agency, concerned school personnel, or juvenile court. Because of the private nature of sexual behavior, offending children and adolescents, like adult offenders, may deny allegations of abuse brought forth by younger children or peers. Parents, concerned about the consequences to their children of being labeled "sexual perpetrators," may readily accept their children's protestations of innocence and may not follow through with treatment recommendations. Therefore, in many cases, as with treatment of adult offenders, successful treatment may require a legal mandate to attend treatment (through either a court proceeding or a child protective services order).

Deblinger and Heflin (1996) describe a therapeutic strategy for sexually abused children who present with sexual problems. The program involves both parents and children and includes the following components: (1) assessing sexual attitudes and knowledge of childhood sexuality; (2) providing education about normal childhood sexuality; (3) teaching parents how to respond to children's questions about sexuality in a calm manner; (4) demystifying inappropriate sexual behavior by discussing ways that sexual behaviors develop; and (5) using behavioral management strategies to address inappropriate sexual behaviors. Behavioral management strategies include three components: (1) open communication between parent and child about sexuality, (2) clear consequences for inappropriate sexual behavior, and (3) development of prosocial behaviors to replace sexual behaviors (e.g., appropriate displays of affection). Cohen and Mannarino (1996a) demonstrated improvements on the CSBI for their CBT-SAP as compared to a nonspecific therapy program; however, because the CBT-SAP combines a number of treatment strategies addressing several adjustment issues, it is difficult to determine those aspects of the program that are responsible for improvements in sexual problem areas.

Because of the impulsive nature of childhood sexual behavior, close monitoring of peer activities and restriction of high-risk activities (e.g., sleepovers with other children) is recommended. Children can "earn" increasing levels of independence from parental supervision by demonstrating adequate self-control. For example, a child may move from constant, direct supervision when around other children to short periods of time with children in places where a supervisor can intermittently check on the children. Although close supervision may feel very restrictive and intrusive, the social consequences of inappropriate sexual behaviors with other children can result in ostracizing by other children and their parents.

Therapy for children with sexual problems can be facilitated through use of several educational materials. The book *Where Did I Come From?* (Mayle, 1995) is an entertaining way of teaching children about sex and sexual feelings. Johnson (n.d.) has developed a game called *Let's Talk about Touching* for educating sexualized children and children who molest.

Family-Based Treatment Approaches

Treatment Programs for
Nonoffending Parents

As noted earlier, social support plays a prominent role in predicting postdisclosure adjustment. In a case of incestuous abuse, the support of the nonoffending parent is crucial (e.g., Everson et al., 1989). Nonetheless, the period after a child's disclosure of father–child incest can be very stressful for the mother, in that she is faced with numerous stressors (e.g., separation from her spouse, managing legal processes) and is left with fewer resources to assist her with coping (e.g., financial pressures, strained relationships with friends and extended family members). Furthermore, the nonoffending parent must manage the behavioral and emotional sequelae resulting from the abuse. Mothers may feel considerable ambivalence between their roles as parents and wives (DeYoung, 1994). Several studies have documented the significant traumatic effects of incestuous abuse disclosure on nonoffending parents (Deblinger, Hathaway, Lippman, & Steer, 1993; Kelly, 1990; Manion et al., 1996; Wolfe, 1991). Cohen and Mannarino (1996b) found that parental emotional distress was predictive of treatment outcome for both a cognitive-behavioral and a nonspecific treatment program.

Deblinger and Heflin (1996) describe a three-part group program for parents of sexually abused children: (1) coping skills training; (2) training in gradual exposure and in ways to assist children with their gradual exposure therapy; and (3) training in behavior management strategies for assisting children with abuse-related sequelae. The coping skills component is designed to assist parents in coping with their own emotional responses to the sexual abuse disclosure. The coping skills sessions have three goals: (1) educating parents about sexual abuse; (2) helping parents express their emotions in healthy ways; and (3) teaching them effective coping skills. Information about the ways perpetrators engage children and reasons why children do not disclose abuse is often helpful in debunking parent's dysfunctional thoughts about their own feelings of guilt and responsibility or attributions of blame toward the children. Cognitive strategies are used to address dysfunctional thoughts that are either inaccurate, nonproductive (e.g., preoccupation with anger toward the perpetrator), or pessimistic.

Gradual exposure sessions focus on two issues: (1) being able to confront and cope with abuse-related discussions, and (2) being able to talk to children directly about the sexual abuse experience. The gradual exposure sessions also teach parents about how to provide sex education and personal safety skill training for their children. Open lines of communication are encouraged, and training is based upon the principles described by Faber and Mazlish (1980). Parents are taught how to maintain open communication about the abuse as the children mature by (1) encouraging questions about the abuse and sex; (2) reinforcing children's efforts to share their problems with the parents; and (3) encouraging their children to express feelings in effective and appropriate ways.

For the behavior management component, parents learn about the ways that children may develop behavioral and emotional problems, particularly problems resulting from sexual abuse. Various behavior management strategies are reviewed, including use of positive reinforcement and praise, principles of differential attention, use of effective instructions, and use of time out. Two specific issues are addressed: sleep problems (sleeping alone, dealing with nightmares) and inappropriate sexual behaviors (masturbation, sexual behavior with peers).

As described earlier, Deblinger et al. (1996) compared child-only treatment with parent-only treatment and combined parent–child treatment. They found that mothers assigned to treatment (parent-only or combined parent-child) described significantly greater decreases in their children's externalizing behaviors and greater improvement in their own parenting skills; their children described significantly greater decreases in their self-reported levels of depression. These findings are particularly encouraging, since some researchers have found that externalizing problems and sexual behavior problems are more resistant to change than some of the other problems related to child sexual abuse (Lanktree & Briere, 1995; Nelki & Waters, 1988).

As noted previously, Cohen and Mannarino (1996b) also included a parent education component in their treatment program for sexually abused preschool children. Although the treatment design did not allow for determining aspects of treatment related to specific effects, given that improvements were found for both the externalizing and sexually inappropriate behaviors, it is highly likely that the parenting aspect (which included contingency management) played a significant role in contributing to treatment effectiveness.

Therapy Issues Specific to Incestuous Abuse

Access between Incestuous Fathers and Their Children. In paternal abuse cases, many children continue to have contact with their incestuous fathers following disclosure, though it is usually supervised by a child protective services agency, a supervised visitation program, or a family member. Supervised access can serve several positive functions (Straus, 1995): (1) helping the child gain a realistic assessment of the parent; (2) serving as a steppingstone to less restricted access; and (3) allowing the child to maintain a relationship with the parent in a safe situation. On the negative side, some children fear their incestuous fathers and visitations stimulate PTSD symptomatology. When legal procedures are ongoing, a child's access to the father may introduce divided loyalties between wanting to please the father and following through with prosecution. Thus, when a therapist is planning postdisclosure access between a child and an incestuous father, care should be taken to balance the child's need for a relationship with his or her parent and the child's need to minimize and manage PTSD symptomatology. Tebbutt et al. (1997), in their longitudinal study of abuse-related sequelae, found that contact between offenders and victims between the 18-month and 5-year follow-up period was predictive of long-term depressive symptoms.

Little is known about the effects of supervised access; in fact, little is known about supervised access practices. Hamilton (1997), in an exploratory study, conducted a review of 40 child protective services files to examine factors associated with father–child access and with positive adjustment to such access. Over half of the fathers had access to their children, with access progressing over time from no access, to access supervised by the child protective services agency, to supervision by mothers or relatives, to unsupervised access. Mothers provided supervision in the majority of cases; only two cases progressed to the point of allowing unsupervised access. Hamilton's (1997) chart review revealed that access supervisors were more likely to note positive adjustment to access when a father (1) had admitted to the abuse, (2) was emotionally supportive of the child, (3) made it clear that he would abide by supervision rules, (4) was highly involved in offender treatment services, and (5) demonstrated positive parenting behaviors during the access visits.

In accord with these findings, some therapists advocate that father–child access should not occur until both the father and child have progressed far enough in therapy to be ready for an abuse clarification session. Abuse clarification requires that the father (1) accept responsibility for the sexual abuse, (2) apologize to the victim and other family members, and (3) agree to abide by a plan to assure the child's safety and security (Swenson & Hanson, 1998). Both father and child must be psychologically ready for the clarification session. The offender must have a good understanding of the reasons for his abusive behavior and must be willing to take full responsibility for the abuse. With the therapist's help and guidance, the offender writes a letter to the victim outlining the following: (1) the offender's "grooming" of the child to initiate the abuse, (2) full admittance of the abuse perpetrated, and (3) a plan to prevent further abusive behavior.

Once the offender's therapist feels that the offender is ready for the abuse clarification session, the child's therapist is contacted to begin readying the child for the meeting. Child preparation includes the following: (1) The child and therapist review the rationale for the meeting (i.e., the offender is to apologize and to listen to what the child has to say); (2) the child and therapist make rules about the meeting (e.g., no touching, no blaming the child or the child's mother); and (3) the child prepares what he or she would like to say to the offender (e.g., how the abuse made him or her feel, the effects of the abuse). The abuse clarification session is usually held in the office of the child's therapist and progresses through the following issues: (1) clarification of the facts; (2) acceptance of responsibility by the offender; (3) agreement about terms of future access; (4) discussion of a safety plan; and (5) discussion of long-term plans for the family (e.g., plans for reunification or permanent separation or divorce).

Family Reunification. Surprisingly little empirical research is available regarding family reunification in cases of incestuous abuse. Early research by Giarretto (1982) describing the Santa Clara Child Sexual Abuse Treatment Program reported high rates of family reunification (85%) with low rates of recidivism (less than 1%). The major feature of the program was a variety of self-help groups broadly defined as Parents United, which included groups for perpetrators, nonoffending parents, couples, and victims (this group was called Daughters and Sons United). Despite impressive gross outcome statistics, no data were produced with regard either to child adjustment or to child satisfaction with family reunification.

O'Connell (1986) described a process of family reunification following the abuse clarification process, which allowed for contingency-based progression from access in public places, to family outings outside the home, to visits at the family home, and finally overnight visits. Specific rules were outlined at each step of increasing access that were designed to insure child safety. For instance, rules for access in public places strictly limited physical contact and restricted conversations related to sexuality, boyfriends, and the sexual abuse. When home visits were initiated, rules included restrictions of time alone between the victim and the offender, enhanced child privacy boundaries, and strict rules about the offender's nighttime behavior and his dress around the child. No research has evaluated the effectiveness of such a reunification strategy in terms of the percentage of families that seek to reunify and those who succeed in carrying out all of O'Connell's steps. Furthermore, no studies have evaluated the effects of reunification on children.

Alexander (1990) described several treatment goals important for incestuous families, particularly those families that plan to reunite: (1) child protection; (2) elimination of secrecy related to the abuse, as well of other family secrets; and (3) acceptance of responsibility for the abuse by the perpetrator, and, where appropriate, by the nonoffending spouse (i.e., for failure to monitor or failure to protect). Family system boundaries were also seen as important therapeutic goals. Physical boundaries related to personal space and property were judged important. Boundaries between parental, marital, and sibling subsystems were also deemed important. In contrast, it was deemed important that the family dismantle existing boundaries between the family and outside societal and social contacts (e.g., social service agencies, child contacts with peers, etc.).

Facilitating Adaptation to Foster Families

Approximately 17% of sexually abused children go into foster care (Finkelhor, 1983). Approximately 30% of children entering the foster care system enter because of a history of sexual abuse; however, once in foster care, many more children disclose a history of sexual abuse. Sexually abused children who go into foster care are more likely to have come from low-SES families, to have experienced multiple abuse episodes, and to have mothers who did not support their abuse allegations (Hunter, Coulter, Runyan, & Everson, 1990; Leifer, Shapiro, & Kassem, 1993). Compared to other reasons for foster placement (e.g., neglect, physical abuse), sexually abused children tend to remain in foster care for shorter durations (approximately 8 months shorter; Lie & McMurtry, 1991).

Most evidence indicates that sexually abused children placed in foster care have significant problems. In fact, two of the factors associated with foster care placement—multiple abuse experiences and nonsupportive mothers—have been shown to be a significant predictor of maladjustment among sexually abused children (Goodman et al., 1992; Wolfe et al., 1989). Clinically significant levels of behavioral and emotional problems are particularly prevalent among sexually abused children in foster care. Thompson, Authier, and Ruma (1994), with a sample of 122 sexually abused children in foster care, found borderline or clinical elevations for a high percentage of the sample on all of the broad-band scales of the CBCL: Social Competence (82%), Internalizing (76%), Externalizing (79%), and Total Behavior Problems (94%). In a separate survey, Thompson et al. (1994) queried foster parents about the types of problems presented by their sexually abused foster children. For preschool and latency-age children, problems with bedwetting, fears, seductive behavior, nightmares, eating, and sleep disturbances, school, and clinging behaviors were identified. For adolescents, problems included suicidal threats and gestures, promiscuous behavior, self-mutilation, school problems, and alcohol and drug use. When queried about reasons for placement breakdowns, the following problems were identified by at least 50% of the respondents: seductive behavior, aggressive behavior, use of alcohol and drugs, suicide attempts, and running away. In addition to the behavioral problems described, Treacy and Fisher (1993) found that sexually abused children had more problems developing harmonious relationships with their foster parents than children who came into foster care for other reasons did.

Questions arise as to whether foster placement has negative effects itself, aside from the premorbid factors related to adjustment prior to placement (i.e., problems in the family of origin, maltreatment experiences, preexisting behavioral problems). Most studies do not indicate significant differences in adjustment between sexually abused children who remain at home and those placed in foster care (Leifer & Shapiro, 1995; Runyan & Gould, 1985a, 1985b). However, because of differences between the samples (sexually abused children placed in foster care would be expected to have more psychological problems, given their chaotic and unsupportive family backgrounds), it is more useful to make within-sample evaluations to determine factors that lead to successful adjustment to foster care. Most studies indicate that stability of placement is of paramount importance when adjustment to foster care is being evaluated (Aldgate, Colton, Chate, & Heath, 1992; Cantos, Gries, & Slis, 1996; Wolkind & Rutter, 1985). Reliable and frequent maternal visits during the period of foster placement are also related to fewer behavior problems among sexually abused children (Cantos, Gries, & Slis, in press; Leifer & Shapiro, 1995). Placement in a kinship foster home (i.e., the home of a child's relative) was also related to better foster care adjustment. Leifer and Shapiro (1995) found no significant improvement in behavioral problems and abuse-specific symptoms over the course of 1 year of placement in foster care. However, children tended to report fewer depressive symptoms and displayed less pathology on the Rorschach inkblot test at the 1-year follow-up.

Not surprisingly, children in foster care are heavy consumers of mental health services (Halfon, Berkowitz, & Klee, 1992; Trupin, Tarico, Low, Jemelka, & McClellan, 1993). Approximately half of all children in the child welfare population exhibit clinically significant problems, and 38% receive mental health services; as a comparison, the general need for children's mental health services within the community at large tends to run between 10% and 20%, with 4% to 12% of the population actually accessing such services (Garland, Landsverk, Hough, & Ellis-MacLeod, 1996). In addition to mental health services, foster children receive psychosocial services through regular contact with their social workers, involvement in therapeutic day care, and involvement with family support programs (Trupin et al., 1993). Halfon et al. (1992) found that children in the child welfare system were 15 times more likely to receive mental health services than a sample of SES-matched children in the community. Garland et al. (1996) found that sexually abused children, compared to other children in foster care, were 4.47 times more likely to receive mental health services. Interestingly, number and intensity of behavioral problems (CBCL Total Behavior Problems score) were not related to whether a child received mental health services: 79% of sexually abused foster children with clinically elevated CBCL scores received mental health services, while 78% of sexually abused foster children without elevated CBCL scores received mental health services.

As noted earlier, stable foster placement appears to be an important predictor of foster care adjustment. However, foster parents typically do not receive specialized training prior to receiving children into their homes, yet are expected to parent children with very serious mental health problems. Although it appears that mental health services are frequently available to these children, the opportunity and responsibility for rehabilitation often lie largely within the foster home. Foster parents' skills in dealing with both internalizing and externalizing problems, without excessive discipline and with understanding, predicts placement success (Doelling & Johnson, 1990).

Several programs have been developed to help foster parents cope with the special needs of sexually abused children. Training issues have included the following (Barth, Yeaton, & Winterfelt, 1994; Treacy & Fisher, 1993): (1) normal development, particularly with regard to sexuality; (2) sexual abuse dynamics and sexual abuse sequelae; (3) strategies for coping with sexual abuse sequelae; (4) strategies for improving behavioral and emotional adjustment; (5) strategies for reducing the number of failed placements; (6) creating a set of specially trained foster parents for sexually abused children; and (7) building a support network among foster parents. Improvements in foster parents' knowledge of child development and recognition of problematic behaviors have been noted with interventions as simple and time-efficient as a quarterly newsletter that provides relevant information about foster care, child maltreatment, and parenting (Rich, 1996). More extensive approaches have demonstrated even more far-reaching effects. Treacy and Fisher (1993) described a five-session (10-hour) program that emphasized five steps for coping with foster children's behavioral problems: (1) observing the children's behavior; (2) determining whether the behavior is normal, atypical, or due to past trauma; (3) considering what the children might be communicating through their behavior; (4) formulating effective parental messages for the children; and (5) setting appropriate limits and using effective discipline strategies. A follow-up evaluation indicated good satisfaction with the program, increased knowledge of sexual development, and increased comfort in coping with problems associated with past sexual abuse. The foster parents also reported feeling more competent and more satisfied in their relationships with their sexually abused foster children.

Barth et al. (1994) reported similar results with a 10-session psychoeducational group program. They highlighted two practicalities that appeared to enhance group attendance: child care and travel expenses. Although Barth et al. (1994) described evidence of foster parents' satisfaction, no changes were found in the children's adjustment. However, given the duration and intensity of the training sessions, significant changes on the outcome measure, the Child Behavior Checklist, were unlikely.

Summary of Tertiary Prevention and Care Interventions

Research has indicated two symptom areas relatively prevalent among sexually abused children: PTSD and sexuality problems. Recent theoretical advances suggest that children who experience repeated, long-term abuse by a family member may show additional problems, such as depression and learned helplessness, dissociative tendencies, and passive rather than active coping styles. Treatment outcome research with sexually abused children has presented many methodological challenges; however, recent studies by Deblinger et al. (1996) and Cohen and Mannarino (1996b) represent remarkable methodological advances. These include (1) selection of participants with clinically significant symptomatology in the areas addressed by the interventions; (2) assessment strategies that documented abuse-specific symptoms; and (3) random assignment to an appropriate comparison group that controlled for the passage of time and therapeutic attention. Deblinger et al. (1996) used an excellent design for demonstrating the effectiveness of parent- and child-based interventions. Both of these studies have demonstrated the effectiveness of abuse-specific interventions. The findings by Deblinger et al. (1996) indicate that child-based gradual exposure interventions may be most effective in reducing PTSD symptoms, whereas parent-based behavior management interventions may be most effective in reducing externalizing problems. Similar methodologically sound research programs are needed to evaluate treatment programs that address other abuse-related sequelae, such as sexuality problems (eroticization, inappropriate sexual play, and molesting of other children) and Type II PTSD symptoms (dissociation, depression, learned helplessness, and passive/avoidant coping). Additional treatment research is needed to address mediators of sexual abuse sequelae, including family and social support and attributional issues (Dalenberg & Jacobs, 1994).

FUTURE DIRECTIONS

In many ways, child protection has become one of the most significant social movements of the 20th century, fueled by changes in women's roles in our culture and by an increasing professionalism among those who work with children and families (Finkelhor, 1996). Finkelhor (1996), noting that all social movements go through stages of development, described the child protection movement as in a transition from its initial stage of gaining public attention and acceptance to a second stage of increasing institutionalization and growing recognition of the need for accountability. The recent flood of interest in empirically validating prevention and intervention programs reflects this transitional stage. Our current knowledge base points the way toward areas where prevention and intervention programs can be improved; in addition, many issues have yet to be explored. These are highlighted below.

Despite current prevention efforts, approximately 70% of sexual abuse goes undetected (Finkelhor, 1994), and approximately 24% of sexual abuse investigations go unconfirmed despite legitimate concerns that sexual abuse may have indeed happened (Jones & McGraw, 1987). Current prevention efforts have been instrumental in increasing the percentage of children who disclose abuse; nevertheless, our current programs fail to reach those children who are most seriously abused (i.e., children abused by family members over long periods of time; Sas et al., 1995). It is also possible that some investigations fail to elicit detailed disclosures, despite what appear to be "state-of-the-art" interview procedures (see Wolfe & Birt, 1997, for a review). Many children fail to disclose abuse because they are concerned about the effects of disclosure. Children are often threatened with violence toward them or toward loved ones if they tell; they are also often led to believe that they will not be believed, that they will go to jail or foster care, or that people will think bad things about them. Most prevention programs do not teach children about the role of child protective services and the process that occurs following disclosure of sexual abuse. Children may need to know that concerted efforts will be made

to assure their safety following abuse disclosure; moreover, they may need to be educated about the lies that perpetrators may use to insure their silence (Conte et al., 1986). Such education may be a necessary component of investigative interviews, especially when suspected perpetrators are known to be violent with other family members (e.g., in cases with concurrent wife assault; Herman & Hirschman, 1981).

Even when children disclose abuse and abuse is confirmed, prosecution occurs in only 50% of cases. Sexual abuse cases involving children under the age of 6 are typically not prosecuted, leaving a large proportion of children particularly vulnerable. Even when prosecution is successful in obtaining convictions, it is questionable whether judicial sentencing results in jail or probation terms sufficient to protect the public, either by assuring adequate treatment for offenders or keeping offenders away from children. Initiatives to inform the public when known offenders live in neighborhoods (Pam Lychner's Sexual Offender Tracking and Identification Act, 1996; Megan's Law, 1994) and laws that keep known sexual predators incarcerated are important for reducing risks to children (*Kansas v. Hendricks,* 1997). Prevention efforts have primarily targeted children; however, future prevention efforts should identify offenders early and provide sufficient treatment or deterrents against further offending. Programs that identify young sex offenders and provide treatment and follow-up will be particularly important.

Once children disclose abuse, it is imperative that efforts be made to reduce the chronic stress that often follows. As discussed in this chapter, efforts to make courtrooms friendly to victims are very important. However, children face other stressors following disclosure. These include multiple investigative interviews by different community professionals (e.g., social workers, police, district attorneys, psychologists). Although videotaping children's disclosures may reduce the number of subsequent interviews (Myers, 1996), some have argued that videotaped investigative interviews can backfire during criminal prosecution (Stern, 1992). Children generally find parental separation difficult; however, issues of custody and access may be hotly debated in incest cases, and children may feel that their voices are unheard. Issues of proving (or failing to prove) the sexual abuse may interfere with making custody and access decisions that are in the "child's best interests." Appointment of a guardian *ad litem* to represent the child's interests may provide representation to the child when the parents' motives appear to be self-serving. When such disputes arise, it is often wise to obtain a custody and access evaluation by a professional who is familiar with sexual abuse and sex offenders.

Sexual abuse often does not occur within a vacuum. Children who have experienced sexual abuse often report histories of other forms of maltreatment, such as physical abuse, psychological maltreatment, neglect, and exposure to family violence (Wolfe et al., 1989). Our literature has only begun to address the issue of the effects of exposure to multiple forms of maltreatment, and has not touched the issue of treatment efficacy for children who have experienced multiple forms of maltreatment.

All of these issues point the way toward the need for further evaluations of prevention and intervention programs. As our prevention efforts become more explicit, the danger of creating undue anxiety and distrust grows. Such efforts run the risk of increasing the probability of false allegations; in addition, more explicit prevention efforts may run the risk of increasing false details within true disclosures, in that children may incorporate such information into their memories of abuse experiences. Community notification programs likewise increase the risk of undue anxiety for children and families, and of unnecessary stigmatization of sex offenders who have been successfully rehabilitated. Evaluation programs should continue to investigate not only the positive effects of prevention and intervention programs, but also possible iatrogenic effects.

Funding of child welfare and child protective services has remained relatively stable over the past several decades, while caseloads and responsibilities have burgeoned (Krugman, 1996). Perhaps with the maturation of the child protection movement, child welfare will receive the level of political and economic support currently dedicated to other social issues, such as health, crime, and education (Finkelhor, 1996).

ACKNOWLEDGMENTS

Preparation of this chapter was supported in part by grants from the Ontario Mental Health Foundation and the National Institutes of Health. I greatly appreciate Jill Jacobson's assistance with the literature review.

REFERENCES

Adams, J., McClellan, J., Douglass, D., McCurry, C., & Storch, M. (1995). Sexually inappropriate behaviours in seriously mentally ill children and adolescents. *Child Abuse and Neglect, 19,* 555–568.

Aldgate, J., Colton, M., Chate, D., & Heath, A. (1992). Educational attainment and stability in long term foster care. *Children and Society, 6,* 91–103.

Alexander, P. C. (1990). Interventions with incestuous families. In S. W. Henggeler & C. M. Borduin (Eds.), *Family therapy and beyond: A multisystemic approach to treating the behavior problems of children and adolescents* (pp. 324–344). Pacific Grove, CA: Brooks/Cole.

Altshuler, J., & Ruble, D. (1989). Developmental changes in children's awareness of strategies of coping with uncontrollable events. *Child Development, 60,* 1337–1349.

American Psychiatric Association. (1994). *Diagnostic and statistical manual of mental disorders* (4th ed.) Washington, DC: Author.

Azrin, N., & Nunn, R. G. (1973). Habit-reversal: A method of eliminating nervous habits and tics. *Behaviour Research and Therapy, 11,* 619–628.

Bagley, C. (1988). *Child sexual abuse in Canada: Further analyses of the 1983 national survey.* Ottawa: Health and Welfare Canada.

Band, E., & Weisz, J. (1988). How to feel better when it feels bad: Children's perspectives on coping with everyday stress. *Developmental Psychology, 24,* 247–253.

Barbaree, H. E., & Marshall, W. L. (1991). Treatment of the adult male child molester. In C. R. Bagley & R. J. Thomlison (Eds.), *Child sexual abuse: Critical perspectives in prevention, intervention, and treatment* (pp. 217–256). Toronto: Wall & Emerson.

Barth, R. P., Yeaton, J., & Winterfelt, N. (1994). Psychoeducational groups with foster parents of sexually abused children. *Child and Adolescent Social Work Journal, 11,* 405–424.

Basta, S., & Peterson, R. (1990). Perpetrator status and the personality characteristics of molested children. *Child Abuse and Neglect, 14,* 555–566.

Berliner, L. (1984). Some issue for prevention of child sexual assault. *Journal of Preventive Psychiatry, 2,* 427–431.

Berliner, L. (1997). Trauma-specific therapy for sexually-abused children. In D. Wolfe, R. McMahon, & R. Peters (Eds.), *Proceedings of the 27th Banff International Conference on Behavioral Sciences.* Thousand Oaks, CA: Sage.

Berliner, L., & Saunders, B. E. (1996). Treating fear and anxiety in sexually abused children: Results of a controlled 2-year follow-up study. *Child Maltreatment, 1,* 294–309.

Berliner, L., & Wheeler, J. R. (1987). Treating the effects of sexual abuse on children. *Journal of Interpersonal Violence, 2,* 415–434.

Berrick, J. D. (1988). Parental involvement in child abuse prevention training: What do they learn? *Child Abuse and Neglect, 12,* 543–553.

Beutler, L. E., Williams, R. E., & Zetzer, H. A. (1994). Efficacy of treatment for victims of child sexual abuse. *The Future of Children, 4, 156–175.*

Binder, R. L., & McNiel, D. E. (1987). Evaluation of a school-based sexual abuse prevention program: Cognitive and emotional effects. *Child Abuse and Neglect, 11,* 497–506.

Birt, J., DiMito, A., & Wolfe, V. V. (1995, March). *Origins of dissociation among sexually abused children.* Poster presented at the biennial meeting of the Society for Research on Child Development, Indianapolis, IN.

Birt, J., & Wolfe, V. V. (1995, November). *Relationship between sexual abuse and anger responses in children.* Poster presented at the annual meeting of the Association for Advancement of Behavior Therapy, Washington, DC.

Borkin, J., & Frank, L. (1986). Sexual abuse prevention for preschoolers: A pilot program. *Child Welfare, 55,* 75–82.

Boudewyns, P. A., & Hyer, L. (1990). Physiological response to combat memories and preliminary treatment outcome in Vietnam veteran PTSD patients treated with direct therapeutic exposure. *Behavior Therapy, 21,* 63–87.

Bowen, G. R., & Lambert, J. A. (1986). Systematic desensitization therapy with Posttraumatic Stress Disorder cases. In C.R. Figley (Ed.). *Trauma and its wake (*Vol. 2, pp. 280–291). New York: Brunner/Mazel.

Boyer, D., & Fine, D. (1991). Sexual abuse as a factor in adolescent pregnancy and child maltreatment. *Family Planning Perspectives, 24,* 4–11.

Brant, E. F., King, C. A., Olson, E., Ghaziuddin, N., & Naylor, M. (1996). Depressed adolescents with a history of sexual abuse: Diagnostic comorbidity and suicidality. *Journal of the American Academy of Child and Adolescent Psychiatry, 34,* 34–41.

Brown, L. K., Kessel, S. M., Lourie, K. J., Ford, H. H., & Lipsitt, L. P. (1997). Influence of sexual abuse on HIV-related attitudes and behaviors in adolescent psychiatry inpatients. *Journal of the American Academy of Child and Adolescent Psychiatry, 35,* 316–322.

Bryant, S. L., & Range, L. M. (1996). Suicidality in college women who report multiple versus single types of maltreatment by parents: A brief report. *Journal of Child Sexual Abuse, 4,* 87–94.

Bulkley, J. (1982). *Recommendations for improving legal intervention in intrafamilial sexual abuse cases.* Washington, DC: American Bar Association, Young Lawyers Division.

Bulkley, J. (1988). Legal proceedings, reforms, and emerging issues in child sexual abuse cases. *Behavioral Sciences and the Law, 6,* 153–180.

California Attorney General's Office. (1988). *California Child Victim Witness Judicial Advisory Committee: final report.* Sacramento: Author.

Canadian Department of Justice. (1992). *Kids in court in the Northwest Territories.* Ottawa: Author.

Cantos, A. L., Gries, L. T., & Slis, V. (1996). Correlates of therapy referral in foster children. *Child Abuse and Neglect, 20,* 921–931.

Cantos, A. L., Gries, L. T., & Slis, V. (in press). Behavioral correlates of parental visiting during family foster care. *Child Welfare.*

Cashmore, J. (1992). *The use of closed circuit television for child witnesses in the ACT.* Sydney: Australian Law Reform Commission.

Ceci, S., & Bruck, M. (1993). Suggestibility of the child witness: An historical review and synthesis. *Psychological Bulletin, 113,* 403–439.

Charney, D. S., Deutch, A. Y., Southwick, S. M., & Krystal, J. H. (1995). Neural circuits and mechanisms of Post-Traumatic Stress Disorder. In M. J. Friedman, D. S. Charney, & A. Y. Deutch (Eds.), *Neurobiological and clinical consequences of stress: From normal adaptation to PTSD* (pp. 271–287). Philadelphia: Lippincott–Raven.

Cohen, J. A., & Mannarino, A. P. (1996a). A treatment outcome study for sexually abused preschooler children: Initial findings. *Journal of the American Academy of Child and Adolescent Psychiatry, 35,* 42–50.

Cohen, J. A., & Mannarino, A. P. (1996b). Factors that mediate treatment outcome of sexually abused preschool children. *Journal of the American Academy of Child and Adolescent Psychiatry, 34,* 1402–1410.

Conte, J., Rosen, C., & Saperstein, L. (1986). An analysis of program to prevent the sexual victimization of children. *Journal of Primary Prevention, 6,* 141–155.

Conte, J. R., Rosen, C., Saperstein, L., & Shermack, R. (1985). An evaluation of a program to prevent the sexual victimization of young children. *Child Abuse and Neglect, 9,* 319–328.

Conte, J., & Schuerman, J. (1987). The effects of sexual abuse on children: A multidimensional view. *Journal of Interpersonal Violence, 2,* 380–390.

Coons, P. M. (1986). Child abuse and Multiple Personality Disorder: Review of the literature and suggestions for treatment. *Child Abuse and Neglect, 10,* 455–462.

Coons, P. M., Bowman, E. S., & Milstein, V. (1988). Multiple Personality Disorder: A clinical investigation of 50 cases. *Journal of Nervous and Mental Disease, 176,* 519–527.

Coons, P. M., Bowman, E. S., Pellow, T. A., & Schneider, P. (1989). Post-traumatic aspects of treatment of victims of sexual abuse and incest. *Psychiatric Clinics of North America, 12,* 325–335.

Coy v. Iowa, 108 S. Ct. 2798, 101 L. Ed. 2d 857; 56 U.S.L.W. 4931 (1988).

Crittenden, P. A. (1996). Research on maltreating families: Implications for intervention. In J. Briere, L. Berliner, J. Bulkley, C. Jenny, & T. Reid (Eds.), *The APSAC handbook on child maltreatment* (pp. 158–174). Thousand Oaks, CA: Sage.

Cunningham, C., & MacFarlane, K. (1991). *When children molest children: Group treatment strategies for young sexual abusers.* Orwell, VT: Safer Society Press.

Dalenberg, C. J., & Jacobs, D. A. (1994). Attributional analyses of child sexual abuse episodes: Empirical and clinical issues. *Journal of Child Sexual Abuse, 3,* 37–50.

Davidson, J. R. T., & van der Kolk, B. A. (1996). The psychopharmacological treatment of Posttraumatic Stress Disorder. In B. A. van der Kolk, A. C. McFarlane, & L. Weisaeth (Eds.), *Traumatic stress: The effects of overwhelming experience on mind, body, and society* (pp. 510–524). New York: Guilford Press.

Davies, G., & Noon, E. (1991). *An evaluation of the Live Link for child witnesses.* London: Home Office.

Davies, G., & Westcott, H. (1995). The child witness in the courtroom: Empowerment or protection? In M. S. Zaragoza, J. R. Graham, G. C. N. Hall, R. Hirschman, & Y. S. Ben-Porath (Eds.), *Memory and testimony in the child witness* (pp. 199–213). Thousand Oaks, CA: Sage.

Davis, N., & Sparks, T. (1988). *Therapeutic stories to heal children* (rev. ed.). Oxon Hill, MD: Psychological Associates.

DeYoung, M. (1994). Women as mothers and wives in paternally incestuous families: Coping with role conflict. *Child Abuse and Neglect, 18,* 73–83.

Deblinger, E., Hathaway, C. R., Lippman, J., & Steer, R. (1993). Psychosocial characteristics and correlates of symptom distress in nonoffending mothers of sexually abused children. *Journal of Interpersonal Violence, 8,* 155–168.

Deblinger, E., & Heflin, A. H. (1996). *Treating sexually abused children and their nonoffending parents: A cognitive-behavioral approach.* Thousand Oaks, CA: Sage.

Deblinger, E., Lippmann, J., & Steer, R. (1996). Sexually abused children suffering posttraumatic stress Symptoms: Initial treatment outcome findings, *Child Maltreatment, 1,* 310–321.

DiLillo, D. K., Long, P. J., & Russell, L. M. (1994). Childhood coping strategies of intrafamilial and extrafamilial female sexual abuse victims. *Journal of Child Sexual Abuse, 3,* 45–65.

DiSavino, P., Turk, E., Massie, E. D., Riggs, D. S., Penkower, D. S., Molnar, C., & Foa, E. B. (1993, November). *The content of traumatic memories: Evaluating treatment efficacy by analysis of verbatim description of the rape scene.* Paper presented at the 27th Annual Meeting of the Association for Advancement of Behavior Therapy, Atlanta, GA.

Doelling, J. L., & Johnson, J. H. (1990). Predicting success in foster placement: The contribution of parent–child temperament characteristics. *American Journal of Orthopsychiatry, 60,* 585–593.

Edwall, G., Hoffman, A., & Harrison, P. (1989). Psychological correlates of sexual abuse in adolescent girls in chemical dependency treatment. *Adolescence, 24,* 279–289.

Elrod, J. M., & Rubin, R. H. (1993). Parental involvement in sexual abuse prevention education. *Child Abuse and Neglect, 17,* 527–538.

Elwell, M. E., & Ephross, P. H. (1987). Initial reactions of sexually abused children. *Social Casework, 68,* 109–116.

Eth, S., & Pynoos, R. S. (1985). Psychiatric interventions with children traumatized by violence. In E. Benedek & D. Schetky (Eds.), *Emerging issues in child psychiatry and the law* (pp. 285–309). New York: Norton.

Everson, M. D., Hunter, W. M., Runyan, D. K., Edelsohn, G. A., & Coulter, M. L. (1989). Maternal support following disclosure of incest. *American Journal of Orthopsychiatry, 59,* 197–207.

Faber, A., & Mazlish, E. (1980). *How to talk so kids will listen and listen so kids will talk.* New York: Avon.

Famularo, R., Kinscherff, R., & Fenton, T. (1988). Propranolol treatment for childhood Posttraumatic Stress Disorder, Acute Type. *American Journal of Diseases of Children, 142,* 1244–1247.

Famularo, R., Kinscherff, R., & Fenton, T. (1990). Symptom differences in acute and chronic presentation of childhood Post-Traumatic Stress Disorder. *Child Abuse and Neglect, 14,* 349–444.

Finkelhor, D. (1979). *Sexually victimized children.* New York: Free Press.

Finkelhor, D. (1983). Removing the child—prosecuting the offender in cases of sexual abuse: Evidence from the National Reporting System for Child Abuse and Neglect. *Child Abuse and Neglect, 7,* 195–205.

Finkelhor, D. (1986). Prevention: A review of programs and research. In D. Finkelhor (Ed.), *A sourcebook on child sexual abuse* (pp. 224–254). Beverly Hills, CA: Sage.

Finkelhor, D. (1990). Early and long-term effects of child sexual abuse: An update. *Professional Psychology: Rearch and Practice, 21,* 325–330.

Finkelhor, D. (1994). Current information on the scope and nature of child sexual abuse. *The Future of Children, 4,* 31–53.

Finkelhor, D. (1996). Introduction. In J. Briere, L. Berliner, J. A. Bulkley, C. Jenny, & T. Reid (Eds.), *The APSAC handbook on child maltreatment* (pp. ix–xiii). Thousand Oaks, CA: Sage.

Finkelhor, D., & Berliner, L. (1995). Research on the treatment of sexually abused children: A review of recommendations. *Journal of the American Academy of Child and Adolescent Psychiatry, 34,* 1408–1423.

Finkelhor, D., & Dziuba-Leatherman, J. (1994). The victimization of children: A national survey. *Pediatrics, 94,* 413–420.

Finkelhor, D., & Dziuba-Leatherman, J. (1995). Victimization prevention programs: A national survey of children's exposure and reactions. *Child Abuse and Neglect, 19,* 129–140.

Finkelhor, D., Gomes-Schwartz, B., & Horowitz, J. (1984). Professionals' responses. In D. Finkelhor (Ed.), *Child sexual abuse: New theory and research* (pp. 200–220). New York: Free Press.

Finkelhor, D., Hotaling, G., Lewis, I. A., & Smith, C. (1990). Sexual abuse in a national survey of adult men and women: Prevalence, characteristics, and risk factors. *Child Abuse and Neglect, 14,* 19–28.

Foa, E. B., & Riggs, D. S. (1993). Posttraumatic Stress Disorder in rape victims. In M. B. Riba & A. Tasman (Eds.), *American Psychiatric Press review of psychiatry,* (vol. 12, pp. 273–303). Washington, DC: American Psychiatric Press.

Foa, E. B., Steketee, G., & Rothbaum, B. O. (1989). Behavioral/cognitive conceptualizations of Post-Traumatic Stress Disorder. *Behavior Therapy, 20,* 155–176.

Foy, D. W., Sipprelle, R. C., Rueger, D. G., & Caroll, E. M. (1984). Etiology of Posttraumatic Stress Disorder in Vietnam veterans: Analysis of premilitary, military, and combat exposure influences. *Journal of Consulting and Clinical Psychology, 52,* 79–87.

Fraser, P. (1985). *Pornography and prostitution in Canada.* Ottawa: Government of Canada.

Friedrich, W. N. (1990). *Psychotherapy of sexually abused children and their families.* New York: Norton.

Friedrich, W. N. (1995). *Psychotherapy with sexually abused boys: An integrated approach.* Thousand Oaks, CA: Sage.

Friedrich, W. N. (1996). An integrated model of psychotherapy for abused children. In J. Briere, L. Berliner, J. Bulkley, C. Jenny, & T. Reid (Eds.), *The APSAC handbook on child maltreatment* (pp. 104–118). Thousand Oaks, CA: Sage.

Friedrich, W. N., Grambsch, P., Broughton, D., Kuiper, J., & Beilke, R. L. (1991). Normative sexual behaviour in children. *Pediatrics, 88,* 456–464.

Friedrich, W. N., Jaworski, T. M., Hexschl, J. E., & Bengston, B. S. (1997). Dissociative and sexual behaviours in children and adolescents with sexual abuse and psychiatric histories. *Journal of Interpersonal Violence. 12,* 155–171.

Friedrich, W. N., & Luecke, W. J. (1988). Young school-age sexually aggressive children. *Professional Psychology: Research and Practice, 19,* 155–164.

Friedrich, W. N., Urquiza, A. J., & Beilke, R. L. (1986). Behavior problems in sexually abused young children. *Journal of Pediatric Psychology, 11,* 47–57.

Fryer, G. E., Kraizer, S. K., & Miyoshi, T. (1987a). Measuring children's retention of skills to resist stranger abduction: Use of the simulation technique. *Child Abuse and Neglect, 11,* 181–185.

Fryer, G. E., Kraizer, S. K., & Miyoshi, T. (1987b). Measuring actual reduction of risk to child abuse: A new approach. *Child Abuse and Neglect, 11,* 173–179.

Garbarino, J. (1987). Children's responses to a sexual abuse prevention program: A study of the Spider-man comic. *Child Abuse and Neglect, 11,* 143–148.

Garland, A. F., Landsverk, J. L., Hough, R. L., & Ellis-MacLeod, E. (1996). Type of maltreatment as a predictor of mental health service use for children in foster care. *Child Abuse and Neglect, 20,* 675–688.

Gershenson, H., Musick, J., Ruch-Ross, H., Magee, V., Rubino, K., & Rosenberg, D. (1989). The prevalence of coercive sexual experience among teenage mothers. *Journal of Interpersonal Violence, 4,* 204–219.

Giarretto, H. (1982). A comprehensive child sexual abuse treatment program. *Child Abuse and Neglect, 6,* 263–278.

Gil, E. (1991). *The healing power of play: Working with abused children.* New York: Guilford Press.

Glod, C. A., & Teicher, M. H. (1996). Relationship between early abuse, Posttraumatic Stress Disorder, and activity levels in prepubertal children. *Journal of the American Academy of Child and Adolescent Psychiatry, 34,* 1384–1393.

Goldstein, J., Freud, A., & Solnit, A. J. (1979). *Before the best interests of the child.* New York: Free Press.

Goodman, G. S., Bottoms, B., Shaver, P. R., & Quas, J. (March, 1995). *Factors affecting children's susceptibility versus resistance to false memory.* Paper presented at the biennial meeting of the Society for Research in Child Development, Indianapolis, IN.

Goodman, G. S., Hirschman, J. E., Hepps, D., & Rudy, L. (1991). Children's memory for stressful events. *Merrill–Palmer Quarterly, 37,* 109–158.

Goodman, G. S., Pyle-Taub, E. P., Jones, D. P. H., England, P., Port, L. K., Rudy, L., & Prado, L. (1992). The effects of criminal court testimony on child assault victims. *Monographs of the Society for Research in Child Development, 57,* 1–163.

Gordon, M. (1987). The family environment of sexual abuse: A comparison of natal and stepfather abuse. *Child Abuse and Neglect, 13,* 121–130.

Gordon, M. (1990). Males and females as victims of childhood sexual abuse: An examination of the gender effect. *Journal of Family Violence, 5,* 321–332.

Gordon, M. A. (1992). Recent Supreme Court rulings on child testimony in sexual abuse cases. *Journal of Child Sexual Abuse, 1,* 61–73.

Halfon, N., Berkowitz, G., & Klee, L. (1992). Mental health service utilization by children in foster care in California. *Pediatrics, 89,* 1238–1244.

Hamilton, L. (1997). *Contact between sexually abused children and their incestuous fathers: Implications for child post-disclosure adjustment.* Senior honors thesis, University of Western Ontario, London, Ontario, Canada.

Harmon, R. J., & Riggs, P. D. (1997). Clonidine for Posttraumatic Stress Disorder in preschool children. *Journal of the American Academy of Child and Adolescent Psychiatry, 35,* 1247–1249.

Harvey, P., Forehand, R., Brown, C., & Holmes, T. (1988). The prevention of sexual abuse: Examination of the effectiveness of a program with kinder-garten-age children. *Behavior Therapy, 19,* 429–435.

Herman, J., & Hirschman, L. (1981). Families at risk for father-daughter incest. *American Journal of Psychiatry, 138,* 967–970.

Hill, P., & Hill, S. (1987). Videotaping children's testimony: An empirical view. *Michigan Law Review, 85,* 809–833.

Holmes, M. R., & St. Lawrence, J. S. (1983). Treatment of rape-induced trauma: Proposed behavioral conceptualization and review of the literature. *Clinical Psychology Review, 2,* 387–408.

Horowitz, M. J. (1993). Stress response syndrome: A review of traumatic stress and adjustment disorders. In J. P. Wilson & B. Raphael (Eds.), *International handbook of traumatic stress syndromes* (pp. 11–60). New York: Plenum Press.

Horton, C. B., Hogan, S., & Cruise, T. K. (1995, March). *Precursors to sexual offending: Group findings and a case studies of sexually reactive children and children who molest.* Paper presented at the biennial meeting of the Society for Research in Child Development, Indianapolis, IN.

Hubert, N., Jay, S., Saltoun, M., & Hayes, M. (1988). Approach-avoidance and distress in children undergoing preparation for painful medical procedures. *Journal of Clinical Child Psychology, 17,* 194–202.

Hunter, W. M., Coulter, M. L., Runyan, D. K., & Everson, M. D. (1990). Determinants of placement for sexually abused children. *Child Abuse and Neglect, 14,* 407–417.

Hyson, M. (1983). Going to the doctor: A developmental study of stress and coping. *Journal of Child Psychology and Psychiatry, 24,* 247–259.

Idaho vs. Wright, 110 S. Ct. 3139 (1990).

Inderbitzen-Pisaruk, H., Sawchuck, C. R., & Hoier, T. S. (1992). Behavioral characteristics of child victims of sexual abuse: A comparison study. *Journal of Clinical Child Psychology, 21,* 14–19.

James, B. (1989). *Treating traumatized children.* Lexington, MA: Lexington Books.

Janoff-Bulman, R. (1989). Assumptive worlds and the stress of traumatic events: Applications of the schema construct. *Social Cognition, 7,* 113–136.

Johnson, D. R. (1987). The role of the creative arts therapies in the diagnosis and treatment of psychological trauma. *The Arts in Psychotherapy, 14,* 7–13.

Johnson, B. K., & Kenkel, M. B. (1991). Stress, coping, and adjustment in female adolescent incest victims. *Child Abuse and Neglect, 15,* 293–305.

Johnson, T. C. (1988). Child perpetrators—children who molest other children: Preliminary findings. *Child Abuse and Neglect, 12,* 219–229.

Johnson, T. C. (1989). Female child perpetrators: Children who molest other children. *Child Abuse and Neglect, 13,* 571–585.

Johnson, T. C. (n.d.). *Let's talk about touching: A therapeutic game for sexualized children and chil-*

dren who molest (2nd ed.). (Available from the author at 1101 Fremont Avenue, Suite 104, South Pasadena, CA 91030)

Johnson, T. C., & Feldmeth, J. R. (1993). Sexual behaviors: A continuum In E. Gil & T. C. Johnson (Eds.), *Sexualized children: Assessment and treatment of sexualized children and children who molest* (pp. 41–52). Rockville, MD: Launch Press.

Joiner, T. E., & Wagner, K. D. (1995). Attributional style and depression in children and adolescents: A meta-analytic review. *Clinical Psychology Review, 15,* 777–798.

Jones, D., & McGraw, E. (1987). Reliable and fictitious accounts of sexual abuse to children. *Journal of Interpersonal Violence, 2,* 27–45.

Jumper, S. A. (1995). A meta-analysis of the relationship of child sexual abuse to adult psychological adjustment. *Child Abuse and Neglect, 19,* 715–728.

Kansas Hendricks, 1997 W.L. 338555 (June 23, 1997).

Katz, L. F., & Gottman, J. M. (1991). Marital discord and child outcomes: A social-psychophysiological approach. In J. Garber & K. A. Dodge (Eds.), *The development of emotion regulation and dysregulation* (pp. 129–155). New York: Cambridge University Press.

Keller, R. A., Cicchinelli, L. F., & Gardner, D. M. (1989). Characteristics of child sexual abuse treatment programs. *Child Abuse and Neglect, 13,* 361–368.

Kelly, S. J. (1990). Parental stress response to sexual abuse and ritualistic abuse of child in day-care centers. *Nursing Research, 39,* 25–29.

Kendall-Tackett, K. A., Williams, L. M., & Finkelhor, D. (1993). Impact of sexual abuse on children: A review and synthesis of recent empirical studies. *Psychological Bulletin, 113,* 164–180.

Kilpatrick, D. G., Veronen, L. J., & Resnick, P. (1979). Assessment of the aftermath of rape: Changing pattern of fear. *Journal of Behavioral Assessment, 1,* 133–148.

Kiser, L. J., Heston, J., Millsap, P. A., & Pruitt, D. B. (1991). Physical and sexual abuse in childhood: Relationship with Post-Traumatic Stress Disorder. *Journal of the American Academy of Child and Adolescent Psychiatry, 30,* 776–783.

Kleemeier, C., Webb, C., Hazzard, A., & Pohl, J. (1988). Child sexual abuse prevention: Evaluation of a teacher training model. *Child Abuse and Neglect, 12,* 555–561.

Kluft, R. P. (1985). Introduction: Multiple Personality Disorder in the 1980's. In R. P. Kluft (Ed.), *Childhood antecedents of multiple personality* (pp. xiii–xiv). Washington, DC: American Psychiatric Press.

Krugman, R. (1996). Epilogue. In J. Briere, L. Berliner, J. A. Bulkley, C. Jenny, & T. Reid (Eds.), *The APSAC handbook on child maltreatment* (pp. 420–422). Thousand Oaks, CA: Sage.

Kolko, D. J. (1988). Educational programs to promote awareness and prevention of child sexual victimization: A review and methodological critique. *Clinical Psychology Review, 8,* 195–209.

Kolko, D. J., Moser, J., Litz, J., & Hughes, J. (1987). Promoting awareness and prevention of child sexual victimization using the red flag/green flag program: An evaluation with follow-up. *Journal of Family Violence, 2,* 11–35.

Koverola, C., Pound, J., Heger, A., & Lytle, C. (1993). Relationship of child sexual abuse to depression. *Child Abuse and Neglect, 17,* 390–400.

Lanktree, C. B., & Briere, J. (1995). Outcome of therapy for sexually abused children: A repeated measures study. *Child Abuse and Neglect, 19,* 1145–1156.

Lanktree, C. B., Briere, J., & Zaidi, L. Y. (1991). Incidence and impact of sexual abuse in a child outpatient sample: The role of direct inquiry. *Child Abuse and Neglect, 15,* 447–453.

Leifer, M., & Shapiro, J. P. (1995). Longitudinal study of the psychological effects of sexual abuse in African American girls in foster care and those who remain home. *Journal of Child Sexual Abuse, 4,* 27–44.

Leifer, M., Shapiro, J. P., & Kassem, L. (1993). The impact of maternal history and behavior upon foster placement and adjustment in sexually abused girls. *Child Abuse and Neglect, 17,* 755–766.

Leippe, M. R., Manion, A. P., & Romanczyk, A. (1992). Discernibility or discrimination?: Understanding jurors' reactions to accurate and inaccurate child and adult eyewitnesses. In G. S. Goodman & B. Bottoms (Eds.), *Child victims, child witnesses: Understanding and improving testimony* (pp. 169–202). New York: Guilford Press.

Liang, B., Bogat, G. A., & McGrath, M. P. (1993). Differential understanding of sexual abuse prevention concepts among preschoolers. *Child Abuse and Neglect, 17,* 641–650.

Lie, G., & McMurtry, S. L. (1991). Foster care for sexually abused children: A comparative study. *Child Abuse and Neglect, 15,* 111–121.

Ligezinska, M., Firestone, P., Manion, I. G., McIntyre, J., Ensom, R., & Wells, G. (1996). Children's emotional and behavioral reactions following disclosures of extrafamilial sexual abuse: Initial effects. *Child Abuse and Neglect, 20,* 111–125.

Lindblad, F., Gustafsson, P. A., Larsson, I., & Lundin, B. (1995). Preschoolers' sexual behavior at daycare centers: An epidemiological study. *Child Abuse and Neglect, 19,* 569–577.

Lipovsky, J. A. (1992). Assessment and treatment of Post-traumatic Stress Disorder in child survivors of sexual assault. In D. Foy (Ed.), *Treating PTSD* (pp. 113–141). New York: Guilford Press.

Lipovsky, J. A., Saunders, B. E., & Murphy, S. M. (1989). Depression, anxiety, and behaviour problems among victims of father-child sexual assault and non-abused siblings. *Journal of Interpersonal Violence, 4,* 452–468.

Lipovsky, J. A., & Stern, P. (1997). Preparing children for court: A multidisciplinary view. *Child Maltreatment, 2,* 150–163.

Lipovsky, J. A., Tidwell, R. P., Kilpatrick, D. G., Saunders, B. E., & Dawson, V. L. (1991, November). *Children as witnesses in criminal court: Is the process harmful?* Paper presented at the 25th Annual Meeting of the Association for Advancement of Behavior Therapy, New York.

Livingston, R., Lawson, L., & Jones, J. (1993). Predictors of self-reported psychopathology in children abused repeatedly by a parent. *Journal of the American Academy of Child and Adolescent Psychiatry, 32,* 948–953.

Love, L. C., Jackson, J. L., & Long, P. J. (1990, November). *Childhood sexual abuse: Correlates of active termination.* Poster presented at the 24th Annual Meeting of the Association for Advancement of Behavior Therapy, San Francisco.

Malinosky-Rummell, R. R., & Hoier, T. S. (1991). Validating measures of dissociation in sexually abused and nonabused children. *Behavioral Assessment, 13,* 341–357.

Manion, I. G., McIntyre, Firestone, P., Ligezinska, M., Ensom, R. & Wells, G. (1996). Secondary traumatization in parents following the disclosure of extrafamilial child sexual abuse: Initial effects. *Child Abuse and Neglect, 20,* 1095–1110.

Martone, M., Jaudes, P. K., & Cavins, M. K. (1996). Criminal prosecution of child sexual abuse cases . *Child Abuse and Neglect, 20,* 457–464.

Maryland v. Craig, 110 S. Ct. 3157; 47 Cr. L. 2258, U. S. Sup. Ct. (1990).

Mayle, P. (1995). *Where did I come from?* New York: Carol.

McClellan, J., McCurry, C., Ronnei, M., Adams, J., Eisner, A., & Storch, M. (1996). Age of onset of sexual abuse: Relationship to sexually inappropriate behaviors. *Journal of the American Academy of Child and Adolescent Psychiatry, 34,* 1375–1383.

McElroy, L. P. (1992). Early indicators of pathological dissociation in sexually abused children. *Child Abuse and Neglect, 16,* 833–846.

McLeer, S. V., Deblinger, E., Atkins, M. S., & Ralphe, D. (1988). Post-Traumatic Stress Disorder in sexually abused children. *Journal of the American Academy of Child and Adolescent Psychiatry, 27,* 650–654.

McLeer, S. V., Deblinger, E., Henry, D., & Orvaschel, H. (1992). Sexually abused children at high risk for Post-Traumatic Stress Disorder. *Journal of the American Academy of Child and Adolescent Psychiatry, 31,* 875–879.

Megan's Law, Pub. L. No. 104–145, 110 Stat. 1345 (1994).

Mennen, F. E., & Meadows, D. (1993). The relationship of sexual abuse to symptom levels in emotionally disturbed girls. *Child and Adolescent Social Work Journal, 10,* 319–328.

Merrick, M. V., Allen, B. M., & Crase, S. J. (1994). Variables associated with positive treatment outcomes for children surviving sexual abuse. *Journal of Child Sexual Abuse, 3,* 67–87.

Miller-Perrin, C. L., & Wurtele, S. K. (1986). The child sexual abuse prevention movement: A critical analysis of primary and secondary approaches. *Clinical Psychology Review, 8,* 313–329.

Miltenberger, R. G., & Thiesse-Duffy, E. (1988). Evaluation of home-based programs for teaching personal safety skills to children. *Journal of Applied Behavior Analysis, 21,* 81–87.

Morrow, K. B. (1991). Attributions of female adolescent incest victims regarding their molestation. *Child Abuse and Neglect, 15,* 477–483.

Moston, S., & Engelberg, T. (1992). The effects of social support on children's eyewitness testimony. *Applied Cognitive Psychology, 6,* 61–75.

Mowrer, O. H. (1960). *Learning theory and behavior.* New York: Wiley.

Myers, J. E. (1996). Taint hearings to attack investigative interviews: A further assault on children's credibility. *Child Maltreatment, 1,* 213–222.

National Film Board of Canada (Producer). (1992). *Good things can still happen* [Film]. Montreal: Producer.

Nelki, J. S., & Waters, J. (1988). A group for sexually abused young children: Unravelling the web. *Child Abuse and Neglect, 13,* 369–377.

Nemerofsky, A. G., Carran, D. T., & Rosenberg, L. A. (1994). Age variation in performance among preschool children in a sexual abuse prevention program. *Journal of Child Sexual Abuse, 3,* 85–102.

Neumann, D. A., Hauskamp, B. M., Pollock, V. E., & Briere, J. (1996). The long-term sequelae of childhood sexual abuse in women: A meta-analytic review. *Child Maltreatment, 1,* 6–16.

Oates, R. K., O'Toole, B. I., Lynch, D. L., Stern, A., & Cooney, G. (1994). Stability and change in outcomes for sexually abused children. *Journal of the American Academy of Child and Adolescent Psychiatry, 33,* 945–953.

O'Connell, M. A. (1986). Reuniting incest offenders with their families. *Journal of Interpersonal Violence, 1,* 374–386.

O'Donohue, W. T., Geer, J. H., & Elliot, A. N. (1992). The primary prevention of child sexual abuse. In W. T. O'Donohue & J. H. Geer (Eds.), *The sexual abuse of children: Clinical issues* (Vol. 2). Hillsdale: Erlbaum.

Ogata, S. M., Silk, K. R., Goodrich, S., Lohr, N. E., Westen, D., & Hill, E. (1990). Childhood sexual and physical abuse in adult patients with Borderline Personality Disorder. *American Journal of Psychiatry, 147,* 1008–1013.

Oldfield, D., Hays, B. J., & Megel, M. E. (1996). Evaluation of the effectiveness of Project Trust: An elementary school-based victimization prevention strategy. *Child Abuse and Neglect, 20,* 821–832.

Ontario Ministry of the Attorney General. (1989). *What's my job in court?* Toronto: Author.

Pam Lychner Sexual Offender Tracking and Identification Act, Pub. L. No. 104–236, 110 Stat. 3093. (1996).

Perry, B. D., Pollard, R. A., Blakley, T. L., Baker, W. L., & Vigilante, D. (1995). Childhood trauma, the neurobiology of adaptation, and use-dependent development of the brain: How states become traits. *Infant Mental Health Journal, 16,* 271–291.

Peters, D. (1990). Confrontational stress and children's testimony: Some experimental findings. In S. Ceci (Chair), *Do children lie? Narrowing the uncertainties.* Symposium conducted at the meeting of the American Psychology and Law Society, Williamsburg, VA.

Peterson, C., & Seligman, M. E. P. (1983). Learned helplessness and victimization. *Journal of Social Issues, 39,* 103–106.

Plummer, C. (1984, April). *Research on prevention: What school programs teach children.* Paper presented at the Third National Conference on Sexual Victimization, Washington, DC. (Available from the author, P. O. Box 421, Kalamazoo, M. 49004–0421)

Pirrelo, V. E. (1994). *Post-traumatic Stress Disorder in sexually abused children.* Unpublished master's thesis, North Carolina State University.

Poche, C., Yoder, P., & Miltenberger, R. (1988). Teaching self protection to children using television techniques. *Journal of Applied Behavior Analysis, 21,* 253–261.

Putnam, F. W. (1994). Dissociation and disturbances of self. In D. Cicchetti & S. L. Toth (Eds.). *Disorders and dysfunctions of the self* (pp. 251–266). Rochester, NY: University of Rochester Press.

Putnam, F. W., Helmers, K., Horowitz, L. A., & Trickett, P. K. (1995). Hypnotizability and dissociativity in sexually abused girls. *Child Abuse and Neglect, 19,* 645–656.

Rainbow House, Children's Resources Center. (1989) *Rainbow Game.* Warner Robins, GA: Author.

Rasmussen, L. A., Burton, J. E., & Christopherson, B. J. (1992). Precursors to offending and the trauma outcome process in sexually reactive children. *Journal of Child Sexual Abuse, 1,* 33–48.

Rasmussen, L. A., & Cunningham, C. (1995). Focused play therapy and nondirective play therapy: Can they be integrated? *Journal of Child Sexual Abuse, 4,* 1–20.

Rich, H. (1996). The effects of a health newsletter for foster parents on their perceptions of the behavior and development of foster children. *Child Abuse and Neglect, 20,* 437–445.

Roesler, T. A., & Wind, T. W. (1994). Telling the secret: Adult women describe their disclosures of incest. *Journal of Interpersonal Violence, 9,* 327–338.

Rohsenow, D., Corbett, R., & Devine, D. (1988). Molested as children: A hidden contribution to substance abuse? *Journal of Substance Abuse Treatment, 5,* 13–18.

Rothbaum, B. O., & Foa, E. B. (1996). Cognitive-behavioral therapy for Posttraumatic Stress Disorder. In B. A. van der Kolk, A. C. McFarlane, & L. Weisaeth (Eds.), *Traumatic stress: The effects of overwhelming experience on mind, body, and society* (pp. 491–509). New York: Guilford Press.

Runyan, D., Everson, M., Edelson, G., Hunter, M., & Coulter, M. L. (1988). Impact of legal interventions on sexually abused children. *Journal of Pediatrics, 113*, 647–653.

Runyan, D. K., & Gould, C. L. (1985a). Foster care for child maltreatment: I. Impact on delinquent behavior. *Pediatrics, 75*, 562–568.

Runyan, D. K., & Gould, C. L. (1985b). Foster care for child maltreatment: II. Impact on school performance. *Pediatrics, 76*, 848–854.

Russell, D. E. H. (1983). The incidence and prevalence of intrafamilial and extrafamilial sexual abuse of female children. *Child Abuse and Neglect, 7*, 133–146.

Russell, D. E. H. (1984). The prevalence and seriousness of incestuous abuse: Stepfathers vs. biological fathers. *Child Abuse and Neglect, 8*, 15–22.

Sansonnet-Hayden, H., Haley, G., Marriage, K., & Fine, S. (1987). Sexual abuse and psychopathology in hospitalized adolescents. *Journal of the American Academy of Child and Adolescent Psychiatry, 26*, 753–757.

Sas, L. D., Cunningham, A. H., Hurley, P., Dick, T., & Farnsworth, A. (1995). *Tipping the balance to tell the secret. Public discovery of child sexual abuse.* London, Ontario, Canada: London Family Court Clinic.

Sas, L., Hurley, P., Austin, G., & Wolfe, D. (1991). *Reducing system-induced trauma for child sexual abuse victims through court preparation, assessment, and follow-up.* Final report to the National Welfare Grants Division, Health and Welfare Canada, Project No. 4555-1-125.

Sas, L., Hurley, P., Hatch, A., Malla, S., & Dick, T. (1993). *Three years after the verdict: A longitudinal study of the social and psychology adjustment of child witnesses referred to the Child Witness Project.* London, Ontario, Canada: London Family Court Clinic.

Saslawsky, D. A., & Wurtele, S. K. (1986). Educating children about sexual abuse: Implications for pediatric intervention and possible prevention. *Journal of Pediatric Psychology, 11*, 235–245.

Saunders, B. E., Kilpatrick, D. G., Resnick, H. S., Hanson, R. A., & Lipovsky, J. A. (1992). *Epidemiological characteristics of child sexual abuse: Results from Wave II of the National Women's Study.* Paper presented at the San Diego Conference on Responding to Child Maltreatment, San Diego, CA.

Saywitz, K. J. (1995). Improving children's testimony. In M. S. Zaragoza, J. R. Graham, G. C. N. Hall, R. Hirschman, & Y. S. Ben-Porath (Eds.), *Memory and testimony in the child witness*. Thousand Oaks, CA: Sage.

Saywitz, K.J., Goodman, G., Nicholas, E., & Moan, S. (1991). Children's memories of a physical examination involving genital touch: Implications for reports of child sexual abuse. *Journal of Consulting and Clinical Psychology, 59*, 682–691.

Saywitz, K. J., & Moan-Hardie, S. (1994). Reducing the potential for distortion of childhood memories. *Consciousness and Cognition, 3*, 257–293.

Saywitz, K. J., & Nathanson, R. (1993). Children's testimony and their perceptions of stress in and out of the courtroom. *Child Abuse and Neglect, 17*, 613–622.

Saywitz, K. J., & Snyder, L. (1996). Narrative elaboration: Test of a new procedure for questioning children. *Journal of Consulting and Clinical Psychology, 64*, 1347–1357.

Saywitz, K. J., Snyder, L., & Lamphear, V. (1996). Helping children tell what happened: A follow-up study of the narrative elaboration procedure. *Child Maltreatment, 1*, 200–212.

Seligman, M., Peterson, C., Kaslow, N., Tanenbaum, R., Alloy, L., & Abramson, L. (1984). Attributional style and depressive symptoms among children. *Journal of Abnormal Psychology, 93*, 235–238.

Shapiro, F. (1995). *Eye movement desensitization and reprocessing: Basic principles, protocols, and procedures*. New York: Guilford Press.

Sigurdson, E., Strang, M., & Doig, T. (1987). What do children know about preventing sexual assault? How can their awareness be increased? *Canadian Journal of Psychiatry, 32*, 551–557.

Silver, R. L., Boon, C., & Stones, M. H. (1983). Searching for meaning in misfortune: Making sense of incest. *Journal of Social Issues, 39*, 81–102.

Silver, R. L., & Wortman, C. (1980). Coping with undesirable life events. In J. Garber & M. Seligman (Eds.), *Human helplessness: Theory and applications* (pp. 279–340). New York: Academic Press.

Sisterman Keeney, K., Amacher, E., & Kastanaskis, J. (1992). The court prep group: A vital part of the court process. In H. Dent & R. Flin (Eds.), *Children as witnesses* (pp. 201–210). Chichester, England: Wiley.

Southwick, S. M., Yehuda, R., & Morgan, C. A. (1995). Clinical studies of neurotransmitter alterations in Post-Traumatic Stress Disorder. In M. J. Friedman, D. S. Charney, & A. Y. Deutch (Eds.), *Neurobiological and clinical consequences of stress: From normal adaptation to Post-Traumatic Stress Disorder* (pp. 335–349). Philadelphia: Lippincott–Raven.

Spectrum South Productions. (1989). *Taking the stand for kids who testify.* (Available from Victim Witness Assistance Program of the 13th Circuit Solicitors Office, Suite 101, Courthouse Annex, Greenville, SC 29601)

Spirito, A., Stark, L., & Williams, C. (1988). Development of a brief coping checklist for use with pediatric populations. *Journal of Pediatric Psychology, 13*, 555–574.

Steiner, H., Garcia, I. G., & Matthews, Z. (1997). Posttraumatic Stress Disorder in incarcerated juvenile delinquents. *Journal of the American Academy of Child and Adolescent Psychiatry, 35,* 357–365.

Stephens, M., Grinnell, R. M., Thomlison, B., & Krysik, J. (1991). Child sexual abuse and police disposition: A Canadian study. *Journal of Child and Youth Care: Special Issue,* 53–63.

Stern, P. (1992). Videotaping child interviews: A detriment to an accurate determination of guilt. *Journal of Interpersonal Violence, 7,* 277–288.

Stern, P. (1993). Preparing a child for court. *Violence Update, 4,* 5–6, 11.

Stilwell, S. L., Lutzker, J. R., & Greene, B. F. (1988). Evaluation of a sexual abuse prevention program for preschoolers. *Journal of Family Violence, 13,* 269–281.

Straus, R. B. (1995). Supervised visitation and family violence. *Family Law Quarterly, 29,* 229–252.

Swenson, C. C., & Hanson, R. F. (1998). Sexual abuse of children: Assessment, research, and treatment. In J. R. Lutzker (Ed.), *Handbook on research and treatment in child abuse and neglect* (pp. 475–499). New York: Plenum Press.

Swim, J., Borgida, E., & McCoy, K. (1992). Videotaped versus in-court witness testimony: Does protecting the child witness jeopardize due process. *Journal of Applied Social Psychology, 23,* 603–631.

Taska, L., & Feiring, C. (1995, November). *Children's adaptation to sexual abuse: The role of shame and attribution.* Poster presented at the 29th Annual Meeting of the Association for Advancement of Behavior Therapy, Washington, DC.

Tebbutt, J., Swanston, H., Oates, R. K., & O'Toole, B. I. (1997). Five years after child sexual abuse: Persisting dysfunction and problems of prediction. *Journal of the American Academy of Child and Adolescent Psychiatry, 35,* 330–339.

Terr, L. C. (1981). "Forbidden games": Post-traumatic child's play. *Journal of the American Academy of Child Psychiatry, 20,* 741–760.

Terr, L. C. (1987, May). *Severe stress and sudden shock—The connection.* Sam Hibbs Award Lecture presented at the annual convention of the American Psychiatric Association, Chicago.

Terr, L. (1991). Childhood traumas: An outline and overview. *American Journal of Psychiatry, 148,* 10–20.

Terr, L. (1997, August 25–29). *The long-term effects of childhood trauma.* Workshop presented at the Cape Cod Institute, Cape Cod, MA.

Tharinger, D. (1990). Impact of child sexual abuse on developing sexuality. *Professional Psychology: Research and Practice, 21,* 331–337.

Thompson, R. W., Authier, K., & Ruma, P. (1994). Behavior problems of sexually abused children in foster care: A preliminary study. *Journal of Child Sexual Abuse, 3,* 7–91.

Timnick, L. (1985, August 25). 22% in survey were child abuse victims. *Los Angeles Times,* pp. 1, 34.

Toby, A. E., Goodman, G. S., Batterman-Faunce, J. M., Orcutt, H. K., & Sachsenmaier, T. (1995). Balancing the rights of children and defendants: The effects of closed-circuit television on children's accuracy and jurors' perceptions. In M. S. Zaragoza, J. R. Graham, G. C. N. Hall, R. Hirschman, & Y. S. Ben-Porath (Eds.), *Memory and testimony in the child witness* (pp. 214–239). Thousand Oaks, CA: Sage.

Treacy, E. C., & Fisher, C. B. (1993). Foster parenting the sexually abused: A family life education program. *Journal of Child Sexual Abuse, 2,* 47–63.

Trupin, E. W., Tarico, V. S., Low, B. P., Jemelka, R., & McClellan, J. (1993). Children on child protective service caseloads: Prevalence and nature of serious emotional disturbance. *Child Abuse and Neglect, 17,* 345–355.

van der Kolk, B. A., McFarlane, A. C., & van der Hart, O. (1996). A general approach to treatment of Posttraumatic Stress Disorder. In B. A. van der Kolk, A. C. McFarlane, & L. Weisaeth (Eds.), *Traumatic stress: The effects of overwhelming experience on mind, body, and society* (pp. 417–440). New York: Guilford Press.

Wells, G. L., Tuttle, J. W., & Luus, C. A. E. (1989). The perceived credibility of child witnesses: What happens when they use their own words. In S. J. Ceci, D. F. Ross, & M. P. Toglia (Eds.), *Perspectives in children's testimony* (pp. 23–36). New York: Springer-Verlag.

Wells, R. D., McCann, J., Adams, J., Voris, J., & Ensign, J. (1995). Emotional, behavioural, and physical symptoms reported by parents of sexually abused, non-abused, and allegedly abused prepubescent females. *Child Abuse and Neglect, 19,* 155–164.

Whitcomb, D. (1992). *When the victim is a child* (2nd Ed.). Washington, DC: National Institute of Justice.

Whitcomb, D., Shapiro, E. R., & Stellwagen, L. D. (1985). *When the victim is a child: Issues for judges and prosecutors.* Washington, DC: National Institute of Justice.

Wolfe, D. A., MacPherson, T., Blount, R. L., & Wolfe, V. (1986). Evaluation of a brief intervention for educating school children in awareness of physical and sexual abuse. *Child Abuse and Neglect, 10,* 85–92.

Wolfe, D. A., Sas, L., & Wekerle, C. (1994). Factors associated with the development of Post Traumatic Stress Disorder among child victims of sexual abuse. *Child Abuse and Neglect, 18,* 37–50.

Wolfe, V. V. (1990b, November). *Type I and Type II PTSD: A conceptual framework for sexual abuse sequelae.* Paper presented at the 24th Annual Meeting of the Association for Advancement of Behavior Therapy, San Francisco.

Wolfe, V. V. (1991, November). *Does a history of child sexual abuse affect maternal responses to their child's abuse?* Paper presented at the 25th Annual Meeting of the Association for Advancement of Behavior Therapy, New York.

Wolfe, V. V. (1990a). Sexual abuse of children. In A. S. Bellack, M. Hersen, & A. E. Kazdin (Eds.), *International handbook of behavior modification and therapy* (2nd Ed., pp. 707–730). New York: Plenum Press.

Wolfe, V. V. (1993, March). *Attributional style and post-traumatic adjustment in sexually abused children.* Paper presented at the biennial convention of the Society for Research in Child Development, New Orleans.

Wolfe, V. V., & Birt, J. (1995). The psychological sequelae of child sexual abuse. In T. H. Ollendick & R. J. Prinz (Eds.), *Advances in clinical child psychology* (Vol. 17, pp. 233–263). New York: Plenum Press.

Wolfe, V. V., & Birt, J. (1997). Child sexual abuse. In E. Mash & L. Terdal (Eds.), Assessment of childhood disorders (3rd ed., pp. 569–623). New York: Guilford Press.

Wolfe, V. V., & Gentile, C. C. (1992). Psychological assessment of sexually abused children. In W. O'Donohue & J. H. Geer (Eds.) *The Sexual Abuse of Children: Clinical Issues, Volume 2* (pp. 143–187). New York: Lawrence Erlbaum.

Wolfe, V. V., Gentile, C. C., & Wolfe, D. A. (1989). The impact of sexual abuse on children: A PTSD formulation. *Behavior Therapy, 20*, 215–228.

Wolfe, V. V., Sas, L., & Wilson, S. K. (1987). Some issues in preparing sexually abused children for courtroom testimony. *The Behavior Therapist, 10*, 107–113.

Wolfe, V. V. & Wolfe, D. A. (1988). The sexually abused child. In E. Mash & L. Terdal (Eds.), *Behavioral assessment of childhood disorders* (2nd ed., pp. 670–714). New York: Guilford Press.

Wolkind, S., & Rutter, M. (1985). *Separation, loss, and family relationships: Child and adolescent psychiatry.* Oxford: Blackwell Scientific.

Wozencraft, T., Wagner, W., & Pellegrin, A. (1991). Depression and suicidal ideation in sexually abused children. *Child Abuse and Neglect, 15,* 505–511.

Wurtele, S. K. (1990). Teaching personal safety skills to four-year-old children: A behavioral approach. *Behavior Therapy, 21*, 25–32.

Wurtele, S. K. (1993). The role of maintaining telephone contact with parents during the teaching of a personal safety program. *Journal of Child Sexual Abuse, 2*, 65–82.

Wurtele, S. K., Currier, L. L., Gillispie, E. I., & Franklin, C. F. (1991). The efficacy of a parent-implemented program for teaching preschoolers body safety skills. *Behavior Therapy, 22*, 69–83.

Wurtele, S. K., Gillispie, E. I., Currier, L. L., & Franklin, C. F. (1992). A comparison of teachers vs. parents as instructors of a personal safety program for preschoolers. *Child Abuse and Neglect, 16*, 127–137.

Wurtele, S. K., Kast, L. C., Miller-Perrin, C. L., & Kondrick, P. A. (1989). A comparison of programs for teaching personal safety skills to preschoolers. *Journal of Consulting and Clinical Psychology, 57,* 505–511.

Wurtele, S. K., Kast, L. C., & Melzer, A. M. (1992). Sexual abuse prevention education for young children: A comparison of teachers and parents as instructors. *Child Abuse and Neglect, 16*, 865–876.

Wurtele, S. K., Kvaternick, M., & Franklin, C. F. (1992). Sexual abuse prevention for preschoolers: A survey of parents' behaviors, attitudes, and beliefs. *Journal of Child Sexual Abuse, 1*, 113–128. 505–511.

Wurtele, S. K., Marrs, S. R., & Miller-Perrin, C. L. (1987). Practice makes perfect?: The role of participant modelling in sexual abuse prevention programs. *Journal of Consulting and Clinical Psychology, 55*, 599–602.

Wurtele, S. K., & Miller-Perrin, C. L. (1987). An evaluation of side effects associated with participation in a child sexual abuse prevention program. *Journal of School Health, 57*, 228–231.

Wurtele, S.K., & Miller-Perrin, C. (1992) *Preventing child sexual abuse: sharing the responsibility.* Lincoln: University of Nebraska Press.

Wurtele, S. K., Saslawsky, D., Miller, C., Marrs, S., & Britcher, J. (1986). Teaching personal safety skills for potential prevention of sexual abuse: A comparison of treatments. *Journal of Consulting and Clincal Psychology, 54*, 688–692

Wyatt, G. E. (1985). The sexual abuse of Afro-American and white American women in childhood. *Child Abuse and Neglect, 9*, 507–519.

Yates, A. (1982). Children eroticized by incest. *American Journal of Psychiatry, 139*, 482–485.

APPENDIX: CHECKLIST FOR USE IN TREATMENT PLANNING

FIGURE 11.1. Symptom checklist for Sexually Abused children.

Patient name_____ **Date**_____ **Treatment phase**_____

The following is a checklist of Type I and Type II PTSD symptoms and sexuality problems often observed in sexually abused children and adolescents. The checklist is designed to be completed by a clinician following a period of assessing the child and consulting with parents and teachers about sexual abuse sequelae. The checklist is intended to help identify treatment goals and objectives, and can be used at various points throughout the therapeutic process to evaluate change and therapeutic effectiveness.

Scoring: Assign an Impairment Index to each individual symptom—that is, rate the symptom's impact on overall impairment of day-to-day functioning, based upon the following scale:

1—No Impairment
2—Minor Impairment
3—Moderate Impairment
4—Significant Impairment
5—Serious Impairment

Calculate the Overall Rating by summing the Impairment Indexes and dividing by the total possible Impair score (e.g., if 3 of 5 items are scored 5, the **Overall Rating** would be 15/25 or 60%).

TYPE I PTSD SYMPTOMS

Hyperarousal/Emotional Dysregulation

1. Difficulty falling or staying asleep

A. Fails to stay in bed   _____
B. Fails to fall asleep alone or in own bed   _____
C. Sleeps all or part of night with parent   _____
D. Requires excessive support to fall asleep   _____
E. Takes a long time to fall asleep   _____
F. Wakes frequently during the night   _____
   Overall Rating   _____

2. Emotional lability

A. Irritable for no reason   _____
B. Moody   _____
C. Excessive temper outbursts   _____
D. Cries easily   _____
   Overall Rating   _____

3. Distractibility/poor concentration

A. Spacey and confused
B. Inattentive   _____
C. Poor concentration in school   _____
D. Noncompliance   _____
   Overall Rating   _____
        _____

4. Hypervigilance/exaggerated startle response

A. Worries about safety of self and others   _____
B. Frequent checking of safety measures (e.g.,
   checking if doors, windows locked)   _____
C. Strong physiological reactions to surprises
   or stress   _____
D. Separation anxiety   _____
   Overall Rating   _____

Fears and Avoidance

1. Abuse-related fears

A. Situations: _____
B. Things: _____   _____
C. People: _____   _____
D. Places: _____   _____
   Overall Rating   _____
        _____

2. Avoidance of reminders of abuse

A. Refuses to talk about abuse
B. Denies abuse, or aspects of abuse   _____
C. Claims no memory of the abuse   _____
   Overall Rating   _____
        _____

3. Sexual anxiety

A. Frightened or upset by thoughts about sex   _____
B. Thinks about sex often   _____
C. Is bothered by sexual scenes on TV or in
   movies (e.g., kissing, embracing, etc.)   _____
D. Finds sex "dirty" or "disgusting"   _____
   Overall Rating   _____

4. Generalized avoidance

A. Detachment or estrangement from others   _____
B. Restricted range of affect   _____
C. Diminished interest in previously
   enjoyed activities   _____
D. Sense of foreshortened future   _____
E. Social withdrawal   _____
   Overall Rating   _____

Reexperiencing

1. Dreams and nightmares

A. Has vivid recollections in dreams that are
   directly related to abuse   _____

B. Has frightening dreams that have symbolic
   content related to abuse   _____

C. Has frightening dreams but cannot describe
   content of dreams   _____
   Overall Rating   _____

2. Intrusive thoughts/reenactments

A. "Out of the blue" conversations about the abuse   _____

B. Bothered by thoughts about abuse   _____

C. During play, acts out aspects of the abuse   _____

D. Talks about abuse to dolls/stuffed animals   _____

E. Physiological reactivity to abuse cues   _____
   Overall Rating   _____

Attributional Mediators (for children 8 or older)

1. Self-blame/guilt

A. Attributes blame to something he or she
   said or did   _____

B. Attributes blame to something about self
   (e.g., too young to do anything about it)   _____

C. Feels guilty about family problems
   following disclosure   _____

D. Feels guilty about not disclosing earlier   _____

E. Feels guilty about effects of disclosure
   on offender   _____

F. Feels embarrassed about the abuse   _____
   Overall Rating   _____

2. Perceptions of world as dangerous

A. Feels adults should not be trusted   _____

B. Fears other children will be abused   _____
   Overall Rating   _____

3. Feelings of vulnerability vs. feelings of empowerment

A. Feels prone to "bad things" or "bad luck"   _____

B. Feels helpless to avoid further abuse   _____

C. Feels unprepared to stop/prevent abuse   _____

D. Not confident that others will protect him or her
   from further victimization   _____
   Overall Rating   _____

TYPE II PTSD SYMPTOMS
Dissociation

1. Excessive fantasy life

A. Imaginary friends

B. Excessive fantasy play with dolls _____

C. Difficulty separating fantasy life from reality _____

D. Reports seeing or hearing usual things
   (e.g., seeing ghosts or hearing voices) _____
   Overall Rating _____

2. "Spaciness" or disorientation

A. Frequent daydreaming _____

B. Excessive dawdling _____

C. Poor attention to environment; problems
   forgetting events, losing possessions,
   getting lost _____

D. Fails to learn from experience _____

E. Poor sense of time _____

F. Cannot recall things for which there is
   evidence of his or her actions (e.g., objects
   moved about in night) _____
   Overall Rating _____

3. Poorly integrated personality

A. Shows relatively rapid changes in mood,
   attitude, and affect _____

B. Refers to self in third person or by
   different names _____

C. Prefers different names from day to day _____

D. Shows changes in skills or abilities from
   day to day _____

E. Regressive behaviors (e.g., 12-year-old
   sucks thumb) _____
   Overall Rating _____

4. Depersonalization

A. Feels as if nothing is real _____

B. Feels/acts as if body is separate from self _____
   Overall Rating _____

Anger

1. Unusually intense anger

A. Common problems evoke strong anger
reactions   _____

B. Anger results in high physiological tension   _____

C. Physiological reactivity persists for a long time _____
Overall Rating   _____

2. Ineffective anger management strategies

A. Displaces anger from source onto others
or things   _____

B. Reacts to anger with violence   _____

C. Reacts to anger with passivity   _____

D. Engages in other ineffective or self-defeating
anger management strategies (e.g.,
overeating, self-harm)   _____

E. Makes self-statements/has fantasies that
exacerbate angry feelings (e.g., imagines
people laughing)   _____
Overall Rating   _____

Depression/Learned Helplessness

1. Self-defeating attributional style

A. Tends to attribute positive events to
external, unstable, specific causes   _____

B. Tends to attribute negative events to
internal, stable, global causes   _____
Overall Rating   _____

2. Depressive symptoms

A. Sadness or irritability   _____

B. Diminished interest in pleasurable activities   _____

C. Sleep or appetite changes   _____

D. Lack of energy, excessive fatigue   _____

E. Slowness in moving or excessive agitation   _____

F. Inability to make decisions   _____

G. Thoughts/actions of self-harm or suicide   _____

H. Feelings of hopelessness   _____

I. Social withdrawal   _____

J. Guilt feelings   _____
Overall Rating   _____

Ineffective Coping

1. "Controllable" situations

A. Overuse of avoidance coping strategies
  (e.g., distraction, distancing self) _____

B. Overuse of emotion-focused coping strategies
  (e.g., seeking social support; internalizing or
  externalizing strategies) _____

C. Underuse of solution-focused strategies
  (e.g., seeking information, problem solving) _____
  Overall Rating _____

2. "Uncontrollable" situations

A. Excessive frustration over uncontrollable
  situations _____

B. Underuse of effective emotion-focused coping
  strategies (e.g., seeking support) _____

C. Underuse of effective distraction strategies _____
  Overall Rating _____

Sexuality Problems

1. Eroticization

A. Excessive masturbation _____

B. Excessive interest in nudity, genitals, and
  sexuality _____

C. Sexual play with dolls and toys _____

D. Noncoercive sexual behavior with peers _____

E. Reenactments of sexual behavior _____

F. Excessive flirtatiousness and seductiveness _____

G. Paraphilias and fetishes _____
  Overall Rating _____

2. Sexual abuse of other children

A. Sexual abuse without elements of coercion
  (offending child at least 5 years older than
  victim child) _____

B. Sexual abuse with coercive elements (e.g.,
  threats, physical coercion, abuse of authority)
  Overall Rating _____

3. Promiscuity and risky sexual behavior

A. Early consensual intercourse _____

B. Indiscriminate sex with multiple partners _____

C. Prostitution _____

D. Failure to protect against pregnancy and sexually
  transmitted diseases _____
  Overall Rating _____

FIGURE 11.2. Checklist for family support of sexually abused children.

Patient name_____ Date_____ Treatment phase_____

The following is a checklist of family factors important to the understanding of the sexually abused child and his or her family. The checklist is designed for completion by a clinician following a period of assessing the child and family and consulting with relevant professionals regarding the child's abuse history and family background. The checklist is intended to help identify family-based treatment goals and objectives, and can be used at various points throughout the therapeutic process to evaluate change and therapeutic effectiveness.

Scoring: Assign an Impairment Index to each specific family issue—that is, a rating of the impact of the family issue on the child's adjustment—in the right-hand column, based upon the following scale:

1—No Impairment
2—Minor Impairment
3—Moderate Impairment
4—Significant Impairment
5—Serious Impairment

Calculate the Overall Rating by summing the Impairment Indexes and dividing by the total possible score (e.g., if 3 of 5 items are scored 5, the **Overall Rating** would be 15/25 or 60%).

Family Functioning

1. Family organization, boundaries, and roles

A. Supervision of children's activities/screening
    of child care providers   _____
B. Sexual boundaries within the home   _____
C. Family's social network   _____
D. Stability of parental relationship   _____
E. Parental abilities to monitor and protect
    children (e.g., absence, youth, physical or
    mental illness, substance use problems)   _____
F. Roles within family (e.g., parentified child;
    siblings responsible for other siblings)   _____
G. Family rules and expectations   _____
    Overall Rating   _____

2. Family cohesion and emotional supportiveness

A. Child management skills   _____
B. Developmental expectations   _____
    Overall Rating   _____

3. *Family adaptability*

A. Problem-solving skills (e.g., negotiation, contracting)

B. Family power structure _____

C. Individual family problems that affect family functioning (e.g., substance use problems, parental dissociative disorders, etc.) _____

Overall Rating _____

Parental Reactions to Disclosure

1. *Parental support of child following abuse disclosure*

A. Emotional support _____

B. Belief of child _____

C. Action toward perpetrator _____

D. Assurance of safety _____

Overall Rating _____

2. *Parental personal reactions following abuse disclosure*

A. Reexperiencing symptoms _____

B. Fears and avoidance _____

C. Hyperarousal _____

D. Issues related to parental history of childhood abuse _____

E. Issues related to parental history of abuse by same offender _____

F. Depression _____

G. Dissociative and avoidance-based coping _____

H. Anger management problems _____

I. Marital discord _____

J. Problems with extended family and social network _____

Overall Rating _____

Family Stress and Disruption Following Abuse Disclosure

1. *Involvement with criminal justice system*

A. Attitude toward decision regarding prosecution _____

B. Mixed alliances regarding prosecution _____

C. Anxiety related to court process _____

D. Resolution of prosecution outcome (i.e., acquittal, conviction, sentencing) _____

Overall Rating _____

2. Involvement with child protective services, family court, and police

A. Attitude regarding investigative process   _____

B. Attitude regarding actions taken by community
   agencies to protect child   _____

C. Attitude regarding actions toward accused   _____

D. Attitude regarding supervision orders   _____

E. Attitude regarding custody and access
   arrangements   _____

F. Satisfaction with child placement   _____
   Overall Rating   _____

3. Financial impact of abuse and abuse disclosure

A. Negative change in financial status   _____

B. Negative change in parental work status   _____

C. Negative change in housing situation   _____
   Overall Rating   _____

4. Social impact of abuse

A. Loss of support within immediate family   _____

B. Loss of support within extended family   _____

C. Loss of support of friends   _____

D. Feeling alienated within the community   _____
   Overall Rating   _____

5. Continued contact with offender

A. Negative effects of contact for victim   _____

B. Conflicting needs for contact with offender
   among family members   _____

C. Unapproved or unsolicited contact by offender
   with victim or other family members   _____
   Overall Rating   _____

Intrafamilial Issues

1. Sibling incest

A. Sexual atmosphere in home   _____

B. Other cases of sexual abuse within home   _____

C. Other types of maltreatment within home   _____

D. Sibling roles in family   _____

E. Parental availability and parental supervision
   of children's care   _____

F. Split parental alliances   _____
   Overall Rating   _____

2. Paternal incest

A. Paternal attachment to child   _____

B. Social isolation/ social skill deficits   _____

C. Sexual preoccupation   _____

D. Marital discord   _____

E. Emotional neediness   _____

F. Pedophilic tendencies   _____

   Overall Rating   _____

3. Maternal factors influencing reaction to incest disclosure

A. Satisfaction with relationship prior to abuse
   disclosure   _____

B. Financial dependency upon offender   _____

C. Emotional dependency upon offender   _____

D. Maternal fear of offender   _____

E. Maternal attachment to child   _____

   Overall Rating   _____

PART VI

PROBLEMS OF ADOLESCENCE

CHAPTER 12

Parent–Adolescent Conflict and Relationship Discord

Sharon L. Foster
California School of Professional Psychology–San Diego

Arthur L. Robin
Wayne State University School of Medicine

Conflict between parents and adolescents frequently accompanies psychological difficulties in adolescence. Conflict is an intrinsic part of the criteria for Oppositional Defiant Disorder in the fourth edition of the *Diagnostic and Statistical Manual of Mental Disorders* (DSM-IV; American Psychiatric Association, 1994), which specify arguments with adults as one of several behaviors that together constitute a pattern of negative, defiant behavior toward others. In addition, the DSM-IV explicitly includes a Parent–Child Relational Problem diagnosis, used when relationship problems are the specific focus of treatment.

Investigators have shown elevated rates of negative family communication to be associated with various externalizing behavior problems, including Conduct Disorder and delinquency (e.g., Alexander, 1973; Hanson, Henggeler, Haefele, & Redick, 1984; Sanders, Dadds, Johnston, & Cash, 1992), Attention-Deficit/Hyperactivity Disorder (ADHD; Barkley, Anas-topoulos, Guevremont, & Fletcher, 1992), and teen alcohol use (Brody & Forehand, 1993). Self-reported problems with communication and conflict also sometimes characterize families with teens with internalizing problems (e.g., Feldman, Rubenstein, & Rubin, 1988; Smith & Forehand, 1986), although these findings are less consistent than those involving externalizing problems, perhaps because studies linking internalizing problems with conflict often fail to consider the overlap between internalizing and externalizing behaviors. Finally, problems in family interactions have also been associated with the diagnoses of schizophrenia-spectrum disorders in adolescence (Doane, West, Goldstein, Rodnick, & Jones, 1981).

The frequent comorbidity between family communication problems and various kinds of adolescent difficulties raises a number of treatment issues. One primary question involves what to treat: the conflictual interaction patterns or the specific problems about which parents and teens disagree. In other words, should the clinician work specifically on reducing conflict with the family of a teenager diagnosed with Conduct Disorder? Or should the therapist instead target such issues as truancy, obedience to home rules, and the like, devising interventions to reduce these problems directly?

The answer to this issue depends in part upon the role that maladaptive parent–adolescent conflict plays in the etiology and maintenance of adolescent disorder. Excessive conflict may, in theory, play several different roles in adolescent disorder.

In the first view, conflict is a primary *cause* of the disorder: Conflict and negative communication precede or put families at risk for the development of problems during adolescence. In the second view, conflict is a *consequence* of the disorder. Thus, the behavior problem itself creates problems in the family, which in turn cause acrimony between parents and adolescent. The third view sees conflict as a variable that maintains disorder. With this view, conflict may or may not be causally implicated in the etiology of the problem, but, once established, it keeps families from resolving their difficulties and thus perpetuates the problem. A fourth view sees conflict as a problem in its own right, independent of its relationship with other disorders.

These views have different implications for how treatment components should be selected and sequenced, and for how treatment outcomes should be assessed. If conflict is a problem in its own right, clinically significant conflict should be addressed directly, and treatment success will be defined by reductions in measures assessing conflict. If conflict maintains family problems, then conflict should be treated to ameliorate other difficulties. The primary measures of treatment success with this model involve measures of conflict and measures of presenting problems, scores on both of which should decline if treatment is effective. If, on the other hand, conflict is a secondary outgrowth of the teen's behavior problems, factors other than conflict maintain the presenting problems. These factors should be treated and assessed, along with measures of the presenting complaints. Conflict should be reduced as a by-product of successful treatment, without needing to be targeted directly for intervention.

Complicating the comorbidity picture further is the fact that conflict may play different roles in different disorders. For example, conflict may be a result of life-threatening weight loss in Anorexia Nervosa but a maintaining variable in

Conduct Disorder. Longitudinal studies examining the etiology of different behavior problems in adolescence will ultimately lead to answers to this question, as will treatment outcome studies comparing different treatment models. At present, however, these relationships remain largely unexplicated. Similarly, despite the proliferation of findings linking family communication difficulties in general with adolescent behavior problems, few theoretical writings explicitly examine the specific role of conflict in the etiology, maintenance, and treatment of specific disorders.

It is beyond the scope of this chapter to review the role of conflict and family communication in every disorder in which they have been implicated. Thus, here we examine treatment strategies that explicitly aim to improve family conflict and communication as a part of treatment. In general, these share a focus on changing family interaction to ameliorate family difficulties. Communication and problem-solving training approaches explicitly attempt to teach parents and/or teenagers the skills that presumably undergird successful communication and conflict resolution, using didactic formats. Other sorts of family interventions are less didactic and focus more broadly on changing family interactional patterns that promote conflict. Rarely do they involve systematic didactic instruction in communication skills, although a therapist and family may discuss communication issues.

In the pages that follow, we first overview issues and practices involved in assessing family conflict, communication, and related dimensions of parent–adolescent relationships. We then survey treatment outcome research related to communication training and family interaction interventions. Finally, we consider general treatment process issues related to engaging and retaining parents and teenagers in family therapy treatments that focus on family interaction and conflict.

ASSESSMENT

Purposes and Goals of Assessment

Assessment of conflict in families can have several purposes in clinical practice, including (1) screening the family for clinically significant levels of conflict and related problems; (2) formulating a conceptual understanding of the family's difficulties and those factors that maintain or exacerbate them; (3) establishing a diagnosis;

(4) selecting and planning an appropriate treatment strategy; and (5) establishing a baseline against which treatment progress can be gauged.

Assessment has important therapeutic as well as informational goals. The therapist meets the family during the assessment phase. Because family members often enter treatment with varying motivation and different concerns, engaging a family in treatment, promoting a shared view of the family's problems, and establishing rapport with family members are crucial clinical goals during this stage of treatment. We discuss these issues in detail later in the chapter.

Selecting assessment tools to gain a picture of family functioning and to assess treatment progress will depend both on the problems the family presents and on the therapist's view of the factors that elicit and maintain conflictual patterns. Rosen and Proctor (1981) describe two types of therapy goals (or outcomes) that are relevant to choice of assessment tools. "Ultimate outcomes" are defined by the clients' goals. Achieving these goals is essential for successful therapy. The clients' goals and wishes, rather than the therapist's framework or theoretical bent, are the primary sources used to define desirable, ultimate outcomes. In the language of science, these can be seen as the crucial "dependent variables" that therapy seeks to improve. In treatment of parent–adolescent conflict, these would be defined in terms of reductions in distressing arguments, and/or changes in satisfaction with the relationship. "Instrumental outcomes," in contrast, are the "independent variables" that the therapist and family must manipulate to produce the ultimate outcomes of treatment. The therapist, not the family, generally selects instrumental outcomes, based on treatment outcome research and the therapist's theoretical framework. For example, communication training approaches assume that if family members learn problem-solving and communication skills, their conflict will diminish. More elaborated variations on this approach, such as behavioral–family systems therapy (Robin & Foster, 1989), further assume that irrational cognition and systemic problems (e.g., couples who fail to work as a team, triangulation, etc.) can contribute to high rates of conflict and should be treated to promote effective conflict resolution. Functional family therapy approaches (Alexander & Parsons, 1982), in contrast, assume that family problems result from the use of maladaptive behaviors to achieve worthwhile functions of interpersonal intimacy, distance, or regulation. Thus, the behavior used

to achieve a particular function must be altered as an instrumental outcome needed to reduce family interaction difficulties. Early therapy sessions and informed consent procedures often focus in part on educating the family about how the instrumental goals of treatment will help the family reach their ultimate goals.

Rosen and Proctor's (1981) framework has several implications for assessment. Because ultimate outcomes are more family-determined than therapist-determined, their assessment should be reasonably independent of the therapist's formulation regarding the factors that promote and maintain conflict. Thus, a behavioral–family systems therapist and a structural family therapist would establish similar ultimate goals for a family presenting with frequent arguments about household rules, school performance, and dating. For both of these therapists, reductions in conflict would constitute therapy success. Assessing these ultimate outcomes before therapy begins and periodically during treatment is crucial for both therapists, whatever interventions they employ.

Instrumental outcomes become the "subgoals" of therapy and are often accomplished and assessed sequentially. For example, in a behavioral–family systems approach, a family that wishes to reduce conflict generally works on mastering communication and problem-solving skills in early sessions, and later addresses cognitive distortions and systemic issues (because these issues are often not apparent until later stages of treatment). In these cases, the therapist should assess problem-solving and communication skills until the family has mastered those steps of treatment, then occasionally check for maintenance. The therapist will shift the assessment focus to cognitive distortions or systemic factors when these become primary instrumental goals, paying particularly close attention to these areas until the family shows sufficient progress to move on to the next goal. Potential instrumental goals should also be assessed early in treatment to help with treatment planning.

Because therapists select instrumental outcomes based on their hypotheses about the factors that promote and maintain conflict, instrumental outcomes will vary depending upon the therapist's theory of conflict. The behavioral–family systems therapist may target and measure specific problem-solving skills and cognitive distortions as contributors to conflict. The structural family therapist, in contrast, may focus on how specific subsystems in the family (parent–child, mother–father) interact, and may attempt to reduce maladaptive coalitions. Instrumental outcomes may also vary from family to family.

Assessing instrumental as well as ultimate outcomes serves several important purposes, both in research studies of treatment outcome and for the individual therapist. First, assessment of ultimate outcomes allows the therapist to assess the social validity of the treatment—its impact as defined in terms of the client's wishes or goals. This demonstration is important for accountability purposes. Second, assessment of both instrumental and ultimate outcomes allows the therapist to test the theoretical mechanisms or premises underlying the therapeutic approach. For example, we (Robin & Foster, 1989) assume that clients who learn good communication skills, master their cognitive distortions, and reduce marital disputes over child rearing and other systemic factors that interfere with family functioning should also show reductions in indicators of conflict. Accomplishing the first without the second means that the therapist (or the theory) overlooked some necessary "independent variable" required for reducing conflict. Change in the second without change in the first may mean that components of the original model are unnecessary, and that other mechanisms besides those the therapist originally proposed may be involved in the change process.

We presume that therapists who treat parent–adolescent conflict need outcome measures primarily geared toward relationship discord and mutual disagreement to assess the ultimate outcomes of treatment. We also assume that (1) assessment should use multiple methods (e.g., observation, self-report, reports from other family members); (2) assessment should utilize instruments and approaches with reliability and validity data that support their relevance for the particular purpose and population with which they are used; (3) measures should be administered periodically to assess treatment impact; and (4) measures should yield information that is sufficiently valuable clinically to compensate for the time spent administering and scoring them. Finally, (5) assessment should follow the "funnel" approach, beginning with broad examination of presenting problems, and comorbid family and individual problems, and then narrow to examine specific factors contributing to those problems. This assessment approach allows the therapist to define the presenting problems with the family in terms of measurable ultimate goals, to select appropriate ways of assessing progress toward these goals, to formulate hypotheses about instrumental goals, and to select

ways of assessing instrumental goals more intensively when they become specific foci of treatment.

Assessing Ultimate Goals

Ultimate goals of treatment with families presenting with high-frequency conflict are likely to include one or more of the following: (1) reductions in specific negative adolescent behaviors that trigger arguments (e.g., disobedience, truancy, homework completion, sibling conflicts); (2) improvements in family interactions and decreases in angry, destructive arguments; and/or (3) improvements in members' overall satisfaction with and positive feelings about family relationships.[1]

It is particularly important in assessing families' goals to distinguish between families in which conflict stems from a single issue (e.g., drugs, dating) and families that argue about many issues. Although both types of families may exhibit similar negative communication patterns when they disagree, the first group of families shows situation-specific conflict, while the second group displays cross-situational interaction problems. Thus, the first group may be more likely to benefit from interventions that directly aim to reduce the problem that prompts disputes, whereas the second group may be better candidates for skills training approaches.

Table 12.1 provides an overview of formal assessment devices available for assessing ultimate goals involving conflict in families with teenagers. Each instrument described in this table has promising psychometric data supporting its use to help in assessing general levels of relationship distress or angry interactions. Table 12.1 describes instruments that are useful for assessing general dimensions of conflict and family relationship satisfaction per se. Table 12.2 (presented later) provides information about assessment tools relevant to specific instrumental goals frequently involved in treatment, including communication and problem-solving skills. Elsewhere (Foster & Robin, 1997), we examine many of these instruments in greater detail.

Measures in Table 12.1 fall into three general categories: questionnaires, interviews, and observation codes. Questionnaire and interview assessments can involve self-reports, reports about the behavior of other family members, or some combination of the two. In general, questionnaires and interviews can provide a wealth of varied information relatively efficiently. They also capture the clients' perspective, which is

TABLE 12.1. Instruments for Assessing Parent–Adolescent Conflict and Relationship Distress

Assessment target	Assessment method	Scale or category name and reference(s)	Description and comments
Topics of conflict	Questionnaire	Issues Checklist (Prinz, Foster, Kent, & O'Leary, 1979; Robin & Foster, 1989)	Family members rate frequency and intensity of discussions of 44 specific topics; often used to select topics for audiotaped discussions in research on conflict.
Topics of conflict	Interview	Unnamed research interview (Smetana, 1989; Smetana, Yau, Restrepo, & Braeges, 1991a, 1991b)	Interviewers ask family members separately about topics about which they disagree; can also inquire about importance, frequency, and severity of disagreements.
Topics of conflict	Telephone interview	Daily telephone interview (Montemayor & Hanson, 1985)	Interviewers ask adolescent to identify and describe any conflict that occurred during previous day; part of 40-minute interview.
Degree of conflict	Questionnaire	Issues Checklist (see above)	Yields scores for frequency, anger intensity, and weighted frequency × anger intensity of discussions.
		Family Environment Scale, Conflict subscale (Moos & Moos, 1981)	Subscale has 9 true–false items; FES has 9 additional subscales.
Degree of conflict	Observation	Oppositional initiations and responses (Vuchinich, 1987; Vuchinich, Emery, & Cassidy, 1988)	Observers identify conflict episodes, which can then be coded for additional elements of conflict (e.g., who sides with whom).
		Extent of agreement, disagreement, and negative behavior (Vuchinich, Vuchinich, & Wood, 1993)	Observers rate videotaped discussion on Likert scale (from 1 to 7); used only with parents, in Vuchinich et al. (1993) study, but could be used with parent–teen dyads or triads as well.
General relationship distress[a]	Questionnaire	Parent–Adolescent Relationship Questionnaire, Global Distress subscale (Robin, Koepke, & Moye, 1990)	Subscale has 15 true–false items; scale contains 14 additional subscales.

[a]The Family Adaptability and Cohesion Scales III (Olson, Portner, & Lavee, 1985) are sometimes used as indicators of general relationship problems in families. We do not include this questionnaire here, however, because item content pertains more to mutual reliance, mutual approval, and decision making than to distress and satisfaction per se. In addition, there is considerable debate over whether these scales have a linear or curvilinear relationship with adaptive functioning (see Foster & Robin, 1997, for more extended discussion of this issue).

important for assessing ultimate goals of therapy. On the other hand, few questionnaire and interview measures assessing family members' portrayals of their behavior have been compared directly with observational measures of the same phenomena. Thus, the extent to which questionnaire and interview reports reflect observable behavior is uncertain.

Observational assessments provide a logical complement to questionnaire and interview as-

TABLE 12.2. Instruments for Assessing Common Instrumental Goals in Treatment of Parent–Adolescent Conflict

Assessment target	Assessment method	Scale or category name and reference(s)	Description and comments
Problem-solving skills	Questionnaire	Parent–Adolescent Relationship Questionnaire, Problem-Solving subscale (Robin, Koepke, & Moye, 1990)	Subscale has 15 true–false items; questionnaire contains 12–14 additional subscales.
		McMaster Family Assessment Device, Problem-Solving subscale (Epstein, Baldwin, & Bishop, 1983)	Subscale 5 items rated on 4-point scales; instrument contains 6 additional subscales.
Problem-solving skills	Observation	Problem-solving categories of Modified Marital Interaction Coding System (Robin & Weiss, 1980)	Used to score taped discussions of family interactions; observers code each thought unit; generally requires extensive observer training to obtain satisfactory interobserver agreement; shortened versions are the Parent–Adolescent Interaction Coding System (Robin & Foster, 1989) and Parent–Adolescent Interaction Coding System—Revised (Barkley, Anastopoulos, Guevremont, & Fletcher, 1992).
		Solving Problems in Family Interaction—II, problem-solving categories and items (Forgatch & Lathrop, 1995)	Used to score taped interactions of family discussions. Has several components: (1) Observers code throught units, using seven problem-solving categories; (2) observers rate their impressions of 11 problem-solving processes at the end of the discussion; (3) family members rate the discussion right after it ends (5 items). Coding thought units requires considerable training.
		Unnamed coding system (Vuchinich, Wood, & Vuchinich, 1994)	Observers rate entire taped family interaction, using 7-point scales (3 categories: quality of solutions, extent of problem resolution, overall problem-solving quality).
		Community Members' Rating Scale, problem-solving categories (Robin & Canter, 1984)	Parents, teens, or clinicians rate taped discussion, using 8 categories related to problem solving; requires large number of raters to get reliable mean ratings; categories same as Modified Marital Interaction Coding System (see above).

(continued)

TABLE 12.2.   (*continued*)

Assessment target	Assessment method	Scale or category name and reference(s)	Description and comments
Communication skills	Questionnaire	Family Environment Scale, Expressiveness subscale (Moos & Moos, 1981)	Subscale has 9 true–false items; questionnaire contains 9 additional subscales.
		Parent–Adolescent Communication Scale (Barnes & Olson, 1985)	Contains two 10-item subscales, Problem Communication and Open Communication; items rated on 5-point scales; teen completes separate versions for mother and father.
		Parent–Adolescent Relationship Questionnaire, Communication subscale (Robin et al., 1990)	Subscale has 15 true–false items; teen reports on mother and father separately; questionnaire contains 12 additional subscales.
		McMaster Family Assessment Device, Communication subscale (Epstein et al., 1983)	Subscale has 6 items rated on 4-point scales; questionnaire contains 6 other subscales.
		Conflict Behavior Questionnaire (Prinz, Foster, Kent, & O'Leary, 1979; Robin & Foster, 1989)	Has 75 yes–no items (73 for teens); teens rate mother and father separately; 44- and 20-item versions available; content assesses conflict, communication, and anger levels, as well as more global perceptions of relationship.
Communication skills	Observation	Modified Marital Interaction Coding System, communication categories (Robin & Weiss, 1990)	See description of general coding system and shortened versions under "Problem-solving skills," above.
		Solving Problems in Family Interaction—II, communication categories (Forgatch & Lathrop, 1995)	Two components address communication skills: (1) Observers code thought units, using 11 communication categories; (2) observers rate their impressions of various communication behaviors, using 4- or 7-point scales.
		Defensive/Supportive Behavior Code (Alexander, 1973)	Observers use 5-second observe, 5-second record observation system to code taped observations.
		Unnamed observation system (Blaske, Borduin, Henggeler, & Mann, 1989; Mann et al., 1990)	Observers count frequencies of some categories and rate others; categories combined into positive communication, supportiveness, and conflict/hostility.

(*continued*)

TABLE 12.2.   (*continued*)

Assessment target	Assessment method	Scale or category name and reference(s)	Description and comments
		Interaction Behavior Code, communication categories (Prinz & Kent, 1978)	Observers rate presence or absence of 29 behaviors and rate 3 others on 3-point scales; scores combined into positive and negative behavior categories; four raters usually evaluate each tape.
		Iowa Family Interaction Scales (Rueter & Conger, 1995b)	Observers rate entire interaction, using 5-point scales; negative and positive communication categories can be derived; how rating scale items are combined has varied from investigation to investigation.
		Community Members' Rating Scale, communication categories (Robin & Canter, 1984)	Contains 15 communication categories; see general description under "Problem-solving skills," above.
Cognition/irrational beliefs	Questionnaire	Family Beliefs Inventory (Vincent Roehling & Robin, 1986)	Parents and teens rate how much they endorse each of 6 types of irrational beliefs (4 for teens) in response to 10 hypothetical situations.
		Parent–Adolescent Relationship Questionnaire, Belief subscales (Robin et al., 1990)	Each subscale includes 8 true–false items for each of 6 irrational beliefs (4 for teens).
		Mother–Adolescent Attribution Questionnaire (Grace, Kelley, & McCain, 1993)	Mothers and teens rate stability, globality, externality of cause of each other's behavior in 8 hypothetical conflicts, using 6-point scales; also rate how much behavior is selfishly motivated, blameworthy, and intentional.
Cognition/irrational beliefs	Video-mediated recall	Unnamed recall task (Sanders & Dadds, 1992)	Family members individually review a tape of family discussion; every 20 seconds, each indicates what he or she was thinking at the moment.
Angry affect	Questionnaire	Issues Checklist (Prinz et al., 1979; Robin & Foster, 1989)	Family members rate anger intensity of discussions of 44 specific topics; sometimes seen as indicator of conflict rather than angry affect.
Angry affect	Observation	Living in Family Environments coding system, aversive affect code (Hops, Davis, & Longoria, 1995)	Real-time coding, using 22 content and 8 affect codes; measures expression of affect.

(*continued*)

TABLE 12.2. (*continued*)

Assessment target	Assessment method	Scale or category name and reference(s)	Description and comments
		Specific Affect Coding System, anger and contempt codes (Gottman & Levenson, 1985, 1986; Capaldi, Forgatch, & Crosby, 1994)	Each thought unit coded, using 11 affect codes; assesses expression of affect.
Angry affect	Self-observation	Experience-sampling method (Larson, 1989)	Participant is supplied with beeper and "beeped" at random times; participant then reports current affect and details of current situation, instrument assesses experience of emotion.
Angry affect	Physiological	Various methods available; see Gottman and Levenson (1985, 1986) for examples with couples	Requires physiological recording equipment, as well as computer linkages for downloading and scoring physiological data; assesses physiological substrate of emotion.
Parental teamwork in child rearing	Questionnaire	Marital Satisfaction Inventory, Conflict Over Child Rearing subscale (Snyder, 1979)	Subscale has 20 true–false items; questionnaire contains 280 items assessing many additional aspects of couple relationship.
		Parenting Alliance Inventory (Abidin & Brunner, 1995)	Has 20 items, each rated on 5-point scale.
Parental teamwork in child rearing	Observation	Unnamed observation system (Vuchinich, Vuchinich, & Wood, 1993)	Observers rate parental agreement and parental conflict in family discussion, using 7-point scales.
Coalitions and alliances	Questionnaire	Parent–Adolescent Relationship Questionnaire, Coalitions subscale (Robin et al., 1990)	Subscale has 30 true–false items assessing mother–teen against father, father–teen against mother, mother–father against teen; questionnaire contains 12 additional subscales.
		Structural Family Interaction Scale—Revised (Perosa & Perosa, 1993)	Has 11 items assessing cross-generational triads, triangulation, and parent–child coalitions.
Coalitions and alliances	Observation	Alliance Coding System (Gilbert, Christensen, & Margolin, 1984)	Observers code each speech act for affective quality and content; codes are combined into positive alliance and negative alliance categories.
		Unnamed coding system (Vuchinich et al., 1993)	Observers rate entire interaction for extent to which mother and father take sides against child, using 7-point scale.

(*continued*)

TABLE 12.2.   (*continued*)

Assessment target	Assessment method	Scale or category name and reference(s)	Description and comments
Triangulation	Questionnaire	Parent–Adolescent Relationship Questionnaire, Triangulation subscale (Robin et al., 1990)	Subscale has 45 true–false items assessing triangulation with mother in the middle, father in the middle, teen in the middle; questionnaire contains 12–14 other subscales.

sessments. One common form of collecting observational data involves asking the parents and teenager to discuss a topic that provokes conflict at home, audiotaping or videotaping the discussion, and later using an established observational measure to score it. The ease of collecting a communication sample in this way is offset, however, by the requirements for scoring it reliably. Although existing observation codes are extremely useful for research purposes, the well-researched codes generally employ highly trained observers, and lengthy amounts of time are needed to code even brief (10-minute) discussions. A few alternative coding schemes require much less training and scoring time, but do so at a price: Agreement between pairs of raters is often quite poor (Robin & Foster, 1989). Researchers avoid this problem by using mean scores based on ratings of several raters (e.g., 4–15; Prinz & Kent, 1978; Robin & Canter, 1984), based on the psychometric principle that the reliability of the mean score will be greater than the reliability of any single rater's score. Although this works well for research purposes, clinicians may be hard pressed to find groups of raters who can evaluate tapes of family interaction routinely.

Another limitation of observational data is reactivity. A certain percentage of family members (between 17% and 50%, depending on the study, the particular member, and the questions used to assess reactivity; Robin & Foster, 1989; Schreer, 1994) report that communication samples in the clinic and research lab differ moderately to markedly from the ways they handle similar situations at home. When asked how samples differ, members generally report that discussions are less angry (Schreer, 1994). This is not surprising, given that family members are in a novel setting away from customary distractions, a relative stranger has instructed them about the task, and they know that their communication will be evaluated.[2]

Investigators have developed surprisingly few approaches that deal effectively with the practicality and generalizability issues posed by customary methods of collecting observational data on family communication in research settings, and that are practical enough to be clinically useful. A few exceptions exist, however. One potentially practical method for gathering data on conflict in the home setting involves conducting brief structured telephone interviews with family members periodically during the week. For example, Montemayor and Hanson (1985) developed a telephone interview about conflicts at home that they administered to family members three times per week. Coders later categorized the responses. A similar method has been used successfully to assess daily reports of problems with younger children (Chamberlain & Reid, 1987). Another strategy involves daily logs in which parents and/or teenagers systematically record aspects of conflict (e.g., the Daily Home Report; Robin & Foster, 1989). Although the latter strategy has the advantage of providing information that might be close to what observers would record in the home, it also requires specific strategies to elicit compliance, such as those described later (see Table 12.3) for promoting completion of therapeutic tasks in general.

The extra effort involved in obtaining and scoring observational data will tempt clinicians to discard formal observational strategies in favor of easier-to-use paper-and-pencil and interview approaches. This is a mistake for several reasons. First, family members' reports of communication patterns diverge frequently enough from what the clinician observes to warrant tentative skepticism about reports of behavior patterns. Second, family members and therapists may label the same communication patterns quite differently, and this misalignment in labels may not be apparent unless the family and the therapist view and discuss the same conversation. Third, most family members are unaware of the microsocial regularities of their interaction—patterns that many therapists are trained to spot. Fourth, observational strategies are crucial for assessing whether family members can demonstrate the skills taught in didactic approaches for improving communication. Although formal coding of communication samples with resource-intensive observation systems may not be feasible in busy practices, less formal coding can be done, as long as the clinician recognizes the probable slippage in the reliability of the scoring system.

In addition to formal assessment approaches described in Table 12.1, less formal ways for evaluating family members' behavior add to the multimethod assessment tool chest. Interviews can be used in various ways to gather information about conflictual patterns. Two important informal methods involve using the clinical interview as a source of information (i.e., for attending to the content of what family members say) and as a vehicle for observing family members' behavior with each other (i.e., for seeing interaction processes). For example, the therapist can ask family members to describe characteristic disputes, to estimate how often they speak calmly versus angrily about family issues, and to indicate which issues routinely cause angry arguments. The therapist can also observe family members' interactions during assessment interviews and therapy sessions, noting how often they agree and disagree about issues that come up during sessions, which issues prompt disagreements, and how angry their discussions become in sessions.

Assessing Instrumental Goals

The literature documents a number of factors associated with family conflict and communication problems. These include problem-solving and communication skills, irrational beliefs, negative (angry) affect, and structural patterns that involve maladaptive patterns of family alignment. Below we briefly describe each of these factors, along with research supporting its role as a correlate of parent–adolescent conflict. Table 12.2 provides an overview of assessment tools for assessing each of these instrumental goals.

Problem-Solving and Communication Skills

Skills-deficit views of parent–adolescent conflict hypothesize that parents and teens experience conflict because they lack or fail to use the skills required to discuss and resolve problems satisfactorily. These skills are sometimes divided into problem-solving skills (which are relatively unique to disagreement situations) and communication skills (which are more cross-situationally applicable). Problem-solving verbal behaviors facilitate arriving at a solution to a specific dispute, and include (1) formulating a clear, succinct, and nonblaming problem definition; (2) generating future-oriented solutions; (3) evaluating the potential consequences of the solutions, then selecting one or more to try; (4) planning the solution; and (5) evaluating whether the solution has worked and renegotiating if necessary. Communication skills facilitate the exchange of information, keep the family on task toward solutions, and heal negative feelings by allowing others to say what is on their mind and by showing others that their views have been understood. In contrast, poor communication interferes with problem solving by eliciting anger from others, sidetracking the conversation, and creating misunderstandings.

A number of studies document a relationship between observations of poor problem-solving skills and other indicators of relationship problems in the family, including referral for mental health services and reports of relationship distress (Robin & Weiss, 1980; Robin, Koepke, & Moye, 1990), and harsh, inconsistent parenting (Rueter & Conger, 1995c). Similarly, investigations show a variety of communication skills to be more prominent in observations of the communication of nondistressed families than in families seeking treatment for adolescent problems associated with conflict. These skills include humor, approval, acceptance of responsibility (Robin & Weiss, 1980), and supportiveness (Alexander, 1973; Mann, Borduin, Henggeler, & Blaske, 1990). In contrast, distressed families display more frequent conflict-hostility (Mann et al., 1990), defensive statements (Alexander, 1973), commands, putdowns, and lack of response (Robin & Weiss, 1980). Furthermore, several studies show correlations between measures of communication skills and measures of problem-solving skills and outcomes (Forgatch, 1989; Robin et al., 1990; Rueter & Conger, 1995a, 1995b; Vuchinich, Wood, & Vuchinich, 1994), supporting the notion that good communication facilitates conflict resolution, whereas negative communication interferes with this process.

A number of established observational systems (see Table 12.2) examine problem-solving and communication skills in brief discussions in which the therapist and family select a hypothetical or real problem for the family to discuss. Several questionnaires (also listed in Table 12.2) assess communication or problem solving generally, although few have the level of behavioral specificity of observational coding schemes. Less standardized clinical procedures can supplement these approaches. These include interview questions about how the family goes about resolving disagreements and about how good and poor discussions differ. Asking the family for a blow-by-blow reconstruction of a past argument can sometimes yield a valuable picture of common interaction sequences, and prompting family members to critique their own strengths and weaknesses can help them to focus on their own contributions to conflict. In addition, the therapist can observe the behaviors and patterns family members display in the session when discord and agreement arise. Observations of in-session behavior not only provide information about patterns of interaction; they also allow the therapist to assess how well family members' descriptions of their interactions match how they actually communicate.

Beliefs and Cognitive Distortions

Proponents of cognitive approaches hypothesize that family members' thoughts about relationship events play important roles in conflictual exchanges. Negative, irrational attributions and expectations for other family members' behavior can disrupt ongoing resolution by polarizing family members into rigid positions on issues, eliciting angry or resentful feelings, and leading to extreme statements and positions. Elsewhere (Robin & Foster, 1989), we have proposed several types of irrational beliefs about others in the family. Irrational beliefs that characterize parents and teens include "ruination" (the unrealistic assumption that catastrophic consequences will follow a particular course of action) and "malicious intent" (the belief that another's negative action was purposefully motivated by a desire to hurt or injure another family member). Among parents, obedience and perfectionistic expectations are other forms of irrational beliefs. "Obedience" involves the belief that a teen should follow a parent's suggestions and adopt the parent's views and values without questioning them, while "perfectionism" refers to excessively high standards for the teen's performance and intolerance for the teen's mistakes. Teen's irrational beliefs about "autonomy" (teens should

be granted as much freedom as they want) and "fairness" (parental rules should always be reasonable, according to the teen's standards) can also interfere with effective conflict resolutions.[3]

Robin and his colleagues have found consistent relationships between teens' ruination beliefs and family distress (Robin et al., 1990; Vincent Roehling & Robin, 1986). Similarly, fathers' reports of ruination, perfectionism, obedience, and malicious intent distinguished distressed from nondistressed fathers in two studies (Robin et al., 1990; Vincent Roehling & Robin, 1986). Results regarding mothers' irrational cognitions and teens' autonomy and fairness beliefs have been mixed, with findings varying depending on the instrument used to assess beliefs.

Additional support for the role played by attributions of malicious intent comes from Grace, Kelley, and McCain's (1993) findings that mothers' and teens' reports of conflict at home correlated significantly with their views that each other's behavior in a hypothetical conflict situation was intentional, selfishly motivated, and blameworthy. Similarly, Baden and Howe (1992) found that mothers of conduct-disordered teens rated child misbehavior as more intentional than did mothers of a non-conduct-disordered group. Mothers who viewed the causes of teen behavior as relatively more stable and cross-situational (global) were more likely to report angrier discussions at home (Grace et al., 1993) and to have conduct-disordered teenagers (Baden & Howe, 1992).

Most ways of assessing cognition use questionnaires that ask parents to endorse beliefs about family relationships or to read hypothetical conflict situations and to indicate how they would think about the situation. One alternative to questionnaire assessment involves videotaping a discussion about a family problem, then replaying it and asking family members to reconstruct their thoughts during the conflict (e.g., Sanders & Dadds, 1992). The therapist can also use a related "stop-action" tactic in treatment by interrupting a particularly negative or otherwise salient interaction and asking family members to describe their thoughts and feelings during the exchange. Both of these methods can provide valuable information on private events that may promote or exacerbate conflictual interaction, and are useful for helping family members see the links among their thoughts, feelings, and behaviors. Family members can also be asked to keep logs of arguments at home, noting their thoughts during each dispute.

Angry Affect

Reports of anger during parent–adolescent discussion are frequent correlates of clinically significant conflict (e.g., Prinz, Foster, Kent, & O'Leary, 1979). We have suggested that the level of acrimony in discussions is one defining feature that should be used to separate clinically significant conflict from its more normative relatives (Foster & Robin, 1997). Anger and hostility levels displayed during discussions of family disputes also correlate negatively with various indicators of problem-solving outcome and effectiveness (Capaldi, Forgatch, & Crosby, 1994; Hops, Davis, & Longoria, 1995), supporting the hypothesis that excessive anger can derail productive family discussion.

Angry affect can be assessed by examining (1) observations of expressions of emotions during family discussions and in therapy sessions; (2) family members' self-reports of anger, either generally or during discussions of problem issues; and (3) physiological reactions that accompany interactions. In addition to the formal assessment devices described in Table 12.2, many informal approaches described earlier for assessing communication skills and cognitive reactions can be used to assess the expression and experience of emotion. Observing interactions in session and inquiring about family members' experience when they look or sound angry is particularly valuable for testing the extent to which expressions and experience of anger converge. In addition, the therapist can ask family members when they are likely to get angry with each other, how they express anger in their interactions, and to what extent their anger disrupts parent–teen interactions.

Structural Factors

Cognitive and affective reactions and communication behaviors are the microsocial variables that form interaction sequences. Structural dimensions of family interaction describe regularities in these interaction sequences at more molar levels, and commonly focus on influence and hierarchical arrangements among family subsystems (e.g., dyads and triads, such as parents, parent–child units, and sibling units). Several of these structural patterns have been empirically related to parent–adolescent conflict.

"Parental teamwork" refers to whether parents or parent figures agree about how to socialize the child and to respond to problem behavior. The teamwork notion also implies reasonable consistency in how parents manage misbehavior. Parents who fail to work as a team may express conflicting ideas about how to respond to the teenager and may argue about child rearing. In some families, these arguments may be part of more general couple conflict about a variety of issues.

Empirical data support the importance of parental teamwork for effective communication and problem solving with children. Vuchinich, Vuchinich, and Wood (1993) showed that both general couple satisfaction and observed agreement between parents during a problem-solving discussion with a preadolescent son correlated with ratings of their problem-solving effectiveness. Similarly, Mann et al. (1990) showed that observations of mother–father conflict/hostility and supportiveness distinguished discussions of families with a delinquent teen from those of families with a well-adjusted adolescent.

Another structural pattern related to conflict involves "parental coalitions," in which the parents join together by directing blame for misbehavior toward the teenager. "Cross-generational coalitions," in contrast, involve a parent and the teen's taking sides against the second parent. In a related pattern, "triangulation," two family members in conflict with each other each recruit a third member as an intermediary. For example, a father and stepdaughter quarrel over rules, and each complains about the other to the child's biological mother, who then intervenes as the peacemaker by calming each person down after an argument. Two studies by Vuchinich et al. (1993, 1994) found that observations of coalitions involving parental blaming directed against a preadolescent son related negatively to ratings of problem solving in a family discussion task. Studies of cross-generational coalitions and triangulation, however, have provided mixed results, with some studies finding that these relate to indicators of conflict and adjustment (e.g., Mann et al., 1990) but others finding no relationship (Schreer, 1994; Vuchinich et al., 1994).

Formal observational and questionnaire methods for gathering information on structural aspects of family interaction are available (see Table 12.2). Supplementing these approaches is a large body of literature describing methods of assessing couple interaction and discord generally (i.e., not specifically in relation to disagreement over child rearing). Weiss and Heyman (1990), Christensen (1987), and Fincham and Bradbury (1987; Bradbury & Fincham, 1987) review many commonly used instruments and approaches.

Interview questions eliciting descriptions of patterns of interaction that describe structural patterns can also provide information for assessing structure. Another valuable tool comes from observations of family interactions in the session. The therapist should be alert for indicators that the parents do or do not agree about how to handle their children's misbehavior. Observations or family members' reports that one parent has a warm relationship with the teen while the other is angry or distant may signal that cross-generational coalitions are present, and can be assessed further with questions about whether one parent "softens" the other's discipline, or whether the teen plays one parent off against another. Similarly, seeing that two family members argue with each other but consistently turn to a third member for assistance in the session provides a clue that triangulation patterns characterize the family's interactions about problem situations.

Comorbidity and Contextual Issues in Assessment

As indicated earlier, parent–adolescent conflict and communication problems have been consistently implicated in a variety of externalizing problems in adolescence, and in internalizing problems to a less consistent extent. These families are likely to present for treatment of the externalizing (or internalizing) problems, and these problems become the primary or ultimate goals of treatment. In these cases, reducing conflict and improving communication may be instrumental goals of treatment. In other cases, families present excessive conflict as the presenting problem, but further assessment reveals significant additional behavior problems or psychopathology in individual members.

In either of these circumstances, conflict and communication patterns should be assessed within the broader context of comorbid conditions. For example, a therapist who sees a family that presents high-frequency conflict with a teenager who engages in delinquent behavior or drug misuse should carefully assess the delin-

quency or drug use problems as well as conflict. Important factors associated with both the delinquency and the drug use should be integrated into a coherent, comprehensive conceptualization of the case and used to formulate a promising treatment plan. Other chapters of this volume and its companion volumes on assessment (Mash & Terdal, 1997) and psychopathology (Mash & Barkley, 1996) address child and adolescent conditions that may present concurrently with parent–adolescent conflict, and these chapters can be consulted for details on specific disorders and their assessment. Likewise, a parent with serious individual problems warrants additional assessment (guided by the literature on the particular form of adult difficulty) to establish how the adult's individual difficulties influence and are influenced by family interaction problems.

It is also important to recognize that family difficulties occur in the broader context of the community in which the family resides. Family ethnicity and related issues (e.g., level of acculturation and acculturation discrepancies between parents and teen; degree of involvement with and attachment to the culture of origin) are significant elements of this context. Cultural norms and influences are especially important to consider in understanding family members' roles, cognitions, and behaviors, in part because many specifics of the skill- and problem-oriented approaches described here were developed and evaluated with primarily white samples from the United States. Their applicability to other populations has not been empirically established. In addition, skill approaches carry the inherent assumptions that the skills taught are "adaptive." These assumptions warrant empirical scrutiny with culturally diverse groups, and should be adopted with caution until these data are available. McGoldrick, Giordano, and Pearce (1996) provide a particularly comprehensive overview of family treatment issues, considering over 30 different ethnic groups in the United States.

Other contextual features that should be considered in assessment involve the family's socioeconomic status (and how day-to-day economic stresses affect family interactions); the neighborhood; the role of friends, kin, and others involved in child rearing (including the presence and role of stepparents); contact with social service agencies; and the teen's school and peer group. These factors may assume greater or lesser importance for different families, depending upon the nature of the difficulties the family presents and what assessment reveals about the connection between those difficulties and family interaction patterns.

TREATMENT STRATEGIES

In the assessment approach described here, the therapist collects information about a variety of factors shown empirically to correlate with parent–adolescent conflict and identifies those that predominate in the interactions of a particular family. The therapist's conceptualization of the case involves generating a series of hypotheses about which factors should constitute the instrumental goals of therapy—the specific "independent" variables that should be altered to produce changes in family interaction and conflict. These instrumental goals vary from family to family, depending upon the interaction patterns the family displays and the number of difficulties the therapist identifies and hypothesizes as relevant to the presenting problems. For example, a therapist may hypothesize that the members of the Magnusson family need to improve their communication and problem-solving skills in order to reduce conflict. In contrast, the same therapist may see the Walkers, a newly blended family, as needing improvements in couple communication about child-rearing issues, improvements in stepfather–daughter communication, reductions in maternal triangulation, and cognitive restructuring of irrational beliefs about obedience and malicious intent.

The fact that the same ultimate goal (reductions in conflict) may require different instrumental goals in different families mandates a modularized approach to treatment. Ideally, the therapist could select an empirically based strategy for addressing each instrumental goal on his or her list, knowing that the particular strategy is generally effective for achieving the particular goal with the particular type of family the therapist is seeing. Although a large body of literature has evaluated didactic approaches to teaching problem-solving and communication skills, investigators have devoted less attention to evaluating strategies for altering other correlates of parent–adolescent conflict. Most of the latter investigations have added components to a form of negotiation or communication training, rather than examining these treatment components in isolation.

Didactic Interventions

Didactic interventions focus on teaching families problem-solving and/or communication skills. They share an explicit focus on skill deficits as an important mechanism that contributes to excessive conflict and family discord. Ordinarily these approaches use systematic curricula and/or skill-building procedures, including instruction, modeling, behavior rehearsal, feedback, and homework assignments to build skills and help families generalize their use to the home. Most are brief approaches, involving 6–12 sessions. Approaches vary, however, in (1) the extent to which they include additional components of treatment (e.g., cognitive restructuring, anger management), (2) whether they provide treatment in family or group formats, (3) the specific content of treatment, and (4) the populations and measures with which investigators have examined treatment impact.

Skills Training Alone

A number of investigations have examined the effects of skills training with few auxiliary interventions. These vary in precise content and formal, but all emphasize improving parent–adolescent communication as a primary goal of treatment. Most train family members in negotiation/problem-solving skills for discussing conflictual issues, and in more general communication skills for use in various situations, including but not limited to conflict.

Elements of Skills Training. Training in problem solving generally includes instruction in a sequence of steps paralleling the problem-solving steps described earlier. The therapist works with the family members to improve their skills in (1) defining the problem in clear, succinct, nonblaming ways; (2) generating solutions by brainstorming, with evaluations and comments specifically prohibited to encourage creativity; (3) evaluating the solutions by discussing their likely effects on all parties involved in the dispute, finally selecting one or more solutions that family members agree is most likely to work; and (4) planning the specific tasks family members must do to put the solution into practice. Table 12.3 provides descriptions of guidelines for and examples of good and poor problem-solving statements relevant to the first three of these steps.

In general, families in individual treatment work on one problem each week. We (Robin & Foster, 1989) recommend addressing less angry and less complex problems in early sessions, to keep high levels of negative affect from interfering with skill acquisition and practice. Less complex problems are also easier to solve successfully, and successful solutions reinforce the problem-solving process as well as treatment attendance. Therapists generally ask families to carry out the solutions they agree upon between sessions. Once family members begin to master problem-solving skills, the therapist asks them to practice components of problem solving at home and becomes less active and directive in guiding discussions. Gradually withdrawing from the family members as their skills improve allows the therapist both to assess the members' skill use without the therapist, and to prepare the family for termination.

Communication training usually accompanies problem-solving training, although some approaches offer communication training without explicit attention to conflictual issues. Among the most common communication skills included in training curricula are the following:

1. Listening skills, often operationalized by asking family members to paraphrase others' statements without adding their own thoughts, reactions, or judgments (e.g., Guerney, 1977; Robin & Foster, 1989). These skills include listening without defensiveness in response to negative feedback. Some also add nonverbal ways of conveying listening, such as making eye contact and conveying attention with one's body posture (Robin & Foster, 1989).

2. Expressing positive and negative feelings in nonaccusatory ways, operationalized by using "I" statements that convey the speaker's feelings or reactions, then describing the antecedent that prompts those reactions (e.g., "I get really mad when you tease your sister and make her cry") (Guerney, 1977; Robin & Foster, 1989).

3. Expressing praise, affection, and positive comments (e.g., Gant, Barnard, Kuehn, Jones & Christopherson, 1981; Openshaw, Mills, Adams, & Durso, 1992).

4. Providing rationales (Gant et al., 1981; Openshaw et al., 1992).

5. Giving specific feedback (Gant et al., 1981).

6. Sticking to the topic under discussion, avoiding digressions and lengthy discussions about past transgressions and conflicts (Robin & Foster, 1989).

7. Making straightforward and tentative instead of absolutist statements, operationalized by using such terms as "sometimes" instead of "always" and "never" (Robin & Foster, 1989).

8. Matching one's verbal and nonverbal messages (Robin & Foster, 1989).

9. Asking questions about others' positions instead of assuming what they think and feel ("mind reading") (Robin & Foster, 1989).

Didactic communication training involves describing the target skill and its rationale, sometimes supplemented by modeling, followed by behavior rehearsal and feedback. As an alternative, the therapist can identify communication skill problems as they arise during family discussion. The latter method has the advantage that family members can generally readily see how the pattern interferes with productive discussion, making them more likely to accept suggestions for change. In addition, the skill being targeted is clearly relevant to the particular family. On the other hand, a few families explode into angry, negative exchanges that quickly spiral out of control when they are asked to discuss a problem. For these families, systematic instruction in communication skills before a problem arises may be more effective than waiting for a situation that may be difficult to defuse once it has begun.

Research on Skills-Training Alone. Many studies that investigate teaching problem-solving and/or communication skills contain components other than skills training. A few studies, however, have examined skills training approaches in isolation. Unfortunately, most of these have been limited by methodological flaws, the most important of which are small sample sizes and the absence of random assignment to treatment conditions.

Openshaw et al. (1992) studied the effects of an 8-week training program in communication and negotiation skills for reducing conflict in a nonclinic population. Either a mother or a father

TABLE 12.3.   Description, Clinical Guidelines, and Examples of Different Steps of Problem Solving

Problem-solving step	Description	Key attributes	Poor examples	Good examples
Problem definition	Definition limits and specifies topic to be discussed. Family members take turns saying what aspect of the problem bothers them, and another member paraphrases the definition.	Be clear, specific, succinct, nonaccusatory.	"You are irresponsible about your schoolwork" (not specific, accusatory). "My problem is that you don't understand me" (not clear, not specific).	"I get really frustrated when you leave your books and assignments in your locker and then I have to drive you to school to get them." "Mom, I really don't like it when I tell you I need to do something and you tell me to do my chores right away anyway, like you didn't care about what I have to do."
Solution listing	Brainstorming provides possible ideas to solve the problems. Family members come up with different ideas for solving the problem; one member writes down the ideas; therapist encourages family to be creative and not to self-censor.	Don't evaluate while listing; be specific; specify positive change; stay future- oriented.	"He should have come home on time last night" (not future-oriented, does not specify positive change). "You should get a better attitude" (not specific).	"He can stay out until 9:00 on weeknights and 11:00 on weekends." "Maybe you could tell me nicely when you don't want to do a chore, and we could see if your brother is willing to trade with you."
Evaluation	Evaluation involves describing the consequences of solutions and selecting a solution. Family members each describe the pluses and minuses of each solution (i.e., what would happen if they adopted it), giving the solution a plus, a minus, or a plus/minus; solutions with pluses from all are candidates to try.	Examine specific solutions; stay consequence-oriented; be specific; consider impact on all involved.	"I don't like any idea that doesn't let me get an allowance" (does not address specific solution, not consequence-oriented, does not consider impact on anyone else). "That's a stupid idea" (not specific, not consequence-oriented).	"I don't think that my just doing my chores would work. That's the rule we have now, and I forget to do them, and Mom gets mad at me." "Getting a maid would work for you, because you wouldn't have to do any extra work. But Dad and I can't afford it."

and a teen participated in a structured training program involving modeling, rehearsal, and homework practice. The experimental group was superior at posttest to a comparison group in role-played performance in hypothetical situations, and reported greater improvement on a seemingly unvalidated measure of trained skills. Parents also reported significant reductions in conflict/hostility (but no reductions in global distress) in the parent–teen relationship, as assessed by a more psychometrically established measure, the Parent–Adolescent Relationship Questionnaire (Robin et al., 1990). Despite these positive results, this study was seriously handicapped by the facts that participants were self-selected into experimental and control groups, and that differential dropout resulted in only seven families in the comparison group.

The absence of random assignment was also a problem in Wood and Davidson's (1993) evaluation of Parent Effectiveness Training, in which parents and teens participated in separate groups and learned active listening, assertiveness, and problem-solving skills. In this study, controls were recruited from the same schools as participants and were matched on age. Observers' ratings of treated parents' and teens' conflict resolution during a very brief (3-minute) discussion of a hypothetical problem improved significantly. Ratings also indicated that treated parents significantly reduced their use of accusational/judgmental confrontation. No differences, however, were reported on questionnaire measures. Unfortunately, none of the measures directly addressed skill use or conflict at home, and the reliability and validity of the questionnaire measures were not clear. The small sample (11 controls, 13 experimental families) further weakened the conclusiveness of the results.

In contrast with the studies above, Riesch et al. (1993) studied the effects of communication training with a very large sample (404 mothers, 188 fathers, 456 teens), using well-established questionnaire and observational measures of family interaction. The sample was prescreened, and families that indicated troubled family or marital relationships (as assessed by the Family Adaptability and Cohesion Scales III or the Dyadic Adjustment Scale) were eliminated from the sample. Unfortunately, as in other investigations, families were self-selected into either the treatment or the control group, based on preference and time availability. Mothers who were self-selected for the intervention reported significantly less satisfaction with family relations before the intervention than the control mothers

did. Participants attended 6 weeks of communication training provided to groups of parents and adolescents together. Communication skills included "problem-ownership, message sending, confrontation, active listening, conflict resolution, and letting go" (Riesch et al., 1993, p. 13); trainers also provided information on young adolescent development. Observational data based on a discussion of a family problem provided by a randomly selected subset of mothers, fathers, and teens indicated no changes in prosocial behavior, but fathers' and teens' antisocial content declined significantly, relative to that of the controls. Mothers, fathers, and teens reported significant improvement in communication or family relations; specific measures that changed depended on the respondents. Absolute magnitudes of change, however, were small.

Other studies of communication/problem-solving didactic approaches with community populations have employed stronger designs involving random assignment. Guerney and colleagues have conducted some of the best evaluations of communication training (Ginsberg, 1971; Guerney, Coufal, & Vogelsong, 1981; Vogelsong, 1975). Their approach, called "relationship enhancement" (RE), is intended as a primary prevention intervention and focuses on communication skills involving expressing views and feelings, listening with empathy, facilitating conversations, and taking turns appropriately (Guerney, 1977). The intervention is delivered to groups of parents in 12–15 weekly sessions. A directive group leader models the skills and directs the participants' skill practice, then provides feedback on performance. The leader also assigns home tasks.

In two studies, Guerney and colleagues showed that families receiving RE displayed consistently better communication skills (as rated by observers) in a task in which parents and teens discussed things they would like to change about themselves or their partners than families who had been randomly assigned to waiting-list control conditions (Ginsberg, 1971; Guerney et al., 1981). Questionnaires assessing family relationships showed similar improvements relative to controls. Vogelsong (1975) provided a portion of the RE group with "booster" intervention consisting of weekly phone calls and meetings every 6 weeks after treatment ended. The RE group that received the booster reported better communication than the RE group that received no booster at a 6-month follow-up. Observed skills were maintained at follow-up and unaffected by the booster intervention.

Guerney et al. (1981) also included a carefully controlled comparison treatment that involved discussion of relationship issues, but lacked the structured didactic focus on communication skills of the RE groups. On all but one measure, this comparison group produced outcomes that were no different from those produced by the waiting-list control. The differences between RE and discussion group findings could not be attributed to therapist differences: The same leaders conducted both interventions, and were rated equally highly on leader characteristics by clients at the end of treatment.

The RE studies are important for several reasons. First, Guerney et al.'s (1981) findings strongly suggest that the structure of their training program, the focus on specific communication skills, or some combination of the two is responsible for positive changes in family interaction. Equally important, the Guerney et al. study shows that simply discussing relationship issues with a supportive group leader is unlikely to have beneficial effects on family interaction. Second, the RE studies indicate that communication training without problem-solving training can have beneficial effects on family relationships, at least in community samples. Note, however, that because Guerney and colleagues specifically addressed communication skills generally, none of their assessments focused on how families communicated during conflictual situations. Thus, whether RE skills generalized to discussions of disagreements is not clear.

Another approach that has been evaluated systematically is "problem-solving communication training" (PSCT; Robin & Foster, 1989), which specifically addresses how family members discuss conflictual situations. The basic components of PSCT involve training individual families in problem-solving and communication skills. Sessions focus on specific family problems, starting with less complex, less anger-provoking issues and progressing to more difficult topics as the family's skills improve. The therapist instructs the family in specific problem-solving skills, models and prompts rehearsal of the skills, provides feedback, guides family members' feedback to each other, and assigns between-session communication and problem-solving tasks to be done at home. These tasks may include implementing solutions the family has agreed upon during a therapy session, prac-

ticing problem-solving or communication skills during the week, or holding a family meeting to discuss a particular issue. Therapists generally work with individual families over the course of 8–12 intervention sessions in outcome studies. (Treatment is longer in clinical practice settings, where intervention may incorporate additional components, such as cognitive restructuring and interventions to change problematic structural aspects of family communication; see Robin & Foster, 1989.)

Several studies using random assignment have evaluated variations on PSCT. Two initial studies (Foster, Prinz, & O'Leary, 1983; Robin, Kent, O'Leary, Foster, & Prinz, 1977) evaluated problem solving with samples recruited via newspaper notices offering treatment for families in conflict. Robin et al. (1977) trained mothers and teens first on hypothetical and then on real problems, and found changes in observations of communication but not in reports of conflict at home. To increase generalization of skills to the home setting, Foster et al. (1983) included fathers in treatment and focused solely on actual problems in the parent–adolescent relationship. In addition, Foster et al. (1983) compared a group that received PSCT alone with an "enhanced generalization" group whose members were also assigned homework discussions and discussed their home use of communication skills with the therapist. In contrast with Robin et al. (1977), Foster et al. (1983) found no evidence of improvement in observed skills, but did find significant improvement in questionnaire measures assessing family relationships. Interestingly, the group that received the "generalization" component of treatment showed no evidence of superior generalization to the home setting; a number of families in the PSCT-only group reported "spontaneous" generalization. In addition, at a 6- to 8-week follow-up, the generalization group showed some declines in outcome, whereas the other group maintained its gains. The findings of both studies—particularly the absence of effects—should be considered in light of samples sizes as low as nine per group, which produce extremely low statistical power.

Together, studies of PSCT suggest that these approaches can change observed family interaction and reports of interactional dimensions of family relationships with community and quasi-clinical (e.g., distressed but recruited via newspaper notices) samples. Several studies have not consistently produced gains in both arenas, however, with some showing limited evidence of home improvement (Openshaw et at., 1992;

Robin et al., 1977; Wood & Davidson, 1993), and others showing stronger suggestions of improvement in family relationships than in acquisition of positive skills (Foster et al., 1983; Riesch et al., 1993). Many of these studies were limited by small samples, however, and correspondingly poor statistical power. In addition, few studies have used these approaches as a sole intervention for clinic populations, although Bry, Conboy, and Bisgay (1986) reported positive effects of a PSCT intervention on drug use and grades with three drug-using teens in a multiple-baseline design.

What ingredients of treatment are essential for families to learn communication skills in didactic interventions? Guerney et al. (1981) showed that structured treatment is required for communication change; discussion of problems in a group setting with a warm, caring therapist produced no changes. Similarly, using a multiple-baseline design, Serna, Schumaker, Hazel, and Sheldon (1986) showed that simply discussing problems did not produce changed communication. Improvements in skills happened only when the therapist introduced specific training procedures.

Studies also provide some empirically based suggestions concerning practices that may improve generalization and maintenance. Vogelsong (1975) showed that booster sessions enhanced maintenance of gains initially produced by this structured treatment. Foster et al. (1983), however, found that giving homework assignments and discussing home use of PSCT skills failed to improve generalization and somewhat impeded maintenance when PSCT failed to produce demonstrable improvements in observed conflict resolution skills. These data are somewhat difficult to interpret, because Robin (1981) used a very similar approach to promote generalization, and found better communication change and maintenance than Foster et al. (1983).

Additional studies with larger samples that can inform therapists of specific treatment components required for immediate and long-term effectiveness are sorely needed in this area. It is particularly important for intervention research to isolate treatment components that promote acquisition, generalization, and maintenance of communication and problem-solving behaviors, and to recognize that different elements of treatment may contribute to each. To do this, studies should assess whether family members can perform the skills under ideal conditions (e.g., discussions in a therapist's office), and whether they use the skills and at what levels at home. Assessing whether these skills affect frequency and intensity of relationship conflict and levels of general relationship satisfaction is also important. Follow-up data are also needed on each of these variables to assess maintenance. Finally, research should examine the relationships among change in each of these variables, to test the explicit and implicit models underlying the use of didactic communication interventions.

Indications and Contraindications of Skills Training Alone.   Communication and problem-solving skills training as a sole intervention is indicated when a family's difficulties seem primarily tied to its communication patterns, with few additional complicating factors. This is most likely to be the case in a mildly to moderately distressed family in which the parents' relationship is satisfactory, the parents work together well as a team, and the teen and parents do not display serious acting-out or internalizing problems (i.e., no clinically significant comorbid conditions exist). Positive results of many communication training programs with community populations also suggest that this approach has some promise as a preventive strategy. Formal, well-designed prevention trials using problem-solving and communication approaches and following individuals over several years have not yet been implemented, however.

In our experience, communication and problem-solving skills training as a sole intervention is unlikely to be effective when additional factors beyond parent–adolescent communication skills contribute to conflict. These include cognitive distortions, problems with parental teamwork or the couple relationship more generally, cross-generational coalitions and triangulation, and functional patterns that lead to important payoffs for conflict for one or more family members. In addition, comorbid conditions (e.g., ADHD or Conduct Disorder in the teenager, Major Depression or Substance Abuse in a parent) often require additional interventions and/or modifications of the approach, although communication and problem-solving skills training may be useful as one component of a multifaceted intervention.

Finally, communication and problem-solving skills training as typically conceptualized in the literature may need modification for use with immigrant families or with families from ethnic groups with values that conflict with the model underlying the skills-training approach. This implicit model emphasizes a democratic or authoritative view of parenting, in which the teenager is allowed considerable participation and voice in decision making. Families from cultures that view the parents as ultimate authorities may find this model difficult to accept, and the approach may need to be altered to downplay the democracy of problem solving and to acknowledge explicitly the parents' senior role and authority in the hierarchy (e.g., with traditional Chinese families—see Lee, 1996). In addition, for a family in which the parents immigrated but the child was born in the new country, a discrepancy between parent and adolescent acculturation (rather than communication problems per se) may be a major factor that promotes and maintains conflict. Although helping the family communicate and resolve arguments may be quite helpful in such a case, intervention should be augmented by helping the family members to attribute their conflicts to natural acculturation pressures, instead of to a "bad child" or "rigid parents."

Using the approach with ethnically diverse families also warrants caution, because the communication and problem-solving skills included in intervention are based on research with predominantly European American families. Adherence to a strict set of rules for what constitutes "good" and "bad" communication among families from diverse groups may lead therapists to ignore communication patterns that are quite functional in these groups. In such a situation, the therapist can (1) study the culture and consult with cultural experts about patterns that are expected versus problematic; (2) assess carefully which communication patterns tend to exacerbate conflict in the family, and target these in particular; and (3) involve the family members in isolating specific, idiographic communication problems by asking them to identify which aspects of other members' communication in session were helpful versus destructive.

Skills Training plus Additional Components

A number of investigators have added components to problem-solving and/or communication skills training. These additions are based on the assumption that the added components address factors that exacerbate or maintain conflict, and that these factors are common to families presenting with conflict. Additional interventions include (1) cognitive restructuring, which addresses irrational cognitions assumed to promote conflict, such as misattributions, parental perfectionism and expectations of obedience, and parents' or teens' fears of ruinous conse-

quences if they pursue a particular solution (Robin & Foster, 1989); (2) anger control training, which teaches methods for dealing with intense negative emotions to reduce the impact of anger on communication and responses to conflictual situations (Stern, 1984); (3) interventions for systemic factors, which include parents' failure to work as a team, cross-generational coalitions, and triangulation (Robin & Foster, 1989); and (4) parent training approaches, which generally target parents' use of consequences (contingency management).

Cognitive Restructuring. Cognitive restructuring approaches address cognitive distortions and misattributions associated with family conflict. Suggestions for dealing with problem cognitions often separate interventions for blaming and attributions of malicious intent from those designed to address such cognitions as rumination, obedience, and fairness.

Clinical descriptions of strategies for dealing with blaming attributions frequently center on ways of reframing the attributions to be more benign (Alexander & Parsons, 1982; Robin & Foster, 1989). Reframing involves suggesting an alternative reason for a negative behavior or characteristic. For example, a therapist might suggest that a teenager's angry outbursts signal unskilled attempts to communicate, rather than attempts to wound a parent; a parent's nagging can be framed as attempts to help a teenager grow up to be a responsible adult, rather than indications that the parent does not trust the teenager. As an alternative to reframing, the therapist can encourage family members to verify or deny the truth of attributional judgments, teaching each family member who voiced a judgment to take the other person at his or her word. The success of reframing depends upon the therapist's coming up with a believable alternative explanation for behavior, whereas the success of the verification intervention depends upon family members' willingness to discuss their thoughts and motivations openly with each other.

We advocate more formal cognitive restructuring to address cognitive distortions (Foster & Robin, 1989; Robin & Foster, 1989). Intervention strategies borrow heavily from the work of Beck and others addressing cognitive components of depression (e.g., Beck, Rush, Shaw, & Emery, 1979), and include (1) providing a rationale explaining how thoughts, communication, and affect (in this case, usually angry feelings) are linked; (2) identifying the specific client belief that promotes communication impasses, anger, or withdrawal in interactions; (3) challenging the belief by examining the logic of the premises that underlie the belief (this is done via exaggerating the belief to absurd proportions, using humor, reframing the belief, or examining evidence for and against the belief); (4) suggesting a more reasonable alternative belief that does not involve unrealistic or absolutist components; and (5) designing and assigning tasks that will undermine or disprove the belief.

An example illustrates this approach. In this case, a mother sought treatment for severe problems involving conflict with her out-of-control adopted son. After a few sessions of problem solving, it became apparent that the mother was unwilling to consider any solutions that involved consequences for the son's misbehavior. As a result, the son readily agreed to various solutions to problems, but failed to follow through on his part of agreements. Further assessment of the mother's reluctance to impose consequences revealed that she believed that because her son was adopted, she should try to satisfy his every wish. If she was hard on him, she believed, he would not love her and she would be a poor adoptive mother. Gentle examination of the rumination components of this belief, together with developmental information about the importance of parental limit setting for development (regardless of the child's adoptive status), persuaded the mother that her assumptions had been incorrect. In this case, the mother needed no formal experiment to disprove the belief. With initial therapist prompting, she began to design and accept solutions that involved consequences for her son's misbehavior. Had such a task been needed, however, the therapist might have asked the mother to talk with other mothers who had good relationships with their adopted children, and specifically to discuss whether these mothers employed limit setting and how they handled issues related to their children's adoptive status.

Three investigations have examined PSCT coupled with cognitive restructuring. In the first, Robin (1981) recruited clients via announcements in newspapers and in various community sites. Robin also included a waiting-list control and a "best alternative treatment," in which therapists used any of a variety of family approaches available at the clinic where the study was conducted. Both treatments produced improvements on questionnaire measures of conflict and family relationships relative to the control conditions, but only PSCT produced significant improvements in observed communication during a problem-solving discussion. Unfortunately, no measures of cognitions were obtained, so the results of the cognitive component of the intervention on cognitive distortions could not be established.

In the second investigation, Nayar (1985) compared PSCT with and without cognitive restructuring and a waiting-list control condition. Treatment involved seven weekly sessions in which two or three families met as a group. Both treated groups improved more than the control group on measures of family conflict, and the cognitive restructuring group was superior to at least one of the other groups on measures of maternal malicious intent and self-blame beliefs. Unfortunately, the study was limited by its small sample size (nine families per group, on average), and thus may not have had sufficient statistical power to detect additional effects of cognitive restructuring (if in fact they were produced) on other family members' cognitions. At the same time, Nayar's findings provide preliminary evidence that cognitive restructuring procedures can produce changes in how mothers think about relationship issues.

Barkley, Guevremont, Anastopoulos, and Fletcher (1992) evaluated PSCT (including a cognitive restructuring component) in one of the few studies to address a clinic-recruited population. They randomly assigned 64 families with adolescents diagnosed with ADHD to either PSCT, behavior management training, or structural family therapy. Contrary to predictions, 8–10 sessions of PSCT produced significant worsening (not evident in the other treatments) in measures of mother perfectionism, obedience, and total irrational beliefs.

Barkley, Guevremont, et al. (1992) provide two possible explanations for these iatrogenic effects: (1) a focus on negative cognition in the absence of positive reframing may exacerbate negative beliefs over the course of treatment; or (2) perhaps cognitive restructuring makes clients more aware of and willing to express their beliefs after treatment. Neither of these hypotheses, however, can explain the discrepancy between Nayar's (1985) and Barkley, Guevremont, et al.'s (1992) results. One factor that could explain the discrepant findings lies in the very different populations in the two studies—one recruited from the community, the other a clinic sample with teenagers diagnosed as having ADHD. In addition, neither Barkley, Guevremont, et al. (1992) nor Nayar (1985) selected families on the basis of cognitive distortions, and thus the cognitive intervention may have been more relevant for some families than for others. Finally, Barkley, Guevremont, et al. found changes only for mothers; yet scores on the measure Barkley and colleagues used (the Family Beliefs Inventory) do not discriminate distressed from nondistressed mothers (Vincent Roehling & Robin, 1986), leading to questions about the validity of this measure for assessing mothers' cognitions. Furthermore, even after treatment, the mean for total irrational beliefs in the Barkley, Guevremont, et al. (1992) study was below the mean for nondistressed mothers in Vincent Roehling and Robin's (1996) sample.

A number of other aspects of Barkley, Guevremont, et al.'s (1992) findings were somewhat paradoxical. Observational measures of a mother–adolescent planning discussion (planning a hypothetical vacation, given unlimited funds) indicated significantly lower proportions of mothers' and teens' problem-solving statements and teens' facilitative statements, and more teen put-down and command statements, after treatment than before. Observations of behavior in conflictual discussions showed no pre–post changes in any of the treatment conditions, except for the structural family therapy group, which produced significant declines in proportions of mothers' facilitative behavior from pre- to posttreatment. Despite these findings, mothers and teenagers in all three groups reported statistically significant declines in the anger intensity of family discussions, as well as significant improvements in family relationships; the three treatments did not differ on these measures. Gains in family report measures were generally sustained during a 3-month follow-up period. The clinical significance of these gains, however, was somewhat limited. Barkley, Guevremont, et al. computed percentages of families who fell into the normal range on reports of numbers and anger intensity levels of family discussions after treatment; they found figures that ranged from 5% to 29%, depending on the specific measure and the treatment condition.

These findings are important for several reasons. First, they imply that brief training in PSCT with ADHD families did not produce significant improvements in observed mother–adolescent communication during discussions of conflictual issues, and could even produce significant worsening of some parental beliefs. This suggests that training procedures that are generally successful in improving the communication of nonclinic populations may warrant modification for use with ADHD families. In addition, a relatively low percentage of families reported conflict in the normal range after treatment. This suggests that PSCT interventions in the context of comorbid circumstances may not be sufficient to propel such a family into the "normal" range of communication and conflict. Rather, as Barkley, Guevremont, et al. (1992) suggest, supplemental treatment components may be required to address additional correlates of ADHD, such as contingency management interventions, study skills training, and psychopharmacological interventions (see Barkley, 1990, and Robin, 1990, for descriptions).

Indications and Contraindications for Cognitive Restructuring. Interventions to alter attributions of malicious intent are generally applicable whenever these arise in therapy, and particularly during early sessions. In fact, some speculate that these interventions are essential for engaging family members in a productive alliance with the therapist and developing a hopeful view of the therapeutic process (e.g., Alexander & Parsons, 1982).

More formal cognitive restructuring interventions may be indicated when therapists encounter treatment impasses, particularly after early treatment success. In particular, therapists should suspect problematic underlying beliefs when family members communicate well about some problems, but become extremely rigid or overreact when discussing other issues. This is a good signal to assess the beliefs that contribute to these unusual reactions, and to intervene with cognitive restructuring if irrational beliefs emerge.

The cognitive interventions described here are contraindicated under several circumstances. The first occurs when an extreme belief is in fact realistic, as, for example, when a parent fears disastrous consequences because of a teen's serious antisocial behavior. In such a case, the belief may in fact be adaptive and spur the parent to the extraordinary efforts that may be required to bring the teen's behavior under control. The second can occur with less acculturated families in which the parents' culture of origin stresses obedience and respect for parental authority. In these cases, conflict is better framed as a discrepancy between the views of the culture of origin and the new culture. Families can be taught that parents and teens are likely to have different views because of their exposure to different cultures, and encouraged to communicate about those differences prior to trying to resolve problems.

A third contraindication occurs when a family member is highly rigid and strongly resists challenging his or her beliefs. A Socratic approach is sometimes sufficient to undermine lesser levels of resistance. With this strategy, the therapist avoids direct challenges, and instead asks a series of questions that prompt the client to draw his or her own conclusions about the belief, its rationality, and its consequences. For example, had the adoptive mother described earlier been resistant to the therapist's attempts at cognitive restructuring, the therapist might have asked the mother about the extent to which she believed adoptive and birth children have different and similar parenting needs; whether she viewed limit setting as important for birth children and why; whether adoptive children are immune from the need for limits; and what messages she thought her son was deriving from the absence of limits and how she knew this. The therapist would gently but relentlessly have pursued this line of questioning until the parent herself began to realize the contradictions or errors in her assumptions.

When the therapist believes that a family member's unwillingness to explore his or her beliefs results from the perceived "challenge" of being questioned in front of other members, a session alone (or, in the case of parents, without the teen present) may prompt the individual to explore his or her thinking more openly. In other cases, the therapist can initially discuss problems about which the family member is flexible; more difficult problems characterized by cognitive distortions can be approached in later sessions, after some progress has been made and the family member shows greater trust of the therapist and the process.

Anger Control Training. Anger control interventions assume that negative interpersonal behavior is often the product of inadequately controlled negative affect. Clinical experience suggests that families' discussions are often derailed when one or more members overreact angrily to the statements of another. In addition, the problem-solving steps taught in many didactic approaches to treating family conflict are quite rational and linear, and their use is inappropriate in conflictual situations in which family members enter the situation already feeling quite angry with one another (e.g., when a teen arrives home an hour after a carefully planned curfew without having called to explain his or

her whereabouts and tardiness). In these cases, other approaches may be needed.

A number of anger control interventions have been implemented with adults and with teenagers (e.g., Deffenbacher, Thwaites, Wallace, & Oetting, 1994; Feindler, 1990; Feinder & Ecton, 1986; Novaco, 1995). Stern (1984) adapted these kinds of anger management approaches and used them with families. She compared a group-delivered version of PSCT with and without anger management training. In the anger management component, therapists gave information about the role of arousal in conflicts; taught family members to notice early signs of arousal and to modify unhelpful thoughts that arose at these times; instructed the family in methods of arousal reduction (relaxation techniques, deep breathing); and prompted use of self-praise to support good emotional control during conflict. Family members also kept logs of angry reactions and were encouraged to physically remove themselves from conflict situations if they were too angry to participate productively in discussions of problems at home.

Results indicated that teens in the group that included anger management were more satisfied with treatment than teens who received PSCT alone. Otherwise, the groups were largely similar on indicators of anger levels at home and observations of conflict in analogue discussions of problem situations. The lack of differentiation between conditions may have been due to the fact that families in the PSCT condition improved significantly in their appraisals of their anger levels during home discussions and in observer ratings of their problem-solving skills. The relatively small sample of the study (8 families in one group, 10 in another) undoubtedly also contributed to the failure to find significant differences between the conditions, although visual inspection of means that did not differ significantly indicated that on some measures of anger, the PSCT group was slightly superior to the anger control group after treatment. Thus, whether additional participants would have changed the pattern of results is not clear.

Indications and Contraindications for Anger Control Training. Despite the intuitive appeal of anger control interventions, it is currently not clear whether their use on a broad scale as part of a package to treat parent–adolescent conflict is warranted. Given the fact that PSCT generally reduces indicators of anger in discussions (e.g.,

Robin, 1981; Stern, 1984), anger management interventions may not be indicated as the sole or initial treatment of choice for parent–adolescent conflict. Instead, these are probably best used as a supplement to or a follow-up for other approaches.

Nonetheless, clinical experience suggests that occasionally parents and teenagers improve their communication but still have occasional angry blowups. In these cases, anger management interventions may be warranted. Family members may also need to be warned that problem solving is unlikely to work when tempers are high. In addition, on rare occasions family members are so angry with one another at the beginning of therapy that they regularly explode angrily during discussions, despite firm therapist attempts to guide and control the sessions. Anger management approaches may be useful for teaching these family members how to calm down sufficiently to engage in rational discussion. In addition, family members who show excessive anger in nonfamilial as well as familial situations may benefit from anger control interventions targeting a range of situations, not just the family-related ones.

Interventions for Systemic Factors. Interventions to alter systemic factors are based on the hypothesis that maladaptive aspects of family systems contribute to conflict. Which interventions are relevant, of course, depends upon the systemic factors believed to play a causal role in eliciting or maintaining conflict. Often systemic interventions are woven into other sorts of treatments designed to alter family interaction.

We (Foster & Robin, 1989; Robin & Foster, 1989) recommend several interventions for improving parental teamwork. These include (1) instructing quarreling parents to discuss the problem and reach common ground in their views before discussing the problem with the teenager; (2) anticipating and troubleshooting problems that may arise in implementing solutions to problems because the parents undermine each other or the teen plays one parent off another; (3) assigning parents the task of discussing together issues that arise at home before either parent unilaterally grants privileges to or imposes consequences on the teenager; (4) blocking the teen from disrupting discussions between parents, or targeting teen interruptions of parent discussions as a communication issue;

(5) working with interparental communication skills directly for a few sessions alone; and/or (6) conducting, or referring the couple for, formal couple therapy.

Limited research has examined the benefits of adding couple interventions to treatment, and the research that does exist focuses on parent training with younger children, not adolescents. Nonetheless, this work generally supports the hypothesis that adding parent-focused interventions to improve couple mutual support and problem solving in regard to child-rearing issues enhances the effects of child management training, particularly if the parents' marriages are generally distressed (Dadds, Schwartz, & Sanders, 1987; Griest et al., 1982).

Even less research has looked at the specific effects of interventions to alter triangulation and cross-generational coalitions. Many interventions designed to strengthen the parental alliance may weaken maladaptive cross-generational alliances by promoting parental teamwork and communication. In addition, cross-generational manipulation and triangulation can be targeted as communication skill problems. This usually entails improving the communication between one of the parents and the teenager. In addition, structural family therapists often suggest tasks to be done at home that are intended to break up patterns of triangulation or cross-generational alliances (see, e.g., Minuchin & Fishman, 1981); specific tasks vary from family to family.

Although a few studies support the efficacy of structural family therapy in general with teenagers with externalizing behavior problems (e.g., Szapocznik, Kurtines, Foote, Perez-Vidal, & Hervis, 1983, 1986), most have not fully specified the nature of the intervention or specifically measured structural aspects of family interaction before and after treatment. One well-controlled study (Mann et al., 1990) measured alliance patterns in families with teenage delinquents, and indicated that multisystemic therapy (described in more detail later) altered these patterns. Specifically, intervention significantly increased supportiveness and decreased conflict/hostility between mothers and fathers and between fathers and adolescents. Because multisystemic therapy is highly individualized (and thus can vary considerably from family to family), however, the specific treatment components responsible for these improvements could not be determined. Clearly, more research is need to ascertain which specific structural interventions effectively alter specific systemic patterns of family interactions such as cross-generational coalitions and triangulation, and whether these alterations produce changes in the ultimate goals of treatment.

Indications and Contraindications for Systemic Interventions. Improvements in parental teamwork should be encouraged when parents are inconsistent, when parents argue unproductively about discipline, or when the teen manipulates one parent against another. Similarly, interventions to reduce triangulation are indicated for families in which conflict and negative relationships between two parties persists in part because a third mediates between them.

Interventions to improve parents' functioning as a team will often be applicable across ethnic groups, particularly when the group in question has a strong tradition supporting parental authority. In some cases, however, the locus of intervention may need to be broadened if adults other than parents share authority for making decisions about and disciplining the children. In these cases, the roles of these adults should be considered in interventions to promote interauthority consistency.

The therapist should use interventions addressing cross-generational coalitions and triangulation with caution (and sometimes not at all) in relatively less acculturated families from cultures in which triangulation and/or cross-generational patterns are normative. For example, Matsui (1996) describes Japanese families as involving the father and eldest son in family executive functioning, and as strongly valuing mother–child relationships. In these cases, discouraging cross-generational relationships would run counter to strong cultural norms. In addition, cross-generational relationships within and outside the family may be important sources of support in cultures that stress community and kinship bonds, such as in African American families (Hine & Boyd-Franklin, 1996). The key in these kinds of cases is to assess the role of coalitions and triangulation in the family very carefully. If these patterns of interaction are not functionally related to conflict or problematic teen behavior, they probably do not warrant changing. If they are functionally related to a family's problems, a therapist should consider methods of intervening that will not clash with cultural traditions that the family holds strongly. For example, if an immigrant grandmother from China forms coalitions with her son and grandson, creating marital problems between a husband and his wife, the therapist might enlist the grandmother's assistance in promoting parental authority over the teen (a value in the grandmother's culture of origin), rather than trying to intervene in the grandmother–grandchild relationship directly.

Parent Training. Parent training approaches are logical additions to communication and problem-solving skills training. Most parent training emphasizes instruction in effective use of consequences (contingency management) to teach appropriate behavior and to reduce inappropriate responding. Parent training typically encourages parents to use rewarding consequences such as praise and acknowledgment, attention, privileges, token or point systems, "Premack principle" contingencies (e.g., "Work first, then play"), and contracts that specify the desired teen behavior and the consequences for performing and not performing it. In place of harsh, inconsistent, or ineffective negative consequences, therapists may encourage parents to withdraw privileges, temporarily limit access to reinforcers (e.g., ground a teen briefly, remove a teen's car keys), impose extra chores, or take away tokens or points. With younger children, therapists also encourage parents to use time out or brief social isolation immediately after negative behaviors. Many parent training programs also emphasize clear parental communication of commands and family rules.

Several features of parent training make it a logical companion to problem-solving and communication skills training approaches. First, both types of interventions often use a didactic format. Second, the success of parent training approaches with younger children suggests that this approach, with appropriate developmental modifications, might be quite useful for helping families with teens who display externalizing problems. Problem solving, with its explicit involvement of the teen in decision making, provides an appropriate developmental bridge between interventions for children and interventions for adults. Finally, parent training explicitly addresses the functions of the child's problem behavior—something missing in many descriptions of communication training.

A few studies have evaluated contingency management or parent training in combination with problem-solving and/or communication skills training. Nangle, Carr-Nangle, and Hansen (1994) presented data from an uncontrolled case study of a teen with severe ADHD and Conduct Disorder, in which the family first participated in contingency management. Although this resulted in some improvements in the boy's behavior, adding problem-solving training led to much higher rates of parent-reported compliance and positive family interactions.

Patterson and Forgatch (1995) examined predictors of outcome of a treatment program that included training in both family management and problem solving with parents and preteen children with serious antisocial behavior problems. Assessments of children's aversive behavior in the home and parents' reports of externalizing behavior problems showed significant declines between pre- and posttreatment assessments. Observer ratings of parental discipline in the home and observations of problem solving in a family discussion of a current dispute showed significant improvements. Interestingly, changes in problem solving significantly predicted reduced arrests during the 2 years following treatment. Perhaps because the focus of the study was on predicting changes over time, and because of the wealth of literature demonstrating the efficacy of parent training over no treatment, no control condition was included.

Gant et al. (1981) and Besalel and Azrin (1981) each evaluated combinations of communication training and contingency management training with families with teenagers using random assignment to treatment versus control groups. Besalel and Azrin (1981) provided parents and teens referred for severe behavior problems with four counseling sessions that focused on setting specific goals, contracting and other reinforcement-based interventions, and communication skills training in providing positive and negative feedback. They reported significant declines in parent- and teen-reported problems immediately after treatment; treated families differed significantly from a waiting-list control group. The waiting-list group showed similar improvement when the same intervention was implemented after the posttreatment assessment. Families maintained these gains at a 6-month follow-up. Unfortunately, this study used only a single self-report measure and provided no evidence of its reliability or validity. In addition, no specific data described the nature of participants' problems prior to intervention, and the absence of measures of instrumental goals made it impossible to assess whether treatment affected parenting and communication behavior.

Gant et al. (1981) also used measures with limited validity evidence, but included measures directly related to change in communication skills. Their intervention targeted court-referred

families, who were randomly assigned to receive usual community services or to participate in a 7-month program that focused on consistent use of consequences; implementation of a token economy program; and improvement in feedback, affection, and negotiation skills. After treatment, treated families showed significantly more constructive communication and less nonconstructive communication than controls in a discussion of parent and child behavior during the last 24 hours. They also rated their communication in the discussion more positively. Unfortunately, measures of behavior at home were not collected.

Dishion and Andrews (1995) conducted one of the best outcome studies evaluating a combination of problem-solving training with training in other parenting skills. Dishion and Andrews randomly assigned 119 families with a 10- to 14-year-old child at risk for antisocial behavior and the development of drug use to either (1) a parent-focused intervention; (2) a teen-focused intervention; (3) an intervention that contained both the parent- and teen-focused components; or (4) a self-directed change condition, in which parents and teens received the newsletters and videotapes describing the content of the other interventions, but had no therapist contact. The parent intervention included 12 group sessions and 3 individual sessions; it focused on problem solving, limit setting, positive reinforcement, and parental monitoring of children's activities and whereabouts. The teen groups emphasized self-regulation and included materials related to self-monitoring, positive goal setting, setting limits with friends, developing friends who would support prosocial behavior, and improving communication and problem solving with parents and peers. Dishion and Andrews also recruited a comparison group of 39 parents and teenagers who met the same criteria as the treated families but did not participate in treatment.

Results immediately after treatment showed that parents and teens in all three of the parent- and teen-focused conditions significantly decreased their negative communication in discussion of home problems, relative to the self-directed control group and to the comparison families. Mothers reported significant changes in conflict at home in only the combined parent- and child-focused intervention, although the use of a relatively unknown instrument to assess conflict somewhat weakens these findings. Teachers reported significantly better Child Behavior Checklist (CBCL) Externalizing behavior scores for the parent-only group relative to the control and comparison groups, but this effect disappeared by a 1-year follow-up. Importantly, the two treatments that involved teen interventions both showed evidence of iatrogenic effects 1 year after treatment, with teens in these groups having significantly higher Externalizing scores on the teacher form of the CBCL than did controls/comparisons. They also reported higher rates of smoking. Dishion and Andrews (1995) suggest that aggregating high-risk young adolescents in groups may have been responsible for these effects. Despite these provocative findings, the results of the parent-focused intervention suggest that group interventions with high-risk parents (supplemented with occasional individual sessions) can improve parent–teen communication without the teen's necessarily being involved in treatment. Although teen-only groups can produce similarly beneficial effects on parent–teen communication, the fact that these interventions did not affect reports of conflict and had possible negative effects on teens' functioning in the school indicate that these groups should be used with caution when they are composed solely of high-risk adolescents. Of course, the curriculum of these teen groups addressed many features of school and family life besides problem solving and communication; whether a sole focus on communication would have yielded the same findings is an empirical question.

Surprisingly little research has connected parent training with communication interventions for adolescents, in light of their logical interrelationships. One particularly potent ingredient of parent training is its explicit focus on the functions of problem behavior. Although we and others (e.g., Alexander & Parsons, 1982; Foster & Robin, 1989) have strongly advocated including an analysis of the functions of teen and parent behavior in comprehensive behavioral–family systems assessment and treatment planning, most communication training programs do not do so, at least not explicitly. Whether this attention significantly improves the effects of intervention awaits further research. In addition, comparative evaluations of the relative contribution of parent training and communication training interventions to different sorts of treatment outcome would be particularly useful for teasing out the relative contributions of problem-solving and family management components. Finally, Dishion and Andrew's (1995) counterintuitive findings also point to the importance of assessing a range of outcomes, both short- and long-term, and of attending in particular to the contexts in which therapists deliver parent and teen interventions.

Indications and Contraindications for Parent Training. Assessment of the consequences parents provide for a teen's adaptive and maladaptive behavior seems warranted in any comprehensive intervention addressing negative family interactions in which teen noncompliance, rule violations, or acting out is the basis for disputes. Similarly, consideration of the functions family members' communication serve for all involved parties (including parents) can provide clues about inadvertent reinforcement and avoidance patterns that may maintain conflictual patterns, as well as punishment that may suppress adaptive responding.

Interventions that alter parents' use of consequences are warranted when parents are inconsistent or erratic in their use of consequences, regularly apply harsh or ineffective discipline, or simply fail to utilize consequences for a teen's problem behavior at all. Consequence-based interventions are also warranted when a teen, in spite of good intentions, consistently fails to follow through with family agreements. In many cases, simply prompting the family to generate and evaluate consequences for rule violations and compliance as part of problem-solving discussions will be sufficient. This has the advantage that the family generally proposes consequences that are part of the parents' repertoire and can be readily made part of the family's routines, promoting maintenance of consequence use in the natural environment. In cases in which the parents or teens lack knowledge of or use bad judgment in selecting consequences (e.g., a family selects a long-term reward for an ADHD teenager), some instruction in appropriate consequences and ways of providing them may be warranted.

Consequence-based parent training interventions can vary considerably in the effort they require parents to make to implement them. In general, interventions that require a great deal of parental effort are contraindicated when less effortful steps to correct the problem will suffice. In addition, highly effortful interventions are contraindicated when parent problems (depression, substance use problems) or skill deficits (lack of consistency in many areas of functioning) make it unlikely that the parent(s) will follow through with the intervention. In these cases, the therapist should either address the problem that leads to parental inconsistency, or help the family arrive at less effortful interventions that are more likely to be implemented at home.

Other Family Interventions

The research described thus far suggests that interventions to address problem solving, communication, and conflict directly can alter those skills and reduce indicators of conflict in the family. In addition, other types of interventions have produced changes in interactions in families with teenagers referred for clinical services. Two well-researched treatment strategies that consistently produce changes in family interactions are functional family therapy (FFT; Alexander & Parsons, 1982; Barton & Alexander, 1981) and multisystemic therapy (MST; Henggeler & Borduin, 1990). Although both have an impressive track record in reducing delinquent behavior and maintaining those improvements, here we specifically concentrate on the effects of these interventions on family communication.

FST and MST approaches resemble didactic approaches in that they share a focus on family processes as key ingredients that maintain problems in teen behavior. They differ, however, in that both MST and FST were developed to reduce delinquent and aggressive behavior rather than to address conflict per se. Perhaps because of this, most outcome studies examining FFT and MST have focused on clinic-referred or juvenile justice populations. In addition, both types of treatment include multiple components, many of which directly address family processes. However, neither includes a lengthy, structured didactic approach to problem solving and communication.

Multisystemic Therapy

MST (Henggeler & Borduin, 1990; Henggeler, Schoenwald, & Pickrel, 1995) uses an empirically based ecosystemic approach to conceptualizing deviant adolescent behavior. Specifically, MST targets the correlates of adolescent antisocial behavior, focusing on the important social and individual systems in which the teen functions. These systems include the teen as an individual, the family, the school, the peer group, and the neighborhood and community. A therapist identifies strengths and weaknesses in each of these areas. Together with the family, the therapist plans an intervention that capitalizes on family, teen, and system strengths, with the goal of placing the teen in contexts that promote adaptive alternatives to delinquent activities. In-

terventions are highly individualized, and borrow whenever possible from approaches documented in previous studies to be effective in producing the instrumental goals of treatment. Thus, a therapist might use cognitive restructuring or pharmacological approaches to reduce a parent's depression, parent training to teach systematic use of consequences, or communication training to help feuding parents come to agreements on how to parent their problem child. Therapists typically deliver treatment in the natural environment whenever possible, and schedule sessions according to client needs. Evaluations of MST in community settings also keep therapist caseloads low, provide consistent supervision, and emphasize engagement as an important goal of treatment (Henggeler, Pickrel, Brondino, & Crouch, 1996). Treatment length is quite variable, but contact lasts 20–25 hours on average (Borduin et al., 1995; Mann et al., 1990).

A number of investigations have examined the effects of multisystemic therapy in treating families of delinquent and drug-using teenagers. These investigations have included relatively large samples of teenagers with serious antisocial behavior problems, and most have employed measures of family interaction. Henggeler et al. (1986), Mann et al. (1990), and Borduin et al. (1995) compared how MST versus alternative treatments affected family communication in unrevealed-differences tasks, in which family members had to reach a consensus about answers to hypothetical questions after individually ranking their preferences. Henggeler et al. (1986) showed improvements in maternal warmth and decreases in adolescent aggression in these interactions relative to those of a comparison group (not randomly assigned) receiving other services in the community. Mann et al. (1990) randomly assigned two-parent families to MST or to individual therapy. They found that MST produced improvements in mother–father and adolescent–father supportiveness, coupled with decreases in father–adolescent and mother–father conflict/hostility. Borduin et al. (1995) reported comparable findings for a sample that included single-parent as well as two-parent families. Although Henggeler et al. (1986) reported no significant changes in reports of family relations in the home, Borduin et al. (1995) and Henggeler, Melton, and Smith (1992) reported significant improvements in family members' reports on the Family Adaptability and Cohesion Scales II, a questionnaire assessing perceptions of family interactions. Mann et al.

(1990) also found that increases in mother–father supportiveness and activity and decreases in parental conflict-hostility were linked to changes in reported symptomatology on the Symptom Checklist—90. This supports the clinical notion that improving parental teamwork and communication may be important to treatment success, at least with families of delinquent teens.

Consistent findings that MST results in changes in observed and reported family interaction suggest that it may be possible to alter family communication without direct training in communication skills. All of the MST investigations cited above likewise found significant changes in indicators of delinquency in the MST group. These findings are consistent with the hypothesis that communication patterns may result from teen delinquent behavior, rather than causing or maintaining it. Several factors, however, make it hard to draw this conclusion from the data currently available. First, the individualized nature of MST makes it possible that some families actually received communication training as part of their intervention. Second, although changes in observational indicators of communication were linked with changes in adolescent symptomatology in one study (Mann et al., 1990), reports of parent–teen relations did not mediate the intervention effect in another (Henggeler et al., 1992). Third, none of these studies directly addressed communication about real-life disagreements, so whether changes occurred in ways of handling conflict was not clear. Finally, it is possible that some third factor, such as improvements in school performance, resulted both in problem reduction and in improvements in family communication. Again, the highly individualized nature of MST makes it quite difficult to ascertain the active ingredients of the intervention package. Regardless of the reason for the changes in communication, MST findings clearly demonstrate that didactic skills training is not the only route to improvements in family communication.

Functional Family Therapy

FFT's proponents (Alexander & Parsons, 1982) hypothesize that child behavior problems result when family members use maladaptive methods of seeking intimacy, distance, or regulation outcomes in their interactions with others. FFT therapists examine family transactions over time, looking for patterns suggesting that a family member desires closeness and contact ("intimacy"), privacy and independence from others

("distance"), or some balance of these two in his or her interactions with others in the family. As therapists conceptualize the functions that problem behaviors and family members' reactions to those behaviors serve for the individuals in the family, they also plan how to help the family members achieve the same outcomes using more adaptive methods. Such interventions might include contracts for handling a problem, consequence systems, and interventions to alter the nature of family communication about the problem (Alexander & Parsons, 1982). Although the form of intervention may vary considerably from family to family, interventions share a focus on changing the topography of family interactions while permitting family members to continue to obtain the same kinds of outcomes their more maladaptive styles promoted. Early sessions of FFT typically focus on engaging families in treatment and on altering problematic attributions and expectations that may interfere with therapeutic processes. To accomplish these goals, therapists typically use strategies that include reframing problem interactions in nonblaming ways and highlighting the interdependence of family members' thoughts, feelings, and behaviors. Later sessions introduce specific strategies designed to alter the nature of family interactions.

Several well-controlled outcome studies have evaluated FFT with teens with status offenses referred by court systems for treatment; later studies have examined delinquent populations with more serious offenses. Alexander and Parsons (1973) and Barton, Alexander, Waldron, Turner, and Warburton (1985) documented improvements in family members' discussions over the course of FFT. These changes were superior to those shown after client-centered therapy and in a no-treatment control condition in the Alexander and Parsons (1993) study. FFT has also produced improvements in recidivism rates, relative to alternative treatment conditions (Alexander & Barton, 1976; Alexander, Barton, Schiavo, & Parsons, 1976; Alexander & Parsons, 1973; Barton et al., 1985).

Data also suggest that improvements in communication are active ingredients in producing reductions in delinquent activity. Alexander et al. (1976) showed that improvements in families' ratio of supportive to defensive communication in therapy sessions correlated positively with therapist judgments of improvement and with reduced recidivism rates. These findings support a focus on family interaction style and suggest that this focus may reduce teenagers' externalizing behaviors. One cannot rule out the possibility, however, that the reverse is true—that changes in teens' behavior produced improved family interactions. These data are limited by the fact that Alexander et al. (1976) assessed changes in communication during therapy sessions, not in home settings or family discussions in the absence of the therapist. It may be that good family communication in therapy is the result of the presence of a skilled therapist who keeps therapy sessions productively focused, rather than an indicator of changed family dynamics in the home.

In addition, FFT therapists—like MST therapists—individualize treatment by drawing from various strategies, which may include but are not limited to communication approaches. As with MST, it is difficult to know which aspects of FFT produce changes in family communication: reductions in problem behavior, changes in communication skills, better-organized family routines, or some combination of these and other factors. Furthermore, evaluations of MST and FFT have not examined whether the observed changes in family interaction patterns are maintained over time. In addition, perhaps because both types of interventions focus on family interaction generally as an instrumental rather than an ultimate goal of treatment, they have rarely assessed family discussions of ongoing family disputes.

In spite of these limitations, studies of both MST and FFT are important for understanding the dynamics of family interaction for several reasons. First, they show that—at least for delinquent teenagers—interventions that focus on here-and-now transactions in the family (FFT, MST), the school and community (MST), and the peer group (MST) can produce changes in communication, apparently without extensive didactic training in problem-solving and communication skills. These findings suggest that technologies in addition to didactic skill training should be explored for changing family communication patterns, particularly with families with comorbid communication problems and teen delinquency.

The results of evaluations of MST and FFT, together with findings that skill-oriented communication approaches and other problem-focused but nondidactic interventions often produce similar effects on reports and/or observations of family interactions (Barkley, Guevremont, et al., 1992; Robin, 1981), challenge behavioral assumptions that deficits in skill knowledge produce conflict. If skill deficits

alone are responsible for conflictual patterns, families should only show improvement after specific training or exposure to the skills they lack. Instead, findings are more consistent with a performance deficit hypothesis, in which at least some families can at times communicate positively and suppress negative behaviors, but fail to do so in conflictual or affectively charged situations. Examination of the mechanisms by which various problem- and interaction-focused approaches produce change in family communication would help fill the gaps in our understanding of the factors that contribute to clinically significant conflict in families and warrant intervention.

TREATMENT PROCESS ISSUES

Clinical writings describing the many different treatment strategies for dealing with families with troublesome adolescents show remarkable similarity in the issues they raise as problems in treating families successfully (e.g., Alexander & Parsons, 1982; Minuchin & Fishman, 1981; Robin & Foster, 1989). One set of issues relates specifically to engaging family members in treatment and eliciting their commitment to a family-oriented intervention process. A second group of issues involves keeping family members involved in treatment and working toward positive changes, dealing with treatment impasses and implementation problems as they arise.

A growing body of research literature has begun to support and add caveats to the clinical lore about working with families with teenagers. In one classic study, Alexander et al. (1976) showed that supervisors' ratings of therapists' relationship skills (warmth, humor, relating the interdependence of affect and behavior) and structuring skills (directiveness and self-confidence) accounted for significant portions of the variance in family therapy outcome. Both sets of behavior differentiated therapists who produced good versus poor outcomes, suggesting that both types of skills are needed to produce changes in families. Investigators have examined in more detail how these skills play out during the course of treatment, both in early treatment sessions and as treatment progresses.

Early Treatment: Engaging Family Members in Treatment

Family members rarely enter treatment equally committed to participating or with similar goals for its outcome. A teenager may discount or deny problems (Phares & Danforth, 1994). Parents may view a teenager as the cause of difficulties, attributing family problems to the teen's personality, negative behavior, or the like. Seen in this light, it is not surprising that parents or teenagers may be reluctant to participate in therapy. Thus, engaging family members in treatment is a key issue during the initial stages of intervention.

Prompting attendance at initial sessions by all involved family members is a first step in engaging the family into the treatment process. Fathers and teenagers generally resist participating more than mothers do (Szapocznik et al., 1988). A number of strategies can be used to gain parents' attendance at initial sessions. These include stating clearly that the therapist would like all family members to attend initial sessions, with the rationale that all parties' views are important to hear. The therapist can also speak directly to a reluctant parent, listen and reflect the parent's concerns, and invite the parent to participate for an initial assessment session, with the understanding that the parent may or may not attend future sessions. Among families from ethnic groups with strong paternal leadership traditions, therapists can appeal to reluctant fathers by discussing a father's role as leader of the family. In addition, tying the need for therapy to the family's own values (e.g., emphasizing concerns about difficulties with schoolwork in families that value achievement) may prompt reluctant members to come for an initial assessment.

Szapocznik and colleagues (e.g., Santisteban et al., 1995; Szapocznik et al., 1988) have systematically studied the effects of engagement strategies such as those just described with Hispanic families containing a drug-using adolescent member. Both Santisteban et al. (1995) and Szapoczak et al. (1988) randomly assigned families to either an engagement-as-usual intervention or an enhanced-engagement intervention in which a therapist raised the level of intervention until he or she had recruited the teen and all adult caretakers into treatment. In the enhanced intervention, therapists were encouraged to make preintake telephone contacts (and, at the most intensive level of engagement intervention, out-of-office visits) with family members, with the goal of establishing rapport/alliances with family members, beginning to restructure family members' views, gathering information about each family, and inquiring about and intervening to encourage attendance at an intake session. In both studies, the enhanced intervention pro-

duced significantly better engagement, defined by Szapocznik et al. as coming to the initial intake and by Santisteban et al. as attending both the intake and an initial treatment session. Once engaged, the number of families that completed treatment did not differ between conditions (Santisteban et al., 1995), nor did the outcomes of the engagement-as-usual and enhanced-engagement approaches differ (Szapocznik et al., 1988). This is not surprising, as therapists in all treatment conditions in both studies utilized identical family treatment procedures once the families came in for treatment. Interestingly, Santisteban et al. (1995) indicated that none of the three families in which therapists used the most intensive engagement intervention (which included out-of-home visits) engaged in treatment, and that Cuban Hispanic families were less responsive to the intervention than were families with origins in other Spanish-speaking countries. Post hoc qualitative analyses suggested that the Cuban families failing to engage in treatment were all characterized by high levels of parent resistance.

Reluctance will not automatically disappear because a therapist has persuaded or otherwise intervened to get reluctant family members to attend an initial session. Additional therapeutic strategies during early sessions can help engage participants more fully in the treatment process. A number of investigations have examined various ways of reducing blaming attributions and other negative exchanges during initial therapy sessions, in the interest of promoting engagement and setting the stage for productive later sessions.

Robbins, Alexander, Newell, and Turner (1996) investigated the relationship between therapist reframing and family members' behavior in an initial therapy session between parents and a delinquent teen. Specifically, coders classified therapist behaviors as reflections (consisting of acknowledgments and restatements of the family member's attributions, but without reframing), organizational statements (i.e., statements that directed family members' behavior in the session, or that explained the treatment or the setting), or reframes (statements that normalized blaming attributions or reconstrued them in nonblaming ways). Additional coders rated the positivity–negativity of family members' immediate responses to each therapist statement. Analyses revealed that mothers responded most positively to organizational statements, whereas teens were least negative following reframing. General statements about the impact of reframing must be interpreted with caution, however: Patterson and Forgatch (1985) found considerable variability in how mothers responded immediately after therapist reframing. Using a single-subject approach to examine interactions throughout parent training therapy, they found that reframing increased noncompliant behavior from some mothers, decreased it for others, and had no effect on a third group.

Another possible way to reduce negative interactions early in treatment is to prompt a family to focus on strengths instead of weaknesses. Melidonis and Bry (1995) used an ABA single-subject reversal design with four families to examine the effects of therapist "exceptions questions," in which the therapist responded to family members' blaming statements by asking family members to describe situations in which the problem was usually present or expected and did not occur. The therapist then inquired further about the nature of these situations. Visual inspection of data indicated that intervention produced declines in blaming and increases in positive behavior, although the timing of intervention in some families coincided with trends in data that made the impact of the intervention difficult to ascertain visually (e.g., the intervention began just after blaming statements showed a declining trend in the baseline condition). Interestingly, behavior quickly reversed once the therapist stopped using exceptions questions, suggesting that repeated therapist intervention may be needed during early sessions to reduce the negativity of family exchanges.

A related intervention that promotes a positive family focus is the "formula first session task" (FFST; de Shazer, 1985). After the first session, the therapist implements the FFST by asking the family members during the coming week to observe one or more aspects of their relationship that they would like to continue. Adams, Piercy, and Jurich (1991) examined the effects of this task by randomly assigning couples and families that came to a treatment center to one of three groups. All three groups received a similar problem-focused initial session and problem-focused structural–strategic therapy after the second session; problem-focused sessions revolved around discussions of problem areas rather than family strengths or positive behavior. The three conditions differed, however, in the task the therapist assigned after the first session and in the nature of the second session. The family-therapy-as-usual group received a problem-focused task and a problem-focused second session. In the second group, the therapist as-

signed the FFST and conducted a second session of solution-focused therapy. Solution-focused therapy involved asking about family strengths and focusing on exceptions to the presenting problem, similar to Melidonis and Bry's (1995) strategies. In the third group, clients received the FFST and a problem-focused second session. Assigning the FFST produced greater compliance than the problem-focused task, along with higher estimates of improvements in presenting problems during and after the second session, but not greater client optimism. These results were consistent regardless of whether observers' ratings of sessions, clients' reports, or therapists' ratings were used to assess the outcome. The three intervention groups did not differ in the results of therapy at the end of treatment.

A number of additional strategies may be helpful in engaging reluctant participants during early stages of treatment, although evidence for their effectiveness is anecdotal rather than empirical. We (Robin and Foster, 1989) and DiGiuseppe, Linscott, and Jilton (1996) advocate making sure teenagers know why they have been brought to therapy, and clarifying misconceptions about the nature of treatment. Liddle (1995) recommends using terms other than "therapy" to reduce stigmas associated with the term. Liddle (1995) and DiGiuseppe et al. (1989) also underscore the importance of eliciting teens' views of changes they would like to see in their lives or families, and using the content of this information to develop treatment goals that address teens' as well as parents' concerns.

The therapist must balance setting goals that recognize a teen's concerns with those that recognize parents' objectives. This is often difficult because, upon first glance, the parents' and teens' goals may seem quite different. Looking for how different goals connect and reflecting these connections can frequently be helpful in gaining mutual agreement on a set of goals for treatment. Therapist reflection and reframing that emphasize the interdependence of family members' behavior, thoughts, and feelings provides one logical way of connecting family members' concerns (Alexander & Parsons, 1982; Robin & Foster, 1989). To do this, the therapist can ask family members to describe their interactions, then reflect their descriptions in ways that highlight reluctant members' unwitting involvement in interaction problems, the connections between these interactions and their concerns, and the potential personal benefits they can gain from participating in therapy. For example, consider the hypothetical Keeler family, in which the teenager denies personal problems despite having been repeatedly suspended from school and complains about parental nagging and the desire for more independence. The parents view the problems as the result of the teen's willfulness, and Mrs. Keeler repeatedly lectures the teen about the need to complete schooling. Mr. Keeler views the problem as a mother–son issue and does not wish to attend therapy. In this case, the therapist might reframe family members' statements to show that (1) the teenager is involved in many unpleasant negative interactions, which he does not enjoy and which lead the parents to refuse him the independence he desires; (2) the parents have been trying their best but their conflict and lecturing have not dealt effectively with the teenager's behavior; (3) the parents' and teen's ways of interacting are driving a wedge between the mother and the father; and (4) the more the father leaves discipline to the mother, the more desperate and angry she becomes and the more she criticizes his lack of involvement, perpetuating the cycle. This reframing communicates that all family members pay a price for the interactions that transpire; that all have something to gain by participating in the therapy; and that changes in the ways family members interact about problem situations are crucial for dealing with the teen's problem behavior effectively, as well as for reducing the number of angry exchanges in the family.

Together, studies of engagement processes show that actively construing attendance and engagement as important phases of therapy, together with such strategies as reframing, asking exceptions questions, and assigning tasks that prompt observations of positive interactions, can have positive effects on indicators of early engagement. However, the few studies that examine whether these early interventions have a lasting impact on therapy outcome have suggested that they do not (Adams et al., 1991; Melidonis & Bry, 1995; Santisteban et al., 1996; Szapocznik et al., 1988), although Szapocznik et al. (1988) did find that enhanced-engagement strategies reduced later treatment dropout. This should not be surprising; engagement is probably a necessary but not a sufficient condition for treatment success. Additional therapist skills may come into play in different stages of therapy and may be important for promoting treatment compliance and reducing dropout later in treatment.

Later Treatment: Dealing with Implementation Problems and Preventing Dropout

In addition to engaging family members in the early stages of intervention, the therapist must keep the members involved until they have accomplished the ultimate goals of treatment. This involves dealing with implementation issues specific to the type of intervention used, as well as preventing premature treatment dropout.

Treatment implementation issues differ, depending upon the type of treatment employed. For example, in a study described earlier, Barkley, Guevremont, et al. (1992) compared PSCT, behavior management, and structural family therapy with families with an ADHD teen. Therapists rated family members' cooperation with treatment after each session. Therapist ratings indicated significantly less cooperation among PSCT families than among families in the other two treatments. This was not an artifact of therapist differences, as the same therapists implemented all three treatments. Barkley, Guevremont, et al. (1992) suggest that the focus on behavior change and home practice in didactic interventions such as PSCT may place more demands on families than other types of interventions may. We too have noted that the ease with which communication interventions are often specified in writing belies the difficulty in implementing them successfully in treatment. Table 12.4 lists implementation problems sometimes encountered in providing communication and problem-solving skill-oriented interventions for families with adolescents, along with suggested solutions. Unfortunately, this information comes more from clinical and supervisory experience than from empirical data.

A few studies have investigated therapy process issues empirically during treatments similar to those described here with younger (mostly preadolescent) children. Patterson and colleagues have examined resistance in parent training in a series of studies (Chamberlain, Patterson, Reid, Kavanagh, & Forgatch, 1984; Patterson & Forgatch, 1985; Stoolmiller, Duncan, Bank, & Patterson, 1993) that are noteworthy for their observations of client behavior in treatment sessions. Although different studies have defined "resistance" slightly differently, in general the resistance category has included such behaviors as confronting the therapist; interrupting; sidetracking the session; and making defensive, hopeless, or blaming statements.

TABLE 12.4. Solutions to Common Implementation Problems Encountered with Didactic Communication and Problem-Solving Approaches

Implementation problem	Possible solutions
Communication approaches	
Family member is reluctant to practice skill in the session.	Avoid labeling practice as "role play"; weave practice naturally into sessions without abrupt transitions; have less reluctant members go first; select issues that are important to reluctant member to discuss.
Family members think communication skill sounds stilted or unnatural.	Get family members to generate alternative ways of communicating in nondefensive, nonjudgmental ways; use family members' feedback to select which skills would be most natural to them.
Family members interrupt each other, argue, get angry, and control the session.	Provide an agenda and stick to it; courteously redirect family back to skill; establish "sessions rules" with family and enforce them; target interruptions, off-task remarks, or expressions of anger as communication skills and intervene directly with these behaviors; use formal cognitive restructuring or anger management training.
Family member reacts defensively when therapist gives feedback on skills.	Get family member to self-evaluate own performance; get family member to solicit feedback from others; videotape performance and play back; target "accepting negative feelings from family members" as communication skill; make sure that therapist feedback was expressed appropriately.
Family members fail to generalize skill use across sessions.	Review previous skills at beginning of session; ask family members to generate personal communication goals for sessions that include past skills; assign home practice of skills in multiple relevant situations; get family to generate ideas for when and how to use the skill in different situations.
Family members fail to comply with assignments to use skills at home.	Clearly specify assignment in advance; write down assignment; get explicit agreement from family members to complete assignment; use term other than "homework," to avoid negative connotations; troubleshoot potential problems with completing assignment; only assign task that has at least an 80% chance of completion and success; praise task completion; brainstorm solutions to completing assignments if family consistently fails to do home tasks.
Problem-solving approaches	
Family member thinks problem solving is too artificial.	Explain that many new skills seem artificial at first; later sessions will adapt skills to family's lifestyle.
Parent protests that using a specific problem definition avoids the real problem.	Explain that problem must be formulated in specific terms for others to understand the problem and to change their behavior; indicate to parent that his or her global concerns arise from specific problem interactions; help the parent formulate general concern (e.g.,"respect") in specific terms that cover the concern fully; frame the parent's thoughts as common but phrased in ways that prevent reaching good solutions.

(continued)

TABLE 12.4. (*continued*)

Implementation problem	Possible solutions
Family and therapist spend too much time on problem definition, no time on solutions.	Ask family members to identify one or two parts of problem that bother them most, prior to stating their problem definitions; target succinct communication if members talk too much generally; accept less-than-perfect problem definitions, especially early in treatment (use shaping to build better and better performance over time); break complex problems into component parts and solve components one by one.
Parent or therapist thinks that problem is too complex for problem solving.	Break problem into component parts; solve each one by one.
Family members try to force others to accept their problem definitions.	Explain that all members have a right to their own problem definitions, that members need to listen to each other's positions but need not agree, and that different definitions are important because they clarify the nature of the conflict.
Family members evaluate solutions while brainstorming.	Remind members they will have a chance to evaluate later; ask critical members to come up with a better solution instead of criticizing.
Solutions are too vague.	Prompt members to be more specific; model.
Too few solutions.	Suggest a crazy idea; ask questions that prompt different classes of solutions (e.g., "Are there any consequences that might help Johnny clean his room?" "Try thinking of some ways to change your routine that might help you . . .").
Too many solutions; evaluation phase drags.	Ask members to review list and eliminate solutions no one likes without discussion.
One family member dominates evaluation.	Ask members to take turns; give dominant member role of asking others for their opinion.
Teenager agrees to everything and does not voice true opinion.	Ask teen to evaluate pros and cons of solutions from parents' perspective, and get parents to voice teen's perspective; examine parental consequences if teen voices negative opinion; target "giving honest opinion" as communication skill.
Members deadlock, with parents supporting one position, teen supporting another.	Brainstorm further solutions; ask family to try one solution (usually teen's) for a week, and to use the other solution if the first does not work.
Member fails to move from initial position.	Assess for possible cognitive distortion; discuss with member how failure to compromise leads to continued problem; assess whether problem situation serves important function for resistant member; insure that family members are willing to discuss different ideas for problem before beginning discussion.
Teenager becomes silent and refuses to participate.	Establish rapport with teen and promote interaction in early sessions; give teen role that prompts speaking (e.g., writing down and reading back solutions); assess when silence began and what prompted it; see teen alone and inquire about conditions in which silence occurs; assess possible important functions of the silence and intervene accordingly.

A number of important findings have emerged from these investigations. First, lag-sequential analyses using videotapes collected throughout treatment showed that therapist teaching and confrontational behaviors significantly increased the likelihood of immediate resistance from most mothers; experimental manipulations of these behaviors established these therapist behaviors as causes of the resistance (Patterson & Forgatch, 1985). Therapist facilitative statements, questions, and supportive remarks decreased the chances that mothers would resist immediately afterwards. Second, those with high levels of resistance early in treatment tended to drop out of treatment (Chamberlain et al., 1984). Third, for many of the clients who stayed in treatment, resistance showed a curvilinear relationship across sessions, rising in the middle of therapy and dropping at the end (Chamberlain et al., 1984; Stoolmiller et al., 1993). Fourth, Stoolmiller et al. (1993) provided data supporting the hypothesis that children in families that showed these increased levels of resistance in the middle of treatment, but whose resistance declined by the end of treatment, were least likely to experience arrests during the 2-year period following treatment. In contrast, families in which the children were arrested after treatment displayed either chronically high or low levels of resistance, or patterns of resistance that increased over time and never declined. Mothers who scored high on measures of antisocial behavior and who displayed poor discipline skills in home observations were most likely to show chronically high levels of resistance. Maternal depressed mood and stress were also correlated with resistance early in treatment. Mothers who were depressed at the outset of treatment, however, were also most likely to show the "struggle-and-work-though" pattern of resistance associated with reduced arrests.

These findings, if replicated with additional samples and types of treatment, suggest that active parental engagement in the therapy process—even it that engagement takes the form of confrontation and negative attitudes—may be a predictable and possibly adaptive process in didactic treatments that call for changes in parenting behavior. Of course, the therapist must be sufficiently skillful to help parents work through resistant reactions; otherwise, chronic resistance or therapy dropout may occur (Chamberlain et at., 1984). We suspect that certain factors (early treatment successes; family members' trust in the therapist; and therapist support, problem solving, and facilitative skills) are particularly important in this process, but these hunches await empirical inquiry.

Dropout from family intervention has also received increasing scientific attention, although, as in other studies of treatment process, most of this investigation has examined parents who received treatment for problems with their preadolescent children. Kazdin, Stolar, and Marciano (1995) examined dropout from outpatient treatment that involved cognitive problem-solving training for children and child management training for parents. Separate examinations of black and white families showed some of the same predictors for both groups. Echoing Stoolmiller et al.'s (1995) findings with resistance, maternal antisocial behavior and negative parenting practices predicted dropout in both white and black families. So did reports of parental stress and parent reports of levels of child antisocial behavior prior to treatment. A number of other factors predicted dropout for white families but not black families, including family socioeconomic disadvantage, maternal youthfulness and single-parent status, and child IQ and involvement with deviant peers. In contrast, only the child's educational performance emerged as an additional predictor for black families. Contrary to findings regarding parent reports of antisocial behavior, families of black children whose teachers reported worse behavior problems were less likely to drop out of treatment than were families of children whose school behavior was less troublesome. The failure to find a greater number of predictors for black families may have been in part a result of the fact that only 1 of 12 therapists who treated the families was black; thus, therapist race could have accounted for some of the dropout in black families.

Although these results speak to the issue of which clients may need dropout prevention efforts, they do not explicate therapist behaviors or therapy characteristics that might be most effective at keeping families engaged in treatment. Kazdin, Holland, and Crowley (1997) examined this issue by developing therapist and client versions of a Barriers to Treatment Scale, with subscales assessing the respondent's views of factors that compete with treatment, treatment demands and issues, treatment relevance for the family, and the therapeutic relationship. An additional Critical Events section asks the respondent to indicate whether any of several potentially disruptive events (e.g., moving, hospitalization) occurred during treatment. Kazdin et al. (1997) evaluated client and therapist reports for families who had completed versus dropped out of the same kinds of family and child interventions employed in the Kazdin et al. (1995) investigation. Clients who completed treatment reported fewer stressors and obstacles during the treatment period, higher perceived relevance of treatment, and better therapeutic relationships than did clients who terminated treatment prematurely; therapist reports were similar. These results should be interpreted cautiously, however, because families and therapists completed the Barriers to Treatment Scale after families had either dropped out or completed treatment, and their retrospective reports may have been biased as a result of knowing each family's dropout status. Nonetheless, among families with demographic factors indicative of risk for dropping out, reports of fewer perceived barriers reduced risk of dropout. Analyses of whether barriers to treatment mediated the relationship between risk factors and dropout suggested at best only a partial mediational role. This is consistent with the notion that therapist skill, and not just characteristics that exist in a family prior to treatment, is important in helping family members to overcome roadblocks to treatment, to see the relevance of treatment for their concerns, and to establish a good working relationship with the therapist.

Prinz and Miller (1994) directly manipulated therapist behaviors that they thought might be responsible for families' staying in treatment versus dropping out of behavioral parent training. Families of 4- to 9-year-old boys with antisocial behavior problems were randomly assigned to one of two conditions. In the standard parent training program, the therapist focused exclusively on parent–child interactions and emphasized use of consequences and skill-building strategies to shape appropriate child behaviors and decrease antisocial responses. In the second condition, families received the same parent training program, accompanied by specific times when the therapist elicited and responded to parental concerns that did not involve parent–child interactional issues. The enhanced treatment protocol lead to a significantly higher percentage of families who completed treatment (71%) than did the standard treatment protocol (53%). Improved retention among families who experienced high levels of adversity (e.g., parental or couple problems, low socioeconomic status, aversive social networks, agency referral) accounted for these benefits; those with lower levels of adversity dropped out of the two conditions at equal rates.

Prinz and Miller (1994) also contacted 67% of the dropouts and inquired about their reasons for stopping treatment. Similar to Kazdin et al. (1997), they found that dropouts reported more situational obstacles, dissatisfaction with treatment, and dissatisfaction with the therapist than those who completed treatment did. Prinz and Miller also compared dropouts in the enhanced and standard conditions, finding that those who dropped out of the standard condition were particularly likely to voice dissatisfaction with the treatment. Overall, those who dropped out were more likely than completers to have children rated as high in aggression at school, to have greater rates of family adversity, and to be agency- rather than self-referred. In treatment, they were more likely to miss appointments without notification, to be late for appointments, and to complete fewer homework assignments. Therapists also rated dropouts' participation in treatment sessions as significantly poorer, although average ratings of both completers and dropouts were in the "adequate" to "good" range.

These studies describe a consistent anatomy of impasses in parent training interventions. Relative to less troubled clients, families that experience high levels of parent economic, personal, and marital problems; that have relatively high levels of child antisocial behavior; and that are referred by agencies rather than self-referred are likely to be less accepting of therapist interventions (Chamberlain et al., 1984), to miss appointments and/or come late (Prinz & Miller, 1994), to drop out of treatment prematurely (Kazdin et al., 1995; Prinz & Miller, 1994), and to ascribe their termination decision to a lack of treatment relevance and to obstacles that got in the way of treatment (Kazdin et al., 1997; Prinz & Miller, 1994). Interventions that specifically address these obstacles by interspersing discussion of parental issues into parent training both improve retention of these families in treatment and enhance their perceptions of the therapeutic process (Prinz & Miller, 1994).

Despite their consistency and importance, these findings have several limitations for understanding therapy process with parents and adolescents. First, all have addressed younger children and parent training interventions; whether these findings generalize to families with teenagers and to different sorts of interventions is unclear. Nonetheless, the results are consistent with Bischoff and Sprenkle's (1993) conclusions in their review of dropout research involving a variety of family and couple interventions. Second, studies have primarily addressed either white or a mixture of black and white families. The one study that compared predictors for white and black families (Kazdin et al., 1995) found several consistencies, but differences as well. This mandates further assessment of generalizability of findings across ethnic groups. In so doing, race/ethnicity of therapists should be examined, particularly in search of important or unique skills that may be required to conduct therapy effectively with members of ethnic and racial groups different from a therapist's own.

In addition, most studies of resistance and dropout in family interventions have examined clinical populations of families treated in individual therapy. This kind of research is clearly essential for understanding how to treat families who come to clinics. At the same time, interventions with parents and adolescents—particularly short-term didactic approaches—are often offered in groups and as preventive efforts. The question of whether treatment process findings generalize to these circumstances is important to assess.

Finally, further examination of specific therapist behaviors and how they affect different clients at different stages of treatment will be particularly useful. Most studies have examined client characteristics and perceptions generally, and few have linked these specifically to therapist behaviors that might reduce, mediate, or moderate negative client reactions to treatment. Developing a list of common "critical impasses" in treatment (such as those described in Table 12.4), and then empirically testing different therapist methods for resolving them, should assist in turning clinical impressions into scientifically based recommendations for dealing with common treatment implementation problems. These examinations should also be linked, of course, with assessments of how resolution of these problems relates to treatment outcomes more generally.

FUTURE DIRECTIONS

Investigators have examined an array of interventions for improving parent–adolescent communication and reducing acrimonious conflict. Findings from these studies generally support the hypothesis that short-term, highly focused, didactic, skill-based approaches can produce positive changes in family communication patterns as assessed by outside observers, and in

family members' reports of communication and family relationships in the home, at least among community samples recruited via notices in newspapers and agencies. Changes are frequently maintained for 3- to 6-month periods after treatment.

Results have nonetheless been limited by several factors. First, samples in outcome studies of communication and problem-solving approaches have often been quite small. Second, several studies have produced changes in observational measures without producing reports of changes at home, whereas others have found the reverse pattern. This points to the need for more precise elaboration of treatment components that are necessary and sufficient to produce skill demonstration, skill use at home (i.e., generalization), and maintenance of changes over time. Third, most studies of short-term communication training have not tested these interventions with clinically referred populations. Barkley, Guevremont, et al. (1992) examined PSCT with ADHD clinic samples and generally found this approach to be no more effective than viable alternative treatments. The relative success of the longer, more individualized, multicomponent MST and FFT interventions for delinquent teens and their families suggests that communication interventions may work best as part of a broader intervention package with seriously distressed clinic families, although simpler interventions may work well on their own as preventive interventions or for relatively uncomplicated cases presenting specifically for treatment of family conflict.

Findings of studies assessing whether additional components add to the effectiveness of communication and problem-solving skills training have produced mixed results. Again, however, these studies have frequently used small samples. This is a particular problem when a generally effective treatment is being compared to the same treatment with components added to enhance its effects, because differences between interventions may be quite subtle and mandate sufficient power to detect small to moderate effect sizes.

In addition, most studies involving additional components have failed to indicate whether families entering treatment in fact show problems or deficiencies in the areas addressed by additional treatment components. Cognitive restructuring, for example, cannot be expected to be effective for family members who fail to show cognitive distortions. Two sets of findings underscore the importance of screening families for cognitive distortions, anger control problems, and the like before implementing interventions designed to change these behaviors. Dadds et al. (1987) found that a couple support intervention enhanced parent training outcome, but only for parents in distressed marriages. Similarly, Prinz and Miller (1994) showed that including therapist–family discussions of extrafamilial issues into parent training prevented dropout, but only for families whose lives were characterized by adversity (and whose extrafamilial interactions presumably impinged on parenting behavior).

Finally, it is important for studies to test whether interventions specifically designed to alter such factors as parental teamwork, contingency use, and irrational cognitions actually produce changes in these variables, independent of their effect on conflict. Developing a repertoire of modularized, empirically based interventions to address various instrumental goals of treatment will only be made possible by compiling systematic evidence about the effects of specific interventions on specific components of family interaction. Yet surprisingly few studies have examined specific procedures for changing family members' thought patterns, improving ways of handling anger during conflict, and altering parental teamwork, triangulation, and cross-generational coalitions.

Attention to the mechanisms by which treatment works should also advance our understanding of treatment process. During the last decade, increased attention to therapist–client interactions, dropout, and barriers to treatment (particularly in family treatments of younger children) has considerably enhanced our data base for understanding the therapeutic relationship. Extension of these investigations to parent–adolescent interventions would provide another step forward in this area.

In addition, studies that link instrumental and ultimate outcomes should likewise improve our theoretical understanding of how effective treatment works. For example, problem- and skill-focused interventions like those described in this chapter can have an effect via two different mechanisms (Foster, 1994). First, as most skills trainers suggest, intervention (when successful) may work because it equips families with the skills needed to interact positively and to resolve conflicts effectively. An alternative explanation, however, is that treatment works because it helps families to resolve their most anger-provoking issues. Thus, family members fight less not because their skills have improved, but because intervention has helped them resolve the issues about which they argued. These disparate impacts are important to untangle, because they speak to where the therapist should focus effort—on solutions to specific problems, or on family process, with reductions in problems occurring as a fortunate (and perhaps essential) by-product of the family's shift from dysfunctional to more adaptive processes.

Unfortunately, research to date has not directly investigated this issue. Findings that treatments that do not directly target conflict resolution skills can produce improvements in communication suggest, however, that problem reduction may have important effects on family process. It is likely, of course, that problem reduction and improved communication processes have reciprocal and synergistic effects: Problem reductions trigger better communication; and better communication reduces anger and promotes understanding; improved family relations equip all members to deal more effectively with conflict. It will be important for future research to test these hypotheses explicitly, however.

Outcome studies could benefit from other improvements to make their findings more clinically relevant. First, it is important to describe each sample in terms of measures or terminology commonly employed in the literature, to facilitate comparison of the study population with the population to which the clinician wishes to generalize. Comorbidity is particularly important to consider and report. With clinical populations, scores on measures like the CBCL or descriptions of diagnoses (at a minimum, referral problems) can be quite useful in this regard. Demographic data are also important to provide; these should include information on race/ethnicity, gender, socioeconomic status, and number of single-parent families, as well as descriptions of which family units participate in treatment.

Second, as indicated earlier, collecting measures that address both instrumental and ultimate goals of treatment is important for testing hypotheses about the mechanisms that underlie successful treatment. When this is done properly, an outcome study contributes to theoretical understanding of the change process and the factors that maintain family conflict, in addition to documenting treatment efficacy. One good example of this kind of study was conducted by Mann et al. (1990), who looked at the role of family coalitions in MST.

Third, specifying whether treatment gains are clinically as well as statistically significant (Jacobson & Truax, 1991) provides important information about the percentage of families for which the intervention is sufficient to produce meaningful change, and the percentage that warrant additional and/or different treatment. Studying who does and does not benefit and why should point investigators toward ways of enhancing the impact of intervention. Comorbidity of conflict and other types of parent and adolescent difficulty will be particularly important to examine in this regard.

Finally, it is important to extend treatment research on parent–adolescent conflict to ethnically diverse populations. This should be done cautiously, with careful attention to the extent to which underlying assumptions and treatment components are inadvertently ethnocentric and warrant adjustment or modification for different populations. Clinicians should be particularly careful in making judgments about whether particular communication behaviors, cognitions, and structural patterns are maladaptive, and should assess their role and function within ethnically diverse clients' home and cultural contexts. Such extensions offer numerous opportunities for extending the range of treatment options for a wide array of families. Furthermore, such extensions may force investigators and clinicians to reevaluate the mechanisms that lead to and maintain conflict in families; such efforts should broaden our understanding of how these processes operate in families, and should ultimately enhance therapeutic and preventive interventions.

NOTES

1. We assume in this chapter that family members present excessive conflict as one of the difficulties that lead them to seek treatment. In these cases, a decrease in conflict is an ultimate goal of treatment. In other cases, family members present with specific issues involving maladaptive teen behavior (e.g., delinquency, truancy, school problems), and the therapist sees conflict as one contributor to these difficulties. In these cases, conflict or communication becomes an instrumental goal of treatment, based on the therapist's assumption that treating the conflict/communication problems will lead to reductions in the teen's problem behavior. All of the approaches described here are relevant both when conflict reduction is an ulti-

mate goal of treatment and when it is an instrumental goal.

2. Although reactivity can be a problem for collecting assessment data that indicate what happens at home, even highly reactive data can be useful clinically. For example, a good discussion in the clinic despite many fights at home may help family members see therapy in a hopeful light, particularly if the therapist reflects the family members' experiences in ways that help them see that discussions can be productive in spite of their negative history with each other. In addition, the therapist can use a reactive discussion to explore factors that differentiated between therapy and home discussions. This can illuminate features of the home environment that may inadvertently promote conflict (e.g., parents' attempts to discuss a problem issue when the teen is busy, rushed, or angry) and that may be useful to discuss in treatment.

3. Initially we also proposed other irrational beliefs, including self-blame and approval. These are irrational beliefs directed toward the self, however, instead of toward others. Other-directed (externalizing) beliefs logically seem likely to produce negative emotions directed toward others (such as anger), whereas self-directed beliefs seem more likely to produce negative emotions directed toward the self (sadness, anxiety, depression). In fact, parental reports of self-blame and approval beliefs and adolescent reports of approval have consistently failed to correlate with indicators of anger and conflict (Robin et al., 1990; Vincent Roehling & Robin, 1986).

REFERENCES

Abidin, R. R., & Brunner, J. F. (I 995). Development of a Parenting Alliance Inventory. *Journal of Clinical Child Psychology, 24,* 31–40.

Adams, J. F., Piercy, F. P., & Jurich, J. A. (1991). Effects of solution focused therapy's "formula first session task" on compliance and outcome in family therapy. *Journal of Marital and Family Therapy, 17,* 277–290.

Alexander, J. F. (1973). Defensive and supportive communications in normal and deviant families. *Journal of Consulting and Clinical Psychology, 40,* 223–231.

Alexander, J. F., & Barton, C. (1976). Behavioral systems therapy for families. In D. H. L. Olson (Ed.), *Treating relationships* (pp. 167–187). Lake Mills, IA: Graphic.

Alexander, J. F., Barton, C., Schiavo, R. S., & Parsons, B. V. (1976). Systems–behavioral intervention with families of delinquents: Therapist characteristics, family behavior, and outcome.

Journal of Consulting and Clinical Psychology, 44, 656–664.

Alexander, J. F., & Parsons, B. V. (1973). Short term behavioral intervention with delinquent families: Impact on family process and recidivism. *Journal of Abnormal Psychology, 81,* 219–225.

Alexander, J. F., & Parsons, B. V. (1982). *Functional family therapy.* Monterey, CA: Brooks/Cole.

American Psychiatric Association. (1994). *Diagnostic and statistical manual of mental disorders* (4th ed.). Washington, DC: Author.

Baden, A. D., & Howe, G. W. (1992). Mothers' attributions and expectancies regarding their conduct-disordered children. *Journal of Abnormal Child Psychology, 20,* 467–485.

Barkley, R. A. (1990). *Attention-deficit hyperactivity disorder: A handbook for diagnosis and treatment.* New York: Guilford Press.

Barkley, R. A., Anastopoulos, A. D., Guevremont, D. C., & Fletcher, K. E. (1992). Adolescents with Attention Deficit Hyperactivity Disorder: Mother–adolescent interactions, family beliefs and conflicts, and maternal psychopathology. *Journal of Abnormal Child Psychology, 20,* 263–288.

Barkley, R. A., Guevremont, D. C., Anastopoulos, A. D., & Fletcher, K. E. (1992). A comparison of three family therapy programs for treating family conflicts in adolescents with Attention Deficit Hyperactivity Disorder. *Journal of Consulting and Clinical Psychology, 60,* 450–462.

Barnes, H. L., & Olson, D. H. (1985). Parent–adolescent communication and the Circumplex Model. *Child Development, 56,* 438–447.

Barton, C., & Alexander, J. F. (1981). Functional family therapy. In A. S. Gurman & D. P. Kniskern (Eds.), *Handbook of family therapy* (pp. 403–443). New York: Brunner/Mazel.

Barton, C., Alexander, J. F., Waldron, H., Turner, C. W., & Warburton, J. (1985). Generalizing treatment effects of functional family therapy: Three replications. *American Journal of Family Therapy, 13,* 16–26.

Beck, A. T., Rush, A. J., Shaw, B. F., & Emery, G. (1979). *Cognitive therapy of depression.* New York: Guilford Press.

Besalel, V. A., & Azrin, N. H. (1981). The reduction of parent–youth problems by reciprocity counseling. *Behaviour Research and Therapy, 19,* 297–301.

Bischoff, R. J., & Sprenkle, D. H. (1993). Dropping out of marriage and family therapy: A critical review of research. *Family Process, 32,* 353–375.

Blaske, D. M., Borduin, C. M., Henggeler, S. W., & Mann, B. J. (1989). Individual, family, and peer characteristics of adolescent sexual and assaultive offenders. *Developmental Psychology, 25,* 846–855.

Borduin, C. M., Mann, B. J., Cone, L. T., Henggeler, S. W., Fucci, B. R., Blaske, D. M,, & Williams, R. A. (1995). Multisystemic treatment of juvenile offenders: Long-term prevention of criminality and violence. *Journal of Consulting and Clinical Psychology, 63,* 569–578.

Bradbury, T. N., & Fincham, F. D. (1987). Assessing the effects of behavior marital therapy: Assumptions and measurement strategies. *Clinical Psychology Review, 7,* 525–538.

Brody, G. H., & Forehand, R. (1993). Prospective associations among family form, family processes, and adolescents' alcohol and drug use. *Behaviour Research and Therapy, 21,* 587–593.

Bry, B. H., Conboy, C., & Bisgay, K. (1986). Decreasing adolescent drug use and school failure: Long-term effects of targeted family problem-solving training. *Child and Family Behavior Therapy, 8,* 43–59.

Capaldi, D. M., Forgatch, M. S., & Crosby, L. (1994). Affective expression in family problem-solving discussions with adolescent boys. *Journal of Adolescent Research, 9,* 28–49.

Chamberlain, P., Patterson, G. R., Reid, J. B., Kavanagh, K., & Forgatch, M. S. (1984). Observation of client resistance. *Behavior Therapy, 15,* 144–155.

Chamberlain, P., & Reid, J. B. (1987). Parent observation and report of child symptoms. *Behavioral Assessment, 9,* 97–109.

Christensen, A. (1987). Assessment of behavior. In K. D. O'Leary (Ed.), *Assessment of marital discord: An integration for research and clinical practice.* Hillsdale, NJ: Erlbaum.

Dadds, M. R., Schwartz, S., & Sanders, M. R. (1987). Marital discord and treatment outcome in behavioral treatment of child conduct disorders. *Journal of Consulting and Clinical Psychology, 55,* 396–403.

Deffenbacher, J. L., Thwaites, G. A., Wallace, T. L., & Oetting, E. R. (1994). Social skills and cognitive-relaxation approaches to general anger reduction. *Journal of Counseling Psychology, 41,* 386–396.

de Shazer, S. (1985). *Keys to solutions in brief therapy.* New York: Norton.

DiGiuseppe, R., Linscott, J., & Jilton, R. (1996). Developing the therapeutic alliance in child–adolescent psychotherapy. *Applied and Preventive Psychology, 5,* 85–100.

Dishion, T. J., & Andrews, D. W. (1995). Preventing escalation in problem behaviors with high-risk adolescents: Immediate and 1-year outcomes. *Journal of Consulting and Clinical Psychology, 63,* 538–548.

Doane, J. A., West, K. L., Goldstein, M. J., Rodnick, E. H., & Jones, J. E. (1981). Parental communication deviance and affective style. *Archives of General Psychiatry, 38,* 679–685.

Epstein, N. B., Baldwin, L. M., & Bishop, D. S. (1983). The McMaster Family Assessment Device. *Journal of Marital and Family Therapy, 9,* 171–180.

Feindler, E. L. (1990). Adolescent anger control: Review and critique. In M. Hersen, R. M. Eisler, & P. M. Miller (Eds.), *Progress in behavior modifica-*

tion (Vol. 26, pp. 11–59). Newbury Park, CA: Sage.

Feindler, E. L., & Ecton, R. B. (1986). *Adolescent anger control: Cognitive-behavioral techniques.* New York: Pergamon Press.

Feldman, S. S., Rubenstein, J. L., & Rubin, C. (1988). Depressive affect and restraint in early adolescents: Relationships with family structure, family process, and friendship support. *Journal of Early Adolescence, 8,* 279–296.

Fincham, F. D., & Bradbury, T. N. (1987). The assessment of marital quality: A reevaluation. *Journal of Marriage and the Family, 49,* 797–809.

Forgatch, M. S. (1989). Patterns and outcome in family problem-solving: The disrupting effect of negative emotion. *Journal of Marriage and the Family, 51,* 115–124.

Forgatch, M. S., & Lathrop, M. (1995). *SPI-FL II: The final version.* Unpublished manual.

Foster, S. L. (1994). Assessing and treating parent–adolescent conflict. In M. Hersen, R. M. Eisler, & P. M. Miller (Eds.), *Progress in behavior modification* (Vol. 29, pp. 53–72). Pacific Grove, CA: Brooks/Cole.

Foster, S. L., Prinz, R. J., & O'Leary, K. D. (1983). Impact of problem-solving communication training and generalization procedures on family conflict. *Child and Family Behavior Therapy, 5,* 1–23.

Foster, S. L., & Robin, A. L. (1989). Parent–adolescent conflict. In E. J. Mash & R. Barkley (Eds.), *Treatment of childhood disorders* (pp. 493–528). New York: Guilford Press.

Foster, S. L., & Robin, A. L. (1997). Family conflict and communication in adolescence. In E. J. Mash & L. G. Terdal (Eds.), *Assessment of childhood disorders* (3rd ed., pp. 627–682). New York: Guilford Press.

Gant, B. L., Barnard, J. D., Kuehn, F. E., Jones, H. H., & Christophersen, E. R. (1981). A behaviorally based approach for improving intrafamilial communication patterns. *Journal of Clinical Child Psychology, 10,* 102–106.

Gilbert, R., Christensen, A., & Margolin, G. (1984). Patterns of alliances in nondistressed and multiproblem families. *Family Process, 23,* 75–87.

Ginsberg, B. G. (1971). *Parent–adolescent relationship development: A therapeutic and preventive mental health program.* Unpublished doctoral dissertation, Pennsylvania State University.

Gottman, J. M., & Levenson, R. W. (1985). A valid measure for assessing self-report of affect in marriage. *Journal of Consulting and Clinical Psychology, 53,* 151–160.

Gottman, J. M., & Levenson, R. W. (1986). Assessing the role of emotion in marriage. *Behavioral Assessment, 8,* 31–48.

Grace, N. C., Kelley, M. L., & McCain, A. P. (1993). Attribution processes in mother–adolescent conflict. *Journal of Abnormal Child Psychology, 21,* 199–211.

Griest, D. L., Forehand, R., Rogers, T., Bremer, J., Furey, W., & Williams, C. A. (1982). Effects of parent enhancement therapy on the treatment outcome and generalization of a parent training program. *Behaviour Research and Therapy, 20,* 429–436.

Guerney, B., Jr. (1977). *Relationship enhancement.* San Francisco: Jossey-Bass.

Guemey, B., Jr., Coufal, J., & Vogelsong, E. (1981). Relationship enhancement versus a traditional approach to therapeutic/preventative/enrichment parent–adolescent programs. *Journal of Consulting and Clinical Psychology, 49,* 927–939.

Hanson, C. L., Henggeler, S. W., Haefele, W. F., & Rodick, J. D. (1984). Demographic, individual, and family relationship correlates of serious and repeated crime among adolescents and their siblings. *Journal of Consulting and Clinical Psychology, 52,* 528–538.

Henggeler, S. W., & Borduin, C. M. (1990). *Family therapy and beyond: A multisystemic approach to treating the behavior problems of children and adolescents.* Pacific Grove, CA: Brooks/Cole.

Henggeler, S. W., Melton, G. B., & Smith, L. A. (1992). Family preservation using multisystemic therapy: An effective alternative to incarcerating serious juvenile delinquents. *Journal of Consulting and Clinical Psychology, 60,* 953–961.

Henggeler, S. W., Pickrel, S. G., Brondino, M. J., & Crouch, J. L. (1996). Eliminating (almost) treatment dropout: Multisystemic therapy using home-based services with substance abusing/dependent delinquents. *American Journal of Psychiatry, 153,* 427–428.

Henggeler, S. W., Redick, J. D., Borduin, C. M., Hanson, C. L., Watson, S. M., & Urey, J. R. (1986). Multisystemic treatment of juvenile offenders: Effects on adolescent behavior and family interaction. *Developmental Psychology, 22,* 132–141.

Henggeler, S. W., Schoenwald, S. K., & Pickrel, S. G. (1995). Multisystemic therapy: Bridging the gap between university- and community-based treatment. *Journal of Consulting and Clinical Psychology, 63,* 709–717.

Hine, P. M., & Boyd-Franklin, N. (1996). African American families. In M. McGoldrick, J. Giordano, & J. K. Pearce (Eds.), *Ethnicity and family therapy* (2nd ed., pp. 66–84). New York: Guilford Press.

Hops, H., Davis, B., & Longoria, N. (1995). Methodological issues in direct observation: Illustrations with the Living in Family Environments (LIFE) coding system. *Journal of Clinical Child Psychology, 24,* 193–203.

Jacobson, N. S., & Truax, P. (1991). Clinical significance: A statistical approach to defining meaningful change in psychotherapy research. *Journal of Consulting and Clinical Psychology, 59,* 12–19.

Kazdin, A. E., Holland, L., & Crowley, M. (1997). Family experience of barriers to treatment and premature termination from child therapy. *Journal of Consulting and Clinical Psychology, 65,* 453–463.

Kazdin, A. E., Stolar, M. J., & Marciano, P. L. (1995). Risk factors for dropping out of treatment among white and black families. *Journal of Family Psychology, 9,* 402–417.

Larson, R. (1989). Beeping children and adolescents: A method for studying time use and daily experience. *Journal of Youth and Adolescence, 18,* 511–530.

Lee, E. (1996). Chinese families. In M. McGoldrick, J. Giordano, & J. K. Pearce (Eds.), *Ethnicity and family therapy* (2nd ed., pp. 249–267). New York: Guilford Press.

Liddle, H. A. (1995). Conceptual and clinical dimensions of a multidimensional, multisystems engagement strategy in family-based adolescent treatment. *Psychotherapy, 32,* 39–58.

Mann, B. J., Borduin, C. M., Henggeler, S. W., & Blaske, D. M. (1990). An investigation of systemic conceptualizations of parent–child coalitions and symptom change. *Journal of Consulting and Clinical Psychology, 58,* 336–344.

Mash, E. J., & Barkley, R. A. (Eds.). (1996). *Child psychopathology.* New York: Guilford Press.

Mash, E. J., & Terdal, L. G. (Eds.). (1997). *Assessment of childhood disorders* (3rd ed.) New York: Guilford Press.

Matsui, W. T. (1996). Japanese families. In M. McGoldrick, J. Giordano, & J. K. Pearce (Eds.), *Ethnicity and family therapy* (2nd ed., pp. 268–280). New York: Guilford Press.

McGoldrick, M., Giordano, J., & Pearce, J. K. (Eds.). (1996). *Ethnicity and family therapy* (2nd ed.). New York: Guilford Press.

Melidonis, G. G., & Bry, B. H. (1995). Effects of therapist exceptions statements on blaming and positive statements in families with adolescent behavior problems. *Journal of Family Psychology, 9,* 451–457.

Minuchin, S., & Fishman, H. C. (1981). *Family therapy techniques.* Cambridge, MA: Harvard University Press.

Montemayor, R., & Hanson, E. (1985). A naturalistic view of conflict between adolescents and their parents and siblings. *Journal of Early Adolescence, 5,* 23–30.

Moos, R. H., & Moos, B. S. (1981). *Family Environment Scale manual.* Palo Alto, CA: Consulting Psychologists Press.

Nangle, D. W., Carr-Nangle, R. E., & Hansen, D. J. (1994). Enhancing generalization of a contingency-management intervention through the use of family problem-solving training: Evaluation with a severely conduct disordered adolescent. *Child and Family Behavior Therapy, 16,* 65–76.

Nayar, M. (1985). *Cognitive factors in the treatment of parent–adolescent conflict.* Unpublished doctoral dissertation, Wayne State University.

Novaco, R. W. (1995). Clinical problems of anger and its assessment and regulation through a stress coping skills approach. In W. O'Donohue & L. Krasner (Eds.), *Handbook of psychological skills training:*

Clinical techniques and applications (pp. 320–338). Needham Heights, MA: Allyn & Bacon.

Olson, D. H., Portner, J., & Lavee, Y. (1985). *FACES III.* St. Paul, MN: Author.

Openshaw, D. K., Mills, T. A., Adams, G. R., & Durso, D. D. (1992). Conflict resolution in parent–adolescent dyads: The influence of social skills training. *Journal of Adolescent Research, 7,* 457–468.

Patterson, G. R., & Forgatch, M. S. (1985). Therapist behavior as a determinant for client noncompliance: A paradox for the behavior modifier. *Journal of Consulting and Clinical Psychology, 53,* 846–851.

Patterson, G. R., & Forgatch, M. S. (1995). Predicting future clinical adjustment from treatment outcome and process variables. *Psychological Assessment, 7,* 275–285.

Perosa, S. L., & Perosa, L. M. (1993). Relationships among Minuchin's structural family model, identity achievement, and coping style. *Journal of Counseling Psychology, 40,* 479–489.

Phares, V., & Danforth, J. S. (1994). Adolescents', parents', and teachers' distress over adolescents' behavior. *Journal of Abnormal Child Psychology, 22,* 721–732.

Prinz, R. J., Foster, S. L., Kent, R. N., & O'Leary, K. D. (1979). Multivariate assessment of conflict in distressed and nondistressed mother–adolescent dyads. *Journal of Applied Behavior Analysis, 12,* 691–700.

Prinz, R. J., & Kent, R. N. (1978). Recording parent–adolescent interactions without the use of frequency or interval-by-interval coding. *Behavior Therapy, 9,* 602–604.

Prinz, R. J., & Miller, G. E. (1994). Family-based treatment for childhood antisocial behavior: Experimental influences on dropout and engagement. *Journal of Consulting and Clinical Psychology, 62,* 645–650.

Riesch, S. K., Tosi, C. B., Thurston, C. A., Forsyth, D. M., Kuenning, T. S., & Kestly, J. (1993). Effects of communication training on parents and young adolescents. *Nursing Research, 42,* 10–16.

Robbins, M. S., Alexander, J. F., Newell, R. M., & Turner, C. W. (1996). The immediate effect of reframing on client attitude in family therapy. *Journal of Family Psychology, 10,* 28–34.

Robin, A. L. (1981). A controlled evaluation of problem-solving communication training with parent–adolescent conflict. *Behavior Therapy, 12,* 593–609.

Robin, A. L. (1990). Training families with ADHD adolescents. In R. A. Barkley, *Attention Deficit Disorder: A handbook for diagnosis and treatment* (pp. 462–497). New York: Guilford Press.

Robin, A. L., & Canter, W. (1984). A comparison of the Marital Interaction Coding System and community ratings for assessing mother–adolescent problem-solving. *Behavioral Assessment, 6,* 303–314.

Robin, A. L., & Foster, S. L. (1989). *Negotiating parent–adolescent conflict: A behavioral–family systems approach.* New York: Guilford Press.

Robin, A. L., Kent, R., O'Leary, K. D., Foster, S. L., & Prinz, R. J. (1977). An approach to teaching parents and adolescents problem-solving communication skills: A preliminary report. *Behavior Therapy, 8,* 639–643.

Robin, A. L., Koepke, T., & Moye, A. (1990). Multidimensional assessment of parent–adolescent relations. *Psychological Assessment, 2,* 451–459.

Robin, A. L., & Weiss, J. G. (1980). Criterion-related validity of behavioral and self-report measures of problem-solving communication skills in distressed and non-distressed parent–adolescent dyads. *Behavioral Assessment, 2,* 339–352.

Rosen, A., & Proctor, E. K. (1981). Distinctions between treatment outcomes and their implication for treatment evaluation. *Journal of Consulting and Clinical Psychology, 49,* 418–425.

Rueter, M. A., & Conger, R. D. (1995a). Antecedents of parent–adolescent disagreements. *Journal of Marriage and the Family, 57,* 435–448.

Rueter, M. A., & Conger, R. D. (1995b). Interaction style, problem-solving behavior, and family problem-solving effectiveness. *Child Development, 66,* 98–115.

Rueter, M. A., & Conger, R. D. (1995c, March). *The interplay between parenting and adolescent problem-solving behavior: Reciprocal influences.* Paper presented at the biennial meeting of the Society for Research in Child Development, Indianapolis, IN.

Sanders, M. R., & Dadds, M. R. (1992). Children's and parents' cognitions about family interaction: An evaluation of video-mediated recall and thought listing procedures in the assessment of conduct disordered children. *Journal of Clinical Child Psychology, 21,* 371–379.

Sanders, M. R., Dadds, M. R., Johnston, B. M., & Cash, R. (1992). Childhood depression and conduct disorder: I. Behavioral, affective, and cognitive aspects of family problem-solving interactions. *Journal of Abnormal Psychology, 101,* 495–504.

Santisteban, D. A., Szapocznik, J., Perez-Vidal, A., Kurtines, W. M., Murray, E. J., & LaPerriere, A. (1995). Efficacy of intervention for engaging youth and families into treatment and some variables that may contribute to differential effectiveness. *Journal of Family Psychology, 10,* 35–44.

Schreer, H. E. (1994). *Communication, problem-solving skills, and cross-generational coalitions as predictors of parent–adolescent conflict.* Unpublished doctoral dissertation, California School of Professional Psychology–San Diego.

Serna, L. A., Schumaker, J. B., Hazel, J. S., & Sheldon, J. B. (1986). Teaching reciprocal social skills to parents and their delinquent adolescents. *Journal of Clinical Child Psychology, 15,* 64–77.

Smetana, J. G. (1989). Adolescents' and parents' reasoning about actual family conflict. *Child Development, 60,* 1052–1067.

Smetana, J. G., Yau, J., Restrepo, A., & Braeges, J. L. (1991a). Adolescent-parent conflict in married and divorced families. *Developmental Psychology, 27,* 1000–1010.

Smetana, J. G., Yau, J., Restrepo, A., & Braeges, J. L. (1991b). Conflict and adaptation in adolescence: Adolescent–parent conflict. In M. E. Colten & S. Gore (Eds.), *Adolescent stress: Causes and consequences* (pp. 43–65). New York: Aldine de Gruyter.

Smith, K. A., & Forehand, R. (1986). Parent–adolescent conflict: Comparison and prediction of the perceptions of mothers, fathers, and daughters. *Journal of Early Adolescence, 6,* 353–367.

Snyder, D. K. (1979). Multidimensional assessment of marital satisfaction. *Journal of Marriage and the Family, 41,* 813–823.

Stern, S. (1984). *A group cognitive-behavioral approach to the management and resolution of parent–adolescent conflict.* Unpublished doctoral dissertation, University of Chicago.

Stoolmiller, M., Duncan, T., Bank, L., & Patterson, G. R. (1993). Some problems and solutions in the study of change: Significant patterns in client resistance. *Journal of Consulting and Clinical Psychology, 61,* 920–928.

Szapocznik, J., Kurtines, W. M., Foote, F. H., Perez-Vidal, A., & Hervis, 0. (1983). Conjoint versus one-person therapy: Some evidence for the effectiveness of conducting family therapy through one person. *Journal of Consulting and Clinical Psychology, 51,* 889–899.

Szapocznik, J., Kurtines, W. M., Foote, F. H., Perez-Vidal, A., & Hervis, O. (1986). Conjoint versus one-person therapy: Further evidence for the effectiveness of conducting family therapy through one person with drug-abusing adolescents. *Journal of Consulting and Clinical Psychology, 54,* 395–397.

Szapocznik, J., Perez-Vidal, A., Brickman, A. L., Foote, F. H., Santisteban, D., Hervis, O., & Kurtines, W. M. (1988). Engaging adolescent drug abusers and their families in treatment: A strategic structural systems approach. *Journal of Consulting and Clinical Psychology, 56,* 552–557.

Vincent Roehling, P., & Robin, A. L. (1986). Development and validation of the Family Beliefs Inventory: A measure of unrealistic beliefs among parents and adolescents. *Journal of Consulting and Clinical Psychology, 54,* 693–697.

Vogelsong, E. L. (1975). *Preventative–therapeutic programs for mothers and adolescent daughters: A follow-up of relationship enhancement versus discussion and booster versus no-booster methods.* Unpublished dissertation, Pennsylvania State University.

Vuchinich, S. (1987). Starting and stopping spontaneous family conflicts. *Journal of Marriage and the Family, 49,* 591–601.

Vuchinich, S., Emery, R. E., & Cassidy, J. (1988). Family members as third parties in dyadic family conflict: Strategies, alliances, and outcomes. *Child Development, 52,* 1293–1302.

Vuchinich, S., Vuchinich, R., & Wood, B. (1993). The interparental relationship and family problem solving with preadolescent males. *Child Development, 64,* 1389–1400.

Vuchinich, S., Wood, B., & Vuchinich, R. (1994). Coalitions and family problem solving with preadolescent children in referred, at risk, and comparison families. *Family Process, 33,* 409–424.

Weiss, R. L., & Heyman, R. E. (1990). Observation of marital interaction. In F. D. Fincham & T. N. Bradbury (Eds.), *The psychology of marriage: Basic issues and applications* (pp. 87–117). New York: Guilford Press.

Wood, C., & Davidson, J. (1993). Conflict resolution in the family: A PET evaluation study. *Australian Psychologist, 28,* 100–104.

CHAPTER 13

Anorexia Nervosa and Bulimia Nervosa

John P. Foreyt
Walker S. Carlos Poston II
Baylor College of Medicine

Allen A. Winebarger
Grand Valley State University,
Allendale, Michigan

Jill K. McGavin
Department of Veterans Affairs Medical Center,
Houston, Texas

Anorexia Nervosa and Bulimia Nervosa are increasingly common, complex disorders that are often perplexing to therapists, frequently resistant to treatment, and often difficult to cure. The purpose of this chapter is to review the history, nature, etiology, assessment, and treatment of these disorders, as well as to provide a brief introduction to the proposed diagnostic category of Binge-Eating Disorder.

Assessment strategies, individual psychotherapy, inpatient approaches, outpatient programs, and specific therapeutic techniques and components are presented. Throughout the chapter, we emphasize that treatment of these disorders is most effective when therapists utilize comprehensive, multicomponent intervention programs. We welcome the growing trend away from treatment by a single therapist in favor of

intervention programs involving many disciplines. We believe that treatments of eating disorders should be considered experimental in nature. However, with the increasing interest in these disorders by researchers and clinicians, we hope that in the near future the merits of some of the methods described in this chapter will be empirically established.

HISTORY

Anorexia Nervosa

Cases of self-inflicted starvation and weight loss were recorded as early as the 4th century A.D. To a young, "well-bred" girl, St. Jerome wrote, "Let your companions be women, pale and thin with fasting" (Lacey, 1982). This young woman's sister, also under St. Jerome's tutelage, died of the regimen. Evidence suggests that in the 11th century, Princess Margaret of Hungary may have had Anorexia Nervosa (Halmi, 1982). There is an account of a nun in the 13th century who claimed to ingest nothing but the Eucharist for 7 years (Hammond, 1879), and a female saint in the 14th century is said to have existed for years on nothing but a small piece of apple (Hammond, 1879). In those times, the women's behavior was not interpreted as indicating the presence of a psychological or physical disorder. The unusual abstinence was seen as a sign of spiritual power and saintly self-denial (Bell, 1985).

Richard Morton's account in 1694 is generally credited as the first clinical description of Anorexia Nervosa. He described a state of "nervous consumption" characterized by decreased appetite, amenorrhea, food aversion, emaciation, and hyperactivity. He wrote:

> I do not remember that I ever did in all my Practice see one, that was conversant with the Living so much wasted with the greatest degree of Consumption (like a Skeleton only clad with skin) yet there was no Fever, but on the contrary a coldness of the whole body. (quoted by Powers & Fernandez, 1984, p. 2)

This patient died 3 months later, after refusing the medication offered.

The disorder gained recognition with the report of Charles Laseque (1873) and the coining of the term "anorexia nervosa" in 1874 by Sir William Gull. Gull noted that the condition typically has its onset in adolescence, occurs predominantly in females, and is characterized by a "morbid mental state." He further discussed the effects of prolonged starvation and calorie depletion on metabolic functioning, and emphasized the importance of timely intervention.

Laseque (1873) independently described the cognitive/perceptual distortions in regard to health and body image, as well as the role of the family. He noted, "The family has but two methods at its service which it always exhausts—entreaties and menaces" (quoted by Strober, 1986, p. 235). He wrote that the family attempts to lead the sufferer to eat by enticing her with delicacies and asking for proof of her affection, and that the "excess of insistence begets an excess of resistance" (quoted by Strober, 1986, p. 236).

The accounts of Gull and Laseque, not surprisingly, provoked a debate regarding the involvement of the family in treatment. Some argued that the patient must be removed from her domestic environment for treatment to be successful (Playfair, 1888); others claimed that such removal constituted unnecessary cruelty and cost too much (Myrtle, 1888).

Views about the disorder changed when, in 1914, Simmonds described a patient who suffered from ill health and malnutrition ("cachexia"). At autopsy, the patient was found to have pituitary destruction. Consequently, in the following 10–20 years there was a tendency to view Anorexia Nervosa as a medical disorder caused by pituitary abnormalities.

With the spread of psychoanalytic thought in the 1940s and 1950s, Anorexia Nervosa came to be seen as a psychiatric disorder. Simmonds's original cases were reanalyzed, and several important distinctions were drawn between "Simmonds disease" and Anorexia Nervosa. Patients with Simmonds disease have only a mild degree of weight loss and are often hypoactive. Furthermore, Simmonds's patients did not have a drive for thinness, deny their illness, show body image disturbance, or make vigorous efforts at weight loss, including purging behavior (Sheehan & Summers, 1949). The two disorders share only two features: amenorrhea and a low basal metabolic rate. With this distinction clarified, Anorexia Nervosa was viewed as a psychological disorder. Within the psychoanalytic tradition, then, Anorexia Nervosa was hypothesized to be related to fixated unconscious conflicts regarding oral–sadistic fears, oral impregnation, regressive wishes, and primitive fantasies.

This viewpoint was challenged by the clinical studies of Hilde Bruch (1973), which spanned three decades. Bruch brought about a major rethinking of the treatment and conceptualization of the disorder. She believed that the falsification of early developmental learning experiences is of primary importance in the etiology of Anorexia Nervosa. The core problems consist of faulty learning regarding the discrimination of internal states and body boundaries, a deep sense of ineffectiveness, and lack of autonomy. Treatment, consequently, should be aimed at girding up and nurturing feelings of effectiveness and autonomy.

Minuchin, Rosman, and Baker (1978) have spurred a more recent conceptual shift in the understanding and treatment of Anorexia Nervosa. Anorexia Nervosa, in their view, is a family disorder that is caused by the family's structure (e.g., boundaries, roles, and alliances) and its inability to establish appropriate conflict resolution strategies. The developmental stasis of such families and the intergenerational difficulties or changes have also been emphasized in Bulimia Nervosa (Schwartz, Barrett, & Saba, 1985).

Cultural factors (e.g., Crisp, Palmer, & Kalucy, 1976; Iancu, Spivak, Ratzoni, Apter, & Weizman, 1994; Schwartz, Thompson, & Johnson, 1982; Wilfley & Rodin, 1995) have received recent emphasis; most significant is the observation that the incidence of these disorders appears to be on the rise (Iancu et al., 1994; Jones, Fox, Babigian, & Hutton, 1980; Wilfley & Rodin, 1995; Willi & Grossman, 1983) and corresponds to pressure placed on women by the society at large to be thin (Schwartz et al., 1982; Wilfley & Rodin, 1995).

Biological theories have also reappeared. These theories focus on hormonal changes that accompany puberty (Garfinkel & Garner, 1982; Leibowitz, 1983; Strober, 1986) and on differences in central nervous system (CNS) and neurotransmitter functioning (Braun & Chouinard, 1992; Brewerton, 1995; Kaye & Weltzin, 1991; Wurtman & Wurtman, 1984). The statistical relationship found between eating disorders and mood disorders in first-degree relatives has been used to argue for a genetic component to the disorders (Hudson, Pope, Jonas, & Yurgelun-Todd, 1983; Steiger, Stotland, Ghadirian, & Whitehead, 1995). Additional preliminary support for the potential role of genetic etiological factors has been found for both Anorexia Nervosa and Bulimia Nervosa (Fichter & Noegel, 1990; Holland, Sicotte, & Treasure, 1988; Hsu, Chesler, & Santhouse, 1990; Treasure & Holland, 1995). However, the data strongly suggest complex gene–environment interactions and genetically based vulnerabilities to psychopathology rather than simple gene–behavior models (Holland, Sicotte, & Treasure, 1988; Kendler et al., 1991; Strober, 1991, 1995). In addition, some of the very preliminary genetic data available for these disorders tend to be overinterpreted, as is the case in much of the behavioral genetics literature concerned with psychological disorders (Poston & Winebarger, 1996).

Bulimia Nervosa and Binge-Eating Disorder

Bulimia and binge eating occur as symptoms of Anorexia Nervosa; in addition, Bulimia Nervosa and Binge-Eating Disorder occur as a syndrome and proposed syndrome, respectively (American Psychiatric Association [APA], 1994). Binge eating varies greatly in terms of severity. Some persons consider any overeating to be "binge eating." Operational definitions are needed in order to clarify the meaning of the term. It is difficult, except in the case of the Binge-Eating/Purging Type of Anorexia Nervosa, to make judgments regarding historical accounts of bulimic behavior. In early Roman times, vomitoria (public places where people went to vomit) were described, and Seneca, a Stoic philosopher who lived about 65 A.D., wrote, "Men eat to vomit and vomit to eat" (quoted in Lowenberg, Todhunter, Wilson, Savage, & Lubawski, 1974, p. 45). The public nature of the vomiting, however, is not consistent with the secretiveness of the purging (and bingeing) of today's bulimics. The Babylonian Talmud (see Kaplan & Garfinkel, 1984), written around 400 A.D., describes bulimia as a symptom of various illnesses. Gull (1874) mentioned that a patient with Anorexia Nervosa had an occasional "voracious" appetite. Janet (1919) noted the occurrence of a cluster of symptoms, including vomiting, bulimia, and mood lability, in one group of anorexic patients. Binswanger's (1958) classic account of Ellen West presents a detailed picture of a life characterized by extreme cycles of gorging and purging, laxative abuse, dramatic vomiting, and violent diarrhea in a woman who was not underweight, although she wished to be. Given that bingeing may also occur in the absence of purging or other inappropriate compensatory behaviors, the fourth edition of the *Diagnostic and Statistical Manual of Mental Disorders* (DSM-IV; APA, 1994) has proposed Binge-Eating Disorder as a tentative diagnostic category worthy of further study.

NATURE OF THE DISORDERS

Definitions and Occurrence

Anorexia Nervosa and Bulimia Nervosa are currently recognized by specific sets of symptoms, according to the DSM-IV (APA, 1994). The diagnostic criteria for Anorexia Nervosa are presented in Table 13.1.

The central characteristic of Anorexia Nervosa is "drive for thinness." Persons with the disorder strive to lose weight beyond the point of social desirability, attractiveness, and good health. At very low weights, they deny that they are too thin and instead declare themselves "too fat." Secondary to this weight loss and near-starvation condition are preoccupation with food, amenorrhea, and a variety of psychological and physiological disturbances. As Table 13.1 indicates, Anorexia Nervosa in the DSM-IV is divided into two specific types: Binge-Eat-

TABLE 13.1.   DSM-IV Criteria for Anorexia Nervosa

A. Refusal to maintain body weight at or above a minimally normal weight for age and height (e.g., weight loss leading to maintenance of body weight less than 85% of that expected; or failure to make expected weight gain during period of growth, leading to body weight less than 85% of that expected).
B. Intense fear of gaining weight or becoming fat, even though underweight.
C. Disturbance in the way in which one's body weight or shape is experienced, undue influence of body weight or shape on self-evaluation, or denial of the seriousness of the current low body weight.
D. In postmenarcheal females, amenorrhea, i.e., the absence of at least three consecutive menstrual cycles. (A woman is considered to have amenorrhea if her periods occur only following hormone, e.g., estrogen, administration.)
   Specify type:
   Restricting Type: during the current episode of Anorexia Nervosa, the person has not regularly engaged in binge-eating or purging behavior (i.e., self-induced vomiting or the misuse of laxatives, diuretics, or enemas)
   Binge-Eating/Purging Type: during the current episode of Anorexia Nervosa, the person has regularly engaged in binge-eating or purging behavior (i.e., self-induced vomiting or the use of laxatives, diuretics, or enemas)

Note. From American Psychiatric Association (1994, pp. 544–545). Copyright 1994 by the American Psychiatric Association. Reprinted by permission.

ing/Purging Type, and Restricting Type. People meeting diagnostic criteria for Anorexia Nervosa, Binge-Eating/Purging Type would most likely have been diagnosed with Anorexia Nervosa and Bulimia Nervosa as concurrent disorders under DSM-III-R criteria (Woodside, 1995). Anorexics are afraid of becoming obese, are often hyperactive, and develop odd eating rituals. Underneath these concerns, according to Bruch (1973), is a deep sense of ineffectiveness and a lack of autonomy. From a feminist perspective, women experiencing this disorder are highly motivated to adhere to socially derived notions of beauty and femininity (i.e., thinness) in response to the sense of ineffectiveness and a lack of autonomy (Striegel-Moore, 1995).

The salient characteristic of Bulimia Nervosa is an excessive intake of food, usually high in calories, in a relatively short period of time, accompanied by "recurrent inappropriate compensatory behavior in order to prevent weight gain" (APA, 1994, p. 549). Such compensatory behaviors may take various forms, as the diagnostic criteria indicate. The binge eating is generally done in secret; bulimics regard their binge eating as shameful and perceive their eating behavior as "out of control" while they are bingeing. The DSM-IV diagnostic criteria for Bulimia Nervosa are presented in Table 13.2.

Binge-Eating Disorder has been included in the "Criteria Sets and Axes Provided for Further Study" appendix of the DSM-IV. Inclusion in this appendix is designed to provide researchers and clinicians with the guidance necessary to evaluate the reliability, validity, and utility of the proposed diagnostic categories. As with Bulimia Nervosa, the salient characteristic of Binge-Eat-

ing Disorder is an excessive intake of food, usually high in calories, in a relatively short period of time. This proposed disorder has been of particular interest to researchers interested in the eating behaviors of obese populations (Brody, Walsh, & Devlin, 1994), and populations engaging in binge eating without a focus on weight or shape control (Woodside, 1995). The key distinction between this proposed syndrome and Bulimia Nervosa is the absence of the inappropriate compensatory behaviors mentioned in Table 13.2. The research criteria for Binge-Eating Disorder are presented in Table 13.3

Anorexia Nervosa begins in early to late adolescence, with a bimodal risk for onset highest at ages 14 and 18 (APA, 1994; Halmi, Casper, Eckert, Goldberg, & Davis, 1979), whereas the mean age of onset for Bulimia Nervosa is 17–19 (Agras & Kirkley, 1986; APA, 1994; Fairburn & Cooper, 1982; Mitchell, Hatsukami, Eckert, & Pyle, 1985). Both disorders occur in females approximately 90% of the time (APA, 1994; Halmi, 1974, 1982; Hay & Leonard, 1979). Anorexia Nervosa is most frequently found in the upper socioeconomic classes, although in recent years there has been a shift toward more equal distribution among classes (Eckert, 1985). Approximately 1% of young women have Anorexia Nervosa (Crisp et al., 1976), with estimates ranging from 0.2% to 1.3% reported in a survey of epidemiological studies (Hoek, 1995; Woodside, 1995; Wakeling, 1996). The prevalence of Bulimia Nervosa is approximately 1%–3% (APA, 1994; Hoek, 1995; Hsu, 1996), but it has been estimated that between 4% and 19% of all young women engage in clinically significant levels of bulimic behavior (Halmi, Falk, &

TABLE 13.2. DSM-IV Criteria for Bulimia Nervosa

A. Recurrent episodes of binge eating. An episode of binge eating is characterized by both of the following:
   (1) eating, in a discrete period of time (e.g., within any 2-hour period), an amount of food that is definitely larger than most people would eat during a similar period of time and under similar circumstances
   (2) a sense of lack of control over eating during the episode (e.g., a feeling that one cannot stop or control what or how much one is eating)
B. Recurrent inappropriate compensatory behavior in order to prevent weight gain, such as self-induced vomiting; misuse of laxatives, diuretics, enemas, or other medications; fasting; or excessive exercise.
C. The binge eating and inappropriate compensatory behaviors both occur, on average, at least twice a week for 3 months.
D. Self-evaluation is unduly influenced by body shape and weight.
E. The disturbance does not occur exclusively during episodes of Anorexia Nervosa.
   Specify type:
   Purging Type: during the current episode of Bulimia Nervosa, the person has regularly engaged in self-induced vomiting or the misuse of laxatives, diuretics, or enemas
   Nonpurging Type: during the current episode of Bulimia Nervosa, the person has used other inappropriate compensatory behaviors, such as fasting or excessive exercise, but has not regularly engaged in self-induced vomiting or the misuse of laxatives, diuretics, or enemas

Note. From American Psychiatric Association (1994, pp. 549–550). Copyright 1994 by the American Psychiatric Association. Reprinted by permission.

Schwartz, 1981; Pyle et al., 1983; Strangler & Printz, 1980), depending upon the restrictiveness of the diagnostic criteria utilized (Edwards & Kerry, 1993). These rates seem to have increased significantly in the past 10–20 years (Ash & Piazza, 1995; Edwards & Kerry, 1993; Jones et al., 1980; Willi & Grossman, 1983). However, with respect to Anorexia Nervosa, it is unclear whether the observed increases in rate "reflect changes in the response to the condition, as opposed to changes in its incidence" (Fombonne, 1995, p. 469). Concern about body weight and fairly reasonable weight control efforts, including dieting, tend to precede the development of eating disorders (Beumont, Booth, Abraham, Griffiths, & Turner, 1983; Woodside, 1995).

Differential Diagnosis

It has been noted that a variety of psychiatric disorders, although they may involve changes in weight and/or eating behavior, should not be considered eating disorders (and particularly should not be confused with Anorexia Nervosa), although some have suggested that eating disorders are simply variants of other disorders (Garfinkel, 1995; Garfinkel & Kaplan, 1986). In conversion disorders, schizophrenia, and depression, changes in appetite and attitudes toward food are sometimes evident. These disorders can usually be distinguished from Anorexia Nervosa by the absence of an intense drive for thinness, a disturbed body image, and an increased activity level. These symptoms are unique to Anorexia

Nervosa and thus are the best discriminators (Woodside, 1995). For example, although both anorexics and schizophrenics may avoid specific foods, anorexics will avoid foods because they are high in caloric content, and schizophrenics may avoid foods because they are thought to be "poisoned." Amenorrhea, on the other hand, may occur in each of the disorders.

A reliable classification system for eating disorders does not exist at present; however, a number of diagnostic labels have been popularized. Labels currently used include "Anorexia Nervosa" (APA, 1994; Casper, Eckert, Halmi, Goldberg, & Davis, 1980), "bulimia" (Mitchell & Pyle, 1982), "Bulimia Nervosa" (APA, 1994; Russell, 1979), "bulimarexia" (Boskind-Lodahl & White, 1978), "binge eating" (Abraham & Beumont, 1982), "binge–purge syndrome" (Hawkins, Fremouw, & Clement, 1984), "self-induced vomiting" (Rich, 1978), "dietary chaos syndrome" (Palmer, 1979), "psychogenic vomiting" (Rosenthal, Webb, & Wruble, 1980), and "laxative abuse syndrome" (Oster, Materson, & Rogers, 1980). The validity of each as a separate syndrome or entity has not been established. The interrelationships between these possible diagnostic entities are not well known. Of these, only Anorexia Nervosa and Bulimia Nervosa are currently listed as diagnoses in the DSM-IV (APA, 1994), with, again, Binge-Eating Disorder being listed as a diagnostic category worthy of further study.

An additional problem inherent in the study of the eating disorders contained in the DSM-IV is the continuing evolution of the diagnostic

TABLE 13.3. DSM-IV Research Criteria for Binge-Eating Disorder

A. Recurrent episodes of binge eating. An episode of binge eating is characterized by both of the following:

    (1) eating, in a discrete period of time (e.g., within any 2-hour period), an amount of food that is definitely larger than most people would eat during a similar period of time and under similar circumstances

    (2) a sense of lack of control over eating during the episode (e.g., a feeling that one cannot stop or control what or how much one is eating)

B. The binge-eating episodes are associated with three (or more) of the following:

    (1) eating much more rapidly than normal

    (2) eating until feeling uncomfortably full

    (3) eating large amounts of food when not feeling physically hungry

    (4) eating alone because of being embarrassed by how much one is eating

    (5) feeling disgusted with oneself, depressed, or very guilty after overeating

C. Marked distress regarding binge eating is present.

D. The binge eating occurs, on average, at least 2 days a week for 6 months.

E. The binge eating is not associated with the regular use of inappropriate compensatory behaviors (e.g., purging, fasting, excessive exercise) and does not occur exclusively during the course of Anorexia Nervosa or Bulimia Nervosa. (pp. 731)

Note. The method of determining frequency differs from that used for Bulimia Nervosa; future research should address whether the preferred method of setting a frequency threshold is counting the number of days on which binges occur or counting the number of episodes of binge eating. From American Psychiatric Association (1994, p. 731). Copyright 1994 by the American Psychiatric Association. Reprinted by permission.

categories. The approximate 16%–47% overlap between Anorexia Nervosa and Bulimia Nervosa (Casper et al., 1980; Theander, 1970), as assessed via the diagnostic criteria contained in the DSM-III-R (APA, 1987), resulted in the creation of two "types" of Anorexia Nervosa in the DSM-IV (APA, 1994). Specifically, those individuals who previously would have been concurrently diagnosed with Anorexia Nervosa and Bulimia Nervosa would most likely qualify for the diagnosis of Anorexia Nervosa, Binge-Eating/Purging Type. Normal-weight and underweight binge eaters tend to be similar on a number of demographic, clinical, and psychometric variables and to differ from non-binge-eating anorexics (Garner, Garfinkel, & O'Shaughnessy, 1983). Compared to nonbingeing anorexics, bingeing anorexics appear to have greater problems with impulsive behavior and self-control in the form of shoplifting, alcohol and other substance misuse, self-mutilation, sexual activity, and lability of mood (Garfinkel, Moldofsky, & Garner, 1980). Bingeing anorexics are more extroverted (Beumont, 1977), whereas non-bingeing anorexics are more socially withdrawn. Bingeing anorexics have histories of obesity both personally and in their families, show greater childhood maladjustment, have higher rates of familial alcoholism and affective illness, and experience greater conflict and negativity in family relationships (Strober, 1986). Not surprisingly, bingeing anorexics are more difficult to treat and have poorer outcomes (Garfinkel et al., 1980). As a group, bingeing anorexics have

not been found to be characterized by low body weight, body image distortion, or marked denial of illness (Casper et al., 1980).

ETIOLOGY

Given that eating disorders generally begin during the adolescent years, most etiological theories incorporate adolescence and its concomitants as causal factors. In addition, culturally defined norms and influences, personality factors and difficulties, and affective difficulties are often looked to as significant etiological factors (Iancu et al., 1994; Striegel-Moore, 1995). "Adolescence" involves biological, social, and psychological changes. Biologically, there are physical changes involving the maturation of the reproductive system, along with a growth spurt. Socially, adolescence is a time of transition between childhood and adulthood. Adolescents begin to assume greater responsibility for their actions and are allowed a larger range of independent action and greater freedom. Not only are they "allowed" greater responsibility and freedom; it is *expected* that they begin to be more self-sufficient and more helpful toward others. New demands and expectations (e.g., a first interpersonal relationship involving sexuality and intimacy, and situations requiring new accomplishments) arise. The impact of these experiences may be thought to be heightened as well, in that, psychologically, adolescence is a time of intense self-scrutiny and awareness. Furthermore, adolescents become more capable of higher levels of abstract thought. It is a time during which identity concerns are of foremost importance; adolescents attempt to answer the question "Who am I?" The biological and social changes and new relationships form a part of the answer to this question. In short, adolescence is a time of great change. Bulimics have a difficult time coping with transitions, including changes in settings, going from school to work, and going from work to home. Certainly the passage from childhood to adulthood (i.e., adolescence) is a time of transition, in a larger sense of the word. Perhaps this is the difficulty of anorexics as well. Many theorists have focused on particular transitions as being problematic for anorexics.

Even the briefest review of the literature on eating disorders illustrates the significant etiological role given to societal factors. Specifically, it is theorized that the traditional definition of femininity has much to do with the development of eating disorders (Iancu et al., 1994; Wilfley & Rodin, 1995). Social norms and mores are asserted to define the self-worth of women in terms of their ability to relate to others (Striegel-Moore, 1995). This relatedness is often associated with the ability of women to appear attractive, which in turn is influenced by the perceived level of femininity that is possessed. This often results in what has been described as an intense fear of becoming fat (Iancu et al., 1994) or as a "fat phobia" (Lee, 1995). From a feminist perspective, women experiencing eating disorders are highly motivated to adhere to socially derived notions of beauty and femininity (i.e., thinness) in response to a sense of ineffectiveness and lack of autonomy (Striegel-Moore, 1995) that results from the continually mixed messages sent to women by the pressures of Western culture (Heinberg, 1996). However, Lee (1995), in a review of cross-cultural studies, asserts that this view may be somewhat ethnocentric in nature. Specifically, the occurrence of significant numbers of non-fat-phobic anorexics found in cross-cultural studies suggest that the application of culturally flexible diagnostic criteria may enhance both the validity and utility of the eating disorder categories (Lee, 1995).

Current research focusing on the role of personality in the development of eating disorders stresses the assertion that the etiological underpinnings of eating disorders are complex, and that the identification of a single etiological factor is unlikely (Leon, Fulkerson, Perry, & Early-Zald, 1995; Strober, 1991, 1995). Anorexic populations have been described as exhibiting

constrictive, conforming, obsessive characteristics (Sohlberg & Strober, 1994; Vitousek & Manke, 1994), and as being socially inhibited, compliant, and emotionally constrained (Wonderlich, 1995). Cloninger (1986, 1988), using a three-dimensional personality model, asserts that anorexic individuals tend to be low in novelty seeking, high in harm avoidance, and high in reward dependence. Less consistent patterns for Bulimia Nervosa suggest that bulimic patients tend to exhibit traits indicative of poor impulse control, chronic depression, acting-out behaviors, low frustration tolerance (Wonderlich, 1995), affective lability, difficult temperament, and inhibition (Vitousek & Manke, 1994). Finally, populations exhibiting eating disorders may exhibit greater than typical rates of personality disorders and personality-disorder-related symptoms (Vitousek & Manke, 1994; Wonderlich, 1995), have been described as experiencing chronic low self-esteem (Silverstone, 1992), and may tend to exhibit poor introceptive awareness (Leon et al., 1995).

The eating disorders have also been reported as being triggered by traumatic separations and losses and familial discord (Garner, Garfinkel, Schwartz, & Thompson, 1980; Hodes & Le Grange, 1993; Kalucy, Crisp, & Harding, 1977; Strober, 1981). These have included the breakup of the parental home, death of a parent, going away to college, summer vacation, parental illness, pregnancy in parent or sibling, "family scandal," parental infidelities, or sibling promiscuity (Beumont, Abraham, Argall, George, & Glaun, 1978; Kalucy, Crisp, & Harding, 1977; Theander, 1970). Imagined or actual instances of personal failure have also been noted to precede Anorexia Nervosa (Dally, 1969; Halmi, 1974; Rowland, 1970). Specific traumas, such as childhood sexual abuse, have also been suggested as potential etiological factors in the development of eating disorders (Everill & Waller, 1995; Wonderlich, Brewerton, Jocic, Dansky, & Abbott, 1997). Currently, the results of studies examining the association between eating disorders and sexual abuse have produced mixed results. For example, some investigators have found higher reported rates of childhood sexual abuse in bulimics than in non-eating-disordered populations (Rorty, Yager, & Rossotto, 1994). In contrast, several well-controlled studies have found that sexual abuse is reported by a minority of bulimic patients; however, it is not a bulimia-specific risk factor, but more often is associated with increased risk for general psychiatric disturbance (Vize & Cooper, 1995; Welch & Fairburn, 1994). These data suggest that childhood sexual abuse is not a primary or specific risk factor for eating disorders, and that the role it does play is due to a complex interaction with other risk factors that is still not well understood (Vize & Cooper, 1995).

Any etiological theory must account for the fact that eating disorders occur predominantly in females. Adolescence is a time of transition for males as well as females, but very few males develop eating disorders. The pressure placed upon females to be thin and attractive may provide a partial explanation; males tend to be evaluated in terms of their actions, or what they do, whereas females tend to be evaluated in terms of their appearance, or how they look. Arguments have also been made regarding the ambivalent, "mixed" messages given females regarding their proper role in society. Although girls are encouraged to be autonomous, they are treated differently from boys from early childhood, and are taught that femininity involves "dependency."

Some physiological conditions may predispose certain individuals toward these extreme conditions, which may then be compounded by societal contingencies for weight control, particularly in females. The relative efficacy of antidepressants in the treatment of Bulimia Nervosa (see "Treatment," below) has led to the development of a serotonin hypothesis for this disorder (Brewerton, 1995; Ericsson, Poston, & Foreyt, 1996; Kaye & Weltzin, 1991; Weltzin, Fernstrom, & Kaye, 1994). This hypothesis states that given the research linking serotonin to carbohydrate consumption and binge eating in both animals and humans, individuals experiencing Bulimia Nervosa may have lower endogenous levels of serotonin in the CNS and may attempt to compensate for the deficiency by eating foods high in tryptophan and relatively low in protein (such as one would obtain via a high-carbohydrate meal). Hence, binge eating may serve as a form of mood regulation and self-medication, which can be replaced by the higher levels of serotonin brought about by the use of antidepressant medications (Advokat & Kutlesic, 1995; Craighead & Agras, 1991). The serotonergic hypothesis also suggests that Anorexia Nervosa may be associated with overactivity in serotonergic activity in the CNS (Brewerton, 1995). This overactivity subsequently leads to decreased food intake with subsequent weight loss. This suggestion is based, in part, on the relative ineffectiveness of medication interventions designed to raise the levels of serotonin

available to the CNS in the treatment of Anorexia Nervosa (Advokat & Kutlesic, 1995). Taken together, these data suggest that serotonin dysregulation may play an important role in the etiology or maintenance of eating disorders (Brewerton, 1995). Disruptions in other neurotransmitter systems have also been implicated in the etiology of eating disorders (Mauri et al., 1996). Some studies have found alterations in noradrenergic and peptide neuromodulator activity in bulimic patients. For example, Kaye et al. (1990) found reduced levels of norepinephrine and serotonin metabolites in the cerebrospinal fluids of bulimic patients. Finally, some investigators have proposed that eating disorders are neuropsychological disorders, with some studies showing differences between eating-disordered patients and controls in brain metabolic functions and hemispheric activity (Braun & Chouinard, 1992).

Although the data from these studies suggest that neurotransmitter dysregulation and neuropsychological dysfunctions may play a role in the etiology or maintenance of eating disorders, they do not point to a definitive causal role. It is possible that these neurochemical changes occur as a *result* of eating-disordered behavior and are not actually causal (Kaye & Weltzin, 1991). Specifically, these neurotransmitter derangements may be the consequence of extremes in dietary intake and purging or other compensatory behaviors. As such, they may be more important in the maintenance of eating-disordered behavior because they propel the eating-disordered patient into a vicious cycle, where pathological eating behaviors promote and maintain pathological purging or restrictive behaviors that contribute to poor treatment outcomes (Kaye & Weltzin, 1991). Another problem with this area of research is that many of these neurotransmitter and neuropeptide modulator alterations are not specific to Bulimia Nervosa or eating disorders in general. For example, similar alterations in serotonin regulation have been found in depression, impulsivity, substance use disorders, and Obsessive–Compulsive Disorder (Jarry & Vaccarino, 1996; Weltzin et al., 1994) and decreased levels of cholecystokinin have been found in both Bulimia Nervosa and Panic Disorder patients (Brambila et al., 1993; Lydiard et al., 1993). Due to this lack of disorder-related specificity, it has been suggested that dysregulation in serotonin and other neurotransmitter systems may be a common pathway for many disorders, rather than being a specific mechanism in eating disorders. A final criticism of the physiological research is that it is often based on small and potentially biased clinical samples, and that it suffers from methodological problems. Gillberg (1994) noted that many findings in the eating disorder literature, particularly in the area of etiology, lack replication and are based on potentially biased and nonrepresentative samples. In addition, some of these studies suffer from methodological and statistical shortcomings. For example, the Kaye et al. (1990) study cited earlier, which found differences between bulimic and control patients in cerebrospinal fluid levels of norepinephrine and serotonin metabolites, was based on a small sample (27 bulimics and 14 controls); the investigators also computed multiple t tests on their data without correcting for potential alpha inflation. In a study of cerebral hemispheric glucose metabolism, differences were found between bulimic patients and controls (Wu et al., 1990). The authors stated that the patterns of metabolism were also different from studies of anorexic and depressed patients (Wu et al., 1990). Unfortunately, the study suffered from a very small sample size (8 bulimic patients and 8 matched controls), and the investigators again performed multiple comparisons without correcting for alpha inflation. If the data from these two studies had applied the Bonferroni correction, or some other method to control alpha inflation (e.g., multivariate analysis), it is questionable whether any of the findings would have remained statistically significant (Ross & Pam, 1995).

In sum, we are doubtful that the occurrence of these complex disorders will be explained without an understanding of many relevant dimensions, including the physiological, societal, familial, psychiatric, and psychological (Ericsson et al., 1996). Furthermore, it is highly probable that no narrow definition of the psychological dimension will suffice; our behavioral–systems view thus includes a recognition and assessment of cognitive factors, emotional regulation and coping skills, and behavioral–environmental contingencies. This view should increase our understanding of the causes of these extreme conditions.

ASSESSMENT

Eating disorders are complex and thus require comprehensive, multimodal assessment (Devlin, 1996; Foreyt & McGavin, 1988; Foreyt & Mikhail, 1997; Lee & Miltenberger, 1997; Tobin, Johnson, Steinberg, Staats, Baker, & Dennis,

1991). There is at present no single standardized instrument that thoroughly evaluates each and every one of the components or determinants of the disorders. Figure 13.1 illustrates the range of factors that seem to be relevant to the disorders.

There are at least four general areas to assess, in addition to eating behavior. Anorexics and bulimics have difficulties with (1) self-regulation, particularly affect regulation (including the identification and expression of feelings); (2) interpersonal skills and relationships; (3) personal identity, self-esteem, and sexual identity; and (4) distorted beliefs and cognitions. These difficulties are generally connected to the disordered eating in rather direct ways. In Bulimia Nervosa, for example, feelings of sadness and anger accompanied by negative, distorted thoughts (self-referential) following negative interpersonal interactions are typical triggers for binges. A thorough analysis of the binge behavior should uncover such associations. In the case of restricting anorexics, thoughts and feelings associated with the need to lose weight and control over food reflect similar, basic difficulties, insofar as self-worth is equated with weight loss and deprivation.

The instruments listed below focus primarily on the macroanalysis and microanalysis of the abnormal eating behavior, and also give some attention to individual differences or "personality" factors. Although some of the instruments are quite comprehensive, normative data are not yet available for many of them.

Eating Disorders Instruments

Several semistructured questionnaires are available to assess the presence and severity of eating disorders. They can be used as self-report or standardized interview instruments. Thus far, there have been no widely available instruments for use with parents or teachers. The Diagnostic Survey for Eating Disorders (DSED) was designed by Johnson (1985) and his colleagues at Northwestern University Medical School. It is a 16-page questionnaire that collects demographic information, as well as information regarding weight and body image, dieting behavior, binge-eating behavior, purging behavior, exercise and related behavior, sexual functioning, menstrual history, and family history. The DSED—Revised (Johnson & Pure, 1986), a somewhat lengthier version (21 smaller-sized pages), is also available. The DSED—Revised contains no new sections, but has additional questions regarding family, feelings during weight loss and

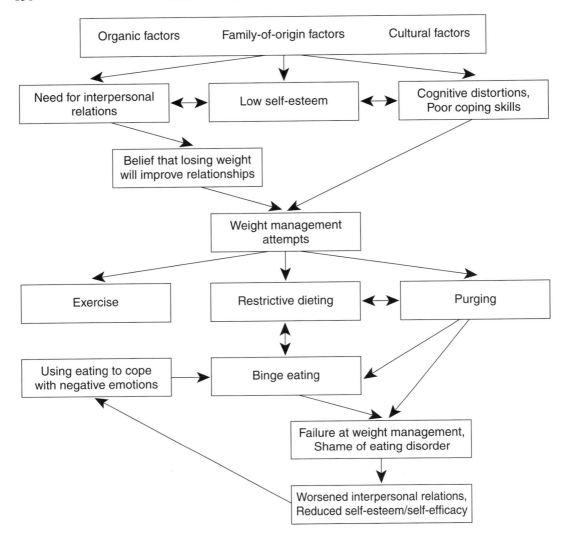

FIGURE 13.1. The vicious cycle of eating disorders.

gain, physical symptoms, and others. The Eating Disorder Examination was designed to compensate for some of the problems inherent in self-report measures and to provide more detailed information than is typically available from self-report measures (Cooper & Fairburn, 1987). This interview appears to have adequate inter-rater reliability and validity, as reported by Williamson, Anderson, Jackman, and Jackson (1995). The Eating Disorders Questionnaire (EDQ) of the University of South Florida (Powers, 1984a) is a 24-page instrument that collects demographic data, weight history, information on binge eating and purging, medical history, social history, weight profile, and autobiographical information. The Eating Attitudes Test (EAT; Garner & Garfinkel, 1979) is also included as a part of the EDQ. The EAT, as reviewed by Williamson et al. (1995), has been normed with Anorexia Nervosa patients, female controls, male controls, and clinically recovered anorexic samples. In addition, the EAT appears to have adequate reliability and validity. Finally, the Yale–Brown–Cornell Eating Disorder Scale (Mazure, Halmi, Sunday, Romano, & Einhorn, 1994; Sunday, Halmi, & Einhorn, 1995) is a promising clinical interview designed to assess process issues in eating disorders.

More specialized self-report instruments for Anorexia Nervosa and Bulimia Nervosa include the Hunger–Satiety Questionnaire by Monello, Seltzer, and Mayer (1965); the Situational Discomfort Scale by Goldberg, Halmi, Casper, Eckert, and Davis (1977); the Goldberg Anorectic Attitude Scale by Goldberg et al. (1980); the Eating Disorder Inventory by Garner, Olmsted, and Polivy (1983), which has been normed on clinical samples, nonclinical samples (Garner, 1991), and adolescents (Shore & Porter, 1990); the Binge Eating Scale by Gormally, Black, Daston, and Rardin (1982); and the Binge Scale by Hawkins and Clement (1980). The Setting Conditions for Anorexia Nervosa Scale appears to demonstrate utility in the prediction of individuals at risk for the development of Anorexia Nervosa (Slade & Dewey, 1986). This instrument, as reported by Williamson et al. (1995), has been normed on a relatively large nonclinical sample and a small clinical population. Additional instruments that appear to demonstrate adequate reliability and validity include the Bulimia Test—Revised (Thelen, Farmer, Wonderlich, & Smith, 1991), an instrument normed on clinical and nonclinical samples; the Eating Questionnaire—Revised (Williamson, Davis, Bennett, Goreczny, & Gleaves, 1989), a symptom checklist designed to assess Bulimia Nervosa; the Bulimic Investigatory Test, Edinburgh (Henderson & Freeman, 1987), an instrument designed to gauge binge eating and the cognitive and behavioral correlates of bingeing behaviors; and the Eating Disorder Evaluation Scale (Vandereycken, 1993), a global assessment measure that may be used in either a self-report or a clinical interview format. A state-of-the-art review of many of these measures is available (Williamson et al., 1995). Many of these instruments have been used only for diagnostic/screening or theoretical/research purposes.

Given the importance of cognitive and emotional characteristics in eating disorders, a number of instruments designed to assess these specific content areas are currently available. The Mizes Anorectic Cognitions Questionnaire (Mizes & Klesges, 1989) is a questionnaire designed to assess the cognitions associated with eating disorders. This instrument appears to demonstrate adequate reliability and validity, and to have remarkable utility (Williamson et al., 1995). The EAT, described above, also focuses on the cognitions that accompany eating disorders. Other measures focusing on the role of cognitions in eating disorders include, but certainly are not limited to, the Modified Distressing Thoughts Questionnaire (Clark, Feldman, & Channon, 1989); the Cognitive Error Questionnaire, as modified by Dritschel, Williams, and

Cooper (1991); and the Food and Weight Cognitive Distortions Survey (Thompson, Berg, & Shatford, 1987). Measures designed to tap into self-efficacy include the Eating Self-Efficacy Scale (Glynn & Ruderman, 1986) and the Self-Efficacy Scale (Schneider, O'Leary, & Agras, 1987).

Given the potential importance of personality factors in the etiology of eating disorders, a number of personality assessment instruments are discussed in the scientific literature. The Tridimensional Personality Questionnaire (TPQ; Brewerton, Hand, & Bishop, 1993) is one such promising measure. The TPQ was designed to tap into the three etiologically important dimensions of personality: harm avoidance, novelty seeking, and reward dependence (Cloninger, 1986). The developers of this instrument assert that its utility is enhanced because Cloninger's (1986) three dimensions are related to serotonin, dopamine, and norepinepherine function. In addition, the Kids Eating Disorder Survey (Childress, Jarrell, & Brewerton, 1993), a measure designed to be administered to middle-school-age populations, may allow the early identification of factors predictive of the development of eating disorders, and may prove to be a useful screening measure in prevention programs.

For clinical purposes, self-monitoring behaviors such as food diaries can be invaluable (Garner, 1995). The Self-Monitoring Form by Johnson and Pure (1986) is an expanded version of a food diary that explores mood, activities, physical state, interpersonal climate, feelings about eating, and alcohol intake, as well as food intake. Patients are encouraged to fill it out four times daily for at least 1 week during the assessment phase of treatment and periodically thereafter.

Two instruments utilize professional reports. The Anorexic Behaviour Scale (ABS) by Slade (1973) is a 22-item scale that requires professionals to make judgments ("yes," "no," or "?") regarding hospitalized patients' resistance to eating, disposal of food, and activity. The Psychiatric Rating Scale for Anorexia Nervosa by Goldberg et al. (1977) is a 14-item scale that is typically completed by nursing or other professional staff members. Most of the items on these scales assume a psychiatric or psychodynamic orientation. The items on the ABS are intended to reflect the major descriptive and psychopathological features of Anorexia Nervosa: denial of illness, fear of fat, thin ideal body image, loss of appetite, selective appetite, fear of becoming a compulsive eater, desire for activity, desire to control, manipulativeness, depression, obsessiveness, immaturity, purgative and diuretic abuse, and exaggerated cheerfulness (Slade, 1973).

Assessment of the Family Environment

The family unit is perhaps the most critical learning place for the development of interpersonal roles and skills. The roles within the family need to change as children grow and mature. As children reach and progress through adolescence, they struggle with identity concerns and need to see themselves as separate, independent persons. In order to do that, they begin to reject childish roles and dependence upon parents and family and to assert themselves. Frequently this happens in a rebellious fashion. This is a difficult time for all concerned, parents as well as children/adolescents. Eating disorders halt or twist this developmental process. The bingeing or food refusal can serve to meet the needs of a child to grow and become more independent, and at the same time can preserve and tighten close parent–child ties. In fact, eating problems typically bring forth increased involvement between parents and children. Conceptualized in this way, eating problems represent a pseudosolution to the task of adolescence.

The question remains, however, why some children (usually girls) who are entering adolescence or progressing from adolescence into young adulthood adopt this pseudosolution while others do not. These families seem to differ from families without eating-disordered adolescents in their cohesiveness, roles, communication style, and conflict resolution (Hodes & Le Grange, 1993; Johnson & Pure, 1986). Thus, it seems prudent to assess these characteristics. "Cohesiveness" refers to how close family members are to one another—how much independence or "separateness" is encouraged/permitted. If family members have little privacy and there is little distinction between their roles and functions, this adds confusion and conflict. Roles and functions should be somewhat different, given the inevitable differences in terms of age and talents of family members. On the other hand, if the boundaries are very rigid and family members have little in common, this can mean little sense of community and, for the children, a

push toward autonomy and independence before they are ready for it. "Communication" refers to the way information is sent and received. Messages can be delivered and responded to directly or indirectly. Indirect communication is often used to invalidate or qualify overt messages. For example, with anorexics, parents may tell their daughters to "grow up" and "obey us" at the same time, perhaps not recognizing that one way of growing up is to become less obedient and more independent. "Conflict resolution" refers to the manner in which conflict is handled; assessment of conflict resolution generally focuses on the conflict within the marital unit. The eating-disordered patient may not know how to cope with conflict in a direct manner and may have been taught to avoid conflict (and anger) at all costs. Parents frequently are in conflict over how to "help" the eating-disordered patient. Fathers frequently take a harsh, disciplinary role, while mothers take a more nurturant, appeasing role. In order to avoid direct conflict, parents may each try to appeal to the child to support their posture ("triangulation"), or parents may set aside their conflicts superficially in order to protect or blame their sick child ("detouring").

Strober and Yager (1985) assess the following factors when meeting with parents and families:

- Individual perceptions of their children (e.g., strengths, weaknesses) and aspects of each child's behavior they admire or find troublesome.
- Their aspirations for the children.
- Their views on adolescence (e.g., emancipation, contacts outside the home, sexuality).
- Impact of the eating disordered child's illness on the family lifestyle, marital relationship, and family relations generally (e.g., activation of separation fears, abandonment, etc.).
- Their own personal–developmental histories (early self-esteem and maturational problems, relationship with parents and siblings, ongoing intergenerational problems).
- Familial psychiatric disorders.
- General organizational structure of the family (e.g., power structure, parental coalitions, clarity of boundaries, efficiency of problem solving and negotiation, clarity of expression of individual thoughts and emotions, responsibility for individual ac-

tions, degree of emotional closeness among members, expressiveness, general emotional tone, degree and intensity of conflict, and degree of empathic responsiveness.

In most cases, the patient's actions and abilities (or inabilities) have considerable impact upon the family, and vice versa. Thus, it is useful for the therapist to entertain the question "How might X symptom function in an adaptive way in this family?" Obviously, the disordered eating of a family member is going to be experienced by or have some impact on the rest of the family. The role the family plays in the maintenance of the problem, and how family members might be involved in treatment, should also be considered. If the problematic behavior is seen to be maintained by the reactions it engenders, or if stimuli for problematic behavior are identified within the family, family therapy should be considered. This may mean that the parents are simply worried about their child's medical status and that worry may play an important role in the parents' marital relationship, or that the problem child may perceive her eating behavior to play a role in their relationship. (Note: Because the vast majority of patients with eating disorders are females, feminine pronouns are used in this chapter to refer to such patients.) More obviously, when parents' willingness to comply with treatment is questionable, family therapy is indicated. Family assessment for patients 18 years of age or younger is essential (Woodside, 1995). Similar to the assessment protocols discussed above, Woodside (1995) assesses the following components of family process and functioning: the reason for referral, overview of the problem, the family's theories about the problem, the family's attempts to help with the problem, membership in the family, significant events in the family history, medical and psychiatric history, and eating habits of the family.

Before we conclude this section, it is crucial to note that the manner in which these dimensions are assessed is of the utmost importance. Families, particularly parents and the afflicted child, are frightened that they are to blame for the disorder. Questions about the areas listed above, if poorly worded or delivered, can arouse thoughts and feelings that are very counterproductive to the establishment of a working therapeutic alliance with patient or parents. Thus, at the outset, the clinician may be wise to tell the

family that he or she does not view them as deserving blame, but that if therapy is to succeed, all of their support and guidance will be needed. Even if they are not part of the "problem," they may be part of the "solution."

Assessment of Relationships and Environment Outside the Family

Although adolescence and adulthood imply leaving the family, they also imply going to or joining outside networks, girlfriends, boyfriends, peers, colleagues, and the world at large. It is reasonable to assume that there is an underinvolvement in this realm corresponding to the overinvolvement at home. Moreover, interpersonal effectiveness outside of one's family of origin may become increasingly important as one enters adolescence and adulthood. There are data to suggest that anorexics and bulimics have serious interpersonal difficulties. Of 102 consecutive patients seen by Crisp, Hsu, Harding, and Hartshorn (1980), 23 were excessively shy, and 43 had few or no friends during childhood. This difficulty may persist during and after the illness. A review of 700 outcome studies of anorexics (Schwartz & Thompson, 1981) found that only 47% of anorexics had married or were maintaining active heterosexual lives. Bulimic patients report that their problems with eating and weight interfere "a great deal" with their social relationships (94%) and school or job performance (84%) (Leon, Carroll, Chernyk, & Finn, 1985). Bulimic behavior also leads to decreased social contact (Johnson & Larson, 1982). If these disorders are to be thoroughly assessed, it consequently becomes important to assess the level and extent of a patient's current social functioning.

Medical Assessment

All eating-disordered patients should be assessed medically. A complete review of the medical assessment of Anorexia Nervosa and Bulimia Nervosa is beyond the scope of this chapter. For such, the reader is referred to excellent comprehensive reviews by Mitchell (1985, 1986a, 1986b) and Kaplan and Garfinkel (1993). A standard medical assessment should include physical examination, standard laboratory tests, multiple-channel chemistry analysis, complete blood count, and urinalysis. The systems that should be reviewed include endocrinological/metabolic, cardiovascular, renal, gastrointestinal, musculoskeletal, dermatological, hematological, and pulmonary (Woodside, 1995). The clinician should be alert to complaints of weakness, tiredness, constipation, and depression, which can be produced by electrolyte abnormalities (Webb & Gehi, 1981)—a complication of vomiting and purgative abuse.

The medical assessment is used, along with other measures, to determine whether hospitalization is necessary. Hospitalization is useful for nutritional rehabilitation and general medical care. Criteria for inpatient treatment have been outlined by Andersen (1986), Andersen, Bowers, and Evans (1997), and Powers (1984b):

- Significant weight loss (15–25% below normal weight or more), particularly if the weight loss has been recent and rapid, and severe starvation symptoms.
- Medical instabilities and metabolic abnormalities, especially hypokalemic alkalosis from bulimic complications.
- Overriding psychiatric problems involving clinical depression and/or thoughts or intents of suicide.
- Nonresponsiveness to outpatient treatment (after 3–4 months).
- Demoralized, nonfunctioning family.
- Lack of outpatient facilities.

TREATMENT

The treatment of eating disorders is an area of ongoing study, with the scientific merit of many approaches remaining to be explored and established. We review approaches that have and have not been rigorously examined, in the hope that future research will be done to validate and refine the methods of some of our experienced clinicians. Treatments range from individual approaches (including individual psychotherapy and psychopharmacology) to family therapy, group psychotherapy, and intensive programs involving all of the preceding plus coping skills training, assertiveness training, training in women's issues, and nutritional education, in inpatient settings, outpatient settings, or both. Team approaches are becoming increasingly popular. The primary issues in each of these modalities, along with adjunctive techniques, are reviewed. Table 13.4 outlines the organization of the treatment overview.

The approaches and techniques described below are designed specifically for the treatment of Anorexia Nervosa, Bulimia Nervosa, and Binge-Eating Disorder, although some have been used with other target problems as well. Although ongoing research in these areas is extensive, more and better studies of the comparative efficacy of these techniques, either combined or used separately, continue to be warranted. We advocate the use of multicomponent, multidisciplinary approaches to the treatment of eating disorders. Although various components of these programs have been highlighted here, readers should not assume that any of these components represents an entire treatment, unless this is stated explicitly. Future research will be needed to refine the use of these techniques.

Ethical issues surrounding assessment and treatment of eating-disordered patients, such as involuntary commitment, tube feeding, consultation with professionals in other disciplines, patients' rights regarding information about treatment, and specialized competency of therapists, have yet to be resolved. Clinicians should not attempt to treat these patients without specific training in these disorders.

Psychosocial Therapies: General Issues

Most types of psychotherapy have been utilized with eating-disordered patients, including individual interventions utilizing behavioral, cognitive-behavioral, psychodynamic, and interpersonal approaches. In addition, group psychotherapy has been attempted with both bulimic and anorexic patients. This section discusses general issues relevant to psychological interventions in eating disorders.

In individual psychotherapy, we believe that the cornerstones of the treatment, both philosophically and pragmatically, are flexibility and sensitivity. Therapeutic programs need to be tailored to individuals in terms of speed, content, and style. Specifically, treatments for eating disorders must be designed to take advantage of the integration of psychosocial interventions, medical management, and the appropriate dietary and rehabilitative services, as well as psychiatric medications when warranted (Yager, 1995). Anorexic patients can be quite recalcitrant or even excessively dependent in therapy. These patients can be especially draining on therapists, particularly on those who carry a heavy caseload. Their treatment is often long-term and may involve periodic regressions. A therapist must respond flexibly to changes in patients' level of organization and maturity (Goodsitt,

TABLE 13.4. Overview of Treatment Modalities

I. Psychosocial therapies: General issues
II. Inpatient approaches
III. Multicomponent outpatient treatment programs
IV. Psychotherapy techniques and therapeutic approaches
  A. Behavioral therapies and techniques
    1. Antecedent control
    2. Aversion techniques
    3. Exposure plus response prevention
    4. Operant conditioning
    5. Response delay
    6. Self-monitoring
    7. Social skills training
    8. Stimulus control
    9. Systematic desensitization
  B. Cognitive and cognitive-behavioral techniques
  C. Supportive–expressive therapy
  D. Interpersonal psychotherapy
  E. Body image work
  F. Emotional regulation training
  G. Family therapy
  H. Feminist approaches
  I. Group therapy
  J. Physical therapy
  K. Positive connotation
  L. Psychoeducational approaches for bulimics
  M. Symptom prescription
V. Pharmacological treatment
VI. Combined modalities: Integrating pharmacology and psychology

withdrawal/alienation, may help establish a common ground between a therapist and an unwilling patient. The therapist should take care to provide a rationale that does not place blame upon either the patient or the patient's family for the disorder. Bruch (1985) told her patients early in therapy that their illness, their preoccupation with eating and weight, was a coverup for their doubt about their own self-worth and value. As Goodsitt (1997) describes it, the therapist explains

> that he (or she) is asking her to give up a major adaptive defense that has served important protective functions for her. The therapist expects her to feel anxious. The therapist asks her to sit with her anxiety while the therapist sits with her. The therapist explains that asking her to give up an adaptive defense (anorexia or bulimia) is like asking a person who cannot swim to let go of the life preserver and try swimming. The person fears that she will drown, but she will not be left alone to sink or swim. The therapist may point out that it is really a choice she must make. She may continue to desperately hold on to what seems a life preserver (i.e., her illness), and continue to feel some temporary relief in not eating. She can also expect to continue her lonely, miserable, suffering life unchanged. On the other hand, the therapist continues, she can choose to let go and take a chance on eating—and life. Clearly, by doing so, she is entering a forbidden unknown. The therapist knows that the patient has little faith in her capacity to relate to others or to live an enjoyable or satisfying life of her own. She may indeed have good reason, based on past experience, not to be optimistic about her future. If this is the case, the therapist should acknowledge that. But the therapist tells the patient that he or she is committed to helping the patient learn the skills (the functions of ego and self) she needs to make her life better. (pp. 219–220)

In addition to supporting the patient by pointing out the positive, and in some ways adaptive, functions of the symptoms, we emphasize an additional five components of therapy: (1) thorough information gathering regarding the parameters and history of the disorder, ranging from concrete data regarding weight and amounts of food consumed to social and family functioning; (2) the need to help the eating-disordered patient learn to become aware of, identify, and express her emotional and inner life in more constructive ways; (3) the need to bolster

1985; 1997). Although patients should be allowed as much independence as they can possibly manage, the therapist should not make the mistake of assuming a false mask of self-sufficiency to be real, and should be ready to step in and take over as necessary.

The therapist must also be continually aware of the trust-building aspects of the relationship (Levenkron, 1983). A patient must experience that the therapist is interested in helping her and listens to what she has to say (Bruch, 1985). If the patient is pressured into therapy by her family, for example, motivation and trust will be essentially nonexistent until the patient sees therapy as helpful to her. Thus, one of the initial steps in the establishment of a therapeutic relationship is the development of a frame for therapy that is acceptable to both the patient and the therapist. This can only be done by listening closely to the patient's concerns and presenting therapy in a way that is perceived as benefiting the client. Inquiry into the side effects of starvation, such as sleep disturbance, irritability, depression, preoccupation with food, and social self-esteem and to take into account the severe self-doubts and low self-esteem of the eating-disordered patient; (4) education of the patient regarding the physiology and psychology of starvation, purging, and binge eating; and (5) a framing of therapy as a way to help the patient get what she wants and thereby minimize issues of coercion and control.

Inpatient Approaches

Hospitalization is not so much an approach as it is a setting in which many therapeutic techniques and procedures can be conducted under close supervision. Hospitalization may be indicated in situations where there are serious physical complications, suicide risk, very low body weight, lack of response to outpatient treatment, lack of available outpatient treatment, severe behavioral disturbances, and/or the need for separation from current living situation (Fichter, 1995). Most hospital programs are multidisciplinary and have many therapeutic components, including outpatient therapy and follow-up services. Psychiatry, psychology, nursing, dietetics, occupational therapy, physical therapy, social services, and general medicine services may be involved with the same patient in a team approach to treatment. There are many excellent eating disorders treatment programs in North America, some of which are free-standing facilities and some of which are operated within university medical schools. The following is a list of some of the more prominent programs that provide inpatient, partial hospitalization, and/or outpatient treatment: The Renfro Center in Philadelphia, PA; Remuda Ranch in Wickenberg, AZ; Laureate in Tulsa, OK; Rogers Memorial Hospital in Oconomowoc, WI; The Menninger Clinic in Topeka, KS; Stanford University Medical School; University of Iowa Medical School; University of New Mexico Medical School; Yale University Medical School; the Neuropsychiatric Institute at the University of California, Los Angeles; Toronto General Hospital and the University of Toronto; University of Cinncinati Medical Center; and the University of Minnesota Medical School.

Each member of the interdisciplinary team contributes to the therapy and management of the patient. In reviewing the different hospital programs, we find, however, that each takes a different approach to the questions of what professions or disciplines are represented on the team and what roles the different professionals

play. The roles are not neatly dictated by disciplines. With this in mind, we present the "roles" of each of the members on a typical treatment team.

1. Psychiatrists prescribe and monitor psychotropic medications, do intake evaluations, and, depending upon training and interest, may provide individual and family therapy. Given the structure and tradition of hospitals, psychiatrists also tend to occupy administrative and directorial positions on such wards.

2. Psychologists provide psychological and family evaluations, devise treatment plans, and conduct individual, group, and family therapy. If behavioral management contracts are developed, it is often a psychologist who does this. However, Powers and Powers (1984) recommend that the person administering the behavioral management program not be responsible for an anorexic's psychotherapy. The anorexic is often very angry about the program and may well have difficulty relating positively to the person administering it.

3. A medical consultant is needed to take careful histories and conduct physical examinations as a part of the evaluation process (especially in cases of atypical presentation), to conduct laboratory screenings and possibly neurological assessments, and to monitor patients' medical stability.

4. The nursing staff implements the treatment plans, enforces the rules, supervises the meals, and monitors the patients after eating (to prevent purging). The nursing staff has the most difficult and often the least rewarding role, and consequently should be given periodic progress reports to foster enthusiasm (Powers & Powers, 1984).

5. Dietitians and nutritionists help patients to plan meals and educate patients regarding nutrition and calories. The role of dietitians can be a problematic one, but not one without solutions. Dietitians, because of the milieu of their profession, tend to endorse a nutritional philosophy very similar to that held by anorexics (Beaumont, Beaumont, Touyz, & Williams, 1997; Kalucy, Gilchrist, McFarlane, & McFarlane, 1985); the profession emphasizes the deleterious effects of being overweight, the "badness" of refined carbohydrates, and the "goodness" of bran, fruit, and fresh vegetables, for example. Kalucy et al. (1985) conclude that dietitians must develop some psychotherapeutic skills and learn to ignore some of the traditional philoso-

phies of their profession. They also point out the danger of hiring a female dietitian—as well as a nurse, social worker, or doctor—who is herself anorexic.

Hospitalization generally lasts between 2 and 4 months (Andersen et al., 1997; Powers, 1984b; Powers & Powers, 1984), and generally consists of the following four phases: preparation, admission and start of treatment, stabilization, and transition from inpatient to outpatient treatment (Fichter, 1995). The preparation phase consists simply of informing the patient about the process, customizing the experience to meet the patient's needs, and facilitating the transition to the admission phase. The admission process involves negotiation with the patient and family. Toward this end, preadmission tours and contracts (Andersen et al., 1997; Powers & Powers, 1984) help to allay concerns and smooth the transition. The program should be clearly explained so that patients and their families know what to expect. They should be given an opportunity to talk with other patients, and should be allowed to ask the staff questions. They should be told what to expect in terms of their diet and its management, in particular. Some programs require that patients sign statements promising that they will comply with all aspects of the programs, and are told that they will be expected to "take food" as if it were a prescribed medication (Andersen et al., 1997). Patients may also be more ready to enter the program if they are assured that the staff will not allow them to become overweight.

Refeeding tends to begin with a diet of 1,200–1,500 calories per day, distributed across three meals. This is gradually increased by 500–750 calories a week to 3,500–5,000 calories per day. Powers (1984b) reports that the University of South Florida program has established limits on the duration of meals, and that if a meal is not consumed in an appropriate amount of time, patients may be given a liquid meal for their next meal. If patients fail to consume the liquid, they can be tube-fed. Andersen et al. (1997) suggest that tube feedings are rarely required with their more than 700 patients; others (Powers, 1984b) report using tube feedings infrequently and almost never more than once with any particular patient. If this procedure is to be used, this plan should be clearly explained to the patient upon admission.

Tuschen and Bents (1995) describe an intensive inpatient treatment for Bulimia Nervosa developed at the University of Marburg in Germany. This program begins with a comprehensive psychological and medical assessment designed to obtain both global and specific measures of function. After a comprehensive cognitive preparation phase, the program begins exposure therapy with cognitive intervention. Specifically, each patient's day is very structured, and during the course of the treatment each patient is repeatedly exposed to "forbidden" food, binge food and binge triggers, actual total body shape, and actual body weight. Cognitive interventions are relatively nonconfrontational, and consist of the facilitation of cognitive dissonance and the development of skills to adaptively utilize and reduce the dissonance. Finally, this inpatient protocol puts a special emphasis on relapse prevention and self-management.

Goal Weights

During the stabilization phase, goal weights grow in importance (Fichter, 1995). Staff members typically set an initial goal weight for a patient by consulting weight charts (e.g., Frisch & McArthur, 1974; Metropolitan Life Insurance Company, 1984). When set, the goal weight takes the form of a 3- to 5-pound range. Andersen et al. (1985; 1997) make this decision as a staff after several weeks of treatment, and they modify the goal weight range depending upon the patient's appearance. However, patients are not informed of their goal weight until they are in the middle of the established range. It is helpful to keep patients hospitalized for approximately 2 weeks after they have reached their goal weight, in order to help them become comfortable maintaining that weight, and to provide a supportive environment when they fear they may continue to gain weight and become obese.

Special Problems

Special problems associated with hospitalization have been discussed in detail by Garfinkel, Garner, and Kennedy (1985), Fichter (1995), and Woodside (1995). These problems are outlined below.

Problems with Patients.

1. Patients may refuse to cooperate with the treatment program, because they feel they have no problem and do not want to change.

2. Patients may believe that others want to control them rather than help them; they may also mistrust themselves for fear that they cannot control themselves.

3. Severe depression may be present.

4. Anorexic patients may compete for staff time or "specialness" by virtue of being the most seriously ill.

5. Attitudes of nonanorexic patients toward anorexic patients may be problematic. Since anorexic patients require more staff time, other patients tend to feel neglected and angry.

6. Medical complications may arise. Anorexic patients are, or can become, seriously physically ill; consequently, they pose special concerns to staff members accustomed to dealing primarily with psychiatric problems.

Problems with Families.
1. Families may encourage the patients to resist treatment or push for a premature discharge.
2. Patients and parents may fear separation.
3. Family members may experience significant levels of guilt and/or fear being blamed for a patient's difficulties.

Staff Problems.
1. Staff members may become frustrated and angry with a patient's resistance and repeat the family's attempt to punish the patient; or, conversely, they may avoid confrontation, may not be consistently firm, or may allow the patient to be manipulative.
2. Staff members may become polarized around various issues because of an anorexic's tendency to view people and situations as "all good" or "all bad."
3. Inexperienced staff members may be provoked by a patient's behaviors and respond in ways similar to those of significant people in the patient's life.

Admission Problems. In general, involuntary admission to inpatient settings should be avoided whenever possible (Fichter, 1995). General problems with admission to the hospital have been discussed by Kalucy et al. (1985). Their group typically conducts preadmission assessments over several weeks, and states that patients and families often try to circumvent this process by presenting in a state of crisis. The support system may have been driven to a state of rage, despair, and impotence, or the patient may feel that she has lost control of her eating and will become obese if not admitted immediately. Kalucy et al. (1985) have found that these families and patients will agree to anything to escape the crisis, but that once hospitalization has occurred and the crisis has been smoothed over, motivation and compliance are minimal.

Thus, except in cases of medical and psychiatric emergencies, they insist that routine assessment procedures be followed. If a patient is in a medical crisis characterized by confusion, disorientation, and memory disturbance, or in a psychiatric emergency (e.g., a suicidal depression), then she is hospitalized on an emergency basis and is stabilized. She is not initially admitted into the eating disorders program; however, after she is stabilized, she is reevaluated and may or may not be admitted to the program. In some cases, patients are discharged with outpatient services.

Some admission problems can be circumvented by not considering hospitalization as an "all-or-none" decision. Kalucy et al. (1985), for example, describe four hospitalization alternatives, each with different aims, ranging from very short-term stays with limited goals to protracted inpatient stays. If a patient is in an extreme state of emaciation, a short-term admission is recommended as a life-saving procedure. A second option is presented to patients whose eating behavior is "substantially out of control" and who are psychologically and socially in a state of chaos. They are considered for a short-term admission in order to stabilize and restore physical and metabolic well-being (e.g., to treat hypokalemia). A third alternative is a 1-month hospitalization, which is used to establish a therapeutic alliance, complete a thorough assessment, and establish a reasonable set of rules about eating and diet for orderly weight gain. This alternative is considered as a prelude to outpatient therapy, as a compromise for patients who need more than a short stay but less than a protracted stay. Finally, the fourth option involves a protracted inpatient stay with strict bed rest until a target weight is reached, followed by progressive mobilization, psychological work, and relaxation of controls dependent upon the quality of the psychotherapeutic relationship. One-third of Kalucy's group's patients (Kalucy et al., 1985) then pursue intensive individual psychotherapy for 6–24 months after hospitalization, while 10% receive longer and more intensive therapy.

Multicomponent Outpatient Treatment Programs

Intensive, multicomponent outpatient treatment programs are becoming increasingly popular for the treatment of Bulimia Nervosa, Anorexia Nervosa, and Binge-Eating Disorder (Agras et al., 1994; Lacey, 1985; Mitchell, Hatsukami, Goff, et al., 1985; Wooley & Kearney-Cooke,

1986). These programs typically combine educational seminars, group psychotherapy, individual psychotherapy, family therapy, and body image therapy, incorporating many of the themes discussed above and utilizing many of the techniques outlined below. These approaches may also be utilized in conjunction with pharmacological interventions (Yager, 1994).

The Eating Disorders Clinic in the Psychiatry Department of the University of Cincinnati Medical Center offers an intensive treatment program (Wooley & Kearney-Cooke, 1986). The women are seen daily for 6–8 hours of therapy, in groups of six, for 3½ weeks while they are housed in a nearby hotel. (The program is designed for women who are from out of town.) One group of 18 patients treated in this program was followed up 12 months after termination; of the 16 patients contacted, 7 were entirely free of binge–purge behaviors. The other 9 showed an average reduction in binge behavior of 85% (range, 63% to 94%). These patients also showed improvement on psychometric tests and general life adaptation.

Psychotherapy Techniques and Therapy Components

Comparisons of therapeutic processes and techniques have failed to identify a clear choice among approaches. Specifically, reviews of the literature tend to find behavioral, cognitive, cognitive-behavioral, and interpersonal therapeutic approaches to perform significantly better than either no treatment or pharmacological interventions alone (Wilson & Fairburn, 1993). However, there is no consistent, clear-cut pattern of differential performance among the above-mentioned theoretical approaches in the scientific literature. In fact, reviews of the literature indicate that almost every type of therapeutic technique has been attempted with eating-disordered patients, and that all have shown some efficacy (Garner & Garfinkel, 1985; 1997). A brief discussion of several types of therapeutic interventions follows.

Behavioral Therapies and Techniques

Antecedent Control. Antecedent control involves the manipulation of factors preceding a binge. These factors often include particular feeling states (e.g., boredom or anxiety), difficulty with interpersonal relationships, and dietary deprivation. These strategies are very similar to coping skills training, which teaches patients to cope with difficult situations.

Aversion Techniques. Aversion techniques were used by Kenny and Solyom (1971) with a female patient who binged and vomited an average of three times daily. The subject formed a mental image of the eight steps leading to a vomiting episode, and raised her finger when each image was clearly perceived. An electric shock at pain threshold intensity was delivered to her middle finger. Each of the eight steps was punished individually, and the procedure was repeated five times each session for 22 sessions. The subject stopped vomiting after 15 sessions; she reported at follow-up 3 months later that she had not resumed vomiting.

Exposure plus Response Prevention. There has been some controversy about the role of exposure plus response prevention (ERP) procedures in the treatment of bulimic behaviors. These procedures were initially studied by Rosen and Leitenberg (1982). They hypothesized that vomiting is a response to overeating that decreases anxiety related to an intense fear of gaining weight. As a result, the individual learns that vomiting after eating leads to anxiety reduction. Rosen and Leitenberg proposed that binge eating might not occur if the bulimic individual were prevented from vomiting afterward. Some studies support the use of ERP procedures (Gray & Hoage, 1990; Kennedy, Katz, Neitzert, Ralveski, & Mendlowitz, 1995; Leitenberg, Rosen, Gross, Nudelman, & Vara, 1988; Williamson, Prather, et al., 1989; Wilson, Rossiter, Kleinfield, & Lindholm, 1986), although several of these studies can be criticized for lack of adequate controls and having small sample sizes. A controlled study by Agras, Schneider, Arnow, Raeburn, and Telch (1989) found that ERP procedures added no benefit to, and potentially detracted from the efficacy of, cognitive-behavioral therapy (CBT). Although proponents of ERP have suggested that the Agras et al. (1989) study suffered from methodological problems, such as not allowing for adequate ERP practice (Leitenberg & Rosen, 1989), more recent studies that attempted to address these problems did not demonstrate any benefit from adding ERP procedures to CBT (Wilson, Eldredge, Smith, & Niles, 1991). In a study that compared ERP alone to CBT alone, 1-year follow-up data suggested that patients assigned to the ERP-alone condition experienced significantly greater relapse, while patients in the CBT-alone group maintained or slightly improved their scores on measures of bulimia-specific psychopathology and more general measures of psychological functioning (Cooper & Steere, 1995). Although Leitenberg and Rosen (1989) argued that ERP procedures are designed to supplement CBT or other treatments and not to replace them, the role of ERP procedures in the treatment of bulimic behaviors is currently unclear.

Operant Conditioning Techniques. Operant conditioning techniques have been used to facilitate weight gain (Bachrach, Erwin, & Mohr, 1965; Lang, 1965; Leitenberg, Agras, & Thompson, 1968; Steinhausen, 1995a) in hospital settings. These techniques use positive and negative contingencies (either social praise, recreational activities, visiting privileges, hospital rewards, and/or earlier or later discharge) in association with a performance criterion (either eating or weight gain). In the case of Anorexia Nervosa, this criterion is generally a predetermined weight. This requires that the therapist have control over the contingencies, and hospitalization is thus necessary. Although it can produce initial and rapid weight gains, this procedure has not been shown to be any more effective than other treatments in long-term weight maintenance, nor to be any better than simple hospital programs with discharge contingent on weight gains (Garfinkel, Moldofsky, & Garner, 1977). Research utilizing these approaches suggests that in terms of treatment efficacy, they are not superior to cognitive-behavioral techniques (e.g., Wilson & Fairburn, 1993). These findings are consistent with the more traditional assertion that operant conditioning techniques are helpful when part of a comprehensive treatment program, but inadequate when used alone (Bemis, 1978; Steinhausen, 1995a). In addition, a study comparing the efficacy of behavior therapy, interpersonal psychotherapy (IPT), and CBT found very high rates of attrition/withdrawal and poorer outcomes among patients receiving the behavior therapy intervention (Fairburn, Jones, Peveler, Hope, & O'Connor, 1993).

Response Delay. Response delay procedures are based on the theory that if an impulse can be delayed it can be resisted, and that at least initially, delaying an act is easier than resisting one. After time has passed, the urge is thought to subside and become more manageable. Furthermore, the sequence or chain of events will be altered by the delay. The delay tactic can involve allowing some predetermined length of time to pass or engaging in some particular activity (Garner, Vitousek, Pike, 1997). For example, a bulimic client may choose to make herself wait 20 minutes before bingeing, call a friend, wash a load of laundry, or perform some other activity. It is important that the activity be selected ahead of time and be something of the client's choosing, perhaps something pleasurable and esteem-building. Garner and Bemis (1985) suggest that some clients find it helpful to have a "mnemonic card" listing prebinge delay tactics, so that they can consult it if and when their thinking becomes confused. They also state that this tactic is particularly helpful with clients who have not yet made a commitment to stop vomiting.

Self-Monitoring Techniques. Self-monitoring techniques are quite helpful, particularly when patients binge. Patients are encouraged to monitor and record the parameters of their binge eating; associated and preceding thoughts, feelings, and events; presence or absence of others; and the particular environment involved. Fairburn (1980) used elaborate self-monitoring in conjunction with cognitive techniques with four severely bulimic women who engaged in vomiting. The self-monitoring was used as a vehicle whereby the clients and therapist could explore ways to increase self-control over eating and to decrease food avoidance. Utilizing similar methods, Agras et al. (1989) compared the effectiveness of self-monitoring alone to that of a complete CBT package (including self-monitoring). Although self-monitoring alone was effective, the CBT package significantly outperformed it. This suggests that though it was important, self-monitoring should been viewed as a meaningful component of CBT, and not as a "treatment" in and of itself.

Social Skills Training. Social role identification and skills training are used to help correct the deficits in social skills, assertiveness, interpersonal communication, and basic problem-solving capabilities frequently observed in both anorexics and bulimics. Improving such skills may be necessary for patients to develop a greater sense of self-control and become more effective in living. A first step is to identify what their basic roles and postures in life are, and what those roles communicate to and elicit from others. Before giving up the old ways of interacting, patients may need to become clearer on how their current nonassertiveness (and aggressiveness) is both beneficial and protective.

Social skills training was used in one study to try to modify the social isolation and interpersonal anxiety of anorexics (Pillay & Crisp, 1981). Some anorexics have difficulty distinguishing their own motivations and desires from the expectations of others; social skills training can be useful in exploring this distinction. In the study, one group of hospitalized anorexics received the social skills training, and another group was placed in a placebo condition. At a l-year follow-up, the social skills group did not differ significantly from the placebo-treated group in terms of weight, but they were less likely to terminate treatment and reported a more rapid decrease in their levels of anxiety, depression, and fear of negative evaluation. Fichter (1995) suggests that the typical targets of social skills training interventions should be incorporated into inpatient treatment interventions for Anorexia Nervosa patients to enhance overall effectiveness and generalization of treatment.

Stimulus Control Strategies.   Stimulus control strategies are used to limit or negate the environmental cues that lead to inappropriate eating. These include removal of binge foods from the household and avoidance of problematic eating situations (e.g., going to particular restaurants or being alone in the house during specific hours). Stimulus control procedures were evaluated in a single case study by Viens and Hranchuk (1993), which found that stimulus control procedures emphasizing minimal therapist contact, in the absence of cognitive therapy, were successful in reducing vomiting frequency in a 35-year-old bulimic female patient. No strong conclusions can be drawn about the efficacy or generalizability of these procedures from this case study, but stimulus control strategies should be further evaluated in larger, controlled investigations to evaluate the benefit of including them in a comprehensive treatment program.

Systematic Desensitization.   Systematic desensitization has been used to decrease anxiety related to fears of gaining weight and/or being criticized (Hallsten, 1965; Lang, 1965; Ollendick, 1979), self-deprecating thoughts (Monti, McCrady, & Barlow, 1977), and changes in physical appearance concomitant with weight gain (Schnurer, Rubin, & Roy, 1973)

Cognitive/Cognitive-Behavioral Techniques

Cognitive retraining or restructuring techniques combat distorted body image, erroneous beliefs and assumptions, and misinterpretations of environmental "messages" (Beck, 1976). Anorexics and bulimics may judge their self-worth solely in terms of shape and weight. Examples of cog-

nitive distortions (Tuschen & Bents, 1995; Fairburn, Cooper, & Cooper, 1986; Fairburn et al., 1993) include the following:

- "To be fat is to be a failure, unattractive, and unhappy."
- "To be thin is to be successful, attractive, and happy."
- "To exert self-control is a sign of strength and discipline."

These ideas are obviously present in Western culture; therapy consequently involves questioning these social values and identifying the dysfunctional or nonadaptive ways that patients apply them to their lives (Pike, Loeb, & Vitousek, 1996). It is helpful to emphasize that these statements are overgeneralizations, and that although they may be true to some degree, they are not absolute or universal truths. Common categories of cognitive disturbances and procedures for facilitating CBT of eating disorders have been detailed by Garner (1986), Garner and Bemis (1982), Fernandez (1984), and Pike et al. (1996). Teaching patients to label cognitive distortions as such can help them combat these thoughts.

An extensive listing of cognitive techniques is provided by Garner et al. (1977). These include articulation of beliefs, decentering, decatastrophizing, challenging the "shoulds," challenging beliefs through behavioral exercises, prospective hypothesis testing, reattribution techniques, palliative techniques (parroting and distraction), and challenging cultural values regarding shape. It is also important to help patients improve their self-esteem by encouraging them to explore their interests and to develop a more complex view of self (Garner & Bemis, 1985; Garner et al., 1997). To accomplish this, these authors praise small signs of independent and competent functioning, including risk taking, reasonable self-expression, assertiveness, flexibility, the pursuit of purely pleasurable activities, and even "healthy" noncompliance. Once deficits in emotions, sensations, and thoughts are identified, new responses are practiced.

Self-monitoring, stimulus control, and cognitive restructuring have been used by Grinc (1982), who reported a case of a 26-year-old normal-weight bulimic woman. Each of the components was introduced sequentially. Treatment lasted 7 months; sessions were weekly at first and became less frequent later. Self-monitoring and stimulus control procedures were introduced in the second session, and vomiting decreased from 12 episodes per week to 3 per week; then, at the fifth session, cognitive restructuring was introduced. Two weeks after this introduction (by week 9), the vomiting had ceased altogether. There were several relapses 3 months later (weeks 1–22), but at a follow-up 1-year after the beginning of therapy (week 52), the patient reported that she had not vomited in 5 months.

Research utilizing approaches combining cognitive and behavioral interventions (CBT) have enjoyed meaningful levels of efficacy (Mitchell, Hoberman, Peterson, Mussell, & Pyle, 1996; Pike et al., 1996). In a study of 50 bulimic patients, CBT was found to be mildly superior to supportive–expressive treatment on measures of vomiting frequency, but the results were much stronger when other symptoms were examined (e.g., concern about eating and weight, depression, and self-esteem) (Garner et al., 1993). CBT techniques, and CBT techniques used in combination with pharmacological interventions, tend to be superior to pharmacological intervention alone in reducing the primary symptoms of Bulimia Nervosa (Agras, 1997; Crow & Mitchell, 1996; Goldbloom et al., 1997). However, relapse, over the long term, was lower in subjects administered a 24-week combined pharmacological–CBT treatment protocol. Current research suggests that the efficacy of CBT approaches may be enhanced by the addition of other techniques, such as "planned binges" in the treatment of Bulimia Nervosa (Steel, Farag, & Blaszczynski, 1995). Specifically, the addition of planned binges that are gradually faded over time, allows a direct approach to the control of bingeing behavior.

CBT also presents a promising approach to the treatment of Anorexia Nervosa, with a primary focus on weight restoration (Wilson & Fairburn, 1993). However, anorexic patients are far more likely to resist attempts to change their eating behavior and/or body weight. Finally, as discussed below, recent studies of CBT approaches indicate that IPT may perform similarly well, but may take a longer time to be effective (Fairburn et al., 1993).

Supportive–Expressive Therapy

Supportive–expressive therapy, originally developed as a brief psychoanalytic therapy (Luborsky, 1984), has also been applied in the treatment of eating disorders. Supportive–expressive therapy posits that eating disorder symptoms disguise underlying interpersonal problems. Therapy is nondirective and interpretive, with a focus on listening to the patient, expressing feel-

ings, and identifying problems and solutions. A primary task during therapy is to explore the past in order to illuminate interpersonal difficulties and establish core conflictual relationship themes that underlie eating disorder symptoms. As noted earlier, supportive–expressive therapy was found to be slightly less effective than CBT in reducing the frequency of self-induced vomiting, but CBT was significantly more effective in ameliorating dysfunctional attitudes about eating and weight, depression, poor self-esteem, and general psychological distress (Garner et al., 1993).

Interpersonal Psychotherapy

Recent trends in the study of the differential efficacy of different types of psychological interventions for eating disorders include the systematic study of the effectiveness of IPT. Specifically, studies of IPT have found it to be as effective as CBT (Fairburn et al., 1995) in the treatment of Bulimia Nervosa. In a related study, IPT was found to perform as well as CBT approaches, but appeared to work somewhat more slowly (Fairburn et al., 1993). This finding has been replicated in several studies (e.g., Garner et al., 1993) and raises the following question: Why does a therapeutic approach that does not focus primarily on eating behaviors result in significant improvements in individuals experiencing Bulimia Nervosa? Agras (1991) proposes that IPT addresses a second mechanism in the development and maintenance of Bulimia Nervosa. This second mechanism consists of the interaction of dissatisfaction with social relationships, difficulties in social functioning, anxiety, depression, general negative affect, and low self-esteem—all typical targets of IPT.

Research addressing the efficacy of IPT with Binge-Eating Disorder patients who have failed in CBT treatment has not found it effective (Agras et al., 1995). Consequently, this finding suggests that patients benefiting from CBT are not significantly different from those who benefit from IPT.

Body Image Work

Body image work helps patients become more accepting of their bodies and more aware of them. Photographs, videotapes, various types of role playing, movement, expressive art, and guided imagery therapies can be employed. Wooley and Kearney-Cooke (1986) discuss the use of a combination of such techniques. In particular, they describe using deep muscle relaxation along with the suggestion of images or guided imagery. They focus on three major vignettes. One is the transition from childhood to puberty. Patients are asked to recall and develop pictures in their minds of what their bodies were like at age 5, first grade, prepuberty, the age when they first menstruated, adolescence, and the age when they first left home. They may be asked to draw these images or to sculpt them in clay. The second concerns early sexual experiences. Patients are asked to recall early sex play with childhood peers, early sex play with adults, sexual encounters during adolescence, and recent sexual experiences. They visualize the actual settings in which these experiences took place and the feelings they had at the time. Again, sculptures and drawings may be used to capture these images. In the third vignette, a patient compares her own body image to that of her mother. The patient is asked to imagine herself as her mother preparing for a social event and then at the actual event, copying her movements and gestures. These exercises help to uncover feelings and beliefs, as well as traumatic experiences that have shaped the lives of these women and their attitudes about their bodies.

Rosen, Reiter, and Orosan (1995) evaluated a body-image-oriented form of CBT with patients diagnosed with Body Dysmorphic Disorder. They found that patients treated with CBT experienced significant decreases in their body image disturbance, compared to no-treatment controls. In addition, remission was achieved in 82% of treated patients at termination and 77% of cases at follow-up (Rosen et al., 1995). It is possible that these cognitive-behavioral methods could be integrated into the treatment of Anorexia Nervosa and Bulimia Nervosa, to more adequately address the needs of eating disorder patients with significant body image disturbance.

Emotional Regulation Training

Emotional regulation training consists of keeping diaries of feelings and the exploration of reasons behind demands and actions. Such diaries can be used to help patients become more aware of their inner experiences. Also, when a therapist takes a patient's thoughts and feelings seriously, this helps the patient to take her own thoughts and feelings seriously. Wooley and Kearney-Cooke (1986) argue that "the central task of therapy is to push patients outside their range of comfort into expressing of meaningful emotion" (p. 486). In order to do this, they employ six strategies: (1) interrupting minimization of problems, (2) exploring ambivalence, (3) exploring relationships, (4) re-enacting past events, (5) dramatizing future events, and (6) amplifying emotional expression with movement.

Family Therapy

Family therapy ranges from supportive, informational counseling to more intensive work focused on changing a family's structural and/or functional patterns. Family therapy has been used as a treatment by itself (Minuchin et al., 1978) and as an element of multicomponent treatment packages (e.g., Strober & Yager, 1985; Dare & Eisler, 1997). Although the goals of both approaches are quite similar, the varieties and techniques are extensive and sometimes mutually exclusive. In general, family therapy as the sole treatment aims at encouraging an anorexic's gradual disengagement from the family, her progress toward adolescence and adulthood, and the realignment of family roles and boundaries along more developmentally appropriate and adaptive lines. The agenda of family therapy as an element of a treatment package (Wooley & Kearney-Cooke, 1986) is to help the patient find a way to achieve the necessary separation from the family without the feared loss of all connection to her family; to help her state personal needs and feelings clearly; to help her get permission from her mother to be separate or different from her; and to facilitate communication between the parents, so that the daughter is not needed as a facilitator.

Dare and Eisler (1995) review several studies focusing on the differential utility of family vs. individual supportive therapy for the treatment of eating disorders. In their review, these authors report that adolescent anorexics receiving family intervention outperformed those receiving individual treatment on measures of maintained body weight at 5-year follow-up. Russell, Szmukler, Dare, and Eisler (1987), in a controlled trial, found that family therapy was superior to individual supportive therapy in patients who started before age 19 and whose illness was not chronic. Crisp et al. (1991) also found family therapy to be an important component of their combined therapy in a study of 90 anorexic patients. Their study compared the efficacy of four treatment modalities: inpatient treatment; outpatient individual therapy coupled with family psychotherapy, plus dietary counseling; outpatient group family therapy plus dietary counseling; and no treatment. Both of the treatment protocols that included family therapy were found to be superior to the no-treatment condition on measures of weight gain, return of menstruation, and aspects of social and sexual adjustment. In contrast, a recent evaluation of behavioral–family systems therapy with adolescent female anorexics found that family therapy and ego-oriented individual therapy, which focuses on improving a patient's ego strength, coping skills, and individuation from the family, were equivalent in producing improvements in eating attitudes, body dissatisfaction, interoceptive awareness, depression, and family conflict (Robin, Siegel, & Moye, 1995; Robin, Siegel, Koepke, Moye, & Tice, 1994). In addition, many of these improvements were maintained 1 year after treatment termination. In fact, the only difference in outcome between the two therapy approaches was that behavioral–family systems therapy produced greater changes in body mass index. Similarly, few differences were found in a study that compared family therapy to separate counseling for the patient and parents (le Grange, Eisler, Dare, & Russell, 1992). Clearly, as Gillberg (1994) has suggested, more research is needed to clarify the role and benefits of family therapy in the treatment of eating disorders.

Feminist Approaches to Treatment

Although the definition of a "feminist approach," with respect to psychological interventions, is continuously evolving and somewhat difficult to articulate, a brief description of the ideas that fall under the umbrella of the term is warranted. Wooley (1995) discusses the importance of considering the social and cultural context in which eating-disordered patients find themselves. Specifically, feminist therapists attempt to focus on patients' difficulties with respect to the metaphorical meaning of the difficulties. Therapeutic approaches are designed to empower patients and help them self-differentiate, as opposed to the application of more traditional techniques, which may result in the retraumatization of some patients. Feminist approaches to treatment take into account the role of culture in etiology (Striegel-Moore, 1995) and discuss the potential impact of sexual abuse on the development of eating disorders in children (Kearney-Cooke & Striegel-Moore, 1994) and adults (Everill & Waller, 1995).

Group Therapy

Group Approaches for Anorexics.   Group therapy for anorexics is rarely advocated, compared to group approaches for normal-weight bulimic patients (Hall, 1985). Conducting group therapy for anorexics can be a lonely, draining experience for therapists and requires many special considerations. Most group therapies are not suitable for many anorexic patients. However, group work may be beneficial for those anorexics who are not severely ill (i.e., who are gaining weight or are stable), are highly motivated, have benefited psychologically from other treatments, are not totally isolated or withdrawn, are psychologically minded, are able to reveal feelings, are sensitive to others, are liked by the therapist, and have the potential to be liked by other group members. Additional considerations are whether other treatments are indicated (inpatient treatment or family therapy) and/or whether it is practical to combine other treatments with group work (Hall, 1985). Careful consideration must also be given to group size and composition, preparation of clients for the group, length of session, duration of treatment, the admittance of new members, and therapist characteristics and tenure (Polivy & Federoff, 1997). From her experience and those of others, Hall has developed very specific guidelines for therapists regarding the structuring of groups through the various stages of treatment—from preparatory phases to the first session, to early stages, and on to termination. Hall also advises against the use of gestalt techniques, such as role plays and other strategies that facilitate emotional expression; such experiences tend to be refused by anorexics because of their self-consciousness, fears of failure, and fears of loss of control.

Experiential Group Therapy for Bulimics.   Experiential group therapy has been advocated for the treatment of normal-weight bulimic women. This type of therapy may incorporate a feminist perspective and take the position that eating disorders are caused in part by the conflicting role demands placed upon today's women. Accordingly, Bulimia Nervosa is considered to be "related to the struggle to achieve a perfect, stereotypic female image in which women surrender most of their self-defining powers to others" (White & Boskind-White, 1981, p. 501). Treatment consequently questions these standards (Boskind-Lodahl & White, 1978). In their earlier report (Boskind-Lodahl & White, 1978), of 12 of 13 women who completed treatment, 4 ceased bingeing, 6 reduced the frequency and length of their binges, and 2 had no change. Follow-up 1 year later suggested that the successes had been maintained. A similar treatment procedure was followed with a separate sample of 14 women (White & Boskind-White, 1981); 6 months after treatment, 3 of the women reported a cessation of binges, 7 reported reduced frequency and decreased duration of binges, and 4 reported little change in binges. All of the 10 women who found the treatment helpful in reducing their binge behavior also reported that they no longer engaged in purge behavior, despite a high frequency of purges prior to treatment.

Physical Therapy

Moderate exercise (walking, stretching) is thought to promote a healthy distribution of weight gain and is a source of encouragement to patients. A graduated exercise program is begun within a week or two after admission at the Johns Hopkins program (Andersen, 1986). However, strenuous exercise (e.g., aerobics) is generally not allowed until near discharge time. The concern is that the exercise may become compulsive and used as a weight reduction strategy. Thus, close supervision of such activities may be necessary.

Positive Connotation

Positive connotation can be used with binge behaviors and interpersonal problems for anorexics and bulimics and their families. Loro (1984) suggests to bulimics that their counterdependency and rebelliousness is "smart when you have to deal with all the undependable people around today" (p. 202). When an undesirable behavior is judged to be positive, it is much easier to approach the frightening topics of vulnerability, rejections, and exposure that dependency may have come to mean. Thus, rather than trying to reduce the counterdependency, the therapist can encourage bulimics to refine their methods for finding dependable people. Positive connotation allows the therapist to tread on sensitive ground without causing the client to feel criticized.

Although Coffman (1984) does not discuss his therapeutic techniques in terms of positive connotation, what he does with his clients could easily be considered to involve positive connotation. He interprets binge behavior as "a statement of determination and integrity" (pp. 216), which is called forth by a significant relationship in which the client is pressured to conform to a controlling "master's" expectations. With this understanding, the client is then encouraged to be her own master, to choose to do whatever she wishes—to eat or not to eat, to binge or not to binge. Emphasis shifts to replacing the goals of the old master with the goals of the new master. Many of the client's desires, wants, needs,

and values may be hidden, and the therapist's help may be needed in order to bring them forth. Johnson, Lewis, and Hagman (1984) emphasize the "adaptiveness" of binge eating as a relatively safe way of regulating tension and being impulsive, aggressive, erotic, oppositional, or "out of control."

Psychoeducational Approaches

Psychoeducational approaches have been viewed as an important part of eating disorders treatment and are based on the idea that maladaptive beliefs and behaviors develop as a result of incorrect or absent information (Olmsted & Kaplan, 1995). Psychoeducation typically consists of providing information to patients about the nature of the disorder and methods for overcoming it with the intention of promoting attitudinal and behavior change. In addition, psychoeducational programs tend to focus on a coaching model of treatment, that is, the patient is empowered with information and methods and that the locus of change is within the patient (Garner, 1997; Olmsted & Kaplan, 1995). Psychoeducational programs cover a wide range of topics, depending on the treatment population and professionals involved. When considering eating disorders, topics may include the multidimensional etiology of Anorexia Nervosa, Bulimia Nervosa, and Binge-Eating Disorder; the negative consequences of dieting; nutritional information; set-point theory; the effects of starvation on behavior; the cultural context of eating disorders; body image and self-esteem issues; cognitive and behavior change strategies; medical complications; and relapse prevention, just to name a few (Garner, 1997; Olmsted & Kaplan, 1995). Finally, psychoeducational programs are most often provided to patients in group formats that facilitate interaction and support and can include family members.

Johnson et al. (1983) and Connors et al. (1984) treated two groups of 10 bulimic women over a 12-week period. Therapy included didactic presentations as well as group process interventions. The didactic presentations focused on challenging beliefs about the value of thinness and distorted ideas about food, weight, and dieting. Subjects were also taught to reduce bingeing and purging by means of behavioral strategies, and to normalize eating by means of self-monitoring and self-graduated goal setting. Binge–purge episodes were reduced by 70% at posttreatment and at a 6-month follow-up. Three subjects had ceased bingeing, eight had reduced their frequency by more than 50%, six had reduced their frequency by between 30% and 50%, and three patients were unchanged.

Olmsted et al. (1991) utilized a sequential cohort design to compare the relative effectiveness of an 18-week CBT intervention for Bulimia Nervosa with that of a 4-week (five-session) group psychoeducational protocol. CBT was found to be significantly more effective for the most seriously ill patients (32% of the sample who reported bingeing more than 42 times in the month prior to treatment) on measures of vomiting frequency. For less severe patients, no significant difference on measures of vomiting frequency between CBT and the psychoeducational intervention was detected. A similar but less robust finding was reported for scores on the Drive for Thinness and Maturity Fears scales included in this study. Though showing differential utility, the results of this study certainly highlight the implications of the relative effectiveness of psychoeducational interventions for the delivery of efficient and cost-effective treatment of Bulimia Nervosa.

Symptom Prescription

"Programmed bingeing" or "symptom prescription" is used to help patients experience their problem behavior in a new and different way (Haley, 1976; Loro, 1984; Weeks & L'Abate, 1982). A therapist and client typically review previous binge behavior and identify preferred binge foods, as well as thoughts and feelings that accompany the binge. The bulimic or bingeing anorexic may be instructed to bring the binge foods into the therapist's office and to consume them in the therapist's presence, or the therapist and client may contract together for the client to go on a binge. Amount of food, time of day of binge, location, and so on may be specified. The client may or may not be directed to keep detailed records of calories consumed, thoughts, and feelings. The client may be encouraged to eat slowly and to think about the number of calories in each bite, the taste of each bite, and the sensations of eating, or to binge-eat in her usual fashion.

Since the binge behavior is typically seen as something over which clients lack control, having clients engage in binge behavior "voluntarily" as opposed to "involuntarily" changes the experience of the binge. Clients typically experience that they have more control than they formerly perceived themselves to have, and that the self-recriminations that generally follow their bingeing are not a necessary consequence of bingeing (they do not blame themselves, because they are merely doing as the therapist requested). Steel et al. (1995) present case study data arguing for the relative utility of planned binges as a means of bringing eating behaviors under a client's control. Furthermore, when the binge behavior loses its "forbidden" status, it sometimes loses its desirability. In Loro's (1984) experience, many clients report being unable to follow through on the binge because they become uninterested in eating or are unable to eat as much as anticipated. Such experiences can be used to identify tactics a client can use later to resist bingeing.

Psychosocial Treatments: Conclusions

Although there appears to be a vast array of potential psychosocial treatments that can be applied to eating-disordered patients, none address all symptoms or produce outcomes that are clearly superior to all other treatments. For example, though CBT appears to produce substantial improvements in symptoms of Bulimia Nervosa and Binge-Eating Disorder, all patients do not benefit (Agras et al., 1995). In fact, as noted above, the evidence for many psychosocial therapies (e.g., family therapy, behavioral techniques, etc.) is weak or equivocal at this time. Patients with eating disorders appear to have high rates of relapse and recurrence, regardless of the treatment modality (Keller, Herzog, Lavori, Bradburn, & Mahoney, 1992; Steinhausen, 1995a); this suggests that current psychosocial treatments are not adequate, and that future efforts should focus on developing new approaches or integrating and evaluating existing therapies.

Pharmacological Treatment

Anorexia Nervosa

Pharmacological treatments have typically been used as one component of multicomponent programs for Anorexia Nervosa, and include neuroleptic antidepressants (Hoffman & Halmi, 1993) and antianxiety medications. For example, Garfinkel and Walsh (1997) suggest that small amounts of a benzodiazepine (e.g., lorezapam) may be helpful for some highly anxious anorexic patients shortly before meals. Andersen et al. (1997) argue that the use of medications to stimulate appetite is misguided, in that appetite is not disturbed in anorexics. They refrain from using antidepressant medications until patients have attained normal weight, and then use them only if a patient meets the criteria for Major Depressive Disorder.

A double-blind inpatient drug study compared cyproheptadine (a weight-inducing antidepressant drug) to amitriptyline hydrochloride (a tricyclic antidepressant) and a placebo (Halmi, Eckert, LaDu, & Cohen, 1986). The overall lack of effect of cyproheptadine on the number of days it took for the anorexic patients to reach a normal weight obscured a differential response to the drug. Cyproheptadine shortened treatment for the nonbulimic anorexic patients and lengthened treatment for the anorexic patients with bulimic symptoms, compared to the amitriptyline- and placebo-treated groups. The authors recommended cyproheptadine as a therapeutic adjunct to a structured milieu and psychotherapeutic treatment program, and emphasized the absence of serious side effects. The study unfortunately failed to comment on the long-term outcome of these patients, and it is not clear that speeding up weight gain (in an absolute sense) is an important treatment goal.

In general, antidepressant medications have shown differential effects for Anorexia Nervosa and Bulimia Nervosa. Specifically, antidepressant medications do not appear to be particularly effective for the treatment of Anorexia Nervosa (Advokat & Kutlesic, 1995; Jimerson, Wolfe, Brotman, & Metzger, 1996), but do show promising effects on Bulimia Nervosa. However, two small uncontrolled studies utilizing the antidepressant fluoxetine in the treatment of Anorexia Nervosa have found some preliminary promising results (Gwirtsman, Guze, Yager, & Gainsley, 1990; Kaye, Weltzin, Hsu, & Bulik, 1991). In addition, Hoffman and Halmi (1993), in their review of the efficacy of antidepressant medications in the treatment of Anorexia Nervosa, described studies in which tricyclic antidepressants (imipramine and amitriptyline) were found to have some impact on weight gain.

Other pharmacological interventions utilized with anorexic populations include the use of neuroleptics and sedatives (benzodiazepines and major tranquilizers). Hoffman and Halmi (1993) discussed the use of neuroleptics over the course of the last 30 years, and the relative absence of controlled studies examining their use. They speculated on the possible effectiveness of dopamine agonists in the treatment of Anorexia Nervosa. Woodside (1995) described the use of sedatives (either benzodiazepines or major tranquilizers) to address mealtime anxiety, but the efficacy of such interventions in anorexic patients has not been empirically established. Finally, Szmukler, Young, Miller, Lichenstein, and Binns (1995) conducted an 8-week randomized, placebo-controlled, double-blind trial with cisapride—a drug shown to improve gastric emptying, which is thought to be impaired in anorexics. Although gastric emptying improved significantly in both the active drug and placebo group over the course of the study, the patients in the active treatment reported increased hunger (Szmukler et al., 1995). Since there were no significant differences in gastric emptying or weight gain between anorexic patients treated with cisapride or placebo, its role in Anorexia Nervosa treatment is unclear.

Bulimia Nervosa

Pharmacological treatment of binge eating with antidepressants and the anticonvulsant medication phenytoin sodium has been explored. Tricyclic antidepressants, monoamine oxidase inhibitors (MAOIs), and atypical antidepressants have all been utilized with bulimic patients. Mitchell, Raymond, and Specker (1993) reviewed the efficacy of antidepressants as reported in 12 different double-blind controlled trials. In the seven studies of tricyclic antidepressants reviewed, their use uniformly led to significant reductions in binge eating and/or vomiting when compared to placebo. The reduction in binge eating ranged from 47% to 91%. Antidepressant medications typically used included releasing agents and reuptake inhibitors, such as imipramine, amitriptyline, desipramine, and fenfluramine.

In conjunction with the serotonin etiological theory discussed earlier in this chapter, the selective serotonin reuptake inhibitor fluoxetine has shown remarkable efficacy in the treatment of Bulimia Nervosa. Advocat and Kutlesic (1995) describe the serotonin hypothesis in the following way: "Bulimia nervosa is the behavioral expression of functional underactivity of serotonin...in the central nervous system" (p. 61); they review two studies utilizing fluoxetine. Both studies, using small samples, reported significant short-term improvement in bingeing and vomiting, along with good long term maintenance of gains. Patients treated with fluoxetine for 16 weeks demonstrated significant reductions in binge eating and vomiting episodes when compared to patients treated with a placebo (Goldstein, Wilson, Thompson, Potvin, & Rampey, 1995). Fluoxetine treatment alone also has produced results similar to the combination of psychodynamically oriented supportive psychotherapy and fluoxetine (Walsh et al., 1997). When compared to cognitive-behavioral therapy, fluoxetine alone produces poorer outcomes and the combination of both is only marginally better than cognitive-behavioral therapy alone (Goldbloom et al., 1997; Walsh et al., 1997). These data have led Agras (1997) to conclude that cognitive-behavioral therapy is more effective than medication in the treatment of Bulimia Nervosa over the long-term, but from a cost perspective, medication is less expensive over an initial 6-month treatment period. Results suggest that a stepped-care model might be appropriate for Bulimia Nervosa patients, with primary care practitioners providing less intensive educational interventions combined with medication and if this treatment fails, referring the patient for cognitive-behavioral treatment, with or without further medication (Agras, 1997).

Fenfluramine has been evaluated in several controlled trials with mixed results. In a 15-week, placebo-controlled, double-blind, crossover study that also evaluated the efficacy of desipramine, the investigators concluded that both drugs had beneficial effects on the frequency of bingeing and vomiting, the urge to binge, and psychological distress when compared to placebo, but that a greater proportion of patients responded to fenfluramine (Blouin et al., 1988). In contrast, Russell, Checkley, Feldman, and Eisler (1988) did not find support for the use of fenfluramine over placebo in the treatment of bulimic patients when they analyzed the data for study completers. They suggested that the lack of differences may have been due to the high attrition rate (38% of the treatment group and 43% of the placebo group), and found some improvements in bulimic symptoms when data from the total sample were analyzed. Unfortunately, given the high dropout rate in the study, it would not seem prudent to draw positive conclusions about the efficacy of fenfluramine in the treatment of Bulimia Nervosa. They were also unable to demonstrate an improvement in depression in the treatment group, and concluded that the clinical usefulness of fenfluramine requires further investigation (Russell et al., 1988). Similarly, a more recent randomized, double-blind, placebo-controlled trial did not find any benefit from the addition of fenfluramine to CBT when compared to CBT and placebo. Abnormal eating behaviors and psychopathology improved in both groups, and the authors concluded that fenfluramine is not an effective treatment for Bulimia Nervosa (Fahy, Eisler, & Russell, 1993). Because of potential serious side effects, including recent data on its

potential associaton with valvular heart disease (CDC, 1997; Connolly et al., 1997; FDA, 1997), fenfluramine and dexfenfluramine were withdrawn from the market in September, 1997.

Another partial serotonin agonist, ipsapirone, was evaluated in an open pilot study with 17 patients. The investigators found that bulimic symptomatology greatly improved during the four weeks of treatment, but since this was not a blinded or placebo-controlled study, it can only be concluded that ipsapirone may be a promising pharmacological intervention (Geretsegger, Greimel, Roed, & Hesselink, 1995).

MAOI antidepressants have been used because of data suggesting a link between Bulimia Nervosa and affective disorders (Hudson, Laffer, & Pope, 1982; Mitchell et al., 1993; Walsh et al., 1982). Results have been mixed. Russell (1979) reported that these antidepressants failed to have an effect on eating behavior. In contrast, Walsh et al. (1982) reported dramatic improvement in both mood and eating behavior in six women who met the DSM-III-R criteria for Bulimia Nervosa as well as Atypical Depression (Liebowitz, Quitkin, & Stewart, 1981). Unfortunately, there was no control group; the sample size was small; the method for measuring improvement was not specified; and follow-up data were not presented. In addition, Walsh et al. (1988), and Kennedy et al. (1988) using MAOIs, found reductions in bingeing behaviors comparable to those typically found with tricyclic antidepressant medication. However, the side effects typically associated with MAOIs indicate that they should not be considered as the first line of treatment for Bulimia Nervosa.

Other studies (Pope & Hudson, 1982; Pope, Hudson, & Jonas, 1983; Stewart, Walsh, Wright, Roose, & Glassman, 1984; Brotman, Herzog, & Woods, 1984) shed further light on the potential use of antidepressant medications for Bulimia Nervosa. Pope and Hudson (1982) reported moderate (defined as 50%) to marked (75%) decreases in bingeing within 3 weeks in six of eight cases treated with tricyclics (mainly imipramine hydrochloride); these improvements were maintained at 2- and 6-month follow-ups. With an expanded sample of 65 bulimic patients, which was reduced to 49 (after those who were judged to have had an inadequate trial of medication were excluded), 10 showed remission, 15 showed marked improvement, 12 showed moderate improvement, and 12 experienced no improvement (Pope et al., 1983). The authors stated, however, that half of the remitted cases reported an occasional binge or cluster of binges. Stewart et al. (1984) reported that 10 of 12 bulimic patients showed a rapid decrease in binges (from 14 to 1 per week on the average) after treatment with MAOIs; 6 of the 12 patients met the DSM-III-R criteria for Major Depressive Disorder, and 4 patients had had a Major Depressive Episode. At follow-up approximately 9 months later, 6 of the initial 10 responders had maintained their improvement; 5 of these had continued to take their medication. Three patients who continued their medication had relapsed within 2–3 months.

Pope et al. (1983) assigned 22 bulimic patients to treatment with imipramine or placebo in a double-blind study. Patients who were suicidal, had Anorexia Nervosa, or had been previously treated with antidepressant drugs were screened out of the study. Of the 22 subjects, 19 completed the 6-week treatment (2 experimental subjects withdrew because of side effect problems, and 1 placebo subject withdrew from the study). The drug group showed a 70% reduction in bingeing at posttreatment, whereas the placebo control group showed no improvement. At follow-up 2–8 months later, 90% continued to report at least a moderate or marked reduction in binge eating, and 35% had ceased binge eating altogether.

Walsh, Stewart, Roose, Gladis, and Glassman (1984) randomly assigned patients to either phenelzine sulfate or placebo for 8 weeks, using a double-blind methodology. Screened out were subjects who were suicidal, had recent alcohol or drug use problems, or were judged to be unable to follow a tyramine-free diet. Of the 35 subjects entered in the study, 15 were excluded from data analysis because they failed to adhere to the diet, keep appointments, or take the medication as instructed, or because they responded to the placebo treatment in the first 2 weeks. Only 15 patients completed the full 8-week course of treatment; however, data were analyzed for all 20 patients. All of the phenelzine-treated patients had reduced their binge eating by 50% or more, and 5 of these 9 patients stopped binge eating entirely. Only 2 of the 11 placebo-treated patients reduced their binge frequency by 50% or more, and none stopped binge eating completely. The selectivity of this sample must be kept in mind, however. At follow-up (between 3 and 15 months), only 3 of the phenelzine-treated group had continued to take the medication. Of those who discontinued the medication, 3 had relapsed and 2 were binge-free; of those who continued the medication, 2 were binge-free and 1 had had a partial relapse.

Sabine, Yonace, Farrington, Barratt, and Wakeling (1983) tested the effects of mianserin hydrochloride compared to placebo on 50 patients with Bulimia Nervosa for 8 weeks, using a double-blind procedure. Although both groups showed significant improvement on attitudes toward eating and bingeing, depression, and anxiety, no changes occurred in the number of days per week that subjects binged.

Desipramine has fewer side effects than the medications described above. An advantage of desipramine is that it does not require that patients be placed on diets with rigid restrictions. Furthermore, in one study using a double-blind, placebo-controlled, partial crossover trial, desipramine hydrochloride reduced binge frequency by 91%, whereas the placebo group showed a 19% increase in binge frequency (Hughes, Wells, Cunningham, & Ilstrup, 1984). Of the 22 patients on the drug, 15 attained complete abstinence from bingeing and purging after 6 weeks of treatment.

Anticonvulsant medications, such as phenytoin sodium, have also been used in the treatment of eating disorders; the rationale for this has been that binge eating may be a symptom of epileptic convulsions. Abnormal electroencephalograms have been found in some individuals with compulsive eating disorders (Green & Rau, 1974; Rau & Green, 1975). Treatment successes as high as 90% have been reported with phenytoin (Green & Rau, 1974); however, the criteria for improvement were unclear, and there were no controls for placebo effects. Wermuth, Davis, Hollister, and Stunkard (1977) used a double-blind crossover study with phenytoin and a placebo (*n* = 19); although binge frequency was significantly reduced during the phenytoin phase compared to placebo, improvement continued during the placebo phase. Overall, only 40% of subjects experienced marked or moderate improvement. Other studies (Weiss & Levitz, 1976; Greenway, Dahms, & Bray, 1977) of the effects of anticonvulsant medication on compulsive eating indicated a lack of response to medication. With further study, Green and Rau (1977) concluded that a neurophysiological element is evident in some, but not all, compulsive eaters.

Combined Modalities: Integrating Pharmacology and Psychology

Newer research in the treatment of eating disorders has focused on the efficacy of combining pharmacological and psychological interventions (Crow & Mitchell, 1996). Of these combinations, those exhibiting the most utility appear to be protocols combining the use of CBT with antidepressant treatments. Agras et al. (1992) compared the antidepressant desipramine alone to CBT alone, and the combination of CBT and antidepressant medication, in the treatment of Bulimia Nervosa. In this study, 71 subjects were randomly assigned to one of the following groups: desipramine withdrawn at 16 weeks; desipramine withdrawn at 24 weeks; combined treatment (medication withdrawn at either 16 or 24 weeks); and 15 sessions of CBT. In general, CBT and combined antidepressant–CBT both outperformed medication alone on measures of binge eating and purging. Most interestingly, the results of this study suggested that continued use of CBT prevented relapse in subjects withdrawn from medication at 16 weeks. In addition, the combination of CBT and medication appears to have decreased levels of associated psychopathology (e.g., dietary preoccupation, hunger).

In a study combining group-administered CBT with tricyclic antidepressant medication, subjects in the combined condition showed a 51% abstinence rate in bulimic behaviors, compared to a 16% abstinence rate in the medication-only condition (Mitchell et al., 1990), again highlighting the potential utility of combining the approaches. In contrast, in a study of the treatment of binge eating as a method of facilitating weight loss in obese patients, the use of desipramine did not lead to greater improvements in binge-eating symptoms when compared to CBT alone; neither CBT, nor CBT with desipramine, improved overall weight loss at the end of treatment or follow-up (Agras et al., 1994). These contradictory findings suggest that the value of augmenting CBT with drug treatment for bulimic or binge eating patients is still unclear and should be further studied (Agras, 1997; Crow & Mitchell, 1994).

Prediction of Outcome

There are very few data suggesting that different treatments have better or worse outcomes, and almost no differential outcome data based upon treatment and symptom characteristics. For the most part, treatment effectiveness has been explored in relationship to *patient*, not *treatment*, characteristics.

Eckert (1985) has provided a concise review of prognostic indicators in Anorexia Nervosa. Favorable long-term prognosis has been found to be related to early age of onset of illness (Halmi, 1974; Halmi, Brodland, & Rigas, 1975; Hsu, Crisp, & Harding, 1979; Morgan & Russell, 1975; Pierloot, Wellens, & Houben, 1975; Sturzenberger, Cantwell, Burroughs, Salkin, & Green, 1977; Theander, 1970). Poor outcomes have been associated with longer duration of illness and previous hospitalizations (Garfinkel et al., 1977; Hsu et al., 1979; Morgan & Russell, 1975; Pierloot et al., 1975; Seidensticher & Tzagournis, 1968); very low weight during illness (Dally, 1969; Hsu et al., 1979; Morgan & Russell, 1975); and the presence of bulimic symptoms, such as vomiting and laxative abuse (Garfinkel et al., 1977; Halmi, 1974; Halmi et al., 1975; Hsu et al., 1979; Theander, 1970).

Less commonly mentioned negative prognosticators include overestimation of body size (Garfinkel et al., 1977; Kalucy, Crisp, Lacy, & Harding, 1977), premorbid personality difficulties and family relations (Dally, 1969; Hsu et al., 1979; Morgan & Russell, 1975), depressive and obsessive–compulsive symptoms (Halmi, Brodland, & Loney, 1973), high rates of physical complaints (Halmi et al., 1973), neuroticism (Dally, 1969; Pierloot et al., 1975), psychological tests suggesting psychosis (Pierloot et al., 1975), and lower social class (Garfinkel et al., 1977; Halmi et al., 1973; Hsu et al., 1979; Seidensticher & Tzagournis, 1968).

Factors predictive of weight gain by anorexic patients during a 35-day treatment program included greater hyperactivity and exercising, less denial of illness, greater expressed anger and appetite, less psychosexual immaturity, less tendency to overestimate actual body size, and less sleep disturbance (Garfinkel et al., 1977).

Strober (1983) discriminated three types of Anorexia Nervosa that were related to outcome at 30, 60, and 90 days. This study was based upon 130 females between the ages of 15 and 19, who were diagnosed as having Anorexia Nervosa and admitted to a hospital for at least 3 months, with a duration of symptoms (indexed as the number of months past onset of compulsive dieting) between 4 and 22 months. Type 1 patients were characterized by a high need to conform and exercise control, but were self-accepting and maintained a sense of well-being without frank psychopathology. Type 2 patients had high levels of anxiety, self-doubt, and social isolation, with premorbid histories of social avoidance and obsessionality, and intermediate levels of intrafamilial tension. Type 3 patients had low ego strength, were impulsive, were prone to addictive behaviors, and had turbulent interpersonal dynamics. There was significant family pathology and disharmony, both present and past, with histories of obesity and binge eating. Outcomes were best for Type 1 and worst for Type 3, with Type 2 falling in the middle.

Research focusing on the 10-year follow-up of a sample of 76 severely ill anorexic females suggests that the disorder can be variable in course, chronic, and even fatal (Eckert, Halmi, Marchi, Grove, & Crosby, 1995). At the 10-year follow-up, 23.7% of the sample had no diagnosis, 35.5 % were diagnosed with Eating Disorder Not Otherwise Specified, 22.4% met diagnostic criteria for Bulimia Nervosa, 9.2% met diagnostic criteria for Anorexia Nervosa, 2.65% met diagnostic criteria for both Anorexia and Bulimia Nervosa, and 6.6% of the sample had died. In addition, the anorexic patients in this sample were found to live alone and remain single longer than typical. Furthermore, the subjects in this sample, when married, had fewer than expected offspring relative to age- and sex-matched populations; this group also appeared to have had a higher than expected level of induced abortions. Wonderlich, Fullerton, Swift, and Klein (1994), in a 5-year outcome study of 30 eating-disordered patients found that patients with personality disorders did not differ in the amount of symptomatic change over time, in a consistent way, from those without personality disorders. Steinhausen (1995b), in a review of 68 outcome studies conducted with anorexic patients from 1953 to 1989, concluded that early age of onset, histrionic personality, conflict-free parent–child relationships, short interval between onset and treatment, short duration of inpatient treatment without readmission, and high socioeconomic status/education were favorable prognostic indicators. Unfavorable prognostic indicators included vomiting and other bulimic symptoms, high loss of weight, chronicity, and premorbid developmental and/or clinical abnormalities.

In a review of outcome studies for individuals meeting diagnostic criteria for Bulimia Nervosa, Hsu (1995) suggested that the most common difficulty at follow-up is subsyndromal bulimia, followed by full Bulimia Nervosa. In general, after receiving CBT, approximately 50% of Bulimia Nervosa patients were asymptomatic at 2- to 10-year follow-up. Normal-weight bulimic patients did not tend to develop Anorexia Nervosa, and their rate of obesity was found to be lower than that of the general population. Herzog et al. (1993) found percent body weight increase and type of eating disorder to be the only variables associated with outcome during a 1-year follow-up. Specifically, patients diagnosed with Bulimia Nervosa tended to fare better than those diagnosed with either Anorexia Nervosa or both Bulimia Nervosa and Anorexia Nervosa (by DSM-III-R criteria). With respect to body weight, each 10% increase in percent body weight was associated with an 18% increase in hazard. Rorty, Yager, and Rossotto (1993) examined the factors that former Bulimia Nervosa patients felt were especially instrumental in their recovery. Responses from 40 female subjects suggested several factors that they perceived as important to their recovery, including a sense of being "fed up" with the disorder, the desire to have a better life, the importance/difficulty of cognitive change, and the development of empathic and caring relationships with others. Factors perceived by the former patients as making recovery more difficult included lack of understanding by important others, insufficient acknowledgment or activity by therapists, and the sabotage of the healing process by family members or others.

Finally, Windauer, Lennerts, Talbot, Touyz, and Beumont (1993) have stressed the importance of validating outcome measures when attempting to evaluate "cured" patients, lest we delude ourselves with invalid indicators that have limited utility.

CONCLUSIONS

This chapter has reviewed the considerable controversy and complexity surrounding the treatment of the eating disorders (i.e., Anorexia Nervosa, Bulimia Nervosa, and Binge-Eating Disorder). The field is currently one of intense activity and interest; yet few questions about these disorders have been answered definitively. Why young women, predominantly, engage in such apparently self-defeating, irrational behaviors centered around such a basic life activity is no longer a complete mystery. There are many indications, perhaps each a part of the "truth." It is now time for a comprehensive view of these disorders—one that recognizes the interplay among biological, social, behavioral, and psychological factors. The importance of cultural factors such as the changing nature of women's roles is increasing, at the same time that biological factors such as neurological functioning are being explored. The *Zeitgeist* encourages clinicians to incorporate recognition of these different spheres in their treatment of clients with eating disorders.

Although eating disorders are very complex and multifactorial, much of the current research suffers from significant deficiencies that makes it difficult to determine the value or importance of many potential etiologies and treatments (Keel & Mitchel, 1997). Several issues need to be addressed in future research to help to clarify this problem.

Issue 1: Are Eating Disorders Distinct Disorders?

Although nosological or syndromal classification is the standard in mental health in general, and for eating disorders in particular, much of the current evidence suggests that eating disorders may not be distinct disorders. For example, it is well known that eating-disordered patients experience a high frequency of comorbid psychological disorders, including depression, anxiety disorders (e.g., Obsesive–Compulsive Disorder), and addictive disorders (Braun & Chouinard, 1992; Cooper, 1995; Holderness, Brooks-Gunn, & Warren, 1994; Wilson, 1995). Among the reasons for this high frequency of comorbidity are overlap in symptoms for the different syndromes, poor interrater reliability of many psychiatric diagnostic categories, and the common biological pathways that have been implicated in these disorders (Brewerton, 1995; Jarry & Vaccarino, 1996; Kaye et al., 1991; van Praag, 1993). For example, most Axis I disorders have kappa coefficients below .70, indicating less than adequate reliability (Kirk & Kutchins, 1992). In addition, the neurotransmitter serotonin is thought to play a role in the etiology or maintenance of eating disorders, substance use disorders, depression, and Obsesive–Compulsive Disorder, indicating a common physiological mechanism, even though they are all supposed to be distinct disorders (Brewerton, 1995). Also, many of the cognitive and behavioral features of each of these disorders are observationally and phenomenologically similar and seem to elicit the same physiological reward mechanisms. Finally, none of these disorders has a distinct and reliable biological marker that is not shared by one of the mentioned comorbid conditions (Gillberg, 1994; Jarry & Vaccarino, 1996). Based on this evidence, some investigators have concluded that

eating disorders may be addictions or on a continuum with Obsesive–Compulsive Disorder (Gold, 1993; Jarry & Vaccarino, 1996; Parham, 1995), although others have noted the poor fit between eating disorders and addictions (Wilson, 1991, 1995). Both of these arguments are problematic because they do not address the underlying issues of syndromal classification, but they do highlight the lack of distinctiveness between eating disorders and several other psychiatric conditions.

Issue 2: Are We Focusing on the Wrong Areas?

In spite of a voluminous literature on the etiology of eating disorders, with a particular focus on physiological and personality factors, the results of treatment outcome studies for eating disorders are less than satisfying. Eating-disordered patients appear to have high relapse rates, experience their disorder for long periods of time, and often suffer from several other comorbid psychiatric conditions (Keller et al., 1992; Kirschenbaum & Fitzgibbon, 1995). One wonders why researchers and clinicians continue to emphasize internal-defect models, rather than focusing on social and cultural explanations (Pate, Pumariega, Hester, & Garner, 1992; Striegel-Moore, 1995). As Poston and Weinbarger (1996) suggested, individual-defect models of behavior help to "solve" pressing social problems by identifying individuals, or culturally defined populations, as constitutionally defective. This allows the redirection of energies and money away from potential social etiologies and fundamental social change. In addition, this approach allows individuals and families to cope better with complex and difficult issues by providing simple causal explanations for problematic behavior. These models also lead to diagnoses that allow individuals to receive services and money, as well as minimizing the role of individual responsibility and of family and environmental factors in the expression of problematic behavior, thus allowing our society to lay the blame on an individual's "bad biology"(Vatz & Weinberg, 1990). Finally, constitutional-deficiency models solve a host of problems for researchers and clinicians, including relieving them from the distress of not solving significant mental health problems with the same speed and efficiency with which medical researchers have controlled many infectious diseases. In effect, these explanations help bolster the credibility of professions that have not made significant progress in solving difficult and complex problems, such as eating disorders and substance use disorders, and allows greater public acceptance and access to research dollars (Leifer, 1990).

Issue 3: What Are We Missing?

There are several deficiencies in the eating disorder literature that must be addressed. First, there is a strong need for epidemiological research with culturally diverse populations and in different countries (Gillberg, 1994; Pate et al., 1992; Study Group on Anorexia Nervosa, 1995). For example, many of the conclusions that have been drawn about the etiology and treatment outcome of eating-disordered patients are based on work with potentially biased samples (e.g., clinic-based or inpatient). In addition, there is very little systematic cross-cultural research on the prevalence or incidence of eating disorders (Pate et al., 1992). It is therefore premature to debate whether the prevalence of eating disorders is increasing or becoming epidemic, because our prevalence estimates are based on nonrepresentative samples (Gillberg, 1994).

Another problem in the science of eating disorders is the lack of prospective and replication studies, adequate sampling and sample sizes, and appropriate analysis in both determinant and treatment outcome studies (Ericsson et al., 1996). Some studies of biological determinants suffer from small sample sizes and uncorrected statistical analyses, which lead to illusory biological differences. There is very little replication of these findings or of potentially important and useful results that may have come from more controlled studies (Gillberg, 1994). Finally, it is possible that some of the lack of reproducibility or reliability of findings lies in the narrow nosological classification system that is currently in favor. A system of functional classification may help to alleviate this problem by making the psychological dysfunction the elementary unit of analysis, rather than a broad and unreliable syndrome (van Praag, 1993). In fact, many biological variables that have low diagnostic specificity when syndromes are considered can be related very strongly to specific psychopathological dimensions (e.g., serotonin disturbance as a moderator for disturbed aggression regulation, because low serotonin has been found to play a role in suicidal behavior, eating disorders, and aggression) (van Praag, 1993). Future research should focus on these issues in order to adequately address the problem of eating disorders.

Issue 4: Treatment and Prevention Needs

One of the most significant issues in the treatment of eating disorders is the growing recognition that a narrow behavioral focus on the disordered eating may not address important core issues that may play a role in the etiology and maintenance of eating disorders. Primary in this area is a recognition that conflictual interpersonal relationships and sociocultural pressures may be at the heart of eating disorders. Thus, there is a need to determine whether focusing on interpersonal relationships might not be more effective than a sole focus on disordered eating. Although IPT did not lead to further improvements in CBT-resistent patients (Agras et al., 1995), Wilfley et al. (1993) found that IPT was as effective as CBT for nonpurging Bulimia Nervosa (Binge-Eating Disorder).

Because eating disorders are associated with poor body image and low self-esteem, research should also focus on determining whether or not exercise can play a role in treatment. Higher levels of physical fitness are associated with positive mental health, enhanced self-esteem, reduced anxiety, and improved body image in women (Grilo, Brownell, & Stunkard, 1993; Salusso-Deonier & Schwarzkopf, 1991). Exercise may also improve eating control through changes in endogenous opioid channels (Brewerton, Lydiard, Laraia, Shook, & Ballenger, 1992). These changes may facilitate improvements in mood and enhanced feelings of energy, which may help reduce eating dyscontrol associated with negative affect. Thus, future research should focus on examining the potential beneficial effects of exercise on Bulimia Nervosa and Binge-Eating Disorder.

Medications are frequently promoted as a primary treatment modality, due to the tendency to view eating disorders as caused by biological defects. This occurs despite the weak evidence for a biological etiology, and the fact that eating disorders occur mainly in women and in cultures emphasizing thinness as a value for women. Although the rewarding effects of eating can be inhibited by opiate antagonists (Marrazzi, Markham, Kinzie, & Luby, 1995), and binge eating and vomiting can be reduced through the administration of selective serotonin reuptake inhibitors (Goldstein, Wilson, Thompson, Potvin, & Rampey, 1995), medications do not address the problems of social isolation and perceived lack of nurturance from interpersonal relationships that many patients suffer from. Indeed, use of prescription medications for the treatment of eating disorders may inappropriately replace needed therapy, because the physician and patient desire quick and easy solutions. Research is needed to determine whether medication can add to the effectiveness of IPT and CBT approaches, and to determine how such medication regimens can be administered in controlled, ethical ways.

Public health measures must be taken to help prevent new cases and to assist those already afflicted. There is currently a serious dearth of information about effective prevention, probably due to the complex nature of eating disorders and the lack of knowledge about risk factors for their development and maintenance (Fairburn, 1995). Future research efforts should focus on changing the cultural attitudes that may cause many women to develop poor self-esteem and body image and may predispose some women to develop eating disorders (Battle & Brownell; 1996; Foreyt et al., 1996). In addition, targeted prevention efforts should be developed for high-risk populations, such as athletes and women with a family history of eating disorders. Although there will always be a role for treatment at the tertiary level, only primary prevention efforts can truly address and reduce the tremendous social impact of eating disorders.

ACKNOWLEDGMENTS

Preparation of this chapter was partially supported by a grant from the National Heart, Lung and Blood Institute (No. HL47052), and by a Minority Scientist Development Award to Dr. Poston from the American Heart Association (AHA) with funds contributed by the AHA, Puerto Rico Affiliate.

REFERENCES

Abraham, S. F., & Beumont, P. J. V. (1982). How patients describe bulimia or binge eating. *Psychological Medicine, 12,* 625–635.

Advokat, C., & Kutlesic, V. (1995). Pharmacotherapy of the eating disorders: A commentary. *Neuroscience and Biobehavioral Reviews, 19,* 59–66.

Agras, W. S. (1991). Nonpharmacologic treatments of bulimia nervosa. *Journal of Clinical Psychiatry, 52*(10, Suppl.), 29–33.

Agras, W. S. (1997). The treatment of bulimia nervosa. *Drugs of Today, 33,* 405–411.

Agras, W. S., & Kirkley, B. G. (1986). Bulimia: Theories of etiology. In K. D. Brownell & J. P. Foreyt (Eds.), *Handbook of eating disorders: Physiology, psychology, and treatment of obesity, anorexia, and bulimia* (pp. 367–378). New York: Basic Books.

Agras, W. S., Rossiter, E. M., Arnow, B., Schneider, J. A., Telch, C. F., Raeburn, S. D., Bruce, B., Perl, M., & Koran, L. M. (1992). Pharmacologic and cognitive-behavioral treatment for Bulimia Nervosa: A controlled comparison. *American Journal of Psychiatry, 149,* 82–87.

Agras, W. S., Schneider, J. A., Arnow, B., Raeburn, S. D., & Telch, C. F. (1989). Cognitive-behavioral and response-prevention treatments for Bulimia Nervosa. *Journal of Consulting and Clinical Psychology, 57,* 215–221.

Agras, W. S., Telch, C. F., Arnow, B., Eldredge, K., Detzer, M. J., Henderson, J., & Marnell, M. (1995). Does interpersonal therapy help patients with Binge Eating Disorder who fail to respond to cognitive-behavioral therapy? *Journal of Consulting and Clinical Psychology, 63,* 356–360.

Agras, W. S., Telch, C. F., Arnow, B., Eldredge, K., Wilfley, D. E., Raeburn, S. D., Henderson, J., & Marnell, M. (1994). Weight loss, cognitive-behavioral, and desipramine treatments in Binge Eating Disorder: An additive design. *Behavior Therapy, 25,* 225–238.

American Psychiatric Association (APA). (1987). *Diagnostic and statistical manual of mental disorders* (3rd ed., rev.). Washington, DC: Author.

American Psychiatric Association (APA). (1994). *Diagnostic and statistical manual of mental disorders* (4th ed.). Washington, DC: Author.

Andersen, A. E., Bowers, W., & Evans, K. (1997). Inpatient treatment of anorexia nervosa. In D. M. Garner & P. E. Garfinkel (Eds.), *Handbook of treatment for eating disorders* (2nd ed., pp. 327–353). New York: Guilford Press.

Andersen, A. E. (1986). Inpatient and outpatient treatment of Anorexia Nervosa. In K. D. Brownell & J. P. Foreyt (Eds.), *Handbook of eating disorders: Physiology, psychology, and treatment of obesity, anorexia, and bulimia* (pp. 333–352). New York: Basic Books.

Ash, J. B., & Piazza, E. (1995). Changing symptomatology in eating disorders. *International Journal of Eating Disorders, 18,* 27–38.

Bachrach, A. J., Erwin, W. J., & Mohr, P. J. (1965). The control of eating behavior in an anorexic by operant conditioning techniques. In L. Ullmann & L. Krasner (Eds.), *Case studies in behavior modification* (pp.153–163). New York: Holt, Rinehart & Winston.

Battle, E. K., & Brownell, K. D. (1996). Confronting a rising tide of eating disorders and obesity: Treatment vs. prevention and policy. *Addictive Behaviors, 21,* 755–765.

Beck, A. (1976). *Cognitive therapy and the emotional disorders.* New York: International Universities Press.

Bell, R. M. (1985). *Holy anorexia.* Chicago: University of Chicago Press.

Bemis, K. M. (1978). Current approaches to the etiology and treatment of Anorexia Nervosa. *Psychological Bulletin, 85*, 593–617.

Beumont, P. J. V. (1977). Further categorization of patients with Anorexia Nervosa. *Australian and New Zealand Journal of Psychiatry, 11*, 223–226.

Beumont, P. J. V., Abraham, S. F., Argall, W. J., George, C. W., & Glaun, D. E. (1978). The onset of Anorexia Nervosa. *Australian and New Zealand Journal of Psychiatry, 12*, 145–149.

Beumont, P. J. V., Beumont, C. C., Touyz, S. W., & Williams, H. (1997). Nutritional counseling and supervised exercise. In D. M. Garner & P. E. Garfinkel (Eds.), *Handbook of treatment for eating disorders* (2nd ed., pp. 178–187). New York: Guilford Press.

Beumont, P. J. V., Booth, A. L., Abraham, S. F., Griffiths, D. A., & Turner, T. R. (1983). A temporal sequence of symptoms in patients with Anorexia Nervosa: A preliminary report. In P. L. Darby, P. E. Garfinkel, D. M. Garner, & D. V. Coscina (Eds.), *Anorexia nervosa: Recent developments in research* (pp. 129–136). New York: Alan R. Liss.

Binswanger, L. (1958). The case of Ellen West. In R. May, E. Angel, & H. F. Ellenberger (Eds.), *Existence: A new dimension in psychiatry and psychology* (pp. 236–363). New York: Basic Books.

Blouin, A. G., Blouin, J. H., Perez, E. L., Bushnik, T., Zuro, C., & Mulder, E. (1988). Treatment of bulimia with fenfluramine and desipramine. *Journal of Clinical Psychopharmacology, 8*, 261–269.

Boskind-Lodahl, M., & White, W. C. (1978). The definition and treatment of bulimarexia in college women: A pilot study. *Journal of the American College Health Association, 27*, 84–86.

Brambila, F., Bellodi, L., Perna, G., Barberi, A., Panerai, A., & Sacerdote, P. (1993). Lymphocyte cholecystokinin concentrations in Panic Disorder. *American Journal of Psychiatry, 150*, 1111–1113.

Braun, C. M. J., & Chouinard, M. J. (1992). Is Anorexia Nervosa a neuropsychological disease? *Neuropsychology Review, 3*, 171–212.

Brewerton, T. D. (1995). Toward a unified theory of serotonin dysregulation in eating and related disorders. *Psychoneuroimmunology, 20*, 561–590.

Brewerton, T. D., Hand, L. D., & Bishop, E. R. (1993). The Tridimensional Personality Questionnaire in eating disorder patients. *International Journal of Eating Disorders, 14*, 213–218.

Brewerton, T. D., Lydiard, R. B., Laraia, M. T., Shook, J. E., & Ballenger, J. C. (1992). CSF beta-endorphin and dynorphin in Bulimia Nervosa. *American Journal of Psychiatry, 149*, 1086–1090.

Brody, M. L., Walsh, B. T., & Devlin, M. (1994). Binge Eating Disorder: Reliability and validity of a new diagnostic category. *Journal of Consulting and Clinical Psychology, 62*, 381–386.

Brotman, A. W., Herzog, D. B., & Woods, S. W. (1984). Antidepressant treatment of bulimia: The relationship between bingeing and depressive symptomatology. *Journal of Clinical Psychiatry, 45*, 7–9.

Bruch, H. (1973). *Eating disorders: Obesity, Anorexia Nervosa and the person within.* New York: Basic Books.

Bruch, H. (1985). Four decades of eating disorders. In D. M. Garner & P. E. Garfinkel (Eds.), *Handbook of psychotherapy for anorexia nervosa and bulimia* (pp. 7–18). New York: Guilford Press.

Casper, R. C., Eckert, E. D., Halmi, K. A., Goldberg, S. C., & Davis, J. M. (1980). Bulimia: Its incidence and clinical importance in patients with Anorexia Nervosa. *Archives of General Psychiatry, 37*, 1030–1040.

Centers for Disease Ccontrol (CDC) (1997). Cardiac valvulopathy associated with fenfluramine or dexfenfluramine: U.S. Department of Health and Human Services Interim Public Health Recommendations, November 1997. *MMWR, 46*, 1061–1066.

Childress, A. C., Jarrell, M. P., & Brewerton, T. D. (1993). The Kids' Eating Disorders Survey (KEDS): Internal consistency, component analysis, and reliability. *Eating Disorders, 1*, 123–131.

Clark, D. A., Feldman, J., & Channon, S. (1989). Dysfunctional thinking in Anorexia and Bulimia Nervosa. *Cognitive Therapy and Research, 13*, 377–387.

Cloninger, C. R. (1986). A unified biosocial theory of personality and its role in the development of anxiety states. *Psychiatric Development, 3*, 167–226.

Cloninger, C. R. (1988). A unified biosocial theory of personality and its role in the development of anxiety states: A reply to commentaries. *Psychiatric Development, 2*, 83–120.

Coffman, D. A. (1984). A clinically derived treatment model for the binge–purge syndrome. In R. C. Hawkins, II, W. J., Fremouw, & P. F. Clement (Eds.). *The binge-purge syndrome: Diagnosis, treatment, and research* (pp. 211–236). New York: Springer.

Connolly, H. M., Crary, J. L., McGoon, M. D., Hensrud, D. D., Edwards, B. S., Edwards, W. D., & Schaff, H. V. (1997). Valvular heart disease associated with fenfluramine–phentermine. *New England Journal of Medicine, 337*, 581–588.

Connors, M. E., Johnson, C. L., & Stuckey, M. K. (1984). Treatment of bulimia with brief psychoeducational group therapy. *American Journal of Psychiatry, 141*, 1512–1516.

Cooper, P. J. (1995). Eating disorders and their relationship to mood and anxiety disorders. In K. D. Brownell & C. G. Fairburn (Eds.), *Eating disorders and obesity: A comprehensive handbook* (pp. 159–164). New York: Guilford Press.

Cooper, P. J., & Steere, J. (1995). A comparison of two psychological treatments for Bulimia Nervosa: Implications for models of maintenance. *Behaviour Research and Therapy, 33*, 875–885.

Cooper, Z., & Fairburn, C. (1987). The Eating Disorders Examination: A semi-structured interview for the assessment of specific psychopathology of eating disorders. *International Journal of Eating Disorders, 6,* 1–8.

Craighead, L. W., & Agras, W. S. (1991). Mechanisms of action in cognitive-behavioral and pharmacological interventions for obesity and Bulimia Nervosa. *Journal of Consulting and Clinical Psychology, 59,* 115–125.

Crisp, A. H., Hsu, L. K., Harding, B., & Hartshorn, J. (1980). Clinical features of Anorexia Nervosa: A study of a consecutive series of 102 female patients. *Journal of Psychosomatic Research, 24,* 179–191.

Crisp, A. H., Norton, K., Gowers, S., Halek, C., Bowyer, C., Yeldham, D., Levett, G., & Bhat, A. (1991). A controlled study of the effect of therapies aimed at adolescent and family psychopathology in Anorexia Nervosa. *British Journal of Psychiatry, 159,* 325–333.

Crisp, A. H., Palmer, R. L., & Kalucy, R. S. (1976). How common is Anorexia Nervosa?: A prevalence study. *British Journal of Psychiatry, 218,* 549–554.

Crow, S. J., & Mitchell, J. E. (1994). Rational therapy of eating disorders. *Drugs, 48,* 372–379.

Crow, S. J., & Mitchell, J. E. (1996). Pharmacological treatments for eating disorders. In J. K. Thompson (Ed.), *Body image, eating disorders, and obesity: An integrative guide for assessment and treatment* (pp. 345–360). Washington, DC: American Psychological Association.

Crow, S. J., & Mitchell, J. E. (1996). Integrating cognitive therapy and medications in treating bulimia nervosa. *Psychiatric Clinics of North America, 19,* 755–760.

Dally, P. D. (1969). *Anorexia nervosa.* New York: Grune & Stratton.

Dare, C., & Eisler, I. (1995). Family therapy and eating disorders. In K. D. Brownell & C. G. Fairburn (Eds.), *Eating disorders and obesity: A comprehensive handbook* (pp. 318–323). New York: Guilford Press.

Dare, C., & Eisler, I. (1997). Family therapy for anorexia nervosa. In D. M. Garner & P. E. Garfinkel (Eds.), *Handbook of treatment for eating disorders* (2nd ed., pp. 307–324). New York: Guilford Press.

Devlin, M. J. (1996). Assessment and treatment of binge-eating disorder. *Psychiatric Clinics of North America, 19,* 761–772.

Dritschel, B. H., Williams, K., & Cooper, P. J. (1991). Cognitive distortions amongst women experiencing bulimic episodes. *International Journal of Eating Disorders, 10,* 547–556.

Eckert, E. D. (1985). Characteristics of Anorexia Nervosa. In J. E. Mitchell (Ed.), *Anorexia nervosa and bulimia: Diagnosis and treatment* (pp. 3–28). Minneapolis: University of Minnesota Press.

Eckert, E. D., Halmi, K. A., Marchi, P., Grove, W., & Crosby, R. (1995). Ten-year follow-up of Anorexia Nervosa: Clinical course and outcome. *Psychological Medicine, 25,* 143–156.

Eckert, E. D., & Labeck, L. (1985). Integrated treatment program for Anorexia nervosa. In J. E. Mitchell (Ed.), *Anorexia Nervosa and bulimia: Diagnosis and treatment* (pp. 152–170). Minneapolis: University of Minnesota Press.

Edwards, M. D., & Kerry, I. (1993). Obesity, anorexia, and bulimia. *Clinical Nutrition, 77,* 899–909.

Ericsson, M., Poston, W. S., & Foreyt, J. P. (1996). Common biological pathways in eating disorders and obesity. *Addictive Behaviors, 21,* 733–743.

Everill, J. T., & Waller, G. (1995). Reported sexual abuse and eating psychopathology: A review of the evidence for a causal link. *International Journal of Eating Disorders, 18,* 1–11.

Fahy, T. A., Eisler, I., & Russell, G. M. (1993). A placebo-controlled trial of d-fenfluramine in Bulimia Nervosa. *British Journal of Psychiatry, 162,* 597–603.

Fairburn, C. G. (1980). Self-induced vomiting. *Journal of Psychosomatic Research, 24,* 193–197.

Fairburn, C. G. (1995). The prevention of eating disorders. In K. D. Brownell & C. G. Fairburn (Eds.), *Eating disorders and obesity: A comprehensive handbook* (pp. 289–293). New York: Guilford Press.

Fairburn, C. G., & Cooper, P. J. (1982). Self-induced vomiting and Bulimia Nervosa: An undetected problem. *British Medical Journal, 284,* 1153–1155.

Fairburn, C. G., Cooper, Z., & Cooper, P. J. (1986). The clinical features and maintenance of Bulimia Nervosa. In K. D. Brownell & J. P. Foreyt (Eds.), *Handbook of eating disorders: Physiology, psychology, and treatment of obesity, anorexia, and bulimia* (pp. 389–404). New York: Basic Books.

Fairburn, C. G., Jones, R., Peveler, R. C., Hope, R. A., & O'Connor, M. (1993). Psychotherapy and Bulimia Nervosa: Longer-term effects of interpersonal psychotherapy, behavior therapy, and cognitive behavior therapy. *Archives of General Psychiatry, 50,* 419–428.

Fairburn, C. G., Norman, P. A., Welch, S. L., O'Connor, M. E., Doll, H. A., & Peveler, R. C. (1995). A prospective study of outcome in Bulimia Nervosa and the long-term effects of three psychological treatments. *Archives of General Psychiatry, 52,* 304–312.

Fernandez, R. C. (1984). Disturbance in cognition: Implications for treatment. In P. S. Powers & R. C. Fernandez (Eds.), *Current treatment of Anorexia Nervosa and bulimia* (pp. 133–142). Basel: Karger.

Fichter, M. M. (1995). Inpatient treatment of Anorexia Nervosa. In K. D. Brownell & C. G. Fairburn (Eds.), *Eating disorders and obesity: A comprehensive handbook* (pp. 336–343). New York: Guilford Press.

Fichter, M. M., & Noegel, R. (1990). Concordance for Bulimia Nervosa in twins. *International Journal of Eating Disorders, 9,* 255–263.

Fombonne, E. (1995). Anorexia Nervosa: No evidence of an increase. *British Journal of Psychiatry, 166,* 462–471.

Food and Drug Administration (FDA) (1997). FDA analysis of cardiac valvular dysfunction with use of appetite suppressants, 9/17/97 (http://www.fda.gov/cder/news/slides/index.htm).

Foreyt, J. P., & McGavin, J. K. (1988). Anorexia Nervosa and bulimia. In E. J. Mash & L. G. Terdal (Eds.), *Behavioral assessment of childhood disorders* (2nd ed., pp. 776–805). New York: Guilford Press.

Foreyt, J. P., & Mikhail, C. (1997). Anorexia nervosa and bulimia nervosa. In E. J. Mash & L. G. Terdal (Eds.) *Assessment of childhood disorders* (3rd ed., pp. 683–716). New York: Guilford Press.

Foreyt, J. P., Poston, W. S., & Goodrick, G. K. (1996). Future directions in obesity and eating disorders. *Addictive Behaviors, 21,* 767–778.

Frisch, R. D., & McArthur, J. W. (1974). Menstrual cycles: Fatness as a determinant of minimum weight for height necessary for their maintenance of onset. *Science, 185,* 949–951.

Garfinkel, P. E. (1995). Classification and diagnosis of eating disorders. In K. D. Brownell & C. G. Fairburn (Eds.), *Eating disorders and obesity: A comprehensive handbook* (pp. 125–134). New York: Guilford Press.

Garfinkel, P. E., & Garner, D. M. (1982). *Anorexia nervosa: A multidimensional perspective.* New York: Brunner/Mazel.

Garfinkel, P. E., Garner, D. M., & Kennedy, S. (1985). Special problems of inpatient management. In D. M. Garner & P. E. Garfinkel (Eds.). *Handbook of psychotherapy for Anorexia Nervosa and bulimia* (pp. 344–362). New York: Guilford Press.

Garfinkel, P. E., & Kaplan, A. S. (1986). Anorexia Nervosa: Diagnostic conceptualizations. In K. D. Brownell & J. P. Foreyt (Eds.), *Handbook of eating disorders: Physiology, psychology, and treatment of obesity, anorexia, and bulimia* (pp. 266–282). New York: Basic Books.

Garfinkel, P. E., Moldofsky, H., & Garner, D. M. (1977). The outcome of Anorexia Nervosa: significance of clinical features, body image and behavior modification. In R. A. Vigersky (Ed.), *Anorexia nervosa* (pp. 315–330). New York: Raven Press.

Garfinkel, P. E., Moldofsky, H., & Garner, D. M. (1980). The heterogeneity of Anorexia Nervosa: Bulimia as a distinct subgroup. *Archives of General Psychiatry, 37,* 1036–1040.

Garfinkel, P. E., & Walsh, B. T. (1997). Drug therapies. In D. M. Garner & P. E. Garfinkel (Eds.), *Handbook of treatment for eating disorders* (2nd ed., pp. 373–380). New York: Guilford Press.

Garner, D. M. (1986). Cognitive therapy for Anorexia Nervosa. In K. D. Brownell & J. P. Foreyt (Eds.), *Handbook of eating disorders: Physiology, psychology, and treatment of obesity, anorexia, and bulimia* (pp. 301–327). New York: Basic Books.

Garner, D. M. (1991). *Eating Disorder Inventory—2 manual.* Odessa, FL: Psychological Assessment Resources.

Garner, D. M. (1995). Measurement of eating disorder psychopathology. In K. D. Brownell & C. G. Fairburn (Eds.), *Eating disorders and obesity: A comprehensive handbook* (pp. 117–121). New York: Guilford Press.

Garner, D. M. (1997). Psychoeducatonal principles in treatment. In D. M. Garner & P. E. Garfinkel (Eds.), *Handbook of treatment for eating disorders* (2nd ed., pp. 145–177), New York: Guilford Press.

Garner, D. M., & Bemis, K. M. (1982). A cognitive-behavioral approach to Anorexia Nervosa. *Cognitive Therapy and Research, 6,* 123–150.

Garner, D. M., & Bemis, K. M. (1985). Cognitive therapy for Anorexia Nervosa. In D. M. Garner & P. E. Garfinkel (Eds.), *Handbook of psychotherapy for anorexia nervosa and bulimia* (pp. 107–146). New York: Guilford Press.

Garner, D. M., & Garfinkel, P. E. (1979). The Eating Attitudes Test: An index of the symptoms of Anorexia Nervosa. *Psychological Medicine, 9,* 273–279.

Garner, D. M., & Garfinkel, P. E. (Eds.). (1985). *Handbook of psychotherapy for anorexia nervosa and bulimia.* New York: Guilford Press.

Garner, D. M., Garfinkel, P. E., & O'Shaughnessy, M. (1983). Clinical and psychometric comparison between bulimia in Anorexia Nervosa and bulimia in normal weight women. In *Understanding Anorexia Nervosa and bulimia: Report of Fourth Ross Conference on Medical Research* (pp. 6–14). Columbus, OH: Ross Laboratories.

Garner, D. M., Garfinkel, P. E., Schwartz, D., & Thompson, M. (1980). Cultural expectations of thinness in women. *Psychological Reports, 47,* 483–491.

Garner, D. M., Olmsted, M. P., & Polivy, J. (1983). Development and validation of a multidimensional Eating Disorder Inventory for Anorexia Nervosa and bulimia. *International Journal of Eating Disorders, 2,* 15–34.

Garner, D. M., Rockert, W., Davis, R., Garner, M. V., Olmsted, M. P., & Eagle, M. (1993) Comparison of cognitive-behavioral and supportive–expressive therapy for Bulimia Nervosa. *American Journal of Psychiatry, 150,* 37–46.

Garner, D. M., Vitousek, K. M., & Pike, K. M. (1997). Cognitive-behavioral therapy for Anorexia Nervosa. In D. M. Garner & P. E. Garfinkel (Eds.), *Handbook of treatment for eating disorders* (2nd ed., pp. 94–144). New York: Guilford Press.

Geretsegger, C., Greimel, K. V., Roed, I. S., & Hesselink, J. M. K. (1995). Ipsapirone in the treatment of Bulimia Nervosa: An open pilot study. *International Journal of Eating Disorders, 17,* 359–363.

Gillberg, C. (1994). Whither research in Anorexia and Bulimia Nervosa? *British Journal of Hospital Medicine, 51,* 209–215.

Glynn, S. M., & Ruderman, A. J. (1986). The development and validation of an Eating Self-Efficacy Scale. *Cognitive Therapy and Research, 10*, 403–420.

Gold, M. S. (1993). Are eating disorders addictions? In E. Ferrari, F. Brambilla, & S. B. Solerte (Eds.), *Primary and secondary eating disorders: A psychoneuroendocrine and metabolic approach* (pp. 455–463). New York: Pergamon Press.

Goldberg, S. C., Halmi, K. A., Casper, R., Eckert, E., & Davis, J. M. (1977). Pretreatment predictors of weight change in Anorexia Nervosa. In R. A. Vigersky (Ed.), *Anorexia nervosa* (pp. 31–42). New York: Raven Press.

Goldberg, S. C., Halmi, K. A., Eckert, E. D., Casper, R. C., Davis, J. M., & Roper, M. (1980). Attitudinal dimensions in Anorexia Nervosa. *Journal of Psychiatric Research, 15*, 129–251.

Goldbloom, D. S., Olmstead, M., Davis, R., Clewes, J., Heinmaa, M., Rockert, W., & Shaw, B. (1997). A randomized controlled trial of fluoxetine and cognitive behavior therapy for Bulimia Nervosa— Short term outcome. *Behaviour Research and Therapy, 35*, 803–811.

Goldstein, D. J., Wilson, M. G., Thompson, V. L., Potvin, J. H., & Rampey, A. H. (1995). Long-term fluoxetine treatment of Bulimia Nervosa: Fluoxetine Bulimia Nervosa Research Group. *British Journal of Psychiatry, 166*, 660–666.

Goodsitt, A. (1985). Self psychology and the treatment of Anorexia Nervosa. In D. M. Garner & P. E. Garfinkel (Eds.), *Handbook of psychotherapy for anorexia nervosa and bulimia* (pp. 55–82). New York: Guilford Press.

Gormally, J., Black, S., Daston, S., & Rardin, D. (1982). The assessment of binge eating severity among obese persons. *Addictive Behaviors, 7*, 47–55.

Gray, J. J., & Hoage, C. M. (1990). Bulimia Nervosa: A group behavior therapy with exposure plus response prevention. *Psychological Reports, 66*, 667–674.

Green, R. S., & Rau, J. H. (1974). Treatment of compulsive eating disturbances with anti-convulsant medication. *American Journal of Psychiatry, 131*, 428–432.

Green, R. S., & Rau, J. H. (1977). The use of diphenylhydantoin in compulsive eating disorders: Further studies. In R. A. Vigersky (Ed.), *Anorexia Nervosa* (pp. 377–382), New York: Raven Press.

Greenway, F. L., Dahms, W. T., & Bray, G. A. (1977). Phenytoin as a treatment of obesity associated with compulsive eating. *Current Therapeutic Research, 21*, 338–342.

Grilo, C. M., Brownell, K. D., & Stunkard, A. J. (1993). The metabolic and psychological importance of exercise in weight control. In A. J. Stunkard & T. A. Wadden (Eds.), *Obesity: Theory and therapy* (2nd ed., pp. 253–273). New York: Raven Press.

Grinc, G. A. (1982). A cognitive-behavioral model for the treatment of chronic vomiting. *Journal of Behavioral Medicine, 5*, 135–141.

Gull, W. W. (1874). Anorexia nervosa (apepsia hysterica, anorexia hysterica). *Transactions of the Clinical Society of London, 7*, 22–28.

Gwirtsman, H. E., Guze, B. H., Yager, J., & Gainsley, B. (1990). Fluoxetine treatment of Anorexia Nervosa: An open clinical trial. *Clinical Psychiatry, 51*, 378–382.

Haley, J. (1976). *Problem-solving therapy.* San Francisco: Jossey-Bass.

Hall, A. (1985). Group therapy for Anorexia Nervosa. In D. M. Garner & P. E. Garfinkel (Eds.), *Handbook of psychotherapy for anorexia nervosa and bulimia* (pp. 213–239). New York: Guilford Press.

Hallsten, E. A. (1965). Adolescent Anorexia Nervosa treated by desensitization. *Behaviour Research and Therapy, 3*, 87–91.

Halmi, K. A. (1974). Anorexia Nervosa: Demographic and clinical features in 94 cases. *Psychosomatic Medicine, 36*, 18–25.

Halmi, K. A. (1982). Pragmatic information on the eating disorders. *Psychiatric Clinics of North America, 5*, 371–377.

Halmi, K. A., Brodland, G., & Loney, J. (1973). Prognosis in Anorexia Nervosa. *Annals of Internal Medicine, 78*, 907.

Halmi, K. A., Brodland, G., & Rigas, C. (1975). A follow-up study of 79 patients with Anorexia Nervosa: An evaluation of prognostic factors and diagnostic criteria. *Life History Research in Psychopathology, 4*, 290–298.

Halmi, K. A., Casper, R. C., Eckert, E. C., Goldberg, S. C., & Davis, J. M. (1979). Unique features associated with age of onset of Anorexia Nervosa. *Psychiatric Research, 1*, 290–215.

Halmi, K. A., Eckert, E., LaDu, T. J., & Cohen, J. (1986). Anorexia Nervosa: Treatment efficacy of cyproheptadine and amitriptyline. *Archives of General Psychiatry, 43*, 177–181.

Halmi, K. A., Falk, J. R., & Schwartz, E. (1981). Binge eating and vomiting: A survey of a college population. *Psychological Medicine, 11*, 697–706.

Hammond, W. A. (1879). *Fasting girls: Their physiology and pathology.* New York: Putnam.

Hawkins, R. C., II, & Clement, P. F. (1980). Development and construct validation of a self-report measure of binge eating tendencies. *Addictive Behaviors, 5*, 219–226.

Hawkins, R. C., II, Fremouw, W. J., & Clement, P. F. (Eds.). (1984). *The binge–purge syndrome: Diagnosis, treatment and research.* New York: Springer.

Hay, G. G., & Leonard, J. C. (1979). Anorexia Nervosa in males. *Lancet, ii*, 574–575.

Heinberg, L. J. (1996). Theories of body image disturbance: Perceptual, developmental, and sociocultural factors. In J. K. Thompson (Ed.), *Body image, eating disorders, and obesity: An integrative guide for assessment and treatment* (pp. 27–47). Washington DC: American Psychological Association.

Henderson, M., & Freeman, C. P. I. (1987). A self-rating scale for bulimia: The "BITE." *British Journal of Psychiatry, 150*, 18–24.

Herzog, D. B., Sacks, N. R., Keller, M. B., Lavori, P. W., von Ranson, K. B., & Gray, H. M. (1993). Patterns and predictors of recovery in Anorexia Nervosa and Bulimia Nervosa. *Journal of the American Academy of Child and Adolescent Psychiatry, 32*, 835–842.

Hodes, M., & Le Grange, D. (1993). Expressed emotion in the investigation of eating disorders: A review. *International Journal of Eating Disorders, 13*, 279–288.

Hoek, H. W. (1995). The distribution of eating disorders. In K. D. Brownell & C. G. Fairburn (Eds.), *Eating disorders and obesity: A comprehensive handbook* (pp. 207–211). New York: Guilford Press.

Hoffman, L., & Halmi, K. (1993). Psychopharmacology in the treatment of Anorexia Nervosa and Bulimia Nervosa. *Psychopharmacology II, 16*, 767–778.

Holderness, C. C., Brooks-Gunn, J, & Warren, M. P. (1994). Co-morbidity of eating disorders and substance abuse: Review of the literature. *International Journal of Eating Disorders, 16*, 1–34.

Holland, A. J., Sicotte, N., & Treasure, J. (1988). Anorexia Nervosa: Evidence for a genetic basis. *Journal of Psychosomatic Research, 32*, 561–571.

Hsu, L. K. (1995). Outcome of Bulimia Nervosa. In K. D. Brownell & C. G. Fairburn (Eds.), *Eating disorders and obesity: A comprehensive handbook* (pp. 238–244). New York: Guilford Press.

Hsu, L. K. (1996). Epidemiology of the eating disorders. *Psychiatric Clinics of North America, 19*, 681–700.

Hsu, L. K., Chesler, B. E., & Santhouse, R. (1990). Bulimia Nervosa in eleven sets of twins: A clinical report. *International Journal of Eating Disorders, 9*, 275–282.

Hsu, L. K., Crisp, A. H., & Harding, B. (1979). Outcome of Anorexia Nervosa. *Lancet, i*, 61–65.

Hudson, J. I., Laffer, P. S., & Pope, H. G. (1982). Bulimia related to effective disorder by family history and response to the dexamethasone suppression test. *American Journal of Psychiatry, 139*, 685–687.

Hudson, J. I., Pope, H. G., Jonas, J. M., & Yurgelun-Todd, D. (1983). Family history study of Anorexia Nervosa and bulimia. *British Journal of Psychiatry, 142*, 133–138.

Hughes, P. L., Wells, L. A., Cunningham, C. J., & Ilstrup, D. M. (1984, May 9). *Treating bulimia with desipramine: A double-blind placebo-controlled study.* Paper presented at the annual meeting of the American Psychiatric Association, Los Angeles.

Iancu, I., Spivak, B., Ratzoni, G., Apter, A., & Weizman, A. (1994). The sociocultural theory in the development of Anorexia Nervosa. *Psychopathology, 27*, 29–36.

Jarry, J. L., & Vaccarino, F. J. (1996). Eating disorder and Obsessive–Compulsive Disorder: Neurochemical and phenomenological commonalities. *Journal of Psychiatry and Neuroscience, 21*, 36–48.

Janet, P. (1919). *Les obsessions et la psychasthenie.* Paris: Alcan.

Jimerson, D. C., Wolfe, B. E., Brotman, A. W., & Metzger, E. D. (1996). Medications in the treatment of eating disorders. *Psychiatric Clinics of North America, 19*, 739–754.

Johnson, C. (1985). Initial consultation for patients with bulimia and Anorexia Nervosa. In D. M. Garner & P. E. Garfinkel (Eds.), *Handbook of psychotherapy for anorexia nervosa and bulimia* (pp. 19–51). New York: Guilford Press.

Johnson, C., Connors, M., & Stuckey, M. (1983). Short-term group treatment of bulimia. A preliminary report. *International Journal of Eating Disorders, 2*, 199–208.

Johnson, C., & Larson, R. (1982). Bulimia: Analysis of moods and behavior. *Psychosomatic Medicine, 44*, 341–353.

Johnson, C., Lewis, C., & Hagman, J. (1984). The syndrome of bulimia: Review and synthesis. *Psychiatric Clinics of North America, 7*, 247–273.

Johnson, C., & Pure, D. L. (1986). Assessment of bulimia: A multidimensional model. In K. D. Brownell & J. P. Foreyt (Eds.), *Handbook of eating disorders: Physiology, psychology, and treatment of obesity, anorexia, and bulimia* (pp. 405–449). New York: Basic Books.

Jones, D. J., Fox, M. M., Babigian, H. M., & Hutton, H. E. (1980). The epidemiology of Anorexia Nervosa in Monroe County, New York: 1960–1976. *Psychosomatic Medicine, 42*, 551–558.

Kalucy, R. S., Crisp, A. H., & Harding, B. (1977). A study of 56 families with Anorexia Nervosa. *British Journal of Medical Psychology, 50*, 381–395.

Kalucy, R. S., Crisp, A. H., Lacey, J. H., & Harding, B. (1977). Prevalence and prognosis in Anorexia Nervosa. *Australian and New Zealand Journal of Psychiatry, 11*, 251–257.

Kalucy, R. S., Gilchrist, P. N., McFarlane, C. M., & McFarlane, A. C. (1985). The evolution of a multi-therapy orientation. In D. M. Garner & P. E. Garfinkel (Eds.), *Handbook of psychotherapy for anorexia nervosa and bulimia* (pp. 458–487). New York: Guilford Press.

Kaplan, A. S., & Garfinkel, A. H. (1984). Bulimia in the Talmud. *American Journal of Psychiatry, 141*, 721.

Kaplan, A. S., & Garfinkel, P. E. (1993). *Medical issues and the eating disorders: The interface.* New York: Brunner/Mazel.

Kaye, W. H., Ballenger, J. C., Lydiard, B., Stuart, G. W., Laraia, M. T., O'Neil, P., Fossey, M. D., Stevens, V., Lesser, S., & Hsu, G. (1990). CSF monoamine oxidase levels in normal-weight bulimia: Evidence for abnormal noradrenergic activity. *American Journal of Psychiatry, 147*, 225–229.

Kaye, W. H., & Weltzin, T. E. (1991). Neurochemistry of Bulimia Nervosa. *Journal of Clinical Psychiatry, 52,* 21–28.

Kaye, W. H., Weltzin, T. E., Hsu, L. K. G., & Bulik, C. M. (1991). An open trial of fluoxetine in patients with Anorexia Nervosa. *Clinical Psychiatry, 52,* 464–471.

Kearney-Cooke, A., & Striegel-Moore, R. (1994). Treatment of childhood sexual abuse in Anorexia Nervosa and Bulimia Nervosa: A feminist psychodynamic approach. *International Journal of Eating Disorders, 15,* 305–319.

Keel, P. K., & Mitchell, J. E. (1997). Outcome in Bulimia Nervosa. *American Journal of Psychiatry, 154,* 313–321.

Keller, M. B., Herzog, D. B., Lavori, P. W., Bradburn, I. S., & Mahoney, E. M. (1992). The naturalistic history of Bulimia Nervosa: Extraordinary high rates of chronicity, relapse, recurrence, and psychosocial morbidity. *International Journal of Eating Disorders, 12,* 1–9.

Kendler, K. S., MacLean, C., Neale, M., Kessler, R., Heath, A., & Eaves, L. (1991). The genetic epidemiology of Bulimia Nervosa. *American Journal of Psychiatry, 148,* 1627–1637.

Kennedy, S. H., Katz, R., Neitzert, C. S., Ralveski, E., & Mendlowitz, S. (1995). Exposure with response prevention treatment of Anorexia Nervosa–bulimic subtype and Bulimia Nervosa. *Behaviour Research and Therapy, 33,* 685–689.

Kennedy, S. H., Piran, N., Warsh, J. J., Prendergast, P., Mainprize, E., Whynot, C., & Garfinkel, P. E. (1988). A trial of isocarboxazid in the treatment of Bulimia Nervosa. *Journal of Clinical Psychopharmacology, 8,* 391–396.

Kenny, F. T., & Solyom, L. (1971). The treatment of compulsive vomiting through faradic disruption of mental images. *Canadian Medical Association Journal, 105,* 1071–1073.

Kirk, S. A., & Kutchins, H. (1992). *The selling of DSM: The rhetoric of science in psychiatry.* New York: Aldine de Gruyter.

Kirschenbaum, D. S., & Fitzgibbon, M. L. (1995). Controversy about the treatment of obesity: Criticisms or challenges? *Behavior Therapy, 26,* 43–68.

Lacey, J. H. (1982). Anorexia Nervosa and a bearded female saint. *British Medical Journal, 285,* 1816–1817.

Lacey, J. H. (1983). Bulimia Nervosa, binge eating, and psychogenic vomiting: A controlled treatment study and long term outcome. *British Medical Journal, 286,* 1609–1613.

Lacey, J. H. (1985). Time-limited individual and group treatment for bulimia. In D. M. Garner & P. E. Garfinkel (Eds.). *Handbook of psychotherapy for anorexia nervosa and bulimia* (pp. 431–457). New York: Guilford Press.

Lang, P. J. (1965). Behavior therapy with a case of Anorexia Nervosa. In L. P. Ullmann & L. Krasner (Eds.), *Case studies in behavior modification* (pp. 217–221). New York: Holt, Rinehart & Winston.

Laseque, C. (1873). On hysterical anorexia. *Medical Times Gazette, 2,* 265–266.

Lee, M. I., & Miltenberger, R. G. (1997). Functional assessment and binge eating. A review of the literature and suggestions for future research. *Behavior Modification, 21,* 159–171.

Lee, S. (1995). Self-starvation in context: Towards a culturally sensitive understanding of Anorexia Nervosa. *Social Science in Medicine, 41,* 25–36.

le Grange, D., Eisler, I., Dare, C., & Russell, G. F. M. (1992). Evaluation of family treatments in adolescent Anorexia Nervosa: A pilot study. *International Journal of Eating Disorders, 12,* 347–357.

Leibowitz, S. F. (1983). Hypothalamic catecholamine systems controlling eating behavior: A potential model for Anorexia Nervosa. In P. L. Darby, P. E. Garfinkel, D. M. Garner, & D. V. Coscina (Eds.), *Anorexia Nervosa: Recent developments in research* (pp. 221–229). New York: Alan R. Liss.

Leifer, R. (1990). Introduction: The medical model as the ideology of therapeutic state. *Journal of Mind and Behavior, 11,* 247–258.

Leitenberg, H., Agras, W. S., & Thompson, L. E. (1968). A sequential analysis of the effect of selective positive reinforcement in modifying Anorexia Nervosa. *Behaviour Research and Therapy, 6,* 211–218.

Leitenberg, H., & Rosen, J. (1989). Cognitive-behavioral therapy with and without exposure plus response prevention in treatment of Bulimia Nervosa: Comments on Agras, Schneider, Arnow, Raeburn, and Telch. *Journal of Consulting and Clinical Psychology, 57,* 776–777.

Leitenberg, H., Rosen, J., Gross, J., Nudelman, S., & Vara, L. S. (1988). Exposure plus response-prevention treatment of Bulimia Nervosa. *Journal of Consulting and Clinical Psychology, 56,* 535–541.

Leon, G. E., Carroll, K., Chernyk, B., & Finn, S. (1985). Binge eating and associated habit patterns within college student and identified bulimic populations. *International Journal of Eating Disorders, 4,* 43–57.

Leon, G. R., Fulkerson, J. A., Perry, C. L., & Early-Zald, M. B. (1995). Prospective analysis of personality and behavioral vulnerabilities and gender influences in the later development of disordered eating. *Journal of Abnormal Psychology, 104,* 140–149.

Levenkron, S. (1983). *Treating and overcoming Anorexia Nervosa.* New York: Warner Books.

Lewis, J. M. (1978). The adolescent and the healthy family. In S. C. Feinstein & P. L. Giovacchini (Eds.), *Adolescent psychiatry* (Vol. 6, pp. 156–170). Chicago: University of Chicago Press.

Liebowitz, M. R., Quitkin, F., & Stewart, J. W. (1981). Phenelzine and imipramine in atypical depression. *Psychopharmacological Bulletin, 17,* 159–161.

Loro, A. D., Jr. (1984). Binge eating: A cognitive-behavioral treatment approach. In R. C. Hawkins II, W. J. Fermouw & P. F. Clement (Eds.), *The binge–purge syndrome: Diagnosis, treatment, and research* (pp. 183–210). New York: Springer.

Lowenberg, M., Todhunter, E., Wilson, E., Savage, J., & Lubawski, J. (1974). *Food and man* (2nd ed.). New York: Wiley.

Luborsky, I. (1984). *Principles of psychoanalytic psychotherapy: A manual for supportive–expressive treatment.* New York: Basic Books.

Lydiard, R. B., Brewerton, T. D., Fossey, M. D., Laraia, M. T., Stuart, G., Beinfeld, M. C., & Ballenger, J. C. (1993). CSF cholecystokinin octapeptide in patients with Bulimia Nervosa and in normal comparison subjects. *American Journal of Psychiatry, 150,* 1099–1101.

Marrazzi, M. A., Markham, K. M., Kinzie, J., & Luby, E. D. (1995). Binge Eating Disorder: Response to naltrexone. *International Journal of Obesity, 19,* 143–145.

Mauri, M. C., Rudelli, R., Somaschini, E., Roncoroni, L., Papa, R., Mantero, M., Longhini, M., & Penati, G. (1996). Neurobiological and psychopharmacological basis in the therapy of bulimia and anorexia. *Progress in Neuro-Psychopharmacology and Biological Psychiatry, 20,* 207–229.

Mazure, C. M., Halmi, K. A., Sunday, S. R., Romano, S. J., & Einhorn, A. M. (1994). Yale–Brown–Cornell Eating Disorder Scale: Development, use, reliability, and validity. *Journal of Psychiatric Research, 28,* 425–445.

Metropolitan Life Insurance Company. (1984). 1983 Metropolitan height and weight tables. *Statistical Bulletin, 64,* 2–9.

Minuchin, S., Rosman, B. L., & Baker, L. (1978). *Psychosomatic families: Anorexia Nervosa in context.* Cambridge, MA: Harvard University Press.

Mitchell, J. E. (1985). Medical complications. In J. E. Mitchell (Ed.), *Anorexia Nervosa and bulimia: Diagnosis and treatment* (pp. 48–77). Minneapolis: University of Minnesota Press.

Mitchell, J. E. (1986a). Anorexia Nervosa: Medical and physiological aspects. In K. D. Brownell & J. P. Foreyt (Eds.). *Handbook of eating disorders: Physiology, psychology, and treatment of obesity, anorexia, and bulimia* (pp. 247–265). New York: Basic Books.

Mitchell, J. E. (1986b). Bulimia: Medical and physiological aspects. In K. D. Brownell & J. P. Foreyt (Eds.), *Handbook of eating disorders: Physiology, psychology, and treatment of obesity, anorexia, and bulimia* (pp. 379–388). New York: Basic Books.

Mitchell, J. E., Hatsukami, D., Eckert, E. D., & Pyle, R. L. (1985). Characteristics of 275 patients with bulimia. *American Journal of Psychiatry, 142,* 482–485.

Mitchell, J. E., Hatsukami, D., Goff, G., Pyle, R. L., Eckert, E., & Davis, L. E. (1985). Intensive outpatient group treatment for bulimia. In D. M. Garner & P. E. Garfinkel (Eds.), *Handbook of psychotherapy for anorexia nervosa and bulimia* (pp. 240–256). New York: Guilford Press.

Mitchell, J. E., Hoberman, H. N., Peterson, C. B., Mussell, M., & Pyle, R. L. (1996). Research on the psychotherapy of Bulimia Nervosa: Half empty or half full. *International Journal of Eating Disorders, 20,* 219–229.

Mitchell, J. E., & Pyle, R. L. (1982). The bulimic syndrome in normal weight individuals: A review. *International Journal of Eating Disorders, 1,* 61–73.

Mitchell, J. E., Pyle, R. L., Eckert, E. D., Hatsukami, D., Pomeroy, C., & Zimmerman, R. (1990). A comparison study of anti-depressants and structured group therapy in the treatment of Bulimia Nervosa. *Archives of General Psychiatry, 47,* 149–157.

Mitchell, J. E., Raymond, N., & Specker, S. (1993). A review of the controlled trials of pharmacotherapy and psychotherapy in the treatment of Bulimia Nervosa. *International Journal of Eating Disorders, 14,* 229–247.

Mizes, J. S., & Christiano, B. A. (1995). Assessment of cognitive variables relevant to cognitive behavioural perspectives on Anorexia Nervosa and Bulimia Nervosa. *Behaviour Research and Therapy, 33,* 95–105.

Mizes, J. S., & Klesges, R. C. (1989). Validity, reliability, and factor structure of the Anorectic Cognitions Questionnaire. *Addictive Behaviors, 14,* 589–594.

Monello, L. F., Seltzer, C. C., & Mayer, J. (1965). Hunger and satiety sensations in men, women, boys and girls: A preliminary report. *Annals of the New York Academy of Sciences, 131,* 493–602.

Monti, P. M., McCrady, B. S., & Barlow, D. H. (1977). Effect of positive reinforcement, informational feedback and contingency contracting on a bulimic anorexic female. *Behavior Therapy, 8,* 258–263.

Morgan, H. G., & Russell, G. F. M. (1975). Value of family background and clinical features as predictors of long-term outcome in Anorexia Nervosa: Four-year follow-up study of 41 patients. *Psychological Medicine, 5,* 355–371.

Morton, R. (1694). *Phthisiologica: Or a treatise of consumptions.* London: S. Smith & B. Walo.

Myrtle, A. S. (1888). Letters to the editor. *Lancet, i,* 899.

Ollendick, T. H. (1979). Behavioral treatment of Anorexia Nervosa: A five-year study. *Behavior Modification, 3,* 124–135.

Olmsted, M. P., Davis, R., Rockert, W., Irvine, J. J., Eagle, M., & Garner, D. M. (1991). Efficacy of a brief group psychoeducational intervention for Bulimia Nervosa. *Behaviour Research and Therapy, 29,* 71–83.

Olmsted, M. P., & Kaplan, A. S. (1995). Psychoeducation in the treatment of eating. In K. D. Brownell & C. G. Fairburn (Eds.), *Eating disorders and obesity: A comprehensive handbook* (pp.299–305). New York: Guilford Press.

Oster, J. R., Materson, B. J., & Rogers, A. I. (1980). Laxative abuse syndrome. *American Journal of Gastroenterology, 74*, 451–458.

Palmer, R. L. (1979). The dietary chaos syndrome: A useful new term? *British Journal of Medical Psychology, 52*, 187–190.

Parham, E. S. (1995). Compulsive eating: Applying a medical addiction model. In T. B. VanItallie, A. P. Simonpoulos, S. P. Gullo, & W. Futterweit (Eds.) *Obesity: New directions in assessment and management*. Philadelphia: Charles Press.

Pate, J. E., Pumariega, A. J., Hester, C., & Garner, D. M. (1992). Cross-cultural patterns in eating disorders: A review. *Journal of the American Academy of Child and Adolescent Psychiatry, 31*, 802–809.

Pierloot, R., Wellens, W., & Houben, M. (1975). Elements of resistance to a combined medical and psychotherapeutic program in Anorexia Nervosa. *Psychotherapy and Psychosomatics, 36*, 101–107.

Pike, K. M., Loeb, K., & Vitousek, K. (1996). Cognitive-behavioral therapy for Anorexia Nervosa and Bulimia Nervosa. In J. K. Thompson (Ed.), *Body image, eating disorders, and obesity: An integrative guide for assessment and treatment* (pp. 253–302). Washington DC: American Psychological Association.

Pillay, M., & Crisp, A. H. (1981). The impact of social skills training within an established in-patient treatment program for Anorexia Nervosa. *Journal of Psychiatry, 139*, 533–539.

Playfair, W. S. (1888). Note on the so-called anorexia nervosa. *Lancet, i*, 817.

Polivy, J., & Federoff, I. (1997). Group psychotherapy. In D. M. Garner & P. E. Garfinkel (Eds.), *Handbook of treatment for eating disorders* (2nd ed., pp. 462–475). New York: Guilford Press.

Pope, H. G., & Hudson, J. (1982). Treatment of bulimia with antidepressants. *Psychopharmacology, 78*, 167–169.

Pope, H. G., Hudson, J. I., & Jonas, J. M. (1983). Antidepressant treatment of bulimia: Preliminary experience and practical recommendations. *Journal of Clinical Psychopharmacology, 3*, 274–281.

Poston, W. S. C., & Winebarger, A. A. (1996). The misuse of behavioral genetics in prevention research, or for whom the "bell curve" tolls. *Journal of Primary Prevention, 17*, 133–147.

Powers, P. S. (1984a). Eating Disorders Questionnaire. In P. S. Powers & R. C. Fernandez (Eds.), *Current treatment of Anorexia Nervosa and bulimia* (pp. 302–325). Basel: Karger.

Powers, P. S. (1984b). Multidisciplinary approach to treatment and evaluation. In P. S. Powers & R. C. Fernandez (Eds.). *Current treatment of Anorexia Nervosa and bulimia* (pp. 166–179). Basel: Karger.

Powers, P. S., & Fernandez, R. C. (1984). Introduction. In P. S. Powers & R. C. Fernandez (Eds.), *Current treatment of Anorexia Nervosa and bulimia* (pp. 1017). Basel: Karger.

Powers, P. S., & Powers, H. P. (1984). Inpatient treatment of Anorexia Nervosa. *Psychosomatics, 25*, 512–527.

Pyle, R. L., Mitchell, J. E., Eckert, E. E., Halverson, P., Neuman, P., & Goff, G. (1983). The incidence of bulimia in freshmen college students. *International Journal of Eating Disorders, 2*, 75–85.

Rau, J. H., & Green, R. S. (1975). Compulsive eating: A neuropsychologic approach to certain eating disorders. *Comprehensive Psychiatry, 16*, 223–231.

Rich, C. L. (1978). Self-induced vomiting: Psychiatric considerations. *Journal of the American Medical Association, 239*, 2688–2689.

Robin, A. L., Siegel, P. T., & Moye, A. (1995). Family versus individual therapy for anorexia: Impact on family conflict. *International Journal of Eating Disorders, 17*, 313–322.

Robin, A. L., Siegel, P. T., Koepke, T., Moye, A. W., & Tice, S. (1994). Family therapy versus individual therapy for adolescent females with Anorexia Nervosa. *Journal of Developmental and Behavioral Pediatrics, 15*, 111–116.

Rorty, M., Yager, J., & Rossotto, E. (1993). Why and how do women recover from Bulimia Nervosa?: The subjective appraisals of forty women recovered for a year or more. *International Journal of Eating Disorders, 14*, 249–260.

Rorty, M., Yager, J., & Rossotto, E. (1994). Childhood sexual, physical, and psychological abuse in Bulimia Nervosa. *American Journal of Psychiatry, 151*, 1122–1126.

Rosen, J. C., & Leitenberg, H. (1982). Bulimia Nervosa: Treatment with exposure and response prevention. *Behavior Therapy, 13*, 117–124.

Rosen, J. C., Reiter, J., & Orosan, P. (1995). Rosen, J. C., Reiter, J., & Orosan, P. (1995). Cognitive-behavioral body image therapy for Body Dysmorphic Disorder. *Journal of Consulting and Clinical Psychology, 63*, 263–269.

Rosenthal, R. H., Webb, W. L., & Wruble, L. D. (1980). Diagnosis and management of persistent psychogenic vomiting. *Psychosomatics, 21*, 722–730.

Ross, C. A., & Pam, A. (1995). *Pseudoscience in biological psychiatry*. New York: Wiley.

Rowland, C. V., Jr. (1970). Anorexia Nervosa: A survey of the literature and review of 30 cases. *International Psychiatric Clinics, 7*, 37–137.

Russell, G. F. M. (1979). Bulimia Nervosa: An ominous variant of Anorexia Nervosa. *Psychological Medicine, 9*, 429–448.

Russell, G. F. M., Checkley, S. A., Feldman, J., & Eisler, I. (1988). A controlled trial of *d*-fenfluramine in Bulimia Nervosa. *Clinical Neuropsychopharmacology, 11*(Suppl. 1), S146-S159.

Russell, G. F. M., Szmukler, G. I., Dare, C., & Eisler, I. (1987). An evaluation of family therapy in Anorexia Nervosa and Bulimia Nervosa. *Archives of General Psychiatry, 44*, 1047–1056.

Sabine, E. J., Yonace, A., Farrington, A. J., Barratt, K. H., & Wakeling, A. (1983). Bulimia Nervosa: A placebo controlled double-blind therapeutic trial of mianserin. *British Journal of Clinical Pharmacology, 15*(Suppl.), 195S-202S.

Salusso-Deonier, C. J., & Scharzkopf, R. J. (1991). Sex differences in body cathexis associated with exercise involvement. *Perceptual and Motor Skills, 73,* 139–145.

Schneider, J. A., O'Leary, A., & Agras, W. S. (1987). The role of perceived self-efficacy in recovery from bulimia: A preliminary examination. *Behaviour Research and Therapy, 25,* 429–432.

Schnurer, A. T., Rubin, R. R., & Roy, A. (1973). Systematic desensitization of Anorexia Nervosa seen as a weight phobia. *Journal of Behavior Therapy and Experimental Psychiatry, 4,* 149–153.

Schwartz, D. M., & Thompson, M. G. (1981). Do anorectics get well?: Current research and future needs. *American Journal of Psychiatry, 138,* 319–323.

Schwartz, D. M., Thompson, M. G., & Johnson, C. L. (1982). Anorexia nervosa and bulimia: The sociocultural context. *International Journal of Eating Disorders, 1,* 20–36.

Schwartz, R. C., Barrett, M. J., & Saba, G. (1985). Family therapy for bulimia. In D. M. Garner & P. E. Garfinkel (Eds.), *Handbook of psychotherapy for anorexia nervosa and bulimia* (pp. 280–310). New York: Guilford Press.

Seidensticher, J. F., & Tzagournis, M. (1968). Anorexia Nervosa: Clinical features and long-term follow-up. *Journal of Chronic Diseases, 21,* 361–367.

Sheehan, H. L., & Summers, V. K. (1949). The syndrome of hypopituitarism. *Quarterly Journal of Medicine, 18,* 319–378.

Shore, R. A., & Porter, J. E. (1990). Normative and reliability data for 11 to 18 year olds on the Eating Disorder Inventory. *International Journal of Eating Disorders, 9,* 201–207.

Silverstone, P. H. (1992). Is chronic low self-esteem the cause of eating disorders? *Medical Hypotheses, 39,* 311–315.

Simmonds, M. (1914). Uber embolische prozesse in der hypophysis. *Archives of Pathology and Anatomy, 217,* 226–239.

Slade, P. D. (1973). A short Anorexic Behaviour Scale. *British Journal of Psychiatry, 122,* 83–85.

Slade, P. D., & Dewey, M. E. (1986). Development and preliminary validation of the SCANS: A screening instrument for identifying individuals at risk for developing Anorexia and Bulimia Nervosa. *International Journal of Eating Disorders, 5,* 517–538.

Sohlberg, S., & Strober, M. (1994). Personality in Anorexia Nervosa: An update and a theoretical integration. *Acta Psychiatrica Scandinavica, 89*(suppl. 378), 1–15.

Steel, Z. P., Farag, P. A., & Blaszcznski, A. P. (1995). Interrupting the binge–purge cycle in bulimia: The use of planned binges. *International Journal of Eating Disorders, 18,* 199–208.

Steiger, H., Stotland, S, Ghadirian, A. M., & Whitehead, V. (1995). Controlled study of eating concerns and psychopathological traits in relatives of eating-disordered probands: Do familial traits exist? *International Journal of Eating Disorders, 18,* 107–118.

Steinhausen, H. C. (1995a). Treatment and outcome of adolescent Anorexia Nervosa. *Hormone Research, 43,* 168–170.

Steinhausen, H. C. (1995b). The course and outcome of Anorexia Nervosa. In K. D. Brownell & C. G. Fairburn (Eds.), *Eating disorders and obesity: A comprehensive handbook* (pp. 234–237). New York: Guilford Press.

Stewart, J. W., Walsh, T., Wright, L., Roose, S. P., & Glassman, A. H. (1984). An open trial of MAO inhibitors in bulimia. *Journal of Clinical Psychiatry, 45,* 217–219.

Strangler, R. S., & Printz, A. M. (1980). DSM-III: Psychiatric diagnosis in a university population. *American Journal of Psychiatry, 137,* 937–940.

Striegel-Moore, R. H. (1995). A feminist perspective on the etiology of eating. In K. D. Brownell & C. G. Fairburn (Eds.), *Eating disorders and obesity: A comprehensive handbook* (pp. 224–229). New York: Guilford Press.

Strober, M. (1981). The significance of bulimia in juvenile Anorexia Nervosa: An exploration of possible etiological factors. *International Journal of Eating Disorders, 1,* 28–43.

Strober, M. (1983). An empirically derived typology of Anorexia Nervosa. In P. L. Darby, P. E. Garfinkel, D. M. Garner, & D. V. Coscina (Eds.), *Anorexia Nervosa: Recent developments in research* (pp. 185–196). New York: Alan R. Liss.

Strober, M. (1986). Anorexia Nervosa: History and psychological concepts. In K. D. Brownell & J. P. Foreyt (Eds.). *Handbook of eating disorders: Physiology, psychology, and treatment of obesity, anorexia, and bulimia* (pp. 231–246). New York: Basic Books.

Strober, M. (1991). Family-genetic studies of eating disorders. *Journal of Clinical Psychiatry, 52*(10, Suppl.), 9–12.

Strober, M. (1995). Family-genetic perspectives on Anorexia and Bulimia Nervosa. In K. D. Brownell & C. G. Fairburn (Eds.), *Eating disorders and obesity: A comprehensive handbook* (pp. 212–218). New York: Guilford Press.

Strober, M., & Yager, J. (1985). A developmental perspective on the treatment of Anorexia Nervosa in adolescents. In D. M. Garner & P. E. Garfinkel (Eds.), *Handbook of psychotherapy for anorexia nervosa and bulimia* (pp. 363–390). New York: Guilford Press.

Study Group on Anorexia Nervosa. (1995). Anorexia Nervosa: Directions for future research. *International Journal of Eating Disorders, 17,* 235–241.

Sturzenberger, S., Cantwell, P. D., Burroughs, J., Salkin, B., & Green, J. K. (1977). A follow-up study of adolescent psychiatric inpatients with Anorexia Nervosa. *Journal of the American Academy of Child Psychiatry, 16*, 703–715.

Sunday, S. R., Halmi, K. A., & Einhorn, A. (1995). The Yale–Brown–Cornell Eating Disorder Scale: A new scale to assess eating disorder symptomatology. *International Journal of Eating Disorders, 18*, 237–245.

Szmukler, G. I., Young, G. P., Miller, G., Lichenstein, M., & Binns, D. S. (1995). A controlled trial of cisapride in Anorexia Nervosa. *International Journal of Eating Disorders, 17*, 347–357.

Theander, S. (1970). Anorexia Nervosa: A psychiatric investigation of 94 female patients. *Acta Psychiatrica Scandinavica, 65*(Suppl. 214), 1–194.

Thelen, M. H., Farmer, J., Wonderlich, S., & Smith, M. (1991). A revision of the Bulimia Test: The BULIT-R. *Psychological Assessment, 3*, 119–124.

Thompson, D. A., Berg, K. M., & Shatford, L. A. (1987). The heterogeneity of bulimic symptomatology: Cognitive and behavioral dimensions. *International Journal of Eating Disorders, 6*, 215–234.

Tobin, D. L., Johnson, C., Steinberg, S, Staats, M., & Baker Dennis, A. (1991). Multifactorial assessment of Bulimia Nervosa. *Journal of Abnormal Psychology, 100*, 14–21.

Treasure, J., & Holland, A. (1995). Genetic factors in eating disorders. In G. I. Szmukler, C. Dare, & J. Treasure (Eds.), *Handbook of eating disorders: Theory, treatment and research* (pp. 65–81). Chichester, England: Wiley.

Tuschen, B., & Bents, H. (1995). Intensive brief inpatient treatment of Bulimia Nervosa. In K. D. Brownell & C. G. Fairburn (Eds.), *Eating disorders and obesity: A comprehensive handbook* (pp. 354–360). New York: Guilford Press.

van Praag, H. M. (1993). *"Make-believes" in psychiatry or the perils of progress.* New York: Brunner/Mazel.

Vandereycken, W. (1993). The Eating Disorder Evaluation Scale (EDES). *Eating Disorders, 1*, 115–122.

Vatz, R. E., & Weinberg, L. S. (1990). The conceptual bind in defining the volitional component of alcoholism: Consequences for public policy and scientific research. *Journal of Mind and Behavior, 11*, 531–544.

Viens, M. J., & Hranchuk, K. (1993). The treatment of Bulimia Nervosa following a surgery using a stimulus control procedure: A case study. *Journal of Behavior Therapy and Experimental Psychiatry, 23*, 313–317.

Vitousek, K., & Manke, F. (1994). Personality variables and disorders in Anorexia Nervosa and Bulimia Nervosa. *Journal of Abnormal Psychology, 103*, 137–147.

Vize, C. M. & Cooper, P. J. (1995). Sexual abuse in patients with eating disorders, patients with depression, and normal controls: A comparative study. *British Journal of Psychiatry, 167*, 80–85.

Wkeling, A. (1996). Epidemiology of Anorexia Nervosa. *Psychiatry Research, 62,* 3–9.

Walsh, B. T., Gladis, M., Roose, S. P., Stewart, J. W., Stetner, F., & Glassman, A. H. (1988). Phenelzine vs. placebo in 50 patients with bulimia. *Archives of General Psychiatry, 45*, 471–475.

Walsh, B. T., Stewart, J. W., Roose, S. P., Gladis, M., & Glassman, A. H. (1984). Treatment of bulimia with phenelzine: A double-blind placebo-controlled study. *Archives of General Psychiatry, 41*, 1105–1109.

Walsh, B. T., Stewart, J. W., Wright, L., Harrison, W., Roose, S. P., & Glassman, A. H. (1982). Treatment of bulimia with monoamine oxidase inhibitors. *American Journal of Psychiatry, 139*, 1629–1630.

Walsh, B. T., Wilson, G. T., Loeb, K. L., Devlin, M. J., Pike, K. M., Roose, S. P., Fleiss, J., & Waternaux, C. (1997). Medication and psychotherapy in the treatment of Bulimia Nervosa. *American Journal of Psychiatry, 154,* 523–531.

Webb, W. L., & Gehi, M. (1981). Electrolyte and fluid imbalance: Neuropsychiatric manifestations. *Psychosomatics, 22,* 199–202.

Weeks, G. R., & L'Abate, L. (1982). *Paradoxical psychotherapy: Theory and practice with individuals, couples, and families.* New York: Brunner/Mazel.

Weiss, T., & Levitz, L. (1976). Diphenylhydantoin treatment of bulimia [Letter to the editor]. *American Journal of Psychiatry, 133,* 1093.

Welch, S. L. & Fairburn, C. G. (1994). Sexual abuse and Bulimia Nervosa: Three integrated case control comparisons. *American Journal of Psychiatry, 151*, 402–407.

Weltzin, T. E., Fernstrom, M. H., & Kaye, W. H. (1994). Serotonin and Bulimia Nervosa. *Nutrition Reviews, 52,* 399–408.

Wermuth, B., Davis, K., Hollister, L., & Stunkard, A. (1977). Phenytoin treatment of the binge-eating syndrome. *American Journal of Psychiatry, 134,* 1249–1253.

White, W. C., & Boskind-White, M. (1981). An experiential–behavioral approach to the treatment of bulimarexia. *Psychotherapy: Theory, Research, and Practice, 18*, 501–597 .

Wilcox, J. A. (1990) Fluoxetine and bulimia. *Journal of Psychoactive Drugs, 22*, 81–82.

Wilfley, D. E., Agras, W. S., Telch, C. F., Rossiter, E. M., Schneider, J. A., Cole, A. G., Sifford, L., & Raeburn, S. D. (1993). Group CBT and group interpersonal psychotherapy for non-purging bulimics: A controlled comparison. *Journal of Consulting and Clinical Psychology, 61,* 296–305.

Wilfley, D. E., & Rodin, J. (1995). Cultural influences on eating disorders. In K. D. Brownell & C. G. Fairburn (Eds.), *Eating disorders and obesity: A comprehensive handbook* (pp. 78–82). New York: Guilford Press.

Willi, J., & Grossman, S. (1983). Epidemiology of Anorexia Nervosa in a defined region of Switzerland. *American Journal of Psychiatry, 140*, 564–567.

Williamson, D. A., Anderson, D. A., Jackman, L. P., & Jackson, S. R. (1995). Assessment of eating disordered thoughts, feelings, and behaviors. In D. B. Allison (Ed.), *Handbook of assessment methods for eating behaviors and weight-related problems* (pp. 347–374). Thousand Oaks, CA: Sage.

Williamson, D. A., Davis, C. J., Bennett, S. M., Goreczny, A. J., & Gleaves, D. H. (1989). Development of a simple procedure for assessing body image disturbances. *Behavioral Assessment, 11,* 433–446.

Williamson, D. A., Prather, R. C., Bennett, S. M., Davis, C. J., Watkins, P. C., & Grenier, C. E. (1989). An uncontrolled evaluation of inpatient and outpatient cognitive-behavior therapy for Bulimia Nervosa. *Behavior Modification, 13,* 340–360.

Wilson, G. T. (1991). The addiction model of eating disorders: A critical analysis. *Advances in Behaviour Research and Therapy, 13,* 27–72.

Wilson, G. T. (1995). Eating disorders and addictive disorders. In K. D. Brownell & C. G. Fairburn (Eds.), *Eating disorders and obesity: A comprehensive handbook* (pp. 165–170). New York: Guilford Press.

Wilson, G. T., Eldredge, K. L., Smith, D., & Niles, B. (1991). Cognitive-behavioral treatment with and without response prevention for bulimia. *Behaviour Research and Therapy, 29,* 575–583.

Wilson, G. T., & Fairburn, C. G. (1993). Cognitive treatments for eating disorders. *Journal of Consulting and Clinical Psychology, 61,* 261–269.

Wilson, G. T., Rossiter, E., Kleinfield, E. I., & Lindholm, L. (1986). Cognitive-behavioral treatment of Bulimia Nervosa: A controlled evaluation. *Behaviour Research and Therapy, 24,* 277–288.

Windauer, U., Lennerts, W., Talbot, P., Touyz, S. W., & Beumont, P. J. V. (1993). How well are 'cured' Anorexia Nervosa patients? An investigation of 16 weight-recovered anorexic patients. *British Journal of Psychiatry, 163,* 195–200.

Wonderlich, S. A. (1995). Personality and eating disorders. In K. D. Brownell & C. G. Fairburn (Eds.), *Eating disorders and obesity: A comprehensive handbook* (pp. 171–175). New York: Guilford Press.

Wonderlich, S. A., Brewerton, T. D., Jocic, Z., Dansky, B. S., & Abbott, D. W. (1997). Relationship of childhood sexual abuse and eating disorders. *Journal of the American Academy of Child and Adolescent Psychiatry, 36,* 1107–1115.

Wonderlich, S. A., Fullerton, D., Swift, W., & Klein, M. H. (1994). Five-year outcome from eating disorders: Relevance of personality disorders. *International Journal of Eating Disorders, 15,* 233–243.

Woodside, D. B. (1995) The review of Anorexia Nervosa and Bulimia Nervosa. *Current Problems in Pediatrics, 25,* 67–89.

Wooley, S. C. (1995). Feminist influences on the treatment of eating disorders. In K. D. Brownell & C. G. Fairburn (Eds.), *Eating disorders and obesity: A comprehensive handbook* (pp. 294–298), New York: Guilford Press.

Wooley, S. C., & Kearney-Cooke, A. (1986). Intensive treatment of bulimia and body-image disturbance. In K. D. Brownell & J. P. Foreyt (Eds.), *Handbook of eating disorders: Physiology, psychology, and treatment of obesity, anorexia, and bulimia* (pp. 476–502). New York: Basic Books.

Wooley, S. C., & Wooley, O. W. (1985). Intensive outpatient and residential treatment for bulimia. In D. M. Garner & P. E. Garfinkel (Eds.), *Handbook of psychotherapy for anorexia nervosa and bulimia* (pp. 391–430). New York: Guilford Press.

Wu, J. C., Hagman, J, Buchsbaum, M. S., Blinder, B., Derrfler, M., Tai, W. Y., Hazlett, E., & Sicotte, N. (1990). Greater left cerebral hemispheric metabolism in bulimia assessed by positron emission tomography. *American Journal of Psychiatry, 147,* 309–312.

Wurtman, R. J., & Wurtman, J. J. (1984). Nutrients, neurotransmitter synthesis, and the control of food intake. In A. J. Stunkard & E. Stellar (Eds.), *Eating and its disorders* (pp. 77–86). New York: Raven Press.

Yager, J. (1994). Psychosocial treatments for eating disorders. *Psychiatry, 57,* 153–164.

Yager, J. (1995). The management of patients with intractable eating disorders. In K. D. Brownell & C. G. Fairburn (Eds.), *Eating disorders and obesity: A comprehensive handbook* (pp. 374–378). New York: The Guilford Press.

CHAPTER 14

Adolescent Substance Use Problems

Mark G. Myers
Sandra A. Brown
University of California at San Diego
Veterans Affairs HealthCare System

Peter W. Vik
Idaho State University

OVERVIEW OF ADOLESCENT SUBSTANCE USE PROBLEMS

History

Adolescent use and misuse of psychoactive substances are not, despite recent attention to the issue, new phenomena. However, it was not until the early 1970s, with the growing prevalence of illicit drug use, that public attention focused on this issue. Prior to the 1970s, alcohol and tobacco were the psychoactive substances predominantly used by adolescents. The late 1960s and early 1970s saw increased acceptance by youths of various other drugs, most notably marijuana. With the increased acceptance and availability of psychoactive substances, the prevalence of experimental and problematic use of alcohol and drugs during adolescence likewise increased. Concern regarding youth substance use and misuse resulted in the implementation of school-based substance use prevention programs in the 1970s. The renewed focus on this issue was further reflected in the implementation by the National Institute on Drug Abuse of two surveys of youth alcohol and drug use: the National Household Survey on Drug Abuse, which began in 1971 and is repeated every 2 to 3 years; and the Monitoring the Future Study, an annual survey of high school students initiated in 1975. Recently published data from the Monitoring the Future Study (U.S. Department of Health and Human Services [DHHS], 1995) details trends in youth alcohol and drug use over the 20 years from 1975 to 1995. This annual survey demonstrates that within this time frame, prevalence of alcohol and drug use among high school seniors peaked in 1979 (88.1% and 54.2% annual prevalence for alcohol and illicit drug use, respectively), reached a low in 1992 (72.7% and 27.1% annual prevalence for alcohol and illicit drug use, respectively), and has been on the increase again since then. Similar recent increases have been observed in the use of alcohol, tobacco, and other drugs among 8th- and 10th-graders (U.S. DHHS, 1995). Further evidence on recent increases in youth substance involvement comes from the most recent annual Household Survey on Drug Abuse (Substance Abuse and Mental Health Services Administration, 1995), which demonstrates substantial increases since 1992. The 1995 survey reports that the incidence (i.e., number of new users) of drug use is rising among youths aged 12–17 years, with rates increasing from 38 per 1,000 person-years in 1991 to 74 per 1,000 person-years in 1994. The bulk of our current knowledge regarding the etiology and progression of substance use derives from information generated in the past two decades and forms the empirical basis for intervention design.

It was not until the late 1970s and early 1980s that adolescent-specific treatment of substance use problems emerged (e.g., Woltzen et al., 1986), based on prevalent adult models of alcoholism treatment (e.g., the Minnesota model; Laundergan, 1982). Until the 1980s the majority of adolescents were treated within adult treatment settings, with little attention provided to critical developmental issues and differences between adolescent and adult addiction (Beschner & Friedman, 1985). The 1980s saw a proliferation of adolescent treatment programs in response to the public perception of "epidemic" drug use by youths. With the introduction of adolescent-specific programs, more comprehensive models of treatment were implemented that included developmentally specific components, such as family therapy, school, and recreation (e.g., Obermeier & Henry, 1985). Despite improvements in attention to adolescent issues, adolescent treatment facilities have typically based their programs on the disease model of addiction—an approach developed primarily from work with adult alcoholics (Institute of Medicine, 1990). A disadvantage of this relatively unitary approach to addiction is that adolescent substance misusers represent a heterogeneous population with diverse problems and needs. Current approaches to adolescent substance use treatment also suffer from a paucity of knowledge regarding what constitutes effective treatment and the process whereby teens succeed or fail following treatment. The appropriateness of existing models of treatment for adolescent substance misuse has generally received little empirical attention, despite the large number of existing programs. In fact, with the exception of a growing body of research on family-based interventions, little treatment outcome research is available to guide the design of an optimal intervention for adolescent substance use problems.

Nature

At the simplest level, a "substance use problem" can be defined as a pathological involvement with alcohol and/or drugs (Bukstein & Kaminer, 1994). A description of the nature of such problems among adolescents rests largely on examination of the consequences of substance involvement on functioning across various life domains, and to a lesser extent reflects absolute levels of involvement with alcohol and other drugs (i.e., quantity and frequency of use). The results of youth substance involvement are most frequently expressed in deterioration in interpersonal relationships, increases in family conflict, declines in academic functioning, higher levels of negative affect (e.g., depression, anxiety), and involvement in various antisocial behaviors (theft, property destruction, truancy, etc.). The diverse nature of adolescent substance use is evident in the difficulties in ascertaining the direction of causality. For example, for some teens substance involvement may escalate in response to certain difficulties (e.g., negative affect, other psychiatric disorders, environmental stressors), ultimately exacerbating the original problem. Alternately, increased involvement with alcohol and other drug use by "normally" functioning youths may precipitate deterioration in psychosocial functioning (e.g., school problems, withdrawal and isolation, legal problems). For yet others, substance use is embedded within a matrix of deviant behaviors and attitudes—a phenomenon described as the "problem behavior" syndrome (Jessor & Jessor, 1977).

The context of adolescent alcohol and drug involvement must be carefully considered in describing the nature of this involvement. One such consideration involves ethnic and cultural background. Research consistently demonstrates that youth substance involvement diverges by ethnicity. In general, it appears that European American and Hispanic youths show the highest rates of alcohol and drug involvement, with African-American and Asian adolescents typically reporting the lowest rates (Bachman et al., 1991). Findings to date suggest that ethnic differences in vulnerability to substance involvement reflect variability in exposure to risk factors. For example, a study by Mahaddian, Bentler, and Newcomb (1988) examined the relationships between 10 risk factors and substance involvement among European American, Hispanic, African American, and Asian adolescents. These authors found that European American and Hispanic youths had similar levels of risk for substance involvement and were comparable in exposure to the risk factors. However, for European Americans youth low religious commitment and early alcohol use were the principal risk factors, while for Hispanics deviance was dominant. African American and Asian adolescents were found to evidence substantially lower exposure to risk factors predictive of substance involvement than were European American and Hispanic youth. For African Americans poor family relationships represented the single most important risk, while among Asians low religiosity, poor self-esteem, poor family relationships, and sensation seeking were important factors. A study examining early initiation of substance use by European American and African American fifth-graders (Catalano et al., 1993) found similar patterns, in that ethnic differences emerged on exposure to risk factors. The African American children exhibited more aggression and delinquency and reported more deviant siblings, whereas the European American children stated higher intentions to use substances and reported less parental use of family management strategies. Thus, it is apparent that ethnic and cultural differences play a role in the divergent trajectories of substance involvement observed for youths of different ethnicities. Although factors influencing the likelihood of substance misuse do not appear to vary substantially by ethnicity, ethnic differences are apparent in the extent of exposure to or presence of these risk factors.

Another particularly important contextual consideration is the observed increase in experimentation and involvement with substances during adolescence, which for some youths reflects "normative" behavior (e.g., Shedler & Block, 1990). Despite the concerns regarding youth substance involvement, there appears to be a discontinuity in school-based samples between substance use during adolescence and during adulthood, such that youth alcohol problems do not strongly predict adult Alcohol Dependence (e.g., Blane, 1976; Newcomb & Bentler, 1988). However, heavy drug use during adolescence has been found to be associated with a variety of negative consequences during early adulthood, including impaired social relationships and physical and psychological disturbances (Newcomb & Bentler, 1988). More recently, information has become available from longitudinal studies of clinical course following treatment for adolescent substance use problems. This research indicates that adolescents return to substance use following treatment at rates similar to those of adults (Brown, Myers, Mott, & Vik, 1994; Brown, Vik, & Creamer, 1989), and that these teens evidence continued difficulties with alcohol and drugs and display high rates of antisocial behaviors as they enter early adulthood (Brown, 1993; Stewart, 1994). Thus, available empirical evidence demonstrates significant differences in the nature of substance misuse for adolescents and adults.

Current Definitions

The assessment and treatment of adolescent substance use problems are compromised by problems of definition. The diagnosis of Substance Abuse and Dependence in adolescents still relies on criteria that were originally developed for adults and that provide no distinctions between adult and adolescent features of the disorders. Unfortunately, few studies have attempted to produce a valid definition of youth substance use problems, and little work has assessed the reliability and validity of existing classification systems as they apply to adolescents (Bukstein & Kaminer, 1994; Stewart & Brown, 1995). The *Diagnostic and Statistical Manual of Mental Disorders,* fourth edition (DSM-IV; American Psychiatric Association, 1994) defines psychoactive Substance Dependence as repeated use resulting in physiological dependence and compulsive substance-taking behavior. A DSM-IV diagnosis of Substance Dependence requires evidence of at least three of seven specified criteria within a 12-month period. The first two criteria reflect physical consequences from use—tolerance (continued use leading to lesser subjective effects from the same quantity of the substance) and withdrawal (unpleasant behavioral, physiological, and cognitive symptoms that occur as concentrations of the substance in the system diminish). The remaining five criteria focus on preoccupation with use, involvement in obtaining the substance, failure to control use, and impaired psychosocial functioning as a consequence of use.

In contrast to Substance Dependence, DSM-IV defines psychoactive Substance Abuse as a milder form of substance involvement that, though producing negative consequences, does not meet dependence criteria. Substance Abuse is defined as a pattern of maladaptive use resulting in clinically significant impairment or distress; the diagnosis requires that one of four symptoms be evident within a 12-month period. This diagnosis focuses on negative consequences of substance involvement, and does not include symptoms of physical dependence (i.e., tolerance and withdrawal).

Although DSM-III-R and DSM-IV criteria are often used with adolescents, several of the existing criteria are not appropriate for teens (Stewart & Brown, 1995; Martin, Kaczynski, Maisto, Bukstein, & Moss, 1995). For example, adolescent substance users typically do not exhibit the type of consequences that correspond with the extensive history of involvement commonly found for adults, such as medical complications and a progression of the disorder (Blum, 1987; Brown, Mott, & Stewart, 1992; Kaminer, 1991). Furthermore, adolescents seen in clinical settings are typically involved with multiple drugs, resulting in patterns of withdrawal and dependence symptoms that are more complex than those associated with the DSM-based diagnostic classification (Stewart & Brown, 1995). In particular, adolescents display fewer psychological withdrawal symptoms but more affective distress. Results of a recent study of DSM-IV Alcohol Abuse and Dependence symptoms and five exploratory domains of problems typical for adolescents (Martin et al., 1995) provided some support for the utility of the DSM-IV definition of Alcohol Dependence. The domains of blackouts, passing out, risky sexual behavior, craving, and declining school grades were found to be specific to a diagnosis of adolescent Alcohol Abuse. However, in the Stewart and Brown (1995) investigation, the presentations for tolerance, withdrawal, and medical problems were found to differ between adults and adolescents. This type of research highlights the need for teen-specific criteria and is essential to the development of valid definitions of adolescent Substance Abuse and Dependence.

Theoretical/Conceptual Formulation

The prevalent psychological conceptualization of addictive behaviors emerges from a biobehavioral perspective, which acknowledges the contribution of biological, psychological, and social factors to the emergence of alcohol and drug use problems (e.g., Donovan, 1988). Within this biobehavioral model, treatment is often conceptualized from a cognitive-behavioral perspective based on a social learning theory understanding of substance misuse (e.g., Marlatt & Gordon, 1985; Monti, Abrams, Kadden, & Cooney, 1989). Although a cognitive-behavioral perspective acknowledges the contributions of multiple domains to the emergence of alcohol and drug use problems, it centers on the influence of environmental forces and of learned beliefs and behaviors.

Modeling by family members, peers, and society is a critical influence in the emergence of alcohol and drug use behaviors. In particular, beliefs regarding the effects of substances evolve through observations of alcohol and drug use in the context of family, peers, and society/culture (Christiansen, Goldman, & Inn, 1982; Goldman, Brown, & Christiansen, 1987). Beliefs formed early in life regarding the effects of alcohol and drug use are important, in that they predict onset and escalation of substance involvement during adolescence (Christiansen, Roehling, Smith, & Goldman, 1989). Expectations that use of alcohol or other drugs will facilitate social interactions, provide relief from stress, promote acceptance within the peer group, or produce the positive feelings associated with being "high" appear to be involved in decisions regarding substance involvement (Goldman, Brown, Christiansen, & Smith, 1991). Adolescents at greater risk for developing substance use problems are typically those who have limited abilities for managing negative mood states, are unskilled in appropriate social interactions, have difficulties experiencing positive feelings without alcohol and drug use, and/or are ineffective in managing social pressures for substance involvement (e.g., Bentler, 1992; Pandina & Schuele, 1983). This perspective on the development of adolescent substance misuse is consistent with recently developed skills-based approaches to substance use treatment (e.g., Monti et al., 1989). The cognitive-behavioral conceptualization of adolescent substance use problems implies that effective treatment for such problems must include skills for managing and changing the circumstances associated with substance use, and must provide sources of reinforcement that can serve as alternatives to alcohol and drug use.

Etiologies

Various risk factors have been identified that precede, and increase the likelihood of developing substance use problems. These risk factors have been variously described, but can be conceptualized broadly as intrapersonal and environmental/contextual. At the intrapersonal level, risk factors include biological liability (family history of substance misuse), individual temperament and psychopathology, and personal attitudes and beliefs regarding substance use.

Extensive research demonstrates that children who have parents with alcohol or drug problems are at increased risk of substance misuse, emotional difficulties, and other problem behaviors (Bennett, Wolin, & Reiss, 1988; Chassin, Rogosch, & Barrera, 1991; Knop, Teasdale, Schulsinger, & Goodwin, 1985; Moos & Billings, 1982; Russell, 1990). Children with an alcohol-misusing parent are found to have poorer emotional, behavioral, and cognitive functioning than children of nonalcoholics (e.g., Tarter & Edwards, 1988). In addition, offspring of alcoholics evidence more academic difficulties, more impulsive and problematic behavior, and more depression and anxiety than children of nonalcoholics. Estimates from studies of the heritability of alcoholism find a four- to sixfold increase in substance use problems among the male offspring of an alcoholic parent. The increased liability for alcoholism among female children of an alcoholic is approximately twice that for females from nonalcoholic families. The literature on genetic factors in alcoholism has been criticized on methodological and conceptual grounds (Searles, 1988); nonetheless, it seems reasonable to conclude that genetic factors exert an influence on risk for alcoholism (McGue, 1994). It is important to note that the bulk of research in this area has focused on male sons of alcoholic fathers, and thus that our knowledge of genetic and biological contributions to alcoholism among females is currently limited. Likewise, the majority of studies have explored alcoholism, and far less is known regarding the genetic and biological factors underlying increased vulnerability to misuse of drugs other than alcohol.

Various temperamental factors, which are presumed to be largely inherited (Tarter & Edwards, 1988), have been found to be predictive of substance use problems. Most notably, poor impulse control and sensation-seeking tendencies have been associated with greater substance involvement (Cloninger, 1987; Shedler & Block, 1990). In addition, externalizing disorders (e.g., Conduct Disorder) are associated with greater lifetime risk for Substance Dependence (Robins & Price, 1991; Vaillant, 1983). These observations suggest that the concordance between various undercontrolled behaviors is partly explained by common genetic influences (McGue, 1994).

Within the domain of environmental influences, nonbiological familial factors play a role in the development of adolescent substance use and misuse. Alcohol- and/or drug-misusing parents model substance use behaviors that play a role in forming children's beliefs and attitudes concerning the anticipated effects of substance use (i.e., expectancies). Significantly, adolescents with an alcohol-misusing parent are found to anticipate more reinforcement from alcohol than do those with no parental alcohol misuse (Brown, Creamer, & Stetson, 1987). This latter point is particularly relevant, since children who hold heightened expectancies for the positive effects of drinking (e.g., for managing negative emotions or facilitating social interactions) are at greater risk for later developing alcohol-related problems (Smith & Goldman, 1994). In addition, parental substance misuse often increases the availability and accessibility of alcohol and drugs for children.

Family factors other than parental substance misuse are found to influence the likelihood of adolescent substance misuse. Parenting style has been found to be related to adolescent substance use problems. For example, parental hostility and lack of warmth have been found to be related to both problematic alcohol use (Johnson & Pandina, 1991) and drug use (Shedler & Block, 1990). Similarly, greater parental support and control have been found to predict lower adolescent alcohol use (Stice, Barrera, & Chassin, 1993). Adolescent alcohol use is also found to increase with greater familial stress and conflict (e.g., Baer, Garmezy, McLaughlin, Pokorny, & Wernnick, 1987; Brown, 1989) and reduced parental monitoring. In sum, parental substance misuse and characteristics of family interactions are found to influence the development of adolescent substance use problems.

Peer relations play an important role in the initiation and progression of adolescent substance use (Bates & Labouvie, 1995; Newcomb & Bentler, 1988; Wagner, 1993). Modeling of substance use within the peer group can create social pressure to engage in these behaviors, and peers then provide reinforcement for conformity. Peer relations may also influence adolescent substance involvement by creating stress and modeling or reinforcing maladaptive coping efforts (Richter, Brown, & Mott, 1991). Difficult interactions with peers may create social anxiety, perceived pressure to drink, and increased interpersonal conflict (e.g., Hundleby & Mercer, 1987). These in turn may enhance the appeal of substance use, particularly for teens who hold expectations that alcohol or drug use will provide relief from social stress or reduce social tension by providing a common behavioral activity. Peer influences probably combine with family factors to determine adolescent substance use (Barnes, 1990). For example, affiliation with deviant peers who model substance use and other deviant behaviors may be more likely for teens whose parents are themselves substance misusers or are less involved in monitoring their children (Patterson, DeBaryshe, & Ramsey, 1989). In general, adolescents invested in relationships with peers who engage in drinking and deviant behavior are found themselves to have increased rates of problem behaviors (Barnes, Farrell, & Banerjee, 1994).

The complexity of etiological pathways to substance misuse is highlighted by the role of familial influences. For example, parental alcoholism may increase the risk for adolescent substance involvement through biological differences in sensitivity to the pharmacological properties of drugs, and/or through environmental influences such as modeling of substance use behaviors and increased availability of alcohol and/or other substances (Sher, 1994). At this time, it is not known which particular risk factors or combinations of factors are most predictive of adolescent drug use. Understanding of the relations between these risk factors and substance use problems is further complicated in that many of the same factors also predict other adolescent problem behaviors, such as delinquent or antisocial behaviors (e.g., Loeber, 1990; Patterson et al., 1989).

Recent conceptual models that incorporate multiple sources of risk have been proposed to enhance efforts to explain the etiology of adolescent alcohol and drug involvement (e.g., Chassin, Pillow, Curran, Molina, & Barrera, 1993; Oetting, Edwards, & Beauvais, 1989; Roosa, Sandler, Gehring, Beals, & Cappo, 1988; Sher, 1994). For example, Chassin and her colleagues (Chassin et al., 1993; Colder & Chassin, 1993) have described a pathway to teen substance use involving negative affect. In this model, children from alcoholic families were found to experience higher levels of negative affect related to increased stress and temperamental emotionality. The relation between negative affect and substance use is in turn influenced by peer use. Other investigators have provided ad-

ditional support for the influence of negative affect, mediated by peer influences, on pathological substance involvement (Oetting et al., 1989; Roosa et al., 1988). This type of model provides an example of the interplay between biological and environmental influences in the development of substance use problems, and highlights the complexities inherent in this process.

ASSESSMENT

Basic Considerations

Assessment of adolescent substance use problems is best conceptualized from a perspective that considers the interactions among the biological, psychological, and social factors influencing the clinical presentation (Donovan & Marlatt, 1988; Vik, Brown, & Myers, 1997). Consideration of the multiple influences on the development and progression of substance misuse is essential to successful treatment outcome (Brown, 1993). Thus, in the course of assessment, each of the following areas should be evaluated: (1) substance involvement characteristics (e.g., use, context, consequences); (2) intrapersonal factors (e.g., coping/social skills, comorbid psychopathology, antisocial tendencies); (3) environmental factors (e.g., family functioning, social support, cultural influences, life stress, peer substance use); and (4) functioning in major life domains (e.g., academics, interpersonal relations, extracurricular activities/hobbies) (Tapert, Stewart, & Brown, in press; Tarter, Ott, & Mezzich, 1991).

A biobehavioral perspective on adolescent substance misuse also emphasizes the value of a broad-spectrum assessment (Donovan, 1988). To the extent possible, information should incorporate adolescent self-reports (e.g., clinical interview, self-administered structured questionnaires, and self-monitoring), reports from significant others (e.g., parents, teachers), and objective measures (e.g., neuropsychological/academic functioning, toxicology screens). Although an ideal assessment includes all possible sources of data, the reality of clinical practice often dictates that reports from the adolescent and family members are the only sources of information.

The assessment process is guided by the ultimate purposes for which this information will be used. A multilevel or sequential approach is typically recommended, which includes initial screening, determining diagnosis, identifying problems and deficits in the domains of psychosocial functioning affected by substance use, and determining the appropriate level and intensity of intervention. In cases where available information clearly indicates problematic substance involvement (e.g., previous history of treatment, drug-related arrests), screening becomes less important, and the clinician can proceed with a broader-based assessment to identify problem domains. A thorough substance use assessment also serves the important dual purposes of (1) providing baseline information, which can be used for assessing progress during the course of treatment; and (2) enhancing motivation for entering treatment and adhering to the selected intervention strategy (Miller & Rollnick, 1991).

As with other adolescent problems, substance misuse is embedded within the developmental context of adolescence. Developmental changes during adolescence are accompanied by normative increases in negative affect, substance use, and other problem behaviors. The biological changes accompanying puberty may often precipitate behavioral and emotional changes that are difficult to separate from the effects of alcohol and drug use (Brown, Mott, & Myers, 1990). Thus, the developmental tasks of adolescence and the stage of development of the individual adolescent are critical factors to consider in developing an accurate clinical picture.

Further complicating assessment is the heterogeneous nature of adolescent substance use problems (Farrell & Strang, 1991). Substance-misusing youths vary in the types of substances used, the frequency with which use occurs, the beliefs regarding the effects and consequences from use, the motivations underlying use, and the nature of factors that precipitate and accompany use (Henly & Winters, 1989). Thus, clinicians involved in the treatment of adolescent substance use problems must be aware that multiple factors influence the development of such problems, and that flexibility is needed in determining the optimal intervention strategy. This latter point is consistent with evidence that multiple pathways exist for the successful resolution of adolescent substance misuse (Brown, 1993).

Instruments for Assessment of Substance Misuse

Until recently, few well-validated standardized measures of adolescent substance involvement were available. As a consequence, clinicians have often relied on their own judgments or utilized measures developed "inhouse" (Owen &

Nyberg, 1983). With the recent introduction of psychometrically validated instruments, standardized assessment has become more feasible and is strongly recommended. Employment of standardized assessment procedures offers various advantages, such as providing a basis for comparing and validating clinical decisions, and protecting against the introduction of rater bias (Henly & Winters, 1989). Standardized assessments have the additional advantage of providing a time-efficient means for gathering large quantities of information. Data gathered from standardized instruments can help inform the clinical interview, during which the clinician can clarify previously obtained information and can verify the accuracy of responses. Although direct observation of adolescent substance use behavior is unrealistic, observation and rating of in-session behavior can provide valuable information. Finally, information regarding intellectual and academic functioning is particularly useful. Since neuropsychological deficits and learning disabilities are often observed among adolescents with substance use problems, this information is essential to selecting appropriate intervention strategies and determining the need for educational compensation or remediation.

Table 14.1 lists several standardized instruments for assessing adolescent substance misuse. In cases where a screening measure is needed, the Personal Experience Screening Questionnaire (PESQ; Winters, 1991) is recommended for its theoretical and psychometric strengths. This measure is quite brief, includes response bias scales that indicate invalid responding, and provides cutoffs and normative values for determining problem severity. At this time, the normative sample for the PESQ contains few minority subjects, and thus results from minority respondents must be interpreted with caution.

Several multidimensional assessment instruments are currently available. These provide information on a variety of domains of functioning consistent with a biobehavioral conceptualization of adolescent substance misuse. The Personal Experience Inventory (PEI; Winters & Henly, 1989a) is a recently developed and well-validated self-report measure. The PEI consists of several subscales assessing problem severity, drug and alcohol use history, and psychosocial adjustment. Another multidimensional measure, the Drug Use Screening Inventory (DUSI; Tarter, 1990), assesses substance use involvement and severity of impairment for nine domains of functioning (e.g., school adjustment, social skills, family functioning). The DUSI is

TABLE 14.1. Measures of Adolescent Alcohol and Other Drug Involvement

Measure	Description
	Screening measures
The Adolescent Drinking Inventory: Drinking and You (Harrell & Wirtz, 1989)	A 24-item questionnaire designed for use by clinicians without specialized training in substance use assessment. Utilizes a multidimensional conceptualization of adolescent drinking and has been shown to possess good psychometric properties.
The Rutgers Alcohol Problem Index (RAPI; White & Labouvie, 1989)	A 23-item measure assessing drinking-related problems. The RAPI includes DSM-III-R criteria required for a diagnosis of Alcohol Abuse. Initial work supports validity, however, further work is needed to establish psychometric properties.
The Drug and Alcohol Problem Quick Screen (Schwartz & Wirtz, 1990)	A 30-item scale designed to detect adolescent substance misuse, from which a 14-item short form has also been developed. Intended for use in primary care settings; however, this measure has not been independently validated, and data have not been published on clinical samples.
The Personal Experience Screening Questionnaire (PESQ; Winters, 1991)	A 40-item questionnaire designed to identify adolescents in need of a drug use assessment referral. The PESQ includes a problem severity scale, two response distortion scales, and a supplemental information section on substance use and psychosocial functioning history. The PESQ has demonstrated excellent psychometric properties with both nonclinical and clinical populations.
	Multidimensional measures
The Personal Experience Inventory (PEI; Winters & Henly, 1989a)	A self-administered interview that includes 276 items divided into 5 sets of scales: basic scales (i.e., substance involvement), clinical scales, validity scales, personal adjustment scales, and family and peer environment scales. The PEI is intended to provide information for identifying problems, planning treatment, and evaluating outcome. This measure has been comprehensively and rigorously evaluated and has been shown to have adequate reliability and validity.
The Drug Use Severity Inventory (DUSI; Tarter, 1990)	A 149-item self-administered questionnaire that profiles substance use involvement in conjunction with the severity of disturbance in nine spheres of everyday functioning. The DUSI yields a needs assessment and diagnostic summary intended to inform treatment planning. Available work shows that the DUSI possesses adequate psychometric properties.
The Customary Drinking and Drug Use Record (CDDR; Brown, Creamer, & Stetson, 1987)	A structured interview with 143 items, the CDDR gathers information as to ages at onset of use; frequency of cigarette, alcohol, and drug use; alcohol and drug withdrawal; DSM-III-R Psychoactive Substance Dependence symptoms (excluding nicotine); and life problems related to alcohol and drug use. The lifetime version of the CDDR obtains lifetime information regarding use of alcohol and other drugs. This structured clinical interview has good reliability and validity for clinical samples of teen substance abusers (Stewart & Brown, 1995; Brown et al., in press).
The Structured Clinical Interview for Adolescents (SCI; Brown, Vik, & Creamer, 1989)	A structured interview that is designed to provide demographic and background information that can inform both research and clinical decision making. The SCI elicits information regarding academic, interpersonal, and psychosocial functioning, including previous treatment for alcohol or other mental health problems, peer substance involvement, motivation for entering treatment, and motivation and efficacy for reducing substance use. In addition, it includes a comprehensive assessment of familial history of alcohol and drug misuse. Several studies suggest that the SCI is valid; however, it has not yet been subjected to extensive psychometric assessment.

(continued)

TABLE 14.1. (*continued*)

Measure	Description
The Teen Addiction Severity Index (T-ASI; Kaminer, Bukstein, & Tarter, 1991; Kaminer, Wagner, Plummer, & Seifer, 1993)	An adaptation of the Addiction Severity Index (McLellan et al., 1980). This semistructured interview yields 7 measures: substance involvement, academic functioning, employment status, family relationships, peer/social status, legal status, and psychiatric disturbance. Limited data suggest adequate reliability for the T-ASI.
Adolescent Diagnostic Interview (ADI; Winters & Henly, 1989b)	A comprehensive structured interview designed to yield DSM-III-R diagnoses for Psychoactive Substance Abuse. In addition to substance use diagnoses, the ADI provides a global rating of functioning, an assessment of severity of psychosocial stressors, and a rating of cognitive functioning. The ADI is thus designed to provide detailed diagnostic information relevant to treatment planning for substance misusing youths. Validity of diagnosis has been demonstrated for white adolescents.

unique in that it is designed to facilitate the application of assessment findings to treatment planning by providing a needs assessment, domain severity scores, and a diagnostic summary. Recent reports have supported the validity and reliability of the DUSI (Kirisci, Mezzich, & Tarter, 1995; Kirisci, Tarter, & Hsu, 1994). Also available is a semistructured interview measure, the Teen Addiction Severity Index (T-ASI; Kaminer, Bukstein, & Tarter, 1991; Kaminer, Wagner, Plummer, & Seifer, 1993), which is an adolescent-specific version of the widely used Addiction Severity Index (McLellan, Luborsky, O'Brien, & Woody, 1980). The T-ASI assesses seven domains of functioning, including substance use; school, employment, family, peer/social, and legal status; and psychiatric disturbance. Although limited at this time, available information suggests that the T-ASI possesses adequate psychometric properties (Kaminer et al., 1991, 1993). Another adolescent version of the Addiction Severity Index has also recently been developed by creators of the original instrument (the Comprehensive Addiction Severity Index for Adolescents; Meyers, McLellan, Jaeger, & Pettinati, 1995). This measure assesses risk factors, symptomatology, and consequences of substance involvement across seven primary areas of functioning: academics, alcohol/drug use, family relationships, peer relationships, legal issues, psychiatric difficulties, and recreation. Initial examination of the reliability and validity of this measure has provided preliminary evidence for its psychometric utility (Meyers et al., 1995).

Finally, the Structured Clinical Interview (SCI; Brown, Creamer, & Stetson, 1987; Brown et al., 1989), which assesses adolescent functioning in major life domains in relation to adolescent substance involvement, is typically used in conjunction with the Customary Drinking and Drug Use Record (CDDR; Brown et al., in press). The latter is a psychometrically sound instrument allowing detailed evaluation of involvement with alcohol and various drug types, as well as withdrawal/dependence and consequences of substance involvement.

In addition to measures that provide an indication of the severity of substance use and its consequences, a few instruments have been developed to evaluate specific features of adolescent substance use involvement. For example, the Inventory of Drug Taking Situations (IDTS; Annis & Martin, 1985) is a 50-item self-report questionnaire that evaluates the frequency of use in various situations. The IDTS includes situations in eight domains, including conflict, social pressure, pleasant social situations, positive and negative emotions, physical discomfort, testing personal control, and urges. The questionnaire is scored to provide a profile of use across the eight areas, and as such allows identification of settings or circumstances associated with frequent substance use, which can then be targeted in the course of treatment. Another useful measure is the Adolescent version of the Alcohol Expectancy Questionnaire (AEQ-A; Christiansen & Goldman, 1983). This self-administered questionnaire measures individual beliefs regarding the anticipated effects of alcohol in seven domains (global positive changes, social and physical pleasure, cognitive and motor enhancement, sexual enhancement, cognitive and behavioral deterioration, arousal, and relaxation/tension reduction). Several studies support the concurrent and predictive validity of the AEQ (see Brown, Christiansen, & Goldman, 1987), which can assist in identifying domains of reinforcement from alcohol that are of particular importance to the adolescent. This information can be used for targeting areas for which alternative means of reinforcement must be developed, and for selecting interventions designed to modify or alter alcohol-related beliefs (Brown, 1993; Smith & Goldman, 1994).

Instruments for Assessment of Domains Related to Substance Misuse

Additional measures can be used to provide supplemental information relevant to the various domains influenced by and/or contributing to adolescent substance misuse. A particularly useful measure is the Child Behavior Checklist (CBCL; Achenbach, 1991a), a parent self-report instrument that assesses a variety of behavior problems and social competence. The CBCL includes three Social Competence scales and nine Behavior Problem scales (including Hyperactivity, Hostility/Withdrawal, and Aggression), and has been extensively investigated with adolescent normative data available for a variety of clinical populations. Two additional measures related to the CBCL are the Teacher's Report Form (TRF; Achenbach, 1991b) and the Youth Self-Report (YSR; Achenbach, 1991c). As its name suggests, the TRF is designed to be completed by teachers, and elicits information regarding academic performance, adaptive functioning, and behavioral and emotional problems. The majority of the TRF items assessing emotional and behavioral problems (93 out of the total 118 items) are identical to those on the CBCL, thus allowing for comparison of these behaviors in different settings. Finally, the YSR is a self-report form that similarly assesses adolescent social competence and behavioral and emotional problems. The YSR items overlap substantially with the CBCL and TRF, except that items are worded in the first person. The similarity of items across these three measures allows for comparison across sources of information, thus alerting the clinician to the convergence and divergence of perceived problems between the adolescent and adults. The multiple sources of information can be particularly useful to the clinician in determining the degree to which an adolescent is likely to be open to intervention for particular problem areas. In addition, information from the CBCL and/or the related measures can be utilized to identify areas for intervention and is especially well suited for assessing progress and treatment outcome. Another recent measure of adolescent behavioral functioning is the Behavioral Assessment System for Children (Reynolds & Kamphaus, 1994). This scale has satisfactory psychometric properties for use with adolescents and includes a normative reference sample for interpreting scores.

A formal diagnostic assessment for the presence of additional psychiatric conditions is recommended because of the high rates of comorbid psychopathology found among substance-misusing youths. This assessment can be conducted in the course of the clinical interview or can rest on information from one of several available structured clinical interviews based on DSM criteria, such as the Diagnostic Interview Schedule for Children version (DISC; Costello, Edelbrock, Dulcan, Kalas, & Klaric, 1987) and the Schedule for Affective Disorders and Schizophrenia for School-Age Children (K-SADS; Puig-Antich & Orvaschel, 1987).

Finally, the issue of tobacco use is one that is often overlooked in the course of substance use treatment, yet represents a significant problem among substance-misusing youths. Cigarette smoking is strongly correlated with alcohol and drug use for adolescents (e.g., Fleming, Leventhal, Glynn, & Ershler, 1989). In fact, examinations of clinical samples of teen substance misusers reveal rates of smoking three to four times higher than those found in the general adolescent population (Myers & Brown, 1994). Of particular concern is evidence that cigarette smoking persists following teen substance use treatment regardless of alcohol or drug use outcome, and that smoking-related health problems are already evident in late adolescence. The extent of risk from smoking by substance misusers is highlighted by recent data that found tobacco use to be the leading cause of death among adults treated for alcoholism (Hurt et al., 1996). A potential consequence of the failure to address nicotine use in the context of substance misuse treatment is that this may inadvertently serve to reinforce tobacco use. Adolescents may perceive this as tacit approval of tobacco use. Importantly, addressing the use of nicotine along with use of alcohol and other drugs during treatment will provide a more consistent message to adolescents regarding addiction. Furthermore, there is probably a substantial overlap in the types of skills and behaviors needed for abstinence from cigarettes, alcohol, and other drugs (e.g., skills for managing temptations, refusal skills, coping in situations with high risk for relapse). As such, it is important to assess the history and extent of cigarette involvement and to explore motivation for smoking cessation by adolescents presenting for substance use treatment. Unfortunately, information about cigarette smoking is not elicited on many of the existing standardized measures of adolescent substance use (e.g., the PEI, the PESQ), with the exception of the CDDR; as such, it often needs to be evaluated separately. However, tobacco use can be assessed very simply by asking about age at first use of cigarettes and other tobacco products (e.g., chewing tobacco), age when the teen began using tobacco regularly (e.g., onset of weekly use), and the current pattern of tobacco use (e.g., how many days per week in the past month, how many times cigarettes or other tobacco products are used per day, and most recent use of tobacco products). Although no empirically supported interventions have yet been shown to be efficacious for adolescent smoking cessation, strategies found helpful for adults may well be useful for adolescents. A recent review and summary recommendations on treatment of smoking cessation finds that providing support for cessation, engaging in problem solving centered around difficulties in maintaining abstinence (i.e., relapse prevention), and encouraging the use of nicotine replacement products are key elements for intervention (U.S. DHHS, 1996). In the case of adolescents, particular attention must be given to peer issues and parental influences in relation to smoking. At this time it is premature to recommend that adolescents be required to abstain from tobacco products in the course of treatment for substance misuse. However, it is important that this issue be addressed and that adolescents receive a clear message that tobacco use is discouraged.

Formulating Treatment Recommendations

Prior to the presenting of treatment recommendations, results from the assessment should be carefully organized. The case formulation rests on detailing the function served by substance use for the individual adolescent, identifying areas for intervention, establishing goals for treatment, and outlining an intervention plan. It is important to conceptualize the data in a manner that permits identification of the factors promoting and maintaining substance use, anticipates obstacles to behavior change, and identifies strengths (personal, familial, environmental) that will facilitate behavior change and maintenance of gains. The case formulation should include detailed feedback to the teen, a list of identified problems, evaluation of motivation for behavior change, the contexts within which use frequently occurs, and available resources for maintaining behavior change.

Case formulation begins with generating feedback on the teen's substance involvement relative to normative samples, and providing a comprehensive problem list that outlines the relationship of substance use to presenting problems and symptoms. A critical issue in determining an appropriate intervention approach is evaluating the presence of concomitant psychopathology. Information from the assessment must be adequate to permit the clinician to determine the presence of conditions other than substance misuse; to evaluate the course of such problems; and to estimate the degree to which they precede, are independent of, or follow from the substance misuse. The nature of the relationship between substance use problems and other psychopathology is often difficult to determine (Brown, Inaba, et al., 1994). However, a condition that predates the onset of substance use or for which symptoms exist during periods of abstinence provides evidence for an independent disorder. Because substance effects can mimic or produce symptoms consistent with other psychiatric problems, the clinician should exercise caution in inferring the presence of a comorbid condition if such symptoms are assessed while the adolescent is still involved in substance use or is in the early stages of withdrawal (approximately the initial 3 weeks of abstinence; Brown & Schuckit, 1988).

Next, the adolescent's motivation for changing substance use patterns and related behaviors must be evaluated. Recent conceptualizations of the process of addictive behavior change (e.g., Prochaska, DiClemente, & Norcross, 1992) highlight the importance of matching interventions to an individual's readiness to undertake a program of change (e.g., Hester & Miller, 1988; Miller & Rollnick, 1991). Consideration of motivation for change is essential to developing short-term treatment goals that will be accepted and adhered to by the adolescent.

The provision of feedback from the assessment to the adolescent and his or her family, and the manner in which the feedback is delivered, are important to eliciting compliance with treatment recommendations. Miller and Rollnick (1991) describe an approach that emphasizes the value of personalized feedback for persuading clients of the necessity for behavior change. The following suggestions are often helpful in insuring the effective communication of assessment findings and treatment recommendations. The clinician should (1) provide a complete description of assessment findings, delivered in a manner that assures comprehension by the adolescent and his or her family; (2) avoid confrontational approaches, as these tend to increase resistance; (3) attend to and reflect everyone's reactions to assessment information; (4) be open to feedback from the adolescent and family; (5) anticipate possible strong emotional reactions; and (6) carefully summarize the feedback session and then solicit input from the adolescent and family.

TREATMENT

Overview

Limited empirical evidence is available to recommend a particular intervention approach for adolescent substance misusers. Because of the complex clinical presentation that typically accompanies substance use problems in youths, treatment programs typically incorporate multiple components designed to address the various affected domains of functioning. Intervention thus must be designed to address the specific problems identified for each adolescent. The heterogeneity of adolescent substance use and variability in developmental stages preclude prescribing a "one size fits all" approach; instead, a client–treatment matching strategy is important. The current status of the field and the nature of adolescent substance use problems dictate a flexible approach to treatment that can be adapted to meet the particular needs and developmental stage of each client. To this end, we subscribe to a cognitive-behavioral skills training intervention as the core of treatment for adolescent substance misuse. This approach is designed to be flexible, and as such can be employed as the sole intervention or can be incorporated within a multicomponent treatment program (e.g., family, etc.). The intervention outlined below focuses on deficits commonly associated with adolescent substance misuse, and is based on a body of research that identifies predictors and correlates of successful outcome following treatment for adolescent substance use

problems. The intervention is described here as an individual-focused intervention; however these techniques are readily translated into a group format.

Empirical Evidence for Treatment Efficacy

As previously noted, adolescent substance use treatment programs have evolved from models designed for the treatment of adult addictions. Current programs generally advertise a broad range of therapeutic components and incorporate age-appropriate components to address school, peer, family, and other issues. These programs are usually based on a medical/disease model of addiction that emerged from the field of adult alcoholism, and little empirical evidence exists for this model's efficacy when applied to adolescents (Brown, Mott, & Myers, 1990; Rahdert, 1988). Initial studies of treatment outcome for substance-misusing youths were primarily descriptive and examined large data bases gathered in the 1970s (Hubbard, Cavanaugh, Graddock, & Rachel, 1983; Rush, 1979; Sells & Simpson, 1979). Some of this information was based on older adolescent participants in adult treatment programs, thus limiting its relevance to current adolescent-specific programs. Furthermore, the data selected for examination were generally designed to evaluate adult treatment and thus may not have included variables relevant to adolescent outcome. Overall, these treatment programs appeared to reduce hard drug use among teens, but had a more limited impact on levels of alcohol and marijuana use. The descriptive nature of the data, the absence of comparison or control groups, and limited information regarding specific treatment components do not allow any conclusions to be drawn regarding the efficacy of specific intervention approaches.

More recently, a few studies have been published that provide evidence for effective approaches to the treatment of adolescent substance misuse; the majority of these are family-based interventions. Family approaches have received increased attention in recent years because of consistent evidence for the role of the family factors in adolescent substance use (for a review, see Denton & Kampfe, 1994). In particular, multicomponent family approaches that are specifically designed for treating adolescent substance misuse and that incorporate components focused on domains beyond the family system (i.e., integrative approaches) are found to be effective in reducing adolescent substance use and problem behaviors (for a review, see Liddle & Dakof, 1995). These integrative approaches incorporate traditional family systems therapy, focused on identifying and changing the interactional patterns within the family that serve to maintain substance use behaviors. Integrative family therapy approaches also draw on other psychotherapeutic techniques to address adolescent peer relationships, school functioning, and legal issues.

For example, Szapocznik and his colleagues (Szapocznik, Kurtines, Foote, Perez-Vidal, & Hervis, 1983, 1986) have published several reports examining the efficacy of a brief strategic family therapy approach, which focuses on interactional patterns within the family system and between the family and the environment. These researchers have demonstrated that this approach is effective with Hispanic participants in engaging families in therapy (Szapocznik et al., 1988); it is also effective in reducing adolescent substance involvement and improving family relations, when either the family (conjoint family therapy) or only the adolescent ("one-person family therapy") is seen in treatment (Szapocznik et al., 1983, 1986). Another pioneering approach to family therapy for adolescent substance use is multidimensional family therapy, developed by Liddle et al. (1992). This approach diverges from traditional family therapies, in that it is a research-based approach specialized to address adolescent substance use and conduct problems; it places more emphasis on the individual, and it focuses on intrapersonal and extrafamilial factors, in addition to family system factors, in treating substance use problems (Liddle et al., 1992). As evidence for efficacy of this approach, adolescents receiving multidimensional family therapy showed greater reductions in drug use at the end of treatment and at a 1-year follow-up than participants in comparison interventions did (Liddle & Dakof, 1992). Other integrative family approaches for which initial findings support efficacy include family systems therapy (Joanning, Quinn, Thomas, & Mullen, 1992), brief family therapy (Lewis, Piercy, Sprenkle, & Trepper, 1990) and multisystemic therapy (Henggeler et al., 1991).

Collectively, these studies suffer from various methodological shortcomings, and cannot at this time be interpreted as firm evidence for the superiority of family-based approaches over other forms of intervention. One of the few studies to examine a behavioral treatment intervention

found better outcomes in terms of substance use, family relations, and emotional and behavior problems, compared with a supportive counseling program (Azrin, Donohue, Besalel, Kogan, & Acierno, 1994). The core components of this behavioral program included stimulus control, urge control, and contracting. Although promising, this initial study is based on a small sample size and thus requires replication with a larger, independent sample before any firm conclusions can be drawn regarding its' efficacy.

In the absence of any clear evidence regarding optimal approaches to adolescent substance use treatment, interventions must be based on the following: sensitivity to adolescent development issues, incorporation of the relevant research literature (e.g., risk factors, predictors of clinical course), a comprehensive conceptualization of adolescent substance use, and a focus on problem behaviors associated with substance use (Liddle & Dakof, 1995).

Empirical Evidence for Predictors and Correlates of Clinical Course

The choice of a cognitive-behavioral intervention for adolescent substance use rests largely on available evidence from studies investigating clinical samples of adolescents treated for substance use problems. In the realm of family factors, poorer treatment outcome is found to be related with greater lifetime exposure to familial substance misuse, less expressiveness by family members, and lower family support as perceived by the adolescent (Brown et al., 1990). In the broader domain of social resources, more satisfaction with social supports and a greater proportion of nonusers in an adolescent's social network were significantly related to less alcohol and drug use following treatment (Richter et al., 1991; Vik, Grizzle, & Brown, 1992). Personal characteristics such as lower self-esteem and more delinquent-type behaviors have also been associated with poorer treatment outcome (Brown, Gleghorn, Schuckit, Myers, & Mott, 1996; Myers, Brown, & Mott, 1995; Richter et al., 1991). Persistence in some type of formal treatment is associated with better outcome for both adolescents (Vik & Brown, 1994) and adults (e.g., Project MATCH Research Group, 1997). Also, an investigation of a subsample of these adolescents found that, along with coping skills, parental socioeconomic status and alcohol effect expectancies assessed during treatment significantly predicted alcohol and drug consumption 6 months after treatment (Myers,

Brown, & Mott, 1993). Finally, we have examined in some detail the role of behaviors and cognitions related to coping with situations presenting temptations for substance use (Myers & Brown, 1990a, 1990b, 1996; Myers et al., 1993). These investigations suggest that strategies for managing situations involving social pressure to use and awareness of negative consequences from substance use predict better treatment outcome for teen substance misusers. Viewed in concert, our studies suggest that strategies targeted at improving personal resources (e.g., improving coping skills, increasing social support, maintaining involvement in treatment, and reducing environmental risk) facilitate long-term success for adolescents with alcohol and other drug problems. Specifically, studies of coping with relapse risk suggest that behavioral strategies specific to managing substance use temptations and awareness of the negative consequences of alcohol and drug use are important aspects of successful outcome for adolescent substance misusers.

As for the clinical course following treatment, an examination of correlates of successful outcome found that adolescents with less posttreatment alcohol and drug use improved on measures of emotional, interpersonal, familial, academic, vocational, and recreational functioning (Brown, Myers, et al., 1994). A noteworthy finding was that improvement in some domains (e.g., family relations) occurred more slowly than in others (e.g., school, interpersonal functioning). This study also demonstrated that a proportion of adolescents who relapsed initially were later able to maintain a stable abstinence. These data reveal that adolescent alcohol and drug problems can be successfully resolved, but the clinician is cautioned to hold realistic expectations for the time course of progress and the likely variability in improvement across domains of functioning.

Cognitive-Behavioral Skills Training: Overview and Rationale

The selection of a cognitive-behavioral skills-based intervention is consistent with the evidence reviewed above for the importance of social resources, coping skills, substance-related attitudes, self-esteem, and family relations as predictors of adolescent treatment outcome. Based on such findings and the underlying biobehavioral theoretical perspective, the intervention described below focuses on identifying the role occupied by alcohol and drug use in the life of the adolescent, and centers on identifying strategies and techniques by which to alter the substance use behaviors directly with the teen.

As they are in treatment for many adolescent problems, family issues may be of particular salience in the therapy of adolescent substance misuse. Recent research provides evidence for the important role of the family in the outcome of treatment for adolescent substance use problems, in that reestablishment of positive family relations appears to play a significant role in successful treatment outcome, particularly for younger teens (Brown, 1993). In addition, improved family functioning follows persistent reductions in posttreatment adolescent substance use (Stewart & Brown, 1994). In general, given the evidence for efficacy of family-based approaches in treating adolescent substance misuse, we recommend that family structure, family functioning, and parenting be assessed and involved in the course of treatment. Whether family involvement consists of an additional family intervention above and beyond the individual or group skills-based intervention, or is limited to inclusion in the regular course of treatment with the teen, should be based on the needs and characteristics of each family. Depending on the presence of parental alcohol and drug misuse or other psychopathology, and on family members' motivation for change, the intervention approach may vary markedly.

Our description of the present intervention focuses primarily on the adolescent. In this context, the initial stages of intervention consist of training and rehearsal in a variety of strategies (e.g., social skills training and affect management) designed to improve functioning in inter- and intrapersonal domains of functioning. The focus during this initial portion of the intervention is on the skills to be improved and/or acquired, rather than on substance use per se.

Strategies for preventing relapse are introduced later in the intervention and focus more specifically on situations and circumstances surrounding previous substance use. Relapse prevention is considered a particularly important component of this intervention. "Relapse" is herein conceptualized in accordance with the cognitive-behavioral model of relapse (Marlatt & Gordon, 1985), which defines it as a process of returning to problematic substance use rather than as a discrete event. From this perspective, single occurrences of alcohol or drug use ("lapses" or "slips") are considered as learning opportunities rather than as failure experiences. This model identifies situations in which substance use previously occurred, and that tax or exceed available coping resources, as representing high risk for relapse. The probability of a lapse in a given situation is related to the extent to which substance use was previously employed to manage similar circumstances, the availability of effective coping strategies, the individual's belief in his or her ability to cope successfully with such situations (self-efficacy), and the individual's motivation to sustain an abstinent lifestyle.

Finally, strategies for maintenance of behavior change must be planned in accordance with information about the clinical course following treatment for adolescent substance misuse. Adolescents evidence high rates of relapse in the initial months following treatment (Brown et al., 1990), with the first 6 months representing the period of greatest risk (Brown, 1993). In additional, this period poses the greatest stress for youths and reports of anxiety and depression are prevalent. Thus, continued intervention contacts appears to be critical to maintaining treatment gains during this period.

Session Structure

Each session within this intervention contains similar elements and proceeds in a similar sequence: review and discussion of previous material and assignments; introduction of new material; practice (i.e., role plays) of new skills; and, finally, selection of skill enhancement assignments.

Given the emergence of independence and need for autonomy during adolescence, it is important for the clinician to solicit feedback from the adolescent about the perceived helpfulness and relevance of all material covered in session. In particular, attention should be given to comprehension of session material and completion of assignments, in order to anticipate and identify barriers to compliance and to determine optimal directions of cooperation. This collaborative strategy is helpful in reducing resistance and facilitates tailoring treatment to the pace, ability, and motivation of each adolescent.

Introduction of new material is preceded by discussion of a rationale, which should conform with the functional analysis framework of the intervention. Comprehension and acceptance of the rationale are enhanced when the clinician can provide examples relevant to the adolescent's personal experience and facilitate the adolescent's generation of personal examples. Also

helpful are handouts that outline each topic area and provide concrete, teen-specific examples relevant to assignments. In general, new material should be introduced briefly so as not to tax the adolescent's attention span. When new skills are being taught, it is useful for the clinician initially to model the relevant skill, and then to engage the adolescent in a role play.

Skill enhancement assignments are important, since these provide an opportunity for practicing skills *in vivo*. Input from the adolescent is important in deciding the details and extent of each assignment. It is generally best to limit the amount of "homework" assigned in order to minimize problems with compliance, since skill enhancement assignments are often perceived as "school-like." In additional, possible barriers to completion (e.g., time constraints, frequency of target situations) should be expected, evaluated, and discussed prior to jointly defining practice exercises. It is particularly important to select assignments that will be successfully executed and result in success, so as to enhance self-efficacy.

Core Sessions

The core sessions of the present intervention are designed to engage the adolescent, to jointly define and prioritize treatment goals and areas for intervention, and to introduce the functional analysis framework that is employed throughout treatment. Although the core sessions are presented at the outset of treatment, the specific skills training modules are designed to be flexible and can be introduced to correspond with the identified needs, goals, and developmental stage of each adolescent.

Motivational Enhancement

Since youths typically enter substance use treatment at the request of someone else (e.g., parents, the school, or a legal authority), motivation is a particularly important issue to address at the outset of therapy. The role of motivation in changing addictive behaviors has recently been afforded much attention, in part because of the difficulty of engaging and retaining individuals in substance use treatment (e.g., Miller & Rollnick, 1991). Motivation is believed to fluctuate over time, and thus it must be constantly monitored and maintained. Strategies to reduce client resistance are particularly important in the case of adolescent substance misusers, who are often rebellious and unconventional by nature or have not yet made a personal decision to change their substance involvement. To this end, an adolescent must be involved in the process of goal setting and identifying problem areas, in order to reduce resistance; compliance and motivation will be improved to the extent that the adolescent has a sense of partnership and control in the treatment process.

A client–treatment matching approach is considered useful for enhancing motivation and compliance (Hester & Miller, 1988). A key principle of this approach is that interventions matched to the adolescent's cognitive style and ability will improve outcomes—an important consideration, given the variability in adolescent cognitive development. Providing choices as to the content of specific intervention components is also important for increasing an adolescent's motivation and commitment. A collaborative approach may additionally serve to reduce resistance to treatment. Within a skills training intervention, the adolescent can be given choices as to specific domains to be addressed and particular techniques and strategies to be employed. In addition, decisions about the extent to which additional elements (e.g., family therapy, intervention for other problem areas) are included in the program of treatment can be made in collaboration with the adolescent and family.

Hester and Miller (1988) have proposed adolescent-specific factors to consider in tailoring an intervention:

1. Severity of substance involvement.
2. Other concurrent psychopathology.
3. Quality of support systems: home, family relationships, community resources, school, and peer relationships.
4. Severity of deviant or antisocial behaviors.
5. Personal characteristics: aggression, impulsivity, self-esteem.
6. Social skills and functioning.
7. Physical health.
8. Academic status.

The client–treatment matching process is based on assessment results and includes negotiating goals of treatment; selecting the intensity of intervention (e.g., inpatient vs. outpatient, frequency of sessions); choosing the modality of intervention (e.g., family therapy, group therapy, individual therapy, etc.); determining maintenance strategies (i.e., identifying and implementing supports for a drug-free lifestyle); and

TABLE 14.2. Cognitive-Behavioral Skills Training Outline

I. Core sessions
    Motivational enhancement
    Introduction of functional analysis
    Cognitive-behavioral skills training modules
II. Interpersonal skills
    Assertiveness
    Giving and receiving criticism; expressing feelings
    Dealing with conflict (anger and frustration)
III. Managing negative emotions
IV. Relapse prevention
    Rationale/identifying high-risk situations
    Coping with high-risk situations
    Refusal skills
    Goal setting/alternative activities

providing posttreatment evaluation and contact (Miller, 1989).

For adolescents, substance use treatment goals should address the various problems identified, rather than focusing exclusively on substance use. It is possible that assessment results may contradict an adolescent's perceptions of problems, thus leading to resistance. Therefore, a motivational approach may be particularly important when problems identified by the adolescent differ from those perceived by the parents and the clinician. One technique for reducing opposition to treatment goals is called "rolling with the resistance," which involves testing adolescent-identified goals or concerns. The notion underlying this strategy is that success in addressing the adolescent's concerns may increase his or her openness to continued intervention. Conversely, failure by the teen to achieve a self-identified goal will serve as evidence for the relevance of other problems identified during the assessment. Often, negotiating for a "trial of abstinence" allows the teen an opportunity to have a positive therapeutic experience and makes potential impediments to lengthening abstinence more salient.

Finally, the process of client–treatment matching should include consideration of important individual characteristics, such as gender, ethnicity, and concomitant psychopathology. Although boys typically display higher levels of substance involvement, adolescents in treatment settings are found to evidence few significant gender-related differences. Several studies have found that girls are more likely than boys to report the use of alcohol to relieve emotional discomfort or stress (Thompson & Wilsnack, 1984; Windle & Barnes, 1988). A large-scale examination of adolescents in treatment settings found few differences by gender; however, girls obtained higher scores on use of drugs to manage emotional discomfort and sensitivity to the emotional effects of drug use (Opland, Winters, & Stinchfield, 1995). The latter findings suggest that treatment content does not need to be dramatically different for girls and boys. However, in intervening with a female adolescent, it may be valuable to pay particular attention to the use of drugs for emotional management and to incorporate appropriate skill enhancement techniques (Opland et al., 1995).

Ethnic differences must be considered in the process of treatment planning and intervention. For example, African American and Hispanic adolescents have been found to be less likely than European American youths to seek treatment for substance use problems (Dembo & Shern, 1982; Windle, Miller-Tutzauer, Barnes, & Welte, 1991). Furthermore, Hispanics were found to have poorer rates of retention than either European American or African American adult participants in a therapeutic community (de Leon, Melnick, Schocket, & Jainchill, 1993). Other authors have suggested that minority involvement in addiction treatment is detrimentally influenced by the perception of Twelve-Step fellowships as exclusive, by misconceptions regarding the principles underlying these self-help groups, and by concerns regarding racism (Smith, Buxton, Bilal, & Seymour, 1993). In general, it is important to keep in mind that the broad ethnic groupings typically employed (i.e., African American, Hispanic, Asian) conceal varied and heterogeneous subgroups, and that it is difficult to prescribe specific strategies for tailoring treatment to each. However, available findings highlight the importance of sensitivity to cultural differences—in particular, the importance of ethnically appropriate discussion and presentation of the intervention plan, so as to enhance engagement and participation in treatment. For example, in Hispanic cultures labels such as "alcoholism" are considered pejorative and may be likely to provoke discontinuation of treatment, and thus should be avoided. Similarly, substance misuse is considered shameful within some Hispanic and Asian families; clinicians working with such populations must be sensitive to this point, both in discussing assessment findings and in formulating treatment recommendations. Another consideration for Asian clients is the common emphasis on the privacy of family problems. This cultural value suggests that for Asians individual or family formats are preferable to group treatment modalities. For African Americans it is often advantageous to utilize community-based resources such as churches or clubs as adjuncts to treatment, in lieu of Twelve-Step groups, which may be perceived as "Eurocentric." More generally, since exposure to substance misuse risk factors is shown to vary by ethnic origin, it is important that assessment findings be interpreted and explained in reference to the appropriate subgroup. To this end, the clinician must pay particular attention to the presence and influence of particular risk factors that may vary by subgroup (e.g., family structure, substance involvement within the home/family and within the community). It may be useful to be forthright and elicit the client's concerns about cultural issues/differences from the onset, thus providing an opportunity to address and discuss these issues.

Additional psychopathology is common among adolescents treated for alcohol and drug problems. Conduct Disorder (CD) and mood disorders are typically the most frequently observed concomitant disorders (e.g., Bukstein, Glancy, & Kaminer, 1992; Stowell & Estroff, 1992). To the extent that additional psychopathology has been identified during the assessment phase, such problems must be addressed in the course of treatment. For example, referral for pharmacotherapy evaluation may be appropriate. Although little is known about the incremental value of medication for concomitant psychopathology among adolescent substance misusers, psychoactive medication is commonly prescribed in substance use treatment settings and may be useful to the extent that such medication has been proven effective for the comorbid condition. For example, a recent preliminary report suggests the utility of pharmacotherapy for Attention-Deficit/Hyperactivity Disorder (ADHD) in the treatment of adolescents with concomitant CD and ADHD (Riggs, Thompson, Mikulich, Whitmore, & Crowley, 1996). Also, given the high incidence of CD and disruptive behaviors among adolescent substance misusers (e.g., Brown et al., 1996), it may be fruitful to incorporate an intervention focused on these problems. For example, several authors describe adolescent and parent conflict resolution and communication skills interventions that may be helpful for youths with CD (e.g., Forgatch & Patterson, 1989; Robin & Foster, 1989). The reader is referred to other chapters in this vol-

Trigger	Thought	Feeling	Behavior	Consequences	
				Positive	**Negative**
1. Gathering with friends, offered drugs	I'll feel left out if I don't use They'll think I'm lame if I say no	Anxious, uncomfortable	Use drugs	Feel comfortable with peers, have a good time, enjoy high	Guilt, feel like failure Hangover Spent money Punishment, loss of privileges Parents upset
2. Argument with parents	They don't listen or understand I'm sick of being blamed for everything	Angry, frustrated	Use drugs	Forget about argument, feel relaxed, feel less angry	Parents more angry Problems not addressed

FIGURE 14.1. Sample behavior chain worksheet.

ume that address treatment for relevant comorbid disorders.

Introduction of Functional Analysis

A functional analysis of alcohol and drug use (McCrady, 1986; McCrady, Dean, Dubreuil, & Swanson, 1985) forms the framework of the intervention and is introduced prior to the skills training modules. The functional analysis format is based on a behavioral conceptualization of alcohol and drug use as a learned behavior. From this perspective, the functions served by alcohol and drug use in the life of an addicted individual must be identified in order for appropriate intervention strategies to be selected and implemented. The functional analysis thus serves as a tool for identifying the stimuli, reinforcement contingencies, cognitions, and behaviors that maintain adolescent alcohol and drug involvement; thus, it helps target the particular strategies and skill domains to be selected for inclusion during the course of treatment.

After the rationale for the functional analysis is provided, the "behavior chain" (see Figure 14.1) is introduced as the tool used in a functional analysis. The behavior chain (consisting of triggers, thoughts, feelings, behavior, and consequences [positive and negative]) is best presented in graphic form on a flipchart or chalk board. Also, the adolescent should be provided with behavior chain worksheets (Figure 14.1) to complete for different precipitants (triggers) of use. First discussed are the antecedents to behavior: triggers, thoughts, and feelings. A "trig-

ger" is broadly defined as a circumstance that increases the probability of substance use. A trigger can be a person, place, or thing that has previously been associated with adolescent substance use (e.g., social situations, offers of alcohol and/or drugs by peers, arguments with friends or family, unpleasant emotions). Once the concept has been introduced to and comprehended by the adolescent, personal examples are elicited.

Following the discussion of triggers, it is usually best to introduce the feelings component of the chain, even though thoughts immediately follow in the behavior chain diagram. This is because adolescents may be unfamiliar with or have difficulty with the notion that thoughts can lead to feelings; they may also be less adept at identifying and labeling affective states (the latter is particularly true for impulsive youths). An adolescent is asked to generate a list of emotions he or she has experienced in response to the triggers previously identified (e.g., an argument may result in anger and frustration; offers of alcohol and drugs may elicit a desire to use [urges or craving]). The idea that thoughts can cause feelings is addressed after the adolescent has identified emotions associated with triggers. The role of thoughts in causing feelings is discussed in the context of Beck's concept of "automatic thoughts," which are thoughts or cognitions that enter consciousness without effort and may escape awareness (Beck, Rush, Shaw, & Emery, 1979). An adolescent-identified trigger is then selected, and the adolescent is asked to identify some thoughts related to the resulting feeling (e.g., an argument with parents may result in thoughts such as "I wish they'd get off my back" or "What's the big deal?"). Because adolescents may have difficulty with this task the clinician must be able to provide examples of thoughts associated with different types of situations. It is also valuable to examine the role of drug-use specific thoughts that may serve to motivate use. For example, Beck, Wright, Newman, and Liese (1993) describe three types of "addictive beliefs" about drugs that develop in addicted individuals and serve to maintain addiction and increase risk for relapse: "anticipatory," "relief-oriented," and "permissive" beliefs. Anticipatory beliefs are those that involve expected positive consequences of using ("It'll be fun at the party"); relief-oriented beliefs refer to expected negative reinforcement from use ("Using will get rid of my cravings," "If I use, I won't feel so stressed any more"); and permissive beliefs are those that are used to justify or "rationalize" use ("I can't focus without using," "I can control my use—there's no problem"). These types of thoughts should be discussed as motivating drug use, and the adolescent should then be asked to generate examples relevant to each type of addictive belief. It should also be pointed out that thoughts in response to a trigger can be either positive or negative (i.e., automatic thoughts are not necessarily "bad"). In order to establish comprehension of the antecedent portion of the behavior chain (triggers, thoughts, and feelings), completion of several examples representing different types of triggers, thoughts, and feelings is recommended.

Discussion of the next link in the chain, behavior, follows presentation of the antecedents. Consistent with a focus on substance use, alcohol and/or drug use behaviors are always noted on the chain in order to highlight the relationship between specific triggers and use. (The behavior portion of the chain is later used to specify adaptive alternative behaviors to use of alcohol and drugs.) An outline of the consequences of alcohol and/or drug use behaviors constitutes the next task to be completed. The positive consequences resulting from use in response to various triggers are discussed first (e.g., use following an argument may provide relief from anger and frustration, use in response to social pressure may facilitate feeling comfortable in a social situation). Acknowledging the positive consequences of use is important for emphasizing the factors that reinforce and maintain substance use, as well as for building credi-

bility with skeptical adolescents, who are usually tired of hearing that drugs are "bad" for them. After the various positive consequences are listed, negative consequences for a particular trigger are outlined, beginning with those most proximal. For example, alcohol or drug use when an adolescent is angry after an argument may lead to temporary relief, but the same negative feelings may eventually return. A more distal consequence is that use to relieve emotions results in avoidance of the issues underlying conflict, thereby assuring that the real issues are never addressed or changed. In the case of substance use in social contexts, intoxication may result in negative interactions (e.g., being belligerent, behaving foolishly) and can thus impair relationships. The adolescent should be encouraged to generate as many personal consequences as possible, and then to elaborate on personal negative consequences, including the long-term effects of substance use (e.g., discomfort interacting with others when not intoxicated, as a result of not having learned or used social skills; not being involved in rewarding activities, because of neglect of alternative activities; parental anger and punishment). Attention to the balance between positive and negative consequences is a useful motivational strategy (i.e., do the overall negative consequences of use outweigh the positives?). This approach can be used to monitor current motivation and to maintain or enhance motivation for change—an issue of particular importance, since motivation tends to fluctuate over time. A written record of the negative consequences of substance use by the adolescent is an effective strategy for providing a concrete reminder of personal motives for change. In discussing consequences the clinician is advised to avoid confrontation and refrain from imposing the opinion that use is "bad"; rather, the adolescent's perception of consequences is of primary importance.

Next discussed is the use of the behavior chain worksheet for identifying means by which to break the chain that leads to alcohol and drug use. Each link in the chain is a potential point where change can occur. For example, the ultimate behavior of alcohol or drug use can be disrupted by avoiding or altering certain triggers. Examination and reframing of perceptions or thoughts in reaction to a trigger may serve to avert emotions that can precipitate use. Finally, alternative means can be learned for managing the feelings that precede alcohol or drug use. In order to enhance the validity of the behavior chain, the clinician and adolescent should generate concrete examples of how alcohol and drug use behaviors can be influenced by acting on each link in the chain. Based on the previously agreed-upon areas for intervention, the adolescent can then be assigned to complete several behavior chain worksheets for the first area chosen to be addressed.

In order to motivate and engage the adolescent, the clinician must project optimism and confidence in the feasibility of this approach. It should be clarified that the behavior chain framework can accommodate a large range of strategies and tools, from which the adolescent can select those best matched to his or her individual needs and abilities. Overall, the introduction of the behavior chain should serve to illustrate how this tool will be used throughout treatment to help identify new skills, strategies, and behaviors for changing the old substance use behaviors or other problem behaviors.

Cognitive-Behavioral Skills Training Modules

The following topics are typically included in a skills training intervention for substance-misusing adolescents. Selection and sequencing of specific skills training modules for inclusion in the intervention are based upon the problem areas identified in the course of assessment, targets of change identified by the adolescent, and treatment goals negotiated with the adolescent. The amount of time devoted to any particular topic is determined by the needs and abilities of each adolescent. The skills modules are organized into three domains: interpersonal skills, managing negative emotions; and relapse prevention.

Interpersonal Skills

Assertiveness. Effective assertive behavior is relevant to various other topics—in particular, those involving interpersonal functioning—and as such is generally introduced first. The utility of assertive behavior for improving interpersonal relationships serves as the rationale for this module: Good relationships help decrease conflict and the resulting negative emotions, and increase self-efficacy, thereby reducing the likelihood of alcohol and drug use to manage these feelings.

Beginning with a general discussion of assertiveness, the clinician should have the adolescent describe his or her understanding of the concept. Assertiveness can be contrasted with aggressiveness and passivity as follows:

1. The assertive person has respect both for the rights of others and for his or her own rights.
2. The passive person respects others' rights at the expense of his or her own rights.
3. The aggressive person respects his or her own rights at the expense of the rights of other people.

After clarifying any questions regarding assertiveness and discussing concrete examples, the clinician outlines basic individual rights. Providing the adolescent with a list of rights and asking for examples of how these rights might be violated are helpful at this point. Personal examples should be elicited (and/or provided from the clinician's observation and knowledge of the adolescent client) of situations where the adolescent had his or her rights violated and instances where he or she violated the rights of others. Individual rights should be highlighted. That is, every person has the following rights:

1. To make his or her own decisions.
2. To have and express his or her own feelings.
3. To have and express his or her own thoughts, beliefs and opinions.
4. To decide whether to agree to or decline a request.
5. To be healthy and safe, and not to be abused (physically, emotionally, or sexually).

The presentation of assertiveness and personal rights is followed by a discussion of passive and/or aggressive behaviors by the adolescent. Once personal passive and aggressive behaviors have been identified, the adolescent is asked to prioritize problems with assertiveness; these are then examined, using the behavior chain in order to demonstrate the negative consequences of these behaviors. Next, the following guidelines for assertive behavior are reviewed, with a focus on those pertinent to the previously completed behavior chains:

1. You can only control your own behavior, not that of others. You can ask others to change their behavior, but they have the right to refuse.
2. It is important to know in advance what you want to get out of a particular situation or circumstance.
3. Communicate clearly and specifically what it is you want.

4. Pay attention to body language; avoid presenting a passive or aggressive posture.

5. The timing of attempts at assertive behavior is important. In particular, make sure you're calm and composed when making a request or having a discussion with someone.

6. It is important to use "I" statements, and avoid words such as "should" and "never."

7. When criticizing someone, address the *behavior* you don't like, rather than characteristics of the *person*.

8. To provide constructive feedback, use the "sandwich" technique: Start with something positive about the issue/person, follow this with criticism/feedback, then end with a positive comment.

9. Be willing to compromise; plan ahead of time what you're willing and unwilling to negotiate.

After these assertive guidelines are reviewed, the behavior chains are reworked, substituting assertive for passive or aggressive behaviors. In particular, the different consequences that result from assertive as opposed to aggressive and/or passive behavior should be emphasized. Finally, a role play of assertive behaviors is undertaken and repeated until the teen demonstrates improved performance and confidence.

Practicing assertive skills in situations that engender success is critical. To this end, initial assignments must be focused on relatively nonthreatening situations for which success is highly likely. The adolescent should be asked to complete a number of behavior chains for triggers relevant to assertive behaviors drawn from daily experiences.

Giving and Receiving Criticism, Expressing Feelings: The next module focuses on situations in which the adolescent has had difficulty accepting or providing criticism, or expressing positive or negative feelings appropriately. The personal examples reviewed as part of treatment need not be substance-use-related, but should be concrete and outlined in detail. In the event that the adolescent has difficulty providing examples, reference can be made to interpersonal conflict items endorsed as common use situations on the IDTS (Annis & Martin, 1985). Family and school examples abound in this domain and can be useful content in the parent or family components of the intervention as well. The adolescent should complete a behavior chain worksheet for each example, followed by a discussion of how the antecedents and behavior in the situation could be changed to produce a more positive outcome. When reviewing alternative behaviors, the clinician should refer the adolescent to the guidelines for assertive behavior, in order to generate strategies for more effective behaviors. Discussion of the behavior chain and alternative behaviors is followed by a role play of the alternative behaviors previously generated.

The adolescent should be assisted in selecting a nonthreatening situation for practicing the skills reviewed. The importance of planning and rehearsal prior to entering the situation should be emphasized: What is the goal, and what responses will be most effective in achieving that goal? Completion of behavior chains for triggers relevant to situations involving the expression of criticism and other feelings drawn from the adolescent's daily experiences is suggested.

Dealing with Conflict (Anger and Frustration). The module on dealing with conflict begins with having the adolescent identify and select recent conflict situations (arguments, fights). Conflicts with friends and peers are examined separately from family conflict situations. A behavior chain worksheet is completed for each trigger, including the antecedents and behaviors that led to anger and/or frustration. Next, the adolescent is asked to identify links in the chain that can be altered to avoid the previously experienced negative consequences. Of particular importance is identification of previous thoughts (perceptions and beliefs about what occurred in the situation) and behaviors that were ineffective in managing conflict. This exercise is followed by generating alternative thoughts and behaviors in response to the trigger situation(s), referring to the assertive behavior guidelines. Discussion of the behavior chain and alternative behaviors is followed by a role play of the alternative behaviors previously generated.

The adolescent should be assisted in selecting a relatively minor, frequently occurring conflict situation for initial practice. It is often helpful to identify a recent unresolved conflict situation that the adolescent can attempt to address (after practicing in session). For future sessions, the adolescent can be assigned to identify additional ongoing conflict situations or anticipated conflicts. Family-related conflicts may be more effectively addressed in the context of a family session, particularly when it is judged that behavior change on the part of the adolescent will be insufficient to alter the outcome of such conflicts.

Managing Negative Emotions

The next skills training domain concentrates on skills and strategies for managing negative emotions, such as depression, anxiety, and anger. Because negative affect increases with the transition through puberty and is frequently associated with substance use, effective means for managing such emotions are particularly important. As a general rule, it is valuable to normalize for the adolescent the experience of negative affect. This can be accomplished through discussing of negative emotions as a normal part of everyday life, and pointing out that such feelings can result in situations where the teen has responded or behaved appropriately (i.e., one can't control other people's feelings).

Once relevant negative emotions and corresponding trigger situations have been identified (based on previous assessment information, the IDTS, etc.), the behavior chain concept is employed to detail the thoughts and behaviors that contribute to and exacerbate the emotions. The selection of specific strategies for managing negative emotions should depend on the particular triggers commonly experienced and the adolescent's level of cognitive ability. Matching strategies to cognitive style is particularly important in this context, since some adolescents are more comfortable with concrete behavioral strategies rather than cognitive approaches (and vice versa). Adolescents may perceive alcohol and/or drug use as effective means for managing negative emotions. As such, it is particularly important to assess these beliefs (e.g., using the AEQ-A) to enhance the adolescent's confidence in the utility of the selected mood management techniques, and to boost his or her self-efficacy for successfully implementing alternative strategies.

Providing a menu of both cognitive and behavioral strategies that will permit the teen to select the skills most relevant to his or her trigger situations and personal style is helpful, as negative affect can emerge across a variety of circumstances. Strategies for managing such feelings as anger, frustration, stress, depression, and boredom should be selected in accordance with identified triggers and clinical judgment regarding the particular needs of each adolescent. Although a detailed outline of strategies for adolescent mood management is beyond the scope of this chapter, several excellent sources describe specific techniques that are easily incorporated within the present framework (e.g., Clarke, Lewinsohn, & Hops, 1990; Burns, 1989).

Once appropriate mood management strategies have been selected in collaboration with the adolescent, the behavior chain is used to illustrate how these strategies function. For example, the clinician can say, "Progressive muscle relaxation is a skill that helps you feel less stressed and anxious. If you feel less stressed, you'll be less likely to use alcohol/drugs to calm yourself." Or, "Being involved in enjoyable activities will help you feel better when you're down and make it less likely that you'll use to deal with being depressed or bored." Or, "Learning to think differently about situations where you get upset can reduce these feelings and help you feel more in control." The adolescent's comprehension of how the selected strategies will help him or her manage unpleasant feelings is essential to motivate compliance. In-session practice and rehearsal are particularly valuable for enhancing compliance with these strategies.

The adolescent should be assisted in identifying upcoming situations that may precipitate negative emotions. Specific strategies are then prescribed for practice. Having the adolescent perform daily mood ratings (e.g., a daily rating of anxiety level on a 1-to-10 scale) can help identify particular emotions to be targeted, and is also useful in providing feedback as to the effectiveness of the strategies employed.

Relapse Prevention

Rationale/Identifying High-Risk Situations. The discussion of relapse prevention for adolescents starts with defining "relapse" as a process of returning to problematic alcohol and drug use, rather than a single, all-or-none event (Marlatt & Gordon, 1985). It is important to clarify that a single occasion of use (a "slip" or "lapse") does not represent a failure or an inevitable return to problematic use. Within this model, one's reaction to a lapse plays a large role in what happens next. Because of the high rate of lapses following treatment for adolescent substance misuse, it is critical that such an event be perceived as a learning experience rather than a failure. The message to be conveyed is that recovery from alcohol and drugs is a gradual process during which setbacks are to be anticipated. It is important to prepare an adolescent for feelings of guilt and failure in the event of a lapse, and to reframe this experience as an opportunity to learn to avoid future lapses. Discussion of a lapse is intended to increase the adolescent's awareness of potential relapse risks and to facilitate planning for such an event. It must be emphasized that discussion of this issue in no way implies permission to use! In the course of discussion of this topic, it is imperative to solicit feedback and reactions from the adolescent regarding the described process of relapse and the meaning of a lapse.

The concept of high-risk situations and the role of coping are introduced following the discussion of relapse. Because many of the triggers discussed in previous sessions represent relapse risk situations, the concept of high-risk situations should be easily comprehended by the adolescent. Although some relapse risk situations are apparent (e.g., being at a party where alcohol and/or drugs are being used), unique risk situations must be identified for each adolescent in order to enhance preparedness and vigilance. The rationale for relapse prevention training rests on the notion that preparation and the availability of specific coping skills are necessary tools for reducing the probability of lapses in high-risk situations. It is helpful to elicit from the adolescent his or her own experiences (if any) at successfully managing temptations to use alcohol and/or drugs. Success experiences in this realm are important for building the adolescent's self-efficacy and confidence for managing relapse risk situations.

The process of identifying personal high-risk situations follows the discussion of the concepts underlying relapse prevention. Because adolescents often underestimate the difficulty of coping successfully with relapse risk situations (e.g., Myers & Brown, 1990a), it is important to examine examples of likely high-risk situations and to highlight the risk involved. Typical adolescent high-risk situations include social situations, social pressure, and family conflict. Additional situations previously identified as triggers during the course of treatment or endorsed on the IDTS (Annis & Graham, 1985) can be utilized as examples. Another measure that may assist in the process of identifying relapse risk situations is the Drug Taking Confidence Questionnaire (DTCQ; Annis & Martin, 1985). This questionnaire is identical in item content to the IDTS, but asks respondents to rate their self-efficacy for abstaining in each situation. An adolescent's responses to the DTCQ can thus serve to identify situations that are perceived as particularly difficult to manage. It is important to convey that it is also important to be prepared to manage less common situations associated with past use, as well as unantici-

pated events. Behavior chains worksheets completed during the course of treatment are a good source for illustrating the broad range of situations that may represent an increased risk for relapse. Once the adolescent's personal high-risk situations are identified, perceived risk of relapse and ability to cope should be assessed for each. This assessment can incorporate a detailed discussion of perceived risk (why might a situation be difficult or easy to handle?) and adolescent-generated strategies for managing various circumstances. Feedback as to the likely accuracy of these perceptions is valuable at this point, along with an emphasis on the importance of being prepared for the unexpected.

The adolescent should be assigned to generate two lists of potential high-risk situations: those that are likely to be encountered in the present, and more distal, future risks. The particular approach taken with regard to relapse will also depend on external constraints (e.g., probation if a teen is on probation, drug testing, etc.). Clear discussions of the impact of these external factors need to take place with teen and parents early in the therapeutic process. Behavior chain worksheets, including coping strategies for avoiding lapses (alternative behaviors), should be completed for a number of the situations (the exact number should be based on negotiation with the adolescent). Asking the adolescent to generate coping strategies can help the clinician to assess his or her abilities and to identify coping efforts the adolescent perceives as useful. An additional useful exercise is to have the adolescent monitor socially sanctioned pressures to drink. This can be done by keeping a log of messages (e.g., television, magazines, newspapers, movies, adult discussions, etc.) designed to promulgate the use of alcohol. The exercise also helps adolescents identify previously unrecognized cues for alcohol involvement.

Coping with High-Risk Situations. Having identified a variety of high-risk situations, the adolescent is assisted in determining which are likely to pose the greatest and most immediate risk for relapse. The extent of risk from a given situation is based on the following considerations: (1) Has the adolescent previously been successful in managing a given type of situation? (2) How skilled is the adolescent in the strategies required to manage a particular situation? (3) What is the adolescent's self-efficacy with respect to avoiding use in a given situation? (4) How realistic is the adolescent's estimate of difficulty for each situation? A review of upcoming events can serve to identify and prioritize particularly risky situations to be worked on in session. Once a list of high-risk situations is completed, a behavior chain worksheet is completed to evaluate each identified situation in detail and to specify alternative behaviors for altering and/or managing the specific circumstances involved.

Planning and rehearsal of strategies are especially important for high-risk situations likely to be encountered in the near future. Once a relapse risk situation occurs, there is little time to think through alternatives; therefore, at least one strategy perceived as effective and feasible by the adolescent must be identified and rehearsed for each type of situation. In-session work should thus focus on planning and rehearsing coping alternatives. The specific strategies discussed will be dictated by the type of situation targeted (e.g., mood management strategies for negative affect, assertive skills for conflict situations, etc.). Avoiding high-risk situations is a useful strategy that is recommended early in treatment, but is unlikely to be effective over the long term. After specific coping techniques are discussed, it is helpful to engage the adolescent in a detailed discussion of how each plan will be executed, how the adolescent and others may react in the situation, and how the adolescent perceives his or her self-efficacy for executing the coping efforts. This discussion serves to anticipate and identify potential barriers to coping. Finally, because of the high frequency of adolescent relapse, it is important to outline a plan of action in the case of a slip, particularly when difficult situations are imminent. Providing the adolescent with a concrete plan that includes clearly specified steps to be followed can decrease the likelihood of a protracted relapse following a slip. A "slip management plan" can include such strategies as contacting the clinician, calling a nonusing friend, attending a support group meeting, discarding any alcohol or drugs in the adolescent's possession, or leaving the use situation. This plan can be reinforced by drawing up, together with the adolescent, a "relapse recovery plan" contract that is then signed by the adolescent. Of course, action to be taken and requirements based on external contingencies must also be considered. Regardless of external factors, repeated slips need to be dealt with aggressively in treatment, as use compromises the teen's cognitive and affective motivation for successful treatment participation.

Practice of coping skills outside of the therapeutic setting is assigned following in-session

practice. Initial practice must be planned for situations presenting minimal risk, with subsequent assignments gradually introducing more difficult circumstances. The primary goal of practice assignments in this phase of treatment is to establish the adolescent's self-efficacy for managing relapse risk situations. In order to insure success, a support person is identified who will accompany the adolescent in high-risk situations. This support person can be a nonusing peer, a parent, or (if appropriate) the clinician. The ultimate goal of these exercises is for the adolescent to attribute success and improvement to his or her own efforts and abilities. To this end, the use of avoidance and reliance on support persons should be gradually faded out in the later stages of treatment.

Refusal Skills. Discussion of refusal skills is particularly important, since adolescents commonly relapse in peer social situations where there is pressure to use alcohol and/or drugs. The importance of addressing this issue is highlighted by the prominent role of peers in modeling and reinforcing alcohol and drug use behaviors during adolescence. It is important that the clinician recognize and acknowledge the difficulty of maintaining abstinence in the face of peer pressure. The extent of this difficulty is evident, in that adolescent experimentation with substances is normative and the prevalence of alcohol and drug use increases throughout adolescence. In this context, abstinence from alcohol and drug use represents a behavior that is at odds with the reality of the adolescent's environment, and thus efforts at abstinence are particularly challenging.

Particularly helpful in the context of refusing offers of substances are review and rehearsal of assertive skills. In addition to behavioral skills, cognitive factors are important for drug refusal. In particular, it is helpful to evaluate the adolescent's perception of what it means to him or her to refuse offers of substance use. For example, the likelihood of attempts at coping may rest on the extent to which the adolescent believes that refusal will influence how he or she is perceived and accepted by others. The forces of social influence can be countered through discussion of the adolescent's concerns regarding peer acceptance, and by examining the accuracy of these perceptions (e.g., cognitive techniques for examining "irrational" thoughts).

Assignments for refusal skills are similar to those described for coping with high-risk situations. Before assigning practice in "real-life" situations, the clinician must ascertain that the adolescent will be able to manage such situations successfully.

Goal Setting/Alternative Activities.   A major concern for many substance misusing adolescents is the fear that life will be dull and uninteresting in the absence of drugs and alcohol. Therefore, identifying and developing enjoyable, non-substance-use-related activities are critical aspects of relapse prevention. Other benefits of rewarding and enjoyable pursuits include enhancing self-esteem, developing a sense of autonomy, developing a non-using peer group and supporting identity development (so critical during adolescence). Since research demonstrates that involvement in alternative activities accompanies the successful resolution of substance use problems for adults and teens (Brown, 1993), this is a particularly useful component of intervention.

Adolescents in treatment generally have limited hobbies or extracurricular interests, often as a consequence of their substance involvement. It is therefore useful to spend time in session for setting goals or identifying possible interests. The process can be initiated by identifying activities in which the adolescent was involved before the onset of substance use. Also helpful for identifying potential areas of interest are presenting a variety of domains (hobbies, recreational activities, sports, social activities, jobs) and exploring the possibilities within each. Another domain worthy of consideration is that of volunteer activities, which place the teen in a position of responsibility and respect. A systematic approach to goal setting/activity planning is recommended. As the first step, it is helpful to provide menus or lists of potential activities. The clinician can facilitate the selection of activities by "brainstorming" specific examples for different types or domains of activities. The adolescent is then assigned to rank activities based on his or her personal interest. Once this is done, a discussion is undertaken to develop a plan for how each activity will be pursued. A focus on making detailed, concrete plans and on identifying potential barriers is important to facilitate adolescent follow-through. The clinician should assist the adolescent in setting specific, attainable goals as homework assignments (e.g., "Goal: Join group *X* by next month. Steps to complete: (1) call to get information, (2) arrange transportation, (3) attend a meeting," etc.). It is important that the selected activities, goals, and plan of action be realistic and attainable, and that they not overwhelm the adolescent.

Evaluating Progress and Treatment Outcome

The success of treatment is evaluated on the basis of improvements across the domains of functioning initially identified as problem areas, rather than defined solely in terms of substance involvement. Assessment of progress and outcome must therefore consider each area addressed during the course of treatment. At a minimum, scales and measures initially used to identify problem areas and affective states during assessment should be readministered at the end of treatment. As suggested, the CBCL and its accompanying version for youths, the YSR, can be utilized throughout the treatment process to evaluate improvement and identify remaining problem areas. Brief screening measures such as the PESQ may prove helpful in assessing substance use status following treatment. Systematic evaluation of progress and treatment outcome is strongly recommended, as it serves to provide positive feedback to the adolescent client, furnishes the clinician with objective evidence for the efficacy of intervention, and assists both client and clinician in anticipating new or continued problems.

Maintenance of Behavior Change

Maintenance of behavior change for adolescent substance misusers is greatly assisted by continued clinical contact following the completion of treatment. Contact during the initial months after treatment (when risk for relapse is highest) and timely responses in the case of lapses function to improve alcohol and drug use outcome. A flexible approach to intervention with adolescents following treatment for substance use problems is recommended. Consistent therapist support is important, even when adolescents initiate activities that vary from those traditionally associated with successful abstinence. The value of such flexibility is supported by evidence for a variety of pathways to successful outcome for adolescent substance misusers. As such, efforts initiated by an adolescent in support of abstinence should be supported as long as these are consistent with treatment goals.

Evidence regarding the clinical course following treatment for adolescent substance use problems suggests strategies that may improve the likelihood of successful outcome. Because the initial 6 months following treatment represent the greatest risk for relapse, relapse prevention efforts should be maintained during this period. Follow-up contacts can consist of office visits and phone calls, scheduled with gradually decreasing frequency. Such contacts provide opportunity for the clinician to assess the maintenance of behavior change, to address any problems that have occurred, and to evaluate the adolescent for the emergence of new clinical symptoms (e.g., depression, anxiety).

Prompt attention to lapse and relapse events is also important to maintaining behavior change. Adolescents differ from adults in that they more often lapse on substances other than their previous "drug of choice," and as many as one-quarter of initial lapses do not result in full-blown relapse. In this context, rapid attention to lapses can interrupt the process of relapse and obstruct a return to previous levels of problematic drug and/or alcohol use. As previously noted, lapse experiences are considered opportunities for learning rather than as failures. Lapse episodes should be reviewed and discussed in a nonjudgmental fashion, and behavior chain worksheets should be employed to examine the reasons underlying a return to substance use. Review of lapse episodes should also be used to highlight the importance of vigilance, preparation, and motivation in the face of relapse risk situations. Furthermore, a prompt reaction to a lapse episode can help temper the feelings of guilt and failure that often accompany such an episode.

Finally, treatment outcome can be enhanced by therapist support for nontraditional efforts at maintaining abstinence. Affiliation with traditional support systems for abstinence (Alcoholics Anonymous/Narcotics Anonymous, recovery support groups) is a strong predictor of long-term abstinence among adolescent substance misusers (Brown, 1993). However, some adolescents successfully utilize alternative supports or efforts, which are equally effective in promoting long-term abstinence (Brown, 1993). For example, younger adolescents not involved in recovery organizations are able to maintain abstinence through increased family involvement. If available, a relatively supportive family unit may be assisted in providing adequate support for continued abstinence through intervention aimed at improving family interactions and communication. Early individuation by older adolescents represents another nontraditional avenue for

success. Adolescents who succeed in maintaining abstinence by this path often have parents with a history of alcohol or drug misuse, and are able to achieve abstinence by gaining independence from their family without involvement in the traditional recovery community. These adolescents usually become involved in activities that provide drug-free environments (e.g., hobbies, work, extracurricular activities) and that enhance independence and self-esteem. Although relatively few adolescents are found to utilize these alternative pathways to abstinence, strategies such as these provide an alternative for those who do not become involved with abstinence-focused support groups.

Problems in Implementation

Substance misusing adolescents can appear to be difficult clients because they seldom enter treatment of their own accord. As discussed throughout the chapter, issues regarding motivation for change, resistance to treatment, and poor compliance with the intervention are of great importance. Another difficult issue encountered in treating adolescent substance use problems is that of continued alcohol and drug use during the course of treatment. Strategies for the detection of substance use (e.g., random toxicology screens) and contingencies in response to episodes of use must be outlined in detail and agreed upon at the outset of treatment. A further factor complicating the therapeutic decision-making process is confidentiality—an issue common to all therapeutic settings in which offspring are treated, either independently of or in concert with parents and family. Although no uniform recommendation is made here, due to the considerable variability in circumstances that may lead an adolescent to treatment, the agreements between therapist and adolescent and between therapist and family must be clearly outlined, preferably in the first session. In situations in which adolescent drug use is to be automatically reported (e.g., drug screens, teen reports, etc.), consequences should be explicitly specified. Even in such situations, confidentiality regarding other information emerging in treatment should be clearly differentiated.

Motivation for and Compliance with Treatment

Adolescent development is a critical consideration when one is designing interventions for enhancing motivation and reducing resistance to treatment. These issues have been addressed throughout the chapter and are briefly reiterated here.

Motivation for change is a critical issue in the treatment of addictive behaviors, and as such should be assessed and addressed throughout the course of treatment. To this end, adolescent developmental issues must be kept in mind: Although they are expected to behave as adults, adolescents usually have little control over day-to-day events or external stressors, and as a consequence often feel powerless or helpless. To this end, engaging an adolescent in a collaborative fashion and involving him or her in the process of treatment planning is particularly important, so as to reduce resistance and enhance compliance (i.e., the adolescent should enter the treatment process with a sense of "ownership").

Adolescents with substance use problems generally present with a wide range of neurocognitive abilities, and attentional difficulties are fairly common. Thus, intervention content must be carefully matched to the cognitive level and abilities of each adolescent. Information should be presented in manageable quantities, and in language that is appropriate for the adolescent's level of comprehension. Overwhelming the adolescent with information or failing to insure that material is comprehended will lead to frustration and a decrease in motivation and compliance. It is important to keep in mind that techniques developed for adults may be inappropriate for use with adolescents. The clinician must be sensitive to this issue and not make any *a priori* assumptions regarding the appropriateness of materials. In evaluating whether a particular technique will be effective, feedback must be sought from the adolescent as to whether the material is acceptable, whether it makes sense, and how comfortable he or she feels with it. This feedback should be elicited in a sensitive manner that does not result in the adolescent's feeling that his or her intelligence or ability is being questioned.

Since tasks that appear "school-like" are often met with resistance, compliance with between-session assignments can be problematic. Such assignments should be referred to as "skill enhancement activities" rather than "homework." In order to reduce resistance, tasks that focus on activities and behaviors rather than on reading and writing are generally assigned. It is often helpful to go over an assignment in detail during the session, in order to identify potential obstacles or difficulties that may impede compliance. The adolescent should make a commitment to attempt this task at the close of each session. In addition, beginning the session with a review of the previous assignment can be useful. Feedback from the adolescent should be elicited as to how helpful the task was and how much it was liked or disliked. This information can then be used to modify subsequent assignments if necessary, and to solve problems regarding resistance and barriers to compliance.

Substance Use during the Course of Treatment

The traditional goal of treatment for substance use problems is complete abstinence from psychoactive substances. To this end, issues of continued use, lapse, and relapse must be addressed and agreed upon at the outset of intervention. Agreement must be reached as to the means by which substance use will be monitored, as well as the consequences of lapses or continued use.

Traditional definitions of abstinence from psychoactive substances typically exclude the use of nicotine (and caffeine). Given that tobacco use is ubiquitous and represents the leading cause of death among individuals previously treated for alcohol problems (Hurt et al., 1996), this is an issue that must be addressed in the course of treatment. Unfortunately, although ample evidence exists to demonstrate that youths often attempt to quit smoking (e.g., Ershler, Leventhal, Fleming, & Glynn, 1989) little is currently known about effective treatment of adolescent nicotine dependence—a situation exacerbated by the fact that the recovery community typically models and condones heavy cigarette involvement. Nonetheless, nicotine should be identified to the adolescent as an addictive substance, and motivation should be assessed for behavior change in this realm. Available research provides evidence for the role of nicotine dependence (Ershler et al., 1989; Hansen, 1983), peer smoking (Ary & Biglan, 1988; Hansen, Collins, Johnson, & Graham, 1985), and parental smoking (Chassin, Presson, & Sherman, 1984) as factors that impede efforts at adolescent smoking cessation. The clinician can provide the adolescent with smoking cessation materials (e.g., pamphlets such as those produced by the American Lung Association, identifying community resources for adolescent smoking cessation). In addition, an excellent resource for clinicians is a recently published U.S. DHHS (1996) booklet of clinical guidelines for smoking cessation, which is free and provides a detailed overview of cessation techniques along with supporting research. In sum, efforts at smoking cessation during the course of intervention should be encouraged and supported to the extent that the adolescent is interested. The message to be conveyed is that although abstinence from tobacco products is not a requirement of treatment, the expectation is that the adolescent will eventually make efforts at smoking cessation.

Substance use can be monitored through a variety of methods, including self-report by the adolescent, parent report, or urine toxicology screening. Urine screening is commonly employed because it is an objective indicator of use, can serve as a deterrent to use, and may encourage honest reporting by the adolescent. The urine-screening procedure is best presented as a standard procedure required of all individuals treated for substance misuse. The adolescent must be provided with a rationale for the employment of urine screens, with an emphasis that the issue is not trust but accountability: Having agreed to a goal of abstinence, the adolescent is responsible for pursuing that goal and being honest about lapses or difficulties with abstinence during the course of treatment. The procedure can also be framed as a means for protecting the adolescent, since continued alcohol and/or drug use may lead to various personal risks or severe adverse consequences. Urine screens can be administered routinely, at random intervals, or at the clinician's discretion. Random screening is difficult to implement in the context of a set treatment schedule (i.e., weekly sessions), and may also be interpreted by the adolescent as a sign of mistrust, since random tests are more difficult to "plan" use around. Regular (e.g., weekly, biweekly, or monthly) urine screens may thus be perceived by the adolescent as less intrusive than random testing. When relatively infrequent urine testing is selected, the clinician must reserve the right to request a urine sample in a situation where evidence suggests unacknowledged alcohol and/or drug use by the adolescent. The clinician should provide examples of the circumstances that may motivate such a request (e.g., behavioral withdrawal symptoms, atypical mood changes, family reports of unusual behavior), and should clarify that if such a circumstance arises, the underlying reasons will be fully discussed with the adolescent. Additional issues pertaining to urine toxicology screening include the cost of the procedure and its potential impact on the therapeutic relationship. The questions of who will have access to the results and what are appropriate and inappropriate reactions on the part of parents or family must be clarified at the outset. In particular, parents should be discouraged from displaying a punitive response in the case of a positive urine screen; rather, they should be encouraged to perceive isolated instances of use as an opportunity for learning, which should be discussed with the adolescent in a supportive and appropriate manner.

A basic rule in working with a substance-misusing adolescent is that the adolescent must not arrive at a session under the influence of alcohol or drugs. It must be made clear that no useful work can be accomplished if the adolescent is "under the influence" during sessions. If such an event does occur, the clinician must carefully assess the situation and decide on appropriate action For example, is the adolescent in any danger? Can the teen be sent home safely? Does this suggest the need for more intensive intervention? Such an occurrence should be followed by a makeup session scheduled as soon as is feasible in order to process the event.

Given that abstinence is the goal of treatment, the expectation that the adolescent not use alcohol or drugs during the course of treatment should be made explicit. In reality, especially in outpatient settings, absolute abstinence throughout the course of treatment is often difficult to achieve. As discussed above, lapse experiences during the course of treatment often represent powerful learning experiences. However, continued alcohol and drug use by the adolescent may also indicate that the selected course and modality of treatment are not effective. Thus, it is incumbent upon the clinician to clearly define the consequences of use episodes. In general, treatment proceeds with the understanding that lapses may occur, but that open and honest discussion of any such lapses is a condition for continued treatment. Repeated denial of lapses in the face of objective evidence or a pattern of continued use that does not diminish with time may indicate the need to seek a different and perhaps more intensive treatment approach.

CASE EXAMPLE

Tim, a 16-year-old high school sophomore, was brought to treatment by his mother and father after being placed in juvenile detention by police for possession of a controlled substance. His parents were extremely distressed by the downward spiral of withdrawal, depression, and irresponsible behavior they had observed in their son over the course of the preceding year. Most recently, Tim had failed to come home on a number of occasions; he had started missing school regularly; and his previously good grades had deteriorated remarkably. Despite their efforts to speak with him of their concerns, Tim remained sullen and uncommunicative. Consequently, the parents increasingly threatened more serious disciplinary action, but found it difficult to carry out their punishment for fear of further alienating their son. In particular, Tim's father, who was a computer software salesman, had become increasingly angry with his son. His preference was to have their son leave home until he "stopped using drugs and cleaned up his act." In contrast, Tim's mother was frightened to have him leave home for fear he would choose to live with his drug-using friends and become involved in more deviant behavior. Furthermore, she felt much empathy for her son's distress, as well as guilt that perhaps her employment or attention to her older (college-age) son might somehow be responsible for Tim's current difficulties.

After a brief meeting with Tim and his parents, Tim was interviewed separately while his parents were asked to complete several self-report measures (the CBCL, the Family Environment Scale). He clearly had no wish to be in treatment and felt that his parents and school officials were becoming unfair to him. His friends, who Tim felt cared about him deeply, likewise thought that his parents were punitive in comparison with their own parents. This group of friends also considered their substance involvement "normal" for males their age. Tim initially did not disclose his level of use, but acknowledged experimenting with alcohol, marijuana, cocaine, and methamphetamines. (He did report being a regular cigarette smoker, but did not want his parents to know about this.) When queried, he stated that he used no more than his peers, and that he did not think his drug use was a problem, as he was still attending school and hadn't ever failed a class. From his perspective, kids who couldn't handle their drug use started stealing for their habit and dropped out of school. He was not like those problem users; he was "not an addict."

Following some discussion of the circumstances that brought him to treatment, including probation-mandated abstinence, Tim agreed to come to treatment to placate his parents and show the judge he was wrong. It was explained to Tim that, with the exception of the results of urine toxicology screens (required as part of his probation), all other material in the session would be held in confidence unless the therapist was legally required by law to release information. After some discussion, Tim agreed to participate in therapy in order to appease the legal system and diminish the conflict at home. Although he clearly underestimated the difficulties of not using during the upcoming week, he agreed that for 1 week he would avoid his usual friends, and that he would generate a list of recreational or special things to be used in the future as rewards for abstinence and compliance. Tim also agreed to complete several self-report questionnaires before the next session, in 2 days. The therapist offered to discuss at the next session the possibility of writing a letter to school officials indicating that Tim had started treatment. Finally, the Mini-Mental Status Exam and Hamilton Rating Scale for Depression were completed to assess the severity of Tim's current depressive symptoms.

The initial session ended with bringing the parents back into the room, discussing the therapist–teen contract, and negotiating a contract between the parents and therapist that was to be honored regardless of Tim's behavior over the next several days. Tim's parents agreed to make a list of things they liked about their son and to specify potential family rewards for Tim's efforts at an alcohol- and drug-free lifestyle. Tim and his parents were then informed about the usual affective, cognitive, and physiological withdrawal symptoms from stimulants and depressants, so as to prepare them for the experiences likely to occur over the next few days and weeks. All parties agreed to meet in 2 days to complete the assessment and treatment-planning process.

At the second session, following a brief discussion of withdrawal symptoms and current family relations, Tim's list of special recreational activities and rewards was reviewed. It was expanded to include low-cost small rewards and substantive rewards for major goals he might set and accomplish himself. Tim's parents presented their list of positive things about their son, and the family activity list was reviewed. All agreed to one family activity, which Tim selected.

Following this, the SCI (Brown, Creamer, & Stetson, 1987) and the CDDR (Brown et al., in press) were completed with Tim. The former made it clear that although Tim was still in school, his previously good grades had deteriorated, substance involvement was prevalent among his closest friends, and he currently engaged in few extracurricular activities. Although his parents never used drugs other than cigarettes and were currently abstaining from alcohol, there was a substantial family history of Alcohol Dependence among both maternal and paternal relatives. Based on Tim's responses to the CDDR, he met criteria for DSM-defined Marijuana, Stimulant, and Nicotine Dependence, and had a history of Alcohol Abuse and experimentation with inhalants and hallucinogens. His preferred drug was methamphetamine, which he obtained from his friends, and its use was related to several life problems (legal, school, family). His use of stimulants was usually followed by alcohol consumption, although he did not consider alcohol a problem.

Not surprisingly, Tim appeared less depressed than when previously seen. With encouragement, he acknowledged anger at his parents, the police, and school officials, and reported feeling "tense" most of the time. Since Tim had difficulty articulating details regarding the topography of his drug use, he was asked to complete the IDTS, which indicated use across both interpersonal and intrapersonal situations. He also completed the AEQ-A and the Cocaine Effects Expectancy Questionnaire, to determine salient dimensions of reinforcement associated with his drug involvement. Tim agreed to have a teacher to whom he felt connected complete the TRF version of the CBCL and gave the therapist permission to contact the teacher, pending parental agreement.

Although the assessment process was not yet complete, motivational interviewing strategies were used to ascertain self-identified concerns for Tim, regardless of his perception of their relation to his substance involvement. Clearly, Tim was motivated to reduce family conflict and sustain his success in school, but he was concerned about the social consequences of changing his drug involvement. However, he was also embarrassed by his recent arrest and determined not to be stereotyped because of his drug-related arrest and probation. The therapist empathized with his concerns and encouraged him to begin to explore ways in which he could accomplish his personal goals.

At the close of the session, a joint discussion was held with Tim and his parents to review the family activity, select a family activity for the upcoming week, and provide the parents an opportunity to discuss their current concerns and efforts to support their son. The previous contracts were renewed until the third session. The therapist described the next session as their planning session, in which the therapist would provide detailed feedback from the assessment process and in which each family member would discuss goals and concerns. The closing expectation was that all family members would be actively engaged in the therapeutic process to accomplish both personal and mutually agreed-upon goals.

A review of the teen, parent, and teacher assessment data indicated no major psychopathology independent of Tim's substance involvement. However, results of the CBCL and TRF did suggest less than optimal social competence. The IDTS and expectancy questionnaires indicated that Tim used substances predominantly in social contexts, and that the greatest anticipated reinforcement for use involved enhanced comfort in social interactions and diminished stress related to such situations.

The third session began with all family members present. The therapist reported negative results of the toxicology screen sent since the last session, and congratulated Tim on his continued success in this area. Assessment feedback was next provided to Tim and his parents about the lack of major psychopathology independent of Tim's substance involvement, but a number of symptoms and life problems appearing secondary to his substance involvement. The findings of social difficulties were next discussed in the context of normal developmental changes of adolescence. In particular, since peer relations become a salient focus in middle adolescence, difficulties in this area may raise anxiety across many settings, leaving the teen with less than optimal confidence for mastering social relations in general. Following a discussion of this issue with Tim, and with the therapist modeling, the parents were able to verbalize a new appreciation for Tim's social concerns. A general agreement was reached that increasing Tim's social comfort and competence was an important objective for therapy.

Tim's parents were given feedback regarding "normal" parental responses when an adolescent is experiencing the difficulties of the type Tim had been displaying. The parents confirmed their frustrations and fears regarding Tim's behavior. In particular, although they believed he was at an age at which more independence in decision making and activities should be unfolding, they felt considerable ambivalence about granting him increasing independence, given his recent difficulties. Since the issue of independence was a primary source of conflict for Tim and his parents, all agreed that the goal of increasing independence was important and that concrete steps needed to be taken in the therapeutic process to insure that this normal developmental transition could unfold, contingent on positive behaviors (a list of which was generated).

Finally, when the therapist asked whether Tim wanted to discuss drug-related issues, Tim indicated that he preferred to deal with these privately with the therapist. He did acknowledge to his parents, however, that he had experimented with marijuana, alcohol, methamphetamine, inhalants, and hallucinogens. Tim's right to deal with this privately was discussed, along with the advantages and disadvantages for the family. His parents arrived at a decision to respect and support his wishes for privacy, so long as they were kept informed of the results from the mandated toxicology screens. The parents agreed that for 1 month they would discuss with Tim only concerns about his behavior, and would discuss their personal concerns regarding drug-related matters (e.g., the family history of alcohol and drug problems) primarily with the therapist. There was a clear understanding that all of the contracts would be reviewed and could be renegotiated if problems arose or if the family members' wishes changed. After some discussion of possible consequences of any future drug use by Tim, his parents agreed to have three discussions at home of the advantages and disadvantages of each consequence, and to have this be a topic for the family portion of the session the following week.

The therapist then met with Tim privately and shared with him detailed results of the substance components of the assessment. Tim acknowledged "feeling dependent on stimulants, marijuana, or alcohol," particularly in social situations, but had never considered cigarettes a problem. He was enthusiastic about wanting to improve his social skills and management of situations where he felt anxious about interpersonal matters. He acknowledged fears about losing important male relationships if he chose not to use with his friends. This opportunity was used to introduce and conduct a functional analysis of his substance involvement with friends. Based on Tim's previous statements, the behavior chain was outlined by the therapist, with Tim filling in and refining all components (e.g., triggers, thoughts, feelings, behavior, short-term and long-term consequences). A role-playing exercise was conducted to help Tim develop a strategy to manage social pressures during the upcoming week. Finally, given Tim's positive response to the functional analysis approach,

he selected a second risk situation and agreed to conduct his own functional analysis, which would be discussed in the next session.

The fourth session began the structured cognitive-behavioral skills training program with the initiation of assertiveness training. Following a review of the functional analysis of a second social pressure situation for use, the rationale for assertive skills was introduced, and Tim chose to focus on this area. Assertion was introduced through a discussion of Tim's understanding of the concept and by generating examples of passive, assertive, and aggressive responses to a generic social offer of marijuana. These responses were used to compare and counteract characteristics of each form of behavior, and to discuss individual rights and general guidelines for deciding on assertive behaviors. With the aid of handouts and worksheets, a nonthreatening situation was identified (i.e., asking for more information about homework). Tim agreed to do a functional analysis of this situation and make at least one assertive clarification request for homework at school each day. The session closed with a brief family discussion of the previous week's family activity, selection of a new activity, and the therapist's roleplaying a clarifying request of the parents for Tim. A discussion of concrete consequences, should Tim experience a lapse, was also held. It was agreed that a lapse would result in immediate family discussion with the therapist and loss of an independence reward. Subsequent sessions continued with a review of previous material, progression to the next content area (e.g., criticism, conflict management, dealing with negative emotions, etc.), and role plays for each. At the end of each session a family discussion was held, reviewing family activities, planning a new activity, and discussing aspects of Tim's behavior that merited either a personal reward or "independence" reward.

On two occasions the parents were seen independently to discuss Tim's progress, their concerns, and improvement/issues regarding family relations. At the ninth session, the first half of the session was devoted to a discussion of a lapse, in which Tim's parents confronted him upon returning home from an outing with friends and smelled alcohol on his breath. Although Tim had not been subject to a random urinanalysis that week, he acknowledged having had one beer with his friends. Tim preferred to discuss the details privately, but listened to his parents' feelings, including disappointment, fear, and reduced trust. Two independence privileges were taken away (i.e., seeing these friends in an unsupervised context and use of the car for 3 weeks). The parents then agreed not to discuss the incident again; however, the next level of consequences was discussed in case a second use episode should occur. When discussing this event individually with the therapist, Tim initially focused on his anger at his parents and their lack of trust in him. However, in response to motivational interviewing techniques used by the therapist, Tim acknowledged the previously agreed-upon consequences for substance use and, subsequently, his difficulties in managing the social situation in which drinking occurred. Since resistance to social pressure from a date had not been a previously evaluated situation, a functional analysis was conducted in the session, and assertive responses were generated and role-played. The therapist discussed the lapse as a learning opportunity, and Tim self-generated several new high-risk situations he had experienced in the previous 2 weeks. He chose to generate his own functional analysis and come to the next session with assertive responses and acceptable coping strategies that could be employed. The therapist and Tim reviewed his general progress in therapy, including markedly improved relations with his parents up to this point, increasing self-confidence in social situations, decreased anxiety, and relative success in staying off alcohol and other substances (except for nicotine). The concept of relapse prevention was discussed, and Tim agreed that he needed a social context with peers in which drug use was discussed. Since he displayed considerable resistance to Alcoholics Anonymous or Narcotics Anonymous, a school-based group was selected. This program, while using the Twelve-Step model, had the advantage of being available on a daily basis at school and would not require involving his parents in transportation (which was a salient issue to him, given the loss of driving privileges).

In order to maintain Tim's motivation, the therapist at one point agreed to a meeting with Tim's counselor at school, and on another occasion met with the probation officer. After several relapse prevention sessions, the focus in therapy shifted for both Tim and his parents with his resumption of extracurricular activities. For the parents, this demonstrated his progress in increasing responsibility; for Tim, it provided increasing opportunities for independence, as well as a gradual transition in his social support network to include more nonusing peers. Finally, to help facilitate a transition in Tim's image of him-

self as lacking social competence, he agreed to volunteer at a senior citizen program run by the city. In this context, in which no one knew of his former substance involvement, he was treated with considerable respect and appreciation. He was also able to practice many competence exercises prior to employing them in peer interactions.

Therapy was reduced to biweekly sessions after 3 months and monthly sessions for an additional 6 months. Near the end of therapy, Tim felt confident enough that he was able to discuss his former use with his parents; they were able both to empathize with his experience and to congratulate him on his success in changing his drug use and becoming more responsible. Consequently, it was easier for them to support his increasing independence. The family members continued to have a family activity or family night at least once per week, to maintain their mutual progress in therapy as well.

Tim was last known to have successfully completed his probationary period, plus 1 additional year of abstinence beyond that, before he left home to begin college.

CONCLUSION

As is obvious, there are multiple pathways to substance misuse for youths. The various risks and resources also influence decisions about optimal forms of intervention for adolescents and their families. When the treatment process includes cognitive and behavioral intervention strategies that provide success experiences for youths and when non-substance-related reinforcers are included in their lives, teens are able to benefit from the therapeutic process. Obviously, decisions regarding the type and intensity of family involvement vary with the resources and limitations that parents bring to this context. Finally, given the critical role that developmental factors play in the value of various activities and rewards, it is critical to have adolescents play an active role in determining the content of the techniques used to facilitate their transition out of a substance-misusing lifestyle.

REFERENCES

Achenbach, T. M. (1991a). *Manual for the Child Behavior Checklist/4–18 and 1991 Profile.* Burlington: University of Vermont, Department of Psychiatry.

Achenbach, T. M. (1991b). *Manual for the Teacher's Report Form and 1991 Profile*. Burlington: University of Vermont, Department of Psychiatry.

Achenbach, T. M. (1991c). *Manual for the Youth Self-Report and 1991 Profile*. Burlington: University of Vermont, Department of Psychiatry.

American Psychiatric Association. (1994). *Diagnostic and statistical manual of mental disorders* (4th ed.). Washington, DC: Author.

Annis, H. M., & Graham, J. M. (1985). *Inventory of Drug Taking Situations*. Toronto: Addiction Research Foundation.

Annis, H. M., & Martin, G. (1985). *Drug Taking Confidence Questionnaire*. Toronto: Addiction Research Foundation.

Ary, D. V., & Biglan, A. (1988). Longitudinal changes in adolescent smoking behavior: Onset and cessation. *Journal of Behavioral Medicine, 11*, 361–382.

Azrin, N. H., Donohue, B., Besalel, V. A., Kogan, E. S., & Acierno, R. (1994). Youth drug abuse treatment: A controlled outcome study. *Journal of Child and Adolescent Substance Abuse, 3*, 1–16.

Bachman, J. G., Wallace, J. M., O'Malley, P. M., Johnston, L. D., Kurth, C. L., & Neighbors, H. W. (1991). Racial/ethnic differences in smoking, drinking, and illicit drug use among American high school seniors, 1976–1989. *American Journal of Public Health, 81*, 372–333.

Baer, P. E., Garmezy, L. B., McLaughlin, R. J., & Pokorny, A. D. (1987). Stress, coping, family conflict, and adolescent alcohol use. *Journal of Behavioral Medicine, 10*, 449–466.

Barnes, G. M. (1990). Impact of the family on adolescent drinking patterns. In R. L. Collins, K. E. Leonard, & J. S. Searles (Eds.), *Alcohol and the family: Research and clinical perspectives* (pp. 137–161). New York: Guilford Press.

Barnes, G. M., Farrell, M. P., & Banerjee, S. (1994). Family influences on alcohol abuse and other problem behaviors among black and white adolescents in a general population sample. *Journal of Research on Adolescence, 4*, 183–201.

Bates, M. E., & Labouvie, E. W. (1995). Personality–environment constellations and alcohol use: A process-oriented study of intraindividual change during adolescence. P*psychology of Addictive Behaviors, 9*, 23–35.

Beck, A. T., Rush, A. J., Shaw, B. F., & Emery, G. (1979). *Cognitive therapy of depression*. New York: Guilford Press.

Beck, A. T., Wright, F. D., Newman, C. F., & Liese, B. S. (1993). *Cognitive therapy of substance abuse*. New York: Guilford Press.

Bennett, L. A., Wolin, S. J., & Reiss, D. (1988). Cognitive, behavioral, and emotional problems among school-age children of alcoholic parents. *American Journal of Psychiatry, 145*, 185–190.

Bentler, P. M. (1992). Etiologies and consequences of adolescent drug use: Implications for prevention. *Journal of Addictive Diseases, 11*, 47–61.

Beschner, G. M., & Friedman, A. S. (1985). Treatment of adolescent drug abusers. *International Journal of the Addictions, 20*, 971–993.

Blane, H. (1976). Middle-aged alcoholics and young drinkers. In, H. Blane & M. Chafetz (Eds.). *Youth, alcohol, and social policy* (pp. 5–38). New York: Plenum Press.

Blum, R. W. (1987). Adolescent substance abuse: Diagnostic and treatment issues. *Pediatric Clinics of North America, 34*, 523–537.

Brown, S. A. (1989). Life events of adolescents in relation to personal and parental substance abuse. *American Journal of Psychiatry, 146*, 484–489.

Brown, S. A. (1993). Recovery patterns in adolescent substance abuse. In, J. S. Baer, G. A. Marlatt, & R. J. McMahon (Eds.), *Addictive behaviors across the lifespan: Prevention, treatment and policy issues* (pp. 161–183). Newbury Park, CA: Sage.

Brown, S. A., Christiansen, B. A., & Goldman, M. S. (1987). The Alcohol Expectancy Questionnaire: An instrument for the assessment of adolescent and adult alcohol expectancies. *Journal of Studies on Alcohol, 48*, 483–491.

Brown, S. A., Creamer, V. A., & Stetson, B. A. (1987). Adolescent alcohol expectancies in relation to personal and parental drinking patterns. *Journal of Abnormal Psychology, 96*, 117–121.

Brown, S. A., Gleghorn, A., Schuckit, M., Myers, M. G., & Mott, M. A. (1996). Conduct Disorder among adolescent substance abusers. *Journal of Studies on Alcohol, 57*, 314–324.

Brown, S. A., Inaba, R., Gillin, J. C., Stewart, M. A., Schuckit, M. A., & Irwin, M. R. (1994). Alcoholism and affective disorder: Clinical course of depressive symptomatology. *American Journal of Psychiatry, 152*, 45–52.

Brown, S. A., Mott, M. A., & Myers, M. G. (1990). Adolescent drug and alcohol treatment outcome. In R. R. Watson (Ed.), *Prevention and treatment of drug and alcohol abuse* (pp. 373–403). Clifton, NJ: Humana Press.

Brown, S. A., Mott, M. A., & Stewart, M. A. (1992). Adolescent alcohol and drug abuse. In C. E. Walker & M. C. Roberts (Eds.). *Handbook of clinical child psychology* (2nd ed., pp. 677–693). New York: Wiley.

Brown, S. A., Myers, M. G., Mott, M. A., & Vik, P. (1994). Correlates of successful outcome following treatment for adolescent substance abuse. *Journal of Applied and Preventive Psychology, 3*, 61–73.

Brown, S. A., Myers, M. G., Lippke, L. F., Stewart, D. G., Tapert, S. F., & Vik, P. (in press). Psychometric evaluation of the Customary Drinking and Drug Use Record (CDDR): A measure of adolescent alcohol and drug involvement. *Journal of Studies on Alcohol*.

Brown, S. A., & Schuckit, M. A. (1988). Changes in depression among abstinent alcoholics. *Journal of Studies on Alcohol, 49*, 412–417.

Brown, S. A., Vik, P. W., & Creamer, V. A. (1989). Characteristics of relapse following adolescent substance abuse treatment. *Addictive Behaviors*, *14*, 291–300.

Bukstein, O. G., Glancy, L. J., & Kaminer, Y. (1992). Patterns of affective comorbidity in a clinical population of dually diagnosed adolescent substance abusers. *Journal of American Academy of Child and Adolescent Psychiatry*, *31*, 1041–1045.

Bukstein, O., & Kaminer, Y. (1994). The nosology of adolescent substance abuse. *American Journal of Addictions*, *3*, 1–13.

Burns, D. (1989). *Feeling good. The new mood therapy.* New York: Signet.

Chassin, L., Pillow, D. R., Curran, P. J., Molina, B. S. G., & Barrera, M. (1993). Relation of parental alcoholism to early adolescent substance use: A test of three mediating mechanisms. *Journal of Abnormal Psychology*, *102*, 3–19.

Chassin, L., Presson, C. C., & Sherman, S. J. (1984). Cognitive and social influence factors in adolescent smoking cessation. *Addictive Behaviors*, *9*, 383–390.

Chassin, L., Rogosch, F., & Barrera, M. (1991). Substance use and symptomatology among adolescent children of alcoholics. *Journal of Abnormal Psychology*, *100*, 449–463.

Catalano, R., Hawkins, J. D., Krenz, C., Gillmore, M., Morrison, D., Wells, E., & Abbott, R. (1993). Using research to guide culturally appropriate drug abuse prevention. *Journal of Consulting and Clinical Psychology, 61*, 804–811.

Christiansen, B. A., & Goldman, M. S. (1983). Alcohol-related expectancies versus demographic/background variables in the prediction of adolescent drinking. *Journal of Consulting and Clinical Psychology*, *51*, 249–257.

Christiansen, B. A., Goldman, M. S., & Inn, A. (1982). Development of alcohol-related expectancies in adolescents: Separating pharmacological from social-learning influences. *Journal of Consulting and Clinical Psychology, 50,* 336–344.

Christiansen, B. A., Roehling, P. V., Smith, G. T., & Goldman, M. S. (1989). Using alcohol expectancies to predict adolescent drinking behavior after one year. *Journal of Consulting and Clinical Psychology*, *57*, 93–99.

Clarke, G., Lewinsohn, P., & Hops, H. (1990). Leader's manual for adolescent goups: Adolescent coping with depression guide. Eugene, OR: Castalia Publishing.

Cloninger, C. R. (1987). Neurogenetic adaptive mechanisms in alcoholism. *Science*, *236*, 410–416.

Colder, C. R., & Chassin, L. (1993). The stress and negative affect model of adolescent alcohol use and the moderating effects of behavioral undercontrol. *Journal of Studies on Alcohol*, *54*, 326–333.

Costello, A. J., Edelbrock, C., Dulcan, M. K., Kalas, R., & Klaric, S. (1987). *Diagnostic Interview Schedule for Children (DISC)*. Pittsburgh: Western Psychiatric Institute and Clinic, University of Pittsburgh School of Medicine.

de Leon, G., Melnick, G., Schoket, D., & Jainchill, N. (1993). Is the therapeutic community culturally relevant?: Findings on race/ethnic differences in retention in treatment. *Journal of Psychoactive Drugs, 25*, 77–86.

Dembo, R., & Shern, D. (1982). Relative deviance and the processes of drug involvement among inner-city youths. *International Journal of the Addictions*, *17*, 1373–1399.

Denlon, R. E. (1994). The relationship between famiy variables and adolescent substance abuse: A literature review. *Adolescence, 29,* 475–495.

Donovan, D. M. (1988). Assessment of addictive behaviors: Implications of an emerging biopsychosocial model. In D. M. Donovan & G. A. Marlatt (Eds.), *Assessment of addictive behaviors* (pp. 3–48). New York: Guilford Press.

Donovan, D. M., & Marlatt, G. A. (Eds.). (1988). *Assessment of addictive behaviors*. New York: Guilford Press.

Ershler, J., Leventhal, H., Fleming, R., & Glynn, K. (1989). The quitting experience for smokers in sixth through twelfth grades. *Addictive Behaviors*, *14*, 365–378.

Farrell, M., & Strang, J. (1991). Substance use and misuse in childhood and adolescence. *Journal of Child Psychology and Psychiatry, 32,* 109–128.

Fleming, R., Leventhal, H., Glynn, K., & Ershler, J. (1989). The role of cigarettes in the initiation and progression of early substance use. *Addictive Behaviors*, *14*, 261–272.

Forgatch, M. S., & Patterson, G. R. (1989). *Parents and adolescents living together: Part 2: Family problem solving.* Eugene, OR: Castalia Publishing.

Goldman, M. S., Brown, S. A., & Christiansen, B. A. (1987). Expectancy theory: Thinking about drinking. In H. T. Blane & K. E. Leonard (Eds.), *Psychological theories of drinking and alcoholism* (pp. 173–220). New York: Guilford Press.

Goldman, M. S., Brown, S. A., Christiansen, B. A., & Smith, G. T. (1991). Alcoholism and memory: Broadening the scope of expectancy research. *Psychological Bulletin*, *110*, 137–146.

Hansen, W. B. (1983). Behavioral predictors of abstinence: Early indicators of a dependence on tobacco among adolescents. *International Journal of the Addictions*, *18*, 913–920.

Hansen, W. B., Collins, L. M., Johnson, C. A., & Graham, J. W. (1985). Self-initiated smoking cessation among high school students. *Addictive Behaviors*, *10*, 265–271.

Harrel, A. V., & Wictz, P. W. (1989). Screening for adolescent problem drinking: Validation of a multi-dimensional instrument for case identification. *Psychological Assessment: A Journal of Consulting and Clinical Psychology, 1,* 61–63.

Henggeler, S. W., Borduin, C. M., Melton, G. B., Mann, B. J., Smith, L. A., Hall, J. A., Cone, L., & Fuccie, B. R. (1991). Effects of multisystemic therapy on drug use and abuse in serious juvenile offenders: A progress report from two outcome studies. *Family Dynamics Addiction Quarterly, 1,* 40–51.

Henly, G. A., & Winters, K. C. (1989). Development of psychosocial scales for the assessment of adolescents involved with alcohol and drugs. *International Journal of the Addictions, 24,* 973–1001.

Hester, R. K., & Miller, W. R. (1988). Empirical guidelines for optimal client-treatment matching. In E. R. Rahdert & J. Grabowski (Eds.), *Adolescent drug abuse: Analyses of treatment research* (DHHS Publication No. ADM 88-1523, NIDA Research Monograph No. 77, pp. 27–38). Washington, DC: U. S. Government Printing Office.

Hubbard, R. L., Cavanaugh, E. R., Graddock, S. G., & Rachel, J. V. (1983). *Characteristics, behaviors and outcomes for youth in TOPS study* (Report submitted to National Institute on Drug Abuse, Contract No. 271-79-3611). Research Triangle Park, NC: Research Triangle Institute.

Hundleby, J. D., & Mercer, G. W. (1987). Family and friends as social environments and their relationship to young adolescents' use of alcohol, tobacco, and marijuana. *Journal of Marriage and the Family, 49,* 151–164.

Hurt, R. D., Offord, K. P., Croghan, I. T., Gomez-Dahl, L., Kottke, T. E., Morse, R. M., & Melton, L. J. (1996). Mortality following inpatient addictions treatment: Role of tobacco use in a community-based cohort. *Journal of the American Medical Association, 275,* 1097–1103.

Institute of Medicine. (1990). *Broadening the base of treatment for alcohol problems.* Washington, DC: National Academy Press.

Jessor, R., & Jessor, S. L. (1977). *Problem behavior and psychosocial development: A longitudinal study of youth.* New York: Academic Press.

Joanning, H., Quinn, W., Thomas, F., & Mullen, R. (1992). Treating adolescent drug abuse: A comparison of family systems therapy, group therapy, and family drug education. *Journal of Marital and Family Therapy, 18,* 345–356.

Johnson, V., & Pandina, R. J. (1991). Effects of the family environment on adolescent substance use, delinquency and coping styles. *American Journal of Alcohol and Drug Abuse, 17,* 71–88.

Kaminer, Y. (1991). Adolescent substance abuse. In R. J. Frances & S. I. Miller (Eds.), *Clinical textbook of addictive disorders* (pp. 320–346). New York: Guilford Press.

Kaminer, Y., Bukstein, O. G., & Tarter, R. E. (1991). The Teen Addiction Severity Index: Rationale and reliability. *International Journal of the Addictions, 26,* 219–226.

Kaminer, Y., Wagner, E. F., Plummer, B. A., & Seifer, R. (1993). Validation of the Teen Addiction Severity Index (T-ASI): Preliminary findings. *American Journal on Addictions, 2,* 250–254.

Kirisci, L., Mezzich, A., & Tarter, R. E. (1995). Norms and sensitivity of the adolescent version of the Drug Use Screening Inventory. *Addictive Behaviors, 20,* 149–157.

Kirisci, L., Tarter, R. E., & Hsu, T. (1994). Fitting a two-parameter logistic item response model to clarify the psychometric properties of the Drug Use Screening Inventory for adolescent alcohol and drug abusers. *Alcoholism: Clinical and Experimental Research, 18,* 1335–1341.

Knop, J., Teasdale, T. W., Schulsinger, F., & Goodwin, D. W. (1985). A prospective study of young men at high risk for alcoholism: School behavior and achievement. *Journal of Studies on Alcohol, 46,* 273–278.

Laundergan, J. C. (1982). *Easy does it: Alcoholism treatment outcomes, Hazelden and the Minnesota model.* Minneapolis: Hazelden Foundation.

Lewis, R. A., Piercy, F. P., Sprenkle, D. H., & Trepper, T. S. (1990). Family-based interventions for helping drug-abusing adolescents. *Journal of Adolescent Research, 5,* 82–95.

Liddle, H. A., & Dakof, G. A. (1992). *Effectiveness of family-based treatment for adolescent substance use.* Paper presented at the annual conference of the Society for Psychotherapy Research, Pittsburgh.

Liddle, H. A., & Dakof, G. A. (1995). Family-based treatment for adolescent drug use: State of the science. In E. Rahdert & D. Czechowics (Eds.). *Adolescent drug abuse: Clinical assessment and therapeutic interventions* (DHHS Publication No. ADM 95-3908, NIDA Research Monograph No. 156). Washington, DC: U.S. Government Printing Office.

Liddle, H. A., Dakof, G. A., Diamond, G., Holt, M., Aroyo, J., & Watson, M. (1992). The adolescent module in multidimensional family therapy. In G. W. Lawson & A. W. Lawson (Eds.), *Adolescent substance abuse: Etiology, treatment, and prevention* (pp. 165–186). Gaithersburg, MD: Aspen.

Loeber, R. (1990). Development and risk factors of juvenile antisocial behavior and delinquency. *Clinical Psychology Review, 10,* 1–41.

Mahaddian, E., Bentler, P. M., & Newcomb, M. D. (1988). Risk factors for substance use: Ethnic differences among adolescents. *Journal of Substance Abuse, 1,* 11–24.

Marlatt, G. A., & Gordon, J. A. (Eds.). (1985). *Relapse prevention: Maintenance strategies in the treatment of addictive behaviors.* New York: Guilford Press.

Martin, C. S., Kaczynski, N. A., Maisto, S. A., Bukstein, O. M., Moss, H. B. (1995). Patterns of DSM-IV Alcohol Abuse and Dependence symptoms in adolescent drinkers. *Journal of Studies on Alcohol, 56,* 672–680.

McCrady, B. S. (1986). Alcoholism. In D. H. Barlow (Ed.), *Clinical handbook of psychological disorders* (pp. 245–298). New York: Guilford Press.

McCrady, B. S., Dean, L., Dubreuil, E., & Swanson, S. (1985). The Problem Drinkers' Project: A programmatic application of social-learning based treatment. In G. A. Marlatt & J. R. Gordon (Eds.), *Relapse prevention: Maintenance strategies in the treatment of addictive behaviors* (pp. 417–471). New York: Guilford Press.

McGue, M. (1994). Why developmental psychology should find room for behavioral genetics. In C. A. Nelson (Ed.). *Minnesota Symposia on Child Psychology: Vol. 27. Threats to optimal development: Integrating biological, psychological, and social risk factors* (pp. 105–119). Hillsdale, NJ: Erlbaum.

McLellan, A. T., Luborsky, L., O'Brien, C. P., & Woody, G. E. (1980). An improved evaluation instrument for substance abuse patients: The Addiction Severity Index. *Journal of Nervous and Mental Disease, 168,* 26–33.

Meyers, K., McLellan, A. T., Jaeger, J. L., & Pettinati, H. M. (1995). The development of the Comprehensive Addiction Severity Index for Adolescents (CASI-A): An interview for assessing multiple problems of adolescents. *Journal of Substance Abuse Treatment, 12,* 181–193.

Miller, W. R. (1989). Matching individuals with interventions. In R. K. Hester & W. R. Miller (Eds.), *Handbook of alcoholism treatment approaches* (pp. 261–272). New York: Pergamon Press.

Miller, W. R., & Rollnick, S. (Eds.). (1991). *Motivational interviewing: Preparing people to change addictive behavior.* New York: Guilford Press.

Monti, P. M., Abrams, D. B., Kadden, R. M., & Cooney, N. L. (1989). *Treating alcohol dependence.* New York: Guilford Press.

Moos, R. H., & Billings, A. G. (1982). Children of alcoholics during the recovery process: Alcoholic and matched control families. *Addictive Behaviors, 7,* 155–163.

Myers, M. G., & Brown, S. A. (1990a). Coping and appraisal in relapse risk situations among substance abusing adolescents following treatment. *Journal of Adolescent Chemical Dependency, 1,* 95–116.

Myers, M. G., & Brown, S. A. (1990b). Coping responses and relapse among adolescent substance abusers. *Journal of Substance Abuse, 2,* 177–190.

Myers, M. G. & Brown, S. A. (1994). Smoking and health in substance abusing adolescents: A two year followup. *Pediatrics, 93,* 561–566.

Myers, M. G., & Brown, S. A. (1996). The Adolescent Relapse Coping Questionnaire: Psychometric validation. *Journal of Studies on Alcohol, 57,* 40–46.

Myers, M. G., Brown, S. A., & Mott, M. A. (1993). Coping as a predictor of adolescent substance abuse treatment outcome. *Journal of Substance Abuse, 5,* 15–29.

Myers, M. G., Brown, S. A., & Mott, M. A. (1995). Preadolescent Conduct Disorder behaviors predict relapse and progression of addiction for alcohol and drug abusing adolescents. *Alcoholism: Clinical and Experimental Research, 19,* 1528–1536.

Newcomb, M. D. & Bentler, P. M. (1988). *Consequences of adolescent drug use.* Beverly Hills, CA: Sage.

Obermeier, G., & Henry, P. (1985). Inpatient treatment of adolescent alcohol and polydrug abusers. *Seminars in Adolescent Medicine, 1,* 293–301.

Oetting, E. R., Edwards, R. W., & Beauvais, F. (1989). Social and psychological factors underlying inhalant abuse. In R. A. Crider & B. A. Rouse (Eds.), *Epidemiology of inhalant abuse: An update* (DHHS Publication No. 89-123278 NIDA Research Monograph No. 85, pp. 172–203). Washington, DC: U.S. Government Printing Office.

Opland, E., Winters, K., & Stinchfield, R. (1995). Gender differences in drug-abusing adolescents. *Psychology of Addictive Behaviors, 9,* 167–175.

Owen, P., & Nyberg, L. (1983). Assessing alcohol and drug problems among adolescents: Current practice. *Journal of Drug Addiction, 13,* 249–254.

Pandina, R. J., & Schuele, J. A. (1983). Psychosocial correlates of alcohol and drug use of adolescent students and adolescents in treatment. *Journal of Studies on Alcohol, 44,* 950–973.

Patterson, G. R., DeBaryshe, B. D., & Ramsey, E. (1989). A developmental perspective on antisocial behavior. *American Psychologist, 44,* 329–335.

Prochaska, J. O., DiClemente, C. C., & Norcross, J. C. (1992). In search of how people change: Applications to addictive behaviors. *American Psychologist, 47,* 1102–1114.

Puig-Antich, J., & Orvaschel, H. (1987). *Schedule for Affective Disorders and Schizophrenia for School-Age Children: Epidemiologic version and Present Episode version.* Pittsburgh: Western Psychiatric Institute and Clinic.

Rahdert, E. R. (1988). Treatment services for adolescent drug abusers: Introduction and overview. In E. R. Rahdert & J. Grabowski (Eds.), *Adolescent drug abuse: Analysis of treatment research.* (DHHS Publication No. ADM 88-1523, pp. 1–3). Washington, DC: U. S. Government Printing Office.

Reynolds, C., & Kamphaus, R. (1994). *Behavioral Assessment System for Children.* Circle Pines, MN: American Guidance Service.

Richter, S. S., Brown, S. A., & Mott, M. A. (1991). The impact of social support and self-esteem on adolescent substance abuse treatment outcome. *Journal of Substance Abuse, 3,* 371–385.

Riggs, P. D., Thompson, L. L., Mikulich, S. K., Whitmore, E. A., & Crowley, T. J. (1996). An open trial of pemoline in drug-dependent delinquents with Attention-Deficit Hyperactivity Disorder. *Journal of the American Academy of Child and Adolescent Psychiatry, 35,* 1018–1024.

Robin, A. L., & Foster, S. L. (1989). *Negotiating parent–adolescent conflict: A behavioral–family systems approach.* New York: Guilford Press.

Robins, L. N., & Price, R. K. (1991). Adult disorders predicted by childhood conduct problems: Results from the NIMH Epidemiologic Catchment Area project. *Psychiatry, 54,* 116–132.

Roosa, M. W., Sandler, I. N., Gehring, M., Beals, J., & Cappo, L. (1988). The Children of Alcoholics Life-Events Schedule: A stress scale for children of alcohol-abusing parents. *Journal of Studies on Alcohol, 49,* 422–429.

Rush, T. V. (1979). Predicting treatment outcomes for juvenile and young adult clients in the Pennsylvania substance-abuse system. In G. M. Beschner & A. S. Friedman (Eds.), *Youth drug abuse: Problems, issues and treatment* (pp. 629–656). Lexington, MA: Lexington Books.

Russell, M. (1990). Prevalence of alcoholism among children of alcoholics. In M. Windle & J. S. Searles (Eds.), *Children of alcoholics: Critical perspectives* (p. 9–38). New York: Guilford Press.

Searles, J. S. (1988). The role of genetics in the pathogenesis of alcoholism. *Journal of Abnormal Psychology, 97,* 153–167.

Sells, S. B., & Simpson, D. D. (1979). Evaluation of treatment outcome for youths in the Drug Abuse Reporting Program (DARP): A followup study. In G. M. Beschner & A. S. Friedman (Eds.), *Youth drug abuse: Problems, issues and treatment* (pp. 571–628). Lexington, MA: Lexington Books.

Schwartz, R. H., & Wirth, P. W. (1990). Potentialsubstance abuse: Detection among adolescent patients: Using the Drug and Alcohol Problem (DAP) Quick Screen, a 30-item questionnaire. *Clinical Pediatrics, 29,* 38–43.

Shedler, J., & Block, J. (1990). Adolescent drug use and psychological health: A longitudinal inquiry. *American Psychologist, 45,* 612–630.

Sher, K. J. (1994). Individual-level risk factors. In R. Zucker, G. Boyd, & J. Howard (Eds.),. *The development of alcohol problems: Exploring the biopsychosocial matrix of risk* (DHHS Publication No. ADM 94-3495, pp. 77–108). Washington, DC: U.S. Government Printing Office.

Smith, D. E., Buxton, M. E., Bilal, R., & Seymour, R.B. (1993). Cultural points of resistance to the 12-step recovery process. *Journal of Psychoactive Drugs, 25,* 97–108.

Smith, G. T., & Goldman, M. S. (1994). Alcohol expectance theory and the identification of high-risk adolescents. *Journal of Research on Adolescence, 4,* 229–247.

Stewart, D. G. (1994). Antisocial behavior and long term outcome of substance abuse treatment. In S. A. Brown (Chair), *Long term outcomes among adolescents following alcohol and drug treatment.* Symposium conducted at the annual meeting of the American Psychological Association, Los Angeles.

Stewart, D. G., & Brown, S. A. (1995). Withdrawal and dependency symptoms among adolescent alcohol and drug abusers. *Addiction, 90,* 627–635.

Stewart, M. A., & Brown, S. A. (1994). Family functioning following adolescent substance abuse treatment. *Journal of Substance Abuse, 5,* 327–339.

Stice, E., Barrera, M., & Chassin, L. (1993). Relation of parental support and control to adolescents' externalizing symptomatology and substance use: A longitudinal examination of curvilinear effects. *Journal of Abnormal Child Psychology, 21,* 609–629.

Stowell, R. J. A., & Estroff, T. W. (1992) Psychiatric disorders in substance-abusing adolescent inpatients: A pilot study. *Journal of the American Academy of Child and Adolescent Psychiatry, 31,* 1036–1040.

Substance Abuse and Mental Health Services Administration. (1996). *Preliminary estimates from the 1995 National Household Survey on Drug Abuse* (Office of Applied Studies Advance Report No. 18). Washington, DC: Author.

Szapocznik, J., Kurtines, W. A., Foote, F., Perez-Vidal, A., & Hervis, O. (1983). Conjoint versus one-person family therapy: Some evidence for the effectiveness of conducting family therapy through one person. *Journal of Consulting and Clinical Psychology, 51,* 889–899.

Szapocznik, J., Kurtines, W. A., Foote, F., Perez-Vidal, A., & Hervis, O. (1986). Conjoint versus one-person family therapy: Further evidence for the effectiveness of conducting family therapy through one person with drug abusing adolescents. *Journal of Consulting and Clinical Psychology, 54,* 395–397.

Szapocznik, J., Perez-Vidal, A., Brickman, A. L., Foote, F., Santisteban, D., Hervis, O., & Kurtines, W. A. (1988). Engaging adolescent drug abusers and their families in treatment: A strategic structural systems approach. *Journal of Consulting and Clinical Psychology, 56,* 552–557.

Tapert, S. F., Stewart, D. G., & Brown, S. A. (in press). Drug abuse in adolescence. In A. J. Goreczny & M. Hersen (Eds.), *Handbook of pediatrics and adolescent health psychology.* Needham Heights, MA: Allyn & Bacon.

Tarter, R. E. (1990). Evaluation and treatment of adolescent substance abuse: A decision tree method. *American Journal of Drug and Alcohol Abuse, 16,* 1–46.

Tarter, R. E., & Edwards, K. (1988). Psychological factors associated with the risk for alcoholism. *Alcoholism: Clinical and Experimental Research, 12,* 471–480.

Tarter, R. E., Ott, P. J., & Mezzich, A. C. (1991). Psychometric assessment. In R. J. Frances & S. I. Miller (Eds.), *Clinical textbook of addictive disorders* (pp. 237–267). New York: Guilford Press.

Thompson, K. M., & Wilsnack, R. W. (1984). Drinking and drinking problems among female adolescents: Patterns and influences. In S. C. Wilsnack & L. J. Beckiman (Eds.), *Alcohol problems in women: Antecedents, consequences, and intervention.* New York: Guilford Press.

U.S. Department of Health and Human Services (DHHS). (1995). *Monitoring the Future Study: Summary of findings through 1995* (DHHS Publication No. ADM 96-4139). Washington, DC: U.S. Government Printing Office.

U.S. Department of Health and Human Services (DHHS). (1996). *Smoking cessation* (Publication No. AHCPR 96–0692,Clinical Practice Guideline No. 18*)*. Washington, DC: U. S. Government Printing Office.

Vaillant, G. E. (1983). *The natural history of alcoholism.* Cambridge, MA: Harvard University Press.

Vik, P. W., & Brown, S. A. (1994). *A process-oriented approach to understanding post-treatment adolescent substance use.* Poster presented at the 28th Annual Meeting of the Association for Advancement of Behavior Therapy, San Diego.

Vik, P. W., Brown, S. A., & Myers, M. G. (1997). Assessment of adolescent substance use problems, In E. J. Mash & L. G. Terdal (Eds.), *Assessment of childhood disorders* (3rd ed., pp. 717–748). New York: Guilford Press.

Vik, P. W., Grizzle, K., & Brown, S. A. (1992). Social resource characteristics and adolescent substance abuse relapse. *Journal of Adolescent Chemical Dependency, 2,* 59–74.

Wagner, E. F. (1993). Delay of gratification, coping with stress, and substance use in adolescence. *Experimental and Clinical Psychopharmacology, 1,* 27–43.

White, H. R. & Labouire, E. W. (1989). Towards the assessment of adolescent problem drinking. *Journal of Studies on Alcohol, 50,* 30–37.

Windle, M., & Barnes, G. M. (1988). Similarities and differences in correlates of alcohol consumption and problem behaviors among male and female adolescents. *International Journal of the Addictions, 23,* 707–728.

Windle, M., Miller-Tutzauer, C., Barnes, G. M., & Welte, J. (1991). Adolescent perceptions of help-seeking resources for substance abuse. *Child Development, 62,* 79–189.

Winters, K. C. (1991). *The Personal Experience Screening Questionnaire.* Los Angeles: Western Psychological Services.

Winters, K. C., & Henly, G. A. (1989a). *The Personal Experience Inventory.* Los Angeles: Western Psychological Services.

Winters, K. C., & Henly. G. A. (1989b). *The Adolescent Diagnostic Interview.* Los Angeles: Western Psychological Services.

Woltzen, M. C., Filstead, W. J., Anderson, C. OL., Anderson, S., Twadell, S., Sisson, C., & Zoch, P. (1986). Clinical issues central to the residential treatment of alcohol and substance misusers. *Advances in Adolescent Mental Health, 2,* 271–282.

Author Index

Subject Index

Note. *t*, table; *f*, figure.